Exceptional
Learners

eighth edition

Exceptional

Allyn and Bacon

BOSTON LONDON TORONTO SYDNEY TOKYO SINGAPORE

Learners

introduction to special education

Daniel P. Hallahan

James M. Kauffman

UNIVERSITY OF VIRGINIA

Senior Editor: Virginia Lanigan
Editor-in-Chief, Education: Paul A. Smith
Editorial Assistant: Karin Huang
Developmental Editor: Alicia R. Reilly
Marketing Manager: Brad Parkins
Production Administrator: Deborah Brown

Editorial-Production Service: Barbara Gracia
Copyeditor: William Heckman
Text Designer: Deborah Schneck
Manufacturing Buyer: Megan Cochran
Cover Administrator: Linda Knowles

Copyright © 2000, 1997, 1994, 1991, 1988, 1982, 1978 by Allyn & Bacon
A Pearson Education Company
160 Gould Street
Needham Heights, MA 02494-2310

Library of Congress Cataloging-in-Publication Data

Hallahan, Daniel P., 1944–
        Exceptional learners: introduction to special education /
Daniel P. Hallahan, James M. Kauffman.—8th ed.
             p.   cm.
        Includes bibliographical references (p.   ) and indexes.
        ISBN 0-205-28779-4 (alk. paper)
        1. Special education—United States. I. Kauffman, James M.
II. Title
LC3981.H34 2000   99-23615
371.9'073--dc21   CIP

Printed in the United States of America
10 9 8 7 6 5 4 3 2 1—VHP—03 02 01 00 99

Cover Credit: *Triple Deckers.* Watercolor on rag paper Carmella Salvucci was born in Brighton, MA in 1951. Her work has been exhibited throughout the Boston area, in New York, and at the Very Special Arts Gallery in Washington, DC. Her work has also been shown in London, England, where it received awards from The Royal Society for Handicapped Children and Adults. She has also received several awards from the Ebensburg Center in Pennsylvania. In 1996 her work was featured in *From the Outside In,* an exhibition at the Fuller Museum of Art in Brockton, MA.

Chapter-Opening Quotes:
pp. 3 and 119 from Richard H. Hungerford, 1950, "On Locusts," *American Journal of Mental Deficiency, 54,* pp. 415–418. **p. 43** from Bob Dylan, "The Times They Are A-Changin'," 1963 Warner Bros., Inc. (Renewed). All rights reserved. Used by permission. International copyright secured. **p. 85** from *The Measure of Our Success* by Marian Wright Edelman. Copyright © 1992 by Marian Wright Edelman. Reprinted by permission of Beacon Press. **p. 159,** reprinted with the permission of Scribner, a Division of Simon & Schuster, from *A Roving Commission: My Early Life* by Winston Churchill. Copyright 1930 by Charles Scribner's Sons; copyright renewed © 1958 by Winston Chruchill. **p. 203** from Heinrich Hoffmann, "The Story of Fidgety Philip" in (Author) *Slovenly Peter or Cheerful Stories and Funny Pictures for Good Little Folks* (Philadelphia: John C. Winston, 1940). **p. 245** from Anonymous, 1994, "First-Person Account: Schizophrenia with Childhood Onset," *Schizophrenia Bulletin, 20,* 287–588. **p. 295** from David Shields, *Dead Languages* (New York: Alfred A. Knopf, Inc., 1989). **p. 341** from Helen Keller, *The Story of My Life* (New York: Doubleday, 1954). **p. 385** from Stephen Kuusisto, *The Planet of the Blind: A Memoir* (New York: The Dial Press, 1998). **p. 425** Excerpt abridged from *Autobiography of a Face* by Lucy Grealy. Copyright © 1994 by Lucy Grealy. Reprinted by permission of Houghton Mifflin Company. All rights reserved. **p. 467** from *The Autobiography of Mark Twain,* edited by Charles Neider. Copyright 1927, 1940, 1958, 1959 by the Mark Twain Company, copyright 1924, 1952, 1955 by Clara Clemens Somossoud, copyright 1959 by Charles Neider. Reprinted by permission of HarperCollins Publishers, Inc. **p. 513** from Christopher Nolan, *Under the Eye of the Clock: the Life Story of Christopher Nolan* (New York: St. Martin's Press, 1989).

Photo Credits:
Gateway Crafts: p. 4; Will Faller: pp. 7, 33, 47, 69, 93, 112, 114, 173, 188, 189, 224, 246, 266, 271, 280, 285, 301, 316, 318, 330, 350, 370, 426, 432, 455, 490; Courtesy of Kathy Buckley: p. 9; Will Hart: pp. 13, 20, 23, 60, 90, 97, 98, 101, 104, 107, 123, 129, 145, 216, 225, 253, 303, 306, 345, 362, 371, 375, 401, 412, 476, 481, 488, 516, 517, 521, 524, 532; Lyrl Ahern: p. 25; North Wind Picture Archive: p. 26; AP/Wide World Photos: pp. 30, 55, 255, 409, 472, 473; Brian Smith: pp. 49, 63, 125, 147, 162, 164, 211, 219, 417, 502; Courtesy of the Carroll Center: pp. 50, 408;

(Photo credits are continued on page 608 and are considered an extension of the copyright page.)

contents

chapter 6

Attention Deficit Hyperactivity Disorder 203

chapter 7

Emotional or Behavioral Disorders 245

chapter 8

Communication Disorders   295

chapter 9

Hearing Impairment   341

chapter **10**

Visual Impairment   385

chapter **11**

Physical Disabilities   425

preface

Exceptional Learners: Introduction to Special Education, 8e is a general introduction to the characteristics of exceptional learners and their education. (*Exceptional* is the term that traditionally has been used to refer to persons with disabilities as well as to those who are gifted.) This book emphasizes classroom practices, as well as the psychological, sociological, and medical aspects of disabilities and giftedness.

We have written this text with two primary audiences in mind: those individuals who are preparing to be special educators and those who are preparing to be general educators. Given the current movement toward including students with disabilities in general education classrooms, general educators must be prepared to understand this special student population and be ready to work with special educators to provide appropriate educational programming for these students. This book also is appropriate for professionals in other fields who work with exceptional learners (e.g., speech-language pathologists, audiologists, physical therapists, occupational therapists, adapted physical educators, and school psychologists).

In Chapter 1, we begin with an overview of exceptionality and special education, including definitions, basic legal requirements, and the history and development of the field. In Chapter 2, we discuss major current issues and trends, such as inclusion, early childhood programming, transition to adulthood programming, inclusion of students with disabilities in general assessments of progress, and discipline of students with disabilities. In Chapter 3, we address multicultural and bilingual aspects of special education. And in the following nine chapters (4 through 12) we examine each of the major categories of exceptionality: mental retardation, learning disabilities, attention deficit hyperactivity disorder, emotional or behavioral disorders, communication disorders, hearing impairment, visual impairment, physical disabilities, and giftedness. Finally, in Chapter 13, we consider the significant issues pertaining to parents and families of persons with disabilities.

We believe that we have written a text that reaches the heart as well as the mind. It is our conviction that professionals working with exceptional learners need to develop not only a solid base of knowledge but also a healthy attitude toward their work and the people whom they serve. Further, we contend that such knowledge and attitudes must *both* evolve to remain relevant and focused. Professionals must constantly challenge themselves to learn more theory, research, and practice in special education and to develop an ever more sensitive understanding of exceptional learners and their families.

Major Changes for this Edition

New Chapter on Attention Deficit Hyperactivity Disorder (ADHD).
One-third to one-half of cases referred to guidance clinics are for ADHD, and most authorities estimate that 3 to 5 percent of the school-age population have ADHD. Although ADHD is not recognized as a separate category of special education by the U.S. Department of Education, more and more students with ADHD obtain special education services under the category of "other health impaired." Given the large numbers of students identified with this condition, as well as the many controversial issues surrounding identification and treatment of ADHD, it is timely and prudent to include a chapter (Chapter 6) on ADHD. We hope you enjoy reading this chapter as much as we enjoyed writing it.

Expanded Coverage of Major Issues. This edition includes new material in Chapter 1 on IDEA 1997, the development of IEPs, and the March '99 federal regulations related to IDEA '97. The Amendments to IDEA in 1997 were significant, and we bring students up to date on the new features of federal law and IEP requirements. In Chapter 2, we have added new sections discussing the inclusion of students with disabilities in general assessments of educational progress and on the discipline of students with disabilities. IDEA 1997 requires appropriate inclusion of students with disabilities in general assessments of educational progress as part of schools' movement toward setting higher academic standards. This requirement raises many questions for most teachers and prospective teachers, and our revisions address the most common of these. Probably the most controversial and adversarial aspect of IDEA 1997 is the law related to disciplinary action involving students with disabilities. For this reason, we included considerable new material on the discipline of students with disabilities in Chapters 2 and 7. Also, in Chapter 2 we end each section with a discussion of issues continuing into the new century. Issues in special education are ever changing, but some controversies and problems will undoubtedly extend well into the next century or even beyond.

Extensive Revisions and Updates

In addition to the new chapter on ADHD, we have made extensive revisions to virtually every aspect of the remaining twelve chapters. We have included 431 new references, virtually all of which bear a 1998–2000 copyright date. Close to 20 percent of the main text in these twelve chapters is new. These chapters also now include 33 new glossary terms, 11 new tables, and 8 new figures.

The unique features of our book that have come to enjoy immense popularity with instructors and students have been retained but have been augmented with new material:

Suggestions for Teaching Students in General Education Classrooms.
Written specifically for general education teachers, this feature provides a variety of teaching ideas and strategies. Each categorical chapter ends with a Suggestions for Teaching section that will serve as an excellent starting place for general education teachers faced with teaching special education students in their classrooms. In addition to many tips and techniques, this feature provides lists of helpful resources, books, and software. The Suggestions for Teaching were prepared

by Professor Jane Nowacek of Appalachian State University and Professor Peggy Tarpley of Longwood College, both of whom are experienced resource teachers currently involved in teacher education.

Myths and Facts Boxes. We start each chapter with a box that juxtaposes several myths and facts about the subject of the chapter. This popular feature serves as an excellent advance organizer for the material to be covered. Although longtime users will be familiar with this feature (it dates back to our first edition in 1978), we have added ten new myths and facts to the twelve retained chapters.

Chapter-Opening Quotes. Also going back to our first edition is the practice of opening each chapter with an excerpt from literature or song. We draw on this quote in the opening paragraphs to begin our discussion of the topics covered in the chapter. Students continue to tell us that they find this use of quotes to be an effective method of grabbing their attention and leading them into some of the issues contained in the text. Two chapters (Learning Disabilities and Visual Impairment) include new chapter-opening quotes.

Special Topics Boxes. Inserted throughout the text are boxes of three types: some highlight research findings and their applicability to educational practice; some discuss issues facing educators in the field; and some present the human side of having a disability. We have added 29 new boxes.

Collaboration: Key to Success. Each categorical chapter contains a feature in which two teachers—one from general education and one from special education—talk about how they collaborate to effectively integrate exceptional learners into general education classrooms. These sections serve as models of best practices for inclusion. In addition to a new collaboration box for the new chapter on ADHD, we have included new collaboration features for the chapters covering mental retardation, emotional/behavioral disorders, communication disorders, and hearing impairment.

Success Stories: Special Educators at Work. Special educators work in a variety of settings, ranging from general education classrooms to residential institutions. Although their main function involves teaching, these professionals also engage in a variety of roles, such as counseling, collaborating, consulting, and so forth. To illustrate this variety, each of the nine categorical chapters includes an example of a special educator at work. Written by Dr. Jean B. Crockett of Virginia Tech University, an experienced special education administrator and teacher educator, each story focuses on a special educator's work with an individual student. These boxes show readers the wide range of challenges faced by special educators, the dynamic nature of their positions, and the competent, hopeful practice of special education. Dr. Crockett has prepared a new Success Story for the ADHD chapter.

Photography. Over half of the photographs for this edition were supplied by Allyn and Bacon's photo library. The photo library is a compilation of images from photo shoots that were set up at schools around the country, including California, Connecticut, Florida, Maryland, Massachusetts, Missouri, New Mexico, Utah, and Canada. Photos for our eighth edition were selected from the most recent photo sessions. Allyn and Bacon's photo department is aware of the rapid changes that are occurring in special education and is committed to reflecting those changes in its library.

Allyn and Bacon solicited our guidance for the shoots. All the photographs we chose are reproduced with the consent of the individual depicted.

Supplements

Student Study Guide. Written by Dr. E. Paula Crowley of Illinois State University, and reviewed by Dan Hallahan and Jim Kauffman, the study guide reinforces for students conceptual and factual text material and includes key points, learning objectives, exercises, practice tests, and enrichment activities.

Companion Website with Online Study Guide. This dynamic, interactive companion site includes an online study guide that provides, on a chapter-by-chapter basis, learning objectives, study questions with text page references, "live" links to relevant websites, and additional enrichment material. [www.abacon.com]

Instructor's Resource Manual and Test Bank. The Instructor's Resource Manual section of this supplement was prepared by Melody Tankersley of Kent State University, along with Dan Hallahan and Jim Kauffman. For each chapter of the text, it provides a Chapter Outline, a Chapter Overview, and an Annotated Outline wherein the major headings of the chapter are summarized in detail. Included in the Annotated Outline are suggestions for Lecture Ideas, Discussion Points, and Activities. The IRM also keys each chapter to appropriate videos, transparencies, and digital images available with this text. Also included are references to Related Media, Films, Journals, and Websites.

The Test Bank section, written by Kerri F. Martin of East Tennessee State University, consists of over 1000 test questions, including multiple choice, true/false, and essay formats. Also included are quizzes and comprehensive tests for each chapter.

Computerized Test Bank. A computerized version of the Test Bank is available in either 3½" or 5¼" disks (IBM or Macintosh).

The "Snapshots" Video Series for Special Education. *Snapshots: Inclusion Video* (c. 1995; 22 minutes) profiles three students of different ages and with various levels of disability in inclusive class settings.

Snapshots 2: Video for Special Education (categorical organization) (c. 1995; 20–25 minutes) is a set of six videotaped segments designed specifically for use in your college classroom. The topics explored are:

- traumatic brain injury
- behavior disorders
- learning disabilities
- mental retardation
- hearing impairment
- visual impairment

Each segment profiles three individuals, their families, teachers, and experiences. These programs will be of great interest to your students. Instructors who have used the tapes in their courses have found that they help in disabusing students of stereotypical viewpoints, and put a "human face" on course material. Teaching notes for both *Snapshots: Inclusion* and *Snapshots 2* are provided in corresponding chapters of the Instructor's Resource Manual.

New from the Allyn and Bacon "Professionals in Action" Video Series Comes "Teaching Students with Special Needs." Available with the 8th edition of the text, the *Professionals in Action* video is approximately two hours in length, consisting of five 15–30 minute modules. These modules present several viewpoints and approaches to teaching students of various disabilities in general education classrooms, separate education settings, and several combinations of the two. Each module explores its topic through actual classroom footage and interviews with students, general and special education teachers, and parents. The five modules are:

1. Working Together: The Individualized Education Plan (IEP)
2. Working Together: The Collaborative Process
3. Instruction and Behavior Management
4. Technology for Inclusion
5. Working with Parents and Families

Transparency Package. The Transparency Package has been revised and expanded for the 8th edition to include approximately 100 acetates, over half of which are full color.

Acknowledgments

We are grateful to those individuals who reviewed the seventh and eighth editions, and to the readers of the drafts of our revised chapters:

Peggy L. Anderson, Metropolitan State College of Denver
William N. Bender, University of Georgia
David F. Conway, University of Nebraska at Omaha
Rhoda Cummings, University of Nevada
Gary A. Davis, University of Wisconsin—Madison
Mary K. Dykes, University of Florida—Gainesville
Laura Gaudet, Towson State University
Herbert Grossman, University of Wisconsin at Platteville
Thomas F. Reilly, Chicago State University
Phillip Waldrop, Middle Tennessee State University
George J. Yard, University of Missouri—St. Louis

We thank Peggy Weiss who oversaw the tedious task of securing permissions for quoted material. And we also thank Karen Santos of James Madison University for her contributions to the five new or revised Collaboration features.

We are thankful for the wonderful support and assistance we have received for this and other editions from the folks at Allyn and Bacon. Alicia Reilly continues to amaze us with her ability to balance family responsibilities while attending to all the details of our book. She is a gem. Deborah Brown's professionalism, as always, brought order to moments of chaos. Karin Huang's responsiveness to our e-mails and phone calls was critical to our meeting our deadlines. And, finally, we are extremely grateful to education editor Ray Short, who came out of retirement to oversee the revision. His unflappable demeanor and confidence in us as authors has always been appreciated. We wish him the best now that he can really retire.

This may well be the most extensive overall revision we have made in the twenty-two-year history of this text. In addition to the new content described above, we also consolidated material throughout so that the total length of the book was not increased substantially. For those loyal users of previous editions, we assure you that we weighed carefully each change or update. We hope you will agree that our revisions reflect the myriad changes in the field of special education over the past few years as well as the information explosion brought about by ever more accessible computer databases and the Internet. We also hope you will agree that we have not failed in our continuing commitment to bring you the best that research has to offer with regard to educating exceptional learners.

DPH
JMK

Special Acknowledgment

Allyn and Bacon is once again privileged to include original artwork from Gateway Crafts. These works, which are paintings and sculpture, appear on the cover and in the chapter openers. In the chapter openers, a brief biography of each artist appears below the painting or sculpture. All of the artists are people with disabilities. The artists chosen for this edition have shown their work throughout the United States and abroad.

Gateway Crafts in Brookline, Massachusetts, is a vocational art service of the nonprofit organization, Vinfen. Adults with developmental and other disabilities attend the program, which has an on-site crafts store and gallery. Gateway participants receive funding from the Massachusetts Department of Mental Retardation, the Massachusetts Rehabilitation Commission, the Massachusetts Department of Mental Health, the Massachusetts Commission for the Blind, the Perkins School for the Blind, and private funding sources.

Exceptional
Learners

cathy
anderson

Untitled (Stairways). Ink, watercolor on paper. 25 x 24 in.

Cathy Anderson died in December 1995 when she was only 29 years old. Her work
has been exhibited at The Gateway Gallery, The Clark Gallery, and Brandeis University
in Massachusetts. In New York her work has been shown at the Outsider Art Fair and Bridges
and Bodell Gallery. She has also shown at the Very Special Arts Gallery in Washington, DC.
She won an award from the Royal Society for Mentally Handicapped Children and Adults in
London, England and from The Ebensburg Center in Pennsylvania. In 1996, her work was
featured in an exhibition at the Fuller Museum of Art called: From the Outside In.

Exceptionality and Special Education

Only the brave dare look
    upon the gray—
upon the things which
    cannot be explained easily,
upon the things which often
    engender mistakes,
upon the things whose cause
    cannot be understood,
upon the things we must
    accept and live with.
And therefore only the brave
    dare look upon difference
without flinching.

RICHARD H. HUNGERFORD
"On Locusts"

The study of exceptional learners is the study of *differences*. The exceptional learner is different in some way from the average. In very simple terms, such a person may have problems or special talents in thinking, seeing, hearing, speaking, socializing, or moving. More often than not, he or she has a combination of special abilities or disabilities. Today, over five million such different learners have been identified in public schools throughout the United States. About one out of every ten students in U.S. schools is considered exceptional. The fact that even many so-called normal students also have school-related problems makes the study of exceptionality very demanding.

The study of exceptional learners is also the study of *similarities*. Exceptional individuals are not different from the average in every way. In fact, most exceptional learners are average in more ways than they are not. Until recently, professionals and laypeople as well, tended to focus on the differences between exceptional and nonexceptional learners, almost to the exclusion of the ways in which all individuals are alike. Today, we give more attention to what exceptional and nonexceptional learners have in common—to similarities in their characteristics, needs, and ways of learning. As a result, the study of exceptional learners has become more complex, and many so-called facts about children and youths with disabilities and those who have special gifts or talents have been challenged.

Students of one of the "hard" sciences may boast of the difficulty of the subject matter because of the many facts they must remember and piece together. The plight of students of special education is quite different. To be sure, they study facts, but the facts are relatively few compared to the unanswered questions. Any study of human beings must take into account inherent ambiguities, inconsistencies, and unknowns. In the case of the individual who deviates from the norm, we must multiply all the mysteries of normal human behavior and development by those pertaining to the person's exceptionalities. Because there is no single accepted theory of normal development, it is not at all surprising that relatively few definite statements can be made about exceptional learners.

There are, however, patches of sunshine in the bleak gray painted by Hungerford (see p. 2). It is true that in the vast majority of cases we are unable to identify the exact reason why a person is exceptional, but progress is being made in determining the causes of some disabilities. In a later chapter, for example, we discuss the detection of causal factors in

The goal of special education is to prepare individuals with disabilities for success and a high quality of life in mainstream society. This woman with several disabilities is a highly successful painter.

misconceptions about Exceptional Children

myth Public schools may choose not to provide education for some students with disabilities.	**fact** Federal legislation specifies that to receive federal funds, every school system must provide a free, appropriate education for every student regardless of any disabling condition.
myth By law, the student with a disability must be placed in the least restrictive environment (LRE). The LRE is always the regular classroom.	**fact** The law does require the student with a disability to be placed in the LRE. However, the LRE is *not* always the regular classroom. What the LRE does mean is that the student shall be separated as little as possible from home, family, community, and the regular class setting while appropriate education is provided. In many but not all instances, this will mean placement in the regular classroom.
myth The causes of most disabilities are known, but little is known about how to help individuals overcome or compensate for their disabilities.	**fact** In most cases, the causes of disabilities are not known, although progress is being made in pinpointing why many disabilities occur. More is known about the treatment of most disabilities than about their causes.
myth People with disabilities are just like everyone else.	**fact** First, no two people are exactly alike. People with disabilities, just like everyone else, are unique individuals. Most of their abilities are much like those of the average person who is not considered to have a disability. Nevertheless, a disability is a characteristic not shared by most people. It is important that disabilities be recognized for what they are, but individuals with disabilities must be seen as having many abilities—other characteristics that they share with the majority of people.
myth A disability is a handicap.	**fact** A *disability* is an inability to do something, the lack of a specific capacity. A *handicap*, on the other hand, is a disadvantage that is imposed on an individual. A disability may or may not be a handicap, depending on the circumstances. For example, the inability to walk is not a handicap in learning to read, but it can be a handicap in getting into the stands at a ball game. Sometimes handicaps are needlessly imposed on people with disabilities. For example, a student who cannot write with a pen but can use a typewriter or word processor would be needlessly handicapped without such equipment.

Down syndrome—a condition resulting in the largest number of children classified as having moderate mental retardation. Likewise, the incidence of **retinopathy of prematurity (ROP)**—at one time a leading cause of blindness—has been greatly reduced since the discovery of its cause. The cause of mental retardation associated with a metabolic disorder—**phenylketonuria (PKU)**—has been discovered. Soon after birth, infants are now routinely tested for PKU so that mental retardation can be prevented if they should have the disorder. More recently, the gene responsible for cystic fibrosis, an inherited disease characterized by chronic respiratory and digestive problems, has been identified. And in the future, the specific genes governing many other diseases and disorders will also likely be located. The location of such genes raises the possibility of gene therapy to prevent or correct many disabling conditions.

Besides these and other medical breakthroughs, research is bringing us a more complete understanding of the ways in which the individual's psychological, social, and educational environments are related to learning. For example, special educators, psychologists, and pediatricians are increasingly able to identify environmental conditions that increase the likelihood that a child will have learning or behavior problems (Hart & Risley, 1995; Patterson, Reid, & Dishion, 1992; Werner, 1986).

Educational methodology has also made strides. In fact, compared to what we know about causes, we know a lot about how exceptional learners can be taught and managed effectively in the classroom. Although special educators constantly lament that all the questions have not been answered, we do know considerably more today about how to educate exceptional learners than we did ten or fifteen years ago.

Before moving to the specific subject of exceptional learners, we must point out that we vehemently disagree with Hungerford on an important point: We must certainly learn to live with disabling exceptionalities, but we must never accept them. We prefer to think there is hope for the eventual eradication of many of the disabling forms of exceptionality. In addition, we believe it is of paramount importance to realize that even individuals whose exceptionalities are extreme can be helped to lead fuller lives than they would without appropriate education.

We must not let people's *disabilities* keep us from recognizing their *abilities*. Many people with disabilities have abilities that go unrecognized because their disabilities become the focus of our concern and we do not give enough attention to what they *can* do. We must study the disabilities of exceptional children and youths if we are to learn how to help them make maximum use of their abilities in school. Some students with disabilities that are not obvious to the casual observer need special programs of education and related services to help them live full, happy, productive lives. However, we must not lose sight of the fact that *the most important characteristics of exceptional learners are their abilities*.

Most exceptional individuals have disabilities, and they have often been referred to as "handicapped" in laws, regulations, and everyday conversations. In this book, we make an important distinction between *disability* and *handicap*. A disability is an inability to do something, a diminished capacity to perform in a specific way. A handicap, on the other hand, is a disadvantage imposed on an individual. Thus, a disability may or may not be a handicap, depending on the circumstances. Likewise, a handicap may or may not be caused by a disability.

For example, blindness is a disability that can be anything but a handicap in the dark. In fact, in the dark, the person who has sight is the one who is handicapped. Needing to use a wheelchair may be a handicap in certain circumstances,

retinopathy of prematurity (ROP). Formerly referred to as *retrolental fibroplasia;* a condition resulting from administration of an excessive concentration of oxygen at birth; causes scar tissue to form behind the lens of the eye.

phenylketonuria (PKU). A metabolic genetic disorder caused by the inability of the body to convert phenylalanine to tyrosine; an accumulation of phenylalanine results in abnormal brain development.

One major challenge for special education is to teach individuals with disabilities—as well as those around them—to focus on abilities: what they can do as opposed to what they cannot.

but the disadvantage may be a result of architectural barriers or other people's reactions, not the inability to walk. Others can handicap people who are different from them (in color, size, appearance, language, and so on) by stereotyping them or not giving them opportunities to do the things they are able to do. When working and living with exceptional individuals who have disabilities, we must constantly strive to separate their disabilities from the handicaps. That is, our goal should be to confine their handicaps to those characteristics and circumstances that cannot be changed, and to make sure that we impose no further handicaps by our attitudes or our unwillingness to accommodate their disabilities.

Educational Definition of Exceptional Learners

For purposes of their education, *exceptional learners are those who require special education and related services if they are to realize their full human potential.* They require special education because they are markedly different from most students in one or more of the following ways: They may have mental retardation, learning disabilities, emotional or behavioral disorders, physical disabilities, disorders of communication, autism, traumatic brain injury, impaired hearing, impaired sight, or special gifts or talents. In the chapters that follow, we define as exactly as possible what it means to have an exceptionality.

Two concepts are important to our educational definition of exceptional learners: (1) diversity of characteristics and (2) need for special education. The concept of diversity is inherent in the definition of exceptionality; the need for special education is inherent in an educational definition.

Consider the case of Kathy Buckley, described in the box on page 9. Kathy obviously has a disability, but her deafness was at one time misdiagnosed as mental retardation. She needed special instruction, but not because her intelligence was impaired. She achieved success in spite of the fact that she received inappropriate education, but such success does not usually come to students with disabilities who do not get special education that is appropriate to their needs. Subsequent cases portray the more typical outcomes of failure to identify students' disabilities and provide appropriate special education. Kathy's experiences illustrate the need for accurate assessment of school problems and the importance of facing the fact of a disability rather than denying it. Her story also illustrates a matter we discuss further in Chapter 2—how some persons with disabilities use their keen wit to break down stereotypes through humor.

Sometimes seemingly obvious disabilities are never identified, and the consequences for the person and his or her family, as well as the larger society, are tragic. Sometimes disabilities are identified but special education is not provided, squandering opportunities for the child's development. The box on page 10 describes two such cases. In spite of federal laws requiring appropriate education and the existence of a special education system, Willie and Anthony received no special education at all or extremely poor special education services. The consequences of the neglect of their need for special education are profoundly negative. Although early identification and intervention hold the promise of preventing many disabilities from becoming worse, preventive action is often not taken (Kauffman, 1999b).

When special education works as it should, a student's disability is identified early and effective special education is provided in the least restrictive environment. The student's parents are involved in the decision about how to address the student's needs, and the outcome of special education is the student's improved achievement and behavior. Consider the case of Alice, presented in the box on page 11.

Students with exceptionalities are an extraordinarily diverse group compared to the general population, and relatively few generalizations apply to all exceptional individuals. Their exceptionalities may involve sensory, physical, cognitive, emotional, or communication abilities or any combination of these. Furthermore, exceptionalities may vary greatly in cause, degree, and effect on educational progress, and the effects may vary greatly depending on the individual's age, sex, and life circumstances. Any individual we might present as an example of our definition is likely to be representative of exceptional learners in some respects but unrepresentative in others.

The *typical* student who receives special education has no immediately obvious disability. He—more than half of the students served by special education are males—is in elementary or middle school and has persistent problems in learning and behaving appropriately in school. His problems are primarily academic and social or behavioral. These difficulties are not apparent to many teachers until they have worked with the student for a period of weeks or months. His problems persist despite teachers' efforts to meet his needs in the regular school program in which most students succeed. He is most likely to be described as having a learning disability or to be designated by an even broader label indicating that his academic and social progress in school are unsatisfactory due to a disability.

By federal law, an exceptional student is not to be identified as eligible for special education until careful assessment indicates that he or she is unable to make satisfactory progress in the regular school program without special services designed to meet his or her extraordinary needs. Federal special education laws and

Laughing Out Loud: Turning a Deaf Ear to Comedy

When it comes to comedy, Kathy Buckley takes center stage. Billed as "America's First Hearing Impaired Comedienne," she was nominated "Best Female Stand-Up Comedienne" for the 1997 American Comedy Awards, the third year in a row Buckley has made the award list.

On a Wing and a Dare

Buckley never aspired to be a comedienne. "I didn't know what I wanted to do," she says. "I wanted to be a nurse when I was a kid, but because of my hearing impairment they said I couldn't." Actually, her performing career started almost by accident.

"I did it on a dare," Buckley admits, speaking of the first time she performed on stage. It was in 1988 at a charity benefit called "Stand-up Comics Take a Stand" in Encino, California. "I was a nervous wreck," she admits. Even though she could not hear the audience's laughter except by feeling the stage floor vibrations, Buckley says what really made her nervous was competing against other comedians with years of experience. Despite that, she won fourth place.

Since then Kathy Buckley has turned the comedy world "on its ear." She is popular at "Catch a Rising Star" in Las Vegas, "The Improv" and "The Comedy Store" in Hollywood, and has appeared several times on HBO comedy specials and such television shows as "The Tonight Show Starring Jay Leno," "The Howard Stern Show," and "Phil Donahue." Much of her comic material is based on her hearing loss.

Kathy Buckley's Humor

On personal relationships: "I haven't had a date in over two and a half years. I don't know if it's just me or because I couldn't hear the phone ring."

On hearing: "One of the first sounds I ever heard were the birds, and I thought 'Birds are hard to lip read, they've got these tiny little beaks!'"

On rehabilitation: "I spent 13 years learning how to talk, and now everyone thinks I'm from New York."

On celebrities: Howard Stern asked me if I would consider dating a man who had a disability and I said, 'Sure, I'd consider dating you.'"

On intimacy: "I love it when a man kisses me on the neck. When he sticks his tongue in my ear he gets electrocuted."

Childhood Diagnosis

Buckley says it is wonderful how parents have learned to embrace a child's disability. She was not so lucky as a child. Her own parents never questioned their daughter's hearing impairment and could not accept that she had a disability.

Buckley recalls the years it took teachers and administrators to realize she was deaf. Her grades were poor; there seemed no way to stimulate her academically. "People weren't educated then," she says. "My parents just did what the doctor told them and never asked any questions." What they were told was to put Buckley in a school for children with mental retardation. It took almost a year after that before doctors realized her disability. "And they called *me* slow?" she laughs.

"My parents went into denial that I even had a problem. The doctors saw I had a problem, but told my parents that this or that device would 'fix' me. I ended up in denial as well because no one ever talked to me about it." Buckley says it was not until she was 34 years old that a specialist explained her condition to her. "It was the first time anyone had talked to me about it."

"You cannot bond or love unconditionally in denial," Kathy says. "The best gift parents can give their children is joy. Teach that to your children."

Embracing Individuality

"My comedy disarms people. I truly believe that the only disability out there today is attitude," she says. "I love to make people laugh, but I love even more if I can teach them something at the same time."

And that is just what she does. In her nightly performances she jokes about what it is like to be hearing impaired and about how others treat her. She performs for many charity events and benefits.

Buckley says that although she tries to entertain and enlighten all kinds of people, her heart belongs to children. "Kids mean everything to me," she says. "Every single child deserves to have a real childhood, and they should have healthy role models to show them that people do care about them deeply."

Source: D'Agostino, D. (1997). Laughing out loud: Turning a deaf ear to comedy. *Exceptional Parent, 27*(3), 44–45. Reprinted by permission.

regulations include definitions of several conditions (categories such as *learning disability, mental retardation, hearing impairment,* and so on) that might create a need for special education. These laws and regulations require that special services be provided to meet whatever special needs are created by a disabling condition and cannot be met in the regular educational program. They do not require that special education be provided simply because a student has a disability.

Prevalence of Exceptional Learners

Prevalence refers to the percentage of a population or number of individuals having a particular exceptionality. The prevalence of mental retardation, for example, might be estimated at 2.3 percent, which means that 2.3 percent of the population, or twenty-three people in every thousand, are assumed to have mental retardation. If the prevalence of giftedness is assumed to be between 3 percent and 5 percent, we would expect somewhere between thirty and fifty people in a sample of a thousand to have special gifts of some kind. Obviously, accurate estimates of prevalence depend on our ability to count the number of people in a given population who have a certain exceptionality.

Where Needs are Great, the Needs Go Untended:
Failings of Special Ed System Extract a High Price

A lost childhood ago, Willie Williamson was forgotten in the D.C. schools. He flunked kindergarten and first grade. His speech was a muddled slur. He never learned to read. He heard his father kill his brother with a shotgun in the next room. His life cried out for help.

Willie was declared mildly retarded when he was 7, tested again at 10 and then never reevaluated for eight years. He was bumped up from grade to grade. Now 18, angry and illiterate, Willie hides in an overlarge jacket and watches the world with suspicion.

"He was lost in the system," said his guardian, Cynthia Savage. "Nobody cared enough to say, 'We will help this child.'"

Fighting for a Grandson

Rosemary McKinney, like many others, has had to learn the jargon and intricacies of the special education system to try to get D.C. schools to provide proper service for her grandson, Anthony.

Born of a mother who used PCP and other drugs, according to school social worker evaluations, Anthony stuttered badly and had a poor attention span. His grandmother helped get him speech therapy in elementary school. For a while, the system was working.

"He was coming along fine—learning his ABC's and counting real good," McKinney said of the 7-year-old. When she moved to the neighborhood served by Webb Elementary School in Northeast Washington in September, she asked the school to enroll him in its special education class. Seven months later, she found school officials had misplaced Anthony's records.

"They just put him in a regular class and left him there," she said "Now, he writes backwards. He doesn't say anything about school. He's missed a whole year, now. I don't know what's going to happen to him."

A request to school authorities for a response from Webb was not answered.

McKinney, who lives with a son and three grandchildren, is often exhausted by the chore of fighting the schools. "You need a lawyer just to get them to do anything."

Source: Struck, D. (1997, February 19). Where needs are great, the needs go untended: Failings of special ed system extract a high price. *The Washington Post,* A1, A9. ©1997, The Washington Post. Reprinted with permission.

An IEP for Alice: What Can Happen When Special Education Works

Alice's first-grade teacher called about five minutes after the educational planner left my room. Both the first-grade teacher and the educational planner informed me that at the eligibility meeting the day before, it was determined that Alice qualified for services in my class for children with mild mental retardation.

"It would be great if you could write the IEP for Alice soon, so we could have her start right after Christmas," her teacher suggested. "She cries so much. I feel so bad for her. She's no problem, but she just *can't* do the work."

Legally, I had thirty days before an educational plan had to be approved by the parents. It was just a few days before Christmas break, all the kids in the school had decided to have a nervous breakdown, and all the teachers were tired and cranky—especially me. And my aide and I had the added fatigue of trying to insure that all the students in my class received some presents for Christmas. I wasn't keen to add to my stress or my responsibilities. But both the supervisor and the first-grade teacher had pleaded with me to arrange a meeting with the parents as quickly as I could.

I spent the evening reading Alice's psychological folder. She had been in the preschool program for three years. The preceding spring, when there had been an eligibility meeting, the school staff felt Alice qualified for services in my class beginning in September. But the parents felt otherwise. *Retardation* is such a dirty word. The present euphemism "class for children with mild mental disabilities" didn't disguise the fact for the parents that this was what some would call the "dummy class."

The father flatly refused to have her placed in my class. "Alice can do the work. I know she can," he said.

So Alice started out the year with new clothes, a smile, and the fine-motor skills of a two-year-old. And although she was from a loving, attentive family that read to her and paid a lot of attention to her, her skills were seriously delayed compared to the other students in the first grade. It wasn't that she didn't learn. She just took *so much longer* than the other children in her class. Even though Alice participated in the resource program, the speech program, the occupational therapy program (all done in the general education classroom and including other classmates in her lessons), she could not keep up with even the slowest group in her class.

It wasn't long before Alice was asking her mother, "Why can't I do what the other kids do? I *want* to do it." Motivation did not seem to be a problem initially, but after a few months, Alice decided not to try to try. Can't say that I much blame her. After a while, she made her misery known to all, both at home and at school. She became a helpless blob that cried most of the time. Her teacher said, "As far as I know, no one in my class has ever been mean to Alice. She just purely hates school now," she sighed. Alice's mother agreed with the teacher. "I've asked her over and over again if anyone has been mean to her. She says no, and I believe her."

After reading her folder and talking with teachers who worked with Alice, I felt bad for her too. The parents and I wrote an educational plan for Alice, stating that she would begin attending my class after Christmas. Dad still wasn't so sure that he approved, but knew that *something* had to be done. "But you have to promise to push her. She can be really manipulative," he warned.

After a few weeks of Alice's placement in my room, the parents and I met again. They seemed much happier. "Alice enjoys coming to school now," they let me know. The dad, much to his credit, wished that he had not denied her services in the fall. "She feels so much better about herself now," he said.

Two years later, Alice's father and I talked about his reaction to the eligibility meeting (the one deciding that Alice qualified for my services). "There were so many people," he said, "and they were all saying that there was something terribly wrong with my daughter. I wondered who in the hell they were talking about! My pretty little girl is so loving and funny. How could they say she was retarded?"

"Does it matter what label they put on her? Isn't she still a pretty, funny, loving little girl?"

"Yeah," he laughed. "Except now she can read!"

Source: Kauffman, J. M., & Pullen, P. L. (1996). Eight myths about special education. *Focus on Exceptional Chidren, 28*(5), 7–8. Reprinted with permission.

At first thought, the task of determining the number of students who have exceptionalities seems simple enough, yet the prevalence of most exceptionalities is uncertain and a matter of considerable controversy. A number of factors make it hard to say with great accuracy and confidence just how many exceptional individuals there are, including vagueness in definitions, frequent changes in

Figure 1.1

Changes in the distribution of specific disablilities for children ages 6–21 served under IDEA.

Sources: U.S. Department of Education, 1992, p. 9; 1997, pp. II–27.

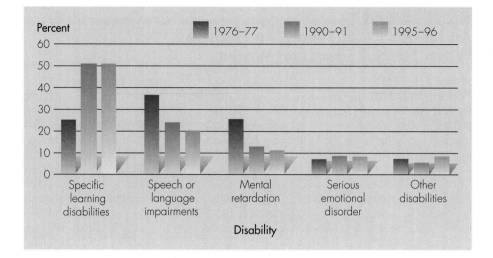

definitions, and the role of schools in determining exceptionality—matters we discuss in later chapters.

Government figures show that about ten students out of every hundred were receiving special education in the late 1990s (U.S. Department of Education, 1998). Beginning in the mid-1970s, there was steady growth in the number of students served by special education, from about 3.75 million in 1976 to about 5 million in the late 1990s. Most of the children and youths served by special education are between the ages of six and seventeen. Although preschoolers and youths eighteen to twenty-one are being identified with increasing frequency as having disabilities, school-age children and youths in their early teens make up the bulk of the identified population.

The distribution of certain disabilities has changed considerably from the mid-1970s to the present. As shown in Figure 1.1, the percentage of students with disabilities in the "specific learning disabilities" category has doubled since the mid-1970s. Figure 1.1 contains data through the 1995–96 school year. The largest increase during the last quarter of the twentieth century was in the percentage categorized as having "specific learning disabilities." In contrast, the percentage of students whose primary disability is "speech or language impairments" has declined substantially, and the percentage identified as having "mental retardation" is now about half of what it was in 1976. No one has an entirely satisfactory explanation of these changes. However, they may in part reflect alterations in definitions and diagnostic criteria for certain disabilities and the social acceptability of the "learning disabilities" label. In subsequent chapters we discuss the prevalence of specific categories of exceptionality.

Definition of Special Education

Special education means specially designed instruction that meets the unusual needs of an exceptional student. Special materials, teaching techniques, or equipment and/or facilities may be required. For example, students with visual impairments may require reading materials in large print or braille; students with hearing impairments may require hearing aids and/or instruction in sign language; those with physical disabilities may need special equipment; those with emotional or behavioral disorders may need smaller and more highly structured classes; and students with special gifts or talents may require access to working professionals. Related services—special transportation, psychological assessment, physical and occupational therapy, medical treatment, and counseling—may be necessary if special education is to be effective. The single most important goal of special education is finding and capitalizing on exceptional students' *abilities*.

Providing Special Education

Several administrative plans are available for the education of exceptional learners, from a few special provisions made by the student's regular teacher to twenty-four-hour residential care in a special facility. Who educates exceptional students and where they receive their education depends on two factors: (1) how and how much the student differs from average students, and (2) what resources are available in the school and community. We describe various administrative plans for education according to the degree of physical integration—the extent to which exceptional and nonexceptional students are taught in the same place by the same teachers.

Beginning with the most integrated intervention, the *regular classroom teacher* who is aware of the individual needs of students and skilled at meeting them may be able to acquire appropriate materials, equipment, and/or instructional methods.

Individuals with disabilities are as diverse a group as any other; thus, a major emphasis of special education is to tailor services to meet individual needs.

At this level, the direct services of specialists may not be required—the expertise of the regular teacher may meet the student's needs.

At the next level, the regular classroom teacher may need consultation with a *special educator* or other professional (e.g., school psychologist) in addition to acquiring the special materials, equipment, or methods. The special educator may instruct the regular teacher, refer the teacher to other resources, or demonstrate the use of materials, equipment, or methods.

Going a step further, a special educator may provide *itinerant services* to the exceptional student and/or the regular classroom teacher. The itinerant teacher establishes a consistent schedule, moving from school to school and visiting classrooms to instruct students individually or in small groups. This teacher provides materials and teaching suggestions for the regular teacher to carry out and consults with the regular teacher about special problems.

At the next level, a *resource teacher* provides services for the students and teachers in only one school. The students being served are enrolled in the regular classroom and are seen by the specially trained teacher for a length of time and at a frequency determined by the nature and severity of their particular problems. The resource teacher continually assesses the needs of the students and their teachers, and usually works with students individually or in small groups in a special classroom where special materials and equipment are available. Typically, the resource teacher serves as a consultant to the regular classroom teacher, advising on the instruction and management of the student in the classroom and perhaps demonstrating instructional techniques. The flexibility of the plan and the fact that the student remains with nondisabled peers most of the time make this a particularly attractive and popular alternative.

Diagnostic-prescriptive centers go beyond the level of intervention represented by resource teachers and rooms. In this plan, students are placed for a short time in a special class in a school or other facility so their needs can be assessed and a plan of action can be determined on the basis of diagnostic findings. After an educational prescription has been written for the pupil, the recommendations for placement may include anything from institutional care to placement in a regular classroom with a particularly competent teacher who can carry out the plan.

Hospital or homebound instruction is most often required by students who have physical disabilities, although it is sometimes employed for those with emotional or behavioral disorders or other disabilities when no alternative is readily available. Typically, the youngster is confined to the hospital or the home for a relatively short time, and the hospital or homebound teacher maintains contact with the regular teacher.

One of the most visible—and in recent years, controversial—service alternatives is the special *self-contained class*. Such a class typically enrolls fifteen or fewer exceptional students with particular characteristics or needs. The teacher ordinarily has been trained as a special educator and provides all or most of the instruction. Those assigned to such classes usually spend most or all of the school day separated from their nondisabled peers. Often students with disabilities are integrated with nondisabled students during part of the day (perhaps for physical education, music, or some other activity in which they can participate well).

Special day schools provide an all-day special placement for exceptional learners. The day school is usually organized for a specific category of exceptional students and may contain special equipment necessary for their care and education. These students return to their homes during nonschool hours.

The final level of intervention is the *residential school*. Here, exceptional students receive twenty-four-hour care away from home, often at a distance from their communities. These children and youths may make periodic visits home or return each weekend, but during the week they are residents of the institution, where they receive academic instruction in addition to management of their daily living environment.

The major features of each type of placement or service alternative, examples of the types of students most likely to be served in each, and the primary roles of the special educators who work with them are shown in Table 1.1 (pp. 16 and 17). Note that although these are the major administrative plans for delivery of special education, variations are possible. For example, special day schools and residential schools may help students make the transition to regular schools as they are able to return. Many school systems, in the process of trying to find more effective and economical ways of serving exceptional students, combine or alter these alternatives and the roles special educators and other professionals play in service delivery. Furthermore, the types of students listed under each service alternative are *examples only;* there are wide variations among school systems in the kinds of placements made for particular kinds of students. Note also that what any special education teacher may be expected to do includes a variety of items not specified in Table 1.1. We discuss these expectations for teachers in the following section.

As noted earlier, special education law requires placement of the student in the **least restrictive environment (LRE).** What is usually meant is that the student should be separated from nondisabled classmates and from home, family, and community as little as possible. That is, his or her life should be as normal as possible, and the intervention should be consistent with individual needs and not interfere with individual freedom any more than is absolutely necessary. For example, students should not be placed in special classes if they can be served adequately by resource teachers, and they should not be placed in institutions if a special class will serve their needs just as well.

Although this movement toward placement of exceptional students in the least restrictive environment is laudable, the definition of *least restrictive* is not as simple as it seems. Cruickshank (1977) has pointed out that greater restriction of the physical environment does not necessarily mean greater restriction of psychological freedom or human potential. In fact, it is conceivable that some students could be more restricted in the long run in a regular class where they are rejected by others and fail to learn necessary skills than in a special class or day school where they learn happily and well. It is important to keep the ultimate goals for the students in mind and to avoid letting "least restrictive" become a hollow slogan that results in shortchanging them in their education (Crockett & Kauffman, 1999; Kauffman, 1995). As Morse has noted, "The goal should be to find the most productive setting to provide the maximum assistance for the child" (1984, p. 120).

Although considerable variation in the placement of students with disabilities is found from state to state and among school systems within a given state, most exceptional students are educated in regular classes. Nationwide, over 40 percent of exceptional children and youths are served primarily in regular classes. Most of these students receive special instruction for part of the school day from special education resource teachers. In the United States, about one-fourth of all students in special education spend most of their school day in a resource room. Most of these students spend a significant part of their school day in regular classes. Slightly over 20 percent of all children and youths with disabilities are placed in

least restrictive environment (LRE). A legal term referring to the fact that exceptional children must be educated in as normal an environment as possible.

Table 1.1 Examples of Service Alternatives for Special Education

Most Physically Integrated ◄──────────────────────────────────►

Type of Placement	Regular Class Only	Special Educator Consultation	Itinerant Teacher	Resource Teacher
Major features of placement alternatives	Regular teacher meets all needs of student; student may not be officially identified or labeled; student totally integrated	Regular teacher meets all needs of student with only occasional help from special education consultant(s); student may not be officially identified or labeled; student totally integrated	Regular teacher provides most or all instruction; special teacher provides intermittent instruction of student and/or consultation with regular teacher; student integrated except for brief instructional sessions	Regular teacher provides most instruction; special teacher provides instruction part of school day and advises regular teacher; student integrated most of school day
Types of students typically served	Student with mild learning disability, emotional/behavioral disorder, or mild mental retardation; student with physical disability	Student with mild learning disability, emotional/behavioral disorder, or mild mental retardation	Student with visual impairment or physical disability; student with communication disorder	Student with mild to moderate emotional/behavioral, learning, or communication disorder or hearing impairment
Primary role of special education teacher	None	To offer demonstration and instruction and to assist regular class teacher as requested	To visit classroom regularly and see that appropriate instruction, materials, and other services are provided; to offer consultation, demonstration, and referral for regular teacher and assessment and instruction of student as needed; to work toward total integration of student	To assess student's needs for instruction and management; to provide individual or small-group instruction on set schedule in regular class or resource room; to offer advice and demonstration for regular teacher; to handle referral to other agencies for additional services; to work toward total integration of student

separate special classes, and many of these students are mainstreamed into regular classes for some part of the school day. Only about 5 percent are placed in separate schools or other special environments (e.g., residential facilities, hospital schools, and homebound instruction; see Figure 1.2 on p. 18). Since the late 1980s, there has been a steady trend toward placing more students with disabilities in regular classes and a corresponding trend toward placing fewer students with disabilities in resource rooms, separate classes, and separate facilities (U.S. Department of Education, 1995, 1997). Placing more students in regular classes and schools reflects educational reform in the 1990s, a topic to which we return later in this chapter and in Chapter 2.

Least Physically Integrated →

Diagnostic-Prescriptive Center	Hospital or Homebound Instruction	Self-Contained Class	Special Day School	Residential School
Special teacher in center provides most or all instruction for several days or weeks and develops plan or prescription for regular or special education teacher; following diagnosis and prescription, student may be partially or totally integrated into regular school or class	Special teacher provides all instruction in hospital or home until student is able to return to usual school classes (regular or special) from which he or she has been temporarily withdrawn; student totally separated from regular school for short period	Special teacher provides most or all instruction in special class of students; regular teacher may provide instruction in regular class for part of school day; student mostly or totally separated from regular class	Special teacher provides instruction in separate school; also may work with teachers in regular or special classes of regular school; student totally or mostly separated from regular school	Same as special day school; special teacher also works with other staff to provide a total therapeutic environment or milieu; student totally or mostly in special setting
Student with mild disability who has been receiving no services or inadequate services	Student with physical disability; student undergoing treatment or medical tests	Student with moderate to severe mental retardation or emotional/behavioral disorder	Student with severe or profound physical or mental disability	Student with severe or profound mental retardation or emotional/behavioral disorder
To make comprehensive assessment of student's educational strengths and weaknesses; to develop written prescription for instruction and behavior management for receiving teacher; to interpret prescription for receiving teacher and assess and revise prescription as needed	To obtain records from student's school of attendance; to maintain contact with teachers (regular or special) and offer instruction consistent with student's school program; to prepare student for return to school (special or regular)	To manage and teach special class; to offer instruction in most areas of curriculum; to work toward integration of students in regular classes	To manage and teach individuals and/or small groups of students with disabilities; to work toward integration of students in regular school	Same as special day school; also to work with residential staff to make certain school program is integrated appropriately with nonschool activities

Children under the age of six less often receive education in regular classes, and more often attend separate schools than do children who have reached the usual school age. Special classes, separate schools, and other environments such as homebound instruction are used more often for older teenagers and young adults than for students of elementary and high school age. We can explain these differences by several facts:

1. Preschoolers and young adults who are identified for special education tend to have more severe disabilities than students in kindergarten through grade 12.

Figure 1.2

Percentage of students with disabilities ages 6–21 served in each educational environment: 1990–91 to 1994–95

Source: U.S. Department of Education, Office of Special Education Programs, Data Analysis System (DANS).

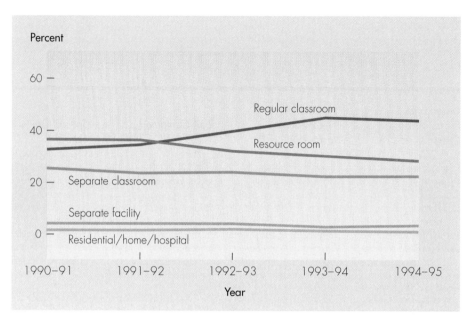

2. Some school systems do not have regular classes for preschoolers and young adults, and thus placements in other than regular classes are typically more available and more appropriate.
3. Curriculum and work-related educational programs for older teens and young adults with disabilities are frequently offered off the campuses of regular high schools.

The environment that is least restrictive depends in part on the individual's exceptionality. There is almost never a need to place in a separate class or separate school a student whose primary disability is a speech impairment. Likewise, most students with learning disabilities can be appropriately educated primarily in regular classes. On the other hand, the resources needed to teach students with severe impairments of hearing and vision may require that they attend separate schools or classes for at least part of their school careers.

Teachers' Roles

We have noted that most students in public schools who have been identified as exceptional are placed in regular classrooms for at least part of the school day. Furthermore, there is good reason to believe that a large number of public school students not identified as disabled or gifted share many of the characteristics of those who are exceptional. Thus, all teachers must obviously be prepared to deal with exceptional students.

The roles of general and special education teachers are not always clear in a given case. Sometimes uncertainty about the division of responsibility can be extremely stressful; for example, teachers may feel uneasy because it is not clear whose job it is to make special adaptations for a pupil or just what they are expected to do in cooperating with other teachers.

Relationship Between General and Special Education

During the 1980s, the relationship between general and special education became a matter of great concern to policymakers, researchers, and advocates for exceptional children. Proposals for changing the relationship between general and special education, including radical calls to restructure or merge the two, came to be known in the 1980s as the **regular education initiative (REI)**. In the 1990s, reform proposals have been called the **inclusive schools movement.** Moderate proponents of reform suggest that general educators take more responsibility for many students with mild or moderate disabilities, with special educators serving more as consultants or resources to regular classroom teachers and less as special teachers. More radical reformers recommend that special education be eliminated as a separate, identifiable part of education. They call for a single, unified educational system in which all students are viewed as unique and special and entitled to the same quality of education. Although many of the suggested reforms have great appeal and some could produce benefits for exceptional students, the basis for the integration of special and general education and the ultimate consequences they might bring have been questioned (Fuchs & Fuchs, 1994; Kauffman, 1995; Lloyd, Singh, & Repp, 1991; Martin, 1995).

One reason behind reform proposals is concern for pupils who are considered at risk. *At risk* is often not clearly defined, but it generally refers to students who perform or behave poorly in school and appear likely to fail or fall far short of their potential. Some advocates of reform suggest that at-risk students cannot be or should not be distinguished from those with mild disabilities. Others argue that the problems of at-risk students tend to be ignored because special education siphons resources from general education. Should special education and general education merge for the purpose of making general education better able to respond to students at risk? Or should special education maintain its separate identity and be expanded to include these students? Should general education be expected to develop new programs for at-risk students without merging with special education? There are no ready answers to these and other questions about the education of students at risk.

We discuss inclusion and its implications further in Chapter 2. Regardless of one's views, the controversy about the relationship between special and general education has made teachers more aware of the problems of deciding just which students should be taught specific curricula, which students should receive special attention or services, and where and by whom these should be provided (Kauffman & Hallahan, 1995, 1997; Ysseldyke, Algozzine, & Thurlow, 1992). There are no pat answers to the questions about how special and general education should work together to see that every student receives an appropriate education. Yet it is clear that the relationship between them must be one of cooperation and collaboration. They must not become independent or mutually exclusive educational tracks. Neither can we deny that general and special educators have somewhat different roles to play. With this in mind, we summarize some of the major expectations for all teachers, and for special education teachers in particular.

regular education initiative (REI). A philosophy that maintains that general education, rather than special education, should be primarily responsible for the education of students with disabilities.

inclusive schools movement. A reform movement designed to restructure general education schools and classrooms so they better accommodate all students, including those with disabilities.

Expectations for All Educators

Regardless of whether a teacher is specifically trained in special education, he or she may be expected to participate in educating exceptional students in any one of the following ways:

1. *Make maximum effort to accommodate individual students' needs.* Teaching in public schools requires dealing with diverse students in every class. All teachers must make an effort to meet the needs of individuals who may differ in some way from the average or typical student. Flexibility, adaptation, accommodation, and special attention are to be expected of every teacher. Special education should be considered necessary only when a teacher's best efforts to meet a student's individual needs are not successful.

2. *Evaluate academic abilities and disabilities.* Although a psychologist or other special school personnel may give a student formal standardized tests in academic areas, adequate evaluation requires the teacher's assessment of the student's performance in the classroom. Teachers must be able to report specifically and precisely how students can and cannot perform in all academic areas for which they are responsible.

3. *Refer for evaluation.* By law, all public school systems must make extensive efforts to screen and identify all children and youths of school age who have disabilities. Teachers must observe students' behavior and refer those they suspect of having disabilities for evaluation by a multidisciplinary team. *We stress here that a student should not be referred for special education unless extensive and unsuccessful efforts have been made to accommodate his or her needs in regular classes. Before referral, school personnel must document the strategies that have been used to teach and manage the student in general education. Referral is justified only if these strategies have failed.* (See the box on p. 21.)

4. *Participate in eligibility conferences.* Before a student is provided special education, his or her eligibility must be determined by an interdisciplinary

Special education referrals very often begin with the recommendations of general education teachers.

What Should I Do Before I Make a Referral?

If you are thinking about referring a student, probably the most important thing you should do is contact his or her parents. If you cannot reach them by phone, try a home visit or ask the visiting teacher (or school social worker, psychologist, or other support personnel) to help you set up a conference. It is very important that you discuss the student's problems with the parents *before* you refer. Parents should never be surprised to find that their child has been referred; they should know well in advance that their child's teachers have noticed problems. One of the most important things you can do to prevent conflict with parents is to establish and maintain communication with them regarding their child's progress.

Before making a referral, check *all* the student's school records. Look for information that could help you understand the student's behavioral or academic problems.

Has the student ever:

- Had a psychological evaluation?
- Qualified for special services?
- Been included in other special programs (e.g., programs for disadvantaged children or speech or language therapy)?
- Scored far below average on standardized tests?
- Been retained?

Do the records indicate:

- Good progress in some areas, poor progress in others?
- Any physical or medical problem?
- That the student is taking medication?

Talk to the student's other teachers and professional support personnel about your concern for him or her.

Have other teachers:

- Also had difficulty with the student?
- Found ways of dealing successfully with the student?

The analysis of information obtained in these ways may help you teach and manage the student successfully, or help you justify to the parents why you believe their child may need special education.

Before making a referral, you will be expected to document the strategies that you have used in your class to meet the student's educational needs. Regardless of whether the student is later found to have a disabling condition, your documentation will be useful in the following ways:

1. You will have evidence that will be helpful to or required by the committee of professionals who will evaluate the student.
2. You will be better able to help the student's parents understand that methods used for other students in the class are not adequate for their child.
3. You will have records of successful and/or unsuccessful methods of working with the student that will be useful to you and any other teacher who works with the student in the future.

Your documentation of what you have done may appear to require a lot of paperwork, but careful record keeping will pay off. If the student is causing you serious concern, then you will be wise to demonstrate your concern by keeping written records. Your notes should include items such as the following:

- Exactly what you are concerned about
- Why you are concerned about it
- Dates, places, and times you have observed the problem
- Precisely what you have done to try to resolve the problem
- Who, if anyone, helped you devise the plans or strategies you have used
- Evidence that the strategies have been successful or unsuccessful

In summary, make certain that you have accomplished the following before you make a referral:

1. Held at least one conference to discuss your concerns with the parents (or made extensive and documented efforts to communicate with the parents)
2. Checked all available school records and interviewed other professionals involved with the child
3. Documented the academic and behavioral management strategies that you have tried

Remember that you should refer a student only if you can make a convincing case that the student may have a disability and probably cannot be served appropriately without special education. Referral for special education begins a time-consuming, costly, and stressful process that is potentially damaging to the student and has many legal ramifications.

team. Therefore, teachers must be ready to work with other teachers and with professionals from other disciplines (psychology, medicine, or social work, for example) in determining a student's eligibility for special education.

5. *Participate in writing individualized education programs.* A written individualized education program (IEP) must be on file in the records of every student with a disability. Teachers must be ready to participate in a conference (possibly including the student and/or parents, as well as other professionals) in which the program is formulated.

6. *Communicate with parents or guardians.* Parents (sometimes surrogate parents) or guardians must be consulted during the evaluation of their child's eligibility for special education, formulation of the individualized education program, and reassessment of any special program that may be designed for their child. Teachers must contribute to the school's communication with parents about their child's problems, placement, and progress.

7. *Participate in due process hearings and negotiations.* When parents, guardians, or students with disabilities themselves are dissatisfied with the school's response to educational needs, they may request a due-process hearing or negotiations regarding appropriate services. Teachers may be called on to offer observations, opinions, or suggestions in such hearings or negotiations.

8. *Collaborate with other professionals in identifying and making maximum use of exceptional students' abilities.* Finding and implementing solutions to the challenges of educating exceptional students is not the exclusive responsibility of any one professional group. General and special education teachers are expected to share responsibility for educating students with special needs. In addition, teachers may need to collaborate with other professionals, depending on the given student's exceptionality. Psychologists, counselors, physicians, physical therapists, and a variety of other specialists may need teachers' perspectives on students' abilities and disabilities, and they may rely on teachers to implement critical aspects of evaluation or treatment.

A high level of professional competence and ethical judgment is required to conform to these expectations. Teaching demands a thorough knowledge of child development and expertise in instruction. Furthermore, teachers are sometimes faced with serious professional and ethical dilemmas in trying to serve the needs of students and their parents, on the one hand, and in attempting to conform to legal or administrative pressures, on the other (Howe & Miramontes, 1992). For example, when there are indications that a student may have a disability, should the teacher refer that student for evaluation and possible placement in special education, knowing that only inadequate or inappropriate services will be provided? Should a teacher who believes strongly that teenage students with mild retardation need sex education refrain from giving students any information because sex education is not part of the prescribed curriculum and is frowned on by the school board?

Expectations for Special Educators

In addition to being competent enough to meet the preceding expectations, special education teachers must attain special expertise in the following areas:

1. *Academic instruction of students with learning problems.* The majority of students with disabilities have more difficulty learning academic skills

than do those without disabilities. This is true for all categories of disabling conditions because sensory impairments, physical disabilities, and mental or emotional disabilities all tend to make academic learning more difficult. Often, the difficulty is slight; sometimes it is extreme. Special education teachers must have more than patience and hope, though they do need these qualities; they must also have the technical skill to present academic tasks so that students with disabilities will understand and respond appropriately.

2. *Management of serious behavior problems.* Many students with disabilities have behavior problems in addition to their other exceptionalities. Some, in fact, require special education primarily because of their inappropriate or disruptive behavior. Special education teachers must have the ability to deal effectively with more than the usual troublesome behavior of students. Besides understanding and empathy, special education teachers must master the techniques that will allow them to draw out particularly withdrawn students, control those who are hyperaggressive and persistently disruptive, and teach critical social skills. Federal law now requires, in fact, that positive, proactive behavior intervention plans be written for all students who receive special education and exhibit serious behavior problems, regardless of their diagnostic label or classification (Bateman & Linden, 1998; Yell, 1998; Yell & Shriner, 1997).

3. *Use of technological advances.* Technology is increasingly being applied to the problems of teaching exceptional students and improving their daily lives. New devices and methods are rapidly being developed, particularly for students with sensory and physical disabilities. Special education teachers need more than mere awareness of the technology available; they must also be able to evaluate its advantages and disadvantages for teaching the exceptional children and youths with whom they work.

4. *Knowledge of special education law.* For good or ill, special education today involves many details of law. The rights of students with disabilities

Educators today must be prepared to address the needs of both general and special education learners simultaneously.

are spelled out in considerable detail in federal and state legislation. The laws, as well as the rules and regulations that accompany them, are constantly being interpreted by new court decisions, some of which have widespread implications for the practice of special education. Special education teachers do not need to be lawyers, but they do need to be aware of the law's requirements and prohibitions if they are to be adequate advocates for students with disabilities (see Bateman & Linden, 1998; Yell, 1998).

The knowledge and skills that every special education teacher is expected to master have been detailed by the primary professional organization of special educators (Council for Exceptional Children, 1998). We caution here that the specific day-to-day expectations for special education teachers vary from school system to school system and from state to state. What are listed here are the general expectations and areas of competence with which every special educator will necessarily be concerned. Nevertheless, we emphasize that special educators have the responsibility to offer not just good instruction but instruction that is highly individualized, intensive, relentless, urgent, and goal directed (Zigmond & Baker, 1995).

Origins of Special Education

There have always been exceptional learners, but there have not always been special educational services to address their needs. During the closing years of the eighteenth century, following the American and French Revolutions, effective procedures were devised for teaching children with sensory impairments—those who were blind or deaf (Winzer, 1986, 1993). Early in the nineteenth century, the first systematic attempts were made to educate "idiotic" and "insane" children—those who today are said to have mental retardation and emotional or behavioral disorders.

In the prerevolutionary era, the most society had offered children with disabilities was protection—asylum from a cruel world into which they did not fit and in which they could not survive with dignity, if they could survive at all. But as the ideas of democracy, individual freedom, and egalitarianism swept America and France, there was a change in attitude. Political reformers and leaders in medicine and education began to champion the cause of children and adults with disabilities, urging that these "imperfect" or "incomplete" individuals be taught skills that would allow them to become independent, productive citizens. These humanitarian sentiments went beyond a desire to protect and defend people with disabilities. The early leaders sought to normalize exceptional people to the greatest extent possible and confer on them the human dignity they presumably lacked.

The historical roots of special education are found primarily in the early 1800s. Contemporary educational methods for exceptional children can be traced directly to techniques pioneered during that era. And many (perhaps most) of today's vital, controversial issues have been issues ever since the dawn of special education. Some contemporary writers feel that the history of special education is critically important to understanding today's issues and should be given more attention for the lessons we can learn from our past (e.g., Kauffman, 1999a; Smith, 1998a, 1998b). In our discussion of some of the major historical events and trends since 1800, we comment briefly on the history of people and ideas, the growth of the discipline, professional and parent organizations, and legislation.

People and Ideas

Most of the originators of special education were European physicians. They were primarily young, ambitious people who challenged the wisdom of the established authorities, including their own friends and mentors (Kanner, 1964; see also Winzer, 1998).

Jean-Marc-Gaspard Itard
(1775–1838)

Jean-Marc-Gaspard Itard (1775–1838), a French physician who was an authority on diseases of the ear and on the education of students who were deaf, is the person to whom most historians trace the beginning of special education as we know it today. In the early years of the nineteenth century, this young doctor began to educate a boy of about twelve who had been found roaming naked and wild in the forests of France. Itard's mentor, Philippe Pinel (1745–1826), a prominent French physician who was an early advocate of humane treatment of insane persons, advised him that his efforts would be unsuccessful because the boy, Victor, was a "hopeless idiot." But Itard persevered. He did not eliminate Victor's disabilities, but he did dramatically improve the wild child's behavior through patient, systematic educative procedures (Itard, 1962).

Itard's student, Édouard Séguin (1812–1880), immigrated to the United States in 1848. Before that, Séguin had become famous as an educator of so-called idiotic children, even though most thinkers of the day were convinced that such children could not be taught anything of significance.

The ideas of the first special educators were truly revolutionary for their times. These are a few of the revolutionary ideas of Itard, Séguin, and their successors that form the foundation for present-day special education:

- *Individualized instruction,* in which the child's characteristics, rather than prescribed academic content, provide the basis for teaching techniques
- *A carefully sequenced series of educational tasks,* beginning with tasks the child can perform and gradually leading to more complex learning
- *Emphasis on stimulation and awakening of the child's senses,* the aim being to make the child more aware of and responsive to educational stimuli
- *Meticulous arrangement of the child's environment,* so that the structure of the environment and the child's experience of it lead naturally to learning
- *Immediate reward for correct performance,* providing reinforcement for desirable behavior
- *Tutoring in functional skills,* the desire being to make the child as self-sufficient and productive as possible in everyday life
- *Belief that every child should be educated to the greatest extent possible,* the assumption being that every child can improve to some degree

So far we have mentioned only European physicians who figured prominently in the rise of special education. Although it is true that much of the initial work took place in Europe, many U.S. researchers contributed greatly during those early years. They stayed informed of European developments as best they could, some of them traveling to Europe for the specific purpose of obtaining firsthand information about the education of children with disabilities.

Among the young U.S. thinkers concerned with the education of students with disabilities was Samuel Gridley Howe (1801–1876), an 1824 graduate of Harvard Medical School. Besides being a physician and an educator, Howe was a political and social reformer, a champion of humanitarian causes and emancipation. He

Thomas Hopkins Gallaudet
(1787–1851)

was instrumental in founding the Perkins School for the Blind in Watertown, Massachusetts, and was also a teacher of students who were deaf and blind. His success in teaching Laura Bridgman, who was deaf and blind, greatly influenced the education of Helen Keller. In the 1840s, Howe was also a force behind the organization of an experimental school for children with mental retardation and was personally acquainted with Séguin.

When Thomas Hopkins Gallaudet (1787–1851), a minister, was a student at Andover Theological Seminary, he tried to teach a girl who was deaf. He visited Europe to learn about educating the deaf and in 1817 established the first American residential school, in Hartford, Connecticut, for students who were deaf (now known as the American School of the Deaf). Gallaudet University in Washington, D.C., the only liberal-arts college for students who are deaf, was named in his honor.

The early years of special education were vibrant with the pulse of new ideas. It is not possible to read the words of Itard, Séguin, Howe, and their contemporaries without being captivated by the romance, idealism, and excitement of their exploits. The results they achieved were truly remarkable for their era. Today special education remains a vibrant field in which innovations, excitement, idealism, and controversies are the norm. Teachers of exceptional children—and that includes, as discussed earlier, *all* teachers—must understand how and why special education emerged as a discipline.

Growth of the Discipline

Special education did not suddenly spring up as a new discipline, nor did it develop in isolation from other disciplines. The emergence of psychology and sociology, and especially the beginning of the widespread use of mental tests in the early years of the twentieth century, had enormous implications for the growth of special education. Psychologists' study of learning and their prediction of school failure or success by means of tests helped focus attention on children with special needs. Sociologists, social workers, and anthropologists drew attention to the ways in which exceptional children's families and communities responded to them and affected their learning and adjustment. Anecdotal accounts of mental retardation or other mental disabilities can be found in the nineteenth-century literature, but they are not presented within the conceptual frameworks that we recognize today as psychology, sociology, or special education (see, for example, Hallahan & Kauffman, 1977; Kauffman, 1976; Richards & Singer, 1998). Even in the early twentieth century, the concepts of disability seem crude by today's standards (see Trent, 1998).

As the education profession itself matured and as compulsory school attendance laws became a reality, there was a growing realization among teachers and school administrators that a large number of students must be given something beyond the ordinary classroom experience. Elizabeth Farrell, a teacher in New York City in the early part of the century, was highly instrumental in the development of special education as a profession. She and the New York City superintendent of schools attempted to use information about child development, social work, mental testing, and instruction to address the needs of children and youths who were being ill served in or excluded from regular classes and schools. Farrell was a great advocate for services for students with special needs (see Safford & Safford, 1998). Her motives and those of the teachers and administrators who worked with her were to see that every student—including every exceptional child or youth—had an appropriate education and received the related health and social services necessary for optimum learning in school (Hendrick & MacMillan, 1989; MacMillan & Hendrick, 1993). In 1922, Farrell and a group of other special educators from across the United States and Canada founded the Council for Exceptional Children, today still the primary professional organization of special educators.

Contemporary special education is a professional field with roots in several academic disciplines—especially medicine, psychology, sociology, and social work—in addition to professional education. It is a discipline sufficiently different from the mainstream of professional education to require special training programs but sufficiently like the mainstream to maintain a primary concern for schools and teaching.

Professional and Parent Organizations

Individuals and ideas have played crucial roles in the history of special education, but it is accurate to say that much of the progress made over the years has been achieved primarily by the collective efforts of professionals and parents. Professional groups were organized first, beginning in the nineteenth century. Effective national parent organizations have existed in the United States only since 1950.

The earliest professional organizations having some bearing on the education of children with disabilities were medical associations founded in the 1800s. With the organization of the Council for Exceptional Children (CEC) and its many divisions, educators had a professional association devoted to special education. Today the CEC has a national membership of over 50,000, including about 10,000 students. There are state CEC organizations and hundreds of local chapters. Divisions of the CEC have been organized to meet the interests and needs of members who specialize in a particular area.

Although parent organizations offer membership to individuals who do not have exceptional children of their own, they are made up primarily of parents who do have such children and concentrate on issues of special concern to them. Parent organizations have typically served three essential functions: (1) providing an informal group for parents who understand one another's problems and needs and help one another deal with anxieties and frustrations; (2) providing information regarding services and potential resources; and (3) providing the structure for obtaining needed services for their children. Some of the organizations that came about primarily as the result of parents' efforts include the ARC (formerly the Association for Retarded Citizens), the National Association for Gifted Children, the Learning Disabilities Association, the Autism Society of America, and the Federation of Families for Children's Mental Health.

Legislation

Laws have played a major role in the history of special education. In fact, much of the progress in meeting the educational needs of children and youths with disabilities is attributable to laws requiring states and localities to include students with special needs in the public education system. We focus here on recent legislation that represents a culmination of decades of legislative history.

A landmark federal law was passed in 1975, the **Education for All Handicapped Children Act,** also commonly known as PL 94–142.* In 1990 this law was amended to become the **Individuals with Disabilities Education Act (IDEA).** In 1997 the law was amended again, but its name was not changed (see Bateman & Linden, 1998, and Yell, 1998, for details). IDEA ensures that all children and youths with disabilities have the right to a free, appropriate public education.

Another landmark federal law, enacted in 1990, is the **Americans with Disabilities Act (ADA).** ADA ensures the right of individuals with disabilities to nondiscriminatory treatment in other aspects of their lives; it provides protections of civil rights in the specific areas of employment, transportation, public accommodations, state and local government, and telecommunications.

IDEA and another federal law focusing on intervention in early childhood (PL 99–457) now mandate a free, appropriate public education for every child or youth between the ages of three and twenty-one regardless of the nature or severity of the disability he or she may have. PL 99–457 also provides incentives for states to develop early intervention programs for infants with known disabilities and those considered at risk. Together, these laws require public school systems to identify all children and youths with disabilities and to provide the special education and related services they may need.

The law we know today as IDEA was revolutionary. It was the first federal law mandating free, appropriate public education for all children with disabilities. Its basic provisions, as amended in 1997, are described in the box on p. 29.

Education for All Handicapped Children Act (PL 94–142). This federal law contains a mandatory provision stating that to receive funds under the act, every school system in the nation must provide a free, appropriate public education for every child between the ages of three and eighteen (now extended to ages three to twenty-one), regardless of how or how seriously he or she may be disabled.

Individuals with Disabilities Education Act (IDEA). The Individuals with Disabilities Education Act of 1990 and its amendments of 1997; replaced PL 94–142.

Americans with Disabilities Act (ADA). Civil rights legislation for persons with disabilities ensuring nondiscrimination in a broad range of activities.

Trends in Legislation and Litigation

Trends in Legislation

Legislation historically has been increasingly specific and mandatory. In the 1980s, however, the renewed emphasis on states' rights and local autonomy, plus a political strategy of federal deregulation, led to attempts to repeal some of the provisions of IDEA (then still known as PL 94–142) and loosen federal rules and regulations. Federal disinvestment in education and deregulation of education programs were hallmarks of the Reagan administration (Clark & Astuto, 1988; Verstegen & Clark, 1988), so it is not surprising that federal mandates for special education came under fire during that time. Dissatisfaction with federal mandates is due in part to the fact that the federal government contributes relatively little to the funding of special education. Although the demands of IDEA are detailed, state and local governments must pay most of the cost of special education programs. Some have characterized the legal history of special education as a long, strange trip (Yell, Rogers, & Rogers, 1998). Special education law is highly controversial; not surprisingly, Congressional battles over IDEA are ongoing.

---

* Legislation is often designated PL (for public law), followed by a hyphenated numeral, the first set of digits representing the number of the Congress that passed the bill and the second set representing the number of that bill. Thus, PL 94–142 was the 142nd public law passed by the 94th Congress.

Major Provisions of IDEA

	Each state and locality must have a plan to ensure:
Identification	Extensive efforts to screen and identify all children and youths with disabilities.
Free, Appropriate Public Education (FAPE)	Every student with a disability has an appropriate public education at no cost to the parents or guardian.
Due Process	The student's and parents' rights to information and informed consent before the student is evaluated, labeled, or placed, and the right to an impartial due process hearing if they disagree with the school's decisions.
Parent/Guardian Surrogate Consultation	The student's parents or guardian are consulted about the student's evaluation and placement and the educational plan; if the parents or guardian are unknown or unavailable, a surrogate parent must be found to act for the student.
Least Restrictive Environment (LRE)	The student is educated in the least restrictive environment consistent with his or her educational needs and, insofar as possible, with students without disabilities.
Individualized Education Program (IEP)	A written individualized education program is prepared for each student with a disability, including levels of functioning, long- and short-term goals, extent to which the student will *not* participate in the general education classroom and curriculum, services to be provided, plans for initiating and evaluating the services, and needed transition services (from school to work or continued education).
Nondiscriminatory Evaluation	The student is evaluated in all areas of suspected disability and in a way that is not biased by his or her language or cultural characteristics or disabilities. Evaluation must be by a multidisciplinary team, and no single evaluation procedure may be used as the sole criterion for placement or planning.
Confidentiality	The results of evaluation and placement are kept confidential, though the student's parents or guardian may have access to the records.
Personnel Development, Inservice	Training for teachers and other professional personnel, including inservice training for regular teachers, in meeting the needs of students with disabilities.

Detailed federal rules and regulations govern the implementation of each of these major provisions. The definitions of some of these provisions—LRE and nondiscriminatory evaluation, for example—are still being clarified by federal officials and court decisions. See Appendix for summary of IDEA '97 regulatory issues and related web sites.

The amendment and continuation of IDEA in 1997 represented a sustained commitment to require schools, employers, and government agencies to recognize the abilities of people with disabilities. IDEA and ADA (the Americans with Disabilities Act) require reasonable accommodations that will allow those who have disabilities to participate to the fullest extent possible in all the activities of daily living that individuals without disabilities take for granted. The requirements of ADA are intended to grant equal opportunities to people with disabilities in employment, transportation, public accommodations, state and local government, and telecommunications.

Professional Golf, Arguing for Cart Blanche

Three years ago a New York attorney named Philip K. Howard published a spirited book called "The Death of Common Sense." Subtitled "How Law is Suffocating America," it was an analysis of the ways in which laws intended to protect citizens' rights and opportunities have produced unforeseen and, in many cases, undesirable effects. One law that drew his attention was the Americans With Disabilities Act, which Howard cited as an instance in which "rights are handed out once and the legislature, basking in the praise of some group, has no clue about what the consequences will be."

Casey Martin

Most of the act's aftereffects on which Howard focused were bureaucratic, i.e., the expenditure of millions upon millions of dollars to make access to public transit "equal" for all riders and to build wheelchair ramps in places rarely if ever used by the disabled. But as we were reminded last week by the engrossing story of Casey Martin, the law has other repercussions that its framers surely could not have envisioned.

Martin is 25 years old and suffers from Klippel Trenaunay Weber Syndrome, an exceedingly rare congenital abnormality affecting the circulatory system. It usually is limited to one limb—in Martin's case, the right leg—and produces a variety of symptoms and complications. For Martin, who is otherwise vigorous, its chief effect is a severe limitation on his ability to walk.

This would be a painful affliction for anyone. It is all the more so for Martin because for much of his young life he has been a golfer, and an uncommonly good one. At Stanford, where his roommate and teammate was Tiger Woods, Martin played on teams that won and finished second in the National Collegiate Athletic Association championship. To make his way around the course he often used a golf cart.

Now that he is through with college, Martin would like to make golf his livelihood. It is here that complications—as well as the disabilities law—enter the picture. Although Martin has as yet not qualified for the Professional Golfers Association Tour, he is playing on a "satellite"—the equivalent of AAA minor-league baseball—called the Nike Tour. He is doing this over the objections of the PGA which mandates that "players and caddies shall not use automotive transportation," but with the endorsement of a federal magistrate in Oregon (where Martin lives), who ordered the PGA to let him play, riding between shots in a cart, until his suit against the PGA is heard next month.

The case is fascinating on two levels. The first is obvious: It is an irresistible human-interest story. Even the PGA's lawyers acknowledged as much, writing that "plaintiff's golf skills and accomplishments may be notable, even inspirational." One would have to be hardhearted indeed to have been unmoved when Martin not merely competed in a Nike Tour competition in Florida a week ago but actually won it, a victory, as he quite accurately pointed out, proving that "I'm capable of playing out here." Three cheers, and a fourth for good measure.

ADA has been as revolutionary for business in the 1990s as PL 94–142 (now IDEA) was for education when it was enacted in the 1970s. ADA has had great implications for many young adults with disabilities as they have left high school for work or higher education, and for the everyday lives of all individuals with disabilities who live in our communities. Yet ADA has not been without controversy. In fact, the controversy was reflected in a special-issue forum in the *Washington Post* on July 18, 1995, called "Year Five of the ADA" (Taylor, 1995). Some critics of ADA have claimed that it has not lived up to its promise of more employment for people with disabilities, whereas others have described it as too expensive and its regulations as too oppressive to business. To some, support for ADA may seem to come primarily from legislators and people with disabilities.

Unfortunately, there is more to the story than a feel-good rush. The PGA's strictures about golf carts are not frivolous, nor is its insistence that "Congress never intended the [disabilities act] to require a private organization such as the PGA Tour to change the rules of its tournaments to accommodate a would-be participant." The PGA has long felt (and most professional golfers seem to agree) that the approximately five miles a player walks in an 18-hole round are part of the game's challenge and thus must be walked by all competitors. It also argues that it is a private organization that has the right to set its own rules of membership and play.

Obviously there is plenty to be debated in all this. The PGA rule appears to have more to do with keeping carts off the course than with leveling the field of play, though it is true that in certain weather walking can be a test in and of itself. Inasmuch as professional golf is to all intents and purposes controlled by the PGA, whether it is actually a "private" entity is, at the least, open to question. The same goes for the legality of the walking rule, which, depending on one's point of view or interpretation of the law, is either a legitimate regulation of play or an act of discrimination.

The betting here is that the courts will find it the latter, though presumably discrimination of a de facto rather than an intentional character. It is just about impossible to imagine that Congress had professional golf in mind when it debated and passed the disabilities act. But history has shown us that what Congress had in mind can count for precious little when the regulatory bureaucracy and the courts get around to interpreting its legislative actions. If a person cannot be denied access to public transit or pedestrian spaces because of a disability, it is a far from illogical next step to conclude that a person cannot be denied the pursuit of happiness because of one; it is in such pursuit that Casey Martin wants to play professional golf.

If the case does go against the PGA, the game of professional golf almost certainly will go on just as before, except that it will enjoy benefits in public interest and media attention that Casey Martin's career quite certainly will afford it; he would, in his fashion, be "the next Tiger Woods," no doubt to the immense profit of many of the rigid traditionalists who are now trying to keep him in the gallery.

But that, though a likely and far from disagreeable outcome, is not the point. The PGA's basic argument—that the rules of the game should be made not by the courts but by "the governing body of the game"—is sound. The principle has been recognized by the courts in many cases, perhaps the most famous being the Supreme Court ruling in 1922, written by Oliver Wendell Holmes, upholding organized baseball's exemption from antitrust laws and in so doing placing baseball, in effect, above the law.

It will, and should, be pointed out that the PGA could have finessed the entire business by acknowledging that Casey Martin's situation is unique and granting him an exemption to the walking rule. This would have been savvy legal strategy, savvy public relations and—dare the words be said?—good sportsmanship. It chose instead to be rigidly literal-minded in its reading of its own rules; the courts, by contrast, may take their own liberties with the disabilities act. If that's what happens, it will be difficult not to conclude that the PGA dug its own grave.

Source: Yardley, J. (1998, January 19) Professioal golf, arguing for cart blanche. *The Washington Post*, p. C–2. © 1998 The Washington Post. Reprinted with permisssion.

However, a 1995 survey by Louis Harris and the National Organization on Disability (NOD) found overwhelming support for ADA among business owners (Taylor, 1995).

The box above illustrates how some of the arguments about the ADA are played out in individual cases. Casey Martin, a golfer with a physical disability, was able to use a golf cart as a college athlete. However, professional golf competition presented a new challenge for him—a rule that competitors must walk the course, regardless of any disability. The ADA was intended to "level the playing field" for people with disabilities in earning their livelihood and participating in community life. Just where the boundaries of fairness are in making accommodations for disabilities will likely be a matter of continuing controversy.

Martin was eventually allowed to use a golf cart and continue competing professionally, but his opportunity to do so would have been extremely unlikely without the ADA.

Relationship of Litigation to Legislation

Legislation requires or gives permission to provide special education, but it does not necessarily result in what legislators intended. Whether the laws are administered properly is a legal question for the courts. That is, laws may have little or no effect on the lives of individuals with disabilities until courts interpret exactly what the laws require in practice. Exceptional children, primarily through the actions of parent and professional organizations, have been getting their day in court more frequently since IDEA and related federal and state laws were passed. Thus, we must examine trends in litigation to complete the picture of how the U.S. legal system may safeguard or undermine appropriate education for exceptional children.

Trends in Litigation

Zelder (1953) noted that in the early days of public education, school attendance was seen as a privilege that could be awarded or withheld from an individual child at the discretion of local school officials. During the late nineteenth and early twentieth centuries, the courts typically found that disruptive children or those with mental retardation could be excluded from school for the sake of preserving order, protecting the teacher's time from excessive demands, and sparing children the "pain" of seeing others who are disabled. In the first half of the twentieth century, the courts tended to defend the majority of school children from a disabled minority. But now the old excuses for excluding students with disabilities from school are no longer thought to be valid. Today the courts must interpret laws that define school attendance as the *right* of every child, regardless of his or her disability. Litigation is now focused on ensuring that every child receives an education *appropriate for his or her individual needs.*

   Litigation may involve legal suits filed for either of two reasons: (1) because special education services are not being provided for students whose parents want them, or (2) because students are being assigned to special education when their parents believe they should not be. Suits filed *for* special education have been brought primarily by parents whose children are unquestionably disabled and are being denied any education at all or are being given very meager special services. The parents who file these suits believe that the advantages of their children's identification for special education services clearly outweigh the disadvantages. Suits *against* special education have been brought primarily by parents of students who have mild or questionable disabilities and who are already attending school. These parents believe that their children are being stigmatized and discriminated against rather than helped by special education. Thus, the courts today are asked to make decisions in which individual students' characteristics are weighed against specific educational programs.

   Parents want their children with disabilities to have a free public education that meets their needs but does not stigmatize them unnecessarily and that permits them to be taught in the regular school and classroom as much as possible. The laws governing education recognize parents' and students' rights to such an education. In the courts today, the burden of proof is ultimately on local and state education specialists, who must show in every instance that the student's abilities and disabilities have been completely and accurately assessed and that appropriate educational procedures are being employed. Much of the special education litigation has involved controversy over the use of IQ and other standardized testing to determine students' eligibility for special education. Although there has been much acrimony in the debate about IQ tests, some scholars have found that IQ scores themselves have not been the primary means of classifying children as eligible for special education (MacMillan & Forness, 1998).

One historic court case of the 1980s deserves particular consideration. In 1982, the U.S. Supreme Court made its first interpretation of PL 94–142 (now IDEA) in *Hudson v. Rowley,* a case involving Amy Rowley, a child who was deaf. The Court's decision was that appropriate education for a deaf child with a disability does not necessarily mean education that will produce the maximum possible achievement. Amy's parents had contended that she might be able to learn more in school if she were provided with a sign language interpreter. But the Court decided that because the school had designed an individualized program of special services for Amy and she was achieving at or above the level of her nondisabled classmates, the school system had met its obligation under the law to provide an appropriate education. Future cases will undoubtedly help to clarify what the law means by *appropriate education* and *least restrictive environment* (Huefner, 1994; Yell, 1998).

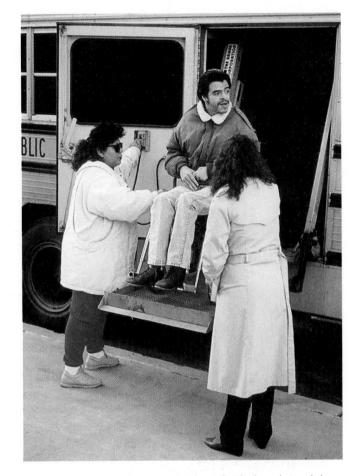

The Individuals with Disabilities Act (IDEA), passed in 1990, and renewed in 1997, requires public schools to provide equal education opportunities for all students with disabilities.

The Intent of Legislation: An Individualized Education Program

The primary intent of the special education laws passed during the past two decades has been to require educators to focus on the needs of individual students with disabilities. The **individualized education program (IEP)** is the most important aspect of this focus; it spells out just what teachers plan to do to meet an exceptional student's needs, and the plan must be approved by the student's parents or guardian. IEPs vary greatly in format and detail and from one school district to another. Some school districts use computerized IEP systems to help teachers determine goals and instructional objectives and to save time and effort in writing the documents. Legally, such cut-and-paste IEPs may be questionable because they lack sufficient attention to the particular needs of individuals (see Bateman & Linden, 1998). Many school systems, however, still rely on teachers' knowledge of students and curriculum to complete handwritten IEPs on the district's forms. Federal and state regulations do not specify exactly how much detail must

individualized education program (IEP). IDEA requires an IEP to be drawn up by the educational team for each exceptional child; the IEP must include a statement of present educational performance, instructional goals, educational services to be provided, and criteria and procedures for determining that the instructional objectives are being met.

Table 1.2 IEP Components	
For All Students:	**For Some Students:**
• Present levels of performance • Measurable goals and objectives • Assessment status • Nonparticipation with nondisabled students • All needed services fully described (amount, frequency, etc.) • Progress reporting	• Transition—including transfer of parental rights to students • Behavior plan • ESL needs • Braille • Communication needs • Assistive technology

Source: Reprinted with permission from Bateman, B. D., & Linden, M. A. (1998). *Better IEPs: How to develop legally correct and educationally useful programs* (3rd ed.). Longmont, CO: Sopris West. All rights reserved.

be included in an IEP, only that it must be a written statement developed in a meeting of a representative of the local school district, the teacher, the parents or guardian, and, whenever appropriate, the child—and that it must include certain elements (see Table 1.2).

The IEPs written in most schools contain much information related to the technical requirements of IDEA in addition to the heart of the plans—their instructional components. Figure 1.3 is an IEP provided by Bateman and Linden (1998). Curt "is a ninth-grade low achiever who was considered by the district to be a poorly motivated disciplinary problem student with a 'bad attitude.' His parents recognized him as a very discouraged, frustrated student who had learning disabilities, especially in language arts" (Bateman & Linden, 1998, p. 126).

As mentioned earlier, there is no standard IEP format used by all schools. An entire IEP may be a document of ten pages or more, depending on the format and the extent and complexity of the student's disabilities. The emphasis should be on writing IEPs that are clear, useful, and legally defensible, not on the IEP format (Bateman & Linden, 1998). Clear and explicit relationships among IEP components are required to make sure that the focus of the individualized program—special, individually tailored instruction to meet unique needs—is not lost. In Curt's IEP (Figure 1.3), the relationships among the components are maintained by the alignment of information across columns. Reading across the form, we first read a description of the unique characteristic or need and present level of performance, then the special services and modifications needed to address that need, and then the annual goals and short-term objectives or benchmarks related to the need.

The process of writing an IEP and the document itself are perhaps the most important features of compliance with the spirit and letter of IDEA. Bateman and Linden (1998) summarize compliance with both the spirit and the letter of the law as the "IDEA Commandments," as shown in Table 1.3 on page 38. When the IEP is prepared as intended by the law, it means that:

- The student's needs have been carefully assessed.
- A team of professionals and the parents have worked together to design a program of education to best meet the student's needs.
- Goals and objectives are clearly stated so that progress in reaching them can be evaluated.

Individualized Education Program

Student: _____Curt_____   Age: __15__   Grade: __9__   Date: __1998__

Unique Educational Needs, Characteristics, and Present Levels of Performance (PLOPs) *(including how the disability affects the student's ability to progress in the general curriculum)*	Special Education, Related Services, Supplemental Aids & Services, Assistive Technology, Program Modifications, Support for Personnel *(including frequency, duration, and location)*	Measurable Annual Goals & Short-Term Objectives or Benchmarks • To enable student to participate in the general curriculum • To meet other needs resulting from the disability *(including how progress toward goals will be measured)*
Present Level of Social Skills: Curt lashes out violently when not able to complete work, uses profanity, and refuses to follow further directions from adults. Social Needs: • To learn anger management skills, especially regarding swearing • To learn to comply with requests	1. Teacher and/or counselor consult with behavior specialist regarding techniques and programs for teaching skills, especially anger management. 2. Provide anger management instruction to Curt. Services 3 times/week, 30 minutes. 3. Establish a peer group which involves role playing, etc., so Curt can see positive role models and practice newly learned anger management skills. Services 2 times/week, 30 minutes. 4. Develop a behavioral plan for Curt which gives him responsibility for charting his own behavior. 5. Provide a teacher or some other adult mentor to spend time with Curt (talking, game playing, physical activity, etc.). Services 2 times/week, 30 minutes. 6. Provide training for the mentor regarding Curt's needs/goals.	<u>Goal:</u> During the last quarter of the academic year, Curt will have 2 or fewer detentions for any reason. Obj. 1: At the end of the 1st quarter, Curt will have had 10 or fewer detentions. Obj. 2: At the end of the 2nd quarter, Curt will have had 7 or fewer detentions. Obj. 3: At the end of the 3rd quarter, Curt will have had 4 or fewer detentions. <u>Goal:</u> Curt will manage his behavior and language in a reasonably acceptable manner as reported by faculty and peers. Obj. 1: At 2 weeks, asked at the end of class if Curt's behavior and language were acceptable or unacceptable, 3 out of 6 teachers will say "acceptable." Obj. 2: At 6 weeks, asked the same question, 4 out of 6 teachers will say "acceptable." Obj. 3: At 12 weeks, asked the same question, 6 out of 6 teachers will say "acceptable." *(continued)*

Figure 1.3

An IEP for Curt.

Source: Reprinted with permission from Bateman, B. D., & Linden, M. A. (1998). *Better IEPs: How to develop legally correct and educationally useful programs* (3rd ed.). Longmont, CO: Sopris West. All rights reserved.

Government regulation of the IEP process has always been controversial. Some of the people who were influential in formulating the basic law (IDEA) have expressed great disappointment in the results of requiring IEPs (Goodman & Bond, 1993, p. 413). Others question whether the requirement of long-term and short-term objectives is appropriate:

> The IEP assumes that instructors know in advance what a child should and can learn, and the speed at which he or she will learn.... This is a difficult projection to make with nondisabled children of school age—for preschool children with cognitive, emotional, and social disabilities, it is near impossible. (Goodman & Bond, 1993, p. 415)

A major problem is that the IEP—the educational *program*—is too often written at the wrong time and for the wrong reason (Bateman & Linden, 1998).

Individualized Education Program (continued)

Unique Educational Needs, Characteristics, and Present Levels of Performance (PLOPs) *(including how the disability affects the student's ability to progress in the general curriculum)*	Special Education, Related Services, Supplemental Aids & Services, Assistive Technology, Program Modifications, Support for Personnel *(including frequency, duration, and location)*	Measurable Annual Goals & Short-Term Objectives or Benchmarks • To enable student to participate in the general curriculum • To meet other needs resulting from the disability *(including how progress toward goals will be measured)*
Study Skills/ Organizational Needs: How to read text Note taking How to study notes Memory work Be prepared for class, with materials Lengthen and improve attention span and on-task behavior **Present Level:** Curt currently lacks skill in all these areas.	1. Speech/lang. therapist, resource room teacher, and content area teachers will provide Curt with direct and specific teaching of study skills, i.e. 　Note taking from lectures 　Note taking while reading text 　How to study notes for a test 　Memorization hints 　Strategies for reading text to retain information 2. Assign a "study buddy" for Curt in each content area class. 3. Prepare a motivation system for Curt to be prepared for class with all necessary materials. 4. Develop a motivational plan to encourage Curt to lengthen his attention span and time on task. 5. Provide aide to monitor on-task behaviors in first month or so of plan and teach Curt self-monitoring techniques. 6. Provide motivational system and self-recording form for completion of academic tasks in each class.	<u>Goal:</u>　At the end of academic year, Curt will have better grades and, by his own report, will have learned new study skills. Obj. 1:　Given a 20–30 min. lecture/oral lesson, Curt will take appropriate notes as judged by that teacher. Obj. 2:　Given 10–15 pgs. of text to read, Curt will employ an appropriate strategy for retaining info.—i.e., mapping, webbing, outlining, notes, etc.—as judged by the teacher. Obj. 3:　Given notes to study for a test, Curt will do so successfully as evidenced by his test score. <u>Goal:</u>　Curt will improve his on-task behavior from 37% to 80% as measured by a qualified observer at year's end. Obj. 1:　By 1 month, Curt's on-task behavior will increase to 45%. Obj. 2:　By 3 months, Curt's on-task behavior will increase to 60%. Obj. 3:　By 6 months, Curt's on-task behavior will increase to 80% and maintain or improve until end of the year.

As illustrated in Figure 1.4 (p. 38), the legal IEP is written following evaluation and identification of the student's disabilities and before a placement decision is made; what the student needs is determined first, and then a decision is made about placement in the least restrictive environment in which the needed services can be provided. Too often, we see the educationally wrong (and illegal) practice of basing the IEP on an available placement; that is, the student's IEP is written *after* available placements and services are considered.

Writing IEPs that meet all the requirements of the law and that are also educationally useful is no small task. Computerized IEPs and those based only on standardized testing or developmental inventories are likely to violate the requirements of the law, or be of little educational value, or both (Bateman & Linden, 1998; Goodman & Bond, 1993). However, much of the controversy

Unique Educational Needs, Characteristics, and Present Levels of Performance (PLOPs) *(including how the disability affects the student's ability to progress in the general curriculum)*	Special Education, Related Services, Supplemental Aids & Services, Assistive Technology, Program Modifications, Support for Personnel *(including frequency, duration, and location)*	Measurable Annual Goals & Short-Term Objectives or Benchmarks • To enable student to participate in the general curriculum • To meet other needs resulting from the disability *(including how progress toward goals will be measured)*
Academic Needs/ Written Language: Curt needs strong remedial help in spelling, punctuation, capitalization, and usage. Present Level: Curt is approximately 2 grade levels behind his peers in these skills.	1. Provide direct instruction in written language skills (punctuation, capitalization, usage, spelling) by using a highly structured, well-sequenced program. Services provided in small group of no more than four students in the resource room, 50 minutes/day. 2. Build in continuous and cumulative review to help with short-term rote memory difficulty. 3. Develop a list of commonly used words in student writing (or use one of many published lists) for Curt's spelling program.	Goal: Within one academic year, Curt will improve his written language skills by 1.5 or 2 full grade levels. Obj. 1: Given 10 sentences of dictation at his current level of instruction, Curt will punctuate and capitalize with 90% accuracy (checked at the end of each unit taught). Obj. 2: Given 30 sentences with choices of usage, at his current instructional level, Curt will perform with 90% accuracy. Obj. 3: Given a list of 150 commonly used words in writing, Curt will spell with 90% accuracy.

Adaptations to Regular Program:
- In all classes, Curt should sit near the front of the class.
- Curt should be called on often to keep him involved and on task.
- All teachers should help Curt with study skills as trained by spelling/language specialist and resource room teacher.
- Teachers should monitor Curt's work closely in the beginning weeks/months of his program.

about IEPs and the disappointment in them appear to result from misunderstanding of the law, or lack of instructional expertise, or both. Within the framework of IDEA and other regulations, it is possible to write IEPs that are both legally correct and educationally useful. Bateman and Linden (1998) summarize do's and don'ts in the form of IEP "sins" and "virtues," as illustrated in Table 1.4 (p. 39).

Legislation and litigation were initially used in the 1960s and 1970s to include exceptional children in public education with relatively little regard for quality. In the 1980s and 1990s, laws and lawsuits have been used to try to ensure individualized education, cooperation, and collaboration among professionals; parental participation; and accountability of educators for providing high-quality, effective programs.

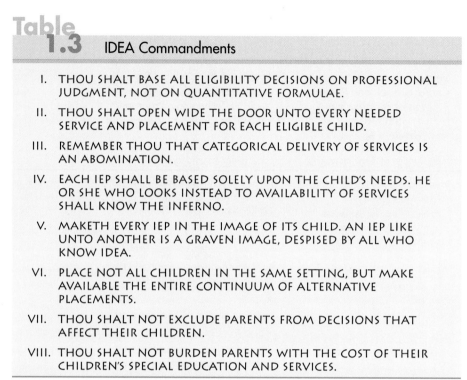

Table 1.3 IDEA Commandments

I.   THOU SHALT BASE ALL ELIGIBILITY DECISIONS ON PROFESSIONAL JUDGMENT, NOT ON QUANTITATIVE FORMULAE.

II. THOU SHALT OPEN WIDE THE DOOR UNTO EVERY NEEDED SERVICE AND PLACEMENT FOR EACH ELIGIBLE CHILD.

III. REMEMBER THOU THAT CATEGORICAL DELIVERY OF SERVICES IS AN ABOMINATION.

IV. EACH IEP SHALL BE BASED SOLELY UPON THE CHILD'S NEEDS. HE OR SHE WHO LOOKS INSTEAD TO AVAILABILITY OF SERVICES SHALL KNOW THE INFERNO.

V.   MAKETH EVERY IEP IN THE IMAGE OF ITS CHILD. AN IEP LIKE UNTO ANOTHER IS A GRAVEN IMAGE, DESPISED BY ALL WHO KNOW IDEA.

VI. PLACE NOT ALL CHILDREN IN THE SAME SETTING, BUT MAKE AVAILABLE THE ENTIRE CONTINUUM OF ALTERNATIVE PLACEMENTS.

VII. THOU SHALT NOT EXCLUDE PARENTS FROM DECISIONS THAT AFFECT THEIR CHILDREN.

VIII. THOU SHALT NOT BURDEN PARENTS WITH THE COST OF THEIR CHILDREN'S SPECIAL EDUCATION AND SERVICES.

Source: Reprinted with permission from Bateman, B. D., & Linden, M. A. (1998). *Better IEPs: How to develop legally correct and educationally useful programs* (3rd ed.). Longmont, CO: Sopris West. All rights reserved.

individualized family service plan (IFSP). A plan mandated by PL 99–457 to provide services for young children with disabilities (under three years of age) and their families; drawn up by professionals and parents; similar to an IEP for older children.

IDEA, for example, is noteworthy for its expansion of the idea of individualized planning and collaboration among disciplines. PL 99–457 mandated an **individualized family service plan (IFSP)** for infants and toddlers with disabilities. An IFSP is similar to an IEP for older children in that it requires assessment and statement of goals, needed services, and plans for implementation. As we discuss in Chapter 2, an IFSP also requires more involvement of the family, coordination of services, and plans for making the transition into preschool. IDEA mandated

Figure 1.4

The wrong and right routes to placement.

Source: Reprinted with permission from Bateman, B. D., & Linden, M. A. (1998). *Better IEPs: How to develop legally correct and educationally useful programs* (3rd ed. p. 66.). Longmont, CO: Sopris West. All rights reserved.

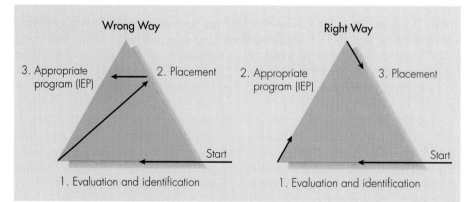

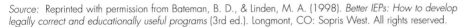

IEP Sins	IEP Virtues
■ Failure to individualize the program to fit the student ■ Failure to address all the student's needs ■ Failure to sufficiently describe and specify all necessary services ■ Failure to write clear, objective, meaningful, and reasonable PLOPs, objectives, and goals	■ Full and equal parental participation ■ Truly individualized to fit the student ■ Present levels of performance (PLOPs) and needs/characteristics carefully specified ■ All services, modifications, and supports to meet the student's needs fully detailed ■ Goals and objectives measurable, real, and taken seriously

Source: Reprinted with permission from Bateman, B. D., & Linden, M. A. (1998). *Better IEPs: How to develop legally correct and educationally useful programs* (3rd ed.). Longmont, CO: Sopris West. All rights reserved.

the inclusion of plans for transition from school to work for older students as part of their IEPs. Other provisions of IDEA are intended to improve the quality of services received by children and youths with disabilities.

A Perspective on the Progress of Special Education

Special education has come a long way since it was introduced into American public education over a century ago. It has become an expected part of the U.S. public education system, a given rather than an exception or an experiment. Much progress has been made since PL 94–142 (now IDEA) was enacted a quarter century ago. Now parents and their children have legal rights to free, appropriate education; they are not powerless in the face of school administrators who do not want to provide appropriate education and related services. The enactment of PL 94–142 was one of very few events in the twentieth century that altered the power relationship between schools and parents (Sarason, 1990).

In spite of the fact that IDEA and related laws and court cases have not resulted in flawless programs for exceptional children, they have done much to move American public schools toward providing better educational opportunities for those with disabilities. Laws like PL 99–457 (see p. 28) help ensure that all infants and toddlers with disabilities will receive early intervention. Laws like ADA (see pp. 28–31) help ensure that young adults will not be discriminated against in U.S. society. Laws and court cases cannot eliminate all problems in our society, but they can certainly be of enormous help in our efforts to equalize opportunities and minimize handicaps for people with disabilities.

We have made much progress in special education, but making it all that we hope for is—and always will be—a continuing struggle. In Chapter 2 we discuss current trends and issues that highlight dissatisfaction with the way things are and represent hope for what special education and related services might become.

Summary

The study of exceptional learners is the study of similarities and differences among individuals. Exceptional learners differ from most others in specific ways, but they are also similar to most others in most respects. Exceptionalities—differences—must not be allowed to obscure the ways in which exceptional learners are like others. We distinguish between an exceptionality that is a disability and one that is a handicap. A *disability* is an inability to do something. A *handicap* is a disadvantage that may be imposed on an individual. A disability may or may not be a handicap.

For purposes of education, *exceptional learners* are defined as those who require special education and related services if they are to realize their full human potential. Special education strives to make certain that students' handicaps are confined to those characteristics that cannot be changed.

Current government figures show that approximately one student in ten is identified as exceptional and receiving special education services. Most children and youths identified as exceptional are between the ages of six and seventeen, although identification of infants and young adults with disabilities is increasing.

Special education refers to specially designed instruction that meets the unusual needs of exceptional learners. The single most important goal of special education is finding and capitalizing on exceptional students' abilities. Special education may be provided under a variety of administrative plans. The regular classroom teacher, sometimes in consultation with other professionals, such as psychologists or teachers with more experience or training, is expected to serve many exceptional students in her or his regular classroom. Some exceptional students are served by an itinerant teacher who moves from school to school or by a resource teacher. Itinerant and resource teachers may teach students individually or in small groups for certain periods of the school day and provide assistance to regular classroom teachers. Sometimes students are placed in a diagnostic-prescriptive center so their special needs can be determined. The special self-contained class is used for a small group of students, who are usually taught in the special class all or most of the day. Special day schools are sometimes provided for students whose disabilities necessitate special equipment and methods for care and education. Hospital and homebound instruction are provided when the student is unable to go to regular classes. Finally, the residential school provides educational services and management of the daily living environment for students with disabilities who must receive full-time care.

Present law requires that every exceptional child and youth be placed in the *least restrictive environment (LRE)* so that educational intervention will be consistent with individual needs and not interfere with individual freedom and the development of potential. Today, therefore, most students with exceptionalities are educated primarily in regular classes.

All teachers need to be prepared to some extent to deal with exceptional students because many of these students are placed for part of the day in regular classrooms. Furthermore, many students not identified as exceptional share some of the characteristics of disability or giftedness. Although the relationship between general and special education must be one of collaboration and shared responsibility for exceptional learners, the roles of special and general educators are not always clear. Both may be involved in educating exceptional students by making maximum efforts to accommodate individual students' needs, evaluating academic abilities and disabilities, referring students for further evaluation, participating in eligibility conferences, writing individualized education programs (IEPs), communicating with parents, participating in due-process hearings, and collaborating with other professionals. In addition, special educators must have particular expertise in instructing students with learning problems, managing serious behavioral problems, using technological aids, and interpreting special education law.

Systematic attempts to educate learners with disabilities, especially those with mental retardation and emotional and behavioral disorders, began in the early 1800s. European physicians like Itard, Pinel, and Séguin pioneered in these educational efforts. Their revolutionary ideas included individualized instruction, carefully sequenced series of educational tasks, emphasis on stimulation and the awakening of the child's senses, meticulous arrangement of the child's environment, immediate reward for correct performance, tutoring in functional skills, and the belief that every child should be educated to the greatest extent possible. Howe and Gallaudet brought special education techniques and ideas to the United States.

Many other disciplines, especially psychology and sociology, were involved in the emergence of special education as a profession. Much of the progress in special education has resulted from the efforts of professional and parent organizations. The Council for Exceptional Children (CEC) is an influential group with many divisions devoted to such things as the study of specific exceptionalities; the administration, supervision, and implementation of special programs; teacher training and placement; and research. Organizations such as the ARC provide parents, schools, and the public with information about exceptionalities and the structure for obtaining needed services.

The legal basis of special education has evolved over the years, from permissive legislation allowing public funding of special programs for exceptional learners, to mandatory legislation requiring such expenditures. The contemporary commitment to the principle that every individual has the right to as normal a life and education as possible prompted much legislation and litigation in the 1970s and 1980s. Special education legislation has historically been increasingly specific and mandatory. The Individuals with Disabilities Education Act (IDEA) mandated that in order to receive funds under the act, *every school system in the country must make provision for a free, appropriate education for every child and youth with a disability.*

Laws and regulations may have little effect until the courts, through litigation, interpret their meanings. Litigation today focuses on ensuring that every exceptional child and youth receives an education that is appropriate for his or her individual needs. Lawsuits *for* special education tend to be filed on behalf of students who are unquestionably disabled but are receiving no education at all or only meager ser-

vices. Lawsuits *against* special education tend to be filed on behalf of students whose disabilities are mild or questionable and for whom special education is thought to be more stigmatizing and discriminatory than helpful. Future court cases will undoubtedly result in clarification of the term *appropriate* with reference to education for exceptional students.

The primary intent of special education legislation has been to require educators to focus on the needs of individual students. Thus, a central feature of IDEA is the requirement that every student receiving special education under the law must have an individualized education program (IEP). An IEP is a written plan, which must be approved by the child's parents or guardian, that specifies the following for each area of disability: (1) the student's current level of performance; (2) annual goals; (3) short-term instructional objectives or benchmarks; (4) special services to be provided and the extent to which the student will participate in regular education; (5) plans for starting services and their expected duration; (6) plans for evaluation; and (7) for older students, the services needed to ensure a successful transition from school to work or higher education. These goals are based on the view that special education must be *individualized, intensive, relentless, urgent, and goal directed.*

Special education has made much progress during the past century. It is now an expected part of American public education, not an exception or experiment. Parents of students with disabilities now have more involvement in their children's education. In part, this progress has occurred because of laws requiring appropriate education and other services for individuals with disabilities.

Sichel 1/97

gabrielle sichel

Next Time. Watermedia on rag paper. 11 × 15 in.

Gabrielle Sichel graduated from the School of the Museum of Fine Arts, Boston, in 1986 and from Tufts University in 1989. Her work has been exhibited at the Gateway Gallery in Brookline, MA; the Federal Reserve Bank of Boston Gallery; the School of the Museum of Fine Arts; galleries in Ipswich and Marshfield, MA; and the Cambridge (MA) Public Library. She has written and illustrated a book of poetry, *Sees and Hears*.

Current Trends and Issues

Come writers and critics
Who prophesy with your pen
And keep your eyes wide,
The chance won't come again.
And don't speak too soon
For the wheel's still in spin
And there's no tellin' who
That it's namin'
For the loser now
Will be later to win
For the times they are a-changin'.

BOB DYLAN
"The Times They Are A-Changin'"

B ob Dylan could have written his song "The Times They Are A-Changin'" (see excerpt on p. 43) for the field of special education, which has a rich history of controversy and change. In fact, controversy and change are what make the teaching and study of people with disabilities so challenging and exciting. The history of special education is replete with unexpected twists and turns. Many of today's events and conditions will undoubtedly have consequences that we do not foresee (see Kauffman, 1999a; Smith, 1998). The 1980s and 1990s have seen especially dramatic changes in the education of people with disabilities, and current thinking indicates that the field is poised for still more changes in the early twenty-first century. One critically important trend and issue for the new century is movement toward multicultural special education. Because this topic is so important, it is the subject of Chapter 3.

In this chapter, we explore five major trends in special education and the related issues that the field will face in the new millenium:

1. Integration of people with disabilities into the larger, nondisabled society
2. Participation of students with disabilities in general assessments of educational progress
3. Early intervention with children who have disabilities
4. Transition from secondary school to adulthood
5. Discipline of students with disabilities

Integration into the Larger Society

The trend of integrating people with disabilities into the larger society began in the 1960s and continues stronger than ever today. Champions of integration are proud of the fact that they have reduced the number of people with disabilities who reside in institutions and the number of special education students who attend special schools and special self-contained classes. Some of today's more radical proponents of integration, however, will not be satisfied until virtually all institutions, special schools, and special classes are eliminated. These proponents recommend that all students with disabilities be educated in regular classes. And even today's more conservative advocates of integration recommend a much greater degree of interaction between students with and without disabilities than was ever dreamed of by most special educators in the 1960s and 1970s.

Philosophical Roots: The Principle of Normalization

A key principle behind the trend toward more integration of people with disabilities into society is normalization. First espoused in Scandinavia (Bank-Mikkelsen, 1969) before being popularized in the United States, **normalization** is the philosophical belief that we should use "means which are as culturally normative as possible, in order to establish and/or maintain personal behaviors and characteristics which are as culturally normative as possible" (Wolfensberger, 1972, p. 28). In other words, under the principle of normalization, both the means and the ends of education for students with disabilities should be as much like those for nondisabled students as possible. Regarding the means, for example, we should place students with disabilities in educational settings as similar to those of nondisabled students as possible. And we should use treatment

normalization. A philosophical belief in special education that every individual, even the most disabled, should have an educational and living environment as close to normal as possible.

misconceptions
about Persons with Disabilities

myth Normalization, the philosophical principle that dictates that the means and ends of education for students with disabilities should be as culturally normative as possible, is a straightforward concept with little room for interpretation.

fact There are many disagreements pertaining to the interpretation of the normalization principle. As just one example, some educators have interpreted it to mean that all people with disabilities must be educated in regular classes, whereas others maintain that a continuum of placements (residential schools, special schools, special classes, resource rooms, regular classes) should remain available as options.

myth All professionals agree that technology should be used to its fullest to aid people with disabilities.

fact Some believe that technology should be used cautiously because it can lead people with disabilities to become too dependent on it. Some professionals believe that people with disabilities can be tempted to rely on technology rather than develop their own abilities.

myth All students with disabilities must now be included in standardized testing and follow the standardized testing routine, just like students without disabilities.

fact Most students with disabilities will be included in standardized testing procedures, but for some a given test will be judged inappropriate. Some students will require adaptations of the testing procedure to accommodate their specific disabilities. However, students with disabilities can no longer be automatically excluded from participation in standardized assessment procedures.

myth Research has established beyond a doubt that special classes are ineffective and that mainstreaming is effective.

fact Research comparing special versus mainstream placement has been inconclusive because most of these studies have been methodologically flawed. Researchers are now focusing on finding ways of making mainstreaming work more effectively.

myth Professionals agree that labeling people with disabilities (e.g., "retarded," "blind," "behavior disordered") is more harmful than helpful.

fact Some professionals maintain that labels help them communicate, explain the atypical behavior of some people with disabilities to the public, and spotlight the special needs of people with disabilities for the general public.

myth People with disabilities are pleased with the way the media portray them, especially in stories about the extraordinary achievements of such persons.

fact Some disability rights advocates are disturbed by what they believe are too frequent overly negative and overly positive portrayals in the media.

myth Everyone agrees that teachers in early intervention programs need to assess parents as well as their children.

fact Some authorities now believe that although families are an important part of intervention programming and should be involved in some way, special educators should center their assessment efforts primarily on the child, not the parents.

myth Everyone agrees that good early childhood programming for students with disabilities should follow the same guidelines as those for nondisabled preschoolers.

fact There is considerable disagreement about whether early intervention programming for children with disabilities should be child directed, as is typical of regular preschool programs, or more teacher directed.

myth Professionals agree that all students with disabilities in secondary school should be given a curriculum focused on vocational preparation.

fact Professionals are in conflict over how much vocational versus academic instruction students with mild disabilities should receive.

myth There are completely different rules of discipline for students with disabilities.

fact In most cases, the same discipline rules apply to students with and without disabilities. However, the law does not allow discontinuation of education for a student with a disability. Even if the student is not allowed to return to the school, education must be provided in an alternative setting.

approaches that are as close as possible to the ones we use with the rest of the student population. Regarding the ends, we should strive to help students with disabilities weave into the larger fabric of society.

Although on its face the principle of normalization seems simple enough, numerous controversies have swirled around the implementation of this important concept. We shall mention four of the more hotly contested issues:

1. The phrase *as culturally normative as possible* is open to interpretation. Even though the originators of the normalization principle saw the need for a variety of service delivery options—including residential institutions, special schools, and special classes—more recently, some have interpreted normalization to mean the abolishment of such separate settings.

2. Some groups of people with disabilities are leery about being too closely integrated with nondisabled society. For example, some people who are deaf, because of their difficulty in communicating with the hearing world, prefer associating with other people who are deaf. For them, normalization does not translate into integration with the larger society (Lord, 1991; Padden & Humphries, 1988). Others have pointed out that a diversity of different settings and groupings of people is itself normative in most societies (Kauffman & Hallahan, 1997).

3. Some disability rights advocates suggest that the assessment of normalization is wrongheaded, as it begins with the idea that nondisabled people should be seen as the norm to which those with disabilities are compared. For example, a representative of the organization Disabled People's International has called for "the elimination of the value concept of normalization as a measurement and the use of non-disabled people as the norm" (Mathiason, 1997, p. 2).

4. Some have questioned whether the rapidly expanding use of technology to assist people with disabilities actually works against the goal of normalization. Certainly, there is little doubt that technology has made it possible for more and more people with disabilities to take part in activities that previously were inaccessible to them. Thus, in many instances, technology serves as a means for achieving normalization. Some people with disabilities, however, have expressed concern that individuals might be too quick to rely on technology instead of working to improve their own abilities. Reliance on artificial means of interacting with the environment when more natural means are possible could jeopardize a person's quest for normalization.

As technology becomes ever more sophisticated, the issue of independence will become ever more important. One general guideline might be that if the technology allows people with disabilities to do something they could not do without it, then the technology is in their best interest. If, however, it allows them to do something new or better but at the same time imposes new limitations, then one might need to rethink the technology's benefits.

Historical Roots: Deinstitutionalization and the Full Inclusion Movement

The idea of integrating people with disabilities into society is hardly new. Professionals have been advocating for and implementing programs of integration for thirty or forty years. Although the amount of interaction between people with and without disabilities has increased relatively steadily over this time, two movements have helped speed up integration: deinstitutionalization and the full-inclusion movement.

Deinstitutionalization.

At one time it was common to place children and adults with retardation and/or mental illness in residential institutions, especially if they had relatively severe problems. The 1960s and 1970s, however, witnessed a systematic drive to move people out of institutions and back into closer contact with the community. Referred to as **deinstitutionalization,** this movement caused more and more

Children with disabilities would become further restricted from exploring their environments and participating in active pursuits if they were kept away from normal activities.

children with disabilities to be raised by their families. Today, smaller facilities, located within local neighborhoods, are now common. Halfway houses exist as placements for individuals with emotional difficulties who no longer need the more isolated environment of a large institution. For people with mental retardation, group homes house small numbers of individuals whose retardation may range from mild to severe. More and more people with disabilities are now working, with assistance from "job coaches," in competitive employment situations.

Some professionals assert that deinstitutionalization has been implemented, in certain cases, without much forethought (Crissey & Rosen, 1986; Landesman & Butterfield, 1987; Zigler, Hodapp, & Edison, 1990). They maintain that although deinstitutionalization has the potential to improve the quality of life for most people who, in previous generations, would have been lifelong residents of institutions, it has failed other people because of poor planning. Some individuals, for instance, have been turned out of institutions onto the streets. Moreover, institutions *can be* humane, effective alternative placements for some individuals.

Research in this area has made it evident that much still needs to be done to improve the quality of life for some persons with disabilities who have been released from institutions (Kauffman & Hallahan, 1992). Studies of deinstitutionalization in California, where it has become a common practice, indicate that mortality (the death rate) is considerably higher among people with mental retardation who have been returned from institutions to community settings than among those who have remained in institutions (Strauss & Kastner, 1996; Strauss, Shavelle, Baumeister, & Anderson, 1998).

deinstitutionalization. A social movement of the 1960s and 1970s whereby large numbers of persons with mental retardation and/or mental illness were moved from large mental institutions into smaller community homes or into the homes of their families; recognized as a major catalyst for integrating persons with disabilities into society.

The Full-Inclusion Movement.   Although there are different conceptualizations of what the term **full inclusion** means (Laski, 1991; Sailor, 1991; Stainback & Stainback, 1992), most definitions contain the following elements:

1. All students with disabilities—no matter the types or severities of disabilities—attend all classes in general education. In other words, there are no separate special education classes.
2. All students with disabilities attend their neighborhood schools (i.e., the ones they would normally go to if they had no disabilities).
3. General education, not special education, assumes primary responsibility for students with disabilities.

With regard to this last point, some full-inclusionists propose the total elimination of special education. Others hold that professionals such as special educators and speech therapists are still needed but that their main duties should be carried out in general education classrooms along with general education teachers.

Current Trends

Integration has involved an array of controversial issues, including whether a continuum of placement options should be maintained, the legitimacy of claims for and against full inclusion, and a variety of arguments regarding the implementation of inclusion, pro and con.

Full Inclusion Versus a Continuum of Alternative Placements. Educational programming for students with disabilities has historically been built on the assumption that a variety of service delivery options need to be available (Crockett & Kauffman, 1999). As mentioned in Chapter 1, special education law stipulates that schools place students with disabilities in the least restrictive environment (LRE). The notion of LRE assumes that there are alternatives along a continuum of restrictiveness, with residential institutions on one end and regular classes on the other. For the most part, special educators have been proud of this **continuum of alternative placements.** They have viewed the LRE concept as the lifeblood of special education, something they fought hard to get enacted into law. Before LRE was enacted into law, school personnel were free to claim that they did not have services for children with disabilities and to deny these children access to regular classes.

> Advocates of full inclusion, however, favor eliminating a continuum of placements: Three generations of children subject to LRE are enough. Just as some institution managers and their organizations—both overt and covert—seek refuge in the continuum and LRE, regional, intermediate unit, and special school administrators and their organizations will continue to defend the traditional and professionally pliable notion of LRE. The continuum is real and represents the status quo. However, the morass created by it can be avoided in the design and implementation of reformed systems by focusing all placement questions on the local school and routinely insisting on the home school as an absolute and universal requirement. In terms of placement, the home-school focus renders LRE irrelevant and the continuum moot. (Laski, 1991, p. 413)

Premises of Full Inclusion.   Those who advocate full inclusion base their position on at least the following four premises:

full inclusion. All students with disabilities are placed in their neighborhood schools in general education classrooms for the entire day; general education teachers have the primary responsibility for students with disabilities.

continuum of alternative placements. The full range of alternative placements, from those assumed to be least restrictive to those considered most restrictive; the continuum ranges from regular classrooms in neighborhood schools to resource rooms, self-contained classes, special day schools, residential schools, hospital schools, and home instruction.

Some advocates of full inclusion feel that all students, regardless of the severity of their disabilities, should be mainstreamed in regular classroom settings.

1. Labeling people is harmful.
2. Special education pull-out programs have been ineffective.
3. People with disabilities should be viewed as a minority group.
4. Ethics should take precedence over empiricism.

We consider each of these premises in the sections that follow.

Labeling Is Harmful.   Some people fear that a "special education" label can cause a child to feel unworthy or to be viewed by the rest of society as a deviant and hence grow to feel unworthy. This fear is not entirely unfounded. Most of the labels used to designate students for special education carry negative connotations. Being so described may lower a person's self-esteem or cause others to behave differently toward him or her. Consequently, advocates for people with disabilities have suggested using different labels or, to the extent possible, avoiding the use of labels altogether.

Antilabeling sentiment is based, in part, on the theory that disabilities are a matter of social perceptions and values, not inherent characteristics. Bogdan (1986) suggests that *disability* is a socially created construct. Its existence depends on social interaction. Only in a very narrow sense, according to Bogdan, does a person *have* a disability. For example, the fact that a person cannot see only sets the stage for his or her being labeled "blind."

Once we call a person "blind," a variety of undesirable consequences occur. Our interactions are different because of the label. That is, we view the person primarily in terms of the blindness. We tend to interpret everything he or she can or cannot do in terms of the blindness, and the label takes precedence over other things we may know about the individual. This labeling opens the door for viewing the person in a stereotypical and prejudicial manner because, once labeled, we tend to think of all people with blindness as being similar to one another but different from the rest of society.

When the use of labels takes precedence over recognizing individual characteristics, labels themselves can become disabling. For instance, if we view these sailors only in terms of their blindness, we might overlook things about them that don't fit our stereotype of blind people.

Research on the effects of labeling has been inconclusive. On the one hand, studies indicate that people tend to view labeled individuals differently from non-labeled ones. People are more likely both to expect deviant behavior from labeled individuals and to see abnormality in nondisabled individuals if told (incorrectly) that nondisabled persons are deviant. On the other hand, labels may also make nondisabled people more tolerant of those with disabilities. That is, labels may provide explanations or justifications for differences in appearance or behavior for which the person with a disability otherwise might be blamed or stigmatized even more (Fiedler & Simpson, 1987). For example, it is probably fairly common for the nondisabled adult to tolerate a certain degree of socially immature behavior in a child with mental retardation while finding the same behavior unacceptable in a nondisabled child.

In addition to serving as an explanation for unusual behavior, the use of labels is defended on other grounds by some special educators. First, they argue that the elimination of one set of labels would only prompt development of another set. In other words, they believe that individuals with special problems will always be perceived as different. Second, these special educators contend that labels help professionals communicate with one another. In talking about a research study, for example, it helps to know with what type of population the study was conducted. Third, they assert that labels help spotlight the special needs of people with disabilities for the general public: "Like it or not, it is a fine mixture of compassion, guilt, and social consequence that has been established over these many years as a conditioned response to the label 'mental retardation' that brings forth ... resources [monies for specialized services]" (Gallagher, 1972, p. 531). The taxpayer is more likely to react sympathetically to something that can be labeled. Finally, they point out that anytime we use an intervention that is not universal—used with all students regardless of their characteristics—we automatically apply a label. That is, labels are an inescapable part of preventive practices that are not universal (Kauffman, 1999b).

Cutting Through Prejudicial Barriers with Humor

Most special education professionals and people with disabilities would agree that there are many ways to break down attitudinal barriers toward those who have disabilities. Humor may be one of the most effective weapons against such prejudices, especially if humor and disability are merely coincidental. In her syndicated cartoon feature "For Better or For Worse," Lynn Johnston occasionally includes a teacher who uses a wheelchair. This teacher experiences the frustrations and successes of any other in managing and teaching students, and her use of a wheelchair is typical of humor in this vein.

Others make frontal attacks on attitudinal barriers through humor in which disability is central, not incidental. One of the best-known cartoonists taking this approach is John Callahan, who is quadriplegic (as a result of an auto accident) and a recovering alcoholic. His cartoons, which often feature so-called black humor about disability, have appeared in *The New Yorker, Penthouse, National Lampoon, American Health,* and a variety of other magazines, newspapers, and books. Callahan's autobiography, *Don't Worry, He Won't Get Far on Foot,* is a book that some may find offensive but others find liberating in its irreverence and ability to make people laugh at disability.

For Better or For Worse®   by Lynn Johnston

Source: "For Better or For Worse." Copyright © United Features Syndicate. (Reprinted by permission.)

Special Education Pull-Out Programs Have Been Ineffective.   Some special educators assert that research shows **pull-out programs** to be ineffective. These educators maintain that students with disabilities have better, or at least no worse, scores on cognitive and social measures if they stay in regular classes than if they are pulled out for all (self-contained classes) or part (resource rooms) of the school day. Adding fuel to this argument are studies showing that the instruction received in pull-out programs is not what one would expect if special education were being implemented appropriately (e.g., Vaughn, Moody, & Schumm, 1998).

Many research studies have compared students with disabilities in more and less segregated settings; over the past thirty years, there have been more than fifty such studies. Results, when taken at face value, have not been very supportive of pull-out programs. Critics of this research, however, argue that taking these investigations at face value is highly questionable (Kauffman & Hallahan, 1992). The biggest problem with this line of research is that most of the studies are methodologically flawed. Furthermore, some studies do show that some students

pull-out programs. Special education programs in which students with disabilities leave the general education classroom for part or all of the school day (e.g., to go to special classes or resource room).

with disabilities make better progress in more specialized settings and that full inclusion does not serve all children best.

> These findings challenge the idea that one type of placement (full inclusion) is best for all children. By limiting placement for special education children to mainstreamed classrooms only, some children may experience a less than optimal learning environment. As Bricker (1995) reminds us, the needs of the child should not be lost in a movement to advocate one type of placement over all other considerations. (Mills, Cole, Jenkins, & Dale, 1998, p. 89)

People with Disabilities as a Minority. Advocates of full inclusion tend to see people with disabilities as members of a minority group, rather than as individuals who have difficulties as an inherent result of their disabilities. In other words, the problems that people with disabilities face are seen as the result of society's discrimination and prejudice. The Stainbacks typify this point of view:

> In the past, educators have assumed a "functional limitations" approach to services. This paradigm locates the difficulty within students with disabilities when they experience problems in learning or adapting in general education classrooms. From this perspective, the primary task of educators is to remediate these students' functional deficits to the maximum extent possible. That is, educators attempt to fix, improve, or make ready the students who are being unsuccessful by providing them with the skills to be able to succeed in a mainstreamed educational environment that is not adapted to meet their particular needs, interests, or capabilities. And if this is not possible, they must be relegated to special, separate learning settings. In the "functional limitations" paradigm the student is expected to fit into the existing or educational environment.
>
> This paradigm is gradually being replaced by a minority group paradigm. The minority group paradigm of school operation locates the principle [*sic*] difficulties of students with disabilities as not residing in the student, but rather in the organization of the general education environment. That is, school failure is the result of such things as educational programs, settings, and criteria for performance that do not meet the diverse needs of students. From this perspective, the problem is with the educational organization or environment that needs to be fixed, improved, or made ready to address the diverse needs of all students. (Stainback & Stainback, 1992, p. 32)

The notion of people with disabilities as a minority is consistent with the views of disability rights activists. These activists are a part of the **disability rights movement,** which is patterned after the civil rights movement of the 1960s. Disability activists claim that they, like African Americans and other ethnic minority groups, are an oppressed minority. They have coined the term *handicapism,* a parallel of racism. **Handicapism** is a "set of assumptions and practices that promotes the differential and unequal treatment of people because of apparent or assumed physical, mental, or behavioral differences" (Bogdan & Biklen, 1977, p. 14).

Although more and more people with disabilities—and nondisabled professionals too—are supporting the disability rights movement, there are several impediments to its achieving the same degree of impact as the civil rights movement. Some believe that the political climate in the United States has not been conducive to fostering yet another rights movement. Whereas the civil rights movement of the 1960s was spawned in an era of liberal ideology, the disability rights movement has coincided with a more conservative climate (Gartner & Joe, 1986).

disability rights movement. Patterned after the civil rights movement of the 1960s, this is a loosely organized effort to advocate for the rights of people with disabilities through lobbying legislators and other activities. Members view people with disabilities as an oppressed minority.

handicapism. A term used by activists who fault the unequal treatment of individuals with disabilities. This term is parallel to the term *racism,* coined by those who fault unequal treatment based on race.

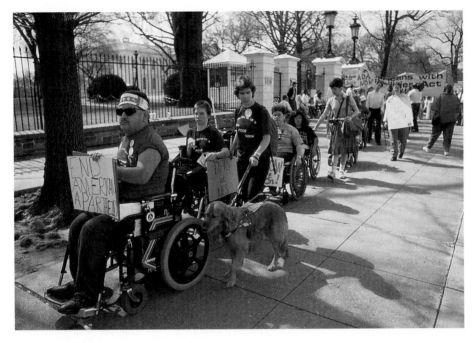

The disability rights movement is now international and is addressing a wide range of issues (see the box on pages 54–55). Like other political or social movements, the disability rights movement includes a spectrum of views on controversial topics, and not every statement of every person with a disability is representative of the majority of people with disabilities. For example, the views expressed in the box on page 54 regarding Christopher Reeve, and the negative sentiments expressed toward finding a "cure" for spinal cord injuries that would allow people with paralysis to walk, are not shared by all people with disabilities. Some find Christopher Reeve's optimism about finding a way to reverse the effects of spinal cord injuries laudable and heartening.

Activists themselves have been unable to agree on the best ways to meet the movement's general goals. For example, some believe that individuals with disabilities should receive special treatment in such things as tax exemptions or reduced public transportation fares. Others maintain that such preferential treatment fosters the image that people with disabilities are dependent on the nondisabled for charity (Gartner & Joe, 1986).

People with disabilities are an incredibly heterogeneous population. Although general goals can be the same for all people with disabilities, specific needs vary greatly, depending to a large extent on the particular type and severity of disability the person has. Clearly, the *particular* problems an adolescent with severe retardation and blindness faces are considerably different from those of a Vietnam veteran who has lost the use of his or her legs. Although activists admit it would not be good for the public to believe that all people with disabilities are alike—any more than they already do (Gartner & Joe, 1986)—this heterogeneity does make it more difficult for people with disabilities to join forces on specific issues.

But perhaps what has been missing most and what is hardest to achieve is a sense of pride. The civil rights movement for African Americans and the women's movement fostered pride in their supporters. For example, there has been no

Ready, Willing, and Disabled

Women at Global Forum Turn the Wheelchairs of Progress

When Laura Hershey wants to move, she breathes into a tube that controls her wheelchair. When she wants to speak, she shifts the tube away with her lips. This is how she painstakingly traverses the world, how she went to college, how she studied in Britain, how she traveled to China.

But she does not want to inspire you. She does not want you to think she is courageous. She does not want your sympathy.

"Disability," the woman from Denver says, "is not a tragedy. It's an exciting thing. It's really powerful."

Ask her what the power is, where it lies, and she says just this: "Look around."

Around her are other women. Women using wheelchairs. Blind women. Deaf women. Women with no arms. Women whose bodies jerk and twitch and whose words sputter out of their mouths. More than 500 people from 80 countries have come to the Bethesda Hyatt Regency for the International Leadership Forum for Women With Disabilities, which runs through tomorrow. They have been meeting all week, listening to such speakers as Secretary of State Madeleine Albright, talking about political organizing and education and sexuality and employment.

To an able-bodied observer (a term many here would find objectionable, but more about that later), it is astonishing: A self-contained world in which wheelchairs are the norm, in which no one nervously averts eyes from faces without chins and arms without hands.

While Barbara Walters and TV viewers across the country cheer and weep for Christopher Reeve, men and women who use wheelchairs grimace at the paralyzed actor's talk about a cure through medical research that they long ago accepted will not come in their lifetimes—and that some say they do not even want. They are not a problem for doctors, or anyone else, to solve. Like Laura Hershey, who spent years insisting her disability didn't matter and said nothing about her, the disability rights movement has changed and radicalized, demanding not only curb cuts and jobs, but a shift in attitude as well. "I hate when people say, 'Oh, you're so competent, I forget you're disabled!'" says Ellen Rubin, an educator from New York. That she is blind is not a fact she strives to overcome, to minimize. "It's part of who I am."

"What we're doing is not just challenging assumptions about disability, but assumptions about life in general," Hershey says. "There's a real pressure to conform, to try to fit a mold, to adhere to a certain standard of beauty and success. We can challenge the standard that says you have to be perfect or you're no good."

The women here wear conference buttons declaring themselves "Loud, Proud and Passionate." They are the activists, the advocates, the ones who talk back. Whenever Rubin hears a parent nervously shush a child who has commented on her electronic cane, she addresses the adult directly: "Don't worry," she says. "I know I'm blind."

Help is not a simple idea. Jenny Kern, a lawyer from San Francisco, has too often felt strangers' hands on her wheelchair, moving her without even asking if she needs assistance. She throws the brake defiantly. Rubin is frequently asked, "Do you know where you're going?" by pedestrians apparently assuming she is lost without their guidance....

A project of the Wheeled Mobility Center at San Francisco State University, Whirlwind Women is still in its infancy. Ralf Hotchkiss, a professor at San Francisco State and co-founder of the Whirlwind Wheelchair Network, has worked with disabled people in the developing world for 15 years, designing and building appropriate chairs. Mechanics trained by the program have made more than

equivalent of the "Black is beautiful" slogan within the disability rights movement, although the movement is attempting to develop a sense of identity and community. One of the vehicles for accomplishing this is a publication, *The Disability Rag,* which highlights disability as a civil rights issue.

People in the disability rights movement have been active on a variety of fronts, ranging from lobbying legislators and employers to criticizing the media for being guilty of representing people with disabilities in stereotypical and inaccurate ways. Disability activists have been particularly critical of television and movies (Klobas, 1985; Longmore, 1985; see also Safran, 1998). They argue that the depictions are typically overly negative or overly positive. On the negative side, electronic media often treat people with disabilities as criminals, monsters, potential suicides, mal-

10,000 wheelchairs, but Hotchkiss estimates 20 million people around the world still don't have needed mobility devices.

The chairs are both practical and symbolic. "Disabled women, for many reasons, are infantilized," says Barbara Duncan, director of communications for Rehabilitation International, one of the sponsors of the forum. "People reach by to pat them on the head. They do not look at them as women who have a future. They don't look at them as women. They look at them as old children."...

Irene Woodell wears silver nail polish on the two fingers that she has, and above her face with its deformed mouth and jaw her hair gleams rusty red with silver bangs.

She refuses to be invisible.

As she walks down the street, Woodell greets each stranger. "If I say 'Hi!' they have to say 'Hi!' back," says the university administrator from Detroit. "They feel uncomfortable but they respond."

Look at me, these women are saying. Listen to me. When you call yourself able-bodied, what are you saying about my abilities? When you tell your child not to stare, what fears are you teaching? When you talk about curing my condition, what are you saying about my right to exist?

Hotchkiss spent years designing super-wheelchairs. He wanted a chair that could climb stairs, that could crouch down, that would make him more like he was before the accident that paralyzed him. Looking back, he sees those chairs as signs that he was still attempting to defy his condition.

"It's just part of a process," says Jenny Kern, the process of adjusting to new realities. And in Christopher Reeve's talk about a cure for spinal cord injuries, she

Positive media portrayals of individuals with disabilities have helped change attitudes, but also may have set unrealistic expectations for these individuals as well.

hears that he is just beginning a journey, the one she traveled in her teens and that others are traveling now.

"There are kids who are putting off their lives today because they're misled by Christopher Reeve's doctors that a cure is around the corner," Hotchkiss says.

"I talked to one the other day, a ballerina," he says. "It took her 2½ years to get past just waiting every day for a cure."

Kern stopped waiting long ago. She has left her law firm to volunteer with Whirlwind Women and raise money for more workshops. She is building a wheelchair herself. This is not a matter of courage.

"Courage to what?" Hotchkiss asks. "Courage to get up in the morning? To decide to live? It's not a courage thing. It's just a different life and moving on."

"It's survival," Kern says.

Source: Kastor, E. (1997, June 19). Ready, willing, and disabled: Women at global forum turn the wheelchairs of progress. *The Washington Post*, p. D-1. © 1997 The Washington Post. Reprinted with permission.

adjusted people, or sexual deviants. These portrayals offer the viewer absolution for any difficulties faced by persons with disabilities and allow the nondisabled to "blame the victims" for their own problems. Rarely do movie themes acknowledge society's role in creating attitudinal barriers for people with disabilities.

When television attempts to portray people with disabilities in a positive light, it often ends up highlighting phenomenal accomplishments—a one-legged skier, a wheelchair marathoner, and so forth. The superhero image, according to some disability activists, is a mixed blessing. It does promote the notion that being disabled does not automatically limit achievement. Such human interest stories, however, may make other more ordinary people with disabilities somehow feel inferior because they have not achieved such superhuman goals. These stories also imply that people with disabilities can prove their worth only by achieving superhuman goals and reinforce "the view that disability is a problem of individual emotional coping and physical overcoming, rather than an issue of social discrimination against a stigmatized minority" (Longmore, 1985, p. 35).

Although disability activists, for the most part, have been extremely displeased with television's handling of disabilities, they have been more complimentary of TV advertising that uses characters with disabilities. Beginning in the mid-1980s, advertisers began to experiment with the use of persons with disabilities. In the last years of the twentieth century, there has been a dramatic increase

Ad Ventures for the Disabled

New Visibility Marks a Change in Attitudes

The Sears commercial is a fast-paced kaleidoscope of beaming customers showing off their new clothes, reaching for tools, painting their houses, videotaping their kids' Easter egg hunts—all while a singer croons about "the many sides of Sears." In one scene, a fisherman relaxes on a dock at sunset with his pals and his dog; the fisherman is in a wheelchair.

Then there's the double-page magazine ad for Saturn that, like all Saturn's advertising, features a real-life car buyer or dealer. The photo shows satisfied customer June Rooks, a 44-year-old Navy research analyst, wearing a broad grin and a bright dress, and balanced on a pair of crutches. "When you've tackled everything else life has thrown your way," the headline says, "a little traffic won't stop you."

And a TV spot for Nike, in which an athletic young man runs picturesquely through the forest and foothills of Malibu Canyon, presents his story in stark white-on-black titles: "Ric Munoz, Los Angeles. 80 miles every week, 10 marathons every year. HIV-positive." Followed by Nike's familiar hortatory slogan: "Just Do It."

After years of lobbying for inclusion in the imagery that penetrates virtually every American home, people with disabilities are becoming far more visible in mainstream advertising. Kellogg's corn flakes commercials, for instance, have starred a deaf teenager (who signs enthusiastically about crunchiness) and a woman in a wheelchair. A Home Depot spot scheduled to air in 20 cities (including Washington) next month feature an employee with a prosthetic arm—70-year-old Henry Gibson of Houston, to be precise—touting hardware. This list of big-budget advertisers whose TV commercials and print spreads incorporate actors and models with disabilities also included AT&T, Toys R Us, McDonald's, Mitsubishi, Target, Nordstrom, Chrysler and Toyota. "This has been a real break-

through," says Barrett Shaw, editor of the Louisville-based magazine the *Disability Rag.*

Advertising historically has been the domain of the perfect, off-limits not only to the disabled but to almost everyone who isn't young, lithe and gorgeous. Sandra Gordon, a former Easter Seal executive who now consults with major corporations on disability issues, remembers in the '70s urging advertisers to include a single wheelchair-user in ads with group photographs. "I was told that I was crazy, that it was a disgusting idea," Gordon recalls. "It would turn consumers off; they might think using the product would make *them* disabled."

It's now more common for executives to talk like Sears marketing chief John Costello: "We are really committed to reflecting the full diversity of our consumer group in our advertising." Sears has one of the largest marketing budgets of any U.S. company. Its "many sides" ad, produced by Young & Rubicam and expected to air nationally in both 30- and 60-second versions throughout the year, marks the first time the company has used a disabled person in an ad. But Costello says, "you can expect to see more."

The ads themselves have also evolved since the first few appeared, with long intervals between them, in the '80s. Probably the most-remembered of the early entries was the spot that introduced Bill Demby, a Vietnam vet and double amputee who was shown vigorously playing basketball on artificial feet developed by DuPont. The ad and Demby were inspiring. But, Gordon notes, "it's very hard, if you're a person who's deaf or blind or uses a wheelchair, to live up to those 'Supergimp' stereotypes."

Current ads are less apt to emphasize heroic conquests, more likely to show people with disabilities in ordinary situations. Editor Shaw, for instance, was particularly impressed with the Saturn ad, which was created by Hal Riney and Partners and has run in the *Atlantic Monthly,*

in actors with disabilities in TV advertising, whether out of corporate America's desire to be more socially responsive or their recognition of the large market of buyers with disabilities. (See the box below.)

Ethics over Evidence. Full-inclusion proponents emphasize that people with disabilities are a minority group who have undergone discrimination. Thus, these proponents tend to approach issues of integration from an ethical, rather than an empirical, evidentiary perspective. Many proponents of full inclusion are not interested in pursuing the question of whether full inclusion is effective. For

---

Gourmet, Essence, Newsweek and *Scientific American,* among other magazines. June Rooks, Shaw notes, "was treated the same way other people in Saturn ads are."

As with other corporate attempts at "diversity," the inclusion of people with disabilities in marketing efforts serves several purposes at once. It shows sensitivity and creates goodwill, and some business executives think it may actually help effect social change. "We believe advertising changes America's attitudes on a lot of fronts," says Ron Hatley, consumer affairs manager at AT&T, which has run several print and TV ads featuring disabled actors. "When we see people of color in ads, we relate to them as individuals, we have a less segregated society. Including people with disabilities in ads will help change attitudes, too." . . .

Beyond the public relations factors, however, companies also have designs on a large and potentially lucrative market. The Census Bureau estimates that a startling 49 million Americans have some degree of disability, meaning that they have "difficulty" performing certain functions or activities; this group, which is disproportionately elderly, could include everyone from the blind or deaf to someone with learning disabilities like dyslexia. Of this group, 24 million describe disabilities that the Census Bureau classifies as "severe." The larger group of 49 million controls $188 billion in discretionary income; the smaller, severely disabled group has a spare $55 billion to spend.

Far from feeling exploited by such wooing, advocates for disabled people say, the market is happy to be courted. "It helps to see people with disabilities as a contributing force in this society—tax-paying citizens who also buy Charmin or Colgate—not just people who are asking for things," says Sandra Gordon.

Source: Span, P. (1995, March 7). Ad Ventures for the disabled. *The Washington Post,* D-1, D-8. © 1995 The Washington Post. Reprinted with permission.

Advertisers in recent years have sought to demonstrate their sensitivity, and to activate potentially lucrative markets, by including diverse societal groups in their print and television advertising, and this trend has not overlooked individuals with disabilities, whose presence in the glossy world of advertising may be at once a reflection and an agent of changing attitudes toward disabilities.

them, empirical data on the comparative effectiveness of full inclusion versus pull-out programs are irrelevant. Apparently, even if one were to find, through well-controlled research, that pull-out programs lead to better academic and social outcomes than do full-inclusion programs, these advocates would still favor full inclusion on ethical grounds. For them,

> by far the most important reason for including all students into the mainstream is that it is the fair, ethical, and equitable thing to do. It deals with the value of EQUALITY. As was decided in the *Brown versus Board of Education* decision, SEPARATE IS NOT EQUAL. All children should be part of the educational and community mainstream.
>
> It is discriminatory that some students, such as those labeled disabled, must earn the right or be prepared to be in the general education mainstream or wait for educational researchers to prove that students with disabilities can profit from the mainstream, when other students are allowed unrestricted access simply because they have no label. No one should have to pass anyone's test or prove anything in a research study to live and learn in the mainstream of school and community life. It is a basic right, not something one has to earn. (Stainback & Stainback, 1992, p. 31)

Arguments Against Full Inclusion. The notion of full inclusion has met with considerable resistance. At least six arguments against full inclusion have been offered:

1. General educators, special educators, and parents are largely satisfied with the current continuum of placements.
2. General educators are unwilling and/or unable to cope with all students with disabilities.
3. Justifying full inclusion by asserting that people with disabilities are a minority is flawed.
4. Full-inclusion proponents' unwillingness to consider empirical evidence is professionally irresponsible.
5. The available empirical evidence does not support full inclusion.
6. In the absence of data to support one service delivery model, special educators must preserve the continuum of placements.

Satisfaction with the Current Continuum of Placements. Defenders of the full continuum point out that, for the most part, teachers, parents, and students are satisfied with the degree of integration into general education now experienced by children with disabilities. Repeated polls, surveys, and interviews have indicated that the vast majority of parents of students with disabilities, as well as students themselves, were satisfied with the special education system and placement options (e.g., Guterman, 1995; Semmel, Abernathy, Butera, & Lesar, 1991). Many students themselves say they prefer pull-out to in-class services, which may be interpreted to support the preservation of a full continuum of placement options (Klinger, Vaughn, Schumm, Cohen, & Forgan, 1998). Although many students are no doubt unhappy with the stigma the label of learning disabilities brings with it, the majority seem not to regret that they are not educated in general education classes. As one student summed up:

> [Full inclusion] would make it worse. Basically it would be embarrassing for that person (a student with learning disabilities). It (an inclusive classroom)

would be egging it more. People would be getting into a lot more fights because somebody is always going to joke around and say something like, "He's a retard." (Guterman, 1995, p. 120)

Critics of full inclusion claim that the idea of full inclusion is being championed by only a few radical special educators.

General Educators Are Unwilling and/or Unable to Cope.   The attitudes of many general educators toward including students with disabilities in regular classes have been less than enthusiastic. In a synthesis of over two dozen surveys of general educators' views on integrating students with disabilities into their classes, only about half thought that integration could provide some benefits (Scruggs & Mastropieri, 1996). Furthermore, only about one-fourth to one-third thought they had sufficient time, skills, training, and resources needed for working with students with disabilities. Most critics of full inclusion sympathize with the classroom teacher's already arduous job. Although some critics blame teachers for their unwillingness to accommodate more students with disabilities, many agree that their hesitation to do so is justified (see Lieberman, 1992).

Justifying Full Inclusion by Asserting That People with Disabilities Are a Minority Is Flawed.   Many critics of full inclusion do not deny that, in many ways, people with disabilities have been treated similarly to oppressed minority groups, such as African Americans, Hispanics, and women. They have experienced discrimination on the basis of their disability and thus can be considered an oppressed minority group.

These critics, however, do not see that this minority group status translates into the same educational placement decisions as it does for African Americans, Hispanics, and women (Dupre, 1997; Hallahan & Kauffman, 1994; Kauffman & Hallahan, 1993; Kauffman & Lloyd, 1995). They argue that for the latter groups, separation from the mainstream cannot be defended on educational grounds, but for students with disabilities, separation can. Students with disabilities are sometimes placed in special classes or resource rooms to accommodate their educational needs better. Placement in separate educational environments is inherently unequal, these critics maintain, when it is done for factors irrelevant to learning (e.g., skin color), but such placements may result in equality when done for instructionally relevant reasons (e.g., student's ability to learn, difficulty of material being presented, preparation of the teacher).

Finally, critics of full inclusion argue that the most important civil right of the minority in question—students with disabilities and their parents—is the right to choose. That is, the Individuals with Disabilities Education Act (IDEA) (discussed in Chapter 1) gives parents and students themselves, when appropriate, the right to choose the environment they, not advocates of total inclusion, consider most appropriate and least restrictive (Crockett & Kauffman, 1998, 1999).

Unwillingness to Consider Empirical Evidence Is Professionally Irresponsible.   Some professionals see as folly the disregard of empirical evidence espoused by some proponents of full inclusion (Fuchs & Fuchs, 1991; Kauffman, 1989, 1999a; Kauffman & Hallahan, 1997; Kauffman, Lloyd, Hallahan, & Astuto, 1995). These professionals believe that ethical actions are always of the utmost importance. They assert, however, that decisions about what is ethical should be informed by research. In the case of mainstreaming, they think it is important to have as much data as possible on its advantages and disadvantages and how best

Critics of full inclusion assert that it is unrealistic to expect the general education system—with its fast, competitive pace and whole-group focus—to provide the individualized attention often required by learners with disabilities.

to implement it before deciding if and how it should be put into practice. Some critics maintain that full-inclusion proponents have gone too far in championing their cause, that they have resorted to rhetoric rather than reason. These critics assert that backers of full inclusion have traded in their credentials as scientific researchers in favor of becoming advocates and lobbyists.

Available Empirical Evidence Does Not Support Full Inclusion.   There are few rigorous studies of full inclusion, but those available suggest that full inclusion has not led to social or academic benefits, according to critics. For example, one study found that students with disabilities in full-inclusion classrooms were not very well liked by their general education peers (Sale & Carey, 1995), another that attempts to implement full inclusion did not produce the expected results (Fox & Ysseldyke, 1997), still another that full inclusion did not serve all children appropriately (Mills et al., 1998). The authors concluded that their results were similar to those of previous studies of students with disabilities who were served in resource rooms. With respect to academics, the combined results of three longitudinal studies indicate that, even after investing tremendous amounts of financial and professional resources, 40 percent of fully included students with learning disabilities "were slipping behind at what many would consider a disturbing rate" (Zigmond et al., 1995, p. 539).

In perhaps the most extensive study of full inclusion, researchers interviewed school personnel and students and observed in classrooms in five full-inclusion sites around the United States (Baker & Zigmond, 1995; Zigmond, 1995; Zigmond & Baker, 1995). Based on their data, the researchers claimed that teachers did not individualize instruction or plan ahead for how to accommodate the needs of students with disabilities. In fact, the individualization that did occur was most often carried out by peers (using peer tutoring—see pp. 64–65) or paraprofessionals (teacher aides). The researchers concluded:

> Regardless of how well prepared a general educator is, the focus of general
> education practice is on the group: managing instruction for a large group

of students, managing behavior within a large group of students, designing assessments suitable for a large group, and so forth. The special educator's focus has always been, and should continue to be, on the individual, providing unique and response-contingent instruction, teaching socially appropriate behavior, designing tailored assessments that are both diagnostic and summative, and so forth. (Zigmond & Baker, 1995, pp. 249–250)

Preserving the Continuum of Placements.   Critics of full inclusion argue that, given that empirical evidence is scant and that what is available does not support any one service delivery option, it is wise to be cautious about changing the current configuration too quickly or drastically. They admit that there are problems with the current special education system and that there may even be a need for more integration of students with disabilities, including the use of full inclusion. They are leery, however, about eliminating the range of service delivery options currently available to school personnel and parents (e.g., Crockett & Kauffman, 1999; Gallagher, 1994; Martin, 1994).

Mainstreaming Practices

Whether or not one supports the concept of full inclusion, the fact is that most special educators are in favor of some degree of **mainstreaming**—integrating students with disabilities with nondisabled students. Educators have devised a number of strategies for implementing mainstreaming. Most of these practices are still in the experimental stages; that is, we do not have a wealth of evidence indicating their effectiveness. However, various authorities have recommended the following four basic strategies:

1. Prereferral teams
2. Collaborative consultation
3. Cooperative teaching
4. Curricula and instructional strategies

In the following sections, we briefly describe each of these approaches.

Prereferral Teams.   Groups of professionals called **prereferral teams (PRTs)** work with general education teachers to recommend different strategies for working with children who exhibit academic and/or behavioral problems. One of the primary goals is to establish "ownership" of these children by general and not special educators. In other words, PRTs try to keep down the number of referrals to special education by stressing that general educators try as many alternative strategies as possible before deciding that difficult-to-teach students need to become the primary responsibility of special educators.

The makeup of PRTs varies from one place to another, sometimes including the school principal or a school psychologist but almost always including a special educator and a general educator. In fact, because of the emphasis on general education's ownership, some have maintained that general educators are the most important team members (Chalfant, Pysh, & Moultrie, 1979; Gerber & Semmel, 1985). A major justification for using classroom teachers to make decisions regarding referral to special education is that they may have information on individual children that is even more important than results of the usual standardized tests: "Teachers observe tens of thousands of discrete behavioral events during each school day. Formal tests of ability and achievement are based on analysis of

mainstreaming. The placement of students with disabilities in general education classes for all or part of the day and for all or only a few classes; special education teachers maintain the primary responsibility for students with disabilities.

prereferral teams (PRTs). Teams made up of a variety of professionals, especially regular and special educators who work with regular class teachers to come up with strategies for teaching difficult-to-teach children. Designed to influence regular educators to take ownership of difficult-to-teach students and to minimize inappropriate referrals to special education.

only small samples of student behavior. Clearly teachers have available to them, if they choose to use it, a far richer and varied sample of student behavior than the typical 'test'" (Gerber & Semmel, 1984, p. 141).

There is very little research on the effectiveness of PRTs (see Hallahan, Kauffman, & Lloyd, 1999; Vaughn, Bos, & Schumm, 1997). The few evaluations that have been done indicate two things: (1) they do cut down on the number of referrals to special education; and (2) team members and administrators report that they are effective (Schram et al., 1984).

Collaborative Consultation.   Cooperation between general and special education is a key concept in providing appropriate special education (Bateman & Linden, 1998). In **collaborative consultation,** the special education teacher or psychologist acts as an expert in providing advice to the general education teacher. The special education teacher may see the child with disabilities in a resource room, or the student may receive all of his or her instruction in the general education class.

Collaborative consultation stresses mutuality and reciprocity: "Mutuality means shared ownership of a common issue or problem by professionals. Reciprocity means allowing these parties to have equal access to information and the opportunity to participate in problem identification, discussion, decision making, and all final outcomes" (West & Idol, 1990, p. 23). In collaborative consultation, then, the special educator and the general educator assume equal responsibility for the student with disabilities, and neither assumes more authority in making recommendations about how to teach the child. Like PRTs, collaborative consultation can be used to keep teachers from referring difficult-to-teach students to special education or after the child has been identified for special education.

Research suggests that collaborative consultation is a promising approach to meeting the needs of many students with disabilities in general education settings. Nevertheless, much remains unknown about what makes consultation effective or ineffective in meeting students' needs.

Cooperative Teaching.   Sometimes referred to as collaborative teaching or co-teaching, **cooperative teaching** takes the notions of mutuality and reciprocity in collaborative consultation one step further (see Vaughn, Schumm, & Arguelles, 1997). In cooperative teaching general educators and special educators jointly teach in the same general education classroom composed of students with and without disabilities. In other words, the special educator comes out of his or her separate classroom (sometimes permanently) to teach in the regular class setting. In addition to promoting the notions of mutuality and reciprocity, one of the advantages that proponents of this model point out is that it helps the special educator know the everyday curricular demands faced by the student with disabilities. The special educator sees the context within which the student must function to succeed in the mainstream. As one teacher, when interviewed, put it:

> I have learned so much about the content itself which has helped me to teach English and math to students in my resource class.... I certainly have gained insights into the students themselves. For instance, when I do observation for [re-evaluations]... I am able to go into a class on one day and that's what I see, how that particular child performed on that particular day. But to be able to see kids on a day-in and day-out basis, I really feel I have a much better sense of who tunes outs [sic] when and why and who plugs away every minute of the day and still has difficulty because he hasn't

collaborative consultation. An approach in which a special educator and a general educator collaborate to come up with teaching strategies for a student with disabilities. The relationship between the two professionals is based on the premises of shared responsibility and equal authority.

cooperative teaching. An approach in which general educators and special educators teach together in the general classroom; it helps the special educator know the context of the regular classroom better.

Proponents of inclusion advocate cooperative learning strategies that pair students with disabilities with nondisabled peers.

understood. I can see their interactions with their peers. I can see their interest in the subject matter. I have a much more complete view of each child. (Nowacek, 1992, p. 275)

Cooperative teaching can vary with regard to who has the primary instructional responsibility in the classroom: the general educator, the special educator, or both. In some arrangements, the general educator assumes primary responsibility for instruction of academic content, while the special educator teaches academic survival skills, such as note taking and organizing homework assignments. This form of cooperative teaching is popular at the secondary level because it is difficult for special educators to have expertise in all content areas (history, biology, chemistry, Spanish, French, and so forth). In another arrangement, which is more popular at the elementary level, the special educator and general educator practice team teaching. They jointly plan and teach all content to all students, taking turns being responsible for different aspects of the curriculum. Under this model, a person walking into the classroom would have a difficult time telling which of the two teachers is the special educator.

Research on cooperative teaching is in its infancy. Researchers are consistently finding, however, that its success is dependent on at least two factors (Reeve & Hallahan, 1994). First, enough time needs to be built into the general and special educators' schedules for cooperative planning. Second, the two teachers' personalities and working styles need to be compatible. As one teacher said:

The biggest drawback I could see to using the collaborative model would be for the school system to say, "We're going to do this. We're going to train you teachers and you two are going to work together." That would not work at all. Carol and I have a relationship where it works. I'm sure there are other teachers that I couldn't work with. I think it's very person-specific. . . . It does take a lot of adjustment for the classroom teacher because we're used to being in control—in charge—and all of a sudden, there's this other person in your room. (Nowacek, 1992, p. 274)

Because of the importance of interpersonal skills in making cooperative teaching and collaborative consultation successful, some researchers have cautioned teachers against neglecting the actual teaching of the *students* (Fuchs & Fuchs, 1992; see also Vaughn, Bos, & Schumm, 1997). In other words, teachers engaged in cooperative teaching or collaborative consultation need to work on getting along together, but not to the neglect of the students they are teaching.

Curricula and Instructional Strategies.   Over several decades, authors have developed curriculum materials to enlighten nondisabled students about students with disabilities. These materials often involve activities constructed to teach children about differences, including disabilities. Some curricula are focused on multicultural differences (e.g., Thompson, 1993). Others are materials produced and disseminated by organizations such as the Easter Seal Society (see Arizona Easter Seal Society). Many of these approaches involve a variety of media and activities. One especially creative approach is "Kids on the Block" (The Kids on the Block, Inc., Alexandria, VA), a puppet show with Muppet-like characters that have different kinds of disabilities (e.g., mental retardation, cerebral palsy, visual impairment, behavior disorders). The show comes with scripts designed to explain basic concepts about children with disabilities and has a variety of curriculum suggestions.

Another curricular approach to improving pupils' attitudes toward their peers who have disabilities is the use of simulations. Some professionals believe that teachers can promote understanding of disabilities by having nondisabled students simulate disabilities in and out of school (Wesson & Mandell, 1989). Walking through the school while blindfolded, wearing glasses smeared with petroleum jelly, or trying to button clothing with hands covered with thick socks, for example, may help students understand and appreciate the disabilities of their peers who have limited vision or mobility.

Although more and more schools are using materials designed to teach children in regular education about students with disabilities, very few efforts have been mounted to evaluate these curricular modifications systematically.

Cooperative learning is an instructional strategy that many proponents of inclusion stress is an effective way of integrating students with disabilities into groups of nondisabled peers. In cooperative learning, students work together in heterogeneous small groups to solve problems or practice responses. The emphasis is on assisting each other in learning rather than on competition. Some educators have suggested that cooperative learning leads to better attitudes on the part of nondisabled students toward their peers with disabilities as well as to better attitudes of students with disabilities toward themselves. However, studies of cooperative groups also indicate that some students with disabilities, particularly those with emotional or behavioral disorders and those with mental impairments, do not work very well with others in groups that demand cooperation (Pomplun, 1997).

Peer tutoring is another recommended method of integrating students with disabilities into the mainstream (Jenkins & Jenkins, 1987). Professionals have advocated using children with disabilities as tutors as well as tutees. When a child with a disability assumes the role of tutor, the tutee is usually a younger peer.

When the whole class is involved, the strategy is referred to as **classwide peer tutoring (CWPT)**. In this procedure, peer tutoring is routinely done by all students in the general education classroom for particular subject matter (e.g., reading). CWPT does not mean that the teacher provides no instruction but that peers

cooperative learning. A teaching approach in which the teacher places students with heterogeneous abilities (for example, some might have disabilities) together to work on assignments.

peer tutoring. A method that can be used to integrate students with disabilities in general education classrooms, based on the notion that students can effectively tutor one another. The role of learner or teacher may be assigned to either the student with a disability or the nondisabled student.

classwide peer tutoring (CWPT). An instructional procedure in which all students in the class are involved in tutoring and being tutored by classmates on specific skills as directed by their teacher.

tutor each other to provide drill and practice (Greenwood, 1996). Researchers are continuing to test new combinations of cooperative learning and peer tutoring (e.g., Klinger & Vaughn, 1998).

Research on the effectiveness of various peer tutoring and cooperative learning strategies suggests that these methods may be very helpful for some students with disabilities and virtually useless for others (see Utley, Mortweet, & Greenwood, 1997). This leads us to emphasize the importance of monitoring carefully the progress of each individual student to assess the effectiveness of any instructional approach.

Partial participation means having students with disabilities participate, on a reduced basis, in virtually all activities experienced by all students in the general education classroom. It questions the assumption that including students with severe mental and physical limitations is a waste of time because they cannot benefit from them in the same way that nondisabled students can. Instead of excluding anyone from these activities, advocates of partial participation recommend that the teacher accommodate the student with disabilities by such strategies as "providing assistance for more difficult parts of a task, changing the 'rules' of the game or activity to make it less difficult, or changing the way in which a task or activity is organized or presented" (Raynes, Snell, & Sailor, 1991, p. 329).

The objectives of partial participation are twofold. First, proponents maintain that it provides exposure to academic content that the student with disabilities might otherwise miss. Second, it helps students with disabilities achieve a greater degree of social interaction with nondisabled peers (Giangreco & Putnam, 1991; Raynes et al., 1991).

Issues Continuing into the New Millennium

As the twenty-first century unfolds, the full-inclusion controversy is being sharpened by emphasis on school reform, especially reforms setting higher standards that all students are expected to meet. The direction the controversy will take is anyone's guess (see Kauffman, 1999a). However, three dimensions of the controversy appear likely to dominate.

First, there is the question of the legitimacy of atypical placements: Do special classes and special schools have a legitimate, defensible place in the alternatives provided to students with disabilities at public expense? If the answer to this question is "yes," then we are likely to see renewed emphasis on the advantages such special placements offer.

Second, if a student is not able to function adequately in the general education curriculum—achieving what is judged to be "success" in general education—then should he or she remain in the general education environment or be taught in an alternative place with students having similar learning needs? If the answer to this question is "remain in the general education environment," then ways must be found to remove the stigma of failure in that environment from both the student and the teacher, who may be judged to have failed to measure up to expectations.

Third, for students placed in alternative environments, increasing attention must be given to the quality of instruction that is provided there. Vaughn et al. (1998) found that the instruction offered in the resource rooms they studied was not the intensive, individualized, relentless, and effective instruction that should characterize special education. Kauffman (1994) suggested that the critical

partial participation. An approach in which students with disabilities, while in the general education classroom, engage in the same activities as nondisabled students but on a reduced basis; the teacher adapts the activity to allow each student to participate as much as possible.

problem of today's special education is not that students with disabilities are taught in separate settings but that special education teachers too seldom use the opportunity of such settings to offer the instruction students need.

Participation in General Assessments of Progress

In the 1990s, state and federal policy makers became very concerned about what they perceived as a general decline in students' educational achievement. As a result, they emphasized "standards-based" reforms. These reforms involve setting standards of learning or achievement that are measured through standardized tests or other assessment procedures. The reformers felt that teachers' expectations have been too low and that *all* students should be held to higher standards of performance.

Current Trends

Because special education is an integral part of the system of public education in America, students with disabilities were included in the concern expressed for higher standards. That is, the feeling was that expectations have been too low for students in special education and that they should not only be expected to learn the general curriculum but be expected to perform at a level comparable to that of students without disabilities on assessments of progress. Moreover, reformers argued, no school or state should be allowed to avoid responsibility for demonstrating that its students with disabilities are making acceptable progress in the general education curriculum.

The standards-based reform movement of the 1990s brought with it a heavy emphasis on *access to the general education curriculum* by students with disabilities. The curriculum for students with disabilities often has been different from the curriculum in general education. Failure to teach students with disabilities the same things that are taught in general education has been interpreted to mean that the expectations for these students are lower, resulting in their low achievement and failure to make a successful transition to adult life.

Furthermore, students with disabilities often have not been included in statewide or national assessments of educational progress. Consequently, we have little information about how they have been progressing compared to the normative group or how education reforms might affect them (Gronna, Jenkins, & Chin-Chance, 1998; Vanderwood, McGrew, & Ysseldyke, 1998). The standards-based reform movement of the 1990s resulted in projects designed to include students with disabilities in national and state assessments of educational progress. The 1997 amendments of the federal Individuals with Disabilities Education Act (IDEA) required the inclusion of students with disabilities in such assessments (Bateman & Linden, 1998; McDonnell, McLaughlin, & Morison, 1997; Yell, 1998; Yell & Shriner, 1997).

Understandably, the standards-based reform movement has generated much controversy: What should the standards be (just how high should they be, and in what areas of the curriculum should they be set)? Who should set the standards? How should achievement of or progress toward the standards be measured?

What should be the consequences for students—and for schools or states—if standards are not met?

For students with disabilities, additional questions arise: Should all standards apply to all students, regardless of their disability? What should be the consequences of failing to meet a given standard if the student has a disability? Under what circumstances are alternative standards appropriate? Under what circumstances should special accommodations be made in assessing progress toward a standard? Answering questions like these requires professional judgment in the individual case, and such judgment is required by law (see Bateman & Linden, 1998; Yell, 1998).

The inclusion of students with disabilities in assessments of progress in the general education curriculum must now be addressed in every IEP. Although the law recognizes that some students with disabilities have educational needs that are not addressed in the general education curriculum, each student's IEP must include:

A statement of measurable annual goals, including benchmarks or short-term objectives related to—

(i) meeting the child's needs that result from the child's disability to enable the child to be involved in and progress in the general curriculum; and

(ii) *meeting each of the child's other educational needs that result from the child's disability* [author's emphasis].

Thus, the IEP team for each child with a disability must make an individualized determination regarding how the child will participate in the general curriculum, and what, if any, educational needs that will not be met through involvement in the general curriculum should be addressed in the IEP. This includes children who are educated in separate classrooms or schools. (Bateman & Linden, 1998, pp. 192–193)

Yell and Shriner (1997) explain further:

The IEP team must document which portions of the curriculum, and therefore which goals and standards, are relevant to each student in special education. It may be that all curricular goals are pertinent regardless of where instruction is provided. In this case, the student should take part in the general state assessment even if accommodations are needed. If the student's instruction addresses only some of the curricular goals, partial participation is indicated. In this case, the student has a modified assessment plan. If the student is working on performance goals and standards unique to his or her situation, because no portion of the curriculum is appropriate (even with modification), participation in the general assessment . . . is the appropriate course in these circumstances. A plan for how the student will be assessed must be part of the IEP. (p. 7)

Accommodations for evaluation procedures might involve altering the time given for responding, changing the setting in which the assessment is done, or using an alternative format for either the presentation of tasks or the type of response required. Examples of the kinds of accommodations that might be made for students with disabilities who are taking tests are shown in Table 2.1. Such accommodations may make a significant difference in how students with some disabilities are able to perform on standardized tests (Tindal, Heath, Hollenbeck, Almond, & Harniss, 1998). Therefore, making sure that students are assessed with appropriate accommodations for their disabilities will be extremely important when they are included in evaluations of progress.

Table 2.1 Examples of Accommodations for Assessments

Flexible Time	Flexible Setting	Alternative Presentation Format	Alternative Response Format
Extended time	Test alone in test carrel or separate room	Braille or large-print edition	Pointing to response
Alternating lengths of test sections (e.g., shorter and longer)	Test in small-group setting	Signing of directions	Using template for responding
More frequent breaks	Test at home (with accountability)	Interpretation of directions	Giving response in sign language
Extended testing sessions over several days	Test in special education classroom	Taped directions	Using a computer
	Test in room with special lighting	Highlighted keywords	Allow answers in test book

Source: Yell, M. L., & Shriner, J. G. (1997). The IDEA amendments of 1997: Implications for special and general education teachers, administrators, and teacher trainers. *Focus on Exceptional Children, 30*(1), p. 8. Reprinted with permission.

Issues Continuing into the New Millennium

No doubt the standards-based reform movement of the 1990s will entail enormous difficulties related to all students, but particularly to those with disabilities. In any area of performance, setting a standard that very few individuals fail will be perceived, eventually, as "low." Setting a standard that many individuals cannot reach will be perceived, at least after a time, as "high." Who will be blamed for a given person's failure to meet a standard—and who will be congratulated when someone meets or exceeds a standard—depends on our assessment of the effort expended by teacher and student.

However, one thing seems certain: Standards will not homogenize achievement or expectations. The consequences of standards-based reform for students with and without disabilities will become clearer during the first decades of the new millennium.

Early Intervention

Many educators and social scientists believe that the earlier in life a disability is recognized and a program of education or treatment is started, the better the outcome for the child (Burchinal, Campbell, Bryant, Wasik, & Ramey, 1997; Odom & Kaiser, 1997). Bricker (1986) states three basic arguments for early intervention:

1. A child's early learning provides the foundation for later learning, so the sooner a special program of intervention is begun, the further the child is likely to go in learning more complex skills.

Public Law 99–457, passed in 1986, stipulates that states must provide preschool services to all children between the ages of three and five who have disabilities. This law also provides incentives for establishing special education programs for infants and toddlers.

2. Early intervention is likely to provide support for the child and family that will help prevent the child from developing additional problems or disabilities.

3. Early intervention can help families adjust to having a child with disabilities; give parents the skills they need to handle the child effectively at home; and help families find the additional support services they may need, such as counseling, medical assistance, or financial aid.

Children whose disabilities are diagnosed at a very young age tend to be those with specific syndromes (Down syndrome, for example) or obvious physical disabilities. Many have severe and multiple disabilities. Up through the primary grades, children with disabilities may be categorized under the broad label **developmental delay** rather than identified as having a more specific disability (e.g., mental retardation, learning disability, or emotional disturbance). Typically, such a child's needs cannot be met by a single agency or intervention, so many professionals must work together closely if the child is to be served effectively. If the child's disabilities are recognized at an early age and intervention by all necessary professionals is well coordinated, the child's learning and development can often be greatly enhanced.

Federal laws now require that a variety of early intervention services be available to all infants and toddlers who are identified as having disabilities. Such services include special education instruction, physical therapy, speech and language therapy, and medical diagnostic services. In addition, laws require the development of an **individualized family service plan (IFSP)** (see Bateman & Linden, 1998). As discussed in Chapter 1, an IFSP is similar to an individualized education program (IEP) for older children, but it broadens the focus to include the family as well as the child. In fact, federal regulations stipulate that the family be involved in the development of the IFSP. Other important requirements are that the IFSP must contain statements of the:

- child's present levels of functioning in cognitive, physical, language and speech, psychosocial, and self-help development

developmental delay. A term often used to encompass a variety of disabilities of infants or young children indicating that they are significantly behind the norm for development in one or more areas such as motor development, cognitive development, or language.

individualized family service plan (IFSP). A plan mandated by PL 99–457 to provide services for young children with disabilities (under three years of age) and their families; drawn up by professionals and parents; similar to an IEP for older children.

- family's resources, priorities, and concerns relating to the child's development
- major expected outcomes for the child and family, including criteria, procedures, and time lines for assessing progress
- specific early intervention services necessary to meet the child's and the family's needs, including frequency, intensity, location, and method of delivery
- projected dates for initiating and ending the services
- name of the case manager
- steps needed to ensure a smooth transition from the early intervention program into a preschool program

Types of Programs

One common way of categorizing the variety of early intervention programs is to consider whether the primary location of the services is in a center, a home, or a combination of the two. The earliest early intervention programs for children with disabilities were center-based. In center-based programs, the child and the family come to the center for training and/or counseling. One advantage to center-based programs is that center staff can see more children. Furthermore, some professionals believe that this program allows center staff to have more influence over what goes on in the interaction between parent and child.

In more recent years, authorities have advocated home-based programs or a combination of center- and home-based approaches. There are several advantages to approaches that take place in the home. A couple of the most important are that (1) with the increase in mothers working outside the home and single-parent families, home-based programs are more convenient for more family members, and (2) skills and techniques learned by children and adults at the center need to be transferred to the home, but when these skills are learned in the natural environment—that is, the home—this transfer is not necessary.

Current Trends

Compared to special education in general, special education for infants, toddlers, and preschoolers has had few controversial issues. This is probably because so many professionals have fought for so long to get the needs of very young children recognized that they have not had time to engage in many debates about specific details concerning early intervention. In a sense, early childhood special educators have been bound together by the common goal of securing legislation and programming for young children with disabilities. Nevertheless, there have been and continue to be some areas of disagreement among early childhood special education professionals (Carta & Greenwood, 1997; Lerner, Lowenthal, & Egan, 1998). Three of the most compelling issues relate to (1) the appropriate role of the family in early intervention, (2) whether it is better to have a child- or a teacher-directed curriculum, and (3) whether full inclusion is best for all young children.

Appropriate Role of the Family.   A significant issue is how the family should be involved in early intervention programming (Lerner et al., 1998; Thompson, Lobb, Elling, Herman, Jurkiewicz, & Hulleza, 1998). One characteristic of recent early intervention programming, and indeed one of the hallmarks of the IFSP, has been the involvement of parents. Federal regulations, however, have not specifically directed how parents should be included in early intervention programming.

For example, some special educators hold that parents should be trained to use intervention techniques with their preschoolers. Research on the effectiveness of this approach is scant, but one team of researchers found that preschoolers with language disorders made comparable progress whether they received intervention from professionals or from their parents who had been trained to deliver the intervention (Eiserman, Weber, & McCoun, 1995). Other educators are concerned that the notion of including parents may be being misinterpreted to mean that professionals should focus more on changing the family than the child. Slentz and Bricker (1992), for example, have pointed out that federal regulations stipulate that any services provided for the family are for the purpose of meeting the needs of the child.

In particular, Slentz and Bricker are opposed to early childhood special educators becoming heavily involved in assessment of family members. If they do, "parents may legitimately question why providing such information is necessary when they thought the purpose of the early intervention program was to help their child. Many families perceive this process as an invasion of privacy" (Slentz & Bricker, 1992, p. 14). Instead, they believe that professionals should take a low-key approach to assessing families. Slentz and Bricker recommend that professionals briefly interview parents to find out the needs of the family and the child, rather than administer a lengthy battery of tests. If parents indicate a need for it, they can be referred for further evaluation.

Closely related to the issue of assessment is the larger issue of who should be in control over decision making for the family. Slentz and Bricker (1992) believe that "in large measure, families should decide on their goals and priorities with the early intervention staff assisting in the attainment of those goals" (pp. 17–18; see also Gallagher, 1992; Lerner et al., 1998)

Child-Directed Versus Teacher-Directed Programs.   For some time, tension has existed between early childhood educators concerned with nondisabled populations and those focused on children with disabilities over the degree of teacher direction that is most appropriate. Heavily influenced by the theories of Piaget, most early childhood teachers are oriented toward a curriculum that allows children to explore their environment relatively freely. These teachers advocate a developmental approach that assumes that children's development will unfold naturally with encouragement, guidance, and support from the teacher (Position Statement of National Association for the Education of Young Children and National Association of Early Childhood Specialists in State Departments of Education, 1991).

Many early interventionists, on the other hand, come from a tradition that assumes children with disabilities need a heavy dose of direction from adults if they are to learn the skills they lack. Furthermore, early childhood special educators have generally had a greater focus on individualizing instruction for preschoolers through task analysis, adaptation of materials and activities, and systematic assessment (Carta, 1995; Carta & Greenwood, 1997). As more and more children with disabilities have been integrated with nondisabled preschoolers, the issues of teacher direction and individualization have come to the fore.

A major task facing early childhood special educators is to reach agreement with mainstream early childhood educators regarding programming for preschoolers with disabilities. Both sides can undoubtedly learn from each other. On the one hand, researchers have known for a long time that preschoolers with disabilities do better in highly structured, teacher-directed, individualized programs (Abt Associates, 1976–1977). On the other hand, authorities have noted that moving from a highly structured preschool intervention program to a traditional kindergarten can present problems:

> The ecology of special education preschool classrooms may preclude opportunities for students to practice skills that foster independence. Students in special education preschools spend more time in small groups of individual instruction, and receive much more teacher prompting than do peers in typical preschool classes. Although these instructional arrangements may facilitate skill acquisition, they may inhibit the acquisition of the very academic support skills that facilitate a successful transition to the academic mainstream. Children in these special education classrooms have few opportunities to acquire or practice the independent skills that are important for success in kindergarten. (Fowler, Schwartz, & Atwater, 1991, p. 138)

Inclusive Education.   Virtually all early childhood educators suggest that children with identifiable disabilities and those considered at risk for school failure should be included in programs designed to serve diverse groups of learners, including young children without disabilities (Bowman, 1994; Katz, 1994; Sainato & Strain, 1993). However, the extent to which the practices in programs for typically developing young children are appropriate for children with disabilities is a matter of considerable controversy (Bricker, 1995; McLean & Odom, 1993).

Bricker's observation that a radical philosophy of inclusive education may not necessarily serve all young children well seems borne out by research (Garrett, Thorp, Behrmann, & Denham, 1998; Mills et al., 1998).

Issues Continuing into the New Millennium

We hope that early childhood education will continue to play an important role in eliminating and lessening the impact of disability on children and their families. We caution, however, not to assume that early intervention alone will mean fewer children with disabilities. Although educators are devising more effective programs of early intervention, the number of children with disabilities is increasing. The reasons for this increase are many and complex and are related to changes in economic and social conditions in the United States. Today, we know that at the beginning of the twenty-first century:

- A high percentage of young children and their mothers live in poverty, have poor nutrition, and are exposed to environmental conditions likely to cause disease and disability.
- Many babies are born to teenage mothers.
- Many babies are born to mothers who receive inadequate prenatal care, have poor nutrition during pregnancy, and abuse substances that can harm the fetus.
- Many babies are born with a low birthweight.
- Environmental hazards, both chemical and social, are increasing.
- Millions of children are subjected to abuse and an environment in which violence and substance abuse are pervasive.

- Substantial cuts in and revisions of social programs have widened the gap between needs and the availability of social services.

These facts prompted the President's Committee on Mental Retardation and the National Coalition on Prevention of Mental Retardation to speak of a new morbidity—a new set of disabilities (Baumeister, Kupstas, & Klindworth, 1990). The new morbidity includes a variety of behavioral, health, and school problems that affect a growing number of U.S. children and are caused by many of the preceding factors. Implementing and expanding services and training the early childhood specialists necessary to provide effective early intervention are major challenges of the twenty-first century.

Early intervention seems to hold great promise for prevention of disabilities, but there are strong forces working against prevention, including the revulsion many people feel for labels and propositions of education reformers that work against identifying problems early and intervening to stop them from getting worse (Kauffman, 1999b). Besides issues surrounding prevention, other issues for the new millennium include the use of computer technology with young children, the changing roles of special educators, emerging philosophies of early childhood education, cultural and linguistic diversity, and access to community resources (Lerner et al., 1998).

Transition from Secondary School to Adulthood

Preparing students for continued education, adult responsibilities, independence, and employment have always been goals of public secondary education. Most students complete high school and find jobs, enter a vocational training program, or go to college without experiencing major adjustment difficulties. We know that dropout and unemployment rates are far too high for all youths, especially in economically depressed communities, but the outlook for students with disabilities may be even worse (Hendrick, MacMillan, & Balow, 1989; Wolman, Bruininks, & Thurlow, 1989; U.S. Department of Education, 1994).

Published figures on dropout rates must be viewed with caution because there are many different ways of defining *dropout* and computing the statistics (MacMillan et al., 1992). Studies of what happens to students with disabilities during and after their high school years strongly suggest, however, that a higher percentage of them, compared to students without disabilities, have difficulty in making the transition from adolescence to adulthood and from school to work. Many students with disabilities drop out of school, experience great difficulty in finding and holding jobs, do not find work suited to their capabilities, do not receive further training or education, or become dependent on their families or public assistance programs (Collet-Klingenberg, 1998; Heal & Rusch, 1995; Sinclair, Christenson, Evelo, & Hurley, 1998; Sitlington, Frank, & Carson, 1992).

Federal Initiatives

Federal laws, including IDEA, now require attention to transition plans for older students, and these must be incorporated in students' IEPs (Bateman & Linden, 1998; Yell, 1998). The federal government defines transition services as:

Students with disabilities must have preparation for life after high school, including further education, work, recreation, and independent living.

a coordinated set of activities for a student, designed within an outcome-oriented process, which promotes movement from school to post-school activities, including post-secondary education, vocational training, integrated employment (including supported employment), continuing and adult education, adult services, independent living, or community participation.

Each student's IEP must contain a statement of needed transition services for him or her, beginning no later than sixteen years of age and annually thereafter. (For students for whom it is appropriate, the statement is to be included in the IEP at a younger age.) In addition, the IEP must include a statement of the linkages and/or responsibilities of each participating agency before the student leaves the school setting.

An important aspect of this legislation is that it recognizes that transition involves more than just employment. The box on page 75 illustrates how multiple agencies and individuals may be involved in planning for the transition of a high school student with disabilities. This broad emphasis on independent living, community adjustment, and so forth has been applauded by many authorities. For example, some have championed the idea that transition programming should be aimed at increasing the quality of life for people with disabilities (Chadsey-Rusch & Heal, 1995; Halpern, 1993; Sands & Kozleski, 1994; Szymanski, 1994). Although quality of life is difficult to define, Halpern (1993) points to personal choice as its underlying principle. He also identifies three important quality-of-life domains: (1) physical and material well-being; (2) performance of adult roles (e.g., employment, leisure, personal relationships, social responsibility); and (3) personal fulfillment (e.g., happiness).

Supported Employment. With the federal mandate for transition services has come an increase in the use of supported employment. In fact, it is cited in the federal definition of transition services as an example of integrated employment (see above). **Supported employment,** designed to assist persons with disabilities who cannot function independently in competitive employment, is a

supported employment. A method of integrating people with disabilities who cannot work independently into competitive employment; includes use of an employment specialist, or job coach, who helps the person with a disability function on the job.

Case Study: Sarah

Sarah is a junior at East Side High School. She was in an accident in 3rd grade that left her with a learning disability and without the use of her legs; she uses a wheelchair for mobility. Sarah has use of both arms and hands, but she experiences weakness in them after prolonged use. Sarah is interested in a career in the retail fashion industry, both in sales and clothing design. She plans to live independently and wants to work with youth programs in her spare time.

Her IEP team this year is headed by one of the school's guidance counselors and consists of Sarah, her parents, her LD teacher, a vocational rehabilitation counselor, the OT/PT, her marketing and distributive education (DE) teacher, and the district's transition specialist. Based on an assessment of Sarah's needs, goals, and preferences, her educational program for 11th grade will consist of the following courses: art (drawing), computers (graphic design), marketing and distribution (two class periods), English, math, and physical education.

The guidance counselor and LD teacher are working with the general academic teachers to assist Sarah in applying strategies to facilitate her learning in these classes. Through her marketing and distributive education class (a regular vocational education cooperative program), Sarah will begin working at the Gap store in the local mall. She will leave school at the end of sixth period and will work 20 hours per week. She will ride the transit system bus from school to work. Her parents will provide transportation home, although Sarah expects to arrange rides with co-workers in the mall once she gets to know them.

The DE teacher has worked with Sarah and her new supervisor to develop a training plan that identifies her work tasks and the competencies she is to develop through the work experience. The VR counselor is helping the employer modify the cashiering station to accommodate Sarah's wheelchair, as well as the storage areas and store aisles. In the future, the VR counselor will assist Sarah in developing a PASS plan (Plan to Achieve Self-Support) to purchase a computer needed for the graphic arts program at the community college—her immediate postschool training goal. The DE teacher has also invited and encouraged Sarah to join the DE club that meets every Wednesday after school.

Through the help of her parents and the district transition specialist, Sarah worked half days during the previous summer, and will do so next year, in the summer youth program doing arts and crafts activities with elementary school children. To help Sarah gain strength in her hands and arms, the OT/PT is working with Sarah and her PE teacher to develop a weight-lifting program. She has also helped to identify strategies that Sarah can use when drawing and working on the computer so that her arms and hands become less fatigued.

At home, Sarah has specific chores and responsibilities involving cleaning, cooking, laundry, and helping to care for the family pet. With her parents' assistance and cooperation, Sarah developed a schedule that fits together school, work, and home responsibilities as well as provides time to just hang out with her friends.

Source: Kohler, P. D. (1998). Implementing a transition perspective of education: A comprehensive approach to planning and delivering secondary education and transition services. In F. R. Rusch & J. G. Chadsey (Eds.), *Beyond high school: Transition from school to work.* © *1998* Belmont, CA: Wadsworth, p. 185. Reprinted with permission.

method of ensuring that they are able to work in integrated work settings. Competitive employment is defined as working at least twenty hours per week. Integrated work settings are defined as:

> settings where (a) most workers are not handicapped and (b) individuals with handicaps are not part of a work group consisting only of others with handicaps, or are part of a small work group of not more than eight individuals with handicaps. Additionally, if there are no co-workers or the only co-workers are members of a small group of not more than eight individuals with handicaps, individuals with handicaps must have regular contact with nonhandicapped individuals, other than personnel who provide support services. Finally, these regulations require that supported employees be provided follow-up services at least twice monthly at the job site, except in the case of chronic mental illness. (Rusch & Hughes, 1990, p. 9)

In a typical supported employment situation, an employment specialist, or **job coach,** places the individual in a job with a business. The job coach then provides

job coach. A person who assists adult workers with disabilities (especially those with mental retardation), providing vocational assessment, instruction, overall planning, and interaction assistance with employers, family, and related government and service agencies.

onsite training that is gradually reduced as the worker is able to function more independently on the job.

Current Trends

Like early intervention programming, little controversy surrounds the basic premise of transition programming for students as they move from school to work. All special educators agree that transition programming is critical for the successful adjustment of adults with disabilities (see Kohler, 1998). However, there is some controversy regarding the specifics of transition. Much of this has to do with trying to meet the diverse requirements of the federal mandate. A few states have achieved a high degree of compliance with federal law and have implemented excellent transition policies, but many others have not (Furney, Hasazi, & DeStefano, 1997). Many IEPs are in technical compliance with the IDEA mandate for transition but lack key elements, reflecting a lack of thoughtful planning (Grigal, Test, Beattie, & Wood, 1997).

Some professionals are debating how best to build a curriculum that covers education, employment, independent living, and community participation. This concern for meeting the diverse needs of students is manifested somewhat differently for students with more severe disabilities than for those with milder disabilities.

Students with Severe Disabilities. For students with severe disabilities, much of the concern focuses on the coordination and linkage of the many agencies outside the school setting (DeStefano & Wermuth, 1992). Many special education personnel are unaccustomed to working with nonschool agencies. For example, the relationship between vocational and special education has traditionally been ambiguous. Federal regulations, however, now require that special education work with vocational education as well as with other agencies in the community.

For a number of years, special educators at the secondary level have been moving toward more involvement in the community, but the federal transition mandate has hastened the need for these outreach efforts. Approaches such as supported employment, for example, require that special educators work with local employers in setting up and instituting training and working environments for students with disabilities. Not all special educators have been trained for this expanded role, however. We are still in the infancy stage of knowing how best to accomplish this interface between the school and community environments. There is a need for experimentation with approaches to educating special educators for this broader role.

Students with Mild Disabilities. For students with mild disabilities, much of the concern centers on attempting to meet their academic as well as their vocational needs. Teachers of secondary students are constantly faced with the decision of how much to stress academics versus vocational preparation. Because their disabilities are milder, many children with learning disabilities, for example, may be able to go on to postsecondary educational institutions, such as community colleges or universities. It is often difficult to tell as early as tenth grade (when such decisions need to be made) whether to steer students with learning disabilities toward college preparatory or more vocationally oriented curricula.

Some authorities believe that too many students with learning disabilities have been "sold short" on how much they can achieve academically. These authorities believe that such students are written off as academic failures who can never achieve at the college level. This diminished expectation for academic success translates into a curriculum that makes few academic demands on students. For example, one study of students in learning disabilities classrooms at the secondary level found an "environmental press against academic content" (Zigmond & Miller, 1992, p. 25); hence the recent emphasis we have already discussed on access to and progress in the general education academic curriculum.

Other authorities maintain that an overemphasis on academics leaves many students with learning disabilities unprepared to enter the world of work upon leaving school. They believe that the learning problems of students with learning disabilities tend to be minimized. These authorities assert that just because students with learning disabilities are characterized as having mild disabilities, they do not necessarily have insignificant learning impairments.

Along these same lines, some professionals think that far too few support services are available to students with mild disabilities. Whereas transition services such as supported employment are available to persons with severe disabilities, individuals with milder disabilities are often left to fend for themselves once they graduate from secondary school (see Zetlin & Hosseini, 1989).

Goals 2000 and Transition Programming for Students with Mild Disabilities.   Adding to the confusion over the debate about academics versus vocational preparation is the current federal emphasis on academics. Beginning in the late 1980s and continuing into the 1990s, a number of national reports have criticized the general educational system in the United States. Pointing to the low achievement levels of American youths, compared with those of other industrialized countries, these reports have resulted in a call for higher standards in the nation's schools, as we mentioned in our earlier discussion of standards-based reform and assessment of educational progress.

In 1994, Congress passed the **Goals 2000: Educate America Act,** which sets eight national goals for the year 2000 (see Table 2.2 on page 78). Critics assert that these goals largely ignore the educational needs of students with disabilities. What's more, they fear that the emphasis on higher standards has taken away the focus from the needs of students with disabilities who are unable to meet such high standards. As one example, critics point to the fact that several states now require students to pass minimum competency tests to receive their high school diplomas. Some special educators have expressed concern that these requirements might be unfair to students with disabilities (Halpern, 1992).

Issues Continuing into the New Millennium

It is still too early to tell how much impact Goals 2000, the related emphasis on standards-based reform, and the inclusion of students with disabilities in general education curriculum and assessment procedures (as mandated by the 1997 amendments to IDEA) will have on students with disabilities. But as we enter the twenty-first century, despite some of the unresolved issues, we can be encouraged by all the attention that special educators have given to the area of transition. A variety of transition opportunities are available now that were unavailable just a few years ago. However, it is increasingly clear that successful transition takes early and sustained effort, and it is not clear just how such support can best be provided (see Collet-Klingenberg, 1998; Sinclair et al., 1988).

In considering transition issues, it is helpful to keep in mind that a smooth and successful transition to adult life is difficult for any adolescent. Individuals find

Goals 2000: Educate America Act. Legislation passed in 1994, aimed at increasing the academic standards in U.S. schools; some educators fear that the focus on high standards may harm students with disabilities.

Table

2.2   Eight Goals Established by Goals 2000: Educate America Act

1	Readiness for school	By the year 2000, all children in the United States will start school ready to learn.
2	High school completion	By the year 2000, the high school graduation rate will have increased to at least 90 percent.
3	Student achievement and citizenship	By the year 2000, all students will leave grades 4, 8, and 12 having demonstrated competency over challenging subject matter (including English, mathematics, science, history, foreign languages, civics and government, economics, arts, and geography), and every school in the U.S. will ensure that all students learn to use their minds well, so they may be prepared for responsible citizenship, further learning, and productive employment in a modern economy.
4	Teacher education and professional development	By the year 2000, the nation's teaching force will have access to programs for the continued improvement of their professional skills and the opportunity to acquire the knowledge and skills needed to instruct and prepare all U.S. students for the next century.
5	Science and mathematics	By the year 2000, U.S. students will be first in the world in science and mathematics achievement.
6	Adult literacy and lifelong learning	By the year 2000, every adult American will be literate and will possess the knowledge and skills necessary to compete in a global economy and exercise the rights and responsibilities of citizenship.
7	Safe, disciplined, and alcohol- and drug-free schools	By the year 2000, every school in the U.S. will be free of drugs and violence and the unauthorized presence of firearms and alcohol, and will offer a disciplined environment conducive to learning.
8	Parental participation	By the year 2000, every school will promote partnerships that increase parental involvement and participation in promoting the social, emotional, and academic growth of children.

Source: U.S. Senate–House Conference, 1994

many different routes to adulthood, and we would be foolish to prescribe a single pattern of transition. Our goal must be to provide the special assistance needed by adolescents and young adults with disabilities that will help them achieve the most rewarding, productive, independent, and integrated adult lives possible. This goal cannot be achieved by assuming that all adolescents and young adults with disabilities, or even all individuals falling into a given special education category, will need the same special transition services or that all will achieve the same level of independence and productivity. One of education's great challenges is to devise an effective array of programs that will meet the individual needs of students on their paths to adulthood.

Discipline of Students with Disabilities

In the 1990s, safe schools and orderly learning environments became paramount concerns of many school administrators and legislators (e.g., U.S. Department of Education, 1998). Dramatic shootings in schools, plus statistics on the presence of weapons, violence, and drugs in schools, led to severe measures intended to improve discipline, decrease violence, and eliminate drugs in schools.

One of the most dramatic and controversial measures involving discipline for serious offenses is known as *zero tolerance*. Zero tolerance was introduced by the federal Gun-Free Schools Act of 1994, which led to corresponding state legislation. Under most of these state laws, school boards and other school administration may choose to use discretion in applying the zero tolerance policy, although sometimes they do not. In the case of discipline, zero tolerance means that the circumstances surrounding a particular incident are not weighed in deciding what the consequences should be; only the act itself is to be questioned. For example, if a student brings a weapon to school, the circumstances leading up to the incident are not considered relevant in determining the punishment.

In many ways, zero tolerance is parallel to **mandatory sentencing** in the legal system. Mandatory sentencing, which requires a particular sentence for a particular offense without consideration of circumstances, was passed into law because judges were thought to be often too lenient. In essence, judges were assumed to be abusing their authority to use discretion, so their discretion was removed by legislators; the judge's only role, under mandatory sentencing laws, is to determine whether or not a particular criminal offense was committed by the defendant. Predictably, mandatory sentencing has resulted in outrageous miscarriages of justice, as judges have no discretion in taking facts other than the commission of the offense into consideration in determining punishment. For example, a defendant might be sentenced to twenty years or more in prison for an offense that he or she did not understand.

Similar observations led to the institution of zero tolerance in school discipline, and the outcomes have been similar. In education, school administrators and teachers have been assumed to abuse their discretion in determining the punishment for certain serious offenses, such as bringing a weapon to school. Therefore, higher authorities (e.g., boards of education) have in many cases removed discretion from the hands of teachers and lower administrators, prescribing a given punishment (e.g, long-term suspension or expulsion) for a particular offense (e.g., bringing a knife or a drug to school) regardless of the circumstances surrounding the act. For example, if an elementary school child accidentally brings a paring knife to school in her lunch box, then she will be expelled. If a high school boy forgets to remove a roofing knife from his pocket and turns it in at the office because he knows he should not have it in school, then he will be expelled. If a toy gun is brought to school by a mentally retarded student who does not understand that a gun is a weapon and even toy weapons are forbidden in school, or if a child is found to possess a single dose of a commonly used nonprescription drug, then he or she will be expelled. Decisions like these have actually been made by school authorities under the zero-tolerance rationale.

Violence, disorder, and drugs in schools are serious problems that must be addressed. However, the current movement toward zero tolerance and standardization of penalties presents particular problems for special education. Special educators recognize the need for schoolwide discipline that brings a high degree of uniformity to consequences for particular acts (e.g., Nelson, Martella, & Galand, 1999; Sugai, 1996). Nevertheless, special educators also argue for, and the 1997 amendments to IDEA require, that exceptions be made based on the relevance of the student's disability to the event in question (Zurkowski, Kelly, & Griswold, 1998).

mandatory sentencing. Laws requiring specific sentences for specific violations, removing the discretion of the judge in sentencing based on circumstances of the defendant or other considerations.

Current Trends

The discipline of students with disabilities is highly controversial, and many teachers and school administrators are confused about what is legal. Special rules apply to managing some of the serious misbehavior of students who are identified as having disabilities. In some cases, the typical school rules apply, but in others they do not (see Bateman & Linden, 1998; Yell, 1998; Yell & Shriner, 1997). In any case, much of the special education advocacy regarding discipline is based on finding alternatives to suspension and expulsion for bringing weapons or drugs to school or for endangering others, as keeping students out of school is not an effective way of helping them learn to behave acceptably (Bock, Tapscott, & Savner, 1998).

Three concepts and related procedures provide the basis for much of the controversy surrounding the discipline of students with disabilities: (1) determining whether the behavior is or is not a manifestation of the student's disability, (2) providing an alternative placement for the student's education for an interim period if temporary removal from the student's present placement is necessary, and (3) developing positive, proactive behavior intervention plans. We discuss these issues further in Chapter 9, as they most frequently arise in the case of students with emotional or behavioral disorders.

Under IDEA, typical rules of discipline apply to the student with disabilities unless (1) the offense involves a weapon or drugs, (2) the student is a danger to self or others, or (3) the consequence of the act is suspension or placement in an alternative setting for more than ten days. If a weapon or drug is involved or the student is found to be dangerous or the school decides to suspend or place the student in an alternative setting for more than ten days, then school officials must make a **manifestation determination** before deciding on the discipline of a student with a disability. If they determine that the student's misbehavior *was* a manifestation of his or her disability, then the typical discipline procedures of the school involving suspension of more than ten days or expulsion will not apply; if they determine that the student's misbehavior *was not* a manifestation of disability, then the same discipline procedures that apply to other students apply to the student with the disability—except that under no circumstances can the education of the student with disability simply be terminated. There are no exceptions to the rule, under IDEA 1997, that the education of a student with a disability must be continued, even if the student goes to prison. Predictably, some educators argue that this gives unequal and unfair protection to students with disabilities.

The use of alternative interim placements for students who violate school rules is another point of controversy. With the emphasis on inclusion in general education, it is understandable that some special educators see any alternative setting for misbehaving students as unwarranted segregation. The issue is balancing the interests of one student against the safety of other students and of judging the nature of the environment in which the student with disabilities is most likely to be educated effectively.

Perhaps the most critical part of the discipline provisions of IDEA 1997 is the requirement that teachers must devise positive behavioral intervention plans for students with disabilities who have behavior problems. The emphasis of this requirement is on creating proactive and positive interventions (Artesani & Millar, 1998; Ruef, Higgins, Glaeser, & Patnode, 1998). When special discipline is in-

manifestation determination.
A procedure in which school officials determine whether a student's behavior is or is not a manifestation of his or her disability.

volved, the school must reevaluate the student's IEP and make efforts to address the misconduct that led to the problem. Also required is a functional assessment of behavior, in which educators attempt to determine and alter the factors that account for the student's misconduct (McConnell, Hilvitz, & Cox, 1998). Although the notion of functional assessment is itself a controversial issue (Nelson, Roberts, Mather, & Rutherford, 1999), it is clear that the intent of the legal requirement is to encourage proactive problem solving rather than reactive punishment of misconduct.

Issues Continuing into the New Millennium

The struggle to resolve discipline issues involving students with disabilities is on-going. On the one hand, school administrators want the highest possible degree of uniformity of expectations (i.e., the same high expectations for all students). On the other hand, special educators and other advocates for students with disabilities see the uniformity of disciplinary rules as failure to accommodate students' individual abilities and needs. The legal requirements regarding discipline, including suspension and expulsion, will continue to evolve as educators find more productive ways of dealing with serious misconduct (see Walther-Thomas & Brownell, 1998).

The twenty-first century will no doubt see efforts to tip the balance of interests one way or the other—toward greater uniformity and fewer exceptions for students with disabilities or toward greater individualization and discretion in determining the punishment for specific infractions of school expectations. We hope that the new century will see a still greater emphasis on proactive intervention and positive behavioral supports for all students.

Some Concluding Thoughts Regarding Trends and Issues

If you are feeling a bit overwhelmed at the controversial nature of special education, then we have achieved our objective. We, too, are constantly amazed at the number of unanswered questions our field faces. It seems that just as we find what we think are the right answers to a certain set of questions about how to educate students with disabilities, another set of questions emerges. And each new collection of questions is as complex and challenging as the last.

It would be easy to view this inability to reach definitive conclusions as indicative of a field in chaos. We disagree. We prefer to view this constant state of questioning as a sign of health and vigor. The controversial nature of special education is what makes it exciting and challenging. We would be worried (and we believe people with disabilities and their families would be worried, too) if the field were suddenly to decide that it had reached complete agreement on most of the important issues. We should constantly be striving to find better ways to provide education and related services for persons with disabilities. In doing this, it is inevitable that there will be differences of opinion.

Summary

Special education has changed dramatically during its history, and the field appears poised for more changes. Five major trends and issues for the new millennium are integration, participation in assessments of progress, early intervention, transition from secondary school to adulthood, and discipline.

The trend toward integration of people with disabilities into the larger society began in the 1960s and continues stronger than ever today. Much of the philosophical rationale for integration comes from the principle of normalization. Normalization dictates that both the means and ends of education for people with disabilities should be as normal as possible. Controversies have surrounded implementation of the normalization principle. There is disagreement about whether it means the abolition of residential programs and special classes. Members of some groups, such as those who are deaf, have questioned whether normalization should mean integration for them. And some have cautioned that the overuse of technology may go against the concept of normalization.

Two important movements in the drive toward more integration have been deinstitutionalization and the full-inclusion movement. Started in the 1960s, deinstitutionalization is a trend to move people with disabilities into closer contact with the community and home. Some researchers question the wisdom of complete deinstitutionalization, as some people who return to community placements do not fare well and the death rate may be higher for these people in community placements than in institutions. Advocates of full inclusion contend that there should be no separate special education classes, that students should attend their neighborhood schools, and that the general education system should have the primary responsibility for all students. Others believe that although mainstreaming should be employed more than is currently the case, what's needed is a continuum of placements (e.g., residential institutions, special schools, special classes, resource rooms, general classes) from which parents and professionals can choose.

Full inclusion is based on four premises: (1) labeling of people is harmful; (2) special education pull-out programs have been ineffective; (3) people with disabilities should be viewed as a minority group; and (4) ethics should take precedence over empiricism.

Sentiment against labeling arose out of the fear that labeling students for special education stigma-tizes them and makes them feel unworthy. Research on the effects of labeling is inconclusive. People do tend to view labeled individuals differently than they do those without labels. Some educators maintain, however, that labels may provide an explanation for atypical behavior.

Over the past thirty years, more than fifty studies have compared outcomes for students with disabilities placed in special education versus regular classes, or resource rooms versus general education classes. The results have not been very supportive of special education. Critics of this research, however, point out that virtually all these studies have been methodologically flawed.

Advocates of full inclusion tend to believe that the problems people with disabilities face are due to their being members of a minority group, rather than the result of their disability. This view is consistent with that of the disability rights movement, whose members have advocated for a variety of civil rights for persons with disabilities and have been influential in lobbying legislators and promoting more appropriate media portrayals of people with disabilities.

Some full-inclusion advocates do not care if full inclusion is more or less effective than pull-out special education programs; they believe in full inclusion because they think it is the ethical thing to do.

Opponents of full inclusion argue that (1) professionals and parents are largely satisfied with the current level of integration; (2) general educators are unwilling and/or unable to cope with all students with disabilities; (3) although equating disabilities with minority group status is in many ways legitimate, it has limitations when it comes to translation into educational programming recommendations; (4) an unwillingness to consider empirical evidence is professionally irresponsible; (5) available empirical evidence does not support full inclusion; and (6) in the absence of data to support one service delivery model, special educators must preserve the continuum of placements.

Even those special educators who do not believe in full inclusion believe there needs to be more integration of students into general classes and more research on better ways to implement mainstreaming. Some of the most popular mainstreaming practices are prereferral teams, collaborative consultation, cooperative teaching, and curricula and instructional strategies. Among the curricula and instructional strategies employed to further inclusion are curricula designed to change attitudes toward disabilities, cooperative learning, peer tutoring, and partial participation.

The standards-based reform movement of the 1990s has been expanded to include students with disabilities. Standards-based reform emphasizes higher expectations for all students and measuring progress toward academic goals through standardized tests or other assessment procedures. Students with disabilities have often been excluded from participation in the general education curriculum and from standardized tests of educational progress. IDEA now requires that students with disabilities have access to the general curriculum studied by nondisabled students and be included in systemwide or statewide assessments of educational progress, with appropriate adaptations or accommodations as necessary. Accommodations for assessment might involve altering the time given to respond, changing the setting of the assessment, or using an alternative format for presenting tasks or responding.

Early intervention programs for children with disabilities and their families are now mandated by law. A cornerstone of early intervention is the individualized family service plan (IFSP). The IFSP is like an IEP, but it broadens the focus to include the family.

There are several types of early intervention programs. A common way of categorizing them is according to whether they are center-based, home-based, or a combination of the two.

Three issues pertaining to early childhood intervention are (1) the appropriate role of the family, (2) whether the curriculum should be teacher or child centered, and (3) whether full inclusion is best for all young children.

Federal law now also stipulates programming for transition from secondary school to adulthood. Transition is defined as including a variety of postschool activities, including postsecondary education, vocational training, integrated employment, continuing and adult education, adult services, independent living, or community participation. The law mandates that transition plans must be incorporated into the IEPs of students with disabilities. The law emphasizes both employment and issues pertaining to the quality of life of people with disabilities.

Supported employment is one way to integrate persons with disabilities into the workplace. In a typical supported employment situation, a job coach provides onsite training, which gradually tapers off as the worker learns to perform the job independently.

Issues pertaining to implementing transition from secondary school to adulthood for people with severe disabilities focus largely on coordinating and linking the many agencies outside the school setting. For people with mild disabilities, many of the issues center on providing programming that balances their vocational and academic needs. Some educators are concerned that the recent press for more rigorous academic standards—articulated by the Goals 2000: Educate America Act passed in 1994—generally will result in the disregard of the needs of students with disabilities.

Concern for safe and orderly schools has resulted in controversial policies related to the discipline of students with disabilities. Much of the controversy regarding discipline has to do with zero tolerance for certain behaviors that might result in the student's suspension or expulsion, such as bringing a weapon or drugs to school. The disciplinary action the school may take might depend on determining whether the student's misbehavior was or was not a manifestation of his or her disability.

In most cases, the same rules of discipline apply to students with disabilities as apply to all other students. However, federal law does not allow the discontinuation of education for students with disabilities, even if they are expelled. If a student with disabilities is disciplined by suspension or expulsion, then his or her education must continue in an alternative setting.

The 1997 amendments to IDEA that relate to discipline empasize problem solving rather than punishment. Educators must develop proactive and positive behavioral intervention plans and complete a functional assessment of the student's behavior designed to solve or prevent problems.

jose
lopes

Welcome to My Igloo. Watercolor on rag paper. 9 × 12 in.

Jose Lopes was born in Portugal in 1958. In 1981, he immigrated to the United States with his family; he recently became an American citizen. He paints on pottery as well as paper and canvas. His paintings have been shown at the Gateway Gallery in Brookline, MA; the Outsider Art Fair in New York; the Sawhill Gallery in Harrisonburg, VA; the Very Special Arts Gallery in Washington, DC; the Ebensburg Center in Pennsylvania; and in Cambridge, England.

chapter 3

Multicultural and Bilingual Aspects of Special Education

Remember and help America remember that the fellowship of human beings is more important than the fellowship of race and class and gender in a democratic society.... All children need [a] pride of heritage and sense of history of their own people and of all the people who make up the mosaic of this great nation. African American and Latino and Asian American and Native American children should know about European history and cultures, and white children should know about the histories and cultures of diverse peoples of color with whom they share a city, a nation, and a world. I believe in integration. But that does not mean I become someone else or ignore or deny who I am. I learned the Negro National anthem, "Lift Every Voice and Sing," at the same time I learned "The Star Spangled Banner" and "America the Beautiful" and I love them all. I have raised you, my children, to respect other people's children, not to become their children but to become yourselves at your best. I hope others will raise their children to respect you.

MARIAN WRIGHT EDELMAN
The Measure of Our Success:
A Letter to My Children and Yours

In the last decade of the twentieth century, many nations and regions have splintered into factions, clans, tribes, and gangs. In some cases, this splintering has been accompanied by extreme cruelty of individuals or groups toward others. Differences—especially those of religion, ethnic origin, color, custom, and social class—are too often the basis for viciousness toward other people. This has been the case throughout human history, and it remains a central problem of humankind. All cultures and ethnic groups of the world can take pride in much of their heritage, but most, if not all, also bear a burden of shame because at some time in their history, they have engaged in the ruthless treatment or literal enslavement of others. Sometimes this treatment has extended to certain members of their own group whose differences have been viewed as undesirable or intolerable.

In virtually every nation, society, religion, ethnic group, tribe, or clan, discrimination exists against those who are different in some dimension of human identity. The discrimination that we practice or experience stems from and perpetuates fear, hatred, and abusive relationships. If a group feels discriminated against or subjugated and sees no hope of becoming valued and being treated fairly, it inevitably will seek to become separate and autonomous, sometimes threatening or subjugating others in the process.

It is critically important, therefore, that we learn and help others learn tolerance. Furthermore, it is necessary for special educators, as well as general educators, to understand the purpose of **multicultural education.** Namely, multicultural education aims to change educational institutions and curricula so that they will provide equal educational opportunities to students regardless of their gender, social class, ethnicity, race, disability, or other cultural identity. It also seeks to socialize students to a multicultural norm—tolerance of and respect for those whose culture is different from one's own.

Our desire as Americans is to build a diverse but just society in which the personal freedom and pride of all cultural groups and respect for others' cultural heritage are the norm, a society in which fear, hate, and abuse are eliminated (see Banks & Banks, 1997; Glazer, 1997, 1998; Spencer, 1997). Working toward this ideal demands a multicultural perspective, one from which we can simultaneously accomplish two tasks. First, as a nation of increasing cultural diversity, we must renew our efforts to achieve social justice and take specific steps to understand and appreciate one another's cultures. Second, in doing so we must pledge our first loyalty to common cultural values that make diversity a strength rather than a fatal flaw. We seek a commitment to our common humanity and to democratic ideals that bind people together for the common good and give all the freedom to revel in a pride of heritage. These two tasks of multicultural education in a multicultural nation are expressed in the words of Marian Wright Edelman in her letter to her children and others (see excerpt on p. 85).

Nevertheless, multicultural education has its critics, some of whom see it as eroding the moral foundations of society and undermining the central purpose of schooling—ensuring the academic competence of students. For example, one newspaper columnist wrote, "For 40 years, American public education has pressed children into a humanistic, secular, multicultural mold" (Thomas, 1998, p. A8). Although multiculturalism may sometimes be distorted into indefensible ideology, we do not understand how the multicultural education we advocate can be anything but helpful in students' academic learning and socialization to American ideals.

Since the civil rights movement of the 1960s, educators have become increasingly aware of the extent to which differences among cultural and ethnic groups af-

multicultural education. Aims to change educational institutions and curricula so they will provide equal educational opportunities to students regardless of their gender, social class, ethnicity, race, disability, or other cultural identity.

misconceptions

about Multicultural and Bilingual Aspects of Special Education

myth Multicultural education addresses the concerns of ethnic minorities who want their children to learn more about their history and the intellectual, social, and artistic contributions of their ancestors.

fact This is a partial truth. In fact, multicultural education seeks to help the children of all ethnic groups appreciate their own and others' cultural heritages—plus our common American culture that sustains multiculturalism.

myth Everyone agrees that multicultural education is critical to our nation's future.

fact Some people, including some who are members of ethnic minorities, believe that multicultural education is misguided and diverts attention from our integration in a distinctive, cohesive American culture.

myth Implementing multicultural education is a relatively simple matter of including information about all cultures in the curriculum and teaching respect for them.

fact Educators and others are struggling with how to construct a satisfactory multicultural curriculum and multicultural instructional methods. Nearly every aspect of the task is controversial—which cultures to include, how much attention to give to each, and what and how to teach about them.

myth Multiculturalism includes only the special features and contributions of clearly defined ethnic groups.

fact Ethnicity is typically the focal point of discussions of multiculturalism, but ethnicity is sometimes a point of controversy if it is defined too broadly (for example, by lumping all Asians, all Africans, or all Europeans together). Besides ethnic groups, other groups and individuals—such as people identified by gender, sexual orientation, religion, and disability—need consideration in a multicultural curriculum.

myth Disproportionate representation of ethnic minorities in special education is no longer a problem.

fact Some ethnic minorities are still underrepresented or overrepresented in certain special education categories. For example, African American students, especially males, are overrepresented in programs for students with emotional disturbance and underrepresented in programs for gifted and talented students.

myth Disability is never related to ethnicity.

fact Some disabilities are genetically linked and therefore more prevalent in some ethnic groups. For example, sickle cell disease (a severe, chronic, hereditary blood disease) occurs disproportionately in children with ancestry from Africa, Mediterranean and Caribbean regions, Saudi Arabia, and India.

myth If students speak English, there is no need to be concerned about bilingual education.

fact Conversational English is not the same as the more formal and sometimes technical language used in academic curriculum and classroom instruction. Educators must make sure that students understand the language used in teaching, not just informal conversation.

fect children's schooling. Gradually, educators and others are coming to understand that the cultural diversity of the United States and the world demands multicultural education. Progress in constructing multicultural education has been slow, however, in part because of the way all cultural groups tend to view themselves as the standard against which others should be judged. Rogoff and Morelli (1989) note that in the United States this view has led to a focus on minority cultures:

> The United States, like many modern nations, is an aggregate of peoples of many cultural backgrounds. However, the role of culture is most noticeable when any of us views the practices of some other group than our own, and so the study of culture has generally focused on minorities in the United States and on people of other nations. It is easy for dominant cultural groups to consider themselves as standard and other groups as variations. (Think of the number of people who comment on other people's accents and insist that they themselves do not have one.) (p. 341)

Education that takes full advantage of the cultural diversity in our schools and the larger world requires much critical analysis and planning. It may be very difficult for all cultural or ethnic groups to find common satisfaction in any specific curriculum, even if they are all seeking what they consider the multicultural ideal. Moreover, some argue that the more important goal is finding the common American culture and ensuring that our children have a common cultural literacy (see Hirsch, 1987, 1996; Kennedy, 1997; Rodriguez, 1982, 1992). Even the metaphors we use for dealing with cultural diversity and cultural unity are points of controversy. The United States has often been called a "cultural melting pot," but some now reject the notion of total melding or amalgamation—they reject the metaphor of an alloy in which metals are dissolved in each other and fused into a new substance (Price, 1992; see also Spencer, 1997). For example, one teacher in a videotaped case study of multicultural education comments about the American melting pot, "I have no desire to melt, but I would love to enrich. But I do not want to melt! ... Back to my stew, if I'm going in as a carrot, I want to be tasted as a carrot and then still add to the flavor of the entire ..." (McNergney, 1992). To continue with the "stew" metaphor, there is controversy regarding how "chunky" our American culture should be.

That racism and discrimination remain serious problems in the United States and most other societies is obvious (Glazer, 1997; Spencer, 1997). These problems have no simple resolution, and they are found among virtually all ethnic groups. People of every cultural description struggle with the meaning of differences that may seem trivial or superficial to some but elicit powerful emotional responses and discrimination from others. Russell (1992) describes color discrimination that is practiced not only between whites and African Americans but also among African Americans of varied hues. Consider the hostilities and suffering associated with differences in color as well as in gender, religion, sexual orientation, abilities and disabilities, and political beliefs. In the box on page 89, the Jewish mother of a black man, James McBride, recalls the racial and religious prejudices she experienced and observed as a child in the 1930s. Anti-Semitism and other racist attitudes still exist in all regions of America, and no cultural group is entirely free of prejudice and other racist sentiments. Consider the experience of Susie Kay, a Jewish teacher in a Washington, D.C., high school where all the students are African American:

> Kay's students say they know about white culture mainly from television shows; hardly any interact regularly with whites—"Caucasians," as they

The Color of Water: School

The Jewish school didn't really count with the white folks, so I went to the white school, Thomas Jefferson Elementary. If it was up to Tateh [my father] he would have kept me out of school altogether. "That gentile school won't teach you anything you can use," he scoffed. He paid for us to take private lessons in sewing and knitting and record keeping from other people. He was tight with his money, but when it came to that kind of thing, he wasn't cheap, I'll say that for him. He would rather pay for us to study privately than to go to school with gentiles, but the law was the law, so I had to go to school with the white folks. It was a problem from the moment I started, because the white kids hated Jews in my school. "Hey, Ruth, when did you start being a dirty Jew?" they'd ask. I couldn't stand being ridiculed. I even changed my name to try to fit in more. My real name was Rachel, which in Yiddish is Ruckla, which is what my parents called me—but I used the name Ruth around white folk, because it didn't sound so Jewish, though it never stopped the other kids from teasing me.

Nobody liked me. That's how I felt as a child. I know what it feels like when people laugh at you walking down the street, or snicker when they hear you speaking Yiddish, or just look at you with hate in their eyes. You know a Jew living in Suffolk when I was coming up could be lonely even if there were fifteen of them standing in the room, I don't know why; it's that feeling that nobody likes you; that's how I felt, living in the South. You were different from everyone and liked by very few. There were white sections of Suffolk, like the Riverview section, where Jews weren't allowed to own property. It said that on the deeds and you can look them up. They'd say "for White Anglo-Saxon Protestants only." That was the law there

and they meant it. The Jews in Suffolk did stick together, but even among Jews my family was low because we dealt with *shvartses* [blacks]. So I didn't have a lot of Jewish friends either.

When I was in the fourth grade, a girl came up to me in the schoolyard during recess and said, "You have the prettiest hair. Let's be friends." I said, "Okay." Heck, I was glad someone wanted to be my friend. Her name was Frances. I'll never forget Frances for as long as I live. She was thin, with light brown hair and blue eyes. She was a quiet gentle person. I was actually forbidden to play with her because she was a gentile, but I'd sneak over to her house anyway and sneak her over to mine. Actually I didn't have to sneak into Frances's house because I was always welcome there. She lived past the cemetery on the other side of town in a frame house that we entered from the back door. It seemed that dinner was always being served at Frances's house. Her mother would serve it on plates she took out of a wooden china closet; ham, bread, and hot biscuits with lots of butter—and I couldn't eat any of it. It was *treyf*, not kosher for a Jew to eat. The first time her mother served dinner I said, "I can't eat this," and I was embarrassed until Frances piped out, "I don't like this food either. My favorite food is mayonnaise on white bread." That's how she was. She'd do little things to let you know she was on your side. It didn't bother her one bit that I was Jewish, and if she was around, no one in school would tease me.

Source: Reprinted by permission of Riverhead Books, a division of Penguin Putnam Inc. from *The Color of Water,* pp. 80–82. Copyright © 1996 by James McBride.

call them. Most have never met a Jewish person, except for Miss Kay, who wears her Star of David necklace every day. Prompting students to ask, "Isn't that the star of the Devil?"

"And what's the difference between a white person and a Jew anyway?" asks another. Both are rich, right? (Horwitz, 1998, p. F1)

The solution is not as simple as becoming sensitized to differences. Too often, Eurocentrism is met with Europhobia, Afrocentrism with Afrophobia, homocentrism with homophobia, sensitivity to difference with hypersensitivity about being different. Nor is the solution to become "blind" to difference, as the box "In Living Black and White" on page 91 illustrates (see Schofield, 1997; Williams, 1998a, 1998b). In discussing people of color, Spencer (1997) concludes that "we need the current racial classifications in order to fight racism, because as soon as we discard the racial classifications black people are still going to be discriminated against" (p. 148). Glazer (1997, 1998) also observes that loss of racial identity in the service of equal opportunity for minorities cannot work. Likewise, eliminating labels for individuals with disabilities inevitably results in the loss of their equal educational opportunity (Hallahan & Kauffman, 1994); we cannot accommodate what we do not see and label. Perhaps the solution must include both engendering sensitivity to differences and building confidence that one's own differences will not be threatened by others'. The solution may also require transforming the curriculum in ways that help students understand how knowledge is constructed and how to view themselves and others from different perspectives (Banks, 1997; Banks & Banks, 1997).

Perhaps we *can* find a uniquely American culture, one that celebrates valued diversities within a framework of clearly defined common values, one that sees "our problems" rather than the problems of particular racial or ethnic groups or other subgroups of our common culture (see Kennedy, 1997). This perspective recognizes that not all diversity is valued, that tolerance has its limits, and that American culture is dynamic and continuously evolving:

> There are limits to cultural tolerance, a lesson the 20th century has repeatedly taught us. There are, among some cultures, deeply held convictions—about women and their bodies; about races; about children; about authority; about lawbreakers, the sick, the weak, the poor and the rich—that we absolutely deplore. The fact is, we need absolutes. Where a plurality of cultures exists, we need an overarching set of values cherished by all. Otherwise what begins as multicultural harmony inevitably descends into balkanization or chaos....
>
> The simple truth, which is either denied or distorted by the prevailing orthodoxies, is that a thriving national culture does exist. It is neither a salad bowl nor static, received tradition, but an ever-evolving national process which selects, unrepresentatively, from the marketplace of raw, particular identities, those that everyone finds it useful and gratifying to embrace and transform into their own. (Patterson, 1993, p. C2)

An individual's membership in any cultural, ethnic, racial, regional, gender, social class, or disability group should not affect what education opportunities are available to him or her.

In Living Black and White

My son used to attend a small nursery school. Over the course of a year, three different teachers in his school assured me that he was colorblind. Resigned to this diagnosis, I took my son to an ophthalmologist who tested him and pronounced his vision perfect. I could not figure out what was going on until I began to listen carefully to what he was saying about color.

As it turned out, my son did not misidentify color. He resisted identifying color at all. "I don't know," he would say when asked what color the grass was; or, most peculiarly, "It makes no difference." This latter remark, this assertion of the greenness of grass making no difference, was such a precociously cynical retort that I began to suspect some social complication in which he somehow was invested.

The long and short of it is that the well-meaning teachers at his predominantly white school had valiantly and repeatedly assured their charges that color makes no difference. "It doesn't matter," they told the children, "whether you're black or white or red or green or blue." Yet upon further investigation, the very reason that the teachers had felt it necessary to impart this lesson in the first place was that it did matter, and in predictably cruel ways: Some of the children had been fighting about whether black people could play "good guys."

My son's anxious response was redefined by his teachers as physical deficiency—illustrative, perhaps, of the way in which the liberal ideal of colorblindness is too often confounded. That is to say, the very notion of blindness about color constitutes an ideological confusion at best, and denial at its very worst. I recognize, certainly, that the teachers were inspired by a desire to make whole a division in the ranks. But there is much overlooked in the move to undo that which clearly and unfortunately matters just by labeling it that which "makes no difference." The dismissiveness, however unintentional, leaves those in my son's position pulled between the clarity of their own experience and the often alienating terms in which they must seek social acceptance.

Source: Excerpt from *Seeing a Color-Blind Future: The Paradox of Race* by Patricia J. Williams. Copyright © 1997 by Patricia J. Williams. Reprinted by permission of Farrar, Strauss & Giroux, Inc.

We are optimistic about multicultural education because it is an opportunity to face our shared problems squarely and to extract the best human qualities from each cultural heritage. Without denying any culture's inhumanity to others or to its own members, we have the opportunity to develop an appreciation of our individual and shared cultural treasures and to engender tolerance, if not love, of all differences that are not destructive of the human spirit. We concur with Price (1992):

> The appropriate antidote for cultural insularity is a culture of inclusiveness that infuses every facet of our society.... Were those who ardently preach American values truly to practice them, then perhaps our collective anxiety about the growing intolerance and insularity in America would, shall we say, melt away. (p. 213)

Multiculturalism is now a specialized field of study and research in education, and its full exploration is far beyond the scope of this chapter (see, for example, Banks, 1997; Banks & Banks, 1997; Winzer & Mazurek, 1998). Of particular concern to special educators is how exceptionalities are related to cultural diversity and the way in which special education fits within the broader general education context in a multicultural society (Artiles & Trent, 1997a, 1997b; Trent & Artiles, 1998). Cultural diversity presents particular challenges for special educators in three areas: (1) assessment of abilities and disabilities, (2) instruction, and (3) socialization. Before discussing each of these challenges, we summarize some of the major concepts about education and cultural diversity that set the context for multicultural and bilingual special education.

Education and Cultural Diversity: Concepts for Special Education

Culture has many definitions. As Banks (1994) points out, however, "Most contemporary social scientists view culture as consisting primarily of the symbolic, ideational, and intangible aspects of human societies" (p. 83). Banks suggests six major components or elements of culture:

1. Values and behavioral styles
2. Languages and dialects
3. Nonverbal communication
4. Awareness (of one's cultural distinctiveness)
5. Frames of reference (normative world views or perspectives)
6. Identification (feeling part of the cultural group)

These elements may together make up a national or shared culture, sometimes referred to as a **macroculture.** Within the larger macroculture are **microcultures**—smaller cultures that share the common characteristics of the macroculture but have their unique values, styles, languages and dialects, nonverbal communication, awareness, frames of reference, and identities. An individual may identify with the macroculture and also belong to many different microcultures, as shown in Figure 3.1. The variety of microcultures to which a person belongs affects his or her behavior.

Macroculture in the United States consists of certain overarching values, symbols, and ideas, such as justice, equality, and human dignity. Microcultures within the U.S. macroculture may share these common values but differ in many additional ways. The number of microcultures represented in U.S. schools has increased in recent decades because of the variety of immigrants from other countries, particularly Southeast Asia. Duke (1990) notes that "these newcomers contribute to a diversity of cultures and languages that probably has not characterized American society since the turn of the [nineteenth to twentieth] century" (pp. 69–70). Students from some microcultures in U.S. society do extremely well in school, but others do not. The factors accounting for the school

Figure 3.1

Individuals belong to many different microcultural groups.
Source: From J. A. Banks, *Multiethnic education: Theory and practice,* 3rd ed., p. 89. Copyright © 1994 by Allyn & Bacon. Reprinted with permission.

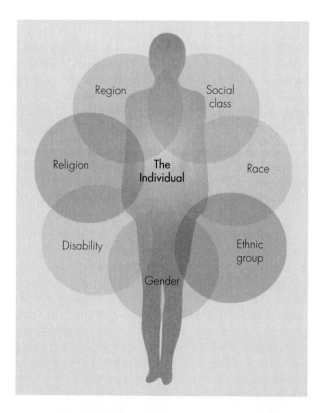

Family support (or the lack thereof) is recognized as a key factor in children's academic success.

performance of microcultural minorities are complex, and social scientists are still searching for the attitudes, beliefs, behavioral styles, and opportunities that foster the success of specific microcultural groups (Jacob & Jordan, 1987).

Researchers have reported that Southeast Asian (Indochinese) refugee families adopting an orientation to certain American values—acquiring material possessions and seeking fun and excitement—have children whose academic performance is lower than that of children from families maintaining traditional Southeast Asian values—persistence, achievement, and family support (Caplan, Choy, & Whitmore, 1992). This finding suggests that schools and teachers may face an impossible task unless changes occur in students' home cultures. "It is clear that the U.S. educational system can work—if the requisite familial and social supports are provided for the students outside school" (Caplan et al., 1992, p. 36). Ogbu (1992) also notes the critical role played by different minority communities in encouraging academic success among their children and youth. He differentiates between immigrant, or *voluntary,* minorities—those who have come to the United States primarily for their own economic and social benefit— and castelike, or *involuntary,* minorities who were originally brought to the United States against their will. Most Chinese and Punjabi Indians, for example, are voluntary minorities; African American children and youths are, for the most part, members of an involuntary minority. Ogbu concludes that "minority children do not succeed or fail only because of what schools do or do not do, but also because of what the community does" (1992, p. 12). He continues:

> At this point in my research I suggest four ways in which the involuntary minority community can encourage academic striving and success among its children. One is to teach the children to separate attitudes and behaviors that lead to academic success from attitudes and behaviors that lead to a loss of ethnic identity and culture or language.... Second, the involuntary minority community should provide the children with concrete evidence that its members appreciate and value academic success as much as they appreciate and value achievements in sports, athletics, and entertainment.

macroculture. A nation or other large social entity with a shared culture.

microculture. A smaller group existing within a larger cultural group and having unique values, style, language, dialect, ways of communicating nonverbally, awareness, frame of reference, and identification.

Third, the involuntary minority community must teach the children to recognize and accept the responsibility for their school adjustment and academic performance....

Finally, the involuntary minority middle class needs to reevaluate and change its role vis-à-vis the community. (1992, p. 12)

Ogbu goes on to describe two ways in which minority individuals who have achieved middle-class status might interact with the minority community. For example, successful, educated, professional people might provide highly visible role models for youths, demonstrating how they can achieve success in the wider society and retain their collective identity and bona fide membership in the minority community. This is the example typically provided by voluntary minorities. Ogbu also notes that:

In contrast, involuntary minorities seem to have a model that probably does not have much positive influence on schooling. Members of involuntary minorities seem to view professional success as "a ticket" to leave their community both physically and socially, to get away from those who have not "made it." People seek education and professional success, as it were, in order to leave their minority community. (1992, p. 13)

Although there is considerable evidence that various ethnic minority communities have a strong influence on students' achievement and school behavior, we offer three cautions:

1. We need to guard against stereotypes—assumptions that one's cultural identity is sufficient to explain academic achievement or economic success. The "Doonesbury" cartoon below makes the point rather well, we feel.
2. The fact that minority communities may have a strong influence on school success does not relieve schools of the obligation to provide a multicultural education. All students need to feel that they and their cultural heritage are included in the mainstream of American culture and schooling.
3. Unless teachers and other school personnel value minority students—see value and promise in them and act accordingly by setting demanding but not unreachable expectations—the support of families and the minority community may be insufficient to improve the academic success of minority students (Steele, 1992). Too often, minority students are devalued in school, regardless of their achievements and behaviors (Boutte, 1992; Steele, 1992).

Doonesbury   BY GARRY TRUDEAU

Source: "Doonesbury." Copyright © 1992 G. B. Trudeau. Reprinted with permission of Universal Press Syndicate. All rights reserved.

The general purposes of multicultural education are (1) to promote pride in one's own cultural heritage and understanding of microcultures different from one's own, (2) to foster positive attitudes toward cultural diversity, and (3) to ensure equal educational opportunities for all students. These purposes cannot be accomplished unless students develop an understanding and appreciation of their own cultural heritage, as well as an awareness and acceptance of cultures different from their own. Understanding and appreciation are not likely to develop automatically through unplanned contact with members of other microcultures. Rather, teachers must plan experiences that teach about culture and provide models of cultural awareness and acceptance and the appreciation of cultural diversity.

On the surface, teaching about cultures and engendering an acceptance and appreciation of cultural diversity appear to be simple tasks. However, two questions immediately complicate the matter when we get below the surface and address the actual practice of multiculturalism in education: (1) Which cultures shall we include? (2) What and how shall we teach about them?

The first question demands that we consider all the microcultures that might be represented in the school and the difficulties inherent in including them all. The United States has more than 100 distinct microcultures based on national origin alone. In some urban school districts with large numbers of immigrant children, more than twenty different languages may be spoken in students' homes. But ethnic or national origin is only one dimension of cultural diversity, one branch of many in the multicultural program. Ethnicity is not the only representation of culture, and there is much variation of culture within any ethnic group (Keogh, Gallimore, & Weisner, 1997). In fact, assuming that all individuals of a particular racial or ethnic group have the same values and perspectives is a form of stereotyping.

Many advocates of multiculturalism consider gender, sexual orientation, religion, disability, and so on to be additional dimensions of cultural diversity that require explicit attention. Moreover, some microcultural groups find the traditions, ceremonies, values, holidays, and other characteristics of other microcultures unacceptable or even offensive. That is, when it comes to what and how to teach about other cultures, the stage may be set for conflict. Treating all cultures with equal attention and respect may present substantial or seemingly insurmountable logistical and interpersonal problems.

One of the most controversial aspects of multicultural education is the use of language. For instance, is it appropriate to refer to a *minority* or *minorities* when the group or aggregates to which we refer constitute half or more of the population in a given school, district, region, or state? What labels and terms are acceptable for designating various groups? What languages or dialects should be used for instruction? With the arrival of many immigrants to the United States, the issue of bilingual education and its relationship to multiculturalism has become increasingly important. The box on page 96 illustrates how controversial the issue of language can be. As we discuss later, bilingual education is of even greater concern when children with disabilities are considered (Gersten, Brengelman, & Jimenez, 1994).

Given the multiplicity of microcultures, each wanting—if not demanding—its precise and fair inclusion in the curriculum, it is not surprising that educators sometimes feel caught in a spiral of factionalism and feuding. Furthermore, additional questions about cultural values inevitably must be addressed: Which cultural values and characteristics should we embrace? Which, if any, should we shun? Would we, if we could, fully sustain some cultures, alter some significantly, and eliminate others? Consider, for example, cultures in which women are

Plan to Teach in Spanish Draws Heat in Arlington

A proposal by Arlington school administrators to teach Spanish-speaking kindergartners at four schools in their native language for two hours a day has drawn heated opposition from some county residents, who say it will make it harder for the children to learn English.

The County's School Board this week postponed voting on the plan after 12 residents spoke against it at a board meeting and two spoke in favor. Only one of the five board members, E. T. "Libby" Garvey, expressed strong support for the bilingual experiment, whose aim is to boost the academic performance of Spanish-speaking children. Other board members said they wanted to learn more about it.

The program would be the first of its kind in the Washington area. Most area public schools put students with weak English skills in English as a Second Language (ESL) classes, which are conducted in English.

Under the Arlington proposal, the special Spanish language classes would be an option for about 120 kindergartners this fall at Barcroft, Barrett, Glencarlyn and Henry elementary schools. The students' families, if they preferred, could instead have their children placed in ESL classes or in regular classes.

The two hours a day of instruction in Spanish would cover basic subjects such as reading concepts, science, math and social studies. The program would continue until the third grade, with more kindergartners being added each year.

Leaders of Arlington's Republican Party have been among the chief critics of the plan. They argue that giving some students Spanish-language instruction would produce the same parental dissatisfaction that has led to a June ballot measure in California designed to kill bilingual education in that state.

"Native-language programs simply trap children in a cycle of government dependency by denying them the opportunity to learn English," Henriette Warfield, chairman of the Arlington Republican Party, told the board.

But Kathleen F. Grove, Arlington's assistant school superintendent for instruction, said the proposed pilot program is simply a small part of the school system's effort to raise the academic achievement level of Spanish-speaking students to match that of their classmates who speak English at home.

On the Stanford 9 test, for example, the average scores of Hispanic students in Arlington are 29 to 40 percentile points lower than the average scores of non-Hispanic white student in the county, depending on the grade level. The test is one of five nationally recognized standardized achievement tests.

Criticisms of the proposal, Grove said, "sounded as if they were motivated more by the desire to identify an inflammatory issue than discuss what is the best thing to do."

In California, many Hispanic parents have objected to instructing children in Spanish. At Tuesday night's Arlington School Board meeting, the residents who criticized the proposal did not include any Spanish-speaking residents with children in the county schools. Grove said she has not notified Hispanic parents about the program. She said she wanted to get board approval first so as not to raise the hopes of parents who might want to try it.

Jose R. Oyola, a member of the Arlington Hispanic Parents Association, said he has read the proposal and thought "it had merit in its structure."

Some studies show bilingual education to be effective, and some do not. In California and other states that have such programs, increasing numbers of educators and Hispanic parents have argued that the Spanish-language lessons, after a year or so, become a crutch that keeps students from developing the English skills they need in high school and college.

A recent report by Wayne Thomas and Virginia Collier, of the Graduate School of Education at George Mason University, noted that the number of students from non-English-speaking families had quadrupled in Arlington in the last two decades. About 31 percent of Arlington public school children are Hispanic.

The GMU researchers found that the county's efforts to build English skills through ESL lessons put most of the students into regular classes fairly quickly. But after that, the students generally lagged far behind native English speakers, particularly in high school, the study said.

Arlington, like several other Washington area school districts, has a voluntary Spanish immersion program, in which all the students at one elementary school are taught in Spanish for about half the school day and taught in English for the other half.

The report by Thomas and Collier recommended more immersion programs, which depend on voluntary participation by significant numbers of English-speaking parents. The report said national studies show that such programs are the most effective approach for students with poor English.

Source: Mathews. J. (1998, April 17) Plan to teach in Spanish draws heat in Arlington. *The Washington Post,* C–1, C–5. © 1998 The Washington Post. Reprinted with permission.

One of the most controversial aspects of multicultural education is whether English and non-English languages should be combined in classrooms and how.

treated as chattel, as well as the drug culture, the culture of street gangs, the culture of poverty. To what extent does every culture have a right to perpetuate itself? How should we respond to some members of the Deaf culture, for example, who reject the prevention of deafness or procedures and devices that enable deaf children to hear, preferring deafness to hearing and wishing to sustain the Deaf culture deliberately? Depending on how we define culture, the values of our own cultural heritage, and our role in multicultural education, we may find ourselves embroiled in serious cultural conflicts. No wonder that some describe the late twentieth century as an era of "culture wars" (Hunter, 1991). To deal effectively with the multicultural challenge, we must focus on the challenges most pertinent to special education.

Implementing Multicultural and Bilingual Special Education

The microcultures of particular importance for special education are ethnic groups and exceptionality groups. Banks (1997) notes that an *ethnic group* "has a historic origin and a shared heritage and tradition" (p. 66). It has value orientations, behavioral patterns, and often political and economic interests that differ from those of other groups in the larger society. An ethnic group may be a majority or a minority of people in a given country or region. We define an *exceptionality group* as a group sharing a set of specific abilities or disabilities that are especially valued or that require special accommodation within a given microculture. Thus, a person may be identified as exceptional in one ethnic group (or other microculture defined by gender, social class, religion, etc.) but not in another. Being unable to read or speak standard English, for example, may identify a student as having a disability in an Anglo-dominated microculture, although the same student would not be considered disabled in a microculture in which

Educators will be more successful in addressing individual needs if they are sensitive to the possibility that attitudes toward disabilities vary among different cultural groups.

English-language skills are unimportant. In certain cultures, children avoid direct eye contact with adults in positions of authority. Given this, a child who does not look directly at the teacher may mistakenly be assumed to be inattentive or oppositional by adults from cultures in which eye contact between the teacher and pupil is expected. This child could be inappropriately identified as having a disability requiring special education.

Ethnicity and exceptionality are distinctly different concepts. In fact, multicultural special education must focus on two primary objectives that go beyond the general purposes of multicultural education:

1. Ensuring that ethnicity is not mistaken for educational exceptionality
2. Increasing understanding of the microculture of exceptionality and its relationship to other microcultures

Ethnicity may be mistaken for exceptionality when one's own ethnic group is viewed as setting the standard for all others. For example, patterns of eye contact, physical contact, use of language, and ways of responding to persons in positions of authority may vary greatly from one ethnic group to another. Members of each ethnic group must realize that what they see as deviant or unacceptable in their own group may be normal and adaptive in another ethnic group. That is, we must not mistakenly conclude that a student has a disability or is gifted just because he or she is different.

Members of minority ethnic groups are more apt to be identified as disabled because their differences are not well understood or valued by others. In part, this higher risk may be a result of prejudice—unreasonable or irrational negative attitudes, feelings, judgments, or behaviors based on ignorance or misunderstanding. Prejudice may cause individuals to be judged as deviant or disabled on the basis of characteristics that are typical for their ethnic group or from stereotyping. That is, an individual's identity as a member of a particular group may result in the automatic assumption that he or she will behave in certain ways.

Students may be particularly likely to be identified or not identified as having certain disabilities depending on their gender and ethnicity. The disproportional representation of males and ethnic minority students in special education is a problem of long standing. Boys make up considerably more than half of the students with certain disabilities (e.g., about 75 percent of those with emotional disturbance), and the percentage of students with certain disabilities who are ethnic minorities is disproportionately high—or, in some cases, disproportionately low. Table 3.1 shows the discrepancies between the percentages of all public school students who are white, black, Asian/Pacific Islander, and Hispanic and the percentages of these minorities identified as having certain disabilities. Although 67 percent of the total school population is white, only 58 percent of students identified as having moderate mental retardation are white. Whites are thus somewhat underrepresented among students with moderate mental retardation. Black students are 16 percent of the total school population, but 32 percent of students identified as having mild mental retardation are black; thus, blacks are highly overrepresented among students with mild mental retardation. We must be careful not to misinterpret such statistics. A common misinterpretation is that 32 percent of black students are identified as having mild mental retardation (see MacMillan & Reschly, 1998). It is also important to recognize that disproportionality is not an equal problem in all schools, localities, or states for any given ethnic group. The problem of overrepresentation is most obvious in locales where ethnic minority students are a substantial percentage of the school population (see Artiles & Zamora-Duran, 1997).

The U.S. Department of Education (1992, 1996, 1997) has shown particular concern about the disproportional representation of ethnic minorities in special

Table 3.1   Percentage of Students of Various Ethnic Groups in the Total School Population and Their Percentage of Those Having Specific Disabilities

	White	Black	Asian/Pacific Islander	Hispanic
Percent of total school population	67	16	3	12
Percent of those with mild mental retardation	61	32	0.9	5
Percent of those with moderate mental retardation	58	29	2	9
Percent of those with emotional disturbance	67	24	0.7	7
Percent of those with specific learning disability	68	18	1	12

Source: U.S. Department of Education. (1997). *Nineteenth annual report to Congress on the implementation of the Individuals with Disabilities Education Act.* Washington, DC: Author, p. I–43.

education. Important civil rights are involved in the issue. On the one hand, children with disabilities have a right to appropriate education regardless of their ethnicity, even if their ethnic group is statistically overrepresented in special education. On the other hand, however, children also have a right to freedom from discrimination and segregation. The disproportional placement of ethnic minority students in special education strongly suggests that in some cases students are misidentified and wrongly placed (and stigmatized and segregated) in special education, while in other cases ethnic minority students' disabilities are ignored (and the students thus denied appropriate education).

The reasons for the disproportional representation of certain groups in special education may involve assessment of students' abilities, but other factors such as community standards and resources may be implicated as well. In commenting on the disproportionately high representation of black students in most special education categories, the Department of Education commented, "It is possible that black youth were more likely than their white counterparts to have experienced poor prenatal, perinatal, or postnatal health care and early childhood nutrition which may have resulted in actual disabilities" (1992, p. 15). In its 1996 report to Congress on the implementation of IDEA, the Department of Education focused on the problems of urban schools and the relationship of urban factors to disproportional placement in special education. It has become clear that the problem of disproportionality is very complex and that there are no simple solutions.

> The complexity of this issue requires an integrated and multifaceted effort to promote greater educational access and excellence for racial/ethnic minority students that involves policy makers, educators, researchers, parents, advocates, students, and community representatives. The disproportionate representation of racial/ethnic minority students in special education programs and classes points to the need to:
>
> - make available strong academic programs that foster success for all students in regular and special education;
>
> - implement effective and appropriate special education policies and procedures for referral, assessment, eligibility, classification, placement, and re-evaluation;
>
> - increase the level of home/school/community involvement in the educational process; and
>
> - use diverse community resources to enhance and implement educational programs. (U.S. Department of Education, 1997, p. I–47)

Disproportionality is not the only multicultural issue in special education. People with certain exceptionalities can develop their own microcultures (Gollnick & Chin, 1994). Those with severe hearing impairments, for example, are described by some as belonging to a Deaf culture that is not well understood by most normally hearing people and that results in feelings of isolation or separation from people with normal hearing (Padden & Humphries, 1988). An important aspect of multicultural special education is developing an increased awareness, understanding, and appreciation of cultural differences involving disabilities. Multicultural special education is not merely a matter of overcoming students' prejudice and stereotyping. We must also educate ourselves as teachers to improve methods of assessment, provide effective instruction, and foster appropriate socialization.

We now turn to specific problems in assessment, instruction, and socialization involving microcultural groups, including students with exceptionalities.

Assessment

Assessment is a process of collecting information about individuals or groups for the purpose of making decisions. In education, assessment ordinarily refers to testing, interviewing, and observing students. The results of assessment should help us decide whether problems exist in a student's education and, if problems are identified, what to do about them (Taylor, 1997). Clearly, assessment often results in important decision about people's lives, and therefore in the U.S. macroculture there is great concern for accuracy, justice, and fairness (Ysseldyke & Marston, 1988).

Unfortunately, the accuracy, justice, and fairness of many educational assessments, especially those involving special education, are open to question (McDonnell, McLaughlin, & Morison, 1997). Particularly when ethnic microcultures are involved, traditional assessment practices have frequently violated the U.S. ideals of fairness and equal opportunity, regardless of ethnic origin, gender, or disability. That is, the assessment practices of educators and psychologists have frequently come under attack as being (1) biased, resulting in misrepresentation of the abilities and disabilities of ethnic minorities and exceptional students, and (2) useless, resulting only in labeling or classification rather than improved educational programming (Council for Exceptional Children, 1997; Ford, 1998; Patton, 1998). Even prereferral practices, in which the objective is to find solutions to educational problems *before* referral for evaluation, are subject to bias (see Katsiyannis, 1994).

The problems of assessing students to qualify for special education are numerous and complex, and there are no simple solutions (Kauffman, Hallahan, & Ford, 1998; MacMillan, & Reschly, 1998; MacMillan, Gresham, Lopez, & Bocian, 1996). Many of the problems are centered on traditional standardized testing approaches to assessment that have serious limitations: (1) they do not take cultural diversity into account, (2) they focus on deficits in the individual alone, and (3) they do not provide information useful in teaching. Although these problems have not been entirely overcome, awareness of them and the use of

An intent of multicultural education is to ensure that children with disabilities are not further disabled by their unique ethnic and cultural background.

more appropriate assessment procedures for diverse learners are increasing (Lopez-Reyna & Bay, 1997). Assessment must not result in the misidentification of children whose language or other characteristics are merely different, but it must also identify those whose differences represent disabilities (Ortiz, 1997; Van Keulen, Weddington, & DeBose, 1998).

Standardized tests may be biased because most of the test items draw on specific experiences that students from different microcultures may not have had. Tests may, for example, be biased toward the likely experiences of white, middle-class students; be couched in language unfamiliar to members of a certain microculture; or be administered in ways that penalize students with impaired vision, hearing, or ability to answer in a standard way. Because test scores are often the basis for deciding that a student qualifies for special education, many scholars suspect that test bias accounts for the disproportionate representation of certain groups in special education, especially males and children of color, and the neglect of many children of color who are gifted (see Artiles & Zamora-Duran, 1997; Ford, 1998; Patton, 1997, 1998, U.S. Department of Education, 1996, 1997).

At best, test scores represent a sample of an individual's ability to respond to a standard set of questions or tasks; they do not tell us *all* the important things an individual has learned or how much he or she *can* learn. Controversy over the biases inherent in standardized tests and the search for so-called culture-free and culture-fair tests continue (Taylor, 1997). Three cautions are in order:

1. Tests give only clues about what a student has learned.
2. Test scores must be interpreted with recognition of the possible biases the test contains.
3. Testing alone is an insufficient basis for classifying a student or planning an instructional program.

Traditional assessment procedures focus on the student, not on the environment in which he or she is being taught. Critics of traditional assessment have decried the assumption that any deficit identified will be a deficit of the student. So in addition to assessing the student's behavior or performance, many educators now suggest assessing the instructional environment. This may involve classroom observation and interviews with the student and teacher. It focuses on such items as whether instruction is presented clearly and effectively, the classroom is effectively controlled, the teacher's expectations are appropriate, appropriate curriculum modifications are made, thinking skills are being taught, effective motivational strategies are used, the student is actively engaged in academic responding and given adequate practice and feedback on performance, and progress is directly and frequently evaluated. The purpose of assessing the instructional environment is to make sure that the student is not mistakenly identified as the source of the learning problem (see Hallahan, Kauffman, & Lloyd, 1999). An underlying assumption is that this approach will decrease the likelihood that cultural differences will be mistaken for disabilities.

Traditional assessment procedures result in test scores that may be useful in helping to determine a student's eligibility for special education or other special services. These testing procedures do not, however, typically provide information that is useful in planning for instruction. A variety of alternative assessment procedures were devised in the late 1980s and early 1990s, focusing on students' performance in the curriculum or on tasks in everyday contexts, as opposed to how well they did on standardized tests (see Rueda, 1997; Rueda & Garcia, 1997). The intent of these procedures is to avoid the artificiality and biased nature of traditional testing and obtain a more fair and instructionally useful assessment of students' abilities. These procedures may be useful in some respects, but they are not a solution to all problems of assessment (Terwilliger, 1997).

One particularly useful alternative approach that emerged in the 1980s is *curriculum-based assessment* (Choate, Enright, Miller, Poteet, & Rakes, 1995; Fuchs & Fuchs, 1997). This method of assessment contrasts sharply with traditional testing, in which students are tested infrequently and may never before have seen the specific items on the test. Curriculum-based assessment involves students' responses to their usual instructional materials; it entails direct and frequent samples of performance from the curriculum in which students are being instructed. (We discuss curriculum-based assessment in more detail in Chapter 5.) This form of assessment is thought to be more useful for teachers than traditional testing and to decrease the likelihood of cultural bias.

Finally, we note that fair and accurate assessment is an issue in identifying special gifts and talents as well as disabilities. Too often, the extraordinary abilities of students of color or other ethnic difference and those with disabilities are overlooked because of bias or ignorance on the part of those responsible for assessment. In Chapter 1, we emphasized the importance of identifying the abilities as well as the disabilities of students. To that we want to add the importance of being aware of culturally relevant gifts and talents and recognizing and valuing the abilities of minority students (Ford, 1998; Patton, 1997).

Instruction

A major objective of multicultural education is ensuring that all students are instructed in ways that do not penalize them because of their cultural differences and that, in fact, capitalize on their cultural heritage. The methods used to achieve this objective are among the most controversial topics in education today. All advocates of multicultural education are concerned with the problem of finding instructional methods that help equalize educational opportunity and achievement for all microcultural groups—that is, methods that break down the inequities and discrimination that have been part of the U.S. public education system. Yet there is considerable debate over the question of what instructional methods are most effective in achieving this goal.

The controversy regarding instruction is generated by what Minow (1985) calls "the dilemma of difference." The dilemma is that either ignoring or recognizing students' linguistic or cultural differences can perpetuate them and maintain inequality of social power and opportunity among ethnic or other microcultural groups. If students' differences are ignored, the students will probably be given instruction that is not suited to their cultural styles or needs. They will then likely fail to learn many skills, which will in turn deny them power and opportunity in the dominant culture. For example, if we ignore non-English-speaking students' language and cultural heritage and force them to speak English, they may have great difficulty in school. "This story [of the harm children experience when their language and cultural differences are not recognized] manifests one half of the difference dilemma: nonacknowledgment of difference reiterates difference" (p. 838).

However, the answer to this problem is not necessarily recognition of students' differences, for instruction geared to individual students' cultural styles may teach only skills valued by their own microcultures. Because the dominant culture does not value these skills, the students' difference will be perpetuated.

Teachers must recognize and confront their own attitudes about people from various cultural groups, or they may inadvertently discriminate against their own students. Achieving this awareness is a key factor in the success or failure of multicultural education.

For example, if non-English-speaking students are taught in their native language and are not required to learn English, their progress in the English-speaking society will be slowed:

> Here … is the other side of the dilemma; acknowledgment of difference can create barriers to important aspects of the school experience and delay or derail successful entry into the society that continues to make that difference matter. Both sides of the dilemma appear and reappear in the history of education for students who are not native English speakers. (Minow, 1985, p. 384)

Should a student who speaks no English be forced to give up his or her native language in school and learn to use only English (ignoring the cultural-linguistic difference)? Or should the student's native language be used as the primary vehicle of instruction, while English is taught as a second language (acknowledging the cultural-linguistic difference) (Gersten & Woodward, 1994; Ovando, 1997)? We could pose similar questions for students with severe hearing impairments: Should we teach them by using primarily sign language or spoken language? And the same dilemma of difference appears in providing instruction for students with other disabilities: To what extent should they be treated as different and provided with special accommodations, and to what extent should they be treated just like everyone else?

To a great extent, the controversy over the dilemma of difference has to do with how students fare in society after their school years, not just how they are treated in school. Delpit (1988, 1995) examines a variety of perspectives on the problem of multicultural education, including the following position:

> Children have the right to their own language, their own culture. We must fight cultural hegemony and fight the system by insisting that children be allowed to express themselves in their own language and style. It is not they, the children, who must change, but the schools. (1988, p. 291)

Delpit's response to this perspective acknowledges both the benefit of recognizing and valuing different cultural styles and the necessity of accepting the realities of the society in which we live:

> I believe in diversity of style, and I believe the world will be diminished if cultural diversity is ever obliterated. Further, I believe strongly ... that each cultural group should have the right to maintain its own language style. When I speak, therefore, of the culture of power, I don't speak of how I wish things to be but of how they are.

> I further believe that to act as if power does not exist is to ensure that the power status quo remains the same. To imply to children or adults ... that it doesn't matter how you talk or how you write is to ensure their ultimate failure. I prefer to be honest with my students. Tell them that their language and cultural style is unique and wonderful but that there is a political power game that is also being played, and if they want to be in on that game there are certain games that they too must play.... They [my colleagues] seem to believe that if we accept and encourage diversity within classrooms of children, then diversity will automatically be accepted at gatekeeping points....

> I believe that will never happen. What will happen is that the students who reach the gatekeeping points ... will understand that they have been lied to and react accordingly. (1988, p. 292)

The gatekeeping points to which Delpit refers are admission to higher education and employment.

Hilliard (1989) also notes the necessity of taking students' cultural styles into account in teaching and the equal necessity of good teaching that prepares students of all cultural groups for the demands of the larger society:

> There is something we can call style—a central tendency that is characteristic of both individuals and groups. This style is cultural—learned. It is meaningful in the teaching and learning interaction. Students' style is not, however, to be used as an excuse for poor teaching or as an index of low capacity. (p. 69)

Clearly, the problem of instruction in multicultural education is not easily resolved, especially for bilingual students in special education (Gersten et al., 1994). Most authorities now agree, however, that accepting and fostering cultural diversity must not be used as an excuse for not teaching students the skills they need to survive and prosper in the larger context of American macroculture.

Among the multicultural controversies of our time are Afrocentric instruction and special African American programs and schools. Afrocentric instruction is an alternative to the Eurocentrism of the prevailing curriculum and methods of instruction; it highlights African culture and seeks distinctively African modes of teaching and learning. Some suggest that Afrocentrism is a regressive practice that detaches students from the realities of their American social environment (Wortham, 1992). Others call for instructional practices that are culturally sensitive—attuned to the particular cultural characteristics of African American learners (Ford, Obiakor, & Patton, 1995; Franklin, 1992; Van Keulen et al., 1998). The assumption underlying culturally sensitive instruction is that students with different cultural backgrounds need to be taught differently, that certain aspects of a student's cultural heritage determine to a significant extent how he or she learns best. For example, Franklin (1992) suggests that African American students differ from others in the cultural values of their homes and families, their language and patterns of movement, their responses to variety and multiplicity of stimulation, and their preference for divergent thinking.

Perhaps it is understandable that when emphasis is placed on differences in the ways students learn, there is also emphasis on devising special programs and schools that cater to these differences. Furthermore, the greater the diversity of cultural backgrounds of students in one class, the greater the difficulty in teaching all students effectively—if we assume that cultural background determines how students are best taught. Of course, we might hypothesize that certain methods of instruction are equally effective for all students in a culturally diverse group (see Singh, Ellis, Oswald, Wechsler, & Curtis, 1997). That is, some instructional approaches (e.g., cooperative learning, peer tutoring, and cross-age grouping) allow teachers to provide culturally sensitive instruction to all members of a diverse group at once.

Nevertheless, the notion that certain curricula and instructional practices are more appropriate for students of one ethnic origin than another may be used to justify distinctive programs, including African American immersion schools, in which all instruction is geared to the presumed particular learning characteristics of a single ethnic group (see Ascher, 1992; Leake & Leake, 1992). Such schools are often said to be segregationist in practice and intent, but Leake and Leake (1992) suggest that their philosophy opposes the concept of segregation:

> True integration occurs naturally when the differences between peers are minimal. Therefore, the bane of segregation is a culturally and ethnically diverse population of academically competent and self-confident individuals. The African-American immersion schools were designed to provide academically challenging and culturally appropriate experiences for their students. It was hoped that the anticipated increase in student achievement would work to vitiate the African-American students' feelings of inadequacy and impotence. (p. 784)

Do special programs designed with specific learning characteristics in mind help students learn more than they otherwise would and increase their self-esteem? This is a central controversy for both special education and multicultural general education, and research has not provided a clear answer for special programs of either type. Given that ethnicity and disability are two separate dimensions of human difference, however, special programming might be much more appropriate and effective for one dimension of difference than the other.

Hilliard (1992) poses the question of differential programming for students with disabilities as follows: "Can learning impediments be overcome or eliminated, allowing the formerly impaired student to perform significantly better than he or she would have without the services, or allowing the student to perform well in the mainstream academic program?" (p. 171). Research does not answer this question resoundingly—either affirmatively or negatively—for any model of delivering special education services. The question remains open as to whether making special education multicultural in its best sense will add to the weight of evidence regarding special education's effectiveness in improving disabled students' academic performance and success in the mainstream.

What is not an open question, however, is this: Must both special and general education adopt instructional programs that value all students and help all to be as successful as possible in American society, regardless of their specific cultural heritage? This question has been answered resoundingly in the affirmative, not by research but by our common commitment to the American values of equality of opportunity and fairness for all (see Singh, 1996). The pursuit of equality and fairness has led educational reformers toward four instructional goals:

1. Teaching tolerance and appreciation of difference
2. Working cooperatively with families
3. Improving instruction for language-minority students
4. Adopting effective teaching practices

Teaching Tolerance and Appreciation.   Noted historian Ronald Takaki (1994), whose grandparents were Japanese immigrant plantation laborers in Hawaii, suggests that the American promise of equality and fairness can become a reality only if we free ourselves from a legacy of racism and prejudice. We can do so by acknowledging the reality of our past and learning more about ourselves and our heritage. Takaki believes that schools have a special responsibility in achieving this:

> I think schools are a crucial—probably the most crucial—site for inviting us to view ourselves in a different mirror. I think schools have the responsibility to teach Americans about who we are and who we have been. This is where it's important for schools to offer a more accurate, a more inclusive multicultural curriculum. The classroom is the place where students who come from different ethnic or cultural communities can learn not only about themselves but about one another in an informed, systematic and non-intimidating way. I think the schools offer us our best hope for working it out. I would be very reluctant to depend upon the news media or the entertainment media, which do not have a responsibility to educate. (1994, p. 15)

Overcoming prejudice and teaching students to appreciate those who are different from themselves will be by no means easy. Moreover, this is not an area in which research can provide definitive guidelines. Yet proposed methods for how teachers can help students learn both self-esteem and tolerance of difference seem promising (Artiles & Zamora-Duran, 1997; Banks, 1997). For example, pupils might study the contributions of other languages and cultures to the development of English in order to understand its multicultural roots (Carnes, 1994), or they might analyze dialects to understand their rules and origins (Adger, Wolfram, & Detwyler, 1993). Students might also correspond with pen

Schools should be places where students from different cultural and ethnic groups can learn about themselves and one another in natural, nonintimidating ways.

pals to dispel regional or other stereotypes (Williams, 1994) or collaborate in small groups or teams to learn social responsibility and conflict resolution.

Teaching tolerance is not, of course, limited to ethnic, regional, or language differences but includes differences of all types, including disabilities. By teaching tolerance, we hope to overcome the kind of prejudice Angie Erickson describes in the box on pages 110–111. In addition, we hope to teach the self-acceptance and pride in identity that Angie articulates.

Working with Families. Schools have always depended, in part, on family involvement and support for their success. The ability of teachers to understand and communicate with their students' parents has been particularly important. The increasing separation of economic and social classes, along with the increasing diversity of racial and ethnic groups in public schools, have created greater demands on teachers' understanding of their students' parents and families. "As the experiential gap between teachers and their students increases, so does teachers' fear of crossing what they perceive as barriers to communication with poor families, and, in particular, families from racial groups other than their own" (Harry, Torguson, Katkavich, & Guerrero, 1993, p. 48).

Teachers should realize that the parents of low-income and minority children may feel alienated from schools, especially if their children have disabilities or histories of school problems. In fact, any parent who associates schools with failure, anxiety, or rejection is likely to shy away from involvement with teachers and avoid participation in school activities. Given this avoidance, teachers may perceive that parents have low expectations for their children. Even in cases in which parents seem unconcerned and do not participate in parent-teacher conferences or other school activities, it is important for teachers to maintain high expectations for students (Sleeter & Grant, 1994). Teachers must reach out to parents—visiting parents' homes, if possible—even if they are skeptical or fearful of what they will encounter (Harry et al., 1993). Building two-way communication, sharing concern for the child's welfare, and focusing on the student's strengths, particularly in initial meetings with parents, are critically important (Kalyanpur & Harry, 1997; Sleeter & Grant, 1994).

Improving Instruction for Language-Minority Students. Students for whom English is a second language face the simultaneous demands of learning a new language and mastering traditional subject matter. Those who have disabilities encounter the third demand of coping with the additional hurdles imposed by their exceptionalities. Bilingual special education is therefore particularly controversial, presenting difficult dilemmas and paradoxes.

We have already discussed the dilemma of difference—the fact that both recognizing and ignoring linguistic or other differences can put children at a disadvantage (Minow, 1985). In addition, language-minority students with disabilities face the paradox of simultaneous overrepresentation and underrepresentation. Ethnic- and language-minority students may be overrepresented in special education if they are referred and misidentified for problems that are not disabilities. At the same time, students from language-minority groups may be underreferred (see Ortiz, 1997). They may "truly need specialized assistance, but ... languish in general education classrooms, benefiting little from conventional instruction" (Gersten & Woodward, 1994, p. 312). Addressing these issues effectively demands that we examine different approaches to second-language instruction.

One approach to teaching language-minority students is to emphasize use of their native languages. In this approach, all academic instruction is initially provided in each student's native language, and English is taught as a separate subject. Later, when the student has demonstrated adequate fluency in English, he or she makes the transition to instruction in English in all academic subjects. A different approach is to offer content-area instruction in English from the beginning of the student's schooling but at a level that is "sheltered," or constantly modified to make sure the student understands it. The goal of this approach is to help the student learn English while learning academic subjects as well.

In the first approach—**native-language emphasis**—students are taught for most of the day in their native languages and later make a transition to English. In the second, **sheltered-English approach,** students receive instruction in English for most of the school day from the beginning of their schooling. The question as to which approach is better for students with disabilities has not been answered, although it is clear that changing from one approach to the other when students change schools creates particular difficulties (Gersten & Woodward, 1994).

Another issue for language-minority instruction is whether an emphasis on the natural uses of language or, alternatively, on skills such as vocabulary and pronunciation is most effective. However, this controversy may be based on a false dichotomy. What students need is an effective balance between skill building and language that is meaningful and relevant to their lives and interests (Ovando, 1997; Van Keulen et al., 1998). Instructional materials must make sense to students and provide explicit links to their own experiences. While teaching specific language skills, teachers must use language and create language variations that students understand. And students must be encouraged to learn to express complex ideas and feelings using increasingly complex sentences as they acquire fluency in English (Gersten & Woodward, 1994). In short, language-minority instruction needs to be constructed in the context of what we know about effective teaching.

Adopting Effective Teaching Practices. In a sense, effective multicultural education requires only that we implement what we know about effective instruction. Namely, effective teaching practices are sensitive to each student's cultural heritage, sense of self, view of the world, and acquired knowledge and skills. Teaching about various cultures, individual differences, and the construction of knowledge should permeate and transform the curriculum (Banks, 1993, 1994, 1997). Nonetheless, for language-minority students—indeed, for all students—we can articulate more specific components of effective teaching. We offer the following description of six components of effective teaching outlined by Gersten et al. (1994, p. 9):

1. *Scaffolding and strategies.* Students learn more efficiently when they are provided a "scaffold," or structure, for ideas and strategies for problem solving. In **scaffolded instruction,** the teacher assists the student in learning a task and then phases out the help as the student learns to use the strategy independently. (See Chapter 5 for further discussion.) Means of helping students learn more easily include stories, visual organizers (e.g., pictures, diagrams, outlines), **mnemonics** (tactics that aid memory, such as rhymes or images), and **reciprocal teaching** (in which the student sees the teacher use a learning strategy and then tries it out).
2. *Challenge.* Too much of education, even special education, is not appropriately challenging for students. All students—including those who are from cultural minorities, who are at high risk for failure, and who have disabilities—need to be given challenging tasks. *Appropriately challenging tasks* are those that a given student finds just manageable. While these

native-language emphasis. An approach to teaching language-minority pupils in which the student's native language is used for most of the day and English is taught as a separate subject.

sheltered-English approach. A method in which language-minority students are taught all their subjects in English at a level that is modified constantly according to individuals' needs.

scaffolded instruction. A cognitive approach to instruction in which the teacher provides temporary structure or support while students are learning a task; the support is gradually removed as the students are able to perform the task independently.

mnemonics. Techniques that aid memory, such as using rhymes, songs, or visual images to remember information.

reciprocal teaching. A method in which students and teachers are involved in a dialogue to facilitate learning.

It's OK to Be Different

Stop Making Fun of My Disability

Why me? I often ask myself. Why did I have to be the one? Why did I get picked to be different? Why are people mean to me and always treating me differently? These are the kinds of questions that I used to ask myself. It took more than 10 years for me to find answers and realize that I'm not more different than anyone else.

I was born on June 29, 1978. Along with me came my twin sister, Stephanie. She was born with no birth defects, but I was born with cerebral palsy. For me, CP made it so I shake a little; when my sister began to walk, I couldn't. The doctors knew it was a minor case of cerebral palsy. But they didn't know if I'd ever walk straight or do things that other kids my age could do.

At first my disability did not bother me, because when you're a toddler, you do things that are really easy. When it took me a little longer to play yard games, because I couldn't run that well, my friends just thought I was slow. My disability was noticed when other children were learning how to write and I couldn't. Kids I thought were my friends started to stay away from me because they said I was different. Classmates began commenting on my speech. They said I talked really weird. Every time someone was mean to me, I would start to cry and I would always blame myself for being different.

People thought I was stupid because it was hard for me to write my own name. So when I was the only one in the class to use a typewriter, I began to feel I was different. It got worse when the third graders moved on to fourth grade and I had to stay behind. I got held back because

the teachers thought I'd be unable to type fast enough to keep up. Kids told me that was a lie and the reason I got held back was because I was a retard. It really hurt to be teased by those I thought were my friends.

After putting up with everyone making fun of me and me crying about it, I started sticking up for myself when I was 10, in fourth grade. I realized if I wanted them to stop, I would have to be the person who made them stop. I finally found out who my real friends were, and I tried to ignore the ones who were mean. Instead of constantly thinking about the things I couldn't do, I tried to think about the things I *could* do, and it helped others, and myself, understand who I really was. When there was something I couldn't do such as play Pictionary, I sat and I watched or I would go find something else to do. A few people still called me names and made fun of me, but after a while, when they saw they didn't get a reaction, they quit, because it wasn't fun anymore. What they didn't know was that it did still hurt me. It hurt me a lot more than they could ever imagine.

When I was 12, my family moved. I kept this fairy tale in my head that, at my next school, no one would be mean to me or would see that I had a disability. I'd always wished I could be someone other than myself. I found out the hard way that I wasn't going to change, that I'd never be able to write and run with no problems. When kids in my new school found out that I couldn't write and my talking and walking were out of the ordinary, they started making fun of me. They never took time to know me.

tasks are not impossible, they do require serious effort and stretch the student's capabilities. Too often, teachers underestimate the capabilities of minority and exceptional students and underteach them (Delpit, 1995; Ford, 1998; Patton, 1997).

3. *Involvement.* Students must be engaged in extended conversations, in which they use complex linguistic structures. Verbal exchanges between teachers and pupils must not always be short, simple, and direct (although such exchanges have their place). Rather, teachers must probe with questions, share experiences, and elicit from pupils the kind of language that demonstrates their active involvement in learning.

4. *Success.* Students at the highest risk of failure and dropping out are those who have low rates of success in daily school activities. *All* students need to experience frequent success, and teachers must present challenging tasks at which *all* students can be successful. Failure should not be perpetuated.

Everything went back to the way it was before. I went back to blaming myself and thinking that, since I was different, I'd never fit in. I would cry all the time, because it was so hard for me to make friends again. I didn't know whether I should trust anyone—I thought that if people knew that I had a disability they would not like me anymore. It took me a long time to understand that I had to return to not caring about what other people say.

People make fun of others because of insecurity. They have to show off to feel better about themselves. When a person made fun of me everyone thought it was just a big joke. After a while I just started laughing along with them or walking away. It really made some kids mad that they weren't getting any reaction out of me. Yeah, it still hurt a lot. I wanted to break down and start crying right then and there, but I knew I didn't want them to get their pleasure out of my hurt feelings. I couldn't cry.

I still get really frustrated when I can't do certain things, and I probably always will. I thought I should give people a better chance to get to know me, but I knew that I would probably get hurt. I never thought that anyone would want to be friends with somebody who had cerebral palsy. At times I have trouble dealing with kids making fun of me, but these are people who need help figuring out things in life and need to be treated better themselves. Maybe then they'll treat others the same. They look disappointed when I walk away or laugh when they try to make fun of me. Perhaps they're hurting more than I am.

It took a lot of willpower on my part and a lot of love from family and friends to get where I am today. I learned that no one was to blame for my disability. I realize that I can do things and I can do them very well. Some things I can't do, like taking my own notes in class or running in a race, but I will have to live with that. At 16, I believe I've learned more than many people will learn in their whole lives. I have worked out that some people are just mean because they're afraid of being nice. They try to prove to themselves and others that they are cool, but, sooner or later, they're going to wish they hadn't said some of those hurtful things. A lot of people will go through life being mean to those with disabilities because they don't know how to act or what to say to them—they feel awkward with someone who's different.

Parents need to teach their children that it's all right to be different and it's all right to be friends with those who are. Some think that the disabled should be treated like little kids for the rest of their lives. They presume we don't need love and friends, but our needs are the same as every other human being's.

There are times when I wish I hadn't been born with cerebral palsy, but crying about it isn't going to do me any good. I can only live once, so I want to live the best I can. I am glad I learned who I am and what I am capable of doing. I am happy with who I am. Nobody else could be the Angela Marie Erickson who is writing this. I could never be, or ever want to be, anyone else.

Source: By Angie Erickson, "It's OK to Be Different," from *Newsweek,* October 24, 1994. © 1994, Newsweek, Inc. All rights reserved. Reprinted by permission.

5. *Mediation and feedback.* Too often, students work for long periods without receiving feedback, or are given feedback that is not comprehensible, or are asked for rote responses to which they attach little or no meaning. Providing frequent, comprehensible feedback on performance is vital to effective teaching, as is focusing on the meanings of responses—how evidence and logic are used to construct questions and their answers.

6. *Responsiveness to cultural and individual diversity.* The content of instruction must be related to students' experiences, including those as individuals and as members of various cultural groups. The issues of cultural and individual diversity cannot be adequately considered in a few special lessons; rather, they must be included routinely in all curriculum areas.

As Banks (1997) points out, a viable multicultural curriculum cannot be created and handed out to teachers. Teachers must be invested in the endeavor, as their values, perspectives, and teaching styles will affect what is taught and how. The effective implementation of a multicultural curriculum requires

Educational programming for all learners must challenge them to stretch their abilities. History warns teachers not to "underteach" minority learners.

teaching strategies that are involvement oriented, interactive, personalized, and cooperative.

This perspective applies to our own teaching and writing as well. In any textbook, the adequate treatment of multicultural issues cannot be confined to a single chapter. A chapter like this one—devoted specifically to multicultural education—may be necessary to ensure that the topic is given sufficient focused attention. Our intention in this book, however, is to prompt consideration of multicultural issues in every chapter.

Socialization

Academic instruction is one of two primary purposes of education. The other, socialization, involves helping students develop appropriate social perceptions and interactions with others and learn how to work for desirable social change.

Destructive and stereotypic social perceptions and interactions among differing microcultural groups are long-standing problems in schools and communities in the United States, particularly when there are cultural differences among students in language and social behavior (Ishii-Jordan, 1997). The most obvious examples involve racial discrimination, although sex discrimination and discrimination against people of differing religions and disabilities are also common in our society. Teachers must become keenly aware of their own cultural heritages, identities, and biases before they can help their students deal with cultural diversity in ways that enhance democratic ideals, such as human dignity, justice, and equality (Banks, 1997). Becoming comfortable with one's own identity as a member of microcultural groups is an important objective for both teachers and students. Depending on the cultural context, accepting and valuing one's identity can be quite difficult. In the box on page 113, Ved Mehta (1989) describes his feelings of discomfort with his identity as a member of several microcultural groups—people from India, people of a particular East Indian culture, and persons who are blind.

Difference in Identity: The Struggle for Acceptance

In the following passage from one of his autobiographical books, Ved Mehta describes his feelings—during his college years—of social isolation and contempt for his identity as a person who is blind and from an Eastern culture. How might his college classmates and instructors have enhanced his feelings of self-worth as a member of these two microcultural groups?

> Mandy went home most weekends. At first, I worried that she never invited me to go with her and meet her family. She never even offered to give me her home address or telephone number. But here, again, far from condemning her behavior, I came to condone it, thinking I should be grateful to her for protecting me from her family's ire. Putting myself in her father's place, I reflected that if I had a daughter who had got herself involved with a handicapped person I would vigorously oppose the romance and try to persuade her not to consider throwing away her life on a handicapped person out of some misguided notion that she could make up for the magnitude of his problems. (Coming from a country with practically no tradition of romantic love, I assumed that dating was tantamount to marriage.) Moreover, I told myself that I was not only handicapped but also a foreigner, who, no matter how superficially Westernized, could never have the same grasp of the English language and American customs that an American had. Just as living in a sighted society was making me contemptuous of everything to do with being blind, studying in America was making me contemptuous of everything to do with being Indian. As a freshman in college, I had taken courses in the history of Western civilization, the philosophy of Western civilization, and the classical music of Western civilization. In Berkeley, I was studying Western economics and American history. (Similar courses in Indian civilization were unheard of.) In the light of this Western education, everything Indian seemed backward and primitive. I remember once listening to a record of Mozart and being awed by the dozens of instruments magically playing in harmony, and then listening to a record of a sitar and being filled with scorn for the twang-twang of the gut.

Source: © Ved Mehta, *The Stolen Light*, p. 260, first published by HarperCollins UK 1989 and W.W. Norton & Co 1989. Reprinted with permission.

Teaching about different cultures and their value may be important in reducing racial and ethnic conflict and promoting respect for human differences. Equally important, however, is structuring classroom interactions to promote the understanding and appreciation of others. One of the most effective ways of breaking down prejudice and encouraging appropriate interaction among students with different characteristics is **cooperative learning** (Johnson & Johnson, 1986; Slavin, 1988). In cooperative learning, students of different abilities and cultural characteristics work together as a team, fostering interdependence. In *Among Schoolchildren,* Tracy Kidder describes this approach to socialization as it was used by a fifth-grade teacher, Chris Zajac:

> Then came fifteen minutes of study, during which teams of two children quizzed each other. Chris paired up good spellers with poor ones. She also made spelling an exercise in socialization, by putting together children who did not seem predisposed to like each other. She hoped that some would learn to get along with classmates they didn't think they liked. At least they'd be more apt to do some work than if she paired them up with friends. Her guesses were good. Alice raised her eyes to the florescent-lit ceiling at the news that she had Claude for a spelling partner. Later she wrote, "Today is the worst day of my life." Clarence scowled at the news that he had Ashley, who was shy and chubby and who didn't look happy either. A little smile collected in one corner of Chris's mouth as she observed the reactions. "Now, you're not permanently attached to that person for the rest of your life," she said to the class. (1989, pp. 28–29)

cooperative learning. A teaching approach in which the teacher places students with heterogeneous abilities (for example, some might have disabilities) together to work on assignments.

Multicultural education may teach us to understand and embrace individual differences, rather than try to erase them.

Teachers of exceptional children and youths must be aware of the variety of microcultural identities their students may be developing and struggling with. Review the multiple aspects of cultural identity suggested by Figure 3.1 (page 92) and reflect on the combinations of these and other subcultures that a given student might adopt. One of the microcultural identities not included in Figure 3.1 is sexual orientation. Yet many children and adolescents, including many with educational exceptionalities, experience serious difficulties with what some have called the "invisible culture" of gay and lesbian youth (McIntyre, 1992a). Students who are "straight" may struggle with their own prejudices against homosexuals, prejudices all too often fostered by both their peers and adults and sometimes given justification by identification with a religious or political microculture. Gay and lesbian students are often harassed and abused verbally and physically in school and may suffer from serious depression or other psychological disorders as a result (McIntyre, 1992a; Uribe & Harbeck, 1992). Consider also that a student might be both gay or lesbian and gifted, physically disabled, mentally retarded, or have any other educational exceptionality.

Our point is that the task of socialization in a multicultural society demands attention to the multitude of identities that students may assume. It also demands an awareness that any of these identities may carry the consequence of social rejection, isolation, and alienation. Our task as educators is to promote understanding of cultural differences and acceptance of individuals whose identities are different from one's own. Building pride in one's cultural identity is a particular concern in teaching exceptional students. As we have noted elsewhere (Hallahan & Kauffman, 1994), many people in the Deaf community prefer to be called "the Deaf," which runs contrary to the current use of terms such as *hearing impaired*. Deaf people and blind people have begun to express pride in their identities and microcultures. In fact, for increasing numbers of people with disabilities, labels are to be embraced, not hidden. For example, one adult with learning disabilities said in an interview, "I need to be proud of myself. As long as I was ashamed of being LD [learning disabled], it was difficult to proceed" (Gerber, Ginsberg, & Reiff, 1992, p. 481).

People from many segments of society, or microcultures—such as parents of children with disabilities, senior citizens, religious groups, recovering alcoholics, and so on—find that congregating for mutual support and understanding enhances their feelings of self-worth. Educators need to consider the possible value of having students with disabilities congregate for specific purposes. As Edgar and Siegel (1995) have noted:

> In a naive and overzealous rush to implement fully inclusive school environments, we risk overlooking and discarding the discovery of identity, common will, and support that comes from the opportunity to congregate with those engaged in struggles that share characteristics of ability, culture, status, or environment. (p. 274)

By trying to avoid labels and insisting that students with disabilities always be placed with those who do not have disabilities, perhaps we risk giving the message that those with have disabilities are less desirable or even not fit to associate with as peers. Bateman (1994) suggests that "something is terribly and not very subtly insulting about saying a bright learning disabled student ought not attend a special school with other students who have learning disabilities because he needs to be with non-disabled students" (p. 516). In striving for true multicultural awareness, we may learn that it is more productive in the long run to embrace identities associated with exceptionalities, while working to increase tolerance and understanding of differences, than it is to avoid labels or refrain from congregating students with specific characteristics.

One of the most difficult tasks of teaching is socializing students through classroom discipline—that is, through the management of classroom behavior. Managing classroom behavior presents a serious challenge for nearly all teachers and a particularly difficult challenge for most special education teachers (Kauffman, Mostert, Trent, & Hallahan, 1998). Two considerations are critical: (1) the relationship between the teacher's approach to classroom discipline and the parents' childrearing practices, and (2) the sensitivity of the teacher to cultural differences in responses to discipline.

Middle-class American teachers may have an approach to classroom discipline that they consider effective and humane but that differs radically from some cultures' accepted childrearing practices. As McIntyre and Silva (1992) point out, educators, like everyone else, are often ethnocentric, believing that their views are correct and those of others are inferior. In the case of discipline involving students of culturally diverse backgrounds, the teacher may face difficult ethical decisions about child abuse or neglect. When do one's own beliefs about the treatment of children demand that a culturally condoned disciplinary practice be confronted as abuse? Answering this question is not easy.

McIntyre (1992b) summarizes some of the cultural differences we might find in expectations regarding classroom behavior. He also describes the cultural sensitivity demanded in managing behavior effectively and humanely. For example, students from different cultures may differ markedly in their pattern of eye contact with the teacher or another authority (especially when being corrected), interpretation of peer assistance on academic work, response to praise or external rewards, touching or being touched, response to deadlines, physical activity level during learning, response to explanations and questions, response to peer pressure, attitude toward corporal punishment, and so on. In selecting classroom management strategies, the teacher must be sensitive to such cultural differences but, at the same time, use an approach that is effective, fair, just, and ethically and legally defensible. This is, to say the least, a highly demanding task.

Finally, we note that education should not merely socialize students to fit into the existing social order. The goals of multicultural education include teaching students to work for social change (Banks, 1997; Banks & Banks, 1997), which entails helping students who are members of oppressed minorities become advocates for themselves and other members of their microcultures.

Summary

Education for cultural diversity involves managing tension between microcultural diversity, on the one hand, and common macrocultural values, on the other. Many microcultures are found in the U.S. macroculture, which values justice, equality, and human dignity. Progress in multicultural education is difficult because each microculture tends to see many of its own values as the standards against which others should be judged. Special educators and general educators alike must understand how to provide an education that gives equal opportunity to students regardless of gender, socioeconomic status, ethnic group, disability, or other cultural identity. Doing so may require that educators change students' knowledge construction of their own and others' cultural identities. Devising a multicultural curriculum that is satisfactory to all groups is difficult, and not everyone agrees that understanding cultural diversity is as important as building the common culture. Although multiculturalism is fraught with conflicts, it offers an opportunity to practice American values of tolerance, justice, equality, and individualism.

Communities and families contribute much to students' attitudes toward education and academic achievement. Minority communities can encourage academic success among students by highlighting values consistent with school achievement. However, we must guard against ethnic stereotypes of achievement or failure and understand that community and family attitudes toward schooling do not excuse educators from their responsibility to provide an effective and multicultural education for all students.

Multicultural education may at first seem a relatively simple matter, but it is complicated by questions about what cultures to include and what and how to teach about them. Many distinct microcultures exist, and some have values or customs that others find un-

acceptable or offensive. Microcultural groups may be distinguished not only by gender and ethnicity but also by religious or political affiliation and sexual orientation. Finding a balance among cultural values and traditions that satisfies all groups is often quite difficult. Moreover, this balance may vary from school to school. Controversy often exists in communities where so-called minorities constitute well over half the school population. Issues such as language differences and bilingual education have become divisive within many such communities.

The types of cultural diversity most relevant to special education are ethnicity and disability or giftedness. We must remember, however, that students may be members of a variety of microcultural groups besides those designating educational exceptionality. Multicultural special education must give special attention to ensuring that ethnicity is not mistaken for educational exceptionality and to increasing the understanding of educational exceptionality and its relationship to other microcultures. Members of ethnic minority groups may be mistakenly identified as disabled or overlooked in attempts to identify special gifts and talents if their cultural practices and languages are not understood by teachers. Disproportional representation of ethnic minority students in special education is a long-standing and complex problem with no obvious solution. Individuals with certain exceptionalities (deafness, for example) may develop their own microcultures, and it is important to help others understand and appreciate these cultures.

Three specific problems in multicultural special education are assessment, instruction, and socialization. Assessment is a particularly critical issue because it forms the basis for decisions about instruction and placement; therefore, it is imperative that assessment be accurate, fair, and directly related to designing effective instruction. Traditional testing procedures, such as standardized tests, are problematic for members of many ethnic minorities. Curriculum-based assessment and performance assessment are gaining wide acceptance as alternatives. Assessment of the learning environment may be as important as assessment of students' skills.

Instruction presents many points of controversy for multicultural and bilingual special education. One of the great and pervasive problems of special education is the dilemma of difference. Recognizing students' differences and providing special services of any kind may be helpful, but identification and special programming may also carry stigmas and perpetuate the differences. Some leading scholars in multicultural education suggest that instruction should help students understand and preserve their own microcultures while at the same time help students learn to function successfully in the American macroculture.

The pursuit of equality and fairness has led educators to four instructional goals: (1) teaching tolerance and appreciation of differences; (2) working cooperatively with families; (3) improving the instruction of language-minority students; and (4) adopting effective teaching practices.

Socialization is an aspect of education that some believe is as important as academic instruction. Multicultural special education must seek to improve students' understanding and acceptance of others' differences and to help students develop pride in their own cultural identities. Teachers may encounter particular multicultural problems in managing classroom behavior because of differences between their own views of discipline and childrearing and those of their students and students' parents.

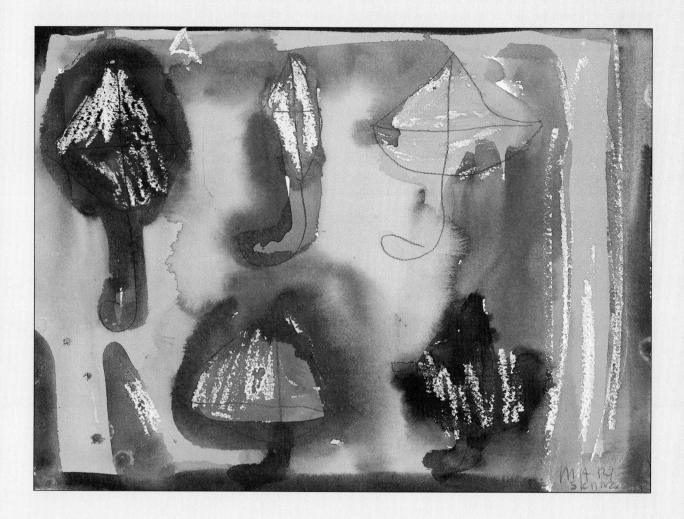

mary skinner

Kites. Watercolor, wax, pencil on rag paper. 11 × 15 in.

Mary Skinner was born in Massachusetts in 1959. She is the youngest of five children and lives with her family in Brighton, MA. Mary is a natural artist who has an ease with paint, using it freely and expressively. Her work is represented by the Gateway Gallery in Brookline, MA. Her work has been shown in New England, Washington, DC, and New York.

chapter 4

Mental Retardation

Everywhere, however, we hear talk of sameness. "All men are created equal" it is declared. And at the ballot box and the subway rush, in Hiroshima and Coney Island it almost seems that way. Moreover, coming back from Staten Island on the ferry, as you see an unkempt bootblack lift his head to gaze at the Manhattan skyline—you know these words of Jefferson are not mere snares for votes and popularity. But standing on the same boat with the hand of your idiot son in one of yours—with mingled love and distaste placing a handkerchief against his drooling mouth—you know that Jefferson's words are not easy to understand.

There is a difference in sameness. Perhaps the days of our years are for the bootblack. But assuredly the nights are for our idiot son.

RICHARD H. HUNGERFORD
"On Locusts"

There is considerable danger in relying on Hungerford's portrayal (p. 119) for our only view of what it is like to have a child who is retarded. Such children may be heartbreakingly different from the children next door in some ways but also like them in others. Many children with mental retardation function like nondisabled children—but nondisabled children at a younger chronological age. Even the differences that do exist need not cause parents a lifetime of constant heartache. Hungerford's statement is valuable, however, because it presents honest feelings. Unlike the romanticized portraits found in many TV dramas, movies, and books, children with retardation can evoke agony, hatred, sorrow, and frustration, as well as love, in their parents.

The Hungerford quote, published in 1950, points out something else as well. It reflects the once-popular stereotype of the person with retardation as a clumsy, drooling, helpless creature. Today we know this is simply not true. First, most children classified as mentally retarded are *mildly* retarded and look like the hypothetical average child living next door. Second, it can be misleading to characterize even those with more severe retardation as helpless. With advanced methods of providing educational and vocational training, people with retardation are capable of leading more independent lives than was previously thought possible. Given appropriate preparation, many are able to live and work with relatively little help from others.

The field of mental retardation has undergone a number of other exciting changes since the time Hungerford wrote. No longer is institutionalization the norm for persons who are severely retarded. More and more students with retardation are spending greater portions of their time in regular classrooms in their neighborhood schools. Terminology, too, is changing. Whereas the term *idiot*, which Hungerford uses, was once acceptable, today professionals use terms that are less stigmatizing.

Perhaps the most significant change since Hungerford wrote "On Locusts" is the fact that designating someone as mentally retarded has become much more difficult. Today, professionals are more reluctant to apply the label of mental retardation than they once were. At least three reasons account for this more cautious attitude toward identification of students as retarded:

1. Professionals became concerned about the misdiagnosis of children from ethnic minority groups as retarded. Twenty to thirty years ago it was much more common for children from ethnic minorities, especially African American and Hispanic students, to be labeled "mentally retarded" because they did not achieve well in school and they scored poorly on intelligence tests.

2. Another reason for using more stringent criteria for determining retardation is related to the fear that the stigma of such a diagnosis can have harmful consequences for the individual. Some believe that the label of mental retardation causes children to have poor self-concepts and to be viewed negatively by others.

3. Some professionals now believe that, to a certain extent, mental retardation is a socially constructed condition. For example, the American Association on Mental Retardation (AAMR) Ad Hoc Committee on Terminology and Classification (1992) has conceived of retardation not as a trait residing in the individual but as the product of the interaction between a person and his or her environment. This point of view has not gone uncontested, with some authorities thinking that the AAMR has gone too far in denying the existence of mental retardation as an essential feature within a person.

misconceptions
about Persons with Mental Retardation

myth Mental retardation is defined by how a person scores on an IQ test.

fact The most commonly used definition specifies that in order for a person to be considered mentally retarded, he or she must meet two criteria: (1) low intellectual functioning *and* (2) low adaptive skills.

myth Once diagnosed as mentally retarded, a person remains within this classification for life.

fact A person's level of mental functioning does not necessarily remain stable; this is particularly true for those individuals who are mildly retarded. With intensive educational programming, some persons can improve to the point that they are no longer retarded.

myth In most cases, we can identify the cause of retardation.

fact In most cases, especially those of people who are mildly retarded or who require less intensive support, we cannot specify the cause. For many children who are mildly retarded, poor environment may be a causal factor, but it is extremely difficult to document.

myth Most mentally retarded children look different from nondisabled children.

fact The majority of children with mental retardation are mildly retarded (or require less intensive support), and most of these look like nondisabled children.

myth We can identify most cases of mental retardation in infancy.

fact Most children with retardation are not identified as such until they go to school, for several reasons: (1) because most children with retardation are mildly retarded; (2) because infant intelligence tests are not very reliable and valid; and (3) because intellectual demands on the child increase greatly upon entrance to school.

myth Persons with mental retardation tend to be gentle people who have an easy time making friends.

fact Because of a variety of behavioral characteristics and because they sometimes live and work in relatively isolated situations, some persons with mental retardation have difficulty making and holding friends.

myth The teaching of vocational skills to students with retardation is best reserved for secondary school and beyond.

fact Many authorities now believe it appropriate to introduce vocational content in elementary school to students with mental retardation.

myth When workers with mental retardation fail on the job, it is usually because they do not have adequate job skills.

fact When they fail on the job, it is more often because of poor job responsibility (poor attendance and lack of initiative) and social incompetence (interacting inappropriately with co-workers) than because of incompetence in task production.

myth Persons with mental retardation should not be expected to work in the competitive job market.

fact More and more persons who are mentally retarded hold jobs in competitive employment. Many are helped through supportive employment situations, in which a job coach helps them and their employer adapt to the workplace.

Definition

A more conservative approach to identifying students as mentally retarded is reflected in changes in definition that have occurred over the years. Since 1950, seven official definitions of mental retardation have been endorsed by the American Association on Mental Retardation (AAMR), the major professional organization dealing with persons with mental retardation.

The AAMR Definition

The current AAMR definition reads:

> *Mental retardation* refers to substantial limitations in present functioning. It is characterized by significantly subaverage intellectual functioning, existing concurrently with related limitations in two or more of the following applicable adaptive skill areas: communication, self-care, home living, social skills, community use, self-direction, health and safety, functional academics, leisure, and work. Mental retardation manifests before age 18. (AAMR Ad Hoc Committee on Terminology and Classification, 1992, p. 5)

In making this definition operational, the professional is to rely on assessment of two areas: intellectual functioning and adaptive skills. **Intellectual functioning,** usually estimated by an IQ test, refers primarily to ability related to academic performance. **Adaptive skills,** usually estimated by adaptive behavior surveys, refers to abilities related to coping with one's environment.

This definition, like each of its predecessors, continues three trends consistent with a more cautious approach to diagnosing students as mentally retarded:

1. A broadening of the definition beyond the single criterion of an IQ score
2. A lowering of the IQ score used as a cutoff for qualification as retarded
3. A conceptualization of retardation as a condition that can be improved and that is not necessarily permanent

intellectual functioning. The ability to solve problems related to academics; usually estimated by an IQ test; one of two major components (the other is adaptive skills) of the AAMR definition.

adaptive skills. Skills needed to adapt to one's living environment (e.g., communication, self-care, home living, social skills, community use, self-direction, health and safety, functional academics, leisure, and work); usually estimated by an adaptive behavior survey; one of two major components (the other is intellectual functioning) of the AAMR definition.

Broadening the Definition

At one time, it was common practice to diagnose individuals as retarded solely on the basis of an IQ score. Today, we recognize that IQ tests are far from perfect and that they are but one indication of a person's ability to function. Professionals came to consider adaptive skills in addition to IQ in defining retardation because they began to recognize that some students might score poorly on IQ tests but still be "streetwise"—able to cope, for example, with the subway system, with an after-school job, with peers.

Lowering the IQ Score Cutoff

It was also common at one time for practitioners to use a cutoff score of 85 on an IQ test as an indicator of mental retardation. This cutoff score was endorsed by the AAMR until the mid-1970s, when they made it more difficult for people to be identified as retarded by establishing a cutoff score of 70 to 75. The current AAMR definition also sanctions this cutoff of 70 to 75. A 5-point spread of 70 to 75 has been established to reinforce the notion that IQ scores should not be regarded as precise measurements, that professionals should use some clinical judgment in interpreting IQ scores.

Adaptive skills refer to abilities related to coping with one's everyday environment, including social skills and the ability to function in different communities.

Retardation as Improvable and Possibly Nonpermanent

At the time of the Hungerford quote (see p. 119), many authorities held little hope for significantly enhancing the functioning of people with retardation and essentially believed retardation to be incurable. Over the years, however, professionals have become more optimistic about the beneficial effects of educational programming. Not only do they believe that the functioning of virtually all persons with retardation can be improved, but they have forwarded the notion that some persons with retardation, especially those with mild retardation, can eventually improve to the point that they are no longer classified as retarded.

In agreement with the notion that mental retardation is improvable and not necessarily permanent, the developers of the latest AAMR definition hold that how well a person with mental retardation functions is directly related to the amount of support he or she receives from the environment. With enough support, he or she can improve and possibly overcome the retardation. The importance of support, in fact, is underscored in the AAMR's classification scheme, to which we now turn.

The AAMR Classification Scheme

Professionals have typically classified persons with mental retardation according to the severity of their problems. For many years, the AAMR promoted the use of the terms **mild, moderate, severe,** and **profound retardation,** with each of these levels keyed to approximate IQ levels. For example, mild mental retardation is from 50–55 to approximately 70, and severe retardation is from 20–25 to 35–40. Most school systems now classify their students with mental retardation using these terms or a close approximation of them.

In 1992, however, the AAMR recommended a radical departure from this system of classification (AAMR Ad Hoc Committee on Terminology and Classification, 1992). Rather than categorize students based on their IQ scores, the AAMR recommended that professionals classify them according to how much

mild retardation. A classification used to specify an individual whose IQ is approximately 55–70.

moderate retardation. A classification used to specify an individual whose IQ is approximately 40–55.

severe retardation. A classification used to specify an individual whose IQ is between approximately 25 and 40.

profound retardation. A classification used to specify an individual whose IQ is below approximately 25.

support they need to function as competently as possible. Table 4.1 depicts these **levels of support.**

The authors of the AAMR classification scheme believe categorization based on support needed is better than categorization based on IQ because it (1) implies that persons with retardation can achieve positive outcomes with appropriate support services, (2) avoids reliance on a single IQ score, and (3) can result in descriptions that are more meaningful when considered in combination with adaptive skills. Rather than saying, for example, that a person has "severe retardation," one might say the person has retardation that requires "extensive supports in self-care, home living, and work."

Criticisms of the AAMR Definition and Classification Scheme. Critics do not agree on which parts of the AAMR definition and classification scheme they find fault with. Some, as we noted above, believe that the notion that mental retardation does not reside in the individual may be too radical. They suggest that believing that retardation is a condition that a person has does not necessarily mean that it is permanent and immutable. Some question the utility of a classification system based on levels of support (MacMillan, Gresham, & Siperstein, 1993; Smith, 1994). They point to the long tradition of classifying individuals on the basis of severity and argue that it is difficult to develop ways of reliably measuring the levels of support different people need. And some question the ability to measure adaptive behavior reliably (Greenspan, 1997).

Concerns about the AAMR definition and classification system have prompted two other definitions that have the backing of several professionals—the American Psychological Association (APA) definition and Greenspan's definition.

The APA Definition

The APA definition reads:

> Mental retardation (MR) refers to (a) significant limitations in general intellectual functioning; (b) significant limitations in adaptive functioning, which exist concurrently; and (c) onset of intellectual and adaptive limitations before the age of 22 years. (Jacobson & Mulick, 1996, p. 13)

Most important, the APA endorses the old AAMR classification terminology of *mild, moderate, severe,* and *profound* based on IQ levels. It is thus a rejection of the idea of classifying persons with mental retardation on the basis of needed levels of support.

Greenspan's Definition

Stephen Greenspan's (1997) definition retains the notion of classification based on levels of support, but it rejects adaptive behavior as a viable construct. Greenspan maintains that adaptive behavior is too vague and difficult to measure. Instead, he thinks the core impairment in mental retardation should be intelligence, but the conceptualization of intelligence should be expanded to include three types of intelligence: conceptual, practical, and social. **Conceptual intelligence** is the traditional view of intelligence, the one assessed primarily by IQ tests. **Practical intelligence** refers to the ability to act independently and manage daily living activities. **Social intelligence** is the ability to interpret the social behavior of others and to interact in a socially appropriate manner.

levels of support. The basis of the AAMR classification scheme; characterizes the amount of support needed for someone with mental retardation to function as competently as possible as (1) intermittent, (2) limited, (3) extensive, or (4) pervasive.

conceptual intelligence. The traditional conceptualization of intelligence emphasizing problem solving related to academic material; what IQ tests primarily assess.

practical intelligence. The ability to solve problems related to activities of daily living; an aspect of the adaptive skills component of the AAMR definition.

social intelligence. The ability to understand social expectations and to cope in social situations; an aspect of the adaptive skills component of the AAMR definition.

Table 4.1 — AAMR Classification Scheme for Mental Retardation Based on Levels of Support

Intermittent	Supports on an "as needed basis." Characterized by episodic nature, person not always needing the support(s), or short-term supports needed during life-span transitions (e.g., job loss or an acute medical crisis). Intermittent supports may be high or low intensity when provided.
Limited	An intensity of supports characterized by consistency over time and time-limited but not of an intermittent nature, may require fewer staff members and less cost than more intense levels of support (e.g., time-limited employment training or transitional supports during the school-to-adult period).
Extensive	Supports characterized by regular involvement (e.g., daily) in at least some environments (such as work or home) and not time-limited (e.g., long-term home living support).
Pervasive	Supports characterized by their constancy, high intensity, provided across environments; potential life-sustaining nature. Pervasive supports typically involve more staff members and intrusiveness than do extensive or time-limited supports.

Source: From AAMR Ad Hoc Committee on Terminology and Classification. (1992). *Mental retardation: Definition, classification, and systems of support.* Copyright © 1992 by American Association on Mental Retardation. Reprinted with permission.

Greenspan's definition reads:

> The term *mental retardation* refers to *persons widely perceived to need long-term supports, accommodations or protections due to persistent limitations in social, practical and conceptual intelligence and the resulting inability to meet the intellectual demands of a range of settings and roles.* These limitations are assumed, in most cases, to result from abnormalities or events occurring during the developmental period, and which have permanent effects on brain development and functioning. Persons with mental retardation may be divided into three sub-categories that indicate degree of overall disability: limited, extensive, and pervasive. These levels are determined by the intensity and pervasiveness of supports needed rather than by degree of intellectual impairment. (Greenspan, 1997, p. 186)

Given the highly sensitive issue of identifying people as retarded, the effort to come up with a definition that will please everyone is perhaps futile. However, virtually all authorities agree on one thing: Mental retardation should not be defined solely on the basis of a single IQ score. That many professionals are now not relying solely on an IQ score is evident from current prevalence figures, to which we now turn.

Critical to how well some individuals with mental retardation function is the level of support that they receive from the people around them.

Prevalence

The average (mean) score on an IQ test is 100. Theoretically, we expect 2.27 percent of the population to fall two standard deviations (IQ = 70 on the Wechsler Intelligence Scale for Children–Revised, or WISC–III) or more below this average. This expectation is based on the assumption that intelligence, like so many other human traits, is distributed along a *normal curve*. Figure 4.1 shows the hypothetical normal curve of intelligence. This curve is split into eight areas by means of standard deviations. On the latest edition of the Wechsler, the WISC–III, where

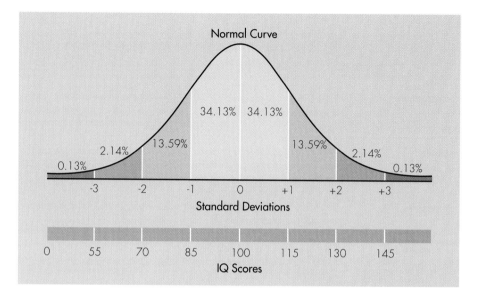

one standard deviation equals 15 IQ points, 2.14 percent of the population scores between 55 and 70 and 0.13 percent scores below 55. Thus it would seem that 2.27 percent should fall between 0 and 70. (See p. 135 for more on intelligence tests.)

However, the actual prevalence figures for students identified as mentally retarded are much lower. In recent years they have been somewhere around 1 to 1.5 percent. Authorities surmise that this lower prevalence figure is due to school personnel considering adaptive behavior or a broader definition of intelligence in addition to an IQ score to diagnose mental retardation. In addition, there is evidence that in cases in which the student's IQ score is in the 70s, thus making identification as retarded a close call, parents and school officials may be more likely to identify children as learning disabled than mentally retarded because "learning disabled" is perceived as a less stigmatizing label (MacMillan, Gresham, Bocian, & Lambros, 1998).

Causes

Many experts estimate that we are able to pinpoint the cause of mental retardation in only about 10 to 15 percent of the cases. Even in this 10 to 15 percent there may still be disagreement in specifying *the* single cause of many cases of retardation, depending on how one defines "cause." As one authority has persuasively argued:

> The term *etiological* [causal] *specificity* is disarmingly simple and should not be regarded as an "either-or" proposition. As an example, just where does mental retardation begin? Does it begin with teen pregnancy, with unhealthy maternal behavior, with intrauterine infection, with premature birthweight, with intracranial bleeds, with an impoverished home environment, with abuse and neglect, with poor school performance, or with a measured low IQ? Etiology is not always a matter of clear identification of some critical agent. Pathogenesis is best regarded as a sequence of events.... (Baumeister, 1997, p. 33)

Although some overlap is evident, for the most part causal factors for persons with mild retardation (requiring less intensive support services) differ from those for persons with more severe retardation (requiring more intensive support services).

Persons with Mild Retardation, or Those Requiring Less Intensive Support

Most individuals identified as retarded are classified as mildly retarded and need less intensive support to function. They typically do not differ in appearance from their nondisabled peers, and they are usually not diagnosed as retarded until they enter school and begin to fall behind in schoolwork. Although there are no definitive data, the estimate of 10 to 15 percent of identifiable causes of all retardation is undoubtedly even lower when considering only persons who are mildly retarded. And the difficulty in pinpointing a specific cause noted above is even more apropos for those with mild retardation.

Professionals often refer to individuals with mild retardation as having **cultural-familial retardation.** Some use this term to refer to a person with a mild degree of retardation who, among other things, (1) has no evidence of brain damage, (2) has parents who are also mildly retarded, (3) has siblings who are mildly retarded (if he or she has siblings), and (4) is likely to produce children who are mildly retarded (Zigler & Hodapp, 1986). Today professionals use the term broadly to indicate mild retardation that may be due to an unstimulating environment (possibly but not necessarily specifically caused by poor parenting) and/or genetic factors. Just which factor is most influential—environment or heredity—has been the subject of debate for years.

cultural-familial retardation. Today, a term used to refer to mild retardation due to an unstimulating environment and/or genetic factors.

The Nature versus Nurture Controversy. In the early part of this century, the predominant viewpoint among educators was that genetics determines intellectual development. The classic study of Skeels and Dye (1939), however, did much to strengthen the position of the environmentalists. Skeels and Dye investigated the effects of stimulation on the development of infants and young children in an orphanage, many of whom were classified as mentally retarded. One group of children remained in the typical orphanage environment, while the other group was given stimulation. For the latter group, nurturance was provided by teenage girls who were retarded. The effects were clearcut: Average IQs for members of the group given stimulation increased, whereas the other children's IQs decreased. Even more dramatic were the results of Skeels's follow-up study, done twenty-one years later (Skeels, 1966). Among other things, the experimental group on average had completed the twelfth grade, with some having one or more years of college and one completing a B.A. degree.

By the 1960s, many educators supported the environmental (nurture) position. During this time, for example, the

Controversy surrounds the issues of whether and to what extent poor social-environmental conditions contribute to retardation.

federal government established the Head Start program, which was based on the premise that the negative effects of poverty could be reduced through educational and medical services during the preschool years.

For many years, theoreticians tended to view the nature-nurture issue from an either/or perspective—either you believed that heredity held the key to determining intellectual development or you held that the environment was the all-important factor. Today, however, most authorities hold that both genetics and the environment are critical determinants of intelligence. Some scientists have tried to discover how much of intelligence is determined by genetics versus the environment, but many view this quest as futile. They assert that genetics and environment do not combine in an additive fashion to produce intelligence. Instead, the interaction between genetics and environment results in intelligence.

The following exchange between a professor of biopsychology and his student points out the importance of viewing intelligence in this way—that is, as the result of an interaction between genetics and experience and not a simple addition of the two:

> Recently, one of my students told me that she had read that intelligence was one-third genetic and two-thirds experience, and she wondered whether this was true. She must have been puzzled when I began my response by describing an alpine experience. "I was lazily wandering up a summit ridge when I heard an unexpected sound. Ahead, with his back to me, was a young man sitting on the edge of a precipice, blowing into a peculiar musical instrument. I sat down behind him on a large sun-soaked rock, and shared his experience with him. Then, I got up and wandered back down the ridge, leaving him undisturbed. I have frequently wondered about the musician, his music, and the powerful effect that it had on me." Then I put the following question to my student: "If I wanted to get a better understanding of the musician, would it be reasonable for me to begin by asking how much of it came from the musician and how much of it came from the instrument?"
>
> "That would be dumb," she said, "The music comes from both; it makes no sense to ask how much comes from the musician and how much comes from the instrument. Somehow the music results from the interaction of the two, and you would have to ask about the interaction."
>
> "That's exactly right," I said. "Now, do you see why..."
>
> "Don't say any more," she interrupted. "I see what you're getting at. Intelligence is the product of the interaction of genes and experience, and it is dumb to try to find how much comes from genes and how much comes from experience." (Pinel, 1993, p. 32)

Persons with More Severe Retardation, or Those Requiring More Intensive Support

Determining causes of retardation is easier in persons whose retardation is more severe than in those who are mildly retarded. Unlike persons with mild retardation, individuals with more severe retardation often do look different from their nondisabled peers and they are often diagnosed in infancy or before entering school. We can divide causes of retardation in persons with more severe retardation into two general categories—genetic factors and brain damage.

Genetic Factors. Mental retardation has a number of genetically related causes. These are, generally, of two types: those resulting from some damage to genetic

---

Down syndrome. A condition resulting from a chromosomal abnormality; characterized by mental retardation and such physical signs as slanted-appearing eyes, hypotonia, a single palmar crease, shortness, and a tendency toward obesity; the most common type of Down syndrome is trisomy 21.

trisomy 21. A type of Down syndrome in which the twenty-first chromosome is a triplet, making forty-seven, rather than the normal forty-six, chromosomes in all.

chromosome. A rod-shaped entity in the nucleus of the cell; contains genes, which convey hereditary characteristics.

amniocentesis. A medical procedure that allows examination of the amniotic fluid around the fetus; sometimes recommended to determine the presence of abnormality.

chorionic villus sampling (CVS). A method of testing the unborn fetus for a variety of chromosomal abnormalities, such as Down syndrome; a small amount of tissue from the chorion (a membrane that eventually helps form the placenta) is extracted and tested; can be done earlier than amniocentesis but the risk of miscarriage is slightly higher.

sonography. A medical procedure in which high-frequency sound waves are converted into a visual picture; used to detect major physical malformations in the unborn fetus.

material, such as chromosomal abnormalities, and those due to hereditary transmission. We discuss five conditions: (1) Down syndrome and (2) Williams syndrome, which result from chromosomal abnormality, and (3) fragile X syndrome, (4) PKU (phenylketonuria), and (5) Tay-Sachs disease, which are all inherited.

Estimated to account for about 5 to 6 percent of all cases of retardation (Beirne-Smith, Ittenbach, & Patton, 1998), **Down syndrome** is associated with a range of distinctive physical characteristics that vary considerably in number from one individual to another. Persons with Down syndrome may have thick epicanthal folds in the corners of the eyes, making them appear to slant upward slightly. Other common characteristics include small stature, decreased muscle tone (hypotonia), hyperflexibility of the joints, a small oral cavity that can result in a protruding tongue, short and broad hands with a single palmar crease, heart defects, and susceptibility to upper respiratory infections and leukemia (Beirne-Smith et al., 1998). There is also evidence of a link between Down syndrome and Alzheimer's disease (see the box on p. 130).

The degree of retardation varies widely among people with Down syndrome; most individuals fall in the moderate range. In recent years, more children with Down syndrome have achieved IQ scores in the mildly retarded range than previously, presumably because of intensive special education programming.

There are several different types of Down syndrome, but the most common by far is **trisomy 21.** In someone with this condition, the twenty-first set of **chromosomes** is a triplet rather than a pair. (The normal human cell contains twenty-three pairs of chromosomes.)

The likelihood of having a child with Down syndrome increases with the age of the mother. For example, for mothers forty-five years of age, there is about a 1 in 30 chance of giving birth to a child with Down syndrome (Beirne-Smith, et al., 1998). In addition to the age of the mother, researchers are pointing to other variables as possible causes, such as age of the father, exposure to radiation, and exposure to some viruses (Beirne-Smith et al., 1998). Research on these factors is still preliminary, however.

Methods are available for screening for Down syndrome and some other birth defects during pregnancy. Four such methods are **amniocentesis, chorionic villus sampling (CVS), sonography,** and **maternal serum screening (MSS):**

- In amniocentesis, the physician takes a sample of amniotic fluid from the sac around the fetus and analyzes the fetal cells for chromosomal abnormalities. In addition, the amniotic fluid can be tested for the presence of proteins that may have leaked out of the fetus's spinal column, indicating the presence of spina bifida (a condition in which the spinal column fails to close properly).
- In CVS, the physician takes a sample of villi (structures that later become the placenta) and tests them for chromosomal abnormalities. One advantage of CVS is that it can be done earlier than amniocentesis.
- In sonography, high-frequency sound waves are converted into pictures of the fetus, allowing the physician to detect physical malformations, such as spina bifida. Although not as accurate as amniocentesis or CVS, sonography also allows detection of Down syndrome through measurements of the spine.

Down syndrome is associated with certain physical characteristics: slightly slanted eyes, decreased muscle tone, and broad hands. Children with Down syndrome have shown an increase in IQ scores into the mildly retarded range since special education programming.

maternal serum screening (MSS). A method of screening the fetus for developmental disabilities such as Down syndrome or spina bifida; a blood sample is taken from the mother and analyzed; if it is positive, a more accurate test such as amniocentesis or CVS is usually recommended.

Down Syndrome and Alzheimer's Disease

It has been well over a century since researchers first noted a high prevalence of senility in persons with Down syndrome (Fraser & Mitchell, 1876, cited in Evenhuis, 1990). And it was in the early twentieth century that postmortem studies of the brains of people with Down syndrome revealed neuropathological signs similar to those of people with Alzheimer's disease (Carr, 1994). It was not until the 1980s and 1990s, however, that scientists started to address this correlation seriously.

Part of the reason for this shift in priority was the observation that the life expectancy for people with Down syndrome had increased dramatically over the twentieth century. In the first half of the century, very few people with Down syndrome lived until adulthood. But today, due to medical advances, the average life expectancy for people with Down syndrome is about fifty years, with many surviving into their sixties (Slomka & Berkey, 1997).

Postmortem studies of the brains of people with Down syndrome indicate that virtually all who reach the age of thirty-five have brain abnormalities very similar to those of persons with Alzheimer's disease (Wisniewski, Silverman, & Wegiel, 1994; Hof et al., 1995). Behavioral symptoms such as memory and speech problems are more difficult to document because of the low cognitive ability of persons with Down syndrome in the first place. However, research generally shows that (1) the prevalence of senility in people with Down syndrome is about 10 to 15 percent for those between the ages of forty and fifty; (2) the average age of onset is about fifty to fifty-five years; and (3) the prevalence is over 75 percent for those between the ages of sixty and seventy (Slomka & Berkey, 1997; Visser et al., 1997).

Findings that link Down syndrome to Alzheimer's disease have made researchers optimistic about uncovering the genetic underpinnings of both conditions. For example, researchers have found that some types of Alzheimer's are related to mutations of the twenty-first pair of chromosomes (Pinel, 1993).

Williams syndrome. A condition resulting from deletion of material in the seventh pair of chromosomes; often results in mild to moderate retardation, heart defects, and elfin facial features; people affected often display surprising strengths in spoken language and sociability while having severe deficits in spatial organization, reading, writing, and math.

fragile X syndrome. A condition in which the bottom of the X chromosome in the twenty-third pair of chromosomes is pinched off; can result in a number of physical anomalies as well as mental retardation; occurs more often in males than females; thought to be the most common hereditary cause of mental retardation.

- In MSS, a blood sample is taken from the mother and screened for the presence of certain elements that indicate the possibility of spina bifida or Down syndrome. If the results are positive, the physician can recommend a more accurate test such as amniocentesis or CVS.

Williams syndrome is caused by the absence of material on the seventh pair of chromosomes. People with Williams syndrome have IQs ranging from about 40 to 100, with a mean around 60 (Lenhoff, Wang, Greenberg, & Bellugi, 1997). In addition, they often exhibit heart defects, an unusual sensitivity to sounds, and "elfin" facial features. Scientists have taken particular interest in people with Williams syndrome because, although they have deficits in reading, writing, math, and especially spatial ability, they have relative strengths in spoken language. In fact, their storytelling ability (see Table 4.2 on page 131), including their ability to modulate the pitch and volume of their voices to interject emotional tone in their stories, together with their sociability and elflike faces, have led some to speculate that people with Williams syndrome are the pixies or fairies depicted in folktales (see box on p. 132).

Fragile X syndrome is thought to be the most common hereditary cause of mental retardation (Baumeister, 1997). It is associated with the X chromosome in the twenty-third pair of chromosomes. In males, the twenty-third pair consists of an X and a Y chromosome; in females, it consists of two X chromosomes. This disorder is called *fragile* X syndrome because in affected individuals the bottom of the X chromosome is pinched off in some of the blood cells. Fragile X occurs less often in females because they have an extra X chromosome, giving them better protection if one of their X chromosomes is damaged. Persons with fragile X syndrome may have a number of physical features, such as a large head; large, flat

Table 4.2	Comparison of Storytelling Ability of a Person with Williams Syndrome and One with Down Syndrome

Task: Invent a story for the pictures

Picture 1: A nighttime scene of a boy and his dog looking at a frog in a jar at the foot of the bed.

Picture 2: The boy and dog are asleep and the frog is climbing out of the jar.

Picture 3: The boy and dog are looking at the empty jar and the frog is nowhere around.

Responses of 17-year-old (IQ = 50) with Williams syndrome

"Once upon a time when it was dark at night, the boy had a frog. The boy was looking at the frog, sitting on the chair, on the table, and the dog was looking through, looking up to the frog in a jar. That night he slept and slept for a long time, the dog did. But the frog was not gonna go to sleep. The frog went out from the jar. And when the frog went out, the boy and the dog were still sleeping. Next morning it was beautiful in the morning. It was bright, and the sun was nice and warm. Then suddenly when he opened his eyes, he looked at the jar and then suddenly the frog was not there. The jar was empty. There was no frog to be found."

Responses of 18-year-old (IQ = 55) with Down syndrome

"The frog is in the jar. The jar is on the floor. That's it. The stool is broke. The clothes is laying there."

Source: Adapted from Williams syndrome and the brain by H. M. Lenhoff, P. P. Wang, F. Greenberg, & U. Bellugi (1997 December) *Scientific American*, p. 71. Copyright © 1997 by Scientific American, Inc. All rights reserved.

ears; long, narrow face; prominent forehead; broad nose; prominent, square chin; large testicles; and large hands with nontapering fingers. Although this condition often results in moderate or severe retardation, the effects are highly variable, with some persons having less severe cognitive deficiencies and some scoring in the normal range of intelligence (Beirne-Smith et al., 1998).

Phenylketonuria (PKU) involves the inability of the body to convert a common dietary substance—phenylalanine—to tyrosine; the accumulation of phenylalanine results in abnormal brain development. All states routinely screen babies for PKU before they leave the hospital. Babies with PKU are immediately put on a special diet. At one time it was thought that the diet could be discontinued in middle childhood. However, authorities now recommend that it be continued indefinitely, for two important reasons: (1) Those who stop the diet are at risk for developing learning disabilities or other behavioral problems. (2) Over 90 percent of babies born to women with PKU who are no longer on the diet will have mental retardation and may also have heart defects (The Arc, 1997).

Tay-Sachs disease, like PKU, can appear when both the mother and father are carriers. It results in progressive brain damage and eventual death. This condition occurs primarily among Ashkenazi Jews—that is, those of East European extraction. The disease, which can be detected *in utero*, has no cure.

Research on the identification and treatment of genetic conditions presents certain moral and ethical concerns. Advances being made by the Human Genome Project are raising a number of thorny issues (see box on p. 134).

phenylketonuria (PKU). A metabolic genetic disorder caused by the inability of the body to convert phenylalanine to tyrosine; an accumulation of phenylalanine results in abnormal brain development.

Tay-Sachs disease. An inherited condition that can appear when both mother and father are carriers; results in death; it can be detected before birth through amniocentesis.

Williams Syndrome: An Inspiration for Some Pixie Legends?

Folktales from many cultures feature magical "little people"—pixies, elves, trolls and other fairies. A number of physical and behavioral similarities suggest that at least some of the fairies in the early yarns were modeled on people who have Williams syndrome. Such a view is in keeping with the contention of historians that a good deal of folklore and mythology is based on real life.

The facial traits of Williams people are often described as pixielike. In common with pixies in folklore and art, many with Williams syndrome have small, upturned noses, a depressed nasal bridge, "puffy" eyes, oval ears and broad mouths with full lips accented by a small chin. Indeed, those features are so common that Williams children tend to look more like one another than their relatives, especially as children. The syndrome also is accompanied by slow growth and development, which leads most Williams individuals to be relatively short.

The "wee, magical people" of assorted folktales often are musicians and storytellers. Fairies are said to "repeat the songs they have heard" and can "enchant" humans with their melodies. Much the same can be said of people with Williams syndrome, who in spite of typically having subnormal IQs,

The children in the photograph, who are unrelated, display elfin facial features that clinicians associate with Williams syndrome.

usually display vivid narrative skills and often show talent for music. (The large pointed ears so often associated with fairies may symbolically represent the sensitivity of those mythical individuals—and of Williams people—to music and to sound in general.)

As a group, Williams people are loving, trusting, caring and extremely sensitive to the feelings of others. Similarly, fairies are frequently referred to as the "good people" or as kind and gentle-hearted souls. Finally, Williams individuals, much like the fairies of legend, require order and predictability. In Williams people this need shows up as rigid adherence to daily routines and a constant need to keep abreast of future plans.

In the past, storytellers created folktales about imaginary beings to help explain phenomena that they did not understand—perhaps including the distinguishing physical and behavioral traits of Williams syndrome. Today researchers turn to Williams people in a quest to understand the unknown, hoping to decipher some of the secrets of how the brain functions.

Source: From Williams syndrome and the brain by H. M. Lenhoff, P. P. Wang, F. Greenberg, & U. Bellugi (1997 December) p. 73. Copyright © 1997 by Scientific American, Inc. All rights reserved.

Brain Damage. Brain damage can result from a host of factors that fall into two general categories—infections and environmental hazards.

Infections. Infections that may lead to mental retardation can occur in the mother-to-be or the infant or young child after birth. **Rubella (German measles), syphilis,** and **herpes simplex** in the mother can all cause retardation in the child. Rubella is most dangerous during the first trimester (three months) of pregnancy. The venereal diseases syphilis and herpes simplex present a greater risk at later stages of fetal development (Hetherington & Parke, 1986). (Herpes simplex, which shows as cold sores or fever blisters, is not usually classified as a venereal disease unless it affects the genitals.)

Three examples of infections in the child that can affect mental development are meningitis, encephalitis, and pediatric AIDS. **Meningitis** is an infection of the covering of the brain that may be caused by a variety of bacterial or viral agents. **Encephalitis,** an inflammation of the brain, results more often in retardation and usually affects intelligence more severely. **Pediatric AIDS** is the fastest-growing

rubella (German measles). A serious viral disease, which, if it occurs during the first trimester of pregnancy, is likely to cause a deformity in the fetus.

syphilis. A venereal disease that can cause mental subnormality in a child, especially if it is contracted by the mother-to-be during the latter stages of fetal development.

infectious cause of mental retardation. The majority of children with this disease obtained their infection from their mothers, who used intravenous drugs or were sexually active with infected men (Baumeister, Kupstas, & Klindworth, 1990).

Infections, as well as other causative factors, can also result in microcephalus or hydrocephalus. **Microcephalus** is a condition characterized by a small head with a sloping forehead. The retardation that results usually ranges from severe to profound. **Hydrocephalus** results from an accumulation of cerebrospinal fluid inside or outside the brain. The blockage of the circulation of the fluid results in a buildup of excessive pressure on the brain and enlargement of the skull. The degree of retardation depends on how early the condition is diagnosed and treated. Treatment consists of surgical placement of a shunt (tube) that drains the excess fluid away from the brain and into a vein behind the ear or in the neck.

Environmental Hazards. Examples of environmental hazards that can result in mental retardation are blows to the head, poisons, radiation, malnutrition, low birthweight or prematurity, and birth injury. Although we are discussing these potential causal agents in this section, which deals with the causes of more severe forms of retardation, there is considerable evidence that a lesser degree of exposure to any of these factors can also result in mild retardation.

It should be obvious that a blow to a child's head can result in mental retardation. The obviousness of this connection, in fact, has served as an impetus for many of the laws requiring the use of child restraints in automobiles. Besides the usual accidents that can lead to brain damage, more and more authorities are citing child abuse as a cause of brain damage that results in mental retardation and other disabilities (see Chapter 11).

Poisoning resulting in mental retardation can occur in the expectant mother or in the child. We are now much more aware of the harmful effects of a variety of substances, from obvious toxic agents, such as cocaine and heroin, to more subtle potential poisons, such as tobacco and alcohol. In particular, researchers have exposed **fetal alcohol syndrome (FAS)** as a significant health problem for expectant mothers who consume large quantities of alcohol and for their unborn children (Baumeister & Woodley-Zanthos, 1996; see also Chapter 11). Children with FAS are characterized by a variety of physical deformities as well as mental retardation. There is evidence that women who drink moderately during pregnancy may have babies who, although not exhibiting full-blown FAS, nevertheless show more subtle behavioral abnormalities.

Although lead in paint is now prohibited, infants still become poisoned by eating lead-based paint chips, particularly in impoverished areas. Lead poisoning varies in its effect on children; high levels can result in death. The federal government now requires that automobile manufacturers produce cars that use only lead-free gasoline to lower the risk of inhaling lead particles from auto exhaust.

We have recognized the hazards of radiation to the unborn fetus for some time. Physicians, for example, are cautious not to expose pregnant women to X rays unless absolutely necessary. Since the mid-to-late 1970s, however, the public has become even more concerned over the potential dangers of radiation from improperly designed or supervised nuclear power plants.

Retardation caused by improper nutrition can occur because the expectant mother is malnourished or because the child, once born, does not have a proper diet.

Low birthweight (LBW) can result in a variety of behavioral and medical problems, including mental retardation. Because most babies with a LBW are premature, the two terms—LBW and premature—are often used synonymously.

herpes simplex. A viral disease that can cause cold sores or fever blisters; if it affects the genitals and is contracted by the mother-to-be in the later stages of fetal development, it can cause mental subnormality in the child.

meningitis. A bacterial or viral infection of the linings of the brain or spinal cord.

encephalitis. An inflammation of the brain; can affect the child's mental development adversely.

pediatric AIDS. Acquired immune deficiency syndrome that occurs in infants or young children; can be contracted by unborn fetuses from the blood of the mother through the placenta or through blood transfusions; an incurable virus that can result in a variety of physical and mental disorders.

microcephalus. A condition causing development of a small head with a sloping forehead; proper development of the brain is prevented, resulting in mental retardation.

hydrocephalus. A condition characterized by enlargement of the head because of excessive pressure of the cerebrospinal fluid.

fetal alcohol syndrome (FAS). Abnormalities associated with the mother's drinking alcohol during pregnancy; defects range from mild to severe.

low-birthweight (LBW). Babies who are born weighing less than 5.5 pounds; usually premature; at risk for behavioral and medical conditions, such as mental retardation.

The Human Genome Project: Ethical Issues Pertaining to Mental Retardation

Started in 1990, the U.S. Human Genome Project is a fifteen-year undertaking of the U.S. Department of Energy and the National Institutes of Health to:

- Identify all the estimated 80,000 genes in human DNA.
- Determine the sequences of the 3 billion chemical bases that make up human DNA, store this information in data bases, and develop tools for data analysis." (Human Genome Management Information System, 1998)

One of the practical benefits noted by the project's administrators is the development of revolutionary ways to diagnose, treat, and eventually prevent genetic conditions. However, such potential breakthroughs have made some authorities uneasy. Although not necessarily opposing the Human Genome Project, many have called for careful consideration of the ethical ramifications of its work. Below are excerpts from an address identifying issues of concern to The Arc of the United States, a national organization on mental retardation:

> More and more people will be able to know whether or not they will develop a disorder or possibly pass a disease gene on to their children. How will having this information impact [sic] society? Do most of us want to know about future genetic information that could change our lives? For example, if you could find out today that you have an 80% to 90% chance of developing a rare and untreatable form of colon cancer in the future, would you want to know?

> Other issues of concern include the following: Must a physician offer prenatal genetic screening to all pregnant women or risk medical malpractice liability if he doesn't? Should a woman have a right to refuse prenatal screening? What if she's already had a child with a serious genetic condition? One of our workshop participants reported that her 3-year-old son's serious genetic condition had already cost more than $1 million, paid for by the state. She expressed her intention to have another child and her

strong belief that she would refuse prenatal screening. What about testing infants and children for genetic conditions when there is no treatment available? . . .

Gene therapy is an experimental treatment in which normal genes are introduced into the body's cells to correct or modify the cell's function.

Arguments in Favor of Gene Therapy. The major argument in favor of gene therapy is based on its potential for treating individuals severely affected by their condition. A perfect example is Lesch-Nyhan disease, which is characterized by communication deficits, writhing movements, and involuntary self-injurious behavior. Males who have this disorder have to be restrained constantly to prevent them from inflicting severe damage on themselves. Most have their teeth removed to keep from biting their lips off. If we have a new medical technology that will cure this condition, don't we have an obligation to use it?

Arguments Against Gene Therapy. A number of arguments are offered against gene therapy, including the concern about the potential for harmful abuse if we don't distinguish between good and bad uses of gene therapy. The eugenics movement of the 1920s to the 1940s found people with mental retardation being involuntarily sterilized, along with others considered less desirable. Another concern is that in mental retardation gene-therapy research, many candidates are likely to be children who are too young or too disabled to understand ramifications of the treatment. Finally, gene therapy is very expensive and may never be sufficiently cost-effective to merit high social priority. Opponents say that if those who can afford gene therapy are the only ones to receive it, the distribution of desirable biological traits will widen the differences among various socioeconomic groups.

Source: Davis, S. (1997). *The Human Genome Project: Examining The Arc's concerns regarding the Human Genome Project's ethical, legal and social implications.* An address presented at the DOE Human Genome Program Contractor-Grantee Workshop VI, posted on the World Wide Web by the Human Genome Management Information System. Retrieved July 5, 1998 from the World Wide Web: http://www.ornl.gov/hgmis/resource/arc.html

---

LBW is usually defined as being 5.5 pounds or lower, and it is associated with a number of factors—poor nutrition, teenage pregnancy, drug abuse, and excessive cigarette smoking. Researchers are also looking at a variety of bacterial infections as possible causes (Baumeister & Woodley-Zanthos, 1996).

Brain injury can also occur during delivery if the child is not positioned properly in the uterus. One problem that sometimes occurs because of difficulty during delivery is **anoxia** (complete deprivation of oxygen).

anoxia. The loss of oxygen; can cause brain injury.

Assessment

Two major areas are assessed to determine whether a person is mentally retarded: intelligence and adaptive skills. To assess intelligence, a professional administers an intelligence test to the person. To assess adaptive skills, a parent or professional who is familiar with the person responds to a survey about different adaptive skills.

Intelligence Tests

There are many types of IQ tests. Because of their accuracy and predictive capabilities, practitioners prefer individually administered tests over group tests. Two of the most common individual IQ tests for children are the Stanford-Binet (4th ed.; Thorndike, Hagen, & Sattler, 1986) and the Wechsler Intelligence Scale for Children–Third Edition (WISC–III) (Wechsler, 1991). Both of these tests are verbal, although the WISC–III is intended to assess both verbal and performance aspects of intelligence. It has a verbal and a performance scale with a number of subtests. The *full-scale IQ*, a statistical composite of the verbal and performance IQ measures, is used when a single overall score for a child is desired.

Another relatively common IQ test is the Kaufman Assessment Battery for Children (K–ABC) (Kaufman & Kaufman, 1983). Some psychologists recommend using the K–ABC with African American students because they believe it is less culturally biased (Kamphaus & Reynolds, 1987).

Although not all IQ tests call for this method of calculation, we can get a rough approximation of a person's IQ by dividing **mental age** (the age level at which a person is functioning) by **chronological age** and multiplying by 100. For example, a ten-year-old student who performs on an IQ test as well as the average eight-year-old (and thus has a mental age of eight years) would have an IQ of 80.

Compared to most psychological tests, IQ tests such as the Stanford-Binet, WISC–III, and K–ABC are among the most reliable and valid. By *reliability*, we mean that a person will obtain relatively similar scores if given the test on two separate occasions that are not too close or far apart in time. *Validity* generally answers the question of whether the instrument measures what it is supposed to measure. A good indicator of the validity of an IQ test is the fact that it is generally considered the best single index of how well a student will do in school. It is wise to be wary, however, of placing too much faith in a single score from any IQ test. There are at least four reasons for caution:

1. Even on very reliable tests, an individual's IQ can change from one testing to another, and sometimes the change can be dramatic.
2. All IQ tests are culturally biased to a certain extent. Largely because of differences in language and experience, persons from minority groups are sometimes at a disadvantage in taking such tests.
3. The younger the child, the less validity and reliability the test has. Infant intelligence tests are particularly questionable.
4. IQ tests are not the absolute determinant when it comes to assessing a person's ability to function in society. A superior IQ does not guarantee a successful and happy life, nor does a low IQ doom a person to a miserable existence. Other variables are also important determinants of a person's coping skills in society. That is why, for example, professionals also assess adaptive skills, to which we now turn. (See also the box on p. 136)

mental age. Refers to the IQ test score that specifies the age level at which an individual is functioning.

chronological age. Refers to how old a person is; used in comparison with mental age to determine IQ:

$$IQ = \frac{\text{mental age}}{\text{chronological age}} \times 100$$

Keeping Tests in Perspective

Most professionals agree that tests, such as IQ tests and adaptive behavior instruments, are necessary. Tests can be helpful in making placement decisions and in evaluating program effectiveness. It is important to keep in mind, however, that they are far from perfect predictors about how a particular individual will function in the real world. The following excerpt from the case study of a woman with mental retardation makes this point nicely:

> When I first saw her—clumsy, uncouth, all-of-a-fumble— I saw her merely, or wholly, as a casualty, a broken creature, whose neurological impairments I could pick out and dissect with precision....
>
> The next time I saw her, it was all very different. I didn't have her in a test situation, "evaluating" her in a clinic. I wandered outside, it was a lovely spring day, with a few minutes in hand before the clinic started, and there I saw Rebecca sitting on a bench, gazing at the April foliage quietly, with obvious delight. Her posture had none of the clumsiness which had so impressed me before. Sitting there, in a light dress, her face calm and slightly smiling, she suddenly brought to mind one of Chekov's young women—Irene, Anya, Sonya, Nina—seen against the backdrop of a Chekovian cherry orchard. She could have been any young woman enjoying a beautiful spring day. This was my human, as opposed to my neurological, vision....

Why was she so de-composed before, how could she be so re-composed now? I had the strongest feeling of two wholly different modes of thought, or of organization, or of being. The first schematic—pattern-seeing, problem-solving—this is what had been tested, and where she had been found so defective, so disastrously wanting. But the tests had given no inkling of anything *but* the deficits, anything, so to speak, *beyond* her deficits.

They had given me no hint of her positive powers, her ability to perceive the real world—the world of nature, and perhaps of the imagination—as a coherent, intelligible, poetic whole: her ability to see this, think this, and (when she could) live this; they had given me no intimation of her inner world, which clearly *was* composed and coherent, and approached as something other than a set of problems or tasks....

It was perhaps fortunate that I chanced to see Rebecca in her so-different modes—so damaged and incorrigible in the one, so full of promise and potential in the other— and that she was one of the first patients I saw in our clinic. For what I saw in her, what she showed me, I now saw in them all.

Source: Reprinted with permission of Simon & Schuster from *The Man Who Mistook His Wife for a Hat and Other Clinical Tales* by Oliver Sacks. Copyright © 1970, 1981, 1983, 1984, 1985 by Oliver Sacks.

Adaptive Skills

Many adaptive skills measures are available. Some of the most commonly used are the Vineland Adaptive Behavior Scales (Sparrow, Balla, & Cicchetti, 1984); the Adaptive Behavior Inventory for Children (Mercer & Lewis, 1982); the AAMR Adaptive Behavior Scale–School, 2nd Edition (Lambert, Nihira, & Leland, 1993); and the AAMR Adaptive Behavior Scale–Residential and Community Edition (Nihira, Leland, & Lambert, 1993). In addition, the Assessment of Adaptive Areas (Bryant, Taylor, & Rivera, 1996) combines the last two and is the only one that covers all ten of the adaptive skills in the AAMR definition (communication, self-care, home living, social skills, community use, self-direction, health and safety, functional academics, leisure, and work). The basic format of these instruments requires that a parent, teacher, or other professional answer questions related to the subject's ability to perform adaptive skills.

Psychological and Behavioral Characteristics

In considering the psychological and behavioral characteristics of persons with mental retardation, we hasten to point out that *individual* persons with mental retardation may not display all the characteristics. There is great variability in the behavior of persons who are retarded, and each person is unique. In this section, we discuss the following characteristics: attention, memory, language development, academic achievement, self-regulation, social development, and motivation.

Attention

The importance of attention for learning is critical. A person must be able to attend to the task at hand before he or she can learn it. For years, researchers have posited that we can attribute many of the learning problems of persons with retardation to attention problems (e.g., Tomporowski & Tinsley, 1997; Zeaman & House, 1963). Often attending to the wrong things, many people who are retarded have difficulty allocating their attention properly.

Memory

One of the most consistent research findings is that persons with mental retardation have difficulty remembering information. Their deficits are widespread, but they often have particular problems with working memory (Bray, Fletcher, & Turner, 1997). **Working memory** involves the ability to keep information in mind while simultaneously doing another cognitive task. Trying to remember an address while listening to instructions on how to get there is an example of working memory.

Language Development

In general, the language of persons who are retarded follows the same developmental course as that of nonretarded persons, but their language development starts later, progresses at a slower rate, and ends up at a lower level of development (Warren & Yoder, 1997). However, considerable variation occurs among those who are retarded, depending on the particular cause of their retardation (Tager-Flusberg & Sullivan, 1998). For example, we noted earlier that those with Williams syndrome, in contrast to those who have Down syndrome, tend to exhibit expressive language well beyond their overall intellectual level.

Academic Achievement

Because of the strong relationship between intelligence and achievement, it is not surprising that students who are mentally retarded perform well below their nonretarded peers in academic achievement. Students who are retarded also tend to be underachievers in relation to expectations based on their intellectual levels (MacMillan, 1982).

Self-Regulation

Self-regulation is a broad term referring to an individual's ability to regulate his or her own behavior. For example, when given a list of words to remember, most people rehearse the list aloud or to themselves in an attempt to keep the words in memory. In other words, they actively regulate their behavior by employing a strategy that will help them remember. People who are retarded are less likely than their nondisabled peers to use self-regulatory strategies such as rehearsal. They also have difficulties with metacognition, which is closely connected to the ability

working memory. The ability to remember information while also performing other cognitive operations.

self-regulation. Refers generally to a person's ability to regulate his or her own behavior (e.g., to employ strategies to help in a problem-solving situation); an area of difficulty for persons who are mentally retarded.

The self-concepts of children with retardation are influenced by their relationships with their peers. Positive personal interaction is as important to these individuals as to anyone.

to self-regulate (Bebko & Luhaorg, 1998). **Metacognition** refers to a person's awareness of what strategies are needed to perform a task, the ability to plan how to use the strategies, and the evaluation of how well the strategies are working. Self-regulation is, thus, a component of metacognition. (We discuss metacognition again in Chapter 5.)

Social Development

Some authorities have argued that retardation should be determined primarily by whether a person is able to fulfill important social roles (e.g., worker and friend) more than by conceptual ability as traditionally measured by IQ tests (Greenspan, Switzky, & Granfield, 1996). What is important, ultimately, is the individual's ability to function in society.

People with mental retardation are candidates for a variety of social problems. They often have problems making and keeping friends, for at least two reasons: First, many do not seem to know how to strike up social interactions with others, and this difference is evident as early as preschool (Kasari & Bauminger, 1998). Second, even when not attempting to interact with others, people who are retarded may exhibit behaviors that "turn off" their peers. For example, they display higher rates of inattention and disruptive behavior than their nonretarded classmates.

Motivation

Many of the problems pertaining to attention, memory, language development, academic achievement, self-regulation, and social development place persons who are retarded at risk to develop problems of motivation. If these individuals have experienced a long history of failure, they can be at risk to develop **learned helplessness**—the feeling that no matter how hard they try, they will still fail. Believing they have little control over what happens to them and that they are primarily controlled by other people and events, some persons with retardation tend to give up easily when faced with challenging tasks. Professionals recognize that a good educational or vocational program for persons with mental retardation needs to contain a component focused on motivational problems.

metacognition. A person's (1) awareness of what strategies are necessary to perform a task and (2) ability to use self-regulation strategies.

learned helplessness. A motivational term referring to a condition wherein a person believes that no matter how hard he or she tries, failure will result.

Educational Considerations

Although there is some overlap, in general the focus of educational programs varies according to the degree of the student's retardation, or how much he or she requires support services. For example, the lesser the degree of retardation, the more the teacher emphasizes academic skills; and the greater the degree of retardation, the more stress there is on self-help, community living, and vocational skills. Keep in mind, however, that this distinction is largely a matter of emphasis; in practice, all students who are retarded, no matter the severity level, need instruction in academic, self-help, community living, and vocational skills.

We now discuss some of the major features of educational programs for students with mental retardation. We focus on the elementary school level here; we discuss preschool and secondary programming in later sections. Although the lines are sometimes blurred, we have divided our coverage into programming for students with mild retardation, or those requiring less intensive support, and students with more severe retardation, or those requiring more intensive support.

Students with Mild Retardation, or Those Requiring Less Intensive Support

Early elementary education is heavily oriented toward providing children who are mildly retarded with **readiness skills:** abilities that are prerequisites for later learning. These include such things as the ability to sit still and attend to the teacher, follow directions, hold a pencil or cut with a pair of scissors, tie shoes, button and unbutton, zip and unzip, use the toilet, and interact with peers in a group situation.

In the later elementary years, emphasis is greater on academics, usually on what are known as **functional academics.** Whereas the nonretarded child is taught academics, such as reading, in order to learn other academic content, such as history, the child with mental retardation is often taught reading in order to learn to function independently. In functional academics, the child learns academics in order to do such things as read a newspaper, read the telephone book, read labels on goods at the store, make change, and fill out job applications.

Although the rudiments of community and vocational living skills are emphasized much more in high school, some children with mild retardation are taught these skills in later elementary school. Many professionals believe that because some students who are retarded take a relatively long time to learn particular skills, it is best to acquaint them with these skills as early as elementary school.

Students with More Severe Retardation, or Those Requiring More Intensive Support

Educational programming for students with mental retardation, especially those with more severe retardation, often includes the following three features: (1) systematic instruction, (2) instruction in *in vivo* settings with real materials, and (3) functional assessment.

Systematic Instruction. **Systematic instruction** involves the use of instructional prompts, consequences for performance, and strategies for the transfer of stimulus control (Davis & Cuvo, 1997).

Instructional Prompts. Students who are retarded often need to be prompted or cued to respond in the appropriate manner. These prompts can be verbal, gestural, physical, or modeling may be used (Davis & Cuvo, 1997). A verbal prompt can be a question, such as, "What do you need to do next?" or a command, such as, "Put your socks in the top dresser drawer." A gestural prompt might involve pointing to the socks and/or the dresser drawer while stating the question or the

readiness skills. Skills deemed necessary before academics can be learned (e.g., attending skills, the ability to follow directions, knowledge of letter names).

functional academics. Practical skills (e.g., reading a newspaper or telephone book) rather than academic learning skills.

systematic instruction. Teaching that involves instructional prompts, consequences for performance, and transfer of stimulus control; often used with students with mental retardation.

success stories
special educators at work

Orono, ME: Thirteen-year-old **Molly Berry** is helpful and energetic, much like her parents, Karen and Dave. As a fifth grader, Molly is a student council representative at her school. Because of her drive (and despite her limitations), the Berrys have advocated for Molly to be included in general education classes since preschool. Special educator Lisa Douville and general educator Mike Morcom are collaborating to maximize Molly's learning before she leaves elementary school.

Karen and Dave Berry agree that Molly is distractible, but they feel she has made significant social gains in the mainstream classroom. Special educator Lisa Douville also sees improvement in Molly's ability to focus. "She has a good attitude and responds without much grumbling! She hasn't needed sticker reinforcement so far this year."

The Berrys have what they call a "healthy adversarial relationship" with Molly's school district. They are strong advocates for parents being closely involved in the educational decisions affecting their children. According to Dave Berry, "When parents and professionals are both well informed, then they're on even ground." The Berrys have received training in individualized education program (IEP) development and how to exercise their rights. Karen Berry says, "I always ask that IEPs be available to all Molly's teachers. Then, I check to see if they are being used."

For the Berrys, the key issue in Molly's education is effective communication and teamwork from year to year. This means that teachers exchange information and that parents and educators listen carefully to each other. "Everyone needs to know it's okay to speak up for the real needs of the child, despite the costs or inconveniences," says Dave Berry. "We've all worked hard to help Molly make progress."

In June, Molly will graduate from the pine-paneled elementary school where she has attended general education classes since grade 1. Triennial testing has been completed and a meeting will soon be held to determine how Molly can best make the transition to middle school for grade 6.

When the Pupil Evaluation Team meets, Lisa Douville and Mike Morcom will attend, along with Dave and Karen Berry. Molly's social goals will be reviewed to determine her progress toward independence in beginning work, attention to task, and use of appropriate behaviors in managing stress. New academic goals will be set and supports will be updated to reflect any changes in modifications,

mike Morcom readied his class for the totem pole project and rehearsed positive behaviors for cooperative learning groups. As Molly listened to reminders about sound levels and cleaning up, she seemed eager to start. "I'm going to make a unicorn for my totem pole," she said, and started to paint an ice-cream container white. She never sat still for long, as she repeatedly left her project to inspect others. She told a friend, "When you finish painting, you'll need some glue."

command. Taking the student's hand and placing it on the socks and/or drawer would be an example of a physical prompt. And the adult might also model putting the socks in the drawer before then asking the student to do it.

Consequences. Research has consistently shown that students who are positively reinforced for correct responses learn faster. Positive reinforcers can range from verbal praise to tokens that can be traded for prizes or other rewards. For students with severe mental retardation, the more immediate the reinforcement,

such as shortened written assignments or notes copied from a sheet on her desk, rather than from the board.

Karen and Dave Berry are committed advocates for Molly and have worked closely with a psychologist to obtain an objective assessment of her abilities and potential for successful inclusion. Together with the team, they have crafted an IEP that describes areas that interfere with Molly's learning:

> Molly exhibits delays in the development of perceptual-motor skills, a mild to moderate phonological disorder, a moderate to severe expressive language delay, and difficulties comprehending complex verbal material. When compared to her peers, Molly has difficulties in the following areas: working independently and initiating and completing tasks. Off-task behaviors consist of unpredictable episodes of physical and visual wandering and ignoring teacher requests. This behavior is compounded in situations when Molly perceives tasks as being difficult. Her levels of performance are consistent with test results and classroom observations.

This year Molly, her best friend Jenny, and two other special-needs students are among the twenty-two members of Mike Morcom's fifth-grade class. "I don't want the kids to patronize Molly, and they don't seem to," says Mike. "We work on building sensitivity to differences and modeling ways of interacting."

Mike acknowledges that it would be hard to manage instructionally without a classroom aide, and he sees this as a key to Molly's success. Janet Metcalf, a certified teacher, has worked as the educational technician with Molly's class for two years. So has special educator Lisa Douville, who supervises Janet, works directly with Molly on reading and math skills in the resource room, and manages her educational plan. Lisa and Mike jointly track Molly's progress.

Molly's math program is carried out by the educational technician in the classroom and guided by individualized packets of materials assembled by Lisa Douville. If the class is working as a group or taking a test, Janet Metcalf will often adapt the activity, pull the next item from Molly's packet, or develop a criterion-referenced test, based on Molly's third-grade-level goals. For social studies and science, Janet adapts Mike Morcom's materials and activities for the special-needs students in the class. Janet also keeps a daily school/home journal with the Berrys.

Like her math program, Molly's reading and spelling programs are directed by Lisa Douville and similarly carried out in the classroom. However, these are areas in which Molly has less confidence and fears failure. She is stronger at receiving information orally but has difficulty decoding words when reading. Says Lisa, "Molly is embarrassed to be seen with the second–third-grade-level books she is able to read. She is aware of her social environment and needs help with handling sensitive issues appropriately."

In reflecting on his daughter's progress, Dave Berry recalls that once Molly was provided with a well-trained aide and resource support, the role of her general educators changed. "We started to work as a team when the second-grade teacher wisely identified the supports Molly needed in the classroom. Her fourth- and fifth-grade teachers have been terrific at working closely with special educators. We don't expect the classroom teachers to do it all, but we do expect them to have help."

As they plan for Molly's future, this team of parents and professionals hopes that she will be able to remain in classes with her nondisabled peers as much as is appropriate for her. Says Dave Berry, "I work with students every day, and I think it must be said that while this approach works for my child, inclusion in a regular class might not be appropriate for someone else's child." Karen Berry agrees: "I don't want Molly just to be *included*. It's what is *done* for her in the classroom that counts."

—By Jean Crockett

the more effective. Once the student demonstrates the desired behavior consistently, the goal is to wean the student from reliance on external reinforcers as soon as possible.

Transfer of Stimulus Control. The goal is to reach a point at which the student does not have to rely on prompts and can be more independent. In order to transfer the control away from the prompts to more naturally occurring stimuli, several techniques are used, including delaying the time between a request and

Collaboration key to success

Maria B. Raynes is a special education teacher at Hugh K. Cassell Elementary School in Augusta County, Virginia; B.S., Special Education, James Madison University; M.Ed., Severe Disabilities, University of Virginia. **Amy C. Michael** is a teacher in a fourth-/fifth-grade multi-age class at Hugh K. Cassell Elementary School in Augusta County, Virginia; B.A., Sociology, Mary Washington College; M.A., Reading, University of Virginia.

Maria Raines

Maria I work with children who have identified needs ranging from mild developmental delays to severe disabilities. These students are members of general education classrooms even though they may have very individualized schedules based on IEP goals. This year, we made a commitment to serve all children who lived in our school's attendance area. This decision was significant in that it encouraged faculty to look at ways to improve collaboration between special and general educators. A specific transition process helps everyone involved with a student to become knowledgeable about the child's individual needs in preparation for the upcoming school year. Based on faculty input, children are matched with appropriate teachers. Classroom teachers visit the students in their current placements and become integrally involved in the IEP process. We will describe our collaboration to meet the needs of a student we'll call Tina.

Amy I teach 24 first graders who have a wide range of skills. It was important for me to observe Tina in her current classroom. Even knowing how challenging Tina would be, I was enthusiastic about working with her. My skepticism, and even fear, revolved around the multi-person team that came with her.

Maria My general education partner has had a great deal of experience with children with a wide range of needs. Her success with these children can be attributed to a classroom culture that emphasizes each student's strengths and value as a member of a community of learners. Our teaming strategies have evolved over the past five years with my level of involvement based on the needs of individual students. In a given day, I may provide whole-group instruction, small-group skill-based lessons, and one-to-one tutorials. In the more successful teaming situations, all the students perceive me as another teacher who shares the instructional responsibilities. Together, the classroom teachers and I set the tone for my involvement in the class. At the beginning of the relationship, Amy shared her knowledge of the curriculum and grade-level expectations. She also has a fuller understanding than I do of issues related to classroom and time management.

Amy Maria shared her knowledge of specifics regarding disabilities. She was excellent at breaking down tasks into workable steps for students. She helped us realize that each step that was accomplished was cause for celebration. Maria also has a gift for creating cohesion among all members of the team and dealing with touchy issues related to territoriality and expertise.

Maria Tina came to us with many challenges—cognitive, motor, and sensory. She entered first grade with very limited readiness skills. She needed assistance in a variety of self-care activities, including toileting as well as fine motor tasks such as cutting and coloring. Academic participation was compromised by Tina's bouts of stubbornness and this would have been a huge issue in many classrooms, but Amy's ability to offer choices rather than ultimatums helped deflect potential power struggles. While Tina presented challenges, she also brought a love of learning and tremendous enthusiasm. She had a refreshing sense of humor and often helped us keep things in perspective.

During the language arts block, I spent part of the morning in Tina's classroom, where I worked with her reading group of seven children. This

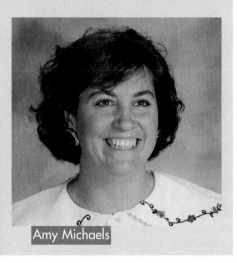
Amy Michaels

gave me an opportunity to see how Tina functioned in a small group and to make suggestions for curricular adaptations. Tina required a great deal of support and modifications in order to be able to participate in classroom activities. A full-time teaching assistant was assigned to the classroom to help with all the students. We were aware of Tina's tendency to become overly dependent on adults as we thought through the role of the teaching assistant.

Amy Having Tina in the classroom forced us to stress community-building skills because of her obvious behavior differences. Tina flapped her arms, jumped, snorted, and continuously played with other students' long hair. We wanted to minimize these behaviors that drew negative attention to Tina and disrupted the class. The key was to channel her energy in a different way. We solicited students' help in modeling appropriate behaviors as well as identifying phrases to use as verbal prompts. Tina responded enthusiastically to the class meeting. We also decided to have a basket of "fidgets" available to offer Tina when her hands needed to move, yet she was required to stay in her own space.

Maria Another aspect of my involvement in Tina's classroom was to provide case management. Amy repeatedly said that dealing with Tina was not as difficult as figuring out all the adults who came as part of the package. These adults are only an asset when they work as part of a coherent team. It was my responsibility to keep everyone focused on the big picture—Tina's IEP goals.

Amy We arrived at the most successful adaptations through a trial-and-error process. We learned through observation that Tina could use both auditory and visual information if it were made relevant to her. To assist with letter recognition and sound-symbol correspondence, we made a pictionary using photographs of some of Tina's favorite people, animals, and places. Eventually she no longer needed the pictures but could recall letter names and sounds with verbal cues. Tina responded to reading materials based on rhythm, predictability, and repetition. One of our math adaptations was based on Tina's ability to remember that the colors of red and yellow mix to make orange. When teaching the basic addition facts, we made a math mat with a

small red circle, a small yellow circle, and a larger orange circle. Tina learned to put one group of manipulatives in each of the smaller circles and combine them to count the total in the larger orange circle.

Maria Always aware that too much dependence on adults was a detriment to Tina, we involved peers in cooperative learning situations. Experience taught us that certain student matches were more successful than others. We had to be cautious that Tina's peers were not always in the helping role and that Tina had a chance to play the role of helper. As we reflected on all that had transpired during the fast-paced year, we realized that Tina had made much growth academically, socially, and behaviorally. She began to tell her mom that she wanted to learn to read. Inappropriate behaviors that had occurred at high rates were now under control. It was also gratifying to see Tina's peer involvement extend beyond the school day. She had peer preferences and was invited to birthday parties and other social events. This was both scary and exciting for her parents.

Amy An unexpected benefit to having many professionals in the classroom was the union of these people, each with his or her own specific strengths. Only through ongoing collaboration did we have the opportunity to truly appreciate individual contributions. The end product was a long-lasting professional relationship based on mutual respect. In our school, it was an end to "my students" versus "your students" and a beginning to "our students." Perhaps the most important benefit was a shared sense of responsibility for each of Tina's successes and failures. We all had taken Tina into our hearts.

> Perhaps the most important benefit was a shared sense of responsibility for each of Tina's successes and failures. We all had taken Tina into our hearts.

the prompt (Browder & Snell, 2000; Wolery & Schuster, 1997). For example, with **constant time delay,** the adult starts by making a request ("Please put your clothes away") and giving a prompt simultaneously ("Put your clothes in the top dresser drawer"). Then the adult might wait a set period of time (e.g., five seconds) between the request and the prompt. With **progressive time delay,** the adult also starts with a simultaneous prompt and request, but then the latency period between the two is increased gradually.

Instruction in *In Vivo* Settings with Real Materials. Instruction can take place in the classroom, under simulated conditions, or in *in vivo* (real-life) settings. For students with severe retardation, as well as for those with mild retardation, it is generally better to teach them daily living skills in the actual, *in vivo* settings where they will be using these skills. Because it is easier to hold instruction in classrooms than in real-life settings, the teacher may start out with instruction in the classroom and then supplement it with *in vivo* instruction (Browder & Snell, 2000). For example, the teacher might use worksheets and photos of various shopping activities in class or set up a simulated "store" with shelves of products and a cash register. These classroom activities could then be supplemented with periodic visits to real grocery stores. Likewise, it is preferable to use real cans of food and real money in teaching students to read product labels and to make change.

Functional Assessment. One of the major reasons some students with severe retardation have difficulty being included in general education classrooms is that they sometimes exhibit inappropriate behavior, such as hitting, biting, or screaming (Horner & Carr, 1997). Authorities recommend that teachers use functional assessment to reduce or eliminate these behaviors. **Functional assessment** involves determining the consequences, antecedents, and setting events that maintain such behaviors (Horner & Carr, 1997). *Consequences* refer to the purpose the behavior serves for the person. For example, some students behave inappropriately in order to gain attention. *Antecedents* refer to things that trigger the behavior. For example, the student might become aggressive only toward certain peers. *Setting events* take into account broader contextual factors. For example, the student might be more likely to exhibit inappropriate behavior when sick or in hot, humid weather. Based on a functional assessment, the teacher can make changes in consequences, antecedents, and/or contextual factors and monitor the effectiveness of these changes.

Service Delivery Models

Placements for school-age students with mental retardation range from general education classes to residential facilities. Although special classes for these students tend to be the norm, more and more students with retardation are being placed in more integrated settings. The degree of integration tends to be determined by the level of severity, with students who are less severely retarded being the most integrated. However, as we discussed in Chapter 2, some professionals believe that all students with retardation should be educated in the general education classroom and that schools should provide the necessary support services (e.g., a special aide or special education teacher) in the class.

Although not all authorities agree on how much inclusion should be practiced, virtually all agree that placement in a self-contained class with no opportunity for interaction with nondisabled students is inappropriate. At the same time, even parents who favor integrated settings often believe that it is good for their children to interact with other children with disabilities, too, and that being

constant time delay. An instructional procedure whereby the teacher makes a request while simultaneously prompting the student and then over several occasions makes the same request and waits a constant period of time before prompting; often used with students with mental retardation.

progressive time delay. An instructional procedure whereby the teacher makes a request while simultaneously prompting the student and then over several occasions gradually increases the latency between the request and the prompt; often used with students with mental retardation.

functional assessment. The practice of determining the consequences (what purpose the behavior serves), antecedents (what triggers the behavior), and setting events (in what contexts the behavior occurs) of inappropriate behavior.

the only student in the class with a disability has its drawbacks (Guralnick, Connor, & Hammond, 1995). The issue of how much interaction is appropriate with nondisabled persons has also surfaced in the highly popular Special Olympics (see the box on pp. 146). And although parents of students with severe retardation enthusiastically believe in the social benefits of having their children in full-inclusion settings, they are more apprehensive about inclusion's impact on the quality of educational programming received by their children (Palmer, Borthwick-Duffy, & Widaman, 1998).

Although large residential facilities for persons with mental retardation still exist, they now tend to include a much higher percentage of residents who are more severely retarded and who have multiple disabilities than they once did. Smaller, community-based facilities (CRFs) are preferred over large residential institutions, and of those living in institutions, many more are now in these community-based facilities rather than in large residential institutions. The **community residential facility (CRF)**, or group home, accommodates small groups (three to ten people) in houses under the direction of "house parents." The level of retardation in people living in CRFs ranges from mild to severe. Placement can be permanent or, with higher-functioning individuals, it can serve as a temporary arrangement to prepare them for independent living. In either case, the purpose of the CRF is to teach independent living skills in a more normal setting than a large institution offers.

Some professionals are questioning whether CRFs go far enough in offering opportunities for integration into the community. They are recommending **supported living,** whereby persons with retardation receive supports to live in more natural, noninstitutional settings, such as their own home or apartment (Howe, Horner, & Newton, 1998; Polloway, Smith, Patton, & Smith, 1996). Supported living means

Community-based instruction focuses on everyday living skills learned in their actual settings.

> rejecting the notion of a continuum of residential services, with its attendant focus on "care and treatment" designed to teach people skills that will result in their moving to the next less restrictive residential setting, in favor of supporting people to experience community presence and participation in homes of their own.... Rather than fitting people into existing residential facilities (e.g., group homes) that offer prepackaged services of a particular kind and level, supported living involves developing support that is matched to a person's specific needs and preferences and changing that support as the person's needs and preferences change.... (Howe, Horner, & Newton, 1998, pp. 1–2)

Early Intervention

We can categorize preschool programs for children with mental retardation as (1) those whose purpose is to prevent retardation and (2) those designed to further the development of children already identified as retarded. In general, the former address children who are at risk for mild retardation, and the latter are for children who are more severely retarded.

Early Childhood Programs Designed for Prevention

The 1960s witnessed the birth of infant and preschool programs for at-risk children and their families. Since the late 1970s, when many of the young children

community residential facility (CRF). A place, usually a group home, in an urban or residential neighborhood where about three to ten adults with retardation live under supervision.

supported living. An approach to living arrangements for those with mental retardation that stresses living in natural settings rather than institutions, big or small.

The Special Olympics: A Good or Bad Idea?

Founded in 1968 by the Joseph P. Kennedy, Jr., Foundation, the Special Olympics was designed as a way of promoting physical fitness, sportsmanship, and feelings of self-worth in persons with mental retardation. If participation and publicity are used as yardsticks, the Special Olympics has achieved great success. There are now more than one million athletes and 1.5 million volunteers, representing more than 140 countries worldwide, and it is estimated that 98 percent of all communities in the United States are involved in the Special Olympics (Special Olympics Michigan, 1998).

Not everyone has been happy with the specialness of the Special Olympics, however. Criticisms have revolved around the segregated nature of the games and the possibility that people who are not disabled will focus on the *differentness* of the athletes. To alleviate these concerns, the Unified Games were introduced in 1989. This competition mixes nondisabled athletes and those with mental retardation on the same teams.

Research on the effects of the Special Olympics, while not definitive, generally supports the event as benefiting athletes and the volunteers. In one study, participants' parents were overwhelmingly satisfied with the traditional Special Olympics, and very few were concerned about

including nondisabled athletes (Klein, Gilman, & Zigler, 1995). In another study, volunteers in the Special Olympics showed improved attitudes about people with retardation, compared to those who did not volunteer. One cautionary finding, however, was that those who had volunteered for several years actually had more stereotypical attitudes than those who were novices (Roper, 1990). A comparison between athletes with mental retardation competing in the Special Olympics and those competing in the Unified Games found little difference in their self-concepts or perceived social acceptance (Riggen & Ulrich, 1993). And in the most extensive investigation to date, three studies suggested positive benefits of the Special Olympics (Dykens & Cohen, 1996). In Study 1, there was a positive relationship between length of time in the Special Olympics and parents' perception of social competence. In Study 2, parents of Special Olympians perceived their children as having higher social competence than a matched group of non-Olympians. In Study 3, the Special Olympians' social competence scores remained high four months after the games.

Although none of these studies is perfect and they all rely heavily on perceptions of behavior rather than observations of behavior, they do not support those who have expressed alarm at the nature of the games.

placed in these programs were reaching their teenage years, we have been able to assess the effects of some of these programs. In 1993, for example, a follow-up study was done on the Perry Preschool Project (Schweinhart & Weikart, 1993). Begun in the early 1960s, the Perry Preschool Project was designed to answer the question: Can high-quality early childhood education improve the lives of low-income children and their families and the quality of life of the community as a whole? A sample of 123 three- and four-year-old African American children from impoverished backgrounds and with IQs between 60 and 90 was randomly assigned either to an experimental group that received two years of a cognitively oriented curriculum or to a control group that received no preschool program. When these students were studied again at age 27, a number of differences favored those who had received the preschool program over those who had not:

- More had completed the twelfth grade
- Fewer had been arrested
- More owned their own homes
- Fewer had ever been on welfare
- They had a lower teenage pregnancy rate
- They earned a better-than-average income
- Classification as disabled or mentally retarded was less likely

Furthermore, a cost–benefit analysis—taking into account such things as costs of welfare and the criminal justice system and benefits on taxes on earnings—showed a return of $7.16 for every dollar invested in the Perry Preschool Project.

One of the best-known infant stimulation programs among those started more recently is the Abecedarian Project (Ramey & Campbell, 1984, 1987). Participants were identified before birth by selecting children from a pool of pregnant women living in poverty. After birth, the infants were randomly assigned to one of two groups: half to a day-care group that received special services, and half to a control group that received no such services. The day-care group participated in a program that provided experiences to promote perceptual-motor, intellectual, language, and social development. The families of these children also received a number of social and medical services. Results of the Abecedarian Project, reported through the end of third grade, indicated that the students from the day-care group had attained higher IQ scores and academic achievement than those from the control group (Campbell & Ramey, 1994).

Early intervention has also been successful in reducing the negative effects of low birthweight. Research suggests that stimulation of these infants in the first year of life, followed by intervention that focuses on the child and the entire family, has the best chance of reducing the incidence of mental retardation in this at-risk population (Blair & Ramey, 1997).

Educators still disagree over the degree to which learners with mental retardation should be integrated in the general education system.

Early Childhood Programs Designed to Further Development

Unlike preschool programs for children at risk, in which the goal is to prevent retardation from developing, programs for infants and preschoolers who are already identified as retarded are designed to help them achieve as high a cognitive level as possible. These programs place a great deal of emphasis on language and conceptual development. Because these children often have multiple disabilities, other professionals—for example, speech therapists and physical therapists—are frequently involved in their education. Also, many of the better programs include opportunities for parent involvement. Through practice with their children, parents can reinforce some of the skills that teachers work on. For example, parents of infants with physical disabilities, such as cerebral palsy, can learn from physical therapists the appropriate ways of handling their children to further their physical development. Similarly, parents can learn appropriate feeding techniques from speech therapists.

Transition

Transition programming for individuals with mental retardation involves two related areas—community adjustment and employment. Most authorities agree that although the degree of emphasis on transition programming should be greater for older than for younger students, such programming should begin in the elementary years. Table 4.3 (see p. 149) depicts some examples of curriculum activities across the school years pertaining to domestic, community living, leisure, and vocational skills.

Community Adjustment

For persons with mental retardation to adjust to living in the community, they need to acquire a number of skills, many of which are in the area of self-help. For example, they need to be able to manage money, use public transportation, and keep themselves well groomed and their living quarters well maintained. They also need to have good social skills so they can get along with persons in the community. In general, research has shown that attempts to train for community survival skills can be successful, especially when the training occurs within the actual setting in which the individuals live.

More and more authorities point to the family as a critical factor in whether persons with mental retardation will be successful in community adjustment and employment (Blacher & Baker, 1992). The majority of adults with mental retardation live with their families (Krauss et al., 1992). And even for those who live away from home, the family can still be a significant source of support for living in the community and finding and holding jobs.

Employment

Traditionally, employment figures for adults with mental retardation have been appalling. For example, in the most thorough national survey, researchers found that three to five years after exiting secondary school only 37 percent of persons with mental retardation were competitively employed (Blackorby & Wagner, 1996).

Even though employment statistics for workers who are retarded have been pessimistic, most professionals working in this area are optimistic about the potential for providing training programs that will lead to meaningful employment for these adults. Research indicates that with appropriate training, persons with retardation can hold down jobs with a good deal of success, measured by such things as attendance, employer satisfaction, and length of employment (Brown et al., 1986; Nietupski, Hamre-Nietupski, VanderHart, & Fishback, 1996; Stodden & Browder, 1986).

When persons with retardation are not successful on the job, the cause more often involves behaviors related to job responsibility and social skills than to job performance per se (Butterworth & Strauch, 1994; Heal, Gonzalez, Rusch, Copher, & DeStefano, 1990; Salzberg, Lignugaris/Kraft, & McCuller, 1988). In other words, the problem is not so much that people with retardation cannot perform the job as it is that they have difficulty with such issues as attendance, initiative, responding to criticism, and interacting socially with co-workers and supervisors. This latter problem—social interaction—most consistently distinguishes workers who are retarded from those who are not.

Table 4.3

Examples of Curriculum Activities across the School Years for Domestic, Community Living, Leisure, and Vocational Skills

Skill Area

Domestic	Community Living	Leisure	Vocational
Elementary School Student: Tim			
Picking up toys	Eating meals in a restaurant	Climbing on swing set	Picking up plate, silverware,
Washing dishes	Using restroom in a local	Playing board games	and glass after a meal
Making bed	restaurant	Playing tag with neighbors	Returning toys to appropriate
Dressing	Putting trash into container	Tumbling activities	storage space
Grooming	Choosing correct change to	Running	Cleaning the room at the end
Eating skills	ride city bus	Playing kickball	of the day
Toileting skills	Giving the clerk money for an		Working on a task for a des-
Sorting clothes	item he wants to purchase		ignated period (15–20
Vacuuming			minutes)
Junior High School Student: Mary			
Washing clothes	Crossing streets safely	Playing volleyball	Waxing floors
Cooking a simple hot meal	Purchasing an item from a	Taking aerobics classes	Cleaning windows
(soup, salad, and	department store	Playing checkers with a	Filling lawn mower with gas
sandwich)	Purchasing a meal at a	friend	Hanging and bagging
Keeping bedroom clean	restaurant	Playing miniature golf	clothes
Making snacks	Using local transportation sys-	Cycling	Bussing tables
Mowing lawn	tem to get to and from	Attending high school or	Working for 1–2 hours
Raking leaves	recreational facilities	local college basketball	Operating machinery (such
Making a grocery list	Participating in local scout	games	as dishwasher, buffer, etc.)
Purchasing items from a list	troop	Playing softball	Cleaning sinks, bathtubs,
Vacuuming and dusting living	Going to neighbor's house	Swimming	and fixtures
room	for lunch on Saturday		Following a job sequence
High School Students: Sandy			
Cleaning all rooms in place	Utilizing bus system to move	Jogging	Performing required janitorial
of residence	about the community	Archery	duties at J.C. Penney
Developing a weekly budget	Depositing checks into bank	Boating	Performing housekeeping
Cooking meals	account	Watching college basketball	duties at Days Inn
Operating thermostat to	Using community department	Video games	Performing grounds keeping
regulate heat or air	stores	Card games (Uno)	duties at VCU campus
conditioning	Using community grocery	Athletic club swimming class	Performing food service at
Doing yard maintenance	stores	Gardening	K St. Cafeteria
Maintaining personal needs	Using community health facili-	Going on a vacation trip	Performing laundry duties at
Caring for and maintaining	ties (physician, pharmacist)		Moon's Laundromat
clothing			Performing photography at
			Virginia National Bank
			Headquarters

Source: Adapted from P. Wehman, M. S. Moon, J. M. Everson, W. Wood, & J. M. Barcus, *Transition from school to work: New challenges for youth with severe disabilities* (Baltimore: Paul H. Brookes, 1988), pp. 140–142. Reprinted with permission.

A variety of vocational training and employment approaches for individuals with mental retardation are available. Most of these are subsumed under two very different kinds of arrangements—the sheltered workshop and supported competitive employment.

sheltered workshop. A facility that provides a structured environment for persons with disabilities in which they can learn skills; can be either a transitional placement or a permanent arrangement.

competitive employment. A workplace that provides employment that pays at least minimum wage and in which most workers are nondisabled.

supported competitive employment. A workplace where adults who are disabled or retarded earn at least minimum wage and receive ongoing assistance from a specialist or job coach; the majority of workers in the workplace are nondisabled.

job coach. A person who assists adult workers with disabilities (especially those with mental retardation), providing vocational assessment, instruction, overall planning, and interaction assistance with employers, family, and related government and service agencies.

individual placement model. A model of supported employment in which a person with mental retardation is placed individually in a business or industry that primarily consists of nonretarded employees; the most common type of supported employment.

mobile work crew model. A model of supported employment in which a small group of workers who are retarded moves from one place to another, such as a janitorial service.

Sheltered Workshops. The traditional job-training environment for adults with mental retardation, especially those classified as more severely retarded, has been the sheltered workshop. A **sheltered workshop** is a structured environment where a person receives training and works with other workers with disabilities on jobs requiring relatively low skills. This can be either a permanent placement or a transitional placement before a person obtains a job in the competitive job market.

Although sheltered workshops remain a relatively popular placement, more and more authorities are voicing dissatisfaction with them. Among the criticisms are the following:

1. Workers make very low wages because sheltered workshops rarely turn a profit. Usually managed by personnel with limited business management expertise, they rely heavily on charitable contributions.
2. There is no integration of workers who are disabled with those who are nondisabled. This restricted setting makes it difficult to prepare workers who are mentally retarded for working side by side with nondisabled workers in the competitive workforce.
3. Sheltered workshops offer only limited job-training experiences. A good workshop should provide opportunities for trainees to learn a variety of new skills. All too often, however, the work is repetitive and does not make use of current industrial technology.

Supported Competitive Employment. In contrast to sheltered employment, **competitive employment** is an approach that provides jobs for at least the minimum wage in integrated work settings in which most of the workers are not disabled. Not surprisingly, workers who are retarded report higher job satisfaction in supported competitive employment than in sheltered workshops (Griffin, Rosenberg, Cheyney, & Greenberg, 1996). Although the ultimate goal for some adults with mental retardation may be competitive employment, many will need supported employment for a period of time or even permanently. In **supported competitive employment,** the person with retardation has a competitive employment position but receives ongoing assistance, often from a **job coach.** In addition to on-the-job training, the job coach may provide assistance in related areas, such as finding an appropriate job, interactions with employers and other employees, use of transportation, and involvement with other agencies.

The use of supported competitive employment has grown dramatically. It is now estimated that there are over 100,000 workers in supported employment; however, this is still far fewer than the estimated 700,000 in sheltered workshops (Nietupski et al., 1996). Researchers have found that movement from sheltered work environments to supported employment has proved cost-effective for society; moreover, this approach has resulted in a 500 percent increase in salaries for workers with mental retardation (McCaughrin, Ellis, Rusch, & Heal, 1993; Revell, Wehman, Kregel, West, & Rayfield, 1994).

There are three main types of supported employment models:

- *Individual placement model.* In the **individual placement model,** the employee with retardation is hired as an individual. The advantages are that it allows maximum flexibility with regard to meeting the worker's job choice and the greatest opportunity for integration (Wehman & Parent, 1996). This is by far the most common type of supported employment model.
- *Mobile work crew model.* In the **mobile work crew model,** there is a crew of about four to eight workers, all of whom are retarded. One common

type is a janitorial service. An advantage is that workers can move from one crew to another and learn a variety of jobs (Wehman & Parent, 1996).

- *Enclave model.* In the **enclave model,** a small group of workers with mental retardation is employed in a business that is primarily made up of workers who are not retarded. The workers in the enclave are allowed to compete for the same benefits and wages as other employees. An advantage of this model is that it allows for integration with nonretarded workers and it allows workers access to the same opportunities as other workers (Wehman & Parent, 1996).

This woman lives in affordable housing developed by Citizens for Independent Living, a group that trains people with mental retardation in living skills and assists them with job placement.

There are two potential problems with the supported competitive employment model. First, clients can become too dependent on the support provided by their job coaches (Lagomarcino, Hughes, & Rusch, 1989). Job coaches need to be skilled at weaning their clients from relying on them for too much. Some authorities also recommend using **self-monitoring** as a way to help develop more independence. Self-monitoring involves workers observing their own performance and then recording it—for example, observing and recording the number of days one is late for work each week. (We talk more about self-monitoring in Chapters 5 and 6.)

Second, the presence of job coaches can inhibit social interactions between workers who are retarded and their nonretarded co-workers (Chadsey, Linneman, Rusch, & Cimera, 1997; Ferguson, McDonnell, & Drew, 1993). Researchers have noted that when job coaches are present, workers may tend to interact with them rather than with co-workers or supervisors. Because workers who are retarded already have difficulties managing appropriate social interactions at work, job coaches should avoid serving as social buffers for them.

Prospects for the Future

Current employment figures and living arrangements for adults with mental retardation may look bleak, but there is reason to be optimistic about the future. Although the sheltered workshop remains the most common work environment for adults who are retarded, placement in competitive employment is increasing (Revell, et al., 1994). Evidence also shows that employers are taking a more favorable attitude toward hiring workers who are mentally retarded (Nietupski et al., 1996). With the development of innovative transition programs, many persons with mental retardation are achieving levels of independence in community living and employment that were never thought possible.

enclave model. A model of supported employment in which a small group of workers who are retarded is employed in a larger business or industry in which the workers are not retarded; the workers in the enclave have the same eligibility for benefits and wages as all other employees.

self-monitoring. A type of cognitive behavior modification technique that requires individuals to keep track of their own behavior.

Summary

Professionals are generally more cautious about identifying students as retarded than they once were because (1) there has been a history of misidentifying students from minority groups, (2) the label "mental retardation" may have harmful consequences for students, and (3) some believe that, to a certain extent, mental retardation is socially constructed. Changes in the definition of the American Association on Mental Retardation over the years reflect this cautious attitude toward identification. The current AAMR definition continues three trends: (1) a broadening of the definition beyond the single criterion of an IQ score (adaptive skills as well as conceptual intelligence are measured), (2) a lowering of the IQ score used as a cutoff, and (3) a view of retardation as a condition that can be improved.

The AAMR has traditionally classified persons as having *mild, moderate, severe,* or *profound* retardation based on their IQ scores. Currently, however, the AAMR recommends classification according to the level of support needed: *intermittent, limited, extensive,* or *pervasive.*

Several authorities have been critical of the AAMR definition on the grounds that (1) it goes too far in denying the existence of retardation within a person, (2) it is more straightforward to classify individuals based on levels of severity, and (3) it is very difficult to measure adaptive behavior reliably. Two other definitions have been offered—the APA definition and Stephen Greenspan's definition. The APA definition promotes the traditional classification of mild, moderate, severe, and profound. Greenspan's definition rejects adaptive behavior as too vague. Instead, it relies on a tripartite notion of intelligence: *conceptual, practical,* and *social.*

From a purely statistical-theoretical perspective, 2.27 percent of the population should score low enough on an IQ test (below about 70) to qualify as retarded. Figures indicate, however, that about 1 to 1.5 percent of the population is identified as mentally retarded. The discrepancy may be due school personnel using low adaptive behavior as well as low IQ as criteria for mental retardation, plus the tendency to prefer to have students labeled "learning disabled" rather than "mentally retarded" because they perceive it as less stigmatizing.

There are a variety of causes of mental retardation. We can actually specify the cause in only a few cases, especially among those with more mild retardation. Most people with mild retardation are considered culturally-familially retarded, a term used to include causes related to poor environmental and/or hereditary factors. Although the nature-nurture debate has raged for years, most authorities now believe that the interaction between heredity and the environment is important in determining intelligence.

We can categorize causes of more severe retardation, or that requiring more intensive support, as due to genetic factors or brain damage. Down syndrome, Williams syndrome, fragile X syndrome, PKU, and Tay-Sachs disease are all examples of genetic causes. Down syndrome and Williams syndrome result from chromosomal abnormalities but are not inherited as such. Fragile X syndrome, PKU, and Tay-Sachs are inherited. Authorities believe that fragile X syndrome is the most common hereditary cause of retardation. Research on genetic engineering is rapidly expanding, raising several moral and ethical dilemmas. Brain damage can result from infectious diseases— for example, meningitis, encephalitis, rubella, and pediatric AIDS—or environmental hazards, such as poisons (e.g., cocaine and alcohol) and excessive radiation. Low birthweight can also result in mental retardation. Using amniocentesis, chorionic villus sampling, sonography, and maternal serum screening, physicians are now able to detect a variety of defects in the unborn fetus.

Two of the most common IQ tests are the Stanford-Binet and the Wechsler Intelligence Scale for Children. The latter has verbal and performance subscales. Some professionals recommend using the Kaufman Assessment Battery for Children (K–ABC) with African American students because they believe it less culturally biased.

There are several cautions in using and interpreting IQ tests: (1) an individual's IQ score can change; (2) all IQ tests are culturally biased to some extent; (3) the younger the child, the less reliable the results; and (4) a person's ability to live a successful and fulfilling life does not depend solely on his or her IQ. In addition to IQ tests, several adaptive behavior scales are available.

Persons with mental retardation have learning problems related to attention, memory (especially working memory), language development, academic achievement, self-regulation, social development, and motivation. An important concept related to self-regulation is *metacognition*—the awareness of what strategies are needed to perform a task and the ability to use self-regulatory mechanisms before, during, and after performing a task.

Educational goals for students with mild retardation emphasize readiness skills at younger ages and functional academics, community adjustment, and vocational training at older ages. Functional academics are for the purpose of enabling the person to function independently. Educational programs for students with more severe retardation are characterized by (1) systematic instruction, (2) instruction in *in vivo* settings with real materials, and (3) functional assessment. Systematic instruction includes instructional prompts, consequences for performance, and transfer of stimulus control, including constant and progressive time delay. *In vivo* instruction using real materials is preferable to instruction that only occurs in the classroom. Functional assessment involves determining the consequences, antecedents, and setting events of behaviors.

Depending to a large extent on the degree of retardation or the need for support, students with mental retardation may be in learning environments ranging from regular classrooms to residential institutions. Although residential institutions still exist and special classes in public schools are common, the trend is to include students who are mentally retarded in more integrated settings. For adults, there is a trend toward supported living arrangements, in which persons with retardation live in more natural settings such as their own home or apartment.

Preschool programs differ in their goals according to whether they are aimed at preventing retardation or furthering the development of children already identified as retarded. For the most part, the former types of programs are aimed at children at risk of developing mild retardation, whereas the latter are for children with more severe retardation. Research supports the clear link between such interventions and success later in life.

Transition programming for individuals with retardation includes goals related to domestic living, community living, leisure, and vocational skills. Although the emphasis on transition programming increases with age, authorities recommend that such efforts begin in elementary school.

The employment picture for workers with retardation is changing. Although sheltered work environments remain popular, authorities have pointed out their weaknesses: (1) wages are very low, (2) there is no integration with nondisabled workers, and (3) they offer only limited job-training experiences. Placement of workers who are retarded in supported competitive employment has increased dramatically since its inception in the early 1980s. The role of the job coach is critical to the success of supported competitive employment arrangements. The job coach provides on-the-job training as well as such things as helping the worker with job selection, interactions with other workers and the employer, use of transportation, and using other agencies. There are three main types of supported employment models: individual placement, mobile work crew, and enclave. Although employment figures are still discouraging, the growth in innovative programs gives reason to be hopeful about the future of community living and employment for adults with mental retardation.

suggestions for teaching

Students with Mental Retardation in General Education Classrooms

By Peggy L. Tarpley

To meet the needs of students with retardation, teachers emphasize instruction that will enable their students to have "meaningful participation" in society (Meyen & Skrtic, 1995; Polloway & Patton, 1997). This type of instruction includes the teaching of functional academics. As the IEP team plans the goals and objectives for the student, it is helpful to consider the projected living situations these students will encounter as adults and determine the most appropriate skills to be taught and mastered. Five content areas are often cited as most appropriate for this curriculum for students with mental retardation. They are:

1. Language—including speaking, listening, comprehending, reading, and writing for everyday personal and social use
2. Mathematics—basic skills necessary for daily living
3. Health and Safety—self-care, health, and community living skills
4. Social Skills—acceptable behaviors
5. Career Education—preparation for employment and leisure activities

Communication is the foundation for success in all academic and social endeavors. Consequently, language is the place to begin any curriculum for students with mental retardation. In any classroom of young students with mental retardation, the students will vary in their ability to communicate. Some will use verbal speech (probably not fluently); others will use a combination of words and gestures; some will only gesture; and some may use a sign language to communicate. Teachers need to teach and use in the classroom a communication system that is compatible with the students' abilities and allows them to meet their needs or get their needs met. Dyer and Luce (1996) suggest that pragmatic communication skills (requesting help or attention, protesting, clarifying directions, taking turns, etc.) should be taught very early through one of several systems: gestural mode, picture communication symbol system, sign language, voice output system, or a verbal system.

The communication system used in the classroom sets the stage for the acquisition of speaking, listening, comprehending, reading, and writing skills. Before the late 1960's it was thought that children with mental retardation could not learn academics and certainly could not learn to read (Oelwein, 1995). We have come a long way in teaching reading to all students. We are overcoming the prejudice that certain people cannot learn this skill and now understand the importance of phonological awareness to learning to read.

Some teachers have seen improvements in language skills and reading skills with the use of a sign language system of communication in the classroom. In a preschool classroom where two students with hearing impairments were included, the teachers decided to teach *all* the students sign language (ASL) (Heller, Manning, Pavur, & Wagner, 1998). To monitor the progress of all students and to compare them with a matched preschool class not using sign language, the students were given the Peabody Picture Vocabulary Test (PPVT), a test of receptive language, at the beginning of the year and again at the end of the year. The results showed that those using sign language in the classroom showed significantly greater gains on the PPVT than those not participating in sign. Like the preschool teachers in this study, elementary teachers have noticed improvements in language acquisition and reading skills when combining sign language and speech in teaching in the classroom (personal conversations with cooperating teachers). Some have suggested that the combination is helpful in getting symbols, information, and concepts into long-term memory.

Other modes of instruction found successful in teaching students with mental retardation are based on teacher-directed, student-directed, and peer-mediated methods.

Teacher-Directed Methods

As you know from reading this chapter, we often use components from applied behavior analysis (antecedents, consequences, reinforcements, etc.) to teach students with mental retardation. Other approaches directed by teachers include cognitive training, direct instruction, and integrated unit instruction. Cognitive training and direct instructional methods also are used with children with learning disabilities and are described more fully in the chapter on learning disabilities.

Cognitive training and direct instruction use such techniques as task analysis, modeling, and scaffolding to teach students concepts, skills, and procedures. These approaches to teaching address the memory deficits and lack of self-generated strategies that are often characteristic of students with mental retardation. First, teachers analyze a given task to determine what skills are needed before the student can be taught that skill (prerequisite skills) and what individual skills are needed to complete the task (component skills). To develop a task analysis, teachers often observe someone who is performing the task and record each step. Then, teachers perform the task using

the steps they have noted to check for accuracy and completeness. Before beginning instruction, they teach any prerequisite skills students do not have. Using the component skills, the teacher creates his or her lesson plans for this skill. The component skills also can be used to teach the student a practical strategy for the task. Teachers will need to use modeling to demonstrate the use of the strategy and scaffolding to "support as needed" the student's efforts at learning the strategy as well as the task. The examples below illustrate modeling, strategy generation, and scaffolding.

Teachers model both observable and nonobservable behavior. By "thinking aloud" as they complete tasks, teachers model their thinking for students. Olson and Platt (1992) provide the following example of a think-aloud used by Mr. Clarke as he taught reading:

> Today, I'd like to share with you a strategy I use when I come to a word that I don't know.... [Mr. Clarke reads the first sentence, "The weatherman said there will be snow flurries."] I know I've heard the word "flurries" before, but I don't know what it means. The word before "flurries" is "snow," so it has something to do with snow... I'll read on. The next sentence says, "When the little boy heard the weather report, he became angry, because he wanted to build a snowman." I think that can help me, because I know that you have to have a lot of snow to build a snowman.... Now, I may know what the word means. I'll bet it means light snow. Let me go back and check. (p. 212)

Frequently, teachers supplement think-alouds by giving students a list of the steps involved in solving the problem. For example, in the think-aloud described above, Mr. Clarke provided students with the following strategy or procedural steps:

1. Read the unknown word in the sentence.
2. See if any other words in the sentence can help you figure out the unknown word.
3. Use any background information you have to help you.
4. Read more of the sentences.
5. Repeat steps 2 and 3.
6. Substitute the new meaning.
7. Reread the sentences to see if the new meaning makes sense. (Olson & Platt, 1992)

Like modeling, scaffolding is a teacher-directed approach that encourages increased student participation as teacher support is decreased. Bos and Vaughn (1997) suggest that scaffolding provides "an adjustable and temporary support that can be removed when no longer necessary" (p. 50). Teachers can use scaffolding in many situations with various techniques. Hendrickson and Frank (1993) give an example using a teacher-questioning sequence known as response-dependent questioning. Moving from full support to no support:

1. The teacher begins with a complete model question, such as: "Lynn bought a new car. Now you tell me what did Lynn do?"
2. Decreasing the support of the complete model in subsequent discussions, the teacher asks yes-or-no questions, such as: "Did Lynn buy a new car?"
3. Next, the teacher asks a restricted alternative question, such as: "Lynn did not watch television or go to the park. What did Lynn do?"
4. The teacher then moves the student toward less support by asking a multiple-choice question, such as: "Did Lynn watch television, go to the park, or buy a car?"
5. Finally, the teacher asks an open question, such as: "What did Lynn do on Saturday?"

The teacher might choose to start the sequence with the open question, building the scaffold as the student's needs dictate toward the full support of the complete model question and then removing the support as the student responds with less prompting or cueing.

Integrated unit instruction (integrated curriculum) addresses the needs of students with mental retardation to learn concepts and skills across the curriculum in real-life situations. For example, map-making skills can be very practical when students make meaningful maps of the area in which they live and the places they need to visit (grocery, doctor, school, etc.). Likewise, math skills are more practical when tied to grocery shopping on a budget. Good nutrition can also be tied into a unit on grocery shopping. As culminating activities for these units, teachers often plan a field trip to the grocery store so that students can show their newly acquired skills of following a map, planning a menu for a nutritious meal, shopping from a list of needed items for the meal, and keeping to a budget.

Student-Directed Procedures

Increasingly, educators are facilitating students' use of self-regulation procedures, such as self-monitoring, self-administering consequences, and self-instruction. These procedures are student directed and promote student independence. Self-monitoring involves teaching students to record their own behaviors so they become aware of their behaviors and regulate them. Self-administering requires students, not teachers, to give themselves predetermined consequences contingent on their own behaviors. A recent review of self-management procedures used to teach persons with mental retardation reported that these two procedures typically are used to increase the occurrence of behaviors students already know how to perform, such as work and daily living skills (Harchik, Sherman, & Sheldon, 1992). Self-instruction, which involves students making directive verbal statements about their own behaviors, is used to teach skills students have not yet mastered, such as academic skills (Harchik et al., 1992). (See Chapter 5 for additional information about these procedures.)

Peer-Mediated Procedures

Given the context of large, heterogeneous classes, teachers often use peer-mediated procedures to provide the additional practice and individual help students with mental retardation need. One such arrangement is peer tutoring, a technique that under certain conditions has been shown to benefit both tutor and tutee academically, behaviorally, and socially. In student tutoring programs, teachers typically provide instruction to all class members. Then students in the class (peer tutors) or older students (cross-age tutors) who have mastered the learning assist those individuals who require additional instruction and practice.

Tutors can take on a variety of responsibilities, such as reviewing lessons, directing and monitoring the performance of newly learned skills, and providing feedback and reinforcement. Planning, supervising, and evaluating a peer-tutoring program requires careful planning and ongoing supervision by the teacher. Several studies and reviews (Gerber & Kauffman, 1981; Jenkins & Jenkins, 1985; Knapczyk, 1989) indicate that several conditions are necessary for effective peer tutoring. They include:

1. Tutors are trained to understand instructional objectives, discriminate between correct and incorrect responses, deliver feedback and reinforcement, and monitor progress and record keeping.
2. Instructional steps are carefully sequenced and clearly outlined in a lesson format that tutors can follow easily.

3. Teachers actively monitor tutor and tutee performance frequently.
4. Teachers provide reinforcement frequently and consistently to the tutor and tutee contingent on their appropriate performances.
5. Tutorial sessions are scheduled for approximately fifteen to thirty minutes at least two or three times each week.

The inclusion of students with severe retardation in general education classrooms has resulted in increased interest among educators in procedures that promote improvement in skills and enhance the social acceptance of these students. Recent reviews of methods for individualizing curriculum and instruction reported by Thousand and Villa (1990) suggest three approaches in addition to peer tutoring: mastery learning, computer-assisted instruction, and cooperative learning.

To implement mastery learning, teachers conduct frequent, brief assessments of each student (e.g., curriculum-based assessment); develop individual objectives and establish specific preset mastery criteria; provide frequent feedback to students regarding their performance and progress toward mastery; and adjust or supplement instruction or practice for students who do not meet their mastery criteria. Individual goals include daily living, social, and vocational skills.

Teachers also use computer-assisted instruction (CAI) in several areas of effective teaching. For students with severe retardation, CAI may be used to introduce new information and to supplement teacher instruction (i.e., tutorials). CAI may also be used to provide the additional drill and practice these students require. Consult with a special educator in your school regarding appropriate software programs that meet the specific needs of your students.

Cooperative learning, an arrangement in which diverse students work in small groups to meet common goals, is a third approach teachers use to enhance learning in social and other skill areas. In Vermont, for example, specialists worked with classroom teachers to form cooperative learning groups that included students needing extensive to pervasive support. To illustrate how these students were integrated into cooperative group activities, Thousand and Villa (1990) described a seventh-grade biology lesson in which Bob, a thirteen-year-old with multiple disabilities, was a participant. This lesson focused on dissecting a frog. Although Bob did not participate directly in the dissection, during this process he worked on his individual goals, which centered on structured communication. Group members helped Bob achieve his lesson objectives as they dissected the frog.

In preparing to integrate special students into general education classes and to promote the social acceptance of these students, Lewis and Doorlag (1999) recommend informing classmates about disabilities. Teachers often introduce this topic by discussing the concept of individual differences. Asking students to think about their own strengths and weaknesses promotes awareness of the fact that each person is unique and possesses different abilities and disabilities. Depending on the grade, teachers frequently follow up this discussion with information about disabilities, either directly or with structured assignments and projects in which students conduct their own research. In addition, teachers provide experiences with people who have disabilities (Lewis & Doorlag, 1999). They invite adults with disabilities into the classroom, arrange visits to special education classes in the school, or use commercially developed materials, such as *Kids on the Block*, which includes puppets portraying children with disabilities. Once students with disabilities are mainstreamed, it is important that teachers provide structured interactions between nondisabled students and students with disabilities, using arrangements such as peer tutoring and cooperative learning.

Helpful Resources

School Personnel

The special educator who also teaches students who are mentally retarded may provide additional instructional suggestions that have been successful in improving performance. This teacher also can recommend and perhaps obtain learning materials designed for special education students and suggest ways in which regular class materials can be adapted to students with retardation. In addition, he or she can recommend books on a variety of subjects that are of high interest to older students and written at lower reading levels. Finally, this teacher and the school psychologist are good resources for specific cognitive and behavioral information about your student.

Instructional Methods

Bos, C. S., & Vaughn, S. (1998). *Strategies for teaching students with learning and behavior problems.* Boston: Allyn & Bacon.

Fowler, G. L., & Davis, M. (1985). The storyframe approach: A tool for improving reading comprehension. *Teaching Exceptional Children, 17,* 296–298.

Hamre-Nietupski, S., McDonald, J., & Nietupski, J. (1992). Integrating elementary students with multiple disabilities into supported regular classes. *Teaching Exceptional Children, 24,* 6–9.

Horton, S. (1983). Delivering industrial arts instruction to mildly handicapped learners. *Career Development for Exceptional Individuals, 6,* 85–92.

Isaacson, S. (1988). Teaching written expression; directed reading and writing; self-instructional strategy training; and computers and writing instruction, *Teaching Exceptional Children, 20,* 32–39.

Jenson, W. R., Sloane, H. N., & Young, K. R. (1988). *Applied behavior analysis in education: A structured teaching approach.* Englewood Cliffs, NJ: Prentice-Hall.

Maheady, L., Harper, G. F., & Sacca, M. K. (1988). Peer-mediated instruction: A promising approach to meeting the diverse needs of LD adolescents. *Learning Disability Quarterly, 11,* 108–113.

Matson, J. L. (Ed.). (1990). *Handbook of behavior modification with the mentally retarded* (2nd ed.). New York: Plenum Press.

McDonnell, J., Wilcox, B., & Hardman, M. L. (1991). *Secondary programs for students with developmental disabilities.* Boston: Allyn & Bacon.

Olson, J., & Platt, J. (2000). *Teaching children and adolescents with special needs* (3rd ed.). Upper Saddle River, NJ: Merrill Prentice-Hall.

O'Shea, L., & O'Shea, D. (1988). Using repeated readings. *Teaching Exceptional Children, 20,* 26–29.

Polloway, E., & Patton, J. (1997). *Strategies for teaching learners with special needs* (6th ed.). Upper Saddle River, NJ: Merrill Prentice-Hall.

Robinson, G. A., & Polloway, E. A. (Eds.). (1987). *Best practices in mental disabilities (Vol. 1).* Des Moines, IA: Iowa State Department of Education Bureau of Special Education.

Schloss, P. J., & Sedlak, R. A. (1982). Behavioral features of the mentally retarded adolescent: Implications for mainstreamed educators. *Psychology in the Schools, 19,* 98–105.

Schultz, J. B., & Carpenter, C. D. (1995). *Mainstreaming exceptional students: A guide for classroom teachers* (4th ed.). Boston: Allyn & Bacon.

Curricula

Agran, M., & Moore, S. C. (1994). *How to teach self-instruction of job skills.* Washington, DC: American Association on Mental Retardation.

Bender, M., & Valletutti, P. J. (1990). *Teaching functional academics.* Austin, TX: Pro-Ed.

Carnine, D., Silbert, J., & Kameenui, E. J. (1990). *Direct instruction reading.* Columbus, OH: Merrill/Macmillan.

Engelmann, S., & Bruner, E. C. (1974). *DISTAR reading.* Chicago, IL: Science Research Associates.

Engelmann, S., & Bruner, E. C. (1983). *Reading mastery.* Chicago, IL: Science Research Associates.

Engelmann, S., Carnine, D., Johnson, G., & Meyers, L. (1988). *Corrective reading: Decoding.* Chicago, IL: Science Research Associates.

Engelmann, S., Carnine, D., Johnson, G., & Meyers, L. (1989). *Corrective reading: Comprehension.* Chicago, IL: Science Research Associates.

Silbert, J., Carnine, D., & Stein, M. (1981). *Direct instruction mathematics* (2nd ed.). Columbus, OH: Merrill.

Valletutti, P. J., Bender, M., & Hoffnung, A. (1996). *A functional curriculum for teaching students with disabilities nonverbal and oral communication (Vol. 2)* (3rd ed.). Austin, TX: Pro-Ed.

Wehman, P., & McLoughlin, P. J. (1990). *Vocational curriculum for developmentally disabled persons.* Austin, TX: Pro-Ed.

Literature about Individuals with Mental Retardation*

Elementary

Anderson, R. (1989). *The bus people.* New York: Henry Holt. (Grades 5–8) (F)

Carrick, C. (1985). *Stay away from Simon!* New York: Clarion. (Ages 8–11) (F)

Clifton, L. (1980). *My friend Jacob.* New York: E. P. Dutton. (Ages 6–10) (F)

Gillham, B. (1981). *My brother Barry.* London: A. Deutsch. (Ages 9–12) (F)

Hasler, E. (1981). *Martin is our friend.* Nashville, TN: Abingdon. (Ages 9–12) (F)

Rabe, B. (1988). *Where's Chimpy?* Berkeley, CA: Gray's Book Company. (Ages 4–7) (F)

Shyer, M. F. (1988). *Welcome home, Jellybean.* New York: Aladdin. (F)

Wright, B. R. (1981). *My sister is different.* Milwaukee, WI: Raintree. (Ages 4–7) (F)

Secondary

Bates, B. (1980). *Love is like peanuts.* New York: Holiday House. (Ages 13–15) (F)

Dougan, T., Isbell, L., & Vyas, P. (1983). *We have been there: A guidebook for families of people with mental retardation.* Nashville, TN: Abingdon. (NF)

Hill, D. (1985). *First your penny.* New York: Atheneum. (F)

Hull, E. (1981). *Alice with golden hair.* New York: Atheneum. (F)

Kaufman, S. Z. (1988). *Retarded isn't stupid, Mom!* Baltimore, MD: Brookes. (NF)

Miner, J. C. (1982). *She's my sister.* Mankato, MN: Crestwood House. (Reading levels: Grades 3–4; Interest level: Grades 7–12) (F)

Rodowsky, C. F. (1996). *What about me?* New York: Viking. (Grades 7–12) (F)

Slepian, J. (1980). *The Alfred summer.* New York: Macmillan. (F)

*F = fiction; NF = nonfiction

Slepian, J. (1981). *Lester's turn.* New York: Macmillan. (F) (A sequel to *The Alfred Summer*)

Software

Alphabet Circus, DLM Teaching Resources, One DLM Park, Allen, TX 75002; call SRA at (800) 843-8855. (Activities focus on letter recognition, alphabetical order, problem solving)

Animal Photo Farm, DLM Teaching Resources, One DLM Park, Allen, TX 75002; call SRA at (800) 843-8855.

Bake and Take, Mindplay, 160 W. Ft. Lowell, Tucson, AZ 85705, (800) 221-7911. (Life skills)

Calendar Skills, Hartley Courseware, 9920 Pacific Heights Boulevard, Suite 500, San Diego, CA 92121, (800) 247-1380.

Clock Works, MECC, 6160 Summit Drive N., Minneapolis, MN 55430-4003, (800) 685-6322. (Time telling on digital and analog clocks).

Comparative Buying Series, MCE, 1800 South 35th Street, Galesburg, MI 49053, (800) 421-4157.

Computer CUP, Amidon Publication, 1966 Benson Avenue, St. Paul, MN 55116, (800) 328-6502 (Nine discs teach basic concepts such as *right-left, as many, beginning*).

Counting Critters, MECC, 6160 Summit Drive N., Minneapolis, MN 55430, (800) 685-6322 (Basic number skills 1–20)

Daily Living Skills, Looking Glass Learning Products, 276 Howard Avenue, Des Plaines, IL 60018-1906, (800) 545-5457. (Reading prescriptions, medical product labels, classified ads, telephone directory, job applications, and paychecks)

Dinosaurs, Advanced Ideas, 591 Redwood Highway, Mill Valley, CA 94941, (415) 388-2430. (Game format teaches matching, sorting, and counting)

Job Success Series, MCE, 1800 South 35th Street, Galesburg, MI 49053, (800) 421-4157.

Library and Media Skills, Educational Activities, P.O. Box 392, Freeport, NY 11520, (800) 645-3739.

Library Skills, Micro Power & Light Company, 8814 Sanshire Avenue, Dallas, TX 75231, (214) 553-0105.

Reader Rabbit, Learning Company, 6493 Kaiser Drive, Fremont, CA 94555, (510) 792-2101.

Spell It!, Davidson & Associates, 19840 Pioneer Avenue, Torrance, CA 90503, (800) 545-7677.

Stickybear Town Builder, Optimum Resource, Inc., 18 Hunter Road, Hilton Head, SC 29926, (888) 784-2592. (Map reading, planning, hypothesizing, problem solving)

Telling Time, Random House School Division, 400 Hahn Road, Westminister, MD 21157, (800) 726-0600.

Vocabulary Challenge, Learning Well, 200 South Service Road, Roslyn Heights, NY 11577, (516) 326-2101.

Vocabulary Game, J & S Software, 14 Vanderventer, Port Washington, NY 11050.

Ways to Read Words, Queue Intellectual Software, 338 Commerce Drive, Fairfield, CT 06432, (800) 232-2224.

Work Habits for Job Success, MCE, 1800 South 35th Street, Galesburg, MI 49053, (800) 421-4157.

Organizations

American Association on Mental Retardation, 444 North Capital Street, N.W., Suite 846, Washington, DC 20001, (202) 387-1968, (800) 424-3688.

ARC, The, 500 E. Border Street, Suite 300, Arlington, TX 76010, (817) 261-6003, fax (817) 277-3491.

Mental Retardation Association of America, 211 E. 300 Street, Suite 212, Salt Lake City, UT 84111, (801) 328-1574.

Mental Retardation Division of the Council for Exceptional Children, 1920 Association Drive, Reston, VA 22091, (703) 620-3660, (888) CEC-SPED.

National Association for Down Syndrome, P.O. Box 4542, Oak Brook, IL 60522, (630) 325-9112.

Bibliography for Teaching Suggestions

Bos, C. S., & Vaughn, S. (1997). *Strategies for teaching students with learning and behavior problems.* Boston: Allyn & Bacon.

Dyer, K., & Luce, S. C. (1996). *Innovations: Teaching practical communication skills* (No. 7). Washington, DC: American Association on Mental Retardation.

Gerber, M., & Kauffman, J. M. (1981). Peer tutoring in academic settings. In P. S. Strain (Ed.). *The utilization of classroom peers as behavior change agents* (pp. 155–187). New York: Plenum Press.

Harchik, A. E., Sherman, J. A., & Sheldon, A. B. (1992). The use of self-management procedures by people with developmental disabilities: A brief review. *Research in Developmental Disabilities, 13,* 211–227.

Heller, I., Manning, D., Pavur, D., & Wagner, K. (1998). Let's all sign! Enhancing language development in an inclusive preschool. *Teaching Exceptional Children,* 51–53.

Hendrickson, J. M., & Frank, A. R. (1993). Engagement and performance feedback: Enhancing the classroom achievement of students with mild mental disabilities. In R. A. Gable & S. F. Warren (Eds.), *Strategies for teaching students with mild to severe mental retardation.* Baltimore: Paul H. Brookes.

Jenkins, J., & Jenkins, L. (1985). Peer tutoring in elementary and secondary programs. *Focus on Exceptional Children, 17,* 1–12.

Knapczyk, D. R. (1989). Peer-mediated training of cooperative play between special and regular class students in integrated play settings. *Education and Training in Mental Retardation, 24,* 255–264.

Lewis, R. B., & Doorlag, D. H. (1999). *Teaching special students in the mainstream* (5th ed.). Upper Saddle River, NJ: Merrill Prentice-Hall.

McCann, S. K., Semmel, M. I., & Nevin, A. (1985). Reverse mainstreaming: Nonhandicapped students in special education classrooms. *Remedial and Special Education, 6,* 13–19.

Meyen, E. L. (Ed.). (1993). *Educating students with mild disabilities.* Denver, CO: Love Publishing Co.

Oelwein, P. L. (1995). *Topics in Down syndrome: Teaching reading to children with Down syndrome: A guide for parents and teachers.* Bethesda, MD: Woodbine House.

Olson, J., & Platt, J. (1992). *Teaching children and adolescents with special needs.* New York: Merrill/Macmillan.

Polloway, E., & Patton, J. (1997). *Strategies for teaching learners with special needs* (6th ed.). Upper Saddle River, NJ: Merrill Prentice-Hall.

Poorman, C. (1980). Mainstreaming in reverse with a special friend. *Teaching Exceptional Children, 12,* 136–142.

Thousand, J. S., & Villa, R. A. (1990). Strategies for educating learners with severe disabilities within their local home schools and communities. *Focus on Exceptional Children, 23*(3), 1–24.

rebecca
bella rich

Flashing Stars from the Sky. Acrylic on canvas. 24 × 34 in.

Rebecca Bella Rich was born in 1960 in Cambridge, MA. She began attending the adult art workshops at Gateway Crafts in Brookline, MA, in 1990. As a woman with learning disabilities, she has struggled to make her uniquely creative voice heard. She draws, paints, and writes poetry. She has also produced an autobiographical performance video, as well as a book of interviews with artists who are challenged with disabilities. Her work has been shown in Massachusetts, New York, Pennsylvania, and England.

chapter 5

Learning Disabilities

I had scarcely passed my twelfth birthday when I entered the inhospitable regions of examinations, through which for the next seven years I was destined to journey. These examinations were a great trial to me. The subjects which were dearest to the examiners were almost invariably those I fancied the least. I would have liked to have been examined in history, poetry, and writing essays. The examiners, on the other hand, were partial to Latin and mathematics. And their will prevailed....

In retrospect these years form not only the least agreeable, but the only barren and unhappy period of my life. I was happy as a child with my toys in my nursery. I have been happier every year since I became a man. But this interlude of school makes a sombre grey patch upon the chart of my journey. It was an unending spell of worries that did not then seem petty, and of toil uncheered by fruition; a time of discomfort, restriction and purposeless monotony....

Harrow was a very good school.... Most of the boys were very happy, and many found in its classrooms and upon its playing-fields the greatest distinction they have ever known in life. I can only record the fact that, no doubt through my own shortcomings, I was an exception. I would far rather have been apprenticed as a bricklayer's mate, or run errands as a messenger boy, or helped my father to dress the front windows of a grocer's shop. It would have been natural; it would have taught me more; and I should have done it much better. Also I should have got to know my father, which would have been a joy to me.... I was on the whole considerably discouraged by my school days. Except in Fencing, in which I had won the Public School Championship, I had achieved no distinction. All my contemporaries and even younger boys seemed in every way better adapted to the conditions of our little world. They were far better both at the games and at the lessons. It is not pleasant to feel oneself so completely outclassed and left behind at the very beginning of the race.

WINSTON CHURCHILL
A roving commission: My early life

Although posthumously diagnosing someone with a learning disability can be unreliable (see Adelman & Adelman, 1987), Churchill's writings (see p. 159) certainly reflect someone with a learning disability on several counts. (See West, 1997, for a detailed analysis of Churchill's learning disabilities.) The struggle Churchill experienced illustrates the frustration felt by virtually all students with learning disabilities, no matter what their particular problems. Even though they may be no less intelligent than their nondisabled classmates, such students have learning difficulties in school. Churchill's feelings of low self-esteem remind us of the many persons with learning disabilities who suffer similarly. He also demonstrates the wide intraindividual differences characterized by such individuals. Churchill was obviously highly skilled, if not gifted, in reading and expressing himself in the English language, but he was woefully inadequate in Latin and mathematics. Finally, and perhaps most important, he was able to capitalize on his strengths to become one of the most highly acclaimed statesmen in the world. Although such achievements should not give false hope to those with learning disabilities, many of whom struggle all their lives with their learning problems, they do underscore the fact that some with learning disabilities are able to achieve fruitful and productive lives.

Professionals, too, have been frustrated by the problems presented by students with learning disabilities. Some of the most intense battles in all of special education have been waged over issues related to educating students with learning disabilities. We can attribute much of the reason for this professional turmoil to two factors:

1. The enigma of children who are not retarded but who have severe academic problems has often led parents of these children, as well as professionals, to seek quick-and-easy "miracle" cures. We now recognize that in most cases learning disability is a lifelong condition with which a person must learn to cope.

2. The field of learning disabilities is a relatively new category of special education, having been recognized by the federal government in 1969. It is also now the largest category, constituting over half of all students identified as eligible for special education. Much professional and popular media exposure has focused on this rapidly expanding category, creating a hotbed in which controversies can ferment.

Although the field of learning disabilities has had to struggle to overcome its penchant for questionable practices and to survive the intense scrutiny of professionals and the lay public, most who work within this field are happy to be part of it. For them, controversy and ambiguity only add excitement to the already challenging task of educating students with learning disabilities.

One controversy that has nagged the field for some time is that of defining learning disabilities. In the next section we look at several common definitions and the criteria they use.

Definitions

At a parents' meeting in New York City in the early 1960s, Samuel Kirk proposed the term *learning disabilities* as a compromise because of the confusing variety of labels then used to describe the child with relatively normal intelligence who was

misconceptions
about Persons with Learning Disabilities

myth IQ–achievement discrepancies are easily calculated.

fact A complicated formula determines a discrepancy between a student's IQ and his or her achievement.

myth All students with learning disabilities are brain damaged.

fact Many authorities now refer to students with learning disabilities as having central nervous system (CNS) *dysfunction*, which suggests a malfunctioning of the brain rather than actual tissue damage.

myth The fact that so many definitions of *learning disabilities* have been proposed is an indicator that the field is in chaos.

fact Although there have been at least eleven definitions proposed at one time or another, professionals have settled on two—the federal definition and the National Joint Committee on Learning Disabilities definition. And although they differ in some ways, these two definitions have a lot in common.

myth The rapid increase in the prevalence of learning disabilities is due solely to sloppy diagnostic practices.

fact Although poor diagnostic practices may account for some of the increase, there are plausible social/cultural reasons for the increase. In addition, there is evidence that school personnel may "bend" the rules to identify students as learning disabled instead of the more stigmatizing identification of "mentally retarded."

myth We know very little about what causes learning disabilities.

fact Although there is no simple clinical test for determining the cause of learning disabilities in individual cases, recent research strongly suggests causes related to neurological dysfunction resulting from genetic, teratogenic, or medical factors.

myth Standardized achievement tests are the most useful kind of assessment for teachers of students with learning disabilities.

fact Standardized achievement tests do not provide much information about *why* a student has achievement difficulties. Formative, informal, and authentic assessment give teachers a better idea of the particular strengths and weaknesses of a student.

myth Math disabilities are relatively rare.

fact Math disabilities are second only to reading as an area of academic difficulty for students with learning disabilities.

myth We need not be concerned about the social-emotional well-being of students with learning disabilities because their problems are in academics.

fact Many students with learning disabilities also develop problems in the social-emotional area.

myth Most children with learning disabilities outgrow their disabilities as adults.

fact Learning disabilities tend to endure into adulthood. Most individuals with learning disabilities who are successful must learn to cope with their problems and make extraordinary efforts to gain control of their lives.

Educators have struggled to formulate a clear and comprehensive definition of the term *learning disability*, which generally describes children of seemingly normal intelligence who, nevertheless, have learning problems.

having learning problems. Such a child was likely to be referred to as *minimally brain injured*, a *slow learner, dyslexic* (a severe impairment in the ability to read), or *perceptually disabled*.

Many parents as well as teachers, however, believed the label "minimal brain injury" to be problematic. **Minimal brain injury** refers to individuals who show behavioral but not neurological signs of brain injury. They exhibit behaviors (e.g., distractibility, hyperactivity, and perceptual disturbances) similar to those of people with real brain injury, but their neurological examinations are indistinguishable from those of nondisabled individuals.

Historically, the diagnosis of minimal brain injury was sometimes dubious because it was based on questionable behavioral evidence rather than on more solid neurological data. Moreover, minimal brain injury was not an educationally meaningful term because such a diagnosis offered little real help in planning and implementing treatment. The term *slow learner* described the child's performance in some areas but not in others—and besides, intelligence testing indicated that the ability to learn existed. *Dyslexic*, too, fell short as a definitive term because it described only reading disabilities, and many of these children had problems in other academic areas such as math. To describe a child as *perceptually disabled* just confused the issue further, for perceptual problems might be only part of a puzzling inability to learn. So the New York parents' group finally agreed on the educationally oriented term *learning disabilities*. Accordingly, they founded the Association for Children with Learning Disabilities, now known as the Learning Disabilities Association of America. A few years later, following the lead of the parents, professionals and the federal government officially recognized the term as well.

The interest in learning disabilities evolved as a result of a growing awareness that a large number of children were not receiving needed educational services. Because they were within the normal range of intelligence, these children did not qualify for placement in classes for children with retardation. And although many of them did show inappropriate behavior disturbances, some of them did not. Thus, it was felt that placement in classes for students with emotional disturbance was inappropriate. Parents of children who were not achieving at their expected potential—children who are learning disabled—wanted their children's academic achievement problems corrected.

minimal brain injury. A term used to describe a child who shows behavioral but not neurological signs of brain injury; the term is not as popular as it once was, primarily because of its lack of diagnostic utility (i.e., some children who learn normally show signs indicative of minimal brain injury).

Factors to Consider in Definitions of Learning Disabilities

Eleven different definitions of learning disabilities have enjoyed some degree of acceptance since the field's inception in the early 1960s (Hammill, 1990). Created by individual professionals and committees of professionals and lawmakers, each definition provides a slightly different slant. Four factors—each of which is included in some definitions, but not all—have historically caused considerable controversy:

1. IQ–achievement discrepancy
2. Presumption of central nervous system dysfunction
3. Psychological processing disorders
4. Learning problems not due to environmental disadvantage, mental retardation, or emotional disturbance

We discuss these factors briefly and then present the two most commonly used definitions.

IQ–Achievement Discrepancy.   A child with an **IQ–achievement discrepancy** is not achieving up to potential as usually measured by a standardized intelligence test. Professionals have used a number of methods to determine such a discrepancy. For many years they simply compared the mental age obtained from an intelligence test to the grade-age equivalent taken from a standardized achievement test. A difference of two years was often considered enough to indicate a learning disability. Two years below expected grade level is not equally serious at different grade levels, however. For example, a child who tests two years below grade 8 has a less severe deficit than one who tests two years below grade 4. So professionals have developed formulas that take into account the relative ages of the students.

Although some states and school districts have adopted different formulas for identifying IQ–achievement discrepancies, many authorities have advised against their use. Some of the formulas are statistically flawed and lead to inaccurate judgments, and those that are statistically adequate are difficult and expensive to implement. Furthermore, they give a false sense of precision. That is, they tempt school personnel to reduce to a single score the complex and important decision of identifying a learning disability.

In addition to the problem of using formulas, some authorities have objected to using an IQ–achievement discrepancy to identify learning disabilities on other conceptual grounds. (See Aaron, 1997, for a review of this research.) For example, some authorities have pointed out that IQ is not a very strong predictor of reading ability. And IQ scores of students with learning disabilities are subject to underestimation because performance on IQ tests is dependent on reading ability, to some extent. In other words, students with poor reading skills have difficulty expanding their vocabularies and learning about the world. As a result, they obtain lower-than-average scores on IQ tests, which lessens the discrepancy between IQ and achievement. Finally, some educators have pointed out that the idea of discrepancy is practically useless in the earliest elementary grades. In the first or second grade, a child is not expected to have achieved very much in reading or math, so it would be difficult to find a discrepancy.

Even with all these problems, many professionals still subscribe to the notion that an IQ–achievement discrepancy is an important characteristic of students

IQ–achievement discrepancy. Academic performance markedly lower than would be expected based on a student's intellectual ability.

with learning disabilities. The support for this notion is probably based on the observation that there continue to be children who have normal intelligence yet do not achieve up to their expected performance. Perhaps the most reasonable position, however, is not to use the IQ–achievement discrepancy as the sole criterion for determining a learning disability (Kavale, 1995) and to shy away from the use of formulas to calculate discrepancies.

Central Nervous System (CNS) Dysfunction. Many of the theoretical concepts and teaching methods associated with the field of learning disabilities grew out of work done in the 1930s and 1940s with children who were mentally retarded and brain injured (Werner & Strauss, 1941). When the field of learning disabilities was emerging, professionals noted that many of these children displayed behavioral characteristics similar to those exhibited by children known to have brain damage (e.g., distractibility, hyperactivity, language problems, perceptual disturbances).

In the case of most children with learning disabilities, however, there is little neurological evidence of physical brain damage. At one time, some professionals were content to attribute brain damage to children with learning disabilities on the basis of behavioral characteristics alone. More recently, there has been a trend away from considering a child to be brain damaged unless the results from a neurological examination provide unquestionable evidence. The term *dysfunction* has come to replace *injury* or *damage*. Thus, a child with learning disabilities is now more likely to be referred to as having central nervous system dysfunction than brain injury. The change in terminology reflects the awareness of how hard it is to diagnose brain damage. Dysfunction does not necessarily mean tissue damage; instead, it signifies a malfunctioning of the brain, or central nervous system.

Psychological Processing Disorders. The field of learning disabilities was founded on the assumption that children with such disabilities have deficits in the ability to perceive and interpret visual and auditory stimuli—that is, they have *psychological processing problems*. These problems are not the same as the visual and auditory acuity problems evidenced in blindness or deafness. Rather, they are difficulties in organizing and interpreting visual and auditory stimuli.

Researchers have found that many students with learning disabilities do indeed have such information-processing problems (see Hallahan, 1975, for a review). Many of the early advocates of this viewpoint, however, also believed that training students in visual- and auditory-processing skills in isolation from academic material would help them conquer their reading problems (Frostig & Horne, 1964; Kephart, 1971; Kirk & Kirk, 1971). For instance, such training might involve finding and tracing figures embedded within other lines or connecting dots as they are drawn on a chalkboard by a teacher.

Researchers ultimately determined that these perceptual and perceptual-motor exercises did not result in benefits for students' reading achievement (see Hallahan & Cruickshank, 1973, for a review); thus, very few teachers use these practices today.

Environmental Disadvantage, Mental Retardation, or Emotional Disturbance. Most definitions of learning disability exclude those children whose learning problems stem from environmental disadvantage, mental retardation, or emotional disturbance. The belief that such an exclusion clause is necessary attests to how difficult it can sometimes be to differentiate between some

Much of the research on learning disabilities has focused on psychological processing problems, or deficits in the ability to perceive and interpret visual and auditory stimuli.

of these conditions. There is ample evidence, for example, that children from disadvantaged backgrounds are more apt to exhibit learning problems, and students with mental retardation or emotional disabilities often display some of the same behavioral characteristics as pupils who are learning disabled. Most definitions assume that children with learning disabilities have intrinsic learning problems because of a central nervous system dysfunction, thus ruling out the environment as the primary causal factor. These definitions state that learning disabilities can occur along with environmental disadvantage, mental retardation, or emotional disturbance, but for children to be considered learning disabled, their learning problems must be primarily the result of their learning disabilities.

We turn now to two of the most popular definitions: The federal definition and the National Joint Committee for Learning Disabilities definition.

The Federal Definition

The majority of states use a definition based on the definition of the federal government (Mercer, Jordan, Allsopp, & Mercer, 1996). This definition, first signed into law in 1977, was—with a few minor wording changes—adopted again in 1997 by the federal government:

A. GENERAL—The term "specific learning disability" means a disorder in one or more of the basic psychological processes involved in understanding or in using language, spoken or written, which disorder may manifest itself in an imperfect ability to listen, think, speak, read, write, spell, or do mathematical calculations.

B. DISORDERS INCLUDED—Such term includes such conditions as perceptual disabilities, brain injury, minimal brain dysfunction, dyslexia, and developmental aphasia.

C. DISORDERS NOT INCLUDED—Such term does not include a learning problem that is primarily the result of visual, hearing, or motor disabilities, of mental retardation, of emotional disturbance, or of environmental, cultural, or economic disadvantage. [Individuals with Disabilities Education Act Amendments of 1997, Sec. 602(26), p. 13.]

The National Joint Committee for Learning Disabilities (NJCLD) Definition

The National Joint Committee on Learning Disabilities (NJCLD), made up of representatives of several professional organizations, has issued an alternative definition:

Learning disabilities is a general term that refers to a heterogeneous group of disorders manifested by significant difficulties in the acquisition and use of listening, speaking, reading, writing, reasoning, or mathematical abilities. These disorders are intrinsic to the individual, presumed to be due to central nervous system dysfunction, and may occur across the life span. Problems in self-regulatory behaviors, social perception and social interaction may exist with learning disabilities but do not by themselves constitute a learning disability.

Although learning disabilities may occur concomitantly with other handicapping conditions (for example, sensory impairment, mental retardation, serious emotional disturbance) or with extrinsic influences (such as cultural differences, insufficient or inappropriate instruction), they are not the result of those conditions or influences. (National Joint Committee on Learning Disabilities, 1989, p. 1)

Similarities and Differences in the Federal and NJCLD Definitions

There are some important similarities in the federal and NJCLD definitions. Both view central nervous system dysfunction as a potential cause; specify that listening, speaking, reading, writing, and math can be affected; and exclude learning problems due primarily to other conditions (e.g., mental retardation, emotional disturbance, cultural differences).

There are also some important differences between the two definitions. The authors of the NJCLD definition point out that it does not use the phrase *basic psychological processes*, which has been so controversial (because such processes are not observable and hence difficult to measure), and does not mention perceptual handicaps, dyslexia, or minimal brain dysfunction, which have been so difficult to define (Hammill, Leigh, McNutt, & Larsen, 1981). Furthermore, the NJCLD definition clearly states that a learning disability may be a lifelong condition.

The federal government's conceptualization of learning disabilities also stresses the notion of an IQ–achievement discrepancy, as discussed earlier. Although such a discrepancy is not part of the definition, the federal regulations for identifying learning disabilities refer to a severe discrepancy between intellectual ability and academic achievement.

Prevalence

According to figures kept by the U.S. government, the public schools have identified as learning disabled between 5 and 6 percent of students six to seventeen years of age. Learning disabilities is by far the largest category of special education. More than half of all students identified by the public schools as needing special education are learning disabled. The size of the learning disabilities category has more than doubled since 1976–1977, when prevalence figures first started being kept by the federal government.

Many authorities maintain that the rapid expansion of the learning disabilities category reflects poor diagnostic practices. They believe that children are being overidentified, that teachers are too quick to label students with the slightest learning problem as "learning disabled" rather than entertain the possibility that their teaching practices are at fault. Some, however, argue that the claim of overidentification has been exaggerated and that there are logical explanations for some of the increase in students with learning disabilities. Some have pointed to social/cultural changes that have raised children's vulnerability to developing learning disabilities (Hallahan, 1992). For example, an increase in poverty has placed children at greater risk for biomedical problems, including central nervous system dysfunction (Baumeister, Kupstas, & Klindworth, 1990). The number of children living in poverty, for example, has grown by 15 to 19 percent since the 1970s (U.S. Department of Education, 1997). Furthermore, even families who are not in poverty are under more stress than ever before, which takes its toll on the time children have for concentrating on their schoolwork and on their parents' ability to offer social support.

Still others maintain that there is a causal relationship between the decrease in the numbers of students being identified as mentally retarded and the increase in the numbers of students being identified as learning disabled. There is suggestive evidence that school personnel, when faced with a student who could qualify as mentally retarded, often "bend" the rules to apply the label of "learning disabilities" rather than the more stigmatizing label of "mental retardation" (MacMillan, Gresham, & Bocian, 1998).

Boys outnumber girls by about three to one in the learning disabilities category (U.S. Department of Education, 1992). Some researchers have suggested that the prevalence of learning disabilities among males is due to their greater biological vulnerability. The infant mortality rate for males is higher than that for females, and males are at greater risk than females for a variety of biological abnormalities. Other researchers have contended, however, that the higher prevalence of learning disabilities among males may be due to referral bias. They suggest that academic difficulties are no more prevalent among boys than among girls, but that boys are more likely to be referred for special education when they do have academic problems because of other behaviors that bother teachers, such as hyperactivity. Research on this issue is mixed (Clarizio & Phillips, 1986; Leinhardt, Seewald, & Zigmond, 1982; Shaywitz, Shaywitz, Fletcher, & Escobar, 1990). So at this point, it is probably safest to conclude that

> some bias does exist but that the biological vulnerability of males also plays a role. For example, the federal government's figures indicate that all disabilities are more prevalent in males, including conditions that are difficult to imagine resulting from referral or assessment bias, such as hearing impairment (53% are males), orthopedic impairment (54% are males), and visual impairment (56% are males). (Hallahan, Kauffman, & Lloyd, 1999, pp. 31–32)

Causes

In many cases, the cause of a child's learning disabilities remains a mystery. For years many professionals suspected that neurological factors were a major cause of learning disabilities. Not all agreed, however, because the evidence for a neurological cause was based on relatively crude neurological measures. In recent years researchers have begun to harness advanced technology to assess brain activity more accurately. The most recent technology being used by researchers to document neurological dysfunction in some persons with learning disabilities includes **computerized axial tomographic (CAT) scans, magnetic resonance imaging (MRI), functional magnetic resonance imaging (fMRI),** and **positron emission tomography (PET) scans.**

- A CAT scan involves placing the patient's head in a large ring and then taking a series of X rays. The X rays are then fed into a computer that plots a series of pictures of the brain (see Figure 5.1).
- An MRI uses radio waves instead of radiation to create cross-sectional images of the brain.
- A fMRI is an adaptation of the MRI. Unlike an MRI or PET scan, it is used to detect changes in brain activity while a person is engaged in a task, such as reading.
- A PET scan, like an fMRI, is used while the person is performing a task. The subject is injected with a substance containing a low amount of radiation,

computerized axial tomographic (CAT) scans. A neuroimaging technique whereby X rays of the brain are compiled by a computer to produce a series of pictures of the brain.

magnetic resonance imaging (MRI). A neuroimaging technique whereby radio waves are used to produce cross-sectional images of the brain; used to pinpoint areas of the brain that are dysfunctional.

functional magnetic resonance imaging (fMRI). An adaptation of the MRI used to detect changes in the brain while it is in an active state; unlike a PET scan, it does not involve using radioactive materials.

positron emission tomography (PET) scans. A computerized method for measuring bloodflow in the brain; during a cognitive task, a low amount of radioactive dye is injected in the brain; the dye collects in active neurons, indicating which areas of the brain are active.

which collects in active neurons. Using a scanner to detect the radioactive substance, researchers can tell which parts of the brain are actively engaged during various tasks.

Using CAT scans and MRIs, researchers have found evidence for a neurological cause in some cases of learning disabilities (Hynd, Marshall, & Gonzalez, 1991; Kushch et al., 1993; Willis, Hooper, & Stone, 1992). Using PET scans and fMRIs, investigators have also found differences in brain metabolism between persons with severe reading disabilities and those who are not disabled (Flowers, 1993; Flowers, Wood, & Naylor, 1991; Gross-Glenn et al., 1991; Hagman et al., 1992; Shaywitz et al., 1998). For example, using fMRIs one team of researchers found that different areas of the brain were activated during reading tasks for adults with dyslexia versus nondyslexics (Shaywitz et al., 1998). See Figure 5.2.

Taken as a whole, these studies are not definitive evidence of a neurological basis for all students identified as learning disabled. Some researchers have noted that, for the most part, the studies have been conducted on individuals with severe learning disabilities. The results, however, have turned many who were formerly skeptical into believers that central nervous system dysfunction may be the cause of many cases of learning disabilities.

Even in cases in which one can be fairly certain that the person with learning disabilities has neurological dysfunction, the question still remains: How did he or she come to have the neurological dysfunction? Possible reasons fall into three general categories: (1) genetic, (2) teratogenic, and (3) medical factors.

Genetic Factors

Over the years, evidence has accumulated that learning disabilities can be inherited. The two most common types of studies used to look at the genetic basis of learning disabilities are familiality studies and heritability studies.

Familiality studies examine the degree to which a certain condition, such as a learning disability, occurs in single family (i.e., the tendency for it to "run in a family"). Researchers have found that about 35 to 45 percent of first-degree relatives of persons with reading disabilities—that is, the immediate birth family (parents and siblings)—have reading disabilities (Hallgren, 1950; Olson, Wise, Conners, Rack, & Fulker, 1989; Pennington, 1990). The same degree of familiality has also been found in families of people with speech and language disorders (Beichtman, Hood, & Inglis, 1992; Lewis, 1992) and spelling disabilities (Schulte-Korne, Deimel, Muller, Gutenbrunner, & Remschmidt, 1996).

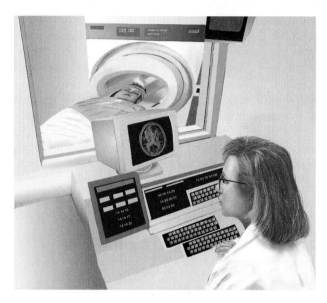

Figure 5.1

The operator views computer-generated pictures of the brain during a CAT scan procedure.

familiality studies. A method of determining the degree to which a given condition is inherited; looks at the prevalence of the condition in relatives of the person with the condition.

heritability studies. A method of determining the degree to which a condition is inherited; a comparison of the prevalence of a condition in identical (i.e., monozygotic, from the same egg) twins versus fraternal (i.e., dizygotic, from two eggs) twins.

teratogens. Agents, such as chemicals, that can disrupt the normal development of the fetus; a possible cause of learning disabilities and other learning and behavioral problems.

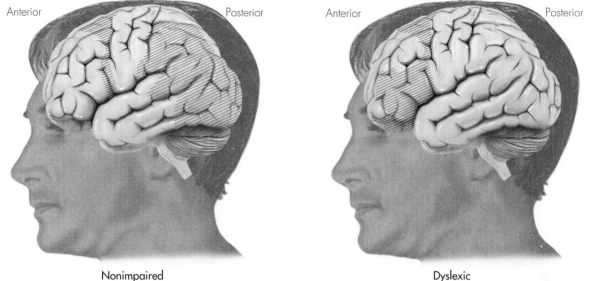

Nonimpaired   Dyslexic

Figure 5.2

The shaded areas represent the parts of the brain that are activated the most in persons with dyslexia versus those without dyslexia when they engage in reading tasks requiring analysis of phonological features—the ability to identify which sounds go with which letters to make up words.

Source: Adapted from Figure 3 of Shaywitz, S. E., Shaywitz, B. A., Pugh, K. R., Fulbright, R. K., Constable, R. T., Mencl, W. E., Shankweiler, D. P., Liberman, A. M., Skudlarski, P., Fletcher, J. M., Katz, L., Marchione, K. E., Lacadie, C., Gatenby, C., & Gore, J. C. (1998). Functional disruption in the organization of the brain for reading in dyslexia. *Proceedings of the National Academy of Sciences, 95,* 2636–2641.

The tendency for learning disabilities to run in families may also be due to environmental factors. For example, it is possible that parents with learning disabilities may pass on their disabilities to their children through their childrearing practices. Given this, a more convincing method of determining whether learning disabilities are inherited is **heritability studies**—comparing the prevalence of learning disabilities in identical (*monozygotic,* from the same egg) versus fraternal (*dizygotic,* from two eggs) twins. Researchers have found that identical twins are more concordant than fraternal twins for reading disabilities and speech and language disorders (DeFries, Gillis, & Wadsworth, 1993; Lewis & Thompson, 1992). In other words, if an identical twin and a fraternal twin each have a learning disability, the second identical twin is more likely to have a learning disability than the second fraternal twin.

There have also been studies attempting to pinpoint the precise gene or genes involved in learning disabilities. Although there is some research implicating genes located on chromosomes 6, 7, and 15, this evidence is only suggestive at this time (Cardon et al., 1994; DeFries et al., 1993; Fisher, Vargha-Khadem, Watkins, Monaco, & Pembrey, 1998; Grigorenko et al., 1997).

Teratogenic Factors

Teratogens are agents that can cause malformations or defects in the developing fetus. In Chapter 4, we discussed fetal alcohol syndrome and lead as two potential causes of mental retardation. Authorities have also speculated that some people may be exposed to levels of these substances that are not high enough to result in mental retardation but do meet a threshold high enough to cause learning disabilities.

Medical Factors

There are several medical conditions that can have such a negative impact on children that they develop learning disabilities. Again, many of these can also result in mental retardation, depending on the severity of the condition. For example, premature birth places children at risk for neurological dysfunction. And pediatric AIDS can also result in neurological damage such that learning disabilities result.

Assessment

Four types of assessment are popular in the field of learning disabilities:

1. Standardized assessment
2. Formative assessment
3. Informal teacher assessment
4. Authentic assessment

Standardized Assessment

Standardized assessment means that the measure has been administered to a large group so that any one score can be compared to the norm, or average. We discuss two types of standardized assessment—achievement tests and a rating scale for identifying learning disabilities.

Standardized Achievement Tests.
Teachers and psychologists commonly use standardized achievement tests with students who are learning disabled because achievement deficits are the primary characteristic of these students. Several standardized achievement tests are currently in use. For example, the Wechsler Individual Achievement Test (WIAT) (The Psychological Corporation, 1992), assesses achievement in all the areas pertaining to the federal definition of learning disabilities: basic reading, reading comprehension, spelling, written expression, mathematics reasoning, numerical operations, listening comprehension, and oral expression. The developers of the WIAT designed the test so it could be used in conjunction with the Wechsler Intelligence Scale for Children (WISC) in order to look for discrepancies between achievement and ability.

The Learning Disabilities Diagnostic Inventory (LDDI).
Teachers can use the LDDI (Hammill & Bryant, 1998) to rate students in six areas identified with most definitions of learning disabilities: listening, speaking, reading, writing, mathematics, and reasoning. Table 5.1 lists sample items from the LDDI.

One limitation to most standardized instruments is that they cannot be used to gain much insight into *why* students have difficulty. Teachers and clinicians use these tests primarily to identify students with learning problems and to provide gross indicators of academic strengths and weaknesses.

The notion of using assessment information to help plan educational strategies has gained much of its popularity from professionals working in the area of learning disabilities. Three methods of assessment—formative assessment, informal teacher assessment, and authentic assessment—are better suited to the philosophy that evaluation is more useful to teachers if it can be translated into educational recommendations. We discuss each in following sections.

Formative Assessment

Formative assessment directly measure a student's behavior to keep track of his or her progress (Choate, Enright, Miller, Poteet, & Rakes, 1995; Deno, 1985; Fuchs,

standardized assessment. A method of evaluating a person that has been applied to a large group so that an individual's score can be compared to the norm, or average.

formative assessment. Measurement procedures used to monitor an individual student's progress; they are used to compare how an individual performs in light of his or her abilities, in contrast to standardized tests, which are primarily used to compare an individual's performance to that of other students.

Table 5.1 — Sample Items from the Learning Disabilities Diagnostic Inventory

		FREQUENTLY			SOMETIMES			RARELY		
		1	2	3	4	5	6	7	8	9
Scale I: Listening	• Has difficulty discriminating among speech sounds. • Confuses simple nouns. • Asks the teacher to repeat directions.									
Scale II: Speaking	• Has slow or labored speech • Is slow to retrieve words. • Has difficulty speaking spontaneously.									
Scale III: Reading	• Has poor memory for letters and words. • Makes errors when reading unfamiliar words aloud. • Cannot break a word into syllables.									
Scale IV: Writing	• Writes awkwardly. • Omits words in sentences. • Spells poorly.									
Scale V: Mathematics	• Does not remember number words or digits. • Disregards decimals. • Has difficulty with word problems.									
Scale VI: Reasoning	• Does not move easily from one idea to another. • Is inconsistent in thinking and makes illogical arguments. • Generalizes with difficulty.									

Source: Hammill, D. D., & Bryant, B. R. (1998). *Learning Disabilities Diagnostic Inventory.* Austin, TX: Pro-Ed.

1986; Fuchs & Fuchs, 1986). Formative evaluation is less concerned with how the student's performance compares with that of other students and more concerned with how the student performs in light of his or her abilities. Although there are a variety of formative evaluation models, at least five features are common to all of them:

1. The assessment is usually done by the child's teacher, rather than a school psychologist or diagnostician.
2. The teacher assesses classroom behaviors directly. For instance, if the teacher is interested in measuring the student's pronunciation of the letter *l*, he or she looks at that particular behavior and records whether the child can pronounce that letter.
3. The teacher observes and records the student's behavior frequently and over a period of time. Most other kinds of tests are given once or twice a year at the most. In formative evaluation, performance is measured at least two or three times a week.
4. The teacher uses formative evaluation to assess the pupil's progress toward educational goals. After an initial testing, the teacher establishes goals for the student to reach in a given period of time. For example, if the student

can orally read 25 words correctly in one minute out of a certain book, the teacher may set a goal, or criterion, of being able to read 100 words correctly per minute after one month. This aspect of formative evaluation is sometimes referred to as *criterion-referenced testing*.

5. The teacher uses formative evaluation to monitor the effectiveness of educational programming. For instance, in the preceding example, if after a few days the teacher realizes it is unlikely that the child will reach the goal of 100 words, the teacher can try a different educational intervention.

Curriculum-Based Assessment. One particular model of formative evaluation is **curriculum-based assessment (CBA)**. Although it draws heavily on earlier research, CBA was largely developed by Deno and his colleagues (Deno, 1985; Fuchs, Deno, & Mirkin, 1984).

Because it is a type of formative evaluation, CBA has the five features just listed. In addition, it has two other distinguishing characteristics:

1. It is designed to measure students' performances on the particular curriculum to which they are exposed. In spelling, for example, a typical CBA assessment strategy is to give children two-minute spelling samples, using dictation from a random selection of words from the basal spelling curriculum. The number of words or letter sequences correctly spelled serves as the performance measure. In math, the teacher may give students two minutes to compute samples of problems from the basal text and record the number of digits computed correctly. Proponents of CBA state that this reliance on the curriculum is an advantage over commercially available standardized achievement tests, which are usually not keyed to the curriculum in any particular school.

2. CBA compares the performance of students with disabilities to that of their peers in their own school or school division. Deno and his colleagues suggest that the teacher take CBA measures on a random sample of nondisabled students so this comparison can be made. Comparison with a local reference group is seen as more relevant than comparison with the national norming groups used in commercially developed standardized tests.

Informal Teacher Assessment

A common method of assessment used by teachers is to ask students to work on their academic assignments and take note of what they do well and where they have difficulty. In the area of reading, for example, teachers can use an **informal reading inventory (IRI)**, a series of reading passages or word lists graded in order of difficulty. The teacher has the student read from the series, beginning with a list or passage that is likely to be easy for the student. The student continues to read increasingly more difficult lists or passages while the teacher monitors his or her performance. After the results of the IRI have been compiled, the teacher can use them to estimate the appropriate difficulty level of reading material for the student.

In using an IRI or other means of informal assessment, the teacher can also do an error analysis of the student's work (Lopez-Reyna & Bay, 1997). Sometimes referred to as miscue analysis, an **error analysis** is a way of pin-

---

curriculum-based assessment (CBA). A formative evaluation method designed to evaluate performance in the particular curriculum to which students are exposed; usually involves giving students a small sample of items from the curriculum in use in their schools; proponents argue that CBA is preferable to comparing students with national norms or using tests that do not reflect the curriculum content learned by students.

informal reading inventory (IRI). A method of assessing reading in which the teacher has the student read progressively more difficult series of passages or word lists; the teacher notes the difficulty level of the material read and the types of errors the student makes.

error analysis. An informal method of teacher assessment that involves the teacher noting the particular kinds of errors a student makes when doing academic work.

Teachers may use the results of informal reading inventories (IRIs) in designing instructional interventions for students.

pointing particular areas in which the student has difficulty. In reading, for example, it might show that the student typically substitutes one vowel for another or omits certain sounds when reading aloud.

Authentic Assessment

Some educators question the authenticity of typical test scores—especially those from standardized tests—asserting that they do not reflect what students do in situations in which they work with, or receive help from, teachers, peers, parents, or supervisors. The purpose behind **authentic assessment** is to assess students' critical-thinking and problem-solving abilities in real-life situations.

Portfolios. An example of authentic assessment is portfolios. **Portfolios** are a collection of samples of a student's work done over time. Portfolios purportedly provide broader-based evidence of students' work (Taylor, 1997). For example, the following might be included:

- Essays or other writing samples, such as letters, instructions, or stories
- Oral discourse, such as recitations, speeches, or oral responses to questions
- Exhibitions, including recitals or other performances
- Experiments and their results or reports (Hallahan, Kauffman, & Lloyd, 1999, p. 110)

Portfolio assessment, however, is more difficult and time consuming than many educators realize (Hallahan et al., 1999). Knowing what to include and how to evaluate it can be challenging. For example, some products, such as written stories, lend themselves more readily to inclusion in portfolios than others, such as oral reading or storytelling. The latter may require videotaping or audiotaping of a student's performance.

authentic assessment. A method that evaluates a student's critical-thinking and problem-solving ability in real-life situations in which he or she may work with or receive help from peers, teachers, parents, or supervisors.

portfolios. A collection of samples of a student's work done over time; a type of authentic assessment.

Psychological and Behavioral Characteristics

Before discussing some of the most common characteristics of persons with learning disabilities, we point out two important features of this population: Persons with learning disabilities exhibit a great deal of interindividual and intraindividual variation.

Interindividual Variation

In any classroom of students with learning disabilities, some will have problems in reading, some will have problems in math, some will have problems in spelling, some will be inattentive, and so on. One term for such interindividual variation is *heterogeneity*. Although heterogeneity is a trademark of children from all the categories of special education, the old adage "No two are exactly alike" is particularly appropriate for students with learning disabilities.

The broad range of disabilities has made it extremely difficult for teachers and researchers to work with and study students with learning disabilities. Teachers have found it difficult to plan educational programs for the diverse group of children they find in their classrooms. Researchers have been faced with the uncertainty of knowing whether inconsistent results from study to study are indeed real or are caused by variations in children selected for one study versus another.

Intraindividual Variation

In addition to differences among one another, children with learning disabilities also tend to exhibit variability within their own profiles of abilities. For example, a child may be two or three years above grade level in reading but two or three years behind grade level in math. Such uneven profiles account for references to specific learning disabilities in the literature on learning disabilities. Some children have specific deficits in just one or a few areas of achievement or development.

Some of the pioneers in the field of learning disabilities alerted colleagues to what is termed *intraindividual* variation. Samuel Kirk was one of the most influential in advocating the notion of individual variation in students with learning disabilities. He developed the Illinois Test of Psycholinguistic Abilities, which purportedly measured variation in processes important for reading. Researchers ultimately found that Kirk's test did not measure processes germane to reading (Hallahan & Cruickshank, 1973; Hammill & Larsen, 1974), and the test is rarely used today. Nonetheless, most authorities still recognize intraindividual differences as a feature of many students with learning disabilities.

We now turn to a discussion of some of the most common characteristics of persons with learning disabilities.

Academic Achievement Problems

Academic deficits are the hallmark of learning disabilities. By definition, if there is no academic problem, a learning disability does not exist.

Reading. Reading poses the most difficulty for most students with learning disabilities. Most authorities believe that this problem is related to deficient language skills, especially **phonological awareness**—the ability to understand the rules of how various sounds go with certain letters to make up words (Lyon & Moats, 1997). It is easy to understand why problems with phonology would be at the heart of many reading difficulties. If a person has problems breaking words into their component sounds, he or she will have trouble learning to read.

Even though phonological problems may be the cause of many reading problems, there is mounting evidence that a small proportion of reading problems may be due to difficulty in processing the *orthographic,* or visual, information from letters (Stanovich, 1991). It is still too early to tell how significant visual/orthographic problems are for persons with reading disabilities.

Written Language. People with learning disabilities often have problems in one or more of the following areas: handwriting, spelling, and composition (Hallahan et al., 1999). Although even the best students can have less-than-perfect handwriting, the kinds of problems manifested by some students with learning disabilities are much more severe. These children are sometimes very slow writers and their written products are sometimes illegible. Spelling can be a significant problem because of the difficulty (noted in the previous section) in understanding the correspondence between sounds and letters.

In addition to the more mechanical areas of handwriting and spelling, students with learning disabilities also frequently have difficulties in the more creative aspects of composition (Englert, 1992; Laughton & Morris, 1989; Montague & Graves, 1992; Montague, Graves, & Leavell, 1991). For example, compared to nondisabled peers, students with learning disabilities:

- Use less complex sentence structures and include fewer types of words
- Write paragraphs that are less well organized
- Include fewer ideas in their written products
- Write stories that have fewer important components, such as introducing main characters, setting scenes, describing a conflict to be resolved (Hallahan et al., 1999, p. 398)

Spoken Language. Many students with learning disabilities have problems with the mechanical (Mann, Cowin, & Schoenheimer, 1989; Vellutino, 1987) and social uses of language (Bryan & Bryan, 1986; Mathinos, 1988). Mechanically, they have trouble with **syntax** (grammar), **semantics** (word meanings), and, as we have already noted, **phonology** (the ability to break words into their component sounds and blend individual sounds together to make words).

With regard to social uses of language—commonly referred to as **pragmatics**—students with learning disabilities are often inept in the production and reception of discourse. In short, they are not very good conversationalists. They are unable to engage in the mutual give-and-take that conversations between individuals require.

For instance, conversations of individuals with learning disabilities are frequently marked by long silences because they do not use the relatively subtle strategies that their nondisabled peers do to keep conversations going. They are not skilled at responding to others' statements or questions and tend to answer their own questions before their companions have a chance to respond. They tend to make task-irrelevant comments and make those with whom they talk

phonological awareness. The ability to understand grapheme-phoneme correspondence—the rules by which sounds go with letters to make up words; generally thought to be the reason for the reading problems of many students with learning disabilities.

syntax. The way words are joined together to structure meaningful sentences (i.e., grammar).

semantics. The study of the meanings attached to words.

phonology. The study of how individual sounds make up words.

pragmatics. The study within psycholinguistics of how people use language in social situations; emphasizes the functional use of language, rather than mechanics.

uncomfortable. In one often-cited study, for example, children with and without learning disabilities took turns playing the role of host in a simulated television talk show (Bryan, Donahue, Pearl, & Sturm, 1981). Analysis of the verbal interactions revealed that in contrast to nondisabled children, children with learning disabilities playing the host role allowed their nondisabled guests to dominate the conversation. Also, their guests exhibited more signs of discomfort during the interview than did the guests of nondisabled hosts. In a similar study, students were asked to assume an Ann Landers–type role and to give advice to others (Hartas & Donahue, 1997). Students with learning disabilities exhibited difficulty in generating solutions to interpersonal problems.

Math. Although disorders of reading, writing, and language have traditionally received more emphasis than problems with mathematics, the latter are now gaining a great deal of attention. Authorities now recognize that math difficulties are second only to reading disabilities as an academic problem area for students with learning disabilities. In one large-scale study of over 1,000 students with learning disabilities, for example, the average math score was at about the 30th percentile (Kavale & Reese, 1992). The types of problems these students have include difficulties with computation of math facts (Cawley, Parmar, Yan, & Miller, 1998) as well as word problems (Cawley & Parmar, 1992); trouble with the latter is often due to the inefficient application of problem-solving strategies.

Perceptual, Perceptual-Motor, and General Coordination Problems

Studies indicate that some children with learning disabilities exhibit visual and/or auditory perceptual disabilities (see Hallahan, 1975, and Willows, 1998, for reviews). A child with visual perceptual problems might, for example, have trouble solving puzzles or seeing and remembering visual shapes, or he or she might have a tendency to reverse letters (e.g., mistake a *b* for a *d*). A child with auditory perceptual problems might have difficulty discriminating between two words that sound nearly alike (e.g., *fit* and *fib*) or following orally presented directions.

Teachers and parents have also noted that some students with learning disabilities have difficulty with physical activities involving motor skills. They de-

The term pragmatics refers to the social uses of language. Individuals with learning disabilities who have problems with pragmatics may find it difficult to carry on conversations.

scribe some of these children as having "two left feet" or "ten thumbs." The problems may involve both fine motor (small motor muscles) and gross motor (large motor muscles) skills. Fine motor skills often involve coordination of the visual and motor systems.

As we noted earlier, several early theorists in the learning disabilities field believed that by training visual-perceptual skills in isolation from academic material, students with learning disabilities would read better. However, researchers have shown that such training does not improve reading ability (see Hallahan & Cruickshank, 1973, for a review).

Disorders of Attention and Hyperactivity

Students with attention problems display such characteristics as distractibility, impulsivity, and hyperactivity. Teachers and parents of these children often characterize them as being unable to stick with one task for very long, failing to listen to others, talking nonstop, blurting out the first things on their minds, and being generally disorganized in planning their activities in and out of school.

Individuals with learning disabilities often have attention problems (Hallahan, Kauffman, & Lloyd, 1999), and they are often severe enough to be diagnosed as having **attention deficit hyperactivity disorder (ADHD)**. ADHD, characterized by severe problems of inattention, hyperactivity, and/or impulsivity, is a diagnosis made by a psychiatrist or psychologist, using criteria established by the American Psychiatric Association (1994). (See Chapter 6 for a full discussion of ADHD.) Although estimates vary, researchers have consistently found an overlap of 10 to 25 percent between ADHD and learning disabilities (Forness & Kavale, in press).

Memory, Cognitive, and Metacognitive Problems

We discuss memory, cognitive, and metacognitive problems together because they are closely related. A person who has problems in one of these areas is likely to have problems in the other two as well. Parents and teachers are well aware that students with learning disabilities have problems remembering such things as assignments and appointments. In fact, they often exclaim in exasperation that they can't understand how a child so smart could forget things so easily. And early researchers in learning disabilities documented that many students with learning disabilities have a real deficit in memory (Hallahan, 1975; Hallahan, Kauffman, & Ball, 1973; Swanson, 1987; Torgesen, 1988; Torgesen & Kail, 1980).

Students with learning disabilities have problems that affect at least two types of memory: **short-term memory (STM)** and **working memory (WM)** (Ashbaker & Swanson, 1996). Problems with STM involve difficulty recalling information shortly after having seen or heard it. A typical STM task requires a person to repeat a list of words presented visually or aurally. Problems with WM affect a person's ability to keep information in mind while simultaneously doing another cognitive task. Trying to remember an address while listening to instructions on how to get there is an example of WM. STM appears to be critical for the early stages of learning to read, such as decoding single words, and WM is relatively more important for later reading skills, such as comprehension (Ashbaker & Swanson, 1996).

attention deficit hyperactivity disorder (ADHD). A condition characterized by severe problems of inattention, hyperactivity, and/or impulsivity; often found in persons with learning disabilities.

short-term memory. The ability to recall information after a short period of time.

working memory. The ability to remember information while also performing other cognitive operations.

Researchers have found that one of the major reasons that children with learning disabilities perform poorly on memory tasks is that, unlike their nondisabled peers, they do not use strategies. For example, when presented with a list of words to memorize, most children will rehearse the names to themselves. They will also make use of categories by rehearsing words in groups that go together. Students with learning disabilities are not likely to use these strategies spontaneously.

The deficiency in the use of strategies on memory tasks also indicates that children with learning disabilities demonstrate problems in cognition. **Cognition** is a broad term covering many different aspects of thinking and problem solving. Students with learning disabilities often exhibit disorganized thinking that results in problems with planning and organizing their lives at school and at home.

Closely related to these cognitive problems are problems in metacognition. **Metacognition** has at least three components—the ability to: (1) recognize task requirements, (2) select and implement appropriate strategies, and (3) monitor and adjust performance (Butler, 1998).

Regarding the first component—ability to recognize task requirements—students with learning disabilities frequently have problems judging how difficult tasks can be. For example, they may approach the reading of highly technical information with the same level of intensity as reading for pleasure.

An example of problems with the second component—ability to select and implement appropriate strategies—is when students with learning disabilities are asked questions such as, "How can you remember to take your homework to school in the morning?" they do not come up with as many strategies (e.g., writing a note to oneself, placing the homework by the front door) as students without disabilities.

An example of the third component of metacognition—ability to monitor or adjust performance—is comprehension monitoring. **Comprehension monitoring** refers to the abilities employed while one reads and attempts to comprehend textual material. Investigators have found that many students with reading disabilities have problems, for example, in being able to sense when they are not understanding what they are reading (Butler, 1998). Good readers are able to sense this and make necessary adjustments, such as slowing down and/or rereading difficult passages. Students with reading problems are also likely to have problems picking out the main ideas of paragraphs. Good readers spend more time and effort focusing on the major ideas contained in the text they read.

Social-Emotional Problems

Although not all, perhaps not even a majority, of children with learning disabilities have significant social-emotional problems, they do run a greater risk than their nondisabled peers of having these types of problems. For those who do experience behavioral problems, the effects can be long-lasting and devastating. In their early years they are often rejected by their peers and have poor self-concepts (Bryan, 1998). And in adulthood, the scars from years of rejection can be painful and not easily forgotten (McGrady & Lerner, in press).

One plausible reason for the social problems of some students with learning disabilities is that they have deficits in social cognition. That is, they misread social cues and may misinterpret the feelings and emotions of others. Most children, for example, are able to tell when their behavior is bothering others. Students with learning disabilities sometimes act as if they are oblivious to the effect their behavior is having on their peers. They also have difficulty taking the perspective of others, of putting themselves in someone else's shoes.

cognition. The ability to solve problems and use strategies; an area of difficulty for many persons with learning disabilities.

metacognition. One's understanding of the strategies available for learning a task and the regulatory mechanisms needed to complete the task.

comprehension monitoring. The ability to keep track of one's own comprehension of reading material and to make adjustments to comprehend better while reading; often deficient in students with learning disabilities.

It may also be that some of these behavioral characteristics of children with learning disabilities annoy others and/or make it difficult for others to interact with them. For example, if a child with learning disabilities has problems with conversational skills, he or she may have difficulty acquiring and maintaining friendships.

Social-skills deficits are among the most difficult to remediate. In fact, many teachers agree that it is easier to improve the academic problems than the social-skills problems of students with learning disabilities. One approach that researchers have found effective is the interpersonal problem-solving intervention of Sharon Vaughn and her colleagues (Vaughn & Sinagub, 1998). See the box on p. 180.

Motivational Problems

Another source of problems for many persons with learning disabilities is their motivation, or feelings about their abilities to deal with life's many challenges and problems. People with learning disabilities may appear content to let events happen without attempting to control or influence them. These individuals have what is referred to as an *external,* rather than an *internal,* **locus of control.** In other words, they believe their lives are controlled by external factors such as luck or fate, rather than by internal factors such as determination or ability (Hallahan, Gajar, Cohen, & Tarver, 1978; Short & Weissberg-Benchell, 1989). People with this outlook sometimes display **learned helplessness:** a tendency to give up and expect the worst because they think that no matter how hard they try, they will fail (Seligman, 1992).

What makes these motivational problems so difficult for teachers, parents, and individuals with learning disabilities to deal with is the interrelationship between cognitive and motivational problems (Montague, 1997). A vicious cycle develops: The student learns to expect failure in any new situation, based on past experience. This expectancy of failure, or learned helplessness, may then cause him or her to give up too easily when faced with a difficult or complicated task. As a result, not only does the student fail to learn new skills; he or she also has another bad experience, reinforcing feelings of helplessness and even worthlessness—and so the cycle goes.

The Child with Learning Disabilities as an Inactive Learner with Strategy Deficits

Many of the psychological and behavioral characteristics we have described can be summed up by saying that the student with learning disabilities is an inactive learner, lacking in strategies for attacking academic problems (Hallahan & Bryan, 1981; Hallahan & Reeve, 1980; Torgesen, 1977). Specifically, research describes the student with learning disabilities as someone who does not believe in his or her own abilities (learned helplessness), has an inadequate grasp of what strategies are available for problem solving (poor metacognitive skills), and has problems producing appropriate learning strategies spontaneously.

The practical implications of this constellation of characteristics is that students with learning disabilities may have difficulties working independently. They are not likely to be "self-starters." Assignments or activities requiring them to work on their own may cause problems, unless the teacher carefully provides an appropriate amount of support. Homework, for example, is a major problem for many students with learning disabilities (Bryan, Nelson, & Mathur, 1995;

locus of control. A motivational term referring to how people explain their successes or failures; people with an internal locus of control believe they are the reason for success or failure, whereas people with an external locus of control believe outside forces influence how they perform.

learned helplessness. A motivational term referring to a condition in which a person believes that no matter how hard he or she tries, failure will result.

An Interpersonal Problem-Solving Intervention

Social skills need to be considered in light of the family, school, environment, classroom, peers, and other relevant issues. Fundamental to this perspective is the belief that teaching social skills in isolation is unlikely to provide significant and long-lasting change. A social strategy training program emphasizing a problem-solving approach has been developed and evaluated by Vaughn and colleagues (McIntosh, Vaughn, & Bennerson, 1995: Vaughn & Lancelotta, 1990: Vaughn et al., 1988; Vaughn et al., 1991). The following procedures outline this model:

1. A school-wide sociometric assessment is performed where each student rates her or his same-sex classmates on the extent to which he or she would like to be friends with them.
2. Students who receive few "friendship" votes and many "no friendship" votes form the rejected group; students with many friendship and few no friendship votes comprise the popular group.
3. Social skills trainers for each participating class include a rejected student with LD and a highly accepted NLD classmate.
4. The social skills trainers are removed from their classrooms several times (e.g., 2–3) each week for approximately 30 minutes each session to learn specific social skills strategies.
5. The first social skills strategy taught is the FAST strategy. The four steps associated with FAST follow (McIntosh et al., 1995):
    a. FREEZE AND THINK! Do not act too quickly. Stop and think: What is the problem?
    b. ALTERNATIVES? What are all of my possible solutions?
    c. SOLUTION EVALUATION. What are the likely consequences of each solution. What would happen next if I do . . . ? Select the best solution(s) for the long run as well as the short run.
    d. TRY IT! What do I need to do to implement the solution? If it does not work, what else can I try?
6. In addition to the FAST strategy, social skills trainers are taught to address solutions in terms of long-run and short-run consequences, and to accept negative feedback by learning the SLAM strategy (McIntosh et al., 1995). Coaching and role-playing are used to promote understanding of the lessons and to practice skills. The four components of the SLAM strategy follow:
    a. STOP! Stop whatever you're doing.
    b. LOOK! Look the person in the eye.
    c. ASK! Ask the person a question to clarify what she or he means.
    d. MAKE! Make an appropriate response to the person.
7. While social skills trainers are learning the social strategies, a problem-solving box (e.g., a decorated shoe box) is put into every classroom. This box is used by all of the students in the classroom to write problems they have with other children, at home, on the playground, and so on. The teacher and social skills trainers explain to the class that the purpose of the problem-solving box is to ask questions about problems they have in the classroom, on the playground, and at home. Problems submitted by students are used by social skills trainers and the entire class to practice their social problem-solving skills and for discussion.
8. After the social skills trainers have learned a particular strategy (e.g.. FAST) and rehearsed it using real-life problems, they present the strategy to their classmates with backup and support from the researcher and classroom teacher.
9. In subsequent weeks, the social skills trainers leave the classroom for only one session per week, and review the skill strategy (e.g., FAST) with classmates at least once per week. These reviews include large-group explanations and small-group problem-solving exercises using the problems from the problem-solving box.
10. Social skills trainers are recognized in front of their classes or schools by the principal. Social skills trainers wear special buttons while at school that indicate that they are social skills trainers for that school. Students in the school are asked to consult these social skills trainers when they have interpersonal difficulties.

Source: Vaughn, S., & Sinagub, J. (1998). Social competence of students with learning disabilities: Interventions and issues. In B. Y. L. Wong (Ed.), *Learning about learning disabilities* (2nd ed., pp. 453–487). San Diego, CA: Academic Press.

Epstein, Polloway, Foley, & Patton, 1993; Epstein et al., 1997). Students' difficulties range from failing to bring home their homework, to being distracted while doing homework, to forgetting to turn in their homework. With the general trend toward increasing homework demands, teachers and parents are often in a quandary about how to accommodate students who are having problems with homework (see the box on p. 182).

Educational Considerations

In this section we consider two major approaches to alleviating the academic problems of students with learning disabilities—cognitive training and Direct Instruction (DI)—as well as service delivery models. Although we look at these approaches individually, in practice they are often combined. In fact, research strongly supports the effectiveness of using cognitive training and DI in combination (Swanson & Hoskyn, in press).

Cognitive Training

The approach termed **cognitive training** involves three components: (1) changing thought processes, (2) providing strategies for learning, and (3) teaching self-initiative. Whereas behavior modification focuses on modifying observable behaviors, cognitive training is concerned with modifying unobservable thought processes, prompting observable changes in behavior. Cognitive training has proven successful in helping a variety of academic problems for many students with learning disabilities (Hallahan et al., 1999).

Authorities give at least two reasons as to why cognitive training is particularly appropriate for students with learning disabilities. Namely, it aims at helping them overcome:

1. Cognitive and metacognitive problems, by providing them with specific strategies for solving problems
2. Motivational problems of passivity and learned helplessness, by stressing self-initiative and involving them as much as possible in their own treatment

A variety of specific techniques and approaches fall under the heading of cognitive training. Here we present two fairly specific techniques—self-instruction and mnemonic strategies—and one general approach, self-regulated strategy development.

Self-Instruction. **Self-instruction** was one of the first cognitive training techniques to be developed. The idea of self-instruction is to make students aware of the various stages of problem-solving tasks while they are performing them and to bring behavior under verbal control (Meichenbaum, 1975; Meichenbaum & Goodman, 1971). All this is usually done gradually. Typically, the teacher first models the use of the verbal routine while solving the problem. Then he or she closely supervises the students using the verbal routine while doing the task, and then the students do it on their own.

One study using self-instruction as an integral feature of instruction involved fifth- and sixth-grade students with learning disabilities solving math word problems (Case, Harris, & Graham, 1992). The five-step strategy the students learned to use involved saying the problem out loud, looking for important words and circling them, drawing pictures to help explain what was happening, writing the math sentence, and writing the answer. Furthermore, students were prompted to use the following self-instructions:

cognitive training. A group of training procedures designed to change thoughts or thought patterns.

self-instruction. A type of cognitive training technique that requires individuals to talk aloud and then to themselves as they solve problems.

Homework: A Major Problem for Students with Learning Disabilities

The combination of calls for higher standards in the schools by general education reformers and for increased inclusion of students who are learning disabled by special education reformers has not mixed well in all respects. One of the problem areas is homework. Unfortunately, a generally passive approach to learning and difficulty in working independently make it hard for many students with learning disabilities to tackle homework. As one parent has put it, "Homework has dominated and ruined our lives for the past eight years" (Baumgartner, Bryan, Donahue, & Nelson, 1993, p. 182).

Many authorities on homework believe that teachers should use it primarily for having students practice proficiency in skills they already possess, rather than for learning new skills. This dictum would appear even more crucial for students with learning disabilities, who are so frequently characterized by their inability to work independently. Asking students to acquire new information during homework only puts students with learning disabilities further behind their peers and jeopardizes the goal of mainstreaming.

Students themselves have definite preferences regarding teachers' homework practices. The following are ratings by middle school students with learning disabilities, from most to least preferred (Nelson, Epstein, Bursuck, Jayanthi, & Sawyer, 1998). (Interestingly, nondisabled students had virtually the same preferences.)

Preferences Rated Above the Mean, or Average

- Give assignments that are finished in school
- Allow extra-credit assignments

- Grade assignments according to effort
- Begin assignments in class and check for understanding
- Give assignments that can be completed without any help
- Allow turn-in of assignments after the due date
- Give more reminders about due dates
- Allow a small group of students to work together to complete assignments

Preferences Rated Below the Mean, or Average

- Give shorter, more frequent assignments
- Give extra help with assignments
- Arrange for another student to help with assignments
- Require use of an assignment notebook
- Allow oral rather than written answers
- Give fewer assignments than given to other students
- Grade assignments easier than other students
- Give different assignments than given to other students

Although it might be tempting to discount students' opinions, figuring they would naturally look for shortcuts, some of the reasons they give for their choices are enlightening. One could discount their first preference as defeating the whole purpose of homework, but they provide some interesting reasons for this choice. For example, many said they would prefer to have assignments they can complete at school because they could get help there more readily. And from the practices they prefer least, it is evident that they do not wish to be singled out or appear different.

1. *Problem definition:* "What do I have to do?"
2. *Planning:* "How can I solve this problem?"
3. *Strategy use:* "The five-step strategy will help me look for important words."
4. *Self-evaluation:* "How am I doing?"
5. *Self-reinforcement:* "Good job. I got it right."

An example of self-instruction used for spelling involved having a boy (1) say the word out loud, (2) say the first syllable of the word, (3) name each of the letters in the syllable three times, (4) say each letter as he wrote it, and (5) repeat steps 2 through 4 for each succeeding syllable (Kosiewicz, Hallahan, Lloyd, & Graves, 1982).

Franklin Pierce (purse)
14 (forking)

Figure 5.3

Mnemonic representation of Franklin Pierce, fourteenth
President of the United States.
Source: Adapted from Mastropieri, M. A., Scruggs, T. E., & Whedon,
C. (1997). Using mnemonic strategies to teach information about U.S.
Presidents: A classroom-based investigation. *Learning Disability
Quarterly, 20,* 13–21. Copyright 1994 by Thomas E. Scruggs and
Margo A Mastropieri.

Mnemonic Strategies. The purpose of **mnemonic strategies** is to develop a more concrete way of taking in information so that it will be easier to remember. By making abstract information more concrete, students are better able to re-member content in a variety of subjects, such as English, history, science, and for-eign languages. Several different types of mnemonic strategies have been used successfully with students ranging from early elementary school to secondary school (Mastropieri & Scruggs, 1998). For example, middle schoolers with learn-ing disabilities used a mnemonic strategy to learn the order of the presidents of the United States (Mastropieri, Scruggs, & Whedon, 1997). Each president was portrayed by a drawing with two components—one associated with his name and one associated with the order of his presidency. For example, for George Washington, the first president, the drawing depicted someone *washing* (Wash-ington) and *buns* (one). For Franklin Pierce, the fourteenth president, the draw-ing showed a *purse* (Pierce) and a *fork* "forking" the purse (see Figure 5.3).

Self-Regulated Strategy Development (SRSD). Developed by Graham and Harris and their colleagues, self-regulated strategy development (SRSD) com-bines several cognitive training techniques, including self-instruction, goal setting, self-monitoring, and scaffolded instruction. Researchers have found SRSD effective in teaching reading comprehension and writing (Graham, Harris, MacArthur, & Schwartz, 1998; Johnson, Graham, & Harris, 1997; Sexton, Harris, & Graham, 1998; Swanson & De La Paz, 1998). As the name implies, goal setting involves having students set goals for themselves. **Self-monitoring,** discussed more fully in Chapter 6, involves students keeping track of their own behavior. In **scaffolded in-struction,** assistance is provided to students when they are first learning tasks and then is gradually reduced, so that eventually students do the tasks independently. For example, in one study, the teacher modeled a three-step strategy for writing, saying the steps aloud:

1. *Think,* who will read this, and why am I writing it?
2. *Plan* what to say using *TREE* (note *Topic* sentence, note *Reasons, Exam-ine* reasons, note *Ending*).
3. *Write* and *Say More.* (Sexton et al., 1998, p. 300)

While modeling the strategy, the students and teacher discussed various aspects of it, and the students gradually memorized the strategy and implemented it on their own.

mnemonic strategies. Cogni-tive training strategies used to help children with mem-ory problems remember cur-riculum content; the teacher transforms abstract informa-tion into a concrete picture that depicts the material in a more meaningful way.

self-monitoring. A type of cognitive training technique that requires individuals to keep track of their own behavior.

scaffolded instruction. A cognitive approach to in-struction in which the teacher provides temporary structure or support while students are learning a task; the support is gradually re-moved as the students are able to perform the task independently.

success stories
special educators at work

San Francisco, CA: Like many students across the country, eleven-year-old **Eliot Danner** attends a private school that does not provide any special education services. His parents had to look elsewhere for specialized training to help him learn to read. They found that help with special educators Nancy Cushen White and Mia Callahan Russell.

Eliot met Nancy Cushen White, a clinical faculty member at the University of California at San Francisco and a learning specialist for the San Francisco City Schools, in the summer before second grade, when he first attended an intense special education program designed to address language disabilities. Up to that point, perceptually oriented therapies had been tried with Eliot, but without clear success. Everyone knew he had trouble reading, but no one was sure what to do about it.

Since kindergarten, Eliot has attended independent schools designed for high academic achievers, not for students with learning disabilities. In the early grades, he had passionate interests and easily memorized stories read to him, but for all his curiosity and interest, Eliot could not read by himself. A psychological evaluation identified problems with spatial orientation, word attack, spelling, and composition skills. After one year of tutoring in phonological awareness to complement his school's whole-language approach, Eliot was still anxious and unsure if he would ever learn to read. "We needed to respond to that, or we feared we would lose him as a reader," says his mother, Nancy Pietrefesa.

Eliot's parents considered enrolling him in another school but kept him in place following an assessment that suggested he would do best in this challenging but relaxed atmosphere. Says Nancy Cullen White, "This wasn't a question of settings but of strategies. Eliot is a child with dyslexia who needed to learn how to read."

"Teaching kids with learning disabilities is not a casual engagement," says Nancy Pietrefesa. She believes her son's success began the summer he met Nancy White and Mia Callahan Russell, both teachers trained to address language disabilities. They could accurately describe Eliot's problems, clearly articulate his strengths and weaknesses, and prescribe intense remedial instruction. Through that process, Eliot assumed greater control and self-acceptance. He began to understand himself as a reader.

It was Nancy White who specifically described his problem:

Scaffolded instruction is supported by Russian psychologist Lev Vygotsky's theory that children learn from their elders in ways that are similar to how apprentices learn their crafts from masters. Although it is far from a panacea (see Pressley, Hogan, Wharton-McDonald, Mistretta, & Ettenberger, 1996, and Stone, 1998, for critical reviews), many instructional theorists have found scaffolding to be an important component of cognitive instruction.

Direct Instruction

Direct Instruction. A method of teaching academics, especially reading and math; emphasizes drill and practice and immediate feedback; lessons are precisely sequenced, fast-paced, and well-rehearsed by the teacher.

The **Direct Instruction (DI)** method focuses on the details of the instructional process. Advocates of Direct Instruction stress a systematic analysis of the concept to be taught, rather than analysis of the characteristics of the student. A critical component of DI is task analysis. **Task analysis** involves breaking down academic problems into their component parts so that teachers can teach the parts

Eliot does not have a weakness in any one modality. He has great difficulty with auditory, visual, and kinesthetic integration, particularly in association with his long-term visual memory. In the summer of 1992, his phonological awareness was poor and he was not able to segment syllables into individual sounds for spelling or to blend sounds into syllables for decoding. In addition, he had difficulties with visual discrimination and both short-term and long-term visual memory for words. Unable to rely on his memory, it all became a jumble when he had to write things down.

That July, eight-year-old Eliot began an intensive regimen of language training and educational therapy that has paid off. Along with a group of ten other students from public and private schools, he attended a three-week summer program for three-and-one-half hours of daily direct instruction in language skills. Says Nancy White, "What some folks learn on their own, these kids need to be taught."

Getting students to think through the process of language is the program's goal. Skills are taught in specific sequence to foster automatic use, and students are given the rationale so they can see how the rules of the English language fit together. "There is emphasis on repetition and practice, much like in sports or in music," says Nancy Pietrefesa. "Have you ever seen how football coaches make kids practice plays over and over?"

Nancy White trains teachers to keep sessions lively. Emphasis is on the active student, self-checking and always thinking. "Nobody should just sit!" she says. "Success hinges on developing the simultaneous association of hearing, saying, seeing, and writing. Students are taught there is a system and they can use it!"

According to Eliot, it was all "fiddle-faddle" until the end of the first summer, when he began to see himself improve. "He was immersed daily," says his mother, "and this intense immersion is what enabled him to see the fruits of his labors." To keep up this pace for grades two and three, a creative schedule was developed with Eliot's private school. Monday through Thursday, he attended classes from 9 to 12 and was tutored at home daily for two and a half hours. He was present for a full day on Friday. Teacher Mia Russell was trained by Nancy White as an educational therapist, and her intensive tutorial work with Eliot was tailored specifically to his individual patterns and errors. After several summers of training, in the fourth grade, Eliot worked with Mia eight hours a week in a room provided for them at his school. The sessions were reduced to three hours a week in grade five. "The staff at the school is very cooperative," says Mia. "They see Eliot as a bright, articulate student who needs specific interventions they are not equipped to offer."

Eliot has worked hard to become an expert on how he learns, and he is eager to start sixth grade. "He has really knocked himself out," says his mom. He is an independent learner, conscious of which strategies he needs to follow to get to what he wants to know. Says Eliot, "Learning that stuff is not fun, but it works!"

—By Jean Crockett

---

separately and then teach the students to put the parts together in order to demonstrate the larger skill.

A variety of DI programs are available for reading, math, and language (Engelmann, Carnine, Engelmann, & Kelly, 1991; Engelmann, Carnine, Johnson, & Meyers, 1988, 1989). These programs consist of precisely sequenced, fast-paced lessons taught to small groups of four to ten. There is a heavy emphasis on drill and practice. The teacher teaches from a well-rehearsed script, and pupils follow the lead of the teacher, who often uses hand signals to prompt participation. The teacher offers immediate corrective feedback for errors and praise for correct responses.

Direct Instruction programs are among the most well-researched commercial programs available for students with learning disabilities. Use of these programs not only results in immediate academic gains but may also bring long-term academic gains (see Lloyd, 1988, for a review of this research).

task analysis. The procedure of breaking down an academic task into its component parts for the purpose of instruction; a major feature of Direct Instruction.

Collaboration key to success

Myla Young Burgess is a learning disabilities specialist; B.S., Communication Disorders, Hampton University; M.Ed., University of North Carolina at Greensboro. **Laura Clark Miles** is a fourth-grade teacher; B.A., Music Education, Longwood College; Elementary certification; M.A., Educational Psychology, University of Virginia.

Myla Young Burgess

Myla Two years ago, Pat Parrot, Chesterfield County's collaborative teaching program facilitator, introduced me to collaborative teaching. She explained that collaborative teaching was an additional service delivery model that would help bridge the gap between special education and regular education.

As my students with learning disabilities experienced difficulties in mainstreaming, it became evident that I should try collaborative teaching. I began by attending a three-day workshop. My principal, Wes Hicks, attended on the day designated for administrators and teachers. After the workshop, he and I agreed we should try collaborative teaching on a small scale at the fourth-grade level.

My first step was to select a co-teacher. I learned in the workshop that co-teachers should choose to work collaboratively and should share common beliefs and goals. With my manual in hand, I excitedly called Laura to ask her to be my co-teacher. She accepted with great enthusiasm. After our principal learned that Laura and I would be co-teaching, he immediately rearranged the fourth-grade rolls so that the five students with learning disabilities we had chosen to participate in the program would all be in Laura's classroom. Having attended the workshop and believing in the philosophy of collaboration, he was more than willing to make these adjustments.

Laura Before the school year started a couple of years ago, Myla called me to tell me about the collaborative teaching

model. She had discussed it with our principal, and plans were under way to implement the program. I was excited by the prospect of participating in this new approach. As a classroom teacher for thirteen years, I had often felt very inadequate in meeting the needs of students with learning disabilities who were mainstreamed into my regular classroom. I was anxious to learn new strategies and techniques to meet their needs.

That September was truly a new beginning for both of us. Our class consisted of five students with learning disabilities and twenty average- to above-average-ability students. We began collaborative teaching using a complementary instruction approach, which allows the general classroom teacher to maintain the primary responsibility for teaching the academic curriculum while the special educator teaches organizational and study skills that students need to master the material. As the year progressed, we moved to a team-teaching approach, which is when the general educator and special educator plan and teach the academic curriculum to all students within the classroom. Under this approach we alternated presenting segments of lessons, with whoever was not teaching being responsible for monitoring student performance and/or behavior. We continued using both approaches throughout the school year.

After Mr. Hicks had closely monitored our classroom the first year and reviewed the progress of all students, he was as committed to this program as we

were. In planning our second year of collaborative teaching, we felt that an increase in collaboration time would better meet the needs of the upcoming fourth-grade students with learning disabilities. To achieve this goal, our first priority was scheduling. Mr. Hicks played a vital role in creating the schedule and determining class size and student placement.

This class consisted of twenty-five students, including ten with learning disabilities, two with language impairment, and thirteen average- to above-average-ability students. We used collaborative teaching for science/social studies, the majority of math, and one hour and fifteen minutes of language arts. All students remained in the regular classroom all day, with the exception of four students with learning disabilities who went to a resource room during language arts. These four students were two or more years below grade level in reading. During this year, we moved almost entirely to the team-teaching approach, with Myla stressing independent learning strategies that benefited all students in the classroom.

Myla We have found several advantages in using the collaborative teaching approach. First, there is more mastery of skills by all students. Two teachers in the classroom allow more individualized help, which enhances mastery of skills. With two teachers, we can give students more instruction, reteaching, and enrichment when needed.

Laura Clark Miles

It is also helpful to have two judgments on assessments, classroom objectives, and lesson presentations. For example, it is good to have two points of view regarding the appropriateness of the format and validity of written tests as well as the appropriateness of alternative assessments for students with disabilities. Sometimes our presentations are not received by students as we had expected. The second teacher can sometimes interpret from a student's point of view what went wrong with the lesson.

We gain from each other's experiences. Each of us is continually attending workshops or classes in our fields. This brings more and more ideas and resources to the classroom. We learn from each other, and the class receives instruction based on the strengths of each of us.

Laura We also have more time to address emotional needs. Students with learning disabilities often have emotional needs that interfere with their academics. With the support of the guidance counselor, school psychologist, and teacher of students with emotional disturbance, individual needs are better met with two teachers in the classroom. For example, while one of us is teaching academics, the other is free to address emotional or attention problems that might interfere, without instruction being interrupted.

Myla Students seem to gain a sense of self-worth and confidence in their own ability by displaying strengths and improving on their weaknesses in a regular

classroom environment. They also have a better sense of belonging because they are with the same students all day and have the same schedule.

Laura Collaborative teaching with flexible groups makes it possible to provide enrichment, practice, reteaching, and teaching at all levels of instruction. Flexible groups means having different groups, determined daily, based on specific instructional and social objectives for a particular day. These groups are set up for cooperative learning activities or station teaching, which is instructional content divided into two parts. Half the group is taught topics such as vocabulary expansion or comprehension. We then switch groups so that all students receive the same instruction. Because it is rare that both of us are absent on the same day, collaborative teaching allows for stability of classroom instruction. Stability of classroom instruction is also increased because there is less time wasted with students traveling to and from the resource room.

We also think that this approach facilitates modeling and the teaching of strategies. We find we draw on each other's strengths to model certain strategies. Myla, because of her training in special education, is familiar with many more strategies. For example, we teach students strategies for paragraph writing, test taking, and a variety of mnemonic strategies.

It has been our experience that this program increases the expectations for students with disabilities. Students' performances have often exceeded our initial expectations. We find it appropriate

> **Students with learning disabilities must know that the expectations held for them are the same as those for regular students.**

to allow students to go as far and as fast as they can. Students with learning disabilities must know that the expectations held for them are the same as those for regular students.

Collaborative teaching also lowers the pupil–teacher ratio. It is very important that the classroom size does not exceed twenty-five students. Too many students create obstacles for a successful program. We believe that students with learning disabilities should not comprise more than half the class and that at least half of the class should be average or above average in ability.

Myla I'd like to describe just one student, who is probably our greatest success story. Mary is a determined and motivated young lady who functions in the low-average range of intellectual ability with skill deficits in visual perception, nonverbal reasoning, and visual-motor integration. She has been in the learning disabilities program since kindergarten. Mary has difficulty with word recognition, word attack, reading comprehension, written language, math concepts, recalling math facts, comprehension of social studies and science concepts, and copying from the board.

As a fourth-grader, Mary's schedule in the morning included science/social studies, which alternated every nine weeks, and math. We taught all these collaboratively. After lunch, she went to the learning disabilities resource room for the remainder of the day for instruction in reading and written language.

We began the school year with many doubts and concerns as to how and to what extent we would be able to meet Mary's needs. Most important, we did not lower our expectations for Mary's performance. Our philosophy was to improve Mary's self-esteem, increase her independence, and have her achieve the highest level of success possible.

Mary far exceeded our original expectations. We worked very closely with her parents, who were very supportive, and the combined effort contributed greatly to her success. Using all the techniques and modifications of the program allowed her to function in the regular classroom, learning the required skills and concepts.

Direct instruction programs, which consist of precisely sequenced, fast-paced lessons taught to small groups of four to ten students, may bring both immediate and long-term academic gains in students with learning disabilities.

Service Delivery Models

For many years, the most common form of educational placement for students with learning disabilities was the resource room. In the mid-1990s, however, in keeping with the trend toward inclusion, the regular classroom surpassed the resource room as the most popular placement. In addition, the number of placements in separate classrooms has gradually diminished (see Figure 5.4).

As we discussed in Chapter 2, more and more schools are moving toward some kind of cooperative teaching arrangement, in which regular and special education teachers work together in the regular classroom. Some believe this model is particularly appropriate for students with learning disabilities, since it allows them to stay in the regular classroom for all or almost all of their instruction.

Because students with learning disabilities make up the largest category of special education and because their academic and behavioral problems are not as severe as those of students with mental retardation or behavior disorders, they are often candidates for full inclusion. However, all the major professional and

Figure 5.4

Percentage of students with learning disabilities, ages 6–21, served in different educational environments during 1992–1993, 1993–1994, 1994–1995.

Sources: U.S. Department of Education (1995, 1996, 1997). *Seventeenth, eighteenth, and nineteenth annual reports to Congress on the implementation of the Individuals with Disabilities Education Act.* Washington, DC: Author.

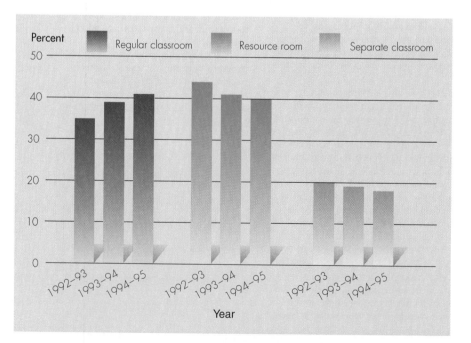

parent organizations have developed position papers against placing *all* students with learning disabilities in full-inclusion settings. And there is evidence that students with learning disabilities themselves prefer resource placements over full inclusion, although many of them also think that inclusion meets their needs (Klingner, Vaughn, Schumm, Cohen, & Forgan, 1998). Research on the effectiveness of inclusion for students with learning disabilities also argues against using full inclusion for all students with learning disabilities (Klingner, Vaughn, Hughes, Schumm, & Elbaum, 1998). In conclusion, evidence indicates that the legal mandate of IDEA requiring the availability of a full continuum of placements is sound policy for students with learning disabilities.

Early Intervention

Very little preschool programming is available for children with learning disabilities because of the difficulties in identifying them at such a young age. When we talk about testing preschool children for learning disabilities, we are really talking about *prediction* rather than *identification* (Keogh & Glover, 1980). In other words, because preschool children do not ordinarily engage in academics, it is not possible, strictly speaking, to say that they are "behind" academically. Unfortunately, all other things being equal, prediction is always less precise than identification.

At least two factors make predicting later learning disabilities particularly difficult at the preschool age:

1. In many cases of learning disabilities, the problems are relatively mild. Many of these children seem bright and competent until faced with a particular academic task, such as reading or spelling. Unlike many other children with disabilities, children with learning disabilities are not so immediately identifiable.
2. It is often difficult to determine what is a true developmental delay and what is merely maturational slowness. Many nondisabled children show slow developmental progress at this young age, but they soon catch up with their peers.

There has been growing sentiment among some professionals not to use the "learning disability" label with preschoolers (Haring et al., 1992). Noting that this label implies deficits in academics, which are not ordinarily introduced until kindergarten or first grade, these professionals favor using more generic labels for preschool children, such as "developmentally delayed" or "at risk." Those who favor using the "learning disability" label argue that the sooner a child's specific problems can be identified, the sooner teachers and parents can make plans for the long-term nature of the condition.

To aid parents and professionals, research is needed on developing better predictive tests at the preschool level. At present, we know that the most accurate predictors are preacademic skills (Foorman, Francis, Shaywitz, Shaywitz, & Fletcher, 1997; Lerner, 1997). **Preacademic skills** are behaviors that are needed before formal instruction can begin, such as identification of numbers, shapes, and colors. A particularly important preacademic skill for reading is phonological awareness, a skill we discussed earlier (see

preacademic skills. Behaviors that are needed before formal academic instruction can begin (e.g., ability to identify letters, numbers, shapes, and colors).

The most accurate predictors of later learning problems are preacademic skills, such as counting and identifying letters, numbers, shapes, and colors.

p. 175). Phonological awareness is the ability to understand the rules by which sounds go with letters to make up words. Nondisabled children generally develop phonological awareness in the preschool years. Preschoolers who exhibit problems in phonological awareness are at risk to have reading disabilities after they enter elementary school.

Transition

Until the late 1970s and early 1980s, relatively little educational programming for students with learning disabilities extended beyond the elementary school years. This attitude of benign neglect probably emanated from the mistaken impression that children with learning disabilities would outgrow them. Although the long-term prognosis for individuals with learning disabilities is generally more positive than that for children with some other disabilities (e.g., behavior disorders), there is still the potential for difficulty. There is a danger, for example, that students with learning disabilities will drop out of school in their teenage years. Also, some run the risk of engaging in delinquent behaviors.

The majority of students with learning disabilities do not engage in delinquent behaviors and/or drop out of school. Nonetheless, their futures can be uncertain. Many adults with learning disabilities have persistent problems in learning, socializing, holding jobs, and living independently (Blackorby & Wagner, 1997; Gerber, 1997; Goldstein, Murray, & Edgar, 1998; Witte, Philips, & Kakela, 1998). And even those individuals who are relatively successful in their transition to adulthood often must devote considerable energy to coping with daily living situations.

For example, in an intensive study of adults with learning disabilities, one of the subjects (S3), an assistant dean of students at a large urban university, found it

> essential that organization and routines remain constant. For example, she recounted that her kitchen is arranged in a specific fashion. Most implements are visible rather than put away because she would not be able to remember where to find them. Once, when her roommate changed the kitchen setup, S3 had great difficulty finding anything, and when she did, she couldn't remember where to return it. She had to reorganize the kitchen to her original plan. When she moved from her home state to the New Orleans area, she kept her kitchen set up in exactly the same way as previously. "I don't know if that's just because I'm stubborn or because it's comfortable."
>
> The need for organization and structure seems to pervade her daily living. She mentioned that she imposes structure on everything from the arrangement of her medicine cabinet to her professional life. She has her work day carefully organized and keeps close track of all her appointments. She has trouble coping with unannounced appointments, meetings or activities. She said that if her work routine is interrupted in such a fashion, "I can't get it together." (Gerber & Reiff, 1991, p. 113)

Factors Related to Successful Transition

How any particular adult with learning disabilities will fare depends on a variety of factors and is difficult to predict. Several researchers have been addressing the topic of what contributes to successful adjustment of adults with learning disabilities (Gerber & Reiff, 1991; Gerber, Ginsberg, & Reiff, 1992; Kavale, 1988;

Murphy, 1992; Reiff & Gerber, 1992; Reiff, Gerber, & Ginsberg, 1997; Spekman, Goldberg, & Herman, 1992). According to successful adults with learning disabilities, the one thing that most consistently sets them apart from their less successful peers is that they have been able to take control of their lives. In interviews with highly successful adults with learning disabilities, researchers have found that:

> As we listened to the highly successful adults in our sample, we were continually reminded of the specific ways that they had reached for control. A noted dentist stated that "I feel most confident when something is in my hands ... when I have total control...." Other comments we heard further substantiate the point about the primacy of control:
>
> "I like to be in control. If things don't work out, okay, but if I lose control, I get terribly anxious."
>
> "Being in control make me most confident."
>
> "I feel the need to control my destiny." (Reiff et al., 1997, pp. 101–102)

Other factors help lead to this sense of control:

- Those who succeed have shown an extraordinary degree of perseverance. As one successful adult asserted, "I've always had a kind of burning feeling ... kind of like being on fire to be successful" (Gerber et al., 1992, p. 480).

- Successful adults with learning disabilities set goals for themselves. As one highly successful individual explained, "Successful people have a plan. You have to have a plan, goals, strategy; otherwise you are flying through the clouds and then you hit the mountain" (Gerber et al., 1992, p. 480).

- Successful individuals have a realistic acceptance of their weaknesses coupled with an attitude of building on their strengths. As one team of researchers concluded, "They seemed to compartmentalize their learning disability and saw it as only one aspect of their identity rather than define themselves entirely by it" (Spekman et al., 1992, p. 167).

- Those who succeed tend to have access to a strong informal network of social support. They have been able to draw on help from parents, husbands, friends, and others at various stages during and after transition to adulthood.

- Adults with learning disabilities are more likely to succeed if they have had intensive and long-term educational intervention (Kavale, 1988). Fortunately, numerous secondary programs are now available for students with learning disabilities, and there has been a blossoming of programs at the college level.

Secondary Programming

Approaches to educating students with learning disabilities at the secondary level differ, depending on whether the goal is to prepare students for college or work. In a college-bound model, for instance, students might receive instruction in content areas (e.g., math, science, foreign language) from general education teachers, and special education teachers consult with these teachers and provide instruction in English/reading courses, survival skills classes, and supervised study halls (Zigmond, 1990).

One team of researchers has proposed the following basic principles for vocationally oriented secondary programming:

- Basic skills instruction, survival skills instruction, academic strategies instruction, and job-related skills must be taught in a vocationally relevant manner....
- Subject matter (i.e., content area) must be integrated with the vocational education curriculum....
- Both in-school mainstream vocational education courses and community-based job experiences must begin in the ninth grade and continue throughout high school....
- Special educators must be responsible for job placement, training, and follow-along before students exit high school....
- Multiple high school re-entry points must be accessible to all youths with learning disabilities, whether they have graduated from high school or not, until they reach age 21. (Grayson, Wermuth, Holub, & Anderson, 1997, pp. 83–85)

Postsecondary Programming

Postsecondary programs include vocational and technical programs as well as community colleges and four-year colleges and universities. More and more individuals with learning disabilities are enrolling in colleges and universities, and more and more universities are establishing special programs and services for these students. One of the major difficulties students with learning disabilities face in the transition from high school to college is the decrease in the amount of guidance provided by adults. Many students find this greater emphasis on self-discipline particularly difficult. The greater demands on writing skills (Gajar, 1989) and note taking also present major problems for many college students with learning disabilities.

Siperstein (1988), believing in a long-range view of programming for college-bound students with learning disabilities, has conceptualized service delivery as consisting of three transitions: (1) high school to college, (2) during college, and (3) college to employment.

During the first stage, high school to college, a major goal is to foster awareness of what college options are available. Because of their frequent experiences with failure, many students with learning disabilities do not aspire to education beyond high school. The emphasis should be on preparing students to make the right choices of colleges as well as on delineating what accommodations they will need in their programs. During this stage, pupils and their families may take advantage of published guides to college programs for students with learning disabilities (Kravets & Wax, 1993; Mangrum & Strichart, 1994; Slovak, 1995; Thomas & Thomas, 1991). Also, students can be made aware of the special accommodations available for students who are learning disabled when they take the Scholastic Aptitude Test (SAT) and the American College Test (ACT).

The second stage of service delivery, which covers the time during college, focuses on enhancing the chances of successfully earning a degree. It includes support services for both academic and social functioning. Section 504 of the Vocational Rehabilitation Act of 1973 (Public Law 93–112) requires that colleges make reasonable accommodations for students with disabilities so that they will not be discriminated against because of their disabilities. Some typical accommodations are extended time on exams, allowing students to take exams in a distraction-free room, providing tape recordings of lectures and books, and assigning volunteer note-takers for lectures.

Another potentially useful skill for college students with learning disabilities can be self-advocacy, the ability to understand one's disability, be aware of one's legal rights, and to communicate one's rights and needs to professors and administrators (Skinner, 1998). Although self-advocacy skills ideally should be taught to students with learning disabilities in secondary school, many students come to college in need of guidance in how to go about advocating for themselves in a confident but nonconfrontational manner.

The third stage, transition from college to employment, is important because even if they survive the rigors of college, many individuals with learning disabilities have difficulties obtaining appropriate employment in the competitive job market. Possible strategies for accomplishing this are workshops for career awareness, job-search strategies, and job-maintenance skills (Siperstein, 1988).

There is little doubt that much remains to be learned about programming effectively for students with learning disabilities at the postsecondary level. However, the field has made great strides in opening windows of opportunity for these young adults. Authorities have noted that many college applicants with learning disabilities attempt to hide their disabilities for fear they will not be admitted (Skinner, 1998). If the burgeoning interest in postsecondary programming for individuals who are learning disabled continues, we may in the near future see the day when students and colleges routinely collaborate to use information concerning students' learning disabilities in planning their programs.

Summary

In the early 1960s, parents and professionals advocated a new category of special education—learning disabilities—to describe individuals who, in spite of normal or near-normal intelligence, have a puzzling array of learning problems. What prompted the creation of this area was the realization that many children with learning problems were not receiving needed educational services.

The four most common factors in definitions of learning disabilities are (1) IQ–achievement discrepancy, (2) presumption of central nervous system (CNS) dysfunction, (3) psychological processing problems, and (4) learning problems not due to environmental disadvantage, mental retardation, or emotional disturbance. The most commonly used definition is that of the federal government, which includes all four factors. Another popular definition, that of the National Joint Committee for Learning Disabilities, does not include psychological processing problems and includes the assertion that learning disabilities may continue into adulthood.

The prevalence of students identified as learning disabled has increased dramatically, more than doubling since 1976–1977. Some believe this growth indicates that teachers are too quick to label students as learning disabled; others argue that social-cultural factors (e.g., increased poverty, increased stress on families) have contributed to the growth of learning disabilities. Boys outnumber girls in the learning disabilities category by three to one; researchers do not agree on the reasons for this difference in prevalence, however.

More and more evidence is accumulating that many persons with learning disabilities have CNS dysfunction. Possible reasons for the CNS dysfunction include genetic, teratogenic, and medical factors.

Practitioners use four general types of assessment with students with learning disabilities: standardized, formative, informal, and authentic assessment. Standardized instruments compare the student with a normative group. Formative evaluation methods have five features: (1) the teacher usually does the assessment; (2) the teacher assesses classroom behaviors directly; (3) the measures are taken frequently and over a period of time; (4) the assessment is done in conjunction with the setting of educational goals; and (5) the teacher uses the assessment information to decide whether the educational program for an individual student is effective. Curriculum-based assessment is a type of formative evaluation. Informal assessment includes having students do academic work in order to analyze where they have problems. Doing an error analysis can help identify what skills need to be remediated. Authentic assessment methods, such as portfolios, evaluate students' critical-thinking and problem-solving abilities in real-life situations.

Persons with learning disabilities exhibit a great deal of inter- and intraindividual variation in their psychological and behavioral characteristics. The interindividual variation is reflected in the heterogeneity of this population. Intraindividual variation means that persons with learning disabilities often have uneven profiles of abilities.

Academic deficits are the hallmarks of learning disabilities. Reading disabilities are often related to poor phonological skills. Students with learning disabilities can also have problems in written or spoken language and math.

Some persons with learning disabilities have problems in perceptual, perceptual-motor, or general coordination. Research has not documented the claim of early theorists that training in these skills would help resolve reading problems.

Persons with learning disabilities often have problems with attention. And some have attentional problems serious enough to also have attention deficit hyperactivity disorder (ADHD).

Many individuals with learning disabilities demonstrate memory deficits. Short-term memory appears to be important for early reading acquisition, and working memory is more important for reading comprehension. They have cognitive problems that lead to disorganization and metacognitive problems that interfere with their ability to recognize task requirements, select and use appropriate strategies, and monitor and adjust performance.

Persons with learning disabilities tend to be rejected by their peers and to have poor self-concepts. In addition, persons with learning disabilities frequently have difficulty being motivated enough to perform. They often have an external locus of control and display learned helplessness.

Some authorities believe that a composite of many of the preceding characteristics indicates that many students with learning disabilities are passive rather than active learners. Many of their problems, such as a propensity to have problems with homework, may be due to this inactive approach to learning.

Educational methods for alleviating the academic problems of students with learning disabilities include cognitive training and Direct Instruction.

Cognitive training focuses on (1) changing thought processes, (2) providing strategies for learning, and (3) teaching self-initiative. Self-instruction and mnemonic strategies are two specific techniques that are examples of cognitive training, and self-regulated strategy development is an example of a general cognitive training approach.

Direct Instruction focuses even more directly on academics than does cognitive training. It concentrates on instructional processes and a systematic task analysis of the concept to be taught, rather than on characteristics of the student.

The regular classroom has surpassed the resource room as the most common placement for students with learning disabilities. Cooperative teaching, in which regular and special education teachers work together in the regular classroom, is gaining in popularity. Students with learning disabilities are often seen as the most likely candidates for full-inclusion programs, although many professional and parent organizations have resisted overuse of this approach.

Most professionals are cautious about establishing programs for children with learning disabilities at the preschool level because it is so hard to predict at that age which children will develop later academic problems. Some prefer to label preschoolers as "at risk" or "developmentally delayed." We do know that certain preacademic skills—such as letter, shape, and color recognition and phonological awareness— are the best predictors of later academic learning.

The importance of educational programming at the secondary level and beyond is underscored by evidence that persons with learning disabilities do not automatically outgrow their problems as adults. Students with learning disabilities are at risk to drop out of school, and evidence suggests a higher prevalence of learning disabilities among juvenile delinquents. The majority who stay in school and do not engage in delinquent behaviors are still at risk of having problems in learning, socializing, holding jobs, and performing daily living skills. The most important factor related to successful transition to adulthood is the ability to take control of one's life. Leading to this sense of control are (1) perseverance, (2) goal setting, (3) realistic acceptance of weaknesses coupled with building on strengths, (4) a supportive social network, and (5) intensive and long-term educational intervention.

Educational programming at the secondary level varies according to whether the goal is preparation for college or work. Service delivery models also differ, depending on the amount and type of instruction delivered by general educators versus special educators.

suggestions
for teaching

Students with Learning Disabilities in General Education Classrooms
By E. Jane Nowacek

As more and more students with mild disabilities are educated exclusively in general education classes, educators acknowledge the importance of individualizing or differentiating instruction (e.g., The 1997–98 Resolutions of the National Education Association; Zigmond et al., 1995). This imperative raises the question: How can classroom teachers differentiate their instruction? One frequently used method is modification. Consider the types and examples of general modifications shown in Table 5.A. We can place these modifications on a continuum (see below) in relation to the curriculum and conceptual level:

Accommodation	Parallel Instruction	Adaptation	Overlapping Instruction
No change in content or conceptual difficulty	No change in content; change in conceptual difficulty	Change in content or conceptual difficulty	Change in content and conceptual difficulty

Informal and ecological assessment along with the contents of the IEP provide a solid basis for determining appropriate modifications for your students with learning disabilities. Key questions you may want to consider as you reflect on possible modifications include (DeBoer & Fister, 1995):

Behavior (Performance) Question: Can the level of cognition be changed? Can, for example, students read for main ideas only or be expected to recall instead of analyze?

Condition Question: Can the amount of time, the setting, the cues, or the circumstances in which the student is to demonstrate learning be changed? For example, can the time be extended, or can oral instead of written assignments be permitted?

Criteria Question: Can the level of competency the student is expected to achieve be altered (e.g., accuracy, mastery, automaticity)? For example, can the number or complexity of ideas on a topic be reduced to accommodate students with learning disabilities?

Product Question: Can the manner in which the student is required to demonstrate understanding be modified? For example, can teachers encourage the use of a word-processing program to complete final written products or allow pictures or drawings to exemplify ideas? Also, can students use manipulatives and/or calculators to complete math problems?

Activity Question: Can the way in which the student participates and completes assignments be altered? Can some assignments, for example, be completed in cooperative groups or with partners, rather than individually?

Examples of specific modifications that address these questions, but do not require changes in curriculum or conceptual level, are plentiful. For example, Wood's (1998) Systematic Approach for Adapting the Learning Environment (SAALE) Model presents modifications to the environment (socioemotional, behavioral, and physical environments); to the instructional environment (lesson plans, techniques, format of content, and media); and to evaluation (student evaluation and grading). The author provides and discusses numerous modifications that you can consider in each of these areas. In addition, Zentall and Stormont-Spurgin's (1995) School Modifications Assessment Checklist presents accommodation categories (i.e., change standards, instructional methods, child involvement, classroom structure, input/output responses, consequences, outside support) and lists individual modifications within each category.

In general, teachers can modify the instructional program in several ways (adapted from Switlick, 1997), including:

Size: Shorten the length of a reading assignment; limit the number of math problems (e.g., assign "evens" or "odds" only).

Time: Lengthen the time allowed to complete an assignment; shorten an activity; divide the activity into two or more parts.

Input: Modify the form of the information given (e.g., use books on tape for students who cannot read the material; provide media and/or graphic organizers to visually represent key concepts; develop cooperative learning groups to support instruction; select computer software programs that allow repetition and practice of skills presented).

Output: Change the form or complexity of the student's response (e.g., allow oral responses, projects, demonstrations instead of written responses; accept drawings, graphs, and charts with explanation).

Conceptual/skill difficulty: Alter the skill or conceptual level (e.g., use high-interest, low-reading-level materials; read for main idea only; require in-depth study by writing a play or composing a song instead of writing a research paper).

Support: Modify the amount of teacher and/or student support available in the classroom (e.g., assign a peer tutor; develop cooperative learning groups; provide cues and strategies that allow students to approach and complete work independently).

Modifying Curriculum

When students with learning disabilities are not able to succeed in the standard curriculum, teachers can adapt the curriculum. One approach to curricular modification is to include IEP goals and objectives as curricular goals. For example, a writing goal in the standard curriculum may become a reading goal for students with learning disabilities, or participation in a cooperative learning group may be a social-skill goal rather than an academic one. In addition, McLaughlin (1993) reports curriculum options for students with special needs that include at least two other adaptations which are reasonable for general education classrooms: learning strategies/study skills curriculum and remedial basic skills curriculum. The first of these options provides students with principles and procedures for approaching and solving academic, social, and learning-to-learn problems. In the second alternative, remedial basic skills curriculum, teachers provide intensive instruction in one or

Table 5.A   Curricular and Instructional Modification

Accommodations

Definition: A modification to the delivery of instruction or method of student performance that does not significantly change the content or conceptual difficulty of the curriculum.

Examples:
- Listening to a taped recording of a novel.
- Circling every other word problem on a math worksheet.
- Providing for oral performance instead of written.

Adaptations

Definition: A modification to the delivery of instruction or method of student performance that changes the content or conceptual difficulty of the curriculum.

Examples:
- Providing picture word cards for key words in a story.
- Using a calculator to complete a math assignment.
- In a story activity the group reports on the main character, plot, subplots, setting, problem, resolution—this student reports on main characters and settings.

Parallel Instruction

Definition: A modification to the delivery of instruction or method of student performance that does not change the content area but does significantly change conceptual difficulty of the curriculum.

Examples:
- Students are reading a story—this student is given a sheet with all or part of the story and asked to circle the A's or perhaps target words.
- Students are completing a math worksheet on fractions—this student is completing a counting from 1 to 10 worksheet.
- Students in citizenship/current events class are orally reading the newspaper and answering questions—this student orally reports three things remembered from listening to the others read.

Overlapping Instruction

Definition: A modification to the student performance expectations while all students take part in a shared activity or delivery of instruction that changes the content area and the conceptual difficulty of the curriculum.

Examples:
- Students are tape recording a rough draft of a play they are creating—this student uses an adaptive switch to activate the recorder and is working on holding up his head for increased amounts of time.
- Students are conducting a chemistry experiment in groups of six—this student is responsible to make sure everyone has a test tube and a worksheet.

Source: Bradley, D. F., King-Sears, M. E., & Tessier-Switlick, D. M. (1997). *Teaching students in inclusive settings: From theory to practice* (p. 240). Boston: Allyn & Bacon. Copyright 1997 by Allyn & Bacon. Reprinted with permission.

more basic skill areas (e.g., reading, mathematics). In the following section, an example is provided of curricular modification using each of these two options. It is important to note that each option may be used to modify other basic skills and content areas.

Written Expression Modification: The Learning Strategies Curriculum When teaching writing, educators often provide opportunities for students to think and talk about their subject before they begin putting their thoughts into words on paper. Teachers also encourage their writers to draft, revise, and edit over an extended period of time and to write for real audiences. Often, however, teachers do not provide strategies that assist students with learning disabilities to address specific aspects of the writing process or specific types of writing assignments. Although there is not one set of strategies that have been developed that will ensure that "learner-authors" write effectively, a learning strategies curriculum may help students with learning disabilities to understand and apply approaches at each step of the writing process. The strategies selected will depend on the individual needs of the students, but as Harris and Graham (1996) point out, modeling, discussion, and collaboration are essential components of any strategy instruction. These ed-

ucators have formalized their recommendations into a six stage process for teachers to follow when introducing and integrating strategy components:

Stage 1: *Develop background knowledge.* During this stage teachers help students to learn necessary preskills in areas related directly to writing (e.g., vocabulary, paragraph development) and to self-regulation (e.g., self instruction in areas relevant to composition, such as teaching an impulsive student to say to himself, "Remember to take my time and go slow").

Stage 2: *Discuss it.* The teacher selects alone, or in collaboration with the student, the specific strategy or set of strategies needed to improve written expression. Together the teacher and learner discuss the importance and benefits of the strategy (or strategies) and the necessity of student effort in learning the strategy. In addition, they discuss the goals of strategy instruction, and the student makes a commitment to master the strategy, which helps to establish motivation as well as purpose. To assist in this process, the student's current performance is discussed, and in order to make goals and progress concrete, the teacher and student may graph student performance on strategy use. As a final step, the teacher describes the writing strategy and discusses with the student how and when to use the strategy.

Stage 3: *Model it.* During this stage teachers model first the writing strategy and then specific types of self-instructions (i.e., things we say to ourselves while we work) that address the individual writer's needs.

Stage 4: *Memorize it.* Here students are expected to memorize the steps in the strategies and the mnemonics used to summarize these steps. This stage is very important for students with learning disabilities who have memory problems.

Stage 5: *Support it.* Teachers support a student's use of strategies in several ways, such as providing prompts, offering guidance, writing collaboratively. As students become more proficient, these supports are withdrawn gradually. Throughout this stage, teachers and students also plan for and begin transfer of the strategy use—for example, by using the strategy in other classrooms.

Stage 6: *Independent performance.* Once students are ready to use strategies independently, plans for maintenance and transfer of strategy use continue, including "booster sessions" if needed, and the teacher and student continue to evaluate the student's strategy performance.

The following are examples of frequently used composition strategies: POWER assists students in remembering and using the steps in the writing process (Englert, Raphael, Anderson, Anthony, & Stevens, 1991):

P = Plan
O = Organize
W = Write
E = Edit/Editor
R = Revise

Another set of strategies, the Three-step Strategy plus PLANS, helps students set goals for their writing and breaks the writing task into several related steps (Harris and Graham, 1996):

The Three-step Strategy

1. **Think**—Who will read this? Why am I writing this?
2. **Plan** what to say
3. **Write** and say more

+

PLANS: P = Pick goals
          L = List ways to meet goals
          A = And make
          N = Notes,
          S = Sequence notes

These strategies, in turn, can be followed by additional strategies that instruct students to write an opinion essay (Harris & Graham, 1996):

TREES: Note Topic sentence
          Note Reasons
          Examine reasons—Will my reader buy this?
          Note Ending

or to write a story (Harris & Graham, 1996):

SPACE: Note Setting
          Note Purpose
          Note Action
          Note Conclusion
          Note Emotions

For other strategies that may address the individual composition needs of your students, see Pressley & Woloshyn (1995). For strategies that teach students to decode as well as comprehend, see Lebzelter and Nowacek (in press). For mathematics strategies, see Miller, Strawser, & Mercer (1996) and Pressley & Woloshyn (1995).

Mathematics Modification: The Remedial Basic Skills Curriculum
With the publication of the National Council of Teachers of Mathematics standards (NCTM, 1989), schools broadened their mathematics curriculum to emphasize areas such as problem-solving, reasoning, and making math connections across the curriculum. These emphases present challenges for students who struggle with reading and writing, and who have difficulty organizing information, selecting appropriate strategies, and self-monitoring (Gurganus and Del Mastro, 1998). Students with learning disabilities, therefore, experience difficulty in math for several reasons including poor understanding of math concepts and lack of prerequisite skills. Although the NCTM does not recommend altering curricular goals, this group does suggest changing the type and speed of instruction. Given the gap between expectations in the classroom and the standards of the NCTM and many students' performance, Carnine (1997) and his colleagues (Carnine, Jones, & Dixon, 1994) recommend the following alternative to current instructional practices:

Teach big ideas: These ideas are concepts and principles (e.g., estimation, proportions) that promote the greatest amount of knowledge acquisition and understanding across the rest of the math content. Teachers are encouraged to organize instruction so that students will be likely to learn big ideas. Before teachers can reorganize their instruction, however, they must consider key questions such as: (1) what skills should the student learn; (2) what are the relationships among these skills; (3) what skills does the student already know; and (4) what procedures/technologies are available for teaching the identified skills.

Teach effective strategies: This instruction is intended to identify and teach rules/approaches to problem solving that will help students solve complex problems. Carnine and his colleagues (1994) caution against selecting strategies that are too broad or too narrow to assist the majority of students most of the time. Teachers should strive to select "medium" or "just right" strategies, those that are specific enough to be useful, but general enough to be used flexibly. Next, teachers map the units of the problem (i.e., components of the problem). Then they require the students to write the known quantities for the units and finally solve for the missing quantity. For example, in the problem:

It takes the attendance office 2 minutes to process 3 tardy students. How long will it take the office to process 11 tardy students?

students map the units as a proportion problem:

minutes / tardy students

Next, they write the known quantities for the units:

$2/3 = x/11$

Then they solve for the missing quantity:

$2/3 \times x/11 = 22/3 = 7\frac{1}{3}$ minutes to process 11 tardy students

Use time efficiently: To help students with learning disabilities "catch up" with their peers, Carnine (1997) recommends four procedures:

1. Abandon low-priority objectives and focus on big ideas: Analyze new information for big ideas and ways in which mathematical knowledge interrelates. Focusing instruction on big ideas, rather than on the individual objectives often presented in basal mathematics texts, reduces the amount of new material to be presented and the likelihood that students will be overwhelmed.

2. Use a strand organization for lessons: The big ideas teachers select for instruction can be organized in a strand format; that is, teachers can plan several consecutive lessons around one big idea and its component concepts. For example, a teacher may develop a lesson in which he or she allocates ten minutes for regrouping (i.e., borrowing); six minutes for estimation, a review applied to subtraction problems; three minutes for a review of math facts to promote fluency and/or automaticity; and the remaining time for work problems that would incorporate all of these components.

3. Ease into complex strategies: Teach complex strategies (i.e., those composed of several components) over time, not in a single lesson. This approach simplifies the communication of the complex strategy without watering down important inherent complexities. If a student becomes confused when using a strategy, it is preferable to reteach the original strategy rather than introducing a new, alternative one.

4. Use manipulatives in a time-efficient manner: Sequence manipulatives after instruction in an algorithm, rather than before, to promote understanding and proficiency.

Provide scaffolded instruction as a transition to self-directed learning and communicate strategies clearly and explicitly: This instruction involves teachers and learners in various forms and amounts of guided practice that help students learn skills and knowledge not yet mastered. Once teachers have determined the skills and knowledge students already have learned, they identify the tasks the student needs to learn to be more competent. They then select a set of instructional examples and activities and determine the type and amount of support that is needed to facilitate learning. Supports include providing definitions of key concepts; explaining the task; giving instructions; modeling the task/strategy; guiding the learner through the task, offering cues and providing consistent corrective feedback. Initially, teachers provide much support; the support is gradually removed as the student becomes more proficient.

If you determine a student needs to learn certain strategies, before beginning strategy instruction, it is important to assess whether all students have prerequisites and/or to determine what prerequisites need to be taught before a strategy is introduced. It is equally as important to provide clear, explicit instruction when introducing and guiding students to use strategies. (See Carnine, 1997, for a scripted example of explicit instruction for introducing proportion word problems.)

Review and practice: Although effective instruction may reduce the amount of practice students need, as a rule teachers need to provide substantial amounts of practice of concepts and skills in meaningful contexts to promote retention for many students with learning disabilities. Because many commercially published mathematics curricula do not include sufficient amounts of practice and review activities for these students, teachers will need to provide supplemental practice. (See Lock, 1996, for additional ways to adapt mathematics instruction in general education classrooms. Also, Jones, Wilson, and Bhojwani, 1997, offer several considerations for mathematics instruction for secondary students with learning disabilities.)

Helpful Resources

Instructional Methods

Algozzine, B., O'Shea, D. J., & O'Shea, L. J. (1998). *Learning disabilities: From theory toward practice.* Upper Saddle River, NJ: Merrill/Prentice-Hall.

Bender, N. (1998). *Learning disabilities: Characteristics, identification, and teaching strategies.* Boston: Allyn & Bacon.

Berdine, W. H., & Cegalka, P. T. (1995). *Effective instruction for students with learning disabilities.* Boston: Allyn & Bacon.

Blair, T. R., Churton, M. W., & Cranston-Gingras, A. M. (1998). *Teaching children with diverse abilities.* Boston: Allyn & Bacon.

Bley, N. S., & Thornton, C. A. (1995). *Teaching mathematics to students with learning disabilities.* Austin, TX: Pro-Ed.

Bos, C. S., & Vaughn, S. (1998). *Strategies for teaching students with learning and behavior problems* (4th ed.). Boston: Allyn & Bacon.

Ciborowski, J. (1995). Using textbooks with students who cannot read them. *Remedial and Special Education, 16,* 90–101.

Deshler, D., Ellis, E., & Lenz, K. (1998). *Teaching adolescents with learning disabilities: Strategies and methods* (3rd ed.). Denver: Love.

Dowdy, C., Patton, J. R., Smith, T. E. C., & Polloway, E. A. (1997). *Attention deficit hyperactivity disorder in the classroom.* Austin, TX: Pro-Ed.

Hammill, D. D., & Bartel, N. R. (1995). *Teaching students with learning and behavior problems* (6th ed.). Boston: Allyn & Bacon.

Hoover, J. J., & Patton, J. R. (1995). *Teaching students with learning problems to use study skills.* Austin, TX: Pro-Ed.

Lerner, J. W., Lowenthal, B., & Lerner, S. R. (1995). *Attention deficit disorders: Assessment and teaching.* Pacific Grove, CA: Brooks/Cole.

Lewis, M. E. H. (1995). *Thematic methods and strategies in learning disabilities.* San Antonio, TX: Psychological Corporation.

Lovitt, T. C. (1995). *Tactics for teaching* (2nd ed.). Englewood Cliffs, NJ: Merrill/Prentice-Hall.

Mercer, C. D., & Mercer, A. R. (1997). *Teaching students with learning problems* (4th ed.). New York: Merrill/Prentice-Hall.

Mercer, A. R., & Mercer, C. D. (1998). *Teaching students with learning problems* (5th ed.). Upper Saddle River, NJ: Merrill/Prentice-Hall.

Miles, D. D., & Forcht, J. P. (1995). Mathematics strategies for secondary students with learning disabilities or mathematics deficiencies: A cognitive approach. *Intervention in School and Clinic, 31,* 91–96.

Polloway, E. A., & Patton, J. R. (1997). *Strategies for teaching learners with special needs* (6th ed.). Englewood Cliffs, NJ: Merrill/Prentice-Hall.

Pressley, M., & Associates. (1995). *Cognitive strategy instruction that really improves children's academic performance.* Cambridge, MA: Brookline Books.

Salend, S. J. (1997). *Effective mainstreaming: Creating inclusive classrooms* (3rd ed.). New York: Macmillan.

Schloss, P. J., Smith, M. A., & Schloss, C. N. (1995). *Instructional methods for adolescents with learning and behavior problems.* Boston: Allyn & Bacon.

Smith, T. E. C., Polloway, E. A., Patton, J. R., & Dowdy, C. A. (1998). *Teaching children with special needs in inclusive settings.* Boston: Allyn & Bacon.

Wineberger, S. (1996). *Teaching kids with learning difficulties in the regular classroom.* Reston, VA: CEC Publications.

Wood, J. W. (1998). *Adapting instruction to accommodate students in inclusive settings* (3rd ed.). Englewood Cliffs, NJ: Merrill/Prentice-Hall.

Curricula and Instructional Materials

Aune, E. P., & Ness, J. E. (1991). *Tools for transition: Preparing students with learning disabilities for postsecondary education.* Circle Pines, MN: American Guidance Services.

Brigance, A. H. (1991). *Victory!* East Moline, IL: LinguiSystem.

Carnine, D., & Kameenui, E. J. (1992). *Higher-order thinking: Designing curriculum for mainstreamed students.* Austin, TX: Pro-Ed.

Carnine, D., Silbert, J., & Kameenui, E. J. (1997). *Direct instruction reading* (3rd ed.). Upper Saddle River, NJ: Merrill/Prentice-Hall.

Cronin, M. E., & Patton, J. R. (1993). *Life skills for students with special needs.* Austin, TX: Pro-Ed.

Deiner, P. L. (1993). *Resources for teaching children with diverse abilities.* Fort Worth, TX: Harcourt Brace Jovanovich.

Englemann, S., Carnine, D., Johnson, G., & Meyers, L. (1988). *Corrective reading: Decoding.* Chicago: Science Research Associates.

Englemann, S., Carnine, D., Johnson, G., & Meyers, L. (1989). *Corrective reading: Comprehension.* Chicago: Science Research Associates.

Hudgins, P. (1998). *The ASSIST Series.* Longmont, CO: Sopris West.

Mercer, C. D., & Miller, S. P. (1991). *Strategic math series.* Lawrence, KS: Edge Enterprises.

Schumaker, J. B., Hazel, J. S., & Pederson, C. S. (1989). *Social skills for daily living.* Circle Pines, MN: American Guidance Service.

Silbert, J., Carnine, D., & Stein, D. (1990). *Direct instructional mathematics* (2nd ed.). Columbus, OH: Merrill.

Literature about Individuals with Learning Disabilities*

Elementary: Ages 5–8 and 9–12

Aiello, B., & Shulman, J. (1988). *Secrets aren't (always) for keeps.* Frederick, MD: Kids on the Block (F)

Cummings, R. W. (1991). *The school survival guide for kids with LD (learning differences).* Minneapolis, MN: Free Spirit. (Ages 9–12) (NF)

Dunn, A. B., & Dunn, K. B. (1993). *Trouble in school: A family story about learning disabilities.* Bethesda, MD: Woodbine House. (Ages 9–12) (F)

Fisher, G., & Cummings, R. (1990). *The survival guide for kids with LD.* Minneapolis, MN: Free Spirit. (Ages 9–12) (NF)

Gehret, J. (1990). *Learning disabilities and the don't give-up kid.* Fairport, NY. Verbal Images (juvenile) (picture book).

Hall D. E., (1993). *Living with learning disability: A guide for students.* Learner Publications Company. (Ages 9–12) (NF)

Hall, L. (1988). *Just one friend.* New York: Collier Books. (F)

Maser, A. (1991). *Don't feed the monster on Tuesday! The children's self-esteem book.* Kansas City, MO: Landmark. (Ages 5–10) (NF)

Richardson, J. (1988). *Bad mood bear.* Hauppauge, NY: Barron's. (Ages 5–8) (F) (picture book)

Roby, C. (1994). *When learning is tough: Kids talk about their learning disabilities.* Concept Books. (Ages 9–12) (NF)

Wolff, V. E. (1988). *Probably still Nick Swansen.* New York: Holt. (F)

Secondary/Adult

Cummings, R. W. (1993). *The survival guide for teenagers with LD (learning differences).* Minneapolis, MN: Free Spirit. (NF)

Gordon, M. (1994). *I would if I could: A teenager's guide to ADHD.* GSI Publications. (Ages 12–18) (NF)

Lauren, J. (1997). *Succeeding with LD: 20 true stories about real people with LD.* Minneapolis, MN: Free Spirit. (NF)

Software

Ace Series, Mindplay, 160 W. Ft. Lowell, Tucson, AZ 85705, (800) 221-7911, Web site: http://www.mindplay.com.

Access to Math, Don Johnston, Inc., 1000 N. Rand Road, Bldg. 115, Wauconda, IL 60084, (800) 999-4660, Web site: http://www.donjohnston.com. (Apple IIe, Apple IIGS) (can be used to create addition, subtraction, multiplication, and division problems)

Alphabetization & Letter Recognition, Milliken Publishing Company, 1100 Research Blvd., St. Louis, MO 63132, (314) 991-4807, Web site: http://www.millikenpub.com. (Apple IIGS)

Arthur's Birthday, Life Science Associates, 1 Fenimore Road, Bayport, NY 11705-2115, (516) 472-2111, Web site: http://www.lifesciassoc@pipeline.com. (Macintosh)

Beamer, Data Command, Inc., 13492 Research Blvd., Ste. 120-215, Austin, TX, (800) 528-7390. (Apple IIe; Apple IIGS)

Blueprint for Decision Making, Lawrence Productions, P.O. Box 458, Galesburg, MD 49053, (800) 421-4157, Web site: http://www.lpi.com. (Apple IIGS; DOS)

Bubblegum Machine, Heartsoft, Inc., P.O. Box 691381, Tulsa, OK 74169-1381, (800) 285-3475, Web site: http://www.thinkology.com. (Apple IIe; Apple IIGS; DOS) (language development)

Calendar Skills, Hartley, 9920 Pacific Heights Blvd., San Diego, CA 92121, (800) 247-1380. (Apple IIe; Apple IIGS; DOS)

Capitalization, Hartley, 9920 Pacific Heights Blvd., San Diego, CA 92121, (800) 247-1380. (Apple IIe; Apple IIGS)

Cat 'n Mouse. Mindplay, 160 W. Ft. Lowell, Tucson, AZ 85705, (800) 221-7911, Web site: http://www.mindplay.com. (Apple IIGS; DOS)

Cause and Effect, Hartley, 9920 Pacific Heights Blvd., San Diego, CA 92121, (800) 247-1380. (Apple IIe; Apple IIGS)

Clock, Hartley, 9920 Pacific Heights Blvd., San Diego, CA 92121, (800) 247-1380. (Apple IIe; Apple IIGS; DOS)

Co:Writer, Don Johnston Inc., 1000 N. Rand Rd., Bldg. 115, Wauconda, IL 60084, (800) 999-4660, Web site: http://www.donjohnston.com. (Macintosh)

Coin Changer, Heartsoft, Inc., P.O. Box 691381, Tulsa, OK 74169-1381, (800) 285-3475, Web site: http://www.thinkology.com. (Apple IIe; Apple IIGS; DOS)

Collaborative Writer, Research Design Associates, Inc., 44-L Jefryn Blvd., Deer Park, NY 11729, (516) 242-5513, (800) 654-8715. (Macintosh) (memos, proposals, reports)

Comprehension Power, Taylor Associates, 200-2 E. 2nd St., Huntington Station, NY 11746, (800) READ-PLUS, Web site: http://www.ta-comm.com. (Apple IIGS; DOS; Macintosh)

Confusing Words, LD Resources, 202 Lake Rd., New Preston, CT 06777, (860) 868-3214, Web site: http://www.ldresources.com. (Macintosh)

*F = fiction; NF = nonfiction

Countdown, Sunburst Communications, 101 Castleton Street, Pleasantville, NY 10570, (800) 321-7511, Web site: http://www.sunburst.com.

Dollars & Cents Series, Attainment Company, Inc., P.O. Box 930160, Verona, WI 53593, (800) 327-4269, Web site: http://www.attainment-inc.com. (Macintosh; Windows)

DragonDictate, Dragon Systems, Inc., 320 Nevada St., Newton, MA 02160, (617) 965-5200, Web site: http://www.dragonsys.com. (Windows)

Edmark Reading Program Series, Edmark Corporation, 6727 185th Avenue NE, Redmond, WA 98052, (800) 426-0856, Web site: http://www.edmark.com. (Apple IIGS)

Essay Ease, Mindplay, 160 W. Ft. Lowell, Tucson, AZ 85705, (800) 221-7911, Web site: http://www.mindplay.com. (Apple IIe; Apple IIGS)

Fact or Opinion, Hartley, 9920 Pacific Heights Blvd., San Diego, CA 92121, (800) 247-1380. (Apple IIe; Apple IIGS; DOS)

Grammar Play with Alps and Droops, Optimal-Ed Learning Materials, 1455 E. Tropicana Ave., Suite 600, Las Vegas, NV 89119, (702) 736-0706. (Apple IIGS)

Graph Club, Sunburst Communications, 101 Castleton Street, Pleasantville, NY 10570, (800) 321-7511, Web site: http://www.sunburst.com.

Hands-on Concepts Series, IntelliTools, 55 Leveroni Ct., Novato, CA 94949, (800) 899-6687, Web site: http://www.intellitools.com. (Macintosh; Apple IIGS; DOS)

How to Read for Everyday Living, Educational Activities, Inc., P.O. Box 392, Freeport, NY 11520, (800) 645-3739, Web site: http://www.edact.com. (Apple IIe; DOS)

How to Write for Everyday Living, Educational Activities, Inc., P.O. Box 392, Freeport, NY 11520, (800) 645-3739, Web site: http://www.edact.com. (Apple IIe; DOS)

Imagination Express Destination Series, Edmark Corporation, 6727 185th Avenue N.E., Redmond, WA 98052, (800) 426-0856, Web site: http://www.edmark.com. (Macintosh; Windows)

Integer/Equations, Hartley, 9920 Pacific Heights Blvd., San Diego, CA 92121, (800) 247-1380.

Jo-Jo's Reading Series. Mindplay, 160 W. Ft. Lowell, Tucson, AZ 85705, (800) 221-7911, Web site: http://www.mindplay.com. (Apple IIGS; DOS)

Learning to Reason Series, Lawrence Productions, P.O. Box 458, Galesburg, MD 49053, (800) 421-4157, Web site: http://www.lpi. (Apple IIGS; DOS)

Map Skills, Optimum Resources, Inc., 18 Hunter Road, Hilton Head, SC 29926, (888) 784-2592.

Math Blaster Plus, Davidson & Associates, Inc., 19840 Pioneer Ave., Torrance, CA 90503, (800) 545-7677, Web site http://www.davd.com.

Money Works, MECC, 6160 Summit Drive N., Minneapolis, MN 55430-4003, (800) 685-6322. (Apple IIe; Apple IIGS)

Mountain Climbing, Mindplay, 160 W. Ft. Lowell, Tucson, AZ 85705, (800) 221-7911, Web site: http://www.mindplay.com. (Apple IIGS; DOS)

Multiply with Balancing Bear, Sunburst Communications, 101 Castleton Street, Pleasantville, NY 10570, (800) 321-7511, Web site: http://www.sunburst.com. (Apple IIe; Apple IIGS; DOS)

Oregon Trail Series, Learning Company School, 6160 Summit Drive N., Minneapolis, MN 55430, (800) 685-6322, Web site: http://www.learningco.com. (Macintosh; Windows)

Phonics Workout, LD Resources, 202 Lake Rd., New Preston, CT 06777, (860) 868-3214, Web site: http://www.ldresources.com. (Macintosh)

Presidents—It All Started with George, IBM: Eduquest, 2929 North Central Avenue, Phoenix, AZ 85012, (602) 217-2702. (DOS)

Quotes, LD Resources, 202 Lake Rd., New Preston, CT 06777, (860) 868-3214, Web site: http://www.ldresources.com. (Macintosh)

Reaching the Hard to Teach Series, Judy Wood Publishing Company, 12411 Southbridge Drive, Midlothian, VA 23113, (804) 379-9430. (Macintosh; Windows; DOS)

Reader Rabbit, Learning Company School, 6160 Summit Drive N., Minneapolis, MN 55430, (800) 685-6322, Web site: http://www.learningco.com. (Apple IIe; Apple IIGS; Macintosh; DOS) (basic reading and spelling skills)

Spelling Machine, SWEPS Educational Software, Inc., 3140 Barker Drive, P.O. Box 1510, Pine, AZ 85544-1510, (520) 476-3433, (800) 880-8812. (Apple IIe; Apple IIGS; DOS)

Special Writer Coach, Tom Snyder Productions, 80 Coolidge Hill Road, Watertown, MA 02472-2817, (800) 342-0236, Web site: http://www.teachtsp.com. (Macintosh)

Stickeybear's Math Town, Optimum Resources, Inc., 18 Hunter Road, Hilton Head, SC 29926, (888) 784-2592, Web site: http://www.stickybear.com. (Macintosh)

Stickeybear Reading, Optimum Resources, Inc., 18 Hunter Road, Hilton Head, SC 29926, (888) 784-2592, Web site: http://www.stickybear.com. (Apple IIe; Apple IIGS; DOS)

Survival Math, Sunburst Communications, 101 Castleton Street, Pleasantville, NY 10570, (800) 321-7511, Web site: http://www.sunburst.com. (Apple IIe; Apple IIGS; DOS)

Swim, Swam, Swum: Mastering Irregular Verbs, Laureate Learning Systems, Inc., 110 E. Spring St., Winooski, VT 05404, (800) 562-6801, Web site: http://www.LaureateLearning.com.

Symbols, LD Resources, 202 Lake Rd., New Preston, CT 06777, (860) 868-3214, Web site: http://www.ldresources.com. (Macintosh)

Type to Learn, Sunburst Communications, 101 Castleton Street, Pleasantville, NY 10570, (800) 321-7511, Web site: http://www.sunburst.com. (Apple IIe; Apple IIGS; Macintosh; DOS)

Vocabulary Skill Builders, Edmark Corporation, 6727 185th Avenue N.E., Redmond, WA 98052, (800) 426-0856, Web site: http://www.edmark.com. (Macintosh; Windows)

What's First? What's Next?, Hartley, 9920 Pacific Heights Blvd., San Diego, CA 92121, (800) 247-1380. (Apple IIe; Apple IIGS) (sequencing)

Word Attack 3, Davidson & Associates, Inc., 19840 Pioneer Ave., Torrance, CA 90503, (800) 545-7677, Web site: http://www.davd.com. (Macintosh; DOS)

Word Parts, LD Resources, 202 Lake Rd., New Preston, CT 06777, (860) 868-3214, Web site: http://www.ldresources.com. (Macintosh)

Word-Processing Programs: No Graphics

Bank Street Writer Plus, Broderbund Software, Inc., 500 Redwood Blvd., P.O. Box 6121, Novato, CA 94948-6121, (415) 382-4400.

Children's Writing and Publishing Center, Learning Company, 6493 Kaiser Drive, Fremont, CA 94555, (510) 792-2101, Web site: http://www.learningco.com.

Dr. Peet's Talking Text Writer, Hartley, 9920 Pacific Heights Blvd., San Diego, CA 92121, (800) 247-1380.

Magic Slate II, Sunburst Communications, 101 Castleton Street, Pleasantville, NY 10570, (800) 321-7511, Web site: http://www.sunburst.com.

Writing Center, Learning Company School, 6160 Summit Drive N., Minneapolis, MN 55430, (800) 685-6322, Web site: http://www.learningco.com. (Macintosh)

Word-Processing Programs: Graphics

Amazing Writing Machine, Broderbund Software, 500 Redwood Blvd., Novato, CA 94948, (415) 382-4400 (Macintosh; Windows)

Bank Street Story Book, Mindscape, 88 Rowland Way, Novato, CA 94945, (415) 895-2000, Web site: http://www.mindscape.com.

Story Board, Data Command, Inc., 13492 Research Blvd., Ste. 120-215, Austin, TX 78750, (800) 528-7390.

Write: OutLoud, Don Johnston Inc., 1000 N. Rand Rd., Bldg. 115, Wauconda, IL 60084, (800) 999-4660, Web site: http://www.donjohnston.com. (Macintosh)

Ultimate Writing and Creativity Center, Learning Company School, 6160 Summit Drive N., Minneapolis, MN 55430, (800) 685-6322, Web site: http://www.learningco.com. (Macintosh; Windows)

Organizations

Council for Exceptional Children, Division for Learning Disabilities, 1920 Association Drive, Reston, VA 22091, (703) 620-3660, (888) CEC-SPED, Web site: www.cec.sped.org.

Council for Learning Disabilities, P.O. Box 40303, Overland Park, KS 66204, (913) 492-8755.

International Dyslexia Association, 8600 LaSalle Road, Chester Bldg., Suite 382, Baltimore, MD 21286-2044, (410) 296-0232.

Learning Disabilities Association of America, 4156 Library Road, Pittsburgh, PA 15234, (412) 341-1515, Web site: http://www.ldnatl.org.

National Adult Literacy and Learning Disabilities Center, Academy for Educational Development, 1875 Connecticut Avenue N.W., Washington DC 20009 (202) 884-8185, (800) 953-2553.

National Center for Learning Disabilities, 381 Park Avenue South, Ste. 1401, New York, NY 10016, (888) 575-7373, (212) 545-7510.

Recording for the Blind and Dyslexic, 20 Roszel Rd., Princeton, NJ 08540, (609) 452-0606, (800) 803-7201.

Bibliography for Teaching Suggestions

Carnine, D. (1997). Instructional design for students with learning disabilities. *Journal of Learning Disabilities, 30,* 130–142.

Carnine, D., Jones, E. D., & Dixon, R. (1994). Mathematics: Educational tools for diverse learners. *School Psychology Review, 23,* 406–428.

DeBoer, A., & Fister, S. (1995). *Working together: Tools for collaborative teaching.* Longmont, CO: Sopris West.

Englert, C. S., Raphael, T. W., Anderson, L. M., Anthony, H. M., & Stevens, D. D. (1991). Making strategies and self-talk visible: Writing instruction in regular and special education classrooms. *American Educational Research Journal, 23,* 337–372.

Gurganus, S., & Del Mastro, M. (1998). Mainstreaming kids with reading and writing problems: Special challenges of the mathematics classroom. *Reading & Writing Quarterly, 14,* 117–126.

Harris, K. R., & Graham, S. (1996). *Making the writing process work: Strategies for composition and self-regulation.* Cambridge, MA: Brookline Books.

Individuals with Disabilities Education Act Amendments of 1997, P.L. 105–17, 105th Congress, 1st session.

Jones, E. D., Wilson, R., & Bhojwani, S. (1997). Mathematics instruction for secondary students with learning disabilities. *Journal of Learning Disabilities, 30,* 151–164.

Lebzelter, S., & Nowacek, E. J. (in press). Reading strategies for secondary students with mild disabilities. *Intervention in School and Clinic.*

Lock, R. H. (1996). Adapting mathematics instruction in the general education classroom for students with mathematics disabilities. *LD Forum, 21,* 19–23.

McLaughlin, V. L. (1993). Curriculum adaptation and development . In B. S. Billingsley (Ed.), *Program leadership for serving students with disabilities.* Richmond, VA: Virginia Department of Education.

Miller, S. P., Strawser, S., & Mercer, C. D. (1996). Promoting strategic math performance among students with learning disabilities. *LD Forum, 21,* 34–40.

National Council of Teachers of Mathematics. (1989). *Curriculum and evaluation standards for school mathematics* (Report No. SE-050-418). Reston, VA: National Council of Teachers of Mathematics. (ERIC Document Reproduction Service No. ED 304 338).

Pressley, M., & Woloshyn, V. (1995). *Cognitive strategy instruction that really improves children's academic performance.* Cambridge, MA: Brookline Books.

Switlick, D. M., & Stone, J. (1997). Team planning for individual student needs. In D. F. Bradley, M. E. King-Sears, & D. M. Tessier-Switlick (Eds.), *Teaching students in inclusive settings from theory to practice.* Boston: Allyn & Bacon.

The 1997–98 resolutions of the National Educational Association. (1997). *NEA Today, 16,* 24–56.

Wood, J. W. (1998). *Adapting instruction to accommodate students in inclusive settings* (3rd ed.). Upper Saddle, NJ: Merrill/Prentice-Hall.

Zentall, S., & Stormont-Spurgin, M. (1995). Educator preferences of accommodations for students with attention deficit hyperactivity disorder. *Teacher Education and Special Education, 18,* 115-123.

Zigmond, N., Jenkins, J., Fuchs, L. S., Deno, S., Fuchs, D., Baker, J. N., Jenkins, L., & Couthino, M. (1995). Special education I restructured schools: Findings form three multi-year studies. *Phi Delta Kappan, 76,* 531–540.

viesia novosielski

Self-Portrait. Acrylic on rag paper. 30 × 22 in.

Viesia Novosielski was born in Somerville, MA, in 1978. She became serious about artwork when, at the age of 12, she was hospitalized for severe depression. Her work has been exhibited at the Gateway Gallery in Brookline, MA; the Federal Reserve Bank of Boston Gallery; and the Ashwell Gallery in Beverly, MA. She has written and illustrated two books: *A Road in Germany,* a book of poems, and *Where They Would Be Safe, They Perish,* a memoir about her hospital experiences.

Attention Deficit Hyperactivity Disorder

Let me see if Philip can

Be a little gentleman.

Let me see, if he is able

To sit still for once at table;

Thus Papa bade Phil behave;

And Mamma look'd very grave.

But fidgety Phil,

He won't sit still;

He wriggles

And giggles,

And then, I declare

Swings backwards and forwards

And tilts up his chair,

Just like any rocking horse;

"Philip! I am getting cross!"

See the naughty restless child

Growing still more rude and wild

Till his chair falls over quite.

Philip screams with all his might.

Catches at the cloth, but then

That makes matters worse again.

Down upon the ground they fall.

Glasses, plates, knives, forks and all.

How Mamma did fret and frown

When she saw them tumbling down!

And Papa made such a face!

Philip is in sad disgrace.

Where is Philip, where is he?

Fairly cover'd up you see!

Cloth and all are lying on him;

He has pull'd down all upon him.

What a terrible to-do!

Dishes, glasses, snapt in two!

Here a knife, and there a fork!

Philip, this is cruel work.

Table all so bare, and ah!

Poor Papa, and poor Mamma

Look quite cross, and wonder how

They shall make their dinner now.

HEINRICH HOFFMANN
"The Story of Fidgety Philip"

Fidgety Phil, the character in the poem by the German physician Heinrich Hoffman (see p. 203) is generally considered one of the first allusions in Western literature to what today is referred to as attention deficit hyperactivity disorder (ADHD) (Barkley, 1998). Phil's lack of impulse control bears an uncanny similarity to today's conceptualization of ADHD as not so much a matter of inattention as primarily a matter of regulating one's behavior. We discuss this conceptualization more fully later, but it is also important to point out here that Phil's excessive motor activity, or hyperactivity, may be characteristic of many children with ADHD, but not all. Interestingly, Hoffman also wrote another poem, "The Story of Johnny Head-in-Air," about a child who fits to a tee children with ADHD who do not have problems with hyperactivity.

The fact that the condition was recognized as early as the mid-nineteenth century, albeit only in the form of a "poetic case study," is important. Today, ADHD is often the subject of criticism, being referred to as a "phantom" or "bogus" condition—sort of a fashionable, trendy diagnosis for persons who are basically lazy and unmotivated. Such thinking is probably behind some of the reasons why ADHD is not recognized as its own separate category (as are mental retardation, learning disabilities, and so forth) by the U.S. Department of Education; students with ADHD are served by special education under the category of "other health impaired."

Although there are undoubtedly a few persons who hide behind an inappropriate diagnosis of ADHD, evidence indicates that the condition is extremely "real" for those who have it. And as we point out in the next section, ADHD is far from a figment of late-twentieth-century imagination.

Brief History

In addition to Hoffman's account of Fidgety Phil, published in the mid-nineteenth century, we have more scientific evidence of the existence of ADHD, dating back to the beginning of the twentieth century.

Still's Children with "Defective Moral Control"

Dr. George F. Still, a physician, is credited with being one of the first authorities to bring the condition we now call ADHD to the attention of the medical profession. Still delivered three lectures to the Royal College of Physicians of London in 1902 in which he described cases of children who displayed spitefulness, cruelty, disobedience, impulsivity, and problems of attention and hyperactivity. He referred to them as having "defective moral control." Moral control involves inhibitory volition—the ability to refrain from engaging impulsively in inappropriate behavior:

> Volition, in so far as it is concerned in moral control, may be regarded as inhibitory; it is the overpowering of one stimulus to activity—which in this connection is activity contrary to the good of all—by another stimulus which we might call the moral idea, the idea of the good of all. There is, in fact, a conflict between stimuli, and in so far as the moral idea prevails the determining or volitional process may be regarded as inhibiting the impulse which is opposed to it. (Still, 1902, p. 1088)

misconceptions
about Persons with Attention Deficit Hyperactivity Disorder

myth All children with ADHD are hyperactive.

fact Psychiatric classification of ADHD includes (1) ADHD, Predominantly Inattentive Type, (2) ADHD, Predominantly Hyperactive-Impulsive Type, or (3) ADHD, Combined Type. Some children with ADHD exhibit no hyperactivity and are classified as ADHD, Predominantly Inattentive.

myth The primary symptom of ADHD is inattention.

fact Although the psychiatric classification includes an Inattentive Type, recent conceptualizations of ADHD place problems with behavioral inhibition and executive functions as the primary behavioral problems of ADHD.

myth ADHD is a fad, a trendy diagnosis of recent times with little research to support its existence.

fact Reports of cases of ADHD go back to the mid-nineteenth century and the beginning of the twentieth century. Serious scientific study of it began in the early and mid-twentieth century. There is now a firmly established research base supporting its existence.

myth ADHD is primarily the result of minimal brain injury.

fact In most cases of ADHD there is no evidence of actual damage to the brain. Most authorities believe that ADHD is the result of neurological dysfunction, which is often linked to hereditary factors.

myth The social problems of students with ADHD are due to their not knowing how to interact socially.

fact Most persons with ADHD know how to interact, but their problems with behavioral inhibition make it difficult for them to implement socially appropriate behaviors.

myth Using psychostimulants, such as Ritalin, can easily turn children into abusers of other substances, such as cocaine and marijuana.

fact There is no evidence that using psychostimulants for ADHD leads directly to drug abuse. However, care should be taken to make sure that children or others do not misuse the psychostimulants prescribed for them.

myth Psychostimulants have a "paradoxical effect" in that they subdue children rather than activate them. Plus, they have this effect only on those with ADHD.

fact Psychostimulants, instead of sedating children, actually *activate* parts of the brain responsible for behavioral inhibition and executive functions. In addition, this effect occurs in persons without ADHD, too.

myth Because students with ADHD react strongly to stimulation, their learning environments should be highly unstructured in order to take advantage of their natural learning styles.

fact Most authorities recommend a highly structured classroom for students with ADHD, especially in the early stages of instruction.

myth ADHD largely disappears in adulthood.

fact Authorities now hold that the majority of children diagnosed with ADHD in childhood will continue to have the condition as adults.

Although Still's words are almost a century old, they still hold currency. For example, one of the most influential current psychological theories is based on the notion that the essential impairment in ADHD is a deficit involving behavioral inhibition (Barkley, 1997, 1998).

Still's cases were also similar to today's population of persons with ADHD in at least five ways:

1. Still speculated that many of these children had mild brain pathology.
2. Many of the children had normal intelligence.
3. The condition was more prevalent in males than females.
4. There was evidence that the condition had a hereditary basis.
5. Many of the children and their relatives also had other psychological and physical problems, such as depression and tics.

We return later to Barkley's theory and to the above five points. Suffice it to say here that Still's children with "defective moral control" today would very likely be diagnosed as having ADHD by itself, or ADHD with **conduct disorder.** (Conduct disorder, which we discuss more fully in Chapter 7, is characterized by a pattern of aggressive, disruptive behavior.)

Goldstein's Brain-Injured Soldiers of World War I

Kurt Goldstein reported on the psychological effects of brain injury in soldiers who had suffered head wounds in combat in World War I. Among other things, he observed in his patients the psychological characteristics of disorganized behavior, hyperactivity, perseveration, and a "forced responsiveness to stimuli" (Goldstein, 1936, 1939). **Perseveration,** the tendency to repeat the same behaviors over and over again, is often cited today by clinicians as a characteristic of persons with ADHD. Goldstein found that the soldiers' forced responsiveness to stimuli was evident in their inability to concentrate perceptually on the "figure" without being distracted by the "ground." For example, instead of focusing on a task in front of them (the figure), they were easily distracted by objects on the periphery (the background).

The Strauss Syndrome

Goldstein's work laid the foundation for the investigations of Heinz Werner and Alfred Strauss in the 1930s and 1940s. Having emigrated from Germany to the United States after Hitler's rise to power, they teamed up to try to replicate Goldstein's findings. Werner and Strauss noted the same behaviors of distractibility and hyperactivity in some children with mental retardation.

In addition to clinical observations, Werner and Strauss also used an experimental task consisting of figure/background slides presented at very brief exposure times. The slides depicted figures (e.g., a hat) embedded in a background (e.g., wavy lines). They found that the children with supposed brain damage, when asked what they saw, were more likely than those without brain damage to say they had seen the background (e.g., "wavy lines") rather than the figure (e.g., "a hat") (Strauss & Werner, 1942; Werner & Strauss, 1939, 1941). After these studies, professionals came to refer to children who were apparently hyperactive and distractible as exhibiting the **Strauss syndrome.**

conduct disorder. A disorder characterized by overt, aggressive, disruptive behavior or covert antisocial acts such as stealing, lying, and fire setting; may include both overt and covert acts.

perseveration. A tendency to repeat behaviors over and over again; often found in persons with brain injury, as well as those with ADHD.

Strauss syndrome. Behaviors of distractibility, forced responsiveness to stimuli, and hyperactivity; based on the work of Alfred Strauss and Heinz Werner with children with mental retardation.

Cruickshank's Work

William Cruickshank, using Werner and Strauss's figure/background task, found that children with cerebral palsy were also more likely to respond to the background rather than the figure (Cruickshank, Bice, & Wallen, 1957). There were two important ways in which this research extended the work of Werner and Strauss. First, whereas Werner and Strauss had largely *assumed* that their children were brain damaged, Cruickshank's children all had cerebral palsy—a condition that is relatively easy to diagnose. **Cerebral palsy** is characterized by brain damage that results in impairments in movement. (See Chapter 11.) Second, the children studied were largely of normal intelligence, thus demonstrating that children without mental retardation could display distractibility and hyperactivity.

Cruickshank was also important, historically, because he was one of the first to establish an educational program for children who today would meet the criteria for ADHD. (We discuss his educational program later in the chapter.) At the time (the late 1950s), however, many of these children were referred to as "minimally brain injured."

Minimal Brain Injury and Hyperactive Child Syndrome

At about the same time as Cruickshank's extension of Werner and Strauss's work to children of normal intelligence, the results of a now classic study were published (Pasamanick, Lilienfeld, & Rogers, 1956). This study of the aftereffects of birth complications revived Still's notion that subtle brain pathology could result in behavior problems, such as hyperactivity and distractibility. Professionals began to apply the label of **minimal brain injury** to children who were of normal intelligence but who were inattentive, impulsive, and/or hyperactive. Although popular in the 1950s and 1960s, the label of minimal brain injury fell out of favor, with professionals pointing out that it was difficult to document actual tissue *damage* to the brain (Birch, 1964).

Minimal brain injury was replaced in the 1960s by the label "hyperactive child syndrome" (Barkley, 1998). **Hyperactive child syndrome** was preferred because it was descriptive of *behavior* and did not rely on vague and unreliable diagnoses of subtle brain damage. This label's popularity extended into the 1970s. By the 1980s, however, it too had fallen out of favor as research began to point out that *inattention*, and not *hyperactivity*, was the major behavioral problem experienced by these children. In fact, some exhibited attention problems without excessive movement.

This recognition of inattention as more important than hyperactivity is reflected in today's definition of ADHD and its immediate predecessors. However, as we discuss later, some authorities are now recommending that deficits in behavioral inhibition replace inattention as the primary deficit in ADHD. In any case, most authorities do not view hyperactivity as the primary deficit in ADHD.

Definition

Most professionals rely on the American Psychiatric Association's (APA's) *Diagnostic and statistical manual of mental disorders (DSM)* for the criteria used to determine whether an individual has ADHD. Over the years, researchers and

cerebral palsy. A condition characterized by paralysis, weakness, incoordination, and/or other motor dysfunction because of damage to the brain before it has matured.

minimal brain injury. A term used to refer to children who exhibit inattention, impulsivity, and/or hyperactivity; popular in the 1950s and 1960s.

hyperactive child syndrome. A term used to refer to children who exhibit inattention, impulsivity, and/or hyperactivity; popular in the 1960s and 1970s.

practitioners have debated whether ADHD was a single syndrome or whether there were subtypes. Partly as a result of this debate the name for the condition has changed from time to time. For example, for several years the APA used the general term *attention deficit disorder (ADD)* to refer to all people with the condition. It then allowed for the subtypes of ADD with Hyperactivity and ADD without Hyperactivity.

The current *DSM* uses ADHD as the general term and subdivides individuals into: (1) ADHD, Predominantly Inattentive Type; (2) ADHD, Predominantly Hyperactive-Impulsive Type; and (3) ADHD, Combined Type (American Psychiatric Association, 1994). See Table 6.1.

Prevalence

ADHD is widely recognized as one of the most frequent reasons, if not the most frequent reason, why children are referred for behavioral problems to guidance clinics. From one-third to one-half of cases referred to guidance clinics are for ADHD (Richters et al., 1995). Most authorities estimate that from 3 to 5 percent of the school-age population have ADHD (National Institutes of Health, 1998). However, because ADHD is not recognized as a separate category of special education by the U.S. Department of Education, it is difficult to estimate how many students with ADHD are served in special education. (See the box on p. 210.)

ADHD occurs much more frequently in boys than girls, with estimates ranging from about 2:1 to 10:1 males to females. The ratios tend to be higher in samples of children referred to clinics, averaging about 6:1, than in samples taken from the population at large, where they average about 3.4:1 (Barkley, 1998). This difference in male:female ratios in clinic-referred versus community samples is often used as evidence of gender-biased referral. Authorities have noted that boys are more likely than girls to exhibit aggressive behavior, which causes them to be referred to the clinics. This has led some to suggest that boys may be over-identified as ADHD and/or that girls may be underidentified as ADHD. Although it is very likely that some referral bias does exist, the fact that boys still outnumber girls by more than three to one in surveys of the community at large suggests that the disparity is also due to real constitutional differences (Barkley, 1998).

Assessment

Most authorities agree that there are three important components to assessing whether a student has ADHD: (1) a medical examination, (2) a clinical interview, and (3) teacher and parent rating scales (Barkley, 1998).

Medical Examination

The medical examination is important in order to rule out other reasons for the child's behavioral problems and to find out if there are any other medical conditions that need to be treated. The child's inattention or hyperactivity may be due to factors other than ADHD. For example, although relatively rare, brain tumors, thyroid problems, seizure disorders, and a variety of other medical

Table 6.1 Diagnostic Criteria for Attention Deficit Hyperactivity Disorder

A. Either (1) or (2):

(1) six (or more) of the following symptoms of *inattention* have persisted for at least 6 months to a degree that is maladaptive and inconsistent with developmental level:

Inattention

(a) often fails to give close attention to details or makes careless mistakes in schoolwork, work, or other activities

(b) often has difficulty sustaining attention in tasks or play activities

(c) often does not seem to listen when spoken to directly

(d) often does not follow through on instructions and fails to finish schoolwork, chores, or duties in the workplace (not due to oppositional behavior or failure to understand instructions)

(e) often has difficulty organizing tasks and activities

(f) often avoids, dislikes, or is reluctant to engage in tasks that require sustained mental effort (such as schoolwork or homework)

(g) often loses things necessary for tasks or activities (e.g., toys, school assignments, pencils, books, or tools)

(h) is often easily distracted by extraneous stimuli

(i) is often forgetful in daily activities

(2) six (or more) of the following symptoms of *hyperactivity-impulsivity* have persisted for at least 6 months to a degree that is maladaptive and inconsistent with developmental level:

Hyperactivity

(a) often fidgets with hands or feet or squirms in seat

(b) often leaves seat in classroom or in other situations in which remaining seated is expected

(c) often runs about or climbs excessively in situations in which it is inappropriate (in adolescents or adults, may be limited to subjective feelings of restlessness)

(d) often has difficulty playing or engaging in leisure activities quietly

(e) is often "on the go" or often acts as if "driven by a motor"

(f) often talks excessively

Impulsivity

(g) often blurts out answers before questions have been completed

(h) often has difficulty awaiting turn

(i) often interrupts or intrudes on others (e.g., butts into conversations or games)

B. Some hyperactive-impulsive or inattentive symptoms that caused impairment were present before age 7 years.

C. Some impairment from the symptoms is present in two or more settings (e.g., at school [or work] and at home).

D. There must be clear evidence of clinically significant impairment in social, academic, or occupational functioning.

E. The symptoms do not occur exclusively during the course of a Pervasive Developmental Disorder, Schizophrenia, or other Psychotic Disorder and are not better accounted for by another mental disorder (e.g., Mood Disorder, Anxiety Disorder, Dissociative Disorder, or a Personality Disorder),

Code Based on Type

314.01 Attention-Deficit/Hyperactivity Disorder, Combined Type: if both Criteria A1 and A2 are met for the past 6 months

314.00 Attention-Deficit/Hyperactivity Disorder, Predominantly Inattentive Type: if Criterion A1 is met but Criterion A2 is not met for the past 6 months

314.01 Attention-Deficit/Hyperactivity Disorder, Predominantly Hyperactive-Impulsive Type: if Criterion A2 is met but Criterion A1 is not met for the past 6 months

Coding note: For individuals (especially adolescents and adults) who currently have symptoms that no longer meet full criteria, "In Partial Remission" should be specified.

How Many Students with ADHD Are Served in Special Education?

Because ADHD is such a prevalent condition, one would think that it would be relatively easy to find out how many students with ADHD receive special education services. Federal law, after all, requires that schools report how many students with a given disability have been identified for special education services. However, when Public Law 94–142 (the Education for All Handicapped Children Act) was passed in 1975, ADHD was not included as one of the separate categories of special education. This was due in part to two interrelated factors: (1) the research on this condition was still in its infancy, and (2) the advocacy base for children with ADHD was not yet well developed. For example, the *Diagnostic and statistical manual of mental disorders* in effect at the time, the *DSM-II* (American Psychiatric Association, 1968), was vague in its criteria for identifying children with these problems. And the major advocacy organization for people with ADHD, CH.A.D.D. (Children and Adults with Attention Deficit Disorder) was not founded until 1987.

By the time of the reauthorization of Public Law 94–142 as the Individuals with Disabilities Education Act (IDEA) in 1990, however, there was substantial research on ADHD, and CH.A.D.D.'s membership was well on its way to its present level of 32,000 members and over 500 chapters nationwide. CH.A.D.D. lobbied hard for ADHD to be included as a separate category, arguing that children with ADHD were being denied services because the only way they could qualify for special education was if they also had another disability, such as learning disabilities or emotional disturbance. Although lobbyists were unsuccessful in getting ADHD included as a separate category in IDEA, the U.S. Department of Education issued a memo, in 1991, stating that students with ADHD should be eligible for special education under the category *other health impaired* (OHI) "in instances where the ADD is a chronic or acute health problem that results in limited alertness, which adversely affects educational performance."

Most members of CH.A.D.D., as well as some professionals, are still disappointed with the decision not to include ADHD as a separate category because they say that using the the OHI category is too roundabout a means of identification. However, the growth of OHI category since 1991 suggests that more and more students with ADHD are being identified as OHI (see figure).

Although numbers in the the OHI category more than doubled in five years, the 0.22 percent reported for 1995–96 is still well below the estimates that 3 to 5 percent of the school-age population have ADHD. The fact that many children who have learning disabilities or emotional disturbance also have ADHD suggests that many students with ADHD are still probably receiving special education services under one of those two categories. By taking the reported degree of coexistence of ADHD with learning disabilities and emotional disturbance as well as the increases in the OHI category, Forness and Kavale (in press) estimated that fewer than half of students with ADHD are receiving special education services. As long as ADHD is not recognized as a separate category of special education, however, it will be virtually impossible to know exactly how many school-age children with ADHD are receiving special education services.

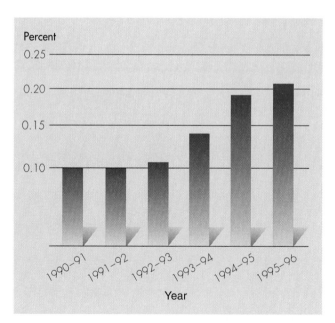

Percentage of students aged 6 to 21 receiving special education services in the category of "other health impaired."
Source: U.S. Department of Education. (1992, 1993, 1994, 1995, 1996, 1997). *Fourteenth, Fifteenth, Sixteenth, Seventeenth, Eighteenth, and Nineteenth annual reports to Congress on the implementation of the Individuals with Disabilities Education Act.* Washington, DC: Author.

Medical exams can rule out other physical reasons for inattention and/or hyperactivity. Clinical interviews by a psychiatrist or psychologist are essential. In addition, rating scales filled out by teachers, parents, and students can help bring some quantification to the process of indentifying children who may have ADHD.

conditions may result in behaviors symptomatic of ADHD. In addition, medications for certain conditions may actually result in inattention and/or hyperactivity (Barkley, 1998).

Clinical Interview

The clinician interviews the parents and the child in order to obtain as much information as possible about the child's physical and psychological characteristics. In addition, the interview can provide important information about how the child's behavior affects the dynamics of the family as well as his or her interactions with peers at school.

Although authorities view the interview as essential to the diagnosis of ADHD, clinicians also need to recognize the subjective nature of the interview situation. This is especially true when it comes to observing the child's behavior. Some children with ADHD can look surprisingly "normal" in their behavior when in the structured and novel setting of a doctor's office. In what could well have been written today, Cantwell's (1979) classic observations of the **doctor's office effect** demonstrate how misleading the behavior of children with ADHD can sometimes be.

Teacher and Parent Rating Scales

In an attempt to bring some quantification to the identification process, researchers have developed rating scales to be filled out by teachers, parents, and in some cases, the child. Inattention, hyperactivity, and impulsivity, for example, are frequently included in rating scales that cover a variety of behavioral problems, such as withdrawn behavior, anxiety, and aggression. In addition, there are several rating scales that focus exclusively on ADHD. Some of the most reliable and popular are the Conners scales and the ADHD-Rating Scale–IV.

One of the first rating scales for ADHD was developed by Conners. There are now several versions of the scale for parents or teachers in use; two of the

doctor's office effect. The observation that children with ADHD often do not exhibit their symptoms when seen by a clinician in a brief office visit.

The "Doctor's Office Effect"

The physician is one of the first professionals parents turn to when they suspect their child might have ADHD. Unfortunately, anecdotes abound about parents who have taken their restless ball of energy to the pediatrician or psychologist only to find that the symptoms have suddenly disappeared. The disparity between the child's behavior at home or at school and at the clinician's has come to be referred to as the "doctor's office effect." The following account of a clinician's encounter with a preschool child is apt:

> When I interviewed his parents, the history they gave was a disaster. They described a small tyrant who ruled the house: he was up all night running around, had learned to unhook the screen door, and had been found walking down Ventura Boulevard in his Pampers, had put himself in the clothes dryer and turned it on, and so on. My next move was to examine the child himself. He appeared abnormal in some minor respects: an articulation problem that made his speech hard to follow, low frustration tolerance, and a mannerism of twirling a tuft of hair and at times pulling it out. Yet he played reasonably quietly with the blocks and with the Fisher-Price dollhouse for some 45 minutes. To his parents and teacher he was a disaster—yet to me he looked pretty good, so I began to wonder what was going on.
>
> The boy then walked outside my office, where there is a group of secretarial desks. One woman was away from her desk, and he climbed up on her chair and started pounding the typewriter. When she returned and asked him to get down, he jumped down, kicked her in the shins, and yelled—because of his articulation problem—"Duck you, bitch!" He then lay down and began kicking and screaming; it took his mother another 45 minutes to calm him sufficiently to take him home.
>
> The main point of this story is ... the relative normality shown in the one-to-one situation with me. This is almost standard in such cases, possibly because the child is somewhat frightened and his adrenal output is up. If he is seen repeatedly, the honeymoon with the doctor will eventually wear off, but a single visit can be misleading. (Cantwell, 1979)

Confirming these anecdotal reports, researchers have also found that clinicians can be at a disadvantage if they rely only on observations in a typical office visit. In a study of ninety-five children who had been rated as hyperactive by teachers, only twenty (21 percent) were rated as hyperactive by physicians on the first office visit (Sleator & Ullman, 1981). Furthermore, three years later the two groups—those rated as hyperactive by both physicians and teachers and those rated as hyperactive only by teachers—were indistinguishable on such things as teachers' ratings of hyperactivity, grade-point average, and the number on medication for ADHD.

most common are the Conners Teacher Rating Scale–39 (Conners, 1989b) and the briefer version, the Conners Teacher Rating Scale–28 (Conners, 1989a).

The ADHD-Rating Scale–IV (DuPaul, Power, Anastopoulos, & Reid, 1998) is based on the *DSM-IV* criteria. Raters, who can be either parents or teachers, rate the child on items pertaining to each of the eighteen criteria listed in the *DSM-IV* (see Table 6.1). For example, for the first item, "Fails to give close attention to details or makes careless mistakes in his/her work," they rate 0 (never or rarely), 1 (sometimes), 2 (often), or 3 (very often), and so forth.

Causes

As noted earlier, authorities in the early and mid-part of the twentieth century attributed problems of inattention and hyperactivity to neurological problems resulting from brain damage. When researchers were unable to verify actual tissue damage in cases of ADHD, many professionals soured on the idea that ADHD was neurologically based. However, as noted in our discussion of learning disabilities (see Chapter 5), the invention of neuroimaging techniques such as MRIs,

PET scans, and fMRIs in the 1980s and 1990s allowed scientists for the first time to obtain more detailed and reliable measures of brain functioning. Using these techniques, researchers have made great strides in documenting the neurological basis of ADHD. Like learning disabilities, the research indicates that ADHD most likely results from neurological dysfunction rather than actual brain damage. Again like learning disabilities, evidence points to heredity as playing a very strong role in causing the neurological dysfunction, with teratogenic and other medical factors also implicated to a lesser degree.

Areas of the Brain Affected:
Frontal Lobes, Basal Ganglia, and Cerebellum

Using neuroimaging techniques, several teams of researchers have found consistent abnormalities in three areas of the brain in persons with ADHD—the frontal lobes, basal ganglia (specifically, the caudate and the globus pallidus), and cerebellum (Aylward et al., 1996; Berquin et al., 1998; Castellanos et al., 1996; Filipek et al., 1997; Hynd, Semrud-Clikeman, Lorys, Novey, & Eliopulos, 1990; Hynd et al., 1993). (See Figure 6.1.) Specifically, researchers have found that the size of each of these areas is smaller in children and adults with ADHD compared to those who are nondisabled. Although not always consistent, several of the studies point to the abnormality occurring on the right side of the brain, especially the right basal ganglia (Castellanos, 1997). In addition, PET scans suggest reduced metabolic activity in the frontal lobes and basal ganglia in persons with ADHD (Lou, Henriksen, & Bruhn, 1984; Lou, Henriksen, Bruhn, Borner, & Nielsen, 1989).

Frontal Lobes. Located in the front of the brain, the **frontal lobes,** and especially the very front portion of the frontal lobes—the **prefrontal lobes**—are responsible for what are referred to as executive functions. Executive functions, among other things, involve the ability to regulate one's own behavior. (We discuss executive functions more fully later.)

frontal lobes. Two lobes located in the front of the brain; responsible for executive functions; site of abnormal development in people with ADHD.

prefrontal lobes. Two lobes located in the very front of the frontal lobes; responsible for executive functions; site of abnormal development in people with ADHD.

Figure 6.1

Areas of the brain (frontal lobes, prefrontal lobes, cerebellum, globus pallidus and caudate of the basal ganglia) identified by some researchers as abnormal in persons with ADHD.

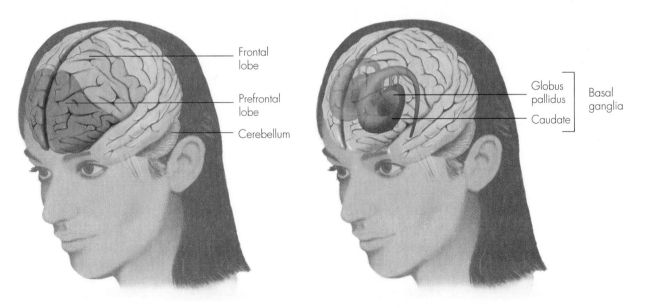

Frontal lobe
Prefrontal lobe
Cerebellum
Globus pallidus
Caudate
Basal ganglia

Basal Ganglia. Buried deep within the brain, the **basal ganglia** consist of several parts, with the **caudate** and the **globus pallidus** being the structures that are abnormal in persons with ADHD. The basal ganglia are responsible for the coordination and control of motor behavior (Pinel, 1997).

Cerebellum. The **cerebellum** is also responsible for the coordination and control of motor behavior. Although it is relatively small, constituting only about 10 percent of the mass of the brain, the fact that it contains more than half of all the brain's neurons attests to its complexity (Pinel, 1997).

Neurotransmitter Involved: Dopamine

Much exciting research is being conducted on what neurotransmitter abnormalities might cause ADHD. **Neurotransmitters** are chemicals that help in the sending of messages between neurons in the brain. One team of researchers, for example, has pointed to **serotonin** as being the key neurotransmitter involved in ADHD (Gainetdinov et al., 1999). Others, however, have identified **dopamine** as being the culprit (Castellanos, 1997; Ernst, Zametkin, Matochik, Jons, & Cohen, 1998; Sagvolden & Sergeant, 1998). Evidence points to the levels of dopamine being too low in the frontal cortex, thus interfering with executive functioning, and too high in the basal ganglia, thus resulting in hyperactivity and impulsivity (Castellanos, 1997). More research is needed to determine if one or both of these neurotransmitters is abnormal in persons with ADHD.

Hereditary Factors

Most authorities agree that there is a hereditary basis to ADHD. Evidence for the genetic transmission of ADHD comes from at least two sources: family studies and twin studies.

Family Studies. Generally, studies indicate that if a child has ADHD, the chance of his or her sibling having ADHD is about 32 percent (Barkley, 1998). And children of adults with ADHD run a 57 percent risk of having ADHD (Biederman et al., 1995).

Twin Studies. There are several studies comparing the prevalence of ADHD in identical (monozygotic, from the same egg) versus fraternal (dizygotic, from two eggs) twins, when one of the members of the pair has ADHD. These studies consistently show that if an identical twin and a fraternal twin each have ADHD, the second identical twin is much more likely to have ADHD than the second fraternal twin (Gillis, Gilger, Pennington, & DeFries, 1992; Sherman, Iacono, & McGue, 1997; Stevenson, 1992).

Teratogenic and Medical Factors

In Chapters 4 and 5 we discussed teratogens—agents that can cause malformations in the developing fetus of a pregnant woman—as the cause of some cases of mental retardation or learning disabilities. Although the evidence is not as strong as it is for heredity, some of these same substances have been shown to be related to ADHD. For example, exposure to lead (Needleman, Schell, Bellinger, Leviton, & Alfred, 1990) and the abuse of alcohol (Aronson, Hagberg, & Gillberg, 1997)

basal ganglia. A set of structures within the brain that include the caudate, globus pallidus, and putamen, with the first two being abnormal in people with ADHD; generally responsible for the coordination and control of movement.

caudate. A structure in the basal ganglia of the brain; site of abnormal development in persons with ADHD.

globus pallidus. A structure in the basal ganglia of the brain; site of abnormal development in persons with ADHD.

cerebellum. An organ at the base of the brain responsible for coordination and movement; site of abnormal development in persons with ADHD.

neurotransmitters. Chemicals involved in sending messages between neurons in the brain.

serotonin. A neurotransmitter, the levels of which may be abnormal in persons with ADHD.

dopamine. A neurotransmitter, the levels of which may be too low in the frontal lobes and too high in the basal ganglia of persons with ADHD.

or tobacco (Milberger, Biederman, Faraone, & Jones, 1998) by pregnant women does place the unborn child at increased risk of developing ADHD.

Other medical conditions may also place children at risk for having ADHD. Again, the evidence is not as strong as it is for heredity, but complications at birth and/or low birthweight are associated with ADHD (Levy, Barr, & Sunohara, 1998; Milberger, Biederman, Faraone, Guite, & Tsuang, 1997).

Psychological and Behavioral Characteristics

One can use the *DSM-IV* criteria discussed earlier (see Table 6.1) to get a sense of some of the typical behaviors of students with ADHD. Although most people think that inattention is the key characteristic of ADHD, there is a growing consensus that inattention, as well as hyperactivity and impulsivity, are actually the result of problems in behavioral inhibition.

Barkley's Model of ADHD

As we noted earlier, Russell Barkley (1997, 1998), in particular, has proposed a model of ADHD in which behavioral inhibition is key. In its simplest form this model proposes that problems in behavioral inhibition set the stage for problems in executive functions, which then disrupt the person's ability to engage in persistent goal-directed behavior.

Behavioral Inhibition. **Behavioral inhibition** refers to the ability to "withhold a planned response; to interrupt a response that has been started; to protect an ongoing activity from interfering activities; and to delay a response" (Rubia, Oosterlaan, Sergeant, Brandeis, & van Leeuwen, 1998). This can be reflected in the ability to wait one's turn, to refrain from interrupting in conversations, to resist potential distractions while working, or to delay immediate gratification in order to work for larger, long-term rewards (Barkley & Murphy, 1998).

Executive Functions. The delay allowed by behavioral inhibition permits the individual to self-regulate his or her behavior. This ability to engage in a variety of self-directed behaviors involves what are referred to as **executive functions.** The fact that there is a wealth of evidence that executive functions are controlled by the prefrontal and frontal lobes of the brain fits nicely with the neuroimaging studies pointing to these areas of the brain being abnormal in persons with ADHD.

In Barkley's model, persons with ADHD can exhibit problems with executive function in four general ways. First, they often have problems with working memory (WM). As we noted in Chapter 5, WM refers to a person's ability to keep information in mind that "can be used to guide one's actions either now or in the near future" (Barkley & Murphy, 1998, p. 2). In the case of students with ADHD, deficiencies in WM can result in forgetfulness, a lack of hindsight and forethought, and problems with time management.

Second, persons with ADHD frequently have delayed inner speech. **Inner speech** is the inner "voice" that allows people to "talk" to themselves about various solutions when in the midst of solving a problem. Students with ADHD who have deficient inner speech have problems in guiding their behavior in situations that demand the ability to follow rules or instructions.

behavioral inhibition. The ability to stop an intended response, to stop an ongoing response, to guard an ongoing response from interruption, and to refrain from responding immediately; allows executive functions to occur; delayed or impaired in those with ADHD.

executive functions. The ability to regulate one's behavior through working memory, inner speech, control of emotions and arousal levels, and analysis of problems and communication of problem solutions to others; delayed or impaired in those with ADHD.

inner speech. An executive function; internal language used to regulate one's behavior; delayed or impaired in those with ADHD.

Poor concentration, distractibility, and an inability to process or follow instructions are common problems for children with ADHD.

Third, children and adults have problems controlling their emotions and their arousal levels. They often overreact to negative or positive experiences. Upon hearing good news, for example, they may scream loudly, unable to keep their emotions to themselves. Likewise, they are often quick to show their temper when confronted with frustrating experiences.

Fourth, children and adults with ADHD have difficulty analyzing problems and communicating solutions to others. They are less flexible when faced with problem situations, often responding impulsively with the first thing that comes to mind.

Persistent Goal-Directed Behavior. The myriad problems with executive functions experienced by persons with ADHD lead to deficits in engaging in sustained goal-directed activities:

> The poor sustained attention that apparently characterizes those with ADHD probably represents an impairment in goal- or task-directed persistence arising from poor inhibition and the toll it takes on self-regulation. And the distractibility ascribed to those with ADHD most likely arises from poor interference control that allows other external and internal events to disrupt the executive functions that provide for self-control and task persistence. The net effect is an individual who cannot persist in effort toward tasks that provide little immediate reward and who flits from one uncompleted activity to another as disrupting events occur. The inattention in ADHD can now be seen as not so much a primary symptom as a secondary one; it is the consequence of the impairment that behavioral inhibition and interference control create in the self-regulation or executive control of behavior. (Barkley, 1997, p. 84)

With diminished self-regulation or executive control abilities, students with ADHD find it exceedingly difficult to stay focused on tasks that require effort or concentration but which are not inherently exciting (e.g., many school-related activities).

Adaptive Skills

The concept of adaptive skills has traditionally been associated with the area of mental retardation. The AAMR definition, for example, stipulates that mental retardation be defined as impairments in intelligence and adaptive behavior (see Chapter 4). Adaptive skills are those abilities needed to adapt to one's living environment (e.g., communication, self-care, home living, social skills, community use, self-direction, health and safety, leisure, and work). In recent years, authorities in the ADHD field have discovered that many children and adults with ADHD also have difficulties in adaptive behavior (Barkley, 1998). Furthermore, those who do have problems with adaptive skills run a much greater risk of having a variety of learning and behavioral problems at school and home (Shelton et al., in press).

Problems Socializing with Peers

Some authorities have argued that the social problems experienced by students with ADHD should be considered the defining characteristic of the condition

(Landau, Milich, & Diener, 1998). Although the evidence may not warrant asserting that all persons with ADHD experience problems getting along with others, it is probably safe to say that the majority experience significant problems in peer relations. In fact, it usually does not take long for others to find students with ADHD uncomfortable to be around. For example, one team of researchers found that after just one day in a summer camp, many children with ADHD were rejected by other campers (Erhardt & Hinshaw, 1994).

Unfortunately, the negative social status experienced by students with ADHD is difficult to overcome and is usually long lasting. The enduring nature of social rejection leads easily to social isolation. The result is that many children and adults with ADHD have few friends even though they may desperately want to be liked. This can set up a vicious circle in which they attempt to win friends by latching onto the least chance for interaction with others. But their frantic need for friendship, coupled with their deficient impulse control, ends up leading them to bother or pester the very persons they are trying to befriend.

Given the problems in behavioral inhibition, it is not surprising that so many children and adults with ADHD end up socially ostracized. Unable to regulate their behavior and emotions, they are viewed as rude by others. It may not be that they do not know how to behave appropriately so much as that they are unable to do so (Landau et al., 1998). In other words, if asked what the appropriate behavior in a given situation should be, they can often give the socially acceptable answer. But when faced with choices in the actual situation, their deficits in behavioral inhibition lead them to make choices impulsively and to overreact emotionally.

Coexisting Conditions

ADHD often occurs simultaneously with other behavioral and/or learning problems, such as learning disabilities, emotional or behavioral disorders, or Tourette's syndrome. In addition, persons with ADHD run a higher risk than the general population for substance abuse.

Learning Disabilities. Studies using careful diagnostic criteria have found an overlap of 10 to 25 percent between ADHD and learning disabilities (Forness & Kavale, in press). And some authorities maintain that the relationship is strongest for students who have ADHD, Primarily Inattentive Type, especially in the case of math disabilities (Marshall, Hynd, Handwerk, & Hall, 1997).

Emotional or Behavioral Disorders. Estimates of the overlap with ADHD vary widely, but it is safe to say that 25 to 50 percent of those with ADHD also exhibit some form of emotional or behavioral disorder (Hallahan & Cottone, 1997; Forness & Kavale, in press). Some persons with ADHD can exhibit aggressive, acting-out behaviors, whereas others can have withdrawn behaviors that accompany anxiety or depression.

Tourette's Syndrome. **Tourette's syndrome** begins in childhood and is characterized by multiple motor tics (repetitive, stereotyped movements) and/or verbal tics (the individual makes strange noises or says inappropriate words or phrases). Authorities agree that Tourette's is caused by neurological problems, and there is suggestive evidence that the area of the brain affected is the caudate and the neurotransmitter involved is dopamine (Wolf et al., 1996)—both of which have been implicated in cases of ADHD. Although Tourette's does not

Tourette's syndrome. A neurological disorder beginning in childhood (about three times more prevalent in boys than in girls) in which stereotyped, repetitive motor movements (tics) are accompanied by multiple vocal outbursts that may include grunting noises or socially inappropriate words or statements (e.g., swearing).

occur with great frequency in people with ADHD, it does occur more often than in the general population. And we do know that about half the people who have Tourette's also have symptoms of ADHD (Biederman, Newcorn, & Sprich, 1991; Lombroso et al., 1995).

Substance Abuse. Adults with ADHD are about twice as likely as the general population to abuse alcohol or to become dependent on drugs, such as cocaine (Biederman, Wilens, Mick, Faraone, & Spencer, 1998; Lambert & Hartsough, 1998). In addition, they are also about twice as likely to be cigarette smokers (Lambert & Hartsough, 1998). Some reports in the popular media have claimed that the treatment of ADHD with psychostimulants such as Ritalin leads children to take up the use of illegal substances. However, there is no research to back up this claim (DuPaul, Barkley, & Connor, 1998).

Exactly why ADHD co-occurs with so many other learning and behavioral disabilities remains largely a mystery. Researchers are just beginning to attempt to tease out which of several possibilities are the most likely reasons for so much overlap between ADHD and other disabilities. For example, does having ADHD put one at risk for developing another disability, such as learning disabilities or depression? Does having a disability, such as Tourette's, lead to symptoms that then result in a diagnosis of ADHD? Or do ADHD and the other disability occur independent of each other? And is there a genetic basis to the coexistence of so many of these conditions? Research over the next few years should begin to provide more definitive answers to these questions.

Educational Considerations

In this section we consider two aspects of effective educational programming for students with ADHD:

- Classroom structure and teacher direction
- Functional assessment and contingency-based self-management

Classroom Structure and Teacher Direction

William Cruickshank, whom we discussed earlier, was one of the first to establish a systematic educational program for children who today would meet the criteria for ADHD. Two hallmarks of Cruickshank's program were: (1) reduction of stimuli irrelevant to learning and enhancement of materials important for learning and (2) a structured program with a strong emphasis on teacher direction.

Because Cruickshank assumed that children with attention problems were susceptible to distraction, irrelevant stimuli were reduced as much as possible. For example, students' workspaces consisted of three-sided cubicles to reduce distractions. On the other hand, teachers were encouraged to use attractive, brightly colored teaching materials.

The emphasis on classroom structure and teacher direction can be summed up by the following:

Specifically, what is meant by a structured program? For example, upon coming into the classroom the child will hang his hat and coat on a given hook—not on any hook of his choice, but on the same hook every day. He will place his lunch box, if he brings one, on a specific shelf each day. He will then go to his cubicle, take his seat, and from that point on follow the teacher's instructions concerning learning tasks, use of toilet, luncheon activities, and all other experiences until the close of the school day. The day's program will be so completely simplified and so devoid of choice (or conflict) situations that the possibility of failure experience will be almost completely minimized. The learning tasks will be within the learning capacity and within the limits of frustration and attention span of the child.... If it is determined that he has an attention span of four minutes, then all teaching tasks should be restricted to four minutes. (Cruickshank, Bentzen, Ratzeburg, & Tannhauser, 1961).

It is rare today to see teachers using all the components of Cruickshank's program, especially the cubicles. Many authorities now believe that not all children with ADHD are distracted by things in their environment. For those who are distractible, however, some authorities recommend the use of such things as cubicles to reduce extraneous stimulation.

The *degree* of classroom structure and teacher direction advocated by Cruickshank is also rarely seen today. First, this intensity of structure could only be achieved in a self-contained classroom. As we discuss later, most students with ADHD are in general education settings. Second, most authorities today believe that a structured program is important in the early stages of working with many students with ADHD but that these students gradually need to learn to be more independent in their learning.

Nevertheless, many of the ideas of Cruickshank are still alive in the educational recommendations of today's professionals. For example:

One of the most common classroom interventions involves moving the hyperactive child's desk away from other children to an area closer to the teacher. This procedure not only reduces the child's access to peer reinforcement of his or her disruptive behavior but also allows the teacher to better monitor the child's behavior.... It may also be beneficial for ADHD children to have individual and separated desks. When children sit very near one another, attention to task often decreases due to disruptions that occur between children....

Physically enclosed classrooms (with four walls and a door) are often recommended for hyperactive children over classrooms that do not have these physical barriers (i.e., "open" classrooms). An open classroom is usually noisier and contains more visual distractions because children can often see and hear the ongoing activities in nearby classes....

Some authorities believe that students with ADHD need considerable classroom structure and teacher direction, especially in the early stages of educational programming.

success stories
special educators at work

Salem, VA: High school sopho-more **Josh Bishop** hopes to play football on a team in the National Collegiate Athletic Association's Division I, despite his struggles with organization and time management. Like many students with ADHD, Josh does not find his school-work difficult to do, but finds it hard to get done. Jane Warner coordinates services for stu-dents with disabilities at a large university with a Division I football team. She guides many students like Josh and encourages all incoming freshman with ADHD to begin their self-advocacy early. Josh's mother, Joni Poff, a spe-cial education supervisor, agrees and encourages her son to seek out structures to support his success.

Special educator Jane Warner coordinates services for postsecondary students with disabilities at Virginia Poly-technic Institute and State University, better known as Virginia Tech. Jane is a proponent of self-advocacy skills and encourages schools to teach students at all grade lev-els about their disabilities. "Students need to know what their disability means, how it affects them academically and socially, and how to articulate this information to

someone else. Students need to understand that disclosing their learning needs is not going to stigmatize them."

Josh Bishop hopes to play football for Virginia Tech and major in engineering. At age sixteen, he has been play-ing football for six years. "I played on the varsity team last year when I was a freshman," he says with pride. As a wrestler, a hurdler, and a discus thrower, Josh is a success-ful high school athlete. In the classroom, he has faced dif-ferent challenges: "I never have been very organized. I got by in elementary school, but middle school was a real wake-up call with much more work to do. In sixth grade, I'd get all my homework done *in* class. In seventh grade, I had homework due for *every* class." According to his mother, Joni Poff, "Josh talked early, but when written language came into play, he had trouble. Written work is what he'll avoid at school."

Josh was diagnosed by his pediatrician with ADHD when he was seven years old. "Josh always had a high activity level," recalls his mother. "In kindergarten, he was put on a behavior contract with stickers as positive reinforcement, but his first-grade teacher didn't follow through with his behavior management." By grade two, medication was recommended and Josh's family moved to a small school district. "The secondary school Josh attends has about 650 students in grades six through twelve, with less than one hundred students at each grade level," says Joni. Josh has not been identified for special services under either IDEA or Section 504. Fortunately for Josh and his family, contact between home and school has been close, but his mother remarks that high school has brought more difficulties. "Josh has made tremendous social gains since elementary school, but as the academic demands have in-creased over the last five to six years, it is harder to deal

The classroom should be well-organized, structured, and predictable, with the posting of a daily schedule and classroom rules. Visual aids are often recommended for ADHD children. Hand signals and brightly colored posters can reduce the need for frequent verbal repetitions of rules....

Varying the presentation format and task materials (e.g., through use of different modalities) also seems to help maintain interest and motivation. When low-interest or passive tasks are assigned, they should be interspersed with high-interest or active tasks....

Academic tasks should be brief (i.e., accommodated to the child's attention span) and presented one at a time rather than all at once ... (Abramowitz, Reid, & O'Toole, 1994)....

with the ADHD issues than when he was younger and more emotionally immature."

Josh keeps an assignment book but admits that he does not use it faithfully. "When I've missed a deadline, sometimes I don't turn the work in at all. I know that I need to do homework and I keep saying I'm going to do it, and then I don't get my homework in and I get a zero. It's not like it's hard; it's just getting it done! I can get work done at school, but I just can't get it done at home." Says Joni, "Josh does better with shorter time segments in a more structured setting. After school, he has trouble following through with sustained work. His pediatrician told me to back off. Josh takes medication during the day and it's harder for him to concentrate in the evening."

Josh mentioned his medication, but did not refer to his difficulties with completing written work, organizational skills, or attentiveness as being out of the ordinary. He would rather not be treated differently from other students, but he acknowledges that only a few teachers have provided the kind of structured instruction that benefits him. "Miss Mauney, in seventh grade, didn't make exceptions. She always made an effort to organize every kid in the class!" added Josh. Joni Poff thinks the most successful teachers for Josh have been those who were very structured and made their expectations very clear. "They weren't wishy-washy. They were sympathetic that some things were difficult for Josh. They understood that he wasn't being purposefully lazy or disrespectful, but they still held high expectations for him," says Joni. "Recently, I've asked Josh to take advantage of a tutor or some structured support, but he seems determined to do it alone."

Doing it alone is not always the answer, says Jane Warner. Students with ADHD frequently need support when they move from high school to college. Says Jane, "Study skills and time management are troublesome for students with ADHD. Things can start to fall apart. Students might miss several classes and think they can never go back, so they just sit out and their grades go down, their self-esteem starts to slip, and they hit the wall." Warner encourages students to disclose their learning needs confidently and make contact with the office for disability services on campus. Students with ADHD who have not received special services in high school are advised to get the documentation they need for colleges to provide them with appropriate accommodations. "We prefer current comprehensive evaluations that have been done by a qualified professional within the previous three years," says Warner. Every accommodation recommended by an evaluator must be accompanied by a rationale based on the student's current level of functioning. "Documentation completed in grade school or middle school doesn't reflect developmental changes or tell us what the student can do now. IEPs are part of the puzzle, but you still can't use an IEP as the only documentation for postsecondary accommodations."

Warner points out that evaluations for students with ADHD can provide a clear picture of their strengths and weaknesses, especially if the professional evaluator explains what the results mean in laymen's terms and makes specific educational recommendations. "Sometime between now and high school graduation," suggests Jane Warner, "getting a current clinical evaluation will be a very important part of fostering self-advocacy for Josh."

—By Jean Crockett

Children's attention span during group lessons may be enhanced by delivering the lesson in an enthusiastic yet task-focused style, keeping it brief, and allowing frequent and active child participation. . . .

Teachers should attempt to schedule as many academic subjects in morning hours as possible, leaving the more active, nonacademic subjects . . . to the afternoon periods. . . .

Other classroom accommodations for written work may include reducing the length of the written assignment (particularly when it is repetitious), using word processors to type reports, and allotting extra time to complete work. (Pfiffner & Barkley, 1998, pp. 480–481)

Collaboration key to success

Ann B. Welch is a special education resource teacher at Virginia L. Murray Elementary School, Abermarle County Schools, Virginia; B.A., Psychology from Simon Fraser University (Canada); Diploma in the Education of Children with Learning and Behavior Disorders, University of British Columbia; M.A., Speech Pathology and Audiology, Western Washington University; M.Ed., Learning Disabilities, George Mason University. **Laurel W. McClurken** is a kindergarten/ 1st grade teacher at Virginia L. Murray Elementary School in Abermarle County, Virginia; A.B., Gettysburg College.

Ann Welch

Ann and **Laurel** We teach in a small school that has both rural and suburban characteristics. Although we are in a country setting, most of our students come from professional families. There is relatively little socioeconomic or cultural diversity. Our school does not have any self-contained special education classes, and it is extremely rare for us to send a student to another setting for a self-contained class. All the children are enrolled in general education classes, and we use a variety of strategies to meet their special education needs.

Ann As the special education teacher in a small elementary school, I have to be a special education "generalist." Sometimes I pull students out to work in the resource room, while at other times I either co-teach in the general education class or a paraeducator assists students in the general education classroom. Some children receive all three types of service, others only one or two. My caseload usually ranges from fifteen to twenty students. Most of the students have learning disabilities, but we also have students with mild mental retardation, autism, and physical disabilities. An increasing number are identified as "other health impaired" due to attention deficit hyperactivity disorder.

Laurel I teach first grade and have responsibility for all subjects except PE and music. The children always have a

wide range of abilities. One of the advantages of the collaborative working relationship Ann and I have is that we brainstorm ways to meet the needs of any of my students, regardless of their current eligibility status.

Ann We're going to describe our work with a student we'll call Jason. Jason was a tall six-year-old boy with immature fine motor skills and some language/ learning problems. He was identified as "developmentally delayed" and received special education services since age two. Jason was an exuberant learner with poor impulse control and organizational problems. Semantic and pragmatic language deficits complicated social interactions. His conversation was tangential and he tended to perseverate on a restricted range of topics. Jason's disabilities contributed to difficulty following directions, but he also had an oppositional streak. We were always trying to figure out how much was "can't" and how much was "won't." Although Jason had all the characteristics of ADHD, he did not receive that label until later. In first grade, neither Jason nor his teachers had the benefit of medication.

Laurel Jason's class was composed of twenty-four students with only one other student eligible for special education services. However, there were several unidentified students who needed additional support in academic as well as social/

emotional areas. As the year progressed, I found myself increasingly grateful for the regular opportunities to brainstorm with Ann about these students also.

Ann I'll never forget Jason's first day in first grade. I had planned to spend most of the day in Laurel's room, because I thought Jason was the student on my caseload who was most likely to have trouble in a new setting. Like many students with ADHD, Jason surprised us by "honeymooning." He was so attracted to exploring Laurel's classroom and meeting his peers that we saw only his cheerful side. Another child was devastated at being separated from his mother, and I spent most of my time with him! We always tell parents that we try to keep the lines between general education and special education "as blurry as the law will let us." Laurel shares ownership for IEP goals and objectives and I share in the responsibility for other students.

Laurel We anticipated that Jason would have academic difficulty in first grade, but he surprised us. Although he did receive individualized language arts instruction, my major concerns were about his behavior and the disruption he caused to the rest of the class. He was easily frustrated. In addition to tantrums, he directed verbal and physical aggression (hitting and kicking) toward me and the other children. When pursuing a task of interest to him, he was quite focused, but when it was a

Laurel McClurken

task of my choosing, the result was often different. Sustaining his attention during a whole-group lesson was particularly difficult. Jason would roll around on the floor and bump into students who were trying to attend.

Ann Laurel and I struggled to find ways to increase positive reinforcement for appropriate behaviors and provide consistent negative consequences for inappropriate behaviors. Jason needed consistency and Laurel needed a system that was easy to manage. After conversations with Jason and his parents, we decided that the three categories of behavior we wanted to increase were "safe," "working," and "considerate." We used broad terms to minimize the number of categories, but we also spent a lot of time identifying specific behaviors as "safe" or "unsafe." We wanted Jason to feel a sense of ownership, so he and his dad painted Popsicle sticks in three different colors to represent the three categories. Laurel taped two small milk cartons to Jason's desk, one for desirable behavior and one for undesirable behavior. Jason started each day with three sticks of each color in the "happy face" container. A stick was moved into the "sad face" container for behavioral infractions. Laurel also gave Jason a "bonus" stick when she noticed a desired behavior.

Laurel I liked the fact that Jason started each day with sticks in the "happy face" container. Ann told Jason

we knew there would be times he would be safe, working, or considerate that I might not notice. Giving him sticks to start the day conveyed our expectation that he would engage in these desirable behaviors. I also liked using the broad categories of behavior. We had tried using more specific target behaviors, but they left too much maneuvering room for Jason to engage in some new kind of misbehavior and argue that it wasn't against the rules. Jason was enthusiastic about the Popsicle stick program and never seemed tempted by dishonesty—luckily for us, or we would have had to devise a different system. He liked the concrete, visual reminders. I liked giving or moving sticks without talking, which preserved instructional time and minimized opportunities for Jason to argue. Although I had responsibility for giving or taking sticks during the day, Ann took the responsibility for recording Jason's performance. I did not have to worry about completing a form or giving rewards at the end of the day, when I was busy trying to help all the students get ready to go home. Jason took the sticks from his "happy face" box and stopped by Ann's resource room on his way to the bus. Ann graphed the number of sticks in each category so he could see his performance over time. She also helped him complete a simple form to take home each day. His parents provided positive or negative consequences. In the morning, Jason would stop by Ann's room and pick up his sticks. Since Jason only took sticks from the "happy face" box to Ann's room, picking them up started off his morning by reminding him of his successes rather than his failures.

> **We tell parents that we try to keep the lines between general education and special education as blurry as the law will let us.**

Ann When Jason touched base with me in the mornings, I could also remind him about other social or academic issues. Sometimes he finished a homework assignment or rehearsed how to ask Laurel for permission to share something he had brought from home. I didn't see Jason every day for pull-out services, so the morning and afternoon check-in times really helped me to stay on top of his program. The other thing that helped was sharing a planning period with Laurel each week. My principal supports the idea that planning is just as important as direct service to children, but some years my schedule is just too crazy to fit in planning with all the teachers who have a child with special needs in their classroom. Without joint planning time, it is very difficult to collaborate. In Jason's case, Laurel and I met once a week to talk about Jason, the other child in her class with special needs, and any other children we were concerned about.

Laurel I always felt supported. We still did what all teachers do; catch one another in the hallways and teachers' lounge, as well as steal moments before, during, or after school. It was the consistent planning time that was critical, however. Although it never felt like enough time, Ann always had her notebook with her so I could flag my concerns and know that weeks wouldn't go by before we tried to address them. We would both be thinking about the same issues, even if we weren't able to come up with solutions during our planning time. When Ann and I do not have a shared planning time, which happens some years, we are not as effective in meeting the needs of the children. Similarly, if she only sees a student in the resource room and doesn't get to know all the children in my class, it's harder to get the full benefit of her expertise. Many children with disabilities are not formally identified in first grade, so I really count on being able to talk to Ann about any child.

Ann I don't know how we would have met Jason's needs without the shared planning time. New issues were always coming up. Laurel and I work really well as a team, but it's difficult to collaborate if you don't see each other.

Teacher-directed general education classes, with colorful visual aids, enclosed teaching areas, and proximity to the teacher have been successful learning environments.

Functional Assessment and Contingency-Based Self-Management

As we noted in Chapter 4, functional assessment is an important aspect of dealing with behavioral problems of students with mental retardation. It is also extremely useful in educational programming for students with ADHD. **Functional assessment** involves determining the consequences, antecedents, and setting events that maintain inappropriate behaviors (Horner & Carr, 1997). Examples of typical functions of inappropriate behavior of students with ADHD are (1) to avoid work and (2) to gain attention from peers or adults (DuPaul & Ervin, 1996).

Contingency-based self-management approaches usually involve having persons keep track of their own behavior and then receive consequences, usually in the form of rewards, based on their behavior (Shapiro, DuPaul, & Bradley-Klug, 1998). For example, the teacher might have students use **self-monitoring** (see Chapter 5) to record how many times they left their seats during a class period.

A combination of functional assessment and contingency-based self-management techniques has proven successful in increasing appropriate behavior of elementary and secondary students with ADHD (DuPaul, Eckert, & McGoey, 1997; Ervin, DuPaul, Kern, & Friman, 1998; Shapiro et al., 1998). In one study, for instance, a combination of functional assessment and contingency-based self-management increased the on-task behavior of two adolescents with ADHD. For example, for one of the students the functional assessment phase consisted of interviews with the teacher and observations in the classroom, which led the researchers and teachers to conclude that an adolescent boy's disruptive behavior was a function of gaining peer attention (Ervin et al., 1998). They based this assumption on evidence that the antecedents to his inattentive behavior consisted of such things as peers looking his way, calling out his name, making gestures toward him, and that the consequences of his inattention were such things as the peers laughing or returning comments to him.

The contingency-based self-management phase involved the student evaluating his on-task behavior on a 5-point scale (0 = unacceptable to 5 = excellent) at the end of each math class. The teacher also rated his behavior, and the student was awarded points based on how closely the ratings matched. During writing

functional assessment.
Evaluation that consists of finding out the consequences (purposes), antecedents (what triggers the behavior), and setting events (contextual factors) that maintain inappropriate behaviors; this information can help teachers plan educationally for students.

contingency-based self-management. Educational techniques that involve having students keep track of their own behavior, for which they then receive consequences (e.g., reinforcement).

self-monitoring. A self-management technique in which students monitor their own behavior, such as attention to task, and then record it on a sheet.

class, the teacher awarded negative or positive points to members of the class depending on whether or not they responded to attention-seeking behaviors from any member of the class. In both classes, the points could be used for privileges.

The Role of Reinforcement. Authorities have pointed to the crucial role that *contingency* plays in contingency-based self-management. In other words, they point out that reinforcement of some kind, such as social praise or points that can be traded for privileges, is especially important in order for self-management techniques to be effective. For example, an extensive review of research found that contingency-based self-management strategies were more effective than self-management strategies without contingencies in leading to positive behavioral changes in students with ADHD (DuPaul & Eckert, 1997). There is, however, one exception to this. Using self-monitoring, in which students keep track of their own on- and off-task behavior without earning reinforcers, has resulted in improvement in the on-task behavior of students with ADHD (see the box on p. 226).

Although the use of behavioral procedures such as reinforcement and punishment is somewhat controversial—that is, there are those who are opposed to their use (Kohn, 1993)—many authorities consider them almost indispensable in working with students with ADHD. For example, they are an integral part of a set of intervention principles advocated by one team of authorities (see Table 6.2 on p. 227).

Medication Considerations

One of the most controversial topics in all of special education is the treatment of ADHD with medication. **Psychostimulants,** which stimulate or activate neurological functioning, are by far the most frequent type of medication prescribed for ADHD. And by far the most common type of psychostimulant used is methylphenidate, or **Ritalin.** The fact that physicians would prescribe a psychostimulant for someone who exhibits hyperactivity is, at first blush, counterintuitive. In fact, for years professionals referred to the **paradoxical effect of Ritalin** because its effects appeared to be the opposite of those one would expect in the case of someone

psychostimulants. Medications that activate dopamine levels in the frontal and prefrontal areas of the brain that control behavioral inhibition and executive functions; used to treat persons with ADHD.

Ritalin. The most commonly prescribed psychostimulant for ADHD; generic name is methylphenidate.

paradoxical effect of Ritalin. The now discredited belief that Ritalin, even though a stimulant, acts to subdue a person's behavior and that this effect of Ritalin is evident in persons with ADHD but not in those without ADHD.

Programs that allow students to monitor their own behavior and performance may encourage them to maintain appropriate behavior at school.

Self-Monitoring of Attention

A team of researchers at the University of Virginia has refined a self-management procedure originally developed by researchers in New Zealand in the early 1970s (Glynn & Thomas, 1974; Glynn, Thomas, & Shee, 1973). This technique, referred to as self-monitoring of attention, has been studied extensively for over twenty years.

The original studies of the Virginia group were conducted with students with learning disabilities nominated by their teachers as having attention problems. Some, but not all, also had a diagnosis of ADHD. (See Lloyd, Hallahan, Kauffman, & Keller, 1998, and Lloyd, Landrum, & Hallahan, 1991, for reviews of these studies.) However, other researchers have found self-monitoring effective with students who have a primary diagnosis of ADHD (Mathes & Bender, 1997).

Self-monitoring of attention involves having students ask themselves "Was I paying attention?" and recording a "yes" or a "no" on a score sheet (see below) every time they hear a tone on a tape recorder. (The time between tones varies randomly from thirty seconds to one and a half minutes.) The following is a set of sample instructions:

"Johnny, you know how paying attention to your work has been a problem for you. You've heard teachers tell you, 'Pay attention,' 'Get to work,' 'What are you supposed to be doing?' and things like that. Well, today we're going to start something that will help you help yourself pay attention better. First, we need to make sure that you know what paying attention means. This is what I mean by paying attention." (Teacher models immediate and sustained attention to task.) "And this is what I mean by not paying attention." (Teacher models inattentive behaviors such as glancing around and playing with objects.)

"Now you tell me if I was paying attention." (Teacher models attentive and inattentive behaviors and requires the student to categorize them.) "Okay, now let me show you what we're going to do. While you're working, this tape recorder will be turned on. Every once in a while you'll hear a little sound like this." (Teacher plays tone on tape.) "And when you hear that tone, quietly ask yourself, 'Was I paying attention?' If you can answer 'yes,' put a check in this box. If you answer 'no,' put a check in this box. Then go right back to work. When you hear the sound again, ask the question, answer it, mark your answer, and go back to work. Now, let me show you how it works." (Teacher models the entire procedure.) "Now, Johnny, I bet you can do this. Tell me what you're going to do every time you hear a tone. Let's try it. I'll start the tape and you work on these papers." (Teacher observes student's implementation of the entire procedure, praises its correct use, and gradually withdraws his or her presence.)

Once the student is able to use the self-monitoring program successfully and consistently, the teacher weans the child off of the tape recorder and the self-recording sheet. For example, the teacher could suggest that Johnny could ask himself "Was I paying attention?" whenever he thought about it, rather than relying on the tones. And once this is successful, the teacher could ask Johnny to answer his "Was I paying attention?" with something like "Yes, good job" or "No, I'd better get back on task."

Research has shown self-monitoring of attention to be effective in increasing on-task behavior of inattentive students in both elementary and secondary school. And although it works best in seatwork situations, it has also been used successfully in group situations.

Date _____

Was I Paying Attention?

	Yes	No		Yes	No
1			21		
2			22		
3			23		
4			24		
5			25		
6			26		
7			27		
8			28		
9			29		
10			30		
11			31		
12			32		
13			33		
14			34		
15			35		
16			36		
17			37		
18			38		
19			39		
20			40		

Table 6.2	**Pfiffner and Barkley's Intervention Principles for ADHD**

1. Rules and instructions must be clear, brief, and often delivered through more visible and external modes of presentation.

2. Consequences must be delivered swiftly and immediately.

3. Consequences must be delivered more frequently [than for students without ADHD].

4. The types of consequences must often be of a higher magnitude, or more powerful [than for students without ADHD].

5. An appropriate and often richer degree of incentives must be provided.

6. Reinforcers, or particularly, rewards must be changed or rotated more frequently.

7. Anticipation is the key. Teachers must be mindful of planning ahead, particularly during phases of transition across activities or classes, to ensure that the children are cognizant of the shift in rules (and consequences) that is about to occur.

Source: Condensed from L. J. Pfiffner & R. A. Barkley, Treatment of ADHD in school settings. In R. A. Barkley, *Attention-deficit hyperactivity disorder: A handbook for diagnosis and treatment,* 2nd ed. (New York: Guilford Press, 1998), p. 354. Reprinted with permission.

without ADHD. Researchers have concluded, however, that Ritalin influences the release of the neurotransmitter dopamine, thus enabling the brain's executive functions to operate more normally (Swanson, Castellanos, Murias, LaHoste, & Kennedy, 1998; Swanson et al., 1998). Furthermore, it is now believed that Ritalin has the same chemical and behavioral effect on persons without ADHD as it does on those with ADHD (Solanto, 1998).

Ordinarily, Ritalin takes about one hour to take effect, with the optimal effect occurring at about two hours. The effects of Ritalin usually wear off after about four hours. Responsiveness to Ritalin is highly individualistic, so the dosage level and number of doses per day vary from person to person.

Opposition to Ritalin

Not all professionals, parents, and laypeople are in favor of using Ritalin. In fact, Ritalin has been the subject of numerous assaults by the media:

There was a well-publicized "media blitz" against [Ritalin] between 1987–1989, in which nationally broadcast television shows such as *Oprah Winfrey, Phil Donahue,* and *Geraldo Rivera* played a large role ... in several civil suits being threatened or actually begun.... Two other particularly well-known examples include the *New York Times* op-ed piece by John Merrow (October 21, 1995) and the *20/20* segment by Tom Jarrell (October 20, 1995) in which a number of other false allegations were made regarding ADHD and [Ritalin]. ADHD has been labeled a "bogus diagnosis" by these media reports, and these reports have also included unfounded allegations concerning the widespread abuse of [Ritalin] by teenagers.... These reports have continued to attack [Ritalin] as having "dangerous" side effects (e.g., permanent brain damage, severe emotional stress, severe depression, psychosis, Tourette's syndrome).... There have also been many anecdotal reports on the internet vilifying [Ritalin] for its deleterious side effects. Protests against [Ritalin] have also come up on such national news shows as *AM America, CBS News,* and *Night Line.* Psychiatric meetings in which ADHD is a topic of discussion are routinely picketed. *The Church of Scientology* has formed a group called the *Citizens for Human Rights* which has filed suit against several physicians. (Kaminester, 1997, p. 108)

The Research Evidence

Effectiveness. Despite all the negative publicity in the media, most authorities in the area of ADHD are in favor of its use. After hundreds of studies, the research is overwhelmingly positive on its effectiveness in helping students have more normalized behavioral inhibition and executive functioning (Barkley, 1998; Crenshaw, Kavale, Forness, & Reeve, 1999; Forness, Kavale, & Crenshaw, in press).

Nonresponders and Side Effects. Ritalin is not effective for everyone. Somewhere around 30 percent of those who take Ritalin do not have a favorable response (Spencer et al., 1996). In addition, some side effects are possible, including insomnia, reduction in appetite, abdominal pain, headaches, and irritability. There has also been speculation on the possibility that in a very small number of cases Ritalin may cause tics or increase their intensity in those who already have tics (DuPaul et al., 1998). There have also been many anecdotal reports of a "rebound effect," in which a child exhibits irritability as the Ritalin wears off. In most cases, these side effects are mild and can be controlled. For example, in the case of the two most common side effects—insomnia and reduction in appetite—care should be taken not to take the Ritalin too close to mealtime or bedtime. In the case of the rebound effect, some physicians recommend using a time-release form of Ritalin.

Cautions Regarding Ritalin

Although the research is overwhelmingly positive on the effectiveness of Ritalin for increasing appropriate behavior, there are still a number of cautions:

- Ritalin should not be prescribed at the first sign of a behavioral problem. Only after careful analysis of the student's behavior and environment should Ritalin be considered. The use of psychostimulants for ADHD in the United States has doubled every four to seven years since 1971 (Wilens & Biederman, 1992). Furthermore, rates of Ritalin usage vary substantially from one country to another. For example, Ritalin is administered in the United States at more than twice the rate of Great Britain and Australia (Kewley, 1998). Although it is possible that the lower rates of Ritalin usage in other countries indicate that many persons with ADHD are not being treated properly, it is also very likely that at least some children in the United States are being medicated inappropriately.

- Although research has demonstrated the effectiveness of Ritalin on behavioral inhibition and executive functions, the results for academic outcomes have not been as dramatic. Although important academic measures, such as work completed or accuracy on assignments, have improved substantially, the impact on achievement tests has been much less (Forness et al., in press). Thus, teachers should not assume that Ritalin will take care of all the academic problems these students face.

- Parents, teachers, and physicians should monitor dosage levels closely so that the dose used is effective but not too strong. Proper dosage levels vary considerably (Hale et al., 1998).
- Teachers and parents should not lead children to believe that the medication serves as a substitute for self-responsibility and self-initiative.
- Teachers and parents should not view the medication as a panacea; they, too, must take responsibility and initiative in working with the child.
- Parents and teachers should keep in mind that Ritalin is a controlled substance. There is the potential for siblings, peers, or the child himself or herself, to attempt to "experiment" with it.
- The final key to the effective use of Ritalin is *communication* among parents, physicians, teachers, and the child himself or herself.

Service Delivery Models

Because ADHD is not recognized as a separate special education category by the U.S. Department of Education, we do not have statistics on how many students are served in different classroom environments. It is safe to assume, however, that one can find students with ADHD across the entire continuum, from residential schools to full inclusion in general education classrooms. But because, as we noted earlier, there is reason to believe that fewer than half receive any special education services (Forness & Kavale, in press), it is logical to assume that most students with ADHD spend most of their time in general education classrooms.

As with all students with disabilities, the best placement for students with ADHD should be determined on an individual basis. Although full inclusion in a general education classroom may be appropriate for some students with ADHD, the estimate that over half do not receive any special education services can be viewed with some concern. This is especially true in light of the fact that studies have shown that positive behavioral changes in students with ADHD are much more likely to occur in special education than in general education settings (DuPaul & Eckert, 1997).

Psychostimulants, especially Ritalin, have sparked a national controversy over the treatment of ADHD. Although Ritalin is not effective for everyone and can have side effects, the bulk of research evidence supports its effectiveness.

Early Intervention

Diagnosis of young children with ADHD is particularly difficult because many children without ADHD tend to exhibit a great deal of motor activity and a lack of impulse control. For the very reason that excessive activity and impulsivity are relatively normal for young children, preschoolers with ADHD can be particularly difficult to manage. Thus, those preschoolers who really do have ADHD are a great challenge to parents and teachers.

Because of the severity of the symptoms of preschoolers who have been diagnosed with ADHD, the importance of the educational principles of classroom structure, teacher direction, functional assessment, and contingency-based self-management that we discussed above are all the more important. Given that even young children without ADHD do not have fully developed self-management skills, most recommend an even stronger emphasis on the use of contingencies in the form of praise, points, and tangible rewards.

In the case of preschoolers with ADHD and high rates of aggression, even implementing very intensive early intervention procedures, including highly structured classrooms with strong contingencies, leads only to limited behavioral and academic improvements that do not endure (Shelton et al., in press). In other words, even high-quality early intervention is not likely to remediate completely the symptoms of children with ADHD and severe aggression. Such children will, undoubtedly, need long-term programming.

Transition to Adulthood

It was not too long ago that most professionals assumed that ADHD diminished in adolescence and usually disappeared by adulthood. Authorities now recognize that the majority of individuals diagnosed with ADHD in childhood will continue to have significant symptoms in adulthood. And with the greater recognition of ADHD by the scientific community as well as by the popular media, many persons are being diagnosed with ADHD in adulthood. The few studies of prevalence that have been conducted report a prevalence rate of about 4 to 5 percent (Barkley, 1998), which mirrors that for children.

Diagnosis in Adulthood

The diagnosis of ADHD in adults is controversial. Because of the long-held assumption that ADHD did not persist into adulthood, there is not a very long history of research on ADHD in adults. Since the late 1980s and 1990s, however, professionals have begun to make progress in identifying and treating ADHD in adults. Because there is no "test" for ADHD, most authorities hold that the person's history is of utmost importance. As one authoritative team has put it:

> This is old-fashioned medicine, not high-tech. This is a doctor talking to a patient, asking questions, listening to answers, drawing conclusions based on getting to know the patient well. These days we often don't respect or trust anything medical that doesn't depend upon fancy technology. Yet the diagnosis of [ADHD] depends absolutely upon the simplest of all medical procedures: the taking of a history. (Hallowell & Ratey, 1994, pp. 195–196)

> The best test for [ADHD] is the oldest test in the history of medicine: the patient's own story.... If possible, the history should always be taken from at least two people—the identified patient plus a parent or spouse or friend. (Hallowell & Ratey, 1996, p. 188)

Two abbreviated histories of adults with ADHD are presented in the box on page 231.

As crucial as the history is, however, its subjective nature does make it vulnerable to misinterpretation. Thus, clinicians have come up with guidelines for diagnosis. Table 6.3 on page 232 is a set of suggested diagnostic criteria for adults. And Figure 6.2 on page 233 is a flowchart of suggested steps for ruling ADHD "in" or "out."

Two Adults with ADHD: Jeremy's Story and Ann's Story

Jeremy's Story

I remember my desk when I was a child. It was usually piled high with papers, toys—whatever I was working on. Once or twice a year my mother would make me clean it up, and it would feel so wonderful.... The fresh start would last maybe a day or two. Then I would start piling my homework on top of my desk and I'd think, oh no, here we go again. The homework would stop as soon as the desk was cluttered again....

Today, my office at home looks like my desk when I was a kid.... It's so cluttered that when my son comes in, he trips on things. My wife, who's the complete opposite of me, [is] embarrassed for people to see it. The fact that I've lived in that kind of environment for *ten years* seems ridiculous.

I feel ashamed. I'm frustrated as hell. I feel like I'm not a grownup yet. On days I have to do paperwork, I make myself sit at my desk and try to get organized.... I pick up a bill, make it out, and start to put a stamp on it. But the stamps are next to the paper clip box and I think it should go in the desk, so I put it in the desk. And I see more pencils than I need, so I throw two of them out. Then the phone rings, and while I'm on the phone I start throwing out junk mail, and there are magazines on the desk, so I take them to the bookcase. In the bookcase there's an old magazine I don't need anymore so I throw that away. Then I realize that the waste basket is full so I empty it. When I go outside to empty the waste basket, I see that there's something going on in the kitchen, so I do something in there. It's like I'm following a trail from one thing to another....

My motivation is always crisis. What gets done is what has to get done.... Bills get paid at the last moment, usually, like reports in school were done at the last minute. I pushed the limits then, and I still push the limits....

I seek immediate gratification with no long term goals. I've got no goal setting at all, really; I can't even set them. I just kind of fell into photography; I never sat down and said, ok, I want to be a photographer.

My file cabinet symbolizes my inadequacy for me. Ten years ago I was going to straighten it out. Now, ten years later, the file cabinet still isn't straightened out. Knowing that I can't organize my file cabinet—telling myself that I'm going to do it and knowing that I can't—drives me nuts....

From society's point of view, I have the potential to accomplish so much more with my life, and I've come to see myself as lazy because I can't do certain tasks. Now I let my wife make the major decisions in my life—whether to buy a house, whether to have kids, how many to have. I just feel like I have no control over my life. Most of the time it doesn't bother me. But sometimes I get angry, really angry, and it comes out uncontrollably at my wife and my professional associates in sarcasm and shouting. I wish I knew what to do.

—Jeremy Southland

Ann's Story

I grew up not feeling very good about myself. In school, it was hard for me to stay on the subject or to finish anything.... Teachers would be on my back. They said I was such a good child—they couldn't understand it. And I tried so hard. I just couldn't finish anything.... I was distracted very easily by practically everything. If someone sneezed, I'd look at him and my mind would go off in a million directions. I'd look out the window, wondering why he had sneezed....

The situation has persisted into adulthood. I'm very disorganized. Take housekeeping, for example. After dinner, when I start the dishes, I'll wash a little, then run and wipe off the table, wipe the cabinet, talk on the phone, and never get anything completed. I have to really concentrate and tell myself "You are going to get the dishes done." Then they get done, but I still get the urge to stop and go wash off the dining room table. Just like someone is pulling me. My closet and drawers are still a mess, just like when I was a kid.

What's really hard is to stay with any kind of paper work—bills, for example. It's my husband's job to do the bills. If it were mine, we'd probably be in jail.... Only recently at age forty-five have I been able to sit down and write a letter. I usually write small postcards.

I'm the most impulsive person in the world. It gets me in trouble. If I see something I know I shouldn't buy, I'll buy it anyway. Or, I'll say something that I know the minute it comes out of my mouth I'm going to regret....

I wish I could just slow down and relax. I have problems sitting still.... People say I make them nervous, but I don't even realize I'm doing anything. That hurts my feelings. I don't want to be different.

My dream has always been to be some kind of counselor, but I felt like I wasn't college material, so I got married and had two children. I have a real estate license now. I don't know how I passed the test. I must have guessed right. What I like about selling is that I'm always on the move and I love people. I'm tuned into them. But I'm too sensitive to have a sense of humor. I think I have a thin skin. I get my feelings hurt easily. When that happens, I cry and go into my shell.

My mood swings from high to low. I either feel very good or very down. I feel up if the house looks good. If I get everything done that I think I should, it makes me feel good about myself. I feel responsible for a lot of people. If my husband is in a bad mood, or if things aren't going right for my kids, my mother, or my sister, I feel bad. I don't know what's wrong with me.

—Ann Ridgley

Source: Weiss, L. (1992). *Attention deficit disorder in adults.* Dallas, TX: Taylor Publishing Co. (pp. 11–14).

Table 6.3   Suggested Diagnostic Criteria for Attention Deficit Disorder in Adults

Note: Consider a criterion met only if the behavior is considerably more frequent than that of most people of the same mental age.

A. A chronic disturbance in which at least twelve of the following are present:

- A sense of underachievement, of not meeting one's goals (regardless of how much one has actually accomplished).
- Difficulty getting organized.
- Chronic procrastination or trouble getting started.
- Many projects going simultaneously; trouble with followthrough.
- A tendency to say what comes to mind without necessarily considering the timing or appropriateness of the remark.
- A frequent search for high stimulation.
- An intolerance of boredom.
- Easy distractibility, trouble focusing attention, tendency to tune out or drift away in the middle of a page or a conversation, often coupled with an ability to hyperfocus at times.
- Often creative, intuitive, highly intelligent.
- Trouble in going through established channels, following "proper" procedure.

- Impatient; low tolerance of frustration.
- Impulsive, either verbally or in action, as in impulsive spending of money, changing plans, enacting new schemes or career plans, and the like; hot-tempered.
- A tendency to worry needlessly, endlessly; a tendency to scan the horizon looking for something to worry about, alternating with inattention to or disregard for actual dangers.
- A sense of insecurity.
- Mood swings, mood lability, especially when disengaged from a person or a project.
- Physical or cognitive restlessness.
- A tendency toward addictive behavior.
- Chronic problems with self-esteem.
- Inaccurate self-observation.
- Family history of ADD or manic-depressive illness or depression or substance abuse or other disorders of impulse control or mood.

B. Childhood history of ADD. (It may not have been formally diagnosed, but in reviewing the history, one sees that the signs and symptoms were there.)

C. Situation not explained by other medical or psychiatric condition.

Source: Hallowell, E. M., & Ratey, J. J. (1995). *Driven to distraction: Recognizing and coping with attention deficit disorder from childhood through adulthood.* New York: Touchstone/Simon & Schuster.

Adult Outcomes

Adults who are diagnosed in childhood with ADHD finish fewer years of formal schooling and obtain jobs of lower social status than those who do not have ADHD (Mannuzza, Klein, Bessler, Malloy, & Hynes, 1997; Mannuzza, Klein, Bessler, Malloy, & LaPadula, 1993; Weiss, Hechtman, Milroy, & Perlman, 1985). Those who have a coexisting condition, such as depression or aggression, tend to have less positive outcomes than those who do not. Although persons with ADHD are at risk for poorer outcomes, it is important to point out that there are many adults with ADHD who have highly successful careers and jobs, and many have happy marriages and families.

Employment.   One of the keys to successful employment for all people, but especially for persons with ADHD, is to select a job or career that maximizes the individual's strengths and minimizes his or her weaknesses. Success is often dependent on pursuing a job that fits a person's needs for structure versus independence. For those who work best with structure, it is recommended that they look for jobs with organizations that have a clear mission and lines of authority, with

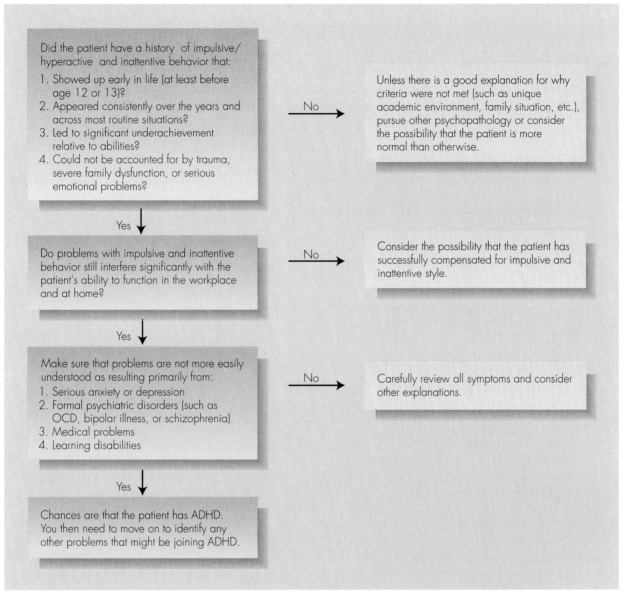

Figure 6.2

The road to a diagnosis of adult ADHD.

Source: Barkley, R. A. (1998),
*Attention-deficit hyperactivity disorder:
A handbook for diagnosis and
treatment* (2nd ed.), p. 354. New
York: Guilford Press.

an emphasis on oversight from supervisors who have an understanding of ADHD. Those who find formal structures too confining should look for work environments that are flexible, have variety, and allow one to be independent (Hallowell & Ratey, 1996).

Marriage and Family. Given some of the behavioral characteristics of ADHD, it is not surprising that husbands and wives of persons with ADHD frequently complain that their spouse is a poor listener, preoccupied, forgetful, unreliable, messy, and so forth (Murphy, 1998). A person's ADHD can have a negative impact on the entire family. Many authorities recommend that the first step to treatment is to have all family members become educated about the facts associated with ADHD. Because ADHD is a family issue, they also recommend that all members of the family should be partners in its treatment:

Unlike some medical problems, [ADHD] touches everybody in the family in a daily, significant way. It affects early-morning behavior, it affects dinner-table behavior, it affects vacations, and it affects quiet time. Let each member of the family become a part of the solution, just as each member of the family has been a part of the problem. (Hallowell & Ratey, 1996, p. 303)

Table 6.4 provides twenty-five tips on the management of ADHD in couples, when one of the partners has ADHD. With current high rates of divorce and

Table 6.4 Twenty-Five Tips on the Management of ADHD in Couples

1. Make sure you have an accurate diagnosis. Once you are sure of the diagnosis, learn as much as you can about ADHD.

2. Keep a sense of humor! At that psychological branch point we all know so well when the split-second options are to get mad, cry, or laugh, go for the laughter. Humor is a key to a happy life with ADHD.

3. Declare a truce. After you have made the diagnosis and have done some reading, take a deep breath and wave the white flag.

4. Set up a time for talking.

5. Spill the beans. Tell each other what is on your mind. Tell each other just how you are being driven crazy, what you like, what you want to change, what you want to preserve. Try to say it all before you both start reacting. People with ADHD have a tendency to bring premature closure to discussions, to go for the bottom line. In this case, the bottom line is the discussion itself.

6. Write down your complaints and your recommendations. Otherwise you'll forget.

7. Make a treatment plan. You may want some professional help with this phase, but it is a good idea to try starting it on your own.

8. Follow through on the plan. Remember, one of the hallmarks of ADHD is insufficient follow-through.

9. Make lists for each other. Try to use them constructively, not as threats or evidence in arguments.

10. Use bulletin boards. Messages in writing are less likely to be forgotten.

11. Put notepads in strategic places such as by your bed, in your car, in the bathroom and kitchen.

12. Consider writing down what you want the other person to do. This must be done in the spirit of assistance, not dictatorship. Keep a master appointment book for both of you.

13. Take stock of your sex lives. ADHD can affect sexual interest and performance. It is good to know the problems are due to ADHD, and not something else.

14. Avoid the pattern of mess-maker and cleaner-upper.

15. Avoid the pattern of pesterer and tuner-outer.

16. Avoid the pattern of the victim and the victimizer. You don't want the ADHD partner to present himself or herself as a helpless victim left at the merciless hands of the all-controlling non-ADHD mate.

17. Avoid the pattern of master and slave. In a funny way it can often be the non-ADHD partner who feels like the slave to his or her mate's ADHD.

18. Avoid the pattern of a sadomasochistic struggle as a routine way of interacting. Many couples spend most of their time attacking and counterattacking each other. One hopes to get past that and into the realm of problem solving. What you have to be aware of is the covert pleasure that can be found in the struggle. Try to vent your anger at the disorder, not at the person.

19. In general, watch out for the dynamics of control, dominance, and submission that lurk in the background of most relationships, let alone relationships where ADHD is involved.

20. Break the tapes of negativity. The "tapes of negativity" can play relentlessly, unforgivingly, endlessly in the mind of the person. They play over and over, grinding noises of "You can't," "You're dumb," "It won't work out." The tapes can be playing in the midst of a business deal, or they can take the place of making love. It is hard to be romantic when you are full of negative thoughts.

21. Use praise freely.

22. Learn about mood management. Anticipation is a great way to help anyone deal with the highs and lows that come along. If you know in advance that when you say "Good morning, honey!" the response you get might be "Get off my back, will you!" then it is easier to deal with that response without getting a divorce.

23. Let the one who is the better organizer take on the job of organization.

24. Make time for each other.

25. Don't use ADHD as an excuse. Each member of the couple has to take responsibility for his or her actions.

Source: From *Answers to Distraction* by Edward M. Hallowell, M.D. & John J. Ratey, M.D. (New York: Bantam Books, 1996), pp. 308–312. Reprinted by permission of Pantheon Books, a division of Random House, Inc.

For learners with ADHD, coaching beyond high school through either a job coach, therapist, or teacher counselor is highly recommended.

single-parent families in the United States, many of these suggestions would also be applicable to the general population.

Importance of Coaching

One highly recommended therapeutic technique is that of coaching (Hallowell & Ratey, 1994). **Coaching** involves identifying someone whom the person with ADHD can rely on for support. The term *coach* is used because this person can be visualized as someone "standing on the sidelines with a whistle around his or her neck barking out encouragement, directions, and reminders to the player in the game" (Hallowell & Ratey, 1994, p. 226). The coach, who can be a therapist or a friend, is someone who spends ten to fifteen minutes each day helping to keep the person with ADHD focused on his or her goals. The coach provides the structure needed to plan for upcoming events and activities, and heaps on praise when tasks are accomplished.

Although ADHD is a lifelong struggle for most people with the condition, with the appropriate combination of medical, educational, and psychological counseling, satisfactory employment and family adjustment is within the reach of most people with ADHD. And now that most authorities recognize that ADHD often continues into adulthood, more and more research will be focused on treatment of ADHD in adults. With this research should come an even more positive outlook for adults with ADHD.

> **coaching.** A technique whereby a friend or therapist offers encouragement and support for a person with ADHD.

Summary

Attention Deficit Hyperactivity Disorder, or ADHD, was first recognized as early as the mid-nineteenth century, though the term ADHD did not appear until over a hundred years later. Early "cases" of the disorder were represented by children described as impulsive, fidgety, or generally lacking in the ability to control their behavior. In 1902, Dr. George F. Still referred to children whose behavior would now be seen as symptomatic of ADHD as having "defective moral control," or an inability to refrain from inappropriate behavior. To this day, ADHD is considered to be primarily a deficit involving behavioral inhibition.

The concept of ADHD has been subject to criticism, often being referred to as a convenient catchall for persons who are simply lazy, disobedient, or unmotivated. ADHD is not recognized as its own special education category, such as mental retardation, learning disabilities, and so forth. However, many students with ADHD are served by special education under the category of "other health impaired."

Research and clinical observations during the middle part of this century suggested compelling evidence for a connection between brain injury and the presence of behaviors now associated with ADHD. Professionals began to apply the label of "minimal brain injury" to children who were inattentive, impulsive, and/or hyperactive. However, while clinical evidence seemed to connect brain injuries and ADHD, actual tissue damage in the brain was difficult to document. Thus, labeling and diagnoses of the disorder continued to rely on behavioral observations, with the primary focus being hyperactivity—the "hyperactive" child. By the 1980s, "inattention" began to be recognized as the primary deficit in cases of ADHD, sometimes accompanied by hyperactivity and sometimes not.

Most professionals rely on the American Psychiatric Association's *Diagnostic and Statistical Manual of Mental Disorders (DSM)* for the criteria used to determine whether an individual has ADHD. The current *DSM* uses ADHD as the general term and subdivides individuals into (1) ADHD, Predominantly Inattentive Type; (2) ADHD, Predominantly Hyperactive-Impulsive Type; and (3) ADHD, Combined Type.

Actual prevalence figures for ADHD are difficult to obtain, though estimates are that 3 to 5 percent of school-age children have ADHD. ADHD is recognized widely as one of the most frequent reasons that children are referred for behavioral problems to guidance clinics. It occurs much more frequently in boys than in girls, though discrepancies between samples of children referred to clinics and samples taken from the population at large, as well as the fact that boys are more likely to exhibit aggressive behavior, and are thus more likely to be referred to clinics, have been cited as evidence that these figures reflect a gender bias. However, the fact that boys still outnumber girls by more than three to one suggests that real constitutional differences exist.

Assessment of whether a student has ADHD should include three components: (1) a medical examination to rule out other reasons for the child's behavior problems; (2) a clinical interview to obtain as much relevant information as possible about the child's physical and psychological characteristics; and (3) teacher and parent rating scales, as a means of quantifying observations. Care must be taken to recognize the subjective nature of interview situations and the fact that persons with ADHD often can behave "normally" in the structured setting of a doctor's office.

Advances in neuroimaging techniques during the 1980s and 1990s allowed scientists to more accurately document the neurological basis of ADHD. Research has found abnormalities in three areas of the brain in persons with ADHD: the frontal lobes, the basal ganglia, and the cerebellum. The frontal lobes are responsible for executive functions, or the abilitiy to regulate one's behavior. The basal ganglia and cerebellum are involved in coordination and control of motor behavior. Research has also revealed abnormal levels of the neurotransmitter dopamine in persons with ADHD, suggesting that levels of dopamine are too low in the frontal cortex, thus interfering with executive functioning, and too high in the basal ganglia, resulting in hyperactivity and impulsivity.

Family studies and twin studies indicate that heredity may also be a significant cause of ADHD. Also involved, though to a lesser degree, are teratogenic factors such as exposure to lead and abuse of alcohol and tobacco, as well as medical factors such as complications at birth and low birthweight.

While the most obvious psychological and behavioral characteristics of ADHD are inattention, hyperactivity, and impulsivity, the more basic problem is the inability to inhibit or regulate one's own behavior. The inability to withhold, interrupt, or delay responses tends to undermine executive functioning. Persons with ADHD find it difficult to engage in a variety of self-directed behaviors or to stay focused on tasks that require sustained effort or concentration.

Children and adults with ADHD also appear to experience problems in adaptive behavior and in their relationships with peers. It is not uncommon for students with ADHD to experience social isolation, though they desperately might want to be liked. ADHD often occurs simultaneously with other behavioral and/or learning disorders, such as learning disabilities, emotional or behavioral disorders, or Tourette's syndrome. Persons with ADHD are also at a higher risk for substance abuse, with adults being twice as likely as the general population to become dependent on alcohol, drugs, or tobocco.

Educational programming for students with ADHD usually has two components: (1) classroom structure and teacher direction; and (2) functional assessment and contingency-based self-management. A high degree of classroom structure and teacher direction, first advocated by William Cruickshank, is rarely seen today, partly because the intensity with which Cruickshank thought it should be practiced cannot practically be delivered in general education settings, where most students with ADHD are placed. In addition, today's educators believe that while a high degree of structure is important in the early stages of working with students with ADHD, the ultimate priority is for them to become independent in their learning.

Functional assessment of students with ADHD involves determining the consequences, antecedents, and setting events that maintain appropriate behaviors (Horner & Carr, 1997). Such approaches might also include self-monitoring or self-management programs, wherein students record their own behaviors. These approaches are often contingency-based, with persons keeping track of their own behavior and then receiving consequences, usually in the form of rewards. Reinforcement in the form of social praise or points that can be traded for privileges plays an important role in the effectiveness of self-management techniques.

The treatment of ADHD with medication is one of the most controversial issues in all of special education, both within and outside the profession. Ritalin, a psychostimulant, is by far the most commonly prescribed medication for ADHD; most scientific studies support its effectiveness, and most authorities in ADHD favor its use. Ritalin stimulates the release of the neurotransmitter dopamine, thereby enabling more normal operation of the brain's executive and motor functions. Responsiveness to Ritalin is highly individualistic, so dosages may vary greatly from person to person. Possible side effects, including insomnia and reduction in appetite, can usually be addressed very simply. Ritalin should not be prescribed at the "first sign" of behavior problems, nor should it be viewed as a panacea for all of a child's academic and social problems.

Early detection of ADHD is difficult, partly because symptoms of ADHD are hard to distinguish from typical behaviors of very young children. Moreover, even high-quality early interventions have not proven to be very effective in the remediation of ADHD. Long-term programming for such children will in most cases still be needed.

The diagnosis of adult ADHD is controversial. For a long time it was assumed that children "outgrew" ADHD, and there has yet to be developed any real "test" for ADHD. Therefore, an interview or history is most crucial in identifying ADHD in adults, though interviews are subjective in nature and might be vulnerable to misinterpretation. Adults with ADHD tend to have less positive outcomes that the general population in terms of employment, marriage and family, and general social well-being, although many exceptions do exist. A recommended therapeutic technique for adults with ADHD is to establish a relationship with a coach, most likely a therapist or a friend, who will spend time regularly with them and help them keep focused on their goals.

suggestions for teaching

Students with Attention Deficit Hyperactivity Disorder in General Education Classrooms

By E. Jane Nowacek

As discussed in the chapter, physicians may prescribe medication for individuals with ADHD. Although teachers may be asked to monitor the academic performance and behavior of students who are taking medication, they do not determine whether or what medication will be used. Therefore, a discussion of medication as an intervention will not be included in this section.

Although no two students with ADHD are identical, many need opportunities during the school day to study away from distractions and to move around the classroom. These students also seem to work best in a structured environment in which novel learning activities are provided. In addition, they often require specific strategies and interventions that help them approach and complete academic tasks and control their behavior. Research with students with learning and behavior problems suggests several techniques that may address their academic and behavioral needs.

Academic Modifications and Interventions

Modifications Before Teaching Consider developing a general plan that addresses some of the needs of students with ADHD (Chesapeake Institute, 1994; Dowdy, Patton, Smith, & Polloway,

1998; Lerner, Lowenthal, & Lerner, 1995; Reid & Maag, 1998; Zentall, 1995; Zentall & Stormont-Spurgin, 1995). For example, think about the physical arrangement of your room. Provide a quiet study area that is located away from high traffic and noise and encourage all students to work in this area or in individual "offices" (study carrels) when they need to concentrate. Establish daily and weekly schedules for classroom activities and display them in the classroom or student planner. There are several ways to modify lessons (e.g., length, format, and difficulty). Consider chunking, or breaking down, each class period into fifteen-minute segments to accommodate short attention spans. Plan various ways students can receive information (input) and ways students can act on information (output). See Figure 6.A for a model of instructional planning.

Build in opportunities for students to move about the classroom by planning activities that encourage students to respond actively, such as working at the board or engaging in role plays, and by encouraging students to follow established classroom routines that allow movement, such as getting and returning materials from designated areas and putting completed assignments in a specified location. Finally, consider what preskills or study skills the academic activities you are planning require and teach these skills directly to students who do not know them.

For example, many students do not know how to take notes. Evans, Pelham, and Grudberg (1994–95) reported a Directed Notetaking Activity (DNA), previously described by Spires and Stone (1989), that improved students' comprehension and disruptive behavior. To begin DNA, as the teacher lectures, he or she provides students with a model of the notes on an overhead and directs them to copy the notes in their notebooks exactly as they appear on the overhead. The teacher explains why some of the information is considered a main idea and why other information is considered detail, and monitors students to be sure all are taking notes. Once students successfully complete this activity for several days, the teacher no longer provides notes, but interrupts the lecture at key points and asks students to give ideas for notes. Using prompts and redirection, the instructor works with the class to generate accurate notes, which are then written on the overhead as a model. During this process the teacher continues to discuss the main ideas, but simply writes the details on the overhead without comment. Gradually the teacher stops writing the details on the overhead model, but continues to discuss and note the main ideas. Several weeks after beginning DNA, the teacher stops using the overhead but answers questions and repeats statements when asked so students can create their own accurate notes. By following DNA, teachers support student learning.

Modifications During Teaching As Montague and Warger (1997) indicate, there are many checklists available for modifying instruction. Most contain the following formats and suggestions:

- Maintain student involvement in group lessons (e.g., keep objectives clear, teach students cognitive strategies such as "think aloud," deliver the lesson at a brisk pace, prompt for student answers after a three- to five-second wait time, model enthusiasm, use meaningful materials, break up presentations with opportunities for students to respond).
- Maintain student involvement in seatwork (e.g., break up long assignments into shorter segments, allow extra time for completing assignments, reduce the number of practice items that students must complete once they have demonstrated mastery).
- Help students engage in learning tasks (e.g., use "to do" lists and checklists, highlight written directions with larger type or color coding, teach students how to use graphic organizers).

In addition, consider providing cues such as time-to-start cues at the beginning of each instructional activity during which students check for and get needed materials and review expectations/goals (Bender & Mathes, 1995), and cues that help students to organize by

Student Input/Output Options						
Output: **Input:**	**Writes**	**Talks**	**Makes**	**Performs**	**Solves**	**Identifies**
Reads						
Listens						
Views						
Does						

Figure 6.A

Student input/output options.

Source: C. A. Dowdy, J. R. Patton, T. E. C. Smith, & E. A. Polloway, *Attention-deficit/hyperactivity disorder in the classroom,* Austin, TX: Pro-Ed, 1998, p. 128. Adapted from J. F. Cawley, A. M. Fitzmaurice-Hayes, and R. A. Shaw, *Mathematics for the mildly handicapped: A guide to curriculum and instruction,* Boston: Allyn & Bacon, 1988, and from P. B. Smith and G. Bentley, *Facilitator manual, Teacher training program: Mainstreaming mildly handicapped students in the regular classroom,* Austin, TX: Education Service Center, Region XII, 1975. Reprinted with permission.

reminding them to record assignments (Chesapeake Institute, 1994).

Interventions During Teaching *Strategy instruction.* DuPaul and Eckert (1998) define strategy instruction as an approach that teaches students to use a set of procedures that specifically address the demands of an academic situation. These investigators report preliminary evidence that suggests strategy instruction can result in short-term improvements in academic performance and on-task behavior and promote independent responsibility for academic outcomes. Educators have developed strategies designed to teach students with learning and behavior problems how to manage themselves, how to learn and study, and how to acquire and demonstrate competence in academic areas such as reading, writing, spelling. See Dowdy, Patton, Smith, and Polloway (1998, p. 108) for a list of many of these strategies. Also see Bos and Vaughn (1998) and Zentall (1993) for techniques useful in teaching specific content areas. This section will focus on some strategies to enhance performance across content areas.

Self-regulation strategies. Self-regulation strategies are promising interventions for students with ADHD because they increase focus, modify impulsive responding, and provide steps and/or self-instructional statements that help students to solve academic and social problems (Dowdy, Patton, Smith, & Polloway, 1998). They involve students in:

- Determining an academic or behavioral goal (self-assessment)
- Observing and recording observations of one's behavior (self-monitoring)
- Instructing or questioning oneself (self-instruction)
- Administering reinforcement to oneself (self-reinforcement)

Bos and Vaughn (1998) report a self-management strategy designed to assist students in setting goals and in keeping track of their process. MARKER, an acronym for this strategy, gives students both a mark to work toward and a marker of their progress. Originally developed by Van Reusen and Bos (1992), this strategy consists of the following steps:

Make a list of goals, set the order, set the date.
Arrange a plan for each goal and predict your success.
Run your plan for each goal and adjust if necessary.
Keep records of your progress.
Evaluate your progress toward each goal.
Reward yourself when you reach a goal, and set a new goal.

For each goal, students use a Goal Planning Sheet on which they answer the following questions:

- Can I describe my goal?
- What is the reason or purpose for the goal?
- Where am I going to work on and complete this goal?
- How much time do I have to complete the goal?
- What materials do I need to complete the goal?
- Can I divide the goal into steps or parts? If so, in what order should I complete each step or part?
- How am I going to keep records of my progress?
- How will I reward myself for reaching my goal?

Learning-to-learn strategies. These strategies, often called "metacognitive" strategies, provide students with specific steps to follow or questions to ask that promote awareness of the skills, strategies, and resources they need to perform a task effectively and enhance their ability to plan, evaluate, check, and remediate.

Think-Aloud strategy. This procedure was designed to assist students to generate questions that help them monitor their understanding as they read (Davey, 1983). To begin, the teacher models the following self-questions in Think-Aloud sessions (Wisconsin Department of Public Instruction, 1989):

Before Reading: "Before I read I ask myself several questions: Why am I reading this selection (purposes)? What will I do with this information? What do I know already about this topic? What do I think I'll learn about this topic (predictions)?"

During Reading: "As I read I ask myself: Am I understanding? Does this make sense to me? Is this what I expected? What parts are similar to and different from my predictions?"

After Reading: "When I finish reading, I wonder: What are the most important points? Which parts of the text support them? How do I feel about this information? What new information did I learn and how does it fit with what I already know? Do I need to go back and reread part so I can understand better?" (p. 158).

After every question, the teacher talks through his or her answer aloud. As a result, Think-Alouds model for students both the strategy of self-questioning and the thought processes used to monitor and regulate comprehension. Gradually, teachers stop modeling this procedure and begin prompting students to "think aloud" on their own. As students become more proficient at using this strategy, instructors stop giving prompts.

Peer Tutoring. All models of peer tutoring have characteristics that enhance the sustained attention of students with ADHD, including: (1) one-to-one work with another individual, (2) instructional pace set by learner, (3) continuous prompting of responses, and (4) frequent and immediate feedback about performance (DuPaul & Eckert, 1998). See the Teaching Suggestions for Students with Mental Retardation following Chapter 4 for a detailed discussion of peer tutoring.

Computer-assisted instruction. As DuPaul and Eckert (1998) point out, there is preliminary evidence that computer-assisted instruction (CAI) may be an effective alternative for some children with ADHD. Because the characteristics of software packages may affect attending behaviors, these educators indicate that software that includes game formats and animation may be more effective than drill and practice or tutorial programs. For more information see *Computer-Assisted Instruction for Students at Risk for ADHD, Mild Disabilities, or Academic Problems* (Bender & Bender, 1996).

Modifications After Teaching
- Plan follow-up lesson(s) or mini-lesson(s) for students who need additional instruction and practice.
- Consider testing accommodations, such as those recommended by Jayanthi, Epstein, Polloway, & Bursuck (1996):
  Use black-and-white copies instead of dittos
  Provide extra space for answering test items
  Give practice questions in a study guide
  Give open-book/notes tests
  Provide individual help with directions during test
  Permit use of aids (such as calculators) during test
  Give extended time to finish tests
  Give fewer questions to answer
  Highlight key words in questions

Read test items to students
Give several quizzes rather than few exams
Simplify wording on test items
Use tests with enlarged print

- Consider grading options. Reflect on the options for evaluation listed in Table 6.A and select those that are suited to the purpose and to your students (Wood, 1998, p. 507).

Behavioral Modifications and Interventions

Reid and Maag (1998) report there are two components of the classroom environment that can be modified to influence students' behavior: (a) antecedents, those events that occur before a student acts; and (b) consequences, those that occur after a student acts. Most classroom modifications focus on antecedents and their intent is to prevent future behavior problems. Interventions, however, are designed to provide students either with reinforcement after an appropriate behavior, or punishment following an inappropriate behavior.

Behavioral Modifications Teachers frequently use modifications that include (Chesapeake Institute, 1994; Dowdy, Patton, Smith, & Polloway, 1998):

- Maintaining an orderly, predictable classroom environment by establishing clear rules that are stated in positive terms so students know exactly what is expected of them. Be sure the rules are enforceable consistently and reward students who follow classroom rules as well as punishing those who do not. Check that all students understand classroom rules. To promote understanding you may decide to take photographs of your students engaged in positive behaviors and display these pictures with the rules or otherwise illustrate each rule.
- Considering the student's activity level by applying classroom rules flexibly (e.g., out-of-seat behavior).
- Giving behavioral prompts to let students know when their behavior is inappropriate (e.g., by making eye contact, moving nearer to the student, calling the student's name, using a primary, prearranged signal word).
- Cueing students when situations will require extra control (e.g., assemblies, fire drills).
- Considering consequence options (e.g., praise effort, give specific compliments for improved behavior).

Behavioral Interventions Once a behavior has occurred and it has been defined in observable terms, teachers can intervene in three ways: positively reinforce the behavior, ignore it, or punish it.

There are various techniques that teachers can use to implement each of these responses. For a discussion of several interventions, including positive reinforcement, see the Teaching Suggestions for Students with Emotional and/or Behavioral Disorders that follows Chapter 7.

Group Contingencies Although there is little research on the use of group contingencies with students with ADHD, if the attention of students in the class is maintaining inappropriate behavior or ignoring appropriate behaviors, a group contingency may be helpful (Reid and Maag, 1998). In this intervention, a group of people, such as a whole class or a cooperative learning group, is treated as one individual. Rewards (i.e., positive reinforcement) are given to everyone in the group based on, or contingent on, the group's meeting specified expectations, such as following classroom rules.

Group contingencies also can combine positive reinforcement and punishment techniques. In an elementary classroom, for example, a teacher used a combined procedure called Stoplight. In this class, when students worked quietly, a green circle was displayed on a cardboard traffic light. If the green light continued to show for a specified period of time, the class was eligible for a reward. When the noise increased and approached an unacceptable level, the teacher covered the green light and exposed the yellow caution light. If the noise level became too loud, the teacher displayed the red light, which signaled the class to stop and also indicated that no reward could be earned for that period of time. In another example, teachers in a middle school initiated a combined procedure that they called Animal Bucks. Here teachers gave each team of students $10 every two weeks. Team members earned bucks by helping peers and lost dollars by not following class rules. At the end of the two-week period, teams that had a specified number of dollars left were allowed to purchase a reward.

Another type of group contingency is peer-mediated contingencies. In this intervention, classmates are trained to praise peers' appropriate behavior and to ignore the inappropriate. There are three types of peer-mediated contingencies (Abramowitz & O'Leary, 1991):

- Interdependent (i.e., the behavior of the entire group receives reinforcement). The Animals Bucks procedure described above is an example of this type of peer-mediated contingency because everyone on the team received rewards if the team met the stated criteria.
- Independent (i.e., each student's behavior determines his or her eligibility to receive the group reward, which is based on a set of contingencies applied to the whole group). For example, Animal Bucks could be implemented so that at the end of the two-week period only those students on the team with the specified number of dollars would be able to purchase a reward.
- Dependent (i.e., the behavior of one or more students determines the reinforcement that is available to the entire group). In Animal Bucks, for example, if one or more team members did not have the required number of bucks left, no one on the team would be able to purchase a reward.

Regardless of the type of contingency selected, Kauffman, Pullen, and Akers (cited in Reid and Maag, 1998) report that teachers need to set a criterion for acceptable performance that all students can achieve; select behaviors that reflect socially appropriate behavior; and keep competition fair by ensuring the students in each group have similar ability and skills. In addition, teachers must monitor group contingencies to be sure that students don't ignore misbehavior because they fear rejection, or become overly punitive (Abramowitz & O'Leary, 1991).

Response Cost Although many educators (e.g., Reid & Maag, 1998) indicate punishment used by itself is not very effective, others (e.g., Abramawitz & O'Leary, 1991) report investigations that suggest some negative consequences, such as reprimands, are important in managing certain behaviors such as the off-task behavior exhibited by many students with ADHD. One intervention that involves punishment, or consequences that reduce the future probability of a behavior, is response cost. In this procedure, predetermined amounts of reinforcers are withdrawn each time a specified inappropriate behavior occurs. There are many ways teachers apply response costs. Bender and Mathes (1995) report one in which a teacher listed the numbers 20 to 1, indicating the amount

Table 6.A	Alternative Approaches to Evaluation
Approach	**Example**
1. *Traditional grading:* letter grades or percentages are assigned.	Students earning 94 percent or greater of the total points available will earn an A.
2. *Pass/fail system:* broad-based criteria are established for passing or failing.	Students who complete all assignments and pass all tests will receive a passing grade for the course.
3. *IEP grading:* competency levels on student's IEP are translated into the school district's performance standards.	If a student's IEP requires a 90 percent accuracy level and the range of 86–93 equals a letter grade of B on the local scale, the student receives a B if he or she attains target accuracy level.
4. *Mastery- or criterion-level grading:* content is divided into subcomponents. Students earn credit when their mastery of a certain skill reaches an acceptable level.	Students who name 38 of the 50 state capitals will receive a passing grade on that unit of the social studies curriculum.
5. *Multiple grading:* the student is assessed and graded in several areas, such as ability, effort, and achievement.	Student will receive 30 points for completing the project on time, 35 points for including all of the assigned sections, and 35 points for using at least four different resources.
6. *Shared grading:* two or more teachers determine a student's grade.	The regular education teacher will determine 60 percent of the student's grade, and the resource room teacher will determine 40 percent.
7. *Point system:* points are assigned to activities or assignments that add up to the term grade.	The student's science grade will be based on a total of 300 points: 100 from weekly quizzes, 100 from lab work in class, 50 from homework, and 50 from class participation.
8. *Student self-comparison:* students evaluate themselves on an individual basis.	If a student judges that he or she has completed the assignment on time, included the necessary sections, and worked independently, then the student assigns him or herself a passing grade for this assignment.
9. *Contracting:* the student and teacher agree on specific activities required for a certain grade.	If the student comes to class regularly, volunteers information at least once during each class, and turns in all required work, then he or she will receive a C.
10. *Portfolio evaluation:* a cumulative portfolio is maintained of each student's work, demonstrating achievement in key skill areas from kindergarten to 12th grade.	Cumulative samples of the handwriting show progress from rudimentary manuscript to legible cursive style from grades 1 to 4.

Source: J. W. Wood, *Adapting instruction to accommodate students in inclusive settings* (3rd ed.). Upper Saddle River, NJ: Merrill/Prentice-Hall, 1998, p. 507. Reprinted with permission.

of time allocated for break. Every time a child blurted out an answer, the targeted behavior, the teacher crossed out the highest number. If, for example, a student blurted out five times during a predetermined period of time, she or he would have fifteen minutes for break instead of the full twenty minutes.

Strategies Educators have developed a variety of strategies to help individuals control their behavior and interact with others appropriately (e.g., social skills training). Bos & Vaughn (1998) report two strategies—FAST and SLAM—designed to promote interpersonal problem solving:

FAST, a strategy that teaches students to reflect on problems before responding to them and to consider options and their consequences.

Freeze and think! (Students are taught to identify the problem.) What is the problem?

Alternatives? (Students are taught to generate solution options.) What are my possible solutions?

Solution evaluation. (Students consider options and select one that is both safe and fair.) Choose the best solution: Safe? Fair?

Try it! (Students rehearse and carry out the solution. If they are unsuccessful, they are taught to go back to the Alternatives.) Slowly and carefully. Does it work?

SLAM, a strategy intended to help students in accepting and assimilating negative feedback and comments from other people (McIntosh, Vaughn, & Bennerson, 1995).

Stop whatever you are doing.

Look the person in the eye.

Ask the person a question to clarify what he or she means.

Make an appropriate response to the person.

Summary of Procedures

Teachers can support students with ADHD in their classrooms in several ways. They can make modifications, many of which seem to benefit the majority of students in the class because they are simply good educational practices. They also can intervene once a student has acted. Multimodal treatment for ADHD includes academic and behavioral interventions and other therapies such as social skills training and impulse control. The bottom line is to help students increase their academic skills and appropriate behavior while decreasing their inappropriate behaviors (Bender & Mathes, 1995). In addition, teachers need to monitor student performance and behavior to determine if modifications and interventions are effective and to make adjustments if they are not. Recording daily frequency of behavior before and then after the intervention is helpful in this process. Tallying the frequency of behaviors is the simplest way to collect data for many behaviors, such as out-of-seat and talking out. These data are helpful not only in scheduling and planning the school day, but in providing important information to the family and other professionals who work with the student. Finally, success is greatly influenced by the commitment of teachers to consistently implement modifications and interventions.

Helpful Resources

Instructional Methods and Materials

Asher, M. J., & Gordon, S. B. (1998). *Meeting the ADD challenge: A practical guide for teachers.* Champaign, IL: Research Press.

Bos, C. S., & Vaughn, S. (1998). *Strategies for teaching students with learning and behavior problems* (4th ed.). Boston: Allyn & Bacon.

Cherkes-Julkowski, M., Sharp, S., & Stolzenberg, J. (1997). *Attention deficit disorders: A radical reconceptualization and its implications for classroom instruction.* Cambridge, MA: Brookline Books.

Chesapeake Institute. (1994). *Teaching strategies: Education of children with attention deficit disorder.* Reston, VA: CEC Publications.

Dowdy, C. A., Patton, J. R., Smith, T. E. C., & Polloway, E. A. (1998). *Attention-deficit/hyperactivity disorder in the classroom: A practical guide for teachers.* Austin, TX: Pro-Ed.

DuPaul, G. J., & Stoner, G. (1994). *ADHD in the schools: Assessment and intervention strategies.* New York: Guilford Press.

Hoover, J. J., & Patton, J. R. (1997). *Curriculum adaptations for students with learning behavior problems.* Reston, VA: CEC Publications.

Hudgins, P. (1998). *The ASSIST Series.* Longmont, CO: Sopris West.

Reif, S. F. (1997). *The ADD/ADHD checklist.* Reston, VA: CEC Publications.

Reif, S. F. (1993). *How to reach and teach ADD/ADHD children: Practical techniques, strategies, and interventions for helping children with attention problems and hyperactivity.* West Nyack, NY: Center for Applied Research in Education.

Rivera, D. P., & Smith, D. D. (1997). *Teaching students with learning and behavior problems* (3rd ed.). Boston: Allyn & Bacon.

Yehle, A. K., & Wambold, C. (1998). An ADHD success story: Strategies for teachers and students. *Teaching Exceptional Children, 30,* 8–13.

Videos

Armstrong, T. (1996). *Beyond the ADD Myth: Classroom Strategies and Techniques.* Port Chester, NY: National Professional Resources.

Asher, M. J., & Gordon, S. B. (1998). *Meeting the ADHD challenge: A practical guide for teachers.* Champaign, IL: Research Press.

Bender, W. N., & McLaughlin, P. J. (1995). *A.D.D. from A to Z.* Reston, VA: CEC Publications.

Chesapeake Institute & The Windmeyer Group. (1995). *Facing the challenges of ADD.* Reston, VA: CEC Publications.

Greenbaum, J., & Markel, G. (1998). *Performance breakthroughs for adolescents with learning disabilities or ADHD.* Champaign, IL: Research Press.

Reif, S. F. (1997). *ADHD: Inclusive instruction and collaborative practices.* Port Chester, NY: National Professional Resources.

Literature about Individuals with Attention Deficit Hyperactivity Disorder*

Elementary

Janover, C. (1997). *Zipper: The kid with ADHD.* Bethesda, MD: Woodbine House. (Ages 9–12) (F)

Morrison, J., & Simpson, C. (1996). *Coping with ADD/ADHD: Attention deficit disorder/attention deficit hyperactivity disorder.* Rosen Publishing Group. (Ages 9–12) (NF)

Moss, D. (1989). *Shelley, the hyperactive turtle.* Bethesda, MD: Woodbine House. (Ages 6+) (F)

Shepherd, E. L. (1997). *Sometimes I drive my mom crazy, but I know she's crazy about me.* Seacaucus, NJ: Genesis Direct. (Ages 9–12) (F)

Secondary

Crist, J. J. (1997). *ADHD: A teenager's guide.* Seacaucus, NJ: Genesis Direct. (Ages 13–18) (NF)

Software

Attention and Memory, Volume I, LocuTour Multimedia, 1130 Grove Street, San Luis Obispo, CA 93401. (800) 777-3166. (Windows; Macintosh)

Attention, Perception, and Discrimination Plus for Windows. Parrot Software, 6505 Pleasant Lake Ct., West Bloomfield, MI 48322. (800) 727-7681. (DOS; Windows)

Captain's Log: Attention Skills, BrainTrain, Inc., 727 Twin Ridge Lane, Richmond, VA 23235. (804) 320-0105. (DOS)

Foundations Series, Psychological Software Services, Inc., 6555 Carrollton Avenue, Indianapolis, IN 46220. (317) 257-9672. (DOS; Windows)

*F = fiction; NF = nonfiction

Hierarchical Attention Training Plus, Parrot Software, 6505 Pleasant Lake Ct., West Bloomfield, MI 48322. (800) 727-7681. (Windows)

Parent Resources

Publications
Barkley, R. A. (1995). *Taking charge of ADHD.* Seacaucus, NJ: Genesis Direct.

Wodrich, D. L. (1994). *Attention deficit hyperactivity disorder: What every parent needs to know.* Baltimore, MD: Paul H. Brookes.

Greenberg, G. S., & Horn, W. F. (1998). *Attention deficit hyperactivity disorder: Questions and answers for parents.* Champaign, IL: Research Press.

Online Resources
AmericaOnline: Adult ADD Support Group ERICNJB@aol.com

Compuserve: Use "GO ADD" command. Send mail to 70006.101@compuserve.com

Prodigy: Adult ADD support groups are listed under Support Groups Medical

Videos
Reif, S. F. (1997). *How to help your child succeed in school: Strategies and guidance for parents of children with ADHD and/or learning disabilities.* San Diego, CA: Educational Resource Specialists.

Trevor, G. H. (1996). *The 3 Rs for special education: Rights, resources, results.* Fair Haven, NJ: Edvantage Media, Inc.

Organizations
National Attention Deficit Disorder Association (ADDA), P.O. Box 972, Mentor, Ohio 44061, (440) 350-9595. Web site: http://www.add.org.

Children and Adults with Attention Deficit Disorders, 499 NW 70th Avenue, Suite 308, Plantation, Florida 33317, (954) 587-3700. Web site: http://www.chadd.org (National CH.A.D.D. has listings for local groups)

Bibliography for Teaching Suggestions

Abramowitz, A. J., & O'Leary, S. G. (1991). Behavioral interventions for the classroom: Implications for students with ADHD. *School Psychology Review, 20,* 220–234.

Bender, R. L., & Bender, W. N. (1996). *Computer-assisted instruction for students at risk for ADHD, mild disabilities, or academic problems.* Boston: Allyn & Bacon.

Bender, W. N., & Mathes, M. Y. (1995). Students with ADHD in inclusive classrooms: Hierarchical approach to strategy selection. *Intervention in School and Clinic, 30,* 226–243.

Bos, C. S., & Vaughn, S. (1998). *Strategies for teaching students with learning and behavior problems* (4th ed.). Boston: Allyn & Bacon.

Chesapeake Institute, Washington DC, with Warger, Eavy, and Associates, Reston, VA, as part of contract #HS92017001 from the Office of Special Programs, Office of Special Education and Rehabilitative Services, United States Department of Education, 1994.

Davey, B. (1983). Think Aloud—Modeling the cognitive processes of reading comprehension. *Journal of Reading, 27,* 44–47.

Dowdy, C. A., Patton, J. R., Smith, T. E. C., & Polloway, E. A. (1998). *Attention-deficit/hyperactivity disorder in the classroom.* Austin, TX: Pro-Ed.

DuPaul, G. J., & Eckert, T. L. (1998). Academic interventions for students with attention-deficit/hyperactivity disorder: A review of the literature. *Reading & Writing Quarterly, 13,* 59–82.

Evans, S. W., Pelham, W., & Grudber, M. V. (1994–95). The efficacy of notetaking to improve behavior and comprehension of adolescents with attention deficit hyperactivity disorder. *Exceptionality, 5,* 1–17.

Jayanthi, M., Epstein, M. H., Polloway, E. A., & Bursuck, W. D. (1996). A national survey of general education teachers' perceptions of testing adaptations. *Journal of Special Education, 30*(1), 99–115.

Landau, S., Milich, R., & Diener, M. B. (1998). Peer relations of children with attention-deficit hyperactivity disorder. *Reading & Writing Quarterly, 14,* 83–105.

Lerner, J. W., Lowenthal, B., & Lerner, S. R. (1995). *Attention deficit disorders: Assessment and teaching.* Pacific Grove, CA: Brooks/Cole.

McIntosh, R., Vaughn, S., & Bennerson, D. (1995). FAST social skills training for students with learning disabilities. *Teaching Exceptional Children, 28,* 37–41.

Montague, M., & Warger, C. (1997). Helping students with attention deficit hyperactivity disorder succeed in the classroom. *Focus on Exceptional Children, 30*(4), 1–16.

Reid, R., & Maag, J. W. (1998). Functional assessment: A method for developing classroom-based accommodations and interventions for children with ADHD. *Reading & Writing Quarterly, 14,* 9–42.

Spires, H. A., & Stone, D. P. (1989). The directed notetaking activity: A self-questioning approach. *Journal of Reading, 33,* 36–39.

Van Reusen, A. K., & Bos, C. S. (1992). *Use of the goal-regulation strategy to improve the goal attainment of students with learning disabilities* (Final Report). Tucson, AZ: University of Arizona.

Wisconsin Department of Public Instruction. (1989). *Strategic learning in the content areas.* Madison, WI: Author.

Wood, J. W. (1998). *Adapting instruction to accommodate students in inclusive settings.* Upper Saddle River, NJ: Merrill/Prentice-Hall.

Zentall, S. S. (1995). Modifying classroom tasks and environments. In S. Goldstein (Ed.), *Understanding and managing children's classroom behavior.* New York: John Wiley & Sons.

Zentall, S. S. (1993). Research on the educational implications of attention deficit hyperactivity disorder. *Exceptional Children, 60,* 143–153.

Zentall, S. S., & Stormont-Spurgin, M. (1995). Educator preferences of accommodations for students with attention deficit hyperactivity disorder. *Teacher Education and Special Education, 18,* 115–123.

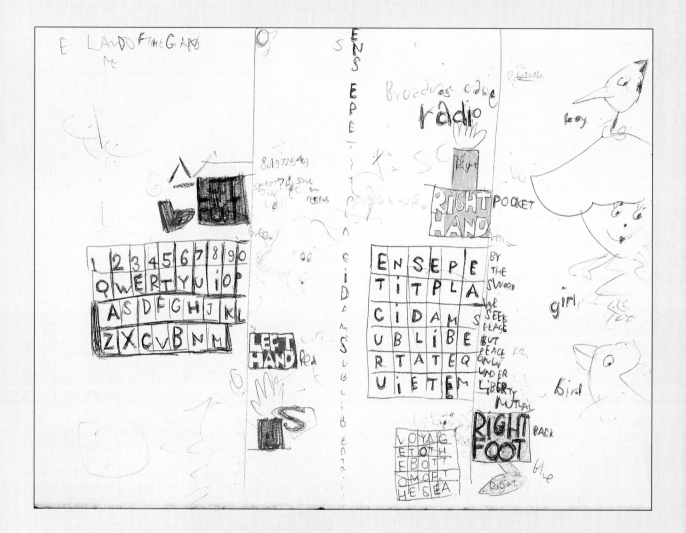

roger swike

Untitled (Left and Right). Ink, marker on rag paper. 11 × 15 in.

Roger Swike was born in Boston in 1962. At an early age he was diagnosed
as having an autistic disorder. He has attended Gateway Crafts, an arts program
for adults with disabilities in Brookline, MA, since July 1995. His work has been
shown at the Gateway Gallery in Brookline; at the Outsider Art Fair in New York;
and in Johnstown, PA, where it received an award from the Ebensburg Center. He
has also been featured in an exhibition at the Fuller Museum of Art in Brockton, MA.

Emotional or Behavioral Disorders

It has always been hard for me to have friends. I want friends, but I don't know how to make them. I always think people are being serious when they are just joking around, but I don't figure that out until a lot later. I just don't know how to adapt.

I get into fights with people all the time. I take their teasing seriously and get into trouble. I don't remember having as much trouble getting along with kids when I was little. They seemed to feel sorry for me or thought I was weird. I used to run away from kids and hide in the bathroom at school or under my desk.

After I got back from the hospital, I really couldn't get along with anyone. That was when kids first began calling me "retard." I am not retarded, but I get confused and can't figure out what is going on. At first I couldn't figure out what they were saying to me. Finally one girl in my special education class became my friend. She kind of took care of me. I had another friend in junior high who was also nice and kind to me. But my best friend is my dog Cindie. Even though I give her a hard time, she is always ready to love me.

I like to play by myself best. I make up stories and fantasies. My mother says it is too bad I have such a hard time writing, because with my imagination and all the stories I have created in my mind I could write a book.

ANONYMOUS

Children and youths who have emotional or behavioral disorders are not typically good at making friends. In fact, their most obvious problem is failure to establish close and satisfying emotional ties with other people. As the youth in the excerpt on page 245 describes, it may be easier for these individuals to hide, both physically and emotionally. If they do develop friendships, it is often with diviant peers (Farmer, Farmer, & Gut, 1999).

Some of these children are withdrawn. Other children or adults may try to reach them, but these efforts are usually met with fear or disinterest. In many cases, this kind of quiet rejection continues until those who are trying to make friends give up. Because close emotional ties are built around reciprocal social responses, people naturally lose interest in individuals who do not respond to social overtures.

Many other children with emotional or behavioral disorders are isolated from others not because they withdraw from friendly advances but because they strike out with hostility and aggression. They are abusive, destructive, unpredictable, irresponsible, bossy, quarrelsome, irritable, jealous, defiant—anything but pleasant. Naturally, other children and adults choose not to spend time with children like this unless they have to, and others tend to strike back at youngsters who show these characteristics. It is no wonder, then, that these children and youths seem to be embroiled in a continuous battle with everyone. The reaction of most other children and adults is to withdraw to avoid battles, but rejected children then do not learn to behave acceptably. "In the case of [the] rejected child, parents, teachers, and peers simply withdraw from the child, and thus 'teaching opportunities' are greatly reduced, along with the opportunity for the rejected child to redeem himself in the eyes of parents, teachers, and mainstream peers" (Ialongo, Vaden-Kiernan, & Kellam, 1998, p. 210).

Where does the problem start? Does it begin with behavior that frustrates, angers, or irritates other people? Or does it begin with a social environment so uncomfortable or inappropriate that the only reasonable response of the child is to withdraw or attack? These questions cannot be answered fully on the basis of current research. The best thinking today is that the problem is not just in the child's

Children with emotional and behavior disorders frequently behave in ways that frustrate adults and others around them.

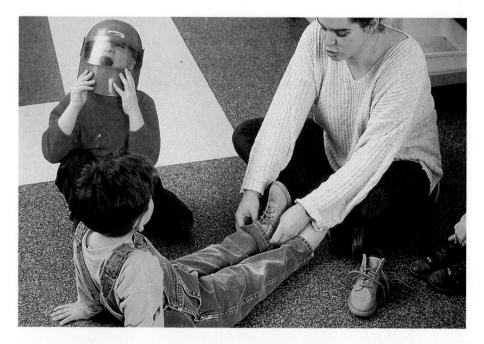

misconceptions about Persons with Emotional or Behavioral Disorders

myth Most children and youths with emotional or behavioral disorders are not noticed by people around them.

fact Although it is difficult to identify the types and causes of problems, most children and youths with emotional or behavioral disorders, whether aggressive or withdrawn, are quite easy to spot.

myth Students with emotional or behavioral disorders are usually very bright.

fact Relatively few students with emotional or behavioral disorders have high intelligence; in fact, most have below-average IQs.

myth Youngsters who exhibit shy, anxious behavior are more seriously impaired than those whose behavior is hyperaggressive.

fact Youngsters with aggressive, acting-out behavior patterns have less chance for social adjustment and mental health in adulthood. Neurotic, shy, anxious children and youths have a better chance of getting and holding jobs, overcoming their problems, and staying out of jails and mental hospitals, unless their withdrawal is extreme. This is especially true for boys.

myth Most students with emotional or behavioral disorders need a permissive environment, in which they feel accepted and can accept themselves for who they are.

fact Research shows that a firmly structured and highly predictable environment is of greatest benefit for most students.

myth Only psychiatrists, psychologists, and social workers are able to help children and youths with emotional or behavioral disorders overcome their problems.

fact Most teachers and parents can learn to be highly effective in helping youngsters with emotional or behavioral disorders, sometimes without extensive training or professional certification. Many of these children and youths do require services of highly trained professionals as well.

myth Undesirable behaviors are only symptoms; the real problems are hidden deep in the individual's psyche.

fact There is no sound scientific basis for belief in hidden causes; the behavior and its social context are the problems. Causes may involve thoughts, feelings, and perceptions.

myth Juvenile delinquency and the aggressive behavior known as conduct disorder can be effectively deterred by harsh punishment, if children and youths know that their misbehavior will be punished.

fact Harsh punishment, including imprisonment, not only does not deter misbehavior but creates conditions under which many individuals become even more likely to exhibit unacceptable conduct.

behavior or just in the environment. The problem arises because *the social interactions and transactions between the child and the social environment are inappropriate.* This is an *ecological* perspective—an interpretation of the problem as a negative aspect of the child *and* the environment in which he or she lives.

Special education for these students is, in many ways, both confused and confusing. The terminology of the field is inconsistent, and there is much misunderstanding of definitions (Forness & Kavale, 1997). Reliable classifications of children's behavior problems have only recently emerged from research. The large number of theories regarding the causes and the best treatments of emotional and behavioral disorders makes it difficult to sort out the most useful concepts. Thus, study of this area of special education demands more than the usual amount of perseverance and critical thinking. In fact, children and youths with emotional or behavioral disorders present some of the most difficult social problems that our society has to solve (Walker, Forness, Kauffman, Epstein, Gresham, Nelson, & Strain, 1998).

Terminology

Many different terms have been used to designate children who have extreme social-interpersonal and/or intrapersonal problems, including *emotionally handicapped, emotionally impaired, behaviorally impaired, socially/emotionally handicapped, emotionally conflicted, having personal and social adjustment problems,* and *seriously behaviorally disabled.* These terms do not designate distinctly different types of disorders; that is, they do not refer to clearly different types of children and youths. Rather, the different labels appear to represent personal preferences for terms and perhaps slightly different theoretical orientations. The terminology of the field is so variable and confusing that it is possible to pick a label of choice simply by matching words from Column A with words from Column B below (and, if it seems appropriate, adding other qualifiers, such as *serious* or *severe*):

Column A	Column B
Emotional	Disturbance
Social	Disorder
Behavioral	Maladjustment
Personal	Handicap
	Impairment

Until 1997, *seriously emotionally disturbed* was the term used in federal special education laws and regulations. *Seriously* was dropped from the terminology in 1997. *Emotionally disturbed* is the term now used in the Individuals with Disabilities Education Act (IDEA), but it has been criticized as inappropriate. *Behaviorally disordered* is consistent with the name of the Council for Children with Behavioral Disorders (CCBD, a division of the Council for Exceptional Children) and has the advantage of focusing attention on the clearly observable aspect of these children's problems—disordered behavior. Many authorities favor terminology indicating that these children may have emotional or behavioral problems or both (Forness & Knitzer, 1992; Kauffman, 1997a).

In 1990, the National Mental Health and Special Education Coalition, representing over thirty professional and advocacy groups, proposed the new terminology *emotional or behavioral disorder* to replace *serious emotional disturbance* in federal laws and regulations (Forness & Knitzer, 1992). It now appears that *emotional or behavioral disorder* may become the generally accepted terminology of the field, although changes in federal and state laws and regulations may be slow in coming.

Definition

Defining emotional and behavioral disorders has always been problematic. Professional groups and experts have felt free to construct individual working definitions to fit their own professional purposes (Forness & Kavale, 1997). For practical reasons, we might say that someone has had an emotional or behavioral disorder whenever an adult authority has said so. Until recently, no one has come up with a definition that is understandable and acceptable to a majority of professionals.

Definitional Problems

There are valid reasons for the lack of consensus regarding definition (Forness & Kavale, 1997; Kauffman, 1997a). Defining emotional and behavioral disorders is somewhat like defining a familiar experience—anger, loneliness, or happiness, for example. We all have an intuitive grasp of what these experiences are, but forming objective definitions is far from simple. The factors that make it particularly difficult to arrive at a good definition of emotional and behavioral disorders are:

- Lack of precise definitions of mental health and normal behavior
- Differences among conceptual models
- Difficulties in measuring emotions and behavior
- Relationships between emotional or behavioral disorder and other disabilities
- Differences in the professionals who diagnose and serve children and youths

Consider each of these problems in turn. Mental health and normal behavior have been hard to define precisely. It is no wonder, then, that the definition of emotional or behavioral disorder presents a special challenge. Professionals who work with youngsters who have emotional or behavioral disorders have been guided by a variety of conceptual models, as we will discuss further. These conceptual models—assumptions or theories about why people behave as they do and what we should do about it—may offer conflicting ideas about just what the problem is. Thus, people who adopt different conceptual models may define emotional or behavioral disorders in very different terms.

Measurement is basic to any definition, and emotions and behavior—the disorders, in this case—are notoriously difficult to measure in ways that make a precise definition possible. Ultimately, subjective judgment is called for, even with the best measurements of emotions and behavior available. Emotional or behavioral disorders tend to overlap a great deal with other disabilities, especially learning disabilities and mental retardation. It is therefore hard to define emotional or behavioral disorders as disabilities clearly distinct from all others.

Finally, each professional group has its own reasons for serving individuals with emotional or behavioral disorders. For example, clinical psychologists, school psychologists, social workers, teachers, and juvenile justice authorities all have their particular concerns and language. Differences in the focuses of different professions tend to produce differences in definition as well (Forness & Kavale, 1997).

Current Definitions

Although the terminology used and the relative emphasis given to certain points vary considerably from one definition to another, it is possible to extract several common features of current definitions. There is general agreement that emotional or behavioral disorder refers to:

- Behavior that goes to an extreme—that is not just slightly different from the usual
- A problem that is chronic—one that does not quickly disappear
- Behavior that is unacceptable because of social or cultural expectations

One definition that must be considered is included in the federal rules and regulations governing the implementation of IDEA. In federal laws and regulations, *emotionally disturbed* has been defined as follows:

(i) The term means a condition exhibiting one or more of the following characteristics over a long period of time and to a marked extent, which adversely affects educational performance:

(A) An inability to learn that cannot be explained by intellectual, sensory, or health factors;

(B) An inability to build or maintain satisfactory relationships with peers and teachers;

(C) Inappropriate types of behavior or feelings under normal circumstances;

(D) A general pervasive mood of unhappiness or depression; or

(E) A tendency to develop physical symptoms or fears associated with personal or school problems.

(ii) The term includes children who are schizophrenic or autistic.* The term does not include children who are socially maladjusted unless it is determined that they are emotionally disturbed. (45 CFR 121a.5[b][8] [1978])

The federal definition is modeled after one proposed by Bower (1981). Bower's definition, however, does not include the statements found in part (ii) of the federal definition. These inclusions and exclusions are, as Bower (1982) and Kauffman (1986, 1997a) point out, unnecessary. Common sense tells us that Bower's five criteria for emotional disturbance indicate that autistic and schizophrenic children *must be included* and that socially maladjusted children *cannot be excluded*. Furthermore, the clause *which adversely affects educational performance* makes interpretation of the definition impossible, unless the meaning of educational performance is clarified. Does educational performance refer only to academic achievement? If so, then children with other characteristics who achieve on grade level are excluded.

---

*The U.S. Department of Education later decided that autism will no longer be included under the category of *emotionally disturbed*. See Bower (1982) for comment on this change. In 1990, autism became a separate category under IDEA.

In recent years the federal definition has been widely criticized, and the federal government has more than once mandated study of it. One of the most widely criticized and controversial aspects of the definition is its exclusion of children who are socially maladjusted but not emotionally disturbed. Strong moves have been made in some states and localities to interpret *social maladjustment* as **conduct disorder**—aggressive, disruptive, antisocial behavior. This is the most common type of problem exhibited by students who have been identified as having emotional or behavioral disorders. Cline (1990) notes that excluding students with conduct disorder is inconsistent with the history of IDEA. Moreover, the American Psychological Association and the CCBD have condemned this practice, which has no empirical basis (Costenbader & Buntaine, 1999). The controversy may be timeless (see Forness & Kavale, 1997; Nelson, Rutherford, Center, & Walker, 1991; Skiba & Grizzle, 1992; Slenkovich, 1992a, 1992b).

A second definition that must be considered is the one proposed in 1990 by the National Mental Health and Special Education Coalition. The coalition's proposed definition is:

(i) The term emotional or behavioral disorder means a disability characterized by behavioral or emotional responses in school so different from appropriate age, cultural, or ethnic norms that they adversely affect educational performance. Educational performance includes academic, social, vocational, and personal skills. Such a disability:

  (A) is more than a temporary, expected response to stressful events in the environment;

  (B) is consistently exhibited in two different settings, at least one of which is school-related; and

  (C) is unresponsive to direct intervention in general education, or the child's condition is such that general education interventions would be insufficient.

(ii) Emotional and behavioral disorders can co-exist with other disabilities.

(iii) This category may include children or youths with schizophrenic disorders, **affective disorder, anxiety disorder,** or other sustained disorders of conduct or adjustment when they adversely affect educational performance in accordance with section (i). (Forness & Knitzer, 1992, p. 13)

The coalition is working to have the proposed definition and terminology adopted in federal laws and regulations; the hope is that states will adopt them as well. Advantages of the proposed definition over the federal definition include the following:

- It uses terminology reflecting current professional preferences and concern for minimizing stigma.
- It includes both disorders of emotions and disorders of behavior and recognizes that they may occur either separately or in combination.
- It is school-centered but acknowledges that disorders exhibited outside the school setting are also important.
- It is sensitive to ethnic and cultural differences.
- It does not include minor or transient problems or ordinary responses to stress.
- It acknowledges the importance of prereferral interventions but does not require slavish implementation of them in extreme cases.
- It acknowledges that children and youths can have multiple disabilities.

conduct disorder. A disorder characterized by overt, aggressive, disruptive behavior or covert antisocial acts such as stealing, lying, and fire setting; may include both overt and covert acts.

affective disorder. A disorder of mood or emotional tone characterized by depression or elation.

anxiety disorder. A disorder characterized by anxiety, fearfulness, and avoidance of ordinary activities because of anxiety or fear.

■ It includes the full range of emotional or behavioral disorders of concern to mental health and special education professionals without arbitrary exclusions.

Classification

Since emotional or behavioral disorders are evidenced in many ways, it seems reasonable to expect that individuals could be grouped into subcategories according to the types of problems they have. Still, there is no universally accepted system for classifying emotional or behavioral disorders for special education.

Psychiatric classification systems have been widely criticized for several decades. Hobbs (1975) commented, "It is important to note that competent clinicians would seldom use for treatment purposes the categories provided by diagnostic manuals; their judgment would be more finely modulated than the classification schemes, and more sensitive than any formal system can be to temporal, situational, and developmental changes" (pp. 58–59). Clearly, the usual diagnostic categories—for example, those found in publications of the American Psychiatric Association—have little meaning for teachers. Many psychologists and educators have recommended relying more on individual assessment of the child's behavior and situational factors than on traditional diagnostic classification.

An alternative to traditional psychiatric classifications is the use of statistical analyses of behavioral characteristics to establish clusters, or *dimensions*, of disordered behavior. Using sophisticated statistical procedures, researchers look for patterns of behavior that characterize children who have emotional or behavioral disorders. By using these methods, researchers have been able to derive descriptive categories that are less susceptible to bias and unreliability than the traditional psychiatric classifications (Achenbach, 1985; Richardson, McGauhey, & Day, 1995).

Achenbach and others (Achenbach, Howell, Quay, & Conners, 1991; Quay, 1986; Walker & Severson, 1990) have identified two broad, pervasive dimensions of disordered behavior: **externalizing** and **internalizing**. Externalizing behavior involves striking out against others. Internalizing behavior involves mental or emotional conflicts, such as depression and anxiety. A variety of more specific dimensions have been found by several researchers. Quay and Peterson (1987), for example, describe six dimensions characterized by the following kinds of behavior:

1. *Conduct disorder*—seeks attention, shows off, is disruptive, annoys others, fights, has temper tantrums
2. *Socialized aggression*—steals in company with others, is loyal to delinquent friends, is truant from school with others, has "bad" companions, freely admits disrespect for moral values and laws
3. *Attention problems–immaturity*—has short attention span and poor concentration; is distractible and easily diverted from task at hand; answers without thinking; is sluggish, slow-moving, and lethargic
4. *Anxiety–withdrawal*—is self-conscious, easily embarrassed, and hypersensitive; feelings are easily hurt; is generally fearful, anxious, depressed, and always sad
5. *Psychotic behavior*—expresses far-fetched ideas, has repetitive speech, shows bizarre behavior
6. *Motor excess*—is restless, unable to sit still, tense, unable to relax, and overtalkative

externalizing. Acting-out behavior; aggressive or disruptive behavior that is observable as behavior directed toward others.

internalizing. Acting-in behavior; anxiety, fearfulness, withdrawal, and other indications of an individual's mood or internal state.

Individuals may show behaviors characteristic of more than one dimension; that is, the dimensions are not mutually exclusive. For instance, a child or youth might exhibit several of the behaviors associated with the attention problems–immaturity dimension (short attention span, poor concentration) and perhaps several of those defining conduct disorder as well (fighting, disruptive behavior, annoying others). Actually, **comorbidity**—the co-occurrence of two or more conditions in the same individual—is the rule, not the exception (Tankersley & Landrum, 1997). Few individuals with an emotional or behavioral disorder exhibit only one type of maladaptive behavior.

Furthermore, children may exhibit characteristic types of behavior with varying degrees of intensity or severity. That is, all dimensions of behavior may be exhibited to a greater or lesser extent; the range may be from normal to severely disordered. For example, an individual might have a severe conduct disorder. The classification of the severe disorders typically called **pervasive developmental disorders** presents particular problems. Children with these disorders exhibit behavior that is qualitatively as well as quantitatively different from that of others (for examples, see Sacks, 1995; Schopler & Mesibov, 1994, 1995; Wenar, Ruttenberg, Kalish-Weiss, & Wolf, 1986). They are often described as inaccessible to others, unreachable, out of touch with reality, or mentally retarded. To the casual observer, their behavior is simply incomprehensible (Prior & Werry, 1986).

Two types of severe childhood disorders are distinguished by most researchers: **autism** and **schizophrenia**. Children with autism are characterized by a lack of responsiveness to other people, major problems in communication (many do not have any useful language), peculiar speech patterns (e.g., parroting what they hear), and bizarre responses (e.g., peculiar interests in or attachments to objects). They often engage in repetitive, stereotyped behavior (Charlop-Christy, Schreibman, Pierce, & Kurtz, 1997). Children with schizophrenia have a severe disorder of thinking. They may believe they are controlled by alien forces or have other delusions or hallucinations. Typically, their emotions are inappropriate for the actual circumstances, and they tend to withdraw into their own private worlds (Asarnow, Tompson, & Goldstein, 1994).

One major difference between autism and schizophrenia is that a child with autism is typically recognized as having a disorder before the age of three years. Childhood schizophrenia is a disorder that typically begins after a normal period of development during early childhood. Autism and schizophrenia in children, then, are differentiated partly on the basis of the child's age at the first appearance of symptoms. There are also other differences between the two conditions, especially these:

1. Children with schizophrenia usually have delusions (bizarre ideas) and hallucinations (seeing or hearing imaginary things), whereas children with autism usually do not.
2. Children with schizophrenia tend to have psychotic episodes interspersed with periods of near-normal behavior, whereas children with autism tend to have persistent symptoms.
3. About 25 percent of children with autism have epileptic seizures, whereas children with schizophrenia seldom have seizures (Rutter & Schopler, 1987).

As mentioned in the discussion of the definition of emotional or behavioral disorders, autism is no longer considered by the U.S. Department of Education under the category "emotionally disturbed" (described in this chapter as emotional or

The causes of autism—a pervasive developmental disorder that may include severe behavioral disorders—are only recently beginning to be understood.

comorbidity. Co-occurrence of two or more conditions in the same individual.

pervasive developmental disorder. A severe disorder characterized by abnormal social relations, including bizarre mannerisms, inappropriate social behavior, and unusual or delayed speech and language.

autism. A disorder characterized by extreme withdrawal, self-stimulation, cognitive deficits, language disorders, and onset before the age of thirty months.

schizophrenia. A disorder characterized by psychotic behavior manifested by loss of contact with reality, distorted thought processes, and abnormal perceptions.

behavioral disorders). There are likely several reasons for this reclassification. First, the parents of children with autism objected—and with good reason—to the blame implied by the term *emotional disturbance,* particularly the explicit blame heaped upon them by prominent psychoanalytical thinking (e.g., Bettelheim, 1950, 1967). And second, autism seems clearly to be caused by a neurological or biochemical dysfunction. Autism is discussed in this chapter and Chapter 8 because of the implications of having autism. For instance, (1) the child exhibits highly problematic emotional and behavioral responses to everyday circumstances; and (2) the child's problems are often centered on difficulty in communicating. Autism is also discussed briefly in Chapter 11 because it involves a brain disorder.

In summary, the most useful classifications of emotional or behavioral disorders describe behavioral dimensions. The dimensions described in the literature involve a wide range of problems, including conduct disorder, socialized aggression, attention problems and immaturity, anxiety and withdrawal, excessive movement, and pervasive developmental disorders. These dimensions include a variety of antisocial conduct, delinquent behavior, substance abuse, depression, and autism and schizophrenia. Nevertheless, because of ambiguity in the federal definition of serious emotional disturbance, controversy persists regarding the classifications that should be included for special education purposes.

Prevalence

Estimates of the prevalence of emotional or behavioral disorders in children and youths have varied tremendously because there has been no standard and reliable definition or screening instrument. For decades, the federal government estimated that 2 percent of the school-age population was emotionally disturbed. The government's estimate was extremely conservative, however. Rather consistently, credible studies in the United States and many other countries have indicated that at least 6 to 10 percent of children and youths of school age exhibit serious and persistent emotional/behavioral problems (Brandenburg, Friedman, & Silver, 1990; Costello, Messer, Bird, Cohen, & Reinherz, 1998; Kauffman, 1997a). Data published by the U.S. Department of Education (1997), however, show that only about 1 percent of schoolchildren in the United States are identified as emotionally disturbed. The Department of Education recognizes that this is an underserved category of special education students whose needs are particularly complex.

The most common types of problems exhibited by students placed in special education for emotional or behavioral disorders are externalizing—that is, aggressive, acting-out, disruptive behavior. Boys outnumber girls in displaying these behaviors by a ratio of 5 to 1 or more. Overall, boys tend to exhibit more aggression and conduct disorder than girls do, although antisocial behavior in girls is an increasing concern (Anderson & Werry, 1994; Kazdin, 1997; Talbott & Callahan, 1997).

Juvenile delinquency and the antisocial behavior known as conduct disorder present particular problems in estimating prevalence. Delinquent youths constitute a considerable percentage of the population. About 3 percent of U.S. youths are referred to a juvenile court in any given year, a disproportionate number of whom are African American males (Miller, 1997). Many others engage in serious antisocial behavior but are not referred to the courts (see Siegel & Senna, 1994). One point of view is that all delinquent and antisocial youths should be thought of as having emotional or behavioral disorders. Some argue that most youths who commit frequent antisocial acts are socially maladjusted, not emotionally disturbed. However, we can not clearly distinguish social maladjustment from emotional disturbance (Costenbader & Buntaine, 1999).

Clearly, disabling conditions of various kinds are much more common among juvenile delinquents than among the general population (Henggeler, 1989). Just as clearly, the social and economic costs of delinquency and antisocial behavior are enormous. Adolescent males account for a disproportionately high percentage of serious and violent crime in U.S. society. Those who exhibit serious antisocial behavior are at high risk for school failure as well as other negative outcomes (Kazdin, 1995, 1997; Walker, Colvin, & Ramsey, 1995; Walker, Forness et al., 1998; Walker, Kavanaugh et al., 1998). If schools are to address the educational problems of delinquent and antisocial children and youths, the number served by special education must increase dramatically.

Some studies have found rates of moderate to serious crime higher among youths with emotional and behavioral disorders. This student from Thurston High School in Springfield, Oregon, is charged with 4 counts of murder including his parents and two classmates.

Causes

The causes of emotional or behavioral disorders have been attributed to four major factors:

1. Biological disorders and diseases
2. Pathological family relationships
3. Undesirable experiences at school
4. Negative cultural influences

Although in the majority of cases there is no conclusive empirical evidence that any of these factors is directly responsible for the disorder, some factors may give a child a predisposition to exhibit problem behavior and others may precipitate or trigger it. That is, some factors, such as genetics, influence behavior over a long time and increase the likelihood that a given set of circumstances will trigger maladaptive responses. Other factors (such as observing one parent beating the other) may have a more immediate effect and may trigger maladaptive responses in an individual who is already predisposed to problem behavior.

Another concept important in all theories is the idea of *contributing factors* that heighten the risk of a disorder. It is extremely unusual to find a *single* cause that has led directly to a disorder. Usually, several factors together contribute to the development of a problem. In almost all cases, the question of what specifically has caused the disorder cannot be answered because no one really knows. However, we often do know the factors that place children at risk—the circumstances or conditions that increase the chances that a child will develop the disorder. Table 7.1 describes factors that place children and youths at risk for conduct disorder, one of the most common and troubling emotional-behavioral problems of young people.

Biological Factors

Behaviors and emotions may be influenced by genetic, neurological, or biochemical factors or by combinations of these. Certainly, there is a relationship between body and behavior, and it would therefore seem reasonable to look for a biological causal factor of some kind for certain emotional or behavioral disorders. But only rarely is it possible to demonstrate a relationship between a specific biological factor and an emotional or behavioral disorder. Many children with emotional or behavioral disorders have no detectable biological flaws that account for their actions, and many behaviorally normal children have serious biological defects. For most children with emotional or behavioral disorders, there simply is no real evidence that biological factors alone are at the root of their problems. For those with severe and profound disorders, however, there is evidence to suggest that biological factors may contribute to their conditions (Asarnow, Asamen, Granholm, Sherman, Watkins, & Williams, 1994; Charlop-Christy et al., 1997; Harris, 1995).

All children are born with a biologically determined behavioral style, or **temperament.** Although children's inborn temperaments may be changed by the way they are reared, some believe that children with so-called difficult temperaments are predisposed to develop emotional or behavioral disorders (Thomas & Chess, 1984). There is no one-to-one relationship between temperament and disorders, however. A difficult child may be handled so well or a child with an easy temperament so poorly that the outcome will be quite different from what one might predict on the basis of initial behavioral style. Other biological factors besides temperament—disease, malnutrition, and brain trauma, for example—may predispose children to develop emotional or behavioral problems (Baumeister, Kupstas, & Klindworth, 1990; Lozoff, 1989). Substance abuse also may contribute to serious emotional and behavioral problems (Gottesman, 1991; Newcomb & Bentler, 1989). Except in rare instances, it is not possible to determine that these factors are direct causes of problem behavior.

As is the case with mental retardation, there is more often evidence of a biological cause among children with severe or profound disabilities. Children with autism or schizophrenia frequently (but not always) show signs of neurological defects (Prior & Werry, 1986). There is convincing evidence that genetic factors contribute to schizophrenia (Gottesman, 1991; Plomin, 1989), although the role of specific biological factors often remains a mystery, even when there is severe and profound disorder (Kauffman, 1997a). It is now generally accepted that autism is a neurological disorder, but the nature and causes of the neurological defect are unknown.

As biological and psychological research has become more sophisticated, it has become apparent that biological factors cause or set the stage for many disorders that formerly were widely assumed to be caused mostly or entirely by social interactions. Schizophrenia and autism are the foremost examples. Another example is **Tourette's syndrome,** which is characterized by multiple motor tics (repetitive, stereotyped movements) and verbal tics (the individual makes strange noises or says inappropriate words or phrases). Although we now understand that autism, schizophrenia, Tourette's disorder, attention deficit hyperactivity dis-

temperament. One's inborn behavioral style, including general level of activity, regularity or predictability, approach or withdrawal, adaptability, intensity of reaction, responsiveness, mood, distractibility, and persistence; is present at birth but may be modified by parental management.

Tourette's syndrome. A neurological disorder beginning in childhood (about three times more prevalent in boys than in girls) in which stereotyped motor movements (tics) are accompanied by multiple vocal outbursts (e.g., grunting or barking noises) or socially inappropriate words or statements.

Table 7.1 — Factors that Place Youth at Risk for the Onset of Conduct Disorder

Child Factors	**Child Temperament.** A more difficult child temperament (on a dimension of "easy-to-difficult"), as characterized by more negative mood, lower levels of approach toward new stimuli, and less adaptability to change.
	Neuropsychological Deficits and Difficulties. Deficits in diverse functions related to language (e.g., verbal learning, verbal fluency, verbal IQ), memory, motor coordination, integration of auditory and visual cues, and "executive" functions of the brain (e.g., abstract reasoning, concept formation, planning, control of attention).
	Subclinical Levels of Conduct Disorder. Early signs (e.g., elementary school) of mild ("subclinical") levels of unmanageability and aggression, especially with early age of onset, multiple types of antisocial behaviors, and multiple situations in which they are evident (e.g., at home, school, the community).
	Academic and Intellectual Performance. Academic deficiencies and lower levels of intellectual functioning.
Parent and Family Factors	**Prenatal and Perinatal Complications.** Pregnancy and birth-related complications including maternal infection, prematurity and low birth weight, impaired respiration at birth, and minor birth injury.
	Psychopathology and Criminal Behavior in the Family. Criminal behavior, antisocial personality disorder, and alcoholism of the parent.
	Parent-Child Punishment. Harsh (e.g., severe corporal punishment) and inconsistent punishment increase risk.
	Monitoring of the Child. Poor supervision, lack of monitoring of whereabouts. and few rules about where children can go and when they can return.
	Quality of the Family Relationships. Less parental acceptance of their children, less warmth, affection, and emotional support, and less attachment.
	Marital Discord. Unhappy marital relationships, interpersonal conflict, and aggression of the parents.
	Family Size. Larger family size, that is, more children in the family.
	Sibling with Antisocial Behavior. Presence of a sibling, especially an older brother, with antisocial behavior.
	Socioeconomic Disadvantage. Poverty, overcrowding, unemployment. receipt of social assistance ("welfare"), and poor housing.
School-Related Factors	**Characteristics of the Setting.** Attending schools where there is little emphasis on academic work, little teacher time spent on lessons, infrequent teacher use of praise and appreciation for school work, little emphasis on individual responsibility of the students, poor working conditions for pupils (e.g.. furniture in poor repair), unavailability of the teacher to deal with children's problems, and low teacher expectancies.

Note: The list of risk factors highlights major influences. The number of factors and the relations of specific factors to risk are more complex than the summary statements noted here.

Source: Kazdin, A. E. (1997). Conduct disorder. In R. J. Morris & T. R. Kratchowill (Eds.), *The practice of child therapy* (3rd ed.) (p. 202). Boston: Allyn & Bacon. Copyright © by Allyn & Bacon. Reprinted by permission.

order (ADHD), some forms of depression, and many other disorders are caused wholly or partly by brain or biochemical dysfunctions, these biological causal factors remain poorly understood. That is, we do not know exactly how genetic, neurological, and other biochemical factors contribute to these disorders, nor do we know how to correct the biological problems involved in these disorders.

It is clear that traumatic brain injury, now a separate category of disability under IDEA, may cause psychosocial problems. Depending on what part of the brain is injured and when the injury occurs during development, the individual may experience serious difficulty in psychosocial behavior—responding appropriately to social circumstances, controlling rage reactions or aggression, showing appropriate affect, and so on.

Four points are important to remember about biological causes:

1. The fact that disorders have biological causes does not mean that they are not emotional or behavioral disorders. An emotional or behavioral disorder can have a physical cause; the biological malfunction is a problem because of the disorder it creates in the individual's emotions or behavior.
2. Causes are seldom exclusively biological or psychological. Once a biological disorder occurs, it nearly always creates psychosocial problems that then also contribute to the emotional or behavioral disorder as well.
3. Biological or medical treatment of the disorder is seldom sufficient to resolve the problem. Medication may be of great benefit, but it is seldom the only intervention that is needed (Sweeney, Forness, Kavale, & Levitt, 1997). The psychological and social aspects of the disorder must also be addressed.
4. Medical or biological approaches are sometimes of little or no benefit and the primary interventions are psychological or behavioral, even though the disorder is known to have primarily a biological cause. Medications do not work equally well for all cases, and for some disorders no generally effective medications are known.

Family Factors

Mental health specialists have been tempted to blame behavioral difficulties primarily on parent-child relationships because the nuclear family—father, mother, and children—has a profound influence on early development. In fact, some advocates of psychoanalysis believe that almost all severe problems of children stem from early negative interactions between mother and child.

However, empirical research on family relationships indicates that the influence of parents on their children is no simple matter and that children with emotional or behavioral disorders may influence their parents as much as their parents influence them. It is increasingly clear that family influences are interactional and transactional and that the effects parents and children have on one another are reciprocal (Patterson, DeBaryshe, & Ramsey, 1989; Patterson, Reid, & Dishion, 1992). Even in cases of severe and profound emotional or behavioral disorders, it is not possible to find consistent and valid research findings that allow the blame for the children's problem behavior to be placed primarily on their parents (Gottesman, 1991).

The outcome of parental discipline depends not only on the particular techniques used but also on the characteristics of the child (Kazdin, 1997; Rutter, 1985). Generalizations about the effects of parental discipline are difficult to make, for as Becker (1964) commented long ago, "There are probably many routes to becoming a 'good parent' which vary with the personality of both the parents and children and with the pressure in the environment with which one must learn to cope" (p. 202). Nevertheless, sensitivity to children's needs, love-oriented methods of dealing with misbehavior, and positive reinforcement (attention and praise) for appropriate behavior unquestionably tend to promote desirable behavior in children. Parents who are generally lax in disciplining their children but are hostile, rejecting, cruel, and inconsistent in dealing with misbehavior are likely to have aggressive, delinquent children. Broken, disorganized homes in which the parents themselves have arrest records or are violent are particularly likely to foster delinquency and lack of social competence (see Reitman & Gross, 1995).

In discussing the combined effects of genetics and environment on behavioral development, Plomin (1989) warns against assuming that the family environment will make siblings similar. "Environmental influences do not operate on a family-by-family basis but rather on an individual-by-individual basis. They are specific to each child rather than general for an entire family" (p. 109). Thus, although we know that some types of family environments (abusive, neglectful, rejecting, and inconsistent, for example) are destructive, we must also remember that each child will experience and react to family relationships in his or her unique way.

In the mid 1990s, Harris (1995) proposed a theory of group socialization, suggesting that the role of parents is minimal in the development of their children's personality or social behavior. Popularization of her theory led many lay persons to the conclusion that family environment has little influence on social development and that the child's peer group is the primary factor in socialization. Although socialization by peers is undeniably an important factor in the development of emotional or behavioral disorders (Farmer et al., 1999), other research already cited indicates that parents and families can have a significant causal influence on some disorders.

Educators must be aware that most parents of youngsters with emotional or behavioral disorders want their children to behave more appropriately and will do anything they can to help them. These parents need support resources—not blame or criticism—for dealing with very difficult family circumstances. The Federation of Families for Children's Mental Health was organized in 1989 to help provide such support and resources, and parents are organizing in many localities to assist each other in finding additional resources (Jordan, Goldberg, & Goldberg, 1991). In the box on page 260, one of the founding members shares her perspective on why parents are so often blamed for their children's emotional or behavioral disorders.

School Factors

Some children already have emotional or behavioral disorders when they begin school; others develop such disorders during their school years, perhaps in part because of damaging experiences in the classroom itself. Children who exhibit disorders when they enter school may become better or worse according to how they are managed in the classroom (Walker, 1995; Walker, Colvin, & Ramsey, 1995). School experiences are no doubt of great importance to children, but as with biological and family factors, we cannot justify many statements regarding how such experiences contribute to the child's behavioral difficulties. A child's temperament and social competence may interact with the behaviors of classmates and teachers in contributing to emotional or behavioral problems. When a child with an already difficult temperament enters school lacking the skills for academic and social success, he or she is likely to get negative responses from peers and teachers (Martin, 1992).

There is a very real danger that such a child will become trapped in a spiral of negative interactions, in which he or she becomes increasingly irritating to and irritated by teachers and peers. The school can contribute to the development of emotional problems in several rather specific ways. For instance, teachers may be insensitive to children's individuality, perhaps requiring a mindless conformity to rules and routines. Educators and parents alike may hold too high or too low

Personal Reflection: Family Factors

Dixie Jordan is the parent of a nineteen-year-old son with an emotional and behavioral disorder, coordinator of the EBD Project at the PACER Center in Minneapolis (a resource center for parents of children with disabilities), and a founding member of the Federation of Families for Children's Mental Health.

Why do you think there is such a strong tendency to hold parents responsible for their children's emotional or behavioral disorders?

I am the parent of two children, the younger of which has emotional and behavioral problems. When my firstborn and I were out in public, strangers often commented on what a "good" mother I was, to have such an obedient, well-behaved, and compliant child. Frankly, I enjoyed the comments, and really believed that those parents whose children were throwing tantrums and generally demolishing their environments were simply not very skilled in child-rearing. I recall casting my share of reproachful glances in those days, and thinking with some arrogance that raising children should be left to those of us who knew how to do it well. Several years later, my second child and I were on the business end of such disdain, and it was a lesson in humility that I shall never forget. Very little that I had learned in the previous 3 years as a parent worked with this child; he was neurologically different, hyperactive, inattentive, and noncompliant even when discipline was consistently applied. His doctors, his neurologist, and finally his teachers referred me to "parenting classes," as though the experiences I had had with my older child were nonexistent; his elementary principal even said that there was nothing wrong that a good spanking wouldn't cure. I expected understanding that this was a very difficult child to raise, but the unspoken message was that I lacked competence in basic parenting skills, the same message that I sent to similarly situated parents just a few years earlier.

Most of us in the world today are parents. The majority of us have children who do not have emotional or behavioral problems. Everything in our experience suggests that when our children are successful and obedient, it is because of our parenting. We are reinforced socially for having a well-behaved child from friends, grandparents, even strangers. It makes sense, then, to attribute less desirable behaviors in children to the failure of their parents to provide appropriate guidance or to set firm limits. Many parents have internalized that sense of responsibility or blame for causing their child's emotional problems, even when they are not able to identify what they might have done wrong. It is a very difficult attitude to shake, especially when experts themselves cannot seem to agree on causation. With most children, the "cause" of an emotional or behavioral disorder is more likely a complex interplay of multiple factors than "parenting styles," "biology," or "environmental influences" as discrete entities, but it is human nature to latch onto a simple explanation—and inadequate parenting is, indeed, a simple explanation. When systems blame parents for causing their child's emotional or behavioral disorders, the focus is no longer on services to help the child learn better adaptive skills or appropriate behaviors, but on rationalizing why such services may not work. When parents feel blamed, their energies shift from focusing on the needs of their child to defending themselves. In either instance, the child is less well served.

Another reason that people hold parents responsible for their children's emotional or behavioral disorders is that parents may be under such unrelenting stress from trying to manage their child's behavior that they may resort to inappropriate techniques because of the failure of more conventional methods. A parent whose 8-year-old hyperactive child smashes out his bedroom window while being timed out for another problem may know that tying the child to a chair is not a good way to handle the crisis, but may be out of alternatives. It may not have been the "right" thing for the parent to do, but [he or she] is hardly responsible for causing the child's problems in the first place. It would be a mistake to attribute the incidence of abuse or neglect as "causing" most emotional or behavioral disorders without consideration that difficult children are perhaps more likely to be abused due to their noncompliant or otherwise difficult behaviors.

Source: Reprinted with the permission of Macmillan Publishing Company from *Characteristics of emotional and behavioral disorders of children and youth* (6th ed.), by James M. Kauffman. Copyright © 1997 by Macmillan Publishing Company.

expectations for the child's achievement or conduct, and they may communicate to the child who disappoints them that he or she is inadequate or undesirable.

Discipline in the school may be too lax, too rigid, or inconsistent. Instruction may be offered in skills for which the child has no real or imagined use. The school environment may be such that the misbehaving child is rewarded with recognition and special attention (even if that attention is criticism or punishment), whereas the child who behaves is ignored. Finally, teachers and peers may be models of misconduct—the child may misbehave by imitating them (Kauffman, 1997a).

In considering how they may be contributing to disordered behavior, teachers must ask themselves questions about their expectations, instructions, and approaches to behavior management (Kauffman, Mostert, Trent, & Hallahan, 1998). Teachers must not assume blame for disordered behavior to which they are not contributing, yet it is equally important that teachers eliminate whatever contributions they may be making to their students' misconduct.

Cultural Factors

Children, their families, and schools are embedded in cultures that influence them (Rogoff & Morelli, 1989; Walker et al., 1995). Aside from family and school, many environmental conditions affect adults' expectations of children and children's expectations of themselves and their peers. Values and behavioral standards are communicated to children through a variety of cultural conditions, demands, prohibitions, and models. Several specific cultural influences come to mind: the level of violence in the media (especially television and motion pictures), the use of terror as a means of coercion, the availability of recreational drugs and the level of drug abuse, changing standards for sexual conduct, religious demands and restrictions on behavior, and the threat of nuclear accidents or war. Peers are another important source of cultural influence, particularly after the child enters the upper elementary grades (Farmer et al., 1999; Harris, 1995).

Undoubtedly, the culture in which a child is reared influences his or her emotional, social, and behavioral development. Case studies of rapidly changing cultures bear this out. Other studies suggest cultural influences on anxiety, depression, and aggression. The level of violence depicted on television and in movies is almost certainly a contributing factor in the increasing level of violence in U.S. society (see Walker et al., 1995).

Garmezy (1987) and Baumeister, Kupstas, and Klindworth (1990) also note the changing cultural conditions in the United States during the 1980s that predisposed children to develop emotional or behavioral disorders and a variety of other disabling conditions. Among these are dramatic increases in the number of children living in poverty. There have also been substantial increases in the number of children born to teenage mothers and to mothers who have abused "crack" cocaine and other substances. At the same time, medical and social services available to poor children and their families have been cut substantially. In short, we are living in an era of enormous affluence for some Americans but also a period in which poverty and related problems continue to grow rapidly. Neglect of the problems of poor children and

The quality of parenting may be a factor causing behavior problems in children, but by itself, it is not an adequate or correct explanation. Children, their families, and schools are embedded in cultures that influence them.

their families has led some to question the importance of the health and welfare of children in U.S. culture (Hodgkinson, 1995; see also Freedman, 1993; Kozol, 1995; Moynihan, 1995).

Abuse and other forms of extreme trauma are known to contribute significantly to the emotional or behavioral disorders of many children in our society today (see Becker & Bonner, 1997; Saigh, 1997). Racial bias and discrimination are also known to be deeply embedded in our culture and to play a part in the disproportionate imprisonment of African American males. Emphasis on imprisonment and punishment, especially for relatively minor offenses, combined with lack of economic and educational opportunities, appear to perpetuate if not exacerbate the harsh conditions of life that contribute to emotional or behavioral disorders and delinquency (Miller, 1997).

Clearly, cultural influences affect how children behave in school. But even when culture is considered as a cause, we must be aware of interactive effects. Schools and families influence culture; they are not simply products of it. Finally, refer back to Chapter 3 and the importance of a multicultural perspective. Consideration of cultural factors in causing emotional or behavioral disorders requires that culturally normative behavior not be construed as disordered.

Identification

It is much easier to identify disordered behaviors than it is to define and classify types and causes of emotional or behavioral disorders. Most students with emotional or behavioral disorders do not escape the notice of their teachers. Occasionally, such students will not bother anyone and thus be invisible, but it is usually easy for experienced teachers to tell when students need help. Teachers often fail to assess the strengths of students with emotional or behavioral disorders. However, it is important to include assessment of students' emotional and behavioral competencies, not just their weaknesses or deficits (Epstein & Sharma, 1997).

The most common type of emotional or behavioral disorder—conduct disorder—attracts immediate attention, so there is seldom any real problem in identification. Immature students and those with personality problems may be less obvious, but they are not difficult to recognize. Students with emotional or behavioral disorders are so readily identified by school personnel, in fact, that few schools bother to use systematic screening procedures. Also, the availability of special services for those with emotional or behavioral disorders lags far behind the need—and there is not much point in screening for problems when there are no services available to treat them.

Children with pervasive developmental disorders are also easily recognized. In fact, the parents of children with autism frequently report that soon after their child's birth, they noticed that he or she was strange or different from most children—unresponsive, rigid, or emotionally detached, for example. Likewise, children with schizophrenia are seldom mistaken for those who are developing normally. Their unusual language, mannerisms, and ways of relating to others soon become matters of concern to parents, teachers, and even many casual observers. But children with these disorders are a small percentage of those with emotional or behavioral disorders, and problems in their identification are not usually encountered.

Even so, do not conclude that there is never any question about whether a student has an emotional or behavioral disorder. The younger the child, the more difficult it is to judge whether his or her behavior signifies a serious problem. And some children with emotional or behavioral disorders are undetected because teachers are not sensitive to their problems or because they do not stand out sharply from other children in the environment who may have even more serious problems. Furthermore, even sensitive teachers sometimes make errors of judgment. Also keep in mind that some students with emotional or behavioral disorders do not exhibit problems at school.

Formal screening and accurate early identification for the purpose of planning educational intervention are complicated by the problems of definition already discussed. In general, however, teachers' informal judgments have served as a fairly valid and reliable means of screening students for emotional or behavioral problems (as compared with judgments of psychologists and psychiatrists). When more formal procedures are used, teachers' ratings of behavior have turned out to be quite accurate.

Walker and his colleagues have devised a screening system for use in elementary schools, based on the assumption that a teacher's judgment is a valid and cost-effective (though greatly underused) method of identifying children with emotional or behavioral disorders (Walker & Severson, 1990; Walker, Severson, & Feil, 1994). Although teachers tend to overrefer students who exhibit externalizing behavior problems (i.e., those with conduct disorders), they tend to underrefer students with internalizing problems (i.e., those characterized by anxiety–withdrawal). To make certain that children are not overlooked in screening but that time and effort are not wasted, a three-step process is used:

1. The teacher lists and ranks students with externalizing and internalizing problems. Those who best fit descriptions of students with externalizing problems and those who best fit descriptions of those with internalizing problems are listed in order from "most like" to "least like" the descriptions.
2. The teacher completes two checklists for the three highest-ranked pupils on each list. One checklist asks the teacher to indicate whether each pupil exhibited specific behaviors during the past month (such as "steals," "has tantrums," "uses obscene language or swears"). The other checklist requires the teacher to judge how often (never, sometimes, frequently) each pupil shows certain characteristics (e.g., "follows established classroom rules" or "cooperates with peers in group activities or situations").
3. Pupils whose scores on these checklists exceed established norms are observed in the classroom and on the playground by a school professional other than the classroom teacher (a school psychologist, counselor, or resource teacher). Classroom observations indicate the extent to which the pupil meets academic expectations; playground observations assess the quality and nature of social behavior. These direct observations of behavior, in addition to teachers' ratings, are then used to decide whether the child has problems that warrant classification for special education. Such carefully researched screening systems may lead to improved services for children with emotional or behavioral disorders. Systematic efforts to base identification on teachers' judgments and careful observation should result in services being directed to those students most clearly in need (Walker et al., 1995).

Psychological and Behavioral Characteristics

Describing the characteristics of children and youths with emotional or behavioral disorders is an extraordinary challenge because disorders of emotions and behaviors are extremely varied. We provide a general picture of these children; however, individuals may vary markedly in intelligence, achievement, life circumstances, and emotional and behavioral characteristics.

Intelligence and Achievement

The idea that children and youths with emotional or behavioral disorders tend to be particularly bright is a myth. Research clearly shows that the average student with an emotional or behavioral disorder has an IQ in the dull–normal range (around 90) and that relatively few score above the bright–normal range. Compared to the normal distribution of intelligence, more children with emotional or behavioral disorders fall into the ranges of slow learner and mild mental retardation. On the basis of a review of the research on the intelligence of students with emotional or behavioral disorders, Kauffman (1997a) hypothesized distributions of intelligence as shown in Figure 7.1.

Of course, we have been referring to children with emotional or behavioral disorders as a group. Some children who have emotional or behavioral disorders are extremely bright and score very high on intelligence tests. We caution, too, that intensive early behavioral intervention may reveal cognitive abilities that have not been apparent. That is, some individuals may have cognitive deficits that early intensive intervention can largely overcome; these individuals may be mistakenly assumed to have permanent cognitive deficits.

There are pitfalls in assessing the intellectual characteristics of a group of children by examining the distribution of their IQs. Intelligence tests are not perfect instruments for measuring what we mean by *intelligence*, and it can be argued that emotional or behavioral difficulties may prevent children from scoring as high as they are capable of scoring. That is, it might be argued that intelligence tests are biased against children with emotional or behavioral disorders and that their true IQs are higher than test scores indicate. Still, the lower-than-normal IQs for these students do indicate lower ability to perform tasks other students

Figure 7.1

Hypothetical frequency distribution of IQ for students with emotional or behavioral disorders as compared to a normal frequency distribution.

Source: Reprinted with the permission of Macmillan Publishing Company from *Characteristics of emotional and behavioral disorders of children and youth* (6th ed.) by James M. Kauffman. Copyright © 1997 by Macmillan Publishing Company.

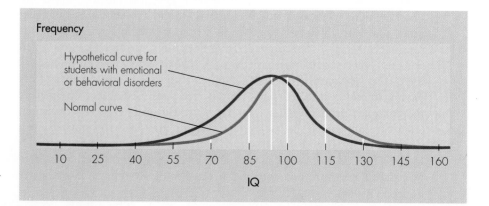

perform successfully, and the lower scores are consistent with impairment in other areas of functioning (academic achievement and social skills, for example). IQ is a relatively good predictor of how far a student will progress academically and socially, even in cases of severe disorders.

Most students with emotional or behavioral disorders are also underachievers at school, as measured by standardized tests (Kauffman, 1997a). A student with an emotional or behavioral disorder does not usually achieve at the level expected for his or her mental age; seldom are such students academically advanced. In fact, many students with severe disorders lack even the most basic reading and arithmetic skills, and the few who seem to be competent in reading or math are often unable to apply their skills to everyday problems. Some children with severe disorders do not even possess basic self-care or daily living skills such as using the toilet, grooming, dressing, and feeding.

Social and Emotional Characteristics

Previously, we described two major dimensions of disordered behavior based on analyses of behavior ratings: externalizing and internalizing. The externalizing dimension is characterized by aggressive, acting-out behavior; the internalizing dimension is characterized by anxious, withdrawn behavior. Our discussion here focuses on the aggressive and withdrawn types of behavior typically exhibited by students with emotional or behavioral disorders.

Although both aggressive and withdrawn behaviors are commonly seen in most children with emotional or behavioral disorders, we discuss the characteristics of severe disorders in a separate section (see p. 270). These children may be qualitatively as well as quantitatively different from others, for certain behavioral features set them apart. Remember, too, that a given student might, at different times, show both aggressive and withdrawn behaviors. Many students with emotional or behavioral disorders have multiple problems (Tankersley & Landrum, 1997; Walker et al., 1995).

At the beginning of this chapter, we said that most students with emotional or behavioral disorders are not well liked or identify with deviant peers. Studies of the social status of students in regular elementary and secondary classrooms indicate that those who are identified as having emotional or behavioral disorders are seldom socially accepted. Early peer rejection as well as aggressive behavior place a child at high risk for later social and emotional problems (Ialongo et al., 1998). Many aggressive students who are not rejected affiliate primarily with others who are aggressive (Farmer et al., 1999). The relationship between emotional or behavioral disorders and communication disorders is increasingly clear (Rogers-Adkinson & Griffith, 1999). Many children and youths with emotional or behavioral disorders have great difficulty in understanding and using language in social circumstances.

Aggressive, Acting-Out Behavior (Externalizing). As noted earlier, conduct disorder is the most common problem exhibited by students with emotional or behavioral disorders. Hitting, fighting, teasing, yelling, refusing to comply with requests, crying, destructiveness, vandalism, extortion—these behaviors, if exhibited often, are very likely to earn a child or youth the label "disturbed." Normal children cry, scream, hit, fight, become negative, and do almost everything else children with emotional or behavioral disorders do, only not so impulsively and often. Youngsters of the type we are discussing here drive adults to distraction.

Children who act out aggressively or impulsively with frequent negative confrontations often are not well liked by their peers.

These youths are not popular with their peers either, unless they are socialized delinquents who do not offend their delinquent friends. They typically do not respond quickly and positively to well-meaning adults who care about them and try to be helpful.

Some of these students are considered to have attention deficit hyperactivity disorder or brain injury. Their behavior is not only extremely troublesome but also appears to be resistant to change through typical discipline. Often they are so frequently scolded and disciplined that punishment means little or nothing to them. Because of adult exasperation and their own deviousness, these youths get away with misbehavior a lot of the time. These are children who behave horribly not once in a while, but so often that the people they must live with or be with cannot stand them. Of course, aggressive, acting-out children typically cannot stand the people they have to live and be with either, and often for good reason. Such children are screamed at, criticized, and punished a lot. The problem, then, is not just the individual children's behavior. What must be examined if the child or anyone else is to be helped is the interaction between the child's behavior and the behavior of other people in his or her environment (Walker, Kavanagh et al., 1998).

Aggression has been analyzed from many viewpoints. The analyses that have the strongest support in empirical research are those of social learning theorists, such as Bandura (1973, 1986), and behavioral psychologists, such as Patterson (Patterson, Reid, & Dishion, 1992). Their studies take into account the child's experience and his or her motivation, based on the anticipated consequences of aggression. In brief, they view aggression as *learned* behavior, and assume that it is possible to identify the conditions under which it will be learned.

Children learn many aggressive behaviors by observing parents, siblings, playmates, and people portrayed on television and in movies. Individuals who model aggression are more likely to be imitated if they are high in social status and are observed to receive rewards and escape punishment for their aggression, especially if they experience no unpleasant consequences or obtain rewards by overcoming their victims. If children are placed in unpleasant situations and they cannot escape from the unpleasantness or obtain rewards except by aggression,

aggression. Behavior that intentionally causes others harm or that elicits escape or avoidance responses from others.

they are more likely to be aggressive, especially if this behavior is tolerated or encouraged by others.

Aggression is encouraged by external rewards (social status, power, suffering of the victim, obtaining desired items), vicarious rewards (seeing others obtain desirable consequences for their aggression), and self-reinforcement (self-congratulation or enhancement of self-image). If children can justify aggression in their own minds (by comparison to the behaviors of others or by dehumanizing their victims), they are more likely to be aggressive. Punishment may actually increase aggression under some circumstances: when it is inconsistent or delayed, when there is no positive alternative to the punished behavior, when it provides an example of aggression, or when counterattack against the punisher seems likely to be successful.

Teaching aggressive children to be less so is no simple matter, but social learning theory and behavioral research do provide some general guidelines. In general, research does not support the notion that it is wise to let children act out their aggression freely. The most helpful techniques include providing examples (models) of nonaggressive responses to aggression-provoking circumstances, helping the child rehearse or role-play nonaggressive behavior, providing reinforcement for nonaggressive behavior, preventing the child from obtaining positive consequences for aggression, and punishing aggression in ways that involve as little counteraggression as possible (e.g., using "time-out" or brief social isolation rather than spanking or yelling) (Walker et al., 1995).

The seriousness of children's aggressive, acting-out behavior should not be underestimated. It was believed for decades that although these children cause a lot of trouble, they are not as seriously disabled as children who are shy, anxious, or neurotic. Research has exploded this myth. When combined with school failure, aggressive, antisocial behavior in childhood generally means a gloomy future in terms of social adjustment and mental health, especially for boys (Ialongo et al., 1998). Neurotic, shy, anxious children are much more likely to be able to get and hold jobs, overcome their emotional problems, and stay out of jails and mental hospitals than are adults who had conduct problems and were delinquent as children (see Kazdin, 1995).

Of course, there are exceptions to the rule. Nonetheless, there is a high probability that the aggressive child who is a failure in school will become more of a social misfit as an adult than will the withdrawn child. When we consider that conduct disorders and delinquency are highly correlated with school failure, the importance of meeting the needs of acting-out and underachieving children is obvious (Kauffman, 1997a; Walker et al., 1995).

Immature, Withdrawn Behavior (Internalizing). In noting the seriousness of aggressive, acting-out behavior, we do not intend to downplay the disabling nature of immaturity and withdrawal. In their extreme forms, withdrawal and immaturity may be characteristics of schizophrenia and autism. Such disorders not only have serious consequences for individuals in their childhood years but also carry a very poor prognosis for adult mental health. The child whose behavior fits a pattern of extreme immaturity and withdrawal cannot develop the close and satisfying human relationships that characterize normal development. Such a child will find it difficult to meet the pressures and demands of everyday life.

All children exhibit immature behavior and act withdrawn once in a while. Children who fit the withdrawn, immature description, however, are typically infantile in their ways or reluctant to interact with other people. They are social isolates who have few friends, seldom play with children their own age, and lack the social skills necessary to have fun. Some retreat into fantasy or daydreaming; some develop fears that are completely out of proportion to the circumstances; some complain constantly of little aches and pains and let their supposed illnesses keep them from participating in normal activities; some regress to earlier stages of development and demand constant help and attention; and some become depressed for no apparent reason (see Rabian & Silverman, 1995; Stark, Ostrander, Kurowski, Swearer, & Bowen, 1995).

As in the case of aggressive, acting-out behavior, withdrawal and immaturity may be interpreted in many different ways. Proponents of the psychoanalytic approach are likely to see internal conflicts and unconscious motivations as the underlying causes. Behavioral psychologists tend to interpret such problems in terms of failures in social learning; this view is supported by more empirical research data than other views (Kauffman, 1997a). A social learning analysis attributes withdrawal and immaturity to an inadequate environment. Causal factors may include overrestrictive parental discipline, punishment for appropriate social responses, reward for isolated behavior, lack of opportunity to learn and practice social skills, and models (examples) of inappropriate behavior. Immature or withdrawn children can be taught the skills they lack by arranging opportunities for them to learn and practice appropriate responses, showing models engaging in appropriate behavior, and providing rewards for improved behavior.

A particularly important aspect of immature, withdrawn behavior is depression. Only recently have mental health workers and special educators begun to realize that depression is a widespread and serious problem among children and adolescents (Guetzloe, 1991; Kaslow, Morris, & Rehm, 1997). Today, the consensus of psychologists is that the nature of depression in children and youths is quite similar in many respects to that of depression in adults. The indications of depression include disturbances of mood or feelings, inability to think or concentrate, lack of motivation, and decreased physical well-being. A depressed child or youth may act sad, lonely, and apathetic; exhibit low self-esteem, excessive guilt, and pervasive pessimism; avoid tasks and social experiences; and/or have physical complaints or problems in sleeping, eating, or eliminating. Sometimes depression is accompanied by such problems as bed-wetting (nocturnal enuresis), fecal soiling (encopresis), extreme fear of or refusal to go to school, failure in school, or talk of suicide or suicide attempts. Depression also frequently occurs in combination with conduct disorder (Kazdin, 1997; McCracken, Cantwell, & Hanna, 1993).

Suicide has increased dramatically during the past decade among those between the ages of fifteen and twenty-four and is now among the leading causes of death in this age group. Depression, especially when severe and accompanied by a sense of hopelessness, is linked to suicide and suicide attempts. Therefore, it is important for all those who work with young people to be able to recognize the signs. Substance abuse is also a major problem among children and teenagers and may be related to depression (Newcomb & Bentler, 1989).

Depression sometimes has a biological cause, and antidepressant medications have at times been successful in helping depressed children and youths overcome their problems (Pomeroy & Gadow, 1997; Sweeney et al., 1997). In many cases, however, no biological cause can be found. Depression can also be caused by environmental or psychological factors, such as the death of a loved one, separation of one's parents, school failure, rejection by one's peers, or a chaotic and punitive home environment. Interventions based on social learning theory—instructing children and youths in social interaction skills and self-control techniques and teaching them to view themselves more positively, for example—have often been successful in such cases (Kaslow et al., 1997).

Characteristics Associated with Traumatic Brain Injury (TBI)

As mentioned earlier, traumatic brain injury (TBI) is a separate category under IDEA, but it may be accompanied by a variety of serious emotional and behavioral effects. Many disturbing behavior patterns, such as violence or other extreme examples of social maladjustment, cannot be connected to brain damage. However, we know that TBI can cause violent aggression, hyperactivity, impulsivity, inattention, and a wide range of other emotional or behavioral problems, depending on just what parts of the brain are damaged (Allison, 1993).

The possible effects of TBI include a long list of other psychosocial problems, some of which include (see Deaton & Waaland, 1994):

- Displaying inappropriate manners or mannerisms
- Failing to understand humor or "read" social situations
- Becoming easily tired, frustrated, or angered
- Feeling unreasonable fear or anxiety
- Being irritable
- Experiencing sudden, exaggerated swings of mood
- Having depression
- Perseveration (persistent repetition of one thought or behavior)

The emotional and behavioral effects of TBI also depend on the person's age at the time of injury and the social environment he or she lived in before and after the injury occurred (Deaton & Waaland, 1994). For instance, home, community, or school environments that are conducive to the misbehavior of any child or youth are extremely likely to exacerbate the emotional or behavioral problems of someone with TBI. In fact, arranging an environment for someone with TBI that is conducive to and supportive of appropriate behavior is one of the greatest challenges of dealing effectively with the effects of brain injury (Bergland & Hoffbauer, 1996; Deaton, 1994). The physical effects of TBI cannot often be undone through medical treatment. Although it may be known that the resulting emotional or behavioral problems are caused by the brain injury, these problems must be addressed primarily through environmental modifications—changing other people's demands, expectations, responses to behavior and adapting the physical surroundings or equipment available for accomplishing various tasks.

TBI often results in a shattered sense of self, and recovery or rehabilitation of identity and behavior may be a slow, painstaking process, requiring multidisciplinary efforts. For students with TBI, effective education and treatment often require not only classroom behavior management but family therapy, medication, and communication training as well (Feeney & Urbanczyk, 1994; see also the discussion of TBI in Chapters 8 and 11). If the student with TBI is to regain an acceptable sense of self and be prepared for transition into the next higher level of education or the workforce, then intensive personal counseling, behavior modification programs, physical modifications of the classroom, vocational training, and academic and personal support systems may be required (Bergland & Hoffbauer, 1996; Pollack, 1994).

Characteristics Associated with Schizophrenia, Autism, and Other Pervasive Developmental Disorders

The characteristics of schizophrenia, autism, and other pervasive developmental disorders are not entirely distinct. Differentiating among these conditions is often difficult, especially in young children. Although autism and schizophrenia are typically distinguished by certain characteristics, particularly age of onset (see page 253), some types of behavior are common among children with a variety of severe disorders. If exhibited to a marked extent and over a long period of time, these behaviors typically carry a poor prognosis; even with early, intensive intervention, a significant percentage of children are unlikely to recover completely (Asarnow, Tompson, & Goldstein, 1994; Charlop-Christy et al., 1997; Werry, McClellan, Andrews, & Ham, 1994).

The following behaviors are typical of individuals with autism and other pervasive developmental disorders (although not all such individuals exhibit all these characteristics):

- *Absent or distorted relationships with people*—inability to relate to people except as objects, inability to express affection, or ability to build and maintain only distant, suspicious, or bizarre relationships
- *Extreme or peculiar problems in communication*—absence of verbal language or language that is not functional, such as **echolalia** (parroting what one hears), misuse of pronouns (e.g., *he* for *you* or *I* for *her*), **neologisms** (made-up, meaningless words or sentences), talk that bears little or no resemblance to reality
- *Self-stimulation*—repetitive, stereotyped behavior that seems to have no purpose other than providing sensory stimulation; this may take a wide variety of forms, such as swishing saliva, twirling objects, patting one's cheeks, flapping one's hands, staring, and the like
- *Self-injury*—repeated physical self-abuse, such as biting, scratching, or poking oneself, head banging, and so on
- *Perceptual anomalies*—unusual responses or absence of responses to stimuli that seem to indicate sensory impairment or unusual sensitivity
- *Apparent cognitive deficits*—inability to respond adequately to intelligence and achievement tests or inability to apply apparent intelligence to everyday tasks
- *Aggression toward others*—severe tantrums or calculated physical attacks that threaten or injure others
- *Lack of daily living skills*—absence or significant impairment of ability to take care of one's basic needs, such as dressing, feeding, or toileting

echolalia. The meaningless repetition (echoing) of what has been heard.

neologism. A coined word that is meaningless to others; meaningless words used in the speech of a person with a mental disorder.

Educational Considerations

Students with emotional or behavioral disorders typically have low grades and other unsatisfactory academic outcomes, have higher dropout and lower graduation rates than other student groups, and are often placed in highly restrictive settings. Moreover, these students are disproportionately from poor and ethnic-minority families and frequently encounter the juvenile justice system (U.S. Department of Education, 1994, 1997). Consequently, their successful education

Educators agree on the importance of collaboration and discussion between the school, community, and family members.

is among the most important and challenging tasks facing special education today. Unfortunately, there is not a consensus among special educators about how to meet the challenge of educating students with emotional or behavioral disorders. Although a national agenda has been written for improving services to students with emotional or behavioral disorders, it is so vaguely worded that it is of little value in guiding the design of interventions (Kauffman, 1997b).

Contrasting Conceptual Models

Several different conceptual models may guide the work of educators. As Kauffman (1997a) points out, few practitioners are guided strictly and exclusively by a single model. Nevertheless, a teacher must have a solid grounding in one conceptual orientation to guide competent practice.

One of two conceptual models, or a combination of the two, guide most educational programs today: the psychoeducational and behavioral models. We illustrate these models in action with actual case descriptions. (See Kauffman, 1997a, for description and case illustrations of other models.)

Psychoeducational Model. The psychoeducational model acknowledges the existence of unconscious motivations and underlying conflicts, yet also stresses the realistic demands of everyday functioning in school, home, and community. One basic assumption of the psychoeducational model is that teachers must understand unconscious motivations if they are to deal most effectively with students' academic failures and misbehaviors. To do so, teachers are not expected to focus on resolving unconscious conflicts, as psychotherapists might. Rather, teachers must focus on how to help students acquire self-control through reflection and planning. Intervention may include therapeutic discussions or *life space interviews (LSIs)*, which are designed to help the youth:

1. Understand that what he or she is doing is a problem
2. Recognize his or her motivations
3. Observe the consequences of his or her actions
4. Plan alternative ways of responding to similar circumstances in the future

The emphasis is on the youngster gaining insight that will result in behavioral change, not on changing behavior directly (see Wood, 1990; Wood & Long, 1991). The following case of Andy, drawn from James and Long (1992), illustrates the psychoeducational model in action:

success stories

special educators at work

Herndon, VA: Fourteen-year-old **Christina Isaacs** attends a special program for students with emotional and behavioral disorders that is attached to a large, public middle school. Special educator Teresa Zutter, principal of this co-facility for seventh- and eighth-graders, knows her sixty students and their families well. She and Christina's mother, Brenda Isaacs, agree that this close community provides Chrissy with the individual support she needs to merge slowly into the mainstream.

Chrissy's goals included increasing academic achievement, reducing reliance on adults, and developing friendships as well as confidence in her abilities and performance. This year, Chrissy was included daily in general classes for PE and teen life and sang with the middle school chorus five days a week. She says with pride, her eyes glancing down at her reflection in the glass-topped table, "I want to do well in the mainstream because I want to be a cheerleader and get a regular high school diploma."

According to Teresa Zutter, Chrissy started seventh grade as a girl in distress, but she took advantage of all the resources available to her. Remembers Zutter, "When I first met Chrissy, she gave the impression of being physically frail and frightened. As we walked around her new school, she grabbed my arm and asked, 'Will I like it here?'" Chrissy admits, "I was nervous last year. The school was so big and beautiful!"

The Herndon Center, a co-facility with Herndon Middle School, is two years old and serves sixty students in grades 7 and 8 who have emotional or behavioral disorders and need individual support to prepare for experiences in the mainstream. Each classroom is equipped with a "hot-line" telephone connected to the main office and a carpeted quiet room that serves as a "time-out" area for angry students. There is also frequent communication between Teresa Zutter and parents, who are alerted to misbehaviors, and, in some instances, called to take their sons or daughters home. Rules and policies are clear for students, teachers, and families. "There is an absolute need for structure and for individualization to get the trust factor going," says Teresa. "We have so many people here to help and to talk to students, no one has to hit to communicate."

The thrust of the program is to offer a low student–teacher ratio to students who need close attention. In

Eighth-grader Chrissy Isaacs stood wide-eyed at the principal's door. "I've called you to my office, Chrissy, because you are a star!" said Teresa Zutter. "In the past year, you have made real progress toward your goals."

At Teresa's invitation, a relieved Chrissy sat down at a dark wooden table and talked about all she had accomplished. "I worked hard last year, and by January, my teachers thought I could join a mainstream drama class. I loved it!" "And she was good!" added Zutter.

Andy

Andy, 14, was referred for special education due to his oppositional and sometimes verbally threatening behavior. In addition to disobeying adults in other ways, he frequently left the classroom without permission and roamed the hallways. He appeared to enjoy confronting his teachers and taunting his peers, especially a deaf peer, Drew, who also had few social skills.

One morning, Drew came to school very agitated, which required that the teacher spend most of her time before lunch calming him down. At lunch, Andy persistently aggravated Drew. When the teacher told Andy to stop and go back to his desk, Andy began yelling that Drew had called him a

addition to Principal Zutter, there are thirteen teachers and a support staff that includes a psychologist, social worker, guidance counselor, health awareness monitor, and conflict resolution teacher. Weekly clinical staff meetings address the needs of individual students and provide a regular forum for educators and support staff to address problems. As described by Teresa, "This is such a spirited staff. We laugh a lot and take care of each other."

The center assumes a treatment model based on the belief that students thrive on positive reinforcement. Nonphysical punishment is employed briefly and only to the degree necessary, while instruction is geared toward remediation and cultivation of coping mechanisms. "Girls and boys who are stressed can be made to feel better," maintains Teresa. "They [do not just have emotional or behavioral disorders] for a while but have entrenched behaviors; it's a life struggle. They won't be okay without interventions and without being taught how to cope with stress."

Most of the students at the Herndon Center are male, a fact Chrissy Isaacs was quick to note. "I'm at that age where I like boys," she says. When she started grade 7, Chrissy had little sense of her own reality; she often gazed at her reflection and slipped into the protection of fantasy. She was also limited in her awareness of social interactions and needed to learn how to respond to various situations. Lost in her own thoughts, she would have tantrums or provoke other students, not understanding the impact these behaviors had on her relationships. She was also becoming oppositional. Academically, Chrissy was below grade level in most areas. Although she could easily decode words, she had problems comprehending what she read and organizing her thoughts.

With frequent reassurance and a great deal of help to stay on task, Chrissy made gains and was performing at grade level in all classes by the end of seventh grade. Speech therapy helped her vocabulary development, particularly in using words with multiple meanings, as used in jokes and riddles. Academic supports included receiving extra adult attention, additional time to complete classwork and tests, shortened assignments, and peer/work helpers and having directions stated several times. Although she daydreamed frequently, Chrissy demonstrated two real strengths: a willingness to work hard and an ability to focus when provided with support. She is now described as a conscientious student who worries about the quality of her work.

As long as she is confronted gently and not embarrassed in front of other students, Chrissy is responsive to correction. She takes great pride in her appearance and talents and is still attracted to anything that captures her image. Socially, she tries to be everybody's friend, but peers are still leery of her erratic behavior, which quickly turns antagonistic. "Chrissy tends to be overly sensitive to what others are saying, whether it relates to her or not," says her mother, Brenda Isaacs. And when she is angry, Chrissy resorts to profanity, inappropriate comments, and even physical threats. This year, to her credit, she has managed to develop some stable friendships with a few girls, which she cherishes.

"With all this support, I see my daughter proud and happy and becoming more mature," says Brenda Isaacs. Teresa Zutter agrees: "Chrissy will always have some difficulties, but with help she can be eased from her world of fantasy. Hopefully, she'll value herself and stay in reality."

—By Jean Crockett

"fag" and that he (Drew) was the one who should return to his desk. The teacher repeated her instruction. Andy then shoved a desk across the room and left the classroom without permission. In the hall, Andy began pacing and disturbing other students. So the teacher and another staff member then escorted Andy to a quiet room, where he went without resistance. In the quiet room, the teacher used LSI techniques to help Andy think through the reasons for his behavior and how he might behave in more adaptive ways.

Through skillful interviewing about the incident with Drew, the teacher was able to help Andy see that he was jealous and resentful of the time she spent with Drew. Andy lived with his mother and an older sister. His sister had multiple disabilities, was very low functioning, and demanded a lot of his mother's attention. His father had left home when Andy was eight, and his mother was not in good health. This meant that Andy had to take on some adult responsibilities at an early age.

The goals of the teacher's LSI about this particular incident were to get Andy to understand that she cared about him and wanted to prevent him from disrupting the group. Most importantly, she wanted Andy to understand that there were similarities in his situation at home and at school that gave rise to similar feelings and behavior.

Andy's teacher used what James and Long (1992) call a "red flag interview," a discussion that addresses the transfer of problems from home to school. A red flag interview follows a predictable sequence in which a student like Andy is helped to understand that:

1. He experiences a stressful situation at home (e.g., a beating, overstimulation, etc.).
2. His experience triggers intense feelings of anger, helplessness, and the like.
3. These feelings are not expressed to the abusive person at home because he is fearful of retaliation.
4. He contains his feelings until he gets on the bus, enters school, or responds to a demand.
5. He acts out his feelings in an environment that is safer and directs his behavior toward someone else.

The LSI may be based on the psychoanalytic notion of defense mechanisms—tactics that people use to avoid dealing with issues, events, or people that may be unpleasant or hurtful. Nonetheless, the LSI also must end with a return to the reality of the situation. In Andy's case, this meant his return to the class and anticipation of future problems. His teacher ended the LSI as follows:

Interviewer: What do you think Drew might do when we walk into the room?

Andy: He will probably point at me and laugh.

Interviewer: That might happen. How can you deal with that?

Andy: I can ignore him.

Interviewer: That will not be easy for you. It will take a lot of emotional strength to control your urge to tease him back. And if you do that and Drew teases you, who is going to get into trouble?

Andy: Drew.

Interviewer: That's right. You are now beginning to think more clearly about your actions. Also, I will set up a behavior contract for you. If you are able to ignore Drew's teasing, you will earn positive one-on-one time with me.

Andy: Agreed. (James & Long, 1992, p. 37)

Behavioral Model. Two major assumptions underlie the behavioral model: (1) The essence of the problem is the behavior itself, and (2) behavior is a function of environmental events. Maladaptive behavior is viewed as inappropriate learned responses to particular demands or circumstances. Therefore, intervention should consist of rearranging antecedent events and consequences to teach more adaptive behavior.

Actually, the behavioral model is a natural science approach to behavior, emphasizing precise definition, reliable measurement, careful control of the variables thought to maintain or change behavior, and establishment of replicable cause–effect relationships. Interventions consist of choosing target responses, measuring their current levels, analyzing probable controlling environmental events, and changing antecedent or consequent events until reliable changes are produced in the target behaviors (see Alberto & Troutman, 1995; Kerr & Nelson, 1998; Walker, 1995; Walker et al., 1995). The following case of Sven, based on a study by Dunlap et al. (1994), illustrates how a behavioral model might guide teaching:

Sven

Sven—an 11-year-old attending a special self-contained class for students with emotional or behavioral disorders—showed inadequate attention to tasks, inappropriate and aggressive talk, and physically aggressive behavior. An observer recorded Sven's behavior during brief (15 second) intervals for 15–30 minutes of his English lesson each day. These observations showed that Sven was engaged in academic tasks less than 60 percent of the time on average and that his behavior was disruptive about 40 percent of the time.

The professionals working with Sven assumed that students who exhibit maladaptive behaviors do so for a variety of reasons, including not only the consequences the behaviors bring but the settings in which they occur and the demands for performance—the antecedents. In this case, the antecedents related to Sven's maladaptive behavior were changed. The antecedents of his off-task, disruptive behavior—what he was assigned to do, especially if it was an assignment he did not like—seemed to be at least as much a problem as the consequences of his behavior. Therefore, the primary strategy used to modify Sven's behavior was to give him his choice of six to eight task options in his English class. The task options were constructed as variations on the work he normally would do, any one of which was acceptable and would lead to the same instructional objective. Under these conditions, Sven engaged in academic tasks about 95 percent of the time, and his disruptive behavior dropped to an average of less than 10 percent.

Clearly, giving Sven assignments about which he had choices—all of them acceptable variations—improved his attention to his tasks and markedly decreased his disruptive behavior. Use of behavioral methods such as rewarding consequences for appropriate behavior and academic performance are critically important. In addition, teachers may also use knowledge of behavior principles to alter the conditions of instruction in ways that defuse task *resistance* and encourage task *attention*.

Balancing Behavioral Control with Academic and Social Learning

Some writers have observed that the quality of educational programs for students with emotional or behavioral disorders is often dismal, regardless of the conceptual model underlying practice. The focus is often on rigid external control of students' behavior, and academic instruction and social learning are often secondary or almost entirely neglected (Knitzer, Steinberg, & Fleisch, 1990). Although the quality of instruction is undoubtedly low in too many programs, examples can be found of effective academic and social instruction for students at all levels (Peacock Hill Working Group, 1991)

Behavioral control strategies are an essential part of educational programs for students with externalizing problems. Without effective means of controlling disruptive behavior, it's extremely unlikely that academic and social learning will occur. Excellent academic instruction will certainly reduce many behavior problems (Gunter, Hummel, & Conroy, 1998; Kauffman et al., 1998; Kerr & Nelson, 1998). Nevertheless, even the best instructional programs will not eliminate the disruptive behaviors of all students. Teachers of students with emotional or behavioral disorders must have effective control strategies, preferably those involving students as much as possible in self-control. In addition, teachers must offer effective instruction in academic and social skills that will allow their students to live, learn, and work with others (Walker et al., 1995).

Importance of Integrated Services

Children and youths with emotional or behavioral disorders tend to have multiple and complex needs. For most, life is coming apart in more ways than one. In addition to their problems in school, they typically have family problems and a variety of difficulties in the community (e.g., engaging in illegal activities, an absence of desirable relationships with peers and adults, substance abuse, difficulty finding and maintaining employment). Thus, children or youths with emotional or behavioral disorders may need, in addition to special education, a variety of family-oriented services, psychotherapy or counseling, community supervision, training related to employment, and so on. No single service agency can meet the needs of most of these children and youths. Integrating these needed services into a more coordinated and effective effort is now seen as essential (Edgar & Siegel, 1995; Nelson & Pearson, 1991).

Strategies That Work

Regardless of the conceptual model that guides education, we can point to several effective strategies. Most are incorporated in the behavioral model, but other models may include them as well. Successful strategies at all levels, from early intervention through transition, balance concern for academic and social skills and provide integrated services. These strategies include the following elements (Peacock Hill Working Group, 1991; see also Walker, Forness et al., 1998):

- *Systematic, data-based interventions*—interventions that are applied systematically and consistently and that are based on reliable research data, not unsubstantiated theory
- *Continuous assessment and monitoring of progress*—direct, daily assessment of performance, with planning based on this monitoring
- *Provision for practice of new skills*—skills are not taught in isolation but are applied directly in everyday situations through modeling, rehearsal, and guided practice
- *Treatment matched to the problem*—interventions that are designed to meet the needs of individual students and their particular life circumstances, not general "formulas" that ignore the nature, complexity, and severity of the problem
- *Multicomponent treatment*—as many different interventions as are necessary to meet the multiple needs of students (e.g., social skills training, academic remediation, medication, counseling or psychotherapy, family treatment or parent training)

- *Programming for transfer and maintenance*—interventions designed to promote transfer of learning to new situations, recognizing that "quick fixes" nearly always fail to produce generalized change
- *Commitment to sustained intervention*—interventions designed with the realization that many emotional or behavioral disorders are developmental disabilities and will not be eliminated entirely or cured.

Service Delivery Models

Only a relatively small percentage of children and youths with emotional or behavioral disorders are officially identified and receive any special education or mental health services. Consequently, those individuals who do receive special education tend to have very serious problems, although most (along with those who have mild mental retardation or learning disabilities) have typically been assumed to have only mild disabilities. That is, the problems of the typical student with an emotional or behavioral disorder who is identified for special education may be more serious than many people have assumed. *Severe* does not apply only to the disorders of autism and schizophrenia; a child can have a severe conduct disorder, for example, and its disabling effects can be extremely serious and persistent (Kauffman, 1997a; Kazdin, 1997; Patterson et al., 1992; Wolf, Braukmann, & Ramp, 1987).

Compared to students with most other disabilities, a higher percentage of students with emotional or behavioral disorders are educated outside regular classrooms and schools, probably in part because students with these disorders tend to have more serious problems before they are identified. Emotional or behavioral disorders include many different types of behavioral and emotional problems, which makes it hard to make generalizations about how programs are administered.

Even so, the trend in programs for students with emotional or behavioral disorders is toward integration into regular schools and classrooms. Even when students are placed in separate schools and classes, educators hope for reintegration into the mainstream. Integration of these students is typically difficult and requires intensive work on a case-by-case basis (Fuchs, Fuchs, Fernstrom, & Hohn, 1991; Kauffman, Lloyd, Baker, & Riedel, 1995; Walker & Bullis, 1991).

Placement decisions for students with emotional or behavioral disorders are particularly problematic (Kauffman, Lloyd, Hallahan, & Astuto, 1995). Educators who serve students with the most severe emotional or behavioral disorders provide ample justification for specialized environments for these children and youths. That is, it is impossible to replicate in the context of a regular classroom in a neighborhood school the intensive, individualized, highly structured environments with very high adult–student ratios offered in special classes and facilities (see Brigham & Kauffman, 1998; Kauffman & Hallenbeck, 1996).

Hence it is extremely important that the full continuum of placement options be maintained for students with emotional or behavioral disorders and that placement decisions be made on an individual basis, after an appropriate program of education and related services has been designed. Students must not be placed outside regular classrooms and schools unless their needs require it. The IDEA mandate of placement in the least restrictive environment (LRE) applies to students with behavioral disorders as well as those in all other categories. In other words, they are to be taught in regular schools and classes and with their nondisabled peers to the extent that doing so is consistent with their appropriate education.

Collaboration key to success

Brenda Baldwin-Marshall is a former high school teacher, Fairfax County Public Schools, Virginia; B.S., Elementary and Special Education, Morgan State University; M.Ed., Special Education, George Washington University. **Fred Amico** is a high school English teacher, Fairfax County Public Schools, Virginia; B.A., English, College of William and Mary.

Brenda Baldwin-Marshall

Brenda Tom is a sixteen-year-old sophomore who has been eligible for special education services since age nine. His initial problems in school were physical aggression toward peers, difficulty staying on task, lack of concentration, poor organizational habits, and, at times, being argumentative with teachers. He also exhibited sudden mood changes and unpredictable outbursts of anger. Furthermore, self-reports and personality assessments indicated low self-esteem, intense feelings of inadequacy, and helplessness. Psychological assessments indicated that his cognitive abilities fell in the average to high average range. With distractibility taken into account, however, his cognitive potential was most likely higher. In the past two years he had also been clinically diagnosed with major depression and obsessive-compulsive disorder (OCD). After seven years of receiving special education services, participating in a social skills group, and involvement in private therapy, his teachers noticed a significant improvement in his behavior and performance.

Our school system offers the following levels of services for students with emotional disabilities: self-contained public day school, a co-facility program (integrated in a regular educational setting), and a general educational program with resource services. Due to Tom's significant progress in a self-contained program for students with emotional disabilities, the IEP team determined that a less restrictive setting such as the co-facility program was appropriate. However, his OCD was becoming more apparent. The IEP team developed a class schedule incorporating team-taught English, U.S. history, and physical education, along with his classes in the special education setting.

The team-taught classes involved both a regular education teacher and a special educator. We planned the curriculum and the adaptations to meet the needs of all students. The students with emotional disabilities were integrated in every possible way to reduce possible stigma.

Fred Tom was enrolled in my team-taught English 10 class. The class consisted of twenty-eight students, including five with emotional disabilities. Although this was not my first year working with special education students, Tom proved to be a great challenge because of the severity of his OCD. Brenda and I followed the county curriculum, making subtle adaptations for specific students if needed. I considered myself equally responsible for the students with emotional disabilities and my general education students. However, I was often struck by how inhibiting emotional disabilities could be. I learned to feel a great deal of empathy for these students. I also realized that regardless of their intellect their emotional disabilities could adversely affect everything they did in school, from social interactions to academic performance.

Brenda As the special education resource teacher, my responsibilities are varied. I am the case manager for twenty-two adolescents with emotional disabilities who are integrated into the general education program. I am involved in determining what classes and teachers are appropriate for these students. Although I know that all special education students have the right to receive their education in the least restrictive setting deemed appropriate to meet their educational needs, I am aware that realistically a select few teachers have the patience, skill, empathy, or desire to teach these students. Many general education teachers have not experienced the personal satisfaction that can be gained from seeing a special education student succeed. I knew Fred would be a good choice for the team-taught class because of his experiences with students with learning disabilities and his philosophy that all students are able to learn and succeed.

After the first week of school, Fred and I noticed that Tom was often unable to complete assignments in a timely manner. We observed Tom exhibiting certain behaviors related to his OCD. He submitted written assignments that reflected his increasing level of anxiety. When given a test or a written assignment, Tom would continuously underline and draw boxes around the words or phrases that were complex or troublesome to him.

Fred As the general education teacher, I noticed that Tom's production and performance suffered with any written assignment. He exhibited great levels of anxiety resulting in perseveration and inability to complete his work. He would also play with his hair, tap his feet, or bite his nails. The problem reached such a crisis that at times Tom would appear to freeze up and become nonfunctional. It was obvious to me that without immediate intervention, Tom's progress would continue to spiral downward.

Brenda My response was to meet with Tom to discuss and find out his perception

Fred Amico

of the English class. Tom did not acknowledge that a problem existed. Fred and I met many times during planning periods and after class to develop strategies to address not only Tom's OCD but also the needs of other students with disabilities.

Prior to meeting with Tom, I requested feedback from his teachers and other staff with whom he interacted. The progress report they filled out dealt with both academic and social/emotional progress. I also spoke to Tom's parents to determine what OCD-related behaviors they were observing, Tom's actions at home, and successful strategies that they used to help him.

Fred In order not to overwhelm or heighten Tom's anxiety, we decided to focus on completing written work. We knew that until he could show some proficiency in the written work, he would continue to feel less than adequate. Some of the options that we presented to Tom included untimed written tests, orally administered tests, shortened written assignments, reduced paper-and-pencil tasks, use of an Alpha Smart (word processor), working with a peer, after-school tutorials with Brenda, and a behavioral contract.

Brenda Initially, Tom was hesitant to accept any assistance; he felt that he was capable of completing the assignments. We reviewed written work as well as previous tests and quizzes and highlighted the areas of difficulty. We expressed to Tom that his abilities were evident but his performance was hampered by his behaviors related to OCD. As we reviewed the written work with Tom, we pointed out specific examples of perseveration and obsessiveness. We

showed him the extraneous highlighting and underlining which were the primary symptoms of his disability. Tom was adamant that this was not a major problem but just a bad habit. Our first major hurdle, therefore, was getting Tom to recognize the compulsive or obsessive behaviors that were hindering his academic performance and, thus, his self-worth. At this point, Fred and I decided to keep anecdotal records. The form was placed in easy proximity for us to unobtrusively record Tom's behaviors. The form highlighted the time the behavior was exhibited, the task Tom was working on, the amount of time taken to work on a task, and the actual behaviors. We kept the running log for two weeks to give Tom a realistic picture of his classroom behavior.

Fred I thought it would be important to involve Tom's parents in helping him to recognize the behaviors and modify them. At the meeting, we encouraged Tom to share his perception of his academic performance and behavior in English class. He felt he was doing better than he truly was. He believed he was earning a B, while in reality he had a low C. When we asked him about his peer relations in other classes, he responded that he felt he got along fine with his peers but didn't feel particularly close to anyone. He also noticed other students stared at him during small-group activities.

Brenda Fred and I realized that this was a very difficult meeting for Tom, but we felt that we couldn't make progress until he was able to acknowledge his behaviors and actual performance. We showed the two-week anecdotal records to Tom and his parents. In a ninety-minute class period, Tom was usually unable to complete assignments that other students completed easily. We highlighted in yellow Tom's actual perseveration marks on his papers. As we examined

the papers it became apparent that the perseveration was prevalent and must be distracting for Tom. It also became apparent that Tom's frustration and anxiety were building. After we showed him his actual grade in the class, he acknowledged that he didn't realize the amount of time spent on the obsessive-compulsive behaviors. Tom asked what we could do to help him succeed in the class. We now knew that we could move on to addressing the issues and implementing our plan of action.

Fred At this time we had to amend the IEP to incorporate most of the strategies that we had decided would be helpful to Tom.

Brenda We implemented a weekly behavioral contract to help him increase his productivity and to decrease his obsessive behaviors. The contract included providing a time frame for completing assignments; seating Tom in close proximity to the teacher, who would cue him regarding behaviors; and giving explicit instruction as well as clear expectations. Tom was also responsible for having a weekly progress report filled out by his teachers to ensure that the reality of his performance matched his perceptions.

Fred In a few weeks Brenda and I noticed a gradual improvement in areas such as his initiating contact with peers, participating in class discussions, and meeting the goals established in the behavioral contract. Although this took a great deal of planning on our part, we were able to get Tom back on task with minimal prompts.

Brenda Tom's first-quarter grade in English was a C+, and although Tom's personal goal was to achieve a B grade, his success could be attributed to the organization of the plan and the consistency of the feedback. I contacted Tom's mother to let her know about his progress and solicit her perceptions of his performance.

Fred We knew that we had reached a major milestone with Tom when he expressed interest in joining an extra-curricular club at the school.

Brenda Ultimately, I think Tom's success was related to an educational program based on teamwork, commitment, and collaboration between the general education teacher and the special education teacher. Neither of us could have done it alone.

> "I think Tom's success was related to an educational program based on teamwork. Neither of us could have done it alone."

Including students with emotional and behavioral disorders in general education classrooms may sometimes be problematic since social interactions are a primary area of concern.

However, students' needs for appropriate education and safety take priority over placement in a less restrictive environment (Bateman & Chard, 1995; Crockett & Kauffman, 1999).

Prior to being identified for special education, many students with emotional or behavioral disorders have been in regular classrooms where they could observe and learn from appropriate peer models. In reality, though, these students usually fail to imitate these models. They are unlikely to benefit merely from being with other students who have not been identified as disabled, as incidental social learning is insufficient to address their difficulties (Hallenbeck & Kauffman, 1995; Kauffman & Pullen, 1996; Rhode, Jensen, & Reavis, 1992). In order for students with emotional or behavioral disorders to learn from peer models of appropriate behavior, most will require explicit, focused instruction about whom and what to imitate. In addition, they may need explicit and intensive instruction in social skills, including when, where, and how to exhibit specific types of behavior (Walker et al., 1995).

The academic curriculum for most students with emotional or behavioral disorders parallels that for most students. The basic academic skills have a great deal of survival value for any individual in society who is capable of learning them; failure to teach a student to read, write, and perform basic arithmetic deprives him or her of any reasonable chance for successful adjustment to the everyday demands of life. Students who do not acquire academic skills that allow them to compete with their peers are likely to be socially rejected (Kauffman, 1997a; Walker, 1995).

Students with emotional or behavioral disorders may need specific instruction in social skills as well. We emphasize two points: (1) effective methods are needed to teach basic academic skills, and (2) social skills and affective experiences are as crucial as academic skills. How to manage one's feelings and behavior and how to get along with other people are essential features of the curriculum for many students with emotional or behavioral disorders. These children cannot be expected to learn such skills without instruction, for the ordinary processes of socialization obviously have failed (Walker et al., 1995).

Students with schizophrenia and other major psychiatric disorders vary widely in the behaviors they exhibit and the learning problems they have. Some may need hospitalization and intensive treatment; others may remain at home and attend regular public schools. Again, the trend today is away from placement in institutions or special schools and toward inclusion in regular public schools. In some cases, students with major psychiatric disorders who attend regular schools are enrolled in special classes.

Educational arrangements for juvenile delinquents are hard to describe in general terms because *delinquency* is a legal term, not an educational distinction, and because programs for extremely troubled youths vary so much among states and localities. Special classes or schools are sometimes provided for youths who have histories of threatening, violent, or disruptive behavior. Some of these classes and schools are administered under special education law, but others are not because the pupils assigned to them are not considered emotionally disturbed. In jails, reform schools, and other detention facilities housing children and adolescents, wide variation is found in educational practices (Nelson, Rutherford, & Wolford, 1987). Education of incarcerated children and youths with learning disabilities is governed by the same laws that apply to those who are not incarcerated, but the laws are not always carefully implemented. Many incarcerated children do not receive assessment and education appropriate for their needs because of lack of resources, poor cooperation among agencies, and the attitude that delinquents and criminals are not entitled to the same educational opportunities as law-abiding citizens (Leone, 1990; Leone, Rutherford & Nelson, 1991).

Given all this, it is clear that teachers of students with emotional or behavioral disorders must be able to tolerate a great deal of unpleasantness and rejection without becoming counteraggressive or withdrawn. Most of the students they teach are rejected by others. If kindness and concern were the only things required to help these students, they probably would not be considered to have disabilities. Teachers cannot expect caring and decency always to be returned. They must be sure of their own values and confident of their teaching and living skills. They must be able and willing to make wise choices for students who choose to behave unwisely (Kauffman, 1997a; Kauffman et al., 1998).

Special Disciplinary Considerations

Disciplining is a controversial topic, especially for students with disabilities, as we discussed in Chapter 2. Many teachers and school administrators are confused about what is legal. Special rules do apply in some cases to students who are identified as having disabilities. In some instances the typical school rules apply, but in others they do not (see Bateman & Linda, 1998; Yell, 1998; Yell & Shriner, 1997). The issues are particularly controversial for students with emotional or behavioral disorders because, although their behavior may be severely problematic, the causes of their misbehavior are often difficult to determine.

Uncertainty or controversy usually involves a change in the student's placement or suspension or expulsion due to very serious misbehavior such as bringing a weapon or illegal drugs to school. The IDEA discipline provisions for students with disabilities are intended to maintain a safe school environment without violating the rights of students with disabilities to fair discipline, taking the effects of their disability into consideration.

> School officials may discipline a student with disabilities in the same manner as they discipline students without disabilities—with a few notable exceptions. If necessary, school officials may unilaterally [without parental approval] change the placement of a student for disciplinary purposes to an

appropriate **interim alternative educational setting (IAES),** another setting, or by suspending the student to the extent that these disciplinary methods are used with students without disabilities. The primary difference is that with students who have a disability, the suspension or placement change may not exceed 10 school days. (Yell & Shriner, 1997, pp. 11–12)

If a student with disabilities brings a weapon or illegal drugs to school or to a school function, then school officials may unilaterally place him or her in an IAES for up to 45 days. If a student with disabilities presents substantial risk to the safety of others, then school authorities may ask for a special hearing about the student's placement. A hearing officer may be asked to consider the evidence that "(a) maintaining the current placement is substantially likely to result in injury to the student or others, (b) the IEP and placement are appropriate, (c) the school has made reasonable efforts to minimize the risk of harm, and (d) the IAES meets the criteria set forth in the IDEA amendments" (Yell & Shriner, 1997, p. 12). If the evidence that all four are true meets the legal definition of "substantial," then the hearing officer may order a change of placement to an IAES for up to 45 days.

If a serious disciplinary situation arises and school officials want to change the student's placement or suspend the student for more than 10 days, or expel the student, then a special review of the relationship between the student's disability and the misbehavior must be made. This is called a **manifestation determination**— school officials must try to decide whether the misconduct was a manifestation of the student's disability.

> A student's IEP team and other qualified personnel must conduct this review, called a manifestation determination. If a determination is made that no relationship exists between the misconduct and disability, the same disciplinary procedures as would be used with students who are not disabled may be imposed on a student with disabilities (i.e., long-term suspension or expulsion). Educational services, however, must be continued. If the team finds a relationship between a student's disability and misconduct, school officials still may seek a change of placement but cannot use long-term suspension or expulsion. (Yell & Shriner, 1997, p. 12)

A student's parents may, of course, challenge the school officials' decision. Those conducting the manifestation determination must consider all relevant information related to the student's misbehavior, including evaluation results, direct observation of the student, and information provided by parents. An IEP team may conclude that misconduct was *not* a manifestation of disability only when all three of the following criteria are met:

1. The student's IEP and placement were appropriate (including the behavior intervention plan) and the IEP was implemented as written;
2. The student's disability did not impair the ability of the student to understand the impact and consequences of the behavior subject to the disciplinary sanction;
3. The student's disability did not impair the student's ability to control the behavior at issue. (Yell & Shriner, 1997, p. 13)

An IAES is an alternative setting chosen by the IEP team that will allow the student to continue participating in the general education curriculum and continue to receive the services described in the IEP. Students must be able to continue working toward their IEP goals and objectives, including those related to the behavior that resulted in placement in the IAES. IAES may include alternative schools, instruction at home ("homebound instruction"), and other special settings. A key requirement of the law is that the student's special education must be continued.

interim alternative educational setting (IAES). An alternative placement (e.g., alternative school, home instruction), chosen by the student's IEP team after the student exhibits serious misconduct (e.g., bringing a weapon or drugs to school), in which the student's education is continued as specified in his or her IEP while school officials make a manifestation determination and find the least restrictive environment in which the student can be educated appropriately.

manifestation determination. A procedure in which school officials determine whether a student's behavior is or is not a manifestation of his or her disability.

Functional Behavioral Assessment

The 1997 amendments to IDEA have raised controversial issues regarding the assessment of behavior. The new law calls for functional analysis or functional assessment of behavior, but the meaning of these terms is not clear in the context of the law (see Nelson, Roberts, Mather, & Rutherford, 1999; Yell & Shriner, 1997). Precisely what the law now requires of special educators and other school personnel is uncertain (see Gable, 1999; Howell & Nelson, 1999; Scott & Nelson, 1999).

One view is that the law simply requires assessment that is meaningful—that helps educators develop effective interventions. Under this assumption, assessment procedures would not need to be changed dramatically in many cases. Educators would need merely to make sure that assessment is meaningfully related to teaching and management. An alternative view is that *functional behavioral assessment* refers to a specific set of procedures designed to pinpoint the *function* of the student's behavior—what the student is communicating through his or her behavior, or what the student is trying to accomplish by exhibiting inappropriate behavior. If this meaning is assumed to be correct, then enormous resources will be required to train educators to apply highly technical procedures. These procedures have been researched almost exclusively with students having severe cognitive disabilities, not with students whose school difficulties fit the classification of emotional or behavioral disorder. The controversy about the exact meaning of *functional behavioral assessment* and similar terms will likely continue until the U.S. Department of Education spells out just what the term does and does not mean.

Early Intervention

Early identification and prevention are basic goals of intervention programs for any category of disability. For students with emotional or behavioral disorders, these goals present particular difficulties—yet they hold particular promise. The difficulties are related to definition and measurement of emotional or behavioral disorders, especially in young children; the particular promise is that young children's social-emotional behavior is quite flexible, so preventive efforts seem to have a good chance of success (see Kauffman, 1999).

As mentioned previously, defining emotional or behavioral disorders in such a way that children can be reliably identified is a difficult task. Definition and identification involving preschool children are complicated by several additional factors:

1. The developmental tasks that young children are expected to achieve are much simpler than those expected of older children, so the range of normal behaviors to be used for comparison is quite restricted. Infants and toddlers are expected to eat, sleep, perform relatively simple motor skills, and respond socially to their parents. School-age children, however, must learn much more varied and complex motor and cognitive skills and develop social relations with a variety of peers and adults.
2. There is wide variation in the childrearing practices of good parents and in family expectations for preschool children's behavior in different cultures, so we must guard against inappropriate norms used for comparison. What is described as *immature, withdrawn,* or *aggressive* behavior in one family may not be perceived as such in another.

3. In the preschool years children's development is rapid and often uneven, making it difficult to judge what spontaneous improvements might occur.
4. The most severe types of emotional or behavioral disorders often are first observed in the preschool years. But it is frequently difficult to tell the difference between emotional or behavioral disorders and other conditions, like mental retardation or deafness. Often the first signs are difficulty with basic biological functions (e.g., eating, sleeping, eliminating) or social responses (e.g., responding positively to a parent's attempts to offer comfort or "molding" to the parent's body when being held). Difficulty with these basic areas or in achieving developmental milestones like walking and talking indicate that the child may have an emotional or behavioral disability. But these difficulties may also be indicators of other conditions, such as mental retardation, sensory impairment, or physical disability.

The patterns of behavior that signal problems for the preschool child are those that bring them into frequent conflict with, or keep them aloof from, their parents or caretakers and their siblings or peers. Many children who are referred to clinics for disruptive behavior when they are seven to twelve years of age showed clear signs of behavior problems by the time they were three or four—or even younger (Loeber, Green, Lahey, Christ, & Frick, 1992). Infants or toddlers who exhibit a very "difficult temperament"—who are irritable; have irregular patterns of sleeping, eating, and eliminating; have highly intense responses to many stimuli and negative reactions toward new situations—are at risk for developing serious behavior problems unless their parents are particularly skillful at handling them. Children of preschool age are likely to elicit negative responses from adults and playmates if they are much more aggressive or much more withdrawn than most children their age. (Remember the critical importance of same-age comparisons. Toddlers frequently grab what they want, push other children down, and throw things and kick and scream when they don't get their way; toddlers normally do not have much finesse at social interaction and often hide from strangers.)

Because children's behavior is quite responsive to conditions in the social environment and can be shaped by adults, the potential for primary prevention—preventing serious behavior problems from occurring in the first place—would seem to be great. If parents and teachers could be taught effective child management skills, perhaps many or most cases could be prevented (Ialongo et al., 1998; Walker et al., 1995; Walker, Kavanagh et al., 1998). Furthermore, one could imagine that if parents and teachers had such skills, children who already have emotional or behavioral disorders could be prevented from getting worse (*secondary prevention*). But as Bower (1981) notes, the task of primary prevention is not that simple. For one thing, the tremendous amount of money and personnel needed for training in child management are not available. For another, even if the money and personnel could be found, professionals would not always agree on what patterns of behavior should be prevented or on how undesirable behavior could be prevented from developing (Kazdin, 1995).

If overly aggressive or withdrawn behavior has been identified in a preschooler, what kind of intervention program is most desirable? Behavioral interventions are highly effective (see also Peacock Hill Working Group, 1991; Strain et al., 1992; Walker et al., 1995; Walker, Forness et al., 1998). A behavioral approach implies defining and measuring the child's behaviors and rearranging the environment (especially adults' and other children's responses to the problem child) to teach and support more appropriate conduct. In the case of aggressive children, social rewards for aggression should be prevented. For example, hitting

Preschool intervention of children with emotional and behavioral disorders has been quite effective in preventing or reducing subsequent problems. However, identifying these disorders between 3 and 5 years can be difficult.

another child or throwing a temper tantrum might result in brief social isolation or "time out" instead of adult attention or getting one's own way.

Researchers are constantly seeking less punitive ways of dealing with problem behavior, including aggression. The best way of handling violent or aggressive play or play themes, for example, would be one that effectively reduces the frequency of aggressive play yet requires minimal punishment. In one study with children between the ages of three and five, violent or aggressive theme play (talk or imitation of weapons, destruction, injury, etc.) was restricted to a small area of the classroom defined by a carpet sample (Sherburne, Utley, McConnell, & Gannon, 1988). Children engaging in imaginative play involving guns, for example, were merely told by the teacher, using a pleasant tone of voice, "If you want to play guns, go over on the rug" (p. 169). If violent theme play continued for more than ten seconds after the teacher's warning, the child or children were physically assisted to the rug. They were not required to stay on the rug for a specific length of time; rather, they merely had to go there if they wanted to engage in aggressive play. This simple procedure was quite effective in reducing violent and aggressive themes in the children's play.

In summary, it is possible to identify at an early age those children who are at high risk for emotional or behavioral disorders (Ialongo et al., 1998; Loeber et al., 1992; Walker et al., 1994; Walker, Kavanagh et al., 1998; Wehby, Dodge, & Valente, 1993). These children exhibit extreme aggression or social withdrawal and may be socially rejected or identify with deviant peers. They should be identified as early as possible, and their parents and teachers should learn how to teach them essential skills and management of their problem behavior using positive, nonviolent procedures (see Timm, 1993; Walker et al., 1995). If children with serious emotional or behavioral disorders are identified very early and intervention is sufficiently comprehensive, intense, and sustained, then there is a good chance that they can recover and exhibit developmentally normal patterns of behavior (cf. Lovaas, 1987; Timm, 1993; Walker et al., 1995).

Nevertheless, research suggests that in practice, early intervention typically does not occur. In fact, intervention does usually not begin until the child has exhibited an extremely disabling pattern of behavior for several years (Duncan, Forness, & Hartsough, 1995). The primary reasons given as to why early, comprehensive, intense, and sustained intervention is so rare include worry about labeling and stigma, optimism regarding the child's development (i.e., the assumption that he or she will "grow out of it"), lack of resources required to address the needs of any but the most severely problematic children, and ignorance about the early signs of emotional or behavioral problems (Kauffman, 1999).

Transition

The programs designed for adolescents with emotional or behavioral disorders have varied widely in aims and structure. Nelson and Kauffman (1977) describe the following types, which remain the basic options today:

- Regular public high school classes
- Consultant teachers who work with regular teachers to provide individualized academic work and behavior management
- Resource rooms and special self-contained classes to which students may be assigned for part or all of the school day
- Work-study programs in which vocational education and job experience are combined with academic study
- Special private or public schools that offer the regular high school curriculum in a different setting
- Alternative schools that offer highly individualized programs that are nontraditional in both setting and content
- Private or public residential schools

Incarcerated youths with emotional or behavioral disorders are an especially neglected group in special education (McIntyre, 1993; Nelson, Rutherford, & Wolford, 1987). One suspects that the special educational needs of many (or most) of these teenagers who are in prison are neglected because incarcerated youths are defined as *socially maladjusted* rather than *emotionally disturbed*. The current federal definition appears to allow denial of special education services to a large number of young people who exhibit extremely serious misbehaviors and have long histories of school failure.

One of the reasons it is difficult to design special education programs at the secondary level for students with emotional or behavioral disorders is that this category of youths is so varied. Adolescents categorized for special education purposes as emotionally disturbed may have behavioral characteristics ranging from autistically withdrawn to aggressively delinquent, intelligence ranging from severely retarded to highly gifted, and academic skills ranging from preschool to college level. Therefore, it is hardly realistic to suggest that any single type of program or model will be appropriate for all such youths. In fact, youths with emotional or behavioral disorders, perhaps more than any other category of exceptionality, need a highly individualized, creative, and flexible education. Programs may range from teaching daily living skills in a sheltered environment to advanced placement in college, from regular class placement to hospitalization, and from the traditional curriculum to unusual and specialized vocational training.

Transition from school to work and adult life is particularly difficult for adolescents with emotional or behavioral disorders. Many of them lack the basic academic skills necessary for successful employment. In addition, they often behave in ways that prevent them from being accepted, liked, and helped by employers, co-workers, and neighbors. It is not surprising that students with emotional or behavioral disorders are among the most likely to drop out of school and among the most difficult to train in transition programs (Carson, Sitlington, & Frank, 1995; Edgar & Siegel, 1995).

Many children and youths with emotional or behavioral disorders grow up to be adults who have real difficulties leading independent, productive lives. The outlook is especially grim for children and adolescents who have conduct disorder. Contrary to popular opinion, the child or youth who is shy, anxious, or neurotic is not the most likely to have psychiatric problems as an adult. Rather, it is the conduct-disordered (hyperaggressive) child or youth whose adulthood is most likely to be characterized by socially intolerable behavior (Kazdin, 1995, 1997). About half the children who are hyperaggressive will have problems that require legal intervention or psychiatric care when they are adults.

Successful transition to adult life is often complicated by neglectful, abusive, or inadequate family relationships. A high percentage of adolescents with conduct disorder have family relationships of this nature. However, the emphasis on punishment and imprisonment, particularly of African American males, appears to be counterproductive. The emphasis on punishment contributes to family deterioration and harsh conditions of life that perpetuate undesirable conduct (Miller, 1997).

Examples of relatively successful high school and transition programs are available, most of which employ a behavioral approach (Edgar & Siegel, 1995; Peacock Hill Working Group, 1991). However, it is important to stress *relatively* because many adolescents and young adults with severe conduct disorder appear to have a true developmental disability that requires intervention throughout their life span (Wolf, Braukmann, & Ramp, 1987). By the time these antisocial youths reach high school, the aim of even the most effective program is to help them accommodate their disabilities. Rather than focusing on remediation of academic and social skills, these programs attempt to teach youths the skills they will need to survive and cope in school and community, to make a transition to work, and to develop vocations (Walker et al., 1995). Well-planned alternative schools appear to offer important options to students at high risk, including those with emotional or behavioral problems (Duke, Griesdorn, & Kraft, 1998).

Summary

Emotional or behavioral disorders are not simply a matter of undesirable or inappropriate behaviors. They involve inappropriate social interactions and transactions between the child or youth and the social environment.

Many different terms have been used for children's emotional or behavioral disorders. In the language of federal laws and regulations, they are *emotionally disturbed*. The term *emotional or behavioral disorder* is becoming widely accepted, due primarily to the work of the National Mental Health and Special Education Coalition, which proposed a new definition and terminology in 1990.

The proposed definition defines *emotional or behavioral disorders* as a disability characterized by behavioral or emotional responses to school so different from appropriate age, cultural, or ethnic norms that they adversely affect educational performance. *Educational performance* is defined as more than academic performance; it includes academic, social, vocational, and personal skills. An emotional or behavioral disorder is more than a temporary or expected response to stressful events. It is exhibited in more than one setting, and it is unresponsive to direct intervention in general education. Finally, the proposed definition notes that the term *emotional or behavioral disorders* covers a wide variety of diagnostic groups, including sustained disorders of conduct or adjustment that adversely affect educational performance and can coexist with other disabilities.

Estimates of the prevalence of emotional or behavioral disorders vary greatly, in part because the definition is not precise. Most researchers estimate that 6 to 10 percent of the child population is affected, but only about 1 percent of the school-age population is currently identified as having emotional or behavioral disorders and is receiving special education services. Most children and youths who are identified for special education purposes are boys, and most exhibit externalizing behavior. About 3 percent of U.S. youths are referred to juvenile court in any given year. Relatively few of these receive special education services for emotional or behavioral disorders.

A single, specific cause of an emotional or behavioral disorder can seldom be identified. In most cases, it is possible only to identify causal factors that contribute to the likelihood that a child will develop a disorder or that predispose him or her to developing a disorder. Major contributing factors are found in biological conditions, family relationships, school experiences, and cultural influences. Possible biological factors include genetics, temperament (i.e., an inborn behavioral style), malnutrition, brain trauma, and substance abuse. Most biological causes are poorly understood, and social as well as medical intervention is almost always necessary.

Family disorganization, parental abuse, and inconsistent discipline are among the most important family factors contributing to emotional or behavioral disorders. However, poor parenting is not always or solely the cause. Furthermore, family factors appear to affect each family member in a different way. School factors that may contribute to emotional or behavioral disorders are insensitivity to students' individuality, inappropriate expectations, inconsistent or inappropriate discipline, unintentional rewards for misbehavior, and undesirable models of conduct. Cultural factors include the influences of the media, values and standards of the community and peer group, and social services available to children and their families. Family, school, and the wider culture create a complex web of cultural causal factors.

Most children and youths with emotional or behavioral disorders—especially those with serious conduct disorder or autism—are easily recognized. Few

schools use systematic screening procedures, partly because services would be unavailable for the many students likely to be identified. The most effective identification procedures use a combination of teachers' rankings and ratings and direct observation of students' behavior. Peer rankings or ratings are often used as well.

The typical student with an emotional or behavioral disorder has an IQ in the dull-normal range. The range of intelligence is enormous: A few are brilliant, and more than in the general population have mental retardation. Most children and youths with emotional or behavioral disorders lack, in varying degrees, the ability to apply their knowledge and skills to the demands of everyday living.

Students who express their problems in aggressive, acting-out behavior are involved in a vicious cycle. Their behavior alienates others so that positive interactions with adults and peers become less likely. Children and youths whose behavior is consistently antisocial have less chance of learning to make social adjustments and of achieving mental health in adulthood than do those who are shy, anxious, or neurotic.

Students with traumatic brain injury (TBI) may have problems related both to the actual brain damage and, depending on the age of onset, to personal adjustment issues. Students with autism or other pervasive developmental disorders often lack basic self-care skills, may appear to be perceptually disabled, and appear to have serious cognitive limitations. Especially evident and important is their inability to relate to other people. In addition, deviations in speech and language abilities, self-stimulation or self-injury, and the tendency to injure others deliberately combine to give these students a poor prognosis. Some of them function permanently at a level of mental retardation and require sustained supervision and care. Recent research brings hope that many may make remarkable progress with early intensive intervention. Some may learn an alternative means of communication.

Special education is typically guided by one of two conceptual models, or a combination of the two: The psychoeducational model focuses on conscious and unconscious motivations; the behavioral model stresses the fact that behavior is learned as a consequence of environmental events. Both models offer valuable insights into teaching students whose behavior is problematic.

Regardless of the conceptual model guiding intervention or the characteristics of the students involved, the following strategies work: using systematic, data-based interventions; assessing and monitoring progress continuously; providing opportunities to practice new skills; providing treatment matched to the student's problem; offering multicomponent treatment to meet all the student's needs; programming for transfer and maintenance of learning; and sustaining intervention as long as it is needed.

A relatively small percentage of children and youths with emotional or behavioral disorders receive special education and related services. Only those with the most severe problems are likely to be identified, one consequence of which is that many are educated outside regular classrooms and schools. The trend, however, is toward greater integration in regular schools and classes. Because difficulty with social interactions is a hallmark of emotional and behavioral disorders, such placements can be particularly problematic.

Special disciplinary considerations are required by the 1997 amendments to IDEA. In most cases, exceptional learners are subject to the same disciplinary procedures as their nondisabled peers. However, in certain cases they can be placed temporarily in an interim alternative educational setting while issues about their behavior are resolved. Also, in some cases it is necessary to determine whether the student's behavior is a manifestation of his or her disability; if it is, then alternative discipline may be required. The issues are especially difficult for students with emotional or behavioral disorders because the causes of their misbehavior are often difficult to determine with confidence.

Functional behavioral assessment is required by the 1997 IDEA amendments, but the meaning of the term is not clearly understood. The term may be interpreted to mean using assessment procedures that are useful. It may also be interpreted to mean pinpointing the function or meaning of behavior, which would require extensive technical training of special educators.

Early identification and prevention are goals of early intervention programs. The problem behavior of many children later referred to clinics for emotional or behavioral disorders is evident early in life. Early intervention has been shown to be highly successful; however, it often does not occur due to worry about labeling and stigma, optimism that the child will "grow out of it," lack of resources, and ignorance about the early signs of problems. With early, intensive intervention, great improvements can be seen in nearly all cases.

Programs of special education for adolescents and young adults with emotional or behavioral disorders are extremely varied and must be highly individualized because of the wide differences in students' intelligence, behavioral characteristics, achievements, and circumstances. Transition from school to work and adult life is particularly difficult for students with emotional or behavioral disorders, and they are among those most likely to drop out of school. The outlook for adulthood is particularly poor for youths with severe conduct disorder; many require intervention throughout their lives.

suggestions
for teaching

Students with Emotional or Behavioral Disorders

By Peggy L. Tarpley

The foundation of good behavior management in the classroom is effective instruction. Kea (1998) states that for students with behavioral difficulties (and I contend *all* students) to make educational and social progress they need teachers who "make a firm personal commitment to using effective instructional procedures" (p. 3). She names and gives examples of nine critical teaching behaviors that research has shown to facilitate learning. Among these are statements that provide an overview (advanced organizer) of what is to be learned, an explanation of the usefulness (rationale) of this learning to the student, communication of specific rules and expectations for behavior and mastery, and review of the facts, concepts, and skills learned (post organizer). Effective teachers also facilitate student independence, promote high rates of on-task behav-

ior, frequently monitor instruction giving positive and/or corrective feedback, and teach to mastery levels of learning.

Given effective teaching principles being used in the classroom, what do you do when students continue to misbehave? Information from your functional behavioral assessment will help you choose an appropriate approach for increasing a behavior, decreasing a behavior, or maintaining a behavior.

Selecting Approaches

An important consideration in choosing a behavior management approach is the degree of intrusiveness and restrictiveness it involves. Intrusiveness refers to the extent to which interventions impinge on students' rights and/or bodies and the degree to which they interrupt educational activities (Kerr & Nelson, 1998). Less intrusive procedures, for example, do not restrict students' movements or interrupt typical, ongoing educational activities. "Restrictiveness refers to the extent to which an intervention inhibits students' freedom to be treated like all other pupils" (Kerr & Nelson, 1998, p. 111).

Although most experts agree it is preferable to begin managing behavior by selecting the least intrusive and restrictive procedure appropriate to the behavior you want to change, they do not agree on the order of these procedures. Kerr and Nelson (1998, p. 111) suggest the following hierarchy, listing from less to more restrictive or intrusive:

Enhancement Procedures	*Reductive Procedures*
Self-regulation	Differential reinforcement
Social reinforcement	Extinction
Modeling	Verbal aversives
Contracting	Response cost
Activity reinforcement	Time-out
Token reinforcement	Overcorrection
Tangible reinforcement	Physical aversives
Edible reinforcement	
Tactile and sensory reinforcement	

It is important to note that some of the procedures listed under "Enhancement Procedures" may be used both to increase and decrease behaviors. For example, teachers may use models to strengthen, weaken, or maintain behavior (Bandura, 1969). However, those listed under "Reductive Procedures" are used only to decrease behaviors. The remainder of the section will discuss the less intrusive and restrictive procedures listed above.

Increasing Appropriate School Behaviors

Reinforcement One strategy teachers use to increase a student's appropriate behavior involves rewarding, or *reinforcing,* that behavior each time the student exhibits it. The reward can take many forms. For instance, it may be a point or token exchangeable at a later time for a special privilege. Because *social reinforcement* is less intrusive and restrictive than other types of reinforcement, teachers typically select it first. Verbal praise, such as "Good work, Tony. It's great that you worked on the math problems by yourself," is an example of social reinforcement. Smiles, handshakes, nods, gentle pats on the back are other examples. However, not all students like the same rewards. You will want to find the one that works with a particular student or group of students.

Activity reinforcement follows the application of the Premack Principle, which also is called "Grandma's law" because it is based on the same idea that prompted Grandma to say, "If you eat your vegetables, then you can have your dessert" (Polloway & Patton, 1993). The Premack Principle makes high-frequency behaviors, such as talking with a friend or playing computer games, contingent on the performance of low-frequency behaviors, such as completing assignments or responding appropriately to adults (cf. Premack, 1959). Some activities that teachers find are reinforcing for their students include being a team leader, receiving extra story time, listening to music, and looking at magazines.

Like social and activity reinforcement, *token reinforcement* is contingent upon the performance of a specific desired behavior. In a token system, or token economy, students receive tokens, such as points or chips, which they can trade at a later time for activity reinforcers, tangible reinforcers (e.g., stickers, certificates, magnets, markers), or edible reinforcers (e.g., pretzels, popcorn). Polloway and Patton (1993) point out that in token reinforcement systems, students earn tokens for appropriate behavior just as adults receive money for their job performance.

Several variables are important in making reinforcers most effective. In *The Tough Kid Book*, Rhode, Jensen, and Reavis (1995) state these as the IFEED-AV rules:

- *I* stands for *immediately.* Timing is very important. The longer the teacher waits to reinforce appropriate behavior, the less effective the reinforcer will be.
- *F* stands for *frequently.* This is especially true when a student is learning a new behavior or skill. A good guideline is to grant three or four positive reinforcers for every one negative consequence (including verbal reprimands).
- The *E*'s stand for how the teacher gives reinforcement. The first *E* stands for *enthusiasm.* The teacher should respond in a manner that shows the student he or she has done something important. The next *E* stands for *eye contact.* By making eye contact, the teacher demonstrates that the student is special and has the teacher's undivided attention.
- *D* stands for *describe* the behavior. Be explicit about what behavior is being reinforced.
- *A* stands for *anticipation.* Building anticipation for the reward (reinforcement) can motivate students to do their best.
- Finally, *V* stands for *variety.* Reinforcers may need to be changed often to keep their potency.

Reinforcement is given on certain schedules (Miltenberger, 1997). Initially, you want to reinforce every incidence of appropriate behavior. This is known as a continuous reinforcement schedule (CRF). Once the student exhibits the desirable behavior regularly, then you can begin gradually to decrease the frequency of the reinforcer until he or she continues to use the behavior at the specified level with less frequent rewards (intermittent reinforcement schedule). The hope is that appropriate behavior also will open other avenues by which the student receives positive reinforcement, ones that are more naturally occurring. The following example illustrates how one teacher used positive reinforcement to increase her student's assignment completion:

Sara is a thirteen-year-old student of average intelligence with behavior disorders who rarely turns in her class assignments. Mrs. Norton, after observing for a week that Sara completed only one out of five assignments (20 percent) each day, wanted to increase that percentage to 80 percent of daily class assignments. Mrs. Norton also observed that during seatwork, Sara often became very upset and then cried. When this happened, Mrs. Norton immediately comforted her by talking individually with her until the crying stopped. In reviewing these observations, Mrs. Norton suspected that her individual attention to Sara was reinforcing the crying; therefore, she decided to use that attention to reward Sara each time she turned in an assignment. The first day she used the reward strategy, Sara completed three out of five assignments (60 percent), and Mrs. Norton talked privately with her after she handed in each paper. Sara did so well that on the third day, with Sara's consent, Mrs. Norton required that Sara complete two assignments before an individual talk with her. Then Mrs. Norton required the completion of three assignments for the individual talk reinforcer. By the eleventh day, Sara had reached the 80 percent criterion level Mrs. Norton established.

Contracting Sometimes the use of reinforcement contingencies are put into the form of a behavioral contract. This written agreement between adult(s) and the student specifies what rewards and consequences will be contingent on the student's performance of a specific behavior. Like any contract, its contents are negotiated and all participants must agree to its terms. A contract states (as adapted from Miltenberger, 1997, and Zirpoli & Melloy, 1997):

- the behavior to be performed, described in specific detail
- the conditions under which the behavior will be performed
- the criterion for successful performance of the behavior
- the reward for performing the behavior
- the consequences of failing to perform the behavior
- the signatures of the contract participants
- the date

The following is an example of a contract negotiated by Mrs. Randolph, Bill, and Bill's parents to decrease his arguing and fighting.

BEHAVIORAL CONTRACT

Mrs. Randolph will check a Good Play card for Bill each time he plays during recess without fighting or arguing with any student. When Bill has earned 10 checks from Mrs. Randolph and has had his card signed by his parents, he may use the computer for 15 minutes. If Bill does not meet this contract within two weeks, Bill will lose one recess period and the contract will be renegotiated.

Signed: _____ (Student)

_____ (Teacher)

_____ (Parents)

Written on (date) _____

Modeling To increase specific behaviors, teachers also may provide a model of the behavior for students to imitate. Students imitate more readily the behavior of models who are similar to themselves in some way, who have high status, and who have been reinforced (Kerr & Nelson, 1998). Both live and vicarious models, such as those shown in videotapes or films, have been effective in altering behavior in public school classrooms. Kerr and Nelson point out that although behavioral procedures such as reinforcement and modeling are often discussed separately in textbooks, in practice they often are used in combination. For example, teachers may model a behavior, such as expressing anger appropriately, and then have students practice this skill in role-plays and reinforce their performance.

Teaching Social Skills The purpose of social skills training is to provide the student who behaves antisocially with the skills needed to avoid interpersonal rejection by peers and adults. Several social skills programs have been developed to address these needs. All follow a similar format, using modeling, role-play, behavioral and metacognitive strategy training (e.g., self-monitoring, self-evaluation, self-reinforcement, etc.), and feedback and reinforcement. Rutherford and Nelson (1995) state that through social skills training, "The student is provided with the tools to evaluate the environment, consider the alternatives, choose prosocial behaviors or strategies, monitor the effects of those behaviors, and adjust his or her behavior accordingly" (p. 10).

Similar to social skills programs are programs for managing anger or replacing aggression. One such program, developed by Goldstein and Glick (1987), teaches students to answer provoca-

tions that in the past ended in anger with a chain of self-awareness/self-control responses that include the following:

1. *Triggers*—The student notes internal and external events that arouse his or her anger.
2. *Cues*—The student identifies physiological factors that indicate anger has been aroused.
3. *Reminders*—The student makes self-statements to reduce anger.
4. *Reducers*—The student uses strategies such as counting backward, deep breathing, and reflecting on consequences of behavior to reduce anger.
5. The student generates and selects alternatives to anger and aggression.
6. The student evaluates the use and results of the anger control sequence.

Decreasing Inappropriate School Behaviors

Just as some students need help increasing appropriate behaviors, others require help in reducing behaviors that are not appropriate for school. Frequently, teachers select *differential reinforcement of incompatible behaviors (DRI)*, which involves reinforcing a behavior that is incompatible with the one the teacher wants to decrease. A related positive approach teachers frequently use is *differential reinforcement of alternate behaviors (DRA)*. During this procedure, teachers reinforce alternatives to the specific behavior targeted for change. For example, if you want to promote a student raising his or her hand instead of talking out in class, you would reinforce handraising.

Although several techniques are effective in decreasing behaviors, many involve using types of punishment. Punishment is defined as consequences that reduce the future probability of a behavior (Kauffman, 1997). When using any form of punishment, teachers should:

1. Combine punishment with positive reinforcement of alternative behaviors
2. Manage punishment procedures carefully and use them consistently and immediately
3. Use punishment only after positive procedures have been unsuccessful

The more restrictive procedures, such as time-out, overcorrection, and physical aversives, should only be used by trained professionals.

Less intrusive punishment procedures include purposeful ignoring of a student's behavior, withholding other rewards, and public postings. Teachers, for example, have used public postings to improve behaviors such as disruptions in the halls (Staub, 1987, cited in Kerr & Nelson, 1998) by recording the daily performance of the class and "best record to date" on a large poster displayed at both ends of a school corridor. One of the most frequently used forms of punishment is reprimands. When using reprimands, make them privately, not publicly; stand near the student while reprimanding; and give him or her direct eye contact before scolding (Kerr & Nelson, 1998).

Prevention of Inappropriate School Behaviors

Because using even mild forms of punishment is less desirable than using positive strategies, teachers may reduce the need to use punishing techniques by preventing many behavior problems. Kerr and Nelson (1998) suggest that the notion of *structuring* is helpful in prevention. They recommend that teachers carefully consider the antecedents of inappropriate behavior to include the use of physical space, daily scheduling, and rules and routines to influence or structure student behavior. As you think about using classroom rules and routines, reflect on the following suggestions made by Lewis and Doorlag (1987):

1. Make rules and routines positive, concrete, and functional, relating them to the accomplishments of learning and order in the classroom (e.g., "Work quietly at the learning centers" rather than "Don't talk when working").
2. Design rules and routines to anticipate potential classroom problems and to manage these situations. For example, teachers may want students to raise their hands when they need help rather than calling out or leaving their seats to locate the teacher.
3. Establish classroom rules and routines at the beginning of the school year by introducing them the first day.
4. Demonstrate or model rules and routines, and continue to provide opportunities for students to practice them until they have mastered them.
5. Associate rules and routines with simple signals that tell students when they are to carry out or stop specific activities and behaviors.
6. Monitor how students follow rules and routines, rewarding students for appropriate behaviors.

Even though you use effective instructional techniques, use appropriate management approaches, and structure the classroom to promote the best behaviors from all students, sometimes (hopefully rarely) a student will not respond to these techniques or will suddenly become aggressive to the point of threatening his or her own safety, your safety, and/or the safety of the students in the classroom. To be prepared for this type of situation, Kerr and Nelson (1998) recommend a class on nonviolent crisis intervention with an annual refresher class and a crisis response plan. Nonviolent crisis intervention classes are offered by police departments, mental health organizations, and sometimes through colleges and universities.

It is very important to devise—with your principal, other teachers, and your students—a crisis plan. This can be presented to your students as a drill like other drills (such as those for fire or dangerous weather) and should be practiced regularly until all those participating respond quickly and efficiently. Your plan may involve a teacher located close to your room, who agrees to come at your signal to assist you by taking your class to another room or calling the office for assistance while you deal with an out-of-control student. It is also a good idea to train an alternate teacher. You will also want to develop a signal to alert a dependable student (and an alternate) in your class to a crisis and train that student as to what the signal calls on him or her to do: get the principal, notify the designated teacher, or tell an adult that you need assistance. Safety of all involved is your first concern.

Helpful Resources

School Personnel

In addition to the school personnel listed in previous chapters, school psychologists may be helpful in understanding and managing students with serious emotional or behavioral disorders. These professionals can provide specific information about students' problems based on their individual evaluations, recommend procedures teachers can use in their classrooms, and offer individual or group counseling for students with emotional or behavioral disorders.

School counselors are valuable in-building resources. They may help when students have behavioral crises. In addition, they are an important link between the classroom teacher and parents. They can provide frequent reports of students' progress and coordinate home-school plans to improve students' behavior and performance.

Instructional Methods

Cartledge, G., & Milburn, J. F. (1995). *Teaching social skills to children and youth: Innovative approaches* (3rd ed.). Boston: Allyn & Bacon.

Center, D. B. (1989). *Curriculum and teaching strategies for students with behavioral disorders.* Englewood Cliffs, NJ: Prentice-Hall.

Cipani, E. (1998). *Classroom management for all teachers: 11 effective plans.* Upper Saddle River, NJ: Prentice-Hall.

Erickson, M. T. (1998). *Behavior disorders of children and adolescents: Assessment, etiology, and intervention.* Upper Saddle River, NJ: Prentice-Hall.

Grossman, H. (1995). *Classroom behavior management in a diverse society* (2nd ed.). Mountain View, CA: Mayfield.

Kauffman, J. M., Mostert, M. P., Trent, S. C., & Hallahan, D. P. (1998). *Managing classroom behavior: A reflective case-based approach* (2nd ed.). Boston: Allyn & Bacon.

Kaplan, J. S., & Drainville, B. (1995). *Beyond behavior modification* (3rd ed.).Austin, TX: Pro-Ed.

Kerr, M. M., & Nelson, C. M. (1998). *Strategies for managing behavior problems in the classroom* (2nd ed.). Upper Saddle River, NJ: Prentice-Hall.

Knowlton, D. (1995). *Managing children with oppositional behavior. Beyond Behavior,* 6(3), 5–10.

Macht, J. (1990). *Managing classroom behavior.* New York: Longman.

Morgan, S. R., & Reinhart, J. A. (1991). *Interventions for students with emotional disorders.* Austin, TX: Pro-Ed.

Nelson, C. M., & Pearson, C. (1991). *Integrating services for children and youth with emotional and behavioral disorders.* Reston, VA: Council for Exceptional Children.

Rhode, G., Jensen, W. R., & Reavis, H. K. (1995). *The tough kid book,* Longmont, CO: Sopris West.

Rockwell, S. (1995). *Back off, cool down, try again: Teaching students how to control aggressive behavior.* Reston, VA: Council for Exceptional Children.

Walker, H. M. (1995). *The acting-out child: Coping with classroom disruption* (2nd ed.). Longmont, CO: Sopris West.

Walker, H. M., Colvin, G., & Ramsey, E. (1995). *Antisocial behavior in schools: Strategies and best practices.* Pacific Grove, CA: Brooks/Cole.

Curricula and Instructional Materials

Dowd, T., & Tierney, J. (1992). *Teaching social skills to youth: A curriculum for child-care providers.* Boys Town, NE: Boys Town Press.

Goldstein, A. P., & Glick, B. (1987). *Aggression replacement training.* Champaign, IL: Research Press.

Goldstein, A. P., Sprafkin, R. P., Greshaw, N. J., & Klein, P. (1980). *Skillstreaming the adolescent: A structural learning approach to teaching prosocial skills.* Champaign, IL: Research Press.

Hazel, J. S., Shumaker, J. B., Sherman, J. A., & Sheldon-Wildgen, J. (1981). *ASSET: A social program for adolescents.* Champaign, IL: Research Press.

Mannix, D. (1990). *I can behave.* Austin, TX: Pro-Ed.

McGinnis, E., & Goldstein, A. P. (1997). *Skillstreaming the elementary school child: A guide for teaching prosocial skills* (rev. ed.). Champaign, IL: Research Press.

Rutherford, R. B., Chipman, J., DiGangi, S. A., & Anderson, K. (1992). *Teaching social skills: A practical instructional approach.* Ann Arbor, MI: Exceptional Innovations.

Stokes, T. F., & Baer, D. M. (1988). *The social skills curriculum.* Circle Pines, MN: American Guidance Service.

Walker, H., McConnell, S., Holms, D., Todis, B., Walker, J., & Golden, N. (1983). *The Walker social skills curriculum: The ACCEPTS program.* Austin, TX: Pro-Ed.

Literature about Individuals with Behavioral Disorders*

Elementary

Berger, T. (1979). *I have feelings, too.* New York: Human Sciences Press. (F)

Sheehan, C. (1981). *The colors that I am.* New York: Human Science Press. (F)

Simon, N. (1974). *I was so mad!* Chicago: A. Whitman. (Middle School) (F)

Hamilton, V. (1971). *The planet of Junior Brown.* New York: Macmillan. (F)

Patterson, K. (1978). *The great Gilly Hopkins.* New York: Cromwell. (F)

Platt, K. (1968). *The boy who could make himself disappear.* Dell. (F)

Secondary/Adult

Berger, G. (1981). *Mental illness.* New York: Franklin Watts. (NF)

Greenfeld, J. (1978). *A place for Noah.* New York: Washington Square Press. (NF)

Greenfeld, J. (1986). *A client called Noah.* San Diego: Harcourt Brace Jovanovich. (NF)

Hayden, T. L. (1980). *One child.* New York: Putnam. (NF)

Heide, F. P. (1976). *Growing anyway up.* Philadelphia: Lippincott. (F)

Hyde, M. O. (1983). *Is this kid "crazy"? Understanding unusual behavior.* Philadelphia: Westminister. (NF)

Videodisc

Interactive Videodisc Social Skills (IVSS) Program, Ron Thorkildsen, Department of Special Education, Utah State University, Logan, UT, 84322–2865, (435)797-3243.

*F = fiction; NF = nonfiction

Organizations

Council for Children with Behavioral Disorders, 1920 Association Dr., Reston, VA 20191, (888) CEC-SPED.

National Consortium for Child Mental Health Services, American Academy of Child and Adolescent Psychiatry, 3615 Wisconsin Avenue N.W., Washington, DC 20016, (202) 966–7300.

Bibliography for Teaching Suggestions

Bandura, A. (1969). *Principles of behavior modification.* New York: Holt, Rinehart, & Winston.

Goldstein, A. P., & Glick, B. (1987). *Aggression replacement training.* Champaign, IL: Research Press.

Individuals with Disabilities Education Act Amendments of 1997, P.L. 105–17, 105th Congress, 1st session.

Kauffman, J. M. (1997). *Characteristics of emotional and behavioral disorders of children and youth* (6th ed.). Upper Saddle River, NJ: Merrill/Prentice-Hall.

Kea, C. (1998). Focus on ethnic and minority concerns: Critical teaching behaviors and instructional strategies for working with culturally diverse students. *Council for Children with Behavioral Disorders Newsletter, 11,* 3–7.

Kerr, M. M., & Nelson, C. M. (1998). *Strategies for managing behavior problems in the classroom* (3rd ed.). Upper Saddle River, NJ: Prentice-Hall.

Lewis, R. B., & Doorlag, D. H. (1999). *Teaching special students in the mainstream* (5th ed.). Upper Saddle River, NJ: Merrill/Prentice-Hall.

Miltenberger, R. (1997). *Behavior modification: Principles and procedures.* Pacific Grove, CA: Brooks/Cole.

Polloway, E. A., & Patton, J. S. (1997). *Strategies for teaching learners with special needs* (6th ed.). Upper Saddle River, NJ: Merrill/Prentice-Hall.

Premack, D., (1959). Toward empirical behavior laws: I. Positive reinforcement. *Psychological Review, 66,* 219–233.

Rhode, G., Jensen, W. R., & Reavis, H. K. (1995). *The tough kid book.* Longmont, CO: Sopris West.

Rutherford, R. B., & Nelson, C. M. (1995). Management of aggressive and violent behavior in the schools. *Focus on Exceptional Children, 27,* 1–15.

Zirpoli, T. J., & Melloy, K. J. (1997). *Behavior management: Applications for teachers and parents* (2nd ed.). Upper Saddle River, NJ: Prentice-Hall.

robert
kirshner

Untitled (Hot Dog Stand). Pencil, crayon, watercolor on rag paper. 11 × 15 in.

Robert Kirshner was born in 1955 and has lived in the Boston area all his life. His work has been shown extensively in and around Boston and at the Outsider Art Fair in New York. He has received awards from The Royal Society for Mentally Handicapped Children and Adults in London, England, and from the Ebensburg Center in Pennsylvania. In 1996 he was featured in *From the Outside In,* an exhibition at the Fuller Museum of Art in Brockton, MA.

Communication Disorders

I said goodbye and turned to go, but she wrapped her purple-green arms around my neck, kissed my cheek, and said, "I love you, Jeremy."

"I'll miss you so much."

"I really, truly love you with all my soul," she said.

"My Dad's waiting. I better go."

She took her arms off me and stepped back, straightened her smock. Then she said, "I've already told you I love you, Jeremy. Can't you say, 'I love you, Faith'?"

"I love you," I said.

"I love you, *Faith*," she insisted.

This little scene in the garage occurred only a few months after my futile attempt to say *Philadelphia* in the living room. Stutterers have a tendency to generalize their fear of one word that begins with a particular sound to a fear of all words that begin with the same sound. In the space of the summer I'd effectively eliminated every *F* from my vocabulary, with the exception of the preposition, "for," which for the time being was too small to incite terror. A few weeks later, my fear of *F* ended when another letter—I think it was *L*—suddenly loomed large. But at the moment, early October 1962, in Faith's garage, I was terrified of *F*s. I simply wasn't saying them. I hadn't called Faith by her first name for nearly a month and had, instead, taken to calling her Carlisle, as if her patronymic had become a term of jocular endearment.

"I can't," I said. "I can't say that."

DAVID SHIELDS
Dead Languages

Communication is such a natural part of our everyday lives that we seldom stop to think about it. Social conversation with families, friends, and casual acquaintances is normally so effortless and pleasant that it is hard to imagine having difficulty with it. Most of us have feelings of uncertainty about the adequacy of our speech or language only in stressful or unusual social situations, such as talking to a large audience or being interviewed for a job. If we always had to worry about communicating, we would worry about every social interaction we had.

Not all communication disorders involve disorders of speech. Not all speech disorders are as handicapping in social interactions as **stuttering,** nor is stuttering the most common disorder of speech. The problem Shields describes (see p. 295) affects only about one person in a hundred, and then usually just during childhood. But stuttering is a mystery, a phenomenon about which theories continue to surface (Culatta & Goldberg, 1995; Hulstijn, Peters, & van Lieshout, 1997). Its causes and cures remain largely unknown, although for many years it captured a large share of speech-language pathologists' attention (Curlee & Siegel, 1997).

In one sense, then, stuttering is a poor example to use in introducing a chapter on communication disorders. It is not the most representative disorder, it is difficult to define precisely, its causes are not fully understood, and few suggestions about how to overcome it can be made with confidence. But in another sense, stuttering is the best example. When people think of speech and language disorders, they tend to think first of stuttering (Owens, 1986). It is a disorder we all have heard and recognized (if not experienced) at one time or another, its social consequences are obvious, and although it *appears* to be a simple problem with obvious logical solutions ("Just slow down"; "Relax, don't worry"; "Think about how to say it"), these seemingly commonsense approaches do not work.

Today, difficulty such as that described by Shields is viewed within the broad context of **communication disorders** because of the obstacle it presents to social interaction, a major purpose of language (Zebrowski, 1995). Jeremy's stuttering was an inability to convey his thoughts and feelings to Faith, not just a problem of being fearful and unable to say certain words. In thinking about communication disorders, the context in which communication occurs must be considered in addition to people's reasons for communicating, and the rules that govern the "games" of discourse and dialogue (Bernstein & Tiegerman-Farber, 1997; Haynes & Pindzola, 1998; Nelson, 1998).

Our points here are simply these: First, all communication disorders carry social penalties. And second, communication is among the most complex human functions, so disorders of this function do not always yield to intuitive or commonsense solutions.

Definitions

Speech and language are tools used for communication. Communication requires *encoding* (sending in understandable form) and *decoding* (receiving and understanding) messages. It always involves a sender and a receiver of messages, but it does not always involve language. Animals communicate through movements and noises, for example, but their communication does not qualify as true language. We are concerned here only with communication through language.

stuttering. Speech characterized by abnormal hesitations, prolongations, and repetitions; may be accompanied by grimaces, gestures, or other bodily movements indicative of a struggle to speak, anxiety, blocking of speech, or avoidance of speech.

communication disorders. Impairments in the ability to use speech or language to communicate.

misconceptions
about Persons with Communications Disorders

myth Children with language disorders always have speech difficulties as well.

fact It is possible for a child to have good speech yet not make any sense when he or she talks; however, most children with language disorders have speech disorders as well.

myth Individuals with communication disorders always have emotional or behavioral disorders or mental retardation.

fact Some children with communication disorders are normal in cognitive, social, and emotional development.

myth How children learn language is now well understood.

fact Although recent research has revealed quite a lot about the sequence of language acquisition and has led to theories of language development, exactly how children learn language is still unknown.

myth Stuttering is primarily a disorder of people with extremely high IQs. Children who stutter become stuttering adults.

fact Stuttering can affect individuals at all levels of intellectual ability. Some children who stutter continue stuttering as adults; most, however, stop stuttering before or during adolescence with help from a speech-language pathologist. Stuttering is primarily a childhood disorder, found much more often in boys than in girls.

myth Disorders of phonology (or articulation) are never very serious and are always easy to correct.

fact Disorders of phonology can make speech unintelligible; it is sometimes very difficult to correct phonological or articulation problems, especially if the individual has cerebral palsy, mental retardation, or emotional or behavioral disorders.

myth There is no relationship between intelligence and communication disorders.

fact Communication disorders tend to occur more frequently among individuals of lower intellectual ability, although they may occur in individuals who are extremely intelligent.

myth There is not much overlap between language disorders and learning disabilities.

fact Problems with verbal skills—listening, reading, writing, speaking—are often central features of learning disabilities. The definitions of language disorders and several other disabilities are overlapping.

myth Children who learn few language skills before entering kindergarten can easily pick up all the skills they need, if they have good peer models in typical classrooms.

fact Early language learning is critical for later language development; a child whose language is delayed in kindergarten is unlikely to learn to use language effectively merely by observing peer models. More explicit intervention is typically required.

language. An arbitrary code or system of symbols to communicate meaning.

speech. The formation and sequencing of oral language sounds during communication.

augmentative communication. Alternative forms of communication that do not use the oral sounds of speech.

speech disorders. Oral communication that involves abnormal use of the vocal apparatus, is unintelligible, or is so inferior that it draws attention to itself and causes anxiety, feelings of inadequacy, or inappropriate behavior in the speaker.

articulation. The movements the vocal tract makes during production of speech sounds; enunciation of words and vocal sounds.

fluency. The flow with which oral language is produced.

language disorders. Oral communication that involves a lag in the ability to understand and express ideas, putting linguistic skill behind an individual's development in other areas, such as motor, cognitive, or social development.

phonology. The study of how individual sounds make up words.

morphology. The study within psycholinguistics of word formation; how adding or deleting parts of words changes their meaning.

syntax. How words are joined together to structure meaningful sentences; grammar.

semantics. The study of the meanings attached to words and sentences.

Language is the communication of ideas through an arbitrary system of symbols used according to certain rules that determine meaning. When people think of language, they typically think of the oral language most of us use. **Speech**—the behavior of forming and sequencing the sounds of oral language—is the most common symbol system used in communication between humans. Some languages, however, are not based on speech. For example, American Sign Language (ASL) does not involve speech sounds; it is a manual language used by many people who cannot hear speech. **Augmentative communication** for people with disabilities involving the physical movements of speech may consist of alternatives to the speech sounds of oral language.

The American Speech-Language-Hearing Association (ASHA, 1993) provides definitions of disorders of communication, including speech disorders, language disorders, and variations in communication (differences or dialects and augmentative systems) that are not disorders (see the box on page 299). **Speech disorders** are impairments in the production and use of oral language. They include disabilities in making speech sounds (**articulation**), producing speech with a normal flow (**fluency**), and producing voice.

Language disorders include problems in comprehending and using language for communication, regardless of the symbol system used (spoken, written, or other). The *form, content,* and/or *function* of language may be involved:

- The form of language includes sound combinations (**phonology**), construction of word forms such as plurals and verb tenses (**morphology**), and construction of sentences (**syntax**).
- The content of language refers to the intentions and meanings people attach to words and sentences (**semantics**).
- Language function is the use to which language is put in communication, and it includes nonverbal behavior as well as vocalizations that form the pattern of language use (**pragmatics**).

Differences in speech or language that are shared by people in a given region, social group, or cultural/ethnic group should not be considered disorders. For example, African American English (Ebonics or Black English Vernacular), Appalachian English, and the New York dialect are varieties of English, not disorders of speech or language. Similarly, the use of augmentative communication systems does not imply that a person has a language disorder. Rather, such systems are used by those who have temporary or permanent inabilities to use speech satisfactorily for communication. Those who use augmentative communication systems may or may not have language disorders in addition to their inability to use speech.

Prevalence

Establishing the prevalence of communication disorders is difficult because they are extremely varied, sometimes difficult to identify, and often occur as part of other disabilities (e.g., mental retardation, traumatic brain injury, learning disability, or autism, see Bernstein & Tiegerman-Farber, 1997; Nelson, 1998). Federal data indicate that about a million children—about one-fifth of all children identified for special education—receive services primarily for language or speech disorders (U.S. Department of Education, 1998). Moreover, speech-language

Definitions of the American Speech-Language-Hearing Association

I. *A communication disorder* is an impairment in the ability to receive, send, process, and comprehend concepts or verbal, nonverbal and graphic symbol systems. A communication disorder may be evident in the processes of hearing, language, and/or speech. A communication disorder may range in severity from mild to profound. It may be developmental or acquired. Individuals may demonstrate one or any combination of communication disorders. A communication disorder may result in a primary disability or it may be secondary to other disabilities.

A. *A speech disorder* is an impairment of the articulation of speech sounds, fluency, and/or voice.

1. *An articulation disorder* is the atypical production of speech sounds characterized by substitutions, omissions, additions, or distortions that may interfere with intelligibility.

2. *A fluency disorder* is an interruption in the flow of speaking characterized by atypical rate, rhythm, and repetitions in sounds, syllables, words, and phrases. This may be accompanied by excessive tension, struggle behavior, and secondary mannerisms.

3. *A voice disorder* is characterized by the abnormal production and/or absences of vocal quality, pitch, loudness, resonance, and/or duration, which is inappropriate for an individual's age and/or sex.

B. *A language disorder* is impaired comprehension and/or use of spoken, written, and/or other symbol systems. The disorder may involve (1) the form of language (phonology, morphology, syntax), (2) the content of language (semantics), and/or (3) the function of language in communication (pragmatics) in any combination.

1. Form of Language
   a. *Phonology* is the sound system of a language and the rules that govern the sound combinations.
   b. *Morphology* is the system that governs the structure of words and the construction of word forms.
   c. *Syntax* is the system governing the order and combination of words to form sentences, and the relationships among the elements within a sentence.

2. Content of Language
   a. *Semantics* is the system that governs the meanings of words and sentences.

3. Function of Language
   a. *Pragmatics* is the system that combines the above language components in functional and socially appropriate communication.

II. *Communication Variations*

A. *Communication difference/dialect* is a variation of a symbol system used by a group of individuals that reflects and is determined by shared regional, social, or cultural/ethnic factors. A regional, social, or cultural/ethnic variation of a symbol system should not be considered a disorder of speech or language.

B. *Augmentative/alternative communication* systems attempt to compensate and facilitate, temporarily or permanently, for the impairment and disability patterns of individuals with severe expressive and/or language comprehension disorders. Augmentative/alternative communication may be required for individuals demonstrating impairments in gestural, spoken, and/or written modalities.

Source: American Speech-Language-Hearing Association. (1993). "Definitions of communication disorders and variations." *ASHA, 35* (Suppl. 10), pp. 40–41. Reprinted with permission.

therapy is one of the most frequently provided related services for children with other primary disabilities (e.g., mental retardation or learning disability).

Table 8.1 outlines the other categories associated with language disorders of children and youths. The outline suggests the multiple, interrelated causes of language disorders and other disabilities:

- *Central factors* refer to causes associated with central nervous system (i.e., brain) damage or dysfunction.

pragmatics. The study within psycholinguistics of how one uses language in social situations; emphasizes the functional use of language rather than its mechanics.

Table 8.1	Categorical Factors Associated with Childhood Language Disorders	
I. Central factors	A. Specific language disability	
	B. Mental retardation	
	C. Autism	
	D. Attention-deficit hyperactivity disorder	
	E. Acquired brain injury	
	F. Others	
II. Peripheral factors	A. Hearing impairment	
	B. Visual impairment	
	C. Deaf-blindness	
	D. Physical impairment	
III. Environmental and emotional factors	A. Neglect and abuse	
	B. Behavioral and emotional development problems	
IV. Mixed factors		

Source: From N. W. Nelson, *Childhood language disorders in context: Infancy through adolescence* (2nd ed.). Copyright © 1998 by Allyn & Bacon. Reprinted by permission.

- *Peripheral factors* refer to sensory or physical impairments that are not caused by brain injury or dysfunction but that nonetheless contribute to language disorders.
- *Environmental and emotional factors* refer to language disorders that have their primary origin in the child's physical or psychological environment.
- *Mixed factors* are included because language disorders often have multiple causes—combinations of central, peripheral, and environmental or emotional factors.

Estimates are that about 10 to 15 percent of preschool children and about 6 percent of students in elementary and secondary grades have speech disorders; about 2 to 3 percent of preschoolers and about 1 percent of the school-age population have language disorders (Matthews & Frattali, 1994). Communication disorders of all kinds are predicted to increase during the coming decades, as medical advances preserve the lives of more children and youths with severe disabilities that affect communication. Thus, there is a need for more speech-language pathologists in the schools as well as for greater knowledge of communication disorders by special and general education teachers and greater involvement of teachers in helping students learn to communicate effectively (Matthews & Frattali, 1994).

Communication disorders cannot be understood and corrected without knowledge of normal language development. So before discussing the disorders of language and speech, we provide a brief description of normal language development. Language disorders are discussed first and more extensively than speech disorders, because the primary focus of speech-language pathologists and other specialists in communicative disorders has shifted from speech to language during the evolution of special education and related services.

The underlying mechanisms that control the development of language—how much is innate and how much is controlled by the environment—are not yet well understood.

Language Development and Language Disorders

The newborn makes few sounds other than cries. The fact that within a few years the human child can form the many complex sounds of speech, understand spoken and written language, and express meaning verbally is one of nature's great miracles. The major milestones in this miraculous ability to use language are fairly well known by child development specialists. The underlying mechanisms that control the development of language are still not well understood, however. What parts of the process of learning language are innate, and what parts are controlled by the environment? What is the relationship between cognitive development and language development? These and many other questions about the origins and uses of language cannot yet be answered definitively (Nelson, 1998).

Comparisons between the language of a normally developing child and one with a language disorder are shown in Table 8.2. Note that, in general, the sequence of development is similar for the two children, but the child with the language disorder reaches milestones at later ages. Although there are other types of language disorders, delayed language—slowness in developing skills and reaching certain milestones—is perhaps the most common type.

No one knows exactly how or why children learn language, but we do know that language development is related in a general way to physical maturation, cognitive development, and socialization. The details of the process—the particulars of what happens physiologically, cognitively, and socially in the learning of language—are still being debated. Carrow-Woolfolk (1988) and Nelson (1998) discuss six theories of language that have dominated the study of human communication at various times. The six theories and research based on them have established the following:

- Language learning depends on brain development and proper brain functioning; language disorders are sometimes a result of brain dysfunction, and ways to compensate for the dysfunction can sometimes be taught. The emphasis is on *biological maturation*.

Table 8.2   Pattern of Development Shown by a Child with a Language Disorder and a Child with Normal Language Development

LANGUAGE-DISORDERED CHILD			NORMALLY DEVELOPING CHILD		
Age	Attainment	Example	Age	Attainment	Example
27 months	First words	*this, mama, bye bye, doggie*	13 months	First words	*here, mama, bye bye, kitty*
38 months	50-word vocabulary		17 months	50-word vocabulary	
40 months	First two-word combinations	*this doggie, more apple, this mama, more play*	18 months	First two-word combinations	*more juice, here ball, more TV, here kitty*
48 months	Later two-word combinations	*Mimi purse, Daddy coat, block chair, dolly table*	22 months	Later two-word combinations	*Andy shoe, Mommy ring, cup floor, keys chair*
52 months	Mean sentence length of 2.00 words		24 months	Mean sentence length of 2.00 words First appearance of -ing	*Andy sleeping*
55 months	First appearance of -ing	*Mommy eating*			
63 months	Mean sentence length of 3.10 words		30 months	Mean sentence length of 3.10 words First appearance of is	*My car's gone.*
66 months	First appearance of is	*The doggie's mad.*	37 months	Mean sentence length of 4.10 words First appearance of indirect requests	*Can I have some cookies?*
73 months	Mean sentence length of 4.10 words				
79 months	Mean sentence length of 4.50 words First appearance of indirect requests	*Can I get the ball?*	40 months	Mean sentence length of 4.50 words	

Source: From L. Leonard, "Language disorders in preschool children," in *Human communication disorders: An introduction* (4th ed.), edited by G. H. Shames, E. H. Wiig, and W. A. Secord. Copyright © 1994 by Allyn & Bacon. Reprinted by permission.

- Language learning is affected by the consequences of language behavior; language disorders can be a result of inappropriate learning, and consequences can sometimes be arranged to correct disordered language. The emphasis is on *behavioral psychology.*
- Language can be analyzed as inputs and outputs related to the way information is processed; faulty processing may account for some language disorders, and more effective processing skills can sometimes be taught. The emphasis is on *information processing.*
- Language is based on linguistic rules; language disorders can be described as failures to employ appropriate rules for encoding and decoding messages, and sometimes these disorders can be overcome by teaching the use of linguistic rules. The emphasis is on *induction of linguistic rules.*

Children with language disorders often have particular difficulty with one dimension of language, be it phonology, morphology, syntax, semantics, or pragmatics.

- Language is one of many cognitive skills; language disorders reflect basic problems in thinking and learning, and sometimes these disorders can be addressed effectively by teaching specific cognitive skills. The emphasis is on *cognitive development*.

- Language arises from the need to communicate in social interactions; language disorders are a breakdown in ability to relate effectively to one's environment, and the natural environment can sometimes be arranged to teach and support more effective interaction. The emphasis is on *social interaction*.

All these theories contain elements of scientific truth, but none is able to explain the development and disorders of language completely. All six theories have advantages and disadvantages for assessing language disorders and devising effective interventions. *Pragmatic* or *social interaction* theory is widely viewed as having the most direct implications for speech-language pathologists and teachers.

Language involves listening and speaking, reading and writing, technical discourse, and social interaction. Language problems are therefore basic to many of the disabilities discussed in this text, especially hearing impairment, mental retardation, learning disability, traumatic brain injury, and autism.

Classification of Language Disorders

Language disorders can be classified according to several criteria. The ASHA (1993) definitions on page 299 provide a classification scheme involving five subsystems of language: *phonology* (sounds), *morphology* (word forms), *syntax* (word order and sentence structure), *semantics* (word and sentence meanings), and *pragmatics* (social use of language). Difficulty with one of these dimensions of language is virtually certain to be accompanied by difficulty with one or more of the others. However, children with language disorders often have particular difficulty with one dimension. Language disorders involving these subsystems are illustrated in the box on pages 304–305.

Disorders of the Five Subsystems of Language

Oral language involves communication through a system of sound symbols. Disorders may occur in one or more of the five subsystems of oral language: *phonology* (sounds and sound combinations), *morphology* (words and meaningful word parts), *syntax* (sequences and combinations of words), *semantics* (meanings or content), and *pragmatics* (use for communication). The following interactions illustrate disorders in each of these subsystems. Note that a given illustration may involve more than a single subsystem.

Phonology

Alvin has just turned 6. He is in kindergarten, but has been receiving speech therapy for 2 years. At 4, his parents sought assistance when his speech and language remained unintelligible and he did not appear to be "growing out" of his problem. He has two older siblings whose speech and language are well within the normal range. Alvin substitutes and omits a number of speech sounds, and in addition, he has difficulty with other subsystems of language as shown in the example below:

Clinician: I'd like you to tell me about some words. Here's something that you may have for breakfast: orange juice. What's orange juice?
Alvin: I doh noh. [I don't know.]
Clinician: See if you can guess. What color is orange juice?
Alvin: Ahnge. N you dink i. [Orange. And you drink it.]
Clinician: That's good. Tell me some more about orange juice.
Alvin: Doh noh.
Clinician: Let's try another. What's sugar? Tell me what sugar is.
Alvin: Yukky.
Clinician: Yukky? Why?
Alvin: Cah i wahtuns yer tee. ['Cause it rottens your teeth.]

Morphology

Children with language disorders in the morphological realm will exhibit difficulty in either understanding or producing morphological inflections. These include the ability to add *-s* to change a word from singular to plural; to include *'s* to make a word a possessive; *-ed* to change the tense of a word from present to past; or to use other inflectional endings to differentiate comparatives and superlatives, among others.

Children with morphological difficulties will use inappropriate suffixes.... Here are a few ... examples, taken from the test protocols of school-age children:

Examiner: Anna, say this after me: *cow.*
Anna: (*age 6*) Cow.
Examiner: Good. Now say *boy.*
Anna: Boy.
Examiner: Now put them together. Say *cowboy.*
Anna: Boy.
Examiner: Frank, find two little words in this big word: *outside.*
Frank: (*age 7*) Outside.
Examiner: Not quite right. We need *two* words.
Frank: (*Shrugs and looks around the room*)
Examiner: Well, if one word is *side*, the other would be ...?
Frank: Be?
Examiner: Jamie, can you tell me a story?
Jamie: (*age 8*) I can't think of none.
Examiner: What if the story began, "One night I walked into a dark haunted house ... and ...
Jamie: I met a ghost. He wanted to kill me. But he couldn't. I ran very, very fastest. And all of a sudden I saw a coffin. I hides in there. And all of a sudden there a ghostes inside there. And I sent out of the coffin. And then there weres a guy named Count. And then he tried to suck my blood. And then he couldn't find me because I hided. And then I met a mummy. And then he wanted to tie me up ... and ... that's all.

Syntax

Marie is 8 years old and in a special first-grade class. Her syntactical difficulties are demonstrated in the following story-telling event:

Clinician: Marie, I want you to listen carefully. I am going to tell you a story; listen, and when I'm done, I want you to tell me the story.

Another way of classifying language disorders is based on the presumed cause or related conditions. The literature on language disorders frequently includes chapters and articles on the particular communication disorders of individuals with other specific disabling conditions, such as autism, traumatic brain injury, mental

Marie: (*interrupting*) I don't know.

Clinician: I haven't told you the story yet. Remember, listen carefully to my story. When I'm done, you are to tell me everything you can remember about the story. One day Mr. Mouse went for a walk. As he was walking, he saw a cat lying in the road. The cat had a stone in his paw so he couldn't walk. Mr. Mouse pulled the stone out of the cat's paw. The cat thanked Mr. Mouse for helping him. They shook hands and walked down the road together.

Marie: Uh, uh, uh . . . Cat was on the road and Mr. Mouse taken out the stone his paw, and then they walked down together the hill and they said thanks, and they walk on the hill, and the mouse chase him.

This task of retelling a story reveals that Marie has difficulty not only in syntax but in the ordering of events and in accurate recall. Indeed, Marie seems unaware that she has modified the story considerably, including giving the story a new ending.

Semantics

Clinician: Burt, tell me about birthday parties.

Burt: (*age 6*) Sing "Happy Birthday," blow away candles, eat a birthday cake, open your presents.

Clinician: All right. Now listen to this story and then say it back to me . . . tell me the whole story: "One day, a little boy went to school. He went up the steps of the school and opened the door. The boy went into his classroom and started playing with his friends. The teacher said, 'Time to come to circle.' The boy put away his toys and sat down on the rug."

Burt: A teacher . . . a boy played with a teacher's toys . . . time for us to come to circle . . . and it's the end.

You will note that Burt does not "blow out" candles; rather, his retrieval of information from semantic memory provides the response "blow away." In addition, it is clear that even the immediate retelling of a story, which in reality represents a string of events well within Burt's everyday experience, is very difficult for Burt. The pauses noted reflect the period of time during which Burt attempted to recall the necessary information.

Pragmatics

Greg, age 7, interacts with his special education teacher. Greg is in a self-contained classroom for mentally retarded children and is one of the more verbal children in the class. Assessment by the speech-language pathologist indicates difficulties in phonology, syntax, morphology, and semantics. He has been identified as suffering from a significant language delay. On most language tests, he functions between 2:7* and 3:6 years of age. His teacher, who has visited his home many times, notes that there are no toys, no books, no playthings, and that there appears to be little communication between Greg and his mother, a single parent. The teacher is eager to draw Greg into conversation and story-telling, and has arranged a "talking and telling time" as part of the daily activities with the seven children who comprise her class.

Teacher: Greg, I'd like you to tell me a story. It can be about anything you like.

Greg: No me.

Teacher: Go ahead, it's your turn.

Greg: (*having had previous instruction on "taking turns"*) No, s'yer turn.

Teacher: You do it. It's your turn.

Greg: I can't. I forget.

Teacher: I bet you can tell me a story about school.

Greg: You eat snack. What we have for snack?

Greg's teacher praises his contribution to the conversation and moves on to another student. She grins to herself; she and Greg have had a running joke about "turns." She feels that Greg tends to use "it's your turn" (when it is inappropriate) to delay the necessity to respond. This time she has enticed him into contributing to the conversation by requesting that he recall something that happens frequently within the school context. Greg attempts to comply, recalling from memory a favored episodic event—a small victory for both Greg and his teacher.

*The age designation 2:7 means "2 years, 7 months" old.

Source: K. G. Butler, *Language disorders in children* (Austin, TX: Pro-Ed, 1986), pp. 13–14, 16–17, 19, 23, 28–29. Reprinted with permission.

retardation, and cerebral palsy (e.g., Owens, 1995; Shames et al., 1994; Szekeres & Meserve, 1995). Owens (1995) discusses seven diagnostic categories of language impairments, each of which tends to present difficulties in particular areas (as shown in Table 8.3): perception, attention, use of symbols, use of language rules,

The causes of communication disorders may be linked to other disabilities; however, many disorders of communication cannot be attributed to specific causes, and must simply be dealt with according to presenting symptoms.

overall mental ability, and social interaction related to communication. In addition, each diagnostic category is characterized by particular problems in the five language subsystems—phonology, morphology, syntax, semantics, and pragmatics—and problems in language comprehension.

Several of the seven conditions included in Table 8.3 are defined in other chapters of this book. **Specific language impairment (SLI)** refers to language disorders that have no identifiable causes. These disorders are not due to mental retardation or to the perceptual problems that characterize language learning disability. Rather, SLI is defined more by the exclusion of other plausible causes than by a clearly defined set of characteristics, and for this reason it is controversial. **Early expressive language delay (EELD)** refers to a significant lag in expressive language that the child will not outgrow (i.e., the child does not have a fifty-word vocabulary or use two-word utterances by age two). About half the children whose language development is delayed at age two *will* gradually catch up developmentally with their age peers; however the other half will not catch up and will continue to have language problems throughout their school years.

A scientific approach to problems demands classification, but human beings and their language are very difficult to categorize. Thus, all classification systems contain ambiguities, and none can account for all cases. Owens (1995) notes:

> Most [college and university] students are in need of a 1-sentence summary statement that once and for all distinguishes each language impairment from the others. Unfortunately, I do not have one forthcoming. We are discussing real human beings who do not like to be placed in boxes and asked to perform in certain ways. (p. 56)

Strategies for Assessment and Intervention

specific language impairment (SLI). A language disorder with no identifiable cause; language disorder not attributable to hearing impairment, mental retardation, brain dysfunction, or other plausible cause; also called specific language disability.

early expressive language delay (EELD). A significant lag in the development of expressive language that is apparent by age two.

Two general strategies of language assessment are (1) to determine, in as much detail as possible, what the child's current language abilities are, and (2) to observe the ease and speed with which the child learns new language skills. The first strategy typically involves use of standardized testing, nonstandardized testing, developmental scales, and behavioral observations. Standardized testing has many dangers and is not always useful in planning an intervention program, but it can sometimes be helpful in making crude comparisons of the child's abilities in certain areas. Development scales are ratings or observations that may be completed by direct observation, or based on memory or records of developmental milestones. Nonstandardized tests and behavioral observations are nonnormative in nature, but they may yield the most important assessment information. The subjective judgment of an experienced clinician based on observation of the child's language in a variety of environments and circumstances may provide the most useful basis for intervention. Because language disorders vary widely in nature and are seen in individuals ranging from early childhood through old age, assessment

Table 8.3 — Language Learning Requirements and the Difficulties of Children with Language Impairment*

	LANGUAGE IMPAIRMENT						
Requirements	Mental Retardation	Language Learning Disability	Specific Language Impairment	Autism	Traumatic Brain Injury	Expressive Language Delay	Neglect/Abuse
Perception	X	X	X	X	X		
Attention		X		X	X		
Use of symbols	X	X	X	X	X	X	X
Use of language rules	X	X	X	X		X	
Overall mental ability	X		X		X		X
Social interaction related to communication				X			

*X's represent problem areas in language learning and use.

Source: From R. E. Owens, *Language disorders: A functional approach to assessment and intervention* (2nd ed.). Copyright © 1995 by Allyn & Bacon. Adapted by permission.

and intervention are never simple and are always idiosyncratic (Nelson, 1998; Owens, 1995).

An intervention plan must consider the content, form, and use of language. That is, it must consider:

1. What the child talks about and should be taught to talk about
2. How the child talks about things and how he or she could be taught to speak of those things more intelligibly
3. How the child uses language and how his or her use of it could be made to serve the purposes of communication and socialization more effectively

In arranging a training sequence, one might base instruction on the normal sequence of language development. Other sequences of instruction might be more effective, however, since children with language disorders obviously have not learned in the normal way and research suggests that different sequences of learning may be more effective. It is more and more apparent that effective language intervention must occur in the child's natural environment and involve parents and classroom teachers, not just speech-language pathologists (Nelson, 1998; Prizant, 1999).

The increasing inclusion of children with all types of disabilities in general education means that all teachers must become aware of how they can address language problems in the classroom. Before discussing the classroom teacher's role in helping students learn to use language more effectively, we consider several special cases: the special communication problems of students with autism, delayed language development, and traumatic brain injury. Other disabilities may present special communication problems as well, and they are discussed in other chapters (see also Rogers-Adkinson & Griffith, 1999).

Language Disorders Associated with Autism

Recall from our discussion in Chapter 7 that autism is a pervasive developmental disability that is typically diagnosed between the ages of eighteen and thirty months. Autism is a poorly understood neurological problem of unknown origin, and the developmental problems associated with it may range from mild to severe. The primary features of autism include impairments of social interaction and communication and restricted interests or activities (Schopler, Misibov, & Hearsey, 1995). The cognitive abilities of children with autism may range from giftedness to severe mental retardation; a high proportion of such children appear to have mental retardation. Children with autism may exhibit repetitive or stereotypic behavior and peculiar patterns of speech as well as problems in learning or using language. Because the inability to communicate effectively is perhaps the single most disabling feature of autism, we focus here exclusively on disorders of speech and language.

A substantial proportion of children with autism—perhaps 50 percent—learn little or no oral language at all, unless they receive intensive language intervention. Some go through periods of apparently normal language development and then regress (Brown & Prelock, 1995). Even many of those who do learn oral language have difficulty learning to use speech to communicate effectively, as their language is qualitatively different from the norm. For example, their speech often has a wooden, robotlike quality or fails to convey appropriate affect. They may exhibit *echolalia*, a parrotlike repetition of words or phrases. Some use jargon or nonsense words that fail to communicate meaning to someone not intimately familiar with the individual's speech. Some children with autism also confuse the use of pronouns (for example, substituting *you* for *I* or *me*) (Lee, Hobson, & Chiat, 1994).

In the 1960s and 1970s, systematic efforts to teach language to nonverbal children with autism consisted of using *operant conditioning* methods. That is, a step-by-step sequence of behaviors approximating functional language was established, and the child's responses at each step in the sequence were rewarded (Koegel, Rincover, & Egel, 1982). A major problem of early research on operant conditioning methods was that few of the children studied acquired truly functional language, even after intensive and prolonged training. Their speech tended to maintain a stereotyped, mechanical quality, and they often could use their language for only very restricted social purposes.

A current trend in language training for nonverbal children—indeed, for all children with language disorders—is to emphasize *pragmatics*, making language more functional in social interactions, and to motivate children to communicate (Koegel & Koegel, 1995). So instead of training children to imitate words in isolation or to use syntactically and grammatically correct forms, instruction might involve training them to use language to obtain a desired result. For example, the child might be taught to say "I want juice" (or a simplified form: "Juice" or "Want juice") in order to get a drink of juice (see Tiegerman-Farber, 1997).

Increasingly, language intervention for people with autism involves structuring opportunities to use language in natural settings (Sigafoos, Kerr, Roberts, & Couzens, 1994). For example, the teacher may set up opportunities for children to make requests by using a missing-item strategy (e.g., giving the child a coloring book but not crayons, prompting a request for crayons), interrupting a chain of behavior (e.g., stopping the child on his or her way out to play, prompting a request to go out), or delaying assistance with tasks (e.g., waiting to help the child put on his or her coat until he or she asks for assistance). This structuring opportunities approach is compatible with today's emphasis on including children with autism in regular preschool and elementary school programs where language serves many practical purposes (Harris, 1995).

Research suggests that people with autism have special difficulty understanding the communication of social and emotional meanings (Happe, 1994; Happe & Frith, 1995; Sigman, 1994). Namely, they may be unable to get a coherent picture of social contexts, use social imagination, accurately attribute mental states or feelings to others, or understand jokes, pretense, lies, or figures of speech. In fact, some believe that the core disability in autism is an absence of a "theory of mind," or the inability to understand the existence of subjective mental states (e.g., beliefs, desires, intentions) and how they help people explain and make sense of behavior (Happe, 1994; Happe & Frith, 1995). Language intervention, then, might focus on helping children with autism understand more about how language is used to communicate about subjective mental states as well as more object-centered social interactions.

Autism is a developmental puzzle that many people would like to solve, for obvious reasons. Perhaps that explains the frequent and often misleading claims of so-called breakthrough interventions. For example, in the early 1990s, claims that normal or extraordinary intelligence and communicative competence was revealed in children and adults with autism using a procedure called *facilitated communication* (discussed further in the section on augmentative and alternative communication; see p. 317) attracted much attention. However, by the mid-1990s, researchers had accumulated overwhelming evidence that facilitated communication is not a reliable means of communication, except perhaps in very rare cases (e.g., Crews et al., 1995; Montee, Miltenberger, & Wittrock, 1995; Shane, 1994; Siegel, 1995).

The language training procedures, based on operant conditioning applied to natural language contexts, have not led to dramatic breakthroughs or a cure for autism. Nonetheless, reliable research, done over a period of decades, now supports their use as a highly effective means of helping children with autism learn to communicate more effectively (e.g., Koegel & Koegel, 1995; Koegel, O'Dell, & Koegel, 1987; Koegel et al., 1982; Lovaas, 1987). To be sure, progress depends on careful, programatic research.

A current trend in language training for nonverbal children is to emphasize pragmatics—making language more practical in natural settings—for example, using a telephone to talk to a friend about something important.

Delayed Language Development

Children with language disorders may follow the same sequence of development as most children but achieve each skill or milestone at a later-than-average age (review Table 8.2). Some children with language disorders reach final levels of development significantly below those of their peers who do not have disabilities. Still other children may be generally delayed in language

development but show great discrepancies in the rate at which they acquire certain features of language.

Some children are "late bloomers" who in time will catch up with their age peers (Owens, 1995; Sowell, 1997). Yet many children whose language development is delayed show a developmental lag that they will not outgrow (Owens, 1997). They are frequently diagnosed as having mental retardation or another developmental disability. Sometimes these children come from environments where they have been deprived of many experiences, including the language stimulation from adults that is required for normal language development, or they have been severely abused or neglected. Regardless of the reasons for a child's delayed language, however, it is important to understand the nature of the delay and to intervene to give him or her the optimal chance of learning to use language effectively.

Some children three years of age or older show no signs that they understand language and do not use language spontaneously. They may make noises, but they use them to communicate in ways that may characterize the communication of infants and toddlers before they have learned speech. In other words, they may use **prelinguistic communication.** For example, they may use gestures or vocal noises to request objects or actions from others, to protest, to request a social routine (e.g., reading), or to greet someone (Ogletree, Wetherby, & Westling, 1992; Warren, Yoder, Gazdag, Kim, & Jones, 1993; Yoder, Warren, Kim, & Gazdag, 1994).

When assessing and planning intervention for children with delayed language, it is important to consider what language and nonlanguage behaviors they imitate, what they comprehend, what communication skills they use spontaneously, and what part communication plays in their lives. It is also important, particularly with young children, to provide intervention in contexts in which language is used for normal social interaction. For example, parents or teachers may use a **milieu teaching** approach, "a naturalistic language intervention designed to teach functional language skills" (Kaiser et al., 1995, p. 40). In this approach, teaching is built around the child's interests. When the child requests some action, object, or activity from the adult, the adult prompts the child's language and makes access to what is requested contingent on an attempt to communicate. Milieu teaching is a naturalistic approach, in that it encourages designing interventions that are similar to the conversational interactions that parents and children ordinarily have.

Early intervention with children who have delayed language is critically important for two primary reasons:

1. The older the child is before intervention is begun, the smaller the chance that he or she will acquire effective language skills (other things being equal).
2. Without having functional language, the child cannot become a truly social being (Warren & Abbaduto, 1992). Of all the skills in which a child may be lagging, language—communication—is the most important, as it is the foundation of academic and social learning.

prelinguistic communication. Communication through gestures and noises before the child has learned oral language.

milieu teaching. A naturalistic approach to language intervention in which the goal is to teach functional language skills in a natural environment.

Language Disorders Associated with Traumatic Brain Injury (TBI)

Most disabling conditions associated with language disorders are developmental in nature. That is, the communication problems are part of a developmental disorder such as cerebral palsy, mental retardation, or autism, and the child's language does not emerge normally. In traumatic brain injury (TBI), the individual may acquire a language disorder after a period of normal development, or he or she may acquire a more severe language disorder than existed prior to the injury. It is important to remember that individuals with TBI are a very diverse population, although "a disproportionate number of students with TBI have a pre-trauma history of learning problems or delayed speech and language" (Ylvisaker, Szekeres, Haarbauer-Krupa, Urbanczyk, & Feeney, 1994; see also Nelson, 1998).

A language disorder resulting from or worsened by TBI can be an extremely frustrating, even devastating, disability. In fact, language disorders may be the greatest complicating factor in most students' return to school following TBI (Blosser & DePompei, 1989). The brain injury may affect the student's speech (as described later in our discussion of speech disorders; see pp. 325–329) or language ability. A loss of ability to understand and formulate language due to brain injury is sometimes referred to as **acquired aphasia** (Swindell, Holland, & Reinmuth, 1994). The student with aphasia may have problems ranging from trouble finding or saying words to being unable to construct sentences that are appropriate for the topic of conversation or social context. Problems like these are a source of frustration, anger, and confusion for some students with TBI (Feenick & Judd, 1994).

The language problems acquired with TBI are primarily related to the cognitive and social demands of communication (Ylvisaker et al., 1994). The student may have problems with tasks that demand responding quickly, organizing, dealing with abstractions, sustaining attention (especially if there are distractions), learning new skills, responding appropriately in social situations, and showing appropriate affect. In fact, TBI can potentially disrupt all aspects of the give-and-take of social interaction that are required for effective communication.

The outcomes of TBI are extremely variable, and careful assessment of the given individual's abilities and disabilities is critically important. Interventions may range from making special accommodations—such as allowing more response time or keeping distractions to a minimum—to focusing on instruction in social skills.

Depending on the site and degree of brain damage, a person with TBI may have motor control problems that interfere with communication, with or without the cognitive and social aspects of communication disorders already discussed. Some students with TBI are not able to communicate orally using the muscles of speech and must rely on alternative or augmentative communication systems, described later (see pp. 317–322).

Language Disorders Associated with Emotional and Behavioral Disorders

Difficulty in using language in social interactions and relationships is now seen as a basic problem in many emotional and behavioral disorders, ranging from social reticence or withdrawal to severe acting out and aggression (Rogers-Adkinson & Griffith, 1999). Young children who have language disorders may have special difficulty in developing skills in social interaction because they do not interpret social circumstances correctly and have difficulty expressing themselves (Guralnick, Connor, Hammond, Gottman, & Kinnish, 1996). Donahue, Hartas, and Cole (1999) provide an example.

> In a kindergarten classroom, there are two adjacent (unisex) bathroom doors, each sporting almost identical pumpkin face posters. Almost invisible to the

acquired aphasia. Loss or impairment of the ability to understand or formulate language because of accident or illness.

adult eye, one pumpkin has the faintest suggestion of eyelashes (instead of triangle eyes, this pumpkin has rectangles with a jagged top). A boy identified as having a language disorder comes out of this bathroom and goes to his table. Another boy approaches him, saying:

Why did you go to the girls' bathroom? (*pointing to the pumpkin face*)

Huh?

You went to the girls' bathroom.

No—no—. That not girls'.

Yes it is.

No way—boys can too. (*voice rising*)

Yeah, there's a girl pumpkin on it.

But—but . . . that not a girl!! (*getting angry*)

Yeah, look at those eyelashes.

But—but . . . NOT! (*Splutters, jumps up and shoves the other boy. The teacher intervenes, and gives the child with the language disorder a time-out for fighting. He sits angrily, muttering to himself, "not a girl!"*) (p. 72)

The communication difficulties of students with emotional or behavioral disorders may require special classroom accommodations or programming. First, it is important for teachers of such students to work closely with a speech-language pathologist. Second, special care must be placed on clear teacher-to-student communication, student-to-student communication, and students' self-talk (Audet & Tankersley, 1999).

Perhaps the most important aspect of working with children who have emotional or behavioral problems related to a language disorder is understanding the child's intentions and helping him or her learn to use language to resolve social conflicts and build social relationships. Sowell (1997) provides an example of how a graduate student working in a classroom was able to do this with Billy, a four-year-old.

Apparently what the graduate student had that the teachers did not always have was common sense and a willingness—and the time—to try to understand a particular child's problem. Billy's biggest problems came out on the playground, where he did not have the skills to negotiate through social encounters. For example, if the graduate student noticed that Billy had his eye on a shovel that another child was using, she would ask him, "Do you want that shovel?" When he nodded, she would then prompt him, "Go ask the child, 'Can I have that shovel please?'" If he was not successful, the graduate student would say, "Ask him, 'Can I have it when you're done?'" Once Billy discovered that using phrases like these in various situations usually got better results than crying, he began to use them on his own. The graduate student also explained to Billy the unspoken social rules of the playground and of life, things that some teachers regard as a nuisance to do. (pp. 59–60)

Language disorders that are associated with emotional or behavioral disorders do not occur only in young children. Older students and adults also may have emotional or behavioral disorders that are in part a consequence of their inability to use language. They may well have language disorders, although their primary diagnosis may be attention deficit hyperactivity disorder, conduct disorder, anxiety disorder, depression, or some other psychiatric designation (Rogers-Adkinson, 1999).

Educational Considerations

Helping children overcome speech and language disorders is not the responsibility of any single profession. Rather, identification is the joint responsibility of the classroom teacher, the speech-language pathologist, and the parents (Nelson, 1997). The teacher can carry out specific suggestions for individual cases. By listening attentively and empathetically when children speak, providing appropriate models of speech and language for children to imitate, and encouraging children to use their communication skills appropriately, the classroom teacher can help not only to improve speech and language but also to prevent disorders from developing in the first place.

The primary role of the classroom teacher is to facilitate the *social use of language*. Phonology, morphology, syntax, and semantics are certainly important. Yet the fact that a student has a language disorder does not necessarily mean the teacher or clinician must intensify efforts to teach the student about the form, structure, or content of language. Rather, language must be taught as a way of solving problems by making oneself understood and making sense of what other people say.

The classroom offers many possibilities for language learning. It should be a place in which there are almost continuous opportunities for students and teachers to employ language and obtain feedback in constructive relationships. Language is the basic medium through which most academic and social learning takes place in school. Nevertheless, the language of school, in both classrooms and textbooks, is often a problem for students and teachers (Nelson, 1998; Owens, 1995).

School language is more formal than the language many children use at home and with playmates. It is structured discourse, in which listeners and speakers or readers and writers must learn to be clear and expressive, to convey and interpret essential information quickly and easily. Without skill in using the language of school, a child is certain to fail academically, and virtually certain to be socially unsuccessful as well.

Teachers need the assistance of speech-language specialists in assessing their students' language disabilities and in devising interventions. Part of the assessment and intervention strategy must also examine the language of the teacher. Problems in classroom discourse involve how teachers talk to students as well as how students use language. Learning how to be clear, relevant, and informative and how to hold listeners' attention are not only problems for students with language disorders but also problems for their teachers. Table 8.4 lists some general guidelines for how parents and teachers should interact with students to facilitate language development.

One example of the role of the teacher's language in classroom discourse is asking questions. Blank and White (1986) note that teachers often ask students questions in areas of their identified weaknesses. For example, a teacher might ask a preschooler who does not know colors to identify colors repeatedly. Unfortunately, teachers may not know how to modify their questions to teach concepts effectively, so their questions merely add to children's confusion.

The following exchange between a teacher and a child diagnosed as having difficulties with problem solving and causal reasoning illustrates this point:

Teacher: How could grass in a jungle get on fire?
Child: 'Cause they (*referring to animals*) have to stay in the jungle.
Teacher: (*in an incredulous tone*) You mean the grass gets on fire because the animals stay in the jungle?

Garden City, NY: College student **Ryan McGarr** has overcome difficulties in speech and language processing as well as problems with memory and organization since being severely injured in a car accident on Thanksgiving Day, 1992. Ryan remained comatose for three days with a traumatic brain injury and fractures to his hip and

legs. "I know it happened," says Ryan, "but I still find it hard to believe." His mother, Kathy McGarr, finds it hard to forget. Although Ryan's physical injuries healed quickly, his residual difficulties in language and cognitive processing presented an academic challenge. Fortunately, an innovative special education project came to his assistance, providing a bridge between rehabilitation services and school reentry.

Special educator Nancy Maher-Maxwell coordinates the New York State Education Department's TBI Project for the Board of Cooperative Educational Services of Nassau County. Hospitals, rehabilitation centers, and school districts know to give her name to families who face the maze of issues following their children's head injuries. Since 1991, the project has coordinated services to support families and train teachers to meet the individual needs of students reentering their classrooms.

Kathy McGarr is grateful that someone at the hospital told her about the project: "Just the trauma and trying to take care of your other children— the whole family tends to fall apart. I didn't have the concentration or anything to deal with this." Nancy Maher-Maxwell understands this: "Research is showing that kids who have this connection between rehabilitation and school reentry, as well as the ongoing staff support once they've returned, have a greater success rate than those who don't. The gulf between rehabilitation and school reentry is too big for families to have to negotiate on their own."

In Ryan's case, several factors combined to make a successful outcome possible, including coordinated services, compensatory instructional strategies, strong support from family and friends, spontaneous neurological recovery, and his own spirit and desire to achieve.

Others were aware of this determination, too. His mother recalls, "The psychologist at the hospital, who evaluated Ryan nine weeks after the accident, told me he would probably never finish school and that I was overwhelming him with academics. But it was what he wanted and I had to let him try to do it." Nancy Maher-Maxwell met Ryan six weeks after the accident and remembers his using crutches and speaking in a slow, monotone voice. He said he was determined to graduate with his class and wanted tutoring.

Child: Yeah.
Teacher: I don't think so. What if there was a fire in somebody's house—
Child: (*interrupting*) Then they're dead, or hurt.
Teacher: Yeah, they'd be hurt. But how would a fire start in somebody's house?
Child: By starting something with matches.
Teacher: A match, okay. Now do you think this could have started with a match?
Child: Yeah.
Teacher: This fire in the jungle? Who would have a match in the jungle? The animals?
Child: A monkey.
Teacher: A monkey would have a match in the jungle?
Child: (*nodding*) I saw that on TV. (Blank & White, 1986, p. 4.)

To start the process, Nancy contacted Ryan's school district. His former English teacher, Maria Webster, agreed to be his home tutor. Despite Ryan's memory problems and slowness in learning, Maria was optimistic; she remembered Ryan as an expressive writer. With Nancy's help, Maria's lessons were individualized, concentrating on vocabulary and word meanings. She used flash cards and, together with Ryan, made up funny sentences using mnemonics to help him remember information. Instead of giving him a chapter to read in history, Maria "chunked" the material to be learned, breaking it into smaller units. Ryan remembers that being helpful: "It used to be that I even had to reread novels two or three times just to get the meaning."

Kathy McGarr recalls that it was hard to tell if Ryan would regain his language abilities. "In speech therapy, he had a terrible time with categorization skills. His therapist asked him to name five green vegetables, and he couldn't do it! What was even more surprising was that he couldn't imagine that anyone could!"

Ryan returned to school part-time in April 1993. He went to an outpatient rehab for therapies in the morning and then to his local public high school in the afternoon for English, social studies, art, and resource room. He returned full-time for his senior year, carrying a full program of academic courses, with resource room support for forty-five minutes daily.

The TBI project coordinated Ryan's reentry into the regular educational environment by providing inservice workshops as well as personal and continual support for his teachers. They were alerted to changes in Ryan's cognitive processing, such as his memory for sequences used in multistep problem solving. Training emphasized Ryan's need to take in new information in a variety of ways, so teachers were shown techniques to reinforce study skills, like taking notes on lectures, outlining chapters, and organizing projects. As Nancy Maher-Maxwell explains, "Often, the typical high school teacher will lecture on the subject, expect the kids to take good notes, and evaluate them on a test. Because of the disruptions in the learning systems of students with TBI, there may be a slower rate in processing, so extended time is often necessary both in teaching and in testing."

TBI is an acquired injury that demands new adjustments. "If I hadn't spoken with Nancy," says Kathy McGarr, "I wouldn't have known to put Ryan in a resource room, since he never needed special education before." Head injuries can also make the future hard to predict. Nancy recalls, "That early neuropsychological evaluation that said he could forget about his academic aspirations never took into account Ryan's determination and the compensatory strategies that special education could provide. It was devastating to everybody—and look how wrong such a prediction can be with TBI!"

Ryan has been fortunate. He spontaneously regained much of his academic strength, and now he can see how far he has come: "When I look back, I realize how slow I was as a result of the head injury." Ryan still finds that he is more easily distracted than he used to be, and he continues to need extended time on some college exams. Nevertheless, he has emerged confident: "I'll succeed in the world doing whatever I want to do. I have no doubts about that."

—By Jean Crockett

After seventeen more exchanges, the teacher gave up.

Alternative question-asking strategies can be used to help students think through problems successfully. When a student fails to answer a higher-order question because it is beyond his or her level of information or skill, the teacher should reformulate the problem at a simpler level. After the intermediate steps are solved, the teacher can return to the question that was too difficult at first, as illustrated by the following dialogue:

Adult: Why do we use tape for hanging pictures?
Child: 'Cause it's shiny.
Adult: Here's a shiny piece of paper and here's a shiny piece of tape. Let's try them both. Try hanging the picture with the shiny paper.
Child: (*does it*)

Adult: Does it work?
Child: No, it's falling.
Adult: Now, try the tape.
Child: (*does it*)
Adult: Does it work?
Child: Yeah, it's not falling.
Adult: So, why do we use the tape for hanging pictures?
Child: It won't fall. (Blank & White, 1986, p. 5)

Teachers sometimes do not clearly express their intent in questioning students or fail to explicitly delimit the topic of their questions. Consequently, students become confused. Teachers must learn to clarify the problems under such circumstances. As Blank and White (1986) note, "Teachers do not establish psychological comfort and eagerness to learn by making students spend as much, if not more, energy deciphering the intent than the content of their questions" (p. 8). Teachers must also give unambiguous feedback to students' responses to their questions. Too often, teachers do not tell students explicitly that their answers are wrong, for fear of showing nonacceptance. Lack of accurate, explicit feedback, however, prevents students from learning the concepts involved in instruction.

Our points here are these:

1. The teacher's role is not merely to instruct students *about* language but also to teach them *how to use it.* More specifically, the teacher must help students learn *how to use language in the context of the classroom.*
2. The teacher's own use of language is a key factor in helping students learn effectively, *especially if students have language disorders.*

Written language is a special problem for many students with language disorders. In fact, as students progress through the grades, written language takes on increasing importance. Students are expected to read increasingly complex and difficult material and understand its meaning. In addition, they are expected to express themselves more clearly in writing. The interactions teachers have with students about their writing—the questions they ask to help students understand how to write for their readers—are critical to overcoming disabilities in written language (Graham, Harris, MacArthur, & Schwartz, 1998; Wong, Wong, Darlington, & Jones, 1991).

Finally, we note that intervention in language disorders employs many of the same strategies used in intervention in learning disabilities (Mann, 1998; Seidenberg, 1997). As discussed earlier, the definitions of *specific language disability* and *specific learning disability* are parallel, if not nearly synonymous. Metacognitive training, strategy training, and other approaches that we discuss in Chapter 6 are typically appropriate for use with students who have language disorders (see also Hallahan, Kauffman, & Lloyd, 1999; Wallach & Butler, 1994).

An attitude of acceptance and openness to a child's language can go a long way in encouraging improvement.

Table 8.4   Guidelines for Parents' and Teachers' Interactive Styles

1	Talk about things in which the child is interested.
2	Follow the child's lead. Reply to the child's initiations and comments. Share his excitement.
3	Don't ask too many questions. If you must, use questions such as *how did/do . . .*, *why did/do . . .*, *and what happened . . .* that result in longer explanatory answers.
4	Encourage the child to ask questions. Respond openly and honestly. If you don't want to answer a question, say so and explain why. (*I don't think I want to answer that question; it's very personal.*)
5	Use a pleasant tone of voice. You need not be a comedian, but you can be light and humorous. Children love it when adults are a little silly.
6	Don't be judgmental or make fun of a child's language. If you are overly critical of the child's language or try to "shotgun" all errors, he will stop talking to you.
7	Allow enough time for the child to respond.
8	Treat the child with courtesy by not interrupting when he is talking.
9	Include the child in family and classroom discussions. Encourage participation and listen to his ideas.
10	Be accepting of the child and of the child's language. Hugs and acceptance can go a long way.
11	Provide opportunities for the child to use language and to have that language work for him to accomplish his goals.

Source: From R. E. Owens, *Language disorders: A functional approach to assessment and intervention* (2nd ed.). Copyright © 1995 by Allyn & Bacon. Adapted by permission.

Augmentative and Alternative Communication

For some individuals, oral language is out of the question; they have physical or cognitive disabilities that preclude their learning to communicate through normal speech. A system of *augmentative* or *alternative communication* (AAC) must be designed for them. AAC includes any manual or electronic means by which such a person expresses wants and needs, shares information, engages in social closeness, or manages social etiquette (Franklin & Beukelman, 1991; Lloyd, Fuller, & Arvidson, 1997).

Students for whom AAC must be designed range in intelligence from highly gifted to profoundly retarded, but they all have one characteristic in common—the inability to communicate effectively through speech because of a physical impairment. Some of these individuals may be unable to make any speech sounds at all; others need a system to augment their speech when they cannot make themselves understood because of environmental noise, difficulty in producing certain words or sounds, or unfamiliarity with the person with whom they want to communicate.

As Franklin and Beukelman (1991) note, manual signs or gestures may be useful for some individuals. But many individuals with severe physical limitations are

Individuals whose motor disabilities prevent them from communicating orally may benefit from augmentative and alternative communication systems; two different types are shown here.

unable to use their hands to communicate through gestures or signs; they must use another means of communication, usually involving special equipment. The problems to be solved in helping these individuals communicate include selecting a vocabulary and giving them an effective, efficient means of indicating elements in their vocabularies. Although the basic ideas behind AAC are quite simple, selecting the best vocabulary and devising an efficient means of indication for many individuals with severe disabilities are extraordinarily challenging.

A variety of approaches to AAC have been developed, some involving relatively simple or so-called low-technology solutions and some requiring complex or high-technology solutions (Lloyd et al., 1997). Many different direct-selection and scanning methods have been devised for AAC, depending on individual capabilities. The system used may involve pointing with the hand or a headstick, eye movements, or operation of a microswitch by foot, tongue, head movement, or breath control. Sometimes, the individual can use a typewriter or computer terminal fitted with a key guard, so that keys are not likely to be pressed accidentally, or use an alternative means for selecting keystrokes. Often, communication boards are used. A *communication board* is an array of pictures, words, or other symbols that can be operated with either a direct-selection or scanning strategy. The content and arrangement of the board will vary, depending on the person's capabilities, preferences, and communication needs.

Speed, reliability, portability, cost, and overall effectiveness in helping a person communicate independently are factors to be considered in designing and evaluating AAC (Lloyd et al., 1997). Some AAC systems are very slow, unreliable (either because of the equipment or a poor match with the abilities of the user), cumbersome, or useful only in very restricted settings. Beukelman (1991) notes that while people typically think of the equipment and material costs involved in AAC, the real costs must include instruction and learning. A communication board will not necessarily be useful just because it is available. And the most sophisticated technological solution to communication is not always the one that will be most useful in the long run.

Today, increasingly innovative and creative technological solutions to the problem of nonvocal communication are being found. At the same time, the importance of making decisions on a highly individual basis has been recognized (Calculator & Jorgensen, 1991). Until rather recently, AAC was seen primarily as a means of allowing users to demonstrate the language skills they have already acquired. But now there is increasing emphasis on how AAC is used as a tool for teaching language—for helping AAC users not only to give voice to what they feel and know about specific tasks but also to acquire increasingly sophisticated language skills (Nelson, 1998).

Researchers are attempting to make it possible for young AAC users to talk about the same kinds of things that other youngsters do (Marvin, Beukelman, Brockhaus, & Kast, 1994). Other efforts are directed at training AAC users to tell those with whom they communicate how to interact with them more effectively— that is, to train AAC users in pragmatics. The box on page 322 summarizes how Vivian, a twelve-year-old sixth grader with quadriplegia due to cerebral palsy, was taught to understand and resolve her friends' problematic styles of interacting with her (Buzolich & Lunger, 1995). Vivian used an AAC device called a Light Talker, which allowed her to select letters and programmed phrases (represented by icons) for output from a computerized display by pointing an infrared light sensor attached to her glasses. Notice how Vivian was taught to recognize communicative problems, such as her friends being positioned where she could not see them, and use explicit language strategies to overcome them.

Users of AAC encounter three particular challenges not faced by natural communicators:

1. AAC is much slower than natural communication—perhaps one-twentieth the typical rate of speech. This can result in great frustration for both the AAC users and natural communicators.
2. Users of AAC who are not literate must rely on a vocabulary and symbols that are selected by others. If the vocabulary and symbols, as well as other features of the system, are not well chosen, AAC will be quite limited in the learning and personal relationships it allows.
3. AAC must be constructed to be useful in a variety of social contexts, allow accurate and efficient communication without undue fatigue, and support the individual's learning of language and academic skills (Franklin & Beukelman, 1991; Lloyd et al., 1997).

Progress in the field of AAC requires that all of these challenges be addressed simultaneously.

The need for AAC is increasing as more people with severe disabilities are surviving and taking their places in the community. As more students with severe disabilities are integrated into regular educational programs at all levels, the availability and appropriate use of AAC in such classrooms become more critical issues (Calculator & Jorgensen, 1991; Lloyd et al., 1997).

The remarkable increase in the power and availability of microcomputers is radically changing our ability to provide AAC. New applications of microcomputers may lead to breakthroughs that will allow people with severe disabilities to communicate more effectively, even if they have extremely limited muscle control. Furthermore, existing microcomputer software suggests ways of encouraging children to use their existing language skills. Technological developments will no doubt revolutionize AAC as we enter the twenty-first century (Quist, Lloyd, & McDowell, 1997).

One type of AAC that burst upon the scene in the early 1990s is called *facilitated communication* (FC), in which a facilitator physically assists the user in typing out messages on a keyboard or in pointing to items on a communication board. Proponents of FC have reported that it reveals unexpected intelligence and literacy in many individuals with severe developmental disabilities, including autism and mental retardation. However, reliable research has not supported the

Collaboration key to success

Julie Bell is a speech-language pathologist, Ashby-Lee Elementary and North Fork Middle Schools, Shenandoah County, Virginia, Public Schools; B.S., Education, Indiana University of Pennsylvania; M.S., Speech-Language Pathology, James Madison University; Certification of Clinical Competence in Speech-Language Pathology, American Speech-Language-Hearing Association. **Stephanie Dysart** is a first/second grade teacher, Ashby-Lee Elementary School, Shenandoah County, Virginia, Public Schools; B.S., Sociology, Bridgewater College; M.Ed., Elementary Education, James Madison University.

Julie Bell

Julie My caseload includes fifty-two children from preschool through eighth grade. The preschool children I serve are a combination of those attending community-based preschools, early childhood special education classes, and home-based programs. School-age children on my caseload are placed in both general and special education classrooms. The types of speech-language disorders I work with include: articulation and phonological disorders, fluency, voice and hearing impairments, as well as language disorders (expressive/receptive language and pragmatics). My roles include evaluation, diagnosis, and remediation. Students are served through monitoring and consultation, resource, or integration in the general education classroom. The Integrated Therapy Model (ITM) allows for team teaching and planning with the regular classroom teacher. I have incorporated this model in grades one through four.

Stephanie My multi-age classroom consists of twenty-five students: twelve first graders and thirteen

second graders. The students are working at various academic levels and are receiving resource services. Seven students participate in a daily language resource program. Ten children receive Title I or reading services, and ten receive speech and language services. Two students in my room participate in gifted and talented education activities. With a large number of students receiving speech/language services, I team teach once a week with Julie. This ITM model helps students generalize their speech and language skills in the general education classroom.

Julie We'll describe our work with Becky, a six-year-old. Our discussion focuses on initial referral, the evaluation process, and the IEP, as well as intervention strategies.

Stephanie Becky came into my classroom as a first-grade student and will "loop" with me to second grade. Throughout her kindergarten year she received remedial services for language arts. She continued to receive these services as a first grader. Becky

demonstrated growth in reading and writing skills, but she continued to have difficulty organizing, recalling, and processing information. For example, Becky cannot retell a story accurately and is challenged by directions requiring two or more steps. In addition, she frequently exhibits difficulty in relaying coherent messages. She often will not refer to the topic and excludes pertinent information. This leaves the listener with the task of probing for information. I held conferences with her father, and he reported observing similar behaviors at home.

Julie Stephanie approached me about her concerns regarding Becky. We decided to complete some observations of Becky while we were team teaching. We found that while Becky is successful with social communication, academic exchanges are difficult for her. Becky is a child who is easily distracted and appears to have difficulty processing information.

Stephanie Before referring Becky for a language evaluation, we tried

Stephanie Dysart

several in-classroom strategies. During class discussions I would present a question to one student and then redirect the same question to Becky. I could then determine if she actually comprehended the information. I also had her repeat directions aloud, used visuals, and provided time for her to complete one step before giving the next step in a series of directions. These same strategies were also used by Becky's resource teacher. Although these strategies seemed to help Becky, I still had concerns about her processing skills.

Julie At this point we decided to recommend a formal language evaluation. Becky's teachers were extremely interested in the types of evaluation tools I planned to use. We met and discussed several assessment tools and the skills they measure. Results of this evaluation confirmed our suspicions of a language processing deficit as well as expressive language difficulties related to coherency of verbal output. We met with Becky's father to review the evaluation results and develop an IEP that would meet Becky's needs.

We colla orated with Becky's father to develop appropriate goals and determine frequency of speech-language services for the upcoming year. We felt that daily services would most benefit Becky. These services would be provided first thing in the morning to prepare her for the upcoming school day. She would also receive services in the classroom. In each daily session, we would practice and review language processing strategies. Since writing is a strength for Becky, we felt a daily log would be appropriate. The log would include Becky's strategies for use in class, as well as assignment sheets.

Stephanie To make this successful for Becky, in addition to our daily contact, Julie and I needed to plan formally once a week. Whether in the hall, on the phone, before or after school, it was important to touch base daily on what was or was not working. We used our weekly planning time to develop units to be team taught and to discuss activities used during Becky's language sessions. We also needed to communicate with Becky's physical education, music, and art teachers to make them aware of strategies being used with Becky. Our purpose was to facilitate her success in all school environments.

> **Through team teaching and collaborative planning, we are able to exchange and model intervention strategies.**

Julie After we had addressed some of the language processing problems, we needed to focus on her coherency skills. Once again, I felt visuals would be helpful to Becky, so I developed a "cue card" for her desk top and notebook. The "cue card" contained pictures that reminded her to express the following key points: who, what, where, and why.

Stephanie In the classroom, my job was to prompt her to use this card by specifying the information needed in her responses. It might have been as simple as a nonverbal cue. I simply pointed to one of the pictures on her cue card to help her organize her thoughts and prepare to respond.

Julie By teaming together, we're not only able to meet students' needs, but we're also finding out that these students make progress in a shorter period of time. Through team teaching and collaborative planning, we are able to exchange and model intervention strategies. We also share and gain information regarding the effects of speech and language skills on students' academic progress. Teaming has made me more aware of how I can incorporate the general education curriculum into my pull-out sessions and what a difference it makes when working with the students. They are able to make connections between their curriculum work and the goals and objectives we are focusing on relative to their speech and language skills.

Stephanie There has to be willingness and dedication on the part of both teachers involved in teaming, as well as the understanding that we both bring expertise to meet our shared goal of helping the student succeed.

321

AAC Pragmatics Training

What Able-Bodied Kids Are Likely to Do When They Talk to You and What You Can Do About It

Friend's Style	System User's Strategy (Vivian)
Friend stands/sits in a position that is uncomfortable for you.	Let your friend know in a nice way that you'd rather have him or her be somewhere else when you're talking. For example, "Can you sit next to me here?" or "Can you come over here where I can see you?"
Friend asks lots of yes/no questions.	Answer yes/no then program additional information on your Talker; e.g., "Yes, I saw *Wayne's World* and I loved it," or answer yes/no then ask partner a question, "No, I didn't. What did you do?"
Friend brings up all the topics.	Switch to a related topic when you finish talking about your friend's topic. Use a phrase such as "Do you know what?" to prepare your friend for a new topic.
Friend does all the talking.	Use a phrase such as "It'll take me a minute to spell what I want to say," "Just a minute," "Wait a second," "I need more time" to alert your friend to use some waiting strategies and give you enough time to talk.
Friend doesn't understand you but acts like he/she does.	Check in with your friend to be sure he/she is understanding you if you suspect he/she isn't: e.g., if your friend doesn't say anything or has a confused look on his/her face, ask him/her, "Did you understand that?" or "Do you know what I mean?" Tell your friend exactly what you are going to do: e.g., "I'll say it again," "Wait, let me say it differently."
Friend watches as you prepare a message but doesn't say anything.	Let your partner know what you want him or her to do as you spell. "Say each letter as I point to it." "Please predict as I spell."

Source: "Empowering system users in peer training," by M. J. Buzolich & J. Lunger, 1995, *Augmentative and Alternative Communication, 11,* p. 41. Reprinted with permission of Decker Periodicals, Inc.

validity or authenticity of FC, and it is not a recommended ACC technique (see Blischak, Loncke, & Waller, 1997; Mesibov, 1995; Montee et al., 1995; Quist, Lloyd, & McDowell, 1997; Shane, 1994; Simpson & Myles, 1995).

In sum, new methods should be developed to allow people with severe disabilities to communicate (Lloyd et al., 1997; Montee et al., 1995). However, any AAC procedure must represent the communication of the user, not someone else. If FC or any other AAC device misrepresents the user's communication, then it demeans the user through pretense. This is not acceptable, as all people with disabilities should be treated with dignity and respect.

Communication Variations

As defined earlier in this chapter (see the box on p. 299), *communication variations* include language that is unique to a particular region, ethnic group, or other cultural group. Thus, the fact that a student does not use the language expected in school does not necessarily mean that he or she has a language disorder. Of course, an individual may both have a language disorder and exhibit a variation that is not a disorder; such an individual will be unable to communicate effectively even with others who use the same language variation (see Battle, 1993).

Encouraging the communication of children whose cultural heritage or language patterns are not those of the professionals' microculture is of increasing concern to classroom teachers and speech-language clinicians. (See Chapter 3 for a discussion of microculture.) On the one hand, care must be taken not to mistake a cultural or ethnic difference for a disorder; on the other hand, disorders existing in the context of a language difference must not be overlooked (Nelson, 1998; Ortiz, 1997; Van Keulen, Weddington, & DeBose, 1998). When assessing children's language, the professional must be aware of the limitations of normative tests and other sources of potential bias.

A child may not have a language disorder yet have a communicative difference that demands special teaching. Delpit (1995), Foster (1986), and Van Keulen et al. (1998) discuss the need for teaching children of nondominant cultures the rules for effective communication in the dominant culture while understanding and accepting the effectiveness of the children's home languages in their cultural contexts. Failure to teach children the skills they need to communicate effectively according to the rules of the dominant culture will deny them many opportunities. In effect, children of minority language groups may need to learn to live in two worlds—one in which their home language is used and one in which school language is used (Westby & Roman, 1995).

Nelson (1998) notes that many students for whom language difference is an issue do not speak entirely different languages, but variations peculiar to certain groups of speakers—that is, *dialects*. For example, one dialect that is different from standard English (and is not a language disorder) is Appalachian English. People in Appalachia speak a variation of English with features not shared by other English dialects. Teachers must understand—and help their students understand—that other dialects are not inferior or limited language systems (Seymour, Champion, & Jackson, 1995; Van Keulen et al., 1998). Furthermore, cultural differences must be recognized regardless of the communication device being used. Multicultural issues arise in all communication interactions, including those in which AAC is used (Soto, Huer, & Taylor, 1997).

Recently, researchers have turned their attention to how the language of different cultural groups is related to school learning. Anderson and Battle (1993) and Westby (1994) note that different cultural groups provide very different language environments for infants and young children. However, these differences are more often matters of social class than ethnicity. "Socioeconomic status is more critical to the development of language than race or ethnicity" (Anderson & Battle, 1993, p. 180).

Families also differ greatly in the ways they talk to children and in the language they expect children to use. Conversational interactions—called **narratives**—differ widely in families. Narratives can be classified as **genres,** which are purposes or plans for discourse—for example, to recount recent events, to explain the reason for doing something, or to tell an imaginative story.

Children's experiences with language prior to coming to school are an important factor in determining how they respond to the language demands of the classroom. Although students may not have language *disorders,* their language *variations* may put them at a disadvantage in using language in an academic context. Consider the cultural variations across narrative genres described by Westby (1994) in Table 8.5. The major implication of these differences is that teachers must be

narrative. Self-controlled, self-initiated discourse; description or storytelling.

genre. A plan or map for discourse; type of narrative discourse.

Table 8.5   Cultural Variations in Narrative Genres

	CULTURE				
Genre	Mainstream	Mexican American	Chinese American	White Working Class	Black Working Class
Recounts (Tell Daddy about our trip to . . .)	Common with young children Open-ended scaffolding Invitations to recount decrease with age	Rare	Rare	Predominant genre Tightly scaffolded	Rare
Accounts (Did you hear what happened to . . .?)	Begun before two years Adults request further explanation Adults suggest alternative outcomes Adults assess attitudes and actions of actor	Frequent Occur especially in family gathering	At home; asked about events of day Not outside the home or with strangers	Not until school Must be accurate Privilege of older adults	Frequent in response to teasing Exaggeration values May be produced cooperatively
Eventcasts (I'm putting the soda in the chest, and then I'll load the car.)	Begun with preverbal Continue throughout the preschool	Almost never in daily events Family may cooperatively plan future events	Occur during on-going activities More frequent for girls than boys	In play with young children In planning family projects with older children	Rare
Stories (Once upon a time . . .)	Frequent story reading Story comprehension negotiated Produce own imaginative stories	Bruja tales Stories about real events embellished with new details and about historical figures and events Children's literature absent	Tales about historical people and events Prefer informational rather than fictional books	Listen to stories read Comprehension not negotiated	No children's storybooks

Source: From C. E. Westby, "The effects of culture and genre, structure, and style of oral and written texts," in *Language learning disabilities in school-age children and adolescents: Some principles and applications,* edited by G. P. Wallach & K. G. Butler. Copyright © 1994 by Allyn & Bacon. Reprinted by permission.

able to understand linguistic variations and help students generate narratives through skillful questioning that will help them comprehend and learn to use the language of school.

A major concern today in both special and general education is teaching children who are learning English as a second language (ESL), who are non–English proficient (NEP), or who have limited English proficiency (LEP). Bilingual education is a field of concern and controversy because of the rapidly changing demo-

The Speech-Language Pathologist

A speech-language pathologist is a highly trained professional capable of assuming a variety of roles in assisting persons who have speech and language disorders. Entering the profession requires rigorous training and demonstration of clinical skills under close supervision. Certification requires completion of a master's degree in a program approved by the American Speech-Language-Hearing Association (ASHA). You may want to write to ASHA, 10801 Rockville Pike, Rockville, MD 20852 for a free booklet, *Careers in Speech-Language Pathology and Audiology.*

Because of the emphasis on *least restrictive environment,* or mainstreaming (see Chapters 1 and 2), speech-language pathologists are doing more of their work in regular classrooms and are spending more time consulting with classroom teachers than they have in the past.

Speech-language pathologists of the future will need more knowledge of classroom procedures and the academic curriculum—especially in reading, writing, and spelling—and will be more involved in the overall education of children with communication disorders. More emphasis will be placed on working as a team member in the schools to see that children with disabilities obtain appropriate educations. Because of legislation and changing population demographics, speech-language pathologists of the future will also probably be more involved with preschool children and those with learning disabilities and severe, multiple disabilities. There will be broader concern for the entire range of communication disorders, including both oral and written communication.

graphics in many American communities (see Crawford, 1992; Nelson, 1998). Spanish-speaking children comprise a rapidly growing percentage of the students in many school districts. Moreover, a large number of Asian/Pacific children have immigrated to the United States during the past decade. Many of these children have no proficiency or limited proficiency in English, and some have disabilities as well. Bilingual special education is "an emerging discipline with a brief history" (Baca & Amato, 1989, p. 168). As we discussed in Chapter 3, finding the best way to teach children to become proficient in English, particularly when they have disabilities as well as language differences, is a special challenge for the new century.

Speech Disorders

As we noted at the beginning of the chapter, speech disorders include disorders of voice, articulation, and fluency. Remember that an individual may have more than one speech disorder and that speech and language disorders sometimes occur together.

We provide only brief descriptions of the major speech disorders for two reasons:

1. Compared to language disorders, speech disorders pose a much smaller problem for classroom teachers.
2. Most speech disorders will be treated primarily by speech-language pathologists, not classroom teachers. Teachers are expected to be aware of possible speech disorders and to refer students they suspect of having such disorders for evaluation by speech-language pathologists. Furthermore, teachers are expected to work with speech-language pathologists to help students correct speech as well as language disorders in the classroom (see the box above).

Voice Disorders

People's voices are perceived as having pitch, loudness, and quality. Changes in pitch and loudness are part of the stress patterns of speech. Vocal quality is related not only to production of speech sounds but also to the nonlinguistic aspects of speech.

Voice disorders, though difficult to define precisely, are characteristics of pitch, loudness, and/or quality that are abusive of the **larynx;** hamper communication; or are perceived as markedly different from what is customary for someone of a given age, sex, and cultural background. Voice disorders can result from a variety of biological and nonbiological causes, including growths in the larynx (e.g., nodules, polyps, or cancerous tissue), infections of the larynx (laryngitis), damage to the nerves supplying the larynx, or accidental bruises or scratches on the larynx (Haynes & Pindzola, 1998). Misuse or abuse of the voice also can lead to a quality that is temporarily abnormal. High school cheerleaders, for example, frequently develop temporary voice disorders (Campbell, Reich, Klockars, & McHenry, 1988). Disorders resulting from misuse or abuse can damage the tissues of the larynx. Sometimes a person has psychological problems that lead to a complete loss of voice (aphonia) or to severe voice abnormalities.

Voice disorders having to do with **resonance**—vocal quality—may be caused by physical abnormalities of the oral cavity (such as **cleft palate**) or damage to the brain or nerves controlling the oral cavity. Infections of the tonsils, adenoids, or sinuses can also influence how the voice is resonated. Most people who have severe hearing loss typically have problems in achieving a normal or pleasingly resonant voice. Finally, sometimes a person simply has not learned to speak with an appropriately resonant voice. There are no biological or deep-seated psychological reasons for the problem; rather, it appears that he or she has learned faulty habits of positioning the organs of speech (Moore & Hicks, 1994).

When children are screened for speech and language disorders, the speech-language pathologist is looking for problems in voice quality, resonance, pitch, loudness, and duration. If a problem is found, referral to a physician is indicated. A medical report may indicate that surgery or other treatment is needed because of a growth or infection. Aside from the medical evaluation, the speech-language pathologist will evaluate when the problem began and how the individual uses his or her voice in everyday situations and under stressful circumstances. Besides looking for how voice is produced and structural or functional problems, the pathologist also looks for signs of infection or disease that may be contributing to the disorder as well as for signs of serious illness.

Articulation Disorders

Articulation disorders involve errors in producing words. Word sounds may be omitted, substituted, distorted, or added. Lisping, for example, involves a substitution or distortion of the [s] sound (e.g., *thunthine* or *shunshine* for *sunshine*). Missing, substituted, added, or poorly produced word sounds may make a speaker difficult to understand or even unintelligible. Such errors in speech production may also carry heavy social penalties, subjecting the speaker to teasing or ridicule.

When are articulation errors considered a disorder? That depends on a clinician's subjective judgment, which will be influenced by his or her experience, the number and types of errors, the consistency of these errors, the age and developmental characteristics of the speaker, and the intelligibility of the person's speech.

larynx. The structure in the throat containing the vocal apparatus (vocal cords); laryngitis is a temporary loss of voice caused by inflammation of the larynx.

resonance. The quality of the sound imparted by the size, shape, and texture of the organs in the vocal tract.

cleft palate. A condition in which there is a rift or split in the upper part of the oral cavity; may include the upper lip (cleft lip).

Young children make frequent errors in speech sounds when they are learning to talk. Many children do not master all the phonological rules of the language and learn to produce all the speech sounds correctly until they are eight or nine years old. Furthermore, most children make frequent errors until after they enter school. The age of the child is thus a major consideration in judging the adequacy of articulation. Another major consideration is the phonological characteristics of the child's community, because children learn speech largely through imitation. For instance, a child reared in the deep South may have speech that sounds peculiar to residents of Long Island, but that does not mean that the child has a speech disorder.

The number of children having difficulty producing word sounds decreases markedly during the first three or four years of elementary school. Among children with other disabilities, especially mental retardation and neurological disorders like cerebral palsy, the prevalence of articulation disorders is higher than in the general population (Schwartz, 1994).

Lack of ability to articulate speech sounds correctly can be caused by biological factors. For example, brain damage or damage to the nerves controlling the muscles used in speech may make it difficult or impossible to articulate sounds (Bernthal & Bankson, 1998: Cannito, Yorkston, & Beukelman, 1998). Furthermore, abnormalities of the oral structures, such as a cleft palate, may make normal speech difficult or impossible. Relatively minor structural changes, such as loss of teeth, may produce temporary errors. Delayed phonological development may also result from a hearing loss.

The parents of a preschool child may refer him or her for assessment if he or she has speech that is really difficult to understand. Most schools screen all new pupils for speech and language problems, and in most cases a child who still makes many articulation errors in the third or fourth grade will be referred for evaluation. Older children and adults sometimes seek help on their own when their speech draws negative attention. A speech-language pathologist will assess not only phonological characteristics but also social and developmental history, hearing, general language ability, and speech mechanism.

Although speech-language pathologists' interest in articulation disorders has appeared to decrease in recent years, with more attention being given to language, persistent articulation disorders may have serious long-term consequences. The decision about whether to include a child in an intervention program will depend on his or her age, other developmental characteristics, and the type and consistency of the articulatory errors. Articulation disorders are often accompanied by other disorders of speech or language; thus, the child may need intervention in multiple aspects of communication (Hodson & Edwards, 1997; Nelson, 1998). The decision will also depend on the pathologist's assessment of the likelihood that the child will self-correct the errors and of the social penalties, such as teasing and shyness, the child is experiencing. If he or she misarticulates only a few sounds but does so consistently and suffers social embarrassment or rejection as a consequence, an intervention program is usually called for.

Fluency Disorders

Normal speech is characterized by some interruptions in speech flow. We occasionally get speech sounds in the wrong order (*revalent* for *relevant*), speak too quickly to be understood, pause at the wrong place in a sentence, use an inappropriate pattern of stress, or become *disfluent*—that is, stumble and backtrack, repeating syllables or words, and fill in pauses with *uh* while trying to think of how to finish what we have to say. It is only when the speaker's efforts are so intense or the interruptions in the flow of speech are so frequent or pervasive that they keep him or her from being understood or draw extraordinary attention that they are considered disorders. Besides, listeners have a greater tolerance for some types of disfluencies than others. Most of us will more readily accept speech-flow disruptions we perceive as necessary corrections of what the speaker has said or is planning to say than disruptions that appear to reflect the speaker's inability to proceed with the articulation of what he or she has decided to say.

The most frequent type of fluency disorder is stuttering. About 1 percent of children and adults are considered stutterers. More boys than girls stutter. Many children quickly outgrow their childhood disfluencies. These children generally use regular and effortless disfluencies, appear to be unaware of their hesitancies, and have parents and teachers who are unconcerned about their speech patterns (Shames & Ramig, 1994). Those who stutter for more than a year and a half or two appear to be at risk for becoming chronic stutterers (Yairi & Ambrose, 1992).

A child who is thought to stutter should be evaluated by a speech-language pathologist. Early diagnosis is important if the development of chronic stuttering is to be avoided. Unfortunately, many educators and physicians do not refer potential stutterers for in-depth assessment because they are aware that disfluencies are a normal part of speech-language development. But nonreferral is extremely detrimental to children who are at risk for stuttering. If their persistent stuttering goes untreated, it may result in a lifelong disorder that affects their ability to communicate, develop positive feelings about self, and pursue certain educational and employment opportunities (Benson, 1995; Bloodstein, 1993; Curlee & Siegel, 1997). "It is now recognized that early intervention is a crucial component of adequate health care provision for stuttering" (Onslow, 1992, p. 983).

Speech Disorders Associated with Neurological Damage

The muscles that make speech possible are under voluntary control. When there is damage to the areas of the brain controlling these muscles or to the nerves leading to them, there is a disturbance in the ability to speak normally. These disorders may involve articulation of speech sounds (**dysarthria**) or selecting and sequencing speech (**apraxia**). Difficulties in speaking happen because the muscles controlling breathing, the larynx, the throat, the tongue, the jaw, and/or the lips cannot be controlled precisely. Depending on the nature of the injury to the brain, perceptual and cognitive functions may also be affected; the individual may have a language disorder in addition to a speech disorder (Brookshire, 1997; Hardy, 1994; Robin, Yorkston, & Beukelman, 1996).

In Chapter 11, we discuss the many possible causes of brain injury. Among them are physical trauma, oxygen deprivation, poisoning, diseases, and strokes. Any of these can cause dysarthria or apraxia. Probably the condition that most frequently accounts for these disorders in children is *cerebral palsy*—brain injury before, during, or after birth that results in muscular weakness or paralysis. Vehicular accidents are a frequent cause of traumatic brain injury in adolescence and young adulthood.

The speech-language pathologist will assess the ability of the person with neurological impairment to control breathing, phonation, resonation, and articulatory movements by listening to the person's speech and inspecting his or her speech mechanism. Medical, surgical, and rehabilitative specialists in the treat-

dysarthria. A condition in which brain damage causes impaired control of the muscles used in articulation.

apraxia. The inability to move the muscles involved in speech or other voluntary acts.

ment of neurological disorders also must evaluate the person's problem and plan a management strategy. In cases in which the neurological impairment makes the person's speech unintelligible, augmentative or alternative communication systems may be required.

Early Intervention

The study of children's early development has shown that the first several years of life are a truly critical period for language learning. Much of children's language and social development depends on the nature and quantity of the language interactions they have with parents or other caregivers. In the homes of children who come to school ready to learn, the language interactions between parents and children have typically been frequent, focused on encouragement and affirmation of the children's behavior, emphasized the symbolic nature of language, provided gentle guidance in exploring things and relationships, and demonstrated the responsiveness of adults to children. By contrast, children who enter school at a disadvantage tend to have experienced much lower rates of language interaction; heard primarily negative, discouraging feedback on their behavior; and heard language that is harsh, literal, and emotionally detached.

Based on extensive observations in homes, Hart and Risley (1995) compared the language experiences of children of professional parents, working-class parents, and parents on welfare. The contrasts in language experiences and the effects observed in children's academic achievement and behavior are stark, but the differences are unrelated to income or ethnicity. Rather, the differences are related to how and how much the parents talked to their children. As summed up by the authors:

> Our data showed that the magnitude of children's accomplishments depends less on the material and educational advantages available in the home and more on the amount of experience children accumulate with parenting that provides language diversity, affirmative feedback, symbolic emphasis, gentle guidance, and responsiveness. By the time children are 3 years old, even intensive intervention cannot make up for the differences in the amount of such experience children have received from their parents. If children could be given better parenting, intervention might be unnecessary. (Hart & Risley, 1995, p. 210)

Thus, it appears that the key to preventing many disabilities related to language development is to help parents improve how they relate to their children when they are infants and toddlers. Nevertheless, for many young children, intervention in the preschool and primary grades will be necessary.

Preschoolers who require intervention for a speech or language disorder occasionally have multiple disabilities that are sometimes severe or profound. Language is closely tied to cognitive development, so impairment of general intellectual ability is likely to have a retarding influence on language development. Conversely, lack of language may hamper cognitive development. Because speech is dependent on neurological and motor development, any neurological or motor problem might impair ability to speak. Normal social development in the preschool years depends on the emergence of language, so a child with language impairment is at a disadvantage in social learning (Prizant, 1999). Therefore, the preschool child's language is seldom the only target of intervention (Nelson, 1998).

The first several years of life are truly critical for language learning.

Researchers have become increasingly aware that language development has its beginning in the earliest mother–child interactions. Concern for the child's development of the ability to communicate cannot be separated from concern for development in other areas. Therefore, speech-language pathologists are a vital part of the multidisciplinary team that evaluates an infant or young child with disabilities and develops an individualized family service plan (IFSP) (see Chapter 2). Early intervention programs involve extending the role of the parent. This means a lot of simple play with accompanying verbalizations. It means talking to the child about objects and activities in the way most mothers talk to their babies. But it also means choosing objects, activities, words, and consequences for the child's vocalizations with great care so the chances that the child will learn functional language are enhanced (Fey, Catts, & Larrivee, 1995; McKnight-Taylor, 1989).

Early childhood specialists now realize that *prelinguistic* intervention is critical for language development—that is, intervention should begin *before* the child's language emerges. The foundations for language are laid in the first few months of life through the nonverbal dialogues infants have with their mothers and other caretakers (Nelson, 1998).

In the early years of implementing IFSPs, emphasis was placed on assessing families' strengths and needs and training parents how to teach and manage their children. More recently, professionals have come to understand that assessing families in the belief that professionals know best is often misguided (Slentz & Bricker, 1992). Parents can indeed be helped by professionals to play an important role in their children's language development (Alpert & Kaiser, 1992). But the emphasis today is on working with parents as knowledgeable and competent partners whose preferences and decisions are respected (see also discussion in Chapter 13).

Intervention in early childhood is likely to be based on assessment of the child's behavior related to the content, form, and especially the use of language in social interaction. For the child who has not yet learned language, assessment and intervention will focus on imitation, ritualized and make-believe play, play with objects, and functional use of objects. At the earliest stages in which the content and form of language are interactive, it is important to evaluate the extent to which the child looks at or picks up an object when it is referred to, does something with an object when directed by an adult, and uses sounds to request or refuse things and call attention to objects. When the child's use of language is considered, the earliest objectives involve him or her looking at the adult during interactions; taking turns in and trying to prolong pleasurable activities and games; following the gaze of an adult and directing the behavior of adults; and persisting in or modifying gestures, sounds, or words when an adult does not respond.

In the preschool, teaching **discourse** (conversation skills) is a critical focus of language intervention. In particular, emphasis is placed on teaching children to use the discourse that is essential for success in school. Children must learn, for example, to report their experiences in detail and to explain why things happen, not just add to their vocabularies. They must learn not only word forms and meanings but also how to take turns in conversations and maintain the topic of a conversation or change it in an appropriate way (Johnston, Weinrich, & Glaser, 1991). Preschool programs in which such language teaching is the focus may include teachers' daily individualized conversations with children, daily reading to individual children or small groups, and frequent classroom discussions.

discourse. Conversation; the skills used in conversation, such as turn taking and staying on the topic.

Current trends are directed toward providing speech and language interventions in the typical environments of young children (Cirrin & Penner, 1995; Nelson, 1998). This means that classroom teachers and speech-language pathologists must develop a close working relationship. The speech-language pathologist may work directly with children in the classroom and advise the teacher about the intervention that he or she can carry out as part of the regular classroom activities. The child's peers may also be involved in intervention strategies. Because language is essentially a social activity, its facilitation requires involvement of others in the child's social environment—peers as well as adults (Audet & Tankersley, 1999; Fey et al., 1995; Prizant, 1999). Normally developing peers have been taught to assist in the language development of children with disabilities by doing the following during playtimes: establishing eye contact; describing their own or others' play; and repeating, expanding, or requesting clarification of what the child with disabilities says. Another intervention strategy involving peers is *sociodramatic play*. Children are taught in groups of three, including a child with disabilities, to act out social roles such as those people might take in various settings (e.g., a restaurant or shoe store). The training includes scripts that specify what each child is to do and say, which may be modified by the children in creative ways.

Transition

In the past, adolescents and adults in speech and language intervention programs generally fell into three categories: (1) the self-referred, (2) those with other health problems, and (3) those with severe disabilities. Adolescents or adults may refer themselves to speech-language pathologists because their phonology, voice, or stuttering is causing them social embarrassment and/or interfering with occupational pursuits. These are generally persons with long-standing problems who are highly motivated to change their speech and obtain relief from the social penalties their differences impose.

Adolescents and adults with other health problems may have experienced damage to speech or language capacities as a result of disease or injury, or they may have lost part of their speech mechanism through injury or surgical removal. Treatment of these individuals always demands an interdisciplinary effort. In some cases of progressive disease, severe neurological damage, or loss of tissues of the speech mechanism, the outlook for functional speech is not good. However, surgical procedures, medication, and prosthetic devices are making it possible for more people to speak normally. Loss of ability to use language is typically more disabling than loss of the ability to speak. Traumatic brain injury may leave the individual with a seriously diminished capacity for self-awareness, goal setting, planning, self-directing or initiating actions, inhibiting impulses, monitoring or evaluating one's own performance, or problem solving (Ylvisaker et al., 1994). Recovering these vital language-based skills is a critical aspect of transition of the adolescent or young adult from hospital to school and from school to independent living.

Individuals with severe disabilities may need the services of speech-language pathologists to help them achieve more intelligible speech. They may also need to be taught an alternative to oral language or given a system of augmented communication. One of the major problems in working with adolescents and adults who have severe disabilities is setting realistic goals for speech and language learning. Teaching simple, functional language—such as social greetings, naming objects, and making simple requests—may be realistic goals for some adolescents and adults.

A major concern of transition programming is ensuring that the training and support provided during the school years are carried over into adult life. To be successful, the transition must include speech-language services that are part of the natural environment. That is, the services must be community based and integrated into vocational, domestic, recreational, consumer, and mobility training activities. Speech-language interventions for adolescents and young adults with severe disabilities must emphasize functional communication—understanding and making oneself understood in the social circumstances most likely to be encountered in everyday life (Nelson, 1998). Developing appropriate conversation skills (e.g., establishing eye contact, using greetings, taking turns, and identifying and staying on the topic), reading, writing, following instructions related to recreational activities, using public transportation, and performing a job are examples of the kinds of functional speech-language activities that may be emphasized (see Nelson, 1998; Rogers-Adkinson & Griffith, 1999).

Identifying Possible Language-Related Problems

Suggestions for Recognizing the Need for Consultation with a Communicative Specialist for Older Children and Adolescents with Moderate-to-Severe Multiple Disabilities

- **Failure to understand instructions.** When a person has difficulty performing essential job or daily living tasks, consider the possibility that the person may not understand the language of instructions and may not have sufficient communicative skill to ask for repetition or clarification.
- **Inability to use language to meet daily living needs.** When individuals can produce enough words to formulate a variety of utterances, including questions, then they can travel independently, shop independently, use the telephone when they need to, and ask for assistance in getting out of problem situations when they arise. If persons cannot function in a variety of working, shopping, and social contexts, consider that communicative impairments may be limiting their independence.
- **Violation of rules of politeness and other rules of social transaction.** The ability to function well in a variety of contexts with friends, acquaintances, and one-time contacts depends on sensitivity to the unspoken rules of social interaction. One of the most frequently cited reasons for failure of workers with disabilities to "fit in" with fellow workers is their inability to engage in small-talk during work breaks. Examples that might cause difficulty are failure to take communicative turns when offered, or conversely, interrupting the turns of others;

saying things that are irrelevant to the topic; not using politeness markers or showing interest in what the other person says; making blunt requests owing to lack of linguistic skill for softening them; failing to shift style of communication for different audiences (e.g., talking the same way to the boss as to co-workers); and any other communicative behavior that is perceived as odd or bizarre. If people seem to avoid interacting with the target person, referral may be justified.
- **Lack of functional ability to read signs and other symbols and to perform functional writing tasks.** The ability to recognize the communicative symbols of the culture enables people to know how to use public transportation, to find their way around buildings, to comply with legal and safety expectations, and to fill out forms or use bank accounts. Communicative specialists may be able to assist in identifying the best strategies for teaching functional reading and writing skills and encouraging the development of other symbol-recognition and use skills.
- **Problems articulating speech clearly enough to be understood, stuttering, or using an inaudible or inappropriate voice.** Other speech and voice disorders may interfere with the person's ability to communicate. When such problems are noted, the individual should be referred to a speech-language pathologist.

Source: N. W. Nelson, *Childhood language disorders in context: Infancy through adolescence* (2nd ed.). Copyright © 1998 by Allyn & Bacon. Reprinted with permission.

Today, much more emphasis is being placed on the language disorders of adolescents and young adults who do not fit into other typical categories of disabilities. Many of these individuals were formerly seen as having primarily academic and social problems that were not language related. But now it is understood that underlying many or most of the school and social difficulties of adolescents and adults are basic disorders of language (Rogers-Adkinson & Griffith, 1999; Wallach & Butler, 1994). These language disorders are a continuation of difficulties experienced earlier in the person's development.

Classroom teachers are in a particularly good position to identify possible language-related problems and request help from a communication specialist. The box on page 332 describes for teachers several characteristics exhibited by older children and adolescents that may indicate a need for consultation and intervention. Addressing problems like these as early and effectively as possible is important in helping youngsters make successful transitions to more complex and socially demanding environments.

Some adolescents and adults with language disorders are excellent candidates for *strategy training,* which teaches them how to select, store, retrieve, and process information (see Hallahan et al., 1999, and Chapter 5). Others, however, do not have the required reading skills, symbolic abilities, or intelligence to benefit from the usual training in cognitive strategies. Whatever techniques are chosen for adolescents and older students, the teacher should be aware of the principles that apply to intervention with these individuals.

Summary

Communication requires sending and receiving meaningful messages. *Language* is the communication of ideas through an arbitrary system of symbols that are used according to specified and accepted rules. *Speech* is the behavior of forming and sequencing the sounds of oral language. Communication disorders may involve language or speech or both. The prevalence of communication disorders is difficult to determine, but disorders of speech and language are among the most common disabilities of children.

Language development begins with the first mother–child interactions. The sequence of language development is fairly well understood, but relatively little is known about how and why children learn language. Some theories of language development include the following major ideas: (1) Language learning depends on brain development and proper brain functioning; (2) language learning is affected by the consequences of language behavior; (3) language is learned from inputs and outputs related to information processing; (4) language learning is based on linguistic rules; (5) language is one of many cognitive (thinking) skills; (6) language arises from the need to communicate in social interactions. Research supports some aspects of all theories, but social interactional or pragmatic theory is now accepted as having the most important implications for speech-language pathologists and teachers.

Language disorders may be classified according to the five subsystems of language: phonology, morphology, syntax, semantics, and pragmatics. They may also be categorized according to the presumed causes of disorders or related conditions. For example, conditions such as mental retardation, traumatic brain injury, and autism are associated with their own respective communication problems.

Assessment and intervention in language disorders require standardized testing and more informal clinical judgments. An intervention plan must consider what the child talks about and should talk about, how the child talks and should speak to become more intelligible, and how the child uses language for communication and socialization. Helping children learn to use language effectively is not the task of any single professional group. Speech-language pathologists now regularly work with classroom teachers to make language learning an integral part of classroom teaching. Recent approaches to addressing communication problems associated with autism, delayed language, and traumatic brain injury have stressed a functional approach, emphasizing social and pragmatic skills that students use frequently.

Augmentative or alternative communication systems are needed for those whose physical or cognitive disabilities preclude oral language. These systems create a way to select or scan an array of pictures, words, or other symbols. Microcomputers have radically changed augmentative communication.

Dialect or native language differences must not be mistaken for language disorders. However, the language disorders of children with communicative differences must not be overlooked. Bilingual special education is an emerging discipline, as more children have little or no proficiency in English. Research has also begun to focus on differences in socioeconomic status and language development.

Children may have more than one type of speech disorder, and disorders of speech may occur along with language disorders. Voice disorders may involve pitch, loudness, and quality of phonation, which may be unpleasant to the listener, interfere with communication, or abuse the larynx. Articulation or phonological disorders involve omission, substitution, distortion, or addition of word sounds, making speech difficult to understand. The most common fluency disorder is stuttering. Neurological damage can affect people's speech by making it difficult for them to make the voluntary movements required.

Children requiring early intervention for speech and language disorders typically have severe or multiple disabilities. A young child's ability to communicate cannot be separated from other areas of development. Children's language and social interactions with parents and caregivers are being looked at as key factors. Consequently, early language intervention involves all social interactions between a child and his or her caretakers and peers and emphasizes functional communication in the child's natural environment.

Adolescents and young adults with speech and language disorders may be self-referred, have health problems, or have multiple and severe disabilities. Transition programming has provided for the carryover of training and support during the school years into adult life. Emphasis today is on functional communication skills taught in naturalistic settings. Language disorders among young children are the basis for academic and social learning problems in later years.

suggestions for teaching

Students with Communication Disorders in General Education Classrooms   By E. Jane Nowacek

Language problems can adversely affect students academically and socially. To understand what teachers can do to facilitate the learning, we must consider the demands students with language disabilities face in school. Conceptually we can place classroom language requirements on a continuum of discourse complexity. Discourse is defined as connected utterances or sustained exchanges combined in a cohesive way to convey a unit of meaning (Merritt, Barton, & Culatta, 1998, p. 144).

Less demanding discourse	Medium demanding discourse	Most demanding discourse
Example: Casual conversations	*Example:* Instructional discourse	*Example:* Unsupported reading/ listening to texts

As Merritt and her colleagues point out, the less demanding types of discourse are supported by reciprocal interactions between the speaker and listener during which adjustments can be made based on feedback. The more demanding forms, such as reading independently and listening to lectures, are nonreciprocal. No adjustments are available to students, without specific modifications. At the midpoint of the continuum is instructional discourse, the type of teacher–student interaction that enhances knowledge, guides understanding, or develops skills. In the following section, techniques are discussed that you can use to address student difficulties in conversations, instructional discourse, and independent literacy activities.

Facilitating Conversational Discourse

Students with language disorders frequently are not able to initiate and manage conversations. Figure 8.A depicts the rules of conversation that individuals need to master in order to converse effectively. Students may find this graphic helpful in understanding the individual skills involved in conversing and their relationship to one another.

To teach key conversation skills, Nelson (1998) and Paul (1995) report the following instructional sequence suggested by Brinton and Fujiki:

Assess: Gather information about the student's conversational strengths and needs.

Plan: Select a skill, based on the student's needs, and develop a plan.

Teach: Model and cue the selected conversational skill. To begin teaching the selected skill, engage the student in conversations with enough support (e.g., models and verbal and nonverbal cues) to ensure success. Gradually reduce the supports to allow the student to take more equal responsibility for managing the conversation. Continue to withdraw the supports as the student becomes more skilled.

Expand: Next, have the student engage a peer in a conversation when the teacher is present to offer cues. As the student becomes able to participate in conversations with fewer and fewer supports, withdraw them until no supports are provided.

Transfer: Structure new opportunities for the student to practice specific foundation skills (e.g., by guiding students to ask each other questions or to give directions and explanations), and highlight the regularities in language (Hoskins, 1994).

For example, an educator might use this sequence to teach the key skill of staying on topic, identified during assessment. The teacher begins by engaging the student in a conversation on a topic of interest (e.g., "I understand you went to the basketball game last night"). If the student begins to wander off topic during the conversation, the teacher provides support to remain on topic (e.g., "It sounds like a great game. What was the most exciting play?"). Gradually the teacher reduces the support to cues such as "Is that what we are talking about?" and then to a nonverbal cue such as a tap on the wrist. Next, the student is asked to have a similar conversation with a classmate when the instructor is present to give the nonverbal cue and to prompt an appropriate comment quietly to the student. As the student becomes skilled in staying on the topic, the teacher gradually eliminates all cues (Paul, 1995).

Providing Supportive Instructional Discourse

Merritt and her colleagues (1998) indicate that the language of the classroom involves talking because talk leads to the creation of meaning. The degree to which students engage in this process depends, in part, on the topics teachers talk about and the discourse strategies they use. According to these professionals, "Classroom discourse will be the most effective for a broad range of students if an overall supportive style is adopted and if some specific teacher-directed discourse strategies are utilized" (p. 150). When should educators use teacher-directed strategies? The main goal of a directive instructional style is to assess students' knowledge of a subject by asking questions and eliciting answers that, in turn, the teacher evaluates for accuracy and completeness. This style, therefore, is appropriate to facilitate the recall of details because the emphasis is on answering specific questions.

Supportive or interactive discourse, on the other hand, facilitates deeper reflection and understanding of the subject matter because it emphasizes elaboration of student thought processes (Merritt et al., 1998). Here the teacher acts as a mediator of the discussion, providing supports for classroom discussions. He or she gives students many opportunities to react to and apply the material being discussed in order to promote their integration of ideas across subject areas and communication channels (i.e., listening, speaking, reading, and writing). Educators can encourage reciprocal interactions essential for supportive instructional discourse and create supportive language environments by:

Teaching students the following active listening strategies (Merritt et al., 1998):

- Prepare to listen (e.g., students think of what they already know about a topic)
- Stay in communication and signal involvement verbally (e.g., "Yes, I understand") and/or nonverbally (e.g., nodding)
- Monitor breakdowns in understanding (e.g., asking self, "Do I understand what is being said?" and asking others, "Do you understand what I am saying?")
- Give constructive feedback (e.g., by acknowledging contributions and extending the dialogue, "That's interesting. Tell me more.")

Providing opportunities for interactions (Schoenbrodt, Kumin, & Sloan 1997):

- Promote frequent interaction by giving students many opportunities to talk and hear talk used for different purposes and in a variety of settings (e.g., create seating arrangements that

Both speaker and listener can
be the stars in a conversation!

Figure 8.A

Rules of Conversation.

Source: Language disorders in older students, by V. L. Larson and N. McKinley, 1995, p. 182. Copyright 1995 by Thinking Publications. Reprinted with permission.

facilitate talk; offer concrete materials such as photographs and materials from nature such as animals, rocks, leaves that relate to the instructional topic to provide students with ideas for conversations)

- Help students to interact and use language as they learn by incorporating discussion into learning activities (e.g., encouraging the sharing of personal experiences related to the instructional topic)
- Encourage students to use language for a variety of purposes and with a variety of audiences to help them "shift" their language (e.g., structure occasions for interactions with older and younger students during which students can use language for different purposes, such as collaborating on school projects or acting out a play);
- Invite students to engage in conversations with the teacher on topics they initiate. During these conversations, it is important that teachers respond positively and use vocabulary and structure that is appropriate to the student.

In addition to adopting a supportive discourse style and language environment and maintaining reciprocal interactions, teachers can use a variety of instructional techniques that facilitate the learning of students with language disabilities (Merritt et al., 1998). These techniques include: (a) defining the objective(s) and focus of the lesson; (b) linking new information to prior knowledge; (c) using visuals to support class discussions; (d) providing examples and connections that are relevant and personal to students; (e) highlighting key points with comments and questions; and (f) asking questions that enhance discussion (e.g., questions that focus on the text and those that focus on student background knowledge).

Providing Instruction for Independent Learning

To help students with language disorders manage the more demanding, nonreciprocal types of classroom discourse, educators can teach the self-talk strategy outlined in Figure 8.B. Self-talk is a form of mediated learning, a process between a learner and an experienced adult during which the adult initially promotes understanding "by asking guiding questions, supplying needed information, directing activity; challenging answers, requiring logical evidence for conclusions, and most important, emphasizing the processes of thinking, learning, and problem solving rather than products" (Haywood, Towery-Woolsey, Arbitman-Smith, & Aldridge, 1988, p. 27). Gradually, students assume the responsibility for talking themselves through each step of the process.

Another strategy teachers can use to promote independent learning is self-questioning. This strategy has been applied to several learning activities, including reading. Nelson (1998) points out that mediated reading is a special type of mediational language intervention in which the teacher focuses the student's attention on whether his or her reading of the text makes sense and then on whether it matches the printed data. The educator teaches students to ask themselves questions such as:

- Does this make sense?
- Does this fit with what we have been reading?
- Does it fit with what we see on the page?
- When you say _____, I expect to see _____. Is that what I see? (Nelson, 1998, p. 431)

Modifying the Instructional Environment

In this final section we suggest several modifications that teachers can make to promote the learning of students with language disorders.

Self-Talk

About Self-Talk:

1. Self-talk is a learning *strategy* or *tool*.
2. People use self-talk when they think out loud.
3. Students can use self-talk to help guide their thinking about school problems by asking and answering questions one step at a time.

Some Ideas for Asking Myself Questions One Step at a Time:

Do I understand what this problem is about?

How can I solve this problem?

What information will help me to solve this problem?

What is the first step I need to do?

What is the next step?

Does the answer seem right?

Am I done?

Note: This self-talk sheet was designed by Adelia Van Meter as a handout for a mini-lesson on self-talk conducted as part of the Language-Based Homework Lab (Nelson, 1997; Nelson & Van Meter, 1996). It was then incorporated in students' looseleaf notebooks, which we call "Tool Books." When a student started working on a school assignment, he or she would open the Tool Book to this page and use it to assist the process of talking himself or herself through each step of the process. © N. W. Nelson and A. VanMeter, 1996. Shared by permission of the authors.

Figure 8.B

Student "Tool Book" Reminder for How to Use Self-Talk

Source: Childhood language disorders in context: Infancy through adolescence, 2nd ed., by N. W. Nelson, 1998, p. 429. Copyright 1998 by Allyn & Bacon. Reprinted with permission.

Providing Appropriate Models Because students imitate the language they hear, classroom teachers must model correct language usage, grammar, and articulation in their own communication. Educators also can provide appropriate language models by reading fiction and nonfiction to students; making audiotapes of content-area material available; and showing selected television programs on videotapes (Gearheart, Weishahn, & Gearheart, 1996).

Using Language Appropriate to Students Being aware of the language used in instruction can help teachers to employ different speaking styles in communicating with their students. For example, teachers may need to slow the rate of speaking for some students to understand main ideas; repeat key phrases; use concrete language when explaining new concepts; and eliminate false starts and digressions that obscure the focus and meaning of their communication (Larson & McKinley, 1995). In addition, it is important that teachers are receptive to student questions, even those that seem irrelevant or repetitive. Larson and McKinley point out that teachers may help students formulate appropriate questions by asking for clarification. For example, teachers may respond to a student's global request by asking "What is confusing you about the directions?" or "What don't you understand?" Finally, they alert teachers to the fact that indirect questions or requests such as "Don't you know that you're suppose to begin silent reading as soon as the bell rings?" may be misunderstood by students with language disorders. To avoid misunderstandings, teachers can make direct requests and/or ask students to explain what is expected of them.

Integrating Curriculum Norris and Hoffman (1993) suggest providing an *integrated curriculum,* in which instruction in all subject areas is based on a single theme (e.g., the weather). For students with less flexible language systems, this approach reduces the demand to address numerous topics in separate subject areas. Furthermore, integrating the curriculum may provide the teacher with an increased opportunity to select materials—at various levels of difficulty—that students can use to explore themes without being stigmatized.

Providing Transitions Another modification involves integrating oral-to-written and written-to-oral activities. For example, teachers may use oral-based activities in composition instruction. Doing so provides a transition between these two forms of communication, a transition that students with disabilities may find difficult to make. Rubin (1994) offers the following suggestions for oral-to-written activities:

- Conduct discussions before students begin writing (e.g., brainstorming, interviews)
- Encourage students to tape-record notes and ideas as a prewriting step (e.g., before doing a first draft)
- Provide time for students to critique each others' writing in peer conferences
- Allow group revising, in which students interested in the same topic talk together and craft a final draft
- Provide opportunities for students to read their writing aloud to various audiences

Meeting the Needs of Students Who Do Not Speak the Language of the Dominant Culture Thorp (1997) points out the fact that the U.S. population is becoming increasingly diverse results in many schools representing several language groups. She recommends several strategies for improving the communication between teacher and culturally and linguistically diverse students and families, to include:

- Find and use a "cultural guide" who can act as a translator or mediator in interactions with children and families.
- Talk with families. Ask questions such as: What are the parents' expectations for formal schooling? What about school is important to them? What is their experience with schools and the community? Persist in communicating with families in order to develop trust and a complete and accurate understanding.
- Examine the classroom environment and practices and create a place where families who want to participate feel welcome. Make sure materials (e.g., bulletin boards, books, resources) reflect the diversity of your students in nonstereotypical ways. For example, see that images reflect students and families as they appear in the United States today, not only in "native" dress as they appeared in history.
- Celebrate diversity throughout the school year, rather than on a designated week or month. Consider what knowledge and experiences families have that can enrich the curriculum and how the stories of students and family members can support literacy (e.g., interviewing parents and listening to and collecting the stories of grandparents).

To these suggestions Gersten and Woodward (1994) add the following recommendations, based on their review of research:

- Provide interesting reading material that makes sense to students who have limited English proficiency and provide explicit links between the student's prior knowledge and the concepts in the story in order for English-language reading to promote the development of English-language competence.
- Ensure that students understand concepts by using redundancy, simple or declarative sentences, and visuals—and check frequently for understanding.
- Encourage students to move from learning and producing limited word translations to using longer sentences and to expressing feelings and more complex ideas.

Helpful Resources

Instructional Methods

Adler, S., & King, D. A. (1994). *Oral communication problems in children and adolescents* (2nd ed.). Boston: Allyn & Bacon.

Bauer, A. M., & Sapona, R. H. (1991). *Managing classrooms to facilitate learning.* Englewood Cliffs, NJ: Prentice-Hall.

Bernstein, D. K., & Tigerman, E. (1997). *Language and communications disorders in children* (4th ed.). Boston: Allyn & Bacon.

Butler, K. G. (Ed.). (1994). *Best practices II: The classroom as an intervention context.* Gaithersburg, MD: Aspen.

Fey, M. E., Windsor, J., & Warren, S. F. (Eds.). (1995). *Language intervention: Preschool through the elementary years.* Baltimore: Paul H. Brookes.

Gruenewald, L. J., & Pollak, S. A. (1990). *Language interaction in curriculum and instruction* (2nd ed.). Austin, TX: Pro-Ed.

Haynes, W. O., Moran, M. J., & Pindzola, R. H. (1994). *Communication disorders in the classroom.* Dubuque, IA: Kendall/Hunt.

Hoggan, K. C., & Strong, C. J. (1994). The magic of "once upon a time": Narrative teaching strategies. *Language, Speech, and Hearing Services in Schools, 25,* 76–89.

LaBlance, G. R., Steckol, K. F., & Smith, V. L. (1994). Stuttering: The role of the classroom teacher. *Teaching Exceptional Children, 27,* 10–12.

Larson, V. L., & McKinley, N. L. (1995). *Communication assessment and intervention strategies for adolescents.* Eau Claire, WI: Thinking Publications.

Lowenthal, B. (1995). Naturalistic language intervention in inclusive environments. *Intervention in School and Clinic, 31,* 114–118.

Merritt, D. D., & Culatta, B. (1998). *Language intervention in the classroom.* San Diego: Singular Publishing.

Nelson, C. D. (1991). *Practical procedures for children with language disorders: Preschool–adolescence.* Austin, TX: Pro-Ed.

Nelson, N. W. (1998). *Childhood language disorders in context: Infancy through adolescence* (2nd ed.). Boston: Allyn & Bacon.

Norris, J. A., & Hoffman, P. R. (1993). *Whole language intervention for school-aged children.* San Diego: Singular Publishing.

Nowacek, E. J. (1997). Spoken language. In E. Polloway and J. Patton (Eds.), *Strategies for teaching learners with special needs* (6th ed.). Upper Saddle River, NJ: Prentice-Hall.

Owens, R. E. (1998). *Language disorders: A functional approach to assessment and intervention* (2nd ed.). Boston: Allyn & Bacon.

Oyer, H. J., Hall, B. J., & Haas, W. H. (1994). Introduction to speech, language, and hearing problems in the schools. In *Speech, language, and hearing disorders: A guide for teachers* (2nd ed.). Boston: Allyn & Bacon.

Polloway, E. A., & Smith, T. E. C. (1992). *Language instruction for students with disabilities* (2nd ed.). Denver: Love.

Paul, R. (1995). *Language disorders from infancy through adolescence.* St. Louis: Mosby.

Reed, V. A. (1994). *An introduction to children with language disorders* (2nd ed.). New York: Merrill/ Macmillan.

Silliman, E. R., & Wilkinson, L. C. (1991). *Communicating for learning: Classroom observation and collaboration.* Gaithersburg, MD: Aspen.

Wallach, G. P., & Butler, K. G. (Eds.). (1994). *Language learning disabilities in school-age children and adolescents: Some principles and applications.* New York: Merrill/Macmillan.

Warren, S. F., & Yoder, P. J. (1994). Communication and language intervention: Why a constructivist approach is insufficient. *Journal of Special Education, 28,* 248–258.

Wiig, E. H., & Semel, E. (1984). *Language assessment and intervention for the learning disabled* (2nd ed.). Columbus, OH: Merrill.

Wood, K. D., & Algozzine, B. (1994). *Teaching reading to high-risk learners: A unified perspective.* Boston: Allyn & Bacon.

Curricular and Instructional Materials

Bloomin' Series (provides activities to improve pragmatics by focusing on such areas as holidays, recipes, experiments, and language arts). LinguiSystems, 3100 Fourth Avenue, East Moline, IL 61244, (800) 776-4332.

Danielson, J., & Sampson, L. (1992). *Question the information: Techniques for classroom listening.* East Moline, IL: LinguiSystems.

Hamersky, J. (1993). *Vocabulary maps.* Eau Claire, WI: Thinking Publications.

Help Series (includes exercises in areas such as language processing, concepts, paraphrasing, problem solving, and pragmatics). LinguiSystems, 3100 Fourth Avenue, East Moline, IL 61244, (800) 776-4332.

Johnston, E. B., Weinrich, B. D., & Glaser, A. J. (1991). *A sourcebook of pragmatic activities: Theory and intervention for language therapy (PK–6)* (Rev. ed.). Tucson, AZ: Communication Skill Builders.

Mannix, D. (1995). *Social skills activities.* Tucson, AZ: Communication Skill Builders.

Marquis, M. A. (1993). *Face to face: Facilitating adolescent communication experiences.* Tucson, AZ: Communication Skill Builders.

Marquis, M. A., & Addy-Trout, E. (1992). *CASE study: Communication and self-esteem.* Eau Claire, WI: Thinking Publications.

Nelson, N. W., & Gillespie, L. L. (1991). *Analogies for thinking and talking.* Tucson, AZ: Communication Skill Builders.

Paul, R. (1992). *Pragmatic activities for language intervention.* Tucson, AZ: Communication Skill Builders.

Strategies for instruction: A handbook of performance activities. (1992). San Antonio, TX: Psychological Corporation (Levels K; Grades 1 & 2; Grades 3 & 4; Grades 5 & 6; Reading, Grades 7–12; Mathematics, Grades 7–12; Language, Grades 7–12; Science/Social Studies, Grades 7–12).

Turnbow, G., & Proctor, D. (1993). *Social language for teens: Tackling real-life situations.* East Moline, IL: LinguiSystems.

Weinrich, B. D., Glaser, A. J., & Johnston, E. B. (1995). *A sourcebook of adolescent pragmatic activities: Theory and intervention for language therapy (grades 7–12 and ESL)* (Rev. ed.). Tucson, AZ: Communication Skill Builders.

Wiig, E. H., & Bray, C. W. (1983). *Let's talk for children.* San Antonio, TX: Psychological Corporation.

Wiig, E. H. (1985). *Words, expression and contexts: A figurative language program.* San Antonio, TX: Psychological Corporation.

Literature about Individuals with Communication Disorders*

Elementary

Brown, A., & Forsberg, G. (1989). *Lost boys never say die.* New York: Delacorte Press. (Ages 9–12) (F)

Bunting, E. (1980). *Blackbird singing.* New York: Macmillan. (Ages 9–12) (F)

Corrigan, K. (1984). *Emily, Emily.* Toronto: Annick Press. (Elementary) (Stuttering) (F)

Cosgrove, S. (1983). *Creole.* Los Angeles: Price Stern Sloan. (Elementary) (Stuttering) (F)

Hague, K. (1985). *The Legend of the Veery bird.* New York: Harcourt, Brace, Jovanovich. (Elementary) (Stuttering) (F)

Kropp, P. (1980). *Wilted.* New York: Coward, McCann & Geoghegan. (Ages 9–12) (F)

Secondary

Berger, G. (1981). *Speech and language disorders.* New York: Franklin Watts. (Ages 13–18) (NF)

Evans, J. (1983). *An uncommon gift.* Philadelphia, PA: Westminster. (Ages 13–18) (NF)

Software

Alphabet Sounds, Data Command Development, Inc., 13492 Research Blvd., Ste. 120-1-215, (800) 528-7390. (Apple IIe; Apple IIGS)

Conceptual Skills, Psychological Software Services, Inc., 6555 Carrollton Avenue, Indianapolis, IN 46220, (312) 257-9672. Web site: http://www.inetdirect.net/pss. (Apple IIe, Atari) (math problem solving)

Conversations, Educational Activities, Inc., 1937 Grand Ave., P.O. Box 392, Freeport, NY 11520, (800) 645-3739. Web site: http://www.edact.com. (DOS)

Dr. Peet's Talkwriter, Hartley Courseware, 9920 Pacific Heights Blvd., Suite 500, San Diego, CA 92121, (800) 247-1380. (Apple IIe; Apple IIGS)

Exploring Vocabulary Series, Laureate Learning Systems, Inc., 110 E. Spring Street, Winooski, VT 05404, (800) 562-6801. Web

*F = fiction; NF = nonfiction

site: http://www.LaureateLearning.com. (Apple IIe; Apple IIGS; Macintosh; DOS)

Fay's Word Rally, Ingenuity Works, 720 Olive Way, Suite 1020, Seattle, WA 98101, (800) 665-0667. Web site: http://www.ingenuityworks.com. (Apple IIe; DOS) (language arts)

Functional Vocabulary Plus for Windows, Parrot Software, 6506 Pleasant Lake Court, West Bloomfield, MI 48322, (800) 727-7681. Web site: http://www.parrotsoft.com. (Windows)

Kid Works 2, Davidson and Associates, Inc., 19840 Pioneer Avenue, Torrance, CA 90503, (800) 545-7677. Web site: http://www.davd.com. (Macintosh; DOS; Windows)

Kid Works 2, Bilingual, Davidson and Associates, Inc., 19840 Pioneer Avenue, Torrance, CA 90503, (800) 545-7677. Web site: http://www.davd.com. (Macintosh) (read stories in English and Spanish)

Mi Escuela, Laureate Learning Systems, Inc., 110 E. Spring Street, Winooski, VT 05404, (800) 562-6801. Web site: http://www.LaureateLearning.com. (Macintosh; DOS) (functional language stimulation program in Spanish)

Muppet Word Book, Sunburst Communications, 101 Castleton Street, Pleasantville, NY 10570, (800) 321-7511. Web site: http://www. sunburst.com. (Apple IIe; Apple IIGS) (language development)

Opposites, Hartley Courseware, 9920 Pacific Heights Blvd., Suite 500, San Diego, CA 92121, (800) 247-1380. (Apple IIe; Apple IIGS; DOS)

Soft Text: Word Study, Continental Press, Inc., 520 E. Bainbridge Street, Elizabethtown, PA 17022, (800) 233-0759. (Apple IIe; Apple IIGS)

Turn-Taking, R. J. Cooper and Associates, 24843 Del Prado, Suite 283, Dana Point, CA 92629, (800) RJ-COOPER (714-240-1912). Web site: http://www.rjcooper.com. (Macintosh, Windows)

Vocabulary Detective, SWEPS Educational Software, Inc., 3140 Barker Drive, P.O. Box 1510, Pine, AZ 85544-1510, (800) 880-8812. (Apple IIe; Apple IIGS; DOS)

Vocabulary Machine, SWEPS Educational Software, Inc., 3140 Barker Drive, P.O. Box 1510, Pine, AZ 85544-1510, (800) 880-8812. (Apple IIe; Apple IIGS; DOS)

Organizations

American Speech-Language-Hearing Association, 10801 Rockville Pike, Rockville, MD 20852, (800) 638-8255, (301) 897-5700. Web site: http://www.asha.org

Division for Children with Communication Disorders, Council for Exceptional Children, 1920 Association Drive, Reston, VA 22091. Web site: http://www.cec.sped.org

National Information Center for Children and Youth with Disabilities, P.O. Box 1492, Washington, DC, (800) 695-0285. Web site: http://www.nichcy.org

Bibliography for Teaching Suggestions

Gearheart, B. R., Weishahn, M. W., & Gearheart, C. J. (1996). *The exceptional student in the regular classroom* (6th ed.). New York: Merrill/Macmillan.

Gersten, R., & Woodward, J. (1994). The language-minority student and special education: Issues, trends, and paradoxes. *Exceptional Children, 60,* 310–322.

Haywood, H. C., Towery-Woolsey, J., Arbitman-Smith, R., & Aldridge, A. (1988). Cognitive education with deaf adolescents: Effects of instrumental enrichment. *Topics in Language Disorders, 8,* 23–40.

Hoskins, B. (1994). Language and literacy: Participating in the conversation. In K. G. Butler (Ed.), *Best practices II: The classroom as an intervention context.* Gaithersburg, MD: Aspen.

Larson, V. L., & McKinley, N. (1995). *Language disorders in older students.* Eau Claire, WI: Thinking Publications.

Merritt, D. D., Barton, J., & Culatta, B. (1998). Instructional discourse: A frame work for learning. In D. D. Merritt & B. Culatta (Eds.), *Language in the classroom.* San Diego: Singular Publishing Group.

Nelson, N. W. (1998). *Childhood language disorders in context: Infancy through adolescence* (2nd ed.). Boston: Allyn & Bacon.

Norris, J. A., & Hoffman, P. R. (1993). *Whole language intervention for school-aged children.* San Diego: Singular Publishing.

Paul, R. (1995). *Language disorders from infancy through adolescence.* St. Louis: Mosby.

Rubin, D. L. (1994). Divergence and convergence between oral and written communication. In K. G. Butler (Ed.), *Best practices I: The classroom as an assessment arena.* Gaithersburg, MD: Aspen.

Schoenbrodt, L., Kumin, L., & Sloan, J. M. (1997). Learning disabilities existing concomitantly with communication disorders, *Journal of Learning Disabilities, 30,* 264–281.

Thorp, E. K. (1997). Increasing opportunities for partnership with culturally and linguistically diverse families. *Intervention in School and Clinic, 32,* 261–269.

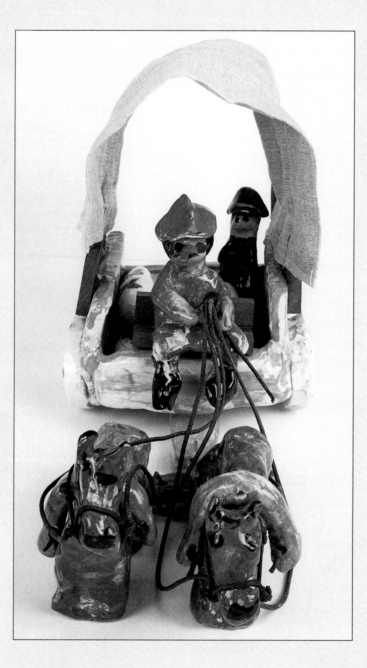

ona
stewart

Covered Wagon. Glazed ceramic and mixed media. 9 × 6 × 12 in.

Ona Stewart, in her own words: "I am deaf and legally blind. It is called Usher's syndrome. I have worked at Gateway [Gateway Crafts, an art program for adults with disabilities in Brookline, MA] since August 1995. At first I was not sure what I should do at Gateway but now I have enjoyed doing it and it helps me create many things. I have taught staff sign language so we can communicate better. I feel confident and comfortable at Gateway."

Hearing Impairment

No deaf child who has earnestly tried to speak the words which he has never heard—to come out of the prison of silence, where no tone of love, no song of bird, no strain of music ever pierces the stillness—can forget the thrill of surprise, the joy of discovery which came over him when he uttered his first word. Only such a one can appreciate the eagerness with which I talked to my toys, to stones, trees, birds and dumb animals, or the delight I felt when at my call Mildred ran to me or my dogs obeyed my commands. It is an unspeakable boon to me to be able to speak in winged words that need no interpretation.

HELEN KELLER
The Story of My Life

Although Helen Keller's achievements were unique in the truest sense of the word, the emotions she conveys here (see page 341) are not. The child who is deaf who does acquire the ability to speak must certainly experience a "joy of discovery" similar to Keller's. Hearing impairment is a great barrier to the normal development of skill in using the English language. As we will see, even if the impairment is not severe enough for the child to be classified as "deaf," but rather as "hard of hearing," the child with a hearing impairment is at a distinct disadvantage in virtually all aspects of English language development. The importance of the English language in U.S. society, particularly in school-related activities, is obvious. Many of the problems that people with hearing impairment have in school are primarily due to their deficiencies in English. We explore this issue in some depth in this chapter.

Another related controversy inherent in Keller's words is the debate concerning whether the child who is deaf should be educated to communicate orally or through manual **sign language**. Keller's opinion is that the ability to speak offers a richer means of communication. But she was extraordinary; extremely few individuals who are deaf attain her level of fluency. Furthermore, because for many years educators exclusively emphasized teaching children who are deaf to speak and actively discouraged their use of sign language, they unwittingly denied these children access to communication. Equal to the poignancy of Keller's breakthrough with verbal language was Lynn Spradley's discovery of communication through sign language after years of frustration with trying to speak:

> "Tom! Bruce! Come quick!" . . .
>
> I jumped up. In an instant we were in Lynn's room.
>
> "Watch!" Louise said, tears streaming down her face. "She said it two times!" Lynn, legs crossed in front of her, sat at the head of her bed. Louise, sitting on the edge, turned back to Lynn.
>
> "I—love—you," her voice came through the tears as she signed. She hugged Lynn, then sat back and waited.
>
> Lynn, beaming, held up two tiny fists, crossed them tightly against her heart, then pointed knowingly at Louise. Without hesitating, she reached out and hugged Louise tightly. The room was blurred; fighting back tears, I picked up Lynn, pulled her close in a long embrace, then sat back on the edge of her bed.
>
> "I—love—you," I signed slowly, my voice quivering as I spoke. I dropped my hands and waited.
>
> "Love you," Lynn signed clearly, confidently, then reached out to hug me. I looked at Louise. There were tears in our eyes.
>
> Bruce hugged his little sister. "I love you," he signed perfectly, a broad smile on his face.
>
> "Love you," Lynn signed back, this time in a more definite exaggerated rhythm.
>
> She had found her voice! (Spradley & Spradley, 1978, pp. 245–246)

sign language. A manual language used by people who are deaf to communicate; a true language with its own grammar.

The oral-versus-manual debate has raged for centuries. For many years there was no middle ground. Although some educators still debate the merits of each, many now have begun to use a method of total communication, which involves a combination of both orientations.

misconceptions
about Persons with Hearing Impairment

myth Deafness is not as severe a disability as blindness.

fact Although it is impossible to predict the exact consequences of a disability on a person's functioning, in general, deafness poses more difficulties in adjustment than does blindness. This is largely due to the effects hearing loss can have on the ability to understand and speak oral language.

myth It is unhealthy for people who are deaf to socialize almost exclusively with others who are deaf.

fact Many authorities now recognize that the phenomenon of a Deaf culture is natural and should be encouraged. In fact, some are worried that too much mainstreaming will diminish the influence of the Deaf culture.

myth In learning to understand what is being said to them, people with hearing impairment concentrate on reading lips.

fact *Lipreading* refers only to visual cues arising from movement of the lips. Some people who are hearing impaired not only read lips but also take advantage of a number of other visual cues, such as facial expressions and movements of the jaw and tongue. They are engaging in what is referred to as *speechreading*.

myth Speechreading is relatively easy to learn and is used by the majority of people with hearing impairment.

fact Speechreading is extremely difficult to learn, and very few people who are hearing impaired actually become proficient speechreaders.

myth American Sign Language (ASL) is a loosely structured group of gestures.

fact ASL is a true language in its own right, with its own set of grammatical rules.

myth ASL can convey only concrete ideas.

fact ASL can convey any level of abstraction.

myth People within the Deaf community are in favor of mainstreaming students who are deaf into regular classes.

fact Some within the Deaf community have voiced the opinion that regular classes are not appropriate for many students who are deaf. They point to the need for a critical mass of students who are deaf in order to have effective educational programs for these individuals. They see separate placements as a way of fostering the Deaf culture.

myth Families in which both the child and the parents are deaf are at a distinct disadvantage compared to families in which the parents are hearing.

fact Research has demonstrated that children who are deaf who have parents who are also deaf fare better in a number of academic and social areas. Authorities point to the parents' ability to communicate with their children in ASL as a major reason for this advantage.

Definition and Classification

There are many definitions and classification systems of hearing impairment. By far the most common division is between *deaf* and *hard of hearing*. This would seem simple enough, except that the two categories are defined differently by different professionals. The extreme points of view are represented by those with a physiological orientation versus those with an educational orientation.

Those maintaining a strictly physiological viewpoint are interested primarily in the *measurable degree* of hearing loss. Children who cannot hear sounds at or above a certain intensity (loudness) level are classified as "deaf"; others with a hearing loss are considered "hard of hearing." Hearing sensitivity is measured in **decibels** (units of relative loudness of sounds). Zero decibels (0 dB) designates the point at which the average person with normal hearing can detect the faintest sound. Each succeeding number of decibels that a person cannot detect indicates a certain degree of hearing loss. Those who maintain a physiological viewpoint generally consider people with hearing losses of about 90 dB or greater to be deaf and people with less to be hard of hearing.

People with an educational viewpoint are concerned with how much the hearing loss is likely to affect the child's ability to speak and develop language. Because of the close causal link between hearing loss and delay in language development, these professionals categorize primarily on the basis of spoken language abilities. Following is the most commonly accepted set of definitions reflecting this educational orientation:

- *Hearing impairment* is a generic term indicating a hearing disability that may range in severity from mild to profound; it includes the subsets of *deaf* and *hard of hearing*.
- A *deaf* person is one whose hearing disability precludes successful processing of linguistic information through audition, with or without a hearing aid.
- A person who is *hard of hearing* generally, with the use of a hearing aid, has residual hearing sufficient to enable successful processing of linguistic information through audition (Brill, MacNeil, & Newman, 1986, p. 67).

Educators are extremely concerned about the age of onset of hearing impairment. Again, the close relationship between hearing loss and language delay is the key here. The earlier the hearing loss occurs in a child's life, the more difficulty he or she will have developing the language of the hearing society (e.g., English). For this reason, professionals frequently use the terms **congenitally deaf** (those who were born deaf) and **adventitiously deaf** (those who acquire deafness at some time after birth).

Two other frequently used terms are even more specific in pinpointing language acquisition as critical: **Prelingual deafness** refers to deafness occurring at birth or early in life prior to the development of speech or language. **Postlingual deafness** is deafness occurring after the development of speech and language. Experts differ regarding the dividing point between prelingual and postlingual deafness. Some believe it should be at about eighteen months, whereas others think it should be lower, at about twelve months or even six months (Meadow-Orlans, 1987).

The following hearing threshold classifications are common: mild (26–54 dB), moderate (55–69 dB), severe (70–89 dB), and profound (90 dB and above). These levels of severity according to loss of hearing sensitivity cut across the broad classifications of deaf and hard of hearing. The broader classifications are not directly

decibels. Units of relative loudness of sounds; zero decibels (0 dB) designates the point at which people with normal hearing can just detect sound.

congenitally deaf. Deafness that is present at birth; can be caused by genetic factors, by injuries during fetal development, or by injuries occurring at birth.

adventitiously deaf. Deafness that occurs through illness or accident in an individual who was born with normal hearing.

prelingual deafness. Deafness that occurs before the development of spoken language, usually at birth.

postlingual deafness. Deafness occurring after the development of speech and language.

dependent on hearing sensitivity. Instead, they stress the degree to which speech and language are affected.

Some authorities object to following any of the various classification systems too strictly. Because these definitions deal with events that are difficult to measure, they are not precise. Thus, it is best not to form any hard-and-fast opinions about an individual's ability to hear and speak solely on the basis of a classification of his or her hearing disability.

In considering issues of definition, it is important to point out that there is growing sentiment among people who are deaf that deafness should not even be considered a disability (Lane, Hoffmeister, & Bahan, 1996; Padden & Humphries, 1988). They argue that deafness only renders a person disabled with respect to acquiring the language of the dominant culture (e.g., English in the United States). Supporters of this view note that deafness does not prohibit a person from learning sign language. Furthermore, they object to labels such as "prelingual" and "postlingual" deafness because such distinctions are keyed to spoken language (Andersson, 1994). Proponents argue that instead of being considered disabled, people who are deaf should be considered a cultural minority with a language of their own—sign language.

Later in the chapter we discuss more thoroughly the issues of sign language as a true language and the nature and purpose of the Deaf culture. For now it is enough to be aware of the challenges that have been raised to the very notion of considering deafness a disability.

Prevalence

Estimates of the number of children with hearing impairment vary considerably. Such factors as differences in definition, populations studied, and accuracy of testing contribute to the varying figures. The U.S. Department of Education's statistics indicate that about 0.14 percent of the population from six to seventeen years of age is identified as deaf or hard of hearing by the public schools. Although the

tympanic membrane (eardrum). The anatomical boundary between the outer and middle ears; the sound gathered in the outer ear vibrates here.

auricle. The visible part of the ear, composed of cartilage; collects the sounds and funnels them via the external auditory canal to the eardrum.

ossicles. Three tiny bones (malleus, incus, and stapes) that together make possible an efficient transfer of sound waves from the eardrum to the oval window, which connects the middle ear to the inner ear.

Department of Education does not report separate figures for the categories of deaf and hard of hearing, some authorities believe that many children who are hard of hearing who could benefit from special education are not being served.

Anatomy and Physiology of the Ear

The ear is one of the most complex organs of the body. The many elements that make up the hearing mechanism are divided into three major sections: the outer, middle, and inner ear. The outer ear is the least complex and least important for hearing; the inner ear is the most complex and most important for hearing. Figure 9.1 shows these major parts of the ear.

The Outer Ear

The outer ear consists of the auricle and the external auditory canal. The canal ends with the **tympanic membrane (eardrum),** which is the boundary between the outer and middle ears. The **auricle** is the part of the ear that protrudes from the side of the head. The part that the outer ear plays in the transmission of sound is relatively minor. Sound is collected by the auricle and is funneled through the external auditory canal to the eardrum, which vibrates, sending the sound waves to the middle ear.

The Middle Ear

The middle ear comprises the eardrum and three very tiny bones (**ossicles**)—called the **malleus** (hammer), **incus** (anvil), and **stapes** (stirrup)—contained within an air-filled space. The chain of the malleus, incus, and stapes conducts the vibrations of

Figure 9.1

Illustration of the outer, middle, and inner ear.

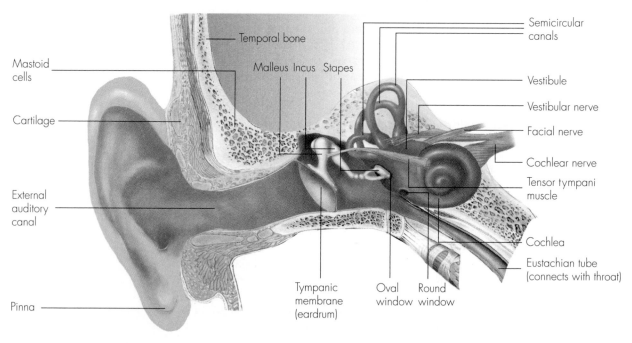

- Temporal bone
- Malleus Incus Stapes
- Semicircular canals
- Vestibule
- Vestibular nerve
- Facial nerve
- Cochlear nerve
- Tensor tympani muscle
- Cochlea
- Eustachian tube (connects with throat)
- Mastoid cells
- Cartilage
- External auditory canal
- Pinna
- Tympanic membrane (eardrum)
- Oval window
- Round window

the eardrum along to the **oval window,** which is the link between the middle and inner ears. The ossicles function to create an efficient transfer of energy from the air-filled cavity of the middle ear to the fluid-filled inner ear.

The Inner Ear

About the size of a pea, the inner ear is an intricate mechanism of thousands of moving parts. Because it looks like a maze of passageways and is highly complex, this part of the ear is often called a *labyrinth.* The inner ear is divided into two sections according to function: the vestibular mechanism and the cochlea. These sections, however, do not function totally independently of each other.

The **vestibular mechanism,** located in the upper portion of the inner ear, is responsible for the sense of balance. It is extremely sensitive to such things as acceleration, head movement, and head position. Information regarding movement is fed to the brain through the vestibular nerve.

By far the most important organ for hearing is the **cochlea.** Lying below the vestibular mechanism, this snail-shaped organ contains the parts necessary to convert the mechanical action of the middle ear into an electrical signal in the inner ear that is transmitted to the brain. In the normally functioning ear, sound causes the malleus, incus, and stapes of the middle ear to move. When the stapes moves, it pushes the oval window in and out, causing the fluid in the cochlea of the inner ear to flow. The movement of the fluid in turn causes a complex chain of events in the cochlea, ultimately resulting in excitation of the cochlear nerve. With stimulation of the cochlear nerve, an electrical impulse is sent to the brain, and sound is heard.

Measurement of Hearing Ability

There are three general types of hearing tests: pure-tone audiometry, speech audiometry, and specialized tests for very young children. Depending on the characteristics of the examinee and the use to which the results will be put, the **audiologist** may choose to give any number of tests from any one or a combination of these three categories.

Pure-Tone Audiometry

Pure-tone audiometry is designed to establish the individual's threshold for hearing at a variety of different frequencies. (Frequency, measured in **hertz (Hz)** units, has to do with the number of vibrations per unit of time of a sound wave; the pitch is higher with more vibrations, lower with fewer.) A person's threshold for hearing is simply the level at which he or she can first detect a sound; it refers to how intense a sound must be before the person can detect it. As mentioned earlier, hearing sensitivity, or intensity, is measured in decibels (dB).

Pure-tone audiometers present tones of various intensities (dB levels) at various frequencies (Hz). Audiologists are usually concerned with measuring sensitivity to sounds ranging from 0 to about 110 dB. A person with average-normal hearing is barely able to hear sounds at a sound-pressure level of 0 dB. The zero decibel level is frequently called the *zero hearing-threshold level (HTL)*, or **audiometric zero.**

malleus. The hammer-shaped bone in the ossicular chain of the middle ear.

incus. The anvil-shaped bone in the ossicular chain of the middle ear.

stapes. The stirrup-shaped bone in the ossicular chain of the middle ear.

oval window. The link between the middle and inner ears.

vestibular mechanism. Located in the upper portion of the inner ear; consists of three soft, semicircular canals filled with a fluid; sensitive to head movement, acceleration, and other movements related to balance.

cochlea. A snail-shaped organ that lies below the vestibular mechanism in the inner ear; its parts convert the sounds coming from the middle ear into electrical signals that are transmitted to the brain.

audiologist. An individual trained in audiology, the science dealing with hearing impairments, their detection, and remediation.

pure-tone audiometry. A test whereby tones of various intensities and frequencies are presented to determine a person's hearing loss.

hertz (Hz). A unit of measurement of the frequency of sound; refers to the highness or lowness of a sound.

audiometric zero. The lowest level at which people with normal hearing can hear.

Hertz are usually measured from 125 Hz (low sounds) to 8,000 Hz (high sounds). Frequencies contained in speech range from 80 to 8,000 Hz, but most speech sounds have energy in the 500 to 2,000 Hz range.

The procedure for testing a person's sensitivity to pure tones is relatively simple. Each ear is tested separately. The audiologist presents a variety of tones within the range of 0 to about 110 dB and 125 to 8,000 Hz until he or she establishes at what level of intensity (dB) the individual can detect the tone at a number of frequencies—125 Hz, 250 Hz, 500 Hz, 1,000 Hz, 2,000 Hz, 4,000 Hz, and 8,000 Hz. For each frequency, there is a measure of degree of hearing impairment. A 50 dB hearing loss at 500 Hz, for example, means the individual is able to detect the 500 Hz sound when it is given at an intensity level of 50 dB, whereas the average person would have heard it at 0 dB.

Speech Audiometry

Because the ability to understand speech is of prime importance, a technique called **speech audiometry** has been developed to test a person's detection and understanding of speech. The **speech reception threshold (SRT)** is the dB level at which one is able to understand speech. One way to measure the SRT is to present the person with a list of two-syllable words, testing each ear separately. The dB level at which he or she can understand half the words is often used as an estimate of SRT level.

Tests for Young and Hard-to-Test Children

A basic assumption for pure-tone and speech audiometry is that the individuals who are being tested understand what is expected of them. They must be able to comprehend the instructions and show with a head nod or raised hand that they have heard the tone or word. None of this may be possible for very young children (under about four years of age) or for children with certain disabilities.

Play Audiometry. With this technique, the examiner establishes rapport with the child and motivates him or her to respond. In a gamelike format, using pure tones or speech, the examiner teaches the child to do various activities whenever he or she hears a signal. The activities are designed to be attractive to the young child. For example, the child may be required to pick up a block, squeeze a toy, or open a book.

Infant Responses to Sound and Reflex Audiometry. Infants as young as three months can be tested by measuring changes in the infant's heart rate or sucking when presented with auditory stimuli (Robinshaw, 1994). In addition, infants normally possess some reflexive behaviors to loud sounds, which are useful for the testing of hearing by **reflex audiometry.** For example, the examiner can test for the *orienting response,* which is evident when the infant turns his or her head and body toward the source of a sound.

Evoked-Response Audiometry. **Evoked-response audiometry** involves measuring changes in brain-wave activity by using an electroencephalograph (EEG). All sounds heard by an individual result in electrical signals within the brain, so this method has become more popular with the development of sophisticated

speech audiometry. A technique that tests a person's detection and understanding of speech, rather than using pure tones to detect hearing loss.

speech reception threshold (SRT). The decibel level at which a person can understand speech.

reflex audiometry. The testing of responses to sounds by observation of such reflex actions as the orienting response.

evoked-response audiometry. A technique involving electroencephalograph measurement of changes in brain-wave activity in response to sounds.

computers. Evoked-response audiometry can be used during sleep, and the child can be sedated and thus not be aware that he or she is being tested.

School Screening

Virtually all children who have severe hearing losses are identified before they reach school, but this is not always the case for children with mild hearing impairments. Many schools, therefore, have routine programs for screening. Hearing screening tests are administered either individually or in groups. These tests, especially those that are group administered, are less accurate than those administered in an audiologist's office. Children detected through screening as having possible problems are referred for more extensive evaluation.

Causes

Conductive, Sensorineural, and Mixed Impairments

Professionals classify causes of hearing loss on the basis of the location of the problem within the hearing mechanism. There are three major classifications: conductive, sensorineural, and mixed hearing losses. A **conductive hearing impairment** refers to an impairment that interferes with the transfer of sound along the conductive pathway of the middle or outer ear. A **sensorineural hearing impairment** involves problems in the inner ear. A **mixed hearing impairment** is a combination of the two. Audiologists attempt to determine the location of the dysfunction. The first clue may be the severity of the loss. A general rule is that hearing losses greater than 60 or 70 dB involve some inner-ear problem. Audiologists use the results of pure-tone testing to help determine the location of a hearing impairment, converting the results to an audiogram—a graphic representation of the weakest (lowest dB) sound the individual can hear at each of several frequency levels. The profile of the audiogram helps determine whether the loss is conductive, sensorineural, or mixed.

Impairments of the Outer Ear

Although impairments of the outer ear are not as serious as those of the middle or inner ear, several conditions of the outer ear can cause a person to be hard of hearing. In some children, for example, the external auditory canal does not form, resulting in a condition known as *atresia*. Children may also develop **external otitis,** or "swimmer's ear," an infection of the skin of the external auditory canal. Tumors of the external auditory canal are another source of impairment.

Impairments of the Middle Ear

Although abnormalities of the middle ear are generally more serious than problems of the outer ear, they, too, usually result in a person's being classified as hard of hearing rather than deaf. Most middle-ear hearing losses occur because the

Hearing can be assessed in infancy by measuring babies' responses to auditory stimuli.

conductive hearing impairment. A hearing loss, usually mild, resulting from malfunctioning along the conductive pathway of the ear (i.e., the outer or middle ear).

sensorineural hearing impairment. A hearing loss, usually severe, resulting from malfunctioning of the inner ear.

mixed hearing impairment. A hearing loss resulting from a combination of conductive and sensorineural hearing impairments.

external otitis. An infection of the skin of the external auditory canal; also called "swimmer's ear."

Routine hearing examinations, conducted in schools, often provide the first identification of mild hearing problems.

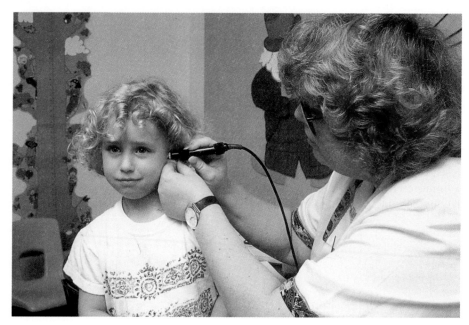

mechanical action of the ossicles is interfered with in some way. Unlike inner-ear impairments, most middle-ear impairments are correctable with medical or surgical treatment.

The most common problem of the middle ear is **otitis media**—an infection of the middle-ear space caused by viral and bacterial factors, among others. It is the second most common disease of childhood, second only to the common cold (Mencher, Gerber, & McCombe, 1997). Otitis media is linked to abnormal functioning of the eustachian tubes. If the eustachian tube malfunctions because of a respiratory viral infection, for example, it cannot do its job of ventilating, draining, and protecting the middle ear from infection (Giebink, 1990). The prevalence of otitis media is much higher in children with Down syndrome or cleft palate because these conditions often result in malformed eustachian tubes. Otitis media can result in temporary conductive hearing loss and, if untreated, can lead to rupture of the tympanic membrane.

Impairments of the Inner Ear

The most severe hearing impairments are associated with the inner ear. Unfortunately, inner-ear hearing losses present the greatest problems for both education and medicine. Troubles other than those related to loss of threshold sensitivity are frequent. For example, sound distortion often occurs. Disorders of the inner ear can result in problems of balance and vertigo along with hearing loss. Also, some individuals with inner-ear impairments may hear roaring or ringing noises.

Causes of inner-ear disorders can be hereditary or acquired. Genetic flaws are a leading cause of deafness in children (Travis, 1998). Acquired hearing losses of the inner ear include those due to bacterial infections (e.g., meningitis, the second most frequent cause of childhood deafness), prematurity, viral infections (e.g., mumps and measles), anoxia (deprivation of oxygen) at birth, prenatal infections of the mother (e.g., maternal rubella, congenital syphilis, and cytomegalovirus),

otitis media. Inflammation of the middle ear.

Rh incompatibility (which can now usually be prevented with proper prenatal care of the mother), blows to the head, unwanted side effects of some antibiotics, and excessive noise levels.

Congenital cytomegalovirus (CMV), a herpes virus, is the most frequent viral infection in newborns, occurring in 1 to 2 percent of all newborns (Hutchinson & Sandall, 1995). CMV can result in a variety of conditions, such as mental retardation, visual impairment, and especially hearing impairment. Estimates vary, but it appears that at least 10 to 15 percent of infants born with CMV will develop hearing impairment.

Psychological and Behavioral Characteristics

Hearing loss can have profound consequences for some aspects of a person's behavior and little or no effect on other characteristics. Consider the question: If you were forced to choose, which would you rather be—blind or deaf? On first impulse, most of us would choose deafness, probably because we rely on sight for mobility and because many of the beauties of nature are visual. But in terms of functioning in an English language–oriented society, the person who is deaf is at a much greater disadvantage than someone who is blind.

English Language and Speech Development

By far the most severely affected areas of development in the person who is hearing impaired and living in the United States are the comprehension and production of the English language. We stress *English* because it is the predominant language in the United States of those who can hear. In other words, people who are hearing impaired are generally deficient in the language used by most people of the hearing society in which they live. The distinction is important, because people who are hearing impaired can be expert in their own form of language. The current opinion is that individuals who use American Sign Language (ASL) produce and comprehend a true language. Furthermore, children who are deaf reach the same language development milestones in sign and do so at the same time as nondisabled children do in spoken language (Lane et al., 1996). For example, they acquire their first words at about 12 to 18 months and two-word phrases at about 18 to 22 months. (We return to a discussion of ASL on p. 365).

Regarding English, however, it is an undeniable fact that individuals with hearing impairment are at a distinct disadvantage. This is true in terms of language comprehension, language production, and speech. With regard to speech, for example, teachers report that 23 percent of students with hearing impairment have speech that is not intelligible, 22 percent have speech that is barely intelligible, and 10 percent are unwilling to speak in public. Speech intelligibility is linked to degree of hearing loss, with 75 percent of children who are profoundly deaf having nonintelligible speech but only 14 percent of children with less-than-severe hearing loss having nonintelligible speech (Wolk & Schildroth, 1986).

In addition, it is much more difficult for children who are prelingually deaf to learn to speak than it is for those who have acquired their deafness, mainly because they do not receive auditory feedback from the sounds they make. They have not heard an adult language model. An interesting research finding is that infants born

congenital cytomegalovirus (CMV). The most frequently occurring viral infection in newborns; can result in a variety of disabilities, especially hearing impairment.

deaf enter the babbling stage at the same time as hearing infants but soon abandon it (Ling & Ling, 1978; Schow & Nerbonne, 1980; Stoel-Gammon & Otomo, 1986). By as early as eight months of age and possibly earlier, babies who are hearing impaired babble less than hearing infants, and the babbling they do is of a qualitatively different nature (Stoel-Gammon & Otomo, 1986). It is thought that these differences occur because hearing infants are reinforced by hearing their own babbling and by hearing the verbal responses of adults. Children who are unable to hear either themselves or others are not reinforced.

The lack of feedback has also been named as a primary cause of poor speech production in children who are deaf. Children who are deaf are handicapped in learning to associate the sensations they receive when they move their jaws, mouths, and tongues with the auditory sounds these movements produce. In addition, these children have a difficult time hearing the sounds of adult speech, which nonimpaired children hear and imitate. As a result, children who are deaf do not have access to an adequate adult model of spoken English.

Table 9.1 gives general examples of the effects that various degrees of hearing loss may have on English language development. This is only a general statement of these relationships, since many factors interact to influence language development in the child with hearing impairment.

Intellectual Ability

Historically, the intellectual ability of children with hearing impairment has been a subject of much controversy. For many years professionals believed that the conceptual ability of individuals who are deaf was deficient because of their deficient spoken language. This belief was erroneous for two reasons:

1. The assumption that language can be equated with cognitive abilities, popularized by famous Russian psychologist Lev Vygotsky (1962), has been largely debunked. Vygotsky assumed that the early speech of children became interiorized as inner speech and that inner speech became the equivalent of thought. Most psychologists now believe that Vygostky's notions of the primary role of language in the development of cognition were misguided.
2. Researchers have warned that we should not assume that persons who cannot speak because they are deaf have no language. They may not have a spoken language, such as English, but if they use American Sign Language, they are using a true language with its own rules of grammar. (Again, we return to this point later.)

Any intelligence testing done with people who are hearing impaired must take into account their English language deficiency. Performance tests, rather than verbal tests, especially if they are administered in sign, offer a much fairer assessment of the IQ of a person with a hearing impairment. When these tests are used, there is no difference in IQ between those who are deaf and those who are hearing (Prinz et al., 1996).

Academic Achievement

Unfortunately, most children with hearing impairment have extreme deficits in academic achievement. Reading ability, which relies heavily on English language skills and is probably the most important area of academic achievement, is most

Table 9.1 Relationship of Degree of Impairment to Understanding of Language and Speech

	Average of the Speech Frequencies in Better Ear	Effect of Hearing Loss on Understanding of Language and Speech
Slight	27–40 dB	• May have difficulty hearing faint or distant speech. • May experience some difficulty with language arts subjects.
Mild	41–55 dB	• Understands conversational speech at a distance of 3–5 feet (face to face). • May miss as much as 50 percent of class discussions if voices are faint or not in line of vision. • May exhibit limited vocabulary and speech anomalies.
Marked	56–70 dB	• Conversation must be loud to be understood. • Will have increased difficulty in group discussions. • Is likely to have defective speech. • Is likely to be deficient in language usage and comprehension. • Will have limited vocabulary.
Severe	71–90 dB	• May hear loud voices about 1 foot from the ear. • May be able to identify environmental sounds. • May be able to discriminate vowels but not all consonants. • Speech and language defective and likely to deteriorate.
Extreme	91 dB or more	• May hear some loud sounds but is aware of vibrations more than tonal patterns. • Relies on vision rather than hearing as primary avenue for communication. • Speech and language defective and likely to deteriorate.

Note: Impairment means medically irreversible conditions and those requiring prolonged medical care.

Source: Adapted from Report of a Committee for a Comprehensive Plan for Hearing-Impaired Children, May 1968, Office of the Superintendent of Public Instruction, Title VI, Elementary and Secondary Education Act, and the University of Illinois, Division of Services for Crippled Children.

affected. Numerous studies paint a bleak picture for the reading achievement of students with hearing impairment (Allen, 1986; Trybus & Karchmer, 1977; Wolk & Allen, 1984). Representative findings are that the growth in reading achievement of students with hearing impairment is about one-third that for hearing students. Upon graduation from high school, it is not at all unusual for students who are deaf to be able to read at no more than a fourth-grade level. Even in math, which is their best academic subject, students with hearing impairment trail their hearing peers by substantial margins.

Several studies have demonstrated that children who are deaf who have parents who are deaf have higher reading achievement than do those who have hearing parents (Kampfe & Turecheck, 1987). Authorities speculate that this is due to the positive influence of sign language. Parents who are deaf may be able to communicate better with their children through the use of ASL, providing the children with needed support. In addition, children who have parents who are deaf are more likely to be proficient in ASL, and ASL may aid these children in learning written English and reading. There is not much research on this topic, but one study did find a relationship between facility in ASL and academic achievement (Prinz et al., 1996).

Social Adjustment

Social and personality development in the hearing population depend heavily on communication—and the situation is no different for those who are deaf. The hearing person has little difficulty finding people with whom to communicate. The person who is deaf, however, may face problems in finding others with whom he or she can converse. Studies have demonstrated that many students who are deaf are at risk for loneliness (Cambra, 1996; Charlson, Strong, & Gold, 1992). Two factors are important in considering the possible isolation of students who are deaf: inclusion and hearing status of the parents.

Researchers have shown that in inclusionary settings, very little interaction typically occurs between students who are deaf and those who are not (Gaustad & Kluwin, 1992). Furthermore, in inclusionary settings, students who are deaf feel more emotionally secure if they have other students who are deaf with whom they can communicate (Stinson & Whitmire, 1992). This is not always possible, however, because of the low prevalence of hearing impairment. Therefore, researchers are trying to come up with programs that directly teach social behaviors to children who are deaf in order to get them to interact with hearing peers (Antia & Kreimeyer, 1997.

Some authorities believe that students who attend residential schools are less likely to experience isolation because they have other students with whom they can easily communicate. At the same time, children in residential schools are prone to feel alienated from their families.

Some authorities believe that the child who is deaf who has hearing parents runs a greater risk of being unhappy than if he or she has parents who are deaf. This is because many hearing parents do not become proficient in ASL and are unable to communicate with their children easily. Given that over 90 percent of children who are deaf have hearing parents, this problem in communication may be critical.

The need for social interaction is probably most influential in leading many persons with hearing impairment to associate primarily with others with hearing impairment. If their parents are deaf, children who are deaf are usually exposed to other deaf families from an early age. Nonetheless, many persons who are deaf end up, as adults, socializing predominantly with others who are deaf, even if they have hearing parents and even if they do not come into contact as children with many other children who were deaf. This phenomenon of socializing with others who are deaf is attributable to the influence of the Deaf culture.

The Deaf Culture. In the past, most professionals viewed isolation from the hearing community on the part of many people who are deaf as a sign of social pathology. But now more and more professionals agree with the many people who are deaf who believe in the value of having their own Deaf culture. They view this culture as a natural condition emanating from the common bond of sign language.

The unifying influence of sign language is the first of six factors noted by Reagan (1990) as demarcating the Deaf community as a true culture: (1) linguistic differentiation, (2) attitudinal deafness, (3) behavioral norms, (4) endogamous marital patterns, (5) historical awareness, and (6) voluntary organizational networks.

Regarding *linguistic differentiation*, most authorities view the Deaf community as bilingual, with individuals possessing varying degrees of fluency in ASL and English (Reagan, 1990). People who are deaf are continually shifting between ASL and English, as well as between the Deaf culture and that of the hearing (Padden, 1996).

Attitudinal deafness refers to whether a person thinks of himself or herself as deaf. It may not have anything to do with a person's hearing acuity. For example, a person with a relatively mild hearing loss may think of himself or herself as deaf more readily than does someone with a profound hearing loss.

The Deaf community has its own set of *behavioral norms*. A few examples of these norms, according to Lane et al. (1996), are that people who are deaf value informality and physical contact in their interactions with one another, often giving each other hugs when greeting and departing. And their departures, or leave-takings, often take much longer than those of hearing society. Also, they are likely to be frank in their discussions, not hesitating to get directly to the point of what it is they want to communicate.

Endogamous marriage patterns are evident from surveys showing rates of ingroup marriage as high as 90 percent. And "mixed marriages" between persons who are deaf and those who are hearing tend to be frowned upon by the Deaf community.

The Deaf community has a long history that has contributed to its *historical awareness* of significant people and events pertaining to people who are deaf. They are often deferential to elders and value their wisdom and knowledge pertaining to Deaf traditions.

Finally, there is an abundance of *voluntary organizational networks* for the Deaf community, such as the National Association of the Deaf, the World Games for the Deaf (Deaf Olympics), and the National Theatre of the Deaf (see the box on p. 356).

Many within the Deaf community and some within professional ranks are concerned that the cultural status of children who are deaf is in peril (Gaustad & Kluwin, 1992; Janesick & Moores, 1992; Lane et al., 1996). They believe that the increase in inclusion is eroding the cultural values of the Deaf culture. In the past, much of Deaf culture was passed down from generation to generation through contacts made at residential schools, but today's children who are deaf may have little contact with other children who are deaf, if they attend local schools. Some authorities have recommended that schools provide classes in Deaf history and culture for students who are deaf who attend local schools. These authorities further recommend that such classes be taught by people who are deaf so they can serve as role models (Drasgow, 1993).

Further evidence of the erosion of the Deaf culture is the fact that Deaf clubs are on the decline (Lane et al., 1996). **Deaf clubs,** common in large metropolitan areas, have traditionally served to forge strong bonds among people who are deaf:

> When school days are over, the club is traditionally the key place for further acculturation and socializing. Older members teach younger ones, explicitly or indirectly, about Deaf values, customs and knowledge, ASL, Deaf stories and jokes, and Deaf history.... In the Deaf clubs, members seek information about the world, the community, employment, friends. They seek relaxation and easy conversation, participation in sports and leisure activities, and entertainment. (Lane et al., 1996, p. 134)

Deaf clubs. Gathering spots where people who are deaf can socialize; on the decline in the United States.

With the increase in inclusion and the growing popularity of the internet as a method of gathering information, it will be interesting to see what the future

The National Theatre for the Deaf

Three Dramatic Decades

The National Theatre of the Deaf is a professional acting company made up of Deaf and hearing actors. Established in 1967, The National Theatre of the Deaf brought Sign Language out of the shadows and placed it in the world spotlight, raising it to the level of an art form. The theatre's signature style, a combination of Sign Language and spoken words, has expanded the boundaries of theatrical expression. This double-sensory style enables audiences to see words as they are spoken in an engaging and compelling art form.

Great literature is brought to life in physical, visually-stunning American Sign Language. For Deaf audiences, the inclusiveness of The National Theatre of the Deaf's style has opened new doors in language and the imagination. For hearing audiences, it offers an expanded view of language and its expression. For all, it is an example of the power of art to transform lives.

The National Theatre of the Deaf has served as a catalyst for dramatic cultural and social changes for the Deaf in this country and abroad for three decades. It has also served as a theatrical role model in the creation of over 40 theatres of the Deaf nationally and internationally.

The National Theatre of the Deaf was the first theatre company to perform in all 50 states and has toured to every continent except Antarctica. The theatre serves as an artistic ambassador for the United States, a shining example to the international community of America's imaginative support, encouragement and celebration of its minorities.

History ...

In 1967, six people bought tickets to see the first performance of The National Theatre of the Deaf (NTD), most of them out of curiosity. Thirty years and one Tony Award later, the NTD has brought audiences to their feet on six continents and has received rave reviews from New York to New Delhi.

The concept of a professional company of deaf performers was formed in the 1950s by Dr. Edna Simon Levine, a psychologist working in the area of deafness. Arthur Penn and Anne Bancroft, the director and leading actress of Broadway's "The Miracle Worker," were approached with the idea and, in turn, brought the idea to David Hays, a Broadway set and lighting designer. With Anne Bancroft, Hays traveled to Gallaudet College where they saw a student production of "Our Town." Hays was immediately struck by the beauty and power of Sign Language on stage. Penn and Bancroft were subsequently unable to be involved due to other commitments; David Hays persisted in his vision of bringing this powerful form of expression to theatre audiences.

A federal grant in 1965 from the U.S. Department of Health, Education and Welfare provided planning funds. In the spring of 1967, a national television program was aired which explored the experimental idea of the NTD. With additional funds from the U.S. Office of Education, the NTD's annual Professional Theatre School began that summer, and the company made its first national tour that fall from a home base it shared with The O'Neill Theatre Center in Waterford, Connecticut. The following year, The Little Theatre of the Deaf, providing theatre for young audiences, was created and began touring.

In 1983, the Company moved to its own home in Chester, CT. In 1992, a Los Angeles-based Little Theatre of the Deaf company was formed which operates in conjunction with the Education Division of The Music Center of Los Angeles County. In 1993, the new Artistic Directors, one deaf and one hearing, joined Artistic Director David Hays, to lead the Company into the next century. In 1995, the National and World Wide Deaf Theatre Conference had its inaugural session, to facilitate communication, techniques, and the work of deaf playwrights from the over 40 theatres of the deaf from around the world that the NTD was instrumental in founding.

Throughout its thirty-year history, the NTD has received critical acclaim for its adaptations of classic literature (Chekhov, Voltaire, Homer, Moliere, Ibsen and Puccini) as well as for original works by the Company. The NTD has put its signature on such creations as a magical adaptation of Philippe de Broca's film, "King Of Hearts" and an adventurous new look at "Hamlet"—Shakespeare from the woman's point of view—in a production titled "Ophelia." The NTD has collaborated with artists such as Chita Rivera, Jason Robards, Arvin Brown, Bill Irwin, Peter Sellars, Tetsuko Kuroyanagi and the late Colleen Dewhurst. The Company appears regularly on national television. The NTD's teleplay of "One More Spring" with the Learning Channel was nominated for an ACE Award.

In thirty years, there have been 59 national tours with visits to all 50 states, 28 international tours to every continent except Antarctica, and over 7,000 performances, earning the NTD its place in theatrical history as the oldest, continually-producing touring theatre company in the United States.

Source: The National Theatre for the Deaf. (1997, October 12). *Three dramatic decades* [Posted on the World Wide Web]. Author. Retrieved May 27, 1998 from the World Wide Web: http://www.ntd.org/about.htm and www.ntd.org/history.htm

holds for Deaf clubs. See Figure 9.2 for an example of a Web site devoted to sharing information among parents, teachers, and students who are deaf.

Even though some may think the Deaf community is in peril of losing its identity, it is still very active in advocating a variety of social, educational, and medical policies. For example, the Deaf Coalition—an alliance of Deaf theater organizations and other groups related to deafness—has been active in promoting the use of actors who are deaf in movies and theater. The coalition maintains that a hearing person could never pass for a native signer, even after years of practice. Moreover, for the Deaf community, seeing a hearing actor playing the role of a person who is deaf is demeaning in the same way that seeing a white actor in "blackface" would be demeaning to an African American.

Another example of Deaf activism occurred in 1988 at Gallaudet University—a liberal arts college for the deaf and hard of hearing—where students and faculty protested the board of trustees' selection of a hearing president. Since its founding in 1864, Gallaudet had never had a deaf president. After students shut down the university for several days, the school's administration acquiesced to their demands for a deaf president and a reconfiguration of the board to include a majority of members who are deaf.

Deaf activists have also been aggressive in attacking what they consider an oppressive medical and educational establishment. An example of just how much this segment of the Deaf community is at odds with many professionals is its opposition to the medical procedure of **cochlear implantation** (see the box on p. 358).

cochlear implantation. A surgical procedure that allows people who are deaf to hear some environmental sounds; an external coil fitted on the skin by the ear picks up sound from a microphone worn by the person and transmits it to an internal coil implanted in the bone behind the ear, which carries it to an electrode implanted in the cochlea of the inner ear.

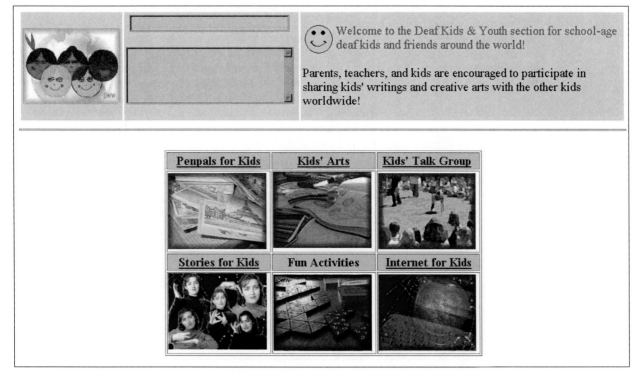

Figure 9.2

Deaf CyberKids

Source: Deaf World Web. (January 15, 1998). *Deaf CyberKids* [Posted on the World Wide Web]. Author. Retrieved from the World Wide Web: http://dww.org/kids (Email: dww@dww.org). Reprinted by permission.

The Controversy Surrounding Cochlear Implants

In 1990, after several years of experimentation, the U.S. Food and Drug Administration (FDA) approved the use of cochlear implants for children as young as two. In Europe, children as young as eight months have been implanted (Arana-Ward, 1997). A cochlear implant involves surgically implanting electronic elements under the skin behind the ear and in the inner ear. A small microphone worn behind the ear picks up sounds and sends them to a small computerized speech processor worn by the person. The speech processor sends coded signals back up to an external coil worn behind the ear, which sends them through the skin to the implanted internal coil. The internal coil then sends the signals to electrodes implanted in the inner ear.

As of the end of 1997, more than 16,500 people worldwide had received cochlear implants, including more than 6,500 children (Cochlear Corporation, 1997). This device is far from a cure-all for deafness, however. A cochlear implant does not automatically enable individuals to understand speech—a significant amount of training is needed to help them make sense of the sounds they may be hearing for the first time (in the case of those who were born deaf). Nonetheless, advocates of implants predict that the procedure will continue to be perfected so that someday it will lead to significant improvements in hearing in many cases.

Whereas the medical community has tended to tout the virtues of cochlear implants, many within the Deaf community see implants as overly zealous medical tinkering. Furthermore, for those who view deafness as leading to a cultural and linguistic difference rather than as a disability, cochlear implants are an assault on the Deaf culture:

> I expect that most Americans would agree that our society should not seek the scientific tools or use them, if available, to change a child biologically so he or she will belong to the majority rather than the minority—even if we believe that this biological engineering might reduce the burdens the child will bear as a member of a minority. Even if we could take children destined to be members of the African American, or Hispanic American, or Native American, or Deaf American communities and convert them with bio-power into white, Caucasian, hearing males—even if we could, we should not. We should likewise refuse cochlear implants for young deaf children even if the devices were perfect. (Lane, 1992, p. 237)

Opponents of cochlear implants are especially negative about using the surgical procedure on young children, particularly those who are prelingually deaf. They assert that research thus far has not demonstrated that the procedure helps children with prelingual deafness to hear and speak significantly better (Lane et al., 1996; Rose, Vernon, & Pool, 1996). Some authorities believe that it will not be until those who were implanted after 1990 start reaching adulthood that definitive statements regarding effectiveness will be able to be made (Arana-Ward, 1997).

Although well-controlled research has not yet demonstrated the widespread effectiveness of cochlear implants with young children, proponents point to several anecdotal accounts of success as reason enough to try the procedure. They think that those who categorically oppose cochlear implants are far too radical and are denying their children potential benefits in their attempts to preserve the Deaf culture.

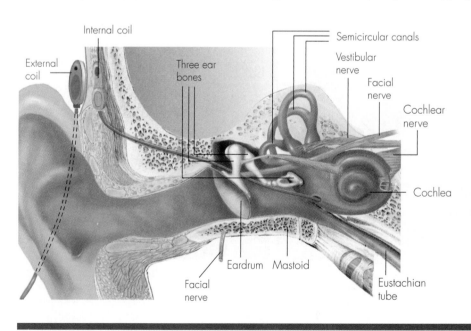

A Cochlear Implant.

Educational Considerations

Formidable problems face the educator working with students with hearing impairment. As we would expect, one major problem is communication. Dating back to the sixteenth century, there has been a raging debate concerning how individuals who are deaf should converse (Lane, 1984). This controversy is sometimes referred to as the **oralism–manualism debate** to represent two very different points of view—one of which advocates teaching people who are deaf to speak and the other, to use of some kind of manual communication. Manualism was the preferred method until the middle of the nineteenth century, when oralism began to gain predominance. Currently, most educational programs involve both oral and manual methods in what is referred to as a **total communication approach** (Meadow-Orlans, Mertens, Sass-Lehrer, & Scott-Olson, 1997). However, many within the Deaf community believe that the total communication approach is inadequate, and they advocate for a **bicultural-bilingual approach,** which promotes (1) American Sign Language (ASL) as a first language, (2) English as a second language, and (3) instruction in the Deaf culture.

We first discuss the major techniques that make up the oral approach and the oral portion of the total communication approach; then we take up total communication, followed by a discussion of the bicultural-bilingual approach.

Oral Approach: Auditory-Verbal Approach and Speechreading

The Auditory-Verbal Approach. The **auditory-verbal approach** stresses using techniques designed to encourage children to make use of what hearing they possess. According to Auditory-Verbal International, Inc. (1998), a major professional organization promoting the auditory-verbal philosophy, some of the principles behind this approach are:

- It is never too early to start auditory-verbal training—ideally it should be introduced in the newborn nursery.
- The majority of children who are hearing impaired have some residual hearing.
- The use of amplification (e.g., hearing aids), starting at an early age, is critical.
- With proper amplification, most children with hearing impairment are able to hear sounds in the frequency range relevant to speech.
- Children should be taught to be active listeners, rather than allowed to rely only on the visual modality.
- Parents do not need to learn sign language.
- Parents, as the primary language models for their children, are a critical component in any treatment plan.

Speechreading. Sometimes inappropriately called lipreading, **speechreading** involves teaching children who are hearing impaired to use visual information to understand what is being said to them. *Speechreading* is a more accurate term than *lipreading* because the goal is to teach students to attend to a variety of stimuli in

oralism–manualism debate. The controversy over whether the goal of instruction for students who are deaf should be to teach them to speak or to teach them to use sign language.

total communication approach. An approach for teaching students with hearing impairment that blends oral and manual techniques.

bicultural-bilingual approach. An approach for teaching students with hearing impairment that stresses teaching American Sign Language as a first language, English as a second language, and promotes the teaching of Deaf culture.

auditory-verbal approach. Part of the oral approach to teaching students who are hearing impaired; stresses teaching the person to use his or her remaining hearing as much as possible; heavy emphasis on use of amplification.

speechreading. A method that involves teaching children to use visual information from a number of sources to understand what is being said to them; more than just lipreading, which uses only visual clues arising from the movement of the mouth in speaking.

Collaboration key to success

Connie Underwood

Cindy Sadonis is a teacher of students who are deaf/hard of hearing, Beverley Manor Elementary School; B.S., Speech and Hearing, Indiana University of Pennsylvania; M.Ed., Hearing Disorders, James Madison University. She was named Teacher of the Year for 1997–98 in Augusta County Schools, Virginia. **Connie Underwood** is a third-grade teacher, Beverley Manor Elementary School, Augusta County Public Schools, Virginia; B.S. in Education, Eastern Nazarene College, Boston.

Connie If you are familiar with the poem "Deaf Donald" by Shel Silverstein, it may give you insight into our approach to collaborative teaching. It hung on both our walls as a reminder of the importance of taking the time to get to know one another.

Cindy I teach nine students with hearing impairments in grades kindergarten through fifth. The students receive a range of special education services, from resource support to more intensive help in a self-contained class, depending on their individual needs. All students, however, are mainstreamed for library, music, P.E., guidance, and special events. The students' hearing losses range from moderate to profound. A total communication approach utilizing speech, speechreading, residual hearing, Cued Speech, and/or Conceptually Accurate Signed English is used within my program. Interpreters, who may also function as paraeducators, accompany the children into general education settings.

Connie I teach a general education third-grade class. This is one of three third-grade classrooms at our school. There are 17 students with reading levels ranging from below grade level to fourth- and fifth-grade reading skills. I incorporate whole language strategies through thematic units which change each month. Centers throughout the room, reading group activities, as well as science and social studies lessons are planned around

the theme for the month. Textbooks are not completely abandoned, but used when appropriate with our theme, or when a specific skill needs targeting.

Cindy I first approached Connie about the possibility of having two of my students in her classroom at the end of the previous school year. The two students were significantly different in both their hearing losses and communication skills. Joe, a child of Korean descent with a partially repaired cleft lip and palate, has hearing thresholds at normal levels with the help of a hearing aid. Sign language was initially introduced in preschool and continued for both receptive and expressive purposes at his parents' request. In the general education classroom, Joe needs the support of a paraeducator rather than an interpreter due to his significant language deficits. He is able to communicate verbally with peers and adults, although restructuring of language complexities is often needed for comprehension. Brittany has a severe-to-profound hearing loss. She simultaneously uses her oral skills and sign skills. To the unfamiliar listener she is approximately 80 percent intelligible. She has more difficulty with receptive communication, especially in group situations. She relies on the interpreter for classroom lecture and discussion, but responds for herself rather than having the interpreter voice for her.

Connie I had worked with students with hearing impairments in my general

education classroom in the past, and although the experiences were positive in many ways, I felt that I was connecting with the students "at a distance." It seemed as though I was teaching a "satellite" class ... getting the information through, but with limited interaction. Ironically, Cindy and I found we both shared some of the same concerns. We did not want this triangular (teacher, interpreter, student) communication approach to be present all the time. I wanted to experience opportunities where I could communicate with the students directly.

Cindy It's important to note that we were both apprehensive despite being friends, co-workers, and experienced teachers. This was new territory, literally and figuratively. I went into Connie's room and she and her third grade students came into my room. It gave me a perspective on what we as special educators request of the general education teachers when we ask them to accommodate "OUR" students. I had to become comfortable teaching a larger group through trial and error while "THEIR" teacher was present. My focus involved incorporating speech and language into everything I did. I found it difficult to let everyone contribute and still have time for accomplishing the instructional objectives. Having a larger group of students affected classroom management, room setup, peer interactions, questioning techniques, as well as my own teaching style.

Cindy Sadonis

Connie Sharing classrooms, although a very simple logistic change, was profound in many ways. Many of my third graders had already asked about what went on in "THEIR" (Cindy's) classroom. My students were entering a new environment but very quickly Joe's and Brittany's room became a familiar, fun place to go for unit time.

I had three main fears. First, was I going to be able to communicate with Joe and Brittany without an interpreter? Yikes! My signing skills were labored, elementary, and painfully wrong at times. But Joe, Brittany, and Cindy were always patient with us ... and sometimes very amused! Feeling vulnerable became less threatening. Second, I faced the ultimate question of all co-teachers—"So how much more planning and time will this take?" I already felt burdened with the myriad new, innovative, teaching strategies that were challenging me in my own classroom. Was this another challenge that would add time demands to my already full schedule? To my surprise, and thanks to Cindy's willingness to take turns, I was teaching what I had already planned for my units and yet I had no added time-consuming responsibilities. When I was lead teacher, Cindy interpreted and observed and was ready the next week with lessons on the same theme. I became a support in her room when she became the lead teacher. With Cindy's help, I became more aware of how difficult it was for the student with a hearing impairment to deal with several tasks at once (e.g, draw this

plant model as I tell you about pollination). I also realized how often I use figurative language and idiomatic expressions. And of course, I developed a true understanding of how important it is to face the student when you speak, rather than speak while writing on the chalkboard. Third, I was concerned about student relationships. Would this collaborative teaching really help our students respond favorably on a social level? Incidental conversations between Joe, Brittany, and my students occurred more and more frequently as the year progressed. Without prompting, our students began signing as they tried to communicate, and by the latter part of the year it was amazing how much communication was going on at the lunch table, in P.E., and even secretively (or so the kids thought) in the classroom. Third graders next door expressed interest in Cindy's early morning sign language lessons, and before long we were moving desks out of the way so more students could join our "cool" sign class.

Cindy Although Joe and Brittany were not mainstreamed into Connie's room for language arts, we did do some collaborative teaching in this area as well. When Joe and Brittany were reading *Rapunzel* we decided to write a play and put it on for various classes within the school. I talked to Connie about having four of her students join Joe and Brittany during this period. Together, the students wrote the play, learned the signs, made the props, and practiced the play. We also included the targeted vocabulary in our morning sign language class so the third graders received additional practice and familiarized themselves with the new words. It was especially rewarding to see a student with weak academic skills from Connie's class just shine on stage.

> I faced the ultimate question of all co-teachers—'So how much more planning and time will this take?'

Connie Sounds hunky-dory, huh? Well, not always. There were times when Brittany and Joe still felt different and when my students found it much easier to engage in conversations with their friends without hearing losses. When Cindy offered to teach me and my class to sign, we quickly became aware that we couldn't learn enough signs to converse fluently by the end of the year, but it felt much better to be able to sign and say, "How are you today?" or "Let's go to P.E." or "Great job!" It was just a small step to help remove that "satellite" feeling. For me, the most moving experience this year was Cindy's invitation to a signing party in her room. The rules were: sign when you enter the door, no voices, and have fun! Of course, any classroom teacher's attention is peaked when you have thirty silent students in one room for half an hour ... silence that is, with the exception of laughter and munching and gulping and small hands moving.

Cindy It is important to note that collaborative teaching to this degree is often difficult, due to schedule. It worked for us this year because of flexibility and modifications in both our schedules. Different years may mean different degrees of collaboration. Positive teacher attitudes are required if inclusion is to succeed. Challenges presented themselves along the way for us, too. Social interaction was always an area of need despite our best efforts. Group situations were difficult for the children with hearing impairments. This is even truer as children get older because peer interactions rely increasingly on verbal communication. As teachers, we have highs and lows too. Working through them has helped us continue to move in the right direction. We've recently set up opportunities for the third-grade students to take turns bringing home our school TTY. This has been an exciting new avenue for Brittany. Her mother recently told us that she was now coming in the door and asking if she had any messages on the answering machine. We've had a great year. The students have grown, but so have we. Time constraints and demands affect everyone; however, collaborative teaching can provide opportunities for each teacher to focus on areas of strength or interest while the other teacher serves as a support teacher.

addition to specific movements of the lips. For example, proficient speechreaders read contextual stimuli so they can anticipate certain types of messages in certain types of situations. They are able to use facial expressions to help them interpret what is being said to them. Even the ability to discriminate the various speech sounds that flow from a person's mouth involves attending to visual cues from the tongue and jaw as well as the lips. For example, to learn to discriminate among vowels, the speechreader concentrates on cues related to the degree of jaw opening and lip shaping.

Cued speech is a method of augmenting speechreading. In cued speech, the individual uses hand shapes to represent specific sounds while speaking. Although it has some devoted advocates, cued speech is not used widely in the United States.

Criticisms of the Oral Approach. Several authorities have been critical of using an exclusively oral approach with students who have hearing impairment (Lane et al., 1996; Padden & Humphries, 1988). In particular, they object to the de-emphasis of sign language in this approach, especially for children who are deaf. These critics assert that for many children with severe or profound degrees of hearing loss, it is unreasonable to assume that they have enough hearing to be of use. As such, denying these children access to ASL is denying them access to a language to communicate.

Critics of the oral approach also point out that speechreading is extremely difficult and good speechreaders are rare. It is easy to overlook some of the factors that make speechreading difficult. For instance, speakers produce many sounds with little obvious movement of the mouth. Another issue is that the English language has many **homophenes**—different sounds that are visually identical when spoken. For example, a speechreader cannot distinguish among the pronunciations of [p], [b], and [m]. There is also variability among speakers in how they produce sounds. Finally, such factors as poor lighting, rapid speaking, and talking with one's head turned are further examples of why good speechreading is a rare skill (Menchel, 1988).

Total Communication

As noted previously, most schools have adopted the total communication approach, a combination of oral and manual methods. The shift from exclusively oral instruction to total communication in the 1970s occurred primarily because researchers found that children who were deaf fared better academically and socially if they had parents who were deaf than if they had hearing parents (Moores & Maestas y Moores, 1981). Investigators attributed this difference to the greater likelihood of signing in families in which children and parents were both deaf.

Signing English Systems. **Signing English systems** are the type of manualism most often used in the total communication approach. Signing English systems refer to approaches that pro-

> **cued speech.** A method to aid speechreading in people with hearing impairment; the speaker uses hand shapes to represent sounds.

> **homophenes.** Sounds that are different but that look the same with regard to movements of the face and lips (i.e., visible articulatory patterns).

> **signing English systems.** Used simultaneously with oral methods in the total communication approach to teaching students who are deaf; different from American Sign Language because they maintain the same word order as spoken English.

A total communication approach blends oral and manual methods.

fessionals have devised for teaching people who are deaf to communicate. There are several such systems—for example, Signing Exact English, Signed English, and Seeing Essential English (Luetke-Stahlman & Milburn, 1996). The fact that teachers use signing English systems instead of ASL has sparked heated debate. **Fingerspelling,** the representation of letters of the English alphabet by finger positions, is also used occasionally to spell out certain words (see Figure 9.3).

The Bicultural-Bilingual Approach

As noted above, the bicultural-bilingual approach consists of using ASL as the primary language in academic instruction and English as the second language. In addition, it includes teaching the history of the Deaf culture. The rationale behind this approach is to provide students who are deaf with a foundation in their natural language, ASL, so that it can serve as a basis for learning English (See the box on page 365).

There are two general models of bilingual education for students who are deaf (Drasgow, 1993). One emphasizes allowing children to acquire ASL naturally from teachers who are deaf or truly bilingual before formally teaching them English. This approach is based on the idea that English will be easier to learn if the child first has a solid ASL foundation. Advocates of the second model do not see an advantage to teaching one language before the other. Instead, they stress exposing the child to both ASL and English from as early an age as possible, as long as the two languages are used consistently in separate contexts or by different people. For example, ASL might be used in some subjects and English in others, or ASL might be used by one teacher and English by another.

The most controversial aspect of the bicultural-bilingual approach is its stress on ASL. Even though the use of ASL in public school classrooms is still rare and those people who employ a total communication approach almost always use a blend of oralism and a signing English system of some sort, there are those within the Deaf community who champion the use of ASL rather than signed English (Drasgow, 1998; Lane, 1987, 1992; Lane et al., 1996; Padden & Humphries, 1988). This small but growing group of advocates asserts that ASL is the natural language of people who are deaf and that it should be fostered because it is the most natural and efficient way for students to learn about the world. To clarify, signing English systems are not true languages, whereas ASL is (see the box on p. 366). Signing English systems have been invented by one or a few people in a short period of time, whereas true sign languages such as ASL have evolved over several generations of users.

One of the most important differences between the two is that signing English systems follow the same word order as spoken English, thus making it possible to sign and speak at the same time; ASL has a different word order, making the simultaneous use of spoken English and ASL extremely difficult. Defenders of signing English systems state that the correspondence in word order between signing English systems and English helps students learn English better. Advocates of ASL assert that the use of signing English systems is too slow and awkward to be of much benefit in learning English. They argue that word order is not the critical element in teaching a person to use and comprehend English. Furthermore, they believe that fluency in ASL provides students with a rich background of information that readies them for the learning of English.

Lending credence to those advocating ASL instruction are studies showing a relationship between ASL usage and academic performance in English (Prinz et

fingerspelling. Spelling the English alphabet by using various finger positions on one hand.

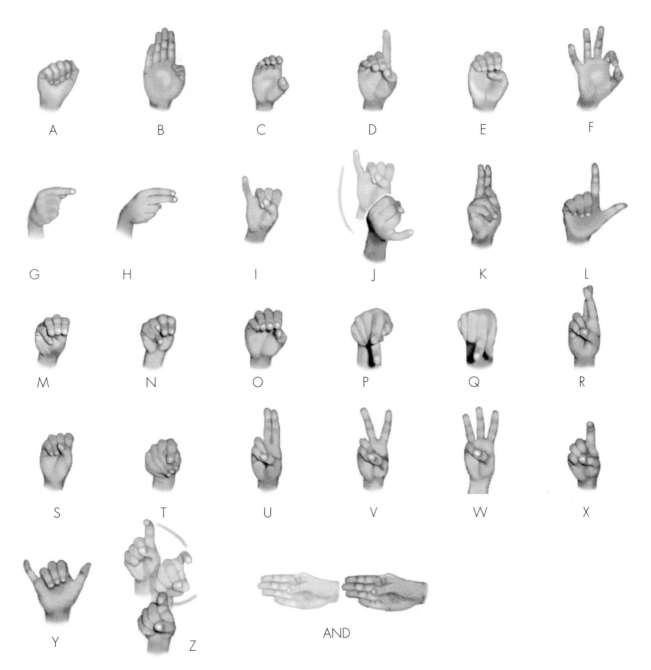

Figure 9.3

Fingerspelling alphabet.
Source: Redrawn from Deaf World Web at http://dww.org. Reprinted by permission.

al., 1996; Strong & Prinz, 1997). That is, students who are exposed to ASL at an early age have better English literacy skills regardless of whether their parents are deaf or hearing. However, research directly bearing on the efficacy of bicultural-bilingual programs is in its infancy. At least one study has found evidence for the effectiveness of bicultural-bilingual programming (Andrews, Ferguson, Roberts, & Hodges, 1997).

It is ironic that, while bicultural-bilingual education is on the rise for students who are deaf, bilingual education for language minorities is under attack in the

New York to Teach Deaf in Sign Language, Then English

In what is being hailed as a landmark change in the education of deaf students, the city's only public school for the deaf will be overhauled so that all teachers will teach primarily in [American Sign Language (ASL)] rather than an English-like sign language ... or other methods like lipreading and pointing....

With the move ... New York City, the nation's largest school system, is embracing an approach that has gained currency among many educators and advocates for the deaf. They say that research shows that the primary language of deaf people is visual, not verbal, and that schools using ... [ASL] educate students better than other schools do.

They say deaf students should be treated as bilingual students, not disabled ones. In their view, students first need a primary language—American Sign Language—before they learn a second language, in this case, English.

The advocacy of bilingual education as a model for deaf people is an integral part of their growing campaign for recognition of a deaf culture with its own rituals and beliefs. Martin Florsheim has been applauded as the first deaf principal in JHS 47's 90-year history.

"I think Public School 47 is in the vanguard of a movement," said Harlan Lane, a Northeastern University professor who teaches deaf culture and was a consultant to JHS 47. "The present system, to put it tersely, is a failure....

But opponents of embracing [ASL] ... contend that it fails to prepare deaf people adequately for a hearing world and that it applies one methodology to a group of people with a wide range of skills.

"The idea that you can learn sign language as your first language and it'll solve problems of education and socialization is utter nonsense," said Arthur Boothroyd, a distinguished professor of speech and learning science at the City University of New York's Graduate Center. "First of all, ASL is not a written language, which limits access to the world's knowledge. I don't want to decry the value, the beauty or the power of sign language, but the issue is how you go about giving a deaf child what they need to have a satisfying and fulfilling life."

Students at the school will for the first time be offered New York State's college-preparatory curriculum and a diploma.... Under the new plan, [ASL] will be used to teach reading and writing English, and all other subjects....

The changes are a culmination of three years of study of deaf education by school alumni and experts from across the nation....

Alumni found that the school had been reflecting the same failures that had left hearing-impaired students behind both academically and socially nationwide....

A handful of state-supported schools in places like California and Indiana have taken the lead in using [ASL] as the language of instruction. Charter schools in Minnesota and Colorado that use ASL primarily have been started in the last five or six years.

Source: Lee, F. R. (1998, March 5). New York to teach deaf in sign language, then English. *The New York Times,* p. B–3. Copyright © 1998 by The New York Times. Reprinted by permission.

United States. For example, in 1998, voters in California chose to eliminate bilingual education in favor of an English-only approach to education. The difference in popular acceptance of bilingualism for those who are deaf versus bilingual teaching of other language minority groups may be due to the fact that the goals for the two are not exactly the same:

> Bilingual/bicultural education for the Deaf child cannot be exactly the same as bilingual/bicultural education for hearing children, primarily because transitional bilingualism, where students move from using their native language to using English all the time, and which is the major goal of bilingual education programs in the U.S., is neither a feasible nor an appropriate goal for Deaf children. The major goal for Deaf children should be maintenance, indeed, cultivation of ASL and ASL literacy, throughout the Deaf child's educational career, with English, as a second language, to be used at specified instructional times. (Lane et al., 1996, pp. 305–306)

American Sign Language as a True Language

Many people, even some of those working in the area of deaf education, have the misconception that ASL and other sign languages are not true languages. (There is no universal sign language; ASL is only one among many. Most of them are nearly as different from each other as the spoken languages of the world.) Some people believe ASL is merely a loosely constructed system of gestures, and some believe that the signs are so highly pictorial in nature that they limit ASL to the representation of concrete, rather than abstract, concepts. Research has demonstrated that ASL's detractors are wrong on both counts.

ASL Has Its Own Grammar

Far from a disorganized system, ASL has its own very complicated grammar. Linguist William Stokoe first submitted that, analogous to the phonemes of spoken English, each sign in ASL consists of three parts: handshape, location, and movement (Stokoe, 1960; Stokoe, Casterline & Croneberg, 1976). He proposed that there are nineteen different handshapes, twelve locations, and twenty-four types of movements. Scoffed at by his colleagues when he first advanced his theory, Stokoe has come to be regarded as a genius for his pioneering work on the structure of ASL (Sacks, 1989; Wolkomir, 1992).

Research since the pioneering work of Stokoe has further confirmed the grammatical complexity of ASL. For example, researchers have found that young children who are deaf make errors in the early stages of learning ASL that are analogous to those made by hearing children learning English (Bellugi & Klima, 1991; Crowson, 1994). For example, children who are deaf make overgeneralization errors similar to those made by hearing children (e.g., using -ed to form past tenses goed or eated).

One team of researchers compared the signing of (1) individuals fluent in ASL to that of (2) a child who was deaf who had, over a period of years, developed a system of gestures for communicating to his hearing parents to that of (3) a group of previously nonsigning hearing adults and children who were asked to communicate with each other nonverbally (i.e., to invent a signing system) (Singleton, Morford, & Goldin-Meadow, 1993). These researchers found that, in contrast to the ASL group, the child and final group did not produce sets of signs that were coherent and systematic. In other words, evidence suggested that it is necessary for a signing system to evolve over time, to be passed down from one generation to another, as ASL has. This evolution is needed in order for the signing system to develop the systematic and internally consistent forms that identify it as a true language.

ASL Can Be Used to Convey Abstract Ideas

The misconception that ASL transmits primarily concrete ideas probably comes from the popular belief that signs are made up mostly of pictorial, or iconic, cues. Actually, the origin of some signs is iconic, but over time, even many of these iconic signs have lost their pictorial qualities (Klima & Bellugi, 1979). Sacks (1989) notes that it is the duality of signing—the use of the abstract and the concrete—that contributes to its vividness and aliveness. The following description captures the beauty of signing:

> The creativity can be remarkable. A person can sculpt exactly what he's saying. To sign "flower growing," you delicately place the fingertips at each side of the nose as if sniffing the flower, then you push the fingertips of one hand up through the thumb and first finger of the other. The flower can bloom fast and fade, or, with several quick bursts, it can be a whole field of daffodils. In spoken English, most people would seem silly if they talked as poetically as some supposedly illiterate deaf people sign. With one handshape—the thumb and little finger stretched out, the first finger pointing forward—you can make a plane take off, encounter engine trouble and turbulence, circle an airport, then come in for a bumpy landing. That entire signed sentence takes a fraction of the time than saying it aloud would. (Walker, 1986, p. 48)

Service Delivery Models

Students with hearing impairment can be found in settings ranging from general education classes to residential institutions. Starting in the mid-1970s, more and more of these students have been attending local schools in self-contained classes, resource rooms, and regular classes. Currently, approximately 70 percent of students with hearing impairment attend local schools, with 21 percent attending residential schools and 8 percent attending day schools (Schildroth & Hotto, 1996). Placement varies considerably, according to severity of hearing loss (students with severest impaiment are more likely to be in residential schools), hearing level of the parents (students with parents who are deaf are more likely to be in residential schools), and age of the students (older students are more likely to be in residential schools) (Holden-Pitt, 1997). For example, 56 percent of high school students with profound hearing loss are in residential schools. And 64 percent of children with profound hearing loss whose parents are deaf are in residential schools.

Many within the Deaf community have been critical of the degree of mainstreaming or inclusion that is occurring (Lane et al. 1996; Padden & Humphries, 1988). They argue that residential schools (and to a lesser extent, day schools) have been a major influence in fostering the concept of a Deaf culture and the use of ASL. Inclusion, they believe, forces students who are deaf to lose their Deaf identity and places them in a hearing and speaking environment in which it is almost impossible to succeed. In particular, critics of inclusion argue that when a student who is deaf is placed in a setting with nondisabled children, he or she is usually the only student with a hearing impairment in the class. This leads to a high degree of social isolation because the student who is deaf lacks peers with whom he or she can communicate (Innes, 1994).

Even professionals who advocate some sort of integration point to the need for a "critical mass" of students who are deaf in order for education to be effective (Higgins, 1992; Holcomb, 1996; Innes, 1994; Kluwin, 1992). As one investigator describes:

> Communication occurs not only between students and teachers. Interaction with peers is crucial to the child's overall development, as is interaction with significant others in the environment. For normal development to occur, deaf children, like all children, must have opportunities for interaction with peers who share their language and mode of communication. The presence of a sufficient number of language-mode peers is an important factor. (Innes, 1994, p. 155)

In order to achieve the critical mass in general education necessary to provide what are considered effective programs, some recommend placing students who are deaf in one building. In addition to consolidating services, authorities suggest an emphasis on extracurricular activities focused on fostering Deaf culture, while at the same time, targeting specific opportunities for interactions with hearing students (Holcomb, 1996).

Studies of students ranging from preschool (Rodriguez & Lana, 1996) to high school age (Holcomb, 1996) have suggested that inclusion in general education classes runs the risk of making students who are deaf feel isolated. For example, a study of high schoolers found that only one in five students who were deaf and in regular schools expressed satisfaction with their levels of participation in school, whereas over half of the students at deaf schools reported being satisfied (Holcomb, 1996).

Even though inclusion may present problems for many students who are deaf, by no means is it a negative experience for all students. Research on the effects of integrating students who are deaf with hearing peers has consistently found that social and academic outcomes vary depending on the individual. For some, full integration is beneficial; for others, a separate setting is best. For example, after conducting an extensive longitudinal study of the effects of mainstreaming on academic outcomes, one researcher concluded:

> Ultimately, we can neither condemn nor support any one type of educational placement for deaf students because multiple factors enter into a

New York, NY: **Najia Elyoumni-Pinedo** will turn six on Christmas Day. Her mother, Esther Pinedo, is from Peru, and her father, Ahmed Elyoumni, is from Morocco. Her parents met in an English language class in Manhattan one year before Najia's birth. When she was two, Najia was diagnosed as profoundly deaf. Since she had no extended family in the United States, a special day school for students who are deaf or hearing impaired became Najia's second home.

It was snack time, and the six kindergarten children decided to crush their cookies and eat crumbs. Their teacher, Wanda Frankel, and her assistant, Maria Diaz-Schwartz, readied chairs for the morning meeting, while Raihiem silently made a mountain. Suddenly, hands flew as another child signed, "Look! Raihiem has the most crumbs!" Warding off further comparisons, Wanda signed for the children to clean up and come to the circle. "Najia," she signed, "What is your job this week?" A dark-haired girl went to get paper towels as she signed back, "To wash the table."

Wanda Frankel is certified as a Teacher of the Deaf. She has taught at the Lexington School for the Deaf for twelve years. Effortlessly, she signs and speaks with her students, using a loud voice to facilitate what hearing some might have. "Usually, I wear a microphone, or an FM system as it's called. Then I don't need to speak so loudly, since I can set the mike to amplify my voice a little louder than other sounds coming through individual hearing aids. Today, it's broken!" Fortunately, there is an audiology repair shop on campus to assist with this and other problems, such as when students' hearing aids fail.

It is this kind of service that Najia's parents, Esther and Ahmed, have come to expect at Lexington. "We want to know everything about deafness," says Esther. "We come here for conferences and for sign language classes. We have cried with other parents and shared our experiences at meetings."

In this specialized setting, Najia has benefited from the intensity of instruction in sign language; from the small classes of six children, one teacher, and one assistant; and from the flexibility of a curriculum that focuses on her needs and interests.

Najia's progress is also linked to the school's resources for parental education and support. The school serves a large immigrant community with many parents like Najia's who must learn both English and sign language. For Najia and her parents, sign is their common language. Many mothers and fathers are also taught new skills as hearing parents of a deaf child. Says Wanda Frankel, "Counseling

complex constellation of relationships. We are, in fact, thrown back to the very basis for special education, that is, the individual consideration of each child and each situation. (Kluwin, 1993, p. 80)

Technological Advances

A number of technological advances have made it easier for persons with hearing impairment to communicate with and/or have access to information from the hearing world. This technological explosion has primarily involved five areas: hearing aids, TV and movies, telephones, computer-assisted instruction, and the Internet.

Hearing Aids. There are three main types of hearing aids—those worn behind the ear, those worn in the ear, and those worn farther down in the canal of the ear. The behind-the-ear hearing aid is the most powerful and is thus used by those with

services addressing unique communication issues are available to help these parents learn to better communicate with their deaf child as well as to help deaf children express their feelings and anger in nonphysical ways."

Najia's progress cannot be separated from her parents' struggle to find her help. Najia was eighteen months old when her father finally became convinced that she was deaf. "He said, 'I clapped, I slammed a door, I made a lot of noise,'" recalls Najia's mother. Before that, other reasons seemed to explain why Najia did not answer to her name. Since Najia and her parents lived with three other Moroccan families and their seven children, Esther and Ahmed thought that she was too busy playing to respond. They also thought it was a foreign language issue. "When Najia was with me and my friends, we spoke Spanish," explains Esther. "At home, her father and the other families spoke Arabic."

Since the Elyoumni-Pinedos had no family members in the United States to provide support, they were helped by an American acquaintance to make appointments at two audiology centers in Manhattan. The first evaluation found that Najia had a severe hearing loss. "I cried, 'No, not Najia,'" remembers Esther. She hoped the second evaluation would prove the initial finding false; instead, the results indicated a profound loss. At that point, the Elyoumni-Pinedos were advised to take Najia to the nearby Lexington School for early intervention services. She was two years old.

Now in kindergarten, Najia receives an intense classroom focus on communication. She has developed a strong language base and is acquiring beginning reading skills. She knows the alphabet and can sight-read the days of the week and names of favorite people. Along with her classmates, she participates in hands-on math readiness activities in basic addition and subtraction. Since there is also a schoolwide emphasis on developing independent learners, children in all grades learn to prepare and to predict through actual problem solving. "Najia comes up with some great solutions," says Wanda Frankel.

At the morning meeting, Najia and her classmates watch Wanda closely, as her lively hands draw their attention. "Listen," she says as she extends her arms and waves her hands, encouraging the children to watch each other. Raihiem is expressive in sign, and his clowning gestures make Najia laugh. She, in turn, signs that she is proud of her body tracing that hangs on the wall. It is decorated in detail and dressed with a feather belt and silver beads for earrings.

"Najia is so artistic," says Wanda. "Last year, she started to draw pictures using perspective! She's very bright." Says Najia's mother, "My husband and I like to think she will be a professional."

The resources of this special school have built a solid foundation for both Najia and her parents. When Esther and Ahmed's second child was born with a hearing loss, the Lexington School was able to provide his evaluation and referral to another program for children with less intense needs.

Esther Pinedo spoke with emotion and her eyes filled as she said, "We are so lucky to have found this school! We are so lucky to be in America!"

—By Jean Crockett

the most severe hearing losses. It is also the one that children most often use because it can be used with FM systems available in some classrooms. With an FM system, the teacher wears a wireless lapel microphone and the student wears an FM receiver (about the size of a cigarette package). The student hears the amplified sound either through a hearing aid that comes attached to the FM receiver or by attaching a behind-the-ear hearing aid to the FM receiver. Whether a student will be able to benefit from a hearing aid by itself depends a great deal on the acoustic qualities of the classroom. Most classrooms have such poor acoustics that an FM system is needed to help the child (Hawkins, 1990).

Although hearing aids are an integral part of educational programming for students with hearing impairment, some children who are deaf cannot benefit from them because of the severity and/or nature of their hearing impairment. Generally, hearing aids make sounds louder, not clearer, so if a person's hearing is distorted, a hearing aid will merely amplify the distorted sound.

The issue of using American Sign Language in general education classrooms becomes even more complex when the needs of non-English-speaking students are to be considered.

For those who can benefit from hearing aids, it is critical for the student, parents, and teachers to work together to ensure the maximum effectiveness of the device. This means that the teacher should be familiar with its proper operation and maintenance.

Television, Video, and Movie Captioning. Several hundred television programs are now captioned for people with hearing impairment. At one time viewers needed a special decoder to access captioned programs. Federal law now requires that TVs over 13 inches must contain a chip to allow one to view captions without a decoder. Many videotapes available from rental stores are captioned as well. And the most recent innovation in captioning is the Rear Window Captioning System, which displays captions on transparent acrylic panels that movie patrons can attach to their seats (National Center for Accessible Media, 1998). The captions are actually displayed in reverse at the rear of the theater, and the viewer sees them reflected on his or her acrylic screen.

Telephone Adaptations. Persons with hearing impairment have traditionally had problems using telephones, either because their hearing loss was too great or because of acoustic feedback (noise caused by closeness of the telephone receiver to their hearing aids). The development of the **teletypewriter (TTY)** has allowed these people access to the telephone. A person can use a TTY connected to a telephone to type a message to anyone else who has a TTY, and a special phone adaptation allows someone without a TTY to use the pushbuttons on his or her phone to "type" messages to someone with a TTY.

The federal government now requires each state to have a relay service for use by people with TTYs. A relay service allows a person with a TTY to communicate with anyone through an operator, who conveys the message to a person who does not have a TTY. The TTY user can carry on a conversation with the non-TTY user, or the TTY user can leave a message. The latter is useful for carrying out everyday

teletypewriter (TTY). A device connected to a telephone by a special adapter; allows communication over the telephone between persons who are hearing impaired and those with hearing.

activities, such as scheduling appointments. More and more people with hearing impairments are also making use of another telephone device—the fax.

Computer-Assisted Instruction (CAI). The explosion of microcomputer and related technology (e.g., videodiscs, CD-ROMs) is expanding learning capabilities for people who are deaf and their families. For example, visual displays of speech patterns on a computer screen can help someone with hearing impairment learn speech. Videodisc programs showing people sign are also available for use in learning ASL.

Visual displays of speech patterns on computer screens can help Individuals with hearing impairment and their families learn speech.

The Internet. The technological advance holding by far the greatest potential for people with hearing impairment is the Internet. The information superhighway has already opened up a variety of communication possibilities for people who are deaf. For example, electronic mail allows people who are deaf to communicate with one another as well as with hearing individuals. People who are deaf may also subscribe to online lists, connect to newsgroups, and participate in "chat rooms" devoted to deafness, along with a multitude of other subjects. The ever-expanding World Wide Web provides access to a variety of information sources.

In addition to providing people who are deaf with a way to access information, educators can also use the internet to help students who are deaf practice reading and writing skills. For instance, teachers can set up newsgroups through which students can communicate with others in the class, the school, or even worldwide.

Early Intervention

Researchers and practitioners have espoused the importance of education for infants and preschoolers with hearing impairments. Because language development is such an issue with children who are hearing impaired and because early childhood is such an important time for the development of language, it is not surprising that many of the most controversial issues surrounding early intervention in the area of deafness focus on language. As indicated in the earlier discussion of oralism versus manualism, some people maintain that English language should be the focus of intervention efforts, and others hold that ASL should be used starting in infancy. Among English language advocates, some professionals recommend a total communication approach, combining spoken English and some kind of signed English system.

Research on children who are deaf who have parents who are deaf versus those with parents who are hearing has consistently found that the latter are at greater risk for a variety of problems (Lane et al., 1996). For example, infants who are deaf who have parents who are deaf develop ASL at a rate similar to the rate at which hearing infants of hearing parents develop English. But infants who are deaf who have hearing parents do not develop either English or ASL at as fast a rate. This may be due to the fact that day-to-day interactions between mothers and infants are more facilitative and natural when both the infant and parents are deaf than when the infant is deaf and the parents are hearing. Hearing mothers of infants who are deaf tend to be more directive in their interactions with their infants—that is, they are more likely to start interactions that are unrelated to the child's activity or expressed interest (Spencer & Meadow-Orlans, 1996).

The frustration that results between young children who are deaf and their hearing parents puts them at risk for behavioral problems. Because they lack a language model, they sometimes resort to physical gestures and other "tricks" (e.g., pulling on clothing, stamping the feet) to try to capture their parents' attention and get what they want (Lane et al., 1996). This frustration in communication is probably the reason why hearing parents of children who are deaf often exhibit high degrees of stress (Meadow-Orlans, 1995). Also, parents who use sign with their children are more likely to have cohesive families, with a high degree of emotional bonding and sharing of interests (Kluwin & Gaustad, 1994).

In addition to facility with ASL, parents who are deaf also have the advantage of being better prepared to cope with their infant's deafness (Meadow-Orlans, 1990). Parents who are hearing are unprepared for the birth of a child with hearing loss, whereas parents who are deaf can draw on their own experiences in order to offer helpful support to their child who is deaf.

Hearing parents, especially if they desire to teach their infants sign language, may need help in understanding the importance of the visual modality in communicating with their infants (Koester & Meadow-Orlans, 1990; MacTurk, Meadow-Orlans, Koester, & Spencer, 1993). Hearing parents need to understand, for example, that the eye gaze of the infant who is deaf is extremely important because it is his or her way of expressing interest and motivation. These parents also need to be aware that, just as hearing babies babble vocally, babies who are deaf engage in babbling with their hands as they begin to acquire sign language (Wolkomir, 1992).

Hearing parents of children who are deaf face a quandary over how to provide their children with appropriate sign language models. Both signed English and ASL, especially the latter, are difficult to learn to a high degree of fluency in a relatively short period of time. And like any language, ASL is harder to acquire as an adult and can rarely be learned to the same degree of fluency as that possessed by a native ASL signer.

The fact that over 90 percent of children who are deaf have parents who are hearing underscores the importance of intervention for many infants who are deaf. In fact, many authorities believe that there is a far greater need for early intervention for families with hearing parents of a child who is deaf than for families where both the parents and the child are deaf (Andrews & Zmijewski, 1997).

Educators have established preschool intervention projects in order to teach the basics of sign language to the parents of children who are deaf as well as to the children themselves. Such projects are generally successful at teaching the rudiments of sign to parents and infants. Once the child is ready to progress beyond one- and two-word signed utterances, however, it is important that native signers be available as models. Authorities recommend a practice that is popular in Sweden—that adults who are deaf be part of early intervention efforts because they can serve as sign language models and can help hearing parents form positive expectations about their children's potential (Lane et al., 1996).

Even though hearing parents may never be able to communicate fluently in sign language, it is important that they continue to sign with their child. Not only does signing allow parents a means of communicating with the child; it also demonstrates that they value the child's language and the Deaf culture. One study found that teenagers whose hearing parents use sign are more likely to have high self-esteem (Desselle, 1994).

Transition

Before the mid-1960s, the only institution established specifically for the postsecondary education of students with hearing impairment was Gallaudet College (now Gallaudet University). Except for this one institution, these students were left with no choice but to attend traditional colleges and universities. However, traditional postsecondary schools were generally not equipped to handle the special needs of students with hearing impairment. It is little wonder, then, that a study by Quigley, Jenne, and Phillips (1968) was able to identify only 224 persons with hearing impairment who were graduates of regular colleges and universities in the United States between 1910 and 1965.

Findings such as these led to the expansion of postsecondary programs. The federal government has now funded a wide variety of postsecondary programs for students with hearing impairment. In 1965, the National Technical Institute for the Deaf (NTID) was established at the Rochester Institute of Technology. The NTID program, emphasizing training in technical fields, complements the liberal arts orientation of Gallaudet University. At NTID, some students with hearing impairment also attend classes with hearing students at the Rochester Institute of Technology.

Following the establishment of NTID, an explosion of postsecondary programs occurred. There are now well over 100 postsecondary programs in the United States and Canada for students with hearing impairment. By law, Gallaudet and NTID are responsible for serving students from all fifty states and territories. Others serve students from several states, from one state only, or from specific districts only.

Although many people who are deaf who enroll in higher education choose to attend Gallaudet, NTID, or colleges with special programs, some go to traditional colleges and universities. These students usually take advantage of the expanding roles of university programs that have been established to facilitate the academic experiences of students with disabilities. One of the accommodations often recommended is to provide sign language interpreters in the classes of students with hearing impairment.

The role of interpreters generates a debate comparable to the one in total communication classrooms concerning ASL versus signed English (discussed earlier). The central conflict is over the use of transliteration, rather than ASL, by the majority of interpreters. **Transliteration,** which is similar to signed English, maintains the same word order as spoken English. ASL, on the other hand, requires the interpreter to digest the meaning of what is said before conveying it through signs. Although interpreters find it more difficult to use ASL, research has shown that it is more effective than transliteration (Livingston, Singer, & Abrahamson, 1994).

Most college instructors have limited, if any, experience in working with sign language interpreters. Even so, it is critical that instructors and interpreters work

transliteration. A method used by sign language interpreters in which the signs maintain the same word order as that of spoken English; although used by most interpreters, found through research not to be as effective as American Sign Language (ASL).

Tips for Working with Sign Language Interpreters

In an article for the journal *College Teaching*, Linda Siple (1993) provides some practical tips for working with sign language interpreters. She notes that first the entire class must have a trusting relationship with the interpreter. His or her job is to translate *everything* that is said in the presence of the student who is deaf, which may include irrelevant or inappropriate comments made during class breaks—even jokes or negative remarks about the student for whom the interpreter is signing.

The interpreter also is expected to maintain confidentiality with regard to sensitive information about the student who is deaf. For example, if the same individual also interprets for the student in other situations (e.g., student health services, financial aid, etc.), any information revealed must be maintained in confidence.

Siple offers the following suggestions for instructors and their classes:

- The interpreter should have copies of all handouts and, if possible, copies of textbooks.
- If a fellow student or the instructor wishes to speak to the student who is deaf, he or she should speak directly to the student, not to the interpreter.

- It is more difficult to interpret in a class in which there is a lot of discussion. Participants should try to talk one at a time, and the instructor should realize that the time lag between what is spoken and when it is signed will put the student who is deaf at a disadvantage during discussion.
- In a lecture class, the instructor should be aware of the pace of his or her delivery, perhaps pausing more frequently than usual.
- If the instructor is comfortable, he or she may request that the interpreter stop the class if something becomes too complicated to interpret. In fact, the interpreter's need to clarify may very well be an indication that the rest of the students do not understand the information either.
- The interpreter should not be considered a participant in the class. Questions for him or her should not be addressed when he or she is not interpreting.

Source: Based on L. A. Siple, "Working with the sign language interpreter in your classroom," *College Teaching*, 41, 139–142, 1993. Reprinted with permission of the Helen Dwight Reid Educational Foundation. Published by Heldref Publications, 1319 Eighteenth St., N.W., Washington, D.C. 20036–1802. Copyright © 1993.

closely together in order to provide the optimum learning experience for students who are deaf, while not disrupting other students in the class (Siple, 1993). The box above provides some tips for working with sign language interpreters.

Sign language interpreters are also used in elementary and secondary schools, where the issues concerning their use are no less severe. There is a tremendous shortage of qualified interpreters for the public schools. And there is often disagreement over role definition. For example, teachers sometimes treat interpreters like teacher aides, asking them to help grade papers and tutor students (Jones, Clark, & Soltz, 1997).

Even though postsecondary programs for persons who are hearing impaired have expanded greatly, there is still considerable room for improvement. In an extensive follow-up (Bullis, Bull, Johnson, & Peters, 1995) of persons three to four years after high school, researchers found that, in comparison with hearing peers, those who were deaf demonstrated a lower rate of attendance at four-year colleges and postsecondary training programs. Individuals who were deaf were also more likely to be unemployed, to earn lower wages, and to have fewer close friends. Even though these data come from only three states in the Pacific Northwest, they generally agree with national statistics on young deaf adults (Blackorby & Wagner, 1996; Valdes, Williamson, & Wagner, 1990).

With regard to raising a family, persons who are deaf often face unique challenges. National statistics indicate that 95 percent of adults who are deaf choose deaf spouses, and 90 percent of the offspring of these marriages have normal hearing (Buchino, 1993). These hearing children often serve as interpreters for their parents. Being called on to interpret for one's parents can help develop self-confidence around adult authority figures (e.g., doctors, lawyers, insurance agents), but it can also force one to face some unpleasant biases, as the following story from a hearing child of deaf parents demonstrates:

> Curled up in the seat, chin dug into my chest, I noticed there was a lull in the conversation. Dad was a confident driver, but Mom was smoking more than usual.
>
> "Something happened? That gas station?" Mom signed to me.
>
> "No, nothing," I lied.
>
> "Are you sure?"
>
> "Everything is fine." Dad and I had gone to pay and get directions. The man behind the counter had looked up, seen me signing and grunted, "Huh, I didn't think mutes were allowed to have driver's licenses." Long ago I'd gotten used to hearing those kind of comments. But I never could get used to the way it made me churn inside. (Walker, 1986, p. 9)

Educational programs for students of all ages and abilities should include opportunities for full expression.

These children also sometimes admit to resenting the fact that being called on to interpret for their parents interfered with their social lives (Buchino, 1993).

There has been a long tradition of preparing students who are deaf for manual trades (Lane, 1992). But today, unskilled and semiskilled trades are fast disappearing from the workforce in favor of jobs requiring higher-level skills. As a result, adults who are deaf face even greater obstacles when they enter the job market. Although the educational, work, and social opportunities for adults who are deaf are often limited, there are reasons to be optimistic about the future. With the continued expansion of transition programming and greater public awareness of the potential of people who are deaf should come a brighter outlook for more adults who are deaf.

Summary

In defining *hearing impairment,* educators are concerned primarily with the extent to which hearing loss affects the ability to speak and understand spoken language. They refer to people with hearing impairment who cannot process linguistic information as *deaf* and those who can as *hard of hearing.* In addition, those who are deaf at birth or before language develops are referred to as having *prelingual deafness,* and those who acquire their deafness after spoken language starts to develop are referred to as having *postlingual deafness.* Professionals favoring a physiological viewpoint define deaf children as those who cannot hear sounds at or above a certain intensity level; they call others with hearing impairment "hard of hearing." Many people who are deaf resent being defined as "disabled" at all; they prefer to be considered a cultural or language minority.

The three most commonly used types of tests for hearing acuity are pure-tone audiometry, speech audiometry, and specialized tests for very young and hard-to-test children. The examiner uses pure tones or speech to find the intensity of sound (measured in decibels) the person can hear at different frequency levels (measured in hertz). Audiologists often test very young children, using play, reflex, or evoked-response audiometry. During the first three months of life, hearing can be measured by changes in heart rate and sucking reflexes in response to auditory stimuli.

Professionals often classify causes of hearing loss according to the location of the problem within the hearing mechanism. *Conductive* losses are impairments that interfere with transfer of sound along the conductive pathway of the ear. *Sensorineural* problems are confined to the complex inner ear and are apt to be more severe and harder to treat.

Impairments of the outer ear are caused by such things as infections of the external canal or tumors. Middle-ear troubles usually occur because of some malfunction of one or more of the three tiny bones called ossicles in the middle ear. Otitis media, a condition stemming from eustachian tube malfunctioning, is the most common problem of the middle ear. The most common inner-ear troubles are linked to hereditary factors. Acquired hearing losses of the inner ear include those due to bacterial infections (such as meningitis), viral infections (such as mumps and measles), prenatal infections of the mother (such as cytomegalovirus, maternal rubella, and syphilis), and deprivation of oxygen at birth.

Impairment of hearing ability can have a profound effect on people, largely because of the emphasis on spoken language in U.S. society. In the past, because they held to the notion that language is the equivalent of thought, professionals believed that deafness led to intellectual inferiority. Researchers now question the theory that thought is dependent on language. Furthermore, authorities now recognize that sign language is as true a language as spoken language. They recommend that people who are deaf be tested in sign language and/or with nonverbal tests of intelligence.

In general, the academic achievement of students with hearing impairment is very low. Even in math, their best academic area, they demonstrate severe underachievement. Several studies have shown that children who are deaf who have parents who are deaf have higher reading achievement than children who are deaf who have hearing parents. This is probably because parents who are deaf are able to communicate more easily with their children through sign language. There is some evidence that students who have more facility with ASL also have higher academic achievement.

Because of problems finding people with whom to communicate, students who are deaf are at risk for loneliness. This problem is particularly acute in inclusive settings, in which there are few students with hearing impairment with whom to communicate. Some authorities also believe that students who are deaf who have hearing parents may experience more unhappiness because of the difficulty they have in communicating with their parents.

Because of these problems in communicating with the larger society, many people who are deaf socialize almost exclusively with others who have hearing impairment. At one time many professionals viewed this tendency toward isolation as negative. More and more authorities are pointing out the potential benefits of a Deaf culture. The Deaf culture is built on six features: linguistic differentiation, attitudinal deafness, behavioral norms, endogamous marriage patterns, historical awareness, and voluntary organizational networks.

Some believe that the cultural status of students who are deaf is vulnerable because of the current emphasis on inclusion in the schools. They cite the decline in Deaf clubs as evidence of the erosion of the Deaf culture. Deaf activists have increasingly decried what they consider to be an oppressive medical and educational establishment, pointing to cochlear implants as an example.

For many years there were two basic approaches to teaching students with hearing impairment: *oralism* and *manualism*. Today, most educators of students who are deaf favor *total communication*, a blend of oralism and manualism. Most educators who use total communication stress the auditory-verbal approach, speechreading, and signing English systems.

Signing English systems are not true languages, in that they follow the word order of spoken English. Proponents of American Sign Language (ASL) argue that it is a grammatically sophisticated, highly evolved language of its own. Moreover, these proponents believe that deaf children should be proficient in ASL and that their education should be based on bilingual models. This *bicultural-bilingual approach* involves using ASL as the primary language in academic instruction and using English as the second language. It also promotes instruction in the history of the Deaf culture.

Students with hearing impairment can be found in a variety of settings, ranging from inclusion in general education classrooms to residential settings. Although the likelihood of inclusion in general education is greater for those with less severe impairment, those who are younger, and those who have parents who are hearing, the overall increase in inclusion has been viewed with skepticism by many in the Deaf community and other professionals.

Numerous technological advances are helping persons with hearing loss. These innovations are occurring primarily in the areas of hearing aids, television and movies, telephones, computer-assisted instruction (CAI), and the Internet.

There are now many programs for infants and preschoolers with hearing impairment. Research indicates that the families of children who are deaf who have hearing parents may be in greater need of intervention than are families of children who are deaf who have parents who are also deaf. One reason for this is that hearing parents generally are not proficient in ASL, which is difficult to learn quickly.

In addition to Gallaudet University and the National Technical Institute for the Deaf, which focus on the education of students who are hearing impaired, there are now several postsecondary programs for students with hearing impairment. Deaf students enrolled in traditional colleges can take advantage of the increasing presence of sign language interpreters and other university programs. Transition programming for students who do not intend to take part in postsecondary programs is also expanding. Unemployment and the number of persons who are overqualified for their jobs among people who are hearing impaired are still exceedingly high.

suggestions for teaching

Students with Hearing Impairment in General Education Classrooms   By E. Jane Nowacek

If a student with hearing loss is to be included in your class, Jaussi (1991) recommends preparing classmates in several ways:

- Lead class discussions about hearing losses, hearing aids, and other amplification devices. Encourage students to talk about their own feelings about deafness.
- Introduce them to persons with hearing impairments by arranging classroom visits with children or adults who are deaf or who have hearing losses.
- Read accounts of persons with hearing impairment. (See the Literature section under Helpful Resources for a list of fiction and nonfiction books about persons with hearing losses.)

In addition, if an educational interpreter will be providing services in the classroom, it is important to introduce him or her to the class and to explain his or her role. Salend and Longo (1994) recommend that the teacher explain that the interpreter is in the room to facilitate communication. If class members understand this responsibility, they may feel more comfortable with having the interpreter assist them in conversing with students with hearing impairment. It is also important that all students understand that the interpreter's role does *not* include assisting with assignments and tests, tutoring, or monitoring behavior. Additional recommendations (Smith, Polloway, Patton, & Dowdy, 1998) are outlined in Figure 9.A.

Students with hearing losses in general education classrooms can be expected to follow the standard curriculum if they have the prerequisite skills (Ross, Brackett, & Maxon, 1991). However, they may require modifications of the physical, instructional, and social environments to benefit fully from education in inclusive classes.

Modifying the Physical Environment

Modifications of the physical environment may involve simple changes in seating, such as moving students away from sources of noise (e.g., open windows and doors) that might be amplified by the student's hearing aid (Lambert, 1994). Adapting seating arrangements so students are located in the front of the room with their chairs or desks turned slightly so they can see the faces of all the other students, permitting free movement around the classroom to reduce the distance between themselves and the speakers, and using flexible seating arrangements that allow students to change seats as activities change promote understanding and participation in class activities (Ross, 1982). In addition, good lighting is critical for speechreading (Lambert, 1994). If the lights are lowered for a video or work on an overhead projector during which the teacher is providing instruction, it is important that the teacher's face be illuminated so all students may benefit from the instruction.

Students with hearing impairments enrolled in general education high school classes offer these suggestions (Nittmann, Gorman, & McGinnis, 1996):

Teachers can ask students to face me (student with hearing loss) or possibly move closer when they speak. I will try to sit in the best spot so that I can see faces. Sometimes I sit facing the class or we sit in a circle so I can follow the discussion. (Vanessa)

Because I have to concentrate so hard in class, I really appreciate being able to have some quiet time (space) by myself. I have a good break in the middle of my day and that helps a lot. (Kim)

Figure 9.A

Interpreters in Educational Settings

General Guidelines

- Include the interpreter as a member of the IEP team to help determine the communication needs of the student.
- Request an interpreter (i.e., do not let parents interpret for their children) for certain important situations (e.g., transition planning meetings).
- Supervise the interpreter if this person is involved with additional classroom tasks.
- Meet with the interpreter regularly to discuss the needs of the student and to review ongoing communication patterns.
- Evaluate the effectiveness of interpreters.

Specific Suggestions

- Allow the interpreter to be positioned so that the student can easily see both the teacher (or media) and the interpreter.
- Prepare the interpreter for the topic(s) that will be covered and the class format that will be followed.
- Provide copies of all visual materials (e.g., overhead transparencies) before class begins.
- Be sensitive to the "time-lag" factor associated with interpreting—the few-word delay that the interpreter lags behind the spoken message.
- Program breaks in lecturing if at all possible.
- Limit movement so that the student can see the interpreter and teacher without difficulty.
- Check student understanding regularly—ensure that the student does not fake understanding.

Source: Teaching students with special needs in inclusive settings (2nd ed.), by T. C. Smith, E. A. Polloway, J. R. Patton, & C. A. Dowdy, 1998, p. 218. Austin, TX: Pro-Ed. Copyright 1998 by Pro-Ed. Inc. Reprinted with permission.

Modifying the Instructional Environment

Instructional modifications also can enhance the learning of students who are hearing impaired. Using teaching formats that include exhibits, demonstrations, experiments, and simulations provides hands-on experiences that tend to promote understanding and are easier to follow than lectures and whole-class discussions.

When you do use lecture and discussion formats, promote understanding (Lambert, 1994; Martin & Clark, 1996; Ross et al., 1991) by:

- Using an overhead projector, instead of the chalkboard, to note important points, key words, directions, and assignments so you can face students while speaking
- Shortening and simplifying verbalizations
- Repeating main points or paraphrasing them in simpler forms
- Repeating questions and answers given by other students

- Providing summaries throughout lectures or discussions
- Using nonverbal cues, such as facial expressions, body movements, and gestures
- Calling speakers' names to reduce time spent locating sources of speech
- Enunciating speech clearly
- Selecting educational films with captions

Additional modifications may be necessary in order to promote success of specific students with hearing impairments. The Program Modification Checklist shown in Figure 9.B lists several items to consider (Luetke-Stahlman, 1996).

In addition, students with hearing impairments suggest the following modifications (Nittmann, Gorman, & McGinnis, 1996):

I like to see pictures, charts and lots of visual aids ahead of time. Then my mind has a map that helps things make sense. (Alana)

It's better to study the words ahead of time and make an outline then I don't waste my time trying to understand the vocabulary and not understand the teacher. I get so tired of carrying around this 30 pound dictionary. (Vanessa)

There's just no way I can follow the class discussion and take notes at the same time! I need to focus all of my energies on following the discussion. (Kim)

Before my class attended the show, *Miss Saigon,* my teacher called the box office and asked them to send a copy of the play to my school. It was wonderful. I knew everything that was going to happen. It's the best thing I ever saw. (Vanessa)

Modifying the Social Environment

To address the social as well as the academic needs of all students, many educators recommend developing small groups and/or cooperative learning groups. Before assigning students with hearing impairments to groups, consider the following points (adapted from Card & Schmider, 1995):

- Smaller groups promote more effective communication because they tend to increase "air time" and decrease background noise. Ideally, group meetings should be scheduled in a quiet place and time.
- Assigning or electing co-leaders, one male and one female, may facilitate communication because some students with mild-to-moderate hearing loss hear certain vocal ranges better than others.
- Seat small groups in a circle. This arrangement helps the student with hearing impairments see the faces of each speaker. If an interpreter is present, seat him or her next to or between the leaders, slightly out of the group, on a higher seat. If the leadership is shared by all members, the interpreters will sit across from the student with a hearing loss.
- Establishing some "rules" for group communication will help students understand and participate in the discussion. Rules might include: (a) speakers signal (e.g., raise hand) before they begin to talk; (b) members do not chew gum during group; (c) the group incorporates visuals, such as writing key points on chart paper, into discussions whenever possible; (d) members signal when information is unclear and/or when it is difficult to understand (Edwards, 1991); (e) students make specific requests for clarification of unclear communications (Caissie & Wilson, 1995); (f) when a request for clarification is made, the speaker revises his or her message rather than repeating it (Caissie & Wilson, 1995).

Figure 9.B

Program Modifications

Mode/Flow of Communication

- Make sure each child has access to all activities
- Provide adequate, appropriate interpreting as needed (oral, cued speech, manual)
- Assess the dominant language system, consider any needed alternatives
- Specify language levels for use of written English, spoken English, ASL in instruction
- Set up an effective method for communication between teachers, interpreters
- Other _____

School Environment

- Establish an ideal listening environment
  –Provide FM equipment as needed
  –Provide quiet rooms without distracting noise
- Modify the physical environment
  –Use sound-deadening carpets, window treatments
  –Install visual alarms
- Classroom Seating
  Make sure deaf students have clear sight lines to teacher, interpreter, blackboard, other students
  If possible, arrange desks in horseshoe configuration
- Learning centers
  Provide access to computers, TTYs, visual and written materials via captioning. interpretation, etc.
- Offer all students ways to experience Deaf Culture
- Other _____

Support Structure

- Hire additional personnel/paraprofessionals as indicated
  –Interpreters
  –Notetakers
- Set up a buddy system with classmate participation
- Offer tutoring
- Establish a resource room
- Other _____

Instructional Formats

- Plan thematic instruction across the curriculum
- Encourage small group interaction
- Structure cooperative learning activities
- Emphasize visual and language-based learning
- Use graphic organizers for classroom work
- Provide relevant information to support learning
- Pay attention to individual learning styles (global, analytical, etc.)
- Use games, simulations, role-plays, etc.
- Other

Mediated/Scaffolded Instruction

- Relate new and previously learned information
- Engage in reciprocal teaching dialogue
- Use a variety of quotation prompts
- Engage in active problem solving
- Teach strategies for acquiring/remembering information

Lesson Planning

- Analyze tasks to determine levels of difficulty
- Teach study skills, use assignment notebooks
- Utilize effective instruction styles, guided practice
- Divide work into small units
- Pace instruction to meet all students' needs

Language Behaviors

- Consider volume and rate of speaking voice
- Present instruction two to four times
- Avoid meaningless hand movements
- Pair common phrases with figurative English
- Use synonyms for words perceived as difficult
- Ask analytical questions

Materials

- Provide study guides, assignments in writing
- Clarify instructions through writing demonstrations
- Read aloud or sign important information rather than relying on student reading
- Rewrite materials as needed for clarity
- Highlight essential information
- Provide duplicate sets of materials for family use

Testing/Grading

- Schedule frequent mini-tests to track progress
- Provide for alternate test response modes if needed
- Consider offering signed videotaped tests
- Provide extra time for students who are acquainted with course content but may need help with test language
- Consider alternative grading methods
  –Curriculum-based tests
  –Criteria-referenced tests
  –Self-referenced tests
  –Pass/fail options
- Provide daily/weekly reports for feedback
- Chart ongoing progress or lack of progress

Please send any feedback or suggestions regarding the checklist and its use in public school programs to:

Barbara Luetke-Stahlman
University of Kansas Medical Center
3901 Rainbow Blvd
Kansas City, KS 66160-7605
e-mail: BLSTAHLMAN@KUMC.edu

Source: "A helpful checklist for schools and students," by B. Luetke-Stahlman, 1996, *Perspectives in Education and Deafness*, 15, 16–17.

Once you have formed groups, you may decide to prepare students for cooperative learning by discussing the concept of cooperation and by role-playing key social skills such as expressing opposition, valuing all members' contributions, managing conflict (Johnson, Johnson, & Holubec, 1994). In addition, the group must understand the expectation that all students will learn and participate in all activities. To facilitate this level of participation, you may assign each member a role, such as coach, checker, reflector, recorder, encourager (Kagan, 1994). Roles tend to reduce the likelihood that one member will dominate, and they provide a means for students to be integrated into the group, an especially important consideration for members with disabilities.

When groups understand the purpose and procedures of cooperative learning, they are ready to begin working together. Given the difficulties students with hearing impairments experience in a discussion format, you may decide to begin group learning with activities that have a visual focus, such as computer activities. A lesson plan might include the following (adapted from Carolina Computer Access Center materials):

Cooperative Computer Use Lesson

Precomputer Phase: State clear objective for the lesson. Demonstrate computer program/activity (see Computer Activities below). Assign or remind students of their roles (including keyboarder) in their group.

Computer Phase: Monitor carefully work at the computer. Schedule a reasonable time frame for group computer work. Encourage use of social skills in group interactions.

Postcomputer Phase: Evaluate actions of the group (e.g., provide feedback on the cooperative learning process). Have groups share their finished products.

Computer Activities that Promote Social Development/Interaction

- Combine text and graphics to make book reports
- Make book jackets for a story or book
- Make a poster to "sell" a book
- Make a travel brochure to advertise a story setting for a vacation
- Publish a classroom newsletter
- Use a word-processing program with graphics to write to a pen pal
- Telecommunicate interesting questions/information to other schools
- Use a crossword puzzle program to study vocabulary words
- Use a crossword puzzle program to practice using descriptors
- Write poems and include graphics
- Use a graphics program to make wordless picture books
- Make a card to send to a character from a book
- Publish cards or notes to send to other classmates
- Create a class book (one page per student)

To further promote social interactions among nonhearing and hearing students, some schools offer American Sign Language as a foreign-language alternative. Others offer sign language classes after school or during special Saturday morning programs (Gearheart, Weishahn, & Gearheart, 1996). The purposes of doing so are to increase the modes of communication for all students, expand the social interactions that occur among students, and reduce miscommunication.

Helpful Resources

Instructional Methods

Bailes, C., Searls, S., Slobodzian, J., & Staton, J. (1997). *It's your turn now! Using dialogue journals with deaf students.* Washington, DC: Gallaudet University Press.

Brackett, D. (1990). Communication management of the mainstreamed hearing impaired student. In M. Ross (Ed.), *Hearing impaired children in the mainstream* (pp. 119–130). Parkton, MD: York Press.

Christopherson, S. (1997). Math: New teaching for an old challenge. *Perspectives in Education and Deafness, 15,* 4–6.

Flexer, C. (1999). *Facilitating hearing and listening in young children* (2nd ed.). San Diego: Singular.

French, M. (1994). Spelling in the real world. *Perspectives in Education and Deafness, 12,* 18–22.

Kluwin, T. N. (1996). Getting hearing and deaf students to write to each other through dialog journals. *Teaching Exceptional Children, 29,* 50–53.

Kluwin, T. N., Moores, D. F., & Gaustad, M. G. (1992). *Toward effective public school programs for deaf students.* New York: Teachers College Press.

Lindsay, J. D. (Ed.). (1993). *Computers and exceptional individuals* (2nd ed.). Austin, TX: Pro-Ed.

Loera, P. A., & Meichenbaum, D. (1993). The potential contribution of cognitive behavior modification for literacy training for deaf students. *American Annals of the Deaf, 138,* 87–95.

Luetke-Stahlman, B. (1994). Research-based language intervention strategies adapted for deaf and hard of hearing children. *American Annals of the Deaf, 138,* 404–410.

Luetke-Stahlman, B., & Luckner, J. (1991). *Effectively educating students with hearing impairments.* White Plains, NY: Longman.

Mangiardi, A. (1993). *A child with a hearing loss in your classroom? Don't panic: A guide for teachers.* Washington, DC: Alexander Graham Bell Association for the Deaf.

Moore, M. S., & Levitan, L. (Eds.). (1993). *For hearing people only: Answers to some of the most commonly asked questions about the deaf community, its culture, and the "deaf reality"* (2nd ed.). Rochester, NY: Deaf Life Press.

Nussbaum, D. (1997). *There's a hearing impaired child in my class* (2nd ed.). Washington, DC: Gallaudet University Press.

Ross, M. (Ed.). (1990). *Hearing-impaired children in the mainstream.* Parkton, MD: York Press.

Ross, M., Brackett, D., & Maxon, A. B. (1991). *Assessment and management of mainstreamed hearing-impaired children: Principles and practices.* Austin, TX: Pro-Ed.

Shirmer, B. R. (1994). *Language and literacy development in children who are deaf.* New York: Merrill/Macmillan.

Yarger, C. C. (1996). Notetaking program: Starting out right! *Perspectives in Education and Deafness, 15,* 6–8, 20–21.

Curricular and Instructional Materials

Cowan, N. (1986). *Preparing for work.* Washington, DC: Gallaudet University Press.

Developmental approach to successful listening (DASL). Circle Pines, MN: American Guidance Services (listening, training materials for preschool–elementary school).

Gillespie, S. (1997). *Kendall Demonstration Elementary School science curriculum guide* (3rd ed.). Washington, DC: Gallaudet University Press.

Gillespie, S., & Miller-Nomeland, M. (1997). *Kendall Demonstration Elementary School deaf students curriculum guide.* Washington, DC: Gallaudet University Press.

Gillespie, S., & Schwarz, D. (1997). *Kendall Demonstration Elementary School health curriculum guide.* Washington, DC: Gallaudet University Press.

Kurlychek, K. (1991). *Software to go.* Washington, DC: Gallaudet University Press (this catalog lists and describes commercial software that may be borrowed by educators of students with hearing impairments).

Mason, V. (1997). *Kendall Demonstration Elementary School mathematics curriculum guide.* Washington, DC: Gallaudet University Press.

Stone, R. (1997). *Let's learn about deafness.* Washington, DC: Gallaudet University Press.

Sunal, D. W., & Sunal, C. S. (1981). *Teachers guide for science— adapted for the hearing impaired: Introduction and Levels 3–7.* Morgantown, WV: West Virginia University (ERIC Document Reproduction Service No. ED JUNRIE).

Curricular guides and materials designed for students who are hearing impaired are available for several subject areas from the bookstore at Gallaudet University. For a free catalogue of current offerings, write or call: Gallaudet Bookstore, 800 Florida Avenue NE, Washington, DC 20002, (202) 651-5271 (voice), (202) 651-5095 (TDD). Lists of captioned videotapes are also available from the Gallaudet bookstore.

Captioned films that address subjects such as business, English, mathematics, and career education are available from: Modern Talking Picture Service, Captioned Films Division, 500 Park Street, St. Petersburg, FL 33709.

Literature about Individuals with Hearing Impairment*

Elementary

Andrews, J. F. (1992). *Hasta leugo, San Diego.* Washington, DC: Gallaudet University Press. (Ages 9–12) (F)

Bornstein, H., & Saulnier, K. L. (1990). *Little Red Riding Hood.* Washington, DC: Gallaudet University Press (signed English drawings to help children with language skills).

Gragg, V. (1998). *What is an audiogram?* Washington, DC: Gallaudet University Press. (Ages 9–12) (NF)

King Midas with selected sentences in American Sign Language. (1990). Washington, DC: Gallaudet University Press.

Levi, D. H. (1989). *A very special friend.* Washington, DC: Kendall Green Publications. (F)

Starowitz, A. M. (1988). *The day we met Cindy.* Washington, DC: Gallaudet University Press. (Ages 5-8) (F)

*F = fiction; NF = nonfiction

Secondary

Bragg, B. (1989). *Lessons in laughter: The autobiography of a deaf actor* (as signed to E. Bergman). Washington, DC: Gallaudet University Press. (Ages 13–Adult) (NF)

Carroll, C. (1992). *Clerc: The story of his early years.* Washington, DC: Gallaudet University Press. (Ages 13–15) (NF)

Flexer, C., Wray, D., & Leavitt, C. (1990). *How the students with hearing loss can succeed in college: A handbook for students, families, and professionals.* Washington, DC: Alexander Graham Bell Association for the Deaf. (Ages 13–18) (NF)

Hepper, C. (1992). *Seeds of disquiet: One deaf woman's experience.* Washington, DC: Gallaudet University Press. (Ages 16–Adult) (NF)

Kisor, H. (1991). *What's that pig outdoors? A memoir of deafness.* New York: Penguin. (Ages 13–Adult) (NF)

Lane, H. (1992). *The mask of benevolence: Disabling the deaf community.* New York: Knopf. (Ages 16–Adult) (NF)

Ogden, P. (1992) *Chelsea: The story of a signal dog.* Boston: Time Warner. (Ages 13–15) (NF)

Schrader, S. L. (1995). *Silent alarm: On the edge with a deaf EMT.* Washington, DC: Gallaudet University Press. (Ages 13–Adult) (NF)

Thomas, S., & Christian, S. (1990). *Silent night.* Washington, DC: Alexander Graham Bell Association for the Deaf. (Ages 13–15) (NF)

Zazove, P. (1993). *When the phone rings, my bed shakes: Memories of a deaf doctor.* Washington, DC: Gallaudet University Press. (NF)

Software

Arthur's Teacher Trouble, Broderbund Software, Inc., 500 Redwood Blvd., Novato, CA 94948, (415) 382-4400. (Macintosh, Windows)

Arump! LocuTour Multimedia, 1130 Grove St., San Luis Obispo, CA 93401, (800) 777-3166. (Macintosh, Windows)

Attention and Memory Volume I, LocuTour Multimedia, 1130 Grove St., San Luis Obispo, CA 93401, (800) 777-3166. (Macintosh, Windows)

BearJam, Dunamis, Inc., 3423 Fowler Blvd., Lawrenceville, GA 30044, (800) 828-2443. (Apple IIGS)

Capitalization, Hartley Courseware, 9920 Pacific Heights Blvd., San Diego, CA 92121, (800) 247-1380. (Apple IIe, Apple IIGS)

Communication Series—Expressions, Dunamis, Inc., 3423 Fowler Blvd., Lawrenceville, GA 30044, (800) 828-2443. (Apple IIGS)

Early Emerging Rules Series: Negation, Plurals, Prepositions, Laureate Learning Systems, Inc., 110 E. Spring St., Winooski, VT 05404, (800) 562-6801, Web site: http://www.LaureateLearning.com (Apple IIe, Apple IIGS, DOS)

EaseTalk, Microflip, Inc., 11213 Petworth Ln., Glen Dale, MD 20769, (301) 262-6020, Web site: http://www.microflip.com (DOS)

First Categories Series, Laureate Learning Systems, Inc., 110 E. Spring St., Winooski, VT 05404, (800) 562-6801, Web site: http://www.LaureateLearning.com (Apple IIe, Apple IIGS, Macintosh, DOS)

Foundations Series, Psychological Software Services, Inc., 6555 Carollton Ave., Indianapolis, IN 46220, (317) 257-9674, Web site: http://www.inetdirect.net/pss (DOS, Windows)

Guided Reading, Taylor Associates, 200-2 E. 2nd St., Huntington Station, NY 11746, (800) READ-PLUS, Web site: http://www.ta-comm.com (Apple IIGS, DOS, Macintosh)

Handi Series, Microsystems Software, Inc., 600 Worcester Rd., Framingham, MA 01702, (800) 828-2600, Web site: http://www.handiware.com (DOS, Windows)

NexTalk for Windows, NXi Communications, Inc., 3191 S. Valley St., Salt Lake City, UT 84109, (801) 466-1258, Web site: http://www.nxicom.com (IBM, Windows)

MicroLADS, Laureate Learning Systems, Inc., 110 E. Spring St., Winooski, VT 05404, (800) 562-6801, Web site: http://www.LaureateLearning.com (Apple IIe, Apple IIGS, Macintosh; DOS)

Sign Language Quiz, Data Assist, 651 Lakeview Plaza Blvd., Suite G, Columbus, OH 43085, (614) 888-8088, Web site: http://www.data.assist.com (DOS)

Speech Viewer, IBM Special Needs Systems, (800) 426-4832 (voice), (800) 426-4833 (TDD), Web site: http://www.austin.ibm.com/sns/ (allows deaf or hearing impaired person to see voice on the screen, then attempt to match proper sounds).

Spell It Plus, Davidson and Associates, Inc., 19840 Pioneer Ave., Torrance, CA 90503, (800) 545-7677, Web site: http://www.davd.com (Apple IIe, Apple IIGS, Macintosh, DOS) (Grades 3–9)

Visuospatial Skills Series, Psychological Software Services, Inc., 6555 Carollton Ave., Indianapolis, IN 46220, (317) 257-9674, Web site: http://www.inetdirect.net/pss (DOS, Windows)

Who, What, Where, Why? Hartley Courseware, 9920 Pacific Heights Blvd., San Diego, CA 92121, (800) 247-1380. (Apple IIe, Apple IIGS, DOS) (Grades 1–4)

Words and Concepts Series, Laureate Learning Systems, Inc., 110 E. Spring St., Winooski, VT 05404, (800) 562-6801, Web site: http://www.LaureateLearning.com

Words Around Me, Edmark Corporation, 6727 185th Ave., NE, Redmond, WA 98052, (800) 426-0856, Web site: http://www.edmark.com (Macintosh, Windows)

Services

Cochlear Implant Hotline/Cochlear Implant Information Center, Cochlear Corporation, 61 Inverness Drive East, Suite 200, Englewood, CO 80112, (800) 458-4999 (voice), (800) 483-3123 (TDD)

ERIC, Educational Resources Information Center Clearinghouse on Disabilities and Gifted Education, The Council for Exceptional Children, 1920 Association Dr., Reston, VA 20191-1589, (800) 328-0272, (703) 264-9449 (TDD), Web site: http://www.cec.sped.org/ericed.htm

National Center for Law and Deafness, Gallaudet University, 800 Florida Ave. NE, Washington, DC 20002, (202) 651-5373 (V/TDD)

National Cued Speech Association, 23970 Hermitage Rd., Cleveland, OH 44122-4008, (800) 459-3529 (V/TDD).

National Information Center on Deafness, Gallaudet University, 800 Florida Ave. NE, Washington, DC 20002, (202) 651-5051 (voice), (202) 651-5052 (TDD), Web site: http://www.gallaudet.edu/~nicd/

National Institute on Deafness and Other Communication Disorders Information Clearinghouse, 1 Communication Ave., Bethesda, MD 20892-3456, (800) 241-1044 (voice), (800) 241-1055 (TDD)

National Rehabilitation Information Center, 8455 Colesville Rd., Suite 935, Silver Spring, MD 20910-3319, (800) 346-2742 (voice), (301) 495-5626 (TDD). Web site: http://www.naric.com/naric

Outreach Services, Pre-College Program, Gallaudet University, 800 Florida Ave. NE, Washington, DC 20002, (800) 526-9105 (V/TDD)

PC PalsTeen Network, Alexander Graham Bell Association for the Deaf, 3417 Volta Place NW, Washington, DC 20007, (202) 337-5220 (V/TDD) (An electronic bulletin board for adolescents who are deaf or hard of hearing)

Organizations

American Graham Bell Association for the Deaf, 3417 Volta Place NW, Washington, DC 20007, (202) 337-5220 (V/TDD)

American Society for Deaf Children, 1820 Tribute Rd., Suite A, Sacramento, CA 95815, (916) 641-6084 (V/TDD)

American Speech-Language-Hearing Association (ASHA), 10801 Rockville Pike, Rockville, MD 20852, (888) 321-ASHA, (301) 897-5700 (voice), (301) 897-0157 (TDD)

National Association of the Deaf, 814 Thayer Ave., Silver Spring, MD 20910, (301) 587-1788 (voice), (301) 587-1789 (TDD)

Self-Help for Hard of Hearing People, Inc., 7910 Woodmont Ave., Suite 1200, Bethesda, MD 20814, (301) 657-2248 (voice) (301) 657-2249 (TDD)

Bibliography for Teaching Suggestions

Caissie, R., & Wilson, E. (1995). Communication breakdown management during cooperative learning activities by mainstreamed students with hearing losses. *The Volta Review, 97,* 105–121.

Card, K. J., & Schmider, L. (1995). Group work with members who have hearing impairments. *Journal of Specialist in Group Work, 20,* 83–91.

Carolina Computer Access Center (1991). *The CompuCID Project: Inclusion, technology, and alternative teaching strategies.* Charlotte, NC: Charlotte Mecklenburg Schools.

Edwards, C. (1991). Assessment and management of listening skills in school-aged children. *Seminars in Hearing, 12,* 389–401.

Flexer, C. (1999). *Facilitating hearing and listening in young children.* San Diego: Singular.

Gearheart, B. R., Weishahn, M. W., & Gearheart, C. J. (1996). *The exceptional student in the regular classroom* (6th ed.). Englewood Cliffs, NJ: Merrill.

Jaussi, K. R. (1991). Drawing the outsiders in: Deaf students in the mainstream. *Perspectives for Teachers of the Hearing Impaired, 9,* 12–15.

Johnson, D. W., Johnson, R. T., & Holubec, E. J. (1994). *The new circles of learning.* Alexandria, VA: Association for Supervision and Curriculum Development.

Kagan, S. (1994). *Cooperative learning.* San Juan Capistrano, CA: Resources for Teachers, Inc.

Lambert, T. (1994). *How to have a winning year teaching the student who is deaf or hard of hearing.* Washington, DC: Alexander Graham Bell Association for the Deaf.

Luetke-Stahlman, B. (1996). A helpful checklist for schools and students. *Perspectives in Education and Deafness, 15,* 16–17.

Martin, F. N., & Clark, J. G. (1996). *Hearing care for children.* Boston: Allyn & Bacon.

Nittmann, V., Gorman, K., & McGinnis, A. (1996). *13 keys to a successful high school experience.* Denver, CO: Educational Audiology Programs, Inc.

Ross, M. (1982). *Hard of hearing children in regular schools.* Englewood Cliffs, NJ: Prentice-Hall.

Ross, M., Brackett, D., & Maxon, A. B. (1991). *Assessment and management of mainstreamed hearing-impaired children.* Austin, TX: Pro-Ed.

Salend, S. J., & Longo, M. (1994). The roles of the educational interpreter in mainstreaming. *Teaching Exceptional Children, 26,* 22–28.

Smith, T. C., Polloway, E. A., Patton, J. R., & Dowdy, C. A. (1998). *Teaching students with special needs in inclusive settings* (2nd ed.). Boston: Allyn & Bacon.

joanne o'connell

Above Average. Ink, watercolor on paper. 17 × 14 in.

O'Connell lives in Brighton, MA, where she was born in 1968. She was left with a number of disabilities, including impaired vision and a seizure disorder, after a near-drowning accident when she was 11. Her work has been shown in and around Boston, in New York, and in Pennsylvania. She has won awards from MENCAP in London, England (1994) and the Ebensburg Center in Pennsylvania (1995). In 1996 her work was featured in *From the Outside In*, an exhibition at the Fuller Museum of Art in Brockton, MA.

chapter 10

Visual Impairment

No two blind people are alike. I, for instance, grew up wearing chains like Houdini, trying to pull off a magic trick. Not everyone with vision loss goes through this long struggle with self-consciousness. There are those who lose their vision suddenly and find tremendous powers of resilience. They give hope to the people around them, both the sighted and the blind.

We are, all of us, ecstatic creatures, capable of joyous mercy to the self and to others. The strong blind move like modern dancers, their every gesture means something. The newly blind or the lifelong blind often possess an art of living, an invisible, delicate vessel they carry. The sighted can have it too: José Carreras comes to mind. After his bout with leukemia, he still sings, and though some critics say that the great tenor's voice is not the same, I say it is more thrilling, touched as it is with buds of darkness. Sometimes roses grow on the sheer banks of the sea cliff.

STEPHEN KUUSISTO
The Planet of the Blind: A Memoir

S tephen Kuusisto's struggle to embrace a blind identity (see quote on p. 385) is not that unusual. Although blind from birth, Kuusisto was well into his adult years before he stopped the charade of trying to "pass" as a sighted person. Once at peace with his blindness, he was able to turn his energies to more productive endeavors, such as being a successful author. As Kuusisto points out, people vary in their response to being blind. Some may actually gain an inner strength from adversity. However, a major impediment to being able to accept one's blindness is society's reactions to people who are blind. Visual impairments seem to evoke more awkwardness than most other disabilities. Why are we so uncomfortably aware of blindness? For one thing, blindness is visible. We often do not realize that a person has impaired hearing, for example, until we actually talk to him or her. The person with visual impairment, however, usually has a variety of symbols—cane, thick or darkened glasses, a guide dog.

Another possible reason for being self-conscious around people who are blind is the role that eyes play in social interaction. Poets, playwrights, and songwriters have long recognized how emotionally expressive the eyes can be for people who are sighted. We all know how uncomfortable it can be to talk with someone who does not make eye contact with us. Think how often we have heard someone say or have ourselves said that we prefer to talk "face to face" on an important matter, rather than over the telephone. We seem to rely a great deal on the expressiveness of people's eyes to judge how they are responding to what we are saying.

Also, research has shown that most of us have a special fear of blindness (Conant & Budoff, 1982). It is reportedly the third most feared condition, with only cancer and AIDS outranking it (Jernigan, 1992). One reason we may be so frightened of becoming blind is that our eyes seem so vulnerable. Our ears feel safely tucked away; eyes seem dangerously exposed. Another reason we fear loss of vision is that the sense of sight is linked so closely with the traditional concept of beauty. We derive great pleasure from our sight. Our feelings about others are often based largely on physical appearances that are visually perceived.

So, despite the fact that blindness is the least prevalent of all disabilities, at least in children, people dread it. With a bit of reflection, however, it becomes obvious that our anxieties about blindness are irrational. Most of our apprehension can be attributed to our lack of experience in interacting with individuals with visual impairment. It is not until we talk to people who are blind or read about their appreciation of sounds, smells, and touch that we begin to realize that sight is not the only sense that enables us to enjoy beauty or interact socially with other people.

Like anyone with a disability, the person who is blind wants to be treated like everyone else. Most people who are blind do not seek pity or unnecessary help. In fact, they can be fiercely protective of their independence.

In this chapter we hope to change the idea that people with visual impairment are all alike in some odd way. We start by presenting a fact that most sighted people do not know: The majority of people who are blind can actually see.

Definition and Classification

The two most common ways of describing visual impairment are the legal and educational definitions. The former is the one laypeople and medical professionals use; the latter is the one educators favor.

misconceptions
about Persons with Visual Impairment

myth People who are legally blind have no sight at all.

fact Only a small percentage of people who are legally blind have absolutely no vision. Many have a useful amount of functional vision.

myth People who are blind have an extra sense that enables them to detect obstacles.

fact People who are blind do not have an extra sense. Some can develop an "obstacle sense" by noting the change in pitch of echoes as they move toward objects.

myth People who are blind automatically develop better acuity in their other senses.

fact Through concentration and attention, individuals who are blind can learn to make very fine discriminations in the sensations they obtain. This is not automatic but rather represents a better use of received sensations.

myth People who are blind have superior musical ability.

fact The musical ability of people who are blind is not necessarily better than that of sighted people; however, many people who are blind pursue musical careers as one way in which they can achieve success.

myth Braille is not very useful for the vast majority of people who are blind; it should only be tried as a last resort.

fact Very few people who are blind have learned braille, primarily due to fear that using it is a sign of failure and to a historical professional bias against it. Authorities acknowledge the utility of braille for people who are blind.

myth Braille is of no value for those who have low vision.

fact Some individuals with low vision have conditions that will eventually result in blindness. More and more, authorities think that these individuals should learn braille to be prepared for when they cannot read print effectively.

myth If people with low vision use their eyes too much, their sight will deteriorate.

fact Only rarely is this true. Visual efficiency can actually be improved through training and use. Wearing strong lenses, holding books close to the eyes, and using the eyes often cannot harm vision.

myth Mobility instruction should be delayed until elementary or secondary school.

fact Many authorities now recognize that even preschoolers can take advantage of mobility instruction, including the use of a cane.

myth The long cane is a simply constructed, easy-to-use device.

fact The National Academy of Sciences has drawn up specifications for the manufacture of the long cane and its proper use.

myth Guide dogs take people where they want to go.

fact The guide dog does not "take" the person anywhere; the person must first know where he or she is going. The dog is primarily a protection against unsafe areas or obstacles.

legally blind. A person who has visual acuity of 20/200 or less in the better eye even with correction (e.g., eyeglasses) or has a field of vision so narrow that its widest diameter subtends an angular distance no greater than 20 degrees.

braille. A system in which raised dots allow people who are blind to read with their fingertips; each quadrangular cell contains from one to six dots, the arrangement of which denotes different letters and symbols.

low vision. A term used by educators to refer to individuals whose visual impairment is not so severe that they are unable to read print of any kind; they may read large or regular print, and they may need some kind of magnification.

cornea. A transparent cover in front of the iris and pupil in the eye; responsible for most of the refraction of light rays in focusing on an object.

aqueous humor. A watery substance between the cornea and lens of the eye.

pupil. The contractile opening in the middle of the iris of the eye.

iris. The colored portion of the eye; contracts or expands, depending on the amount of light striking it.

lens. A structure that refines and changes the focus of the light rays passing through the eye.

vitreous humor. A transparent, gelatinous substance that fills the eyeball between the retina and the lens of the eye.

Legal Definition

The legal definition of *visual impairment* involves assessment of visual acuity and field of vision. A person who is **legally blind** has visual acuity of 20/200 or less in the better eye even with correction (e.g., eyeglasses) or has a field of vision so narrow that its widest diameter subtends an angular distance no greater than 20 degrees. The fraction 20/200 means that the person sees at 20 feet what a person with normal vision sees at 200 feet. (Normal visual acuity is thus 20/20.) The inclusion of a narrowed field of vision in the legal definition means that a person may have 20/20 vision in the central field but severely restricted peripheral vision. Legal blindness qualifies a person for certain legal benefits, such as tax advantages and money for special materials.

In addition to this medical classification of blindness, there is also a category referred to as *partially sighted*. According to the legal classification system, persons who are partially sighted have visual acuity falling between 20/70 and 20/200 in the better eye with correction.

Educational Definition

Many professionals, particularly educators, have found the legal classification scheme inadequate. They have observed that visual acuity is not a very accurate predictor of how people will function or use whatever remaining sight they have. Although a small percentage of individuals who are legally blind have absolutely no vision, the majority are able to see. For example, an extensive study of students who were legally blind found that only 18 percent were totally blind (Willis, 1976).

Many of those who recognize the limitations of the legal definition of blindness and partial sightedness favor the educational definition, which stresses the method of reading instruction. For educational purposes, individuals who are blind are so severely impaired they must learn to read braille or use aural methods (audiotapes and records). (**Braille,** a system of raised dots by which blind people read with their fingertips, consists of quadrangular cells containing from one to six dots whose arrangement denotes different letters and symbols.) Educators often refer to those individuals with visual impairment who can read print, even if they need magnifying devices or large-print books, as having **low vision.**

Prevalence

Blindness is primarily an adult disability. Most estimates indicate that blindness is approximately one-tenth as prevalent in school-age children as in adults. Only about .05 percent of the population ranging from six to seventeen years of age is classified by the federal government as "visually impaired." This makes visual impairment one of the least prevalent disabilities in children.

Anatomy and Physiology of the Eye

The anatomy of the visual system is extremely complex, so our discussion here will focus only on basic characteristics. Figure 10.1 shows the functioning of the eye. The physical object being seen becomes an electrical impulse sent through

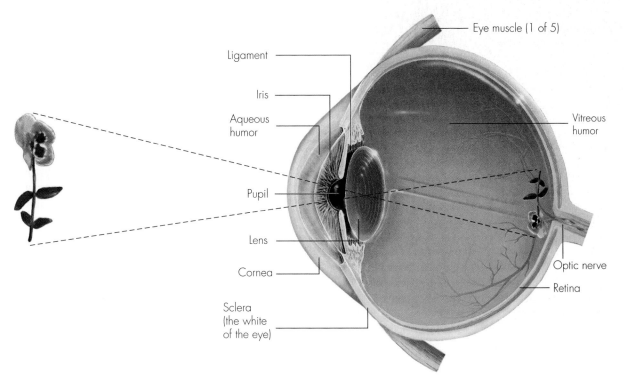

Ligament

Iris

Aqueous humor

Pupil

Lens

Cornea

Sclera (the white of the eye)

Eye muscle (1 of 5)

Vitreous humor

Optic nerve

Retina

Figure 10.1

The basic anatomical features of the eye and the visual process.

the optic nerve to the visual center of the brain, the occipital lobes. Before reaching the optic nerve, light rays reflecting off the object being seen pass through several structures within the eye. The light rays:

1. pass through the **cornea** (a transparent cover in front of the iris and pupil), which performs the major part of the bending (refraction) of the light rays so that the image will be focused.
2. pass through the **aqueous humor** (a watery substance between the cornea and lens of the eye).
3. pass through the **pupil** (the contractile opening in the middle of the **iris,** the colored portion of the eye that contracts or expands, depending on the amount of light striking it).
4. pass through the **lens,** which refines and changes the focus of the light rays before they pass through the **vitreous humor** (a transparent gelatinous substance that fills the eyeball between the retina and lens).
5. come to a focus on the **retina** (the back portion of the eye, containing nerve fibers connected to the optic nerve).

Measurement of Visual Ability

Visual acuity is most often measured with the **Snellen chart,** which consists of rows of letters (for individuals who know the alphabet) or Es (for the very young and for those who cannot read). In the latter case, the Es are arranged in various positions, and the person's task is to indicate in what direction the "legs" of the Es face. Each row corresponds to the distance at which a person with normal vision can

retina. The back portion of the eye, containing nerve fibers connected to the optic nerve.

Snellen chart. Used in determining visual acuity; consists of rows of letters or Es arranged in different positions; each row corresponds to the distance at which a normally sighted person can discriminate the letters; does not predict how accurately a child will be able to read print.

discriminate the directions of the Es. (There are eight rows, one corresponding to each of the following distances: 15, 20, 30, 40, 50, 70, 100, and 200 feet.) People are normally tested at the 20-foot distance. If they can distinguish the direction of the letters in the 20-foot row, they are said to have 20/20 central visual acuity for far distances. If they can distinguish only the much larger letters in the 70-foot row, they are said to have 20/70 central visual acuity for far distances.

Although the Snellen chart is widely used and can be very useful, it has at least three limitations.

1. It measures visual acuity for distant but not near objects—which is why it is necessary to report the results in terms of central visual acuity for *far* distances. Many educational activities, particularly reading, require visual acuity at close distances, and there are a variety of methods available for measuring it. The results of some of these methods can be used to estimate what kinds of reading material the person will be able to read (e.g., store catalogs, children's books, or high school texts).

2. Visual acuity, as measured by the Snellen chart, does not always correspond with visual efficiency. **Visual efficiency** refers to the ability, for example, to control eye movement, discriminate objects from their background, and pay attention to important details. Barraga and colleagues have developed the Diagnostic Assessment Procedure (DAP) to assess visual efficiency (Barraga, 1983; Barraga & Collins, 1979).

3. Some persons, although not totally blind, have so little vision that the Snellen chart is essentially useless. Professionals often assess visual function in these individuals. **Visual function** refers to the degree of useful vision a person has (Hatton, Bailey, Burchinal, & Ferrell, 1997). For example, a person may be said to have *light perception*—the ability to detect light—or to have *object perception*—the ability to detect objects in the environment.

There are screening tests more thorough than the Snellen (Rathgeber, 1981). Using these screening tests, teachers can identify children in need of more complete eye exams. Unfortunately, some schools use only the Snellen chart as a screening procedure. Because it does not pick up all possible types of visual problems, teachers should be alert to other signs that children might have visual impairment. Prevent Blindness America (1998) has listed a number of signs of possible eye problems on their Web site (see the box on p. 391).

Causes

The most common visual problems are the results of errors of refraction. **Myopia** (nearsightedness), **hyperopia** (farsightedness), and **astigmatism** (blurred vision) are examples of refraction errors that affect central visual acuity. Although each can be serious enough to cause significant impairment (myopia and hyperopia are the most common impairments of low vision), wearing glasses or contact lenses usually can bring vision within normal limits.

Myopia results when the eyeball is too long. In this case, the light rays from the object in Figure 10.1 would be in focus in front of, rather than on, the retina. Myopia affects vision for distant objects, but close vision may be unaffected. When the eyeball is too short, hyperopia (farsightedness) results. In this case, the light rays from the object in the diagram would be in focus behind, rather than on, the retina.

visual efficiency. A term used to refer to how well one uses his or her vision, including such things as control of eye movements, attention to visual detail, and discrimination of figure from background; believed by some to be more important than visual acuity alone in predicting a person's ability to function visually.

visual function. A term that refers to a person's useful vision such as the ability to detect light or to detect objects in the environment.

myopia. Nearsightedness; vision for distant objects is affected; usually results when the eyeball is too long.

hyperopia. Farsightedness; vision for near objects is affected; usually results when the eyeball is too short.

astigmatism. Blurred vision caused by an irregular cornea or lens.

Signs of Possible Eye Troubles in Children

It is possible for your child to have a serious vision problem without your being aware of it. Any concern about abnormalities in the appearance of the eyes or vision should be investigated. If you have any questions about your child's vision, see an eye doctor. In any case, start early to provide your child with a regular schedule of professional eye exams.

Signs of possible eye trouble in children include:

Behavior

- Rubs eyes excessively
- Shuts or covers one eye
- Tilts or thrusts head forward
- Has difficulty with reading or other close-up work
- Holds objects close to eyes
- Blinks more than usual or is irritable when doing close-up work
- Is unable to see distant things clearly
- Squints eyelids together or frowns

Appearance

- Crossed or misaligned eyes
- Red-rimmed, encrusted or swollen eyelids

- Inflamed or watery eyes
- Recurring styes (infections) on eyelids
- Color photos of eyes show white reflection instead of typical red or no reflection

Complaints

- Eyes itch, burn, or feel scratchy
- Cannot see well
- Dizziness, headaches or nausea following close-up work
- Blurred or double vision

If a child exhibits one or more of these signs, please seek professional eye care. A professional eye exam is recommended shortly after birth, by six months of age, before entering school (four or five years old) and periodically throughout school years. Regular eye exams are important since some eye problems have no signs or symptoms.

Source: Retrieved April 20, 1998 from the World Wide Web: http://www.prevent-blindness.org/children/trouble_signs.html. Reprinted with permission from Prevent Blindness America®. Copyright © 1997.

Hyperopia affects vision for close objects, but far vision may be unaffected. If the cornea or lens of the eye is irregular, the person is said to have astigmatism. In this case, the light rays from the object in the figure would be blurred or distorted.

Among the most serious impairments are those caused by glaucoma, cataracts, and diabetes. These conditions occur primarily in adults, but each, particularly the latter two, can occur in children.

Glaucoma is a condition in which there is excessive pressure in the eyeball. Left untreated, the condition progresses to the point at which the blood supply to the optic nerve is cut off and blindness results. The cause of glaucoma is presently unknown (although it can be caused secondarily by other eye diseases), and its onset can be sudden or very gradual. Because its incidence increases dramatically after age thirty-five and because it can be prevented if detected early, it is often strongly recommended that all adults have periodic eye examinations after age thirty-five. A common complaint during the early stages of glaucoma is that lights appear to have halos around them (Thomas, 1985).

Cataracts are caused by a clouding of the lens of the eye, which results in blurred vision. In children, the condition is called *congenital cataracts,* and distance and color vision are seriously affected. Surgery can usually correct the problems caused by cataracts. Diabetes can cause **diabetic retinopathy,** a condition resulting from interference with the blood supply to the retina.

Several other visual impairments primarily affect children. Visual impairments of school-age children are often due to prenatal causes, many of which are

glaucoma. A condition of excessive pressure in the eyeball; the cause is unknown; if untreated, blindness results.

cataracts. A condition caused by clouding of the lens of the eye; affects color vision and distance vision.

diabetic retinopathy. A condition resulting from interference with the blood supply to the retina; the fastest-growing cause of blindness.

Consider how people with certain visual impairments see the world: (a) Diabetic retinopathy, which occurs when diabetes is poorly controlled, completely blocks out many parts of an image. (b) Tunnel vision is a late-stage complication of retinitis pigmentosa.

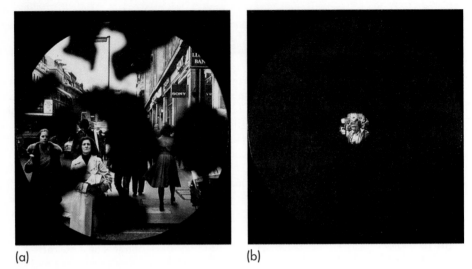

(a)　　　　　　　　　　　　　　　　(b)

hereditary. We have already discussed congenital (meaning *present at birth*) cataracts and glaucoma. Another congenital condition is retinitis pigmentosa, a hereditary disease resulting in degeneration of the retina. **Retinitis pigmentosa** usually causes the field of vision to narrow and also affects one's night vision. Also included in the "prenatal" category are infectious diseases that affect the unborn child, such as syphilis and rubella.

Another childhood condition, apparently on the increase, is **cortical visual impairment (CVI)**. Cortical visual impairment is not well understood, but it is thought to be due to dysfunction in the visual cortex of the brain. Children who have it are characterized by wide fluctuations from day to day in their visual abilities. In addition, children with CVI often have other conditions, such as mental retardation (Hatton et al., 1997).

One of the most dramatic medical discoveries of a cause of blindness involved a condition now referred to as **retinopathy of prematurity (ROP)**. ROP, which results in scar tissue forming behind the lens of the eye, began to appear in the 1940s in premature infants. In the 1950s, researchers determined that excessive concentrations of oxygen often administered to premature infants were causing blindness. The oxygen was necessary to prevent brain damage, but it was often given at too high a level. Since then, hospitals have been careful to monitor the amount of oxygen administered to premature infants. When the cause of ROP was discovered, some authorities thought its occurrence would be drastically reduced, but this has not happened. In fact, there appears to be a resurgence of ROP (Hatton et al., 1997). With medical advances, many more premature babies are surviving, but they need very high levels of oxygen.

Two other conditions resulting in visual problems can be grouped because both are caused by improper muscle functioning. **Strabismus** is a condition in which one or both eyes are directed inward (crossed eyes) or outward. Left untreated, strabismus can result in permanent blindness because the brain will eventually reject signals from a deviating eye. Fortunately, most cases of strabismus are correctable with eye exercises or surgery. Eye exercises sometimes involve the person wearing a patch over the good eye for periods of time in order to force use of the eye that deviates. Surgery involves tightening or loosening the muscles that control eye

retinitis pigmentosa. A hereditary condition resulting in degeneration of the retina; causes a narrowing of the field of vision and affects night vision.

cortical visual impairment (CVI). A poorly understood childhood condition that apparently involves dysfunction in the visual cortex; characterized by large day-to-day variations in visual ability.

retinopathy of prematurity (ROP). A condition resulting from administration of an excessive concentration of oxygen at birth; causes scar tissue to form behind the lens of the eye.

strabismus. A condition in which the eyes are directed inward (crossed eyes) or outward.

movement. **Nystagmus** is a condition in which there are rapid involuntary movements of the eyes, usually resulting in dizziness and nausea. Nystagmus is sometimes a sign of brain malfunctioning and/or inner-ear problems.

Psychological and Behavioral Characteristics

Language Development

Most authorities believe that lack of vision does not have a very significant effect on the ability to understand and use language. They point to the many studies showing that students who are visually impaired do not differ from sighted students on verbal intelligence tests. Because auditory more than visual perception is the sensory modality through which we learn language, it is not surprising that studies have found that people who are blind are not impaired in language functioning. The child who is blind is still able to hear language and may even be more motivated than the sighted child to use language because it is the main channel through which he or she communicates with others.

There are, however, a few subtle differences in the way in which language usually develops in children, especially infants, who are visually impaired. There appears to be a delay in the very earliest stages of language for some infants with visual impairment, their first words tend to come later. Once they start producing words, however, their vocabulary expands rapidly. Some have theorized this initial delay is because it takes them a little longer to discover that words have a symbolic function, that they can represent objects and people (McConachie & Moore, 1994).

Intellectual Ability

Performance on Standardized Intelligence Tests. Samuel P. Hayes pioneered the intelligence testing of people who are blind (Hayes, 1942, 1950). He took verbal items from a commonly used IQ test of his time—the Stanford-Binet—to assess individuals with blindness. His rationale was that people without sight would not be disadvantaged by a test that relied on verbal items: therefore, this kind of test would be a more accurate measure of intelligence than tests containing items of a visual nature.

Since the work of Hayes, professionals have continued to use verbal IQ tests with individuals with visual impairment, but they have also emphasized the importance of measuring areas of intelligence related to spatial and tactual abilities. Many professionals advocate the use of intelligence tests that assess spatial and tactual skills because these abilities have a direct bearing on how well persons with visual impairment can traverse their environment and read braille. Several intelligence tests that emphasize these nonverbal areas are now available.

At one time it was popular for researchers to compare the intelligence of sighted persons with that of persons with blindness. Most authorities now believe that such comparisons are virtually impossible because finding comparable tests is so difficult (Warren, 1984). From what is known, there is no reason to believe that blindness results in lower intelligence.

nystagmus. A condition in which there are rapid involuntary movements of the eyes; sometimes indicates a brain malfunction and/or inner-ear problems.

Conceptual Abilities. It is also very difficult to assess the performance of children with visual impairment on laboratory-type tasks of conceptual ability. Many researchers, using conceptual tasks originally developed by noted psychologist Jean Piaget, have concluded that children who are blind lag behind their sighted peers (e.g., Davidson, Dunn, Wiles-Kettenmann, & Appelle, 1981; Stephens & Grube, 1982). But these comparisons are questionable because, like comparisons on IQ tests, it is virtually impossible to find equivalent tasks for people with and without sight.

Nevertheless, some important differences exist between how those with and without sight perceive the world, most of which are due to the difference between tactual and visual experiences. Persons who are blind rely much more on tactual and auditory information to learn about the world than do those who are sighted, who obtain a great deal of information through sight. As one person who is blind described it, he "sees with his fingers" (Hull, 1990).

An important difference between individuals with and without sight is that the latter need to take much more initiative in order to learn what they can from their environment. Sighted infants and children can pick up a lot of visual information incidentally. In a sense, the world comes to them, whereas children who are visually impaired need to extend themselves out to the world in order to pick up some of the same information. Exploring the environment motorically, however, does not come easily for some infants and young children with visual impairment; they often need encouragement to do so (Wheeler, Floyd, & Griffin, 1997). In addition, one way they can compensate for not being able to explore their environment easily is by becoming adept at obtaining concepts through what they hear from others (Groenveld & Jan, 1992).

We also know that the degree of visual impairment and the age of its onset are important determinants of how the child will explore his or her environment. Children whose blindness was present at birth will generally rely more on their tactual sense to learn about the world than will those who acquire their blindness later. Likewise, children who are totally blind will depend more on the tactual sense for concept development than will those with low vision.

Little is known about the tactual sense of children who are blind and how best to develop it, but we do know that good tactual perception, like good visual perception, relies on being able to use a variety of strategies (Berla, 1981; Griffin & Gerber, 1982). The child with blindness who compares a pencil and ruler, for example, by using such strategies as comparing the length of each to body parts and listening to differences in pitch when each is banged against a table will have an advantage in understanding the differences and similarities between these two objects. Research has shown that the earlier the child with visual impairment is trained to use such strategies, the more beneficial the training will be for his or her tactual development (Berla, 1981).

Mobility

A very important ability for the successful adjustment of many people with visual impairment is their mobility—their skill in moving about in their environments. Mobility skills depend to a great extent on spatial ability. The spatial abilities of persons who are blind continue to develop throughout childhood and adolescence; full development does not occur until well into the teenage years (Ochaita & Huertas, 1993). Authorities have identified two ways in which persons with visual impairment process spatial information—as a sequential route, or as a map depicting the general relation of various points in the environment (Bigelow, 1991; Herman, Chatman, & Roth, 1983; Rieser, Guth, & Hill, 1982). The latter method, referred to as **cognitive mapping,** is preferable because it offers more flexibility in navigating. Consider three sequential points—A, B, and C. A sequential mode of processing spatial information restricts a person's movement so he or she can move from A to C only by way of B. But a person with a cognitive map of points A, B, and C can go from A to C directly without going through B. Mobility skills vary greatly among people with visual impairment. (And even the best of travelers who are blind occasionally run into problems in navigating; see the box below for an account of how *not* to help someone who is blind when he or she is lost.) It is surprisingly difficult to predict which individuals will be the best travelers. For example, common sense seems to tell us that mobility would be better among those who have more residual vision and those who lose their vision later in life, but this is not always the case (McLinden, 1988; Warren & Kocon, 1974). A critical variable appears to be *motivation*. Some authorities have noted that people who have more residual vision and those who become visually impaired later in life may tend to become more frustrated by their loss of vision and less motivated to acquire mobility skills.

> **cognitive mapping.** A nonsequential way of conceptualizing the spatial environment that allows a person who is visually impaired to know where several points in the environment are simultaneously; allows for better mobility than does a strictly sequential conceptualization of the environment.

How Not to Help a Person Who Is Blind and Lost

When people who are sighted encounter someone who is lost, their natural inclination is to ask the person where he or she is headed. As the following entry in the diary of John M. Hull indicates, this question can lead to confusion when the person lost happens to be blind.

Getting Lost   **8 November**

I think it is David Scott Blackhall, in his autobiography *The Way I See Things* (London, Baker, 1971), who remarks how annoying he found it when people refused to answer his question about where he was and insisted on asking him where he was trying to get to. I share this experience.

Going home the other night I was turned out of my way by some construction work on one of the footpaths. By mistake I turned along a side street, and after a block or so, when I realized I had made a mistake somewhere, I was not sure exactly where I was. There were some chaps working on a car parked on the roadside. "Excuse me," I said. "Could you tell me please where I am? What is the name of this street?"

The chap replied, "Where are you trying to get to?"

With what I hoped was a good-humored laugh, I said, "Never mind about that, just tell me, please, what street this is?"

"This is Alton Road. You usually go up Bournbrook Road, don't you? It's just a block further along."

I thanked him, and explained that I needed now to know exactly whereabouts on Alton Road I was so that I could get to Bournbrook Road. "Which side of Alton Road am I on? If I face that way, am I looking towards Bristol Road or is it the other way?"

"You live high up Bournbrook Road, don't you? Well, if you take the next road to the left you'll be OK."

But which way is "left"? Does he mean me to cross the road or to stay on this side? At this point, the blind and sighted enter into mutual bafflement.

When a sighted person is lost, what matters to him or her is not where he is, but where he is going. When he is told that the building he is looking for lies in a certain direction, he is no longer lost. A sighted person is lost in the sense that he does not know where the building he is looking for is. He is never lost with respect to what street he is actually on; he just looks at the street sign on the corner of the block. It is his direction he has lost, rather than his position. The blind person lost has neither direction nor position. He needs position in order to discover direction. This is such a profound lostness that most sighted people find it difficult to imagine.

Source: From *Touching the rock* by John Hull, pp. 144–145. Copyright © 1990 by John M. Hull. Reprinted by permission of Pantheon Books, a division of Random House, Inc.

A bas-relief bronze wall at the FDR Memorial includes braille characters that many people find unreadable because they are too big.

Obstacle Sense. For some persons who are blind, the ability to detect physical obstructions in the environment is a large part of their mobility skills. Walking along the street, they often seem able to sense an object in their path. This ability has come to be known as the **obstacle sense**—an unfortunate term in some ways, because many laypeople have taken it to mean that people who are blind somehow develop an extra sense. It is easy to see why this misconception exists. Even people who are blind have a very difficult time explaining the phenomenon (Hull, 1990). A number of experiments have shown that, with experience, people who are blind come to be able to detect subtle changes in the pitches of high-frequency echoes as they move toward objects. Actually, they are taking advantage of the **Doppler effect,** a physical principle that says the pitch of a sound rises as a person moves toward its source.

Although obstacle sense can be important for the mobility of someone without sight, by itself it will not make its user a highly proficient traveler. It is merely an aid. Extraneous noises (traffic, speech, rain, wind) can render obstacle sense unusable. Also, it requires walking at a fairly slow speed to be able to react in time.

The Myth of Sensory Acuteness. Along with the myth that people with blindness have an extra sense is the general misconception that they automatically develop better acuity in their other senses. However, people who are blind do not have lowered thresholds of sensation in touch or hearing. What they are able to do is make better use of the sensations they obtain. Through concentration and attention, they learn to make very fine discriminations.

Another common belief is that people who are blind automatically have superior musical talent. Some do follow musical careers, but this is because music is an area in which they can achieve success.

Academic Achievement

Most professionals agree that direct comparisons of the academic achievement of students who are blind with that of sighted students must be interpreted cautiously because the two groups must be tested under different conditions. There are, however, braille and large-print forms of some achievement tests. The few studies that have been done suggest that both children with low vision and those who are blind are behind their sighted peers (Rapp & Rapp, 1992). There is speculation that the low achievement of some students who are blind may be due to low expectations and lack of exposure to braille, not necessarily to actual ability.

obstacle sense. A skill possessed by some people who are blind, whereby they can detect the presence of obstacles in their environments; research has shown that it is not an indication of an extra sense, as popularly thought; it is the result of being able to detect subtle changes in the pitches of high-frequency echoes.

Doppler effect. A term used to describe the phenomenon of the pitch of a sound rising as the listener moves toward its source.

Memorial's Braille Letters Pose a Sizable Problem for the Blind

The new Franklin Delano Roosevelt Memorial may have been designed with the disabled in mind, but a problem has emerged with the Braille lettering on what is meant to be the monument's most inviting sculpture.

Most blind people find it unreadable.

"It doesn't say anything!" Linda Kipps said after running her fingers over the raised dots on the piece titled "Social Programs."

The sculpture, a massive bronze wall of bas-relief in the monument's "second room," features 54 images and, beside them, raised Braille dots. But Kipps, a blind District resident visiting the memorial just two weeks after it opened, added her voice to those complaining that what the dots mostly communicate to a visually impaired visitor is frustration.

"If they're going to go to the trouble to put the dots there, it would be helpful if there were actually something you could read," Kipps said.

According to the sculptor and at least one blind visitor, the dots are genuine Braille. They spell out the initials of WPA, CCC and other "alphabet agencies" that Roosevelt championed, programs that put the human figures in the sculpture back to work. The initials (complete with periods) are followed on the bronze by the full name of the agency, then its date of inception.

The main problem is the size of the dots. The characters, or cells, they form are too big to fit under a fingertip.

"The dots are about five times normal size," said Charlie Hodge, another blind visitor. "And the spacing of the dots within a cell and between cells, because of the enlargement, is screwed up.

"It's an additional irritation on top of the controversy over not depicting FDR as the disabled person we know he was."

Gail Snider, public education coordinator at Volunteers for the Blind, said she could read the sculpture's Braille only with great effort.

"Imagine if print letters were so large that you couldn't read each one without eye movement—you couldn't get a single whole letter within your field of vision without eye movement. That would be the equivalent of what this is like," Snider said. "I appreciate artistic license and so on, but it doesn't make it very readable if you magnify it like that."

Sculptor Robert Graham acknowledged that license was taken.

"My concept of that piece was to have Braille as a kind of invitation to touch, more than anything," Graham said from his California studio.

"Braille is not much different than touching a face or anything else," he said. "That was kind of the graphic idea, the layering of many faces coming out and the layering of the Braille and the layering of several tactile surfaces.

"Nothing is life-size in the piece, so you very much have to adjust yourself to the scale."

Graham declined to accept responsibility for a second problem. The sculptor said it was the decision of the memorial's overall architect, Lawrence Halprin, to mount the bronze at a height that put at least a third of the Braille about eight feet off the ground—well beyond reach. "I didn't design the monument," Graham said.

An aide to Halprin called the elevation necessary.

"The idea is you hang the pieces so they can be appreciated from a distance, so they can draw you into them." said Dee Mullen, speaking from Halprin's San Francisco office.

The people running the memorial are as confused as any visitor about the Braille. One National Park Service ranger on duty at the monument . . . said the script was not meant to be read. A Park Service spokeswoman agreed. "It was just supposed to give the illusion of a message," she said. But a second ranger was under the opposite impression.

And Sen. Daniel K. Inouye (D–Hawaii), the FDR Memorial Commission's co-chairman, said while defending the monument's design amid the wheelchair controversy that the bas-relief would include "Braille for the sight-impaired."

Hodge said, "It's a nice idea that's gone awry."

The confusing reality has distressed even some sighted visitors. Washington resident S. Paul Kramer left the monument "astonished at the insensitivity of our monumentalists" after seeing an elderly blind man run his fingertips over the Braille lettering in vain. Kramer said that when he asked what it said, the man replied: "It says nothing, nothing at all. It must be a fake."

"I simply took it as a piece of either callousness or swindle," Kramer said. "And obviously the people in charge of the monument must be upset, if they know about it."

Source: Vick, K. (1997, May 20). Memorial's braille letters pose a sizable problem for the blind. *The Washington Post*, B–1, B–8. © 1997 The Washington Post. Reprinted with permission.

Collaboration key to success

Ricki Curry is an itinerant teacher for students with visual impairment, Piedmont Regional Education Program; A.B., Experimental Psychology, Brown University; M.Ed., Special Education for the Visually Impaired, University of Virginia. Jenny Garrett is a fourth-grade teacher, Stone-Robinson Elementary School, Albemarle, Virginia; B.A. English, College of William and Mary; M.Ed., Curriculum and Instruction, University of Virginia.

Ricki Curry

Ricki In a regional program serving children with low-incidence disabilities in six rural localities, my students were in general education classes, using some variation of the inclusion model, and received itinerant services from one to four times a week. Dennis, one of my students with severe visual impairment, was fully included in Jenny's class.

Jenny My fourth-grade class consisted of twenty-three nine- and ten-year-old students, including two children with learning disabilities: one student with severe behavior disorders and Dennis. They began the year reading anywhere from a first- to a sixth-grade level.

Ricki Although he has some usable vision, Dennis can see no details from a distance of more than about two feet and uses large-print texts for reading. Dennis comes from a very highly educated family and is a very bright, verbal, curious child. Although academically he is right on or above grade level, his independent work skills are very poor.

Jenny Dennis has some difficulty making friends because of his immaturity, his compulsive talking, and his inability to listen. On the other hand, Dennis has a good sense of humor and is quick with language. He loves to take things apart and fiddle with anything mechanical. Dennis is amazingly agile and navigates the classroom, school corridors, and

playground with ease. It is often easy to forget the severity of his visual handicap, but when we venture out of the school environs, he clings to the chaperone's hand and is markedly less self-confident.

Ricki Dennis had been included in this school since kindergarten, but the early grades are extremely developmental in approach, and this was the first year that things were going to get really academic for him. Both Jenny and I had concerns about his ability to be a functioning member of the class.

Jenny Dennis was in my class all day long for every academic subject. Ricki worked with him at the back of the room during a large chunk of the language arts block, teaching braille. She would come to school during the last half of my planning period, which gave us a daily opportunity to discuss assignments, homework, curricular adaptations, equipment, and the like. Homework was an enormous issue. For the first time, Dennis had challenging nightly assignments. Ricki helped him set up a notebook with a homework contract enclosed and a special highlighter, which he used to mark off completed assignments. He had to write down the assignments himself, remember to take the notebook home, complete the assignments, get a parent's signature, and get it back to school. Homework was extremely stressful for Dennis and his parents, both of whom worked full-time. Ricki often

played the "bad cop" when assignments were not returned and was always calm, matter-of-fact, but hard nosed about consequences.

Ricki I've always felt that ownership is a very important issue in successfully including students. If I present a student with visual impairment to a classroom teacher as "mine," then that teacher has every right to abdicate responsibility for the student and expect me to create a program that somehow will fit the student into the class. The student is always seen as an "extra" and not as a real member of the class. If I can communicate to a teacher that I'm only there to help and that the student "belongs" to the classroom teacher, the inclusion process goes much more smoothly. This can be a tricky relationship to establish because I don't want to look as though I'm trying to get away with doing a minimum job—presenting myself as a helper instead of the leader of our little two-person team. But if I come on too strong, as knowing a lot about the student and trying to influence decisions about the student's program, a teacher will often feel intimidated and defer to me about everything, giving up responsibility for the student's inclusion.

Jenny The hardest part of working with Dennis was the start-up period. I had to get to know him, his visual capabilities, his strengths and weaknesses, his coping strategies. I began adapting my

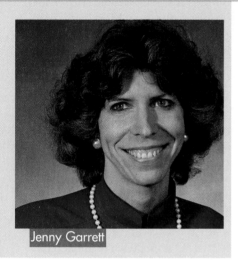
Jenny Garrett

teaching style, using an easel rather than the blackboard so that he could scoot up to it. I had to decide how hard to push, what to expect from his parents, and what to demand from Dennis. Part of the start-up stress was getting to know and trust Ricki. When someone spends an hour a day in your classroom, they see it all! Thankfully, we were a good match, and there were respect and trust on both ends.

Ricki I often found myself overwhelmed by the number of things that Jenny and/or Dennis needed help with in the short time that I was in the building. And so many things seemed to go wrong in the time between when I left one day and arrived again the next day! Dennis couldn't seem to keep track of his papers or get his homework done and back into school, or he'd hit someone on the bus or he'd come into school in tears and refuse to talk to anyone about what was going on. I knew Jenny really didn't have time to deal with the intensive care that Dennis seemed to require, but it was hard for me to come up with effective ways of dealing with his behavioral issues when I usually wasn't around when things happened or when consequences needed to be applied. I would end up getting Jenny's side of the story, trying to figure out from what Dennis said what he thought the situation was, and then trying to come up with a plan of action. I often felt that all I could really do was

produce a "Band-aid" solution. All this mediation and problem solving also took up a lot of the time I had with Jenny and Dennis, so instructional issues got less time than they needed.

Jenny The most rewarding aspect of this collaboration was being part of an inclusion model that worked beautifully! Ricki was like a fairy godmother, continually pulling out material resources to enable Dennis to participate in activities, whether it was sewing our quilt with a darning needle and lab goggles or adapting the computer with a magnification program. Her attitude was: How can I make it work? What can I do? She was creative with her solutions and ideas, energetic, and appreciative of my efforts. It was wonderful to have a colleague in the room to laugh and work with. (Teachers are often extremely isolated from other adults.) Ricki was invaluable in helping Dennis deal with organizational and homework demands. She added so much to the life of the classroom, helping me plan a New Year's party and teaching a unit on braille. While Dennis was brailling and was working with reading groups at the front of the room, other students would quietly go to Ricki for help with their classwork. She was our cheerleader, Dennis's advocate, and a huge plus for our room.

Ricki Although I was frustrated by the limitations imposed by time constraints, the beauty of the inclusion model was that I was very aware of the true gestalt of Dennis's program and knew exactly what he was involved in all the time. Had I been taking him out to do an hour of braille in isolation four times a week, I would never have been aware of all the management issues Jenny had to deal with—getting Dennis to keep track

of his magnifiers and finding his large-print books quickly when he needed them; getting his spelling work, which was done on the computer, printed and hole-punched and put in his notebook on time, instead of being half-finished or left under the computer cart; crying when another student accidentally bumped into him; eating snacks while everyone else was back at work; rummaging through his desk, completely out of touch, while the class was being given the daily assignments. I knew when Jenny came to me with a problem that she wasn't just imagining it or being overly picky! I was able to see for myself how difficult a time Dennis was having being a regular fourth-grader and how much support he needed to grow toward that goal. Seeing Jenny at work also made it clear to me that she truly didn't have time to deal with all Dennis's problems and that she wasn't abdicating responsibility or just whining when she asked for my direct help. Had I not had an almost daily view of Dennis's classroom performance, I might not have believed how hard it was to integrate this very bright, verbal, personable child into Jenny's class. I admired Jenny tremendously for persisting, and in spite of the stress Jenny and I went through, I think Dennis's inclusion was one of the most successful I've seen.

Jenny Collaboration works best when there is match of personalities as well as energy, enthusiasm for teaching, and professionalism. Both of us genuinely like children and enjoy the learning process. During the last several weeks of school, Dennis was absent because of medical problems. Frankly, I was surprised by how much easier it was. I didn't have to be constantly remembering to enlarge assignments or pop over to his desk to check on him or to present every assignment so that he could have maximum visual advantage. In retrospect, teaching Dennis was enriching and stressful, challenging and difficult. His mother wrote at the end of the year, "You have been the turning point for Dennis. He has come a long way this year, and he still has a long way to go. You really gave him a badly needed structure and 'push.'"

> "**Ownership is a very important issue in successfully including students.**"

Social Adjustment

At one time the prevailing opinion of professionals was that people with visual impairment were at risk to exhibit personality disturbances. Most authorities now agree that personality problems are not an inherent condition of blindness. What social difficulties may arise are more likely due to society's inappropriate reaction to blindness than to personality flaws of people without sight.

Much of this inappropriateness may be caused by the average person's unfamiliarity with people who are blind. Because we do not have many acquaintances who are blind, we are not used to their usual patterns of social interaction. Social skills that come naturally to the sighted may be difficult for some people with visual impairment. One good example is smiling. Smiling is a strong visual cue used by sighted people to provide feedback to one another. For some people with visual impairment, however, smiling is not as spontaneous a social response as it is for those who are sighted. John M. Hull, whose eyesight deteriorated gradually over several years, kept a diary of his experiences. The following entry pertains to smiling:

> Nearly every time I smile, I am conscious of it. I am aware of the muscular effort; not that my smiles have become forced, as if I were pretending, but it has become a more or less conscious effort. Why is this? It must be because there is no reinforcement. There is no returning smile.... Most smiling is responsive. You smile spontaneously when you receive a smile. For me it is like sending dead letters. Have they been received, acknowledged? Was I even smiling in the right direction? (Hull, 1990, p. 34)

An important point to keep in mind is that even though people with visual impairment differ from the sighted in how they interact socially, this does not mean that they are socially maladjusted. It does mean, however, that initial interactions between people with and without sight may be strained. We emphasize *initial,* because once sighted individuals and those without sight become acquainted, these problems in communication largely disappear (Fichten, Judd, Tagalakis, Amsel, & Robillard, 1991).

Another important point is that it should not only be up to people who are visually impaired to change their ways of interacting socially. Sighted people should also be responsible for instances of faulty communication with people who are blind. For example:

> While giving a lift to an acquaintance who was blind, the driver [who was sighted] remarked, "We're at the junction you specified. Which house is it—the one with the brown or yellow balconies?" The response to this innocent, but inappropriate query was delivered with a chuckle, "I don't know about brown or yellow balconies; take me to the building on the right." (Fichten et al., 1991, p. 371)

Not only may some people with visual impairment profit from instruction in using appropriate visually based cues (e.g., facial expressions, head nods, and gestures), but sighted people also can learn to use their natural telephone skills when communicating with persons who are blind. Two sighted people talking on the telephone use a variety of auditorially based cues to help them communicate, even though they cannot see each other (e.g., assenting with "uh-hum" or "yeah," asking for more information, adjusting tone of voice) (Fichten et al., 1991). If sighted individuals consciously try to use these strategies when interacting with people who are blind, communication may be smoother.

Stereotypic Behaviors. An impediment to good social adjustment for some students with visual impairment is **stereotypic behaviors:** repetitive, stereotyped

stereotypic behaviors. Any of a variety of repetitive behaviors (e.g., eye rubbing) that are sometimes found in individuals who are blind, severely retarded, or psychotic; sometimes referred to as *stereotypies* or *blindisms.*

movements such as body rocking, poking or rubbing the eyes, repetitive hand or finger movements, and grimacing. For many years, the term **blindisms** was used to refer to these behaviors because it was thought that they were manifested only in people who are blind; however, they are also sometimes characteristic of children with normal sight who are severely retarded or disturbed.

Several competing theories concern the causes of stereotypic behaviors. Most involve the notion that these behaviors are physiological attempts to stabilize one's level of arousal (Baumeister, 1978). For example, one position holds that children with low levels of sensory stimulation, such as those without sight, make up for this deprivation by stimulating themselves in other ways (Thurrell & Rice, 1970). Another theory holds that, even with adequate sensory stimulation, social isolation can cause individuals to seek added stimulation through stereotypic behaviors (Warren, 1981, 1984).

Stereotypic behaviors can be manifested as early as a few months of age. Researchers have found that eye poking and body rocking are among the most prevalent types of stereotypic behaviors and the most difficult to eliminate (Bambring & Troster, 1992). Most authorities agree that it is important to eliminate stereotypic behaviors. In addition to being socially stigmatizing and possibly physically damaging, they can interfere with the child's ability to learn (Bambring & Troster, 1992). Engaging in such behaviors means less time for active learning.

The reduction of stereotypic behaviors can be very difficult. In recent years, researchers have tried cognitive and metacognitive training as ways of decreasing the frequency of such behaviors (Estevis & Koenig, 1994; McAdam, O'Cleirigh, & Cuvo, 1993; Ross & Koenig, 1991; Van Reusen & Head, 1994). One team of researchers, for example, had a student clasp his hands together and tell himself that he did not want to rock whenever he began to rock. This procedure resulted in reduced rocking, presumably due to the student's exerting cognitive control over his behavior.

A stereotypic view of people who are blind is that they do not adjust well socially. This stereotype is no more valid than any other stereotype.

Educational Considerations

Lack of sight can severely limit a person's experiences because a primary means of obtaining information from the environment is not available. What makes the situation even more difficult is that educational experiences in the typical classroom are frequently visual. Nevertheless, most experts agree that students who are visually impaired should be educated in the same general way as sighted children. Teachers need to make some modifications, but they can apply the same general educational principles. The important difference is that students with visual impairment will have to rely on other sensory modalities to acquire information.

The student with little or no sight will possibly require special modifications in four major areas: (1) braille, (2) use of remaining sight, (3) listening skills, and (4) mobility training. The first three pertain directly to academic education, particularly reading; the last refers to skills needed for everyday living.

Braille

In nineteenth-century France, Louis Braille introduced a system of writing for people who, like him, were blind. That system was based on a military method of writing messages using raised-line characters that could be read in the dark

blindisms. Repetitive, stereotyped movements (e.g., rocking or eye rubbing) characteristic of some persons who are blind, severely retarded, or psychotic; more appropriately referred to as *stereotypic behaviors.*

Figure 10.2

Examples of symbols from braille.

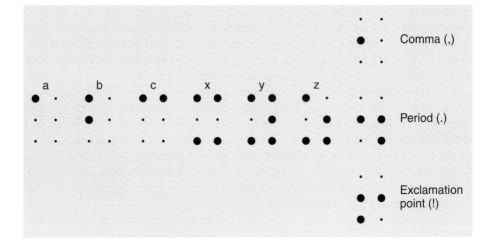

using the sense of touch, not sight. The basic system created by braille is still used today, although the raised-line characters have been replaced by various patterns of raised dots.

One braille code, called *literary braille*, is used for most everyday situations; other codes are available for more technical reading and writing. Some people support adoption of a Unified Braille Code that would combine these several codes into one. These proponents argue that in our ever more technological society most people, sighted or blind, often need to read and write using technical as well as everyday language (Sullivan, 1997). At this point it is not clear how accepting persons who are blind would be of a Unified Braille Code.

The basic unit of braille is a quadrangular *cell*, containing from one to six dots (see Figure 10.2). Different patterns of dots represent letters, numbers, and even punctuation marks. Generally, the best method of reading braille involves using both hands, "with the left reading from the beginning of the line as the right returns from reading the end of the previous line and both meeting in approximately the middle of the line and then separating" (Wormsley, 1996, p. 280).

Two basic means of writing in braille are the Perkins Brailler and the slate and stylus. The **Perkins Brailler** has six keys, one for each of the six dots of the cell (see Figure 10.3). When depressed simultaneously, the keys leave an embossed print on the paper. More portable than the Perkins Brailler is the **slate and stylus** (see Figure 10.4). The stylus—a pen-shaped instrument—is pressed through the opening of the slate, which holds the paper between its two halves. Using this method, the braille cells are written in reverse order, which makes the slate and stylus more difficult to use than the Perkins Brailler.

Perhaps the most hotly debated topic in the field of visual impairment concerns whether students who are blind should be taught to use braille or one of the other methods of communication, such as a tape recorder or voice-activated computer. At one time, it was fairly common for students with blindness to use braille, but over the past several years, its usage has declined dramatically. For example, the percentage of students who are blind who use braille has steadily declined since the mid-1960s, when nearly half used braille; the most recent statistics indicate that fewer than 10 percent now use braille (Schroeder, 1996).

Many within the community of blind people are alarmed at the reduced availability of braille and assert that it has led to a distressing rate of illiteracy

Perkins Brailler. A system that makes it possible to write in braille; has six keys, one for each of the six dots of the cell, which leave an embossed print on the paper.

slate and stylus. A method of writing in braille in which the paper is held in a slate while a stylus is pressed through openings to make indentations in the paper.

(Foulke, 1996; Hatlen, 1993; Ianuzzi, 1992; Omvig, 1997; Raeder, 1991; Schroeder, 1990, 1992). They charge that too few sighted teachers are proficient in braille and that they do little to discourage the notion held by some that using braille indicates inferiority.

Figure 10.3

A Perkins Brailler.

Whether a person is comfortable in identifying himself or herself as blind is critical to whether that person will be motivated to learn braille:

> Legally blind children who regard themselves as blind may find that braille facilitates and intensifies group identification and thus leads to the development of self-confidence and self-esteem.... Children who do not regard themselves as blind may reject braille because of its relationship to blindness. (Schroeder, 1996, 217)

Advocates of braille point out that it is essential for most students who are legally blind to learn braille in order to lead independent lives. Bolstering their argument is research indicating that adults who had learned braille in childhood as their primary medium for reading were employed at twice the rate of those who had used print as their primary medium (Ryles, 1996). Supporters of braille argue that although tape recorders, computers, and other technological devices can contribute much to reading and acquiring information, these devices cannot replace braille. For example, finding a specific section of a text or "skimming" are difficult with a tape recording, but these kinds of activities are possible when using braille. Taking notes for class, reading a speech, or looking up words in a dictionary is easier when using braille than when using a tape recorder (Maurer, 1991). Braille proponents are especially concerned that the slate and stylus be preserved as a viable method of taking notes (Walhof, 1993). They point out that just as computers have not replaced the pen and pencil for people who are sighted, neither can they take the place of the slate and stylus for people who are blind.

Many authorities now recommend that some students with low vision who are able to read large print or print with magnification should also be taught braille (Holbrook & Koenig, 1992). There are many students with low vision whose condition dictates that their visual acuity will worsen over the years. Learning braille at an early age would prepare them for the time when their eyesight no longer allowed them to read print. The vignette in the box on page 406

Figure 10.4

A slate and stylus in use.

success stories

special educators at work

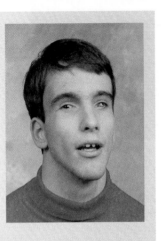

Charlottesville, VA: Nineteen-year-old **Patrick Pugh** has no vision in his left eye and only partial sight in his right. His speech is slurred, and he does not have functional use of his left arm or leg. Patrick's disabilities were caused by being born prematurely. For fourteen years, Patrick's mother, Audrey Pugh, and special educator Ricki Curry have been partners in Patrick's education. They know that, over time, parents and professionals must collaborate and compromise to help students meet their goals.

Patrick Pugh likes to read braille and translate printed sentences with a unimanual brailler. Now, instead of awkwardly holding a book two inches from his right eye, he reads with a relaxed posture as his fingers scan the brailled page of his easy reader. Ricki Curry, an itinerant teacher of students with visual impairment, taught Patrick to braille two years ago. She is proud of his achievements. "Patrick keeps exceeding everybody's expectations. Every time we've taught him something, he's had some success in learning it. We've come to believe in him, and to set our expectations higher, as a result."

This description of her second son does not surprise Audrey Pugh. "Opportunity is the main thing," she says. "All I want anyone to do is give Patrick a fair chance. I think it would be easier if he were either blind or physically disabled, but he's both, and that makes it even harder."

Patrick's progress is the result of his own persistence, the collaboration of his family and teachers, and the continuity of specialized personnel, instruction, and equipment over many years. Ricki and Audrey also credit much of Patrick's progress to a key ingredient: time. Patrick's story is an example of special education not as a fix-it model or cure-all but as a means of providing services over time to persons whose abilities often take much longer than usual to develop.

Patrick started vision and physical therapy when he was two years old. "The physical therapist asked me why he didn't have therapy before," recalls Audrey, "but no one ever told us it was available to infants or that Patrick needed it."

Ricki remembers the youngster whose eyes would lift aimlessly to the ceiling, not using what vision he had. "Our basic goal was for Patrick to learn to use his sight by tracking objects and looking at pictures, but as a five-year-old he was stubborn, difficult, and noncompliant." Despite his reluctance, Patrick successfully learned literal information and concrete routines. To be sure, he was highly distractible and progress was very slow. His parents hoped all he

braille bills. Legislation passed in several states to make braille more available to students with visual impairment; specific provisions vary from state to state, but major advocates have lobbied for (1) making braille available if parents want it, and (2) ensuring that teachers of students with visual impairment are proficient in braille.

demonstrates how important braille instruction can be for these students and how social stigma can get in the way of learning braille.

Another way of ensuring that braille becomes more readily available is through **braille bills.** As of July 1997, twenty-eight states had braille bills on the books (Maurer, 1997). Although the specific provisions of these bills vary from state to state, the National Federation of the Blind, a major proponent of braille bills, has drafted a model bill that specifies two important components:

1. Braille must be available for students if any members of the individualized program (IEP) team, including parents, indicate that it is needed.
2. Teachers of students with visual impairment need to be proficient in braille.

Federal law now reinforces the first component above. The amendments to the Individuals with Disabilities Education Act (IDEA) of 1997 specify that

needed was extra time, so he stayed in a preschool for children with special needs until he was seven.

Audrey had problems with the school district when Patrick was ready for first grade. "They told me there was no place for him in the public schools, so I said, 'Well, find one!'" Patrick was placed in a self-contained class for children with learning disabilities in the nearest physically accessible elementary school. Ricki continued to provide weekly sessions and to supervise Patrick's vision services. He was also given a personal aide to assist with mobility and visual modifications. As Ricki points out, "In some ways, kids with personal aides never have any problems, so they don't learn any problem-solving skills! On the other hand, there are some effective strategies that can be used with close attention." Since Patrick's hand use is limited, Ricki trained his aide to assist him as a scribe. In addition, Patrick's math was broken down into small steps, his reading was individualized, and he was taught to write using a large-print word processor.

Patrick finished elementary school two years older than most of his classmates. Yet he was only able to do rote math and was similarly concrete in reading; he could decode text but remained literal in his understanding of the material. "He could answer factual questions, but he couldn't make that leap to the abstract," recalls Ricki. "Patrick was in a middle school science class, learning about mitochondria. That's when it really hit me: Sure, he could learn the definition of mitochondria, but was this functional for him? He'd never use this word again!"

Patrick was thirteen when his mother was told that he needed a class that emphasized functional academics, such as money skills. Audrey agreed to the placement, but it was devastating because it seemed an admission that her son was mentally retarded. "At that point, we all knew this was what he needed," says Ricki. "Patrick has multiple learning needs, and it takes him a long time to learn; it takes intensive care and a lot of specific teaching. This class gave him the right information at the right pace. We forgot about the mitochondria and were now reading for *comprehension*."

Patrick started high school when he was seventeen, and a creative program was crafted for him, blending functional academics, work experience, and independent living skills. He spent his mornings in two periods of functional English and math. He then boarded a van for the vocational center three afternoons a week, where he ate lunch with co-workers. He spent two afternoons a week at an independent living center, learning to clean, shop, and travel about the community.

Patrick works with Ricki sixty minutes a day on braille skills that are geared toward vocational goals. Ricki is optimistic. "I think there's a job out there for Patrick. We've got two years to get those skills really sharp."

Patrick's odyssey has not been easy for his mother, Audrey. She knows Ricki respects her high expectations, yet she has come to trust that alternate routes hold promise for Patrick's future. Audrey says, "I'd like to think of him living happily in a group home someday, with friends, and, of course, with some supervision and support. I think it's only realistic to imagine he'd need that."

—By Jean Crockett

braille services and instruction are to be a part of the IEP, unless all members of the team, including parents, agree that braille should not be used.

To provide a way of determining the braille proficiency of licensed teachers of students who are blind, the Library of Congress is in the process of developing a National Braille Literacy Competency Test, which it hopes to have completed by the end of 1999. Several states are considering this test as an option for people to demonstrate competency in braille.

Use of Remaining Sight

For many years there was a great deal of resistance to having children with visual impairment use their sight in reading and some other activities. Many myths contributed to this reluctance, including beliefs that holding books close to the eyes is harmful, strong lenses hurt the eyes, and using the eyes too much injures them.

Braille Is Not Just for People Who Are Blind

There are many individuals whose visual impairment is not severe enough in childhood to require learning braille but whose condition will worsen in time to the point where using braille will be a desirable option. For these students, it makes sense to start braille instruction before they actually need to rely on it extensively. Unfortunately, as the following vignette shows, one of the barriers to beginning braille instruction with these students is the social stigma attached to using braille:

> I grew up in a small farming town in Iowa. By the time I was fifteen years of age, I was so blind that I could no longer even pretend to function successfully in the public school, so I was enrolled in the Iowa Braille and Sight-Saving School to complete my last three-and-a-half years of high school.
>
> Unbelievable as it sounds, even though I could read no more than fifteen or twenty words a minute of very large-print material for no more than fifteen or twenty minutes

at a sitting and, further, even though everyone knew I would be totally blind one day, I was not taught Braille at this remarkable institution. The attitude of the school was "Let him be normal (sighted) as long as he can."

My parents knew, of course, that I would be totally blind one day, so they were justifiably concerned about my lack of training. However, when my mother wrote to the school requesting that I be taught Braille, she was told, "He can always learn Braille when he really needs it."

Therefore, since I was unable to read my own school books and papers, I got through high school by having literate students (using either Braille or print) read aloud to me. By the time I graduated, I was nearly totally blind and therefore could read neither print nor Braille at all. (p. 724)

Source: Omvig, J. H. (1997, November) From bad philosophy to bad policy: The American braille illiteracy crisis. *Braille Monitor,* pp. 723–728. Reprinted with permission from the National Federation of the Blind.

At one time, classes for students with low vision were called *sight conservation* or *sight-saving* classes, reflecting the popular assumption that using the eyes too much caused them to deteriorate. It is now recognized that this is true only in very rare conditions. In fact, some professionals believe teachers can actually train students to use what visual abilities they do have to better advantage (Barraga & Collins, 1979; Collins & Barraga, 1980). Even though some question the efficacy of such vision training (Ferrell & Muir, 1996), most agree on the importance of encouraging people with visual impairment to use what sight they do have, but not to the exclusion of braille for those who need it.

Two visual methods of aiding children with visual impairment to read print are large-print books and magnifying devices. **Large-print books** are simply books printed in larger-size type. The text in this book, printed primarily for sighted readers, is printed in 10-point type. Figure 10.5 on page 407 shows print in 18-point type, one of the most popular sizes for large-print materials. Type sizes for readers with visual impairment may range up to 30-point type.

The major difficulty with large-print books is that they are bigger than usual and thus require a great deal of storage space. In addition, they are of limited availability, although, along with the American Printing House for the Blind, a number of commercial publishers are now publishing and marketing large-print books.

Magnifying devices range from glasses and handheld lenses to closed-circuit television scanners that present enlarged images on a TV screen. These devices can be used with normal-size type or large-print books.

Listening Skills

The importance of listening skills for children who are blind cannot be overemphasized. The less a child is able to rely on sight for gaining information from the

large-print books. Books that are printed in a type size that is larger than usual so that people with visual impairment can read them; disadvantages are that they take up more space and some materials are not available in large print.

This is an example of 10-pt. type.

This is an example of 18-pt. type.

This is an example of 24-pt. type.

Figure 10.5

Typefaces come in various sizes. Large-print books often use 18-point type and 24-point type.

environment, the more crucial it is that he or she become a good listener. Some professionals still assume that good listening skills will develop automatically in children who are blind. This belief is unfortunate, for it is now evident that children do not spontaneously compensate for poor vision by magically developing superior powers of concentration. In most cases, they must be taught how to listen. A variety of curriculum materials and programs are available to teach children listening skills (e.g., Bischoff, 1979; Swallow & Conner, 1982).

Listening skills are becoming more important than ever because of the increasing accessibility of recorded material. The American Printing House for the Blind and the Library of Congress are major sources for these materials. Listeners can simply play the material at normal speed, or they can use a compressed-speech device that allows them to read at about 250 to 275 words per minute. This method works by discarding very small segments of the speech. Some of the more sophisticated compressed-speech devices use a computer to eliminate those speech sounds that are least necessary for comprehension.

Mobility Training

How well individuals cope with a visual disability depends to a great extent on how well they are able to move about. And whether a person withdraws from the social environment or becomes independent depends greatly on mobility skills. Four general methods are available to aid the mobility of people with visual impairment: (1) the long cane, (2) guide dogs, (3) human guides, and (4) electronic devices.

The Long Cane. Professionals most often recommend the long cane for those individuals with visual impairments in need of a mobility aid. It is called a **long cane** because it is longer than the canes typically used for support or balance. Research has determined that the long cane should extend at least from the floor to the user's

long cane. A mobility aid used by individuals with visual impairment, who sweep it in a wide arc in front of them; proper use requires considerable training; the mobility aid of choice for most travelers who are blind.

Computer monitors that provide large-print images can aid some individuals with visual impairments.

It usually takes considerable training to learn how to use a long cane.

armpit (Plain-Switzer, 1993). Most authorities recommend the long cane as the most efficient mobility aid for most persons who are blind. By moving the cane along the ground, the user is provided with auditory and tactual information about the environment. It can alert the user to drop-offs, such as potholes or stairs, and can help protect the lower part of the body from collision with objects.

Although the long cane looks like a simple device, scientists, mobility specialists, and others working under the auspices of the National Academy of Sciences have drawn up specifications for its construction. And although watching a skilled user of the long cane may give the impression that it is easy to manipulate, extensive training in its proper use is often required. The traveler holds the butt or crook of the long cane at about the height of the navel and sweeps it in an arc wide enough to protect the body, lightly touching the ground in front with the cane tip (Plain-Switzer, 1993). Considerable coordination between the sweeping of the cane and the movement of the feet is required for proper touch technique.

At one time, orientation and mobility teachers thought that young children were not old enough to be taught mobility skills. Before 1980 it was very difficult for the parents of a preschooler with visual impairment to find him or her a cane. Parents, especially sighted parents, also may have reinforced some of this negative reaction toward the use of canes with young children. In the past, parents may have seen the use of a cane as too stigmatizing. As one person who is blind said:

> When I was growing up, you didn't get a cane when you were six or four or three years old. The cane was the thing that my parents put off for as long as they could, and they did it with the support of educators. For them the cane was the symbol. It transformed me from being their blind son—which was okay—to being somebody who might grow up to be a blind man. That wasn't okay. So I didn't see a cane until I was about eleven years old. (Wunder, 1993, p. 568)

Today, however, more and more preschoolers are learning cane techniques (Cheadle, 1991; Dykes, 1992). In fact, many professionals recommend that cane training be initiated as soon as the child is walking independently with only minor irregularities in balance and gait (Skellenger & Hill, 1991).

Currently, there is considerable debate about whether people who are themselves blind should be allowed to be mobility instructors. Those who oppose this practice mainly focus on safety concerns, asking, for example, whether instructors who are blind would be able to warn their students of potential dangers in the environment such as hanging tree limbs, icy sidewalks, or construction sites (Millar, 1996). Those in favor of instructors who are blind view such concerns as overprotection. They state that such potential dangers are part of the frequently faced realities of cane travel, and that instructors who are blind are more likely to allow their pupils to encounter such obstacles in training and thereby learn to cope with them (Hill, 1997).

Guide Dogs. Contrary to popular notions, the use of a **guide dog** is not recommended very often for people with visual impairment. Extensive training is required to learn how to use guide dogs properly. The extended training—as well as the facts that guide dogs are large, walk relatively fast, and need to be cared for—make them particularly questionable for children. Also contrary to what most people think, the guide dog does not "take" the person who is blind anywhere. The person must first know where he or she is going; the dog is primarily a safeguard against walking into dangerous areas.

For some adults, however, guide dogs have proven to be valuable aides and companions. Some users of guide dogs point out that the dogs are able to alert their owners to important things in the environment—such as stairways, entrances, exits, and elevators—sooner than can be detected by a cane (Gabias, 1992). One person who has found a guide dog especially rewarding is author Stephen Kuusisto (see the box on p. 410).

People who are sighted should keep in mind a few guidelines pertaining to guide dogs and their owners (Ulrey, 1994):

- Although it may be tempting to pet a guide dog, you should do so only after asking the owner's permission. Guide dogs are not just pets—they are working for their owner.

- If someone with a guide dog appears to need help, approach on his or her right side (guide dogs are almost always on the left side) and ask if he or she needs assistance.

- Do not take hold of the dog's harness, as this may confuse the dog and the owner.

Human Guides. Human guides undoubtedly enable people with visual impairment to have the greatest freedom in moving about safely, but this arrangement is

guide dog. A dog specially trained to help guide a person who is blind; not recommended for children and not used by very many adults who are blind because the user needs special training in how to use the dog properly.

The guide dog is still used with success by some individuals, although using a guide dog requires extensive training and would be difficult for children.

Stephen Kuusisto and His Guide Dog, Corky

Stephen Kuusisto has been almost totally blind since birth as the result of retinopathy of prematurity (ROP). In his memoir, *Planet of the Blind,* Kuusisto chronicles how he spent all of childhood and much of adult life in denial of his blindness. Instrumental in his eventual acceptance of a blind identity has been the freedom of mobility provided by Corky, his guide dog. Kuusisto has also discovered that "guide dogs are still wondrous creatures in the public's imagination, and more than fifty years after their introduction to the United States, they remain a novelty." This novelty serves to attract numerous interactions with the public. Although these interactions are usually positive, at times they highlight the misunderstandings that the sighted have about people who are blind:

Stephen Kuusisto and his guide dog Corky.

How strange it is, sometimes, to be Corky's human appendage. Often people stop our forward progress and speak only to her, as if I do not exist, then, after much baby talk, they vanish. Others are drawn to us because we are totemic. Early one morning I meet two boys with developmental disabilities.

"Hi!" one says. "I knew a blind guy, but he died!"

"He was bigger than you," the other adds. "He had a heart attack!" Then they sweep away down the sidewalk on their Rollerblades, and through it all Corky advances without distraction, my familiar, my Pavlova.

In the supermarket we're spotted by a small child.

"Look, Mommy, there's a dog in the store!"

"Shhhh! Be quiet, dear!"

"But Mommy, that man has a *dog!"*

"That's a blind man! The dog helps him."

"Is the dog blind too?"

"No, the dog sees for the man!"

"What happens if the dog is blind?"

"The dog isn't blind, honey, the dog can see. It's the man who can't see!"

"The man can't see?"

"That's right, blind people can't see."

"If he can't see, how does he know when it's morning?"

"Shhhh! Be quiet! The man gets up because he has to have breakfast!"

The woman hurries her little boy down the cleaning products aisle. I hear his thin voice from some distance.

"How does he eat?"

I'm standing beside an enormous pyramid of cans. Corky has decided to sit down. I have an evangelical desire, a need to reassure these two. I want to recite something from Psalms to them: "The Lord is gracious, and full of compassion; slow to anger, and of great mercy."

I want to follow this mother and child through the tall laundry soap displays and tell them that the world doesn't end. I imagine telling them that the blind are not hungry for objects. I want to take strangers by the hand and tell them there is no abyss.

Source: From *Planet of the blind: A memoir* by Stephen Kuusisto, 1998, New York: The Dial Press, pp. 176–177, 179–180. Copyright © 1998 by Stephen Kuusisto. Used by permission of The Dial Press/ Dell Publishing, a division of Bantam Doubleday Dell Publishing Group, Inc.

not practical in most cases. Furthermore, too much reliance on another person causes a dependency that can be harmful. Even people who are blind who are highly proficient travelers have noted that a certain degree of independence is sacrificed when walking accompanied by a sighted person (Hull, 1990). In order to converse with the companion, for instance, the person without sight can be distracted from paying attention to the cues he or she needs to travel efficiently and may come to rely on the sighted companion. This also can give the sighted individual the false impression that the person who is blind does not have good mobility skills.

Most people who travel unaccompanied do not need help from those around them. However, if a person with visual impairment looks as though he or she needs assistance, you should first ask if help is wanted. If physical guidance is required, allow the person to hold onto your arm above the elbow and to walk a half-step behind you. Sighted people tend to grasp the arms of persons without sight and to sort of push them in the direction they are heading.

Electronic Devices. Researchers are working on a number of sophisticated electronic devices for sensing objects in the environment. Most are still experimental, and most are expensive. Representative examples that have been under development for some time are the laser cane and the Sonic Pathfinder. These devices operate on the principle that human beings can learn to locate objects by means of echoes, much as bats do.

The laser cane can be used in the same way as the long cane or as a sensing device that emits three beams of infrared light (one up, one down, and one straight ahead), which are converted into sound after they strike objects in the path of the traveler (Farmer, 1975). The *Sonic Pathfinder,* which is worn on the head, emits ultrasound and converts reflections from objects into audible sound (Heyes, 1998). It provides advance warning of objects in the traveler's path.

Researchers are also working on acoustic signaling systems for people who are blind. For example, Talking Signs uses an infrared beam system. When the user points a receiver toward a transmitter, he or she receives a message identifying the location (Bentzen & Mitchell, 1995).

A word of caution is in order in considering the use of electronic mobility devices: Because of their amazing technology, it is easy to be too optimistic about them. They are best viewed as potential secondary mobility aids for people who are blind. They are not appropriate as substitutes for the long cane, for example.

Technological Aids

In recent years, a technological explosion has resulted in the creation of new electronic devices for use by people with visual impairment. The **Kurzweil Omni 1000** converts print with practically any typeface into synthesized speech (Kurzweil, 1996). The user places the material on a scanner that reads the material with an electronic voice. There are also PC-based reading machines that scan a page of print and convert the text to synthesized speech, braille, or large-print output. Because they are PC-based, these machines also have the advantage of being usable with other typical computer software (Andrews, 1995).

Portable **braille notetakers,** such as BrailleMate and Braille 'n Speak, can serve the same function as the Perkins Brailler or slate and stylus but offer additional speech-synthesizer and word-processing capabilities. The user enters information with a braille keyboard and can transfer the information into a larger computer, review it using a speech synthesizer or braille display, or print it in braille or text (American Foundation for the Blind, 1998).

As computers have moved more and more toward graphic displays of information on the screen, users with visual impairments have become concerned about how this affects their access to that information. For example, a graphics-based interface requires the user to move a mouse to a relatively precise position on the screen in order to click on the desired function. The explosion of visually oriented information now being placed on the World Wide Web also presents problems for those who are blind. Researchers have developed software and hardware adaptations so that those who are blind can access the information nonvisually, but getting these adaptations implemented has proven difficult (Chong, 1997). The

Kurzweil Omni 1000. A computerized device that converts print into speech for persons with visual impairment; the user places the printed material over a scanner that then reads the material aloud by means of an electronic voice.

braille notetakers. Portable devices that can be used to take notes in braille, which are then converted to speech, braille, or text.

A popular electronic braille device for taking notes is the Braille 'n Speak. It has full word processing capabilities and notes can be printed out in braille or in print. The device can also review the brailled notes for the user by reading them aloud.

National Federation of the Blind has drafted model technology bills (similar to the braille bills) that insist on the use of these adaptations (National Federation of the Blind, 1997). It is too soon to tell how successful these efforts to increase accessibility to information presented via computers will be.

Similar to closed captioning for people with hearing impairment, a service is now available for making television more accessible to people with visual impairment. The **Descriptive Video Service**, developed by National Public Radio Station WGBH in Boston, is available for several public television programs. A narrated description of key visual features of the program is inserted between lapses in the dialogue. Also, the National Federation of the Blind has been involved in the development of Newsline for the Blind Network, which delivers newspapers such as the *New York Times, USA Today,* and the *Chicago Tribune* to users via synthetic speech over the telephone.

Service Delivery Models

Descriptive Video Service. A service for use by people with visual impairment that provides audio narrative of key visual elements; available for several public television programs.

itinerant teacher services. Services for students who are visually impaired, in which the special education teacher visits several different schools to work with students and their general education classroom teachers; the students attend their local schools and remain in general education classrooms.

The four major educational placements for students with visual impairment, from most to least segregated, are (1) residential school, (2) special class, (3) resource room, and (4) regular class with itinerant teacher help. Many professionals argue for this continuum of placements. For example, the American Foundation for the Blind endorses a full array of placement options as a high priority (Corn, Hatlen, Huebner, Ryan, & Siller, 1995). In practice, however, most students with visual impairment are educated either in residential schools or in regular classes with itinerant teacher services (especially the latter). The fact is, there are so few students with visual impairment that most schools find it difficult to provide services through special classes or resource rooms (Hatlen, 1993). Both residential institutions and **itinerant teacher services**—wherein a special education teacher visits several different schools to work with students and their general education classroom teachers—make more efficient use of professionals than do resource rooms or special classes. Residential institutions allow for a concentration of specialized services in one place, and itinerant teacher services allow for a distribution of services over several different areas.

In the early 1900s virtually all children who were blind were educated in residential institutions, but today itinerant teacher services to general education classrooms is the most popular placement for students with visual impairment. Far fewer children who are blind are now placed in residential schools, unless they have additional disabilities such as mental retardation or deafness. In the past, most children who were blind attended institutions for several years; today some may attend on a short-term basis, e.g., one to four years. Also, residential institutions are moving toward encouraging students to go home on weekends (Hatlen, 1996).

The prevailing philosophy of integrating children with visual impairments with the sighted is also reflected in the fact that many residential facilities have established cooperative arrangements with local public schools (Cronin, 1992; Erin, 1993; Hatlen, 1996). In these arrangements, students who are visually impaired may come on a regular basis (e.g., once per week) to the institution as day students. Or they may enroll in short-term (e.g., one- or two-week) intensive courses as residential students. The staff of the residential facility usually concentrates on training for independent living skills such as mobility, personal grooming, and home management, while local school personnel emphasize academics. Also, support services such as speech and physical therapy are sometimes better delivered by personnel from institutions because they have had more experience working with children who are blind. And as some point out, given the low prevalence of blindness, having these children come to residential sites periodically affords them an opportunity to interact with other children who have the same types of disabilities (Cronin, 1992).

Early Intervention

For many years psychologists and educators believed that the sighted infant was almost totally lacking in visual abilities during the first half-year or so of life. We now know that the young sighted infant is able to take in a great deal of information through the visual system. This fact makes it easy to understand why professionals are usually eager to begin intensive intervention as early as possible to help the infant with visual impairment begin to explore the environment.

An area of particular importance in early intervention for children with visual impairment is *mobility* (Palazesi, 1986). Some infants who are totally blind are late to crawl, which authorities speculate is due to the fact that they have not learned that there are things in their environments worth pursuing (Fraiberg, 1977). Infants who cannot see may not be as motivated as sighted infants to explore their extended environments because they are more engaged in examining things close to their bodies. Parents can sometimes contribute to their infants' lack of exploration. Concerned for the safety of their infants who are blind, some parents are reluctant to let them investigate their surroundings. By about six months of age, the sighted child spontaneously reaches out to visually perceived objects. Without specific training, the infant who is totally blind may not reach out to things he or she hears until late in the first year.

Children with visual impairment should be given many opportunities to explore and learn about their environments. Touchtown is a program used to develop children's sense of orientation and to stimulate all their senses by providing a "palpable city."

Today most authorities agree that mobility training should be a critical component of preschool programming. In addition to introducing cane techniques to children as soon as they are able to walk relatively well, some researchers are experimenting with methods of encouraging infants at the crawling stage to explore their environments more actively. For example, one study

was successful in increasing the exploratory behaviors of infants who were blind, using a specially constructed room containing a variety of tactile and auditory stimuli (Nielsen, 1991).

Most authorities agree that it is extremely important to involve parents of infants with visual impairment in early intervention efforts. Parents can become actively involved in working at home with their young children, helping them with fundamental skills such as mobility and feeding, as well as being responsive to their infants' vocalizations (Chen, 1996). Parents, too, sometimes need support in coping with their reactions to having a baby with visual impairment. There may be an overwhelming sense of grief. Professionals working in early intervention programs for infants who are blind often recommend that initial efforts should focus on helping parents cope with their own reactions to having a child who is blind (Maloney, 1981).

Transition

Two closely related areas are difficult for some adolescents and adults with visual impairment—independence and employment.

Independent Living

When working with adolescents and adults with visual impairment, it is extremely important to keep in mind that achieving a sense of independence is often difficult for them. Many authorities point out that much of the problem of dependence is because of the way society treats persons without sight. A common mistake is to assume that such individuals are helpless. Many people think of blindness as a condition to be pitied. People with visual impairment have a long history of arguing against paternalistic treatment by sighted society. The National Federation of the Blind has for several years argued fiercely that they want jobs, not handouts:

> What we need most is not, as the professionals would have it, medical help or psychological counseling but admission to the main channels of daily life and citizenship, not custody and care but understanding and acceptance. Above all, what we need is not more government programs or private charitable efforts. Instead, we want jobs, opportunity, and full participation in society. (Jernigan, 1985, p. 388)

Many people who are blind point to the Federal Aviation Administration (FAA) policy toward airline travelers who are blind as an example of a paternalistic attitude. For years the National Federation of the Blind has battled with the FAA and the airline industry over the right for people who are blind to sit by exits on airplanes. The FAA currently stipulates that a person must be able to receive visual directions and be able to assess escape paths outside the aircraft. Individual airlines have varied in how they have interpreted these policies. Some have allowed people who are blind to take seats in exit rows, while others have insisted that persons be able to see well enough, for example, to read the safety directions printed on the card in the seat pocket. The following is the reaction of a spokesperson for the National Federation of the Blind:*

*Source: Jernigan, K. (1991, January). Airline safety: What happens when you see fire on the wing? *Braille Monitor.* Reprinted with permission from the National Federation of the Blind.

It is not enough to show that a given blind person in a given instance may block an exit or pose a safety hazard. Blind persons are just as diverse and variable in their behavior and characteristics as sighted persons are.... It must be shown that they are not being held to a higher standard of conduct than others ... and that there is something about blindness that makes the blind less capable....

If safety is the only consideration, no one at all will fly. But just as in using automobiles, there are tradeoffs, and we are willing to accept a certain amount of risk....

The next fallback position for maximum safety in air travel would probably be to place trained, healthy airline officials in the exit rows, but the airlines say this is unacceptable because of the lost revenue....

If we go to the next fallback position for maximum safety, it would probably be to widen the exit row aisles and have no one sit in them at all.... Again the airlines are not willing—and again for the same reason, economics....

Then perhaps the airlines could at least refuse to sell liquor to people who sit in the exit rows or ask for volunteers to sit there who do not intend to drink anyway. They decline to do the first of these things because of lost revenue and the second because of concern about frightening the passengers by reminding them of possible crashes or in-flight emergencies.

Of course, none of this makes the case for permitting blind persons to sit in the exit rows, but it does demonstrate that safety is not the only (or perhaps even the prime) factor being considered....

Blind persons are either a greater hazard than others seated in exit rows or they aren't. If they are, they shouldn't sit there—and any blind person with any sense wouldn't want to. If they aren't a greater safety hazard than others, then prohibiting them from sitting in the exit row is discrimination....

So where does this leave us? Never in the history of commercial aviation has there been a single recorded instance of a blind person's blocking an exit, slowing an evacuation, or contributing to an accident. But there are recorded instances to the contrary. At night or when the cabin has been filled with smoke, blind persons have on more than one occasion found the exits and led others out. (Jernigan, 1991, pp. 51–53)

No matter which side one takes on the issue of airline seating, there is little doubt that the public has, at times, been at fault in creating an environment that fosters dependency in people with blindness. The accomplished author Ved Mehta has written several books dealing with his adjustment to blindness and going to school in the United States (Mehta, 1982, 1984, 1985, 1989). In the book dealing with his adolescent years at the Arkansas School for the Blind, he talks about experiences that people who are blind typically have to face, experiences that undoubtedly can foster dependence:

I decided that I didn't like going to coffee shops. I had generally eaten at a table, either with my family or with students and staff at a school, and eating alone at a counter filled me with sadness. Moreover, there were always incidents in the coffee shops that would leave me shaken. The waitresses would shout out the menu to me as if I were half deaf, and so attract the attention of everyone in the coffee shop. Even when they got to know me and treated me normally, I would have to contend with customers who didn't know me. I remember that once when I asked for my bill the waitress said, "A man already took care of it."

"I insist on paying for myself."

The waitress refused to accept the money. "The man done gone," she said to the coffee shop. "What does the kid want me to do—take money twice for the same ham sandwich? He should be thankful there are nice people to pay for him." I felt anything but thankful, however. I thought that I'd been an object of pity.

I remember that another time Tom took me to a new coffee shop. The waitress, instead of asking me for my order, turned to him and asked, "What does he want to eat?"

"A ham sandwich," I said, speaking up for myself. She brought me the ham sandwich, but throughout lunch she ignored me, talking to Tom as if I weren't there. (Mehta, 1985, pp. 198–199)

The following letter to "Dear Abby" from the president of the American Foundation for the Blind lists some appropriate ways that the sighted can interact with those who are blind. Suggestions such as these are designed to help avoid awkward social interactions such as those experienced by Mehta, and to help decrease feelings of dependency on the part of those who are blind:

Dear Abby:

You recently ran a letter from a woman who gave a few tips on what sighted people should do when they meet a blind person. As president of the American Foundation for the Blind, and a blind person myself, I believe I can add a few more points of etiquette your readers may find helpful.

1. Speak to people who are blind or visually impaired using a natural conversational tone and speed. Do not speak loudly and slowly unless the person also has a hearing impairment.

2. Address blind people by name when possible. This is especially important in crowded places.

3. Immediately greet blind people when they enter a room or service area. This lets them know you are present and ready to assist.

4. Indicate the end of a conversation with a blind person in order to avoid the embarrassment of leaving a person speaking when no one is actually there.

5. Feel free to use words that refer to vision when conversing with blind people. Words such as "look," "see," "watching TV" are part of everyday communication. The words "blind" and "visually impaired" are also acceptable in conversation.

6. Do not leave a blind person standing in "free space" when you serve as a guide. Also, be sure that the person you guide has a firm grasp on your arm or is leaning against a chair or a wall if you have to be separated momentarily.

7. Be calm and clear about what to do if you see a blind person about to encounter a dangerous situation. For example, if the person is about to bump into something, calmly and firmly call out, "Wait there for a moment; there is an obstruction in your path." . . .

Carl R. Augusto
President
American Foundation for the Blind
New York

Many independent living skills that are learned incidentally by sighted people need to be taught explicitly to those who are visually impaired. The National

Federation of the Blind publishes a book that can be useful in this regard (Jernigan, 1994). It has chapters, for example, on cooking, sewing, marking dials and tactile labeling, and shopping ideas.

In some ways it is more important for people with visual impairment to learn to be independent than it is for those who are sighted. Adults with visual impairment often find that they need to take more initiative to achieve the same level of success as people who are sighted. As one job counselor put it when speaking to a group of college students with visual impairment: "As blind students, you will need to spend time on activities your sighted peers never think about—recruiting and organizing readers, having textbooks prepared in alternative media, getting an early start on term papers" (Rovig, 1992, p. 239).

Employment

Many working-age adults with visual impairment are unemployed, and those who do work are often overqualified for the jobs they hold. For example, the employment rate for adults aged 21 to 64 who have severe functional limitation in seeing (defined as being unable to see words and letters) was only 26 percent (Kirchner & Schmeidler, 1997). Some authorities attribute this unfortunate situation to inadequate transition programming at the secondary school level (Hanley-Maxwell, Griffin, Szymanski, & Godley, 1990; Sacks & Pruett, 1992). Even well-educated adults with visual impairment, when surveyed, indicated that they had not received training to meet their career development needs (Wolffe, Roessler, & Schriner, 1992).

Reports of adults with visual impairment who achieve successful independent living and employment are becoming more and more common—although they are still not as common as one would hope. Innovative programs are being developed to meet the transition needs of students with visual impairment. For example, one successful program involves having adolescents and young adults with visual impairment come together with professionals for a three-week summer training session devoted to issues of transition (Sacks & Pruett, 1992). Among other things, this project uses "job shadowing," in which each student is paired with an adult with a similar visual disability and a job that matches the student's interest. The students spend a couple of days with their partners, observing them on the job.

High on the list of ways to improve employment possibilities for those who are blind are job accommodations. Employees who are blind report that relatively minor adjustments can go a long way toward making it easier for them to function in the workplace. A sample of suggested adaptations are improved transportation (such as carpools), better lighting, tinted office windows to filter light, prompt snow removal, regularly scheduled fire drills to ensure spatial orientation, hallways free of obstacles, and computer software (such as screen magnification

Obtaining gainful, fulfilling employment should not be an unrealistic goal for someone with visual impairment.

programs) and PC-based reading machines that convert print into braille (Rumrill, Roessler, Battersby-Longden, & Schuyler, 1998; Rumrill, Schuyler, & Longden, 1997).

Visual impairment no doubt poses a real challenge for adjustment to everyday living, but remember Stephen Kuusisto's comments in the introduction to the chapter (p. 385). People with visual impairment share many similarities with people in the rest of society. Special and general educators need to achieve the delicate balance between providing special programming for students with visual impairment and treating them in the same manner as they do the rest of their students.

Summary

There are two definitions of *visual impairment*—legal and educational. The legal definition depends on the measurement of visual acuity and field of vision. A person who is legally blind has visual acuity of 20/200 or less in the better eye, even with correction, or has a very narrow (less than 20 degrees) field of vision. Individuals who are partially sighted have visual acuity between 20/70 and 20/200 in the better eye with correction.

Educators, however, prefer to define *blindness* according to how well the person functions, especially in reading. For the educator, blindness indicates the need to read braille or use aural methods. Those who can read print, even though they may need magnification or large-print books, have *low vision*. The majority of those who are legally blind have some vision. Many students who are legally blind are not educationally blind because they can read print.

Blindness is one of the least prevalent disabling conditions in childhood but is much more prevalent in adults.

The Snellen chart, consisting of rows of letters or of Es arranged in different positions, measures visual acuity for far distances. Special charts measure visual acuity for near distances. In addition to these measures of acuity, educators are often interested in students' visual efficiency and visual function.

Most visual problems are the results of errors of refraction. That is, because of faulty structure and/or malfunction of the eye, light rays do not focus on the retina. The most common visual impairments are myopia (nearsightedness), hyperopia (farsightedness), and astigmatism (blurred vision). Eyeglasses or contact lenses can usually correct these problems. More serious impairments include glaucoma, cataracts, diabetic retinopathy, retinitis pigmentosa, cortical visual impairment (CVI), retinopathy of prematurity (ROP),

strabismus, and nystagmus. Most serious visual impairments in school-age students are due to hereditary factors. When scientists first discovered that ROP was caused by high levels of oxygen administered to premature newborns, incidents of this condition decreased. Research indicates, however, that ROP is on the rise due to medicine's efforts to keep more premature babies alive.

Most authorities believe that visual impairment may result in a few subtle language differences but not in deficient language skills. Also, blindness does not result in intellectual retardation. There are some differences in language and conceptual development because children with visual impairment rely more on touch to learn about the world. They also need to be more vigilant to pick up information from their environment. Research has shown that early training in the use of strategies helps children who are blind use their sense of touch more efficiently.

A very important ability for the successful adjustment of people with visual impairment is mobility. There is no one-to-one relationship between the age at onset and the degree of visual loss and mobility skills. Mobility is greatly affected by motivation. Mobility skills depend largely on spatial ability. Those who are able to conceptualize their environments as cognitive maps have better mobility skills than do those who process their environments sequentially.

People who are blind do not, as is commonly thought, have an inherent obstacle sense. But some can develop the ability to detect obstacles by detecting changes in the pitches of echoes as they approach obstacles. Another myth is that people who are blind automatically develop better acuity in other senses. What they actually do is become adept at picking up other sensory cues in their surroundings, thus making better use of their intact senses.

Comparing the academic achievement of students with visual impairment to that of students who are sighted is difficult because the two are tested under different conditions. Evidence suggests, however, that students with visual impairment are behind their sighted peers in achievement. Some believe that this is due to a lack of early exposure to braille.

Personality problems are not an inherent condition of visual impairment. Any social adjustment problems that students with visual impairment have are usually due to society's reaction to blindness. The stereotypic behaviors (e.g., eye poking and body rocking) exhibited by a few persons who are blind can be an impediment to social acceptance, but researchers are working on developing techniques to diminish their occurrence.

Educational experiences in regular classrooms are frequently visual. But with some modifications, teachers can usually apply the same general principles of instruction to both students with and without visual impairment. Since the mid-1960s there has been a sharp decline in the use of braille. Many professionals are now decrying this decrease because they believe it has led to a high rate of illiteracy. The National Federation of the Blind has lobbied for braille bills to increase the availability of braille and to establish braille competency for all teachers of students with visual impairment. Braille is now also being recommended for those whose low vision might worsen over the years.

In addition to braille, large-print books and audiotapes are available. Also, scientists are developing a number of technological devices; examples are the Kurzweil Omni 1000 and braille notetakers.

Mobility training can involve the use of the long cane, guide dogs, human guides, and electronic devices. Most mobility instructors recommend the long cane for the majority of individuals who are blind. At one time, mobility instruction for children did not begin until elementary or secondary school. Now most authorities recommend that mobility instruction should begin in preschool.

The four basic educational placements for students with visual impairment, from most to least segregated, are residential school, special class, resource room, and regular class with itinerant teacher services. Residential placement, at one time the most popular alternative, is now recommended much less frequently than regular classrooms with itinerant services. And many residential schools have adopted a more inclusive philosophy. For example, students are often encouraged to go home on weekends. And some residential schools coordinate their programs with local public schools. The relatively low incidence of visual impairment makes the use of resource rooms and special classrooms less practical.

Without special attention, infants with visual impairment may have restricted interaction with their environment and mobility, in particular, may be affected. Early intervention often focuses on parental interaction with the child and parental reaction to the child's disability.

Education for the adolescent and adult stresses independent living and employment skills. Independence is a particularly important area because society often mistakenly treats people with visual impairment as helpless. Many adults with visual impairment are unemployed or overqualified for their jobs. Professionals are attempting to overcome the bleak employment picture by using innovative approaches. Job accommodations—for example, better transportation and computer software applications—can greatly improve the employment outlook for those who are visually impaired.

suggestions
for teaching

Students with Visual Impairment in General Education Classrooms   By Peggy L. Tarpley

Adapting Educational Materials

From reading the chapter, you know that the primary educational difference between students with low vision and students who are blind is their ability to read print. Students who have low vision can read print, although they may use magnifying devices and require materials written in large print. Individuals who are blind, however, must be instructed by using materials written in braille and by aural methods, including records, cassettes, and CDs. Therefore, one required modification for students who are mainstreamed is adaptation of instructional materials.

Although the itinerant or resource teacher will prepare or provide instructional materials written in braille, you may find that tape-recording instructional lessons, assignments, and tests saves time and reduces the need for planning far in advance. In addition, several organizations, such as the Library of Congress and the American Printing House for the Blind, provide audiotapes and records of a variety of textbooks and materials for pleasure reading. Other organizations, such as Recording for the Blind, also make a large selection of books available to students and have readers who will record specially requested materials.

In addition to adapted printed materials, there are a variety of other aids that your students may find useful in your classroom (Gearheart, Mullen, & Gearheart, 1993, pp. 301–302):

Science aids
- braille thermometers
- insect identification kits
- machine kits, including working models (e.g., pulleys and levers)

Mathematical aids
- a Cranmer abacus (pocket-sized)
- compasses, rulers, and protractors with braille markings
- handheld models of geometric area and of volume
- form boards for manipulation of whole and fractional parts
- calculators with voice output

Writing aids
- raised-line checkbooks
- signature guides

Geography aids
- braille atlases
- embossed relief and landform maps
- enlarged or textured maps

Physical education aids
- audible balls
- audible goal locators
- raised drawings and models of various sport fields or courts

Other sources for materials are the itinerant or resource teachers who are trained to work with students who are visually impaired. They can advise you about curricula specifically designed for these students, such as *Science Activities for the Visually Impaired* or *Project MAVIS*, a curriculum for social studies. They also may suggest ways to modify your existing instructional materials, such as:

1. Using real objects or tactile models in place of pictures whenever possible
2. Selecting materials with clear type and pictures
3. Printing or typing handouts in large print (Alumnae of the Visually Impaired Program at the University of British Columbia, 1994).

Similarly, when selecting computer software programs, teachers should consider the clarity and size of the text and graphics. Large-size print and boldface type options are desirable features. A simple guideline to selecting print size is to be sure that students can see individual letters (Rogow, 1994). One way to accurately assess the student's ability to see or read materials is to say "Tell me what you see," rather than "Can you see?" Students may pretend to see or assume they are seeing what you want them to see (Alberta Education, 1996).

To illustrate how these modifications can be implemented, let's look into a typical primary-grade classroom. Here, the teacher often reads "big books" and stories to the class. When students with visual impairment cannot see the illustrations by sitting close to the reader, the teacher may provide them with their own copies of the book or reproduce the story, enlarging the print. To promote independent reading, the teacher may select and cut out large pictures and place them in a notebook, so the children can "read" these picture books. Or the teacher may transcribe students' stories and enlarge the print, so the children can read their own work. In addition, the teacher may encourage students to create books by using real objects that are placed in felt pockets and glued to the page. Finally, the teacher may create interactive storyboards with real objects or with simple, enlarged pictures to use during story discussions (Rogow, 1994).

You may need some basic items to assist you in adapting materials. The Edmonton, Alberta Special Education Branch (Alberta Education, 1996) suggests this list for your school to purchase:

1. A tracing wheel and rubber mat
2. Colored glue
3. Raised-line or bold graph paper
4. Braille and large-print measuring devices
5. Self-adhesive felt dots
6. Yarn for tactile illustrations

Adapting Instructional Methods

Besides selecting and adapting materials, you will want to modify some of your usual interactions with students to accommodate the student with visual impairment (Alberta Education, 1996). For instance, facial expressions or body language will not caution or reinforce a student with a visual impairment. Voice your praise or disapproval or use a hand on the shoulder to reassure. Your language will need to be very specific when describing the location of people or objects. Avoid using terms like "here" or "there," but do not hesitate to use words like "look" and "see" as the student is used to hearing them.

You also can modify instruction and instructional procedures to enhance learning for students with visual impairment. For example, identify potentially difficult concepts and provide firsthand experiences, such as hands-on learning and concrete materials (Best, 1991). One teacher, for instance, created clay models to illustrate geological features and provided raised diagrams by drawing lines on construction paper with airplane glue (Travis, 1990). Encourage listening and oral communication skills through instruction with multisensory materials and in activities such as storytelling and small-group projects. Verbally describe classroom demonstrations and exhibits, and, when possible, encourage students to touch exhibits. For laboratory work, assign partners.

In order to provide time for students with visual impairment to prepare and read printed information, give them advance lists of assignments and lecture notes. Similarly, allow them extra time to complete tests. Giving tests orally or via tape recorder are also helpful modifications, as is permitting students to respond to test items orally (Alumnae, 1994). Furthermore, consider alternating activities that require close eye work with those that are less visually demanding (Alberta Education, 1996). Finally, make a notebook available that contains the information displayed in the classroom, such as bulletin board announcements and classroom rules, to ensure that all students have access to this information (MacCuspie, 1992).

Adapting the Classroom Environment

When students with visual impairment first enter your class, they will require orientation to the physical arrangement of the room that includes learning the location of materials, desks, activity areas, teacher's desk, and exits. For safety purposes, be sure that doors and drawers are kept consistently open or closed. Low-hanging objects, such as signs, and items that protrude from the walls should be pointed out. Rugs and mats should be taped firmly to the floor, and students should be reminded to push chairs underneath desks and tables (Alumnae, 1994). It is important for safety and for respect of the student that you ask the student's permission before physically assisting him or her. Remind students and teachers to identify themselves by name when speaking to the student or passing him or her in the hall, and teach the student caution about talking to strangers or volunteering personal information (Alberta, 1996).

Once students are oriented to the classroom, they should become familiar with the school and surrounding grounds, learning the locations of the main office, gym, library, restrooms, cafeteria, water fountains, and playground. Keep students informed of changes in and additions to the classroom or school arrangements. Although you should encourage them to move about without the aid of sighted guides, you may want to assign a guide for special events and activities that occur outside the classroom, such as fire drills, assemblies, and field trips.

In addition to providing an orientation to the school and classroom, Best (1991) suggests making sure that work surfaces in the class are glare-free and large enough to accommodate a Brailler, that desks are positioned near the chalkboard and demonstrations, and that the lighting is appropriate. Natural light should come from behind or the side of the student, and a lamp should be available to illuminate the work surface, if needed. Modifications also may be necessary when using videotapes, filmstrips, and films. Torres and Corn (1990) recommend asking another student to read subtitles aloud to the class; using a rear-screen projector, which allows students who are visually impaired to sit right in front of the screen, when possible; and permitting students to view the material before or after the class to ensure they understood all the visual concepts presented.

As educators have pointed out, students with visual impairment deserve the same instruction in all content areas as their nondisabled classmates. However, they also deserve instruction in skill areas re-

quired to meet their specific needs, such as social, sensory-motor, independent, and daily living skills, and orientation and mobility training (Curry & Hatlen, 1988; Sacks, Kekelis, & Gaylord-Ross, 1992). Although other professionals will conduct this training, you can play an important role by being aware of the times your mainstreamed students will receive instruction outside your class and by scheduling, whenever possible, new learning and special events when all students are in your room.

Helpful Resources

Catalogues of Appliances, Aids, and Books

American Foundation for the Blind, 11 Penn Plaza, Suite 300, New York, NY 10001, (212) 502-7600, (800) 232-5463.

American Printing House for the Blind, Inc., 1939 Frankfort Avenue, Louisville, KY 40206, (502) 895-2405, (800) 223-1839.

Braille Book Review, National Library Service for the Blind and Physically Handicapped, 1291 Taylor Street N.W., Washington, DC 20542, (202) 707-5100.

Carroll Center for the Blind, 770 Centre Street, Newton, MA 02649, (617) 969-6200, (800) 852-3131.

HeARRSay, National Association of Radio Reading Services, 2100 Wharton Street, Suite 140, Pittsburgh, PA 15203, (800) 280-5325.

Independent Living Aids, 27 East Mall, Plainview, NY 11803-4404, (516) 752-8080.

National Association for Visually Handicapped, 22 West 21st Street, New York, NY 10010, (212) 889-3141.

Sensory Access Foundation, 1142 West Evelyn Avenue, Sunnyvale, CA, (408) 245-7330.

Talking Book Topics, National Library Service for the Blind and Physically Handicapped, Library of Congress, 1291 Taylor Street N.W., Washington, DC 20542, (202) 707-5100 (lists recorded books and magazines that are available through a national network of cooperating libraries).

Books and Records

Books on Tape, Inc., P.O. Box 7900, Newport Beach, CA 92658, (800) 626-3333.

Braille Book Bank of the National Braille Association, 3 Townline Circle, Rochester, NY 14623, (716) 427-8260.

Braille Institute of America, 741 North Vermont Avenue, Los Angeles, CA 90029, (800) 272-4553.

Computerized books for the blind and print handicapped, University of Montana, 33 N. Corbin Hall, Missoula, MT 59812.

IBM National Support Center for Persons with Disabilities, P.O. Box 2150, Atlanta, GA 30301.

Library Reproduction Service, The Microfilm Company of California, Inc., 1977 South Los Angeles Street, Los Angeles, CA 90011, (213) 749-2463.

National Braille Press, Inc., 88 St. Stephen Street, Boston, MA 02115, (617) 266-6160, (800) 548-7323.

Recording for the Blind, Inc., 20 Roszel Road, Princeton, NJ 08540, (800) 221-4792.

Regional Libraries of the Library of Congress.

Taping for the Blind, 3935 Essex Lane, Houston, TX 77027, (713) 622-2767.

Vision Community Services, 818 Mt. Auburn Street, Watertown, MA 02172, (617) 926-4232.

Toys and Games

Gallagher, P. (1978). *Educational games for visually handicapped children.* Denver: Love Publishing.

Services

Associated Services for the Blind, 919 Walnut Street, Philadelphia, PA 19107, (215) 627-0600.

Blind and Visually Impaired Division, U.S. Department of Education, Office of Special Education and Rehabilitative Services, 330 C Street S.W., Washington, DC 20202, (202) 205-9317.

Blind Outdoor Leisure Development, P.O. Box M, Aspen, CO 81612, (970) 925-9511, (800) 530-3901.

Directory of services for blind and visually impaired persons in the United States (24th ed.), American Foundation for the Blind, 15 West 16th Street, New York, NY 10011.

Guide Dog Foundation for the Blind, 371 East Jericho Turnpike, Smithtown, NY 11787, (516) 265-2121, (800) 548-4337.

Guiding Eyes for the Blind, 611 Granite Springs Road, Yorktown Heights, NY 10598, (914) 245-4024, (800) 942-0149.

Jewish Guild for the Blind, 15 West 65th Street, New York, NY 10023, (212) 769-6200.

Job Accommodation Network (JAN), West Virginia University, P.O. Box 6080, Morgantown, WV 26506-6080, (800) 526-7234.

Lighthouse International, 111 East 59th Street, New York, NY 10022, (800) 829-0500.

National Braille Association, 3 Townline Circle, Rochester, NY 14623, (716) 427-8260, (800) 244-5797.

VISIONS, Services for the Blind and Visually Impaired, 500 Greenwich Street, 3rd Floor, New York, NY 10013, (212) 625-1616.

Instructional Methods

Asen, S. (1994). *Teaching and learning with technology* (Teacher's Guide). Alexandria, VA: Association for Supervision and Curriculum Development.

Barraga, N. C., & Erin, J. N. (1992). *Visual handicaps and learning* (3rd ed.). Austin, TX: Pro-Ed.

Best, A. B. (1991). *Teaching children with visual impairments.* Philadelphia: Open University Press.

Chapman, E. K., & Stone, J. M. (1988). *The visually handicapped child in your classroom.* London: Cassell.

Haring, N., & Romer, L. (Eds.). (1995). *Welcoming students who are deaf-blind into typical classrooms: Facilitating school participating, learning, friendships.* Baltimore: Paul H. Brookes.

Hazekamp, J., & Huebner, K. M. (Eds.). (1989). *Program planning and evaluation for blind and visually impaired students.* New York: American Foundation for the Blind.

Hill, J. L. (1990). Mainstreaming visually impaired children: The need for modifications. *Journal of Visual Impairment and Blindness, 84,* 354–360.

Koenig, A. J. (1992). A framework for understanding the literacy of individuals with visual impairments. *Journal of Visual Impairment and Blindness, 86,* 277–284.

Koenig, A. J., & Holbrook, M. C. (1991). Determining the reading medium for visually impaired students via diagnostic teaching. *Journal of Visual Impairment and Blindness, 85,* 61–68.

Lander, C. R. (1992). *Developing positive attitudes about disabilities.* Ballwin, MO: Claymont School.

Lewis, R. (1993). *Special education technology: Classroom applications.* Pacific Grove, CA: Brookes/Cole.

Lewis, R., & Doorlag, D. H. (1995). *Teaching special students in the mainstream* (4th ed.). Englewood Cliffs, NJ: Merrill/Prentice-Hall.

Liedtke, W. W., & Stainton, L. B. (1994). Fostering the development of number sense: Selected ideas for the blind. *B.C. Journal of Special Education, 18,* 24–32.

McCoy, K. A. (1995). *Teaching special learners in the general education classroom.* Denver, CO: Love Publishing.

Rogow, S. M. (1994). Literacy and children with severe visual problems. *B.C. Journal of Special Education, 18,* 101–108.

Sacks, S. K., Kekelis, L. S., & Gaylord-Ross, R. J. (Eds.). (1992). *The development of social skills by blind and visually impaired students.* New York: American Foundation for the Blind.

Spenciner, L. J. (1992). Mainstreaming the child with a visual impairment. In L. G. Cohen (Ed.), *Children with exceptional needs in regular classrooms* (pp. 82–97). Washington, DC: National Education Association.

Torres, I., & Corn, A. L. (1990). *When you have a visually handicapped child in your classroom: Suggestions for teachers* (2nd ed.). New York: American Foundation for the Blind.

Trief, E. (Ed.). (1992). *Working with visually impaired young students: A curriculum guide for birth to 3 year olds.* Springfield, IL: Charles C. Thomas.

Wisconsin Department of Public Instruction. (1990). *A guide to curriculum planning in education for the visually impaired.* Milwaukee: Wisconsin Department of Public Instruction.

Software

2 + 2, R. J. Cooper and Associates, 24843 Del Prado, Suite 283, Dana Point, CA 92629, (800) RJ-COOPER (714-240-1912). (Macintosh; Windows)

Arithmetic Critters, MECC, 6160 Summit Drive N., Minneapolis, MN 55430–4003, (800) 685-6322. (Apple IIe; Apple IIGS)

Beginning Reading Skills, MicroEd, 5602 Dalrymple Road, Edina, MN 55424, (612) 929-2242.

Big Book Maker: Letters, Numbers, and Shapes, Pelican/Toucan, a division of Queue, Inc., 768 Farmington Avenue, Farmington, CT 06032, (800) 232-2224.

Big Book Maker: Myths and Legends, Pelican/Toucan, a division of Queue, Inc., 768 Farmington Avenue, Farmington, CT 06032, (800) 232-2224.

Big Book Maker: Tall Tales and American Folk Heroes, Pelican/Toucan, a division of Queue, Inc., 768 Farmington Avenue, Farmington, CT 06032, (800) 232-2224.

Elementary Volume 1: Mathematics, American Printing House for the Blind, P.O. Box 6085, 18339 Frankfort Avenue, Louisville, KY 40206-0085, (800) 223-1839. (Apple IIe; Apple IIGS) (requires ECHO speech synthesizer)

Food Facts, American Printing House for the Blind, P.O. Box 6085, 18339 Frankfort Avenue, Louisville, KY 40206-0085, (800) 223-1839. (Apple IIe; Apple IIGS) (requires ECHO speech synthesizer)

Illustrations Picture Disks, Access Unlimited, 3535 Briarpark Drive, Suite 102, Houston, TX 77042-5235, (800) 848-0311. (Apple IIe; Apple IIGS)

Jo-Jo's Reading Circus, Mindplay, 160 W. Ft. Lowell, Tucson, AZ 85705, (800) 221-7911. (Macintosh) (interactive reading)

Keys to Success: Computer Keyboard Skills for Blind Children, Life Science Associates, 1 Fenimore Road, Bayport, NY 11705-2115, (516) 472-2111. (Apple IIe) (requires ECHO II speech synthesizer)

Language Experience Recorder, Teacher Support Software, 3542 N.W. 97th Boulevard, Gainesville, FL 32606, (800) 228-2871. (Apple IIe; Apple IIGS; Macintosh; DOS)

LetterTalk, American Printing House for the Blind, P.O. Box 6085, 18339 Frankfort Avenue, Louisville, KY 40206-0085, (800) 223-1839. (Apple IIe; Apple IIGS) (requires ECHO) (typing tutor)

Pix Cells, Raised Dot Computing, Inc., 408 S. Baldwin Street, Madison, WI 53703, (800) 347-9594.

Milt's Math Drills, Hartley Courseware, Jostens Learning Corp., 9920 Pacific Heights Boulevard, Suite 500, San Diego, CA 92121, (800) 247-1380. (Apple IIe; Apple IIGS)

Noteworthy, GW Micro, Inc., 725 Airport North Office Park, Fort Wayne, IN 46825, (219) 489-3671. (DOS) (a note-taking program)

Perfect Scribe, Arts Computer Products, Inc., 33 Richdale Avenue, P.O. Box 604, Cambridge, MA 02140, (617) 547-5320. (WordPerfect 5.1 and 6.0 tutorial)

Prefixes, American Printing House for the Blind, P.O. Box 6085, 18339 Frankfort Avenue, Louisville, KY 40206-0085, (800) 223-1839. (Apple IIe; Apple IIGS)

Story Board, Data Command, Inc., 13492 Research Boulevard, Suite 120-215, Austin, TX 78750, (800) 528-7390. (Apple IIe; Apple IIGS) (interactive writing program)

Texttalker, American Printing House for the Blind, P.O. Box 6085, 18339 Frankfort Avenue, Louisville, KY 40206-0085, (800) 223-1839. (Apple IIe; Apple IIGS) (a text-to-speech program for many Apple programs—requires ECHO speech synthesizer)

Word-Processing Programs

Dr. Peet's Talkwriter, Hartley Courseware, Jostens Learning Corp., 9920 Pacific Heights Boulevard, Suite 500, San Diego, CA 92121, (800) 247-1380. (Apple IIe; Apple IIGS) (requires speech synthesizer)

Magic Slate II, Sunburst Communications, 101 Castleton Street, Pleasantville, NY 10570, (800) 321-7511. (Apple IIe; Apple IIGS)

Large-Print Programs

1-2-3 Sequence Me, Sunburst Communications, 101 Castleton Street, Pleasantville, NY 10570, (800) 321-7511. (Apple IIe; Apple IIGS; Macintosh) (beginning readers sequence pictures or words to create a story)

Big Book Maker: Favorite Fairy Tales and Nursery Rhymes, Pelican/Toucan, a division of Queue, Inc., 768 Farmington Avenue, Farmington, CT 06032, (800) 232-2224. (prints strips that tape together to create "big books")

Big Book Maker: Letters, Numbers, and Shapes, Pelican/Toucan, a division of Queue, Inc., 768 Farmington Avenue, Farmington, CT 06032, (800) 232-2224.

Big Book Maker: Tall Tales and American Folk Heroes, Pelican/Toucan, a division of Queue, Inc., 768 Farmington Avenue, Farmington, CT 06032, (800) 232-2224.

Big Book Maker: Feeling Good about Yourself, Pelican/Toucan, a division of Queue, Inc., 768 Farmington Avenue, Farmington, CT 06032, (800) 232-2224.

Cotton Tales, Mindplay, 160 W. Ft. Lowell, Tucson, AZ 85705, (800) 221-7911. (Apple IIe; Apple IIGS; Macintosh; DOS)

Letter Recognition, Hartley Courseware, Jostens Learning Corp., 9920 Pacific Heights Boulevard, San Diego, CA 92121, (800) 247-1380. (Apple IIe; Apple IIGS)

Math Tri-Pack, Dataflo Computer Services, Inc., 531 U.S. Rt. 4, Enfield, NH 03748, (603) 448-2223. (Apple IIe; Apple IIGS; DOS)

Railroad Snoop, Sunburst Communications, 101 Castleton Street, Pleasantville, NY 10570, (800) 321-7511. (Apple IIe; Apple IIGS) (requires Magic Slate 11 40-column) (story writing for fifth–seventh grades)

Schoolcraft Games I, Kidsview Software, P.O. Box 98, Warner, NH 03278, (800) 542-7501. (Apple IIe; Apple IIGS)

Schoolcraft Math I, Kidsview Software, P.O. Box 98, Warner, NH 03278, (800) 542-7501. (Apple IIe; Apple IIGS)

Schoolcraft Word I, Kidsview Software, P.O. Box 98, Warner, NH 03278, (800) 542-7501. (Apple IIe; Apple IIGS)

Ready-Set-Read, Continental Press, Inc., 520 E. Bainbridge Street, Elizabethtown, PA 17022, (800) 233-0759. (Apple IIe; Apple IIGS)

Organizations

American Council of the Blind, 1155 15th Street N.W., Suite 720, Washington, DC 20005, (202) 467-5081, (800) 424-8666.

American Council of the Blind—Parents, c/o American Council of the Blind, 1155 15th Street N.W., Suite 720, Washington, DC 20005, (202) 467-5081, (800) 424-8666.

American Foundation for the Blind, 11 Penn Plaza, Suite 300, New York, NY 10001, (212) 502-7600, (800) 232-5463.

Association for Education and Rehabilitation of the Blind and Visually Impaired, 4600 Duke Street, Suite 430, P.O. Box 22397, Alexandria, VA 22304, (703) 823-9690.

Division on Visual Impairments, Council for Exceptional Children, 1920 Association Drive, Reston, VA 22091, (703) 620-3660, (888) CEC-SPED.

National Federation of the Blind, 1800 Johnson Street, Baltimore, MD 21230, (410) 659-9314.

United States Association of Blind Athletes, 33 N. Institute Street, Brown Hall, Suite 015, Colorado Springs, CO 80903.

Bibliography for Teaching Suggestions

Alberta Education, Special Education Branch. (1996). *Teaching students with visual impairments.* Edmonton, Alberta: Author.

Alumnae of the Visually Impaired Program, Faculty of Education, University of British Columbia. (1994). Visually impaired children in regular classrooms: A guide for resource and classroom teachers. *B.C. Journal of Special Education, 18,* 173–180.

Best, A. B. (1991). *Teaching children with visual impairments.* Philadelphia: Open University Press.

Curry, S. A., & Hatlen, P. H. (1988). Meeting the unique educational needs of visually impaired pupils through appropriate placement. *Journal of Visual Impairment and Blindness, 82,* 417–424.

Gearheart, B., Mullen, R. C., & Gearheart, C. J. (1993). *Exceptional individuals.* Pacific Grove, CA: Brooks/Cole.

Leong, S. (1996). Preschool orientation and mobility: A review of the literature. *Journal of Visual Impairment and Blindness, 90,* 145–153.

MacCuspie, A. (1992). Tips for teachers. *DVH Quarterly, 27,* 11.

Project MAVIS. (1979). Boulder, CO: Social Science Education Consortium.

Rogow, S. M. (1994). Literacy and children with severe visual problems. *B.C. Journal of Special Education, 18,* 101–108.

Sacks, S. Z., Kekelis, L. S., & Gaylord-Ross, R. J. (1992). *The development of social skills by blind and visually impaired students.* New York: American Foundation for the Blind.

Science activities for the visually impaired. (1977). Berkeley, CA: Lawrence Hall of Science, University of California.

Scott, E. P. (1982). *Your visually impaired student: A guide for teachers.* Baltimore: University Park Press.

Torres, I., & Corn, A. L. (1990). *When you have a visually handicapped child in your classroom: Suggestions for teachers.* New York: American Foundation for the Blind.

Travis, J. W. (1990). Geology and the visually impaired student. *Journal of Geological Education, 38,* 41–49.

john
colby

Untitled. Ink, crayon, watercolor on rag paper. 15 × 22 in.

John Colby was born in the Boston area in 1955. At age 18, he sustained a head injury and multiple body traumas. He spent many years in therapeutic rehabilitation before attending Gateway Crafts, an art program for adults with disabilities in Brookline, MA, in 1990. His work has been shown at the Gateway Gallery and other galleries in Massachusetts and was selected for exhibit at the Outsider Art Fair in New York in 1999. He writes poetry as well as draws and paints.

Physical Disabilities

My friend Stephen and I used to do pony parties together.... We were invariably late for the birthday party, a result of loading the ponies at the last minute, combined with our truly remarkable propensity for getting lost....

Once we reached the party, there was a great rush of excitement. The children, realizing that the ponies had arrived, would come running from the backyard in their silly hats; their now forgotten balloons, bobbing colorfully behind them, would fly off in search of some tree or telephone wire....

My pleasure at the sight of the children didn't last long, however. I knew what was coming. As soon as they got over the thrill of being near the ponies, they'd notice me. Half my jaw was missing, which gave my face a strange triangular shape, accentuated by the fact that I was unable to keep my mouth completely closed. When I first started doing pony parties, my hair was still short and wispy, still growing in from the chemo. But as it grew I made things worse by continuously bowing my head and hiding behind the curtain of hair, furtively peering out at the world like some nervous actor. Unlike the actor, though, I didn't secretly relish my audience, and if it were possible I would have stood behind that curtain forever, my head bent in an eternal act of deference. I was, however, dependent upon my audience. Their approval or disapproval defined everything for me, and I believed with every cell of my body approval wasn't written into my particular script. I was fourteen years old.

LUCY GREALY
Autobiography of a Face

In Western culture, people are almost obsessed with their bodies. They don't just want to be healthy and strong; they want to be beautiful—well formed and attractive to others. In fact, some people seem to be more concerned about the impression their bodies make than they are about their own well-being. They may even endanger their health in an effort to become more physically alluring. It is not really surprising, then, that people with physical disabilities must fight two battles—the battle to overcome the limitations imposed by their physical conditions and the battle to be accepted by others.

Individuals with physical disabilities or differences are often stared at, teased, socially rejected, or in other ways treated with cruelty. In the excerpt from her autobiography (see p. 425), Lucy Grealy—who at the age of eight had cancer, necessitating disfiguring surgery and chemotherapy—describes the lack of acceptance and approval she felt from others. The reactions of others are major barriers to the social and educational development of children and youths with physical differences or disabilities.

Children with physical disabilities often face more than the problem of acceptance, however. For many, accomplishing the seemingly simple tasks of everyday living is a minor—or major—miracle.

Definition and Classification

In this chapter, we consider children whose primary distinguishing characteristics are health or physical problems. For the purposes of this book, *children with physical disabilities* are defined as those whose physical limitations or health problems interfere with school attendance or learning to such an extent that special services, training, equipment, materials, or facilities are required. Children who have physical disabilities may also have other disabilities of any type, or special gifts or talents. Thus, the characteristics of children with physical disabilities are extremely varied. The child's physical condition is the proper concern of the medical profes-

In the past, physical disabilities kept children from engaging in many everyday activities, but today they are encouraged to participate to the fullest extent possible.

misconceptions
about Persons with Physical Disabilities

myth Cerebral palsy is a contagious disease.

fact Cerebral palsy is not a disease. It is a nonprogressive neurological injury. It is a disorder of muscle control and coordination caused by injury to the brain before or during birth or in early childhood.

myth Physical disabilities of all kinds are decreasing because of medical advances.

fact Because of advances in medical technology, the number of children with severe disabilities is increasing. The number of survivors of serious medical conditions who develop normally or have mild impairments, such as hyperactivity and learning disabilities, is also increasing.

myth The greatest educational problem involving children with physical disabilities is highly specialized instruction.

fact The greatest educational problem is teaching people without disabilities about what it is like to have a disability and how disabilities can be accommodated.

myth The more severe a person's physical disability, the lower his or her intelligence.

fact A person may be severely physically disabled by cerebral palsy or another condition but have a brilliant mind.

myth People with epilepsy are mentally ill.

fact People with epilepsy (seizure disorder) are not any more or less disposed to mental illness than those who do not have epilepsy.

myth Arthritis is found only in adults, particularly those who are elderly.

fact Arthritic conditions are found in people of any age, including young children.

myth People with physical disabilities have no need for sexual expression.

fact People with physical disabilities have sexual urges and need outlets for sexual expression.

myth The effects of traumatic brain injury are not distinguishable from those of other disabilities, such as mental retardation, learning disabilities, and emotional or behavioral disorders.

fact A person who has had traumatic injury to the brain may indeed show cognitive, social, emotional, and behavioral characteristics much like those associated with other disabilities. However, the causes of these characteristics, their prognosis and course, and their management may be quite different from those of other disabilities.

sion—but when physical problems have obvious implications for education, teaching specialists are needed.

The fact that the primary distinguishing characteristics of children with physical disabilities are medical conditions, health problems, or physical limitations highlights the necessity of interdisciplinary cooperation. There simply must be communication between physicians and special educators to maintain the child's health and at the same time develop whatever capabilities he or she has (Bigge, 1991; Heller, Alberto, Forney, & Schwartzman, 1996; Kurtz, Dowrick, Levy, & Batshaw, 1996).

There is a tremendous range and variety of physical disabilities. Children may have **congenital anomalies** (defects they are born with), or they may acquire disabilities through accident or disease after birth. Some physical disabilities are comparatively mild and transitory; others are profound and progressive, ending in total incapacitation and early death. It is difficult to discuss physical disabilities in general, so this chapter is organized around specific conditions falling under one of three categories: neuromotor impairments, orthopedic and musculoskeletal disorders, and other conditions affecting health or physical ability.

Prevalence and Need

About 200,000 students in U.S. public schools—less than 0.5 percent of the school population—are being served under three special education categories related to physical disabilities. About half of these have multiple disabilities (e.g., cerebral palsy and mental retardation), about one-fourth have an orthopedic impairment without other serious complications, and about a fourth have a chronic health condition (see U.S. Department of Education, 1998). The needs of many students with physical disabilities appear to be unmet for a number of reasons, including the fact that the population of children and youths with physical disabilities is growing but the availability of health and social service programs is not (see Heller, Alberto, Forney, & Schwartzman, 1996; Martin, 1992).

Part of the increase in the prevalence of physical disabilities may be due to improvements in the identification of, and medical services to, children with certain conditions. Ironically, medical advances have not only improved the chances of preventing or curing certain diseases and disorders; they have also assured the survival of more children with severe medical problems (Blum, 1992; Brown, 1993; Kurtz et al., 1996). Many children with severe and multiple disabilities and those with severe, chronic illnesses or severe injuries, who in the past would not have survived long, today can have a normal lifespan. So declining mortality rates do not necessarily mean there will be fewer individuals with disabilities. Moreover, improvements in medical care may not lower the number of individuals with disabilities unless there is also a lowering of risk factors in the environment—factors such as accidents, toxic substances, poverty, malnutrition, disease, and interpersonal violence (Baumeister, Kupstas, & Klindworth, 1990; Pless, 1994).

Neuromotor Impairments

congenital anomaly. An irregularity (anomaly) present at birth; may or may not be due to genetic factors.

Neuromotor impairments are the result of injury to the brain (neurological damage) that also affects the ability to move parts of one's body (motor impairment). It may be associated with injury to the brain before, during, or after birth.

Traumatic Brain Injury (TBI)

In Chapter 1, we noted that IDEA (the Individuals with Disabilities Education Act of 1990) created the category of **traumatic brain injury (TBI),** under which students may be found eligible for special education and related services. TBI is an increasingly frequent cause of neurological impairment in children and youths. It presents unique educational problems that have been poorly understood and often mismanaged. Recent medical advances have greatly improved its diagnosis and treatment.

Definition, Prevalence, and Variety of Causes. The definition of TBI specifies that:

1. There is injury to the brain caused by an external force.
2. The injury is not caused by a degenerative or congenital condition.
3. There is a diminished or altered state of consciousness.
4. Neurological or neurobehavioral dysfunction results from the injury (Begali, 1992; Heller, Alberto, Forney, & Schwartzman, 1996; Snow & Hooper, 1994).

TBI may involve *open* head injuries—in which there is a penetrating head wound—from such causes as a fall, gunshot, assault, vehicular accident, or surgery. TBI may involve *closed* head injuries, in which there is no open head wound but brain damage is caused by internal compression, stretching, or other shearing motion of neural tissues within the head (see Christensen, 1996; Savage & Wolcott, 1994). Closed injuries may be caused by a variety of events, including a fall, accident, or abuse such as violent shaking.

Brain injury can be acquired from a variety of nontraumatic causes, as well: **hypoxia** (reduced oxygen to the brain, as might occur in near drowning), infection of the brain or its linings, stroke, tumor, metabolic disorder (such as may occur with diabetes, liver disease, or kidney disease), or toxic chemicals or drugs.

The educational definition of TBI focuses on impairments in one or more areas important for learning, such as cognition, language, speech, memory, information processing, attention, reasoning, abstract thinking, judgment, problem solving, perceptual abilities, psychosocial behavior, and physical abilities (Tyler & Colson, 1994; White, 1998). The various **sequelae** (consequences) of TBI create a need for special education; the injury itself is a medical problem.

The exact prevalence of TBI is difficult to determine, but we do know that TBI occurs at an alarming rate among children and youths. Estimates are that each year about 0.5 percent of school-age children acquire a brain injury. And by the time they graduate from high school, nearly 4 percent of students may have TBI (Begali, 1992; Savage & Wolcott, 1994). Moreover, estimates of the percentages of students receiving special education who sustained TBI at some time before they were found eligible for special education range from 8 percent to 20 percent (Begali, 1992).

Males are more prone to TBI than females, and the age range in which TBI is most likely to occur for both males and females is late adolescence and early adulthood (Christensen, 1996). Under age five, falls are the dominant cause of TBI, with vehicular accidents and child abuse causing substantial injuries as well. After age five, and increasingly through adolescence, vehicular accidents (including accidents involving pedestrians, bicycles, and motorcycles) account for the overwhelming majority of TBI; assaults and gunshot wounds are increasingly prevalent among youths at older ages (Snow & Hooper, 1994).

traumatic brain injury (TBI). Injury to the brain (not including conditions present at birth, birth trauma, or degenerative diseases or conditions) resulting in total or partial disability or psychosocial maladjustment that affects educational performance; may affect cognition, language, memory, attention, reasoning, abstract thinking, judgment, problem solving, sensory or perceptual and motor disabilities, psychosocial behavior, physical functions, information processing, or speech.

hypoxia. A reduction of oxygen in the blood, which can result in brain damage.

sequelae. After effects, secondary effects, or consequences of a disease or injury.

Savage (1988) refers to TBI as a "pervasive epidemic in our children and young adults" (p. 2), and Bigge (1991) notes that although the assessment and treatment of TBI have improved dramatically in recent years, "the sheer number of cases is depressing" (p. 13). The prevalence is all the more depressing because so many of the causes of TBI are entirely preventable or avoidable (see Christensen, 1996).

The effects of TBI may range from very mild to profound and may be temporary or permanent (Heller, Alberto, Forney, & Schwartzman, 1996; Savage & Wolcott, 1994; Snow & Hooper, 1994). In fact, effects may not be seen at all immediately after the injury; some effects may appear months or even years afterward (Allison, 1992; Mira & Tyler, 1991). About half the children and youths who experience serious TBI will require special education, and those who return to regular classes will require modifications if they are to be successful (Mira & Tyler, 1991).

Educational Implications. The educational implications of TBI can be extremely varied, depending on the nature and severity of the injury and the age and abilities of the individual at the time of injury. The box on page 431 summarizes choices educators and parents must face in the light of research on TBI. A significant issue in educating someone who has experienced TBI is helping family members, teachers, and peers respond appropriately to the sudden and sometimes dramatic changes that may occur in the student's academic abilities, appearance, behavior, and emotional states. Both general and special education teachers need training about TBI and its ramifications if students are to be reintegrated successfully into the schools and classrooms they attended before the injury.

Savage (1988) suggests that the following characteristics are essential features of appropriate education for students with TBI:

1. Transition from a hospital or rehabilitation center to the school requires that both institutions be involved; information must be shared to ensure a smooth transition.
2. The school must use a team approach, involving regular and special educators, other special teachers, guidance counselor, administrators, and the student's family.
3. The individualized education program (IEP) for the student must be concerned with cognitive, social/behavioral, and sensorimotor domains.
4. Most students with TBI experience problems in focusing and sustaining attention for long periods, remembering previously learned facts and skills, and learning new things. These students tend to have difficulty with organization, abstraction, and flexible thinking. They often lose basic academic skills and learning strategies and experience high levels of frustration, fatigue, and irritability. They also may have difficulty reestablishing associations with peers and controlling appropriate social behavior.
5. Programs for students with TBI must emphasize the cognitive processes through which academic skills are learned, as well as curriculum content.
6. The school needs to consider the student's long-term needs in addition to his or her annual IEP goals, but initial IEP goals should be reviewed at least every six weeks because rapid changes sometimes take place early in recovery (Savage, 1988; see also Tyler & Mira, 1993).

Some types of neurological impairment occur before, during, or soon after birth and do not involve sudden changes in a person's abilities. TBI is a special case of neurological impairment, in which there is a sudden alteration in abilities; this

What Does the Research Say About Traumatic Brain Injury?

Choices Facing Educators—and Parents

The most essential issue facing schools and parents is not the procedural determination of special education qualification. The key educational task and responsibility involves having the knowledge and skill to construct appropriate instructional learning experiences for children with TBI. Complicating the entire instructional issue is the reality of recognizing that *every student with brain injury is unique.* Two "comparable" cases with similar causes and damage may evidence highly discrepant symptoms and behavioral outcomes....

Even when adequate knowledge of neural development and processing exists, educators and related service providers are limited in fully understanding or predicting what a student with brain injury can and will do in the classroom. Careful review and analysis of clinical cases, as well as careful observation of behavior across settings, can provide useful information for teaching professionals and parents to identify effective learning and coping strategies.

Source: White, R. (1998). Meet Bob: A student with traumatic brain injury. *Teaching Exceptional Children, 30*(3), p. 57.

---

can often cause frustration in the student and teachers who must cope with this loss. The student must undergo medical treatment to address the biophysical aspects of the injury, and it is critical that educators understand the implications of the injury for structuring the student's psychological and social environments in school (Heller, Alberto, Forney, & Schwartzman, 1996; Savage & Mishkin, 1994). For further information, you may want to visit the web site of the Brain Injury Association, Inc. at www.BIAUSA.org.

Other Neurological Impairments

TBI involves brain damage with an identifiable external cause: trauma. However, in many cases of brain damage, it is impossible to identify the exact cause of the impairment. The important point is that *when a child's nervous system is damaged, no matter what the cause, muscular weakness or paralysis is almost always one of the symptoms.* And because these children cannot move about like most others, their education typically requires special equipment, special procedures, or other accommodations for their disabilities. We turn now to some additional types of neurological impairments for which the causes are often unknown.

Cerebral Palsy. **Cerebral palsy (CP)** is not a disease. It is not contagious, it is not progressive (except that improper treatment may lead to complications), and there are no remissions. Although it is often thought of as a motor problem associated with brain damage at birth, it is actually more complicated. For practical purposes, cerebral palsy can be considered part of a syndrome that includes motor dysfunction, psychological dysfunction, seizures, or emotional or behavioral disorders due to brain damage.

Some individuals with CP show only one indication of brain damage, such as motor impairment; others may show combinations of symptoms. The usual definition of CP refers to a condition characterized by paralysis, weakness, lack of coordination, and/or other motor dysfunction because of damage to the child's brain before it has matured (Batshaw & Perret, 1986; Capute & Accardo, 1996a, 1996b). Symptoms may be so mild that they are detected only with difficulty, or

cerebral palsy (CP). A condition characterized by paralysis, weakness, incoordination, and/or other motor dysfunction; caused by damage to the brain before it has matured.

Advances in medical and rehabilitation technology offer increasing hope of overcoming disabilities associated with cerebral palsy.

so profound that the individual is almost completely incapacitated.

Although there is no cure for CP, advances in medical and rehabilitation technology offer increasing hope of overcoming the disabilities imposed by neurological damage. For example, intensive long-term physical therapy in combination with a surgical procedure called *selective posterior rhizotomy*—in which the surgeon cuts selected nerve roots below the spinal cord that cause spasticity in the leg muscles—allow some children with spastic CP to better control certain muscles. Such treatment allows some nonambulatory children to walk and helps others walk more normally (Dyar, 1988).

Causes and Types. Anything that can cause brain damage during the brain's development can cause CP. Before birth, maternal infections, chronic diseases, physical trauma, or maternal exposure to toxic substances or X rays, for example, may damage the brain of the fetus. During the birth process, the brain may be injured, especially if labor or birth is difficult or complicated. Premature birth, hypoxia, high fever, infections, poisoning, hemorrhaging, and related factors may cause harm following birth. In short, anything that results in oxygen deprivation, poisoning, cerebral bleeding, or direct trauma to the brain can be a possible cause of CP.

Although CP occurs at every social level, it is more often seen in children born to mothers in poor socioeconomic circumstances. Children who live in such circumstances have a greater risk of incurring brain damage because of such factors as malnutrition of the mother, poor prenatal and postnatal care, environmental hazards during infancy, and low birthweight (see Baumeister et al., 1990; Nelson, 1996; Stanley & Blair, 1994).

The two means of classification that have been most widely accepted specify the limbs involved and the type of motor disability. Classification according to the extremities involved applies not just to CP but to all types of motor disability or paralysis. The most common classifications may be summarized as follows:

- **Hemiplegia:** One-half (right or left side) of the body is involved.
- **Diplegia:** Legs are involved to a greater extent than arms.
- **Quadriplegia:** All four limbs are involved.
- **Paraplegia:** Only the legs are involved.

hemiplegia. A condition in which one half (right or left side) of the body is paralyzed.

diplegia. A condition in which the legs are paralyzed to a greater extent than the arms.

quadriplegia. A condition in which all four limbs are paralyzed.

paraplegia. A condition in which both legs are paralyzed.

CP may involve problems of voluntary movement or **spasticity**—stiffness or tenseness of muscles and inaccurate voluntary movement. Other types are characterized by abrupt, involuntary movements and difficulty maintaining balance, known as **choreoathetoid** movements, or muscles that give the appearance of floppiness, known as **atonic** muscles. Some individuals have a mixture of various types of CP.

The important point about CP is that the brain damage affects strength and the ability to move parts of the body normally. The difficulty of movement may involve the limbs as well as the muscles used to control facial expressions and speech. As a result, someone with CP may have difficulty moving or speaking or may exhibit facial contortions or drooling. But these results of brain damage do not necessarily mean that the person's intelligence or emotional sensitivity has been affected by the damage affecting muscle control.

Associated Disabilities and Educational Implications. Research during the past few decades has made it clear that CP is a developmental disability—a multidisabling condition far more complex than a motor disability alone (Capute & Accardo, 1996b; Heller, Alberto, Forney, & Schwartzman, 1996). When the brain is damaged, sensory abilities, cognitive functions, and emotional responsiveness as well as motor performance are usually affected. A high proportion of children with CP are found to have hearing impairments, visual impairments, perceptual disorders, speech problems, emotional or behavioral disorders, mental retardation, or some combination of several of these disabling conditions, in addition to motor disability. They may also exhibit such characteristics as drooling or facial contortions.

Some individuals with CP have normal or above-average intellectual capacity, and a few test within the gifted range. The average tested intelligence of children with CP, however, is clearly lower than the average for the general population (Batshaw & Perret, 1986). However, we must be very cautious in interpreting the test results of children with CP, as many standardized tests of intelligence and achievement may be inappropriate for individuals with special difficulties in perception, movement, or response speed. Furthermore, the movement problems of a child with CP may become more apparent in a state of emotional arousal or stress; this can complicate using typical testing procedures, which tend to be demanding and stressful.

The educational problems of children who have CP are as multifaceted as their disabilities. Not only must special equipment and procedures be provided because the children have physical disabilities, but the same special educational procedures and equipment required to teach children with vision, hearing, or communication disorders, learning disabilities, emotional or behavioral disorders, or mental retardation are often needed. Careful and continuous educational assessment of the individual child's capabilities is particularly important. Teaching the child who has CP demands competence in many aspects of special education and experience in working with a variety of disabling conditions in a multidisciplinary setting (Bigge, 1991; Heller, Alberto, Forney, & Schwartzman, 1996; Tyler & Colson, 1994).

Seizure Disorder (Epilepsy).
A person has a **seizure** when there is an abnormal discharge of electrical energy in certain brain cells. The discharge spreads to nearby cells, and the effect may be loss of consciousness, involuntary movements, or abnormal sensory phenomena. The effects of the seizure will depend on the location of the cells in which the discharge starts and how far the discharge spreads.

spasticity. Characterized by muscle stiffness and problems in voluntary movement; associated with spastic cerebral palsy.

choreoathetoid. Characterized by involuntary movements and difficulty with balance; associated with choreoathetoid cerebral palsy.

atonic. Characterized by lack of muscle tone; associated with atonic cerebral palsy.

seizure (convulsion). A sudden alteration of consciousness, usually accompanied by motor activity and/or sensory phenomena; caused by an abnormal discharge of electrical energy in the brain.

People with **epilepsy** have recurrent seizures (Engel, 1995). About 6 percent of the population will have a seizure at some time during life, but most of them will not be diagnosed as having epilepsy because they do not have repeated seizures (Batshaw & Perret, 1986). Seizures reflect abnormal brain activity, so it is not surprising that they occur more often in children with developmental disabilities (e.g., mental retardation or cerebral palsy) than in children without disabilities (Coulter, 1993; Vining & Freeman, 1996).

Causes and Types. Seizures apparently can be caused by almost any kind of damage to the brain. The most common causes include lack of sufficient oxygen (hypoxia), low blood sugar (hypoglycemia), infections, and physical trauma. Certain conditions, like those named, tend to increase the chances that neurochemical reactions will be set off in brain cells (Vining & Freeman, 1996). In many cases, the causes are unknown. Some types of seizures may be progressive; that is, they may damage the brain or disrupt its functioning in such a way that having a seizure increases the probability of having another (Girvin, 1992). Even though the cause of seizures is not well understood, it is important to note that with proper medication most people's seizures can be controlled.

Seizures may take many forms and differ along at least the following dimensions:

- *Duration:* They may last only a few seconds or for several minutes.
- *Frequency:* They may occur as frequently as every few minutes or only about once a year.
- *Onset:* They may be set off by certain identifiable stimuli or be unrelated to the environment, and they may be totally unexpected or be preceded by certain internal sensations.
- *Movements:* They may cause major convulsive movements or only minor motor symptoms (e.g., eye blinks).
- *Causes:* They may be caused by a variety of conditions, including high fever, poisoning, trauma, and other conditions mentioned previously; but in many cases the causes are unknown.
- *Associated disabilities:* They may be associated with other disabling conditions or be unrelated to any other medical problem or disability.
- *Control:* They may be controlled completely by drugs, so that the individual has no more seizures, or they may be only partially controlled.

Educational Implications. About half of all children with seizure disorders have average or higher intelligence. Among those without mental retardation, however, there seems to be a higher-than-usual incidence of learning disabilities (Besag, 1995; Westbrook, Silver, Coupey, & Shinnar, 1991). Although many children who have seizure disorders have other disabilities, some do not. Consequently, both general and special education teachers may expect to encounter children who have seizures (see Spiegel, Cutler, & Yetter, 1996). Besides obtaining medical advice regarding management of the child's particular seizure disorder, teachers should know first aid for epileptic seizures (see the box on page 435). Ignorance about the causes of seizures and about first aid are among the most common misconceptions about epilepsy (Gouvier, Brown, Prestholdt, Hayes, & Apostolas, 1995).

Seizures are primarily a medical problem and require primarily medical attention. Educators are called on to deal with the problem in the following ways:

epilepsy. A pattern of repeated seizures.

First Aid for Epileptic Seizures

A major epileptic seizure is often dramatic and frightening. It lasts only a few minutes, however, and does not require expert care. These simple procedures should be followed:

- Remain calm. You cannot stop a seizure once it has started. Let the seizure run its course. Do not try to revive the child.
- If the child is upright, ease him to the floor and loosen his clothing.
- Try to prevent the child from striking his head or body against any hard, sharp, or hot objects; but do not otherwise interfere with his movement.
- Turn the child's face to the side so that saliva can flow out of his mouth.
- *Do not insert anything between the child's teeth.*

- Do not be alarmed if the child seems to stop breathing momentarily.
- After the movements stop and the child is relaxed, allow him to sleep or rest if he wishes.
- It isn't generally necessary to call a doctor unless the attack is followed almost immediately by another seizure or the seizure lasts more than ten minutes.
- Notify the child's parents or guardians that a seizure has occurred.
- After a seizure, many people can carry on as before. If, after resting, the child seems groggy, confused, or weak, it may be a good idea to accompany him or her home.

Source: Courtesy of Epilepsy Foundation of America.

1. General and special teachers need to help dispel ignorance, superstition, and prejudice toward people who have seizures and provide calm management for the occasional seizure the child may have at school (Spiegel et al., 1996).
2. Special education teachers who work with students with severe mental retardation or teach children with other severe developmental disabilities need to be prepared to manage more frequent seizures as well as to handle learning problems. The teacher should record the length of a child's seizure and the type of activity the child was engaged in before it occurred. This information will help physicians in diagnosis and treatment. If a student is being treated for a seizure disorder, the teacher should know the type of medication and its possible side effects.

Some children who do not have mental retardation but have seizures exhibit learning and behavior problems (Huberty, Austin, Risinger, & McNelis, 1992; Westbrook et al., 1991). These problems may result from damage to the brain that causes other disabilities as well, or they may be the side effects of anticonvulsant medication or the result of mismanagement by parents and teachers. Teachers must be aware that seizures of any type may interfere with the child's attention or the continuity of education (McCarthy, Richman, & Yarbrough, 1995). Brief seizures may require the teacher to repeat instructions or allow the child extra time to respond. Frequent major convulsions may prevent even a bright child from achieving at the usual rate.

Children with seizure disorders have emotional or behavioral problems more often than most children (Freeman, Jacobs, Vining, & Rabin, 1984; Hoare, 1984). However, the school adjustment of students with seizure disorders can be improved dramatically if they are properly assessed, placed, counseled, taught about seizures, and given appropriate work assignments (Heller, Alberto, Forney, & Schwartzman, 1996).

Spina Bifida and Other Spinal Cord Injuries. Neurological damage may involve only the spinal cord, leaving the brain unaffected. Spinal cord injury may occur before or after birth, affecting the individual's ability to move or control bodily functions below the site of the injury.

During early fetal development, the two halves of the embryo grow together or fuse at the midline. When the closure is incomplete, a congenital midline defect is the result. Cleft lip and cleft palate are examples of such midline defects (see Chapter 8). **Spina bifida** is a congenital midline defect resulting from failure of the bony spinal column to close completely during fetal development. The defect may occur anywhere from the head to the lower end of the spine. Because the spinal column is not closed, the spinal cord (nerve fibers) may protrude, resulting in damage to the nerves and paralysis and/or lack of function or sensation below the site of the defect.

Spina bifida is often accompanied by paralysis of the legs and of the anal and bladder sphincters because nerve impulses are not able to travel past the defect. Surgery to close the spinal opening is performed in early infancy, but this does not repair the nerve damage. Although spina bifida is one of the most common birth defects resulting in physical disability, its causes are not known.

Spinal cord injuries resulting from accidents after birth are also a major cause of paralysis. The basic difference between spina bifida and other spinal cord injuries is that the individual who is injured after birth has gone through a period of normal development and must adjust to an acquired disability.

Educational Implications. The extent of the paralysis resulting from a spinal cord injury depends on how high or low on the spinal column it is. Some children with spinal cord injuries are able to walk independently, some need braces, and others have to use wheelchairs. Lack of sensation and ability to control bodily functions, too, will depend on the nature of the injury. Thus, the implications for education are extremely varied.

Some children will have acute medical problems, which may lead to repeated hospitalizations for surgery or treatment of infections. Lack of sensation in certain areas of the skin may increase the risk of burns, abrasions, and pressure sores. The child may need to be positioned periodically during the school day and monitored carefully during some activities in which there is risk of injury. Because the student has deficiencies in sensation below the defect, he or she may have particular problems in spatial orientation, spatial judgment, sense of direction and distance, organization of motor skills, and body image or body awareness. Lack of bowel and bladder control in some children will require periodic **catheterization.** Many children can be taught to do the procedure known as *clean intermittent catheterization* themselves, but teachers should know what to do or obtain help from the school nurse.

Autism and Other Neurological Disorders Not Causing Paralysis. **Autism** is a relatively rare neurological disorder that typically affects a child's ability to communicate, form social relationships, and perform normally on tests of intelligence and academic achievement (Charlop-Christy, Schreibman, Pierce, & Kurtz, 1997; Farber, 1996; Schopler & Mesibov, 1994, 1995). Most students with autism require intensive intervention in communication, social, and academic skills. However, some individuals with autism are highly talented, intellectually superior, and able to communicate the experience of autism with great clar-

spina bifida. A congenital midline defect resulting from failure of the bony spinal column to close completely during fetal development.

catheterization. The insertion of a tube into the urethra to drain the bladder.

autism. A developmental disability characterized by extreme social withdrawal, cognitive deficits, language disorders, self-stimulation, and onset before the age of thirty months.

ity (see Blondis & Lord, 1996; Grandin, 1995; Sacks, 1995). Children with **Asperger syndrome** show normal language development but are slow in developing motor skills and have impairments in emotional and social development that may be much like those in autism (Blondis & Lord, 1996).

The cause or causes of autism and Asperger syndrome and the exact nature of the neurological problem remain mysteries. Likewise, a variety of other neurological disorders that may affect behavior but not result in muscle weakness or paralysis have causes that are known to be brain related. Yet scientists do not know exactly what happens in the brain to cause the symptoms. **Tourette's syndrome** is an example. The behavioral symptoms of Tourette's—sudden repetitive movements known as *tics*, often accompanied by vocalizations of a socially inappropriate nature—are known to be caused by neurological dysfunction, but the exact nature of that dysfunction is unknown (Heller, Alberto, Forney, & Schwartzman, 1996; Sacks, 1995; Singer, 1996).

Orthopedic and Musculoskeletal Disorders

Some children are physically disabled because of defects or diseases of the muscles or bones. Even though they do not have neurological impairments, their ability to move is affected. Most of the time, muscular and skeletal problems involve the legs, arms, joints, or spine, making it difficult or impossible for the child to walk, stand, sit, or use his or her hands. The problems may be congenital or acquired after birth, and the causes may include genetic defects, infectious diseases, accidents, or developmental disorders.

Two of the most common musculoskeletal conditions affecting children and youths are muscular dystrophy and juvenile rheumatoid arthritis. **Muscular dystrophy** is a hereditary disease that is characterized by progressive weakness caused by degeneration of muscle fibers (Batshaw & Perret, 1986). The exact biological mechanism responsible for muscular dystrophy is not known, nor is there any cure at present. **Juvenile rheumatoid arthritis** is a potentially debilitating disease in which the muscles and joints are affected; the cause and cure are unknown (Bigge, 1991). It can be a very painful condition and is sometimes accompanied by complications such as fever, respiratory problems, heart problems, and eye infections. Among children with other physical disabilities, such as cerebral palsy, arthritis may be a complicating factor that affects the joints and limits movement. These and other conditions can significantly affect a student's social and academic progress at school.

A wide variety of other congenital conditions, acquired defects, and diseases also can affect the musculoskeletal system, such as spinal curvature known as **scoliosis** or missing or malformed limbs (see Bigge, 1991; Heller, Alberto, Forney, & Schwartzman, 1996). In all these conditions, as well as in cases of muscular dystrophy and arthritis, the student's intelligence is unaffected, unless there are additional associated disabilities. Regarding the musculoskeletal problem itself, special education is necessary only to improve the student's mobility, to see that proper posture and positioning are maintained, to provide for education during periods of confinement to hospital or home, and otherwise to make the educational experience as normal as possible.

Asperger syndrome. A developmental disability in which language and cognitive development are normal but the child may show a lag in motor development and impairment in emotional and social development.

Tourette's syndrome. A neurological disorder beginning in childhood (about three times more prevalent in boys than in girls) in which stereotyped motor movements (tics) are accompanied by multiple vocal outbursts that may include grunting or barking noises or socially inappropriate words or statements.

muscular dystrophy. A hereditary disease characterized by progressive weakness caused by degeneration of muscle fibers.

juvenile rheumatoid arthritis. A systemic disease with major symptoms involving the muscles and joints.

scoliosis. An abnormal curvature of the spine

Other Conditions Affecting Health or Physical Ability

In addition to those discussed so far, an extremely wide array of diseases, physiological disorders, congenital malformations, and injuries may affect students' health and physical abilities and create a need for special education and related services. The cataloging of these conditions is not important, but special educators should understand the range of physical disabilities and the types of accommodations that may be necessary to provide an appropriate education and related services.

Congenital malformations and disorders may occur in any organ system, and they may range from minor to fatal flaws in structure or function. In many cases, the cause of the malformation or disorder is not known, but in others it is known to be hereditary or caused by maternal infection or substance use by the mother during pregnancy. For instance, **fetal alcohol syndrome (FAS),** which is now one of the most common syndromes involving malformations and mental retardation, is caused by the mother's use of alcohol during pregnancy.

More children die in accidents each year than are killed by all childhood diseases combined. Millions of children and youths in the United States are seriously injured and disabled temporarily or permanently in accidents each year. Many of those who do not acquire TBI receive spinal cord injuries that result in partial or total paralysis below the site of the injury. Others undergo amputations or are incapacitated temporarily by broken limbs or internal injuries.

Acquired immune deficiency syndrome (AIDS) is often thought to be a disease that merely makes one susceptible to fatal infections. However, children with AIDS often acquire neurological problems as well, including mental retardation, cerebral palsy, seizures, and emotional or behavioral disorders (Rudigier, Crocker, & Cohen, 1990). As children and youths with AIDS live longer due to improved medical treatments, there will be an increasing need for special education and related services. Teachers should be aware that if reasonable procedures are followed for preventing infections, there is no serious concern regarding transmission of HIV (the virus that causes AIDS) in the classroom (Heller, Alberto, Forney, & Schwartzman, 1996; Lerner, Lowenthal, & Egan, 1998; Rudigier et al., 1990).

We have already mentioned fetal alcohol syndrome, which results in disabilities acquired by children of mothers who abuse alcohol during pregnancy. The abuse of other substances by mothers also has negative implications for their children. If the mother is a substance abuser, then there is also a high probability of neglect and abuse by the mother after her baby is born. Many women who are intravenous drug users not only risk chemical damage to their babies but also give them venereal diseases such as syphilis, which can result in disabilities. If the number of substance-abusing mothers increases, then the number of infants and young children with severe and multiple disabilities will increase as well. In spite of the multiple causal factors involved, the prospects of effective early intervention with children exposed prenatally to drugs are much better than previously thought. Although the consequences of any drug use during pregnancy may be serious, the near hysteria of the 1980s about the irreversible effects of crack cocaine on infants was not justified (see Hanson, 1996; Lerner et al., 1998; Lockhart, 1996). True, many children exposed prenatally to drugs will have developmental disabilities. Like the developmental disabilities having other causes, however, those of children exposed before birth to drugs are amenable to modi-

fetal alcohol syndrome (FAS). Abnormalities associated with the mother's using alcohol during pregnancy; defects range from mild to severe, including growth retardation, brain damage, mental retardation, hyperactivity, anomalies of the face, and heart failure; also called *alcohol embryopathy.*

acquired immune deficiency syndrome (AIDS). A virus-caused illness resulting in a breakdown of the immune system; currently, no known cure exists.

fication (Heller, Alberto, Forney, & Schwartzman, 1996; Lerner et al., 1998; Lockhart, 1996).

Children who are medically fragile have special health needs that demand immediate attention to preserve life or to prevent or retard further medical deterioration. Delicate medical conditions may arise from a variety of diseases and disorders, and it is important to make distinctions among students whose conditions are *episodic, chronic,* and *progressive:*

> These students include those with special health needs who are having a temporary medical crisis, those who are consistently fragile, and those whose diseases are progressive in nature and will eventually lead to a fragile state. The concept that must be remembered is that any student with a special health need can be fragile at times, but only a small portion of those who are fragile will remain fragile. (Bigge, 1991, p. 71)

Programs for students who are medically fragile must be particularly flexible and open to revision. Daily health care plans and emergency plans are essential, as are effective lines of communication among all who are involved with the student's treatment, care, and schooling. Decisions regarding placement of these students must be made by a team including health care providers and school personnel as well as the student and his or her parents.

An increasing number of children are returning home from hospitalization able to breathe only with the help of a ventilator (a mechanical device forcing oxygen into the lungs through a tube inserted into the trachea). Many of these children are also returning to public schools, sometimes with the assistance of a full-time nurse. It is debatable as to which conditions are appropriate for children who are dependent on ventilators or other medical technology to attend regular classrooms. Educators and parents together must make decisions in each individual case, weighing medical judgment regarding danger to the child as well as the interest of the child in being integrated into as many typical school activities as possible with his or her peers (see Heller, Alberto, Forney, & Schwartzman, 1996).

Prevention of Physical Disabilities

Although some physical disabilities are not preventable by any available means, many or most are. For instance, failure to wear seat belts and other safety devices accounts for many disabling injuries. Likewise, driving under the influence of alcohol or other drugs, careless storage of drugs and other toxic substances, use of alcohol and other drugs during pregnancy, and a host of unsafe and unhealthful practices that could be avoided cause many disabilities (Hanson, 1996).

Teenage mothers are more likely than older women to give birth to premature or low-birthweight babies, and these babies are at high risk for a variety of psychological and physical problems when they reach school age (McCormick, Brooks-Gunn, Workman-Daniels, Turner, & Peckham, 1992). Thus, preventing adolescent pregnancies would keep many babies from being born with disabilities. Inadequate prenatal care, including maternal infections and inadequate maternal nutrition during pregnancy, also contributes to the number of babies born with disabilities. And for young children, immunization against preventable childhood diseases could lower the number of those who acquire disabilities (Hanson, 1996).

Child abuse is a significant contributing factor in creating physical disabilities in the United States, and its prevention is a critical problem. Many thousands of

Teenage girls are more likely than older women to give birth to premature or low-birthweight babies, who will be at high risk for learning problems when they reach school age.

children, ranging in age from newborns to adolescents, are battered or abused each year. They are beaten, burned, sexually molested, starved, or otherwise neglected or brutalized by their parents, stepparents, or other older persons. The consequences of child abuse may be permanent neurological damage, other internal injuries, skeletal deformity, facial disfigurement, sensory impairment, or death. Psychological problems are an inevitable outcome of abuse. Abuse and neglect by adults is now a leading cause of injury—both physical and psychological—and death among children (Deden, 1993). There is a need for better understanding of the nature and extent of the problems among both the general public and professionals. Education for parenting and child management, including family life education in the public schools, is an obvious need in society. In perhaps as many as 50 percent of cases of serious child mistreatment, the adults responsible for the child's welfare have substance abuse problems (Murphy et al., 1991). Thus, progress in preventing child abuse and neglect may be partly limited by the extent of progress in lowering the prevalence of substance abuse in the United States.

Teachers can play an extremely important role in detecting, reporting, and preventing child abuse and neglect because, next to parents, they are the people who spend the most time with children. If they suspect abuse or neglect, teachers must report it to child protective services under state and local regulations. These vary from one area and state to another, but ordinarily the teacher is required to report suspected cases of child abuse or neglect to a school administrator, law enforcement officer, or social services official. A professional who fails to report child abuse or neglect may be held legally liable.

Children who are already disabled physically, mentally, or emotionally are more at risk for abuse than are nondisabled children (Crosse, Kaye, & Ratnofsky, n.d.; Grayson, 1992). Because children with disabilities are more vulnerable and dependent, abusive adults find them easy targets. The poor social judgment and limited experience of many children with disabilities make them even more vulnerable to sexual abuse. Moreover, some of the characteristics of children with disabilities are sources of additional stress for their caretakers and may be contributing factors in physical abuse—they often require more time, energy, money, and patience than children without disabilities. Parenting any child is stressful; parenting a child with a disability can demand more than some parents are prepared to give. It is not surprising that children with disabilities are disproportionately represented among abused children and that the need for training is particularly great for parents of children with disabilities.

Psychological and Behavioral Characteristics

Academic Achievement

It is impossible to make many valid generalizations about the academic achievement of children with physical disabilities because they vary so widely in the nature and severity of their conditions. The environmental and psychological factors that determine what a child will achieve academically also are extremely varied (Heller, Alberto, & Meagher, 1996).

Many students with physical disabilities have erratic school attendance because of hospitalization, visits to physicians, the requirement of bed rest at home, and so on. Some learn well with ordinary teaching methods; others require special methods because they have mental retardation or sensory impairments in addition to physical disabilities. Because of the frequent interruptions in their schooling, some fall considerably behind their age-mates in academic achievement, even though they have normal intelligence and motivation. The two major effects of a physical disability, especially if it is severe or prolonged, are that a child may be deprived of educationally relevant experiences and that he or she may not be able to learn to manipulate educational materials and respond to educational tasks the way most children do.

Some children with mild or transitory physical problems have no academic deficiencies at all; others have severe difficulties. Some students who have serious and chronic health problems still manage to achieve at a high level. Usually these high-achieving children have high intellectual capacity, strong motivation, and teachers and parents who make every possible special provision for their education. Children with neurological impairments are, as a group, most likely to have intellectual and perceptual deficits and therefore to be behind their age-mates in academic achievement (see Bigge, 1991; Heller, Alberto, Forney, & Schwartzman, 1996).

Personality Characteristics

Research does not support the notion that there is a certain personality type or self-concept associated with any physical disability (Llewellyn & Chung, 1997). Children and youths with physical disabilities are as varied in their psychological characteristics as nondisabled children, and they are apparently responsive to the same factors that influence the psychological development of other children. How children adapt to their physical limitations and how they respond to social-interpersonal situations greatly depends on how parents, siblings, teachers, peers, and the public react to them (Bigge, 1991; Lerner et al., 1998; Heller, Alberto, & Meagher, 1996; Myers, 1996).

Public Reactions. Public attitudes can have a profound influence on how children with physical disabilities see themselves, and on their opportunities for psychological adjustment, education, and employment. If the reaction is one of fear, rejection, or discrimination, they may spend a great deal of energy trying to hide their stigmatizing differences. If the reaction is one of pity and an expectation of helplessness, people with disabilities will tend to behave in a dependent manner. To the extent that other people can see children with physical disabilities as persons who have certain limitations but are otherwise just like everyone else, children and youths with disabilities will be encouraged to become independent and productive members of society (see Powers et al., 1996).

Depending on the age of onset of traumatic brain injury (TBI), personal adjustment problems may be a major concern. Even after recovering, victims may live in fear of injuring themselves again, as is the case with this young boy.

Several factors seem to be causing greater public acceptance of people with physical disabilities. Professional and civic groups encourage support and decrease fear of people who are disabled through information and public education. Government insistence on the elimination of architectural barriers that prevent citizens with disabilities from using public facilities serves to decrease discrimination. Programs to encourage hiring workers with disabilities help the public see those with physical disabilities as constructive, capable people. Laws that protect every child's right to public education bring more individuals into contact with people who have severe or profound disabilities (Biehl, 1996; Cooke, 1996). But there is no doubt that many children with physical disabilities are still rejected, feared, pitied, or discriminated against. The more obvious the physical flaw, the more likely it is that the person will be perceived in negative terms by the public.

Public policy regarding children's physical disabilities has not met the needs of most such children and their families (Baumeister et al., 1990). Particularly, as successful medical treatment prolongs the lives of more and more children with severe, chronic illnesses and other disabilities, issues of who should pay the costs of treatment and maintenance (which are often enormous) and which children and families should receive the limited available resources are becoming critical.

Children's and Families' Reactions. As suggested earlier, children's reactions to their own physical disabilities are largely a reflection of how they have been treated by others. Shame and guilt are learned responses; children will have such negative feelings only if others respond to them by shaming or blaming them (and those like them) for their physical differences. Children will be independent and self-sufficient (within the limits of their physical disabilities), rather than dependent and demanding, only to the extent that they learn how to take care of their own needs. And they will have realistic self-perceptions and set realistic goals for themselves only to the extent that others are honest and clear in appraising their conditions.

However, certain psychological reactions are inevitable for the child with physical disabilities, no matter how he or she is treated. The wish to be nondisabled and participate in the same activities as most children and the fantasy that the disability will disappear are to be expected. With proper management and help, the child can be expected eventually to accept the disability and live a happy life, even though he or she knows the true nature of the condition. Fear and anxiety, too, can be expected. It is natural for children to be afraid when they are separated from their parents, hospitalized, and subjected to medical examinations and procedures that may be painful. In these situations, too, proper management can minimize emotional stress. Psychological trauma is not a necessary effect of hospitalization. The hospital environment may, in fact, be better than the child's home in the case of abused and neglected children.

Other important considerations regarding the psychological effects of a physical disability include the age of the child and the nature of the limitation (e.g., whether it is congenital or acquired, progressive or not). But even these factors are not uniform in their effects. A child with a relatively minor and short-term physical disability may become more maladjusted, anxious, debilitated, and disruptive than another child with a terminal illness because of the way the child's behavior and feelings are managed. Certainly, understanding the child's and the family's feelings about the disability are important. But it is also true that managing the consequences of the child's behavior is a crucial aspect of education and rehabilitation.

The box on page 444 illustrates how family support, school experiences, medical treatment, and public attitudes affect the life of a child with a chronic health problem (diabetes). Besides the school and society at large, the family and its cultural roots are important determinants of how and what children with physical disabilities will learn; thus, it is important to take cultural values into account in teaching children not only about the academic curriculum but about their disability as well (Walker, 1995).

Prosthetics, Orthotics, and Adaptive Devices for Daily Living

Many individuals with physical disabilities use prosthetics, orthotics, and other adaptive devices to help them better function on a daily basis. A **prosthesis** is an artificial replacement for a missing body part (e.g., an artificial hand or leg); an **orthosis** is a device that enhances the partial function of a part of a person's body (a brace or a device that allows a person to do something). **Adaptive devices** for daily living include a variety of adaptations of ordinary items found in the home, office, or school—such as a device to aid bathing or handwashing or walking— that make performing the tasks required for self-care and employment easier for the person who has a physical disability.

prosthesis. A device designed to replace, partially or completely, a part of the body (e.g., artificial teeth or limbs).

orthosis. A device designed to restore, partially or completely, a lost function of the body (e.g., a brace or crutch).

adaptive devices. Special tools that are adaptations of common items to make accomplishing self-care, work, or recreation activities easier for people with physical disabilities.

Overcoming a Health Challenge

Jessie Skinner

I was 3 when I was first diagnosed with diabetes. My Mom gave me my shots until I was 8. The first few times I gave myself shots, it was scary! It got easier as I got older. I went to camp and everyone else was doing their own shots, so I decided to start doing it myself.

My diabetes is hard to control. I remember being in the hospital when I was in seventh grade because my blood sugar was high. Close to the end of seventh grade I changed doctors because I didn't feel comfortable adjusting my own insulin. My new doctor was really nice when my Mom was in the room; she'd always compliment me. But when my Mom left the room, she'd tell me, "You'd better start taking your insulin!" I'd tell her, "I *am* taking my insulin!" I never really felt that she believed me. Once when I was in the hospital, the same thing happened—my blood sugar was really high, but *they* were doing my shots for me. From that point on, she believed that I was doing my shots on a regular basis.

Once my doctor started believing me, we got closer and I could talk to her better. I wasn't afraid to tell her that I forgot my insulin on a day. Now she wants me to write some things down to help other kids with hard-to-control diabetes. One suggestion is for kids to always tell the truth about skipping their insulin. I learned that the hard way. One day I was mad at my Mom and I skipped my insulin, thinking that I was going to hurt her. The only one I hurt was myself. I got really sick and ended up in the hospital. Then I had to tell the truth.

If your doctors say that you're skipping your insulin and you're not, keep telling them that you aren't—sooner or later, they'll listen! Also, try to be involved in the decisions about your insulin. They tried to get me to four shots a day, but I told them I only wanted to do three. I would rather do the regular shots less often and the booster shots more often.

I think it's important for kids to learn to take care of their medical issues because it makes you more responsible and it helps you to better understand what you have. If you need help, don't be afraid to ask. For me, if my blood sugar is really high, my vision isn't very good. It's good to take a break once in a while and let someone else do the shot, to make sure it's the right dosage. I'll sometimes ask the nurse at school for help.

Another suggestion I have is in dealing with adults who don't understand. My softball coach found out that I had diabetes. This changed my relationship with her a whole lot. The positions that I was good at she no longer let me play. She put me in right field where no balls ever come. I think she was scared and didn't know anything about diabetes. I ended up talking to her and asking her what her problem was. Her response was, "Your diabetes." I asked her why she was holding me back, because it was something that I couldn't help. She told me that she didn't realize that she was treating me any differently than the other kids. Talking with her turned our relationship around. Now we're best friends. We even go skiing together! And now I play all the positions on my softball team.

When kids feel that they're being treated differently, I suggest they talk to the person and ask what's bothering him or her. Don't give up! I didn't, even though I wanted to give up. I now feel good that I didn't. I was so nervous when I approached my coach, because I thought she was going to kick me off the team. I'm afraid to tell other people that I have diabetes because I'm afraid they'll treat me differently. Even though I have a good relationship with my coach now, I still wonder if she looks at me differently.

Health professionals need to be honest with teens. For example, they need to help teens schedule their medications based on their own personal lifestyles. If a teen is a late sleeper on weekends, let her take her medications later on Friday evening, so she can sleep late the next day. Another suggestion is to believe in your patient. Help build a relationship with the person you're treating. If possible, provide a mentor for the teenager who had similar problems when she was her age, because it helps kids realize they're not the only ones who are going through problems.

Employers need to recognize people as individuals. If you find that an employee has a health challenge, DON'T treat him any differently than you would if he didn't have the challenge! My boss recently found out that I have diabetes. Since then, he's been driving me crazy by calling me to the front of the store every half hour to ask me if I'm feeling okay. If kids learn to be responsible for their medical care and other people listen to and respect what kids say they need and don't need, managing a health challenge will be a lot easier for everyone.

Source: Powers, L. E., Singer, G. H. S., & Sowers, J. (Eds.). (1996). *On the road to autonomy: Promoting self-competence in children and youth with disabilities.* Baltimore: Paul H. Brookes, pp. 255–256. Reprinted with permission.

The most important principles to keep in mind are use of residual function, simplicity, and reliability. For example, the muscles of the arm, shoulder, or back operate an artificial hand. This may be too complicated or demanding for an infant or young child with a missing or deformed upper limb. Depending on the child's age, the length and function of the amputated limb, and the child's other abilities, a passive "mitt" or a variety of other prosthetic devices might be more helpful (Gover & McIvor, 1992). Choice of the most useful prosthesis will depend on careful evaluation of each individual's needs. A person without legs may be taught to use his or her arms to move about in a wheelchair, or to use his or her torso and arms to get about on artificial legs (perhaps using crutches or a cane in addition). Again, each individual's abilities and preferences must be evaluated in designing the prosthesis (see Heller, Alberto, Forney, & Schwartzman, 1996).

Two points regarding prosthetics, orthotics, and residual function must be kept in mind:

1. Residual function is often important even when a prosthesis, orthosis, or adaptive device is not used. For example, it may be crucial for the child with cerebral palsy or muscular dystrophy to learn to use the affected limbs as well as possible without the aid of any special equipment because using residual function alone will make the child more independent and may help prevent or retard physical deterioration. Moreover, it is often more efficient for a person to learn not to rely completely on a prosthesis or orthosis, as long as he or she can accomplish a task without it.

2. Spectacular technological developments often have very limited meaning for the immediate needs of the majority of individuals with physical disabilities. It may be years before expensive experimental equipment is tested adequately and marketed at a cost most people can afford, and a given device may be applicable only to a small group of individuals with an extremely rare condition (Moore, 1985). Even though the device described in the box on page 476 has given Stephanie Hergert greater ability to participate in ordinary childhood activities, the current cost of such devices is clearly a barrier to their common use. Thus, for a long time to come, common standby prostheses, orthoses, and other equipment adapted to the needs of individuals will be the most practical devices.

We do not mean to downplay the importance of technological advances for people with physical disabilities. Advances in computer technology and applications have provided extraordinary help for many students with disabilities (DeFord, 1998). Our point here is that the greatest significance of a

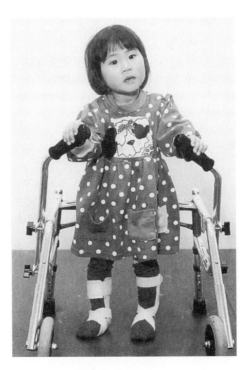

Examples of thermoform leg braces. The braces are molded to fit the contour of the wearer's leg and hold the knee, ankle, and/or foot in a more correct or acceptable position. The orthoses are lighter in weight, more functional, and cosmetically more acceptable than older-style braces and can be worn with a variety of footwear.

Taking Big Steps

Stephanie Hergert, a talkative 7-year-old, was fitted with her first orthotic device at age 18 months. Born with spina bifida, she is paralyzed from the rib cage down.

Stephanie uses a wheelchair at the Coronado elementary school she attends, but at home she uses an orthotic device designed by Saxton, an owner of Southern California Orthotics and Prosthetics (SCOPe), which has five patient-care centers in San Diego County. Saxton said he created the device by combining an Orlau Swivel Walker and a Rochester Parapodium. The parapodium holds Stephanie upright in a rigid, stable frame, and the base of the frame is mounted on swiveling foot plates.

By leaning forward and swinging her arms, Stephanie can move forward, Saxton explained. By leaning backward and swinging her arms, she can move backward. "Five years ago, someone like Stephanie would not have had the opportunity to stand upright," said Stephanie's mother, Robin Hergert.

Indeed, the fact that her daughter can stand, let alone move with the aid of a brace, is more than Hergert ever expected.

"When she was born, the picture was grim," Hergert said. Doctors were very discouraging.

However, she said therapists and orthotists "gave us more hope."

Though the technology is available to custom-design devices such as Stephanie's, the cost to fund such devices is quite another matter.

Stephanie's brace cost close to $7,000. And Saxton said neither the state nor most managed health organizations cover the cost of high-technology devices, only basic or prefabricated devices.

Source: Sharon F. Griffin, "Taking big steps," *The San Diego Union-Tribune,* February 13, 1994, pp. D–1, D–2. Reprinted with permission.

technological advance often lies in how it changes seemingly ordinary items or problems. For example, technological advances in metallurgy and plastics have led to the design of much more functional braces and wheelchairs. The heavy metal-and-leather leg braces formerly used by many children with cerebral palsy or other neurological disorders—cumbersome, difficult to apply, and not very helpful in preventing deformity or improving function—have been largely supplanted by braces constructed of thermoform plastic. Wheelchairs are being built of lightweight metals and plastics and redesigned to allow users to go places inaccessible to the typical wheelchair (see Figure 11.1). And an increasing number of computerized devices are improving the movement and communication abilities of people with disabilities.

Figure 11.1

Rehabilitation engineers are redesigning wheelchairs for use in off-the-street recreational and work environments: (a) chairs suitable for use at the beach or in other soft terrain; (b) a chair specially designed for racing.

(a)

(b)

The greatest problem today is not devising new or more sophisticated assistive technology but rather accurately evaluating children and youths to determine what would be most useful and then making that technology available. As Lynne Anderson-Inman has noted, "The potential for using technology is way beyond what's used in most schools" (quoted in DeFord, 1998, p. 30). Many children and youths who need prostheses or other assistive devices, such as computers, special vehicles, and self-help aids, are not carefully evaluated and provided with the most appropriate equipment (Heller, Alberto, Forney, & Schwartzman, 1996; Parette & VanBiervliet, 1991).

Educational Considerations

Too often, we think of people who have physical disabilities as being helpless or unable to learn. It is easy to lower our expectations for them because we know that they are indeed unable to do some things. We forget, though, that many people with physical disabilities can learn to do many or all the things most nondisabled persons do, although sometimes they must perform these tasks in different ways (e.g., a person who does not have the use of the hands may have to use the feet or mouth). Accepting the limitations imposed by physical disabilities without trying to see how much people can learn or how the environment can be changed to allow them to respond more effectively is an insulting and dehumanizing way of responding to physical differences.

Educating students with physical disabilities is not so much a matter of special instruction for children with disabilities as it is of educating the nondisabled population. People with physical disabilities solve many of their own problems, but their lives are often needlessly complicated because the nondisabled give no thought to what life is like for someone with specific physical limitations. Design adaptations in buildings, furniture, household appliances, and clothing can make it possible for someone with a physical disability to function as efficiently as a nondisabled person in a home, school, or community.

The objectives of educators and other professionals who work with children and youths with physical disabilities should include autonomy and self-advocacy (Powers, Singer, & Sowers, 1996). Children with physical disabilities typically want to be self-sufficient, and they should be encouraged and taught the skills needed to take care of themselves to the maximum extent possible. This requires knowledge of the physical limitations created by the disability and sensitivity to the child's social and academic needs and perceptions—understanding of the environmental and psychological factors that affect classroom performance and behavior. The box on page 448 illustrates how adaptations can be made in the classroom to accommodate the needs of a student with a chronic health impairment in ways that encourage achievement, self-advocacy, and psychological growth.

Individualized Planning

Students with complex physical disabilities typically require a wide array of related services as well as special education. The IEPs (individualized education programs) for such students tend to be particularly specific and detailed. The instructional goals and objectives often include seemingly minute steps, especially

Accommodations and Self-Advocacy in the Classroom

Tonya is 8 years old and has juvenile rheumatoid arthritis. The primary environmental factor affecting her performance is pain and the primary psychological factor affecting performance is self-advocacy. Due to her condition, Tonya is unable to sit for long periods of time without experiencing pain upon getting up from her chair to go to another class. Tonya would try to hide the fact that she was in pain and minimize her arm movement, which only worsened the condition. Her lack of participation in writing, art, and activities requiring arm movement was erroneously attributed to a motivational problem. The staff was given an inservice as to her condition; upon identifying she was in pain, a specific pain management plan was written. In the plan are given activities that she is to engage in at regular intervals that encourage her to use her affected joints, such as helping to get materials, passing papers out in class, and sharpening pencils. This is programmed in such a way so that she is not singled out, but other students are performing the same tasks. If she is in pain, she is to move a special item to the corner of her desk. Tonya prefers this method to decrease drawing attention to herself. After Tonya signals the teacher with the special item, the teacher comes over and the treatment plan is followed. A specific time has been arranged for teaching Tonya any missed material. In the area of self-advocacy, a teacher certified in orthopedic impairments spends time with Tonya role playing situations to assist her in explaining her condition and her needs to significant others.

Source: Heller, K. W., Alberto, P. A., & Meagher, T. M. (1996). The impact of physical impairments on academic performance. *Journal of Developmental and Physical Disabilities, 8,* p. 243.

for young children with severe disabilities (see Hanson, 1996; Heller, Alberto, Forney, & Schwartzman, 1996; Lerner et al., 1998). Many of the children under the age of three years who need special education and related services are children with physical disabilities. These children are required by law to have an **individualized family service plan (IFSP)** rather than an IEP. These plans must specify how the family will be involved in intervention as well as what other services will be provided.

Educational Placement

Children with physical disabilities may be educated in any one of several settings, depending on the type and severity of the condition, the services available in the community, and the medical prognosis for the condition. If such children ordinarily attend regular public school classes but must be hospitalized for more than a few days, they may be included in a class in the hospital itself. If they must be confined to their homes for a time, a visiting or homebound teacher may provide tutoring until they can return to regular classes. In these cases—which usually involve children who have been in accidents or who have conditions that are not permanently and severely disabling—relatively minor, commonsense adjustments are required to continue the children's education and keep them from falling behind their classmates. At the other extreme—usually involving serious or permanent disabilities—the child may be taught for a time in a hospital school or a special public school class designed specifically for children with physical disabilities. Today, most are being integrated into the public schools because of advances in medical treatment: new developments in bioengineering, allowing them greater mobility and functional movement; decreases in or removal of ar-

individualized family service plan (IFSP). A plan for services for young children with disabilities (under three years of age) and their families; drawn up by professionals and parents; similar to an IEP for older children; mandated by PL 99–457.

chitectural barriers and transportation problems; and the movement toward public education for all children (Bigge, 1991; Hanson, 1996; Heller, Alberto, Forney, & Schwartzman, 1996; Lerner et al., 1998).

Educational Goals and Curricula

It is not possible to prescribe educational goals and curricula for children with physical disabilities as a group because their individual limitations vary so greatly. Even among children with the same condition, goals and curricula must be determined after assessing each child's intellectual, physical, sensory, and emotional characteristics. A physical disability, especially a severe and chronic one that limits mobility, may have two implications for education: (1) the child may be deprived of experiences that nondisabled children have, and (2) the child may find it impossible to manipulate educational materials and respond to educational tasks the way most children do. For example, a child with severe cerebral palsy cannot take part in most outdoor play activities and travel experiences and may not be able to hold and turn pages in books, write, explore objects manually, or use a typewriter without special equipment.

For children with an impairment that is only physical, curriculum and educational goals should ordinarily be the same as for nondisabled children: reading, writing, arithmetic, and experiences designed to familiarize them with the world about them. In addition, special instruction may be needed in mobility skills, daily living skills, and occupational skills. That is, because of their physical impairments, these children may need special, individualized instruction in the use of mechanical devices that will help them perform tasks that are much simpler for those without disabilities. For children with other disabilities in addition to physical limitations, curricula will need to be further adapted (Hanson, 1996; Heller, Alberto, Forney, & Schwartzman, 1996).

Educational goals for students with severe or profound disabilities must be related to their functioning in everyday community environments. Only recently have educators begun to address the problems of analyzing community tasks (e.g., crossing streets, using money, riding public transportation, greeting neighbors) and planning efficient instruction for individuals with severe disabilities. Efficient instruction in such skills requires that teaching occur in the community environment itself.

The range of educational objectives and curricula for children with physical disabilities is often extended beyond the objectives and curricula typically provided for other students in school. For example, very young children and those with severe neuromuscular problems may need objectives and curricula focusing on the most basic self-care skills (e.g., swallowing, chewing, self-feeding). Older students may need not only to explore possible careers in the way all students should, but to consider the special accommodations their physical limitations demand for successful performance as well.

Although all students may profit from a discussion of death and dying, education about these topics may be particularly important in classrooms in which a student has a terminal illness. Teachers should be direct and open in their discussion of death and dying. Death should not be a taboo subject, nor should teachers deny their own feelings or squelch the feelings of others. Confronted with the task of educating a child or youth with a terminal illness, teachers should seek available resources and turn to professionals in other disciplines for help (Heller, Alberto, Forney, & Schwartzman, 1996).

Albertson, NY: Sixteen-year-old **David Womack** is in the ninth grade at an academic day school for students with severe physical disabilities. He has been dependent on a ventilator since a spinal cord injury nine years ago. A collaborative team of teachers and therapists work closely with David and his parents, Brenda and David Womack, Sr., to maximize his independence through technology.

On the second day of second grade, seven-year-old David Womack was hit by a car as he stepped from the school bus in front of his home. The accident injured David's spinal cord, leaving him a quadriplegic, with no movement below his neck and no ability for spontaneous respiration.

During David's two-year rehabilitation in a Baltimore hospital, his father, David Womack, Sr., traveled four hours every other weekend to be with his son and his wife, Brenda, who rented a nearby apartment. Their twelve-year-old daughter stayed behind with her grandmother in the Long Island community that rallied in support to raise funds for a home computer system for David and to help his family buy and renovate an accessible home.

Upon David's release from the hospital, his parents and educators from their school district made the decision to enroll nine-year-old David in Henry Viscardi School, a special day school for students with intense medical and physical needs. Unlike most schools, Viscardi is equipped with a large medical and therapeutic staff. Nurses as well as physical and occupational therapists team with teachers, so that students benefit from closely monitored physical and instructional management.

In 1989, David was the first student dependent on a ventilator to attend the school. He made his third-grade entrance in a large electronic "sip-and-puff" wheelchair, directed by airflow he provided through a strawlike mouthpiece. "The vent," as this life-support system is also called, was mounted on the back of his chair and detected by its rhythmic sound. Never more than several feet away was a private-duty nurse, who monitored him at all times. "It was so scary," recalls Brenda Womack. "I could tell everybody was nervous."

The school's task included helping all the Womacks adjust to a different life and stimulating David to discover his new potential. Before the first day of school, staff occupational therapist Ginette Howard worked closely with David to ready him for classroom technology, as well as with his teachers, all of whom were certified in both special and general education. Even though the staff was experienced in dealing with difficult physical issues, David presented a challenge, and the presence of the ventilator, necessary equipment, and private nurse emphasized his fragility. Says Ginette, "Before long, we realized we had to raise everybody's expectations and start treating David like a student instead of a patient!"

David's progress has been built slowly but steadily on a foundation of trust, and his achievements are the result of both sophisticated instructional technology and effective collaboration among teachers, therapists, nurses, and his home community. It was the school's team approach to technology that supported David's classroom learning. Ginette Howard and computer teacher Maryann Cicchillo combined their knowledge of instructional software and sophisticated electronics to provide David with the tools to read, write, and compute. Classroom teachers followed their lead, and so did his nurse, Gail Nolan, who was committed to his academic and social growth.

Links with Other Disciplines

In the opening pages of this chapter we made two points: (1) children with physical disabilities have medical problems, and (2) interdisciplinary cooperation is necessary in their education. It is important for the teacher to know what other disciplines are involved in the child's care and treatment and to be able to com-

"The first year, we needed to overcome fear and develop trust," recalls Ginette Howard. David was frightened to leave the hospital, so the first task was to secure his ventilator equipment for school mobility and classroom use. "We made sure there was a plastic casing over the dials since he was afraid someone might play with the settings," Ginette explains. The second year, David became more confident and was willing to try out new pieces of educational technology. Over six years, Ginette and Maryann have seen David progress from being withdrawn and fearful, to trusting, to finally developing real interest in computer applications. Providing him with computer access has been the challenge.

"David has chin supports to keep his head erect, and he can move his mouth," says Ginette. She and Maryann selected a small alternative-access keyboard, worked by an electronic mouthstick called a *wand*. With much effort, David would clench the mouthstick in his teeth and gently tap the attached wand on the miniature impulse-sensitive keyboard set on a height-adjustable table in front of him. The classroom computer would directly respond, and Maryann ensured that appropriate software was available to David's teacher through the school's network. Very gradually, David became accustomed to the awkwardness of the mouthstick and to the expectation that he was independently responsible for his schoolwork. As Ginette remembers, "David is extremely artistic, and he increased his facility by using adapted paintbrushes. By his second and third year, I was making mouthsticks like you wouldn't believe!"

Now in ninth grade, David no longer needs the adapted access of the miniature system, since he has developed greater facial mobility. Having used mouthsticks for numerous functional tasks, he has the flexibility and range of motion to use one with an angled standard keyboard. "My goal for David is for him to become an independent thinker via technology," says his science teacher, Dorothy Vann. "This direct keyboard access gives him much more freedom in class."

Since David tires easily, he uses a word-prediction and abbreviation/expansion program to reduce the number of keystrokes and increase his speed in writing assignments. He also has started to use a laptop computer with a trackball, further challenging his accuracy and increasing his speed. David's technology sessions have been used to increase his independence as a student. "I can't tell you how many times we've explored technology to support homework assignments, to take tests, or complete a paper," says Maryann. "Last year, we used the word-prediction and abbreviation/expansion program to write formal letters," recalls Ginette Howard. "David learned to program the abbreviations for salutations and common phrases, such as 'DS' for 'Dear Sir,' or 'YT' for 'Yours Truly.' When he keyed in the abbreviations, the phrases would appear."

"Science is my favorite subject," says David, now a quiet young man who speaks in a soft, breathy voice. Dorothy Vann's science lab is fully accessible to him, with adjustable tables and low sinks; it is also equipped with instructional technology that David needs to fully participate. In biology, he views slides through a stereo microscope, which utilizes a small attached video camera to project images onto a TV monitor. "I knew David was capable of doing more than he initially showed us," says Dorothy. "Now he uses the video microscope in labs, and in the future, he will use the computerized video laser disc player for independent research on science topics."

Working with David has been an evolving process for each of the collaborators. "When some teachers see and hear that ventilator, their tendency is to pamper the child," observes Brenda Womack. "But I have a sixteen-year-old son and I want him treated like any other student."

In reflecting on their work with David, Ginette Howard and Maryann Cicchillo think there is a breaking-in period, in which teachers and the child who is newly ventilator dependent have to overcome their fears. Says Dorothy Vann, "It also takes a while for the child to accept goals for achievement and believe in his or her own success."

—By Jean Crockett

municate with professionals in these areas about the child's physical, emotional, and educational development.

It goes almost without saying that knowing the child's medical status is crucial. Many children with physical disabilities will need the services of a physical therapist and/or occupational therapist. Both can give valuable suggestions about helping the child use his or her physical abilities to the greatest possible extent,

Collaboration key to success

Jo Dillenbeck is a special education teacher in New York City; B.S., Special Education/Elementary, Long Island University, C. W. Post Campus, Long Island, New York; M.S., Special Education, Adelphi University, Long Island, New York. **Charlotte Norris** is a regular education teacher in New York City; B.A., Journalism, New York University, New York, New York; M.S., Early Childhood Education, Queens College, Queens, New York.

Jo Dillenbeck

Jo The kids in my class were five and six years old. There were ten in all: four had cerebral palsy and one had spina bifida. There were language needs that emerged with their reading, and they had some emotional and learning issues as well, but they were certainly ambulatory. In terms of their gross motor development, they were all age appropriate. They really enjoyed experiential learning and were especially engaged when we used manipulatives and brought real-life experiences into the classroom, or brought them out of the classroom into their neighborhoods or environments. Basically, I didn't have a lot of behavioral problems.

Charlotte I had ten boys and eighteen girls, all roughly kindergarten age, so they matched up pretty well with Jo's group. My kids were a very mixed group in terms of their academic level. I had children who were new to school and had never been in any kind of school setting, which was certainly a challenge. This was actually a good mix because the students who were at a somewhat higher level were able to help out a lot with the students who were at lower levels, especially in group learning situations.

Jo One very successful collaboration experience that Charlotte and I have had was with a student named Sunita. She's a good example because she was a real

median, right there in the middle as far as capability goes. She had spina bifida, so she wasn't ambulatory, but she could scamper around the floor like you wouldn't believe. She was a very high-spirited kid. Whenever it was her turn to be calendar monitor, I would ask if she wanted to do it from the chair or if she wanted to sit on my lap, and she wanted no part of that: She just really wanted me to get away from the calendar so she could run the show! We would have parents come and observe the class, and I'd bet that some of the kids that are in that class this year are there because the parents just fell in love with Sunita.

Charlotte Sunita was so alive, so bright, so friendly, so vivacious—you couldn't help but want to know her. I think it was very easy for my students to relate to her because she so easily related to them. Sunita could talk, she could say what she was thinking, and she could write or draw what she was thinking with ease. I think that my children could see that even though she may not have been able to walk or run like them, she could do so much *like* them.

Jo Sunita's verbal skills were really superior, even to those of the other children. I think that the hands-on kinds of activities we were doing, especially in science and music, were good for Sunita and all the children in that setting. The differences were not so apparent. We

combined the children into two groups, A and B. Each group was made up of half my children and half of Jo's children. We'd occasionally put the two groups together—for instance, when we went to the fish store or on an exploration out in the schoolyard. I became an expert in a certain content area. I taught it to two groups and Charlotte did the same.

Charlotte Our classes are scheduled for music together because of our collaboration. We had a music teacher come in who taught music to both classes as a large group; however, Jo and I did stay in the classroom to facilitate management needs because it was such a large group for one teacher to handle. In fact, we had to teach the music teacher some management ideas. It was a little overwhelming for someone to come in here with a new teacher and to be faced with thirty-eight children with such a diverse range of skills and abilities and actual needs. The music teacher selected a song and said, "Okay, now we're going to interpret it by wiggling our bodies on the floor." Jo and I looked at each other as if to say, "Oh, no!" She didn't think about the special needs, so it really pointed out that you need to consider how everyone can share and participate in particular activities.

Jo The music teacher wasn't used to David, for instance, who has spastic

Charlotte Norris

quadriplegia. Her affect was a little inappropriate; when he was participating in the song, she overpraised him. Singing is one of his strengths, and I wasn't surprised at all that he could stay on key and that he could get involved. We wanted to be delicate and kind with her, yet let her know that David is one of us. He's one of the guys!

Charlotte It was a good experience for her; she was able to see how you can work with a range and variety of children. It's important to find someone who has a similar philosophy and treats children the way you do, but it also must be someone you can get along with, who has the same tolerance that you do. Had we not been friendly, liked each other, and respected the way each other did things, we would not have been successful. We have seen collaborations that were not as successful as ours because they did not develop out of commonalities.

Jo One of the most demanding things about our collaboration was keeping up with the kids, keeping them on pace, and trying to make it valuable for them educationally. As much as I want this very worthwhile social experience for my special-needs kids, am I giving them the multisensory nuts-and-bolts special education that they need? I constantly have to try and strike a balance between the social needs of the children and the intense requirements of their special needs.

Charlotte The most demanding thing about our collaboration was not working together ourselves, but effectively meeting the needs of the children. That's really the most demanding thing: living up to them. When you're in your own classroom, working in isolation, if something doesn't happen, only you really know about it. But when you work with someone else in collaboration, that forces you to keep your end of the bargain at all times. That's demanding but wonderful.

Jo The rewarding part of our collaboration is that our kids, disabled or not, see one another as comrades, as peers. They know one another on the playground. They seek each other out on the playground. I really feel good about my teaching. I feel as though I am this superb professional. I feel that I can learn something new every day right in the classroom, that I really have my own hands-on laboratory with a very, very fine teacher. It keeps me engaged. Yes, it's hard work, but the personal and professional rewards are really there constantly, and they're immeasurable.

Charlotte I'm going to sound like Jo, but it's true: The most rewarding thing about our work together is hearing my children call those children by name in the lunchroom and seeing them wave to one another at the tables.

Jo I have to talk about what Erica's mother said! (Erica's one of Charlotte's kids.) She was just so thrilled with this collaboration process, and she said, "I'm so happy that Charlotte's her teacher because I really think she has gotten the best in a teacher in a teaching situation. But what's *most* important to me is I overheard her talking to her two-year-old sister the other day. Erica was writing her name and playing with sentences and her sister was trying to do the very same thing. So Erica went over to her sister and said, 'Oh, I see you're making your very best zero. I'm so proud of you.'" Erica's mother continued, "That didn't come from me. That didn't sound like me. I know that came from the school. And to me, that's as important as how she's going to succeed in math and writing and academics. Erica's really a good person. I really have to give credit to the program, to what you two did." It made my heart stop. I was really just so thrilled.

Charlotte I see what we've learned about people carry over in our classroom from year to year. The sensitivity to others, that people are different, and that we do all learn to read differently, to write differently. What's easy for one is hard for another and vice versa. In fact, I had that conversation with them today. Somebody said the math group was just too easy, and you know, we really had to talk about that—that at the same time it was hard for others and that although we're so similar, in some things we're not.

Jo I remember when they weren't understanding the directions, for instance. When Charlotte's kids were off and about and involved in the project, they needed a little bit of coaching. We worked in groups of four so children would be partners or would have to work with three other kids. The demands were to keep children's behaviors appropriate to what the group was doing, not to splash the water around, for instance. We had some younger kids—not in age so much as developmentally. They sometimes acted inappropriately with the materials, and we had to kind of teach them what to do. The kids in Charlotte's class have learned to use the right words—instead of saying, "Don't do this," they say, "Well, let's try this." "How about if we do this?" When you remember how little these kids are—five and six years old—that is really remarkable.

> **You need to consider how *everyone* can share and participate in special activities.**

Prosthetic devices have broadened the range of activities possible for individuals who have lost limbs.

continuing therapeutic management in the classroom, and encouraging independence and good work habits. The teacher should be particularly concerned about how to handle and position the child so that the risk of further physical disability will be minimized and independent movement and manipulation of educational materials can be most efficiently learned.

Specialists in prosthetics and orthotics design and build artificial limbs, braces, and other devices that help individuals who are physically disabled function more conventionally. By conferring with such specialists, the teacher will get a better grasp of the function and operation of a child's prosthesis or orthosis and understand what the child can and cannot be expected to do.

Social workers and psychologists are the professionals with whom most teachers are quite familiar. Cooperation with them may be particularly important in the case of a child with a physical disability. Work with the child's family and community agencies is often necessary to prevent lapses in treatment. The child may also be particularly susceptible to psychological stress, so the school psychologist may need to be consulted to obtain an accurate assessment of intellectual potential.

Speech-language therapists are often called on to work with children with physical disabilities, especially those with cerebral palsy. The teacher will want advice from the speech-language therapist on how to maximize the child's learning of speech and language.

Individuals of all ages need access to play and recreation, regardless of their physical abilities. Any adequate program for children or youths with physical disabilities will provide toys, games, and physical exercise to stimulate, amuse, and teach recreation skills and provide the youngster with options for productive leisure (Murphey, 1996). Physical education that is adapted to the abilities and disabilities of students is an important part of every sound school program.

Early Intervention

All who work with young children with physical disabilities have two concerns: (1) early identification and intervention, and (2) development of communication (see Hanson, 1996). Identifying signs of developmental delay so intervention can begin as early as possible is important in preventing further disabilities that can result from lack of teaching and proper care. Early intervention is also important for maximizing the outcome of therapy. Communication skills are difficult for some children with physical disabilities to learn, and they are one of the critical objectives of any preschool program (see Chapter 8). For young children with TBI, the ultimate level of functioning they are able to attain is very difficult to predict, and appropriate early intervention is critical (Savage & Mishkin, 1994).

Probably the first and most pervasive concerns of teachers of young children with physical disabilities, in addition to communication, should be handling and positioning. Handling refers to how the child is picked up, carried, held, and assisted; positioning refers to providing support for the child's body and arranging instructional or play materials in certain ways. Proper handling makes the child more comfortable and receptive to education. Proper positioning maximizes physical efficiency and ability to manipulate materials; it also inhibits undesirable motor responses while promoting desired growth and motor patterns (Bigge, 1991; Heller, Alberto, Forney, & Schwartzman, 1996; Kurtz et al., 1996).

What constitutes proper positioning for one child may not be appropriate for another. It is important that teachers of children who are physically disabled be aware of some general principles of positioning and handling; in addition, they must work closely with physical therapists and physicians so that each child's particular needs are met. The physical problems that most often require special handling and positioning involve muscle tone. Some children have **spastic** muscles—that is, chronic increased muscle tone. As a result, their limbs may be either flexed or extended all the time. If nothing is done to counteract the effects of the chronic imbalance of muscle tone, the child develops **contractures,** permanent shortening of muscles and connective tissues that results in deformity and further disability. Other children have *athetosis,* or fluctuating muscle tone, that results in almost constant uncontrolled movement. If these movements are not somehow restrained, the child cannot accomplish many motor tasks successfully. Still other children have muscles that are **hypotonic.** These children appear floppy, as their muscles are flaccid and weak. The hypotonia may prevent them from learning to hold up their heads or to sit or stand. All these muscle tone problems can occur together in the same child, they can occur with varying degrees of severity, and they can affect various parts of the body differently.

The teacher of young children with physical disabilities must know how to teach gross motor responses—such as head control, rolling over, sitting, standing, and walking—and understand how abnormal reflexes that may be a part of developmental disabilities may interfere with learning basic motor skills. If the child has severe neurological and motor impairments, the teacher may need to begin by focusing on teaching the child to eat (e.g., how to chew and swallow) and to make the oral movements required for speech (Hanson, 1996; Heller, Alberto, Forney, & Schwartzman, 1996). Fine motor skills, such as pointing, reaching, grasping, and releasing, may be critically important. These

spastic. A term describing a sudden, involuntary contraction of muscles that makes accurate, voluntary movement difficult.

contractures. Permanent shortenings of muscles and connective tissues and consequent distortion of bones and/or posture because of neurological damage.

hypotonic. A term describing low muscle tone that sometimes occurs as a result of cerebral palsy.

Children with physical disabilities need to engage in healthful physical activities from an early age as much if not more than anyone else.

motor skills are best taught in the context of daily lessons that involve self-help and communication. That is, motor skills should not be taught in isolation but as part of daily living and learning activities that will increase the child's communication, independence, creativity, motivation, and future learning.

Motor and communication skills necessary for daily living are not the only areas in which the teacher must provide instruction. Learning social responsiveness, appropriate social initiation, how to play with others, and problem solving, for example, are important goals for which the teacher must develop instructional strategies. Some children who are well beyond the typical preschooler's age may still be functioning at a very early developmental level. Consequently, the muscle tone, posture, and movement problems discussed here (as well as the approach to teaching just described) apply to some older students too.

Transition

Transition involves a turning point, a change from one situation or environment to another. When special educators speak of transition, they typically refer to change from school to work or from adolescence to adulthood. For children with physical disabilities, however, transition is perhaps a more pervasive concern than it is for children with other disabilities. It may involve discharge from intensive care or transition from hospital to home at any age. Neisworth and Fewell (1989) note that "in an era of increasingly sophisticated medical technology, transition begins for some families at or shortly after the birth of a child" (p. xi). Nevertheless, we focus here on the transition concerns of adolescents and young adults with physical disabilities.

Two areas of concern for transition stand out clearly for adolescents and young adults with physical disabilities: careers and sociosexuality. Adolescents begin contemplating and experimenting with jobs, social relations, and sexuality in direct and serious ways. For the adolescent with a physical disability, these questions and trial behaviors are often especially perplexing, not just to themselves but to their families as well: Can I get and hold a satisfying job? Can I become independent? Will I have close and lasting friendships? Will anyone find me physically attractive? How can I gratify my sexual needs? Ordinary adolescents have a hard time coming to grips with these questions and the developmental tasks they imply; adolescents with physical disabilities often have an even harder time.

As we pointed out in discussing psychological characteristics, there is no formula for predicting the emotional or behavioral problems a person with a given physical disability will have. Much depends on the management and training the person has received. So it is particularly important to provide both career education and sociosexual education for students with physical disabilities.

Choosing a Career

For the adolescent or young adult with physical disabilities, career considerations are extremely important (Condeluci, 1994; Johnson, 1996; Ward, 1996). In working out an occupational goal, it is vital to realistically appraise the individual's specific abilities and disabilities and to assess motivation carefully. Postsecondary education must be considered in light of the individual's interests, strengths, demands, and accessibility (Norlund, 1994). Some disabilities clearly rule out certain occupational choices. With other disabilities, high motivation and full use of residual function may make it possible to achieve unusual professional status.

One of the greatest problems in dealing with adolescents who have physical disabilities is helping them attain a realistic employment outlook. Intelligence, emotional characteristics, motivation, and work habits must be assessed at least as carefully as physical limitations. Furthermore, the availability of jobs and the demands of certain occupations must be taken into account. The child who has moderate mental retardation and severe spastic quadriplegia, for instance, is highly unlikely to have a career as a lawyer, a laboratory technician, or a clerk-typist. But what of one who has severe spastic quadriplegia and a bright mind? Such a person may well overcome both the physical limitation and the associated social stigma and be successful in a wide variety of fields in which the work is more mental than physical.

There are no simple conclusions regarding the occupational outlook for students with physical disabilities. Those with mild or transitory disabling conditions may not be affected at all in their occupational choices. Yet some with relatively mild physical disabilities may be unemployed or even unemployable because of inappropriate social and emotional behavior or poor work habits; they may need vocational rehabilitation training to function even in a vocation with limited demands. Some people with severe physical disabilities are able to use their intelligence, social skills, and residual physical abilities to the fullest and become competitive employees (or employers) in demanding occupations.

The outlook for employment of students with physical or multiple and severe disabilities has been improved dramatically by legislation and research and demonstration projects. As mentioned in Chapter 1, the Americans with Disabilities Act (ADA) of 1990 requires that reasonable accommodations be made to create equal employment opportunities for people with disabilities. More accessible transportation and buildings, increased skill in using technology to allow people to accomplish tasks at work, and greater commitment to preparing people with disabilities for work are resulting in more personal independence, economic self-sufficiency, and social acceptance—which benefit not only people with disabilities but the economy and society as well.

We now recognize that preparing for work begins in childhood. Long before adolescence, children—including those with physical disabilities—need to be taught about and to explore various careers. They need to be thinking about what they like to do, as well as what they are particularly good at, and the demands and rewards of various kinds of jobs. The objective should be to help students select training and enter a career that makes maximum use of their abilities in ways that they find personally gratifying.

Supported employment for people with severe disabilities is a relatively new concept that is being adopted widely. In this approach, a person with a severe disability works in a regular work setting. He or she becomes a regular employee, performs a valued function in the same workplace as nondisabled employees, and receives fair remuneration. Training and continued support are necessary; hence the term *supported* employment. Trach (1990) describes the distinguishing features of a supported employment program:

> Notably, these procedures include surveying the community for jobs, identifying and analyzing the requisite skills of potential employment sites, assessing the current skill levels of supported employees, matching jobs to prospective employees, providing systematic training in job-related skills, and providing follow-up training and maintenance of learned skills, satisfying employers, and coordinating related services. (p. 79)

New technologies, especially in computing and other electronic devices, offer great promise for enabling students with physical disabilities to achieve personal

Figure 11.2

A keyboard positioned for efficient use with a headstick.

Source: Bigge, June L., *Teaching individuals with physical and multiple disabilities,* 3rd ed., Copyright © 1991, p. 486. Reprinted by permission of Prentice-Hall, Upper Saddle River, New Jersey.

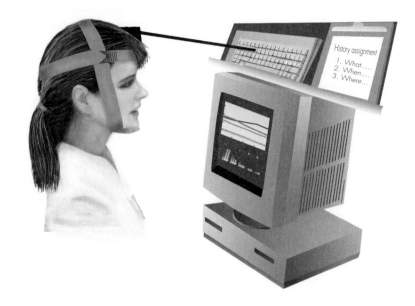

independence, to acquire education and training that will make them employable, and to find employment. Following is one example:

> Last year Justin Dolan, an 18-year-old junior at Falls Church High School, began using a computer that takes dictation, in addition to using an AlphaSmart word processor for class notes. Dolan, who has cerebral palsy and is in a wheelchair, has so improved his ability to keep up with classwork that he's thinking about going to college. "I have a better shot than I did three or four years ago," he said. (DeFord, 1998, p. 30)

In some cases, the technology is readily available and educators need only to become aware of the software (e.g., software that allows the functions of keys to be altered), find ways in which keystrokes can be saved through subprogramming routines (e.g., macro or find-and-replace features in word processing), or provide substitutions for physical manipulation of materials (e.g., computer graphics programs as substitutes for paper paste-ups or model construction) (Heller, Alberto, Forney, & Schwartzman, 1996).

Sometimes an individual's ability to use standard equipment is greatly enhanced by a simple modification such as orientation or location. Figure 11.2 shows how simply placing a keyboard in a vertical position over a monitor may enhance the ability of someone who uses a headstick to use a computer. A headstick is an adaptive device that allows someone who cannot use hands or feet, but who has control of neck muscles, to use a computer or accomplish other tasks. Teachers must always look for simple, virtually cost-free ways to facilitate the performance of students with disabilities—to prevent an environment designed for people without disabilities from handicapping those who must do things a different way. Overlooking the seemingly obvious is perhaps the way in which we most frequently handicap people with disabilities.

Sociosexuality

Until fairly recently, physical disabilities were assumed to cancel human sexuality (see Edmonson, 1988). People who were not normal physically, especially if they had limited mobility, were thought of as having no sex appeal for anyone and as having little or no ability or right to function sexually.

Fortunately, attitudes and experiences are changing. It is now recognized that people with disabilities have a right to family life education, including sex education, and to a full range of human relationships, including appropriate sexual expression. Sociosexual education for students with physical disabilities, as with such education for all other children and youths, should begin early, continue through adulthood, and include information about the structures and functions of the body, human relationships and responsibilities, and alternative modes of sexual gratification (Bigge, 1991).

Youths with physical disabilities need to experience close friendships and warm physical contact that is not sexually intimate. But it is neither realistic nor fair to expect people with physical disabilities to keep all their relationships platonic or to limit themselves to fantasy. Most physical disability, even if severe, does not in itself kill sexual desire or prevent sexual gratification, nor does it preclude marriage and children. The purpose of special education and rehabilitation is to make exceptional individuals' lives as full and complete as possible. In the case of youths with physical disabilities, this may involve teaching or providing alternative means of sexual stimulation and accepting sexual practices and relationships that are different from the norm. With sensitive education and rehabilitation, satisfying sociosexual expression can be achieved by all but a small minority (DeLoach & Greer, 1981; Edmonson, 1988).

Summary

Children with physical disabilities have physical limitations or health problems that interfere with school attendance or learning to such an extent that special services, training, equipment, materials, or facilities are required. They may have disabilities they are born with (congenital disabilities) or acquire disabilities through accident or disease. These children may also have other disabilities, such as mental retardation and emotional or behavioral disorders, or they may have special gifts or talents. The medical nature of the problem highlights the need for interdisciplinary cooperation in special education.

Less than 0.5 percent of the child population in the United States receives special education and related services for physical disabilities. About half of these students have multiple disabilities, about one-fourth have orthopedic impairments, and about a fourth have chronic health problems. Because of advances in medical technology, more children with severe disabilities are surviving and many more are living with disease or injury with mild impairments, such as hyperactivity and learning disabilities. Three major categories of physical disabilities are (1) neuromotor impairments, (2) orthopedic and musculo-skeletal disorders, and (3) other conditions affecting health or physical ability.

Individuals with neuromotor impairments have experienced damage to the brain that affects their ability to move parts of the body. The injury may occur prior to, during, or after birth. The causes of neuromotor impairments include trauma, infections, diseases, hypoxia, poisoning, congenital malformations, and child abuse.

An increasingly frequent cause of neuromotor impairment is traumatic brain injury (TBI), which may range from mild to profound. Medical and educational personnel must work together as a team to provide transition from the hospital or rehabilitation center to school. Frequent educational problems are focusing or sustaining attention, remembering, and learning new skills. Emotional, behavioral, and social problems may also be apparent.

Other neurological impairments include cerebral palsy (CP), a condition characterized by paralysis, weakness, uncoordination, and/or other motor dysfunction. It is nonprogressive brain damage that occurs before or during birth or in early childhood. Classification of CP is generally made according to the limbs involved and the type of motor disability. The educational problems associated with CP are varied because of the multiplicity of symptoms; a careful clinical appraisal must be made of each individual to determine the type of special education needed.

Seizures are caused by abnormal discharges of electrical energy in the brain. Recurrent seizures are referred to as epilepsy. Most people with seizure disorders are able to function normally, except when having seizures. Intelligence is not directly affected by a seizure disorder, so educational procedures consist chiefly of attaining knowledge of the disorder and how to manage seizures, as well as a commitment to help dispel the ignorance and fear connected with seizures.

Spina bifida is a congenital midline defect resulting from failure of the bony spinal column to close completely during fetal development. The resulting damage to the nerves generally causes paralysis and lack of sensation below the site of the defect. The cause of spina bifida is not known. Educational implications of spina bifida are determined by the extent of the paralysis and medical complications as well as the child's cognitive and behavioral characteristics.

Other neurological disorders may not cause paralysis. These include such rare and poorly understood conditions as autism, Asperger syndrome, and Tourette's syndrome.

Some physical disabilities are orthopedic or musculoskeletal disorders, in which there are defects or diseases of the muscles or bones. Children with such disabilities have a range of difficulties in walking, standing, sitting, or using their hands. Muscular dystrophy is a degenerative disease causing a progressive weakening and wasting away of muscle tissues. Juvenile rheumatoid arthritis is a disease that causes acute inflammation around the joints and may cause chronic pain and other complications. These and other musculoskeletal conditions do not cause lowered intelligence, so educational considerations include overcoming the child's limited mobility so that he or she can continue learning in as normal a way as possible.

A wide variety of other conditions may affect health and physical ability, including congenital malformations, diseases, and injuries. Fetal alcohol syndrome (FAS), which is now one of the most common causes of malformation and mental retardation, is caused by the mother's abuse of alcohol during pregnancy. Although maternal substance abuse during pregnancy may have serious consequences for the fetus, the near hysteria of the 1980s about the irreversible effects of crack cocaine was not justified. Accidents that result in neurological impairment, disfigurement, or amputation are an important cause of

physical disabilities among children and youths. AIDS, a life-threatening viral infection, also involves neurological complications such as mental retardation, seizures, cerebral palsy, and emotional or behavioral disorders.

Children who are medically fragile or dependent on ventilators are being returned home from hospitals in increasing numbers. Many of these children are returning to public schools. Careful consideration of the mainstreaming of these children is required.

Many physical disabilities—including those that result from accidents, substance use, and poisoning—are fully preventable. Preventing adolescent pregnancies also would reduce the number of children born with disabilities. Teenage mothers are more likely than older women to give birth to premature or low-birth-weight babies, and the babies of teens will remain at risk for developing a range of physical and psychological problems when they reach school age. Abused and neglected children represent a large number of those with physical disabilities. Children who already have disabilities are more likely to be abused than those without disabilities. Teachers must be especially alert to signs of possible child abuse and neglect, and must be aware of reporting procedures in their states.

As a group, children with physical disabilities represent the total range of impairment, and their behavioral and psychological characteristics vary greatly. The necessity for hospitalization, bed rest, prosthetic devices, and so on means that their academic achievement depends on individual circumstances, motivation, and the caliber of care received both at home and at school. A child with a physical disability may be deprived of educationally relevant experiences or not be able to learn to manipulate educational materials and respond to educational tasks the way most children do.

There does not appear to be a certain personality type associated with any particular physical disability. The reactions of the public, family, peers, and educational personnel—as well as the child's own reactions to the disability—are all closely interwoven in the determination of his or her personality, motivation, and progress. Given ample opportunity to develop educationally, socially, and emotionally in as normal a fashion as possible, many children with physical disabilities are able to make healthy adjustments to their impairments.

Many individuals with physical disabilities use prosthetics, orthotics, and other adaptive devices to improve functioning. A *prosthesis* replaces a missing body part. An *orthosis* is a device that enhances the partial function of a body part. An *adaptive device* aids a person's daily activity. Important considerations in choosing prostheses, orthoses, and adaptive devices are simplicity, reliability, and the use of residual function. Advances in technology are providing more useful devices for those with physical disabilities. The greatest problem is accurately evaluating needs and making existing technology available.

Education for students with physical disabilities must focus on making the most of their assets. The student's individual characteristics (intellectual, sensory, physical, and emotional) must be considered when developing educational plans. Plans for young children must include services for the family.

Increasingly, students with physical disabilities are being placed in regular classrooms. The problem of educating students with physical disabilities is often a problem of educating students *without* disabilities about the needs of people with disabilities. Along with scholastic education, the child may need special assis-tance in daily living, mobility, and occupational skills. Education should serve the goals of autonomy and self-advocacy. The major considerations are to help each child become as independent and self-sufficient in daily activities as possible, to provide basic academic skills, and to prepare him or her for advanced education and work. Links with other disciplines are crucial.

Besides early identification and intervention to develop communication, handling and positioning are important considerations. Motor skills must be taught as part of daily lessons in self-help and communication.

Career choice and sociosexuality are two primary concerns of youths with physical disabilities. Career considerations must include careful evaluation of the young person's intellectual, emotional, and motivational characteristics as well as physical capabilities. Young people with physical disabilities have the right to the social relationships and modes of sexual expression afforded others in society.

suggestions for teaching

Students with Physical Disabilities in General Education Classrooms

By Peggy L. Tarpley

Along with coordinating services for the student with physical disabilities, scheduling times for these services, and communicating with parents, other teachers, and outside agencies, you will need to modify curricula and accommodate your classroom for students with various needs and abilities. As with children who exhibit other disabilities, students with physical disabilities will need to be encouraged and allowed to be as independent as possible. Providing this kind of environment will give these students the confidence to try new experiences, rejoice in accomplishments, and cope with disappointments.

The educational interventions required for students with physical disabilities will vary greatly, depending on the type and severity of their conditions. Some students may require specialized assistance or training in areas such as mobility or communications. Others may need additional support to manage the sensory, learning, and behavioral disorders that can accompany some physical disabilities (see appropriate chapters for these interventions). Still others may require no modifications or only minimal adjustments. For example, teachers simply may need to increase the length of time students have to complete assignments when they are absent or fatigued by their illnesses or the treatment of their illnesses.

In fact, many students with physical and health impairments attend regular education classes for at least a part of the school day and generally are expected to progress through the same curricular materials as nondisabled students. Many of these students, however, re-quire some adaptation of instructional materials and activities in order to succeed in school and to maximize their independence.

Adapting Instructional Methods

Heller, Dangel, and Sweatman (1995) provide teachers with a system for selecting appropriate physical and behavioral adaptations for students with muscular dystrophy and other physically degenerative conditions. It would seem that this system could be used for students with other physical disabilities as well. First, you should watch the student's performance of a particular activity to assess his or her skills and deficits. The assessment should include comparing the skills needed to complete the activity (which is called a task analysis) by a student *without* physical disabilities with the performance (of the same activity) by the student with physical disabilities. Given this information, you now are able to pinpoint the area of difficulty—physical, sensory, communication, learning, or behavioral (such as motivation)—for the student with physical impairment. Next, after having received input from parents and other appropriate school or medical personnel, you can select and implement the appropriate adaptations. The final step is for you, along with the parents and others involved in the student's education, to evaluate the adaptation and then make modifications or choose new adaptations.

Heller and her colleagues (1995, p. 258) define three types of adaptations that might be used in the classroom:

1. Adaptations that allow access to the task (e.g., the use of adapted devices, behavior management strategies, or personal aids; changes in the physical environment; or changes in how the student responds)
2. Adaptations in how the teacher teaches the task (i.e., modified instruction)
3. Adaptations in part or all of the task (i.e., alter the material, activity, or curriculum)

One of the most common adaptations teachers make for students with physical disabilities is of the first type: adapting access to the task, which includes modifying response patterns, using adaptive devices, and employing people as assistants or partners.

Adapting Response Patterns and Using Adaptive Devices

Written Responses
To complete written activities, some students need simple modifications, such as assistance in stabilizing and selecting appropriate materials. These adaptations include (Bigge, 1991):

Stabilization Techniques
- Writing on a pad of paper, rather than on loose sheets
- Using masking tape (two-inch width is strongest) or a clipboard to secure loose papers
- Placing a rubber strip on the back of a ruler or using a magnetic ruler to prevent slipping when measuring or drawing lines
- Using adhesive-backed Velcro to attach items to a desk or wheelchair laptray

Modifying/Selecting Appropriate Materials
- Using pens (felt tip) and pencils (soft lead) that require less pressure
- Twisting a rubber band around the shaft of the pen or pencil or slipping corrugated rubber, a foam hair curler, or a golf practice ball over the writing instrument to make it easier to hold
- Using an electronic typewriter, word processor, or computer
- Using typing aids, such as a pointer stick attached to a headpiece or mouthpiece to strike the keys; a keyboard guard that prevents striking two keys at once; and line spacers that hold written materials while typing
- Audiotaping assignments, lectures, and other instructional activities that require extensive writing. Tape recorders can be modified so students can operate them with a single switch.

For students who have limited strength, muscular control, or mobility, selecting and designing instructional materials that require no word formation may simplify their responding to written tasks. For example, numbering problems and coding possible answers with letters allow students to write single-letter responses (Bigge, 1991). Using worksheets and tests that direct students to put lines through the correct answers requires no letter formation. It is important, however, to provide enough space between the answer alternatives so that students can indicate their choices without marking other responses accidentally.

Still other adaptations do not require students to hold pencils or pens. Bigge (1991) indicates that students can respond to matching, sorting, classifying, and sequencing tasks by manipulating objects. For example, they can move magnetic letters and numbers on a metal cookie sheet to indicate their responses or put wooden blocks on top of their answer choices. In addition, students may indicate their comprehension of content-area reading by matching a set of picture cards

with a set of cards with sentences or paragraphs written on them by pushing the two correct card sets together. Students also can use this response method in practicing vocabulary, especially homonyms, synonyms, and antonyms. Similarly, they can indicate the sequence of historical events, plot episodes from literary works, and organize steps in scientific experiments by placing cards in the correct order that have pictures or sentences describing each event.

In addition, special input devices for computers facilitate student response. Computers, for example, can be equipped with a variety of switches that allow students to operate them with a single movement. Selection of the type of switch will depend on the type of movement the student can best perform. The Adaptive Firmware Card (AFC), available from Don Johnston Developmental Equipment, Inc., is a computer peripheral that permits students to use any commercial software program (Lewis & Doorlag, 1999). The AFC provides a line of letters and symbols called a *scanning array* on the computer screen that students select by pressing a switch. This array allows them to spell words, indicate numbers, and operate the computer. Alternate keyboards (e.g., Unicorn Expanded Keyboard) offer several features, such as providing a larger response area than standard keyboards and removing the need for simultaneous key pressing. Consequently, they offer another means by which students with limited muscular control can use computers. Touch-sensitive screens also enable students to respond to instructions and questions by touching specific areas of the screen. Still other input devices allow students to bypass keyboards completely by talking or by making consistent sounds into a microphone and by making muscular movements (Cavalier & Ferretti, 1996).

Oral Responses
Speech synthesizers voice the responses that students with severe speech impairments type on the computer and enable them to participate in class discussions and ask questions immediately. Less expensive communication boards (charts of pictures, symbols, numbers, or words) allow students to indicate their responses to specific items represented on the charts. To facilitate communication using these boards, Bigge (1991) recommends that listeners name the pictures or say the letters or words quickly, so the conversation moves along more rapidly. Teachers have found creative and less involved response adaptations useful during oral activities. For example, you can give students color-coded objects (such as blocks of wood that are easy to handle and that do not slip) to indicate their response to polar questions, such as true/false; agree/disagree/don't know; or same/different (Bigge, 1991).

Reading Tasks
In addition to response modifications, students with physical disabilities often require equipment that facilitates reading. These devices include book holders; reading stands that adjust to reclining, sitting, and standing positions; and page turners that range from pencil erasers to electric-powered devices that can be operated with minimal mobility. Furthermore, "talking" books enable students who cannot hold books to tape lectures and to enjoy a variety of recorded novels, textbooks, and magazines. This equipment is available at no cost from the Library of Congress. For more information about these and other materials see Suggestions for Teaching Students with Visual Impairment at the end of Chapter 10.

In addition to these devices, instructional materials can be adapted to facilitate student use during reading and thinking activities. For example, try using photo albums that have sticky backings and plastic cover sheets and plastic photo cubes to hold instructional materials, such as pictures or words cards. This latter adaptation allows students to move the cubes to respond to a variety of tasks.

Using Personal Assistants

Some students with physical disabilities have personal assistants who work with them in their classrooms. In these cases, it is important that the assistant aid the student *only* when he or she is unable to perform a task without help. An assistant or peer can also assist with physical components of a task. Heller and colleagues (1995) suggest that a peer might help a student with limited head/arm use with the mechanics of dissecting a frog, while they verbally select and plan the sequence of steps together. Another scenario might be that a student with physical impairments might read the directions for a physical task to a peer who has difficulty with reading. These interactions may promote social interaction between students and foster positive attitudes between students with disabilities and those without.

Helpful Resources

School Personnel

Because students with health impairments and physical disabilities often require the expertise of a variety of professionals, several individuals may provide services to your student. Understanding the role of each is important in coordinating instructional and medical interventions. In addition to what you learned in the chapter, the following list describes the functions of some of the professionals typically involved in the treatment of these students (adapted from Dykes & Venn, 1983):

- *Physicians* are licensed medical doctors who provide services that include diagnosing; prescribing medication; making referrals for physical therapy, occupational therapy, and orthopedic treatment; and recommending the extent and length of various activities and treatments. Specialized physicians include orthopedists (specialists in diagnosing and treating joint, bone, and muscle impairments), neurologists (specialists in diagnosing and treating impairments to the nervous system, such as cerebral palsy and muscular dystrophy), and radiologists (specialists in using X rays and radioactive substances to diagnose and treat conditions such as cancer).
- *School nurses* have varying responsibilities, depending on the school system in which they are employed. Often, they administer medications at school, treat medical emergencies, provide medical information to students and staff, and help identify community health agencies for families.
- *Occupational therapists* provide medically prescribed assistance to help individuals manage their disabilities. They may teach various self-help, daily living, prevocational, leisure time, and perceptual-motor skills. They may also provide instruction in the use of adaptive devices.
- *Rehabilitation counselors* perform a range of services related to vocational training and employment. For example, they may conduct vocational assessment and counseling and arrange for work training and experience. Typically they are employed by the state vocational rehabilitation agency rather than the school district.
- *Physical therapists* provide services designed to restore or improve physical functioning and engage in such activities as exercising to increase coordination, range of motion, and movement.

Instructional Methods, Materials, and Resources

American Software, Inc. (1996). *Adaptive device locator system.* Lexington, KY: Author. (computer program)

Alliance for Technology Access. (1996). *Computer resources for people with disabilities: A guide to exploring today's assistive technology* (2nd ed.). Alameda, CA: Hinter House.

Bigge, J. L. (1989). *Curriculum-based instruction for special education students* (2nd ed.). Mountain View, CA: Mayfield.

Bigge, J. L. (1991). *Teaching individuals with physical and multiple disabilities* (3rd ed.). New York: Merrill/Macmillan.

Fraser, B. A., Hensinger, R. N., & Phelps, J. A. (1990). *Physical management of multiple handicaps: A professional's guide.* Baltimore: Paul H. Brookes.

Hanson, M. J. (Ed.). (1996). *Atypical infant environment* (2nd ed.). Austin, TX: Pro-Ed.

Heller, K. W., Alberto, P. A., Forney, P. E., & Schwartzman, M. N. (1996). *Understanding physical, sensory, and health impairments: Characteristics and educational implications.* Pacific Grove, CA: Brooks/Cole.

Kurtz, L. A., Dowrick, P. W., Levy, S. E., & Batshaw, M. L. (Eds.). (1996). *Handbook of developmental disabilities: Resources for interdisciplinary care.* Gaithersburg, MD: Aspen.

Lerner, J. W., Lowenthal, B., & Egan, R. (1998). *Preschool children with special needs: Children at-risk, children with disabilities.* Boston: Allyn & Bacon.

Lloyd, L. L., Fuller, D. R., & Arvidson, H. H. (1997) (Eds.), *Augmentative and alternative communication: A handbook of principles and practices.* Boston: Allyn & Bacon.

Orelove, F. P., & Sobsey, D. (1996). *Educating children with multiple disabilities: A transdisciplinary approach.* Baltimore: Paul H. Brookes.

Speigel, G. L., Cutler, S. K., & Yetter, C. I. (1996). What every teacher should know about epilepsy. *Intervention in School and Clinic, 32,* 34–38.

Literature about Individuals with Physical Disabilities*

Elementary

Aiello, B., & Shulman, J. (1989). *A portrait of me.* Frederick, MD: Twenty-First Century Books. (Ages 9–12, diabetes) (F; includes factual information about diabetes and its treatment)

Aiello, B., & Shulman, J. (1989). *Friends for life.* Frederick, MD: Twenty-First Century Books. (Ages 9–12, AIDS) (NF)

Aiello, B., & Shulman, J. (1989). *Hometown hero.* Frederick, MD: Twenty-First Century Books. (Ages 9–12; asthma) (F; includes factual information about asthmatic episodes)

Aiello, B., & Shulman, J. (1989). *Trick or treat or trouble.* Frederick, MD: Twenty-First Century Books. (Ages 9–21; epilepsy) (F; includes factual information about responding to seizures)

Arnold, K. (1983) *Anna joins in.* New York: Abingdon. (Ages 5–8; cystic fibrosis) (F)

Auch, M. J. (1990). *Kidnapping Kevin Kolwalski.* New York: Holiday House. (Grades 3–6; brain injury) (F)

Bergman, T. (1989). *On our own terms: Children living with physical handicaps.* Milwaukee, WI: Gareth Stevens. (Grades 3–5; spina bifida, cerebral palsy, and spinal injuries) (NF)

Bernstein, J. E., & Fireside, B. (1991). *Special parents, special children.* Chicago: Albert Whitman. (Grades 4–7; parents with physical disabilities) (NF)

Blair, M. (1989). *Kids want to know about AIDS.* Rockville, MD: National AIDS Information Clearinghouse. (Grades 4–7; AIDS) (NF)

*F = fiction; NF = nonfiction

Bunnett, R. (1993). *Friends in the park*. New York: Checkerboard. (Preschool–Grade 1; various disabilities including physical disabilities) (F)

Butler, B. (1993). *Witch's fire*. New York: Dutton. (Grades 4–6; adjusting to a wheelchair) (F)

Carlson, N. (1990). *Arnie and the new kid*. New York: Viking. (K–Grade 2; wheelchair use) (F)

Caseley, J. (1991). *Harry and Willy and Carrothead*. New York: Greenwillow. (Grades K–2; prosthetic hand) (F)

Cowen-Fletcher, J. (1993). *Mama zooms*. New York: Scholastic. (Preschool–Grade 2; mother in a wheelchair) (F)

Damrell, L. (1991). *With the wind*. New York: Orchard House. (Preschool–Grade 3; wheelchair) (F)

Dwight, L. (1992). *We can do it!* New York: Checkerboard. (Preschool–Grade 2; various disabilities) (NF)

Frevert, P. D. (1983). *Patty gets well*. Mankato, MN: Creative Education. (Grades 4–7; Leukemia) (NF)

Krementz, J. (1992). *How it feels to live with a physical disability*. New York: Simon & Schuster. (Grades 6–9; various disabilities including missing limbs and cerebral palsy) (NF)

Powers, M. E. (1986). *Our teacher's in a wheelchair*. Chicago: Albert Whitman. (Preschool–Grade 1; teacher with a physical disability) (NF)

Rabe, B. (1981). *The balancing girl*. New York: Dutton. (Grades K–3) (F)

Rabe, B. (1986). *Margaret's moves*. New York: Dutton. (Grades 4–6) (F)

Russo, M. (1992). *Alex is my friend*. New York: Greenwillow. (Preschool–Grade 2) (F)

Slepian, J. (1980). *The Alfred summer*. New York: Macmillan. (Grades 4–7; cerebral palsy) (F)

Thompson, M. (1992). *My brother Matthew*. Frederick, MD: Woodbine House. (Grades K–3) (F)

Secondary

Blos, J. W. (1985). *Brothers of the heart: A story of the old northwest, 1837–1839*. New York: Scribner's. (Grades 4–9) (F)

Calvert, P. (1993). *Picking up the pieces*. New York: Scribner's. (Grades 5–8; wheelchair) (F)

Crutcher, C. (1987). *The crazy horse electric game*. New York: Greenwillow. (Grades 8–12; brain injury) (F)

Ferguson, K. (1991). *Stephen Hawking: Quest for a theory of the universe*. New York: Watts. (Grades 7–12; Lou Gehrig's disease) (NF)

Haldane, S. (1991). *Helping hands: How monkeys assist people who are disabled*. New York: Dutton. (Grades 3–6) (NF)

Hall, L. (1990). *Halsey's pride*. New York: Scribner's. (Grades 6–8; epilepsy) (F)

Kriegsman, K. H. (1992). *Taking charge: Teenagers talk about life and physical disabilities*. Frederick, MD: Woodbine House. (Grades 7–12; various disabilities) (NF)

Metzger, L. (1992). *Barry's sister*. New York: Atheneum. (Grades 6–9; cerebral palsy) (F)

Miklowitz, G. D. (1987). *Good-bye tomorrow*. New York: Delacorte Press. (Grades 8–12; AIDS) (F)

Radley, G. (1984). *CF in his corner*. Soquel, CA: Four Winds Press. (Grades 7–10; cystic fibrosis) (F)

Sirof, H. (1993). *Because she's my friend*. New York: Atheneum. (Grades 7–10) (F)

Thiele, C. (1990). *Jodie's journey*. New York: HarperCollins. (Grades 4–7; arthritis) (F)

Voight, C. (1986). *Izzy, willy-nilly*. New York: Atheneum. (Grades 7–10; amputation) (F)

Software

The following programs may be operated by adaptive switch or touch-sensitive screens:

Academics with scanning: Language arts, ACS Software, University of Washington, Department of Speech and Hearing Sciences JG-15, Seattle, WA 98195, (206) 543-7974. (Program includes phonics and word attack)

Academics with scanning: Math, ACS Software, University of Washington, Department of Speech and Hearing Sciences JG-15, Seattle, WA 98195, (206) 543-7974. (Does not provide instruction, but allows students to use the computer as pencil/paper to complete math problems)

Adventures of Jimmy-Jumper, Exceptional Children's Software, P.O. Box 487, Hays, KS 67601, (913) 625-9281. (Prepositions; speech synthesizer required)

Counting Critters, MECC, 6160 Summit Drive N., Minneapolis, MN 55430-4003, (800) 685-6322.

Exploratory Plan, PEAL Software, 5000 North Parkway Calabasas, Ste. 105, Calabasas, CA 91302, (818) 883-7849. (Communication)

First Verbs, Laureate Learning Systems, 110 East Spring Street, Winooski, VT 05404, (800) 562-6801. (Speech synthesizer required)

First Words I and II, Laureate Learning Systems, 110 East Spring Street, Winooski, VT 05404, (800) 562-6801. (Speech synthesizer required)

Interaction Games, Don Johnston, Inc., 1000 North Rand Road, Building 115, P.O. Box 639, Wauconda, IL 60084, (800) 999-4660. (Row and column scanning)

Keyboarding for the Physically Handicapped, Gregg/ McGraw-Hill, 1221 Avenue of the Americas, New York, NY 10020, (800) 262-4729.

Keyboarding with One Hand, Educational, computability Corporation, 40000 Grand River, Ste. 109, Novi, MI 48375, (800) 433-8872.

Keytalk, PEAL Software, 5000 North Parkway Calabasas, Ste. 105, Calabasas, CA 91302, (818) 325-2001. (Electronic communication aid)

My Words, Hartley Courseware, Jostens Learning Corp., 9920 Pacific Heights Boulevard, San Diego, CA 92121, (800) 247-1380. (Combines a language experience approach with a talking word-processing program)

Muppet Slate, Sunburst Communications, 101 Castleton Street, Pleasantville, NY 10570, (800) 321-7511.

Rabbit Scanner, Exceptional Children's Software, P.O. Box 487, Hays, KS 67601, (913) 625-9281. (Scanning trainer)

Representational Play, PEAL Software, 5000 North Parkway Calabasas, Ste. 105, Calabasas, CA 91302, (818) 883-7849. (Communication)

Single Switch Game Library, Arthur Schwartz, 12622 Cedar Road, Cleveland, OH 44106, (216) 687-6990.

Sunny Days, Don Johnston, Inc., 1000 North Rand Road, Building 115, P.O. Box 639, Wauconda, IL 60084, (800) 999-4660. (Word recognition, spelling, and reading skills)

Touch and Match, Exceptional Children's Software, P.O. Box 487, Hays, KS 67601, (913) 625-9281.

Organizations

AIDS

National Association of People with AIDS, 1413 K Street N.W., 7th Floor, Washington, DC 20005, (202) 898-0414.

Arthritis

American Juvenile Arthritis Organization, 1330 W. Peachtree Street, Atlanta, GA 30309, (404) 872-7100, (800) 283-7800.

Birth (Congenital) Defects

March of Dimes Birth Defects Foundation, 1275 Marmaroneck Avenue, White Plains, NY 10605, (914) 997-4555.

Cancer

American Cancer Society, 1599 Clifton Road N.E., Atlanta, GA 30329, (404) 320-3333, (800) ACS-2345.

Cancer Information Service, 9000 Rockville Pike, Building 31, Room 10A-16, Bethesda, MD 20892, (301) 496-8664.

Cerebral Palsy

United Cerebral Palsy Associations, 1660 L Street N.W., Suite 700, Washington, DC 20036, (202) 726-0406, (800) 872-5827.

Child Abuse

American Association for Protecting Children, c/o American Humane Association, 63 Inverness Drive E., Englewood, CO 80112, (303) 792-9900.

Childhelp USA, Inc., 15757 N. 78th Street, Scottsdale, AZ 85260, (602) 922-8212.

Diabetes

American Diabetes Association, National Service Center, P.O. Box 25757, 1660 Duke Street, Alexandria, VA 22313, (800) 342-2383.

Epilepsy

Epilepsy Foundation of America, 4351 Garden City Drive, Landover, MD 20785, (301) 459-3700, (800) EFA-1000.

Muscular Dystrophy

Muscular Dystrophy Association, 3300 E. Sunrise Drive, Tucson, AZ 85718, (602) 529-2000, (800) 572-1717.

Multiple Sclerosis

National Multiple Sclerosis Society, 733 Third Avenue, New York, NY 10017, (212) 986-3240, fax (212) 486-7981.

Spina Bifida

Spina Bifida Association of America, 4590 MacArthur Boulevard N.W., Suite 250, Washington, DC 20007, (800) 621-3141.

Other

Brain Injury Association, Inc., 105 N. Alfred St., Alexandria, VA 22314, (703) 236-6000. www.BIAUSA.org

National Spinal Cord Injury Association, 8300 Colesville Road, Suite 551, Silver Spring, MD 20910, (301) 558-6959, (800) 962-9629.

Bibliography for Teaching Suggestions

Bigge, J. L. (1991). *Teaching individuals with physical and multiple disabilities* (3rd ed.). New York: Merrill/Macmillan.

Cavalier, A. R., & Ferretti, R. P. (1996). Talking instead of typing: Alternate access to computers via speech recognition technology. *Focus on Autism and Other Developmental Disabilities, 11,* 79–85.

Dykes, M. K., & Venn, J. (1983). Using health, physical, and medical data in the classroom. In J. Umbreit (Ed.), *Physical disabilities and health impairments: An introduction.* Columbus, OH: Merrill/Macmillan.

Heller, K. W., Dangel, H., & Sweatman, L. (1995). Systematic selection of adaptations for students with muscular dystrophy. *Journal of Developmental and Physical Disabilities, 7*(3), 253–265.

Lewis, R. B., & Doorlag, D. H. (1999). *Teaching special students in the mainstream* (5th ed.). Merrill/Prentice-Hall.

ruby
pearl

Turning Point. Acrylic on rag paper. 30 × 22 in.

Ruby Pearl was born in Weymouth, MA, in 1949 and won her first art award at the age of 4. She is a prolific painter and collage artist whose work continues to receive awards. She has been exhibited at the Little House Studio in Connecticut; 4th Floor Artists in Rockland, MA; the Healing and Arts Gallery in Boston; and the Governors Gallery in Quincy, MA. Her work enjoys considerable demand. All of her successes have come in spite of a long struggle with mental illness. In 1999 Ruby joined a distinguished group of artists whose work has been incorporated into a 54-foot-long banner that is hung across Route 9 in front of the Chestnut Hill Mall in Newton, Massachusetts.

Special Gifts and Talents

I think Jim Gillis was a much more remarkable person than his family and his intimates ever suspected. He had a bright and smart imagination and it was of the kind that turns out impromptu work and does it well, does it with easy facility and without previous preparation, just builds a story as it goes along, careless of whither it is proceeding, enjoying each fresh fancy as it flashes from the brain and caring not at all whether the story shall ever end brilliantly and satisfactorily or shan't end at all. Jim was born a humorist and a very competent one. When I remember how felicitous were his untrained efforts, I feel a conviction that he would have been a star performer if he had been discovered and had been subjected to a few years of training with a pen. A genius is not very likely to ever discover himself; neither is he very likely to be discovered by his intimates; they are so close to him that he is out of focus to them and they can't get at his proportions; they cannot perceive that there is any considerable difference between his bulk and their own. They can't get a perspective on him and it is only by a perspective that the difference between him and the rest of their limited circle can be perceived.

The Autobiography of Mark Twain

P eople who have special gifts, or at least have the potential for gifted performance, can go through life unrecognized. As Mark Twain pointed out (see p. 467), they may seem unremarkable to their closest associates. Sometimes children and youths with special talents or gifts are not discovered because their families and intimates simply place no particular value on their special abilities. And sometimes they are not recognized because they are not given the necessary opportunities or training. Especially in the case of individuals who are poor or members of minority groups, children with extraordinary gifts or talents may be deprived of chances to demonstrate and develop their potential (Ford, 1998; Ford, Baytops, & Harmon, 1997; Frasier, 1997). How many more outstanding artists and scientists would we have if every talented child had the opportunity and the training necessary to develop his or her talents to the fullest possible extent? There is no way of knowing, but it is safe to say we would have more.

Unlike mental retardation and other disabling conditions, giftedness is something to be fostered deliberately. Yet giftedness is not something a child can show without risk of stigma and rejection. Many people have a low level of tolerance for those who eclipse the ordinary individual in some area of achievement. A child who achieves far beyond the level of his or her average peers may be subject to criticism or social isolation by other children or their parents (Cross, 1997; Swiatek, 1998). Had Jim Gillis been discovered, given a few years of training with a pen, and become a gifted writer, it is possible that some of his intimates would have found his giftedness hard to accept.*

Some of the problems presented by giftedness parallel those presented by the disabling conditions discussed in the other chapters of this book. For instance, the definition and identification of children with special gifts or talents involve the same sort of difficulties that exist in the case of children with mental retardation or emotional or behavioral disorders. But there is an underlying philosophical question regarding giftedness that makes us think differently about this exceptionality: Most of us feel a moral obligation to help those who are at some disadvantage compared to the average person, who have a difference that prevents them from achieving ordinary levels of competence unless they are given special help. But in the case of a person who is has special gifts, we may wonder about our moral obligation to help someone who is already advantaged become even better, to distinguish himself or herself further by fulfilling the highest promise of his or her extraordinary resources. It is on this issue—the desirability or necessity of helping the most capable children become even better—that special education for students who have special gifts or talents is likely to founder (Gallagher, 1994, 1997a; Howley, Howley, & Pendarvis, 1995; Kaufman, 1998). Today, the emphasis is on programs to develop the talents of *all* students, with less special attention to those who may be identified as gifted or talented (see Feldhusen, 1998; Fulkerson & Horvich, 1998; Gallagher, 1998; Treffinger, 1998).

Definition

Children with special gifts excel in some way compared to other children of the same age. Beyond this almost meaningless statement, however, there is little agreement about how giftedness should be defined (Gallagher & Gallagher, 1994).

---

*We are indebted to Dr. Carolyn M. Callahan of the University of Virginia for her invaluable assistance in preparing this chapter.

misconceptions
about Persons With Special Gifts or Talents

myth People with special intellectual gifts are physically weak, socially inept, narrow in interests, and prone to emotional instability and early decline.

fact There are wide individual variations, and most individuals with special intellectual gifts are healthy, well adjusted, socially attractive, and morally responsible.

myth Those who have special gifts or talents are in a sense superhuman.

fact People with special gifts or talents are not superhuman; rather, they are human beings with extraordinary gifts in particular areas. And like everyone else, they may have particular faults.

myth Children with special gifts or talents are usually bored with school and antagonistic toward those who are responsible for their education.

fact Most children with special gifts like school and adjust well to their peers and teachers, although some do not like school and have social or emotional problems.

myth People with special gifts or talents tend to be mentally unstable.

fact Those with special gifts or talents are about as likely to be well adjusted and emotionally healthy as those who do not have such gifts.

myth We know that 3 to 5 percent of the population has special gifts or talents.

fact The percentage of the population that is found to have special gifts or talents depends on the definition of *giftedness* used. Some definitions include only 1 or 2 percent of the population; others, over 20 percent.

myth Giftedness is a stable trait, always consistently evident in all periods of a person's life.

fact Some of the remarkable talents and productivity of people with special gifts develop early and continue throughout life; in other cases, a person's gifts or talents are not noticed until adulthood. Occasionally, a child who shows outstanding ability becomes a nondescript adult.

myth People who have special gifts do everything well.

fact Some people characterized as having a special gift have superior abilities of many kinds; others have clearly superior talents in only one area.

myth A person has special intellectual gifts if he or she scores above a certain level on intelligence tests.

fact IQ is only one indication of one kind of giftedness. Creativity and high motivation are as important as indications as general intelligence. Gifts or talents in some areas, such as the visual and performing arts, are not assessed by IQ tests.

myth Students who have a true gift or talent for something will excel without special education. They need only the incentives and instruction that are appropriate for all students.

fact Some children with special gifts or talents will perform at a remarkably high level without special education of any kind, and some will make outstanding contributions even in the face of great obstacles to their achievement. But most will not come close to achieving at a level commensurate with their potential unless their talents are deliberately fostered by instruction that is appropriate for their advanced abilities.

Local school systems often have widely differing practices regarding the education of students with special gifts or talents, as "gifted" has no clear-cut definition (Mathews, 1998). In describing how giftedness has been treated in American culture, Resnick and Goodman (1994) noted that "as to 'giftedness' itself, there is no tight definition, no single agreed-on meaning. It is a flexible construct which is part of the debate over culture and policy" (p. 109).

The disagreements about definition are due primarily to differences of opinion regarding the following questions:

1. *In what ways do children with a special gift or talent excel?* Do they excel in general intelligence, insight, creativity, special talents, and achievements in academic subjects or in a valued line of work, moral judgment, or some combination of such factors? Perhaps nearly everyone is gifted in some way or other. What kind of giftedness is most important? What kind of giftedness should be encouraged?

2. *How is giftedness measured?* Is it measured by standardized tests of aptitude and achievement, teacher judgments, past performance in school or everyday life, or by some other means? If it is measured in one particular way, some individuals will be overlooked. If past performance is the test, giftedness is being defined after the fact. What measurement techniques are valid and reliable? What measurements will identify which children have the potential to develop special gifts or talents?

3. *To what degree must a child excel to be considered to have a special gift or talent?* Must the child do better than 50 percent, 80 percent, 90 percent, or 99 percent of the comparison group? The number of individuals with special gifts will vary depending on the criterion (or criteria) for giftedness. What percentage of the population should be considered to have special gifts?

4. *Who should make up the comparison group?* Should it be every child of the same chronological age, the other children in the child's school, all children of the same ethnic or racial origin, or some other grouping? Almost everyone is the brightest or most capable in some group. What group should set the standard?

5. *Why should students with special gifts be identified?* What social or cultural good is expected to come from their identification? Is it important to meet individual students' educational needs? Are national economic or security issues at stake? Does identifying these individuals maintain an elite group or social power? By providing special educational opportunities for these students, will others reap personal or social benefits? What criteria will be used to judge whether identifying students with special gifts or talents pays off?

You may have concluded already that giftedness or talentedness is whatever we choose to make it, just as mental retardation is whatever we choose to make it. Someone can be considered gifted (or retarded) one day and not the next, simply because an arbitrary definition has been changed. There is no inherent rightness or wrongness in the definitions professionals use. Some definitions may be more logical, more precise, or more useful than others, but we are still unable to say they are more correct in some absolute sense. We have to struggle with the concepts of gift and talent and the reasons for identifying individuals with these gifts or talents before we can make any decisions about definition (Borland, 1997; Callahan, 1997). Our definition of giftedness will be shaped, to a large extent, by what our culture believes is most useful or necessary for its survival. Giftedness is invented, not discovered (Howley et al., 1995; Sternberg & Davidson, 1986).

Even the terminology of giftedness can be rather confusing. Besides the word *gifted*, a variety of other terms have been used to describe individuals who are superior in some way: *talented, creative, insightful, genius,* and *precocious,* for example.

- **Precocity** refers to remarkable early development. Many children with extraordinary gifts show precocity in particular areas of development, such as language, music, or mathematical ability, and the rate of intellectual development of all children with special intellectual gifts exceeds that for typically developing children.
- **Insight** may be defined as separating relevant from irrelevant information, finding novel and useful ways of combining relevant bits of information, or relating new and old information in a novel and productive way.
- **Genius** has sometimes been used to indicate a particular aptitude or capacity in any area. More often, it has been used to indicate extremely rare intellectual powers (extremely high IQ or creativity).
- **Creativity** refers to the ability to express novel and useful ideas, to sense and elucidate novel and important relationships, and to ask previously unthought of, but crucial, questions.
- **Talent** ordinarily has been used to indicate a special ability, aptitude, or accomplishment.
- **Giftedness,** as we use the term in this chapter, refers to cognitive (intellectual) superiority (not necessarily of genius caliber), creativity, and motivation in combination and of sufficient magnitude to set the child apart from the vast majority of age-mates and make it possible for him or her to contribute something of particular value to society (Renzulli, Reis, & Smith, 1981).

Federal and State Definitions

No federal law requires special education for students with special gifts or talents as it does for students with disabilities. Federal legislation does, however, encourage states to develop programs for such students and support research.

Most states have mandatory programs for students with special gifts or talents. Each state has its own definition of giftedness. The most common elements of state definitions are (1) general intellectual ability, (2) specific academic aptitude, (3) creative thinking ability, (4) advanced ability in the fine arts and performing arts, and (5) leadership ability (Council of State Directors of Programs for the Gifted, 1991).

Changes in the Definition of Giftedness

Intelligence is far more complex than can be measured by the relatively narrow focus of standard intelligence tests.* Furthermore, giftedness seems to be characterized by qualitative differences in thinking and insightfulness, which may not be clearly reflected by performance on intelligence tests (see Reis, 1989; Sternberg,

---

*Recall that the limitations of IQ have become obvious also in the definition of mental retardation. An exceptionally low IQ by itself is no longer sufficient to define mental retardation but must be accompanied by deficits in adaptive behavior.

precocity. Remarkable early development.

insight. The ability to separate and/or combine various pieces of information in new, creative, and useful ways.

genius. A word sometimes used to indicate a particular aptitude or capacity in any area; rare intellectual powers.

creativity. The ability to express novel and useful ideas, to sense and elucidate new and important relationships, and to ask previously unthought-of but crucial questions.

talent. A special ability, aptitude, or accomplishment.

giftedness. Refers to cognitive (intellectual) superiority, creativity, and motivation of sufficient magnitude to set the child apart from the vast majority of age-mates and make it possible for him or her to contribute something of particular value to society.

People of Many Different Intelligences

Oprah Winfrey, a producer, actress, TV talk host, and promoter of writers and readers in her book club on the air, has been a major cultural influence worldwide for the last 20 years.

Mark McGwire and Sammy Sosa, baseball heroes of 1998, broke Babe Ruth's home run record of 60 in a single season by each hitting over 65 home runs.

Scott Adams, creator of the cartoon strip *Dilbert,* is read by millions of Americans every day.

Judah Folkman is pioneering an experimental cancer treatment that destroys tumors.

1996, 1998). Table 12.1 illustrates some of the myths and countermyths about intelligence and its measurement and offers truths to replace these myths.

The field of special education is beginning to appreciate the many different ways in which giftedness can be expressed in various areas of human endeavor (Karnes & Bean, 1996; Sternberg, 1998). Likewise, educators are starting to acknowledge the extent to which the meaning of giftedness is rooted in cultural values.

Whereas the usual tests of intelligence assess the ability to think deductively and arrive at a single answer that can be scored right or wrong, tests of creativity suggest many different potential answers. Recognizing the many facets of human

Jose Saramago, winner of the 1998 Nobel Prize for Literature, is a Portuguese storyteller who because of strong political beliefs lives on the Spanish island Lanzarote.

Julie Taymor won 2 Tony awards in 1998 for director and costumer of *The Lion King*.

Alan Greenspan, Federal Reserve Board chairman, has kept the nation's economic growth on a steady path for the last ten years.

Mary Robinson, former president of Ireland, is the UN High Commissioner for Human Rights.

John Glenn, astronaut and former U.S. Senator from Ohio, repeated his historic space mission in 1998 at the age of 76.

intelligence led to dissatisfaction with previous conceptualizations of general intelligence or primary mental abilities (Gardner & Hatch, 1989). Today many researchers conclude that giftedness cannot possibly be captured by a single measurement (Sternberg, 1997).

For example, Sternberg (1997) describes a theory of intelligence that suggests three main kinds of giftedness: analytic, synthetic, and practical.

- *Analytic giftedness* involves being able to take a problem apart—to understand the parts of a problem and how they are interrelated, which is a skill typically measured by conventional intelligence tests.

Table 12.1   Myths, Mythical Countermyths, and Truths About Intelligence

Myth	Mythical Countermyth	Truth
Intelligence is one thing, g (or IQ)	Intelligence is so many things you can hardly count them.	Intelligence is multidimensional but scientifically tractable.
The social order is a natural outcome of the IQ pecking order.	Tests wholly create a social order.	The social order is partially but not exclusively created by tests.
Intelligence cannot be taught to any meaningful degree.	We can perform incredible feats in teaching individuals to be more intelligent.	We can teach intelligence in at least some degree, but cannot effect radical changes at this point.
IQ tests measure virtually all that's important for school and job success.	IQ tests measure virtually nothing that's important for school and job success.	IQ tests measure skills that are of moderate importance in school success and of modest importance in job success.
We are using tests too little, losing valuable information.	We're overusing tests and should abolish them.	Tests, when properly interpreted, can serve a useful but limited function, but often they are not properly interpreted.
We as a society are getting stupider because of the dysgenic effects of stupid superbreeders.	We have no reason at all to fear any decline in intellectual abilities among successive generations.	We have some reason to fear loss of intellectual abilities in future generations, but the problem is not stupid superbreeders.
Intelligence is essentially all inherited except for trivial and unexplainable variance.	Intelligence is essentially all environmental except for trivial and unexplainable variance.	Intelligence involves substantial heritable and environmental components in interaction.
Racial differences in IQ clearly lead to differential outcomes.	Racial differences in IQ have nothing to do with differential environmental outcomes.	We don't really understand the relationships among race, IQ, and environmental outcomes.
We should write off stupid people.	There's no such thing as a stupid person. Everyone is smart.	We need to rethink what we mean by "stupid" and "smart."

Source: Sternberg, R. J. (1996). Myths, countermyths, and truths about intelligence. *Educational Researcher, 25*(2), p. 12. Copyright 1996 by the American Educational Research Association. Reprinted by permission of the publisher.

- *Synthetic giftedness* involves insight, intuition, creativity, or adeptness at coping with novel situations, skills typically associated with high achievement in the arts and sciences.
- *Practical giftedness* involves applying analytic and synthetic abilities to the solution of everyday problems, the kinds of skills that characterize people who have successful careers.

Other researchers are finding evidence of multiple intelligences, such as logical-mathematical, linguistic, musical, spatial, bodily-kinesthetic, interpersonal and intrapersonal (Gardner & Hatch, 1989; Ramos-Ford & Gardner, 1997). However, the concept of multiple intelligences is sometimes misunderstood and misused to indicate that everyone is equally intelligent (Delisle, 1996; White & Breen, 1998). Whether intelligence should be considered as a general characteristic or identified as having distinctive qualities is an ongoing debate with significant implications for defining giftedness (Bower, 1995). Others have pointed out that intelligence is really a developing form of expertise in a given area, not a static characteristic or trait that can be measured accurately by a test (Sternberg, 1998). Regardless of how the debate is ultimately resolved, it is clear that we have come a long way since the invention of the IQ in conceptualizing human intelligence.

Old stereotypes of giftedness die hard. For example, many still hold the myth that people with special gifts or talents are superior in every way, that they comprise a distinct category of human beings. This myth may account, in part, for the general public's fascination with particularly creative people and the tendency to fawn over those who distinguish themselves in glamorous lines of work.

Today most experts in education of those with special gifts and talents suggest that giftedness refers to superior abilities in specific areas of performance, which may be exhibited under some circumstances but not others (see Gallagher & Gallagher, 1994). So even though giftedness is believed to be a remarkable ability to do something valued by society, it is not an inherent, immutable trait that a person necessarily carries for life. Moreover, having a special gift at one thing does not mean that a person is good at everything.

Another significant issue in reconceptualizing giftedness is recognizing that it, like beauty, is something defined by cultural consensus. Accordingly, Sternberg and Zhang (1995) propose five criteria for judging whether someone exhibits giftedness:

1. *Excellence,* meaning that the individual must be superior to the peer group in one or more specific dimensions of performance
2. *Rarity,* meaning that very few members of the peer group exhibit the characteristic or characteristics
3. *Demonstrability,* meaning that the person must be able to actually exhibit the excellent and rare ability through some type of valid assessment (i.e., he or she cannot just claim to have it)
4. *Productivity,* meaning that the person's performance must lead to or have the potential to lead to producing something
5. *Value,* meaning that the person's performance is highly valued by society

Sternberg and Zhang also suggest that most people intuitively believe that each of these five criteria is necessary and all five together are sufficient to define giftedness. Similar intuitive, consensual definitions appear to have existed in all cultures throughout history (see Hunsaker, 1995; Tannenbaum, 1993).

Regardless of the consensual definition used, we may assume that a person may exhibit giftedness if the conditions are right for gifted performance—that is, if besides possessing above-average ability and creativity, the person is given opportunities and incentives to perform at an extraordinarily high level. Given this perspective, perhaps we should speak of people who exhibit gifted *behavior,* rather than of gifted *people,* because people typically demonstrate special gifts only under particular circumstances (Renzulli & Reis, 1997).

Prevalence

It has been assumed in federal reports and legislation that 3 to 5 percent of the U.S. school population could be considered to have special gifts or talents. Obviously the prevalence of giftedness is a function of the definition chosen. If giftedness is defined as the top *x* percent on a given criterion, the question of prevalence has been answered. Of course, if x percent refers to a percentage of a national sample, the prevalence of gifted pupils in a given school or cultural group may vary from that of the comparison group regardless of the criteria used to measure performance.

Origins of Giftedness

As defined today, giftedness is not something that sets people apart in every way from those who are average. Instead, it refers to specific, valued, and unusual talents that people may exhibit during some periods of their lives. Therefore, the main factors that contribute to giftedness are really much the same as those that foster any type of behavior, whether typical or exceptional:

1. Genetic and other biological factors, such as neurological functioning and nutrition
2. Social factors, such as family, school, the peer group, and community

We are all combinations of the influences of our genetic inheritances and social and physical environments; to say otherwise is to deny reality (see Sternberg, 1998). Having said this, we must decide what to make of these influences—what to emphasize and what to do about them. In a society such as that of the United States (or in any humane and democratic society), the social and physical environments that foster gifted performance must be emphasized without denying that genetics and neurological factors are involved in creating virtually every human characteristic.

As one proponent of special education for students with special gifts suggested, attempts to assign racial or class superiority or inferiority are unacceptable and have no place in a society in which equal opportunity and justice are valued: "In an interdependent, pluralistic, complex and multifaceted world, we are all our brothers' keepers" (Roeper, 1994, p. 150). Although giftedness may be determined in part by one's genetic inheritance, whatever genetic combinations are involved are exceedingly complex and not distributed by race or social class. Genetic differences in abilities apply within various ethnic groups and social classes, not between them (see Plomin, 1997; Thompson & Plomin, 1993).

Children who are gifted may have superior cognitive abilities that allow them to compete with adults of average intellect.

Regardless of how it is defined, the fact that giftedness is partly inherited should not be misinterpreted as an indication that social factors are unimportant. Although genetic influences on the development of superior abilities cannot be denied, these biological influences are clearly no more important (and are probably a lot less important) than the environments in which children are nurtured. Biological factors that are not genetic may also contribute to the determination of intelligence. Nutritional and neurological factors, for example, may partially determine how intellectually competent a child becomes. In previous chapters we pointed out that severe malnutrition in infancy or childhood, as well as neurological damage at any age, can result in mental retardation. But it does not follow that good nutrition and normal neurological status early in life will lead to or are necessary for giftedness. We do know that malnutrition or neurological damage can prevent giftedness from developing, however (Brown & Pollitt, 1996).

Families, schools, peer groups, and communities obviously have a profound influence on the development of giftedness (Clark, 1997; Subotnik & Arnold, 1994; Tannenbaum, 1997). Stimulation, opportunities, expectations, demands, and rewards for performance all affect children's learning (see Sternberg, 1998). For decades, researchers have found a correlation between socioeconomic level and IQ, undoubtedly in part because the performances measured by standard intelligence tests are based on what families, schools, and communities of the upper classes expect and teach. As definitions of intelligence and giftedness are broadened to include a wider range of skills and abilities that are not so specific to socioeconomic class, we will no doubt see changes in how environmental effects on giftedness are viewed.

How can families, schools, and the larger culture nurture children's giftedness? Research has shown that parents differ greatly in their attitudes toward and management of the giftedness of their children. Some parents view having a child with special gifts as positive, some as negative; fathers appear to see their children as having special gifts less often than mothers (Cornell, 1983; see also Silverman, 1997). A study of individuals who have been successful in a variety of fields has shown that the home and family, especially in the child's younger years, are extremely important (Bloom, 1982; Bloom & Sosniak, 1981; see also Subotnik & Arnold, 1994). The following were found to occur in the families of highly successful persons:

- Someone in the family (usually one or both parents) had a personal interest in the child's talent and provided great support and encouragement for its development.
- Most of the parents were role models (at least at the start of their child's development of talent), especially in terms of lifestyle.
- There was specific parental encouragement of the child to explore, to participate in home activities related to the area of developing talent, and to join the family in related activities. Small signs of interest and capability by the child were rewarded.
- Parents took it for granted that their children would learn in the area of talent, just as they would learn language.
- Expected behaviors and values related to the talent were present in the family. Clear schedules and standards for performance appropriate for the child's stage of development were held.
- Teaching was informal and occurred in a variety of settings. Early learning was exploratory and much like play.

- The family interacted with a tutor/mentor and received information to guide the child's practice. Interaction included specific tasks to be accomplished, information or specific points to be emphasized or problems to be solved, a set time by which the child could be expected to achieve specific goals and objectives, and the amount of time to be devoted to practice.

- Parents observed practice, insisted that the child put in the required amount of practice time, provided instruction where necessary, and rewarded the child whenever something was done especially well or when a standard was met.

- Parents sought special instruction and special teachers for the child.

- Parents encouraged participation in events (recitals, concerts, contests, etc.) in which the child's capabilities were displayed in public.

In sum, children who realize most fully their potential for accomplishment have families that are stimulating, directive, supportive, and rewarding of their abilities. This appears to be true regardless of the family's ethnic or cultural identification (Ford, 1994a; Hine, 1994; Robinson, 1993b). Robinson (1993b) described parenting young children with special gifts as "labor intensive," and the same could be said for parenting older children with such characteristics as well. Families in which children with special gifts or talents thrive are not laissez-faire in their approach to childrearing. Research does not indicate much else about how families encourage gifted performance. Moreover, the stresses and needs of families of these children are poorly understood (Silverman, 1997).

Different nations and cultural groups have different ways of structuring schooling and supporting children's learning that have implications for giftedness (Passow, 1997). In spite of severe socioeconomic disadvantages, some microcultural groups in the United States are able to foster high academic achievement in schools in which most other students perform very poorly (Caplan, Choy, & Whitmore, 1992). Overall, high-ability students in the United States do not compare favorably to high-ability students in most other industrialized countries of the world (Callahan, 1994). There are no simple answers to questions about why students in many other countries outperform American students. It appears, though, that one contributing factor may be the much smaller emphasis that American students place on effort in explaining their achievement (Stevenson, Lee, Chen, Kato, & Londo, 1994). Students in the United States appear less likely to attribute extraordinary achievement to hard work and more likely to attribute it to native ability.

Students from countries that outperform American students academically usually credit their high achievement to hard work, rather than native ability; American students, however, typically believe the opposite.

How schools may nurture children's giftedness has received too little attention. Yet the ways in which schools identify giftedness, group children for instruction, design curricula, and reward performance have a profound effect on what the most able students achieve. When schools facilitate the performance of all students who are able to achieve at a superior level in specific areas, giftedness is found among children of all cultural and socioeconomic groups (Feldhusen, 1989, 1998; Fulkerson & Horvich, 1998; Mills, Stork, & Krug, 1992; Renzulli, 1994).

In summary, environmental influences have much to do with how a child's genetic endowment is expressed in performance. But neither environment nor genetics can be entirely responsible for performance, whether an individual has special gifts or retardation. Genetic factors apparently determine the range within which a person will function, and environmental factors determine whether the individual will function in the lower or upper reaches of that range.

Identification of Giftedness

Measurement of giftedness is a complicated matter. Some components cannot be assessed by traditional means; in addition, the particular definition of giftedness will determine how test scores are interpreted. But if it is indeed important to identify giftedness early so that children with special talents will achieve self-fulfillment and be aided in the development of their special potential to make a unique and valuable contribution to society, it is important that appropriate methods be used.

The most common methods of identification include IQ (based on group or individual tests), standardized achievement test scores, teacher nominations, parent nominations, peer nominations, self-nominations, and evaluations of students' work or performances. Typically, some combination of several of these methods is used. Identification practices have been extremely controversial, and best practices have frequently been ignored (Feldhusen, 1998; Ford, 1998; Renzulli, 1997).

In devising identification procedures that are fair to individuals from all cultural and ethnic groups and all social classes, educators must take into account the varied definitions of giftedness and recognize the effects of cultural variation on children's behavior (Ford, 1994b, 1998; Frasier & Passow, 1994; Hunsaker & Callahan, 1995; Patton & Baytops, 1995; Patton & Townsend, 1997). In addressing multicultural differences, it is important to recognize the variations of socioeconomic status, language, and values that occur within various ethnic and cultural groups, not just between them. Hunsaker and Callahan (1995) propose eight general identification principles that will help ensure fairness:

1. Assessments go beyond a narrow conception of talent.
2. Separate and appropriate identification strategies are used to identify different aspects of giftedness.
3. Reliable and valid instruments and strategies are used to assess talent.
4. Appropriate instruments are employed for underserved populations.
5. Each child is viewed as an individual, recognizing the limits of a single score on any measure.
6. A multiple-measure/multiple-criteria approach is followed.
7. Appreciation is shown for the value of the individual case study and the limitations of combinations of scores.
8. Identification and placement are based on individual students' needs and abilities rather than on the numbers who can be served.

The focus of identification methods should be on balancing concern for identifying only those students whose capabilities are markedly above average with concern for including all who show promise for gifted performance.

Physical, Psychological, and Behavioral Characteristics

Giftedness has been recognized in some form in every society throughout recorded history (Hunsaker, 1995; Morelock & Feldman, 1997). In many societies, individuals with special gifts have been stereotyped in one of two ways: (1) as physically weak, socially inept, narrow in interests, and prone to emotional instability and early decline or, in the opposite direction, (2) as superior in intelligence, physique, social attractiveness, achievement, emotional stability, and moral character and immune to ordinary human frailties and defects. Although it may be possible to find a few individuals who seem to fit one stereotype or the other, the vast majority of people with special gifts or talents fit neither.

The box on pages 482–483 summarizes some of what we know about the development of child **prodigies**—children whose development and accomplishments meet or exceed those of adults with extraordinary talent. The article by Burge (1998) illustrates that giftedness occurs in many different fields of performance and among students of both sexes and all cultural identities. Besides those prodigies depicted in the box, Burge (1998) describes Chris Sharma (who won the World Cup in rock climbing at age fifteen), Jennifer Baybrook (who became the first female national yo-yo champion at age seventeen), Alexandra Nechita (who at age twelve showed her paintings in fifty galleries), Sara Chang (who at age eight was a guest violin soloist with Zubin Mehta and the New York Philharmonic), and Justin Miller (a globe-trotting gourmet who by age eight had cooked three times on the David Letterman show).

Students with special gifts tend to be far ahead of their age-mates in specific areas of academic performance. Most children carrying the label "gifted" learn to read easily, often before entering school. They may be far advanced in one area, such as reading or math, but not in another, such as writing or art (e.g., skills requiring manual dexterity). Contrary to popular opinion, most such students are not constantly bored with and antagonistic toward school, if they are given work that is reasonably challenging for them (Gallagher & Gallagher, 1994). Some, however, become uninterested in school and perform poorly in the curriculum or drop out (Baker, Bridger, & Evans, 1998). Not surprisingly, they become upset and maladjusted when they are discriminated against and prevented from realizing their full potential. But such a reaction is not unique to any group of children, exceptional or average, along any dimension.

Perhaps it should not be surprising that the majority of students who show giftedness enter occupations that demand greater-than-average intellectual ability, creativity, and motivation. Most find their way into the ranks of professionals and managers, and many distinguish themselves among their peers in adulthood (Gallagher & Gallagher, 1994; Perrone, 1991). But not all such students enjoy occupational success in demanding jobs; some choose career paths that do not make use of their talents or otherwise fail to distinguish themselves.

The self-concepts, social relationships, and other psychological characteristics of students with special gifts or talents have been matters of considerable interest. Many of these students are happy, well liked by their peers, emotionally stable, and self-sufficient. They may have wide and varied interests and perceive themselves in positive terms (Coleman & Fultz, 1985; Ford & Harris, 1997; Janos & Robinson, 1985). However, the links between many aspects of self-concept and giftedness are uncertain (Hoge & Renzulli, 1993). For example, placing students in homogeneous

prodigy. A child whose development and accomplishments meet or exceed those of adults with extraordinary talent.

classes, in which all students are selected because of their advanced abilities, appears to lower academic self-concept but not self-concept related to such things as appearance and peer relations (Marsh, Chessor, Craven, & Roche, 1995). Students with intellectual gifts are often acutely sensitive to their own feelings and those of others and highly concerned about interpersonal relationships, intrapersonal states, and moral issues (Gruber, 1985; Hague, 1998; Piechowski, 1997; Silverman, 1994). Using their advanced cognitive abilities appears to help many of these children de-

Contrary to myth, most students who are gifted are not constantly bored with and antagonistic toward school, if they are given work that is challenging.

velop at a young age the social and emotional adjustment strategies used by most adults (Sowa, McIntire, May, & Bland, 1994). In short, many (but not all) students with high intellectual gifts are self-aware, self-assured, and socially skilled.

It is important to realize that giftedness includes a wide variety of abilities and degrees of difference from average. Moreover, the nature and degree of an individual's giftedness may affect his or her social and emotional adjustment and educational and psychological needs. Consider, for example, that categorizing only people with IQs of 180 or higher as "gifted" is roughly like categorizing as "mentally retarded" only those individuals with IQs of 20 or less (Zigler & Farber, 1985). In fact, children who are exceptionally precocious—those whose talents are extremely rare—may constitute a group for which extraordinary adaptations of schooling are required (just as extraordinary adaptations are required for children with very severe mental retardation) (see Gross, 1992, 1993; Lovecky, 1994).

Cultural Values Regarding Students with Special Gifts or Talents and Their Education

In American culture, it is relatively easy to find sympathy for children with disabilities but more than a little difficult to turn that sympathy into public support for effective educational programs. However, for children with special gifts, especially intellectual gifts, it is difficult to elicit sympathy and next to impossible to arrange sustained public support for education that meets their needs (Clark, 1997).

This is not a peculiarly American problem, but there is something self-limiting, if not self-destructive, about a society that refuses to acknowledge and nourish the special talents of its children who have the greatest gifts (see Tannenbaum, 1993). Hunsaker (1995) has examined the perception and treatment of giftedness in

Prodigies

The Scientist

Considering her predicament, Carrie Shilyansky's phone voice is surprisingly amiable. "I've got some frozen slugs in my hand, so let me just put them in the freezer quick," she says. As her nonchalance testifies, Carrie knows sea slugs. At 16, she has already studied the creatures for three years, and her research has given scientists insight into the cellular processes behind memory and learning.

Her work with the mollusk—*Aplysia californica* when she talks to her lab buddies—won her second place at the national level in the prestigious Westinghouse Science Talent Search last year. "She is absolutely brilliant," says John Armstrong of Westinghouse. In October, Carrie presented her research, which she hopes eventually to publish, at an annual meeting among thousands of neuroscientists in New Orleans. "It was just amazingly exciting," says Carrie, who lives in San Marino, California.

Her interest in memory began as a child, when she started reading scientific literature to understand how memory works and how information is stored. "People always talk about information and memory," she says. "But they're just sort of these general concepts floating around." She started sitting in on neurobiology seminars at the California Institute of Technology when she was 11. Last fall, when she showed up as a freshman at CalTech, Carrie's advisor remembered her face. "You're the little kid who always used to come sit up front," she said when she met Carrie again.

Carrie began studying sea slugs at a CalTech laboratory where she worked weekends and during breaks at her high school. The creatures, with their simple central nervous systems, make ideal neurobiology subjects. Carrie wanted to study how memory was encoded in the slugs' nervous systems. She tapped them, causing their gills to retract, until they learned the taps weren't harmful. When she changed the frequency of the taps, however, she observed that the slugs had to learn again that the taps were harmless. Scientists had previously thought that only the strength of stimuli such as taps, and not the frequency, affected learning.

Despite her success, Carrie has learned that a young life built around science has its drawbacks. "A big, huge chunk of your social life is just gone because you don't have the time," she says. "There are a lot of times I need to be there for friends and I can't because I need to be in the lab."

The Humanitarian

When Emily Kumpel was 9, her humanitarian career was born from a newspaper article. As a reporter for the now-defunct WBZ radio show "Kid Company,' she was researching a piece about apartheid in South Africa. She came across a newspaper story that detailed how book shortages in South Africa prevented many black children from getting an education. Then she learned about Dr. Wayne Dudley, a Salem (Massachusetts) State College history professor, who was organizing a book drive for South African children. She joined his effort, eventually becoming the national youth coordinator. In the past four years, she has collected 60,000 books for South African students.

Her motive was simple: "I figured that we have had the opportunity to learn, so why shouldn't they?"

Emily started small. She recruited a few friends to help host a bake sale and collect unused books from their school. Then they performed a skit about South Africa in local elementary schools. Their work won them a $3,000 grant, which they used to pay to ship the first books to South Africa. Emily continued to collect books, writing letters to local newspapers asking for donations. She stored the books in a shed behind her house, until the floors began to buckle beneath the weight of 6,000 books. Last year, after a letter-writing campaign, she convinced a local trucking company to transport her books from her home in Wakefield, Massachusetts, to ships in Boston Harbor free of charge. Until then, she had been recruiting relatives to help her move the books, load by load, in her grandparents' Suburban.

Still, there were setbacks. It was hard to find a company willing to move the books from shed to harbor. And whenever she heard, too late, about schools throwing out old textbooks, her heart sank. Still, she says, "It's kind of an infectious thing." She continues to collect books, but she is thinking ahead to future projects. "My dream is to someday get South Africa hooked up to the Internet," she says, "so our school can talk to them."

The Publisher

When Jason Crowe's grandmother died in 1996, he looked for a way to turn his grief into a meaningful tribute to her. Since his grandmother had always read to him and listened to his stories, he decided a newspaper would be fitting, giving a voice to other children the way his grandmother had nurtured his own voice. Besides, he says, "I was on an entrepreneurial kick, and a newspaper was about the only thing I hadn't done."

Jason, now 11, knocked on his neighbors' doors, telling them about his grandmother and the newspaper. (His mother, haunted by visions of angry neighbors demanding their money back if the paper didn't pan out, convinced Jason to begin with three-month subscriptions.) *The Informer* started as a newspaper for the neighborhood, written by kids and for kids. But as the paper began to find its way far from his hometown of Newburgh, Indiana, Jason began writing about broader issues: global warming., euthanasia, racial harmony. His work on *The Informer*, now read in 24 states, the District of Columbia, and four foreign countries, has already won him a $10,000 scholarship. As a tribute to his grandmother, half his profits from the paper go to the American Cancer Society. By the end of this subscription cycle he will have contributed about $170.

Jason does most of the newspaper work himself, although his parents help with spelling, organizing ideas, and photocopying. "It's a lot more fun than most people would think," he says. "You get to get inside people when you interview them. You get to walk into different parts of humanity." The newspaper also gives him school credit. His mother, Cindy Crowe, began home-schooling him when school officials said he was hyperactive—his IQ was off the charts—and suggested the drug Ritalin. "He drove the teachers at regular school crazy because he just has all these ideas and they just keep coming out," she says.

Jason has also won attention for another project: raising money to create a statue of a cellist from Sarajevo who refused to stop playing publicly during the war in Bosnia. Jason has already organized two local events, including a concert, in the cellist's honor. Now he has enlisted former Indiana Congressman Frank McCloskey in his statue project. The two may travel to Sarajevo later this year. "To Jason, it's kind of like food for the soul," says his mother.

The Orator

Adults learned Ayinde Jean-Baptiste had a way with words when he recited part of a sermon by Martin Luther King Jr. to his first-grade class. He was 4 years old. His performance was so powerful that it immediately led to his first gig: delivering the King sermon to a Chicago-area church. In the decade since Ayinde first took the podium, requests for speaking engagements have continued to pour into his Evanston, Illinois, home. He has twice shared a podium with President Clinton—at a celebration of Martin Luther King's birthday and at the inauguration of Kweisi Mfume as president of the National Association for the Advancement of Colored People. At the Million Man March in Washington, D.C., Ayinde addressed hundreds of thousands of men, exhorting them to build their communities and commit themselves to their families.

His speaking, which has helped win him a host of awards—including a $10,000 scholarship and the Chicago NAACP President's Award—takes him around the country to about 25 engagements a year. Said one woman who heard him speak at an awards ceremony: "After two or three sentences, I thought, 'He's really good.' After four or five sentences, he could have sold me swampland."

Ayinde, 15, who has never taken a speech class, practices at home before his family. He memorizes all the speeches he delivers, a strategy (used by the ancient Greeks) that he believes allows the words to flow through him more powerfully. "I enjoy the feeling that I get when people respond to me," he says. "I enjoy being able to spread positivity."

One of the most moving responses came from a young man who approached Ayinde after a 1995 speech in New York City. The man, who remembered Ayinde's talk at the Million Man March, said that in the months after the rally he had conquered his drug addiction and reclaimed his role as a young father.

Ayinde often exhorts young people to value education and to avoid drugs and gangs. "I think the reason that I'm an effective speaker, especially with youth, is that sometimes we listen to each other more readily than we do to adults," he says. "If we're talking with each other about things that we face, it stays with us longer."

Source: K. Burge (1998, April). *Prodigies*. U.S. Airways Attaché, 82–84.

traditional West African, Egyptian, Greco-Roman, Semitic, Chinese, Mesoamerican, and European Renaissance cultures. He found that few of these cultures used the term *gifted*; however, as in contemporary American society, individuals with advanced abilities were viewed with ambivalence:

> They were considered exceptional because of the hopes people had that they would ensure the continued existence of their culture. Their ability was seen as a divine or inherited gift. Great efforts personally and societally were needed to develop their abilities, and special opportunities were generally not available to the socially disadvantaged. Finally, the exceptional were the objects of ambivalent feelings directed toward them as persons and toward their knowledge. Beliefs and feelings about individuals of exceptional ability have not changed a great deal from those we inherited from other cultures. (Hunsaker, 1995, pp. 265–266)

Gallagher (1986) describes American society's attitude toward students with special gifts or talents as a love–hate relationship. Our society loves the good things that people with extraordinary gifts produce, but it hates to acknowledge superior intellectual performance. Opponents of special education for students with special gifts argue that it is inhumane and un-American to segregate such students for instruction, and to allocate special resources for educating those who are already advantaged; also, there is the danger of leaving some children out, when only the ablest are selected for special programs (see, for example, Kaufman, 1998; Margolin, 1994; Sapon-Shevin, 1994; Treffinger, 1998). It would seem, however, impossible to argue against special education for students with special gifts and talents without arguing against special education in general, for all special education involves recognizing individual differences and accommodating those differences in schooling (see Clark, 1997; Gallagher, 1998).

Unlike students with disabilities, those with special gifts or talents do not have a federally guaranteed right to an appropriate education. However, in 1989, the Jacob K. Javits Gifted and Talented Students Education Act provided federal funding for a limited number of model educational projects and for the National Research Center on the Gifted and Talented. Similarly, in the 1980s most states increased their support of programs for students with special gifts. However, federal and state laws still fail to provide adequate safeguards for the educational rights of students with special gifts and talents (Ford, Russo, & Harris, 1995; Gallagher, 1995; Karnes & Marquardt, 1997).

Although it can be argued on the basis of sound logic, common sense, and anecdotal reports that special education should be provided for children with extraordinary abilities, few controlled research studies showing the effects of such education have been done. Callahan (1986) suggests that the wrong questions are often asked in evaluating programs. When the primary objective of a program is to provide education that is appropriate for the capabilities of the students, the major evaluation questions should involve the appropriateness of the education provided, not the outcome of producing more productive citizens (Callahan, 1993). In a study of over 1,000 elementary students, researchers found that students in programs for students with special gifts showed higher achievement and self-perception of scholastic ability than their equally able peers who were not in special programs (Delcourt, Loyd, Cornell, & Goldberg, 1994).

Special programs for students with special gifts and talents remain highly controversial (Feldhusen, 1998; Gallagher, 1998; Kaufman, 1998; Treffinger, 1998; VanTassel-Baska, 1998). Even among the students identified as having special gifts or talents there are differences of opinion about what is helpful and what is not (Delisle, 1987).

The Educational Reform Movement and Controversy Regarding the Education of Students with Special Gifts or Talents

The educational reform movement of the 1990s holds both promise and danger for education of our most able students (Clark, 1997; Gallagher, 1991a, 1997b, 1998; Renzulli & Reis, 1991; Treffinger, 1991, 1998; VanTassel-Baska, 1991a, 1998). The promise and danger are perhaps most clearly evident when reformers emphasize both excellence and heterogeneous grouping for instruction. To the extent that the emphasis of school reform is on improving the quality of instruction and encouraging the highest performance of which students are capable, the movement holds promise for all students, including those with special gifts or talents. To the extent that reformers reject the idea of grouping students for instruction in specific curriculum areas, based on their knowledge of and facility in the subject matter, however, the movement may mean disaster—not only for students with special gifts and talents but also for those with special difficulties in learning. Table 12.2 presents a summary of the possible effects that five popular reforms of the 1990s might have on students who have extraordinary abilities.

Ability grouping is one of the most controversial topics related to school reform, largely because it is seen by some as a way of perpetuating racial or ethnic inequalities in achievement and social class. Some researchers suggest that ability grouping of virtually any kind is discriminatory and ineffective and should be abolished (Oakes, 1985, 1992). Others find that ability grouping across grades and within classes has beneficial effects (Kulik & Kulik, 1992, 1997; see also Clark, 1997; Feldhusen, 1998; Gallagher, 1998; Treffinger, 1998). Grouping students for instruction based on their level of interest and achievement in specific curriculum areas should not be confused with a rigid tracking system. Flexible grouping in which students are not locked into groups or tracks but have opportunities for learning in a variety of homogeneous and heterogeneous groups is seen as highly desirable by most advocates for students with special gifts (Fiedler, Lange, & Winebrenner, 1993; Tomlinson, 1994a; VanTassel-Baska, 1992, 1998).

Many school reformers have suggested that students of all ability levels learn best in heterogeneous groups, in which cooperative learning and peer tutoring are used as strategies for meeting individual needs. Cooperative learning, peer tutoring, and other arrangements for addressing individual differences in heterogeneous groups may meet the needs of most students. However, students who are truly gifted in specific curriculum areas are very poorly served by these strategies. Advocates for students with special gifts and talents argue that these students need instruction that is conceptually more complex and abstract than most learners of similar chronological ages can handle (Feldhusen, 1998; Feldhusen & Moon, 1992; Renzulli & Reis, 1997; VanTassel-Baska, 1998).

Creating a truly "gifted-friendly" classroom in which there is a very great range of abilities among students is actually quite difficult. Furthermore, some students who have special gifts are not well served in regular classrooms (Kennedy, 1995a, 1995b). Tomlinson (1994b) describes the "easy lie" about giftedness and excellence: that it is possible to achieve excellence without challenging each individual to do his or her best. Maintaining the challenge for and demanding excellence of *all* students is an extraordinary challenge in extremely heterogeneous groups, and many teachers may find it overwhelming. The typical classroom often appears to be an acutely restrictive placement for students with special gifts or talents, not the least restrictive environment (see Gallagher, 1997b).

Table 12.2   Educational Reform Devices and Impact on Gifted Students

Middle Schools	This strong movement to replace the junior high school stresses many similar goals to education of gifted students, such as stressing interdisciplinary curriculum, instruction in thinking strategies, emphasis on counseling, team teaching, and individualization. Many proponents also stress heterogeneous grouping, which threatens to exacerbate the lack of challenge that many of these students feel.
Site-Based Management	This drive to bring educational decision making back to the local school level is a reaction to excessive control of activities by a distant central administration or state department of education. How well gifted students will do will depend on who at the site knows about the special needs of gifted students. This is basis for some concern.
Cooperative Learning	This is an instructional strategy that has become quite popular. It stresses small-group activities around a central goal, with the team being evaluated by the performance of all of the members of the team. The stress on heterogeneous grouping in the small groups has caused some distress among teachers of the gifted, who admit to liking the approach if it is used with groups of gifted students.
Outcome-Based Learning	Outcome-based learning emphasizes products (demonstrated learning) as the basis for evaluating programs, as opposed to input measures (e.g., teachers employed) or process information (e.g., number of reports made). This movement could be of some stimulus for programs for gifted students if the expectations of performance are placed high enough to challenge this student group.
Accountability	All educators will be required to demonstrate how effective they have been in helping students to learn. Special programs, such as gifted education, would be required to demonstrate, with some tangible evidence, that the program achieves more than the regular program and justifies the additional expense and resources assigned to it.

Source: From J. Gallagher & S. A. Gallagher, *Teaching the gifted child* (4th ed.). Copyright © 1994 by Allyn & Bacon. Reprinted by permission.

Neglected Groups of Students with Special Gifts or Talents

There has been recent concern for neglected groups of children and youths with special gifts and talents—those who are disadvantaged by economic needs, racial discrimination, disabilities, or gender bias—and it is not misplaced. Two facts cannot be ignored:

1. Children from higher socioeconomic levels already have many of the advantages—such as more appropriate education, opportunities to pursue their interests in depth, and intellectual stimulation—that special educators recommend for those with special gifts or talents.
2. There are far too many individuals with special gifts or talents who are disadvantaged by life circumstances or disabilities and who have been overlooked and discriminated against, resulting in a tremendous waste of human potential (Howley et al., 1995; Treffinger, 1998; Whitmore, 1986).

Underachievers with Special Gifts or Talents

Students may fail to achieve at a level consistent with their abilities for a variety of reasons. Many females achieve far less than they might because of social or cultural barriers to their selection or progress in certain careers. Students who are members of racial or ethnic minorities also are often underachievers because of bias in identification or programming for their abilities. Likewise, students with obvious disabilities are frequently overlooked or denied opportunities to achieve.

Still, underachievement cannot be explained simply by discrimination; many male, nonminority, and nondisabled students also are underachievers. Underachievement of children with special gifts or talents can result from any of the factors that lead to underachievement in any group, such as emotional conflicts or a chaotic, neglectful, or abusive home environment. A frequent cause is inappropriate school programs—schoolwork that is unchallenging and boring because these students have already mastered most of the material or because teachers have low expectations or mark students down for their misbehavior (Ford, 1998; Kolb & Jussim, 1994). A related problem is that underachievers with special gifts or talents often develop negative self-images and negative attitudes toward school (Delisle, 1982; Gallagher & Gallagher, 1994). And when a student shows negative attitudes toward school and self, any special abilities he or she may have will likely be overlooked.

Whitmore (1986) suggests that lack of motivation to excel is usually a result of a mismatch between the student's motivational characteristics and opportunities provided in the classroom. Students are typically highly motivated when (1) the social climate of the classroom is nurturant, (2) the curriculum content is relevant to students' personal interests and challenging, and (3) the instructional process is appropriate to students' natural learning styles.

One way of preventing or responding to underachievement is allowing students to skip grades or subjects so school becomes more nurturing and provides greater interest and challenge. However, acceleration is not always appropriate, nor is it typically sufficient by itself to address the problems of the underachieving student with exceptional abilities (Jones & Southern, 1991; Rimm & Lovance, 1992). Counseling, individual and family therapy, and a variety of supportive or remedial strategies may be necessary alternatives or additions to acceleration (Gallagher, 1991b; VanTassel-Baska, 1990, 1998).

Underachievement must not be confused with nonproductivity (Delisle, 1981). A lapse in productivity does not necessarily indicate that the student is underachieving. The student with extraordinary ability should not be expected to be constantly producing something remarkable. But this points up our difficulty in defining giftedness: How much time must elapse between episodes of creative productivity before we say that someone no longer exhibits giftedness or has become an underachiever? We noted earlier that giftedness is in the performance, not the person. Yet we know that the unrelenting demand for gifted performance is unrealistic and can be inhumane.

Students with Special Gifts from Cultural- and Ethnic-Minority Groups

Three characteristics may be used to define students who have both extraordinary abilities and unique needs because of their cultural or minority status: cultural diversity, socioeconomic deprivation, and geographic isolation (Baldwin, 1985). These characteristics may occur singly or in combination. For example, Swanson (1995) describes the problems of serving African American students in rural areas who have special gifts or talents, and Kitano and Espinosa (1995) discuss the complications of working with such students who are learning English as a second language. Each group has unique needs for different reasons.

Children from minority cultural groups may be viewed negatively, or the strengths and special abilities valued in their cultures may conflict with those of the majority. Children reared in poverty may not have toys, reading materials, opportunities for travel and exploration, good nutrition and medical care, and many other advantages typically provided by more affluent families. Lack of basic necessities and opportunities for learning may mask intelligence and creativity. Children living in remote areas may not have access to many of the educational resources that are typically found in more populated regions.

Among the greatest challenges in the field today are identifying culturally diverse and disadvantaged students with special abilities and including and retaining these students in special programs. Some cultural and ethnic groups have been sorely neglected in programs for students with special gifts or talents. For example, Ford (1998) and Patton and Baytops (1995) note that although African American students comprise about 16 percent of public school enrollment, they make up only about 8 percent of those enrolled in programs for those with special gifts or talents. Frasier (1991) observes that addressing the underrepresentation of cultural or ethnic groups is a task with many proposed solutions, none of which has yet been entirely successful.

The desegregation of public schooling following the landmark 1954 decision of the U.S. Supreme Court in *Brown v. Board of Education* has not yet resulted in racial balance in programs for students with special gifts or talents (Ford & Webb, 1994). Bias in testing and referral practices—as well as a tendency of educators to focus on the deficits, rather than the strengths, of minority students—contribute to the underrepresentation of some ethnic groups in education programs for students with special gifts or talents (Ford, 1998; Frasier, Garcia, & Passow, 1995). Many African American students with special gifts or talents remain underachievers, even if they recognize the importance of achievement in American society (Ford, 1993, 1998). And some, perhaps many, students of color who have exceptional ability feel misunderstood by peers, family, and teachers, who are not trained to respond competently to cultural differences in giftedness (see Cropper, 1998; Ford, 1994b). However, African American students identified as having special gifts or talents have been found to have more positive attitudes toward achievement and to be more optimistic about their futures than are their African American peers who have not been so identified (Ford & Harris, 1996).

Appropriate identification and programming for students with special gifts or talents will result in including approximately equal proportions of all ethnic groups. This proportionality will likely be achieved only if renewed efforts are made to:

Many gifted individuals have been disadvantaged by life circumstances or other disabilities and thus overlooked and discriminated against, resulting in a tremendous waste of potential.

- Devise and adopt culturally sensitive identification criteria
- Provide counseling to raise the educational and career aspirations of students in underrepresented groups
- Make high-achieving models from all ethnic groups available
- Retain underrepresented ethnic students in programs
- Adopt a workable system to ensure the inclusion of underrepresented groups
- Build relationships with the families of minority children

Ultimately, the larger social-environmental issue of making families and communities safe, as well as intellectually stimulating, for children and youths of all cultural and ethnic backgrounds must be addressed (Cropper, 1998; Feldhusen, 1998; Gallagher, 1998). Equal opportunity for development outside the school environment would help address the underrepresentation of minority students in programs for students with extraordinary abilities.

Students with Disabilities and Special Gifts or Talents

The education of students with both disabilities and special gifts or talents is just emerging as a field. The major goals of the field are identification of exceptional students with specific disabilities, research and development, preparation of professionals to work with such children and youths, improvement of interdisciplinary cooperation for the benefit of such children and youths, and preparation of students for adult living.

Whitmore and Maker (1985) note that our stereotypic expectations of people with disabilities frequently keep us from recognizing their abilities. For example, if a child lacks the ability to speak or to be physically active or presents the image associated with intellectual dullness (e.g., drooling, slumping, dull eyes staring), we tend to assume that he or she has mental retardation. The fact is, students with physical characteristics typically associated with severe mental retardation may be intellectually brilliant; unless this is acknowledged, however, the talents of students with cerebral palsy and other physical disabilities may be easily overlooked (Willard-Holt, 1994). Students with special gifts or talents and impaired hearing also may be overlooked if their communication skills are poorly developed, if their teachers are not looking for signs of talent, or if they are taught by teachers who have limited competence in communicating with people who are deaf (Rittenhouse & Blough, 1995). Some students with learning disabilities have extraordinarily high intellectual abilities, yet their talents will be missed if those abilities are not properly assessed (Baum, Olenchak, & Owen, 1998; Gallagher, 1998; Hannah & Shore, 1995; Reis, Neu, & McGuire, 1995).

In fact, giftedness can occur in combination with disabilities of nearly every description, as depicted in cases described by Sacks (1995) and as illustrated in the following:

"Alec (a pseudonym) reads. He reads all the time."

"What does he read?"

"*Scientific American, National Geographic, Omni, Air and Space,* Isaac Asimov."

Alec's mother paused briefly. "For hours at a time he just disappears into books and magazines. He comprehends well. His science vocabulary is incredible."

Students whose disabilities prevent them from speaking or physically expressing themselves may have potential that is not obvious through casual observation.

"How old did you say he is?"

"Eleven."

"And he doesn't go to school?"

"We've kept him home because of his health problems."

As the case conference progressed, it became apparent that Alec was an extraordinary child. His disabilities included asthma, severe food and chemical sensitivities, poor motor skills, difficulties with perception and orientation, hyperactivity, and learning disabilities. In spite of all these problems, Alec had special verbal gifts. (Moon & Dillon, 1995, p. 111)

Consider also the individuals featured in the box on page 491. Evelyn Glennie, a deaf percussionist, and Timothy Cordes, a blind medical student, do not fit the stereotypes we hold of people who are deaf or blind. True, they are not typical of people with their disabilities, or of people who do not have their disabilities, for that matter. Fortunately, their disabilities were not allowed to preclude their pursuit of their areas of special talent.

We do not want to foster the myth that giftedness is found as often among students with disabilities as among those who do not have disabilities. But clearly, students with special gifts or talents and disabilities have been a neglected population. Whitmore and Maker (1985) estimate that at least 2 percent of children with disabilities, excluding those with mental retardation, may have extraordinary abilities as well.

VanTassel-Baska (1991b) summarizes what is known about students with disabilities and special gifts or talents:

> We know that these learners exist, many times hidden inside their specific disabling condition, and we know because of their discrepant pattern, they are difficult to find and identify. Moreover, we also know that these learners require more extensive services in order to develop their potential. (pp. 261–262)

The more extensive services to which VanTassel-Baska refers can seldom be provided by single teachers or schools. So a key factor in meeting these students' needs is the collaboration of a variety of disciplines and institutions to provide appropriate technology and training (Johnson, Karnes, & Carr, 1997).

Females with Special Gifts or Talents

Clearly, females comprise the largest group of neglected students with special gifts or talents. As Callahan (1991) and Kerr (1997) point out, some aspects of the way females are treated in U.S. society are undergoing rapid change. Females with extraordinary capabilities today have many opportunities for education and choice of careers that were denied to females a generation ago. "Yet, there is certainly convincing data that suggest that this particular group of students with special gifts or talents is facing inequities, they are still not achieving at the levels we would expect, and they are not choosing career options commensurate with their abilities" (Callahan, 1991, p. 284).

Disabilities Do Not Preclude Giftedness

The Unbeatable Drummer

For those who would experience the ultimate synthesis of mental, physical and musical harmony, let me prescribe the Evelyn Glennie Workout—if you can keep up with her, you're in terrific shape. On Thursday night at the Kennedy Center, Glennie played the Washington premiere of Joseph Schwantner's Percussion Concerto with the National Symphony Orchestra under Leonard Slatkin and she was magnificent—a thrilling, hyperkinetic wild woman racing about the stage, striking her many and variegated instruments with the ritualized, poetic violence of a martial artist.

Over the course of the concerto's 20 minutes, Glennie leapt repeatedly from one instrument to another—now rapid-fire ostinato patterns for marimba, now a bright explosion of chimes, now a series of mortal whacks to the guts of the tuned drums. Still, for all of Glennie's stamina, dexterity and strength, her sheer musicianship is what lingers in the memory—the subtle gradations of sound and color she brings to every phrase, the assurance with which she controls the whole vast tintinnabulation.

The concerto itself makes an extraordinarily exciting first impression; how well it will stand up to repeated listenings—without the spectacle of Glennie's physical presence—is, to this taste, still open to question. Fortunately, we shall have an opportunity to find out, as RCA Red Seal is recording this series of concerts for release on disc next year.[1]

Blind Valedictorian Is Headed to Med School

Sure but sightless, Timothy Cordes arrived on the University of Notre Dame's campus four years ago, an 18-year-old freshman from Eldridge, Iowa, who wanted to enroll in the biochemistry program. Faculty members tried, politely, to dissuade him. Just how, they wondered aloud, could a blind student keep up with the rigorous courses and demanding laboratory work of biochemistry?

Cordes graduated today from Notre Dame with a degree in biochemistry and a 3.991 grade-point average. He was the last of Notre Dame's 2,000 seniors to enter the crowded auditorium for commencement. His German shepherd, Electra, led him to the lectern to deliver the valedictory speech as his classmates rose, cheered, applauded and yelled his name affectionately.

Cordes starts medical school in two months, only the second blind person ever admitted to a U.S. medical school. He does not plan to practice medicine. His interest is in research, he said: "I've just always loved science."

His life has been both an act of open, mannerly defiance and unshakable faith. And this unassuming, slightly built young man with a choirboy's face awes acquaintances and friends.

Armed with Electra, a high-powered personal computer and a quick wit, Cordes managed a near-perfect academic record, an A-minus in a Spanish class the only blemish. Two weeks ago, he earned a black belt in the martial arts tae kwon do and jujitsu.

"He is really a remarkable young man," said Paul Helmquist, a Notre Dame biochemistry professor. Helmquist at first had doubts but ultimately recommended Cordes for medical school. "He is by far the most brilliant student I've ever come across in my 24 years of teaching," Helmquist said.

If others find some noble lessons in his life, Cordes perceives it more prosaically: He's merely shown up for life and done what was necessary to reach his goals.

"I don't see myself as some sort of 'Profiles in Courage' story," he said. "If people are inspired by what I've done, that's great, but the truth is that I did it all for me. It was just hard work. It's like getting the black belt. It's not like I just took one long lesson. It was showing up every day, and sweating and learning and practicing. You have your bad days and you just keep going." ...

Cordes has Leber's disease, a genetic condition that gradually diminished his vision until he was blind at age 14.

When doctors at the University of Iowa first diagnosed the disease when he was 2, "it was the saddest moment of my life." said his mother, Therese, 50.

"The doctors ... told us: 'He won't be able to do this, and don't expect him to be able to do this,'" Therese Cordes recalled. "So I went home and just ignored everything they said."

The ability to conceptualize images has greatly helped Cordes in his studies, Helmquist said. The study of biochemistry relies heavily on graphics and diagrams to illustrate complicated molecular structures. Cordes compensated for his inability to see by asking other students to describe the visual aides or by using his computer to re-create the images in three-dimensional forms on a special screen he could touch.

Cordes applied to eight medical schools. Only the University of Wisconsin accepted him. (The first blind medical student was David Hartman who graduated from Temple in 1976 and is a psychiatrist in Roanoke, Va.)[2]

Source: (1) Page, T. (1996, October 12). The unbeatable drummer. *The Washington Post.* C–1; (2) Jeter, J. (1998, May 18). Blind valedictorian is headed to med school. *The Washington Post*, A–6. © 1996, 1998 The Washington Post. Reprinted with permission.

Cultural factors work against the development and recognition of females with special gifts or talents (Eccles, 1985). Females simply have not been provided with equal opportunity and motivation to enter many academic disciplines or careers that have, by tradition, been dominated by males, such as chemistry, physics, medicine, and dentistry. When females have entered these fields, they have often been rewarded inappropriately (according to irrelevant criteria or with affection rather than promotion) for their performance. English literature has tended to portray females as wives, mothers, or "weaker" sisters, who are either dependent on males or sacrifice themselves for the sake of males who are dominant. These barriers to giftedness in females have only recently been brought forcefully to public attention.

Females lag behind males in many measures of achievement and aptitude (e.g., professional and career achievement, standardized test scores, grades) and tend not to pursue courses of study or careers involving science and math (Hedges & Nowell, 1995; Junge & Dretzke, 1995; Terwilliger & Titus, 1995). In short, they are underrepresented in many fields of advanced study and in professions and careers that carry high status, power, and pay. We can only presume to know the reasons for their underrepresentation (Callahan, 1991). Factors contributing to the situation may include lower parental expectations for females, overemphasis on and glamorization of gender differences, school and societal stereotypes of gender roles, and educational practices detrimental to achievement (e.g., less attention to high-achieving girls, expectations of less independence of girls).

Research reviewed by Callahan (1991) and Kerr (1997) suggests that the problems of neglect and underrepresentation of females with exceptional abilities are much more complex than previously believed. Like underrepresentation of ethnic and cultural minorities, the problems involving females are closely tied to cultural, social, and political issues, and they do not have simple or easy solutions. Nevertheless, the education of females with special gifts or talents might be improved by encouraging females to take risks by enrolling in challenging courses, to make career choices appropriate for their abilities, and to explore avenues that break stereotypical female roles.

Educational Considerations

Today the focus of education is on talent development across the full spectrum of abilities in particular areas of functioning (see Clark & Zimmerman, 1998; Feldhusen, 1998; Kelly & Moon, 1998; Treffinger 1998; VanTassel-Baska, 1998). However, this point of view includes the recognition by many that special education for some is necessary to provide equity for students with special gifts or talents.

> It is undesirable to identify some students as "gifted" and the rest as "ungifted." All students at all ages have relative talent strengths, and schools should help students identify and understand their own special abilities. Those whose talents are at levels exceptionally higher than those of their peers should have access to instructional resources and activities that are commensurate with their talents. The one-size-fits-all mentality that is at least partly an outgrowth of the inclusion movement reflects a mistaken view of human development. Highly talented young people suffer boredom and negative peer pressure in heterogeneous classrooms. Students at all ages and grade levels are entitled to challenging and appropriate instruction if they are to develop their talents fully. (Feldhusen, 1998, p. 738)

The common belief that students with special gifts or talents do not need education designed for their needs works against talent development. "Contrary to popular belief, talented individuals do not make it on their own. Not only is the process of talent development lengthy and rigorous, but the need for support from others is crucial for ultimate success" (VanTassel-Baska, 1998, p. 762). As noted earlier (see also the box on page 491), family support plays a crucial role in the development of talent. However, special school supports as well are needed for many students if they are to achieve to their full potential. The consensus of leaders in the field is that special education for students with special gifts or talents should have three characteristics:

1. A curriculum designed to accommodate the students' advanced cognitive skills
2. Instructional strategies consistent with the learning styles of students with extraordinary abilities in the particular content areas of the curriculum
3. Administrative arrangements facilitating appropriate grouping of students for instruction (see Feldhusen, 1998; Maker & Nielson, 1996; VanTassel-Baska, 1993, 1998)

States and localities have devised a wide variety of plans for educating students with special gifts or talents. Generally, the plans can be described as providing **enrichment** (additional experiences provided to students without placing them in a higher grade) or **acceleration** (placing the students ahead of their age-mates).

Many variations of enrichment and acceleration have been invented, however, ranging from regular classroom placement, with little or no assistance for the teacher, to special schools offering advanced curricula in special areas such as science and mathematics or the arts. Between these extremes are consulting teacher programs, resource rooms, community mentor programs (in which highly talented students work individually with professionals), independent study programs, special classes, and rapid advancement of students through the usual grades, including early admission to high school or college.

Not every community offers all possible options. In fact, there is great variation in the types of services offered within the school systems of given states and from state to state (Passow & Rudnitski, 1993). As one might expect, large metropolitan areas typically offer more program options than small towns or rural areas. New York City, for example, has a long history of special high schools for students with extraordinary gifts and talents.

Some of the educational options for students with high ability are extremely controversial. For example, the extent to which these students should be served in general education classrooms is hotly debated in the literature (e.g., Maker, 1993). Some educators argue that when students with extraordinary abilities are pulled out of regular classes, there is a negative impact on the attitudes and perceptions of the students who are not pulled out (e.g., Sapon-Shevin, 1994); research findings contradict this assumption, however (Shields, 1995). Others have found that offering a variety of program options for students with special gifts and talents produces good outcomes and that no single type of program option meets the needs of all such students (Delcourt et al., 1994; Feldhusen, 1998).

Ideally, assessment, identification, and instruction are closely linked, whether students have disabilities or special gifts and talents. Sternberg has proposed a model that uses the three kinds of intelligence he has identified—analytic, synthetic, and practical (see pages 473–474)—as the basis for assessing, identifying, and

enrichment. An approach in which additional learning experiences are provided for students with special gifts or talents while they remain in the grade levels appropriate for their chronological ages.

acceleration. An approach in which students with special gifts or talents are placed in grade levels ahead of their age peers in one or more academic subjects.

success stories

special educators at work

Palo Alto, CA: **Noshua Watson** is enrolled in the Ph.D. program in economics at Stanford University. Just eighteen years old, she recently completed high school and college through a residential acceleration program for students with special gifts or talents. Along with her parents, Aremita and Rudy Watson, and program

director Celeste Rhodes, Noshua is satisfied that, for her, this educational alternative makes sense.

At age thirteen, Noshua Watson enrolled in the Program for the Exceptionally Gifted, known as PEG, which is an acceleration program at Mary Baldwin College in Virginia. "The intellectual challenges I had as a young teenager blew my mind. It was so exciting to realize what I could do!" she remembers. "It was the first time I felt part of a school community."

Noshua's parents saw her academically challenged beyond what was possible with the high school curriculum and in a supportive environment that encouraged her personal growth. Noshua thrived on the stimulation of campus activities, including lacrosse, theater, music, and the college's judicial review board. She assisted with institu-

tional research and helped to teach an economics course during her senior year.

"Acceleration programs like PEG challenge our culture," says Celeste Rhodes, the program's director. "Parents and students must be courageous in their ability to accept uniqueness." Noshua's mother, Aremita Watson, explains, "My husband and I feel it's our responsibility to provide opportunities for our girls, and PEG was something Noshua really wanted to do. Most children don't get the chance to be their best because too often we teach them to be like others, instead of encouraging them to be motivated by a belief about life that can shape their dreams and aspirations."

Celeste describes this ten-year-old program as an alternative for the motivated student who may have teenage interests but demonstrates what she calls "a serious sense of purpose." "You see it in the interviews," she says. "There is an energy, a spark, a drive."

To Celeste, giftedness is not defined narrowly by IQ but includes multiple measures, including consistent achievement over time. "We are accelerating students by four years. That requires a history of discipline, hard work, and high grades." Through a lengthy essay and interview process, an optimal match is sought between student and program. Explains Celeste, "Since we are residential, emotional stability is extremely important." Noshua agrees. "As PEG students, we were ready and eager for the academic rigors, but emotionally and physically we were not as mature. We were still teenagers with a lot of special needs."

In this acceleration program, Noshua was supported by an individualized, integrated curriculum that addressed her advanced cognitive skills. Small-group instruction with college students and PEG peers was combined with personal mentoring and alternatives such as independent

teaching students who have special gifts (Sternberg & Clinkenbeard, 1995). According to this model, students' ability to exhibit the three types of intelligence would be assessed, and those who showed extraordinary facility in using a particular form of intelligence in a given area of the curriculum then would be provided instruction that emphasized their unusual strengths. Although this three-dimensional model might be applicable to all program options and areas of the curriculum, its validity for program design has not yet been established.

Advances in telecommunications, the presence of microcomputers in the home and classroom, and the call for excellence in American education are three developments with implications for educating the most able students. Tele-

study and accelerated pacing. According to Noshua, "I was intellectually challenged, but I could socially mature at my own rate, and for me, that was really key."

For her first two years in the program, Noshua lived in a special dormitory for younger PEG students, along with residential coordinators sensitive to the needs of adolescents. Social activities were sponsored and friendships nurtured through residence life, and the coordinators also served as academic advisors to first-year students. Noshua was free to choose among the college's liberal arts offerings but was required to take two specific PEG-level courses: one in literature and one in mathematics. She also took several study skills workshops. Celeste explains, "Study skills is taught by older PEG students and directed toward how to organize for college-level learning. These tutors, or 'near peers,' help acculturate the younger students to life at the college." For her last two years, Noshua lived independently in a regular dorm, and her academic advisor was a faculty member in her chosen major of economics.

Selecting educational alternatives is a familiar practice for Noshua and her family. As a youngster, she attended a magnet school and was described as an avid learner who was strong willed and knew her own mind. Her first experience with education for students with special gifts or talents came from a centralized public school program for third- through fifth-graders. Noshua remembers hoping that when the family moved, she would attend a similar school, but there were no separate programs in her new district. Enrichment classes were held before and after school, but her parents opted not to enroll her because of transportation problems.

Aremita Watson remembers that junior high was not a positive experience for her daughter, who has bad memories. "I was frustrated academically because my guidance counselor said if I wanted to take both French and Span-ish, I also had to take an honors math course one level beyond my grade. Socially, I was frustrated because most kids at school just wanted to 'hang out.' My parents wouldn't allow me to do this, and it was hard for me to relate. I guess you could say I was sort of a geek!"

Through a talent search at a local university, Noshua discovered a residential camp for gifted students and happily attended for three summers. "I felt I could finally be myself," she says. In eighth grade, a national search service identified programs offering alternatives to conventional high schools. "That's where I heard about PEG, and so did a fellow camper. We graduated from college together last June."

Noshua is the recipient of a National Science Foundation Graduate Fellowship. As a doctoral student, she is part of a minority on several counts: At eighteen, she is younger than her peers and considered to be gifted. She is also female and African American. Undaunted, her voice is filled with energy when she says, "I just love being at Stanford! I have more in common with graduate students, since most people my age are just starting to live away from home for the first time. My life experience has been different, and I'm used to a lot more independence."

For Noshua, getting an early start on education and career has been satisfying. But as the oldest of three sisters, she believes that everyone has to make her own choices. Her sister Tenea is now a PEG student, and twelve-year-old Cambria will decide soon if she wants to take the same route. "My parents never pressure us to do things the same way," says Noshua. "They've done so much to provide us with unique experiences."

—By Jean Crockett

communications—including instructional television, telephone conferencing, and electronic mail—are technological means of facilitating the interaction of particularly able students and their teachers over wide geographical areas. These communication systems are important for extending appropriate education to students with special gifts or talents who live in rural and remote areas. The possible uses of microcomputers for enhancing the education of extraordinarily high-performing students are enormous. Using software tutorials, accessing data banks, playing or inventing computer games that are intellectually demanding, writing and editing in English and foreign languages, learning computer languages, and solving advanced problems in mathematics are only a few of the possibilities.

Acceleration

Acceleration involves moving a student ahead of her or his age peers in one or more areas of the curriculum. It may mean skipping one or more grades or attending classes with students in higher grades for one or a few specific subjects. Acceleration has not been used frequently, especially in rural areas (Jones & Southern, 1992). It has been used primarily with students who are extremely intellectually precocious (i.e., those scoring 160 or higher on individually administered intelligence tests). Radical acceleration of extremely precocious students, combined with enrichment at each stage of their school careers, appears to offer many of these students the best social experiences as well as academic progress commensurate with their abilities (Charlton, Marolf, & Stanley, 1994; Gross, 1992).

Opponents of acceleration fear that children who are grouped with older students will suffer negative social and emotional consequences or that they will become contemptuous of their age peers. Proponents of acceleration argue that appropriate curricula and instructional methods are available only in special schools or in regular classes for students who are older than the child with special gifts or talents. Furthermore, proponents argue that by being grouped with other students who are their intellectual peers in classes in which they are not always first or correct, students acquire more realistic self-concepts and learn tolerance for others whose abilities are not so great as their own.

Research on the effects of acceleration does not clearly indicate that it typically has negative effects, but neither does it clearly indicate benefits in all cases (Jones & Southern, 1991). Acceleration appears to be a plan that can work very well but demands careful attention to the individual case and to specific curriculum areas.

Enrichment

Renzulli and his colleagues have developed an enrichment model based on the notion that children exhibit gifted behaviors in relation to particular projects or activities to which they apply their above-average ability, creativity, and task commitment (Olenchak & Renzulli, 1989; Renzulli, 1994; Renzulli & Reis, 1985; 1997). Students selected into a "talent pool" through case-study identification methods are engaged in enrichment activities that involve individual or small-group investigation of real-life problems; they become practicing pollsters, politicians, geologists, editors, and so on. The teacher (1) helps students translate and focus a general concern into a solvable problem, (2) provides them with the tools and methods necessary to solve the problem, and (3) assists them in communicating their findings to authentic audiences (i.e., consumers of information). Students may stay in the enrichment program as long as they have the ability, creativity, and motivation to pursue productive activities that go beyond the usual curriculum for students their age. The model has become known as the *schoolwide enrichment model*. An experimental study of the schoolwide enrichment model in elementary schools by Olenchak and Renzulli (1989) found an improved learning environment for all students and better attitudes of students and teachers toward the education of those with extraordinary abilities. Special programming for students who have such abilities became a more integral part of general education.

Teachers of Students with Special Gifts or Talents

Teaching students who are exceptionally able may at first thought seem easy. Who would not like to teach students who are particularly bright, creative, and motivated? In reality, teachers of these students, just like other special and general education teachers, are vulnerable to burnout (Dettmer, 1982). Students with special gifts or talents often challenge the system of school, and they can be verbally caustic. Their superior abilities and unusual or advanced interests demand teachers who are highly intelligent, creative, and motivated. Simply leading a productive discussion with such a student is a demanding task for even a master teacher (see Coleman, 1992). Teachers who are successful in fostering the creativity of students have developed their own creative competencies and are able to use creative teaching procedures with great skill (Esquivel, 1995).

Teachers of students with special gifts or talents must be adept at assessing students' abilities, interests, and commitment to tasks and skilled at helping other teachers recognize the characteristics that indicate students could profit from special education (Clark, 1998). Frequent communication with regular teachers, observation, interpretation of test scores, and interviews with students, parents, and other professionals are required to identify students who have exceptional abilities. Only teachers with broad interests, extensive information, and abundant creative energy will be able to accomplish the identification, instruction, and guidance of students with special gifts or talents.

In many ways, excellent teachers of students with special gifts or talents are very similar to excellent teachers of all other types of students (Baldwin, 1993). In fact, all good teachers probably share certain core characteristics. Nevertheless, students with special gifts or talents obviously pose a particular challenge for teachers in terms of the breadth and level of information and the degree of creativity they must bring to the classroom, and many teachers do not make these accommodations (Feldhusen, 1997). Whitlock and DuCette (1989) suggest that the following characteristics distinguish outstanding teachers of these students:

- Enthusiasm for and dedication to work with students who have special gifts or talents
- Self-confidence in their ability to be effective
- Facilitation of other people as resources and learners
- Ability to apply knowledge of theory to practice
- Strong achievement orientation

Early Intervention

The giftedness of young children presents special problems of definition, identification, programming, and evaluation (Jackson & Klein, 1997). Biological research suggests that the period from one to three years of age is particularly critical in the development of special gifts and talents (Henderson & Ebner, 1997). Karnes and Johnson (1991) point out that although progress has been made in building model programs and providing better services for young children with

Collaboration key to success

Bessie R. Duncan is a Supervisor, Gifted and Talented Education, Detroit Public Schools; B.S., Medical Technology and M.A., Special Education, Wayne State University. **Louis Carney** is an English teacher, Mackenzie High School, Detroit, Michigan; B.S., Speech and English and M.A., Education Administration, Eastern Michigan University; M.S., Mathematics Education, University of Detroit.

Bessie R. Duncan

Bessie This is my eighth year as Supervisor of Gifted and Talented Education for the Detroit Public Schools. I'm responsible for planning and implementing programs for students with a variety of talents. Before 1985, we had no gifted and talented education department. Rather, everyone was responsible for identifying and nurturing bright students. I'm a very creative person. So, when the position was created, I convinced my supervisor to continue the tradition and allow me to make gifted education part of the fabric of the education of all children rather than a separate program. I wanted to avoid labeling students and creating a "we" and a "they." One part of our program identifies students who may have undiscovered special talent. Another part of our program provides direct services for the needs of identified children in a variety of areas—academic talents, visual and performing arts, and leadership. A part of our philosophy is that when programs are developed and implemented collaboratively with others we guard against these programs' demise because of their being person-dependent. When more people are involved, you have more champions for the program; they feel some personal ownership of the program and want to sustain it and see it grow. So the middle school debate program first evolved in this context. Initially, I went to the supervisor of Communication Arts because, again, I don't develop programs in isolation; I always collaborate with another curriculum department. That's when I first met Lou. I had heard a lot about Lou—that he was a very fine fellow with lots of talent. So, I thought, he sounds just like the person we need—someone who cares a lot about kids, who is gentle and will help us get this program started.

Lou Bessie and Sterling Jones, the supervisor of Communication Arts, were really enthusiastic about the success of the high school debate program. They believed that the traditional cross-examination debate format could also be effective in the middle school. The intent of the program is to promote the intellectual development of middle school students by accelerating and differentiating the curriculum through debate. Debate becomes a vehicle for stimulating middle school students' learning and encouraging them to view the world in more global terms. Reaching the goal of this program depends on a collaborative learning philosophy. Success is linked to the middle school teachers' acceptance of ownership for all decisions and bylaws. We guide them in keeping the program enthusiastic and fair for all participants. We have developed four workshops for interested middle school teachers. The first centers on basic debate terminology. Teachers receive materials describing generative thinking strategies that they can share with their students. The second workshop focuses on defining the resolution, in which the teachers write in the roles of the team members. These plans are made in collaboration with the high school science and social studies teachers. In the third workshop, teachers work in debate squads. Their task is to write a brief based upon a partial brief with supporting literature supplied by me. The opposing squad is also furnished with research to counter the brief. The goal is to redefine what they know and share this with their students. The final workshop is a practice debate among the teachers to review the format. Teachers who are seasoned debate veterans are paired with the first-year debate coaches. Rules and procedures are finalized by the coaches. The first debate is a practice meet. Students are not judged in terms of winning or losing. Instead they are critiqued and walked through the format. They are given suggestions on strengthening their stance by high school debate students, who serve as judges. All judges are given an informal inservice on format and suggestions on evaluating middle school students.

Bessie I want to enlarge on what Lou just brought up—our high school debaters serving as judges. These students have to be released from their classes, and many times their coaches will come to sort of cheer them on. So it's really a collaborative project that has many layers. The collaboration is among administrators, administrators and teachers, teachers and students, and among students. I think that's what makes for the richness of the program, and I think that

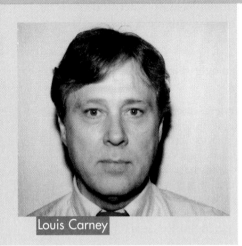
Louis Carney

explains why it's so celebrated by everybody. Problems do arise, but because everybody likes the program, they work around them—arranging transportation to the meet or covering classes for coaches, for example.

Lou I want to comment further on the high school debaters. When they debate, they often complain and are frustrated at times by judges. In competition, they sometimes don't feel that they deserve *this* or they should've received *that.* "I don't understand why the judge didn't vote for us," they say. So now they're the judges for the middle school kids. All of a sudden they're wearing a different hat and they have to make those decisions on winning or losing and balloting for speaker points. They're required to justify their ballots and give the details in the synopsis of their decision. This changes their perspective. It gives them a comprehensive understanding of the debate process and makes their competitions more palatable. They understand that an issue might be interpreted a different way by a different listener. It seems to make them better debaters.

Bessie I'll look at it from the perspective of another group of students—the seventh- and eighth-graders who participate in this project. We have heard many success stories about students who chose to participate. As I said earlier, middle school debate is a collaborative project that's used to identify middle school stu-

dents who have leadership abilities. It's certainly done that. For many of the students who have strong thinking and language skills that emerge in debate, teachers have observed that they have shown increased achievement, better attendance, and a change in their aspirations in terms of what they are going to do next. Many of the high schools who learn about these strong debate teams are courting the middle school students to come and be part of their high school debate teams, or the students choose a high school based on the strength of its debate team. In our first year, we started with five or six schools. In the second year we had fourteen, and now we're up to eighteen schools with debate teams with three others watching and getting ready. That's out of a total of sixty middle schools. So, we predict that in the next three or four years we may have a pretty high ratio of our students participating. That's a reason for celebration for all of us. Living in an urban area, self-management skills are a key to students being successful in school as well as outside of school. For students involved in debate, another payoff is that even when they're upset they are able to choose, more often, appropriate responses to stress because of their thinking and language skills.

Lou Some middle school teachers are not comfortable with the win/lose outcome of debates. They accept the fact that in basketball games there are winners and losers; in chess games, too, there are winners and losers; and in academic games there are winners and losers. But when it comes to debate, there is concern about winning and losing. The majority of people involved in

the program, though, believe that what we are doing is great. They see this activity as being designed to be low-risk and low in stress, and students share their stories with their peers in the school, including faculty and administrators. It seems that the enthusiasm generated by the debate program is developing and growing within the schools, and so as far as the little frustrations go I think the success of the program has outweighed them.

Bessie I certainly agree with that. We really don't have many major frustrations, and I know when I speak to people about Detroit they find it just unfathomable that we are in a district that is very friendly toward identifying and nurturing bright children. But we've done it for years even when there was no centralized leadership for gifted and talented. So it's just part of the way we look at students, and I think that that willingness to accommodate and to do things that would help to develop talent makes everyone just very cooperative and willing to be flexible. It's had terrific benefits for students. The students have gotten involved in community service projects as a result of the topics that they've discussed and debated. For example, they gave a wonderful play on homelessness that really just mirrored all the things that they had learned.

Lou One last point is that this debate program has also extended the collaborative effort at my high school, and I receive a lot of support from my fellow English teacher, Ellen Harcourt. In addition, several teachers in science and social studies and English are collaborating on writing across the curriculum. A collaborative class is currently being initiated at our school using teachers from various disciplines, and this is supported by funds from Bessie's office. These students will be using their debate skills and legal terminology to write a bill and, we hope, introduce it in the state legislature. Again, this program has transcended the departmentalized atmosphere of a high school, and if it continues to nourish talent and flourish, we will be way ahead of the game.

> Self-management skills are a key to students being successful in school as well as outside school.

special gifts, negative attitudes toward such efforts persist. Barriers inhibiting the development of better education for these children include lack of parental advocacy, lack of appropriate teacher training, an emphasis on older students of extraordinary ability, financial constraints, and legal roadblocks such as laws preventing early admission to school.

The barriers to early identification and programming for students with special gifts or talents include school policies and ideologies that Robinson and Weimer (1991) refer to as "the tyranny of the calendar":

> Very few districts pay systematic heed to kindergartners who have already mastered the goals of the curriculum, leaving it up to their already burdened teachers to make provisions. Because many districts favor only enrichment programs, special planning for advanced students does not begin until late into the elementary school years, after basic skills have been mastered. Leaving these students locked into standard grade-level curriculum, which does not match their learning pace or interest level, means that children with advanced conceptual and academic skills, so eager at first to enter school, are in clear danger of becoming casualties of the system. (p. 30)

Many questions regarding the education of young children who have special gifts remain unanswered. Relatively little is known about how advantageous it is to identify and program for such children before they are in third or fourth grade or how best to train parents and teachers to work with preschoolers with special abilities. Yet some statements can be made with a high degree of confidence, as Karnes and Johnson (1991) point out:

1. We have not been committed to early identification and programming for the young gifted.
2. We have few advocates for young gifted children.
3. We do not have institutions of higher learning training personnel in gifted education to work with our young gifted children.
4. We are in need of financial resources to: conduct research with young gifted children and their families, develop more effective and efficient procedures and instruments for screening and assessing young gifted children, determine the most effective strategies for meeting their unique needs, including ways of differentiating instruction, and follow-up data that will give us insights into the effectiveness of our identification and programming.
5. We don't have the legislation we need to permit public schools to serve young gifted children below the age of five, nor to help public schools finance programming.
6. There is little awareness among educators and parents alike of the importance of early identification and programming for the gifted.
7. Procedures and instruments for identification of children who are handicapped and those who come from low income homes must compare children of like kind rather than expect children to demonstrate or score on instruments at the level of their more affluent or non-handicapped peers.
8. Identification of young gifted children must be an ongoing process. This is particularly true for children from low-income and minority groups as well as children with handicapping conditions because these children need time and the opportunity to display their special gifts and talents. (pp. 279–280)

Although not a panacea, early admission to school and acceleration through grades and subjects offer significant advantages for some young students with special gifts or talents. What many young children with special abilities need most is the freedom to make full and appropriate use of school systems as they now exist. They need the freedom to study with older children in specific areas where their abilities are challenged. Such children need to be able to get around the usual eligibility rules so they can go through the ordinary curriculum at an accelerated rate. Unfortunately, relatively few preschoolers with special gifts receive the kind of educational programming appropriate for their abilities. This is especially the case for young children with extraordinary abilities who are also from minority or poor families or have disabilities (Gallagher & Gallagher, 1994).

Preschoolers with special gifts or talents may be intellectually superior and have above-average adaptive behavior and leadership skills, as well. Their advanced abilities in many areas, however, do not mean that their development will be above average across the board. Emotionally, they may develop at an average pace for their chronological age. Sometimes their uneven development creates special problems of social isolation, and adults may have unrealistic expectations for their social and emotional skills because their cognitive and language skills are so advanced (see the box below). They may require special guidance by sensitive adults who not only provide appropriate educational environments for them but also discipline them appropriately and teach them the skills required for social

The Gifted Preschooler: Chris and Jonathan

Chris came running into the house, bubbling over with excitement, "Mommy, mommy. I did it! I put the bird back together. Its bones were scattered all around. Look. I have a skeleton of a bird! I guess I am a paleontologist for real! Let's go to the library and find out what species it is."

Chris, only 4, resembles Stephen Gould, world renowned paleontologist whose interest also began at an early age. A visit to the dinosaur exhibit at the American Museum of Natural History inspired both to the world of paleontological inquiry. Will Chris eventually become a paleontologist? Chris has both advanced knowledge and an all-consuming interest in paleontology.

From this scenario we can attest readily to his superior levels in vocabulary development and comprehension skills. Intense interest, in-depth knowledge, and accelerated development in language provide positive evidence of giftedness. But more important, these characteristics strongly imply that Chris has educational needs different from most 4-year-olds.

Will these special needs be met within the school setting? Unfortunately there are a limited number of educational programs adequately equipped to address the unique requirements of children like Chris. Chris' parents, like most parents of bright preschoolers, voice their concern since many of these youngsters are already reading, composing original stories, and computing simple addition and subtraction problems on their own.

One would only have to listen and watch children like Chris to confirm the need for such services. These children frequently demonstrate advanced vocabularies and often an early ability to read. In addition, they seem to learn easily and spontaneously. Logic appears early in some bright youngsters, often to the embarrassment of adults.

For instance, Jonathan, at 3, requested a grilled cheese sandwich at a restaurant. The waitress explained that grilled cheese was not on the menu. Jonathan, determined to have his way, queried, "Do you have cheese and bread?" The waitress nodded, "We do...." "Then," Jon blurted, "do you have a pan?" Jon got his sandwich. When the sandwich arrived, the waitress took beverage orders. Jonathan ordered a milkshake, but this time the waitress was one step ahead. "Jonathan, we have milk and ice cream, but I'm sorry we don't have any syrup." To which Jon asked, "Do you have a car?"

Other youngsters may show advanced abilities in number concepts, maps, telling time, and block building. Their skills in such activities far exceed that of their agemates. Not only do these characteristics define gifted preschoolers but they also provide a rationale and structure for intervention.

Source: Baum, S. (1986). "The gifted preschooler: An awesome delight," *Gifted Child Today, 9*(4), 42–43. Reprinted with permission.

competence (Baum, 1986; Roedell, 1985). They may need help, for example, in acquiring self-understanding, independence, assertiveness, sensitivity to others, friend-making skills, and social problem-solving skills (Robinson, 1993a).

Transition

For students with special gifts or talents who are achieving near their potential and are given opportunities to take on adult roles, the transitions from childhood to adolescence to adulthood and from high school to higher education or employment are typically not very problematic. In many ways, transitions for these youths tend to mirror the problems in transitions faced by adolescents and young adults with disabilities.

Consider the case of Raymond Kurzweil, inventor of the Kurzweil Reading Machine for blind persons (see Chapter 10).

> A summer job, at age 12, involved statistical computer programming. Could a kid comprehend IBM's daunting Fortran manual? He very well could. Soon, in fact, IBM would be coming to young Kurzweil for programming advice. By the time he was graduated from high school, the whiz kid had earned a national reputation, particularly for a unique computer program that could compose original music in the styles of Mozart and Beethoven, among others. After carefully weighing all his options, Kurzweil decided to enroll in the Massachusetts Institute of Technology so that he could mingle with the gurus of the then-emerging science of artificial intelligence. Kurzweil was in his element. He was also rather quickly in the chips. (Neuhaus, 1988, p. 66)

Today, at middle age, Kurzweil is a highly successful entrepreneur who is chairman of several high-tech corporations he founded.

Not all adolescents and young adults with special gifts or talents take transitions in stride. Many need personal and career counseling and a networking system that links students to school and community resources (Clifford, Runions, & Smyth, 1986; Delisle, 1992). Some are well served by an eclectic approach that employs the best features of enrichment and acceleration (Feldhusen & Kolloff, 1986).

If there is a central issue in the education of adolescents with special gifts or talents, it is that of acceleration versus enrichment. Proponents of enrichment feel that these students need continued social contact with their age peers. They argue that such students should follow the curriculum of their age-mates and study topics in greater depth. Proponents of acceleration feel that the only way to provide challenging and appropriate education for those with special gifts and talents is to let them compete with older students. These educators argue that since the cognitive abilities of such students are advanced beyond their years, they should proceed through the curriculum at an accelerated pace.

Acceleration for adolescents with special gifts or talents may mean early entrance to college or enrollment in college courses while attending high school. Acceleration programs,

Accelerated educational programs, particularly in mathematics, have been evaluated favorably and may support early college entrance for some students who are gifted.

particularly in mathematics, have been evaluated very favorably (Brody & Stanley, 1991; Kolitch & Brody, 1992). In fact, early entrance to college on a full-time or part-time basis appears to work very well for the vast majority of these adolescents, as long as it is done with care and sensitivity to the needs of individual students (Brody & Stanley, 1991; Noble & Drummond, 1992). As Buescher (1991) points out, "Talented adolescents are *adolescents* first and foremost. They experience fully the regression, defensiveness, and relational fluctuations of normal adolescence" (p. 399). Thus, it is important to provide counseling and support services for students who enter college early to ensure that they have appropriate, rewarding social experiences that enhance their self-esteem, as well as academic challenges and successes in the courses they take.

Beyond acceleration and enrichment, adolescents with special gifts or talents need attention to social and personal development if they are to make successful and gratifying transitions to adulthood and careers. Like other groups of students with special characteristics and needs, they may benefit from opportunities to socialize and learn from other students who have similar characteristics and face similar challenges. They may be able to obtain particular benefit from reflecting on the nature and meaning of life and the directions they choose for themselves. Given proper supports, they can often make use of self-determination and survival skills (Galbraith & Delisle, 1996). Delisle (1992) discusses six realities that adults might use in guiding adolescents with special gifts or talents who are in transition:

1. *Remember that the real basics go beyond reading, writing, and arithmetic.* (They include play and relaxation.) . . .
2. *You can be good at something you don't enjoy doing.* (Just because you're good at something doesn't mean you have to plan your life around doing it.) . . .
3. *You can be good at some things that are unpopular with your friends.* (It's a good idea to connect with others who share your preferences, beliefs, and experiences and to guard against stereotyping yourself or others.) . . .
4. *Life is not a race to see who can get to the end the fastest.* (Don't become preoccupied with performance, work, or success, and don't be afraid to try something at which you might not succeed.) . . .
5. *You have the ability to ask questions that should have answers but don't.* (Look and listen to the world around you, and become involved in making the world a better place.) . . .
6. *It's never too late to be what you might have been.* (Remember that you always have career options and pursue those goals that you want most.) (pp. 137–145)

Summary

Disagreements about how to define giftedness center on the questions of exactly how children excel; how this excellence is measured; the degree to which the individual must excel to be considered to have special abilities; who should make up the comparison group; and why giftedness should be identified at all. Even the terms used can be confusing: *Precocity* indicates remarkable early development; *insight* involves separating relevant from irrelevant information and combining information in novel and productive ways; *genius* refers to rare intellectual powers; *creativity* has to do with the ability to express novel and useful ideas, to see novel relationships, to ask original and crucial questions; and *talent* indicates a special ability within a particular area.

The use of individually administered intelligence tests as the only basis for defining giftedness has met with increasing dissatisfaction. First, traditional intelligence tests are limited in what they measure. Second, intelligence is being reconceptualized. Whether intelligence should be considered a general characteristic or distinguished according to unique areas is an ongoing controversy. Third, children exhibit gifted performance in specific domains. For example, a child with a physical disability might show giftedness in any area not impaired by his or her other specific disability.

A consistent myth is that individuals who show giftedness in particular areas are superior beings. Current thinking suggests that individuals may have extraordinary talents in specific areas but ordinary talents in others. Giftedness is no longer considered to be a fixed human characteristic. Moreover, giftedness may be present or not present at different times in an individual's life. Thus, prevalence figures are difficult to establish.

As with some other exceptionalities, the causes of gifted behavior are varied and most likely represent a combination of biological and environmental factors. Although genetic inheritance may be a factor, giftedness is not specific to any socioeconomic or cultural or ethnic-minority group. Current research suggests that one's collection of genes sets limits of performance, but the actual performance within those limits is determined by environmental factors.

A culturally consensual definition of giftedness includes five criteria: excellence, rarity, demonstrability, productivity, and value. For the purposes of education this definition would be expanded to include high ability, high creativity, and high task commitment.

Identification and selection of students for special programs must be based on multiple criteria to avoid bias against neglected groups of students with special gifts or talents. To ensure fairness, principles of identification must take into account the varied definitions of giftedness and recognize the effects of cultural variation—both among and within cultures—on children's behavior.

Giftedness has been recognized in every society throughout history, and individuals with special gifts and talents have been stereotyped as either physically and socially inept or as superhuman. Most individuals with special gifts fit neither category. Identification of giftedness based on IQ scores has often been flawed or biased in favor of physically superior or economically privileged children. Students with special gifts or talents tend to be far ahead of their age-mates in specific areas of academic performance, and the majority of students who show giftedness enter occupations that demand greater-than-average intellectual ability, creativity, and motivation.

The link between giftedness and self-concept is uncertain. Many students who have special gifts or tal-

ents are self-aware, self-assured, and socially skilled. Those who have truly unusual gifts or talents or who are precocious children may constitute a group for which extraordinary adaptations of schooling are required.

American societal attitudes toward giftedness reflect a love–hate relationship: We love the good things giftedness can produce but hate to acknowledge superior intelligence. This is in contrast to some other cultures, in which advanced abilities are seen as a divine gift to be nurtured.

Educational reforms during the 1990s hold both promise and danger for the education of students with special gifts and talents. One of the most controversial reform topics is that of ability grouping, which some believe to be discriminatory. Five popular reforms of the 1990s with potential impact on students with extraordinary abilities are middle schools, site-based management, cooperative learning, outcome-based learning, and teacher accountability.

Neglected groups of students with special gifts and talents include underachievers—those who fail to achieve at a level consistent with their abilities, for whatever reason. Underachievement is often a problem of minority students and those with disabilities, whose special abilities tend to be overlooked because of biased expectations and/or the values of the majority. Students who display physical characteristics typically associated with severe mental retardation may be intellectually brilliant; unless this is acknowledged, however, the talents of students with cerebral palsy and other physical disabilities may be easily overlooked. Females of extraordinary ability are the largest single group of neglected students with special gifts or talents.

Education of students with special gifts or talents should be based on three characteristics: (1) curriculum designed to accommodate advanced cognitive skills, (2) instructional strategies consistent with learning styles in particular curriculum areas, and (3) administrative facilitation of grouping for instruction. Programs and practices in the education of students with special gifts and talents are extremely varied and include special schools, acceleration, special classes, tutoring, and enrichment during the school year or summer. Administrative plans for modifying the curriculum include enrichment in the classroom, use of consultant teachers, resource rooms, community mentors, independent study, special classes, and special schools.

Acceleration has not been a popular plan for educating exceptionally able students, although considerable research supports it. Enrichment includes a schoolwide plan in which students continue to engage in enrichment activities for as long as they are able to go beyond the usual curriculum of their age-mates. This model is designed to improve the learning environment for all students.

Teachers of students who have special gifts or talents should exhibit characteristics that are desirable for all teachers. However, they also must be particularly intelligent, creative, energetic, enthusiastic, and committed to excellence.

Early intervention entails early identification of special abilities, providing stimulation to preschool children to foster giftedness, and special provisions such as acceleration to make education appropriate for the young child's advanced skills. Young children with special gifts appear to have particular skills much like those of older children who do not have such special abilities. Special care is needed not to assume that a child's emotional and social development are advanced just because his or her language and cognitive skills are advanced.

Transitions to adolescence, adulthood, and higher education and employment are typically not the problems for high-achieving children that they are for children with disabilities. Nevertheless, many highly talented adolescents do need personal and career counseling and help in making contacts with school and community resources. A major issue is acceleration versus enrichment. Programs of acceleration (especially in mathematics, in which students skip grades or complete college-level work early) have been evaluated very positively.

suggestions for teaching

Students Who Are Gifted and Talented in General Education Classrooms
By Peggy L. Tarpley

Just as individual school systems have different definitions and eligibility criteria, they also have different ways of meeting the educational needs of gifted students. In some schools, classroom teachers alone provide programming for their students who are gifted. Other schools offer resource classes, taught by teachers trained in gifted education, that students attend for specified periods of time each week. Still other school systems offer a variety of specialized programs, including honor classes, advanced placement courses, and special schools for students gifted in math or science or the arts. In all these arrangements (except special schools), classroom teachers assume the responsibility for providing educational experiences for their gifted students during most of the school day (Milgrim, 1989).

As educators of students who are gifted and talented continue to reflect on what teaching practices best encourage the potential of these students, they find that the content, process, product, and learning environment that comprise best practices for gifted and talented students are the same as those that comprise best practices for all students. It is important that all learners experience concepts at higher levels of thinking, interact with real-life problems, and generate products that require integrating skills and demonstrate understanding of the concepts. As is true of students with other exceptionalities, the assessment of learner needs and capabilities is what leads to identifying appropriate activities for individual learners.

Tomlinson (1995) illustrates the basic elements of effective practice and the variables that can be manipulated to produce the instructional differentiation necessary to meet the needs of a variety of gifted students. She suggests that the learning environment should have an active orientation, in which flexible groupings take place based on the activity, the process, and/or the product desired. Both students and teachers should have escalating expectations about learning, and teachers should continually assess progress and adapt environments accordingly.

Given this learning environment:

- The *content* of learning will be rooted in basic principles such as high relevance, purposefulness, and transferability.
- The *process* of learning will balance critical and creative thought, be driven by concepts and generalizations, and promote cognition and metacognition.
- The *product* of learning will center on concepts and issues, use multiple modes of expression, and reflect real problems for which real audiences are interested in the solutions.

Instructional differentiation for individual learners comes in finding each student's "balance" on nine variables impacting content, process, and product. Finding this "balance" is described by Tomlinson (1995) as similar to the controls on a fine audio system. You as the teacher must assess, based on the ways in which students act on or interact with information, ideas, materials, decision making, planning, and products/solutions, where on the "equalizer" continuum to instruct these students. The variables are mediated on continua from foundational to transformational; from concrete to abstract; from simple to complex; from fewer facets to multifacets; from a smaller leap in understanding to a greater leap; from more structured to more open-ended; from clearly defined to vaguely defined; from less independent to more independent; and from slower to faster.

What follows is a sampling of the ways you can differentiate for gifted learners in the areas of content, process, and product.

Tomlinson (1995) lists many more and suggests that individual teachers (like you) will be able to add to the lists:

Content
Multiple texts
Compacting
Interest/learning centers

Process
Learning centers
Simulation
Tiered assignments
Graphic organizers
Problem-based learning
Multiple-intelligences assignments

Product
Tiered products assignments
Independent study
Negotiated criteria

An example of an appropriate task for an advanced learner would be one that is at a level of transformation, abstractness, complexity, multifacetedness, mental leap, openness, and ambiguity such that it causes the learner to stretch a moderate amount beyond his or her comfort zones in areas such as understanding, insight, skill, cognition, metacognition, production, and self-awareness. Again, pacing and the amount of independence required for the task should be "balanced" according to the nature of the task and the learner's characteristics (Tomlinson, 1995). Instructional differentiation in the classroom is an example of true individualization of education. As such, it can be used with any number of approaches to teaching students with gifts and talents in the general education classroom.

Multiple-Intelligences-Based Orientation

Through acceleration, enrichment, and independent learning, teachers strive to meet the unique needs of gifted learners. For these learners, as well as other exceptional learners, a "one-size-fits-all" approach is not recommended. Among the techniques from which teachers may select are curriculum compacting, mastery learning, problem-based learning, higher-level thinking, critical thinking, self-directed learning, learning centers, independent study, and contracts.

Curriculum Compacting

One means by which curricula are accelerated is by curriculum compacting (Reis & Renzulli, 1993). This is a procedure in which the teacher, through the use of pretesting for mastery, organizing instruction around broad themes, and using less time for drill and practice, moves more rapidly through the required curriculum content to provide additional time for students who are gifted to pursue alternate learning activities. To make these modifications, first identify the academic strengths of your gifted students, using a variety of information sources, such as school records, previous teacher recommendations, standardized and informal test results, and observation. Then, decide what curricular area(s) is most appropriate for compacting (moving through rapidly), considering the following questions:

1. What does the student already know?
2. What does the student need to learn?
3. What activities will meet the student's learning needs?

Next, outline learning experiences, based on your student's strengths and interests. Then decide how to provide these educational activities to meet the required content and skill acquisition of the grade level and how to enrich the learning in the extra time created by compacting.

Mastery Learning

Teachers also use mastery learning to provide time for advanced study. In one application of mastery learning, students with high ability move sequentially through a body of knowledge at their own pace (Eby & Smutny, 1990). If these students demonstrate mastery of a new skill on a pretest, they progress immediately to the next skill in the sequence. Some schools extend the use of mastery learning from individual classrooms to a schoolwide system to eliminate students' being retaught mastered skills from year to year. Mastery learning may be managed in a variety of ways. Eby and Smutny (1990) report that in some schools, one classroom teacher has the responsibility for managing the schoolwide system and for teaching the nongraded material to all students. In other buildings, teachers from different grade levels team teach and students move from classroom to classroom. In order to implement either program, however, the school day must be scheduled so that certain subjects are taught to all students in the school at the same time of day. The key is to provide alternate learning experiences appropriate for gifted students once they have progressed through grade-level materials.

Problem-Based Learning

This approach uses either an ill-structured or vague problem or a clearly stated problem as the basis of student investigations. Teachers act as facilitators and tutors, rather than information givers. Students must employ planning, resource-gathering, and especially creative- and critical-thinking skills. This approach gives gifted students practice in attacking problems just as professionals in the field might do. In fact, this approach is currently used in a number of medical schools.

Shreiver and Maker (1990, as cited in Maker & King, 1996) developed a problem continuum to be used with a matrix. With this matrix, teachers create problem-solving situations that can be presented either as choices in learning centers, optional small-group activities, or required experiences for the entire group. It is important that the problem-solving situations are created at varying levels of difficulty and require differing degrees of independence to solve so as to accommodate the levels of abilities of the students. The matrix can be used with units or themes of instruction and is based on the seven intelligences of Gardner (1993).

In the matrix, five types of problems are possible based on the structure noted in the problem, method, and solution. For example, a Type I problem is highly structured, presented clearly, and a standard method of solving and a correct solution are known to the solver and the presenter (of the problem). For a class studying weather, "Choose words that relate to seasons and weather cycles," is a Type I linguistic problem. Type II problems are presented clearly, but the solver must find or create the method and solution. A Type III problem again is presented clearly, but instead of only one method and one correct solution, several are possible. The solver must select a method and reach a correct solution. Using the weather theme, a bodily-kinesthetic problem could be "Pantomime a scene depicting a season or weather cycle."

Type IV problems are clearly stated but have unlimited appropriate methods and solutions. The student/solver must develop a method and apply it until a reasonable (by his or her reasoning) solution is reached. An example of a Type IV problem from the interpersonal intelligence domain is "Create a weather cycle (your choice of cycles) game. Teach your game to some younger students, and play it with them." Finally, a Type V problem is a real-life situation and is therefore vague. This calls on the student/ solver to define the problem before he or she can determine a method and solution. An example from the music domain might be "Create a musical product that calls to mind moods of the desert." Another Type V problem might be a challenge: "Using any of the materials or people in the classroom, demonstrate what you know about weather cycles."

This method as presented here can easily employ the differentiation method of teaching advocated by Tomlinson (1995) and uses many of the components of higher-level thinking.

Higher-Level Thinking

This approach is based on Benjamin Bloom's *Taxonomy of Educational Objectives* (Bloom et al., 1956), which outlines six levels of thinking: the lower levels of knowledge and comprehension and the higher levels of application, analysis, synthesis, and evaluation. Teachers enrich gifted students' learning by providing educational experiences at the four higher levels of the taxonomy. For example:

> The primary social studies curriculum usually includes content on the topic of "communities." While textbooks cover the basic knowledge and comprehension levels on this topic by providing students with definitions and main ideas, a gifted curriculum can be developed on the topic by writing educational objectives at the higher levels.
>
> At the application level, students can be asked to draw a map of their own community.
>
> At the analysis level, students can compare and contrast two or more communities.
>
> At the synthesis level, students can create a play about important people in the community.
>
> At the evaluation level, students can share their opinions about their own community's services. (Eby & Smutny, 1990, p. 171)

In general, developing higher-level thinking skills means that students spend time exploring ideas, testing the applicability of theories, synthesizing ideas into original solutions, and judging the quality of these solutions (Feldhusen et al., 1989). Consult the gifted education specialist in your building or school system for assistance in developing higher-level thinking skills.

Critical Thinking

Although there are many types of thinking skills in addition to the cognitive skills represented in Bloom's taxonomy (e.g., creative-thinking skills and metacognitive skills), "teaching children to think critically has been perhaps the most popular, fastest growing part of the thinking skills movement" (French & Rhoder, 1992, p. 183).

Ennis (1985) defines critical thinking as "reflective and reasonable thinking that is focused on deciding what to believe or do" (p. 45). It includes skills such as judging information and making decisions. Raths and his colleagues (1986) provide examples of the following critical-thinking skills:

Judging/Examining Assumptions

1. When we hear our class is getting a new student—a girl from Vietnam—what assumptions might we make?
2. When we fill a thermos with hot soup and seal the thermos,

what assumptions are we making?

Making Decisions

1. Give students a flashlight. Ask them to design investigations to show what they can find out about light.
2. When Michael sees Sarah throwing trash from her lunch on the playground, what should Michael do? What are his responsibilities?

As Eby and Smutny (1990) point out, many educators do not advocate adding new critical-thinking programs but rather suggest that teachers remodel existing programs so that students apply critical-thinking strategies to the subject matter they study. In addition, Chaffee (1987, cited in Eby and Smutny, 1990) recommends that students apply problem-solving and critical-thinking strategies to real problems in their own lives, rather than to puzzles and simulated problems. Vaughn, Bos, and Schumm (1997) give an example of using real-life situations for critical thinking. A teacher had become discouraged because of the number of students writing on their desks. She presented this problem to the students along with a discussion of defacing school property and how that property is bought through local taxes. She asked the students to come up with solutions. They came up with the idea of wide masking tape placed around the perimeter of their desks to be used for writing instead of the desk surface. They called them "reference borders" and wrote frequently misspelled words or items to remember. When the students realized that the borders could be used to cheat on tests, the students set up rules about their use.

Several teachers together could generate problems needing critical-thinking skills to have a ready supply. These problems also may be integrated across subject and theme areas to provide continuity of learning and instruction.

Self-Directed Learning

One model of self-directed learning is Renzulli's *enrichment triad curriculum model* (Renzulli, 1977), which is designed to develop student interest in topics and higher-order thinking skills and to enable gifted students to conduct investigations in areas of interest. For more information on this model, see Renzulli and Reis's book *The triad reader* (1986).

Treffinger developed another independent study curriculum called *self-directed learning*. Treffinger and Barton (1988) believe the process of self-directed learning culminates in students being able to "initiate plans for their own learning, identify resources, gather data, and develop and evaluate their own products and projects" (p. 30). Teachers use a variety of techniques—such as learning centers, independent study, and contracting—to promote self-directed learning in regular education classes.

Learning Centers

Teachers often use learning centers to provide enrichment activities for their students. To promote self-directed learning, however, these centers must offer instructional opportunities in areas that are specifically designed and sequenced to encourage student independence.

Teachers in Richland County, Ohio, found they could offer activities in regular education classes that developed the productivity and creativity of their gifted students by designing interest development centers (IDCs) (Burns, 1985). Unlike traditional learning centers, which help students master basic curriculum skills, IDCs facilitate students' independent explorations of a wide range of topics not included in the regular curriculum. The teachers stocked their centers with manipulative, media, and print materials along with several suggestions for examining and experimenting in special-interest areas. In keeping with the Renzulli model, they also included methodological resources that helped promote interest in long-term research. For example, one teacher developed a center about bicycling that contained materials on how to create a bike path and how to approach the city council for permission to build bike racks near businesses that students frequented. For additional information and specific independent learning center resources and ideas, see Burns (1985).

For young children, Maker and King (1996) observed a second-grade classroom set up specifically for exploration. This classroom uses Gardner's (1993) multiple intelligences for the themes of the learning centers. In addition to free exploration of the materials available in each of the centers, individual, small-group, and large-group activities are guided or facilitated by the teacher. Figure 12.A lists the centers and some of the materials that are a part of each center.

Independent Study

Sometimes students will develop and/or maintain great interest in topics they have explored. When this happens, you may decide to help them conduct an independent study on a topic. Independent study involves not only exploring a topic in depth but also producing an original product that is disseminated to an appropriate audience. Because directing an independent study project is time consuming and requires an understanding of the topic, teachers often solicit the help of the gifted resource teacher or another person who is knowledgeable about the subject and willing to participate in the project (Pendarvis, Howley, & Howley, 1990). The role of the teacher and resource person(s) is not to direct the study but rather to serve as assistants who help the student define and frame the problem, establish realistic goals and time lines, become aware of a variety of available usable resources, identify both the product that the study will produce and an audience for the product, and evaluate the study. In addition, the adults involved in the project must reinforce the student's work throughout the study and provide methodological help when necessary.

Contracts

You also can facilitate self-directed learning by providing individualized exploration and instruction in the form of student contracts. Like business contracts, these documents are negotiated with the student and describe the area he or she will study and the procedures and resources he or she will use in the investigation. When contracts are used to guide independent study, they also can specify the intended audience, the means of dissemination, deadlines for stages or steps in the study, and dates and purposes of periodic meetings with the teacher (Tuttle, Becker, & Sousa, 1988).

Helpful Resources

School Personnel

In the pursuit of ideas, information, and materials to use in self-directed learning activities, the school media specialist can be a valuable resource. He or she can orient students to the variety of materials that are available, including yearbooks; geographical, political, and economic atlases; career files; subject-related dictionaries; periodical indexes; bibliographic references and databases; and information available on microfilm and microfiche. Specialists also can help students learn how to evaluate resource materials by assessing such factors as the purpose of the work and its intended audience; the au-

thor's (or editor's) credentials; completeness of index and reference citations; and accuracy and completeness of charts, statistics, graphs, time lines, and other illustrative materials (Flack, 1986, p. 175).

For students involved in independent study, media specialists may be helpful resources in creating research products by instructing students in the use of such processes as videotaping, laminating, and making transparencies. Media specialists also may encourage and facilitate the dissemination of the products. For example, a second-grade student decided to write a children's talking book on Tchaikovsky that was intended for other elementary students and that would be housed permanently in his school's library (Reis & Cellerino, 1983).

Instructional Methods and Materials

Adams, D. M., & Hamm, M. E. (1989). *Media and literacy: Learning in an electronic age—Issues, ideas, and teaching strategies.* Springfield, IL: Charles C. Thomas.

Clark, B. (1997). *Growing up gifted: Developing the potential of children at home and at school* (5th ed.). Upper Saddle River, NJ: Merrill/Prentice-Hall.

Cook, C., & Carlisle, J. (1985). *Challenges for children: Creative activities for gifted and talented primary students.* West Nyack, NY: Center for Applied Research in Education.

Cox, J., Daniel, N., & Boston, B. O. (1985). *Educating able learners: Programs and promising practices.* Austin, TX: University of Texas Press.

Cushenbery, D. C. (1987). *Reading instruction for the gifted.* Springfield, IL: Charles C. Thomas.

Davis, G. A., & Rimm, S. B. (1998). *Education of the gifted and talented* (4th ed.) Boston: Allyn & Bacon.

Dirkes, M. A. (1988). Self-directed thinking in the curriculum. *Roeper Review, 11,* 92–94.

Feldhusen, J., VanTassel-Baska, J., & Seeley, K. (1989). *Excellence in educating the gifted.* Denver: Love.

French, J. N., & Rhoder, C. (1992). *Teaching thinking skills: Theory and practice.* New York: Garland.

Gallagher, J. J. (1994). *Teaching the gifted child* (4th. ed.). Boston: Allyn & Bacon.

Greenlaw, M. J., & McIntosh, M. E. (1988). *Educating the gifted.* Chicago: American Library Association.

Kondziolka, G., & Normandeau, P. (1986). Investigation: An interdisciplinary unit. *Gifted Child Today, 9,* 52–54.

Lewis, R. B., & Doorlag, D. H. (1999). *Teaching special students in the mainstream* (5th ed.). Upper Saddle River, NJ: Merrill/Prentice-Hall.

Lukasevich, A. (1983). Three dozen useful information sources on reading for the gifted. *Reading Teacher, 36,* 542–548.

Milgrim, R. M. (1989). *Teaching gifted and talented learners in regular classrooms.* Springfield, IL: Charles C. Thomas.

Parker, B. N. (1989). *Gifted students in regular classrooms.* Boston: Allyn & Bacon.

Parker, J. P. (1989). *Instructional strategies for teaching the gifted.* Boston: Allyn & Bacon.

Pendarvis, E. D., Howley, A. A., & Howley, C. B. (1990). *The abilities of gifted children.* Englewood Cliffs, NJ: Prentice-Hall.

Romey, W. D., & Hibert, M. L. (1988). *Teaching the gifted and talented in the science classroom* (2nd ed.). Washington, DC: National Education Association.

Schlichter, C. L. (1988). Thinking skills instruction for all classrooms. *Gifted Child Today, 11,* 24–28.

Linguistic
Picture books
Books in two languages
Books written by children
Puppets
Cards with pictures and words
Books on tapes or records
Wooden letters
Wooden blocks with letters
Tape recorder for listening to and telling stories
Mirror
Chart paper
Thesauruses/dictionaries (three different levels)
Sand drawing/colored sands
Individual chalkboards
Taped books
Good earphones
Dress-up supplies
Miniature objects

Logical-Mathematical
Dice
Playing cards
Tangrams
Tangram puzzles of varying levels of difficulty
Unifix cubes
Abacus
Puzzles
Wooden numbers
Wooden blocks with numbers
Play money
Attribute blocks
Calculator
Flashcards
Math games and puzzles
Water table/sand table
Bauhaus blocks
Sticks and circles
Microscope

Magnifying glasses: small, medium, large
Spin tips
Gyroscopes
Mirrors

Spatial
Tissue paper
Drawing paper and brushes
Large floor map
Globe
Geography maps
Various colored pencils
Watercolors
Tempera
Play-Doh and/or clay
Scissors (also left-handed)
Glue
Legos, Tinkertoys, Lincoln Logs, and other materials for construction
Capsels
Large wooden or plastic blocks
Things to take apart and put back together
Watercolor paper
Easels and aprons
Chalk pastels (hard)
Oil pastels
Posterboard
Very fine brushes
Origami paper
Stencils
Clay hammers (for indenting and embossing)
Wet sands and models for sand
Graph paper

Musical
Music from different cultures and in various styles
Flutes (wooden or plastic)
Keyboards

Household items for making different sounds
Bottles to fill with water and make different pitches
Tape recorder/player
Guitar
Xylophone
Rhythm instruments such as maracas and drums
Pentatonic bells and harp
Tapes
Sing-along tapes/records

Bodily-Kinesthetic
Giant bubble maker
Mirrors
Sewing kits
Clothes for dress-up and creative drama
Spin tops
Pictures of exercises and simple yoga positions
Sand trays for drawing or writing
Magic wand
Mosaics
Blocks and sandpaper
Wood scraps
Intrapersonal/Interpersonal
Rocking chair
Charts for record keeping and self-evaluation
Books/pictures of families
Self-portraits drawn by classmates
Videotapes/ audiotapes of class activities
Quiet place
Duplo bricks and people, farms, animals
Got To Be Me cards
Blank books

Combined with self-discovery in these learning centers will be individual, small-group, and large-group activities to develop a well-rounded educational experience.

Figure 12.A

Multiple Intelligences Learning Center Materials

Shore, B. M., Cornell, D. G., Robinson, A., & Ward, V. S. (1991). *Recommended practices in gifted education*. New York: Teachers College Press.

Sisk, D. (1987). *Creative teaching of the gifted*. New York: McGraw-Hill.

Curricular Models, Adaptations, and Materials

Beyer, B. K. (1991). *Teaching thinking skills: A handbook for secondary school teachers*. Boston: Allyn & Bacon.

Betts, G. T. (1985). *Autonomous learner model for the gifted and talented*. Greeley, CO: Autonomous Learning Publications and Specialists.

Bloom, B. J., et. al. (1956). *Taxonomy of educational objectives—Handbook I: Cognitive domain*. New York: McKay.

Clausen, R. E., & Clausen, D. R. (1990). *Gifted and talented students*. Milwaukee, WI: Department of Public Instruction.

Feldhusen, J. F. (1988). *Purdue creative thinking program*. West LaFayette, IN: Purdue University Media-Based Services.

Feldhusen, J. F., & Kolloff, M. B. (1988). A three-stage model for gifted education. *Gifted Child Today, 11*, 14–18.

Guilford, J. P. (1967). *The nature of human intelligence*. New York: McGraw-Hill.

Juntune, J. J. (1986). *Successful programs for the gifted and talented*. St. Paul, MN: National Association for Gifted Children.

Maker, C. J., & Nielson, A. B. (1995). *Teaching models in education of the gifted* (2nd ed.). Austin, TX: Pro-Ed.

Maker, C. J., & Orzechowski-Harland, D. (1993). *Critical issues in gifted education: Vol. III. Programs for the gifted in regular classrooms*. Austin, TX: Pro-Ed.

Renzulli, J. (1977). *The enrichment triad model*. Mansfield Center, CT: Creative Learning Press.

Renzulli, J. S. (Ed.). (1986). *Systems and models for developing programs for the gifted and talented*. Mansfield Center, CT: Creative Learning Press.

Renzulli, J. S., & Callahan, C. M. (1986). *New directions in creativity*. Mansfield Center, CT: Creative Learning Press.

Renzulli, J. S., & Reis, S. (1985). *The schoolwide enrichment model: A comprehensive plan for educational excellence*. Mansfield Center, CT: Creative Learning Press.

Robinson, A. (1986). Elementary language arts for the gifted: Assimilation and accommodation in the curriculum. *Gifted Child Quarterly, 30*, 178–181.

Udall, A. J., & Daniels, M. A. (1991). *Creating the thoughtful classroom: Strategies to promote student thinking*. Tucson, AZ: Zephyr Press.

VanTassel-Baska, J. (Ed.). (1994). *Comprehensive curriculum for gifted learners* (2nd ed.). Boston: Allyn & Bacon.

Literature about Individuals Who Are Gifted and Talented*

Elementary

Aliki. (1984). *Feelings*. New York: Greenwillow. (NF)

Berger, G. (1980). *The gifted and talented*. New York: Franklin Watts. (NF)

Calvert, P. (1980). *The snowbird*. New York: Charles Scribner's Sons. (F)

Cooney, B. (1982). *Miss Rumphius*. New York: Viking. (F)

Fitzgerald, J. D. (1967). *The great brain*. New York: Dial Press. (F)

Fitzhugh, L. (1984). *Harriet the spy*. New York: Harper & Row. (F)

Greenwald, S. (1987). *Alvin Webster's surefire plan for success (and how it failed)*. Boston: Little, Brown. (F)

Hassler, J. (1981). *Jemmy*. New York: Atheneum. (F)

Heide, F. (1985). *Tales for the perfect child*. New York: Lothrop, Lee, and Shepard. (F)

Manes, S. (1982). *Be a perfect person in just three days!* Boston: Houghton Mifflin. (F)

Oneal, Z. (1980). *The language of goldfish*. New York: Viking Press. (F)

Sobol, D. J. (1963). *Encyclopedia Brown: Boy detective*. New York: Thomas Nelson. (F)

Middle and High School

Evernden, M. (1985). *The dream keeper*. New York: Lothrop, Lee & Shepard. (F)

Pfeffer, S. B. (1989). *Dear dad, love Laurie*. New York: Scholastic. (F)

Voight, C. (1982). *Tell me if the lovers are losers*. New York: Atheneum. (F)

Voight, C. (1983). *Solitary blue*. New York: Atheneum. (F)

Zindel, P. (1989). *A begonia for Miss Applebaum*. New York: Harper & Row. (F)

Software

Analogies, Hartley Courseware, 9920 Pacific Heights Blvd., Suite 500, San Diego, CA 92121, (800) 247-1380.

Animate, Broderbund Software, Inc., 500 Redwood Blvd., Novato, CA 94948-6121, (415) 382-4400.

AppleWorks, Apple Computer, 1 Infinite Loop, Cupertino, CA 95014, (800) 795-1000. (Word processing)

Astronomy, The Voyager Company, Learn Technologies Interactive, 361 Broadway, Suite 600, New York, NY 10013, (212) 334-2225.

Bank Street Music Writer, Mindscape, Inc., 88 Rowland Way, Novato, CA 94945, (415) 895-2000.

Bank Street School Filer Databases, Sunburst Communications, 101 Castleton Street, Pleasantville, NY 10570, (800) 321-7511.

Creativity Unlimited, Sunburst Communications, 101 Castleton Street, Pleasantville, NY 10570, (800) 321-7511.

Dazzle Draw, Broderbund Software, Inc., 500 Redwood Blvd., Novato, CA 94948-6121, (415) 382-4400.

Dinosaurs, Advanced Ideas, Inc., 591 Redwood Highway, Mill Valley, CA 94941, (415) 388-2430.

Electronic Encyclopedia, Grolier Electronic Publishing, Inc., 90 Sherman Turnpike, Danbury, CT 06816, (203) 797-3530.

Fermi-Pico-Bagel Logo Game, Royal Fireworks Press, 1 First Avenue, P.O. Box 399, Unionville, NY 10928, (914) 726-4444.

Gears, Sunburst Communications, 101 Castleton Street, Pleasantville, NY 10570, (800) 321-7511.

Incredible Laboratory, Sunburst Communications, 101 Castleton Street, Pleasantville, NY 10570, (800) 321-7511.

Mathware, Royal Fireworks Press, 1 First Avenue, P.O. Box 399, Unionville, NY 10988, (914) 726-4444.

National Gallery of Art, The Voyager Company, Learn Technologies Interactive, 361 Broadway, Suite 600, New York, NY 10013, (212) 334-2225.

Operation Fog, Scholastic, Inc., 2931 East McCarty, Jefferson City, MO 65102, (573) 636-5271.

Planetary Construction Set, Sunburst Communications, 101 Castleton Street, Pleasantville, NY 10570, (800) 321-7511.

*F = fiction; NF = nonfiction

Print Shop, Broderbund Software, Inc., 500 Redwood Blvd., Novato, CA 94948-6121, (415) 382-4400.

Science Tool Kit, Broderbund Software, Inc., 500 Redwood Blvd., Novato, CA 94948-6121, (800) 521-6263.

Slide Show, Videodiscovery, 1700 Westlake Avenue N., Suite 600, Seattle, WA 98109, (800) 548-3472.

Organizations

Association for the Gifted, the Council for Exceptional Children, 1920 Association Drive, Reston, VA 20191, (888) CEC-SPED.

Gifted Child Society, 190 Rock Road, Glen Rock, NJ 07452, (201) 444-6530.

National Association for Gifted Children, 1707 L Street N.W., Suite 550, Washington, DC 20036, (202) 785-4268.

Bibliography for Teaching Suggestions

Bloom, B. J., et al. (1956). *Taxonomy of educational objectives—Handbook I: Cognitive domain.* New York: McKay.

Burns, D. E. (1985). Land of opportunity. *Gifted Child Today, 37,* 41–45.

Clark, B. (1997). *Growing up gifted: Developing the potential of children at home and school* (5th ed.). Upper Saddle River, NJ: Merrill/Prentice-Hall.

Eby, J. W., & Smutny, J. F. (1990). *A thoughtful overview of gifted education.* New York: Longman.

Ennis, R. H. (1985). A logical basis for measuring critical thinking skills. *Educational Leadership, 43,* 44–48.

Feldhusen, J., VanTassel-Baska, J., & Seeley, K. (1989). *Excellence in educating the gifted.* Denver: Love.

Flack, J. D. (1986). A new look at a valued partnership: The library media specialist and gifted students. *School Library Media Quarterly, 14,* 174–179.

French, J. N., & Rhoder, C. (1992). *Teaching thinking skills: Theory and practice.* New York: Garland.

Gardner, H. (1993). *Frames of mind: The theory of multiple intelligences.* New York: Basic Books.

Maker, C. J., & King, M. A. (1996). *Nurturing giftedness in young children.* Reston, VA: Council for Exceptional Children.

Maker, C. J., & Nielson, A. B. (1996). *Teaching models in education of the gifted* (2nd ed.). Austin, TX: Pro-Ed.

Milgrim, R. M., (1989). *Teaching gifted and talented learners in regular classrooms.* Springfield, IL: Charles C. Thomas.

Pendarvis, E. D., Howley, A. A., & Howley, C. B. (1990). *The abilities of gifted children.* Englewood Cliffs, NJ: Prentice-Hall.

Raths, L. E., Wassermann, S., Jonas, A., & Rothstein, A. (1986). *Teaching for thinking: Theory, strategies, and activities for the classroom* (2nd ed.). New York: Teachers College, Columbia University.

Reis, S. M., & Cellerino, M. (1983). Guiding gifted students through independent study. *Teaching Exceptional Children, 15,* 136–139.

Renzulli, J. S. (1977). *The enrichment triad model.* Mansfield Center, CT: Creative Learning Press.

Renzulli, J. S. (1981). *The revolving door identification model.* Mansfield Center, CT: Creative Learning Press.

Renzulli, J. S., & Reis, S. M. (Eds.). (1993). *The triad reader.* Mansfield Center, CT: Creative Learning Press.

Starko, A. (1995). *Creativity in the classroom: Schools of curious delight.* White Plains, NY: Longman.

Tomlinson, C. A. (1995). *Good teaching for one and all: Does gifted education have an instructional identity?* Unpublished manuscript, University of Virginia.

Treffinger, D. J., & Barton, B. L. (1988). Foster independent learning. *Gifted Child Today, 11,* 28–30.

Tuttle, F. B., Becker, L. A., and Sousa, J. A. (1988). *Program design and development for gifted and talented students* (3rd ed.). Washington, DC: National Education Association

VanTassel-Baska, J. (Ed.). (1994). *Comprehensive curriculum for gifted learners* (2nd ed.). Boston, MA: Allyn & Bacon.

Vaughn, S., Bos, C., & Schumm, J. S. (1997). *Teaching mainstreamed, diverse, and at-risk students in the general education classroom.* Boston, MA: Allyn & Bacon.

susan jean
semple

Remnants of a Life Too Well Known. Watercolor, pencil, collage on found book cover. 22 x 14 in.

Susan Jean Semple grew up in Oklahoma. She took up oil painting at 18 and earned a Bachelor of Fine Arts from the University of Oklahoma. She traveled around the country as an itinerant portraitist before settling in Cambridge, MA. Since 1997 her work has been shown at the Gateway Gallery in Brookline, MA, and in galleries in Washington state. She has also participated in Brookline Open Studios and exhibited her quilts at the Quaker Meetinghouse in Cambridge.

chapter 13

Parents and Families

Sun shone that day long ago in Corcloon. Asleep in his blue bed Joseph looked the picture of pleasant childlike thimblework. Nora serenely simpered as she lifted him. He gazed his hurt gaze, lip protruding, eyes busy in conversation. He ordered her to look out the window at the sunshine. He looked hard at her ear ordering her to listen to the birds singing. Then jumping on her knees he again asked her to cock her ear and listen to the village children.... He showed her his arms, his legs, his useless body. Looking at his mother he blamed her, he damned her, he mouthed his cantankerous why, why, why me?... she tried to distract him. Lifting him in her arms she brought him outside into the farmyard. "Come on till I show you the calves," she coaxed. His lonely tears rushed even faster. He knew why she tried to divert his boyish questioning.... "All right," she said, "we'll go back inside and talk." ... she then sat down and faced her erstwhile boy.... Meanwhile he cried continuously, conning himself that he had beaten her to silence. "I never prayed for you to be born crippled," she said. "I wanted you to be full of life, able to run and jump and talk.... Listen here Joseph, you can see, you can hear, you can think, you can understand everything you hear, you like your food, you like nice clothes, you are loved by me and Dad. We love you just as you are."... She got on with her work while he got on with his crying. The decision arrived at that day was burnt forever in his mind. He was only three years in age but he was now fanning the only spark he saw, his being alive and more immediate, his being wanted just as he was.

CHRISTOPHER NOLAN

Under the Eye of the Clock: The Life Story of Christopher Nolan

A fertile ground for conflict or harmony, the family—especially the family with a member who has a disability—is the perfect locale for studying the interplay of human emotion and behavior. Think of your own family as you were growing up. Think of the dynamics of interaction among you and your siblings and parents. These interactions were no doubt carried out within the full range of human emotions. Now add to this mixture of human interaction a dose of disability. Consider how much more complex living in your family would have been if you had had a brother like Joseph, with severe cerebral palsy (see p. 513).

In addition to underscoring the complexities of living with a family member with disabilities, the autobiographical account of Joseph and his mother also demonstrates how resilient some families can be in the face of extreme difficulties. A child with disabilities does not always threaten the well-being of a family. Reactions of family members to the individual with a disability can run the gamut from absolute rejection to absolute acceptance, from intense hate to intense love, from total neglect to overprotection. In fact, some parents and siblings assert that having a family member with a disability has actually strengthened the family. As highlighted by the interaction between Joseph and his mother, however, coping with the stress of raising and living with a child who has a disability rarely comes easily.

In this chapter we explore the dynamics of families with children who are disabled and discuss parental involvement in their treatment and education. Before proceeding further, however, it is instructive to consider the role of parents of children who are disabled from a historical perspective.

Professionals' Changing Views of Parents

Today, knowledgeable professionals who work with exceptional learners are aware of the importance of the family. They now recognize that the family of the person with a disability, especially the parents, can help in their educational efforts. To ignore the family is shortsighted because it can lessen the effectiveness of teaching.

Even though we now recognize how crucial it is to consider the concerns of parents and families in treatment and educational programs for individuals who are disabled, this was not always the case. Professionals' views of the role of parents have changed dramatically. In the not too distant past, some professionals looked to the parents primarily as a cause of some of the child's problems or as a place to lay blame when practitioners' interventions were ineffective. According to one set of authorities, negative views of parents were in some ways a holdover from the **eugenics movement** of the late nineteenth and early twentieth centuries (Turnbull & Turnbull, 1997). Professionals associated with the eugenics movement believed in the selective breeding of humans. For example, they proposed sterilization of people with mental retardation because they erroneously believed that virtually all causes of mental retardation were hereditary.

Although the eugenics movement had largely died out by the 1930s and few professionals any longer blamed disabilities primarily on heredity, the climate was ripe for some of them to blame a variety of disabilities, especially emotional problems, on the childrearing practices of parents. For example, until the 1970s and 1980s, when research demonstrated a biochemical basis for autism, it was quite popular to pin the blame for this condition on the parents, especially the mother. The leading proponent of this viewpoint, Bruno Bettelheim, asserted that

eugenics movement. A popular movement of the late nineteenth and early twentieth centuries that supported the selective breeding of humans; resulted in laws restricting the marriage of individuals with mental retardation and sterilization of some of them.

misconceptions about Parents and Families of Persons with Disabilities

myth Parents are to blame for many of the problems of their children with disabilities.

fact Parents can influence their children's behavior, but so, too, can children affect how their parents behave. Research shows that some children with disabilities are born with difficult temperaments, which can affect parental behavior.

myth Parents must experience a series of reactions—shock and disruption, denial, sadness, anxiety and fear, and anger—before adapting to the birth of a child with a disability.

fact Parents do not go through emotional reactions in lockstep fashion. They may experience some, or all, of these emotions but not necessarily in any particular order.

myth Many parents of infants with disabilities go from physician to physician, "shopping" for an optimistic diagnosis.

fact Just the opposite is often true. Parents frequently suspect that something is wrong with their baby but are told by professionals not to worry—that the child will outgrow the problem. Then they seek another opinion.

myth The father is unimportant in the development of the child with a disability.

fact Although they are frequently ignored by researchers and generally do experience less stress than mothers, fathers can play a critical role in the dynamics of the family. The father's role has become more important, but research indicates that his role is still often indirect, that is, the father can influence the mother's reactions to the child.

myth Siblings are usually unaffected by the addition of a child with a disability to the family.

fact Siblings often experience the same emotional reactions as parents, and their lack of maturity can make coping with these emotions more difficult.

myth The primary role of the early intervention professional should be to provide expertise for the family.

fact Many authorities now agree that professionals should help parents become more involved in making decisions for the family.

myth The typical family in the United States has two parents, is middle class, and has only the father working outside the home.

fact Demographics are changing rapidly. There are now many more families with both parents working as well as more single-parent families and families living in poverty.

myth Parents who elect not to be actively involved (e.g., attending and offering suggestions at IEP meetings or visiting the school frequently) in their child's education and treatment are neglectful.

fact Although it is desirable for parents to be involved, it is sometimes very difficult for them to do so because of their commitments to other family functions (e.g., work and child care).

myth Professionals are always in the best position to help families of people with disabilities.

fact Informal sources of support, such as extended family and friends, are often more effective than formal sources of support, such as professionals and agencies, in helping families adapt to a family member with a disability.

myth Teachers should respect the privacy of parents and communicate with them only when absolutely necessary—for example, when their child has exhibited serious behavior problems.

fact Teachers should initiate some kind of contact with parents as soon as possible, so that if something like a serious behavior infraction does occur, some rapport with the parents will already have been established.

mothers who were cold and unresponsive toward their children—"refrigerator moms"—produced autism in their children (Bettelheim, 1950, 1967).

In the late 1970s and early 1980s, professionals became less likely to blame parents automatically for the problems of their children. There were at least two reasons for this more positive view:

1. Richard Bell forwarded the notion that the direction of causation between child and adult behavior is a two-way street (Bell & Harper, 1977). Sometimes the parent changes the behavior of the child or infant; sometimes the reverse is true. With specific regard to children who are disabled, some researchers point out that these children, even as infants, sometimes possess difficult temperaments, which influence how parents respond to them (Brooks-Gunn & Lewis, 1984; Mahoney & Robenalt, 1986). Some infants who are disabled, for example, are relatively unresponsive to stimulation from their parents, making it more difficult to interact with them. With an understanding of the reciprocal nature of parent–child interaction, we are thus more likely, for example, to sympathize with a mother's frustration in trying to cuddle an infant with severe retardation or a father's anger in attempting to deal with his teenager who has an emotional or behavior disorder.

2. Professionals began to recognize the potentially positive influence of the family in the educational process. Although at first many authorities tended to think that parents needed training to achieve a positive effect on their children, more and more now have recognized that parents often have as much, or more, to offer than professionals regarding suggestions for the treatment of their children. The prevailing philosophy now dictates that, whenever possible, professionals should seek the special insights that parents can offer by virtue of living with their children. Furthermore, authorities today are less likely to view the purpose of early intervention to be training parents to assume the role of quasi-therapist or quasi-teacher (Berry & Hardman, 1998). Instead, many believe the goal should be to develop and preserve the natural parent–child relationship as much as possible. In sum, a healthy parent–child relationship is inherently beneficial.

individualized family service plan (IFSP). A plan for services for young children with disabilities (under three years of age) and their families; drawn up by professionals and parents; similar to an IEP for older children; mandated by PL 99–457.

Federal law stipulates that schools must make a concerted effort to involve parents and families in the education of their children with disabilities.

Recognizing the importance of the family, Congress has passed several federal laws stipulating that schools make a concerted effort to involve parents and families in the education of their children with disabilities. Current law, reflected in the Amendments to the Individuals with Disabilities Education Act (IDEA, PL 105–17) of 1997, mandates that schools attempt to include parents in crafting their children's individualized education programs (IEPs) (see Chapter 1). In the case of children under three years of age, schools must involve parents in developing **individualized family service plans (IFSPs).** The focus of the IFSP is to be family-centered. In other words, the IFSP not only addresses the needs of the individual child who has a disability, but it also focuses on his or her family by specifying what services the family needs to enhance the child's development.

Evidence clearly documents that the parents of children with disabilities undergo more than the average amount of stress. The parents who are well adjusted and happily married before the birth of their disabled child stand the best chance of coping with the challenges they face.

The Effects of a Child with a Disability on the Family

The birth of any child can have a significant effect on the dynamics of the family. The parents and other children must undergo a variety of changes to adapt to the presence of a new member. The effects on the family of the birth of a child who has a disability can be even more profound.

The everyday routines that most families take for granted are frequently disrupted in families with children who are disabled (Bernheimer & Keogh, 1995). For example, the child with a disability may require alterations in housing (e.g., the family may decide to move closer to therapists), household maintenance schedules (e.g., chores may not be done as quickly because of lack of time), and even parents' career goals (e.g., a parent may pass up a promotion in order to spend more time with the child).

Moreover, the child with a disability can have an impact on both parents and siblings and in different ways. We discuss parental reactions first and then sibling reactions.

Parental Reactions

A Stage Theory Approach. Traditionally, researchers and clinicians have suggested that parents go through a series of stages after learning they have a child with a disability. Some of these stages parallel the proposed sequence of responses that accompany a person's reactions to the death of a loved one. Based on interviews of parents of infants with serious physical disabilities, a representative set of stages includes shock and disruption, denial, sadness, anxiety and fear, anger, and finally adaptation (Drotar, Baskiewicz, Irvin, Kennell, & Klaus, 1975).

Several authorities have questioned the wisdom of this stage approach in understanding parental reactions. It is clear that parents should not be thought of as marching through a series of stages in lockstep fashion. It would be counter-productive, for example, to think, "This mother is now in the anxiety and fear stage; we need to encourage her to go through the anger stage, so she can finally adapt."

One argument against a strict stage model comes from the fact that many parents report that they do *not* engage in denial. In fact, they are often the first to suspect a problem. It is largely a myth that parents of children who are disabled go from physician to physician, "shopping" for a more favorable diagnosis. In fact, all too frequently they have to convince the doctor that there is something wrong with their child.

Although parents may not go through these reactions in a rigid fashion, some do experience some or all these emotions at one time or another. A commonly reported reaction is guilt.

The Role of Guilt. The parents of a child with a disability frequently wrestle with the terrifying feeling that they are in some way responsible for their child's condition. Even though in the vast majority of cases there is absolutely no basis for such thoughts, guilt is one of the most commonly reported feelings of parents of exceptional children.

The high prevalence of guilt is probably due to the fact that the primary cause of so many disabilities is unknown. Uncertainty about the cause of the child's disability creates an atmosphere conducive to speculation by the parents that they themselves are to blame. Mothers are particularly vulnerable. As Featherstone (1980), the mother of a boy who was blind and had hydrocephaly, mental retardation, cerebral palsy, and seizures, stated:

> Our children are wondrous achievements. Their bodies grow inside ours. If their defects originated in utero, we blame our inadequate bodies or inadequate caution. If ... we accept credit for our children's physical beauty (and most of us do, in our hearts), then inevitably we assume responsibility for their physical defects.
>
> The world makes much of the pregnant woman. People open doors for her, carry her heavy parcels, offer footstools and unsolicited advice. All this attention seems somehow posited on the idea that she is creating something miraculously fine. When the baby arrives imperfect, the mother feels she has failed not only herself and her husband, but the rest of the world as well.
>
> Soon this diffuse sense of inadequacy sharpens. Nearly every mother fastens on some aspect of her own behavior and blames the tragedy on that. (pp. 73–74)

Dealing with the Public. In addition to ambivalence concerning the cause of the child's disability, parents can feel vulnerable to criticism from others about how they deal with their child's problems. Parents of children with disabilities sometimes sense, whether deservedly or not, that others are scrutinizing their decisions about their child's treatment, educational placement, and so forth.

The public sometimes can be cruel in their reactions to people with disabilities. People with disabilities—especially those who have disabilities that are readily observable—are inevitably faced with inappropriate reactions from those around them. John Hockenberry (1995), holder of an Emmy award and currently a correspondent for *Dateline NBC* and MSNBC.com, who has been in a wheelchair since the age of nineteen years due to an automobile accident, talks about how total strangers sometimes ask him inappropriate questions:

Once on a very hot day on the Washington, D.C., subway a woman sat looking at me for a long time. She was smiling. I suspected that she knew me from the radio, that she had some picture of me somewhere. I am rarely recognized in public, but it was the only plausible explanation for why she kept watching me with a look of some recognition. Eventually, she walked up to me when the train stopped, said hello, then proceeded in a very serious voice.

"Your legs seem to be normal."

"They are normal, I just can't move them."

"Right, I know that. I mean, I can see that you are paralyzed." I was beginning to wonder where she was going with this. "Why aren't you shriveled up more?" she asked, as though she was inquiring about the time of day. "I notice that your legs aren't shrunken and all shriveled up. Why is that?" I was wearing shorts. She looked at my legs as though she was pricing kebab at the market. "I mean, I thought paralyzed legs got all shriveled up after a while. Were you injured recently?"

"Uh ... twelve years ago."

This was a line of questioning I was unprepared for. I continued to smile and listen. I wondered under what circumstances I would ever roll up to a perfect stranger and ask the question, "Why aren't you shriveled up more?" ...

Perhaps the correct answer to the woman ... was to take a deep breath and calmly explain the details of my legs and muscles as I understood them. Yet to do so I would have had to admit that there was a category of shriveled-up people, and that I was not one of them. I would also have had to concede that it was perfectly permissible for her to walk up to me and say something outrageous when that was the last thing I believed. (Hockenberry, 1995, pp. 93–95)

Hockenberry, an adult, had a difficult time knowing how to handle interactions with insensitive people. So think about how much more difficult it would be for a child. Understandably, parents often assume the burden of responding to inappropriate or even cruel reactions from the public. Even people who are well meaning can sometimes offend parents of children with disabilities (see the box on p. 520).

Dealing with the Child's Feelings. In addition to dealing with the public's reactions to their child's disability, parents are also faced with the delicate task of talking with their child about his or her disability. This can be a difficult responsibility because the parents need to address the topic without making the disability seem more important than it actually is. In other words, the parents do not want to alarm the child or make him or her more concerned about the disability than is necessary.

Nevertheless, the child with a disability usually has questions about it: How did I get it? Will it go away? Will it get worse? Will I be able to live independently as an adult? If possible, parents should wait for the child to ask specific questions to which they can respond, rather than lecturing about generalities. However, it is a good idea for parents to talk with the child at as early an age as possible, especially before the teenage years, when so many parents and children have problems communicating. Finally, most authorities recommend that parents be honest in their responses. Here is advice from an adult with cerebral palsy:

Some parents have a tendency to hold back information, wanting to spare their son's or daughter's feelings. What they fail to realize is that, in the long

Here's the Beef

Whack! The first door at the fast food place smacks me in the bottom as the second door pinches Edwin between it and Katie's chair. Pushing the wheelchair buried under a diaper bag, a purse, and coats, we bump and weave our way to a table in the corner. Edwin orders our meal and hot water to make Katie's "fish food," dehydrated flakes reconstituted to make "gourmet" stew—or so says the label. At least we have found something she will eat.

Meanwhile, I'm doing my drill—putting on Katie's bib and moving the stuff from the back of the chair to make room for passage. Gargling, she protests that we are taking too long. Back and forth she sways. It's called "self-stimulation," and we are supposed to stop her. But I do nothing. At least she's stopped gargling and she is comforted by the motion. Finally, Edwin returns with our food and we begin to eat.

Swallowing a bite, Edwin leans over and whispers, "Warning, warning, intruder approaching from the left. It's your turn." I nudge him under the table and tell him he owes me one.

As she draws closer, the woman begins, "I've been watching your daughter..."

No kidding, I think.

"... and I just wanted to tell you what special people you are for God to have chosen you to have this child." We put down our burgers. I turn and listen politely.

"How old is the little angel?" she inquires as she leans down and ruffles Katie's hair. Katie, hating to have her head touched, begins to wail loudly, squirming to escape being touched. Now that we have the attention of the entire restaurant, the monologue continues.

"I have a friend whose niece is a Mongoloid and she says that her niece can sort objects and clothes at Goodwill. It's so nice that now these people can live like everyone else, being out in public and all. And what's wrong with her?" she demands, pointing to Katie.

Diving in, I begin my public education spiel, "Katie is developmentally delayed." At her quizzical look, I continue, "What most people think of as mentally retarded.

She is nine but she functions like a one-year-old." I pick up my frosted desert and swirl the melting mess around with my spoon.

"Well, I'm sure she'll grow out of it," the woman pronounces with another pat on Katie's head. "You never know what these children will do. Look at Stevie Wonder, he's blind! You are just so special and she's God's gift to you!"

"At least Stevie had some brain cells to work with. Katie can't control her hands to play the piano but she does sway back and forth. Does that count?" I quip back at her. Sometimes, public education is just too much for me. "At one time, I cried because I thought Katie was just blind." I continued conversationally, "You know, if Katie had Down syndrome, like your friend's niece has, that would be great. Then she could clean tables at the mall and meet people like you."

A tentative smile appears on the woman's face. Uncertain, she backs away a step. "Well, I know that she'll be fine and God will watch over you. Bless you."

As the woman pulls her coat together, adjusts her purse on her arm and waddles away, Edwin and I dissolve into helpless laughter. We survey our lunch, congealed cheese on cold burgers, melted ice cream, and limp fries. At least Edwin managed to get most of Katie's lunch into her, one spoon at a time.

"Our little Stevie Wonder." Edwin strokes Katie's cheek. "Shall we adjourn?" he asks.

"Yeah. And next time, we'll use the drive-thru, or else you do the talking." Now why didn't we think of that before?

Bernadette Weih, a full time judge, is the mother of three children, Katie 10, Becca 6, and Hans 3. Together with her husband, Edwin, she maintains llamas and Angora goats on a 15-acre ranch in the mountains of Oregon.

Source: Weih, B. (1998). Here's the beef. *Exceptional Parent, 28*(5), 70–71. Reprinted with permission.

term, being given correct information at an early age is very good for healthy development. And, if kids are informed, they can answer questions themselves, rather than depending on Mom or Dad to speak up for them. (Pierro, 1995, p. 92)

Parental Adjustment. Evidence is abundant that parents of children with disabilities undergo more than the average amount of stress (Beckman, 1991; Duis, Summers, & Summers, 1997; Dumas, Wolf, Fisman, & Culligan, 1991; Dyson,

1997; Gavidia-Payne & Stoneman, 1997). The stress usually is not the result of major catastrophic events but rather the consequence of daily responsibilities related to child care. A single event, such as a family member coming down with a serious illness, may precipitate a family crisis, but its effects will be even more devastating if the family was already under stress because of a multitude of "daily hassles."

There is not a clear consensus on whether mothers and fathers of children with disabilities experience the same degree of stress. Earlier studies suggested that fathers are not under as much stress as mothers, but as fathers have assumed more child-care responsibilities than was once the case, there appears to be a trend toward fathers and mothers experiencing relatively equal amounts of stress (Dyson, 1997).

Today, fathers' roles in families with children with disabilities are acknowledged to be more significant than was traditionally thought.

There is no universal parental reaction to the added stress of raising a child with a disability. Although one would think that stress would be strongly related to the severity of the disability, there is little evidence to support this assumption. For example, parents of children with more severe disabilities may have greater child-care burdens, but parents of children with milder disabilities may be more likely to experience additional stress related to that felt by parents of children without disabilities (e.g., stress pertaining to school achievement, dating, driving a car).

The three factors that appear to be most predictive of how parents will cope with the stress are (1) their prior psychological makeup and marital happiness, (2) the quality and degree of informal support they receive from others, and (3) the coping strategies they use. Although there are exceptions, it is fair to say that parents who were well adjusted and happily married before the birth of the child have a better chance of coping with the situation than those who were already having psychological or marital problems.

Social support that parents receive from each other, extended family members, friends, and others can be critical in helping them cope with the stress of raising a child with a disability (D'Asaro, 1998; Duis et al., 1997; Gavidia-Payne & Stoneman, 1997). The support can be physical, such as offering child care, or it can be psychological. Just having someone to talk to about problems can be helpful.

Parents who engage in "thinking-oriented" coping strategies are also more likely to come to terms with their child's disability. For example, parents who are able to say such things as "I need to take this one day at a time" or "Although my child has problems, he could be much worse" are more likely to resolve the initial trauma of finding out that their child has a disability (Pianta, Marvin, Britner, & Borowitz, 1996).

Some parents report that adding a child with a disability to the family actually has some unanticipated positive results. Some parents note, for example, that they have become more concerned about social issues and are more tolerant of differences in other people than they were before. Moreover, some parents claim that the birth of their child with a disability has brought the family closer together. This is not to minimize the fact that the added stress a child with a disability often brings can have a devastating impact on the stability of the family. It is dangerous to assume, though, that the birth of a child with a disability automatically spells doom for the psychological well-being of the parents or for the stability of their marriage.

Sibling Reactions

Although a relatively large body of literature pertains to parental reactions, there is much less information about siblings of persons with disabilities. What is available, however, indicates that siblings can and frequently do experience the same emotions—fear, anger, guilt, and so forth—that parents do. In fact, in some ways, siblings may have an even more difficult time than their parents in coping with some of these feelings, especially when they are younger. Being less mature, they may have trouble putting some of their negative sensations into proper perspective. And they may be uncomfortable asking their parents the questions that bother them. Table 13.1 provides examples of sibling concerns.

Although some feelings about their siblings' disabilities may not appear for many years, a substantial number of accounts indicate that nondisabled siblings are aware at an amazingly early age that their brothers or sisters are different in some way. Jewell (1985), for example, recounts how her sister would make allowances for her cerebral palsy by playing a special version of "dolls" with her, a version in which all the dolls had disabilities. Even though young children may have a vague sense that their siblings with disabilities are different, they may still have misconceptions about the nature of their siblings' conditions, especially regarding what caused them.

As nondisabled siblings grow older, their concerns often become more focused on how society views them and their siblings who are disabled. Adolescence can be a particularly difficult period. Teens, fearing rejection by peers,

Table 13.1   Examples of Sibling Concerns

Concerns about a Sibling with a Disbility	• What caused the disability? • Why does my brother behave so strangely? • Will my sister ever live on her own?
Concerns about Parents	• Why do they let my brother get away with so much? • Why must all their time be given to my sister? • Why do they always ask me to babysit?
Concerns about Themselves	• Why do I have such mixed feelings about my sister? • Will I catch the disability? • Will we have a normal brother-sister relationship?
Concerns about Friends	• How can I tell my best friend about my brother? • Will my friends tell everyone at school? • What should I do when other kids make fun of people with disabilities?
Concerns about School and the Community	• What happens in special education classes? • Will I be compared with my sister? • What should I tell strangers?
Concerns about Adulthood	• Will I be responsible for my brother when my parents die? • Do I need genetic counseling? • Should I join a parents' and/or siblings' group?

Source: Adapted from *Brothers & sisters—A special part of exceptional families* (2nd ed.), by T. H. Powell & P. A. Gallagher, 1993, Baltimore, MD: Paul H. Brookes (P. O. Box 10624, Baltimore, MD 21285–0624).

My True Best Friend

Tall, small, man you're clumsy,
My brother Paul, please don't fall!
Disabled, but still able to help.
Helps me through it when no one
else cares.
Paul you're my brother,
and you're my twin, you help me
through school,
you help me with friends,
Paul you're my brother and my best friend.

Stay with me forever.
Never pass away.
Bro I'll always love you
and I'll care for you.
We are two, but we are one.
One in a trillion you are, and you're fun.

They said we wouldn't live, they said
that you'd be dumb.
Even though you can't talk,
No one is as wise as the one.
The one I call Brother, friend, and twin.
I would share all of my riches with you.
My Brother forever, my best friend.
—Patrick Cannon, 15

Patrick (on the right) is in the eighth grade and has attention deficit disorder (ADD) and hyperactivity. He enjoys drawing, playing basketball, soccer, and baseball. This poem was written for his twin brother, Paul, who has cerebral palsy, is spastic quadriplegic, and has mental retardation. Paul plays baseball for the Challenger Division of Little League Baseball, and Patrick is his "Buddy." Patrick wants his poem to show other people what a great friend his brother is to him.

Source: Cannon, P. (1998). My true best friend. *Exceptional Parent, 28*(6), 84. Reprinted by permission.

often do not want to appear different. And having a sibling with a disability can single a person out.

One area virtually unexplored by researchers is the impact on adjustment when two or more siblings are disabled. Although one might expect that interactions between two siblings with disabilities would be potentially problematic, it is also possible that the shared experience of having a disability would draw the siblings closer. (Perhaps this is why Patrick Cannon, who has attention deficit hyperactivity disorder, has such positive feelings about his brother Paul, who has severe cerebral palsy and mental retardation—see the box above.)

Siblings' Adjustment. Children, like parents, can adapt well or poorly to having family members with disabilities. Research indicates that some siblings have trouble adjusting, some have no trouble adjusting, and some actually appear to benefit from the experience. Like parents, however, siblings of children with disabilities are at a greater risk than siblings of nondisabled children to have difficulties in adjustment.

Why some individuals respond negatively, whereas others do not, is not completely understood. Although not definitive, there is some evidence that birth order, gender, and age differences between siblings have some bearing on adjustment (Berry & Hardman, 1998). A nondisabled girl who is older than her sibling who has a disability is likely to have a negative attitude when she reaches adolescence

Siblings of children with disabilities often recount being aware at a very early age that something was different about their brothers or sisters. Siblings' attitudes change at different stages of their own lives; for example, adolescents become more concerned about public perception of themselves and their siblings with disabilities.

because she often has to shoulder child-care responsibilities. Siblings of the same gender and siblings who are close in age are more likely to experience conflicts. Perhaps the similarity in age, or the fact that the two siblings are of the same gender, makes the differences in ability between the two siblings more obvious.

Access to information is one key to adjustment for siblings of children with disabilities. As noted earlier in Table 13.1, siblings have myriad questions pertaining to their sibling's disability. Straightforward answers to these questions can help them cope with their fears. See the box on p. 525 for an example of how one sibling's understanding of her brother's autism helped her to cope with her embarrassment and to appreciate his strengths.

Teachers, as well as parents, can provide answers to some of these questions. Teachers, for example, can talk with students about the materials and contents of programs for their siblings with disabilities (Powell & Gallagher, 1993). Another excellent resource for providing information and support to siblings is **"sibshops"** (Meyer & Vadasy, 1994). Sibshops are workshops specifically designed to help siblings of children with disabilities.

Family Involvement in Treatment and Education

As noted earlier, today's professionals are more likely to recognize the positive influence parents can have on their exceptional children's development. This more positive attitude toward parents is reflected in how parents are now involved in the treatment and education of their children.

At one time, most early intervention programs for families who had children with disabilities operated according to the philosophy that the *professionals* had the expertise and that the families needed that expertise to function. Most authorities today, however, advocate a **family-centered model,** whereby the professionals work *for* the family, looking for ways to increase the decision-making power of the family and to encourage them to obtain nonprofessional (e.g., family members and friends) as well as formal sources of support. Much of the philosophy behind the family-centered approach is based on the recognition that the family's engagement with the child is long-term, whereas the professional's involvement is relatively temporary.

A family-centered approach has two major goals (Mahoney & Wheeden, 1997):

1. To help the family become capable of dealing with the many burdens and stresses that accompany raising a child with disabilities.
2. To maximize individual family members' abilities to influence their child's development.

Another way of describing the family-centered approach is to say that it is a model in which the professionals work *for* the family. The use of family-centered models reflects a change from viewing parents as passive recipients of profes-

sibshops. Workshops for siblings of children with disabilities; designed to help siblings answer questions about the disability and learn to adjust to having a sister or brother with a disability.

family-centered model. A type of early intervention program; consumer-driven in that professionals are viewed as working for families; views family members as the most important decision makers.

Pete's World

My little brother, Pete, has been "my baby" since the day he was born. But holding and loving Pete was not always easy. He pulled away from hugs, and whenever I tried to pick him up, he would run away.

I always knew that my brother had autism, but it was nothing more than a word to me. When my friends would ask me to describe him, I would talk about his physique and never mention his neurological disorder.

I remember when my second grade teacher called on me, asking me to tell everyone about my brothers. She asked what grades they were in and where they went to school. I told her that my older brothers, Tom and Joseph, were in middle school and that my younger brother did not go to school. Suddenly, I felt the stares of my classmates as my palms began to sweat and my stomach tightened. My teacher asked me why Pete was not in school. I couldn't explain it and I began to cry. Though my parents had tried to explain to me that Pete's disability affected him in many different ways, I guess I never truly understood.

Understanding Pete

When my parents enrolled Pete in a pre-kindergarten class, he couldn't handle it and he acted out. He threw cups of water, blocks, and crayons whenever his teacher or a classmate tried to show him a different way of doing things.

Specialists told my parents that they should give up on Pete and give him away, because he would never get better. However, my parents refused to give up and they began doing a lot of research on how Pete's disorder affected him. After that, they decided to re-enroll him in a special needs elementary school class.

At times he would become agitated and his anger often resulted in kicking and screaming. It was these fits that also em-

Pete

Pete's sister Becky

barrassed me. I was in the third grade then, and the other kids would watch Pete and say things like, "Why does that dumb kid act like that?" and "That kid is really weird." I would pretend that I did not know who Pete was.

Although I didn't understand and I was embarrassed, I did learn about my brother and his autism. I learned that his disability places him in a world where he is often happy and carefree until confusion begins to surround him. Pete needs a routine that must be followed, or he becomes extremely agitated. Thinking back, I realized that when Pete was acting out or being disobedient it was because he just could not understand why people were tying to change his routine. I also learned why my brother did not like to be hugged. It was part of his autism and had nothing to do with his feelings for me or the rest of the family.

Finally, I learned about Pete's strengths and gifts. Pete loves to write phrases he hears on television and he knows how to type on computers. He also has an amazing memory. In fact, I explain to anyone who asks that Pete is just like the character Dustin Hoffman plays in the movie, *Rain Man*. Just as the character remembered numbers he heard only once, when asked, Pete can do the same thing. My brother has such an amazing memory that he even helped me get in touch with a lost friend. Although I took down her new phone number, I had lost it. Pete had been in the room and heard me repeating the new number back to my friend as I wrote it down. It was years later but, Pete gave me her number from memory!

Now, whenever my friends ask me about Pete, I always take pride in my brother's accomplishments.

Source: Davenport, B. (1998). Pete's world. *Exceptional Parent, 28*(5), 92. Reprinted with permission.

sional advice to equal partners in the development of treatment and educational programs for their children. The notion is that, when professionals do not just provide direct services but encourage the family to help themselves and their children, the family takes more control over their own lives and avoids the dependency sometimes associated with typical professional–family relationships. Situations in which the family looks to professionals for all its help can result in family members becoming dependent on professionals and losing their feelings of competence and self-esteem.

Research into the effectiveness of family-centered models is in its early stages, but so far the results suggest that they increase parents' perceptions of personal control over their families' problems (Thompson et al., 1997; Trivette, Dunst, Boyd, & Hamby, 1995). However, research also indicates that, although many give lip service to the concept of family-centered services, the actual implementation of such services has been slow in coming (Mahoney & Bella, 1998; McWilliam et al., 1998).

The effort to build professional–parent partnerships is consistent with the thinking of child development theorists who stress the importance of the social context within which child development occurs. Urie Bronfenbrenner (1979, 1995), a renowned child development and family theorist, has been most influential in stressing that an individual's behavior cannot be understood without understanding the influence of the family on that behavior. Furthermore, the behavior of the family cannot be understood without considering the influence of other social systems (e.g., the extended family, friends, and professionals) on the behavior of the family. The interaction between the family and the surrounding social system is critical to how the family functions. A supportive network of professionals (and especially friends) can be beneficial to the family with a child who has a disability.

Current approaches to involving families in treating and educating their children take into account how the family fits within the broader societal context. We now discuss one such family-centered theory, the family systems framework of the Turnbulls (Turnbull & Turnbull, 1997).

The Family Systems Theory

The family systems theory holds that all parts of the family are interrelated, so that events affecting any one family member also affect the others. It follows that the more treatment and educational programs take into account the relationships and interactions among family members, the more likely they will be successful. The Turnbulls' model includes four interrelated components: **family characteristics, family interaction, family functions,** and **family life cycle** (Turnbull & Turnbull, 1997).

Family Characteristics. Family characteristics provide a description of basic information related to the family. They include characteristics of the exceptionality (e.g., the type and severity), characteristics of the family (e.g., size, cultural background, socioeconomic status, and geographic location), personal characteristics of each family member (e.g., health and coping styles), and special conditions (e.g., child or spousal abuse, maternal depression, and poverty). Family characteristics help determine how family members interact with themselves and with others outside the family. It will probably make a difference, for example, whether the child with a disability is mentally retarded or hearing impaired, whether he or she is an only child or has five siblings, whether the family is upper middle class or lives in poverty, and so forth.

Recent trends in U.S. society make it even more important for teachers and other professionals who work with families to take into account family characteristics. In addition to wider diversity with regard to ethnicity, there are also increases in the numbers of families in which both parents work outside the home, single-parent families, and families who are living in poverty.

family characteristics. A component of the Turnbulls' family systems model; includes type and severity of the disability as well as such things as size, cultural background, and socioeconomic background of the family.

family interaction. A component of the Turnbulls' family systems model; refers to how cohesive and adaptable the family is.

family functions. A component of the Turnbulls' family systems model; includes such things as economic, daily care, social, medical, and educational needs.

family life cycle. A component of the Turnbulls' family systems model; consists of birth and early childhood, childhood, adolescence, and adulthood.

Coupled with these demographic changes—and to a certain extent influenced by them—families today live under a great deal more stress. For one thing, today's parents have less leisure time than ever before. Compared to parents in the late 1960s, for example, today's mothers and fathers between the ages of eighteen and thirty-nine put in 241 and 189 more annual hours of work, respectively (Leete-Guy & Schor, 1992).

A result of these demographic changes and more stressful living conditions may be that a reduced amount of support is available from parents for children with disabilities (Hallahan, 1992). Parents today are so consumed with meeting their own needs that they are unable to provide as much support to their children as was once the case. A counselor with over twenty years' experience in working with families with and without members who have disabilities has observed:

> It has only been recently that I have observed so much anger, insecurity, and despair among all families.... Families are experiencing a great deal of fatigue, and lack energy to advocate like they used to on behalf of their son or daughter, brother or sister. Both parents are working, they have no leisure time, and many are barely able to take care of their own responsibilities. (Stark, 1992, pp. 248–249)

These dramatic societal changes present formidable challenges for teachers and other professionals working with families of children with disabilities. As the configuration of families changes, professionals will need to alter their approaches. For example, the same approaches that are successful with two-parent families may not be suitable for single mothers. Also, professionals need to understand that today's parent is living under more and more stress and may find it increasingly difficult to devote time and energy to working on behalf of his or her child.

Family Interaction. Family members can have a variety of functional and dysfunctional modes of interaction. Some authorities point to the quality of parent–child interactions as being the key ingredient in any family-centered approach; they assert that it largely determines how well the child will develop, especially in the early childhood years (Guralnick, 1998). An important indicator of high-quality interaction is the degree of responsiveness of the parent to the child (Mahoney, Boyce, Fewell, Spiker, & Wheeden, 1998). The more the parent responds appropriately to the young child's body language, gestures, facial expressions, and so forth, the more the child's development will flourish.

In the Turnbulls' model, they point to family cohesion and adaptability as important determinants of how family members interact with each other. In general, families are healthier if they have moderate degrees of cohesion and adaptability.

Cohesion. *Cohesion* refers to the degree to which an individual family member is free to act independently of other family members. An appropriate amount of family cohesion permits the individual to be his or her own person while at the same time allowing him or her to draw on other family members for support as needed. Families with low cohesion may not offer the child with a disability the necessary support, whereas the overly cohesive family may overprotect the child and not allow him or her enough freedom.

It is frequently very difficult for otherwise healthy families to find the right balance of cohesion. They sometimes go overboard in wanting to help their children and, in so doing, limit their children's independence. A particularly stressful time can be adolescence, when the teenager strives to break some of the bonds that have tied him or her to the family. This need for independence is normal behavior. What makes the situation difficult for many families of children with disabilities is that the child, because of his or her disability, has often by necessity been more protected by parents. In fact, there is research to suggest that, in the early years, the more supportive the parent is with the child the better. For example, in one study mothers of toddlers with Down syndrome who during play engaged in more helpful behaviors such as steadying objects and otherwise making it more likely that the children would experience success had children who were more likely to play and vocalize (Roach, Barratt, Miller, & Leavitt, 1998).

As the child matures, however, the issue of independence usually takes on more importance. One way to help children feel more connected to the family, without infringing on their freedom, is to give them family-based responsibilities such as chores. For some children with physical limitations, this may mean making accommodations so they can perform the tasks successfully.

Cohesion can also be an issue for adults with disabilities. For example, adults with mental retardation, especially those who live at home, often have special problems finding the right degree of independence from their families. Compared with those who live in the community, adults with mental retardation who live at home have a narrower range of social contacts outside their families but do experience more support from them, as well (Krauss, Seltzer, & Goodman, 1992).

When adults with disabilities live away from home, their parents are often concerned about providing enough support so that their grown children do not become socially isolated. One mother who was interviewed about future living arrangements for her daughter, who is severely retarded, explained:

> I would like to see her live fairly close so that she can come over and visit when she wants to or if she needed help. She's going to have to have some support, I know that. There are lots of apartments close by that I think she can handle ... and I would like to see her close enough so that we always have the constant, not constant, [sic] but we will always be there if she needs us. And both Tim and I agree that that's something we will always do. We will be here. But, on the other hand, if we want to go away for a month, we'll know there are other people that can be called upon to give her the support she needs. (Lehmann & Baker, 1995, p. 30)

Current thinking dictates two principles that are sometimes difficult to coordinate (Blacher & Baker, 1992): (1) adults with disabilities should live in the community, if at all possible; and (2) family support is critical across the lifespan. Achieving the right degree of independence from the family, while also encouraging family involvement, can be a difficult challenge.

Adaptability. *Adaptability* refers to the degree to which families are able to change their modes of interaction when they encounter unusual or stressful situations. Some families are so chaotic that it is difficult to predict what any one member will do in a given situation. In such an unstable environment, the needs of the family member who is disabled may be overlooked or neglected. At the other end of the continuum are families characterized by extreme rigidity. Each family member has his or her prescribed role in the family. Such rigidity makes it difficult for the family to adjust to the addition of a member with a disability. The addition of any child requires adjustment on the part of the family, but it is even more important if the child has special needs. For example, it may be that the mother's involvement in transporting the child with a disability from one therapy session to another will necessitate that the father be more involved than previously in household chores and taking care of the other children.

Family Functions. Family functions are the numerous routines in which families engage to meet their many and diverse needs. Economic, daily care, social, medical, and educational needs are just a few examples of the functions to which families need to attend.

An important point for teachers to consider is that education is only one of several functions in which families are immersed. And for some students, especially those with multiple disabilities, several professionals may be vying for the time of the parents. It is only natural, of course, that teachers should want to involve parents in the educational programming of their children as much as possible. Teachers know the positive benefits that can occur when parents are part of the treatment program. At the same time, however, teachers need to respect the fact that education is just one of the many functions to which families must attend. If the child has chronic medical problems, for example, the family may be consumed by decisions regarding medical treatment (Martin, Brady, & Kotarba, 1992).

Several authorities have reported that many families of students with disabilities prefer a passive, rather than active, degree of involvement in their children's education (Turnbull & Turnbull, 2000). Parents often have very legitimate reasons for playing a more passive role. For example, in their culture, it may be customary for parents to refrain from interfering with the roles of school personnel in educational matters. Furthermore, some parents may simply be so busy attending to other family functions that they are forced to delegate most of the educational decisions for their children to teachers. Respecting the parents' desire to play a relatively passive role in their child's education does not mean that teachers should discourage or discount parental involvement. Teachers should encourage involvement for those families who want to be involved. Also, it may be that parents who desire not to be involved at one time will want to take a more active role later.

Family Life Cycle. Several family theorists have noted that the impact of a child with a disability on the family changes over time (Berry & Hardman, 1998; Turnbull & Turnbull, 1997). For this reason, some have pointed to the value of looking at families with children with a disability from a life-cycle perspective. Turnbull and Turnbull (1997), for example, have presented four major life-cycle stages that are representative of other family theorists: (1) early childhood, (2) childhood, (3) adolescence, and (4) adulthood.

Transitions between stages in the life cycle are particularly stressful for families, especially families with children who are disabled. We have already mentioned the difficulties facing families at the transition point when their child, as an adult, moves into more independent work and living settings. A particularly difficult issue for some parents of children with disabilities who are entering adulthood is that of mental competence and guardianship. These parents must struggle with how much self-determination to allow their children given their ability to make reasoned choices (Berry & Hardman, 1998). Parents who decide that their children are not competent to make rational choices without endangering themselves, can go through legal channels to obtain guardianship of their children. **Guardianship** means that one person has the authority, granted by the courts, to make decisions for another person. There are three types of guardianship: full, limited, and temporary.

> *Full guardianship* involves one person's full control over the decisions made in another person's life.... *Limited guardianship* allows an individual to keep some control over life decisions while giving another person authority in some areas consistent with the needs of the individual.... *Temporary*

guardianship. A legal term that gives a person the authority to make decisions for another person; can be full, limited, or temporary; applies in cases of parents who have children who have severe cognitive disabilities.

guardianship is applicable under special circumstances and within a limited time frame. An example of a special circumstance may be a reaction to drugs that renders an individual mentally and physically incapacitated. In this case, family members can seek temporary guardianship to deal effectively with this emergency situation. Once the emergency is over, the guardianship is no longer applicable. (Berry & Hardman, 1998, pp. 253–254)

Another particularly troublesome transition can be from the relatively intimate confines of an infant or preschool program to the larger context of a kindergarten setting. For the child, the transition often requires a sudden increase in independent functioning (Fowler, Schwartz, & Atwater, 1991). For the parents, it often means giving up a sense of security for their child. As one parent relates:

As my daughter's third birthday approached, I lived in dread, not wishing to leave the familiar, comfortable environment of her infant program. The infant program had become home away from home for me. It was supportive and intimate. I had made some lifelong friendships, as well as having established a comfortable routine in our lives. I saw making the transition to a preschool program in the school district as an extremely traumatic experience, second only to learning of Amy's diagnosis.

What were my fears? First, I was concerned that my husband and I, along with professionals, would be deciding the future of our child. How could we play God? Would our decisions be the right ones? Second, I feared loss of control, as I would be surrendering my child to strangers—first to the school district's intake assessment team and then to the preschool teacher. The feeling of being at the mercy of professionals was overwhelming. In addition, I had more information to absorb and a new system with which to become familiar. Finally, I feared the "label" that would be attached to my child and feared that this label would lower the world's expectations of her. (Hanline & Knowlton, 1988, p. 116)

Transitions between stages are difficult because of the uncertainty that each new phase presents to the family. One of the reasons for the uncertainty pertains to replacements of the professionals who work with the child who is disabled. In particular, parents of a child with multiple disabilities, who requires services from multiple professionals, can be anxious about the switches in therapists and teachers that occur many times throughout the child's life, especially at transition points. Table 13.2 presents tips for parents at the various transition points throughout the family life cycle.

Social Support for Families

Authorities now recognize that families can derive tremendous benefit from social support provided by others (Dunst & Trivette, 1994; Dunst, Trivette, & Jodry, 1997). **Social support** refers to emotional, informational, or material aid provided to persons in need. In contrast to assistance that comes from professionals and agencies, social support is informal, coming from such sources as extended family, friends, church groups, neighbors, and social clubs. We discuss two methods of providing social support: parental support groups and the Internet.

social support. Emotional, informational, or material aid provided to a person or a family; this informal means of aid can be very valuable in helping families of children with disabilities.

Parental Support Groups. One common type of social support, especially for parents of recently diagnosed children, is parental support groups that consist of parents of children with the same or similar disabilities. Such groups can be relatively unstructured, meeting infrequently with unspecified agendas, or they can

Table 13.2 Tips for Enhancing Successful Transitions

Early Childhood	• Begin preparing for the separation of preschool children by periodically leaving the child with others. • Gather information and visit preschools in the community. • Encourage participation in Parent to Parent programs. (Veteran parents are matched in one-to-one relationships with parents who are just beginning the transition process.) • Familiarize parents with possible school (elementary and secondary) programs, career options, or adult programs so they have an idea of future opportunities.
Childhood	• Provide parents with an overview of curricular options. • Ensure that IEP meetings provide an empowering context for family collaboration. • Encourage participation in Parent to Parent matches, workshops, or family support groups to discuss transitions with others.
Adolescence	• Assist families and adolescents to identify community leisure-time activities. • Incorporate into the IEP skills that will be needed in future career and vocational programs. • Visit or become familiar with a variety of career and living options. • Develop a mentor relationship with an adult with a similar exceptionality and an individual who has a career that matches the student's strengths and preferences.
Adulthood	• Provide preferred information to families about guardianship, estate planning, wills, and trusts. • Assist family members in transferring responsibilities to the individual with an exceptionality, other family members, or service providers as appropriate. • Assist the young adult or family members with career or vocational choices. • Address the issues and responsibilities of marriage and family for the young adult.

Source: Turnbull, A. P., & Turnbull, H. R. (1997). *Families, professionals, and exceptionality: A special partnership* (3rd ed.). Upper Saddle River, NJ: Prentice-Hall, p. 149.

be more structured. In any case, parental groups can provide a number of benefits, "including (1) alleviating loneliness and isolation, (2) providing information, (3) providing role models, and (4) providing a basis for comparison" (Seligman & Darling, 1989, p. 44).

Parental support groups, however, are not of benefit to everyone. Some parents may actually experience more stress from sharing problems and listening to the problems of others (Berry & Hardman, 1998). The impact of support groups on parents is probably dependent on the particular personalities of the parents involved.

Internet Resources for Parents. The Internet has turned into an excellent resource for parents of children with disabilities. Dozens of electronic mailing lists, newsgroups, and World Wide Web sites are now devoted to disability-related topics. Through mailing lists and newsgroups, parents of children with disabilities can communicate with each other, with people who have disabilities, and with professionals concerning practical as well as theoretical issues. Lists and newsgroups are available regarding specific disabilities (e.g, Down syndrome, attention deficit hyperactivity disorder, cerebral palsy, cystic fibrosis) as well as more general ones.

Via Web sites, parents can access information on disabilities. A good example is The Office of Special Education, based at the University of Virginia. (The address for this site is http://curry.edschool.virginia.edu/curry/dept/cise/ose/.) This site provides information and links to other Web sites on such topics as legislation,

Parent support groups provide help to many parents of children with disabilities.

legal issues, documented teaching techniques, parent resources, and upcoming articles in special education journals. Table 13.3 lists several examples of Web sites that contain information for families of persons with disabilities.

Communication Between Parents and Professionals

Virtually all family theorists agree that, no matter what particular approach one uses to work with parents, the key to the success of a program is how well parents and professionals are able to work together. Even the most creative, well-conceived model is doomed to fail if professionals and parents are unable to communicate effectively.

Unfortunately, special education does not have a long tradition of excellent working relationships between parents and teachers (Michael, Arnold, Magliocca, & Miller, 1992). This is not too surprising, considering the ingredients of the situation. On the one hand, there are the parents, who may be trying to cope with the stresses of raising a child with a disability in a complex and changing society. On the other hand, there are the professionals—teachers, speech therapists, physicians, psychologists, physical therapists, and so forth—who may be frustrated because they do not have all the answers to the child's problems.

One of the keys to avoiding professional–parent misunderstandings is *communication*. It is critical that teachers attempt to communicate with the parents of their students. There are advantages to receiving information from parents as well as imparting information to them. Given that the parents have spent considerably more time with the child and have more invested in the child emotionally, they can be an invaluable source of information regarding his or her characteristics and interests. And by keeping parents informed of what is going on in class, teachers can foster a relationship in which they can call on parents for support should the need arise. Even those parents mentioned earlier, who do not want to be actively involved in making decisions regarding their child's educational program, should receive periodic communication from their child's teacher.

Table
13.3 Web Sites for Families of Persons with Disabilities

Web Site	URL
Ability Online Support Network	http://www.ablelink.org/
Autism Society of America	http://www.autism-society.org
C.H.A.D.D.	http://www.chadd.org/
Division for Learning Disabilities of the Council for Exceptional Children	http://edhd.bgsu.edu/DLD/
Family Education Network	http://www.familyeducation.com/
International Dyslexia Association	http://www.interdys.org
Internet Resources for Special Children (IRSC)	http://www.irsc.org/
LD Online	http://www.ldonline.org/
Learning Disabilities Association of America (LDA)	http://www.ldanatl.org
National Adult Literacy and Learning Disabilities Center	http://novel.nifl.gov/nalldtop.htm
National Center for Learning Disabilities, Inc.	http://www.ncld.org
National Parent Network on Disabilities	http://www.npnd.org
PACER Center	http://www.pacer.org
Parents Place Co.	http://www.parentsplace.com/
The ARC	http://www.thearc.org
The Family Village School	http://laran.waisman.wisc.edu/fv/www/education/pti.html
United Cerebral Palsy	http://www.UCPA.org

One area in particular that requires the cooperation of parents is homework. For mainstreamed students who are disabled, homework is often a source of misunderstanding and conflict (Bryan, Nelson, & Mathur, 1995; Mims, Harper, Armstrong, & Savage, 1991; Salend & Gajria, 1995). To avoid this often requires that the regular educator stay in close communication with the parents of the student with a disability. Table 13.4 lists recommendations for the respective roles of general education teachers and parents with regard to homework.

Most authorities agree that the communication between the teacher and parents should take place as soon as possible and that it should not be initiated only by negative behavior on the part of the student. Parents, especially those of students with behavior disorders, often complain that the only time they hear from school personnel is when their child has misbehaved (Kauffman, Mostert, Trent, & Hallahan, 1998). To establish a degree of rapport with parents, some teachers make a practice of sending home a brief form letter at the beginning of the school year, outlining the goals for the year. Others send home periodic newsletters or make occasional phone calls to parents. Even if teachers do not choose to use some of these techniques, authorities recommend that they be open to the idea of communicating with parents as soon as possible in the school year. By establishing a line of communication with parents early in the year, the teacher is in a better position to initiate more intensive and focused discussions should the need arise. Three such methods of communication are parent–teacher conferences, home-note programs, and traveling notebooks.

Table 13.4 Suggested Responsibilities of General Education Teachers and Parents with Regard to Homework

Suggestions for General Educators	• Establish a method of record keeping. This can be accomplished by maintaining a homework notebook or chart. • Ensure that all homework is at the child's academic functional level. • Inform parents and students in advance when special materials or resources are required for homework completion (e.g., study guides, a calculator, or a stopwatch). • Make homework a review of skills that are currently being taught. • Avoid homework that requires new knowledge or skills that have not been presented previously. • Allow time for homework at the end of class when appropriate. If time is available for homework in class, the teacher can answer questions. • Consider the attention span and functional level of the child when assigning homework. Lower-functioning children should not be required to complete the same amount of work as those who are higher functioning.
Suggestions for Parents	• Establish a scheduled time and place for homework to be completed. • Decide who will supervise the homework. This does not mean that the person will always check every problem or every sentence. • Provide an atmosphere conducive to learning. Make sure the area is well lighted and ample work space is provided. • Monitor the noise level. • Provide appropriate supplies. • Provide a tutor for subject areas with which parents are unfamiliar.

Source: Adapted from A. Mims, C. Harper, S. W. Armstrong, & S. Savage, "Effective instruction in homework for students with disabilities," *Teaching Exceptional Children, 24*(1), 42–44. Copyright © 1991 by The Council for Exceptional Children. Reprinted with permission.

Parent–Teacher Conferences. Parent–teacher conferences can be an effective way for teachers to share information with parents. Likewise, they are an opportunity for teachers to learn from parents more about the students from the parents' perspective. In addition to regularly scheduled meetings open to all parents, teachers may want to hold individual conferences with the parents of particular students. Most authorities agree that a key to conducting successful parent–teacher conferences is planning (Turnbull & Turnbull, 1997). How the teacher initiates the meeting, for example, can be crucial. Some recommend that the first contact be a telephone call that proposes the need for the meeting, without going into great detail, followed by a letter reminding the parents of the time and place of the meeting (Kauffman et al., 1998).

Teachers should also be comfortable holding conferences with parents from diverse backgrounds. Table 13.5 presents some suggestions for effective parent–teacher conferences, with special reference to cultural differences.

If the focus of the meeting is the student's poor work or misbehavior, the teacher will need to be as diplomatic as possible. Most authorities recommend that the teacher find something positive to say about the student, while still providing an objective account of what the student is doing that is troubling. The teacher needs to achieve a delicate balance of providing an objective account of the student's transgressions or poor work while demonstrating advocacy for the student. Conveying only bad or good news can lose the parents' sense of trust:

> Conveying only good news skews their perspective ... just as much as conveying only negative information. If a serious incident arises, they have no sense of background or warning. [This] may lead them to conclude that the

teacher is withholding information and provoke a sense of mistrust. When telling parents unpleasant information, it helps not only to be as objective as possible, but also state the case in a way that clearly conveys your advocacy of the student. When it is obvious to the parents that the teacher is angry or upset with their child, parents become apprehensive about the treatment the child may receive. A common response to this sense of dread is a defensiveness which polarizes parent–teacher relationships. (Kauffman et al., 1998, pp. 139–140)

Home-Note Programs. Sometimes referred to as *home-contingency programs,* **home-note programs** are a way of communicating with parents and having them reinforce behavior that occurs at school (Cottone, 1998; Kelley, 1990; Kelley & McCain, 1995; McCain & Kelley, 1993). By having parents dispense the reinforcement, the teacher takes advantage of the fact that parents usually have a greater number of reinforcers at their disposal than do teachers.

There are a number of different types of home-notes. A typical one consists of a simple form on which the teacher records "yes," "no," or "not applicable" to certain categories of behavior (e.g., social behavior, homework completed, homework accurate, in-class academic work completed, in-class academic work accurate). The form also may contain space for the teacher and the parents to write a few brief comments. The student takes the form home, has his or her parents sign it, and returns it the next day. The parents deliver reinforcement for the student's performance. The teacher often starts out sending a note home each day and gradually decreases the frequency until he or she is using a once-a-week note.

Although home-note programs have a great deal of potential, researchers have pointed out that they require close communication between the teacher and

home-note program. A system of communication between the teacher and parents; the teacher evaluates the behavior of the student using a simple form, the student takes the form home, gets the parents' signatures, and returns the form the next day.

Table 13.5 Tips for Effective Teacher–Parent Conferences

Planning for the Conference	• If possible, make an informal contact before the formal conference. • Invite both parents and extended family, if appropriate. • Allot an adequate amount of time for the conference. • Use a comfortable, private setting to facilitate conversation. • Consider using the student's home for the conference, but only if the parents are agreeable.
Family and Family Roles	• View parents as partners. • Acknowledge parents as the student's primary advocate.
Cultural Awareness	• Learn the customs and traditions of the family's culture.
Clear and Constructive Communication	• Be sensitive to natural parental reactions, such as denial, anger, embarrassment, or blame. • With regard to language differences, consider using an interpreter, but avoid using the student as the interpreter because it can confuse the role of the parent and child. • Avoid jargon. • Try to use descriptive data about the child (e.g., the number of times the student engages in an inappropriate behavior).
Closure and Follow-Up	• At the end of the meeting, summarize the main points. • Agree on a mutually acceptable plan of action.

Source: Adapted from Jordan, L., Reyes-Blanes, M. E., Peel, B. B., Peel, H. A., & Lane, H. (1998). Developing teacher–parent partnerships across cultures: Effective parent conferences. *Intervention in School and Clinic, 33,* 141–147.

parents (Cottone, 1998). Additionally, both teachers and parents need to agree philosophically with a behavioral approach to managing student behavior. If either is opposed to using reinforcement as a means of shaping behavior, the home-note program is unlikely to succeed.

Traveling Notebooks. Less formal than home-notes and particularly appropriate for students who see multiple professionals are traveling notebooks. A **traveling notebook** goes back and forth between school and home. The teacher and other professionals, such as the speech and physical therapists, can write brief messages to the parents and vice versa. In addition, a traveling notebook allows the different professionals to keep up with what each is doing with the student. See Figure 13.1 for excerpts from a traveling notebook of a two-year-old with cerebral palsy.

Another important way that parents and other family members can communicate with professionals is through advocacy. **Advocacy** is action that results in benefit to one or more persons (Alper, Schloss, & Schloss, 1996). Advocacy can be a way of gaining needed or improved services for children while helping parents gain a sense of control over outcomes for their children. Although sometimes associated with the notion of confrontations between parents and professionals, advocacy need not be adversarial. In fact, ideally, parents and professionals should work together in their advocacy efforts.

Parents can focus their advocacy on helping their own children, as well as other persons with disabilities. The latter may involve volunteering for advisory posts with schools and agencies as well as political activism—for example, campaigning for school board members who are sympathetic to educational issues pertinent to students with disabilities.

One of the most common ways of advocating for one's own child is by means of the IEP meeting. Table 13.6 lists several ways that parents can help make IEP meetings more effective. And the box on p. 538 offers suggestions on how parents can prepare themselves to advocate for their child.

As important as advocacy is, not all parents have the personalities or the time to engage in such activities. Also, engaging in advocacy may be more or less suitable to some parents at various stages in their child's development. For example, some parents may be heavily involved in such efforts when their children are young but become exhausted over the years and, thus, reduce their involvement. Likewise, some parents may not see the need for intervening on behalf of their children until they encounter problems later on—for example, in transition programming in the teenage years. The best advice for teachers is to encourage parents to be advocates for their children but respect their hesitancy to take on such responsibilities.

traveling notebook. A system of communication in which parents and professionals write messages to each other by way of a notebook or log that accompanies the child to and from school.

advocacy. Action that is taken on behalf of oneself or others; a method parents of students with disabilities can use to obtain needed or improved services.

In Conclusion

Today's knowledgeable educators recognize the tremendous impact a child with a disability can have on the dynamics of a family. They appreciate the negative as well as the positive influence such a child can exert. Today's knowledgeable educators also realize that the family of a child with a disability can be a bountiful reservoir of support for the child as well as an invaluable source of information for the teacher. Although tremendous advances have been made, we are just beginning to tap the potential that families have for contributing to the development

Figure 13.1

A traveling notebook. These short excerpts are taken at random from a notebook that accompanies two-year-old Lauren, who has cerebral palsy, back and forth to her special class for preschoolers. The notebook provides a convenient mode for an ongoing dialogue among her mother, Lyn; her teacher, Sara; her occupational therapist, Joan; and her speech therapist, Marti. As you can see from this representative sample, the communication is informal but very informative in a variety of items relating to Lauren.

Lyn,   9/7

Lauren did _very_ well — We had several criers, but — She played & worked very nicely. She responds so well to instruction — that's such a plus!

She fed herself crackers & juice & did a good job. She was very vocal & enjoyed the other children too. She communicated with me very well for the 1st day. Am pleased with her first day.

Sara

Sara,   9/15

Please note that towel, toothbrush/paste and clean clothes may be removed from bag today — Wed. We witnessed an apparently significant moment in her oral communication: She'll try to say "all done" after a meal. The execution is imperfect, to say the least, but she gets an "A" for effort. Could you please reinforce this after snack? Just ask her, "What do you say after you finish your snack?"

Thanks,
Lyn

9/28

Lauren had an esp. good day! She was jabbering a lot! Being very expressive with her vocalness & jabbering. I know she said "yes," or an approximate thereof, several times when asked if she wanted something. She was so cute with the animal sounds esp. pig & horse — she was really trying to make the sounds. It was the first time we had seen such a response. Still cruising a lot! She walked with me around the room & in the gym. She used those consonant and vowel sounds: dadada, mamama — her jabbering was just so different & definitely progressive. I am sending her work card with stickers home tomorrow for good working.

Several notes:

1. Susie (VI) came today & evaluated Lauren. She will compile a report & be in touch with you and me. She seemed very pleased with Lauren's performance.

2. Marti (speech) will see Lauren at 11 AM for evaluation. She'll be in touch afterwards.

3. Susie informed me about the addition to the IEP meeting on Mon. Oct. 4 at 10 AM here at Woodbrook.

How are the tape & cards working at home? I know you both are pleased with her jabbering. She seems so ready to say "_something_" — we are very, very pleased. See you tomorrow.

Sara

9/29

Lauren was a bit fussy during O.T. today — she stopped fussing during fine motor reaching activities (peg board, block building) but wasn't too pleased with being handled on the ball. She did a great job with the peg board & and readily used her left hand.

I want to bring in some different spoons next week to see if she can become more independent in scooping with a large handle spoon or a spoon that is covered.

Joan

Joan —   10/1

Although Lauren would very much approve of your idea for making her more independent during feeding, we'd rather not initiate self-feeding with an adaptive spoon at this time. Here's why:

1. When I feed Lauren or get her to grip a spoon and then guide her hand, I can slip the entire bowl of the spoon into her mouth and get her to close her lips on it. When Lauren uses a spoon without help, she turns it upside-down to lick it or inserts just the tip of it into her mouth and then sucks off the food . . .

2. Lauren has always been encouraged to do things "normally." She never had a special cup or a "Tommy Tippee," for instance. Of course it took a year of practice before she could drink well from a cup, and she still dribbles a little occasionally; but she's doing well now. We really prefer to give Lauren practice in using a regular spoon so that she doesn't get dependent on an adaptive utensil.

I'd like to assure you that we appreciate your communication about sessions with Lauren and ideas for her therapy. Coordinating her school, home, and CRC programs is going to be a challenge, to say the least.

Lyn

2/26

Good news! Lauren walked all the way from the room to the gym & back — She also walked up & down the full length of the gym!

Several other teachers saw her and were thrilled. She fell maybe twice! But picked herself right up —

Sara

3/2

Lauren had a great speech session! We were playing with some toys and she said "I want help" as plain as day. Later she said "I want crackers" and at the end of the session, she imitated "Cindy, let's go." Super!

Marti

Advocacy in Action: You Can Advocate for Your Child

Get All the Information You Can

The first step to successful advocacy is to gather information. Learn what is happening in the school; get copies of school records, as well as information about any tests or evaluations affecting your child; and talk with your child's teacher to learn his or her view of areas of concern.

You should also learn about special education law and its protections. You can obtain this information from the school's special education or guidance director, state departments of education, or parent information and training centers, as well as organizations such as CEC (Council for Exceptional Children). Because the law can be complex and difficult to understand, you might want to work with a parent advocate, who can explain the law, as well as special education procedures.

Last but not least, talk with your child to learn his or her view of the situation and what he or she thinks will help. Even young children have a keen sense of their stress points and what could be done to make it easier for them to succeed.

What Do You Want the School to Do?

As your child's advocate, you need to be clear about what you want the school to do. Be able to explain what you are happy with, unhappy with, what you want changed, and how you want it changed. For example, if a child is having difficulty completing homework, you should say whether you would like the assignment to be changed or for it to be provided on tape.

To learn about the different options available, you could talk with other parents who have children with similar problems. Ask the school for contact names.

Be a Good Communicator

Communicating well with your child's teacher and other school personnel is essential to your advocacy efforts. Keep in mind that the school's interest is the same as yours—you both want the best for your child. In your dealings with the school, be honest and develop a positive relationship with the teacher and other staff. Start where the concern is, usually the classroom teacher. Only move up the chain of command if you must.

Being diplomatic can be hard when you are concerned about your child's welfare—you want to get feisty. But, get feisty only if that is what it takes.

Bring a Companion to Meetings

Bring a companion, a friend or advocate, with you to school meetings. This person can help you listen, take notes so you are free to concentrate on what is happening, and help you understand what happened afterwards. In addition, your companion can help slow you down if things get too emotional.

Don't Be Afraid to Say No

Don't be pressured into making a bad decision. You can always say no, ask for more information, or for more time to consider a proposed solution. Take the time to consult with experts and people you trust in the community, then get back to the school with your decision.

Due Process

If your child has a disability, you can use due process to resolve disputes with the school, but it should be a last resort. Often, due process proceedings turn the school and parents into adversaries. It is much more beneficial to maintain a positive relationship with the individuals who will work with your child.

Making Your Voice Stronger

One of the best ways to make your voice stronger is to band together with other parents facing similar situations. To learn of other parents who share your concern, give the school a sheet of labels containing your name and address and a statement that you would like to meet other parents facing a similar issue.

When you meet with other parents, share your experiences. As a group, develop some proposals to solve the problem. The parents should then meet with the individual(s) who will be affected. For example, a group of parents who wanted to get computers in the resource room would meet first with the resource room teacher. This approach allows the parents to build a strong partnership with the teachers. Then teachers and parents can build an alliance, which can be particularly effective in creating change.

Source: Osher, T. (1997). Advocacy in action: You can advocate for your child! *CEC Today, 4*(4).

of their children with disabilities. We are just beginning to enable families to provide supportive and enriching environments for their children. And we are just beginning to harness the expertise of families so we can provide the best possible programs for their children.

Table 13.6 Hints for a More Effective IEP Meeting

- Take the initiative to set the date, time, and place of the meeting. Consider holding the meeting in your own home or in a community setting that feels comfortable to you.

- Before the meeting, ask the organizer to clarify the purpose and provide you with information you may need ahead of time. Also, find out who will be attending the meeting so that you may suggest other potential team members.

- Call the organizers to let them know what items you would like to have included on the agenda.

- Write down ideas about your child's present and future goals, interests, and needs, and bring these with you to share at the meeting.

- During the meeting, ask to have discussion items and lists of actions written down on large pieces of flip-chart paper so that all team members can see them.

- Be a "jargon buster"—ask to have unfamiliar terms clarified for you and other team members during the meeting.

- Ask team members to set a regular meeting schedule (e.g., monthly, bimonthly, semiannually, etc.) for the purpose of reviewing and evaluating your child's progress.

- After the meeting, ask to have the minutes sent to you and other team members.

- Help promote ongoing communication by asking other team members to call or write you on a regular basis.

Source: Salembier, G. B., & Furney, F. S. (1998). Speaking up for your child's future. *Exceptional Parent,* 28(7), 62–64.

Summary

At one time the prevailing attitude toward parents of persons with disabilities was negative. Professionals viewed them as causes of their children's problems, at worst, or as roadblocks to educational efforts, at best. Two factors have contributed to a much more positive attitude toward parents: First, current theory dictates that children, even young infants, can cause changes in adults' behavior. Professionals now view adult–child interaction as a two-way street—sometimes adults affect children, and sometimes the reverse is true. Second, professionals began to see parents as a potential source of information about how to educate their children. Most authorities now believe that parents should not be viewed as quasi-therapists or quasi-teachers—the goal should be to preserve the natural parent–child relationship. Current law also recognizes the central role the family plays—in particular, individualized family service plans (IFSPs) stress the need for family-centered programming.

Many theorists believe that parents go through a series of stages after learning that they have a child with a disability. There are limitations to a stage approach, however, including the tendency to view all parents as going through all the stages in the same order. Nevertheless, many parents do have emotional reactions; for example, guilt.

Parents of children with disabilities must deal with a number of sources of stress, including the reactions of the public toward them and the feelings of the children themselves. How parents cope with the stress varies. Although very few experience major psychological disturbances, they are at risk for mild forms of depression. How well they deal with stress is dependent upon three factors: (1) their prior psychological makeup and marital satisfaction, (2) the quality and degree of informal support, and (3) the degree to which they engage in "thinking-oriented" coping strategies. There is not clear consensus on whether the impact of having a child with a disability results in the same amount of stress in mothers and fathers, but there is apparently a trend for fathers to have more stress than was once the case.

Siblings of children with disabilities experience some of the same emotions that parents do. Because they are less mature, may not have a broad base of people with whom to talk, and may be hesitant to talk over sensitive issues with their parents, siblings may have a difficult time coping with their emotions. There is suggestive evidence that birth order, gender, and age differences interact to influence how well one adjusts to having a sibling with disabilities. Nondisabled older girls, siblings of the same gender, and siblings close in age appear to have more difficulties. As they grow older, children's feelings often become centered on how society views them and their family. Like their parents, most children are able to adjust to siblings with disabilities.

Current family practitioners advocate a family-focused or family-centered approach, in which professionals work for families, helping them obtain access to nonprofessional (e.g., family and friends) as well as formal sources of support. Families are encouraged to be active in decision making. Current theorists also stress the influence of the social context on child development. They note that the family, as a whole, affects individual family members and that society affects the family. Family systems theory is a family-centered approach to families that considers the social context.

The family systems model includes four components: family characteristics, family interaction, family functions, and family life cycle. *Family characteristics* comprise the type and severity of the disability as well as such things as the size, cultural background, and socioeconomic background of the family. *Family interaction* refers to how cohesive and adaptable the family is. *Family functions* include such things as economics, daily care, social, medical, and educational needs. It is important for teachers to keep in mind that education is just one of many needs to which the family must attend; some parents prefer more passive than active involvement in educational programming. The *family life cycle* is made up of birth and early childhood, childhood, adolescence, and adulthood. Transitions between stages, especially between preschool and school and between adolescence and adulthood, can be very difficult for families with children who are disabled. With regard to the latter, some families must deal with the complex issue of guardianship. The

model suggests that the impact on the family of a child with a disability as well as the impact of the family on the child are determined by the complex interactions within and between the four stages.

Current family-centered approaches stress the importance of social support—the emotional, informational, or material aid provided informally by such persons as the extended family, friends, neighbors, and church groups. One source of social support is that of parent support groups, made up of parents who have children with similar disabilities. The Internet has grown into an excellent resource for parents, as well. A social systems program is built on the assumption that it is better to enable families to help themselves than to provide only direct services to them.

Family theorists agree that the key to working with and involving parents is *communication*. The parent–teacher conference is one of the most common avenues, and preparation is the key to a successful conference. Teachers need to consider preconference, conference, and postconference planning. A home-note program, in which teachers send home brief checklists of students' behavior that they have filled out, can keep parents informed and involve them in reinforcing the students' behavior. A traveling notebook is a log that accompanies the child to and from school, in which the parent, teacher, and other professionals can write messages to one another concerning the child's progress.

appendix

Summary of IDEA '97 Regulatory Issues

In March, 1999, after much controversy and many delays, the U.S. Department of Education published the federal regulations related to the 1997 reauthorization of IDEA, which is known as *IDEA '97*. Here, we summarize some of the issues about which people frequently raise questions.

1. *IEPs and the general education curriculum.* IEPs must now include statements about how the student will *not* be involved in the general education classroom and curriculum.
2. *Inclusion in state and district assessments.* Students with disabilities must now be included, with appropriate accommodations and modifications, in general assessments of educational progress mandated by the state or district.
3. *Involvement of general education teachers.* At least one general education teacher must be involved in IEP development and informed of his or her responsibilities related to implementing the IEP.
4. *Graduation and diplomas.* The right to FAPE (free, appropriate public education) ends if the student graduates from high school with a regular diploma, but not if the student receives another type of diploma or certificate.
5. *Discipline.* The school may remove a child for up to 10 school days at a time for any violation of school rules, as long as there is not a pattern of such removal. Students with disabilities can not be suspended long-term or expelled for any behavior that is a manifestation of disability. Special education services must be continued for students with disabilities who are suspended (excepting the first 10 days of suspension in a school year) or expelled, regardless whether the misbehavior is a manifestation of disability. If a student with disabilities has a weapon or drugs on school property or is substantially likely to injure others, then the school may move him or her to an interim alternative educational placement for up to 45 days
6. *Functional behavioral assessment and positive behavioral intervention plans.* If a student with disabilities, is removed from school for more than 10 consecutive school days, then the IEP team must conduct a functional behavioral assessment and design a positive behavioral intervention plan to address the student's behavior.
7. *Charter schools.* IDEA and its regulations apply to all public agencies, including public charter schools.

We caution that legislation is subject to change by Congress, regulations to change by administrative departments, both legislation and regulation to reinterpretation or to clarification by courts. For more complete and current information regarding regulations, see one or more of the following web sites:

http://www.ed.gov/offices/OSERS/IDEA
http://ocfo.ed.gov/fedreg/finrule.htm

glossary

acceleration. An approach in which students with special gifts or talents are placed in grade levels ahead of their age peers in one or more academic subjects.

acquired aphasia. Loss or impairment of the ability to understand or formulate language because of accident or illness.

acquired immune deficiency syndrome (AIDS). A virus-caused illness resulting in a breakdown of the immune system; currently, no known cure exists.

adaptive devices. Special tools that are adaptations of common items to make accomplishing self-care, work, or recreation activities easier for people with physical disabilities.

adaptive skills. Skills needed to adapt to one's living environment (e.g., communication, self-care, home living, social skills, community use, self-direction, health and safety, functional academics, leisure, and work); usually estimated by an adaptive behavior survey; one of two major components (the other is intellectual functioning) of the AAMR definition.

adventitiously deaf. Deafness that occurs through illness or accident in an individual who was born with normal hearing.

advocacy. Action that is taken on behalf of oneself or others; a method parents of students with disabilities can use to obtain needed or improved services.

affective disorder. A disorder of mood or emotional tone characterized by depression or elation.

aggression. Behavior that intentionally causes others harm or that elicits escape or avoidance responses from others.

Americans with Disabilities Act (ADA). Civil rights legislation for persons with disabilities ensuring nondiscrimination in a broad range of activities.

amniocentesis. A medical procedure that allows examination of the amniotic fluid around the fetus; sometimes recommended to determine the presence of abnormality.

anoxia. The loss of oxygen; can cause brain injury.

anxiety disorder. A disorder characterized by anxiety, fearfulness, and avoidance of ordinary activities because of anxiety or fear.

apraxia. The inability to move the muscles involved in speech or other voluntary acts.

aqueous humor. A watery substance between the cornea and lens of the eye.

articulation. The movements the vocal tract makes during production of speech sounds; enunciation of words and vocal sounds.

Asperger syndrome. A developmental disability in which language and cognitive development are normal but the child may show a lag in motor development and impairment in emotional and social development.

astigmatism. Blurred vision caused by an irregular cornea or lens.

atonic. Characterized by lack of muscle tone; associated with atonic cerebral palsy.

attention deficit hyperactivity disorder (ADHD). A condition characterized by severe problems of inattention, hyperactivity, and/or impulsivity; often found in persons with learning disabilities.

audiologist. An individual trained in audiology, the science dealing with hearing impairments, their detection, and remediation.

audiometric zero. The lowest level at which people with normal hearing can hear.

auditory-verbal approach. Part of the oral approach to teaching students who are hearing impaired; stresses teaching the person to use his or her remaining hearing as much as possible; heavy emphasis on use of amplification.

augmentative communication. Alternative forms of communication that do not use the oral sounds of speech.

auricle. The visible part of the ear, composed of cartilage; collects the sounds and funnels them via the external auditory canal to the eardrum.

authentic assessment. A method that evaluates a student's critical-thinking and problem-solving ability in real-life situations in which he or she may work with or receive help from peers, teachers, parents, or supervisors.

autism. A developmental disability characterized by extreme withdrawal, cognitive deficits, language disorders, self-stimulation, and onset before the age of thirty months.

basal ganglia. A set of structures within the brain that include the caudate, globus pallidus, and putamen, with the first two being abnormal in people with ADHD; generally responsible for the coordination and control of movement.

behavioral inhibition. The ability to stop an intended response, to stop an ongoing response, to guard an ongoing response from interruption, and to refrain from responding immediately; allows executive functions to occur; delayed or impaired in those with ADHD.

bicultural-bilingual approach. An approach for teaching students with hearing impairment that stresses teaching American Sign Language as a first language, English as a second language, and promotes the teaching of Deaf culture.

blindisms. Repetitive, stereotyped movements (e.g., rocking or eye rubbing) characteristic of some persons who are blind, severely retarded, or psychotic; more appropriately referred to as *stereotypic behaviors.*

braille. A system in which raised dots allow people who are blind to read with their fingertips; each quadrangular cell contains from one to six dots, the arrangement of which denotes different letters and symbols.

braille bills. Legislation passed in several states to make braille more available to students with visual impairment; specific provisions vary from state to state, but major advocates have lobbied for (1) making braille available if parents want it, and (2) ensuring that teachers of students with visual impairment are proficient in braille.

braille notetakers. Portable devices that can be used to take notes in braille, which are then converted to speech, braille, or text.

cataracts. A condition caused by clouding of the lens of the eye; affects color vision and distance vision.

catheterization. The insertion of a tube into the urethra to drain the bladder.

caudate. A structure in the basal ganglia of the brain; site of abnormal development in persons with ADHD.

cerebellum. An organ at the base of the brain responsible for coordination and movement; site of abnormal development in persons with ADHD.

cerebral palsy (CP). A condition characterized by paralysis, weakness, incoordination, and/or other motor dysfunction; caused by damage to the brain before it has matured.

choreoathetoid. Characterized by involuntary movements and difficulty with balance; associated with choreoathetoid cerebral palsy.

chorionic villus sampling (CVS). A method of testing the unborn fetus for a variety of chromosomal abnormalities, such as Down syndrome; a small amount of tissue from the chorion (a membrane that eventually helps form the placenta) is extracted and tested; can be done earlier than amniocentesis but the risk of miscarriage is slightly higher.

chromosome. A rod-shaped entity in the nucleus of the cell; contains genes, which convey hereditary characteristics.

chronological age. Refers to how old a person is; used in comparison with mental age to determine IQ:

$$IQ = \frac{\text{mental age}}{\text{chronological age}} \times 100$$

classwide peer tutoring (CWPT). An instructional procedure in which all students in the class are involved in tutoring and being tutored by classmates on specific skills as directed by their teacher.

cleft palate. A condition in which there is a rift or split in the upper part of the oral cavity; may include the upper lip (cleft lip).

coaching. A technique whereby a friend or therapist offers encouragement and support for a person with ADHD.

cochlea. A snail-shaped organ that lies below the vestibular mechanism in the inner ear; its parts convert the sounds coming from the middle ear into electrical signals that are transmitted to the brain.

cochlear implantation. A surgical procedure that allows people who are deaf to hear some environmental sounds; an external coil fitted on the skin by the ear picks up sound from a microphone worn by the person and transmits it to an internal coil implanted in the bone behind the ear, which carries it to an electrode implanted in the cochlea of the inner ear.

cognition. The ability to solve problems and use strategies; an area of difficulty for many persons with learning disabilities.

cognitive mapping. A nonsequential way of conceptualizing the spatial environment that allows a person who is visually impaired to know where several points in the environment are simultaneously; allows for better mobility than does a strictly sequential conceptualization of the environment.

cognitive training. A group of training procedures designed to change thoughts or thought patterns.

collaborative consultation. An approach in which a special educator and a general educator collaborate to come up with teaching strategies for a student with disabilities. The relationship between the two professionals is based on the premises of shared responsibility and equal authority.

communication disorders. Impairments in the ability to use speech or language to communicate.

community residential facility (CRF). A place, usually a group home, in an urban or residential neighborhood where about three to ten adults with retardation live under supervision.

comorbidity. Co-occurrence of two or more conditions in the same individual.

competitive employment. A workplace that provides employment that pays at least minimum wage and in which most workers are nondisabled.

comprehension monitoring. The ability to keep track of one's own comprehension of reading material and to make adjustments to comprehend better while reading; often deficient in students with learning disabilities.

computerized axial tomographic (CAT) scans. A neuroimaging technique whereby X rays of the brain are compiled by a computer to produce a series of pictures of the brain.

conceptual intelligence. The traditional conceptualization of intelligence emphasizing problem solving related to academic material; what IQ tests primarily assess.

conduct disorder. A disorder characterized by overt, aggressive, disruptive behavior or covert antisocial acts such as stealing, lying, and fire setting; may include both overt and covert acts.

conductive hearing impairment. A hearing loss, usually mild, resulting from malfunctioning along the conductive pathway of the ear (i.e., the outer or middle ear).

congenital anomaly. An irregularity (anomaly) present at birth; may or may not be due to genetic factors.

congenital cytomegalovirus (CMV). The most frequently occurring viral infection in newborns; can result in a variety of disabilities, especially hearing impairment.

congenitally deaf. Deafness that is present at birth; can be caused by genetic factors, by injuries during fetal development, or by injuries occurring at birth.

constant time delay. An instructional procedure whereby the teacher makes a request while simultaneously prompting the student and then over several occasions makes the same request and waits a constant period of time before prompting; often used with students with mental retardation.

contingency-based self-management. Educational techniques that involve having students keep track of their own behavior, for which they then receive consequences (e.g., reinforcement).

continuum of alternative placements. The full range of alternative placements, from those assumed to be least restrictive to those considered most restrictive; the continuum ranges from regular classrooms in neighborhood schools to resource rooms, self-contained classes, special day schools, residential schools, hospital schools, and home instruction.

contractures. Permanent shortenings of muscles and connective tissues and consequent distortion of bones and/or posture because of neurological damage.

cooperative learning. A teaching approach in which the teacher places students with heterogeneous abilities (for example, some might have disabilities) together to work on assignments.

cooperative teaching. An approach in which general educators and special educators teach together in the general classroom; it helps the special educator know the context of the regular classroom better.

cornea. A transparent cover in front of the iris and pupil in the eye; responsible for most of the refraction of light rays in focusing on an object.

cortical visual impairment (CVI). A poorly understood childhood condition that apparently involves dysfunction in the visual cortex; characterized by large day-to-day variations in visual ability.

creativity. The ability to express novel and useful ideas, to sense and elucidate new and important relationships, and to ask previously unthought-of but crucial questions.

cued speech. A method to aid speechreading in people with hearing impairment; the speaker uses hand shapes to represent sounds.

cultural-familial retardation. Today, a term used to refer to mild retardation due to an unstimulating environment and/or genetic factors.

curriculum-based assessment (CBA). A formative evaluation method designed to evaluate performance in the particular curriculum to which students are exposed; usually involves giving students a small sample of items from the curriculum in use in their schools; proponents argue that CBA is preferable to comparing students with national norms or using tests that do not reflect the curriculum content learned by students.

Deaf clubs. Gathering spots where people who are deaf can socialize; on the decline in the United States.

decibels. Units of relative loudness of sounds; zero decibels (0 dB) designates the point at which people with normal hearing can just detect sound.

deinstitutionalization. A social movement of the 1960s and 1970s whereby large numbers of persons with mental retardation and/or mental illness were moved from large mental institutions into smaller community homes or into the homes of their families; recognized as a major catalyst for integrating persons with disabilities into society.

Descriptive Video Service. A service for use of people with visual impairment that provides audio narrative of key visual elements; available for several public television programs.

detectable warnings. Rubberized strips with raised bumps; designed to help people who are blind detect railway and subway platform edges; mandated by ADA.

developmental delay. A term often used to encompass a variety of disabilities of infants or young children indicating that they are significantly behind the norm for development in one or more areas such as motor development, cognitive development, or language.

diabetic retinopathy. A condition resulting from interference with the blood supply to the retina; the fastest-growing cause of blindness.

diplegia. A condition in which the legs are paralyzed to a greater extent than the arms.

Direct Instruction. A method of teaching academics, especially reading and math; emphasizes drill and practice and immediate feedback; lessons are precisely sequenced, fast-paced, and well-rehearsed by the teacher.

disability rights movement. Patterned after the civil rights movement of the 1960s, this is a loosely organized effort to advocate for the rights of people with disabilities through lobbying legislators and other activities. Members view people with disabilities as an oppressed minority.

discourse. Conversation; the skills used in conversation, such as turn taking and staying on the topic.

doctor's office effect. The observation that children with ADHD often do not exhibit their symptoms when seen by a clinician in a brief office visit.

dopamine. A neurotransmitter, the levels of which may be too low in the frontal lobes and too high in the basal ganglia of persons with ADHD.

Doppler effect. A term used to describe the phenomenon of the pitch of a sound rising as the listener moves toward its source.

Down syndrome. A condition resulting from a chromosomal abnormality; characterized by mental retardation and such physical signs as slanted-appearing eyes, hypotonia, a single palmar crease, shortness, and a tendency toward obesity; the most common type of Down syndrome is trisomy 21.

dysarthria. A condition in which brain damage causes impaired control of the muscles used in articulation.

early expressive language delay (EELD). A significant lag in the development of expressive language that is apparent by age two.

echolalia. The meaningless repetition (echoing) of what has been heard.

Education for All Handicapped Children Act (PL 94–142). This federal law contains a mandatory provision stating that to receive funds under the act, every school system in the nation must provide a free, appropriate public education for every child between the ages of three and eighteen (now extended to ages three to twenty-one), regardless of how or how seriously he or she may be disabled.

encephalitis. An inflammation of the brain; can affect the child's mental development adversely.

enclave model. A model of supported employment in which a small group of workers who is retarded is employed in a larger business or industry in which the workers are not retarded; the workers in the enclave have the same eligibility for benefits and wages as all other employees.

enrichment. An approach in which additional learning experiences are provided for students with special gifts or talents while they remain in the grade levels appropriate for their chronological ages.

epilepsy. A pattern of repeated seizures.

error analysis. An informal method of teacher assessment that involves the teacher noting the particular kinds of errors a student makes when doing academic work.

eugenics movement. A popular movement of the late nineteenth and early twentieth centuries that supported the selective breeding of humans; resulted in laws restricting the marriage of individuals with mental retardation and sterilization of some of them.

evoked-response audiometry. A technique involving electroencephalograph measurement of changes in brain-wave activity in response to sounds.

executive functions. The ability to regulate one's behavior through working memory, inner speech, control of emotions and arousal levels, and analysis of problems and communication of problem solutions to others; delayed or impaired in those with ADHD.

external otitis. An infection of the skin of the external auditory canal; also called "swimmer's ear."

externalizing. Acting-out behavior; aggressive or disruptive behavior that is observable as behavior directed toward others.

familiality studies. A method of determining the degree to which a given condition is inherited; looks at the prevalence of the condition in relatives of the person with the condition.

family characteristics. A component of the Turnbulls' family systems model; includes type and severity of the disability as well as such things as size, cultural background, and socioeconomic background of the family.

family functions. A component of the Turnbulls' family systems model; includes such things as economic, daily care, social, medical, and educational needs.

family interaction. A component of the Turnbulls' family systems model; refers to how cohesive and adaptable the family is.

family life cycle. A component of the Turnbulls' family systems model; consists of birth and early childhood, childhood, adolescence, and adulthood.

family-centered model. A type of early intervention program; consumer-driven in that professionals are viewed as working for families; views family members as the most important decision makers.

fetal alcohol syndrome (FAS). Abnormalities associated with the mother's drinking alcohol during pregnancy; defects range from mild to severe, including growth retardation, brain damage, mental retardation, hyperactivity, anomalies of the face, and heart failure; also called *alcohol embryopathy*.

fingerspelling. Spelling the English alphabet by using various finger positions on one hand.

fluency. The flow with which oral language is produced.

formative assessment. Measurement procedures used to monitor an individual student's progress; they are used to compare how an individual performs in light of his or her abilities, in contrast to standardized tests, which are primarily used to compare an individual's performance to that of other students.

fragile X syndrome. A condition in which the bottom of the X chromosome in the twenty-third pair of chromosomes is pinched off; can result in a number of physical anomalies as well as mental retardation; occurs more often in males than females; thought to be the most common hereditary cause of mental retardation.

frontal lobes. Two lobes located in the front of the brain; responsible for executive functions; site of abnormal development in people with ADHD.

full inclusion. All students with disabilities are placed in their neighborhood schools in general education classrooms for the entire day; general education teachers have the primary responsibility for students with disabilities.

functional academics. Practical skills (e.g., reading a newspaper or telephone book) rather than academic learning skills.

functional assessment. Evaluation that consists of finding out the consequences (purposes), antecedents (what triggers the behavior), and setting events (contextual factors) that maintain inappropriate behaviors; this information can help teachers plan educationally for students.

functional magnetic resonance imaging (fMRI). An adaptation of the MRI used to detect changes in the brain while it is in an active state; unlike a PET scan, it does not involve using radioactive materials.

genius. A word sometimes used to indicate a particular aptitude or capacity in any area; rare intellectual powers.

genre. A plan or map for discourse; type of narrative discourse.

giftedness. Refers to cognitive (intellectual) superiority, creativity, and motivation of sufficient magnitude to set the child apart from the vast majority of age-mates and make it possible for him or her to contribute something of particular value to society.

glaucoma. A condition of excessive pressure in the eyeball; the cause is unknown; if untreated, blindness results.

globus pallidus. A structure in the basal ganglia of the brain; site of abnormal development in persons with ADHD.

Goals 2000: Educate America Act. Legislation passed in 1994, aimed at increasing the academic standards in U.S. schools; some educators fear that the focus on high standards may harm students with disabilities.

guardianship. A legal term that gives a person the authority to make decisions for another person; can be full, limited, or temporary; applies in cases of parents who have children who have severe cognitive disabilities.

guide dog. A dog specially trained to help guide a person who is blind; not recommended for children and not used by very many adults who are blind because the user needs special training in how to use the dog properly.

handicapism. A term used by activists who fault the unequal treatment of individuals with disabilities. This term is parallel to the term racism, coined by those who fault unequal treatment based on race.

hemiplegia. A condition in which one half (right or left side) of the body is paralyzed.

heritability studies. A method of determining the degree to which a condition is inherited; a comparison of the prevalence of a condition in identical (i.e., monozygotic, from the same egg) twins versus fraternal (i.e., dizygotic, from two eggs) twins.

herpes simplex. A viral disease that can cause cold sores or fever blisters; if it affects the genitals and is contracted by the mother-to-be in the later stages of fetal development, it can cause mental subnormality in the child.

hertz (Hz). A unit of measurement of the frequency of sound; refers to the highness or lowness of a sound.

home-note program. A system of communication between the teacher and parents; the teacher evaluates the behavior of the student using a simple form, the student takes the form home, gets the parents' signatures, and returns the form the next day.

homophenes. Sounds that are different but that look the same with regard to movements of the face and lips (i.e., visible articulatory patterns).

hydrocephalus. A condition characterized by enlargement of the head because of excessive pressure of the cerebrospinal fluid.

hyperactive child syndrome. A term used to refer to children who exhibit inattention, impulsivity, and/or hyperactivity; popular in the 1960s and 1970s.

hyperopia. Farsightedness; vision for near objects is affected; usually results when the eyeball is too short.

hypotonic. A term describing low muscle tone that sometimes occurs as a result of cerebral palsy.

hypoxia. A reduction of oxygen in the blood, which can result in brain damage.

inclusive schools movement. A reform movement designed to restructure general education schools and classrooms so they better accommodate all students, including those with disabilities.

incus. The anvil-shaped bone in the ossicular chain of the middle ear.

individual placement model. A model of supported employment in which a person with mental retardation is placed individually in a business or industry that primarily consists of nonretarded employees; the most common type of supported employment.

individualized education program (IEP). IDEA requires an IEP to be drawn up by the educational team for each exceptional child; the IEP must include a statement of present educational performance, instructional goals, educational services to be provided, and criteria and procedures for determining that the instructional objectives are being met.

individualized family service plan (IFSP). A plan mandated by PL 99–457 to provide services for young children with disabilities (under three years of age) and their families; drawn up by professionals and parents; similar to an IEP for older children.

Individuals with Disabilities Education Act (IDEA). The Individuals with Disabilities Education Act of 1990 and its amendments of 1997; replaced PL 94–142.

informal reading inventory (IRI). A method of assessing reading in which the teacher has the student read progressively more difficult series of passages or word lists; the teacher notes the difficulty level of the material read and the types of errors the student makes.

inner speech. An executive function; internal language used to regulate one's behavior; delayed or impaired in those with ADHD.

insight. The ability to separate and/or combine various pieces of information in new, creative, and useful ways.

intellectual functioning. The ability to solve problems related to academics; usually estimated by an IQ test; one of two major components (the other is adaptive skills) of the AAMR definition.

interim alternative educational setting (IAES). An alternative placement (e.g., alternative school, home instruction), chosen by the student's IEP team after the student exhibits serious misconduct (e.g., bringing a weapon or drugs to school), in which the student's education is continued as specified in his or her IEP while school officials make a manifestation determination and find the least restrictive environment in which the student can be educated appropriately.

internalizing. Acting-in behavior; anxiety, fearfulness, withdrawal, and other indications of an individual's mood or internal state.

IQ–achievement discrepancy. Academic performance markedly lower than would be expected based on a student's intellectual ability.

iris. The colored portion of the eye; contracts or expands, depending on the amount of light striking it.

itinerant teacher services. Services for students who are visually impaired, in which the special education teacher visits several different schools to work with students and their general education classroom teachers; the students attend their local schools and remain in general education classrooms.

job coach. A person who assists adult workers with disabilities (especially those with mental retardation), providing vocational assessment, instruction, overall planning, and interaction assistance with employers, family, and related government and service agencies.

juvenile rheumatoid arthritis. A systemic disease with major symptoms involving the muscles and joints.

Kurzweil Omni 1000. A computerized device that converts print into speech for persons with visual impairment; the user places the printed material over a scanner that then reads the material aloud by means of an electronic voice.

language. An arbitrary code or system of symbols to communicate meaning.

language disorders. Oral communication that involves a lag in the ability to understand and express ideas, putting linguistic skill behind an individual's development in other areas, such as motor, cognitive, or social development.

large-print books. Books that are printed in a type size that is larger than usual so that people with visual impairment can read them; disadvantages are that they take up more space and some materials are not available in large print.

larynx. The structure in the throat containing the vocal apparatus (vocal cords); laryngitis is a temporary loss of voice caused by inflammation of the larynx.

learned helplessness. A motivational term referring to a condition wherein a person believes that no matter how hard he or she tries, failure will result.

least restrictive environment (LRE). A legal term referring to the fact that exceptional children must be educated in as normal an environment as possible.

legally blind. A person who has visual acuity of 20/200 or less in the better eye even with correction (e.g., eyeglasses) or has a field of vision so narrow that its widest diameter subtends an angular distance no greater than 20 degrees.

lens. A structure that refines and changes the focus of the light rays passing through the eye.

levels of support. The basis of the AAMR classification scheme; characterizes the amount of support needed for someone with mental retardation to function as competently as possible as (1) intermittent, (2) limited, (3) extensive, or (4) pervasive.

locus of control. A motivational term referring to how people explain their successes or failures; people with an internal locus of control believe they are the reason for success or failure, whereas people with an external locus of control believe outside forces influence how they perform.

long cane. A mobility aid used by individuals with visual impairment, who sweep it in a wide arc in front of them; proper use requires considerable training; the mobility aid of choice for most travelers who are blind.

low vision. A term used by educators to refer to individuals whose visual impairment is not so severe that they are unable to read print of any kind; they may read large or regular print, and they may need some kind of magnification.

low-birthweight (LBW). Babies who are born weighing less than 5.5 pounds; usually premature; at risk for behavioral and medical conditions, such as mental retardation.

macroculture. A nation or other large social entity with a shared culture.

magnetic resonance imaging (MRI). A neuroimaging technique whereby radio waves are used to produce cross-sectional images of the brain; used to pinpoint areas of the brain that are dysfunctional.

mainstreaming. The placement of students with disabilities in general education classes for all or part of the day and for all or only a few classes; special education teachers maintain the primary responsibility for students with disabilities.

malleus. The hammer-shaped bone in the ossicular chain of the middle ear.

mandatory sentencing. Laws requiring specific sentences for specific violations, removing the discretion of the judge in sentencing based on circumstances of the defendant or other considerations.

manifestation determination. A procedure in which school officials determine whether a student's behavior is or is not a manifestation of his or her disability.

maternal serum screening (MSS). A method of screening the fetus for developmental disabilities such as Down syndrome or spina bifida; a blood sample is taken from the mother and analyzed; if it is positive, a more accurate test such as amniocentesis or CVS is usually recommended.

meningitis. A bacterial or viral infection of the linings of the brain or spinal cord.

mental age. Refers to the IQ test score that specifies the age level at which an individual is functioning.

metacognition. A person's (1) awareness of what strategies are necessary to perform a task and (2) ability to use self-regulation strategies.

microcephalus. A condition causing development of a small head with a sloping forehead; proper development of the brain is prevented, resulting in mental retardation.

microculture. A smaller group existing within a larger cultural group and having unique values, style, language, dialect, ways of communicating nonverbally, awareness, frame of reference, and identification.

mild retardation. A classification used to specify an individual whose IQ is approximately 55–70.

milieu teaching. A naturalistic approach to language intervention in which the goal is to teach functional language skills in a natural environment.

minimal brain injury. A term used to describe a child who shows behavioral but not neurological signs of brain injury; the term is not as popular as it once was, primarily because of its lack of diagnostic utility (i.e., some children who learn normally show signs indicative of minimal brain injury).

mixed hearing impairment. A hearing loss resulting from a combination of conductive and sensorineural hearing impairments.

mnemonic strategies. Cognitive training strategies used to help children with memory problems remember curriculum content; the teacher transforms abstract information into a concrete picture that depicts the material in a more meaningful way.

mnemonics. Techniques that aid memory, such as using rhymes, songs, or visual images to remember information.

mobile work crew model. A model of supported employment in which a small group of workers who are retarded moves from one place to another, such as a janitorial service.

moderate retardation. A classification used to specify an individual whose IQ is approximately 40–55.

morphology. The study within psycholinguistics of word formation; how adding or deleting parts of words changes their meaning.

multicultural education. Aims to change educational institutions and curricula so they will provide equal educational opportunities to students regardless of their gender, social class, ethnicity, race, disability, or other cultural identity.

muscular dystrophy. A hereditary disease characterized by progressive weakness caused by degeneration of muscle fibers.

myopia. Nearsightedness; vision for distant objects is affected; usually results when the eyeball is too long.

narrative. Self-controlled, self-initiated discourse; description or storytelling.

native-language emphasis. An approach to teaching language-minority pupils in which the student's native language is used for most of the day and English is taught as a separate subject.

neologism. A coined word that is meaningless to others; meaningless words used in the speech of a person with a mental disorder.

neurotransmitters. Chemicals involved in sending messages between neurons in the brain.

normalization. A philosophical belief in special education that every individual, even the most disabled, should have an educational and living environment as close to normal as possible.

nystagmus. A condition in which there are rapid involuntary movements of the eyes; sometimes indicates a brain malfunction and/or inner-ear problems.

obstacle sense. A skill possessed by some people who are blind, whereby they can detect the presence of obstacles in their environments; research has shown that it is not an indication of an extra sense, as popularly thought; it is the result of being able to detect subtle changes in the pitches of high-frequency echoes.

oralism–manualism debate. The controversy over whether the goal of instruction for students who are deaf should be to teach them to speak or to teach them to use sign language.

orthosis. A device designed to restore, partially or completely, a lost function of the body (e.g., a brace or crutch).

ossicles. Three tiny bones (malleus, incus, and stapes) that together make possible an efficient transfer of sound waves from the eardrum to the oval window, which connects the middle ear to the inner ear.

otitis media. Inflammation of the middle ear.

oval window. The link between the middle and inner ears.

paradoxical effect of Ritalin. The now discredited belief that Ritalin, even though a stimulant, acts to subdue a person's behavior and that this effect of Ritalin is evident in persons with ADHD but not in those without ADHD.

paraplegia. A condition in which both legs are paralyzed.

partial participation. An approach in which students with disabilities, while in the general education classroom, engage in the same activities as nondisabled students but on a reduced basis; the teacher adapts the activity to allow each student to participate as much as possible.

pediatric AIDS. Acquired immune deficiency syndrome that occurs in infants or young children; can be contracted by unborn fetuses from the blood of the mother through the placenta or through blood transfusions; an incurable virus that can result in a variety of physical and mental disorders.

peer tutoring. A method that can be used to integrate students with disabilities in general education classrooms, based on the notion that students can effectively tutor one another. The role of learner or teacher may be assigned to either the student with a disability or the nondisabled student.

Perkins Brailler. A system that makes it possible to write in braille; has six keys, one for each of the six dots of the cell, which leave an embossed print on the paper.

perseveration. A tendency to repeat behaviors over and over again; often found in persons with brain injury, as well as those with ADHD.

pervasive developmental disorder. A severe disorder characterized by abnormal social relations, including bizarre mannerisms, inappropriate social behavior, and unusual or delayed speech and language.

phenylketonuria (PKU). A metabolic genetic disorder caused by the inability of the body to convert phenylalanine to tyrosine; an accumulation of phenylalanine results in abnormal brain development.

phonological awareness. The ability to understand grapheme-phoneme correspondence—the rules by which sounds go with letters to make up words; generally thought to be the reason for the reading problems of many students with learning disabilities.

phonology. The study of how individual sounds make up words.

portfolios. A collection of samples of a student's work done over time; a type of authentic assessment.

positron emission tomography (PET) scans. A computerized method for measuring bloodflow in the brain; during a cognitive task, a low amount of radioactive dye is injected in the brain; the dye collects in active neurons, indicating which areas of the brain are active.

postlingual deafness. Deafness occurring after the development of speech and language.

practical intelligence. The ability to solve problems related to activities of daily living; an aspect of the adaptive skills component of the AAMR definition.

pragmatics. The study within psycholinguistics of how people use language in social situations; emphasizes the functional use of language, rather than mechanics.

preacademic skills. Behaviors that are needed before formal academic instruction can begin (e.g., ability to identify letters, numbers, shapes, and colors).

precocity. Remarkable early development.

prefrontal lobes. Two lobes located in the very front of the frontal lobes; responsible for executive functions; site of abnormal development in people with ADHD.

prelingual deafness. Deafness that occurs before the development of spoken language, usually at birth.

prelinguistic communication. Communication through gestures and noises before the child has learned oral language.

prereferral teams (PRTs). Teams made up of a variety of professionals, especially regular and special educators who work with regular class teachers to come up with strategies for teaching difficult-to-teach children. Designed to influence regular educators to take ownership of difficult-to-teach students and to minimize inappropriate referrals to special education.

prodigy. A child whose development and accomplishments meet or exceed those of adults with extraordinary talent.

profound retardation. A classification used to specify an individual whose IQ is below approximately 25.

progressive time delay. An instructional procedure whereby the teacher makes a request while simultaneously prompting the student and then over several occasions gradually increases the latency between the request and the prompt; often used with students with mental retardation.

prosthesis. A device designed to replace, partially or completely, a part of the body (e.g., artificial teeth or limbs).

psychostimulants. Medications that activate dopamine levels in the frontal and prefrontal areas of the brain that control behavioral inhibition and executive functions; used to treat persons with ADHD.

pull-out programs. Special education programs in which students with disabilities leave the general education classroom for part or all of the school day (e.g., to go to special classes or resource room).

pupil. The contractile opening in the middle of the iris of the eye.

pure-tone audiometry. A test whereby tones of various intensities and frequencies are presented to determine a person's hearing loss.

quadriplegia. A condition in which all four limbs are paralyzed.

readiness skills. Skills deemed necessary before academics can be learned (e.g., attending skills, the ability to follow directions, knowledge of letter names).

reciprocal teaching. A method in which students and teachers are involved in a dialogue to facilitate learning.

reflex audiometry. The testing of responses to sounds by observation of such reflex actions as the orienting response.

regular education initiative (REI). A philosophy that maintains that general education, rather than special education, should be primarily responsible for the education of students with disabilities.

resonance. The quality of the sound imparted by the size, shape, and texture of the organs in the vocal tract.

retina. The back portion of the eye, containing nerve fibers connected to the optic nerve.

retinitis pigmentosa. A hereditary condition resulting in degeneration of the retina; causes a narrowing of the field of vision and affects night vision.

retinopathy of prematurity (ROP). A condition resulting from administration of an excessive concentration of oxygen at birth; causes scar tissue to form behind the lens of the eye.

Ritalin. The most commonly prescribed psychostimulant for ADHD; generic name is methylphenidate.

rubella (German measles). A serious viral disease, which, if it occurs during the first trimester of pregnancy, is likely to cause a deformity in the fetus.

scaffolded instruction. A cognitive approach to instruction in which the teacher provides temporary structure or support while students are learning a task; the support is gradually removed as the students are able to perform the task independently.

schizophrenia. A disorder characterized by psychotic behavior manifested by loss of contact with reality, distorted thought processes, and abnormal perceptions.

scoliosis. An abnormal curvature of the spine

seizure (convulsion). A sudden alteration of consciousness, usually accompanied by motor activity and/or sensory phenomena; caused by an abnormal discharge of electrical energy in the brain.

self-instruction. A type of cognitive training technique that requires individuals to talk aloud and then to themselves as they solve problems.

self-monitoring. A self-management technique in which students monitor their own behavior, such as attention to task, and then record it on a sheet.

self-regulation. Refers generally to a person's ability to regulate his or her own behavior (e.g., to employ strategies to help in a problem-solving situation); an area of difficulty for persons who are mentally retarded.

semantics. The study of the meanings attached to words and sentences.

sensorineural hearing impairment. A hearing loss, usually severe, resulting from malfunctioning of the inner ear.

sequelae. After effects, secondary effects, or consequences of a disease or injury.

serotonin. A neurotransmitter, the levels of which may be abnormal in persons with ADHD.

severe retardation. A classification used to specify an individual whose IQ is between approximately 25 and 40.

sheltered workshop. A facility that provides a structured environment for persons with disabilities in which they can learn skills; can be either a transitional placement or a permanent arrangement.

sheltered-English approach. A method in which language-minority students are taught all their subjects in English at a level that is modified constantly according to individuals' needs.

short-term memory. The ability to recall information after a short period of time.

sibshops. Workshops for siblings of children with disabilities; designed to help siblings answer questions about the disability and learn to adjust to having a sister or brother with a disability.

sign language. A manual language used by people who are deaf to communicate; a true language with its own grammar.

signing English systems. Used simultaneously with oral methods in the total communication approach to teaching students who are deaf; different from American Sign Language because they maintain the same word order as spoken English.

slate and stylus. A method of writing in braille in which the paper is held in a slate while a stylus is pressed through openings to make indentations in the paper.

Snellen chart. Used in determining visual acuity; consists of rows of letters or Es arranged in different positions; each row corresponds to the distance at which a normally sighted person can discriminate the letters; does not predict how accurately a child will be able to read print.

social intelligence. The ability to understand social expectations and to cope in social situations; an aspect of the adaptive skills component of the AAMR definition.

social support. Emotional, informational, or material aid provided to a person or a family; this informal means of aid can be very valuable in helping families of children with disabilities.

sonography. A medical procedure in which high-frequency sound waves are converted into a visual picture; used to detect major physical malformations in the unborn fetus.

spastic. A term describing a sudden, involuntary contraction of muscles that makes accurate, voluntary movement difficult.

spasticity. Characterized by muscle stiffness and problems in voluntary movement; associated with spastic cerebral palsy.

specific language impairment (SLI). A language disorder with no identifiable cause; language disorder not attributable to hearing impairment, mental retardation, brain dysfunction, or other plausible cause; also called *specific language disability*.

speech. The formation and sequencing of oral language sounds during communication.

speech audiometry. A technique that tests a person's detection and understanding of speech, rather than using pure tones to detect hearing loss.

speech disorders. Oral communication that involves abnormal use of the vocal apparatus, is unintelligible, or is so inferior that it draws attention to itself and causes anxiety, feelings of inadequacy, or inappropriate behavior in the speaker.

speech reception threshold (SRT). The decibel level at which a person can understand speech.

speechreading. A method that involves teaching children to use visual information from a number of sources to understand what is being said to them; more than just lipreading, which uses only visual clues arising from the movement of the mouth in speaking.

spina bifida. A congenital midline defect resulting from failure of the bony spinal column to close completely during fetal development.

standardized assessment. A method of evaluating a person that has been applied to a large group so that an individual's score can be compared to the norm, or average.

stapes. The stirrup-shaped bone in the ossicular chain of the middle ear.

stereotypic behaviors. Any of a variety of repetitive behaviors (e.g., eye rubbing) that are sometimes found in individuals who are blind, severely retarded, or psychotic; sometimes referred to as *stereotypies* or *blindisms*.

strabismus. A condition in which the eyes are directed inward (crossed eyes) or outward.

Strauss syndrome. Behaviors of distractibility, forced responsiveness to stimuli, and hyperactivity; based on the work of Alfred Strauss and Heinz Werner with children with mental retardation.

stuttering. Speech characterized by abnormal hesitations, prolongations, and repetitions; may be accompanied by grimaces, gestures, or other bodily movements indicative of a struggle to speak, anxiety, blocking of speech, or avoidance of speech.

supported competitive employment. A workplace where adults who are disabled or retarded earn at least minimum wage and receive ongoing assistance from a specialist or job coach; the majority of workers in the workplace are nondisabled.

supported employment. A method of integrating people with disabilities who cannot work independently into competitive employment; includes use of an employment specialist, or job coach, who helps the person with a disability function on the job.

supported living. An approach to living arrangements for those with mental retardation that stresses living in natural settings rather than institutions, big or small.

syntax. The way words are joined together to structure meaningful sentences; grammar.

syphilis. A venereal disease that can cause mental subnormality in a child, especially if it is contracted by the mother-to-be during the latter stages of fetal development.

systematic instruction. Teaching that involves instructional prompts, consequences for performance, and transfer of stimulus control; often used with students with mental retardation.

talent. A special ability, aptitude, or accomplishment.

task analysis. The procedure of breaking down an academic task into its component parts for the purpose of instruction; a major feature of Direct Instruction.

Tay-Sachs disease. An inherited condition that can appear when both mother and father are carriers; results in death; it can be detected before birth through amniocentesis.

teletypewriter (TTY). A device connected to a telephone by a special adapter; allows communication over the telephone between persons who are hearing impaired and those with hearing.

temperament. One's inborn behavioral style, including general level of activity, regularity or predictability, approach or withdrawal, adaptability, intensity of reaction, responsiveness, mood, distractibility, and persistence; is present at birth but may be modified by parental management.

teratogens. Agents, such as chemicals, that can disrupt the normal development of the fetus; a possible cause of learning disabilities and other learning and behavioral problems.

total communication approach. An approach for teaching students with hearing impairment that blends oral and manual techniques.

Tourette's syndrome. A neurological disorder beginning in childhood (about three times more prevalent in boys than in girls) in which stereotyped, repetitive motor movements (tics) are accompanied by multiple vocal outbursts that may include grunting noises or socially inappropriate words or statements (e.g., swearing).

transliteration. A method used by sign language interpreters in which the signs maintain the same word order as that of spoken English; although used by most interpreters, found through research not to be as effective as American Sign Language (ASL).

traumatic brain injury (TBI). Injury to the brain (not including conditions present at birth, birth trauma, or degenerative diseases or conditions) resulting in total or partial disability or psychosocial maladjustment that affects educational performance; may affect cognition, language, memory, attention, reasoning, abstract thinking, judgment, problem solving, sensory or perceptual and motor disabilities, psychosocial behavior, physical functions, information processing, or speech.

traveling notebook. A system of communication in which parents and professionals write messages to each other by way of a notebook or log that accompanies the child to and from school.

trisomy 21. A type of Down syndrome in which the twenty-first chromosome is a triplet, making forty-seven, rather than the normal forty-six, chromosomes in all.

tympanic membrane (eardrum). The anatomical boundary between the outer and middle ears; the sound gathered in the outer ear vibrates here.

vestibular mechanism. Located in the upper portion of the inner ear; consists of three soft, semicircular canals filled with a fluid; sensitive to head movement, acceleration, and other movements related to balance.

visual efficiency. A term used to refer to how well one uses his or her vision, including such things as control of eye movements, attention to visual detail, and discrimination of figure from background; believed by some to be more important than visual acuity alone in predicting a person's ability to function visually.

visual function. A term that refers to a person's useful vision such as the ability to detect light or to detect objects in the environment.

vitreous humor. A transparent, gelatinous substance that fills the eyeball between the retina and the lens of the eye.

Williams syndrome. A condition resulting from deletion of material in the seventh pair of chromosomes; often results in mild to moderate retardation, heart defects, and elfin facial features; people affected often display surprising strengths in spoken language and sociability while having severe deficits in spatial organization, reading, writing, and math.

working memory. The ability to remember information while also performing other cognitive operations.

references

Chapter 1

Bateman, B. D., & Linden, M. A. (1998). *Better IEPs: How to develop legally correct and educationally useful programs* (3rd ed.). Longmont, CO: Sopris West.

Clark, D. L., & Astuto, T. A. (1988). *Education policy after Reagan—What next?* Occasional paper No. 6, Policy Studies Center of the University Council for Educational Administration, University of Virginia, Charlottesville.

Council for Exceptional Children. (1998). *What every special educator must know* (3rd ed.). Reston, VA: Author.

Crockett, J. B., & Kauffman, J. M. (1999). *The least restrictive environment: Its origins and interpretations in special education.* Mahwah, NJ: Erlbaum.

Cruickshank, W. M. (1977). Guest editorial. *Journal of Learning Disabilities, 10,* 193–194.

Fuchs, D., & Fuchs, L. S. (1994). Inclusive schools movement and the radicalization of special education reform. *Exceptional Children, 60,* 294–309.

Goodman, J. F., & Bond, L. (1993). The individualized education program: A retrospective critique. *Journal of Special Education, 26,* 408–422.

Hallahan, D. P., & Kauffman, J. M. (1977). Labels, categories, behaviors: ED, LD, and EMR reconsidered. *Journal of Special Education, 11,* 139–149.

Hart, B., & Risley, T. R. (1995). *Meaningful differences in the everyday experience of young American children.* Baltimore: Paul H. Brookes.

Hendrick, I. G., & MacMillan, D. L. (1989). Selecting children for special education in New York City: William Maxwell, Elizabeth Farrell, and the development of ungraded classes, 1900–1920. *Journal of Special Education, 22,* 395–417.

Howe, K. R., & Miramontes, O. B. (1992). *The ethics of special education.* New York: Teachers College Press.

Huefner, D. S. (1994). The mainstreaming cases: Tensions and trends for school administrators. *Educational Administration Quarterly, 30,* 27–55.

Hungerford, R. (1950). On locusts. *American Journal of Mental Deficiency, 54,* 415–418.

Itard, J. M. G. (1962). *The wild boy of Aveyron.* (George & Muriel Humphrey, Trans.). Englewood Cliffs, NJ: Prentice-Hall.

Kanner, L. (1964). *A history of the care and study of the mentally retarded.* Springfield, IL: Charles C. Thomas.

Kauffman, J. M. (1976). Nineteenth century views of children's behavior disorders: Historical contributions and continuing issues. *Journal of Special Education, 10,* 335–349.

Kauffman, J. M. (1995). Why we must celebrate a diversity of restrictive environments. *Learning Disabilities Research and Practice, 10,* 225–232.

Kauffman, J. M. (1999a). Today's special education and its messages for tomorrow. *Journal of Special Education, 32,* 244–254.

Kauffman, J. M. (1999b). How we prevent the prevention of emotional and behavioral disorders. *Exceptional Children, 65,* 448–468.

Kauffman, J. M., & Hallahan, D. P. (Eds.). (1995). *The illusion of full inclusion: A comprehensive critique of a current special educational bandwagon.* Austin, TX: Pro-Ed.

Kauffman, J. M., & Hallahan, D. P. (1997). A diversity of restrictive environments: Placement as a problem of social ecology. In J. W. Lloyd, E. J. Kameenui, & D. Chard (Eds.), *Issues in educating students with disabilities* (pp. 325–342). Hillsdale, NJ: Erlbaum.

Lloyd, J. W., Singh, N. N., & Repp, A. C. (Eds.). (1991). *The regular education initiative: Alternative perspectives on concepts, issues, and models.* Sycamore, IL: Sycamore Publishing.

MacMillan, D. L., & Forness, S. R. (1998). The role of IQ in special education placement decisions: Primary and determinative or peripheral and inconsequential? *Remedial and Special Education, 19,* 239–253.

MacMillan, D. L., & Hendrick, I. G. (1993). Evolution and legacies. In J. I. Goodlad & T. C. Lovitt (Eds.), *Integrating general and special education.* Columbus, OH: Merrill/Macmillan.

Martin, E. W. (1995). Case studies of inclusion: Worst fears realized. *Journal of Special Education, 29,* 192–199.

Morse, W. C. (1984). Personal perspective. In B. Blatt & R. Morris (Eds.), *Perspectives in special education: Personal orientations.* Glenview, IL: Scott, Foresman.

Patterson, G. R., Reid, J. B., & Dishion, T. J. (1992). *Antisocial boys.* Eugene, OR: Castalia.

Richards, P. L., & Singer, G. H. S. (1998). "To draw out the effort of his mind": Educating a child with mental retardation in early-nineteenth-century America. *Journal of Special Education, 31,* 443–466.

Safford, P. L., & Safford, E. H. (1998). Visions of the special class. *Remedial and Special Education, 19,* 229–238.

Sarason, S. B. (1990). *The predictable failure of educational reform: Can we change course before it's too late?* San Francisco: Jossey-Bass.

Smith, J. D. (1998a). Histories of special education: Stories from our past, insights for our future. *Remedial and Special Education, 19,* 196–200.

Smith, J. D. (Ed.). (1998b). The history of special education: Essays honoring the bicentennial of the work of Jean Itard. [Special issue]. *Remedial and Special Education, 19*(4).

Taylor, H. (1995, July 18). Louis Harris/N.O.D. survey finds employers overwhelmingly support the ADA–and jobs. *The Washington Post,* A10.

Trent, J. W. (1998). Defectives at the World's Fair: Constructing disability in 1904. *Remedial and Special Education, 19,* 201–211.

U.S. Department of Education. (1992). *Fourteenth annual report to Congress on implementation of the Individuals with Disabilities Education Act.* Washington, DC: Author.

U.S. Department of Education. (1995). *Seventeenth annual report to Congress on implementation of the Individuals with Disabilities Education Act*. Washington, DC: Author.

U.S. Department of Education. (1997). *Nineteenth annual report to Congress on implementation of the Individuals with Disabilities Education Act*. Washington, DC: Author.

U.S. Department of Education. (1998). *Twentieth annual report to Congress on implementation of the Individuals with Disabilities Education Act*. Washington, DC: Author.

Verstegen, D. A., & Clark, D. L. (1988). The diminution of federal expenditures for education during the Reagan administration. *Phi Delta Kappan, 70,* 134–138.

Werner, E. E. (1986). The concept of risk from a developmental perspective. In B. K. Keogh (Ed.), *Advances in special education: Vol. 5. Developmental problems in infancy and the preschool years.* Greenwich, CT: JAI Press.

Winzer, M. A. (1986). Early developments in special education: Some aspects of Enlightenment thought. *Remedial and Special Education, 7*(5), 42–49.

Winzer, M. A. (1993). *The history of special education: From isolation to integration.* Washington, DC: Gallaudet University Press.

Winzer, M. A. (1998). A tale often told: The early progression of special education. *Remedial and Special Education, 19,* 212–218.

Yell, M. L. (1998). *The law and special education.* Upper Saddle River, NJ: Prentice-Hall.

Yell, M. L., Rogers, D., & Rogers, E. L. (1998). The legal history of special education: What a long, strange trip it's been! *Remedial and Special Education, 19,* 219–228.

Yell, M. L., & Shriner, J. G. (1997). The IDEA amendments of 1997: Implications for special and general education teachers, administrators, and teacher trainers. *Focus on Exceptional Children, 30*(1), 1–19.

Ysseldyke, J. E., Algozzine, B., & Thurlow, M. L. (1992). *Critical issues in special education* (2nd ed.). Boston: Houghton Mifflin.

Zelder, E. Y. (1953). Public opinion and public education for the exceptional child—Court decisions 1873–1950. *Exceptional Children, 18,* 187–198.

Zigmond, N., & Baker, J. M. (1995). Concluding comments: Current and future practices in inclusive schooling. *Journal of Special Education, 29,* 245–250.

Chapter 2

Abt Associates. (1976–1977). *Education as experimentation: A planned variation model* (Vol. 3A and 4). Cambridge, MA: Author.

Arizona Easter Seal Society. (n.d.). *The first step. Friends who care. Friends who count.* Phoenix, AZ: Author.

Artesani, A. J., & Millar, L. (1998). Positive behavior supports in general education settings: Combining person-centered planning and functional analysis. *Intervention in School and Clinic, 34,* 33–38.

Baker, J. M., & Zigmond, N. (1995). The meaning and practice of inclusion for students with learning disabilities: Themes and implications from the five cases. *Journal of Special Education, 29,* 163–180.

Bank-Mikkelsen, N. E. (1969). A metropolitan area in Denmark: Copenhagen. In R. B. Kugel & W. Wolfensberger (Eds.), *Changing patterns of residential services for the mentally retarded* (pp. 227–254). Washington, DC: President's Committee on Mental Retardation.

Bateman, B. D., & Linden, M. A. (1998). *Better IEPs: How to develop legally correct and educationally useful programs* (3rd ed.). Longmont, CO: Sopris West.

Baumeister, A. A., Kupstas, F., & Klindworth, L. M. (1990). New morbidity: Implications for prevention of children's disabilities. *Exceptionality, 1*(1), 1–16.

Bock, S. J., Tapscott, K. E., & Savner, J. L. (1998). Suspension and expulsion: Effective management for students? *Intervention in School and Clinic, 34,* 50–52.

Bogdan, R. (1986). The sociology of special education. In R. J. Morris & B. Blatt (Eds.), *Special education: Research and trends* (pp. 344–359). New York: Pergamon Press.

Bogdan, R., & Biklen, D. (1977). Handicapism. *Social Policy, 7*(5), 14–19.

Bowman, B. T. (1994). The challenge of diversity. *Phi Delta Kappan, 76,* 218–225.

Bricker, D. D. (1986). An analysis of early intervention programs: Attendant issues and future directions. In R. J. Morris & B. Blatt (Eds.), *Special education: Research and trends* (pp. 28–65). New York: Pergamon Press.

Bricker, D. (1995). The challenge of inclusion. *Journal of Early Intervention, 19,* 179–194.

Burchinal, M. R., Campbell, F. A., Bryant, D. M., Wasik B. H., & Ramey, C. T. (1997). Early intervention and mediating processes in cognitive performance of children of low-income African American families. *Child Development, 68,* 935–954.

Carta, J. J. (1995). Developmentally appropriate practice: A critical analysis as applied to young children with disabilities. *Focus on Exceptional Children, 27*(8), 1–14.

Carta, J. J., & Greenwood, C. R. (1997). Barriers to the implementation of effective educational practices for young children with disabilities. In J. W. Lloyd, E. J. Kameenui, & D. Chard (Eds.), *Issues in educating students with disabilities* (pp. 261–274). Mahwah, NJ: Erlbaum.

Chadsey-Rusch, J., & Heal, L. W. (1995). Building consensus from transition experts on social integration outcomes and interventions. *Exceptional Children, 62,* 165–187.

Chalfant, J. C., Pysh, M. V., & Moultrie, R. (1979). Teacher assistance teams: A model for within-building problem solving. *Learning Disability Quarterly, 2,* 85–96.

Collet-Klingenberg, L. L. (1998). The reality of best practices in transition: A case study. *Exceptional Children, 65,* 67–78.

Crissey, M. S., & Rosen, M. (Eds.). (1986). *Institutions for the mentally retarded: A changing role in changing times.* Austin, TX: Pro-Ed.

Crockett, J. B., & Kauffman, J. M. (1998). Taking inclusion back to its roots. *Educational Leadership, 56*(2), 74–77.

Crockett, J. B., & Kauffman, J. M. (1999). *The least restrictive environment: Its origins and interpretations in special education.* Mahwah, NJ: Erlbaum.

DeStefano, L., & Wermuth, T. R. (1992). IDEA (P.L. 101–476): Defining a second generation of transition services. In F. R. Rusch, L. DeStefano, J. Chadsey-Rusch, L. A. Phelps, & E. Szymanski (Eds.), *Transition from school to adult life* (pp. 537–549). Sycamore, IL: Sycamore Publishing.

Dupre, A. P. (1997). Disability and the public schools: The case against "inclusion." *Washington Law Review, 72,* 775–858.

Eiserman, W. D., Weber, C., & McCoun, M. (1995). Parent and professional roles in early intervention: A longitudinal comparison of the effects of two intervention configurations. *Journal of Special Education, 29,* 20–44.

Fiedler, C. R., & Simpson, R. L. (1987). Modifying the attitudes of nonhandicapped high school students toward handicapped peers. *Exceptional Children, 53,* 342–349.

Fowler, S. A., Schwartz, I., & Atwater, J. (1991). Perspectives on the transition from preschool to kindergarten for children with disabilities and their families. *Exceptional Children, 58*(2), 136–145.

Fox, N., & Ysseldyke, J. E. (1997). Implementing inclusion at the middle school level: Lessons from a negative example. *Exceptional Children, 64,* 81–98.

Fuchs, D., & Fuchs, L. S. (1991). Framing the REI debate: Abolitionists versus conservationists. In J. W. Lloyd, N. N. Singh, & A. C. Repp (Eds.), *The regular education initiative: Alternative perspectives on concepts, issues, and models* (pp. 241–255). Sycamore, IL: Sycamore Publishing.

Fuchs, D., & Fuchs, L. S. (1992). Limitations of a feel-good approach to consultation. *Journal of Educational and Psychological Consultation, 3,* 93–97.

Furney, K. S., Hasazi, S. B., & DeStefano, L. (1997). Transition policies, practices, and promises: Lessons from three states. *Exceptional Children, 63,* 343–355.

Gallagher, J. J. (1972). The special education contract for mildly handicapped children. *Exceptional Children, 38,* 527–535.

Gallagher, J. J. (1992). The roles of values and facts in policy development for infants and toddlers with disabilities and their families. *Journal of Early Intervention, 16*(1), 1–10.

Gallagher, J. J. (1994). The pull of societal forces on special education. *Journal of Special Education, 27,* 521–530.

Garrett, J. N., Thorp, E. K., Behrmann, M. M., & Denham, S. A. (1998). The impact of early intervention legislation: Local perceptions. *Topics in Early Childhood Special Education, 18,* 183–109.

Gartner, A., & Joe, T. (1986). Introduction. In A. Gartner & T. Joe (Eds.), *Images of the disabled/disabling images.* New York: Praeger.

Gerber, M. M., & Semmel, M. I. (1984). Teacher as imperfect test: Reconceptualizing the referral process. *Educational Psychologist, 19,* 137–148.

Gerber, M. M., & Semmel, M. I. (1985). Microeconomics of referral and reintegration: A paradigm for evaluation of special education. *Studies in Educational Evaluation, 11*(1), 13–29.

Giangreco, M. F., & Putnam, J. W. (1991). Supporting the education of students with severe disabilities in regular education environments. In L. H. Meyer, C. A. Peck, & L. Brown (Eds.), *Critical issues in the lives of people with severe disabilities* (pp. 245–270). Baltimore, MD: Paul H. Brookes.

Greenwood, C. R. (1996). Research on the practices and behavior of effective teachers at the Juniper Gardens Children's Project: Implication for the education of diverse learners. In D. L. Speece & B. K. Keogh (Eds.), *Research on classroom ecologies: Implications for inclusion of children with learning disabilities* (pp. 39–67). Mahwah, NJ: Erlbaum.

Grigal, M., Test, D. W., Beattie, J., & Wood, W. M. (1997). An evaluation of transition components of individualized education programs. *Exceptional Children, 63,* 357–372.

Gronna, S. S., Jenkins, A. A., & Chin-Chance, S. A. (1998). Who are we assessing: Determining state-wide participation rates for students with disabilities. *Exceptional Children, 64,* 407–418.

Guterman, B. R. (1995). The validity of categorical learning disabilities services: The consumer's view. *Exceptional Children, 62,* 111–124.

Hallahan, D. P., & Kauffman, J. M. (1994). Toward a culture of disability in the aftermath of Deno and Dunn. *Journal of Special Education, 27,* 496–508.

Hallahan, D. P., Kauffman, J. M., & Lloyd, J. W. (1999). *Introduction to learning disabilities* (2nd ed.). Boston: Allyn & Bacon.

Halpern, A. S. (1992). Transition: Old wine in new bottles. *Exceptional Children, 58*(3), 202–211.

Halpern, A. S. (1993). Quality of life as a conceptual framework for evaluating transition outcomes. *Exceptional Children, 59,* 486–498.

Heal, L. W., & Rusch, F. R. (1995). Predicting employment status for students who leave special education high school programs. *Exceptional Children, 61,* 472–487.

Hendrick, I. G., MacMillan, D. L., & Balow, I. H. (1989, April). *Early school leaving in America: A review of the literature.* Riverside: University of California, California Educational Research Cooperative.

Jenkins, J. R., & Jenkins, L. M. (1987). Making peer tutoring work. *Educational Leadership, 44*(6), 64–68.

Katz, L. G. (1994). Perspectives on the quality of early childhood programs. *Phi Delta Kappan, 76,* 200–205.

Kauffman, J. M. (1989). The regular education initiative as a Reagan-Bush education policy: A trickle-down theory of education of the hard-to-teach. *Journal of Special Education, 23*(3), 256–278.

Kauffman, J. M. (1994). Places of change: Special education's power and identity in an era of educational reform. *Journal of Learning Disabilities, 27,* 610–618.

Kauffman, J. M. (1999a). Today's special education and its messages for tomorrow. *Journal of Special Education, 32,* 244–254.

Kauffman, J. M. (1999b). How we prevent the prevention of emotional and behavioral disorders. *Exceptional Children, 65,* 448–468.

Kauffman, J. M., & Hallahan, D. P. (1992). Deinstitutionalization and mainstreaming exceptional children. In M. C. Alkin (Ed.), *Encyclopedia of educational research* (6th ed.) (Vol. 1, pp. 299–303). New York: Macmillan.

Kauffman, J. M., & Hallahan, D. P. (1993). Toward a comprehensive delivery system: The necessity of identity, focus, and authority for special education and other compensatory programs. In J. I. Goodlad & T. C. Lovitt (Eds.), *Integrating general and special education* (pp. 73–102). Columbus, OH: Merrill.

Kauffman, J. M., & Hallahan, D. P. (1997). A diversity of restrictive environments: Placement as a problem of social ecology. In J. W. Lloyd, E. J. Kameenui, & D. Chard (Eds.), *Issues in educating students with disabilities* (pp. 325–342). Hillsdale, NJ: Erlbaum.

Kauffman, J. M., & Lloyd, J. W. (1995). A sense of place: The importance of placement issues in contemporary special education. In J. M. Kauffman, J. W. Lloyd, D. P. Hallahan, & T. A. Astuto (Eds.), *Issues in educational placement: Students with emotional and behavioral disorders* (pp. 3–19). Hillsdale, NJ: Erlbaum.

Kauffman, J. M., Lloyd, J. W., Hallahan, D. P., & Astuto, T. A. (1995). Toward a sense of place for special education in the twenty-first century. In J. M. Kauffman, J. W. Lloyd, D. P. Hallahan, & T. A. Astuto (Eds.), *Issues in educational placement: Students with emotional and behavioral disorders* (pp. 379–385). Hillsdale, NJ: Erlbaum.

Klinger, J. K., & Vaughn, S. (1998). Using collaborative strategic reading. Teaching *Exceptional Children, 30*(6), 32–37.

Klinger, J. K., Vaughn, S., Schumm, J. S., Cohen, P., & Forgan, J. W. (1998). Inclusion or pull-out: Which do students prefer? *Journal of Learning Disabilities, 31,* 148–158.

Klobas, L. (1985, January–February). TV's concept of people with disabilities: Here's lookin' at you. *The Disability Rag,* pp. 2–6. Louisville, KY: Advocado Press.

Kohler, P. D. (1998). Implementing a transition perspective of education: A comprehensive approach to planning and delivering secondary education and transition services (pp. 179–205). In F. R. Rusch & J. G. Chadsey (Eds.), *Beyond high school: Transition from school to work*. Belmont, CA: Wadsworth.

Landesman, S., & Butterfield, E. C. (1987). Normalization and de-institutionalization of mentally retarded individuals: Controversy and facts. *American Psychologist, 42*, 809–816.

Laski, F. J. (1991). Achieving integration during the second revolution. In L. H. Meyer, C. A. Peck, & L. Brown (Eds.), *Critical issues in the lives of people with severe disabilities* (pp. 409–421). Baltimore, MD: Paul H. Brookes.

Lerner, J. W., Lowenthal, B., & Egan, R. (1998). *Preschool children with special needs: Children at-risk, children with disabilities.* Boston: Allyn & Bacon.

Lieberman, L. M. (1992). Preserving special education ... for those who need it. In W. Stainback & S. Stainback (Eds.), *Controversial issues confronting special education: Divergent perspectives* (pp. 13–25). Boston: Allyn & Bacon.

Longmore, P. K. (1985). Screening stereotypes: Images of disabled people. *Social Policy, 16*, 31–37.

Lord, W. (1991, November). Parent point of view: What is the least restrictive environment for a deaf child? *Michigan Statewide Newsletter*, p. 4.

MacMillan, D. L., Widaman, K. F., Balow, I. H., Borthwick-Duffy, S., Hendrick, I. G., & Hemsley, R. E. (1992). Special education students exiting the educational system. *Journal of Special Education, 26*(1), 20–36.

Martin, E. W. (1994). Case studies on inclusion: Worst fears realized. *Journal of Special Education, 29*, 192–199.

Mathiason, C. S. (1997, February 15). *DPI advocates for a "disability-friendly" International Classification of Impairment, Disability and Handicap (ICIDH)* [Posted on the World Wide Web]. Available: http://www.escape.ca/~dpi/icicdh.html.

McConnell, M. E., Hilvitz, P. B., & Cox, C. J. (1998). Functional assessment: A systematic process for assessment and intervention in general and special education classrooms. *Intervention in School and Clinic, 34*, 10–20.

McDonnell, L. M., McLaughlin, M. J., & Morison, P. (Eds.). (1997). *Educating one and all: Students with disabilities and standards-based reform*. Washington, DC: National Academy Press.

McLean, M. E., & Odom, S. L. (1993). Practices for young children with and without disabilities: A comparison of DEC and NAEYC identified practices. *Topics in Early Childhood Special Education, 13*, 274–292.

Mills, P. E., Cole, K. N., Jenkins, J. R., & Dale, P. S. (1998). Effects of differing levels of inclusion on preschoolers with disabilities. *Exceptional Children, 65*, 79–90.

Nelson, J. R., Martella, R., & Galand, B. (1998). The effects of teaching school expectations and establishing a consistent consequence on formal office disciplinary actions. *Journal of Emotional and Behavioral Disorders, 6*, 153–161.

Nelson, J. R., Roberts, M., Mather, S., & Rutherford, R. J. (1999). Has public policy exceeded our knowledge base? A review of the functional behavioral assessment literature. *Behavioral Disorders, 24*, 169–179

Nowacek, E. J. (1992). Professionals talk about teaching together: Interviews with five collaborating teachers. *Intervention in School and Clinic, 27*(5), 262–276.

Odom, S. L., & Kaiser, A. P. (1997). Prevention and early intervention during early childhood: Theoretical and empirical bases for practice. In W. E. MacLean (Ed.), *Ellis' handbook of mental deficiency, psychological theory, and research* (pp. 137–172). Mahwah, NJ: Erlbaum.

Padden, C., & Humphries, T. (1988). *Deaf in America: Voices from a culture*. Cambridge, MA: Harvard University Press.

Pomplun, M. (1997). When students with disabilities participate in cooperative groups. *Exceptional Children, 64*, 49–58.

Position Statement of National Association for the Education of Young Children and National Association of Early Childhood Specialists in State Departments of Education. (1991). *Young Children, 46*(3), 21–38.

Raynes, M., Snell, M., & Sailor, W. (1991). A fresh look at categorical programs for children with special needs. *Phi Delta Kappan, 73*(4), 326–331.

Reeve, P. T., & Hallahan, D. P. (1994). Practical questions about collaboration between general and special educators. *Focus on Exceptional Children, 26*(7), 1–10, 12.

Ruef, M. B., Higgins, C., Glaeser, B. J. C., & Patnode, M. (1998). Positive behavioral support: Strategies for teacher. *Intervention in School and Clinic, 34*, 21–32.

Rusch, F. R., & Hughes, C. (1990). Historical overview of supported employment. In F. R. Rusch (Ed.), *Supported employment: Models, methods, and issues* (pp. 5–14). Sycamore, IL: Sycamore Publishing.

Safran, S. P. (1998). Disability portrayal in film: Reflecting the past, directing the future. *Exceptional Children, 64*, 227–238.

Sailor, W. (1991). Special education in the restructured school. *Remedial and Special Education, 12*(6), 8–22.

Sainato, D. M., & Strain, P. S. (1993). Increasing integration success for preschoolers with disabilities. Teaching *Exceptional Children, 25*(2), 36–37.

Sale, P., & Carey, D. M. (1995). The sociometric status of students with disabilities in a full-inclusion school. *Exceptional Children, 62*, 6–19.

Sands, D. J., & Kozleski, E. B. (1994). Quality of life differences between adults with and without disabilities. *Education and Training in Mental Retardation and Developmental Disabilities, 29*, 90–101.

Schram, L., Semmel, M. I., Gerber, M. M., Bruce, M. M., Lopez-Reyna, N., & Allen, D. (1984). Problem solving teams in California. Unpublished manuscript, University of California at Santa Barbara.

Scruggs, T. E., & Mastropieri, M. A. (1996). Teacher perceptions of mainstreaming/inclusion, 1958–1995: A research synthesis. *Exceptional Children, 63*, 59–74.

Semmel, M. I., Abernathy, T. V., Butera, G., & Lesar, S. (1991). Teacher perceptions of the regular education initiative. *Exceptional Children, 58*(1), 9–24.

Sinclair, M. F., Christenson, S. L., Evelo, D. L., & Hurley, C. M. (1998). Dropout prevention for youth with disabilities: Efficacy of a sustained school engagement procedure. *Exceptional Children, 65*, 7–21.

Sitlington, P. L., Frank, A. R., & Carson, R. (1992). Adult adjustment among high school graduates with mild disabilities. *Exceptional Children, 59*, 221–233.

Slentz, K. L., & Bricker, D. (1992). Family-guided assessment for IFSP development: Jumping off the family assessment bandwagon. *Journal of Early Intervention, 16*(1), 11–19.

Smith, J. D. (Ed.). (1998). The history of special education: Essays honoring the bicentennial of the work of Jean Itard [Special issue]. *Remedial and Special Education, 19*(4).

Stainback, S., & Stainback, W. (1992). Schools as inclusive communities. In W. Stainback & S. Stainback (Eds.), *Controversial issues confronting special education: Divergent perspectives* (pp. 29–43). Boston: Allyn & Bacon.

Strauss, D., & Kastner, T. A. (1996). Comparative mortality of people with mental retardation in institutions and the community. *American Journal on Mental Retardation, 101,* 26–40.

Strauss, D., Shavelle, R., Baumeister, A., & Anderson, T. W. (1998). Mortality in persons with developmental disabilities after transfer into community care. *American Journal on Mental Retardation, 102,* 569–581.

Sugai, G. (1996). Providing effective behavior support to all students: Procedures and processes. *SAIL, 11*(1), 1–4.

Szymanski, E. M. (1994). Transition: Life-span and life-space considerations for empowerment. *Exceptional Children, 60,* 402–410.

Thompson, B. (1993). *Words can hurt you: Beginning a program of anti-bias education.* Reading, MA: Addison-Wesley.

Thompson, L., Lobb, C., Elling, R., Herman, S., Jurkiewicz, T., & Hulleza, C. (1998). Pathways to family empowerment: Effects of family-centered delivery of early intervention services. *Exceptional Children, 64,* 99–113.

Tindal, G., Heath, B., Hollenbeck, K., Almond, P., & Harniss, M. (1998). Accommodating students with disabilities on large-scale tests: An experimental study. *Exceptional Children, 64,* 439–450.

U.S. Department of Education. (1994). *Sixteenth annual report to Congress on implementation of the Individuals with Disabilities Education Act.* Washington, DC: Author.

U.S. Department of Education. (1998). *Early warning, timely response: A guide to safe schools.* Washington, DC: Author.

Utley, C. A., Mortweet, S. L., & Greenwood, C. R. (1997). Peer-mediated instruction and interventions. *Focus on Exceptional Children, 29*(5), 1–23.

Vanderwood, M., McGrew, K. S., & Ysseldyke, J. E. (1998). Why we can't say much about students with disabilities during education reform. *Exceptional Children, 64,* 359–370.

Vaughn, S., Bos, C., & Schumm, J. S. (1997). *Teaching mainstreamed, diverse, and at-risk students in the general education classroom.* Boston: Allyn & Bacon.

Vaughn, S., Moody, S. W., & Schumm, J. S. (1998). Broken promises: Reading instruction in the resource room. *Exceptional Children, 64,* 211–225.

Vaughn, S., Schumm, J. S., & Arguelles, M. E. (1997). The ABCDEs of co-teaching. Teaching *Exceptional Children, 30*(2), 4–10.

Walther-Thomas, C., & Brownell, M. T. (1998). An interview with Dr. Mitchell Yell: Changes in IDEA regarding suspension and expulsion. *Intervention in School and Clinic, 34,* 46–49.

Wesson, C., & Mandell, C. (1989). Simulations promote understanding of handicapping conditions. *Teaching Exceptional Children, 22*(1), 32–35.

West, J. F., & Idol, L. (1990). Collaborative consultation in the education of mildly handicapped and at-risk students. *Remedial and Special Education, 11*(1), 22–31.

Will, M. C. (1986). Educating children with learning problems: A shared responsibility. *Exceptional Children, 52,* 411–415.

Wolfensberger, W. (1972). *The principle of normalization in human services.* Toronto: National Institute on Mental Retardation.

Wolman, C., Bruininks, R., & Thurlow, M. (1989). Dropouts and drop out programs: Implications for special education. *Remedial and Special Education, 10*(5), 6–20, 50.

Yell, M. L. (1998). *The law and special education.* Upper Saddle River, NJ: Prentice-Hall.

Yell, M. L., & Shriner, J. G. (1997). The IDEA amendments of 1997: Implications for special and general education teachers, administrators, and teacher trainers. *Focus on Exceptional Children, 30*(1), 1–19.

Zetlin, A. G., & Hosseini, A. (1989). Six postschool case studies of mildly learning handicapped young adults. *Exceptional Children, 55,* 405–411.

Zigler, E., Hodapp, R. M., & Edison, M. R. (1990). From theory to practice in the care and education of mentally retarded individuals. *American Journal on Mental Retardation, 95*(1), 1–12.

Zigmond, N. (1995). An exploration of the meaning and practice of special education in the context of full inclusion of students with learning disabilities. *Journal of Special Education, 29,* 109–115.

Zigmond, N., & Baker, J. M. (1995). Concluding comments: Current and future practices in inclusive schooling. *Journal of Special Education, 29,* 245–250.

Zigmond, N., Jenkins, J., Fuchs, L. S., Deno, S., Fuchs, D., Baker, J. N., Jenkins, L., & Couthino, M. (1995). Special education in restructured schools: Findings from three multi-year studies. *Phi Delta Kappan, 76,* 531–540.

Zigmond, N., & Miller, S. E. (1992). Improving high school programs for students with learning disabilities: A matter of substance as well as form. In F. R. Rusch, L. DeStefano, J. Chadsey-Rusch, L. A. Phelps, & E. Szymanski (Eds.), *Transition from school to adult life* (pp. 17–31). Sycamore, IL: Sycamore Publishing.

Zurkowski, J. K., Kelly, P. S., & Griswold, D. E. (1998). Discipline and IDEA 1997: Instituting a new balance. *Intervention in School and Clinic, 34,* 3–9.

Chapter 3

Adger, C. T., Wolfram, W., & Detwyler, J. (1993). Language differences: A new approach for special educators. *Teaching Exceptional Children, 26*(1), 44–47.

Artiles, A. J., & Trent, S. C. (Eds.). (1997a). Building a knowledge base on culturally diverse students with learning disabilities: The need to enrich research with a sociocultural perspective [Special issue]. *Learning Disabilities Research and Practice, 12*(2).

Artiles, A., & Trent, S. C. (1997b). Forging a research program on multicultural preservice teacher education in special education: A proposed analytic scheme. In J. W. Lloyd, E. J. Kameenui, & D. Chard (Eds.), *Issues in educating students with disabilities* (pp. 275–304). Mahwah, NJ: Erlbaum.

Artiles, A. J., & Zamora-Duran, G. (Eds.). (1997). *Reducing disproportionate representation of culturally diverse students in special education.* Reston, VA: Council for Exceptional Children.

Ascher, C. (1992). School programs for African-American males . . . and females. *Phi Delta Kappan, 73,* 777–782.

Banks, J. A. (1993). *Introduction to multicultural education.* Boston: Allyn & Bacon.

Banks, J. A. (1994). *Multiethnic education: Theory and practice* (3rd ed.). Boston: Allyn & Bacon.

Banks, J. A. (1997). *Teaching strategies for ethnic studies* (6th ed.). Boston: Allyn & Bacon.

Banks, J. A., & Banks, C. A. M. (Eds.). (1997). *Multicultural education: Issues and perspectives* (3rd ed.). Boston: Allyn & Bacon.

Bateman, B. D. (1994). Who, how, and where: Special education's issues in perpetuity. *Journal of Special Education, 27,* 509–520.

Boutte, G. S. (1992). Frustrations of an African-American parent: A personal and professional account. *Phi Delta Kappan, 73,* 786–788.

Caplan, N., Choy, M. H., & Whitmore, J. K. (1992, February). Indochinese refugee families and academic achievement. *Scientific American, 266*(2), 36–42.

Carnes, J. (1994). An uncommon language: The multicultural making of American English. *Teaching Tolerance, 3*(1), 56–63.

Choate, J. S., Enright, B. E., Miller, L. J., Poteet, J. A., & Rakes, T. A. (1995). *Curriculum-based assessment programming* (3rd ed.). Boston: Allyn & Bacon.

Council for Exceptional Children. (1997). Making assessments of diverse students meaningful. *CEC Today, 4*(4), 1, 9.

Delpit, L. D. (1988). The silenced dialogue: Power and pedagogy in educating other people's children. *Harvard Educational Review, 58,* 280–298.

Delpit, L. (1995). *Other people's children: Cultural conflict in the classroom.* New York: New Press.

Duke, D. L. (1990). *Teaching: An introduction.* New York: McGraw-Hill.

Edgar, E., & Siegel, S. (1995). Postsecondary scenarios for troubled and troubling youth. In J. M. Kauffman, J. W. Lloyd, D. P. Hallahan, & T. A. Astuto (Eds.), *Issues in educational placement: Students with emotional and behavioral disorders* (pp. 251–283). Hillsdale, NJ: Erlbaum.

Ford, B. A., Obiakor, F. E., & Patton, J. M. (Eds.). (1995). *Effective education of African American exceptional learners: New perspectives.* Austin, TX: Pro-Ed.

Ford, D. Y. (1998). The under-representation of minority students in gifted education: Problems and promises in recruitment and retention. *Journal of Special Education, 32,* 4–14.

Franklin, M. E. (1992). Culturally sensitive instructional practices for African-American learners with disabilities. *Exceptional Children, 59,* 115–122.

Fuchs, L. S., & Fuchs, D. (1977). Use of curriculum-based measurement in identifying students with disabilities. *Focus on Exceptional Children, 30*(3), 1–16.

Gerber, P. J., Ginsberg, R., & Reiff, H. B. (1992). Identifying alterable patterns in employment success for highly successful adults with learning disabilities. *Journal of Learning Disabilities, 25,* 475–487.

Gersten, R., Brengelman, S., & Jimenez, R. (1994). Effective instruction for culturally and linguistically diverse students: A reconceptualization. *Focus on Exceptional Children, 27*(1), 1–16.

Gersten, R., & Woodward, J. (1994). The language-minority student and special education: Issues, trends, and paradoxes. *Exceptional Children, 60,* 310–322.

Glazer, N. (1997). *We are all multiculturalists now.* Cambridge, MA: Harvard University Press.

Glazer, N. (1998). In defense of preference. *The New Republic, 342*(4), 18–21, 24–25.

Gollnick, D. M., & Chinn, P. C. (1994). *Multicultural education in a pluralistic society* (4th ed.). New York: Macmillan.

Hallahan, D. P., & Kauffman, J. M. (1994). Toward a culture of disability in the aftermath of Deno and Dunn. *Journal of Special Education, 27,* 496–508.

Hallahan, D. P., Kauffman, J. M., & Lloyd, J. W. (1999). *Introduction to learning disabilities* (2nd ed.). Boston: Allyn & Bacon.

Harry, B., Torguson, C., Katkavich, J., & Guerrero, M. (1993). Crossing social class and cultural barriers in working with families. Teaching *Exceptional Children, 26*(1), 48–51.

Hilliard, A. G. (1989). Teachers and cultural styles in a pluralistic society. *NEA Today, 7*(6), 65–69.

Hilliard, A. G. (1992). The pitfalls and promises of special education practice. *Exceptional Children, 59,* 168–172.

Hirsch, E. D. (1987). *Cultural literacy: What every American needs to know.* Boston: Houghton Mifflin.

Hirsch, E. D. (1996). *The schools we need and why we don't have them.* New York: Doubleday.

Horwitz, S. (1998, April 5). Lessons in black and white; crossing color lines in room 406 with Miss Kay and her kids. *Washington Post,* F1.

Hunter, J. D. (1991). *Culture wars: The struggle to define America.* New York: Basic Books.

Ishii-Jordan, S. (1997). When behavior differences are not disorders. In A. J. Artiles & G. Zamora-Duran (Eds.), *Reducing disproportionate representation of culturally diverse students in special and gifted education* (pp. 27–46). Reston, VA: Council for Exceptional Children.

Jacob, E., & Jordan, C. (Eds.). (1987). Explaining the school performance of minority students [Special issue]. *Anthropology and Education Quarterly, 18*(4).

Johnson, D. W., & Johnson, R. (1986). Mainstreaming and cooperative learning strategies. *Exceptional Children, 52,* 553–561.

Kalyanpur, M., & Harry, B. (1997). A posture of reciprocity: A practical approach to collaboration between professionals and parents of culturally diverse backgrounds. *Journal of Child and Family Studies, 6,* 487–509.

Katsiyannis, A. (1994). Pre-referral practices: Under Office of Civil Rights scrutiny. *Journal of Developmental and Physical Disabilities, 6,* 73–76.

Kauffman, J. M., Hallahan, D. P., & Ford, D. Y. (1998). Editors' introduction. *Journal of Special Education, 32,* 3.

Kauffman, J. M., Mostert, M. P., Trent, S. C., & Hallahan, D. P. (1998). *Managing classroom behavior: A reflective case-based approach* (2nd ed.). Boston: Allyn & Bacon.

Kennedy, R. (1997). My race problem—and ours. *Atlantic Monthly, 279*(5), 55–66.

Kidder, J. T. (1989). *Among schoolchildren.* Boston: Houghton Mifflin.

Keogh, B. K., Gallimore, R., & Weisner, T. (1997). A sociocultural perspective on learning and learning disabilities. *Learning Disabilities Research and Practice, 12,* 107–113.

Leake, D., & Leake, B. (1992). African-American immersion schools in Milwaukee: A view from inside. *Phi Delta Kappan, 73,* 783–785.

Lopez-Reyna, N. A., & Bay, M. (1997). Enriching assessment using varied assessments for diverse learners. Teaching *Exceptional Children, 29*(4), 33–37.

MacMillan, D. L., & Reschly, D. J. (1998).Overrepresentation of minority students: The case for greater specificity or reconsideration of the variables examined. *Journal of Special Education, 32,* 15–24.

MacMillan, D. L., Gresham, F. M., Lopez, M. F., & Bocian, K. M. (1996). Comparison of students nominated for prereferral interventions by ethnicity and gender. *Journal of Special Education, 30,* 133–151.

McBride, J. (1996). *The color of water: A black man's tribute to his white mother.* New York: Riverhead Books.

McDonnell, L. M., McLaughlin, M. J., & Morison, P. (Eds.). (1997). *Educating one and all: Students with disabilities and standards-based reform.* Washington, DC: National Academy Press.

McIntyre, T. (1992a). The "invisible culture" in our schools: Gay and lesbian youth. *Beyond Behavior, 3*(3), 6–12.

McIntyre, T. (1992b). The culturally sensitive disciplinarian. In R. B. Rutherford & S. R. Mathur (Eds.), *Monograph in behavioral disorders: Severe behavior disorders of children and youth, 15,* 107–115.

McIntyre, T., & Silva, P. (1992). Culturally diverse childrearing practices: Abusive or just different? *Beyond Behavior, 4*(1), 8–12.

McNergney, R. F. (1992). *Teaching and learning in multicultural settings: The case of Hans Christian Anderson School.* Video cassette. Boston: Allyn & Bacon.

Mehta, V. (1989). *The stolen light.* New York: W. W. Norton.

Minow, M. (1985). Learning to live with the dilemma of difference: Bilingual and special education. In K. T. Bartlett & J. W. Wegner (Eds.), *Children with special needs* (pp. 375–429). New Brunswick, NJ: Transaction Books.

Ogbu, J. U. (1992). Understanding cultural diversity and learning. *Educational Researcher, 21*(8), 5–14.

Ortiz, A. A. (1997). Learning disabilities occurring concomitantly with linguistic differences. *Journal of Learning Disabilities, 30,* 321–332.

Ovando, C. J. (1997). Language diversity and education. In J. A. Banks & C. A. M. Banks (Eds.), *Multicultural education: Issues and perspectives* (3rd ed., pp. 272–296). Boston: Allyn & Bacon.

Padden, C., & Humphries, T. (1988). *Deaf in America: Voices from a culture.* Cambridge, MA: Harvard University Press.

Patterson, O. (1993, February 7). Black like all of us: Celebrating multiculturalism diminishes blacks' role in American culture. *The Washington Post,* C2.

Patton, J. M. (1997). Disproportionate representation in gifted programs: Best practices for meeting this challenge. In A. J. Artiles & G. Zamora-Duran (Eds.), *Reducing disproportionate representation of culturally diverse students in special and gifted education* (pp. 59–85). Reston, VA: Council for Exceptional Children.

Patton, J. M. (1998). The disproportionate representation of African Americans in special education: Looking behind the curtain for understandings and solutions. *Journal of Special Education, 32,* 25–31.

Price, H. B. (1992). Multiculturalism: Myths and realities. *Phi Delta Kappan, 74,* 208–213.

Rodriguez, R. (1982). *Hunger of memory: The education of Richard Rodriguez. An autobiography.* Boston: D. R. Godine.

Rodriguez, R. (1992). *Days of obligation: An argument with my Mexican father.* New York: Viking.

Rogoff, B., & Morelli, G. (1989). Culture and American children. *American Psychologist, 44,* 341–342.

Rueda, R. (1997). Changing the context of assessment: The move to portfolios and authentic assessment. In A. J. Artiles & G. Zamora-Duran (Eds.), *Reducing disproportionate representation of culturally diverse students in special and gifted education* (pp. 7–25). Reston, VA: Council for Exceptional Children.

Rueda, R., & Garcia, E. (1997). Do portfolios make a difference for diverse students? The influence of type of data on making instructional decisions. *Learning Disabilities Research and Practice, 12,* 114–122.

Russell, K. Y. (1992). *The color complex: The "last taboo" among African Americans.* San Diego, CA: Harcourt Brace Jovanovich.

Schofield, J. W. (1997). Causes and consequences of the colorblind perspective. In J. A. Banks & C. A. M. Banks (Eds.), *Multicultural education: Issues and perspectives* (3rd ed., pp. 251–271). Boston: Allyn & Bacon.

Singh, N. N. (1996). Cultural diversity in the 21st century: Beyond E Pluribus Unum. *Journal of Child and Family Studies, 5,* 121–136.

Singh, N. N., Ellis, C. R., Oswald, D. P., Wechsler, H. A., & Curtis, W. J. (1997). Value and address diversity. *Journal of Emotional and Behavioral Disorders, 5,* 24–35.

Slavin, R. E. (1988). Cooperative learning and student achievement. *Educational Leadership, 46*(2), 31–33.

Sleeter, C. E., & Grant, C. A. (1994). *Making choices for multicultural education: Five approaches to race, class, and gender* (2nd ed.). New York: Macmillan.

Spencer, J. M. (1997). *The new colored people: The mixed-race movement in America.* New York: New York University Press.

Steele, C. M. (1992, April). Race and the schooling of black Americans. *Atlantic Monthly,* 68–78.

Takaki, R. (1994). Interview: Reflections from a different mirror. *Teaching Tolerance, 3*(1), 11–15.

Taylor, R. L. (1997). *Assessment of exceptional students: Educational and psychological procedures* (4th ed.). Boston: Allyn & Bacon.

Terwilliger, J. (1997). Semantics, psychometrics, and assessment reform: A close look at "authentic" assessments. *Educational Researcher, 26*(8), 24–27.

Thomas, C. (1998, April 22). Do we education our children or preserve an institution? *The Charlottesville Daily Progress,* p. A8.

Trent, S. C., & Artiles, A. J. (Eds.). (1998). Multicultural teacher education in special education [Special issue]. *Remedial and Special Education, 19*(1).

Uribe, V., & Harbeck, K. M. (1992). *Coming out of the classroom closet: Gay and lesbian students, teachers, and curricula.* Binghamton, NY: Hayworth Press.

U.S. Department of Education. (1992). *Fourteenth annual report to Congress on the implementation of the Individuals with Disabilities Education Act.* Washington, DC: Author.

U.S. Department of Education. (1996). *Eighteenth annual report to Congress on the implementation of the Individuals with Disabilities Education Act.* Washington, DC: Author.

U.S. Department of Education. (1997). *Nineteenth annual report to Congress on the implementation of the Individuals with Disabilities Education Act.* Washington, DC: Author.

Van Keulen, J. E., Weddington, G. T., & DeBose, C. E. (1998). *Speech, language, learning, and the African American child.* Boston: Allyn & Bacon.

Williams, E. (1994). North meets South: Pen pals in Alabama and New York discover shared interests, dispel regional stereotypes. *Teaching Tolerance, 3*(1), 17–19.

Williams, P. J. (1998a). In living black and white. *The Washington Post Magazine,* pp. 19–20, 30.

Williams, P. J. (1998b). *Seeing a color-blind future.* New York: Noonday Press.

Winzer, M., & Mazurek, K. (1998). *Special education in multicultural contexts.* Columbus, OH: Merrill.

Wortham, A. (1992, September). Afrocentrism isn't the answer for black students in American society. *Executive Educator, 14,* 23–25.

Ysseldyke, J. E., & Marston, D. (1988). Issues in the psychological evaluation of children. In V. B. Van Hasselt, P. S. Strain, & M. Hersen (Eds.), *Handbook of developmental and physical disabilities* (pp. 21–37). New York: Pergamon.

Chapter 4

AAMR Ad Hoc Committee on Terminology and Classification. (1992). *Mental retardation: Definition, classification, and systems of support* (9th ed.). Washington, DC: American Association on Mental Retardation.

The Arc. (1997, September 18). *Phenylketonuria (PKU)* [Posted on the World Wide Web]. Author. Retrieved June 19, 1998 from the World Wide Web: http://www.thearc.org/faqs/pku.html

Baumeister, A. A. (1997). Behavioral research: Boom or bust? In W. E. MacLean (Ed.), *Ellis' handbook of mental deficiency, psychological theory, and research* (pp. 3–45). Mahwah, NJ: Erlbaum.

Baumeister, A. A., Kupstas, F., & Klindworth, L. M. (1990). New morbidity: Implications for prevention of children's disabilities. *Exceptionality, 1,* 1–16.

Baumeister, A. A., & Woodley-Zanthos, P. (1996). Prevention: Biological factors. In J. W. Jacobson & J. A. Mulick (Eds.), *Manual of diagnosis and professional practice in mental retardation* (pp. 229–242). Washington, DC: American Psychological Association.

Bebko, J. M., & Luhaorg, H. (1998). The development of strategy use and metacognitive processing in mental retardation: Some sources of difficulty. In J. A. Burack, R. M. Hodapp, & E. Zigler (Eds.), *Handbook of mental retardation and development* (pp. 382–407). New York: Cambridge University Press.

Beirne-Smith, M., Ittenbach, R. F., & Patton, J. R. (1998). *Mental retardation* (5th ed.). Upper Saddle River, NJ: Merrill.

Blacher, J., & Baker, B. L. (1992). Toward meaningful family involvement in out-of-home placement settings. *Mental Retardation, 30*(1), 35–41.

Blackorby, J., & Wagner, M. (1996). Longitudinal postschool outcomes of youth with disabilities: Findings from the National Longitudinal Transition Study. *Exceptional Children, 62,* 399–413.

Blair, C., & Ramey, C. T. (1997). Early intervention for low-birth-weight infants and the path to second-generation research. In M. J. Guralnick (Ed.), *The effectiveness of early intervention* (pp. 77–97). Baltimore: MD: Paul H. Brookes.

Bray, N. W., Fletcher, K. L., & Turner, L. (1997). Cognitive competencies and strategy use in individuals with mental retardation. In W. E. MacLean (Ed.), *Ellis' handbook of mental deficiency, psychological theory, and research* (pp. 197–217). Mahwah, NJ: Erlbaum.

Browder, D., & Snell, M. E. (2000). Teaching functional academics. In M. E. Snell & F. Brown (Eds.), *Instruction of students with severe disabilities.* Columbus, OH: Merrill.

Brown, L., Shiraga, B., Ford, A., Nisbet, J., Van Deventer, P., Sweet, M., York, J., & Loomis, R. (1986). Teaching severely handicapped students to perform meaningful work in nonsheltered vocational environments. In R. J. Morris & B. Blatt (Eds.), *Special education: Research and trends* (pp. 131–189). New York: Pergamon Press.

Bryant, B. R., Taylor, R. L., & Rivera, D. P. (1996). *Assessment of Adaptive Areas.* Austin, TX: Pro-Ed.

Butterworth, J., & Strauch, J. D. (1994). The relationship between social competence and success in the competitive work place for persons with mental retardation. *Education and Training in Mental Retardation and Developmental Disabilities, 29,* 118–133.

Campbell, F. A., & Ramey, C. T. (1994). Effects of early intervention on intellectual and academic achievement: A follow-up study of children from low-income families. *Child Development, 65,* 684–698.

Carr, J. (1994). Annotation: Long term outcome for people with Down's syndrome. *Journal of Child Psychology and Psychiatry, 35,* 425–439.

Chadsey, J. G., Linneman, D., Rusch, F. R., & Cimera, R. E. (1997). The impact of social integration interventions and job coaches in work settings. *Education and Training in Mental Retardation and Developmental Disabilities, 32,* 281–292.

Davis, P. K., & Cuvo, A. J. (1997). Environmental approaches to mental retardation. In D. M. Baer & E. M. Pinkerston (Eds.), *Environment and behavior* (pp. 231–242). Boulder, CO: Westview Press.

Dykens, E. M., & Cohen, D. J. (1996). Effects of the Special Olympics International on social competence of persons with mental retardation. *Journal of the American Academy of Child and Adolescent Psychiatry, 35,* 223–229.

Evenhuis, H. M. (1990). The natural history of dementia in Down's syndrome. *Archives of Neurology, 47,* 263–267.

Ferguson, B., McDonnell, J., & Drew, C. (1993). Type and frequency of social interaction among workers with and without mental retardation. *American Journal on Mental Retardation, 97,* 530–540.

Fraser, J., & Mitchell, A. (1876). Kalmuc idiocy: Report of a case with autopsy, with notes on sixty-two cases. *Journal of Mental Science, 22,* 161–179.

Greenspan, S. (1997). Dead manual walking? Why the 1992 AAMR definition needs redoing. *Education and Training in Mental Retardation and Developmental Disabilities, 32,* 179–190.

Greenspan, S., Switzky, H. N., & Granfield, J. M. (1996). Everyday intelligence and adaptive behavior: A theoretical framework. In J. W. Jacobson & J. A. Mulick (Eds.), *Manual of diagnosis and professional practice in mental retardation* (pp. 127–135). Washington, DC: American Psychological Association.

Griffin, D. K., Rosenberg, H., Cheyney, W., & Greenberg, B. (1996). A comparison of self-esteem and job satisfaction of adults with mild mental retardation in sheltered workshops and supported employment. *Education and Training in Mental Retardation and Developmental Disabilities, 31,* 142–150.

Guralnick, M. J., Connor, R. T., & Hammond, M. (1995). Parent perspectives of peer relationships and friendships in integrated and specialized programs. *American Journal on Mental Retardation, 99,* 457–476.

Heal, L. W., Gonzalez, P., Rusch, F. R., Copher, J. I., & DeStefano, L. (1990). A comparison of successful and unsuccessful placements of youths with mental handicaps into competitive employment. *Exceptionality, 1,* 181–195.

Hetherington, E. M., & Parke, R. D. (1986). *Child psychology: A contemporary viewpoint* (3rd ed.). New York: McGraw-Hill.

Hof, P. R., Bouras, C., Perl, D. P., Sparks, L., Mehta, N., & Morrison, J. H. (1995). Age-related distribution of neuropathologic changes in the cerebral cortex of patients with Down's syndrome. *Archives of Neurology, 52,* 379–391.

Horner, R. H., & Carr, E. G. (1997). Behavioral support for students with severe disabilities: Functional assessment and comprehensive intervention. *Journal of Special Education, 31,* 84–104.

Howe, J., Horner, R. H., & Newton, J. S. (1998). Comparison of supported living and traditional residential services in the state of Oregon. *Mental Retardation, 36,* 1–11.

Human Genome Management Information System. (1998, July 5). *Human genome project information* [Posted on the World Wide Web]. Author. Retrieved July 5, 1998 from the World Wide Web: wysiwyg://11/http://www.ornl.gov/TechResources/Human_Genome/home.html

Jacobson, J. W., & Mulick, J. A. (1996). Definition of mental retardation. In J. W. Jacobson & J. A. Mulick (Eds.), *Manual of diagnosis and professional practice in mental retardation* (pp. 13–53). Washington, DC: American Psychological Association.

Kamphaus, R. W., & Reynolds, C. R. (1987). *Clinical and research applications of the K-ABC.* Circle Pines, MN: American Guidance.

Kasari, C., & Bauminger, N. (1998). Social and emotional development in children with mental retardation. In J. A. Burack, R. M. Hodapp, & E. Zigler (Eds.), *Handbook of mental retardation and development* (pp. 411–433). New York: Cambridge University Press.

Kaufman, A. S., & Kaufman, N. L. (1983). *Kaufman Assessment Battery for Children.* Circle Pines, MN: American Guidance Service.

Klein, T., Gilman, E., & Zigler, E. (1995). Special Olympics: An evaluation by professionals and parents. *Mental Retardation, 31,* 15–23.

Krauss, M. W., Seltzer, M. M., & Goodman, S. J. (1992). Social support networks of adults with mental retardation who live at home. *American Journal on Mental Retardation, 96,* 432–441.

Lagomarcino, T. R., Hughes, C., & Rusch, F. R. (1989). Utilizing self-management to teach independence on the job. *Education and Training of the Mentally Retarded, 24,* 139–148.

Lambert, N., Nihira, K., & Leland, H. (1993). *AAMD Adaptive Behavior Scale–School, 2nd Edition.* Austin, TX: Pro-Ed.

Lenhoff, H. M., Wang, P. P., Greenberg, F., & Bellugi, U. (1997, December). Folktales from any cultures … Secrets of how the brain functions. *Scientific American,* 68–73.

MacMillan, D. L. (1982). *Mental retardation in school and society* (2nd ed.). Boston: Little, Brown.

MacMillan, D. L., Gresham, F. M., & Siperstein, G. N. (1993). Conceptual and psychometric concerns about the 1992 AAMR definition of mental retardation. *American Journal of Mental Retardation, 98,* 325–335.

MacMillan, D. L., Gresham, F. M., Bocian, K. M., & Lambros, K. M. (1998). Current plight of borderline students: Where do they belong? *Education and Training in Mental Retardation and Developmental Disabilities, 33,* 83–94.

MacMillan, D. L., & Reschly, D. J. (1997). Issues of definition and classification. In W. E. MacLean (Ed.), *Ellis' handbook of mental deficiency, psychological theory, and research* (pp. 47–74). Mahwah, NJ: Erlbaum.

McCaughrin, W. B., Ellis, W. K., Rusch, F. R., & Heal, L. W. (1993). Cost-effectiveness of supported employment. *Mental Retardation, 31,* 41–48.

Mercer, J. R., & Lewis, J. F. (1982). *Adaptive Behavior Inventory for Children.* San Antonio, TX: Psychological Corporation.

Nietupski, J., Hamre-Nietupski, S., VanderHart, N. S., & Fishback, K. (1996). Employer perceptions of the benefits and concerns of supported employment. *Education and Training in Mental Retardation and Developmental Disabilities, 31,* 310–323.

Nihira, K., Leland, H., & Lambert, N. (1993). *AAMR Adaptive Behavior Scale–Residential and Community,* (2nd ed.). Austin, TX: Pro-Ed.

Palmer, D. S., Borthwick-Duffy, S. A., & Widaman, K. (1998). Parent perceptions of inclusive practices for their children with significant cognitive disabilities. *Exceptional Children, 64,* 271–282.

Pinel, P. J. (1993). Biopsychology (2nd ed.). Boston: Allyn & Bacon.

Polloway, E. A., Smith, J. D., Patton, J. R., & Smith, T. E. C. (1996). Historic changes in mental retardation and developmental dis-

abilities. *Education and Training in Mental Retardation and Developmental Disabilities, 31,* 3–12.

Ramey, C. T., & Campbell, F. A. (1984). Preventive education for high-risk children: Cognitive consequences of the Carolina Abecedarian Project. *American Journal of Mental Deficiency, 88,* 515–523.

Ramey, C. T., & Campbell, F. A. (1987). The Carolina Abecedarian Project: An educational experiment concerning human malleability. In J. J. Gallagher & C. T. Ramey (Eds.), *The malleability of children* (pp. 127–139). Baltimore, MD: Paul H. Brookes.

Revell, W. G., Wehman, P., Kregel, J., West, M., & Rayfield, R. (1994). Supported employment for persons with severe disabilities: Positive trends in wages, models, and funding. *Education and Training in Mental Retardation and Developmental Disabilities, 29,* 256–264.

Riggen, K., & Ulrich, D. (1993). The effects of sport participation on individuals with mental retardation. *Adapted Physical Activity Quarterly, 10,* 42–51.

Roper, P. A. (1990). Special Olympics volunteers' perceptions of people with mental retardation. *Education and Training in Mental Retardation, 25,* 164–175.

Salzberg, C. L., Lignugaris/Kraft, B., & McCuller, G. L. (1988). Reasons for job loss: A review of employment termination studies of mentally retarded workers. *Research in Developmental Disabilities, 9,* 153–170.

Schweinhart, L. J., & Weikart, D. P. (1993). Success by empowerment: The High/Scope Perry Preschool Study through age 27. *Young Children, 49,* 54–58.

Skeels, H. M. (1966). Adult status of children with contrasting early life experiences. *Monographs of the Society for Research in Child Development, 31* (Ser. No. 105). University of Chicago Press.

Skeels, H. M., & Dye, H. B. (1939). A study of the effects of differential stimulation on mentally retarded children. *Convention Proceedings, American Association on Mental Deficiency, 44,* 114–136.

Slomka, G. T., & Berkey, J. (1997). Aging and mental retardation. In P. D. Nussbaum (Ed.), *Handbook of neuropyschology and aging* (pp. 331–347). New York: Plenum Press.

Smith, J. D. (1994). The revised AAMR definition of mental retardation: The MRDD position. *Education and Training in Mental Retardation and Developmental Disabilities, 29,* 179–183.

Sparrow, S. S., Balla, D. A., & Cicchetti, D. V. (1984). *Vineland Adaptive Behavior Scales.* Circle Pines, MN: American Guidance Service.

Special Olympics Michigan. (1998, March 17). *About Special Olympics Michigan* [Posted on the World Wide Web]. Author. Retrieved July 12, 1998 from the World Wide Web: http://www.miso.org/mso2.html

Stodden, R. A., & Browder, P. M. (1986). Community-based competitive employment preparation of developmentally disabled persons: A program description and evaluation. *Education and Training of the Mentally Retarded, 21,* 43–53.

Tager-Flusberg, H., & Sullivan, K. (1998). Early language development in children with mental retardation. In J. A. Burack, R. M. Hodapp, & E. Zigler (Eds.), *Handbook of mental retardation and development* (pp. 208–239). New York: Cambridge University Press.

Thorndike, R. L., Hagen, E. P., & Sattler, J. M. (1986). *Technical manual, Stanford-Binet Intelligence Scale* (4th ed.). Chicago: Riverside.

Tomporowski, P. D., & Tinsley, V. (1997). Attention in mentally retarded persons. In W. E. MacLean (Ed.), *Ellis' handbook of mental deficiency, psychological theory, and research* (pp. 219–244). Mahwah, NJ: Erlbaum.

Visser, F. E., Aldenkamp, A. P., vanHuffelen, A. C., Kuilman, M., Overweg, J., & vanWijk, J. (1997). Prospective study of the prevalence of Alzheimer-type dementia in institutionalized individuals with Down syndrome. *American Journal on Mental Retardation, 101,* 400–412.

Warren, S., & Yoder, P. J. (1997). Communication, language, and mental retardation. In W. E. MacLean (Ed.), *Ellis' handbook of mental deficiency, psychological theory, and research* (pp. 379–403). Mahwah, NJ: Erlbaum.

Wechsler, D. (1991). *Wechsler Intelligence Scale for Children* (3rd ed.). San Antonio, TX: Psychological Corporation.

Wehman, P., & Parent, W. (1996). Supported employment. In P. J. McLaughlin & P. Wehman (Eds.), *Mental retardation and developmental disabilities* (pp. 317–338). Austin, TX: Pro-Ed.

Wisniewski, H. M., Silverman, W., & Wegiel, J. (1994). Aging, Alzheimer disease, and mental retardation. *Journal of Intellectual Disability Research, 38,* 233–239.

Wolery, M., & Schuster, J. W. (1997). Instructional methods with students who have significant disabilities. *Journal of Special Education, 31,* 61–79.

Zeaman, D., & House, B. J. (1963). The role of attention in retardate discrimination learning. In N. R. Ellis (Ed.), *Handbook of mental deficiency.* New York: McGraw-Hill.

Zigler, E., & Hodapp, R. M. (1986). *Understanding mental retardation.* New York: Cambridge University Press.

Chapter 5

Aaron, P. G. (1997). The impending demise of the discrepancy formula. *Review of Educational Research, 67,* 461–502.

Adelman, K. A., & Adelman, H. S. (1987). Rodin, Patton, Edison, Wilson, Einstein: Were they really learning disabled? *Journal of Learning Disabilities, 20,* 270–279.

American Psychiatric Association. (1994). *Diagnostic and statistical manual of mental disorders* (4th ed.). Washington, DC: Author.

Ashbaker, M. H., & Swanson, H. L. (1996). Short-term memory and working memory and their contribution to reading in adolescents with and without learning disabilities. *Learning Disabilities Research and Practice, 11,* 206–213.

Baumeister, A. A., Kupstas, F., & Klindworth, L. M. (1990). New morbidity: Implications for prevention of children's disabilities. *Exceptionality, 1,* 1–16.

Baumgartner, D., Bryan, T., Donahue, M., & Nelson, C. (1993). Thanks for asking: Parent comments about homework, tests, and grades. *Exceptionality, 4,* 177–185.

Beichtman, J. H., Hood, J., & Inglis, A. (1992). Familial transmission of speech and language impairment: A preliminary investigation. *Canadian Journal of Psychiatry, 37,* 151–156.

Blackorby, J., & Wagner, M. (1997). The employment outcomes of youth with learning disabilities: A review of findings from NLTS. In P. J. Gerber & D. S. Brown (Eds.), *Learning disabilities and employment* (pp. 57–74). Austin, TX: Pro-Ed.

Bryan, T. (1998). Social competence of students with learning disabilities. In B. Y. L. Wong (Ed.), *Learning about learning disabilities* (2nd ed., pp. 237–275). San Diego, CA: Academic Press.

Bryan, T. H., & Bryan, J. H. (1986). *Understanding learning disabilities.* Palo Alto, CA: Mayfield.

Bryan, T. H., Donahue, M., Pearl, R., & Sturm, C. (1981). Learning disabled children's conversational skills—The "TV Talk Show." *Learning Disability Quarterly, 4,* 250–260.

Bryan, T., Nelson, C., & Mathur, S. (1995). Homework: A survey of primary students in regular, resource, and self-contained classrooms. *Learning Disabilities Research and Practice, 10,* 85–90.

Butler, D. L. (1998). Metacognition and learning disabilities. In B. Y. L. Wong (Ed.), *Learning about learning disabilities* (2nd ed., pp. 277–307). San Diego, CA: Academic Press.

Cardon, L. R., Smith, S. D., Fulker, D. W., Kimberling, W. J., Pennington, B. F., & DeFries, J. C. (1994, October 14). Quantitative trait locus for reading disability on Chromosome 6. *Science, 266,* 276–279.

Case, L. P., Harris, K. R., & Graham, S. (1992). Improving the mathematical problem-solving skills of students with learning disabilities. *Journal of Special Education, 26,* 1–19.

Cawley, J. F., & Parmar, R. S. (1992). Arithmetic programming for students with disabilities: An alternative. *Remedial and Special Education, 13*(3), 6–18.

Cawley, J. F., Parmar, R. S., Yan, W., & Miller, J. H. (1998). Arithmetic computation performance of students with learning disabilities: Implications for the curriculum. *Learning Disabilities Research and Practice, 13,* 68–74.

Choate, J. S., Enright, B. E., Miller, L. J., Poteet, J. A., & Rakes, T. A. (1995). *Curriculum-based assessment programming* (3rd ed.). Boston: Allyn & Bacon.

Churchill, W. S. (1930). *A roving commission: My early life.* New York: Charles Scribner's Sons.

Clarizio, H. F., & Phillips, S. E. (1986). Sex bias in the diagnosis of learning disabled students. *Psychology in the Schools, 23,* 44–52.

DeFries, J. C., Gillis, J. J., & Wadsworth, S. J. (1993). Genes and genders: A twin study of reading disability. In A. M. Galaburda (Ed.), *Dyslexia and development: Neurological aspects of extra-ordinary brains* (pp. 187–294). Cambridge, MA: Harvard University Press.

Deno, S. L. (1985). Curriculum-based measurement: The emerging alternative. *Exceptional Children, 52,* 219–232.

Engelmann, S., Carnine, D., Engelmann, O., & Kelly, B. (1991). *Connecting math concepts.* Chicago: Science Research Associates.

Engelmann, S., Carnine, L., Johnson, G., & Meyers, L. (1988). *Corrective reading: Decoding.* Chicago: Science Research Associates.

Engelmann, S., Carnine, L., Johnson, G., & Meyers, L. (1989). *Corrective reading: Comprehension.* Chicago: Science Research Associates.

Englert, C. S. (1992). Writing instruction from a sociocultural perspective: The holistic, dialogic, and social enterprise of writing. *Journal of Learning Disabilities, 25,* 153–172.

Epstein, M. H., Polloway, E. A., Buck, G. H., Bursuck, W. D., Wissinger, L. M., Whitehouse, F., & Jayanthi, M. (1997). Homework-related communication problems: Perspectives of general education teachers. *Learning Disabilities Research and Practice, 12,* 221–227.

Epstein, M. H., Polloway, E. A., Foley, R. M., & Patton, J. R. (1993). Homework: A comparison of teachers' and parents' perceptions of the problems experienced by students identified as having behavioral disorders, learning disabilities, or no disabilities. *Remedial and Special Education, 14*(5), 40–50.

Fisher, S. E., Vargha-Khadem, F., Watkins, K. E., Monaco, A. P., & Pembrey, M. E. (1998). Localisation of a gene implicated in a severe speech and language disorder. *Nature Genetics, 18,* 168–170.

Flowers, D. L. (1993). Brain basis for dyslexia: A summary of work in progress. *Journal of Learning Disabilities, 26,* 575–582.

Flowers, D. L., Wood, F. B., & Naylor, C. E. (1991). Regional cerebral blood flow correlates of language processes in reading disability. *Archives of Neurology, 48,* 637–643.

Foorman, B. R., Francis, D. J., Shaywitz, S. E., Shaywitz, B. A., & Fletcher, J. M. (1997). The case for early reading intervention. In B. Blachman (Ed.), *Foundations of reading acquisition and dyslexia: Implications for early intervention* (pp. 243–264). Mahwah, NJ: Erlbaum.

Frostig, M., & Horne, D. (1964). *The Frostig program for the development of visual perception: Teacher's guide.* Chicago: Follett.

Fuchs, L. S. (1986). Monitoring progress among mildly handicapped pupils: Review of current practice and research. *Remedial and Special Education, 7(5),* 5–12.

Fuchs, L., Deno, S. L., & Mirkin, P. K. (1984). The effects of frequent curriculum-based measurement and evaluation of pedagogy, student achievement and student awareness of learning. *American Educational Research Journal, 24,* 449–460.

Fuchs, L. S., & Fuchs, D. (1986). Effects of systematic formative evaluation: A meta-analysis. *Exceptional Children, 53,* 199–208.

Gajar, A. H. (1989). A computer analysis of written language variables and a comparison of compositions written by university students with and without learning disabilities. *Journal of Learning Disabilities, 22,* 125–130.

Gerber, P. J. (1997). Life after school: Challenges in the workplace. In P. J. Gerber & D. S. Brown (Eds.), *Learning disabilities and employment* (pp. 3–18). Austin, TX: Pro-Ed.

Gerber, P. J., Ginsberg, R., & Reiff, H. B. (1992). Identifying alterable patterns in employment success for highly successful adults with learning disabilities. *Journal of Learning Disabilities, 25,* 475–487.

Gerber, P. J., & Reiff, H. B. (1991). *Speaking for themselves: Ethnographic interviews with adults with learning disabilities.* Ann Arbor, MI: University of Michigan Press.

Goldstein, D. E., Murray, C., & Edgar, E. (1998). Employment earning and hours of high school graduates with learning disabilities through the first decade after graduation. *Learning Disabilities Research and Practice, 13,* 53–64.

Graham, S., Harris, K. R., MacArthur, C., & Schwartz, S. (1998). Writing instruction. In B. Y. L. Wong (Ed.), *Learning about learning disabilities* (2nd ed., pp. 391–423). San Diego, CA: Academic Press.

Grayson, T. E., Wermuth, T. R., Holub, T. M., & Anderson, M. L. (1997). Effective practices of transition from school to work for people with learning disabilities. In P. J. Gerber & D. S. Brown (Eds.), *Learning disabilities and employment* (pp. 77–99). Austin, TX: Pro-Ed.

Grigorenko, E. L., Wood, F. B., Meyer, M. S., Hart, L. A., Speed, W. C., Shuster, A., & Pauls, D. L. (1997). Susceptibility loci for distinct components of developmental dyslexia on Chromosomes 6 and 15. *American Journal of Human Genetics, 60,* 27–39.

Gross-Glenn, K., Duara, R., Barker, W. W., Loewenstein, D., Chang, J., Yoshii, F., Apicella, A. M., Pascal, S., Boothe, T., Sevush, S., Jallad, B. J., Novoa, L., & Lubs, H. A. (1991). Positron emission tomographic studies during serial word-reading by normal and dyslexic adults. *Journal of Clinical and Experimental Neuropsychology, 13,* 531–544.

Hagman, J. O., Wood, F., Buchsbaum, M. S., Tallal, P., Flowers, L., & Katz, W. (1992). Cerebral metabolism in adult dyslexic subjects assessed with positron emission tomography during performance on an auditory task. *Archives of Neurology, 49,* 734–739.

Hallahan, D. P. (1975). Comparative research studies on the psychological characteristics of learning disabled children. In W. M. Cruickshank & D. P. Hallahan (Eds.), *Perceptual and learning disabilities in children. Vol. 1: Psychoeducational practices.* Syracuse, NY: Syracuse University Press.

Hallahan, D. P. (1992). Some thoughts on why the prevalence of learning disabilities has increased. *Journal of Learning Disabilities, 25,* 523–528.

Hallahan, D. P., & Bryan, T. H. (1981). Learning disabilities. In J. M. Kauffman & D. P. Hallahan (Eds.), *Handbook of special education.* Englewood Cliffs, NJ: Prentice-Hall.

Hallahan, D. P., & Cruickshank, W. M. (1973). *Psychoeducational foundations of learning disabilities.* Englewood Cliffs, NJ: Prentice-Hall.

Hallahan, D. P., Gajar, A. H., Cohen, S. B., & Tarver, S. G. (1978). Selective attention and locus of control in learning disabled and normal children. *Journal of Learning Disabilities, 4,* 47–52.

Hallahan, D. P., Kauffman, J. M., & Ball, D. W. (1973). Selective attention and cognitive tempo of low achieving and high achieving sixth grade males. *Perceptual and Motor Skills, 36,* 579–583.

Hallahan, D. P., Kauffman, J. M., & Lloyd, J. W. (1999). *Introduction to learning disabilities* (2nd ed.). Boston: Allyn & Bacon.

Hallahan, D. P., & Reeve, R. E. (1980). Selective attention and distractibility. In B. K. Keogh (Ed.), *Advances in special education. Vol. 1: Basic constructs and theoretical orientations.* Greenwich, CT: J.A.I. Press.

Hallgren, B. (1950). Specific dyslexia (congenital word blindness: A clinical and genetic study). *Acta Psychiatrica et Neurologica, 65,* 1–279.

Hammill, D. D. (1990). On defining learning disabilities: An emerging consensus. *Journal of Learning Disabilities, 23,* 74–84.

Hammill, D. D., & Bryant, B. R. (1998). *Learning Disabilities Diagnostic Inventory.* Austin, TX: Pro-Ed.

Hammill, D. D., & Larsen, S. (1974). The effectiveness of psycholinguistic training. *Exceptional Children, 41,* 5–15.

Hammill, D. D., Leigh, J. E., McNutt, G., & Larsen, S. C. (1981). A new definition of learning disabilities. *Learning Disability Quarterly, 4,* 336–342.

Haring, K. A., Lovett, D. L., Haney, K. F., Algozzine, B., Smith, D. D., & Clarke, J. (1992). Labeling preschoolers as learning disabled: A cautionary position. *Topics in Early Childhood: Special Education, 12,* 151–173.

Hartas, D., & Donahue, M. L. (1997). Conversational and social problem-solving skills in adolescents with learning disabilities. *Learning Disabilities Research and Practice, 12,* 213–220.

Hynd, G. W., Marshall, R., & Gonzalez, J. (1991). Learning disabilities and presumed central nervous system dysfunction. *Learning Disability Quarterly, 14,* 283–296.

Individuals with Disabilities Education Act (IDEA) Amendments of 1997. Public Law 105–17.

Johnson, L., Graham, S., & Harris, K. R. (1997). The effects of goal setting and self-instruction on learning a reading comprehension strategy: A study of students with learning disabilities. *Journal of Learning Disabilities, 30,* 80–91.

Kavale, K. A. (1988). The long-term consequences of learning disabilities. In M. C. Wang, M. C. Reynolds, & H. J. Walberg (Eds.), *Handbook of special education: Research and practice. Vol. 2: Mildly handicapped conditions.* New York: Pergamon Press.

Kavale, K. A. (1995). Setting the record straight on learning disability and low achievement: The tortuous path of ideology. *Learning Disabilities Research and Practice, 10,* 145–152.

Kavale, K. A., & Reese, J. H. (1992). The character of learning disabilities: An Iowa profile. *Learning Disability Quarterly, 15,* 74–94.

Keogh, B. K., & Glover, A. T. (1980, November). Research needs in the study of early identification of children with learning disabilities. *Thalamus* (Newsletter of the International Academy for Research in Learning Disabilities).

Kephart, N. C. (1971). *The slow learner in the classroom* (2nd ed.) Columbus, OH: Merrill.

Kirk, S. A., & Kirk, W. D. (1971). *Psycholinguistic learning disabilities: Diagnosis and remediation.* Urbana: University of Illinois Press.

Klingner, J. K., Vaughn, S., Hughes, M. T., Schumm, J. S., & Erlbaum, B. (1998). Outcomes for students with and without learning disabilities in inclusive classrooms. *Learning Disabilities Research and Practice, 13,* 153–161.

Klingner, J. K., Vaughn, S., Schumm, J. S., Cohen, P., & Forgan, J. (1998). Inclusion or pull-out: Which do students prefer? *Journal of Learning Disabilities, 31,* 148–158.

Kosiewicz, M. M., Hallahan, D. P., Lloyd, J. W., & Graves, A. W. (1982). Effects of self-instruction and self-correction procedures on handwriting performance. *Learning Disability Quarterly, 5,* 71–78.

Kravets, M., & Wax, I. F. (1993). *The K & W guide to colleges for the learning disabled* (2nd ed.). New York: HarperCollins.

Kushch, A., Gross-Glenn, K., Jallad, B., Lubs, H., Rabin, M., Feldman, E., & Duara, R. (1993). Temporal lobe surface area measurements on MRI in normal and dyslexic readers. *Neuropsychologia, 31,* 811–821.

Laughton, J., & Morris, N. T. (1989). Story grammar knowledge of learning disabled students. *Learning Disabilities Research, 4,* 87–95.

Leinhardt, G., Seewald, A., & Zigmond, N. (1982). Sex and race differences in learning disabilities classrooms. *Journal of Educational Psychology, 74,* 835–845.

Lerner, J. W. (1997). *Learning disabilities: Theories, diagnosis, and teaching strategies* (7th ed.). Boston: Houghton Mifflin.

Lewis, B. A. (1992). Pedigree analysis of children with phonology disorders. *Journal of Learning Disabilities, 25,* 586–597.

Lewis, B. A., & Thompson, L. A. (1992). A study of development of speech and language disorders in twins. *Journal of Speech and Hearing Research, 35,* 1086–1094.

Lloyd, J. W. (1988). Direct academic interventions in learning disabilities. In M. C. Wang, M. C. Reynolds, & H. J. Walberg (Eds.), *Handbook of special education: Research and practice. Vol. 2: Mildly handicapped conditions.* New York: Pergamon Press.

Lopez-Reyna, N. A., & Bay, M. (1997). Enriching assessment using varied assessments for diverse learners. *Teaching Exceptional Children, 29*(4), 33–37.

Lyon, G. R., & Moats, L. C. (1997). Critical conceptual and methodological considerations in reading intervention research. *Journal of Learning Disabilities, 30,* 578–588.

MacMillan, D. L., Gresham, F. M., & Bocian, K. M. (1998). Discrepancy between definitions of learning disabilities and school practices: An empirical investigation. *Journal of Learning Disabilities, 31,* 314–326.

Mangrum, C. T., & Strichart, S. S. (Eds.) (1994). *Peterson's colleges with programs for students with learning disabilities* (4th ed.). Princeton, NJ: Peterson's.

Mann, V. A., Cowin, E., & Schoenheimer, J. (1989). Phonological processing, language comprehension, and reading ability. *Journal of Learning Disabilities, 22,* 76–89.

Mastropieri, M. A., & Scruggs, T. E. (1998). Constructing more meaningful relationships in the classroom: Mnemonic research into practice. *Learning Disabilities Research and Practice, 13,* 138–145.

Mastropieri, M. A., Scruggs, T. E., & Whedon, C. (1997). Using mnemonic strategies to teach information about U.S. presidents: A classroom-based investigation. *Learning Disability Quarterly, 20,* 13–21.

Mathinos, D. A. (1988). Communicative competence of children with learning disabilities. *Journal of Learning Disabilities, 21,* 437–443.

McGrady, H. J., & Lerner, J. W. (in press). The educational lives of young adults with learning disabilities. In P. Rodis, A. Garrod, & M. L. Boscardin (Eds.), *Learning disabilities and life stories.* New York: Teachers College Press.

McIntosh, R., Vaughn, S., & Bennerson, D. (1995). FAST social skills with a SLAM and a RAP. Teaching *Exceptional Children, 28,* 37–41.

Meichenbaum, D. H. (1975, June). Cognitive factors as determinants of learning disabilities: A cognitive-functional approach. Paper presented at the NATO Conference on the Neuropsychology of Learning Disorders: Theoretical Approaches, Korsor, Denmark.

Meichenbaum, D. H., & Goodman, J. (1971). Training impulsive children to talk to themselves: A means of developing self-control. *Journal of Abnormal Psychology, 77,* 115–126.

Mercer, C. D., Jordan, L., Allsopp, D. H., & Mercer, A. R. (1996). Learning disabilities definitions and criteria used by state education departments. *Learning Disability Quarterly, 19,* 217–232.

Mercer, C. D., & Miller, S. P. (1992). Teaching students with learning problems in math to acquire, understand, and apply basic math facts. *Remedial and Special Education, 13*(3), 19–35, 61.

Montague, M. (1997). Student perception, mathematical problem solving, and learning disabilities. *Remedial and Special Education, 18,* 46–53.

Montague, M., & Graves, A. (1992). Teaching narrative composition to students with learning disabilities. In M. Pressley, K. Harris, & J. T. Guthrie (Eds.), *Promoting academic competence and literacy in schools* (pp. 261–276). New York: Academic Press.

Montague, M., Graves, A., & Leavell, A. (1991). Planning, procedural facilitation, and narrative composition of junior high students with learning disabilities. *Learning Disabilities Research and Practice, 6,* 219–224.

Murphy, S. T. (1992). *On being L.D.: Perspectives and strategies of young adults.* New York: Teachers College Press.

National Joint Committee on Learning Disabilities. (1989, September 18). Letter from NJCLD to member organizations. Topic: Modifications to the NJCLD definition of learning disabilities. Washington, DC: Author.

Nelson, J. S., Epstein, M. H., Bursuck, W. D., Jayanthi, M., & Sawyer, V. (1998). The preferences of middle school students for homework adaptations made by general education teachers. *Learning Disabilities Research and Practice, 13,* 109–117.

Olson, R., Wise, B., Conners, F., Rack, J., & Fulker, D. (1989). Specific deficits in component reading and language skills: Genetic and environmental influences. *Journal of Learning Disabilities, 22,* 339–348.

Pennington, B. F. (1990). Annotation: The genetics of dyslexia. *Journal of Child Psychology and Child Psychiatry, 31,* 193–201.

Pressley, M., Hogan, K., Wharton-McDonald, R., Mistretta, J., & Ettenberger, S. (1996). The challenges of instructional scaffolding: The challenges of instruction that supports student thinking. *Learning Disabilities Research and Practice, 11,* 138–146.

Psychological Corporation (1992). *Wechsler Individual Achievement Test.* San Antonio, TX: Author.

Reiff, H. B., & Gerber, P. J. (1992). Adults with learning disabilities. In N. N. Singh & D. L. Beale (Eds.), *Current perspectives in learning disabilities: Nature, theory, and treatment* (pp. 170–198). New York: Springer-Verlag.

Reiff, H. B., Gerber, P. J., & Ginsberg, R. (1997). *Exceeding expectations: Successful adults with learning disabilities.* Austin, TX: Pro-Ed.

Riccio, C. A., Gonzalez, J. J., & Hynd, G. W. (1994). Attention-deficit hyperactivity disorder (ADHD) and learning disabilities. *Learning Disability Quarterly, 17,* 311–322.

Schulte-Korne, G., Deimel, W., Muller, K., Gutenbrunner, C., & Remschmidt, H. (1996). Familial aggregation of spelling disability. *Journal of Child Psychology and Psychiatry, 37,* 817–822.

Seligman, M. E. (1992). *Helplessness: On depression, development and death.* San Francisco: W. H. Freeman.

Sexton, M., Harris, K. R., & Graham, S. (1998). Self-regulated strategy development and the writing process: Effects on essay writing and attributions. *Exceptional Children, 64,* 295–311.

Shaywitz, S. E., & Shaywitz, B. A. (1987). Attention deficit disorder: Current perspectives. Paper presented at National Conference on Learning Disabilities, National Institutes of Child Health and Human Development (NIH), Bethesda, MD.

Shaywitz, S. E., Shaywitz, B. A., Fletcher, J. M., & Escobar, M. D. (1990). Prevalence of reading disability in boys and girls: Results of the Connecticut Longitudinal Study. *Journal of the American Medical Association, 264,* 998–1002.

Shaywitz, S. E., Shaywitz, B. A., Pugh, K. R., Fulbright, R. K., Constable, R. T., Mencl, W. E., Shankweiler, D. P., Liberman, A. M., Skudlarski, P., Fletcher, J. M., Katz, L., Marchione, K. E., Lacadie, C., Gatenby, C., & Gore, J. C. (1998). Functional disruption in the organization of the brain for reading in dyslexia. *Neurobiology, 95,* 2636–2641.

Short, E. J., & Weissberg-Benchell, J. (1989). The triple alliance for learning: Cognition, metacognition, and motivation. In C. B. McCormick, G. E. Miller, & M. Pressley (Eds.), *Cognitive strategy research: From basic research to educational applications* (pp. 33–63). New York: Springer-Verlag.

Siperstein, G. N. (1988). Students with learning disabilities in college: The need for a programmatic approach to critical transitions. *Journal of Learning Disabilities, 21,* 431–436.

Skinner, M. E. (1998). Promoting self-advocacy among college students with learning disabilities. *Intervention in School and Clinic, 33,* 278–283.

Slovak, I. (Ed.). (1995). BOSC directory: Facilities for people with learning disabilities. Congers, NY: BOSC.

Spekman, N. J., Goldberg, R. J., & Herman, K. L. (1992). Learning disabled children grow up: A search for factors related to success in the young adult years. *Learning Disabilities Research and Practice, 7,* 161–170.

Stanovich, K. E. (1991). Reading disability: Assessment issues. In H. L. Swanson (Ed.), *Handbook of assessment of learning disabilities: Theory, research, and practice* (pp. 147–175). Austin, TX: Pro-Ed.

Stone, C. A. (1998). The metaphor of scaffolding: Its utility for the field of learning disabilities. *Journal of Learning Disabilities, 31,* 344–364.

Swanson, H. L. (Ed.). (1987). *Memory and learning disabilities: Advances in learning and behavioral disabilities.* Greenwich, CT: J.A.I. Press.

Swanson, H. L., & Hoskyn, M. (in press). Experimental intervention research for students with learning disabilities: A meta-analysis of treatment outcomes. *Review of Educational Research.*

Swanson, P. N., & De La Paz, S. (1998). Teaching effective comprehension strategies to students with learning and reading disabilities. *Intervention in School and Clinic, 33,* 209–218.

Taylor, R. L. (1997). *Assessment of exceptional students: Educational and psychological procedures* (4th ed.). Boston: Allyn & Bacon.

Thomas, C. H., & Thomas, J. L. (Eds.). (1991). *Directory of college facilities and services for people with learning disabilities* (3rd. ed.). Phoenix, AZ: Oryx Press.

Torgesen, J. K. (1977). The role of nonspecific factors in the task performance of learning disabled children: A theoretical assessment. *Journal of Learning Disabilities, 10,* 27–34.

Torgesen, J. K. (1988). Studies of children with learning disabilities who perform poorly on memory span tasks. *Journal of Learning Disabilities, 21,* 605–612.

Torgesen, J. K., & Kail, R. V. (1980). Memory processes in exceptional children. In B. K. Keogh (Ed.), *Advances in special education. Vol. 1: Basic constructs and theoretical orientations.* Greenwich, CT: J.A.I. Press.

U.S. Department of Education. (1992). *Fourteenth annual report to Congress on the implementation of the Individuals with Disabilities Education Act.* Washington, DC: Author.

U.S. Department of Education. (1997). *Nineteenth annual report to Congress on the implementation of the Individuals with Disabilities Education Act.* Washington, DC: Author.

Vaughn, S., & Lancelotta, G. X. (1990). Teaching interpersonal social skills to low accepted students: Peer-pairing versus no peer-pairing. *Journal of School Psychology, 28,* 181–188.

Vaughn, S., Lancelotta, G. X., & Minnis, S. (1988). Social strategy training and peer involvement: Increasing peer acceptance of a female, LD student. *Learning Disabilities Focus, 4,* 32–37.

Vaughn, S., McIntosh, R., & Spencer-Rowe, J. (1991). Peer rejection is a stubborn thing: Increasing peer acceptance of rejected students with learning disabilities. *Learning Disabilities Research and Practice, 6,* 83–88.

Vaughn, S., & Sinagub, J. (1998). Social competence of students with learning disabilities: Interventions and issues. In B. Y. L. Wong (Ed.), *Learning about learning disabilities* (2nd ed., pp. 453–487). San Diego, CA: Academic Press.

Vellutino, F. R. (1987). Dyslexia. *Scientific American, 256*(3), 34–41.

Werner, H., & Strauss, A. A. (1941). Pathology of figure-background relation in the child. *Journal of Abnormal and Social Psychology, 36,* 236–248.

West, T. G. (1997). *In the mind's eye: Visual thinkers, gifted people with dyslexia and other learning difficulties, computer images and the ironies of creativity.* Amerherst, NY: Prometheus Books.

Willis, W. G., Hooper, S. R., & Stone, B. H. (1992). Neurological theories of learning disabilities. In N. N. Singh & D. L. Beale (Eds.), *Current perspectives in learning disabilities: Nature, theory, and treatment* (pp. 201–245). New York: Springer-Verlag.

Willows, D. M. (1998). Visual processes in learning disabilities. In B. Y. L. Wong (Ed.), *Learning about learning disabilities* (2nd ed., pp. 203–236). San Diego, CA: Academic Press.

Witte, R. H., Philips, L., & Kakela, M. (1998). Job satisfaction of college graduates with learning disabilities. *Journal of Learning Disabilities, 31,* 259–265.

Zigmond, N. (1990). Rethinking secondary programs for students with learning disabilities. *Focus on Exceptional Children, 23*(1), 1–22.

Chapter 6

Abramowitz, A. J., Reid, M. J., & O'Toole, K. (1994). *The role of task timing in the treatment of ADHD.* Paper presented at the Association for Advancement of Behavior Therapy, San Diego, CA.

American Psychiatric Association. (1994). *Diagnostic and statistical manual of mental disorders* (4th ed.). Washington, DC: Author.

Aronson, M., Hagberg, B., & Gillberg, C. (1997). Attention deficits and autistic spectrum problems in children exposed to alcohol during gestation: A follow-up study. *Developmental Medicine and Child Neurology, 39,* 583–587.

Aylward, E. H., Reiss, A. L., Reader, M. J., Brown, J. E., & Denckla, M. B. (1996). Basal ganglia volumes in children with attention-deficit hyperactivity disorder. *Journal of Child Neurology, 11,* 112–115.

Barkley, R. A. (1997). Behavioral inhibition, sustained attention, and executive functions: Constructing a unifying theory of ADHD. *Psychological Bulletin, 121,* 65–94.

Barkley, R. A. (1998). *Attention-deficit hyperactivity disorder: A handbook for diagnosis and treatment.* New York: Guilford Press.

Barkley, R. A., & Murphy, K. R. (1998). *Attention-deficit hyperactivity disorder: A clinical workbook* (2nd ed.). New York: Guilford Press.

Berquin, M. D., Giedd, J. N., Jacobsen, L. K., Hamburger, S. D., Krain, A. L., Rapoport, J. L., & Castellanos, F. X. (1998). Cerebellum in attention-deficit hyperactivity disorder. *Neurology, 50,* 1087–1093.

Biederman, J., Faraone, S. V., Mick, E., Spencer, T., Wilens, T., Kiely, K., Guite, J., Ablon, J. S., Reed, E., & Warburton, R. (1995). High risk for attention deficit hyperactivity disorder among children of parents with childhood onset of the disorder: A pilot study. *American Journal of Psychiatry, 152,* 431–435.

Biederman, J., Newcorn, J., & Sprich, S. (1991). Comorbidity of attention deficit hyperactivity disorder with conduct, depressive, anxiety, and other disorders. *American Journal of Psychiatry, 148,* 564–577.

Biederman, J., Wilens, T., Mick, E., Faraone, S. V., & Spencer, T. (1998). Does attention-deficit hyperactivity disorder impact the developmental course of drug and alcohol abuse and dependence? *Biological Psychiatry, 44,* 269–273.

Birch, H. G. (1964). Brain damage in children: The biological and social aspects. Baltimore: Williams & Wilkins.

Cantwell, D. P. (1979). The "hyperactive child." *Hospital Practice, 14,* 65–73.

Castellanos, F. X. (1997). Toward a pathophysiology of attention-deficit/hyperactivity disorder. *Clinical Pediatrics, 36,* 381–393.

Castellanos, F. X., Giedd, J. N., Marsh, W. L., Hamburger, S. D., Vaituzis, A. C., Dickstein, D. P., Sarfatti, S. E., Vauss, Y. C., Snell, J. W., Lange, N., Kaysen, D., Krain, A. L., Ritchie, G. F., Rajapakse, J. C., & Rapoport, J. L. (1996). Quantitative brain magnetic resonance imaging in attention-deficit hyperactivity disorder. *Archives of General Psychiatry, 53,* 607–616.

Conners, C. K. (1989a). *Conners Teacher Rating Scale–28.* Tonawanda, NY: Multi-Health Systems.

Conners, C. K. (1989b). *Conners Teacher Rating Scale–39.* Tonawanda, NY: Multi-Health Systems.

Crenshaw, T. M., Kavale, K. A., Forness, S. R., & Reeve, R. E. (1999). Attention deficit hyperactivity disorder and the efficacy of stimulant medication: A meta-analysis. In T. Scruggs & M. Mastropieri (Eds.), *Advances in learning and behavioral disabilities, Vol. 13.* (pp. 135–165). Greenwich, CT: JAI Press.

Cruickshank, W. M., Bentzen, F. A., Ratzeburg, F. H., & Tannhauser, M. T. (1961). *A teaching method of brain-injured and hyperactive children.* Syracuse, NY: Syracuse University Press.

Cruickshank, W. M., Bice, H. V., & Wallen, N. E. (1957). *Perception and cerebral palsy.* Syracuse: Syracuse University Press.

DuPaul, G. J., Barkley, R. A., & Connor, D. F. (1998). Stimulants. In R. A. Barkley (Ed.), *Attention-deficit hyperactivity disorder: A handbook for diagnosis and treatment* (pp. 510–551). New York: Guilford Press.

DuPaul, G. J., & Eckert, T. L. (1997). The effects of school-based interventions for attention deficit hyperactivity disorder: A meta-analysis. *School Psychology Review, 26,* 5–27.

DuPaul, G. J., Eckert, T. L., & McGoey, K. E. (1997). Interventions for students with attention-deficit/hyperactivity disorder: One size does not fit all. *School Psychology Review, 26,* 369–381.

DuPaul, G. J., & Ervin, R. A. (1996). Functional assessment of behaviors related to attention-deficit hyperactivity disorder: Linking assessment to intervention design. *Behavior Therapy, 27,* 601–622.

DuPaul, G. J., Power, D. T. J., Anastopolous, A. D., & Reid, R. (1998). *ADHD Rating Scale–IV: Checklists, norms, and clinical interpretations.* New York: Guilford Press.

Erhardt, D., & Hinshaw, S. P. (1994). Initial sociometric impressions of attention-deficit hyperactivity disorder and comparison boys: Predictions from social behaviors and from nonbehavioral variables. *Journal of Consulting and Clinical Psychology, 62,* 833–842.

Ernst, M., Zametkin, A. J., Matochik, J. A., Jons, P. H., & Cohen, R. M. (1998). DOPA decarboxylase activity in attention deficit hyperactivity disorder adults. A [fluorine–18]fluorodopa positron emission tomographic study. *The Journal of Neuroscience, 18,* 5901–5907.

Ervin, R. A., DuPaul, G. J., Kern, L., & Friman, P. C. (1998). Classroom-based functional and adjunctive assessments: Proactive approaches to intervention selection for adolescents with attention deficit hyperactivity disorder. *Journal of Applied Behavior Analysis, 31,* 65–78.

Filipek, P. A., Semrud-Clikeman, M., Steingard, R. J., Renshaw, P. F., Kennedy, D. N., & Biederman, J. (1997). Volumetric MRI analysis comparing subjects having attention-deficit hyperactivity disorder with normal controls. *Neurology, 48,* 589–601.

Forness, S. R., Kavale, K. A. (in press). Impact of ADHD on school systems. In P. Jensen & J. R. Cooper (Eds.), *NIH consensus conference on ADHD.*

Forness, S. R., Kavale, K. K., & Crenshaw, T. M. (in press). Stimulant medication revisited: Effective treatment of children with ADHD. *Journal of Emotional and Behavioral Disorders.*

Gillis, J. J., Gilger, J. W., Pennington, B. F., & DeFries, C. (1992). Attention deficit disorder in reading-disabled twins: Evidence for a genetic etiology. *Journal of Abnormal Child Psychology, 20,* 303–315.

Glynn, E. L., & Thomas, J. D. (1974). Effect of cueing on self-control of classroom behavior. *Journal of Applied Behavior Analysis, 7,* 299–306.

Glynn, E. L., Thomas, J. D., & Shee, S. M. (1973). Behavioral self-control of on-task behavior in an elementary classroom. *Journal of Applied Behavior Analysis, 6,* 105–113.

Goldstein, K. (1936). The modification of behavior consequent to cerebral lesions. *Psychiatric Quarterly, 10,* 586–610.

Goldstein, K. (1939). *The organism.* New York: American Book.

Hale, J. B., Hoeppner, J. B., DeWitt, M. B., Coury, D. L., Ritacco, D. G., & Trommer, B. (1998). Evaluating medication response in ADHD: Cognitive, behavioral, and single-subject methodology. *Journal of Learning Disabilities, 31,* 595–607.

Hallahan, D. P., & Cottone, E. A. (1997). Attention deficit hyperactivity disorder. In T. E. Scruggs & M. A. Mastropieri (Eds.), *Advances in learning and behavioral disabilities, Vol. 11* (pp. 27–67). Greenwich, CT: JAI Press.

Hallowell, E. M., & Ratey, J. J. (1994). *Driven to distraction.* New York: Touchstone.

Hallowell, E. M., & Ratey, J. J. (1996). *Answers to distraction.* New York: Bantam Books.

Hoffmann, H. (1865). Die Geschichte vom Zappel-Philipp [The Story of Fidgety Philip]. *Der Struwwelpeter.* Germany: Pestalozzi-Verlag.

Horner, R. H., & Carr, E. G. (1997). Behavioral support for students with severe disabilities: Functional assessment and comprehensive intervention. *Journal of Special Education, 31,* 1–11.

Hynd, G. W., Hern, K. L., Novey, E. S., Eliopulos, D., Marshall, R., Gonzalez, J. J., & Voeller, K. K. (1993). Attention deficit hyperactivity disorder and asymmetry of the caudate nucleus. *Journal of Child Neurology, 8,* 339–347.

Hynd, G. W., Semrud-Clikeman, M., Lorys, A. R., Novey, E. S., & Eliopulos, D. (1990). Brain morphology in developmental dyslexia and attention deficit/hyperactivity. *Archives of Neurology, 47,* 919–926.

Kaminester, D. D. (1997). Attention deficit hyperactivity disorder and methylphenidate: When society misunderstands medicine. *McGill Journal of Medicine, 3,* 105–114.

Kewley, G. D. (1998). Personal paper: Attention deficit hyperactivity disorder is underdiagnosed and undertreated in Britain. *British Medical Journal, 316,* 1594–1596.

Kohn, A. (1993). *Punished by rewards: The trouble with gold stars, incentive plans, A's, praise, and other bribes.* Boston: Houghton Mifflin.

Lambert, N. M., & Hartsough, C. S. (1998). Prospective study of tobacco smoking and substance dependencies among samples of ADHD and non-ADHD participants. *Journal of Learning Disabilities, 31,* 533–544.

Landau, S., Milich, R., & Diener, M. B. (1998). Peer relations of children with attention-deficit hyperactivity disorder. *Reading & Writing Quarterly: Overcoming Learning Difficulties, 14,* 83–105.

Levy, F., Barr, C., & Sunohara, G. (1998). Directions of aetiologic research on attention deficit hyperactivity disorder. *Australian & New Zealand Journal of Psychiatry, 32,* 97–103.

Lloyd, J. W., Hallahan, D. P., Kauffman, J. M., & Keller, C. E. (1998). Academic problems. In R. J. Morris & T. R. Kratochwill (Eds.), *The practice of child therapy* (pp. 167–198). Boston: Allyn & Bacon.

Lloyd, J. W., Landrum, T. J., & Hallahan, D. P. (1991). Self-monitoring applications for classroom intervention. In G. Stoner, M. R. Shinn, & H. M. Walker (Eds.), *Interventions for achievement and behavior problems* (pp. 201–239). Silver Spring, MD: National Association of School Psychologists.

Lombroso, P. J., Scahill, L. D., Chappell, P. A., Pauls, D. L., Cohen, D. J., & Leckman, J. F. (1995). Tourette's syndrome: A multigenerational, neuropsychiatric disorder. In W. J. Weiner & A. E. Lang (Eds.), *Behavioral neurology of movement disorders* (pp. 305–318). New York: Raven Press.

Lou, H. C., Henriksen, L., & Bruhn, P. (1984). Focal cerebral hypoperfusion in children with dysphasia and/or attention deficit disorder. *Archives of Neurology, 41,* 825–829.

Lou, H. C., Henriksen, L., Bruhn, P., Borner, H., & Nielsen, J. B. (1989). Striatal dysfunction in attention deficit and hyperkinetic disorder. *Archives of Neurology, 46,* 48–52.

Mannuzza, S., Klein, R. G., Bessler, A., Malloy, P., & Hynes, M. E. (1997). Educational and occupational outcome of hyperactive boys grown up. *Journal of the American Academy of Child and Adolescent Psychiatry, 36,* 1222–1227.

Mannuzza, S., Klein, R. G., Bessler, A., Malloy, P., & LaPadula, M. (1993). Adult outcome of hyperactive boys. *Archives of General Psychiatry, 50,* 565–576.

Marshall, R. M., Hynd, G. W., Handwerk, M. J., & Hall, J. (1997). Academic underachievement in ADHD subtypes. *Journal of Learning Disabilities, 30,* 635–642.

Mathes, M. Y., & Bender, W. N. (1997). The effects of self-monitoring on children with attention-deficit/hyperactivity disorder who are receiving pharmacological interventions. *Remedial and Special Education, 18,* 121–128.

Milberger, S., Biederman, J., Faraone, S. V., Guite, J., & Tsuang, M. T. (1997). Pregnancy, delivery and infancy complications and attention deficit hyperactivity disorder: Issues of gene-environment interaction. *Biological Psychiatry, 41,* 65–75.

Milberger, S., Biederman, J., Faraone, S. V., & Jones, J. (1998). Further evidence of an association between maternal smoking during pregnancy and attention deficit hyperactivity disorder: Findings from a high-risk sample of siblings. *Journal of Clinical Child Psychology, 27,* 352–358.

Murphy, K. R. (1998). Psychological counseling of adults with ADHD. In R. A. Barkley (Ed.), *Attention-deficit hyperactivity disorder: A handbook for diagnosis and treatment.* (pp. 582–591). New York: Guilford Press.

National Institutes of Health (November, 1998). Diagnosis and treatment of attention deficit hyperactivity disorder. *NIH Consensus Statement, 16*(2).

Needleman, H. L., Schell, A., Bellinger, D. C., Leviton, A., & Alfred, E. D. (1990). The long-term effects of exposure to low doses of lead in childhood: An 11-year follow-up report. *New England Journal of Medicine, 322,* 83–88.

Pasamanick, B., Lilienfeld, A. M., & Rogers, M. E. (1956). Pregnancy experience and the development of behavior disorders in children. *American Journal of Psychiatry, 112,* 613–617.

Pfiffner, L. J., & Barkley, R. A. (1998). Treatment of ADHD in school settings. In R. A. Barkley (Ed.), *Attention-deficit hyperactivity disorder: A handbook for diagnosis and treatment* (pp. 458–490). New York: Guilford Press.

Pinel, J. P. J. (1997). *Biopsychology* (3rd ed.). Boston: Allyn & Bacon.

Richters, J. E., Arnold, L. E., Abikoff, H., Conners, C. K., Greenhill, L. L., Hechtman, L., Hinshaw, S. P., Pelham, W. E., & Swanson, J. M. (1995). NIMH collaborative multisite multimodal treatment study of children with ADHD: Background and rationale. *Journal of the Academy of Child and Adolescent Psychiatry, 34,* 987–1000.

Rubia, K., Oosterlann, J., Sergeant, J. A., Brandeis, D., & vanLeeuwen, T. (1998). Inhibitory dysfunction in hyperactive boys. *Behavioral Brain Research, 94,* 25–32.

Sagvolden, T., & Sergeant, J. A. (1998). Attention deficit/hyperactivity disorder—from brain dysfunctions to behaviour. *Behavioural Brain Research, 94,* 1–10.

Shapiro, E. S., DuPaul, G. J., & Bradley-Klug, K. L. (1998). Self-management as a strategy to improve the classroom behavior of adolescents with ADHD. *Journal of Learning Disabilities, 31,* 545–555.

Shelton, T. L., Barkley, R. A., Crosswait, C., Moorehouse, M., Fletcher, K., Barrett, M. S., Jenkins, L., & Metevia, L. (in press). Early intervention with preschool children with aggressive and hyperactive-impulsive behavior: Two-year post-treatment follow-up. *Journal of Abnormal Child Psychology.*

Sherman, D. K., Iacono, W. G., & McGue, M. K. (1997). Attention-deficit hyperactivity disorder dimensions: A twin study of inattention and impulsivity-hyperactivity. *Journal of the American Academy of Child and Adolescent Psychiatry, 36,* 745–753.

Sleator, E. K., & Ullmann, R. K. (1981). Can the physician diagnose hyperactivity in the office? *Pediatrics, 67,* 13–17.

Solanto, M. V. (1998). Neuropsychopharmacological mechanisms of stimulant drug action in attention-deficit hyperactivity disorder: A review and integration. *Behavioural Brain Research, 94,* 127–152.

Spencer, T., Biederman, J., Wilens, T., Harding, M., O'Donnell, D., & Griffin, S. (1996). Pharmacotherapy of attention-deficit hyperactivity disorder across the life cycle. *Journal of the American Academy of Child and Adolescent Psychiatry, 35,* 409–432.

Stevenson, J. (1992). Evidence for a genetic etiology in hyperactive children. *Behavior Genetics, 22,* 337–344.

Still, G. F. (1902). Some abnormal psychical conditions in children. *The Lancet, 1,* 1008–1012, 1077–1082, 1163–1168.

Strauss, A. A., & Werner, H. (1942). Disorders of conceptual thinking in the brain-injured child. *Journal of Nervous and Mental Disease, 96,* 153–172.

Swanson, J., Castellanos, F. X., Murias, M., LaHoste, G., & Kennedy, J. (1998). Cognitive neuroscience of attention deficit hyperactivity disorder and hyperkinetic disorder. *Current Opinion in Neurobiology, 8,* 263–271.

Swanson, J. M., Sergeant, J. A., Taylor, E., Sonuga-Barke, E. J. S., Jensen, P. S., & Cantwell, D. P. (1998). Attention-deficit hyperactivity disorder and hyperkinetic disorder. *The Lancet, 351,* 429–433.

Weiss, G., Hechtman, L., Milroy, T., & Perlman, T. (1985). Psychiatric status of hyperactives as adults. *Journal of the American Academy of Child and Adolescent Psychiatry, 24,* 211–220.

Werner, H., & Strauss, A. A. (1939). Types of visuo-motor activity in their relation to low and high performance ages. *Proceedings of the American Association on Mental Deficiency, 44,* 163–168.

Werner, H., & Strauss, A. A. (1941). Pathology of figure-background relation in the child. *Journal of Abnormal and Social Psychology, 36,* 236–248.

Wilens, T. E., & Biederman, J. (1992). Pediatric psychopharmacology: The stimulants. *Pediatric Clinics of North America, 15*(1), 191–222.

Wolf, S. S., Jones, D. W., Knable, M. B., Gorey, J. G., Lee, K. S., Hyde, T. M., Coppola, R., & Weinberger, D. R. (1996). Tourette syndrome: Prediction of phenotypic variation in monozygotic twins by caudate nucleus D2 receptor gene. *Science, 273,* 1225–1227.

Chapter 7

Achenbach, T. M. (1985). *Assessment and taxonomy of child and adolescent psychopathology.* Newbury Park, CA: Sage.

Achenbach, T. M., Howell, C. T., Quay, H. C., & Conners, C. K. (1991). National survey of problems and competencies among four- to sixteen-year-olds: Parents' reports for normative and clinical samples. *Monographs of the Society for Research in Child Development, 56*(3, Serial No. 225).

Alberto, P., & Troutman, A. (1995). *Applied behavior analysis for teachers* (4th ed.). Columbus, OH: Merrill/Macmillan.

Allison, M. (1993). Exploring the link between violence and brain injury. *Headlines, 4*(2), 12–17.

Anderson, J., & Werry, J. S. (1994). Emotional and behavioral problems. In I. B. Pless (Ed.), *The epidemiology of childhood disorders* (pp. 304–338). New York: Oxford University Press.

Asarnow, R. F., Asamen, J., Granholm, E., Sherman, T., Watkins, J. M., & Williams, M. E. (1994). Cognitive/neuropsychological studies of children with a schizophrenic disorder. *Schizophrenia Bulletin, 20,* 647–669.

Asarnow, J. R., Tompson, M. C., & Goldstein, M. J. (1994). Childhood-onset schizophrenia: A follow-up study. *Schizophrenia Bulletin, 20,* 599–617.

Bandura, A. (1973). *Aggression: A social learning analysis.* Englewood Cliffs, NJ: Prentice-Hall.

Bandura, A. (1986). *Social foundations of thought and action: A social cognitive theory.* Englewood Cliffs, NJ: Prentice-Hall.

Bateman, B. D., & Chard, D. J. (1995). Legal demands and constraints on placement decisions. In J. M. Kauffman, J. W. Lloyd, D. P. Hallahan, & T. A. Astuto (Eds.), *Issues in educational placement: Students with emotional and behavioral disorders* (pp. 285–316). Hillsdale, NJ: Erlbaum.

Bateman, B. D., & Linden, M. A. (1998). *Better IEPs: How to develop legally correct and educationally useful programs* (3rd ed.). Longmont, CO: Sopris West.

Baumeister, A. A., Kupstas, F., & Klindworth, L. M. (1990). New morbidity: Implications for prevention of children's disabilities. *Exceptionality, 1,* 1–16.

Becker, J. V., & Bonner, B. (1997). Sexual and other abuse of children. In R. J. Morris & T. R. Kratochwill (Eds.), *The practice of child therapy* (3rd ed., pp. 367–389). Boston: Allyn & Bacon.

Becker, W. C. (1964). Consequences of different kinds of parental discipline. In M. L. Hoffman & L. W. Hoffman (Eds.), *Review of child development research* (Vol. 1). New York: Russell Sage Foundation.

Bergland, M., & Hoffbauer, D. (1996). New opportunities for students with traumatic brain injuries. *Teaching Exceptional Children, 28*(2), 54–56.

Bettelheim, B. (1950). *Love is not enough.* New York: Macmillan.

Bettelheim, B. (1967). *The empty fortress.* New York: Free Press.

Bower, E. M. (1981). *Early identification of emotionally handicapped children in school* (3rd ed.). Springfield, IL: Charles C. Thomas.

Bower, E. M. (1982). Defining emotional disturbance: Public policy and research. *Psychology in the Schools, 19,* 55–60.

Brandenburg, N. A., Friedman, R. M., & Silver, S. E. (1990). The epidemiology of childhood psychiatric disorders: Prevalence findings from recent studies. *Journal of the American Academy of Child and Adolescent Psychiatry, 29,* 76–83.

Brigham, F. J., & Kauffman, J. M. (1998). Creating supportive environments for students with emotional or behavioral disorders. *Effective School Practices, 17*(2), 25–35.

Carson, R. R., Sitlington, P. L., & Frank, A. R. (1995). Young adulthood for individuals with behavioral disorders: What does it hold? *Behavioral Disorders, 20,* 127–135.

Charlop-Christy, M. H., Schreibman, L., Pierce, K., & Kurtz, P. F. (1997). Childhood autism. In R. J. Morris & T. R. Kratochwill (Eds.), *The practice of child therapy* (3rd ed., pp. 271–389). Boston: Allyn & Bacon.

Cline, D. H. (1990). A legal analysis of policy initiatives to exclude handicapped/disruptive students from special education. *Behavioral Disorders, 15,* 159–173.

Costello, E. J., Messer, S. C., Bird, H. R., Cohen, P., & Reinherz, H. Z. (1998). The prevalence of serious emotional disturbance: A re-analysis of community studies. *Journal of Child and Family Studies, 7,* 411–432.

Costenbader, V., & Buntaine, R. (1999). Diagnostic discrimination between social maladjustment and emotional disturbance: An empirical study. *Journal of Emotional and Behavioral Disorders, 7,* 1–10.

Crockett, J. B., & Kauffman, J. M. (1999). *The least restrictive environment: Its origins and interpretations in special education.* Mahwah, NJ: Erlbaum.

Deaton, A. V. (1994). Changing the behaviors of students with acquired brain injury. In R. C. Savage & G. F. Wolcott (Eds.), *Educational dimensions of acquired brain injury* (pp. 257–276). Austin, TX: Pro-Ed.

Deaton, A. V., & Waaland, P. (1994). Psychosocial effects of acquired brain injury. In R. C. Savage & G. F. Wolcott (Eds.), *Educational dimensions of acquired brain injury* (pp. 239–255). Austin, TX: Pro-Ed.

Duke, D. L., Griesdorn, J., & Kraft, M. (1998, March). *A school of their own: A status check of Virginia's alternative high schools for at-risk students.* Charlottesville, VA: Thomas Jefferson Center for Educational Design.

Duncan, B. B., Forness, S. R., & Hartsough, C. (1995). Students identified as seriously emotionally disturbed in school-based day treatment: Cognitive, psychiatric, and special education characteristics. *Behavioral Disorders, 20,* 238–252.

Dunlap, G., dePerczel, M., Clarke, S., Wilson, D., Wright, S., White, R., & Gomez, A. (1994). Choice making to promote adaptive behavior for students with emotional and behavioral challenges. *Journal of Applied Behavior Analysis, 27,* 505–518.

Edgar, E., & Siegel, S. (1995). Postsecondary scenarios for troubled and troubling youth. In J. M. Kauffman, J. W. Lloyd, D. P. Hallahan, & T. A. Astuto (Eds.), *Issues in educational placement: Students with emotional or behavioral disorders* (pp. 251–283). Hillsdale, NJ: Erlbaum.

Epstein, M. H., & Sharma, J. (1997). *Behavioral and Emotional Rating Scale (BERS): A strength-based approach to assessment.* Austin, TX: Pro-Ed.

Farmer, T. W., Farmer, E. M. Z., & Gut, D. (1999). Implications of social development research for school based intervention for aggressive youth with emotional and behavioral disorders. *Journal of Emotional and Behavioral Disorders, 7*(3).

Feeney, T. J., & Urbanczyk, B. (1994). Behavior as communication. In R. C. Savage & G. F. Wolcott (Eds.), *Educational dimensions of acquired brain injury* (pp. 277–302). Austin, TX: Pro-Ed.

Forness, S. R., & Kavale, K. A. (1997). Defining emotional or behavioral disorders in school and related services. In J. W. Lloyd, E. J. Kameenui, & D. Chard (Eds.), *Issues in educating students with disabilities* (pp. 45–61). Mahwah, NJ: Erlbaum.

Forness, S. R., & Knitzer, J. (1992). A new proposed definition and terminology to replace "serious emotional disturbance" in Individuals with Disabilities Act. *School Psychology Review, 21,* 12–20.

Freedman, J. (1993). *From cradle to grave: The human face of poverty in America.* New York: Atheneum.

Fuchs, D., Fuchs, L. S., Fernstrom, P., & Hohn, M. (1991). Toward a responsible reintegration of behaviorally disordered students. *Behavioral Disorders, 16,* 133–147.

Gable, R. A. (1999). Functional assessment in school settings. *Behavioral Disorders.*

Garmezy, N. (1987). Stress, competence, and development: Continuities in the study of schizophrenic adults, children vulnerable to psychopathology, and the search for stress-resistant children. *American Journal of Orthopsychiatry, 57,* 159–174.

Gottesman, I. I. (1991). *Schizophrenia genesis: The origins of madness.* New York: W. H. Freeman.

Guetzloe, E. C. (1991). *Depression and suicide: Special education students at risk.* Reston, VA: Council for Exceptional Children.

Gunter, P. L., Hummel, J. H., & Conroy, M. A. (1998). Increasing correct academic responding: An effective intervention strategy to decrease behavioral problems. *Effective School Practices, 17*(2), 36–54.

Hallenbeck, B. A., & Kauffman, J. M. (1995). How does observational learning affect the behavior of students with emotional or behavioral disorders? A review of research. *Journal of Special Education, 29,* 45–71.

Harris, J. R. (1995) Where is the child's environment? A group socialization theory of development. *Psychological Review, 102,* 458–489.

Harris, S. L. (1995). Autism. In M. Hersen & R. T. Ammerman (Eds.), *Advanced abnormal child psychology* (pp. 305–317). Hillsdale, NJ: Erlbaum.

Henggeler, S. W. (1989). *Delinquency in adolescence.* Newbury Park, CA: Sage.

Hobbs, N. (1975). *The futures of children.* San Francisco: Jossey-Bass.

Hodgkinson, H . L. (1995). What should we call people? Race, class, and the census for 2000. *Phi Delta Kappan, 77,* 173–179.

Howell, K. W., & Nelson, K. L. (1999). Has public policy exceeded our knowledge base? This is a two part question. *Behavioral Disorders.*

Ialongo, N. S., Vaden-Kiernan, N., & Kellam, S. (1998). Early peer rejection and aggression: Longitudinal relations with adolescent behavior. *Journal of Developmental and Physical Disabilities, 10,* 199–213.

James, M., & Long, N. (1992). Looking beyond behavior and seeing my needs: A red flag interview. *Journal of Emotional and Behavioral Problems, 1*(2), 35–38.

Jordan, D., Goldberg, P., & Goldberg, M. (1991). *A guidebook for parents of children with emotional or behavioral disorders.* Minneapolis: Pacer Center.

Kaslow, N. J., Morris, M. K., & Rehm, L. P. (1997). Childhood depression. In R. J. Morris & T. R. Kratochwill (Eds.), *The practice of child therapy* (3rd ed., pp. 48–90). Boston: Allyn & Bacon.

Kauffman, J. M. (1986). Educating children with behavior disorders. In R. J. Morris & B. Blatt (Eds.), *Special education: Research and trends* (pp. 249–271). New York: Pergamon Press.

Kauffman, J. M. (1997a). *Characteristics of emotional and behavioral disorders of children and youths* (6th ed.). New York: Merrill/Macmillan.

Kauffman, J. M. (1997b). Conclusion: A little of everything, a lot of nothing is an agenda for failure. *Journal of Emotional and Behavioral Disorders, 5,* 76–81.

Kauffman, J. M. (1999). How we prevent the prevention of emotional and behavioral disorders. *Exceptional Children, 65,* 448–468.

Kauffman, J. M., & Hallenbeck, B. A. (Eds.). (1996). Why we need to preserve specialized placements for students with emotional or behavioral disorders [Special issue]. *Canadian Journal of Special Education, 11*(1).

Kauffman, J. M., Lloyd, J. W., Baker, J., & Riedel, T. M. (1995). Inclusion of all students with emotional or behavioral disorders? Let's think again. *Phi Delta Kappan, 76,* 542–546.

Kauffman, J. M., Lloyd, J. W., Hallahan, D. P., & Astuto, T. A. (Eds.). (1995). *Issues in educational placement: Students with emotional and behavioral disorders.* Hillsdale, NJ: Erlbaum.

Kauffman, J. M., Mostert, M. P., Trent, S. C., & Hallahan, D. P. (1998). *Managing classroom behavior: A reflective case-based approach* (2nd ed.). Boston: Allyn & Bacon.

Kauffman, J. M., & Pullen, P. L. (1996). Eight myths about special education. *Focus on Exceptional Children, 28*(5), 1–16.

Kazdin, A. E. (1995). *Conduct disorders in childhood and adolescence* (2nd ed.). Newbury Park, CA: Sage.

Kazdin, A. E. (1989). Developmental psychopathology: Current research, issues, and directions. *American Psychologist, 44,* 180–187.

Kazdin, A. E. (1997). Conduct disorder. In R. J. Morris & T. R. Kratochwill (Eds.), *The practice of child therapy* (3rd ed., pp. 199–270). Boston: Allyn & Bacon.

Kerr, M. M., & Nelson, C. M. (1998). *Strategies for managing behavior problems in the classroom* (3rd ed.). Upper Saddle River, NJ: Prentice-Hall..

Knitzer, J. (1982). *Unclaimed children: The failure of public responsibility to children and adolescents in need on mental health services.* Washington, DC: Children's Defense Fund.

Knitzer, J., Steinberg, Z., & Fleisch, F. (1990). *At the schoolhouse door: An examination of programs and policies for children with behavioral and emotional problems.* New York: Bank Street College of Education.

Kozol, J. (1995, October 1). The kids that society forgot. *The Washington Post,* pp. C1, C4.

Leone, P. E. (Ed.). (1990). *Understanding troubled and troubling youth.* Newbury Park, CA: Sage.

Leone, P. E., Rutherford, R. B., & Nelson, C. M. (1991). *Special education in juvenile corrections.* Reston, VA: Council for Exceptional Children.

Loeber, R., Green S. M., Lahey, B. B., Christ, M. A. G., & Frick, P. J. (1992). Developmental sequences in age of onset of disruptive child behaviors. *Journal of Child and Family Studies, 1,* 21–41.

Lovaas, O. I. (1987). Behavioral treatment and normal educational and intellectual functioning in young autistic children. *Journal of Consulting and Clinical Psychology, 55,* 3–9.

Lozoff, B. (1989). Nutrition and behavior. *American Psychologist, 44,* 231–236.

Martin, R. P. (1992). Child temperament effects on special education: Process and outcomes. *Exceptionality, 3,* 99–115.

McCracken, J. T., Cantwell, D. P., & Hanna, G. L. (1993). Conduct disorder and depression. In E. Klass & H. S. Koplewica (Eds.), *Depression in children and adolescents* (pp. 121–132). New York: Harwood.

McIntyre, T. (1993). Behaviorally disordered youth in correctional settings: Prevalence, programming, and teacher training. *Behavioral Disorders, 18,* 167–176.

Miller, J. G. (1997). African American males in the criminal justice system. *Phi Delta Kappan, 79,* K1-K12.

Moynihan, D. P. (1995, September 21). "I cannot understand how this could be happening." *The Washington Post,* p. A31.

Nelson, C. M., & Kauffman, J. M. (1977). Educational programming for secondary school age delinquent and maladjusted pupils. *Behavioral Disorders, 2,* 102–113.

Nelson, C. M., & Pearson, C. A. (1991). *Integrating services for children and youth with emotional and behavioral disorders.* Reston, VA: Council for Exceptional Children.

Nelson, C. M., Rutherford, R. B., Center, D. B., & Walker, H. M. (1991). Do public schools have an obligation to serve troubled children and youth? *Exceptional Children, 57,* 406–415.

Nelson, C. M., Rutherford, R. B., & Wolford, B. I. (Eds.). (1987). *Special education in the criminal justice system.* Columbus, OH: Merrill/Macmillan.

Nelson, J. R., Roberts, M., Mather, S., & Rutherford, R. J. (1999). Has public policy exceeded our knowledge base? A review of the functional behavioral assessment literature. *Behavioral Disorders.*

Newcomb, M. D., & Bentler, P. M. (1989). Substance use and abuse among children and teenagers. *American Psychologist, 44,* 242–248.

Patterson, G. R., DeBaryshe, B. D., & Ramsey, E. (1989). A developmental perspective on antisocial behavior. *American Psychologist, 44,* 329–335.

Patterson, G. R., Reid, J. B., & Dishion, T. J. (1992). *Antisocial boys.* Eugene, OR: Castalia.

Peacock Hill Working Group. (1991). Problems and promises in special education and related services for children and youth with emotional or behavioral disorders. *Behavioral Disorders, 16,* 299–313.

Plomin, R. (1989). Environment and genes: Determinants of behavior. *American Psychologist, 44,* 105–111.

Pollack, I. W. (1994). Reestablishing an acceptable sense of self. In R. C. Savage & G. F. Wolcott (Eds.), *Educational dimensions of acquired brain injury* (pp. 303–318). Austin, TX: Pro-Ed.

Pomeroy, J. C., & Gadow, K. D. (1997). In R. J. Morris & T. R. Kratochwill (Eds.), *The practice of child therapy* (3rd ed., pp. 419–470). Boston: Allyn & Bacon.

Prior, M., & Werry, J. S. (1986). Autism, schizophrenia, and allied disorders. In H. C. Quay & J. S. Werry (Eds.), *Psychopathological disorders of childhood* (3rd ed.). New York: Wiley.

Quay, H. C. (1986). Classification. In H. C. Quay & J. S. Werry (Eds.), *Psychopathological disorders of childhood* (3rd ed.). New York: Wiley.

Quay, H. C., & Peterson, D. R. (1987). *Manual for the revised behavior problem checklist.* Coral Gables, FL: Author.

Rabian, B., & Silverman, W. K. (1995). Anxiety disorders. In M. Hersen & R. T. Ammerman (Eds.), *Advanced abnormal child psychology* (pp. 235–252). Hillsdale, NJ: Erlbaum.

Reitman, D., & Gross, A. M. (1995). Familial determinants. In M. Hersen & R. T. Ammerman (Eds.), *Advanced abnormal child psychology* (pp. 87–104). Hillsdale, NJ: Erlbaum.

Rhode, G., Jensen, W. R., & Reavis, H. K. (1992). *The tough kid book: Practical classroom management strategies.* Longmont, CO: Sopris West.

Richardson, G. A., McGauhey, P., & Day, N. L. (1995). Epidemiologic considerations. In M. Hersen & R. T. Ammerman (Eds.), *Advanced abnormal child psychology* (pp. 37–48). Hillsdale, NJ: Erlbaum.

Rogers-Adkinson, D., & Griffith, P. (Eds.). (1999). *Communication disorders and children wih psychiatric and behavioral disorders.* San Diego: Singular.

Rogoff, B., & Morelli, G. (1989). Perspectives on children's development from cultural psychology. *American Psychologist, 44,* 343–348.

Rutter, M. (1985). Family and school influences on behavioral development. *Journal of Child Psychology and Psychiatry, 26,* 349–368.

Rutter, M., & Schopler, E. (1987). Autism and pervasive developmental disorders: Concepts and diagnostic issues. *Journal of Autism and Developmental Disabilities, 17,* 159–186.

Sacks, O. (1995). *An anthropologist on Mars: Seven paradoxical tales.* New York: Knopf.

Saigh, P. A. (1997). Posttraumatic stress disorder. In R. J. Morris & T. R. Kratochwill (Eds.), *The practice of child therapy* (3rd ed., pp. 390–418). Boston: Allyn & Bacon.

Schopler, E., & Mesibov, G. B. (Eds.). (1994). *Behavioral issues in autism.* New York: Plenum Press.

Schopler, E., & Mesibov, G. B. (Eds.). (1995). *Learning and cognition in autism.* New York: Plenum Press.

Scott, R. M., & Nelson, C. M. (1999). Functional behavioral assessment: Implications for training and staff development. *Behavioral Disorders.*

Sherburne, S., Utley, B., McConnell, S., & Gannon, J. (1988). Decreasing violent and aggressive theme play among preschool children with behavior disorders. *Exceptional Children, 55,* 166–172.

Siegel, L. J., & Senna, J. J. (1994). *Juvenile delinquency: Theory, practice, and law* (5th ed.). St. Paul, MN: West.

Skiba, R., & Grizzle, K. (1992). Qualifications v. logic and data: Excluding conduct disorders from the SED definition. *School Psychology Review, 21,* 23–28.

Slenkovich, J. E. (1992a). Can the language "social maladjustment" in the SED definition be ignored? *School Psychology Review, 21,* 21–22.

Slenkovich, J. E. (1992b). Can the language "social maladjustment" in the SED definition be ignored? The final words. *School Psychology Review, 21,* 43–44.

Stark, K. D., Ostrander, R., Kurowski, C. A., Swearer, S., & Bowen, B. (1995). Affective and mood disorders. In M. Hersen & R. T. Ammerman (Eds.), *Advanced abnormal child psychology* (pp. 253–282). Hillsdale, NJ: Erlbaum.

Strain, P. S., McConnell, S. R., Carta, J. J., Fowler, S. A., Neisworth, J. T., & Wolery, M. (1992). Behaviorism in early intervention. *Topics in Early Childhood Special Education, 12*(1), 121–141.

Sweeney, D. P., Forness, S. R., Kavale, K. A., & Levitt, J. G. (1997). An update on psychopharmacologic medication: What teachers, clinicians, and parents need to know. *Intervention in School and Clinic, 33,* 4–21, 25.

Talbott, E., & Callahan, K. (1997). Antisocial girls and the development of disruptive behavior disorders. In J. W. Lloyd, E. J. Kameenui, & D. Chard (Eds.), *Issues in educating students with disabilities* (pp. 305–322). Mahwah, NJ: Erlbaum.

Tankersley, M., & Landrum, T. J. (1997). Comorbidity of emotional and behavioral disorders. In J. W. Lloyd, E. J. Kameenui, & D. Chard (Eds.), *Issues in educating students with disabilities* (pp. 153–173). Mahwah, NJ: Erlbaum.

Thomas, A., & Chess, S. (1984). Genesis and evolution of behavioral disorders: From infancy to early adult life. *American Journal of Psychiatry, 141,* 1–9.

Timm, M. A. (1993). The Regional Intervention Program: Family treatment by family members. *Behavioral Disorders, 19,* 34–43.

U.S. Department of Education. (1994). *Sixteenth annual report to Congress on implementation of the Individuals with Disabilities Education Act.* Washington, DC: Author.

U.S. Department of Education. (1997). *Nineteenth annual report to Congress on implementation of the Individuals with Disabilities Education Act.* Washington, DC: Author.

Walker, H. M. (1995). *The acting-out child: Coping with classroom disruption.* Longmont, CO: Sopris West.

Walker, H. M., & Bullis, M. (1991). Behavior disorders and the social context of regular class integration: A conceptual dilemma? In J. W. Lloyd, N. N. Singh, & A. C. Repp (Eds.), *The regular education initiative: Alternative perspectives on concepts, issues, and models.* Sycamore, IL: Sycamore Publishing.

Walker, H. M., Colvin, G., & Ramsey, E. (1995). *Antisocial behavior in school: Strategies and best practices.* Pacific Grove, CA: Brooks/Cole.

Walker, H. M., Forness, S. R., Kauffman, J. M., Epstein, M. H., Gresham, F. M., Nelson, C. M., & Strain, P. S. (1998). Macrosocial validation: Referencing outcomes in behavioral disorders to societal issues and problems. *Behavioral Disorders, 24,* 7–18.

Walker, H. M., Kavanagh, K., Stiller, B., Golly, A., Severson, H., & Feil, E. G. (1998). First Step to Success: An early intervention approach for preventing school antisocial behavior. *Journal of Emotional and Behavioral Disorders, 6,* 66–80.

Walker, H. M., & Severson, H. H. (1990). *Systematic screening for behavior disorders (SSBD): A multiple gating procedure.* Longmont, CO: Sopris West.

Walker, H. M., Severson, H. H., & Feil, E. G. (1994). *The early screening project: A proven child-find process.* Longmont, CO: Sopris West.

Wehby, J. H., Dodge, K. A., & Valente, E. (1993). School behavior of first grade children identified as at-risk for development of conduct problems. *Behavioral Disorders, 19,* 67–78.

Wenar, C., Ruttenberg, B. A., Kalish-Weiss, B., & Wolf, E. G. (1986). The development of normal and autistic children: A comparative study. *Journal of Autism and Developmental Disorders, 16,* 317–333.

Werry, J. S., McClellan, J. M., Andrews, L. K., & Ham, M. (1994). Clinical features and outcome of child and adolescent schizophrenia. *Schizophrenia Bulletin, 20,* 619–630.

Wolf, M. M., Braukmann, C. J., & Ramp, K. A. (1987). Serious delinquent behavior as part of a significantly handicapping condition. *Journal of Applied Behavior Analysis, 20,* 347–359.

Wood, F. H. (Ed.). (1990). When we talk with children: The life space interview [Special section]. *Behavioral Disorders, 15,* 110–126.

Wood, M. M., & Long, N. J. (1991). *Life space intervention: Talking with children and youth in crisis.* Austin, TX: Pro-Ed.

Yell, M. L. (1998). *The law and special education.* Upper Saddle River, NJ: Prentice-Hall.

Yell, M. L., & Shriner, J. G. (1997). The IDEA amendments of 1997: Implications for special and general education teachers, administrators, and teacher trainers. *Focus on Exceptional Children, 30*(1), 1–19.

Chapter 8

Alpert, C. L., & Kaiser, A. P. (1992). Training parents as milieu language teachers. *Journal of Early Intervention, 16*(1), 31–52.

American Speech-Language-Hearing Association (ASHA). (1993). Definitions of communication disorders and variations. *ASHA, 35*(Suppl. 10), 40–41.

Anderson, N. B., & Battle, D. E. (1993). Cultural diversity in the development of language. In D. E. Battle (Ed.), *Communication disorders in multicultural populations* (pp. 158–185). Boston: Andover Medical Publishers.

Audet, L. R., & Tankersley, M. (1999). Implications of communication and behavioral disorders for classroom management: Collaborative intervention techniques. In D. Rogers-Adkinson & P. Griffith (Eds.), *Communication disorders and children with psychiatric and behavioral disorders* (pp. 403–440). San Diego: Singular.

Baca, L., & Amato, C. (1989). Bilingual special education: Training issues. *Exceptional Children, 56,* 168–173.

Battle, D. E. (Ed.). (1993). *Communication disorders in multicultural populations.* Boston: Andover Medical Publishers.

Benson, B. (1995). *Knotted tongues: Stuttering in history and the quest for a cure.* New York: Simon & Schuster.

Bernstein, D. K., & Tiegerman-Farber, E. (1997). *Language and communication disorders in children* (4th ed.). Boston: Allyn & Bacon.

Bernthal, J. E., & Bankson, N. W. (1998). *Articulation and phonological disorders* (4th ed.). Boston: Allyn & Bacon.

Beukelman, D. R. (1991). Magic and cost of communicative competence. *Augmentative and Alternative Communication, 7,* 2–10.

Blank, M., & White, S. J. (1986). Questions: A powerful form of classroom exchange. *Topics in Language Disorders, 6*(2), 1–12.

Blischak, D. M., Loncke, F., & Waller, A. (1997). Intervention for persons with developmental disabilities. In L. L. Lloyd, D. R. Fuller, & H. H. Arvidson (Eds.), *Augmentative and alternative communication: A handbook of principles and practices* (pp. 299–339). Boston: Allyn & Bacon.

Bloodstein, O. (1993). *Stuttering: The search for a cause and cure.* Boston: Allyn & Bacon.

Bloom, L. (1991). *Language development from two to three.* New York: Cambridge University Press.

Blosser, J. L., & DePompei, R. (1989). The head-injured student returns to school: Recognizing and treating deficits. *Topics in Language Disorders, 9*(2), 67–77.

Brookshire, R. H. (1997). *Introduction to neurogenic communication disorders* (5th ed.). St. Louis: Mosby.

Brown, J., & Prelock, P. A. (1995). The impact of regression on language development in autism. *Journal of Autism and Developmental Disorders, 25,* 305–309.

Buzolich, M. J., & Lunger, J. (1995). Empowering system users in peer training. *Augmentative and Alternative Communication, 11,* 37–45.

Calculator, S. N., & Jorgensen, C. M. (1991). Integrating AAC instruction into regular education settings: Expounding on best practices. *Augmentative and Alternative Communication, 7,* 204–212.

Campbell, S. L., Reich, A. R., Klockars, A. J., & McHenry, M. A. (1988). Factors associated with dysphonia in high school cheerleaders. *Journal of Speech and Hearing Disorders, 53,* 175–185.

Cannito, M. P., Yorkston, K. M., & Beukelman, D. R. (Eds.). (1998). *Neuromotor speech disorders: Nature, assessment, and management.* Baltimore: Paul H. Brookes.

Carrow-Woolfolk, E. (1988). *Theory, assessment and intervention in language disorders: An integrative approach.* Philadelphia: Grune & Stratton.

Cirrin, F. M., & Penner, S. G. (1995). Classroom-based and consultative service delivery models for language intervention. In M. E. Fey, J. Windsor, & S. F. Warren (Eds.), *Language intervention: Preschool through the elementary years* (pp. 333–362). Baltimore: Paul H. Brookes.

Crawford, J. (1992). *Hold your tongue: Bilingualism and the politics of "English only."* Reading, MA: Addison-Wesley.

Crews, W. D., Sanders, E. C., Hensley, L. G., Johnson, Y. M., Bonaventura, S., & Rhodes, R. D. (1995). An evaluation of facilitated communication in a group of nonverbal individuals with mental retardation. *Journal of Autism and Developmental Disorders, 25,* 205–213.

Culatta, R., & Goldberg, S. A. (1995). *Stuttering therapy: An integrated approach to theory and practice.* Boston: Allyn & Bacon.

Curlee, R. F., & Siegel, G. M. (Eds.). (1997). *Nature and treatment of stuttering: New directions* (2nd Ed.). Boston: Allyn & Bacon.

Delpit, L. (1995). *Other people's children: Cultural conflict in the classroom.* New York: New Press.

Donahue, M. L., Hartas, D., & Cole, D. (1999). Research on interactions among oral language and emotional/behavioral disorders. In D. Rogers-Adkinson & P. Griffith (Eds.), *Communication disorders and children with psychiatric and behavioral disorders* (pp. 69–97). San Diego: Singular.

Feenick, J. J., & Judd, D. (1994). Physical interventions and accommodations. In R. C. Savage & G. F. Wolcott (Eds.), *Educational dimensions of acquired brain injury* (pp. 367–390). Austin, TX: Pro-Ed.

Fey, M. E., Catts, H. W., & Larrivee, L. S. (1995). Preparing preschoolers for academic and social challenges of school. In M. E. Fey, J. Windsor, & S. F. Warren (Eds.), *Language intervention: Preschool through the elementary years* (pp. 3–37). Baltimore: Paul H. Brookes.

Foster, H. L. (1986). *Ribin', jivin', and playin' the dozens* (2nd ed.). Cambridge, MA: Ballinger.

Franklin, K., & Beukelman, D. R. (1991). Augmentative communication: Directions for future research. In J. F. Miller (Ed.), *Research on child language disorders: A decade of progress* (pp. 321–337). Austin, TX: Pro-Ed.

Graham, S., Harris, K. R., MacArthur, C., & Schwartz, S. (1998). Writing instruction. In B. Y. L. Wong (Ed.), *Learning about learning disabilities* (2nd ed., pp. 391–424). San Diego: Academic Press.

Guralnick, M., Connor, R., Hammond, M., Gottman, J., & Kinnish, K. (1996). The peer relations of preschool children with communication disorders. *Child Development, 67,* 471–489.

Hallahan, D. P., Kauffman, J. M., & Lloyd, J. W. (1999). *Introduction to learning disabilities* (2nd ed.). Boston: Allyn & Bacon.

Happe, F. G. E. (1994). An advanced test of theory of mind: Understanding of story characters' thoughts and feelings by able autistic, mentally handicapped, and normal children and adults. *Journal of Autism and Developmental Disorders, 24,* 129–154.

Happe, F. G. E., & Frith, U. (1995). Theory of mind in autism. In E. Schopler & G. B. Mesibov (Eds.), *Learning and cognition in autism* (pp. 177–197). New York: Plenum Press.

Hardy, J. C. (1994). Cerebral palsy. In G. H. Shames, E. H. Wiig, & W. A. Secord (Eds.), *Human communication disorders: An introduction* (4th ed., pp. 563–604). New York: Merrill/Macmillan.

Harris, S. L. (1995). Educational strategies in autism. In E. Schopler & G. B. Mesibov (Eds.), *Learning and cognition in autism* (pp. 293–309). New York: Plenum Press.

Hart, B., & Risley, T. R. (1995). *Meaningful differences in the everyday experience of young American children.* Baltimore: Paul H. Brookes.

Haynes, W. O., & Pindzola, R. H. (1998). *Diagnosis and evaluation in speech pathology* (5th ed.). Boston: Allyn & Bacon.

Hodson, B. W., & Edwards, M. L. (1997). *Perspectives in applied phonology.* Gaithersburg, MD: Aspen.

Hulstijn, W., Peters, H. F. M., & van Lieshout, P. H. H. M. (Eds.). (1997). *Speech production: Motor control, brain research and fluency disorders.* Amsterdam: Elsevier.

Johnston, E. B., Weinrich, B. D., & Glaser, A. J. (1991). *A sourcebook of pragmatic activities: Theory and intervention for language therapy* (PK–6) (Rev. ed.). Tucson, AZ: Communication Skill Builders.

Kaiser, A. P., Hemmeter, M. L., Ostrosky, M. M., Alpert, C. L., & Hancock, T. B. (1995). The effects of training and individual feedback on parent use of milieu teaching. *Journal of Childhood Communication Disorders, 16,* 39–48.

Koegel, R. L., O'Dell, M. C., & Koegel, L. C. (1987). A natural language teaching paradigm for nonverbal autistic children. *Journal of Autism and Developmental Disabilities, 17,* 187–200.

Koegel, L. K., & Koegel, R. L. (1995). Motivating communication in children with autism. In E. Schopler & G. B. Mesibov (Eds.), *Learning and cognition in autism* (pp. 73–87). New York: Plenum Press.

Koegel, R. L., Rincover, A., & Egel, A. L. (1982). *Educating and understanding autistic children.* San Diego: College-Hill Press.

Lee, A., Hobson, R. P., & Chiat, S. (1994). I, you, me, and autism: An experimental study. *Journal of Autism and Developmental Disorders, 24,* 155–176.

Lloyd, L. L., Fuller, D. R., & Arvidson, H. H. (Eds.). (1997). *Augmentative and alternative communication: A handbook of principles and practices.* Boston: Allyn & Bacon.

Lovaas, O. I. (1987). Behavioral treatment and normal educational and intellectual functioning in young autistic children. *Journal of Consulting and Clinical Psychology, 55,* 3–9.

Mann, V. (1998). Language problems: A key to early reading problems. In B. Y. L. Wong (Ed.), *Learning about learning disabilities* (2nd ed., pp. 163–202). San Diego: Academic Press.

Marvin, C. A., Beukelman, D. R., Brockhaus, J., & Kast, L. (1994). "What are you talking about?" Semantic analysis of preschool children's conversational topics in home and preschool settings. *Augmentative and Alternative Communication, 10,* 75–86.

Matthews, J., & Frattali, C. (1994). The professions of speech-language pathology and audiology. In G. H. Shames, E. H. Wiig, & W. A. Secord (Eds.), *Human communication disorders: An introduction* (4th ed., pp. 2–33). New York: Merrill/Macmillan.

McKnight-Taylor, M. (1989). Stimulating speech and language development of infants and other young children. In P. J. Valletutti, M. McKnight-Taylor, & A. S. Hoffnung (Eds.), *Facilitating communication in young children with handicapping conditions: A guide for special educators.* Boston: Little, Brown.

Mesibov, G. B. (1995). Facilitated communication: A warning for pediatric psychologists. *Journal of Pediatric Psychology, 20,* 127–130.

Montee, B. B., Miltenberger, R. G., & Wittrock, D. (1995). An experimental analysis of facilitated communication. *Journal of Applied Behavior Analysis, 28,* 189–200.

Moore, G. P., & Hicks, D. M. (1994). Voice disorders. In G. H. Shames, E. H. Wiig, & W. A. Secord (Eds.), *Human communication disorders: An introduction* (4th ed., pp. 292–335). New York: Merrill/Macmillan.

Nelson, N. W. (1997). Language intervention in school settings. In D. K. Bernstein & E. Tiegerman-Farber (Eds.), *Language and communication disorders in children* (4th ed., pp. 324–381). Boston: Allyn & Bacon.

Nelson, N. W. (1998). *Childhood language disorders in context: Infancy through adolescence* (2nd ed.). Boston: Allyn & Bacon.

Ogletree, B. T., Wetherby, A. M., & Westling, D. L. (1992). Profile of the prelinguistic intentional communicative behaviors of children with profound mental retardation. *American Journal on Mental Retardation, 97,* 186–196.

Onslow, M. (1992). Choosing a treatment procedure for early stuttering: Issues and future directions. *Journal of Speech and Hearing Research, 35,* 983–993.

Ortiz, A. A. (1997). Learning disabilities occurring concomitantly with linguistic differences. *Journal of Learning Disabilities, 30,* 321–332.

Owens, R. E. (1986). Communication, language, and speech. In G. H. Shames & E. H. Wiig (Eds.), *Human communication disorders* (2nd ed., pp. 27–79). Columbus, OH: Merrill/Macmillan.

Owens, R. E. (1995). *Language disorders: A functional approach to assessment and intervention* (2nd ed.). Boston: Allyn & Bacon.

Owens, R. E. (1997). Mental retardation: difference and delay. In D. K. Bernstein & E. Tiegerman-Farber (Eds.), *Language and communication disorders in children* (4th ed., pp. 457–523). Boston: Allyn & Bacon.

Prizant, B. M. (1999). Early intervention: Young children with communication and emotional/behavioral problems. In D. Rogers-Adkinson & P. Griffith (Eds.), *Communication disorders and children with psychiatric and behavioral disorders* (pp. 295–342). San Diego: Singular.

Quist, R. W., Lloyd, L. L., & McDowell, K. C. (1997). Professional concerns and issues. In L. L., Lloyd, D. R. Fuller, & H. H. Arvidson (Eds.), *Augmentative and alternative communication: A handbook of principles and practices* (pp. 367–388). Boston: Allyn & Bacon.

Robin, D. A., Yorkston, K. M., & Beukelman, D. R. (Eds.). (1996). *Disorders of motor speech: Assessment, treatment, and clinical characterization.* Baltimore: Paul H. Brookes.

Rogers-Adkinson, D. L. (1999). Psychiatric disorders in children. In D. Rogers-Adkinson & P. Griffith (Eds.). *Communication disorders and children with psychiatric and behavioral disorders* (pp. 39–68). San Diego: Singular.

Rogers-Adkinson, D., & Griffith, P. (Eds.). (1999). *Communication disorders and children with psychiatric and behavioral disorders.* San Diego: Singular.

Schopler, E., Misibov, G. B., & Hearsey, K. (1995). Structured teaching in the TEACCH system. In E. Schopler & G. B. Mesibov (Eds.), *Learning and cognition in autism* (pp. 243–268). New York: Plenum Press.

Schwartz, R. G. (1994). Phonological disorders. In G. H. Shames, E. H. Wiig, & W. A. Secord (Eds.), *Human communication disorders: An introduction* (4th ed., pp. 251–290). New York: Merrill/Macmillan.

Seidenberg, P. L. (1997). Understanding learning disabilities. In D. K. Bernstein & E. Tiegerman-Farber (Eds.), *Language and communication disorders in children* (4th ed., pp. 411–456). Boston: Allyn & Bacon.

Seymour, H. N., Champion, T., & Jackson, J. (1995). The language of African American learners: Effective assessment and instructional programming for children with special needs. In B. A. Ford, F. E. Obiakor, & J. M. Patton (Eds.), *Effective education of African American exceptional learners* (pp. 89–121). Austin, TX: Pro-Ed.

Shames, G. H., & Ramig, P. R. (1994). Stuttering and other disorders of fluency. In G. H. Shames, E. H. Wiig, & W. A. Secord (Eds.). *Human communication disorders: An introduction* (4th ed., pp. 336–386). New York: Merrill/Macmillan.

Shames, G. H., Wiig, E. H., & Secord, W. A. (Eds.). (1994). *Human communication disorders: An introduction* (4th ed.). New York: Merrill/Macmillan.

Shane, H. C. (Ed.). (1994). *Facilitated communication: The clinical and social phenomenon.* San Diego: Singular Publishing Group.

Siegel, B. (1995). Assessing allegations of sexual molestation made through facilitated communication. *Journal of Autism and Developmental Disorders, 25,* 319–326.

Sigafoos, J., Kerr, M., Roberts, D., & Couzens, D. (1994). Increasing opportunities for requesting in classrooms serving children with developmental disabilities. *Journal of Autism and Developmental Disorders, 24,* 631–645.

Sigman, M. (1994). What are the core deficits in autism? In S. H. Broman & J. Grafman (Eds.), *Atypical cognitive deficits in developmental disorders: Implication for brain function* (pp. 139–157). Hillsdale, NJ: Erlbaum.

Simpson, R. L., & Myles, B. S. (1995). Effectiveness of facilitated communication with children and youth with autism. *Journal of Special Education, 28,* 424–439.

Slentz, K. L., & Bricker, D. (1992). Family-centered assessment for IFSP development: Jumping off the family assessment bandwagon. *Journal of Early Intervention, 16*(1), 11–19.

Soto, G., Huer, M. B., & Taylor, O. (1997). Multicultural issues. In L. L. Lloyd, D. R. Fuller, & H. H. Arvidson (Eds.), *Augmentative and alternative communication: A handbook of principles and practices* (pp. 406–413). Boston: Allyn & Bacon.

Sowell, T. (1997). *Late-talking children.* New York: Basic Books.

Stoel-Gammon, C. (1991). Issues in phonological development and disorders. In J. F. Miller (Ed.), *Research on child language disorders: A decade of progress* (pp. 255–265). Austin, TX: Pro-Ed.

Swindell, C. S., Holland, A. L., & Reinmuth, O. M. (1994). Aphasia and related adult disorders. In G. H. Shames, E. H. Wiig, & W. A. Secord (Eds.), *Human communication disorders: An introduction* (4th ed., pp. 521–560). New York: Merrill/Macmillan.

Szekeres, S. F., & Meserve, N. F. (1995). Collaborative intervention in schools after traumatic brain injury. *Topics in Language Disorders, 15*(1), 21–36.

Tiegerman-Farber, E. (1997). Autism: Learning to communicate. In D. K. Bernstein & E. Tiegerman-Farber (Eds.), *Language and communication disorders in children* (4th ed., pp. 524–573). Boston: Allyn & Bacon.

U.S. Department of Education. (1998). *Twentieth annual report to Congress on the implementation of the Individuals with Disabilities Education Act.* Washington, DC: Author.

Van Keulen, J. E., Weddington, G. T., & DeBose, C. E. (1998). *Speech, language, learning, and the African American child.* Boston: Allyn & Bacon.

Wallach, G. P., & Butler, K. G. (Eds.). (1994). *Language learning disabilities in school-age children and adolescents: Some principles and applications.* New York: Merrill/Macmillan.

Warren, S. F., & Abbaduto, L. (1992). The relation of communication and language development to mental retardation. *American Journal on Mental Retardation, 97,* 125–130.

Warren, S. F., Yoder, P. J., Gazdag, G. E., Kim, K., & Jones, H. A. (1993). Facilitating prelinguistic communication skills in young children with developmental delay. *Journal of Speech and Hearing Research, 36,* 83–97.

Westby, C. E. (1994). The effects of culture and genre, structure, and style of oral and written texts. In G. P. Wallach & K. G. Butler (Eds.), *Language learning disabilities in school-age children and adolescents: Some principles and applications* (pp. 180–218). New York: Merrill/Macmillan.

Westby, C. E., & Roman, R. (1995). Finding the balance: Learning to live in two worlds. *Topics in Language Disorders, 15*(4), 68–88.

Wong, B. Y. L., Wong, R., Darlington, D., & Jones, W. (1991). Interactive teaching: An effective way to teach revision skills to adolescents with learning disabilities. *Learning Disabilities Research and Practice, 6,* 117–127.

Yairi, E., & Ambrose, N. (1992). A longitudinal study of stuttering in children: A preliminary report. *Journal of Speech and Hearing Research, 35,* 755–760.

Ylvisaker, M., Szekeres, S. F., Haarbauer-Krupa, J., Urbanczyk, B., & Feeney, T. J. (1994). Speech and language intervention. In R. C. Savage & G. F. Wolcott (Eds.), *Educational dimensions of acquired brain injury* (pp. 185–235). Austin, TX: Pro-Ed.

Yoder, P. J., Warren, S. F., Kim, K., & Gazdag, G. E. (1994). Facilitating prelinguistic communication skills in young children with developmental delay II: Systematic replication and extension. *Journal of Speech and Hearing Research, 37,* 841–851.

Zebrowski, P. M. (Issue Ed.). (1995). Language and stuttering in children: Perspectives on an interrelationship. *Topics in Language Disorders, 15*(3).

Chapter 9

Allen, T. E. (1986). Patterns of achievement among hearing-impaired students: 1974 and 1983. In A. N. Schildroth & M. A. Karchmer (Eds.), *Deaf children in America* (pp. 161–206). San Diego, CA: College-Hill Press.

Andersson, Y. (1994). Comment on Turner. *Sign Language Studies, 83,* 127–131.

Andrews, J. F., Ferguson, C., Roberts, S., & Hodges, P. (1997). What's up, Billy Jo? Deaf children and bilingual-bicultural instruction in East-Central Texas. *American Annals of the Deaf, 142,* 16–25.

Andrews, J. F., & Zmijewski, G. (1997). How parents support home literacy with deaf children. *Early Child Development and Care, 127,* 131–139.

Antia, S. D., & Kreimeyer, K. H. (1997). The generalization and maintenance of the peer social behaviors of young children who are deaf or hard of hearing. *Language, Speech, and Hearing Services in Schools, 28,* 59–69.

Arana-Ward, M. (1997, May 11). As technology advances, a bitter debate divides the deaf. *The Washington Post,* pp. A1, A20–21.

Auditory-Verbal International. (1998, April 29). *About the auditory-verbal philosophy* [Posted on the World Wide Web]. Author. Retrieved June 1, 1998 from the World Wide Web: http://www.auditory-verbal.org/about.htm#philosophy

Bellugi, U., & Klima, E. (1991). What the hands reveal about the brain. In D. S. Martin (Ed.), *Advances in cognition, education, and deafness.* Washington, DC: Gallaudet University Press.

Blackorby, J., & Wagner, M. (1996). Longitudinal postschool outcomes of youth with disabilities: Findings from the National Longitudinal Transition Study. *Exceptional Children, 62,* 399–413.

Brill, R. G., MacNeil, B., & Newman, L. R. (1986). Framework for appropriate programs for deaf children. *American Annals of the Deaf, 131,* 65–77.

Buchino, M. A. (1993). Perceptions of the oldest hearing child of deaf parents. *American Annals of the Deaf, 138,* 40–45.

Bullis, M., Bull, B., Johnson, B., & Peters, D. (1995). The school-to-community transition experiences of hearing young adults and young adults who are deaf. *Journal of Special Education, 28,* 405–423.

Cambra, C. (1996). A comparative study of personality descriptors attributed to the deaf, the blind, and individuals with no sensory disability. *American Annals of the Deaf, 141*, 24–28.

Charlson, E., Strong, M., & Gold, R. (1992). How successful deaf teenagers experience and cope with isolation. *American Annals of the Deaf, 137*, 261–270.

Cochlear Corporation. (November 25, 1997). *Patients and parents: hearing and cochlear implants* [Posted on the World Wide Web]. Author. Retrieved May 30, 1998 from the World Wide Web: http://www.cochlear.com/papHearCI.htm

Crowson, K. (1994). Errors made by deaf children acquiring sign language. *Early Child Development and Care, 99*, 63–78.

Desselle, D. D. (1994). Self-esteem, family climate, and communication patterns in relation to deafness. *American Annals of the Deaf, 139*, 322–328.

Drasgow, E. (1993). Bilingual/bicultural deaf education: An overview. *Sign Language Studies, 80*, 243–266.

Drasgow, E. (1998). American Sign Language as a pathway to linguistic competence. *Exceptional Children, 64*, 329–342.

Gaustad, M. G., & Kluwin, T. N. (1992). Patterns of communication among deaf and hearing adolescents. In T. N. Kluwin, D. F. Moores, & M. G. Gaustad (Eds.), *Toward effective public school programs for deaf students: Context, process, & outcomes* (pp. 107–128). New York: Teachers College Press.

Giebink, G. S. (1990). Medical issues in hearing impairment: The otitis media spectrum. In J. Davis (Ed.), *Our forgotten children: Hard-of-hearing pupils in the schools* (pp. 49–55). Bethesda, MD: Self-Help for Hard of Hearing People.

Hawkins, D. B. (1990). Amplification in the classroom. In J. Davis (Ed.), *Our forgotten children: Hard-of-hearing pupils in the schools* (pp. 39–47). Bethesda, MD: Self Help for Hard of Hearing People.

Higgins, P. C. (1992). Working at mainstreaming. In P. M. Ferguson, D. L. Ferguson, & S. J. Taylor (Eds.), *Interpreting disability* (pp. 103–123). New York: Teachers College Press.

Holcomb, T. K. (1996). Social assimilation of deaf high school students: The role of the school environment. In I. Parasnis (Ed.), *Cultural and language diversity and the deaf experience* (pp. 181–198). Cambridge, England: Cambridge University Press.

Holden-Pitt, L. (1997). A look at residential school placement patterns for students from deaf- and hearing-parented families: A ten-year perspective. *American Annals of the Deaf, 142*, 108–114.

Hutchinson, M. K., & Sandall, S. R. (1995). Congenital TORCH infections in infants and young children: Neurodevelopmental sequelae and implications for intervention. *Topics in Early Childhood and Special Education, 15*, 65–82.

Innes, J. J. (1994). Full inclusion and the deaf student: A deaf consumer's review of the issue. *American Annals of the Deaf, 139*, 152–156.

Janesick, V. J., & Moores, D. F. (1992). Ethnic and cultural considerations. In T. N. Kluwin, D. F. Moores, & M. G. Gaustad (Eds.), *Toward effective public school programs for deaf students: Context, process, & outcomes* (pp. 49–65). New York: Teachers College Press.

Jones, B. E., Clark, G. M., & Soltz, D. F. (1997). Characteristics and practices of sign language interpreters in inclusive education programs. *Exceptional Children, 63*, 257–268.

Kampfe, C. M., & Turecheck, A. G. (1987). Reading achievement of prelingually deaf students and its relationship to parental method of communication: A review of the literature. *American Annals of the Deaf, 132*, 11–15.

Klima, E. S., & Bellugi, U. (1979). *The signs of language.* Cambridge, MA: Harvard University Press.

Kluwin, T. N. (1992). What does "local public school" mean? In T. N. Kluwin, D. F. Moores, & M. G. Gaustad (Eds.), *Toward effective public school programs for deaf students: Context, process, & outcomes* (pp. 30–48). New York: Teachers College Press.

Kluwin, T. N. (1993). Cumulative effects of mainstreaming on the achievement of deaf adolescents. *Exceptional Children, 60*, 73–81.

Kluwin, T. N., & Gaustad, M. G. (1994). The role of adaptability and communication in fostering cohesion in families of deaf adolescents. *American Annals of the Deaf, 139*, 329–335.

Koester, L. S., & Meadow-Orlans, K. P. (1990). Parenting a deaf child: Stress, strength, and support. In D. F. Moores & K. P. Meadow-Orlans (Eds.), *Educational and developmental aspects of deafness* (pp. 299–320). Washington, DC: Gallaudet University Press.

Lane, H. (1984). *When the mind hears: A history of the deaf.* New York: Random House.

Lane, H. (1987, July 17). Listen to the needs of deaf children. *The New York Times.*

Lane, H. (1992). *The mask of benevolence: Disabling the Deaf community.* New York: Knopf.

Lane, H., Hoffmeister, R., & Bahan, B. (1996). *A journey into the Deaf world.* San Diego, CA: Dawn Sign Press.

Ling, D., & Ling, A. (1978). *Aural habilitation.* Washington, DC: Alexander Graham Bell Association for the Deaf.

Livingston, S., Singer, B., & Abrahamson, T. (1994). Effectiveness compared: ASL interpretation vs. transliteration. *Sign Language Studies, 82*, 1–54.

Luetke-Stahlman, B., & Milburn, W. O. (1996). A history of Seeing Essential English (SEE I). *American Annals of the Deaf, 141*, 29–33.

MacTurk, R. H., Meadow-Orlans, K. P., Koester, L. S., & Spencer, P. E. (1993). Social support, motivation, language, and interaction. *American Annals of the Deaf, 138*, 19–25.

Meadow-Orlans, K. P. (1987). An analysis of the effectiveness of early intervention programs for hearing-impaired children. In M. J. Guralnick & F. C. Bennett (Eds.), *The effectiveness of early intervention for at-risk and handicapped children* (pp. 325–362). New York: Academic Press.

Meadow-Orlans, K. P. (1990). Research on developmental aspects of deafness. In D. F. Moores & K. P. Meadow-Orlans (Eds.), *Educational and developmental aspects of deafness* (pp. 283–298). Washington, DC: Gallaudet University Press.

Meadow-Orlans, K. P. (1995). Sources of stress for mothers and fathers of deaf and hard of hearing infants. *American Annals of the Deaf, 140*, 352–357.

Meadow-Orlans, K. P., Mertens, D. M., Sass-Lehrer, M. A., & Scott-Olson, K. (1997). Support services for parents and their children who are deaf or hard of hearing. *American Annals of the Deaf, 142*, 278–288.

Menchel, R. S. (1988). Personal experience with speechreading. *Volta Review, 90*(5), 3–15.

Mencher, G. T., Gerber, S. E., & McCombe, A. (1997). *Audiology and auditory dysfunction.* Boston: Allyn & Bacon.

Moores, D. F., & Maestas y Moores, J. (1981). Special adaptations necessitated by hearing impairments. In J. M. Kauffman & D. P. Hallahan (Eds.), *Handbook of special education.* Englewood Cliffs, NJ: Prentice-Hall.

National Center for Accessible Media. (1998, April 7). *Motion picture access* [Posted on the World Wide Web]. Author. Retrieved June 5, 1998 from the World Wide Web: http://www.wgbh.org/wgbh/pages/ncam/currentprojects/mopix.html

Padden, C. A. (1996). Early bilingual lives of Deaf children. In I. Parasnis (Ed.), *Cultural and language diversity and the Deaf experience.* (pp. 99–116). Cambridge, England: Cambridge University Press.

Padden, C., & Humphries, T. (1988). *Deaf in America: Voices from a culture.* Cambridge, MA: Harvard University Press.

Prinz, P. M., Strong, M., Kuntze, M., Vincent, M., Friedman, J., Moyers, P., & Helman, E. (1996). A path to literacy through ASL and English for Deaf children. In C. E. Johnson & J. H. V. Gilbert (Eds.), *Children's language* (Vol. 9, pp. 235–251). Mahwah, NJ: Erlbaum.

Quigley, S., Jenne, W., & Phillips, S. (1968). *Deaf students in colleges and universities.* Washington, DC: Alexander Graham Bell Association for the Deaf.

Reagan, T. (1990). Cultural considerations in the education of deaf children. In D. F. Moores & K. P. Meadow-Orlans (Eds.), *Educational and developmental aspects of deafness* (pp. 73–84). Washington, DC: Gallaudet University Press.

Robinshaw, H. M. (1994). Deaf infants, early intervention and language acquisition. *Early Child Development and Care, 99,* 1–22.

Rodriguez, M. S., & Lana, E. T. (1996). Dyadic interactions between deaf children and their communication partners. *American Annals of the Deaf, 141,* 245–251.

Rose, D. E., Vernon, M., & Pool, A. F. (1996). Cochlear implants in prelingually deaf children. *American Annals of the Deaf, 141,* 258–261.

Sacks, O. (1989). *Seeing voices: A journey into the world of the deaf.* Berkeley: University of California Press.

Schildroth, A. N., & Hotto, S. A. (1996). Changes in student and program characteristics, 1984–85 and 1994–95. *American Annals of the Deaf, 141,* 68–71.

Schow, R., & Nerbonne, M. (Eds.). (1980). *Introduction to aural rehabilitation.* Baltimore: University Park Press.

Singleton, J. L., Morford, J. P., & Goldin-Meadow, S. (1993). Once is not enough: Standards of well-formedness in manual communication created over three different timespans. *Language, 69,* 683–715.

Siple, L. (1993). Working with the sign language interpreter in your classroom. *College Teaching, 41,* 139–142.

Spencer, P. E., & Meadow-Orlans, K. P. (1996). Play, language, and maternal responsiveness: A longitudinal study of deaf and hearing infants. *Child Development, 67,* 3176–3191.

Spradley, T. S., & Spradley, J. P. (1978). *Deaf like me.* Washington, DC: Gallaudet University Press.

Stinson, M. S., & Whitmire, K. (1992). Students' views of their social relationships. In T. N. Kluwin, D. F. Moores, & M. G. Gaustad (Eds.), *Toward effective public school programs for deaf students: Context, process, & outcomes* (pp. 149–174). New York: Teachers College Press.

Stoel-Gammon, C., & Otomo, K. (1986). Babbling development of hearing-impaired and normally hearing subjects. *Journal of Speech and Hearing Disorders, 51,* 33–41.

Stokoe, W. C. (1960). *Sign language structure.* Silver Spring, MD: Linstok Press.

Stokoe, W. C., Casterline, D. C., & Croneberg, C. G. (1976). *A dictionary of American Sign Language on linguistic principles* (2nd ed.). Silver Spring, MD: Linstok Press.

Strong, M., & Prinz, P. M. (1997). A study of the relationship between American Sign Language and English literacy. *Journal of Deaf Studies and Deaf Education, 2,* 37–46.

Travis, J. (1998, January 17). Genes of silence: Scientists track down a slew of mutated genes that cause deafness. *Science News, 153,* 42–44.

Trybus, R. J., & Karchmer, M. A. (1977). School achievement scores of hearing impaired children. National data on achievement status and growth patterns. *American Annals of the Deaf, 122,* 62–69.

Valdes, K., Williamson, C., & Wagner, M. (1990). *The national longitudinal transition study of special education students* (Vol. 1). Palo Alto, CA: SRI International.

Vygotsky, L. S. (1962). *Thought and language.* New York: Wiley.

Walker, L. A. (1986). *A loss for words: The story of deafness in a family.* New York: Harper & Row.

Wolk, S., & Allen, T. E. (1984). A five-year follow-up of reading comprehension achievement of hearing-impaired students in special education programs. *Journal of Special Education, 18,* 161–176.

Wolk, S., & Schildroth, A. N. (1986). Deaf children and speech intelligibility: A national study. In A. N. Schildroth & M. A. Karchmer (Eds.), *Deaf children in America* (pp. 139–159). San Diego: College-Hill Press.

Wolkomir, R. (1992). American Sign Language: "It's not mouth stuff—it's brain stuff." *Smithsonian, 23*(4), 30–38, 40–41.

Chapter 10

American Foundation for the Blind. (1998, January 14). *Braille technology* [Posted on the World Wide Web]. New York: Author. Retrieved March 1, 1998 from the World Wide Web: http://www.afb.org/afb/tc_bra.html

Andrews, D. (1995, January). The other half of the equation: PC-based reading systems—a comparative review. *Braille Monitor,* 27–39.

Bambring, M., & Troster, H. (1992). On the stability of stereotyped behaviors in blind infants and preschoolers. *Journal of Visual Impairment and Blindness, 86,* 105–110.

Barraga, N. C. (1983). *Visual handicaps and learning* (Rev. ed.). Austin, TX: Exceptional Resources.

Barraga, N. C., & Collins, M. E. (1979). Development of efficiency in visual functioning: Rationale for a comprehensive program. *Journal of Visual Impairment and Blindness, 73,* 121–126.

Baumeister, A. A. (1978). Origins and control of stereotyped movements. In C. E. Meyers (Ed.), *Quality of life in severely and profoundly retarded people: Research foundations for improvement* (pp. 353–384). Washington, DC: American Association on Mental Deficiency.

Bentzen, B. L., & Mitchell, P. A. (1995). Audible signage as a wayfinding aid: Verbal landmark versus talking signs. *Journal of Visual Impairment and Blindness, 89,* 494–505.

Berla, E. P. (1981). Tactile scanning and memory for a spatial display by blind students. *Journal of Special Education, 15,* 341–350.

Bigelow, A. (1991). Spatial mapping of familiar locations in blind children. *Journal of Visual Impairment and Blindness, 85,* 113–117.

Bischoff, R. W. (1979). Listening: A teachable skill for visually impaired persons. *Journal of Visual Impairment and Blindness, 73,* 59–67.

Cheadle, B. (1991, October). Canes and preschoolers: The eight-year revolution. *Braille Monitor,* 533–538.

Chen, D. (1996). Parent-infant communication: Early intervention for very young children with visual impairment or hearing loss. *Infants and Young Children, 9*(2), 1–12.

Chong, C. (1997, December). Microsoft takes a big step backward. *Braille Monitor*, 782–793.

Collins, M. E., & Barraga, N. C. (1980). Development of efficiency in visual functioning: An evaluation process. *Journal of Visual Impairment and Blindness, 74*, 93–96.

Conant, S., & Budoff, M. (1982). The development of sighted people's understanding of blindness. *Journal of Visual Impairment and Blindness, 76*, 86–90.

Corn, A. L., Hatlen, P., Huebner, K. M., Ryan, F., & Siller, M. A. (1995). *The national agenda for the education of children and youths with visual impairments, including those with multiple disabilities.* New York: American Foundation for the Blind.

Cronin, P. J. (1992). A direct service program for mainstreamed students by a residential school. *Journal of Visual Impairment and Blindness, 86*, 101–104.

Davidson, P. W., Dunn, G., Wiles-Kettenmann, M., & Appelle, S. (1981). Haptic conservation of amount in blind and sighted children: Exploratory movement effects. *Journal of Pediatric Psychology, 6*, 191–200.

Detectable warnings debate continues. (1993, December). *Braille Monitor*, 1084–1093.

Dykes, J. (1992). Opinions of orientation and mobility instructors about using the long cane with preschool-age children. *RE:view, 24*, 85–92.

Erin, J. N. (1993). The road less traveled: New directions for schools for students with visual impairments. *Journal of Visual Impairment and Blindness, 87*, 219–223.

Estevis, A. H., & Koenig, A. J. (1994). A cognitive approach to reducing stereotypic body rocking. *RE:view, 26*, 119–125.

Farmer, L. W. (1975). Travel in adverse weather using electronic mobility guidance devices. *New Outlook for the Blind, 69*, 433–451.

Ferrell, K. A., & Muir, D. W. (1996). A call to end vision stimulation training. *Journal of Visual Impairment and Blindness, 90*, 364–366.

Fichten, C. S., Judd, D., Tagalakis, V., Amsel, R., & Robillard, K. (1991). Communication cues used by people with and without visual impairments in daily conversations and dating. *Journal of Visual Impairment and Blindness, 85*, 371–378.

Foulke, E. (1996, November). Is it too late for Braille literacy? *Braille Monitor*, 588–600.

Fraiberg, S. (1977). *Insights from the blind.* New York: Basic Books.

Gabias, P. (1992, July). Unique features of guide dogs: Backtracking and homing. *Braille Monitor*, 392–399.

Griffin, H. C., & Gerber, P. J. (1982). Tactual development and its implications for the education of blind children. *Education of the Visually Handicapped, 13*, 116–123.

Groenveld, M., & Jan, J. E. (1992). Intelligence profiles of low vision and blind children. *Journal of Visual Impairment and Blindness, 86*, 68–71.

Hanley-Maxwell, C., Griffin, S., Szymanski, E. M., & Godley, S. H. (1990). Supported and time-limited transitional employment services. *Journal of Visual Impairment and Blindness, 84*, 160–166.

Hatlen, P. H. (1993). A personal odyssey on schools for blind children. *Journal of Visual Impairment and Blindness, 87*, 171–174.

Hatlen, P. (1996, October). The continuing evolution of the Texas School for the Blind and Visually Impaired. *Braille Monitor*, 472–477.

Hatton, D. D., Bailey, D. B., Burchinal, M. R., & Ferrell, K. A. (1997). Developmental growth curves of preschool children with vision impairments. *Child Development, 68*, 788–806.

Hayes, S. P. (1942). Alternative scales for the mental measurement of the visually handicapped. *Outlook for the Blind and the Teachers Forum, 36*, 225–230.

Hayes, S. P. (1950). Measuring the intelligence of the blind. In P. A. Zahl (Ed.), *Blindness.* Princeton, NJ: Princeton University Press.

Herman, J. F., Chatman, S. P., & Roth, S. F. (1983). Cognitive mapping in blind people: Acquisition of spatial relationships in a large-scale environment. *Journal of Visual Impairment and Blindness, 77*, 161–166.

Heyes, T. (1998, February 18). *The Sonic Pathfinder: An electronic travel aid for the vision impaired.* [Posted on the World Wide Web]. Retrieved March 1, 1998 from the World Wide Web: http://ariel.ucs.unimelb.EDU.AU:80/~heyes/pf_blerb.html

Hill, A. (1997, April). Teaching can travel blind? *Braille Monitor*, 222–225.

Holbrook, M. C., & Koenig, A. J. (1992). Teaching braille reading to students with low vision. *Journal of Visual Impairment and Blindness, 86*, 44–48.

Hull, J. M. (1990). *Touching the rock.* New York: Pantheon Books.

Ianuzzi, J. W. (1992, May). Braille or print: Why the debate? *Braille Monitor*, 229–233.

Jernigan, K. (1985, August–September). Blindness: The pattern of freedom. *Braille Monitor*, 386–398.

Jernigan, K. (1991, January). Airline safety: What happens when you can see fire on the wing? *Braille Monitor*, 51–54.

Jernigan, K. (1992, June). Equality, disability, and empowerment. *Braille Monitor*, 292–298.

Jernigan, K. (1994). *If blindness comes.* Baltimore, MD: National Federation of the Blind.

Kirchner, C., & Schmeidler, E. (1997). Prevalence and employment of people in the United States who are blind or visually impaired. *Journal of Visual Impairment and Blindness, 91*, 508–511.

Kurzweil, R. (1996, November). Why I am building reading machines again. *Braille Monitor*, 568–581.

Kuusisto, S. (1998). *The planet of the blind: A memoir.* New York: Dial Press.

Maloney, P. L. (1981). *Practical guidance for parents of the visually handicapped preschooler.* Springfield, IL: Thomas.

Maurer, M. (1991, May 20). *All children should learn braille: Here's why.* Scripps Howard News Service.

Maurer, M. (1994, June). Who wants braille on the money? *Braille Monitor*, 345–348.

Maurer, M. (1997, August). Presidential report: National Federation of the Blind. *Braille Monitor*, 538–551.

McAdam, D. B., O'Cleirigh, M., & Cuvo, A. J. (1993). Self-monitoring and verbal feedback to reduce stereotypic body rocking in a congenitally blind adult. *RE:view, 24*, 163–172.

McConachie, H. R., & Moore, V. (1994). Early expressive language of severely visually impaired children. *Developmental Medicine and Child Neurology, 36*, 230–240.

McLinden, D. J. (1988). Spatial task performance: A metaanalysis. *Journal of Visual Impairment and Blindness, 82*, 231–236.

Mehta, V. (1982). *Vedi.* New York: W.W. Norton.

Mehta, V. (1984). *The ledge between the streams.* New York: W.W. Norton.

Mehta, V. (1985). *Sound-shadows of the new world.* New York: W.W. Norton.

Mehta, V. (1989). *The stolen light: Continents of exile.* New York: W.W. Norton.

Millar, D. (1996). A consumer's perspective. *Journal of Visual Impairment and Blindness, 90*, 9.

National Federation of the Blind. (1997, December 7). *Information technology access state model bill* [Posted on the World Wide Web]. Baltimore, MD: Author. Retrieved March 1, 1998 from the World Wide Web: http://www.nfb.org/techbill.htm

Nielsen, L. (1991). Spatial relations in congenitally blind infants. *Journal of Visual Impairment and Blindness, 85,* 11–16.

Ochaita, E., & Huertas, J. A. (1993). Spatial representation by persons who are blind: A study of the effects of learning and development. *Journal of Visual Impairment and Blindness, 87,* 37–41.

Omvig, J. H. (1997, November). From bad philosophy to bad policy: The American braille illiteracy crisis. *Braille Monitor, 723–728.*

Palazesi, M. A. (1986). The need for motor development programs for visually impaired preschoolers. *Journal of Visual Impairment and Blindness, 80,* 573–576.

Plain-Switzer, K. (1993). A model for touch technique and computation of adequate cane length. *International Journal of Rehabilitation Research, 16,* 66–71.

Prevent Blindness America. (1998, April 9). *Signs of possible eye trouble in children* [Posted on the World Wide Web]. Author. Retrieved April 14, 1998 from the World Wide Web: http://www.prevent-blindness.org/children/trouble_signs.html

Raeder, W. M. (1991, July–August). Overcoming roadblocks to literacy for blind children. *Braille Monitor, 363–365.*

Rapp, D. W., & Rapp, A. J. (1992). A survey of the current status of visually impaired students in secondary mathematics. *Journal of Visual Impairment and Blindness, 86,* 115–117.

Rathgeber, A. J. (1981). Manitoba vision screening study. *Journal of Visual Impairment and Blindness, 75,* 239–243.

Rieser, J. J., Guth, D. A., & Hill, E. W. (1982). Mental processes mediating independent travel: Implications for orientation and mobility. *Journal of Visual Impairment and Blindness, 76,* 213–218.

Ross, D. B., & Koenig, A. J. (1991). A cognitive approach to reducing stereotypic head rocking. *Journal of Visual Impairment and Blindness, 85,* 17–19.

Rovig, L. (1992, May). Ideas for increasing your chance of job success while still in college. *Braille Monitor, 238–244.*

Rumrill, P. D., Roessler, R. T., Battersby-Longden, J. C., & Schuyler, B. R. (1998). Situational assessment of the accommodation needs of employees who are visually impaired. *Journal of Visual Impairment and Blindness, 92,* 42–54.

Rumrill, P. D., Schuyler, B. R., & Longden, J. C. (1997). Profiles of on-the-job accommodations needed by professional employees who are blind. *Journal of Visual Impairment and Blindness, 91,* 66–76.

Ryles, R. (1996). The impact of braille reading skills on employment, income, education, and reading habits. *Journal of Visual Impairment and Blindness, 90,* 219–226.

Sacks, S. Z., & Pruett, K. M. (1992). Summer transition training project for professionals who work with adolescents and young adults. *Journal of Visual Impairment and Blindness, 86,* 211–214.

Schroeder, F. K. (1990, January). Literacy: The key to opportunity. *Braille Monitor, 33–41.*

Schroeder, F. K. (1992, June). Braille bills: What are they and what do they mean? *Braille Monitor, 308–311.*

Schroeder, F. K. (1996). Perceptions of braille usage by legally blind adults. *Journal of Visual Impairment and Blindness, 90,* 210–218.

Skellenger, A. C., & Hill, E. W. (1991). Current practices and considerations regarding long cane instruction with preschool children. *Journal of Visual Impairment and Blindness, 85,* 101–104.

Stephens, B., & Grube, C. (1982). Development of Piagetian reasoning in congenitally blind children. *Journal of Visual Impairment and Blindness, 76,* 133–143.

Sullivan, J. E. (1997, October). A perspective on braille unification. *Braille Monitor, 648–657.*

Swallow, R. M., & Conner, A. (1982). Aural reading. In S. S. Mangold (Ed.), *A teachers' guide to the special educational needs of blind and visually handicapped children.* New York: American Foundation for the Blind.

Thomas, C. L. (Ed.). (1985). *Taber's cyclopedic medical dictionary* (15th ed.). Philadelphia: F.A. Davis.

Thurrell, R. J., & Rice, D. G. (1970). Eye rubbing in blind children: Application of a sensory deprivation model. *Exceptional Children, 36,* 325–330.

Ulrey, P. (1994). When you meet a guide dog. *RE:view, 26,* 143–144.

Van Reusen, A. K., & Head, D. N. (1994). Cognitive and metacognitive interventions: Important trends for teachers of students who are visually impaired. *RE:view, 25,* 153–162.

Walhof, R. (1993, September–October). Braille: A renaissance. *Braille Monitor, 971–977.*

Warren, D. H. (1981). Visual Impairments. In J. M. Kauffman & D. P. Hallahan (Eds.), *Handbook of special education.* Englewood Cliffs, NJ. Prentice-Hall.

Warren, D. H. (1984). *Blindness and early childhood development* (2nd ed.). New York: American Foundation for the Blind.

Warren, D. H., & Kocon, J. A. (1974). Factors in the successful mobility of the blind: A review. *Research Bulletin: American Foundation for the Blind 28,* 191–218.

Wheeler, L. C., Floyd, K., & Griffin, H. C. (1997). Spatial organization in blind children. *RE:view, 28,* 177–181.

Willis, D. H. (1976). *A study of the relationship between visual acuity, reading mode, and school systems for blind students—1976.* Louisville, KY: American Printing House for the Blind.

Wolffe, K. E., Roessler, R. T., & Schriner, K. F. (1992). Employment concerns of people with blindness or visual impairments. *Journal of Visual Impairment and Blindness, 86,* 185–187.

Wormsley, D. P. (1996). Reading rates of young braille-reading children. *Journal of Visual Impairment and Blindness, 90,* 278–282.

Wunder, G. (1993, March). Mobility: Whose responsibility is it? *Braille Monitor, 567–572.*

Chapter 11

Allison, M. (1992). The effects of neurologic injury on the maturing brain. *Headlines, 3*(5), 2–10.

Batshaw, M. L., & Perret, Y. M. (1986). *Children with handicaps: A medical primer.* Baltimore: Paul H. Brookes.

Baumeister, A. A., Kupstas, F., & Klindworth, L. M. (1990). New morbidity: Implications for prevention of children's disabilities. *Exceptionality, 1,* 1–16.

Begali, V. (1992). *Head injury in children and adolescents* (2nd ed.). Brandon, VT: Clinical Psychology Publishing.

Besag, F. M. C. (1995). Epilepsy, learning, and behavior in children. *Epilepsia, 36,* 58–63.

Biehl, R. F. (1996). Legislative mandates. In A. J. Capute & P. J. Accardo (Eds.), *Developmental disabilities in infancy and childhood* (2nd ed.). *Vol. I: Neurodevelopmental diagnosis and treatment* (pp. 513–518). Baltimore: Paul H. Brookes.

Bigge, J. L. (1991). *Teaching individuals with physical and multiple disabilities* (3rd ed.). Columbus, OH: Merrill/Macmillan.

Blondis, T. A., & Lord, C. (1996). The continuum of high-functioning autism. In A. J. Capute & P. J. Accardo (Eds.), *Developmental disabilities in infancy and childhood* (2nd ed.). *Vol. 2: The spectrum of developmental disabilities* (pp. 365–377). Baltimore: Paul H. Brookes.

Blum, R. W. (1992). Chronic illness and disability in adolescence. *Journal of Adolescent Health, 13,* 364–368.

Brown, R. T. (1993). An introduction to the special series: Pediatric chronic illness. *Journal of Learning Disabilities, 26,* 4–6.

Capute, A. J., & Accardo, P. J. (Eds.). (1996a). *Developmental disabilities in infancy and childhood* (2nd ed.). *Vol. I: Neurodevelopmental diagnosis and treatment.* Baltimore: Paul H. Brookes.

Capute, A. J., & Accardo, P. J. (Eds.). (1996b). *Developmental disabilities in infancy and childhood* (2nd ed.). *Vol. 2: The spectrum of developmental disabilities.* Baltimore: Paul H. Brookes.

Charlop-Christy, M. H., Schreibman, L., Pierce, K., & Kurtz, P. F. (1997). Childhood autism. In R. J. Morris & T. R. Kratochwill (Eds.), *The practice of child therapy* (3rd ed., pp. 271–389). Boston: Allyn & Bacon.

Christensen, J. R. (1996). Pediatric traumatic brain injury. In A. J. Capute & P. J. Accardo (Eds.), *Developmental disabilities in infancy and childhood* (2nd ed.). *Vol. I: Neurodevelopmental diagnosis and treatment* (pp. 245–260). Baltimore: Paul H. Brookes.

Condeluci, A. (1994). Transition to employment. In R. C. Savage & G. F. Wolcott (Eds.), *Educational dimensions of acquired brain injury* (pp. 519–542). Austin, TX: Pro-Ed.

Cooke, R. E. (1996). Ethics, law, and developmental disabilities. In A. J. Capute & P. J. Accardo (Eds.), *Developmental disabilities in infancy and childhood* (2nd ed.). *Vol. I: Neurodevelopmental diagnosis and treatment* (pp. 609–618). Baltimore: Paul H. Brookes.

Coulter, D. L. (1993). Epilepsy and mental retardation: An overview. *American Journal on Mental Retardation, 98,* 1–11.

Crosse, S. B., Kaye, E., & Ratnofsky, A. C. (n.d.). *A report on the maltreatment of children with disabilities.* Washington, DC: National Center on Child Abuse and Neglect.

Deden, S. (1993, September/October). Why your hospital needs a child abuse team. *Headlines,* 22.

DeFord, S. (1998, July 26). High tech for the disabled. *The Washington Post Education Review, 4,* 30.

DeLoach, C., & Greer, B. G. (1981). *Adjustment to severe physical disability: A metamorphosis.* New York: McGraw-Hill.

Dyar, S. E. (1988). A step in the right direction. *Helix: The University of Virginia Health Sciences Quarterly, 6*(3), 5–11.

Edmonson, B. (1988). Disability and sexual adjustment. In V. B. Van Hasselt, P. S. Strain, & M. Hersen (Eds.), *Handbook of developmental and physical disabilities* (pp. 91–106). New York: Pergamon Press.

Engel, J. (1995). Concepts of epilepsy. *Epilepsia, 36,* 23–29.

Farber, J. M. (1996). Autism and other communication disorders. In A. J. Capute & P. J. Accardo (Eds.), *Developmental disabilities in infancy and childhood* (2nd ed.). *Vol. 2: The spectrum of developmental disabilities* (pp. 347–364). Baltimore: Paul H. Brookes.

Freeman, J. M., Jacobs, H., Vining, E., & Rabin, C. E. (1984). Epilepsy and the inner city schools: A school-based program that makes a difference. *Epilepsia, 25,* 438–442.

Girvin, J. P. (1992). Is epilepsy a progressive disorder? *Journal of Epilepsy, 5,* 94–104.

Gover, A. M., & McIvor, J. (1992). Upper limb deficiencies in infants and young children. *Infants and Young Children, 5*(1), 58–72.

Gouvier, W. D., Brown, L. M., Prestholdt, P. H., Hayes, J. S., & Apostolas, G. (1995). A survey of common misconceptions about epilepsy. *Rehabilitation Psychology, 40,* 51–59.

Grandin, T. (1995). How people with autism think. In E. Schopler & G. B. Mesibov (Eds.), *Learning and cognition in autism* (pp. 137–156). New York: Plenum Press.

Grayson, J. (1992, Fall). Child abuse and developmental disabilities. *Virginia Child Protection Newsletter, 37*(1), 3–7, 10, 12–13, 16.

Hanson, M. J. (Ed.). (1996). *Atypical infant development* (2nd ed.). Austin, TX: Pro-Ed.

Heller, K. W., Alberto, P. A., Forney, P. E., & Schwartzman, M. N. (1996). *Understanding physical, sensory, and health impairments: Characteristics and educational implications.* Pacific Grove, CA: Brooks/Cole.

Heller, K. W., Alberto, P. A., & Meagher, T. M. (1996). The impact of physical impairments on academic performance. *Journal of Developmental and Physical Disabilities, 8,* 233–245.

Hoare, P. (1984). The development of psychiatric disorder among schoolchildren with epilepsy. *Developmental Medicine and Child Neurology, 26,* 3–13.

Huberty, T. J., Austin, J. K., Risinger, M. W., & McNelis, A. M. (1992). Relationship of selected seizure variables in children with epilepsy to performance on school-administered achievement tests. *Journal of Epilepsy, 5,* 10–16.

Johnson, C. P. (1996). Transition in adolescents with disabilities. In A. J. Capute & P. J. Accardo (Eds.), *Developmental disabilities in infancy and childhood* (2nd ed.). *Vol. I: Neurodevelopmental diagnosis and treatment* (pp. 549–564). Baltimore: Paul H. Brookes.

Kurtz, L. A., Dowrick, P. W., Levy, S. E., & Batshaw, M. L. (Eds.). (1996). *Handbook of developmental disabilities: Resources for interdisciplinary care.* Gaithersburg, MD: Aspen.

Lerner, J. W., Lowenthal, B., & Egan, R. (1998). *Preschool children with special needs: Children at risk, children with disabilities.* Boston: Allyn & Bacon.

Llewellyn, A., & Chung, M. C. (1997). The self-esteem of children with physical disabilities—Problems and dilemmas of research. *Journal of Developmental and Physical Disabilities, 9,* 265–275.

Lockhart, P. J. (1996). Infants of substance-abusing mothers. In A. J. Capute & P. J. Accardo (Eds.), *Developmental disabilities in infancy and childhood* (2nd ed.). *Vol. I: Neurodevelopmental diagnosis and treatment* (pp. 215–229). Baltimore: Paul H. Brookes.

Martin, D. A. (1992). Children in peril: A mandate for change in health care policies for low-income children. *Family and Community Health, 15*(1), 75–90.

McCarthy, A. M., Richman, L. C., & Yarbrough, D. (1995). Memory, attention, and school problems in children with seizure disorders. *Developmental Neuropsychology, 11,* 71–86.

McCormick, M. C., Brooks-Gunn, J., Workman-Daniels, K., Turner, J., & Peckham, G. J. (1992). The health and developmental status of very low-birth-weight children at school age. *Journal of the American Medical Association, 267,* 2204–2208.

Mira, M. P., & Tyler, J. S. (1991). Students with traumatic brain injury: Making the transition from hospital to school. *Focus on Exceptional Children, 23*(5), 1–12.

Moore, J. (1985). Technology is not magic. *Exceptional Parent, 15*(7), 41–42.

Murphy, J. M., Jellinek, M., Quinn, D., Smith, G., Poitrast, F. G., & Goshko, M. (1991). Substance abuse and serious child mistreatment: Prevalence, risk, and outcome in a court sample. *Child Abuse and Neglect, 15,* 197–211.

Murphey, K. H. (1996). Play and recreation. In L. A. Kurtz, P. W. Dowrick, S. E. Levy, & M. L. Batshaw (Eds.), *Handbook of developmental disabilities: Resources for interdisciplinary care* (pp. 605–617). Gaithersburg, MD: Aspen.

Myers, B. A. (1996). Coping with developmental disabilities. In A. J. Capute & P. J. Accardo (Eds.), *Developmental disabilities in infancy and childhood* (2nd ed.). *Vol. I: Neurodevelopmental diagnosis and treatment* (pp. 473–483). Baltimore: Paul H. Brookes.

National Head Injury Foundation. (1988). *An educator's manual: What educators need to know about students with traumatic brain injury.* Southborough, MA: Author.

Neisworth, J. T., & Fewell, R. R. (Eds.). (1989). Transition. *Topics in Early Childhood Special Education, 9*(4).

Nelson, K. B. (1996). Epidemiology and etiology of cerebral palsy. In A. J. Capute & P. J. Accardo (Eds.), *Developmental disabilities in infancy and childhood* (2nd ed.). *Vol. 2: The spectrum of developmental disabilities* (pp. 73–79). Baltimore: Paul H. Brookes.

Norlund, M. R. (1994). Transition to postsecondary education. In R. C. Savage & G. F. Wolcott (Eds.), *Educational dimensions of acquired brain injury* (pp. 507–518). Austin, TX: Pro-Ed.

Parette, H. P., & VanBiervliet, A. (1991). Rehabilitation assistive technology issues for infants and young children with disabilities: A preliminary examination. *Journal of Rehabilitation, 57*(3), 27–36.

Pless, I. B. (Ed.). (1994). *The epidemiology of childhood disorders.* New York: Oxford University Press.

Powers, L. E., Singer, G. H. S., & Sowers, J. (Eds.). (1996). *On the road to autonomy: Promoting self-competence in children and youth with disabilities.* Baltimore: Paul H. Brookes.

Rudigier, A. F., Crocker, A. C., & Cohen, H. J. (1990). The dilemmas of childhood: HIV infection. *Children Today, 19,* 26–29.

Sacks, O. (1995). *An anthropologist on Mars: Seven paradoxical tales.* New York: Knopf.

Savage, R. C. (1988). Introduction to educational issues for students who have suffered traumatic brain injury. *An educator's manual: What educators need to know about students with traumatic brain injury.* Southborough, MA: Author.

Savage, R. C., & Mishkin, L. (1994). A neuroeducational model for teaching students with acquired brain injuries. In R. C. Savage & G. F. Wolcott (Eds.), *Educational dimensions of acquired brain injury* (pp. 393–411). Austin, TX: Pro-Ed.

Savage, R. C., & Wolcott, G. F. (1994). (Eds.). *Educational dimensions of acquired brain injury.* Austin, TX: Pro-Ed.

Schopler, E., & Mesibov, G. B. (Eds.). (1994). *Behavioral issues in autism.* New York: Plenum Press.

Schopler, E., & Mesibov, G. B. (Eds.). (1995). *Learning and cognition in autism.* New York: Plenum Press.

Singer, H. S. (1996). Tourette syndrome. In A. J. Capute & P. J. Accardo (Eds.), *Developmental disabilities in infancy and childhood* (2nd ed.). *Vol. 2: The spectrum of developmental disabilities* (pp. 497–510). Baltimore: Paul H. Brookes.

Snow, J. H., & Hooper, S. R. (1994). *Pediatric traumatic brain injury.* Thousand Oaks, CA: Sage.

Spiegel, G. L., Cutler, S. K., & Yetter, C. I. (1996). What every teacher should know about epilepsy. *Intervention in School and Clinic, 32,* 34–38.

Stanley, F. J., & Blair, E. (1994). Cerebral palsy. In I. B. Pless (Ed.), *The epidemiology of childhood disorders* (pp. 473–497). New York: Oxford University Press.

Trach, J. S. (1990). Supported employment program characteristics. In F. R. Rusch (Ed.), *Supported employment: Models, methods, and issues* (pp. 65–81). Sycamore, IL: Sycamore Publishing.

Tyler, J. S., & Colson, S. (1994). Common pediatric disabilities: Medical aspects and educational implications. *Focus on Exceptional Children, 27*(4), 1–16.

Tyler, J. S., & Mira, M. P. (1993). Educational modifications for students with head injuries. *Teaching Exceptional Children, 25*(3), 24–27.

U.S. Department of Education. (1998). *Twentieth annual report to Congress on the implementation of the Individuals with Disabilities Education Act.* Washington, DC: Author.

Vining, E. P. G., & Freeman, J. M. (1996). Epilepsy and developmental disabilities. In Capute, A. J., & Accardo, P. J. (Eds.). (1996b). *Developmental disabilities in infancy and childhood* (2nd ed.). *Vol. 2: The spectrum of developmental disabilities* (pp. 511–520). Baltimore: Paul H. Brookes.

Walker, B. (1995, June). African-American fathers: In raising a child with disabilities, believe only the best, demand only the best, give only the best. *Pacesetter,* 14–15.

Ward, K. M. (1996). School-based vocational training. In L. A. Kurtz, P. W. Dowrick, S. E. Levy, & M. L. Batshaw (Eds.), *Handbook of developmental disabilities: Resources for interdisciplinary care* (pp. 237–248). Gaithersburg, MD: Aspen.

Westbrook, L. E., Silver, E. J., Coupey, S. M., & Shinnar, S. (1991). Social characteristics of adolescents with ideopathic epilepsy: A comparison to chronically ill and nonchronically ill peers. *Journal of Epilepsy, 4,* 87–94.

White, R. (1998). Meet Bob: A student with traumatic brain injury. *Teaching Exceptional Children, 30*(3), 56–60.

Chapter 12

Baker, J. A., Bridger, R., & Evans, K. (1998). Models of underachievement among gifted preadolescents: The role of personal, family, and school factors. *Gifted Child Quarterly, 42,* 5–15.

Baldwin, A. Y. (1985). Programs for the gifted and talented: Issues concerning minority populations. In F. D. Horowitz & M. O'Brien (Eds.), *The gifted and talented: Developmental perspectives* (pp. 251–295). Washington, DC: American Psychological Association.

Baldwin, A. Y. (1993). Teachers of the gifted. In K. A. Heller, F. J. Monks, & A. H. Passow (Eds.), *International handbook of research and development of giftedness and talent* (pp. 621–629). New York: Pergamon Press.

Baum, S. (1986). The gifted preschooler: An awesome delight. *Gifted Child Today, 9*(4), 42–45.

Baum, S. M., Olenchak, F. R., & Owen, S. V. (1998). Gifted students with attention deficits: Fact and/or fiction? Or, can we see the forest for the trees? *Gifted Child Quarterly, 42,* 96–104.

Bloom, B. S. (1982). The role of gifts and markers in the development of talent. *Exceptional Children, 48,* 510–522.

Bloom, B. S., & Sosniak, L. A. (1981). Talent development vs. schooling. *Educational Leadership, 39,* 86–94.

Borland, J. H. (1997). The construct of giftedness. *Peabody Journal of Education, 72*(3&4), 6–20.

Bower, B. (1995). IQ's evolutionary breakdown: Intelligence may have more facets than testers realize. *Science News, 147,* 220–222.

Brody, L. E., & Stanley, J. C. (1991). Young college students: Assessing factors that contribute to success. In W. T. Southern & E. D. Jones (Eds.), *The academic acceleration of gifted children* (pp. 102–132). New York: Teachers College Press.

Brown, J. L., & Pollitt, E. (1996). Malnutrition, poverty and intellectual development. *Scientific American, 274*(2), 38–43.

Buescher, T. M. (1991). Gifted adolescents. In W. T. Southern & E. D. Jones (Eds.), *The academic acceleration of gifted children* (pp. 382–401). New York: Teachers College Press.

Burge, K. (1998, April). Prodigies. *U.S. Airways Attache, 80–87.*

Callahan, C. M. (1986). Asking the right questions: The central issue in evaluating programs for the gifted and talented. *Gifted Child Quarterly, 30,* 38–42.

Callahan, C. M. (1991). An update on gifted females. *Journal for the Education of the Gifted, 14,* 284–311.

Callahan, C. M. (1993). Evaluation programs and procedures for gifted education: International problems and solutions. In K. A. Heller, F. J. Monks, & A. H. Passow (Eds.), *International handbook of research and development of giftedness and talent* (pp. 605–618). New York: Pergamon Press.

Callahan, C. M. (1994). The performance of high ability students in the United States on national and international tests. In P. O. Ross (Ed.), *National excellence: A case for developing America's talent. An anthology of readings* (pp. 5–26). Washington, DC: U.S. Department of Education, Office of Educational Research and Improvement.

Callahan, C. M. (1997). The construct of talent. *Peabody Journal of Education, 72*(3&4), 21–35.

Caplan, N., Choy, M. H., & Whitmore, J. K. (1992, February). Indochinese refugee families and academic achievement. *Scientific American, 266*(2), 36–42.

Charlton, J. C., Marolf, D. M., & Stanley, J. C. (1994). Follow-up insights on rapid educational acceleration. *Roeper Review, 17,* 123–130.

Clark, B. (1997). *Growing up gifted: Developing the potential of children at home and at school* (5th ed.). Upper Saddle River, NJ: Prentice-Hall.

Clark, C. (1998). The professional development of teachers working with more able learners. *Gifted Child International, 12,* 145–150.

Clark, G., & Zimmerman, E. (1998). Nurturing the arts in programs for gifted and talented students. *Phi Delta Kappan, 79,* 747–751.

Clifford, J. A., Runions, T., & Smyth, E. (1986). The Learning Enrichment Service (LES): A participatory model for gifted adolescents. In J. S. Renzulli (Ed.), *Systems and models for developing programs for the gifted and talented.* Mansfield, CT: Creative Learning Press.

Coleman, J. M., & Fultz, B. A. (1985). Special class placement, level of intelligence, and the self-concepts of gifted children: A social comparison perspective. *Remedial and Special Education, 6*(1), 7–12.

Coleman, L. J. (1992). The cognitive map of a master teacher conducting discussions with gifted students. *Exceptionality, 3,* 1–16.

Cornell, D. G. (1983). Gifted children: The impact of positive labeling on the family system. *American Journal of Orthopsychiatry, 53,* 322–335.

Council of State Directors of Programs for the Gifted. (1991). The 1990 state of the states gifted and talented education report. Washington, DC: Author.

Cropper, C. (1998). Fostering parental involvement in the education of the gifted minority student. *Gifted Child Today, 21*(1), 20–24, 46.

Cross, T. L. (1997). Psychological and social aspects of educating gifted students. *Peabody Journal of Education, 72*(3&4), 180–200.

Delcourt, M. A. B., Loyd, B. H., Cornell, D. G., & Goldberg, M. D. (1994, October). *Evaluation of the effects of programming arrangements on student learning outcomes.* Storrs, CT: National Research Center on the Gifted and Talented, University of Connecticut.

Delisle, J. (1981). The non-productive gifted child: A contradiction. *Roeper Review, 3,* 20–22.

Delisle, J. (1982). The gifted underachiever: Learning to underachieve. *Roeper Review, 4,* 16–18.

Delisle, J. R. (1987). *Gifted kids speak out.* Minneapolis, MN: Free Spirit Publishing.

Delisle, J. R. (1992). *Guiding the social and emotional development of gifted youth: A practical guide for educators and counselors.* New York: Longman.

Delisle, J. R. (1996). Multiple intelligences: Convenient, simple, wrong. *Gifted Child Today, 19*(6), 12–13.

Dettmer, P. (1982, January–February). Preventing burnout in teachers of the gifted. *Gifted/Creative/Talented,* pp. 37–41.

Eccles, J. S. (1985). Why doesn't Jane run? Sex differences in educational and occupational patterns. In F. D. Horowitz & M. O'Brien (Eds.), *The gifted and talented: Developmental perspectives.* Washington, DC: American Psychological Association.

Esquivel, G. B. (1995). Teacher behaviors that foster creativity. *Educational Psychology Review, 7,* 185–202.

Feldhusen, J. F. (1989). Synthesis of research on gifted youth. *Educational Leadership, 46*(6), 6–11.

Feldhusen, J. F. (1997). Educating teachers for work with talented youth. In N. Colangelo & G. A. Davis (Eds.), *Handbook of gifted education* (2nd ed., pp. 547–552). Boston: Allyn & Bacon.

Feldhusen, J. F. (1998). Programs for the gifted few or talent development for the many? *Phi Delta Kappan, 79,* 735–738.

Feldhusen, J. F., & Kolloff, P. B. (1986). The Purdue secondary model for gifted and talented youth. In J. S. Renzulli (Ed.), *Systems and models for developing programs for the gifted and talented.* Mansfield, CT: Creative Learning Press.

Feldhusen, J. F., & Moon, S. M. (1992). Grouping students: Issues and concerns. *Gifted Child Quarterly, 36,* 63–67.

Fiedler, E. D., Lange, R. E., & Winebrenner, S. (1993). The concept of grouping in gifted education. *Roeper Review, 16,* 4–7.

Ford, D. Y. (1993). An investigation of the paradox of underachievement among gifted black students. *Roeper Review, 16,* 78–84.

Ford, D. Y. (1994a). Nurturing resilience in gifted black youth. *Roeper Review, 17,* 80–85.

Ford, D. Y. (1994b, September). *The recruitment and retention of African-American students in gifted education programs: Implications and recommendations.* Storrs, CT: National Research Center on the Gifted and Talented, University of Connecticut.

Ford, D. Y. (1998). The under-representation of minority students in gifted education: Problems and promises in recruitment and retention. *Journal of Special Education, 32,* 4–14.

Ford, D. Y., Baytops, J. L., & Harmon, D. A. (1997). Helping gifted minority students reach their potential: Recommendations for change. *Peabody Journal of Education, 72*(3&4), 201–216.

Ford, D. Y., & Harris, J. J. (1996). Perceptions and attitudes of black students toward school, achievement, and other educational variables. *Child Development, 67,* 1141–1152.

Ford, D. Y., & Harris, J. J. (1997). A study of the racial identity and achievement of black males and females. *Roeper Review, 20,* 105–110.

Ford, D. Y., Russo, C. J., & Harris, J. J., III. (1995). Meeting the educational needs of the gifted: A legal imperative. *Roeper Review, 17,* 224–231.

Ford, D. Y., & Webb, K. S. (1994). Desegregation of gifted educational programs: The impact of Brown on underachieving children of color. *Journal of Negro Education, 63,* 358–375.

Frasier, M. M. (1991). Disadvantaged and culturally diverse gifted students. *Journal for the Education of the Gifted, 14,* 234–245.

Frasier, M. M. (1997). Gifted minority students: Reframing approaches to their identification and education. In N. Colangelo & G. A. Davis (Eds.), *Handbook of gifted education* (2nd ed., pp. 498–515). Boston: Allyn & Bacon.

Frasier, M. M., Garcia, J. H., & Passow, A. H. (1995, February). *A review of assessment issues in gifted education and their implications for identifying gifted minority students.* Storrs, CT: National Research Center on the Gifted and Talented, University of Connecticut.

Frasier, M. M., & Passow, A. H. (1994, December). *Toward a new paradigm for identifying talent potential.* Storrs, CT: National Research Center on the Gifted and Talented, University of Connecticut.

Fulkerson, J., & Horvich, M. (1998). Talent development: Two perspectives. *Phi Delta Kappan, 79,* 756–759.

Galbraith, J., & Delisle, J. (1996). *The gifted kids' survival guide: A teen handbook* (rev. ed.). Minneapolis: Free Spirit Publishing.

Gallagher, J. J. (1986). Our love-hate affair with gifted children. *Gifted Child Today, 9*(3), 47–49.

Gallagher, J. J. (1991a). Educational reform, values, and gifted students. *Gifted Child Quarterly, 35,* 12–19.

Gallagher, J. J. (1991b). Personal patterns of underachievement. *Journal of the Education of the Gifted, 14,* 221–233.

Gallagher, J. J. (1994). Current and historical thinking on education for gifted and talented students. In P. O. Ross (Ed.), *National excellence: A case for developing America's talent. An anthology of readings* (pp. 83–107). Washington, DC: U.S. Department of Education, Office of Educational Research and Improvement.

Gallagher, J. J. (1995). Education of gifted students. A civil rights issue? *Phi Delta Kappan, 76,* 408–410.

Gallagher, J. J. (1997a). Issues in the education of gifted students. In N. Colangelo & G. A. Davis (Eds.), *Handbook of gifted education* (2nd ed., pp. 10–23). Boston: Allyn & Bacon.

Gallagher, J. J. (1997b). Least restrictive environment and gifted students. *Peabody Journal of Education, 72*(3&4), 153–165.

Gallagher, J. J. (1998). Accountability for gifted students. *Phi Delta Kappan, 79,* 739–742.

Gallagher, J. J., & Gallagher, S. A. (1994). *Teaching the gifted child* (4th ed.). Boston: Allyn & Bacon.

Gardner, H., & Hatch, T. (1989). Multiple intelligences go to school: Educational implications of the theory of multiple intelligences. *Educational Researcher, 18*(8), 4–9.

Gross, M. U. M. (1992). The use of radical acceleration in cases of extreme intellectual precocity. *Gifted Child Quarterly, 36,* 91–99.

Gross, M. U. M. (1993). *Exceptionally gifted children.* London: Routledge.

Gruber, H. E. (1985). Giftedness and moral responsibility: Creative thinking and human survival. In F. D. Horowitz & M. O'Brien (Eds.), *The gifted and talented: Developmental perspectives* (pp. 301–330). Washington, DC: American Psychological Association.

Hague, W. J. (1998). Is there moral giftedness? *Gifted Education International, 12,* 170–174.

Hannah, C. L., & Shore, B. M. (1995). Metacognition and high intellectual ability: Insights from the study of learning-disabled gifted students. *Gifted Child Quarterly, 39,* 95–109.

Hedges, L. V., & Nowell, A. (1995). Sex differences in mental test scores, variability, and numbers of high-scoring individuals. *Science, 269,* 41–45.

Henderson, L. M., & Ebner, F. F. (1997). The biological basis for early intervention with gifted children. *Peabody Journal of Education, 72*(3&4), 59–80.

Hine, C. Y. (1994, August). *Helping your child find success at school: A guide for Hispanic parents.* Storrs, CT: National Research Center on the Gifted and Talented, University of Connecticut.

Hoge, R. D., & Renzulli, J. S. (1993). Exploring the link between giftedness and self-concept. *Review of Educational Research, 63,* 449–465.

Howley, C. B., Howley, A., & Pendarvis, E. D. (1995). *Out of our minds: Anti-intellectualism and talent development in American schooling.* New York: Teachers College Press.

Hunsaker, S. L. (1995). The gifted metaphor from the perspective of traditional civilizations. *Journal for the Education of the Gifted, 18,* 255–268.

Hunsaker, S. L., & Callahan, C. M. (1995). Creativity and giftedness: Published instrument uses and abuses. *Gifted Child Quarterly, 39,* 110–114.

Jackson, N. E., & Klein, E. (1997). Gifted preformance in young children. In N. Colangelo & G. A. Davis (Eds.), *Handbook of gifted education* (2nd ed., pp. 460–474). Boston: Allyn & Bacon.

Janos, P. M., & Robinson, N. M. (1985). Psychosocial development in intellectually gifted children. In F. D. Horowitz & M. O'Brien (Eds.), *The gifted and talented: Developmental perspectives* (pp. 149–195). Washington, DC: American Psychological Association.

Johnson, L. J., Karnes, M. B., & Carr, V. W. (1997). Providing services to children with gifts and disabilities: A critical need. In N. Colangelo & G. A. Davis (Eds.), *Handbook of gifted education* (2nd ed., pp. 516–527). Boston: Allyn & Bacon.

Jones, E. D., & Southern, W. T. (1991). Conclusions about acceleration: Echoes of debate. In W. T. Southern & E. D. Jones (Eds.), *The academic acceleration of gifted children* (pp. 223–228). New York: Teachers College Press.

Jones, E. D., & Southern, W. T. (1992). Programming, grouping, and acceleration in rural school districts: A survey of attitudes and practices. *Gifted Child Quarterly, 36,* 112–117.

Junge, M. E., & Dretzke, B. J. (1995). Mathematical self-efficacy gender differences in gifted/talented adolescents. *Gifted Child Quarterly, 39,* 22–28.

Karnes, F. A., & Marquardt, R. G. (1997). The fragmented framework of legal protection for the gifted. *Peabody Journal of Education, 72*(3&4), 166–179.

Karnes, M. B., & Bean, S. M. (1996). Leadership and the gifted. *Focus on Exceptional Children, 29*(1), 1–12.

Karnes, M. B., & Johnson, L. J. (1991). The preschool/primary gifted child. *Journal for the Education of the Gifted, 14,* 267–283.

Kaufman, M. (1998, February 2). The best for the brightest. *The Washington Post Magazine,* 18–20, 32–35.

Kelly, K. R., & Moon, S. M. (1998). Personal and social talents. *Phi Delta Kappan, 79,* 743–746.

Kennedy, D. M. (1995a). Glimpses of a highly gifted child in a heterogeneous classroom. *Roeper Review, 17,* 164–168.

Kennedy, D. M. (1995b). Plain talk about creating a gifted-friendly classroom. *Roeper Review, 17,* 232–234.

Kerr, B. (1997). Developing talents in girls and young women. In N. Colangelo & G. A. Davis (Eds.), *Handbook of gifted education* (2nd ed., pp. 475–482). Boston: Allyn & Bacon.

Kitano, M. K., & Espinosa, R. (1995). Language diversity and giftedness: Working with gifted English language learners. *Journal for the Education of the Gifted, 18,* 234–254.

Kolb, K. J., & Jussim, L. (1994). Teacher expectations and underachieving gifted children. *Roeper Review, 17,* 26–30.

Kolitch, E. R., & Brody, L. E. (1992). Mathematics acceleration of highly talented students: An evaluation. *Gifted Child Quarterly, 36,* 78–86.

Kulik, J. A., & Kulik, C. C. (1992). Meta-analytic findings on grouping programs. *Gifted Child Quarterly, 36,* 73–77.

Kulik, J. A., & Kulik, C. C. (1997). Ability grouping. In N. Colangelo & G. A. Davis (Eds.), *Handbook of gifted education* (2nd ed., pp. 230–242). Boston: Allyn & Bacon.

Lovecky, D. V. (1994). Exceptionally gifted children: Different minds. *Roeper Review, 17,* 116–120.

Maker, C. J. (Ed.). (1993). *Critical issues in gifted education: Programs for the gifted in regular classrooms.* Austin, TX: Pro-Ed.

Maker, C. J., & Nielson, A. B. (1996). *Curriculum development and teaching strategies for gifted learners.* Austin, TX: Pro-Ed.

Margolin, L. (1994). *Goodness personified: The emergence of gifted children.* New York: Aldine de Gruyter.

Marsh, H. W., Chessor, D., Craven, R., & Roche, L. (1995). The effects of gifted and talented programs on academic self-concept: The big fish strikes again. *American Educational Research Journal, 32,* 285–319.

Mathews, J. (1998, June 7). Across area, "gifted" has no clear-cut definition: School guidelines mystify many parents. *The Washington Post,* A1, A16.

Mills, C. J., Stork, E. J., & Krug, D. (1992). Recognition and development of academic talent in educationally disadvantaged students. *Exceptionality, 3,* 165–180.

Moon, S. M., & Dillon, D. R. (1995). Multiple exceptionalities: A case study. *Journal for the Education of the Gifted, 18,* 111–130.

Morelock, M. J., & Feldman, D. H. (1997). High IQ children, extreme precocity, and savant syndrome. In N. Colangelo & G. A. Davis (Eds.), *Handbook of gifted education* (2nd ed., pp. 439–459). Boston: Allyn & Bacon.

Neuhaus, C. (1988). Genius at work. *US Air, 10*(2), 64–68.

Noble, K. D., & Drummond, J. E. (1992). But what about the prom? Students' perceptions of early college entrance. *Gifted Child Quarterly, 36,* 106–111.

Oakes, J. (1985). *Keeping track: How schools structure inequality.* New Haven, CT: Yale University Press.

Oakes, J. (1992). Can tracking research inform practice? Technical, normative, and political considerations. *Educational Researchers, 22*(4), 12–21.

Olenchak, F. R., & Renzulli, J. S. (1989). The effectiveness of the schoolwide enrichment model on selected aspects of elementary school change. *Gifted Child Quarterly, 33*(1), 36–46.

Passow, A. H. (1997). International perspective on gifted education. In N. Colangelo & G. A. Davis (Eds.), *Handbook of gifted education* (2nd ed., pp. 528–535). Boston: Allyn & Bacon.

Passow, A. H., & Rudnitski, R. A. (1993, October). *State policies regarding education of the gifted as reflected in legislation and regulation.* Storrs, CT: National Research Center on the Gifted and Talented, University of Connecticut.

Patton, J. M., & Baytops, J. L. (1995). Identifying and transforming the potential of young, gifted African Americans: A clarion call. In B. A. Ford, F. E. Obiakor, & J. M. Patton (Eds.), *Effective education of African American exceptional learners: New perspectives* (pp. 27–67). Austin, TX: Pro-Ed.

Patton, J. M., & Townsend, B. L. (1997). Creating inclusive environments for African American children and youth with gifts and talents. *Roeper Review, 20,* 13–17.

Perrone, P. A. (1991). Career development. In N. Colangelo & G. A. Davis (Eds.), *Handbook of gifted education* (pp. 321–327). Boston: Allyn & Bacon.

Piechowski, M. M. (1997). Emotional giftedness: The measure of intrapersonal intelligence. In N. Colangelo & G. A. Davis (Eds.), *Handbook of gifted education* (2nd ed., pp. 366–381). Boston: Allyn & Bacon.

Plomin, R. (1997). Genetics and intelligence. In N. Colangelo & G. A. Davis (Eds.), *Handbook of gifted education* (2nd ed., pp. 67–74). Boston: Allyn & Bacon.

Ramos-Ford, V., & Gardner, H. (1997). Giftedness from a multiple intelligences perspective. In N. Colangelo & G. A. Davis (Eds.), *Handbook of gifted education* (2nd ed., pp. 54–66). Boston: Allyn & Bacon.

Reis, S. M. (1989). Reflections on policy affecting the education of gifted and talented students: Past and future perspectives. *American Psychologist, 44,* 399–408.

Reis, S. M., Neu, T. W., & McGuire, J. M. (1995, January). *Talents in two places: Case studies of high ability students with learning disabilities who have achieved.* Storrs, CT: National Research Center on the Gifted and Talented, University of Connecticut.

Renzulli, J. S. (1994). *Schools for talent development: A practical plan for total school improvement.* Mansfield Center, CT: Creative Learning Press.

Renzulli, J. S. (1997). The total talent portfolio: Looking at the best in every student. *Gifted Child International, 12,* 58–63.

Renzulli, J. S., & Reis, S. M. (1985). *The schoolwide enrichment model: A comprehensive plan for educational excellence.* Mansfield Center, CT: Creative Learning Press.

Renzulli, J. S., & Reis, S. M. (1991). The reform movement and the quiet crisis in gifted education. *Gifted Child Quarterly, 35,* 26–35.

Renzulli, J. S., & Reis, S. M. (1997). The schoolwide enrichment model: New directions for developing high-end learning. In N. Colangelo & G. A. Davis (Eds.), *Handbook of gifted education* (2nd ed., pp. 136–154). Boston: Allyn & Bacon.

Renzulli, J. S., Reis, S. M., & Smith, L. H. (1981). *The revolving door identification model.* Mansfield Center, CT: Creative Learning Press.

Resnick, D. P., & Goodman, M. (1994). American culture and the gifted. In P. O. Ross (Ed.), *National excellence: A case for developing America's talent. An anthology of readings* (pp. 109–121). Washington, DC: U.S. Department of Education, Office of Educational Research and Improvement.

Rimm, S. B., & Lovance, K. J. (1992). The use of subject and grade skipping for the prevention and reversal of underachievement. *Gifted Child Quarterly, 36,* 100–105.

Rittenhouse, R. K., & Blough, L. K. (1995). Gifted students with hearing impairments: Suggestions for teachers. *Teaching Exceptional Children, 27*(4), 51–53.

Robinson, N. M. (1993a). Identifying and nurturing gifted, very young children. In K. A. Heller, F. J. Monks, & A. H. Passow (Eds.), *International handbook of research and development of giftedness and talent* (pp. 507–524). New York: Pergamon Press.

Robinson, N. M. (1993b, November). *Parenting the very young, gifted child.* Storrs, CT: National Research Center on the Gifted and Talented, University of Connecticut.

Robinson, N. M., & Weimer, L. J. (1991). Selection of candidates for early admission to kindergarten and first grade. In W. T. Southern & E. D. Jones (Eds.), *The academic acceleration of gifted children* (pp. 29–50). New York: Teachers College Press.

Roedell, W. C. (1985). Developing social competence in gifted preschool children. *Remedial and Special Education, 6*(4), 6–11.

Roeper, A. (1994). Gifted education must take a stand on *The Bell Curve. Roeper Review, 17,* 150.

Sacks, O. (1995). *An antropologist on Mars: Seven paradoxical tales.* New York: Knopf.

Sapon-Shevin, M. (1984). The tug-of-war nobody wins: Allocation of educational resources for handicapped, gifted, and "typical" students. *Curriculum Inquiry, 14,* 57–81.

Sapon-Shevin, M. (1994). *Playing favorites: Gifted education and the disruption of community.* Albany: State University of New York Press.

Shields, C. M. (1995). A comparison study of student attitudes and perceptions in homogeneous and heterogeneous classrooms. *Roeper Review, 17,* 234–238.

Silverman, L. K. (1994). The moral sensitivity of gifted children and the evolution of society. *Roeper Review, 17,* 110–116.

Silverman, L. K. (1997). Family counseling with the gifted. In N. Colangelo & G. A. Davis (Eds.), *Handbook of gifted education* (2nd ed., pp. 382–397). Boston: Allyn & Bacon.

Sowa, C. J., McIntire, J., May, K. M., & Bland, L. (1994). Social and emotional adjustment themes across gifted children. *Roeper Review, 17,* 95–98.

Sternberg, R. J. (1996). Myths, countermyths, and truths about intelligence. *Educational Researcher, 25*(2), 11–16.

Sternberg, R. J. (1997). A triarchic view of giftedness: Theory and practice. In N. Colangelo & G. A. Davis (Eds.), *Handbook of gifted education* (2nd ed., pp. 43–53). Boston: Allyn & Bacon.

Sternberg, R. J. (1998). Abilities are forms of developing expertise. *Educational Researcher, 27*(3), 11–20.

Sternberg, R. J., & Clinkenbeard, P. R. (1995). The triarchic model applied to identifying, teaching, and assessing gifted children. *Roeper Review, 17,* 255–260.

Sternberg, R. J., & Davidson, J. E. (Eds.) (1986). *Conceptions of giftedness.* New York: Cambridge University Press.

Sternberg, R. J., & Zhang, L. (1995). What do we mean by giftedness? A pentagonal implicit theory. *Gifted Child Quarterly, 39,* 88–94.

Stevenson, H. W., Lee, S., Chen, C., Kato, K., & Londo, W. (1994). Education of gifted and talented students in China, Taiwan, and Japan. In P. O. Ross (Ed.), *National excellence: A case for developing America's talent. An anthology of readings* (pp. 27–60). Washington, DC: U.S. Department of Education, Office of Educational Research and Improvement.

Subotnik, R. F., & Arnold, K. D. (Eds.). (1994). *Beyond Terman: Contemporary longitudinal studies of giftedness and talent.* Norwood, NJ: Albex.

Swanson, J. D. (1995). Gifted African-American children in rural schools: Searching for the answers. *Roeper Review, 17,* 261–266.

Swiatek, M. A. (1998). Helping gifted adolescents cope with social stigma. *Gifted Child Today, 21*(1), 42–46.

Tannenbaum, A. J. (1993). History of giftedness and "gifted education" in world perspective. In K. A. Heller, F. J. Monks, & A. H. Passow (Eds.), *International handbook of research and development of giftedness and talent* (pp. 3–27). New York: Pergamon Press.

Tannenbaum, A. J. (1997). The meaning and making of giftedness. In N. Colangelo & G. A. Davis (Eds.), *Handbook of gifted education* (2nd ed., pp. 27–42). Boston: Allyn & Bacon.

Terwilliger, J. S., & Titus, J. C. (1995). Gender differences in attitudes and attitude changes among mathematically talented youth. *Gifted Child Quarterly, 39,* 29–35.

Thompson, L. A., & Plomin, R. (1993). Genetic influence on cognitive ability. In K. A. Heller, F. J. Monks, & A. H. Passow (Eds.), *International handbook of research and development of giftedness and talent* (pp. 103–113). New York: Pergamon Press.

Tomlinson, C. A. (1994a). Gifted learners: The boomerang kids of middle school? *Roeper Review, 16,* 177–182.

Tomlinson, C. A. (1994b). The easy lie and the role of gifted education in school excellence. *Roeper Review, 16,* 258–259.

Treffinger, D. J. (1991). School reform and gifted education—Opportunities and issues. *Gifted Child Quarterly, 35,* 6–11.

Treffinger, D. J. (1998). From gifted education to programming for talent development. *Phi Delta Kappan, 79,* 752–755.

VanTassel-Baska, J. (Ed.). (1990). *A practical guide to counseling the gifted in a school setting* (2nd ed.). Reston, VA: Council for Exceptional Children.

VanTassel-Baska, J. (1991a). Gifted education in the balance: Building relationships with general education. *Gifted Child Quarterly, 35,* 20–25.

VanTassel-Baska, J. (1991b). Serving the disabled gifted through educational collaboration. *Journal for the Education of the Gifted, 14,* 246–266.

VanTassel-Baska, J. (1992). Educational decision making on acceleration and grouping. *Gifted Child Quarterly, 36,* 68–72.

VanTassel-Baska, J. (1993). Theory and research on curriculum development for the gifted. In K. A. Heller, F. J. Monks, & A. H. Passow (Eds.), *International handbook of research and development of giftedness and talent* (pp. 365–386). New York: Pergamon Press.

Van Tassel-Baska, J. (1998). The development of academic talent: A mandate for educational best practice. *Phi Delta Kappan, 79,* 760–763.

White, D. A., & Breen, M. (1998). Edutainment: Gifted education and the perils of misusing multiple intelligences. *Gifted Child Today, 21*(2), 12–17.

Whitlock, M. S., & DuCette, J. P. (1989). Outstanding and average teachers of the gifted: A comparative study. *Gifted Child Quarterly, 33,* 15–21.

Whitmore, J. R. (1986). Understanding a lack of motivation to excel. *Gifted Child Quarterly, 30,* 66–69.

Whitmore, J. R., & Maker, C. J. (1985). *Intellectual giftedness in disabled persons.* Rockville, MD: Aspen.

Willard-Holt, C. (1994, September). *Recognizing talent: Cross-case study of two high potential students with cerebral palsy.* Storrs, CT: National Research Center on the Gifted and Talented, University of Connecticut.

Zigler, E., & Farber, E. A. (1985). Commonalities between the intellectual extremes: Giftedness and mental retardation. In F. D. Horowitz & M. O'Brien (Eds.), *The gifted and talented: Developmental perspectives* (pp. 378–408). Washington, DC: American Psychological Association.

Chapter 13

Alper, S., Schloss, P. J., & Schloss, C. N. (1996). Families of children with disabilities in elementary and middle school: Advocacy models and strategies. *Exceptional Children, 62,* 261–270.

Beckman, P. J. (1991). Comparison of mothers' and fathers' perceptions of the effect of young children with and without disabilities. *American Journal on Mental Retardation, 95,* 585–595.

Bell, R. Q., & Harper, L. V. (1977). *Child effects on adults.* Hillsdale, NJ: Erlbaum.

Bernheimer, L. P., & Keogh, B. K. (1995). Weaving interventions into the fabric of everyday life: An approach to family assessment. *Topics in Early Childhood and Special Education, 15,* 415–433.

Berry, J. O., & Hardman, M. L. (1998). *Lifespan perspectives on the family and disability.* Boston: Allyn & Bacon.

Bettelheim, B. (1950). *Love is not enough.* New York: Macmillan.

Bettelheim, B. (1967). *The empty fortress.* New York: Free Press.

Blacher, J., & Baker, B. L. (1992). Toward meaningful family involvement in out-of-home placement settings. *Mental Retardation, 30,* 35–43.

Bronfenbrenner, U. (1979). *The ecology of human development: Experiments by nature and design.* Cambridge, MA: Harvard University Press.

Bronfenbrenner, U. (1995). Developmental ecology through space and time: A future perspective. In P. Moen, G. H. Elder, & K. Luscher (Eds.), *Examining lives in context: Perspectives on the ecology of human development* (pp. 619–647). Washington, DC: American Psychological Association.

Brooks-Gunn, J., & Lewis, M. (1984). Maternal responsivity in interactions with handicapped infants. *Child Development, 55,* 858–868.

Bryan, T., Nelson, C., & Mathur, S. (1995). Homework: A survey of primary students in regular, resource, and self-contained classrooms. *Learning Disabilities Research and Practice, 10,* 85–90.

Cottone, E. (1998). *Home-school collaboration: Evaluating the effectiveness of a school-home note program for children with ADHD.* Unpublished doctoral dissertation, University of Virginia, Charlottesville.

D'Asaro, A. (1998). Caring for yourself is caring for your family: Methods of coping with the everyday stresses of care giving. *Exceptional Parent, 28*(6), 38–40.

Drotar, D., Baskiewicz, A., Irvin, N., Kennell, J., & Klaus, M. (1975). The adaptation of parents to the birth of an infant with a congenital malformation: A hypothetical model. *Pediatrics, 56,* 710–717.

Duis, S. S., Summers, M., & Summers, C. R. (1997). Parent versus child stress in diverse family types: An ecological approach. *Topics in Early Childhood and Special Education, 17,* 53–73.

Dumas, J. E., Wolf, L. C., Fisman, S. N., & Culligan, A. (1991). Parenting stress, child behavior problems, and dysphoria in parents of children with autism, Down syndrome, behavior disorders, and normal development. *Exceptionality, 2,* 97–110.

Dunst, C. J., & Trivette, C. M. (1994). Aims and principles of family support programs. In C. J. Dunst, C. M. Trivette, & A. Deal (Eds.), *Supporting and strengthening families: Vol. 1. Methods, strategies, and practices* (pp. 30–48). Cambridge, MA: Brookline Books.

Dunst, C. J., Trivette, C. M., & Jodry, W. (1997). Influences of social support on children with disabilities and their families. In M. J. Guralnick (Ed.), *The effectiveness of early intervention* (pp. 499–522). Baltimore: Paul H. Brookes.

Dyson, L. L. (1997). Fathers and mothers of school-age children with developmental disabilities: Parental stress, family functioning, and social support. *American Journal on Mental Retardation, 102,* 267–279.

Featherstone, H. (1980). *A difference in the family: Life with a disabled child.* New York: Basic Books.

Fowler, S. A., Schwartz, I., & Atwater, J. (1991). Perspectives on the transition from preschool to kindergarten for children with disabilities and their families. *Exceptional Children, 58,* 136–145.

Gavidia-Payne, S., & Stoneman, Z. (1997). Family predictors of maternal and paternal involvement in programs for young children with disabilities. *Child Development, 68,* 701–717.

Guralnick, M. J. (1998). Effectiveness of early intervention for vulnerable children: A developmental perspective. *American Journal on Mental Retardation, 102,* 319–345.

Hallahan, D. P. (1992). Some thoughts on why the prevalence of learning disabilities has increased. *Journal of Learning Disabilities, 25,* 523–528.

Hanline, M. F., & Knowlton, A. (1988). A collaborative model for providing support to parents during their child's transition from infant intervention to preschool special education public school programs. *Journal of the Division for Early Childhood, 12,* 116–125.

Hockenberry, J. (1995). *Moving violations: War zones, wheelchairs, and declarations of independence.* New York: Hyperion.

Jewell, G. (1985). *Geri.* New York: Ballantine Books.

Kauffman, J., Mostert, M., Trent, S., & Hallahan, D. (1998). *Managing classroom behavior: A reflective case-based approach.* Boston: Allyn & Bacon.

Kelley, M. L. (1990). *School-home notes: Promoting children's classroom success.* New York: Guilford Press.

Kelley, M. L., & McCain, A. P. (1995). Promoting academic performance in inattentive children. *Behavior Modification, 19,* 357–375.

Krauss, M. W., Seltzer, M. M., & Goodman, S. J. (1992). Social support networks of adults with mental retardation who live at home. *American Journal on Mental Retardation, 96,* 432–441.

Leete-Guy, L., & Schor, J. B. (1992). *The great American time squeeze: Trends in work and leisure, 1969–1989.* Briefing paper, Economic Policy Institute, Washington, DC.

Lehmann, J. P., & Baker, C. (1995). Mothers' expectations for their adolescent children: A comparison between families with disabled adolescents and those with non-labeled adolescents. *Education and Training in Mental Retardation and Developmental Disabilities, 30,* 27–40.

Mahoney, G., & Bella, J. M. (1998). An examination of the effects of family-centered early intervention on child and family outcomes. *Topics in Early Childhood and Special Education, 18,* 83–94.

Mahoney, G., & Robenalt, K. (1986). A comparison of conversational patterns between mothers and their Down syndrome and normal infants. *Journal of the Division for Early Childhood, 10,* 172–180.

Mahoney, G., & Wheeden, C. A. (1997). Parent-child interaction—the foundation for family-centered early intervention practice: A response to Baird and Peterson. *Topics in Early Childhood and Special Education, 17,* 165–184.

Mahoney, G., Boyce, G., Fewell, R. R., Spiker, D., & Wheeden, C. A. (1998). The relationship of parent-child interaction to the effectiveness of early intervention services for at-risk children and children with disabilities. *Topics in Early Childhood and Special Education, 18,* 5–17.

Martin, S. S., Brady, M. P., & Kortarba, J. A. (1992). Families with chronically ill children: The unsinkable family. *Remedial and Special Education, 13,* 6–15.

McCain, A. P., & Kelley, M. L. (1993). Managing the classroom behavior of an ADHD preschooler: The efficacy of a school-home note intervention. *Child and Family Behavior Therapy, 15*(3), 33–44.

McWilliam, R. A., Ferguson, C., Harbin, G. L., Porter, P., Munn, D., & Vandiviere, P. (1998). The family-centeredness of individualized family service plans. *Topics in Early Childhood and Special Education, 18,* 69–82.

Meyer, D. J., & Vadasy, P. F. (1994). *Sibshops: Workshops for siblings of children with special needs.* Baltimore: Paul H. Brookes.

Michael, M. G., Arnold, K. D., Magliocca, L. A., & Miller, S. (1992). Influences on teachers' attitudes of the parents' role as collaborator. *Remedial and Special Education, 13,* 24–30, 39.

Mims, A., Harper, C., Armstong, S. W., & Savage, S. (1991). Effective instruction in homework for students with disabilities. *Teaching Exceptional Children, 24*(1), 42–47.

Nolan, C. (1987). *Under the eye of the clock: The life story of Christopher Nolan.* New York: St. Martin's Press.

Pianta, R. C., Marvin, R. S., Britner, P. A., & Borowitz, K. C. (1996). Mothers' resolution of their children's diagnosis: Organized patterns of caregiving representations. *Journal of Infant Mental Health, 17,* 239–256.

Pierro, C. (1995). Talking with your child about disabilities. *Exceptional Parent, 25*(6), 92.

Powell, T. H., & Gallagher, P. A. (1993). *Brothers & sisters—A special part of exceptional families* (2nd ed.). Baltimore: Paul H. Brookes.

Roach, M. A., Barratt, M. S., Miller, J. F., & Leavitt, L. A. (1998). The structure of mother-child play: Young children with Down syndrome and typically developing children. *Developmental Psychology, 34,* 77–87.

Salend, S. J., & Gajria, M. (1995). Increasing the homework completion rates of students with mild disabilities. *Remedial and Special Education, 16,* 271–278.

Seligman, M., & Darling, R. B. (1989). *Ordinary families, special children: A systems approach to childhood disability.* New York: Guilford Press.

Stark, J. (1992). Presidential Address 1992: A professional and personal perspective on families. *Mental Retardation, 30,* 247–254.

Thompson, L., Lobb, C., Elling, R., Herman, S., Jurkiewicz, T., & Hulleza, C. (1997). Pathways to family empowerment: Effects of family-centered delivery of early intervention services. *Exceptional Children, 64,* 99–113.

Trivette, C. M., Dunst, C. J., Boyd, K., & Hamby, D. W. (1995). Family-oriented program models, helpgiving practices, and parental control appraisals. *Exceptional Children, 62,* 237–248.

Turnbull, A. P., & Turnbull, H. R. (1997). *Families, professionals, and exceptionality: A special partnership* (3rd ed.). Upper Saddle River, NJ: Prentice-Hall.

Turnbull, A. P., & Turnbull, H. R. (2000). Fostering family-professional partnerships. In M. E. Snell & F. Brown (Eds.), *Instruction of students with severe disabilities.* Columbus, OH: Merrill/Prentice-Hall.

name index

subject index

Photo Credits (continued):
Cynthia Johnson/Gamma Liaison: p. 53; Courtesy of Toys R Us and the Saturn
Corporation: p. 57; Robert Harbison: pp. 74, 127, 176, 235, 261, 309, 440, 446 (right);
Courtesy of Williams Syndrome Association: p. 132; Jim Pickerell: p. 138; Courtesy of
Jean Gibson/ The South Brunswick Citizens for Independent Living: p. 151; Courtesy of
Time Magazine: p. 229; James King Holmes/Science Source/ Photo Researchers: p. 349;
Argentum/Science Source/Photo Researchers: p. 392; Thresher/TWP: p. 396; John
Bunting/Impact Visuals: p. 403 (top); Wyman/Monkmeyer: p. 407; Marion Ettlinger:
p. 410; Paul S. Howell/Gamma Liasion: p. 413; Stephen Marks: p. 442; Courtesy of James
Koefler/Children's Orthopedic Surgery Foundation: p. 445; Courtesy of Surf Chair: p. 446
(left); Rogers/Monkmeyer: p. 454; John Nordell/Picture Cube: p. 478.